African American National Biography

African American National Biography

SECOND EDITION

HENRY LOUIS GATES JR.

EVELYN BROOKS HIGGINBOTHAM

Editors in Chief

VOLUME 11: TABORN, EARL "MICKEY" – WHEELER, EMMA ROCHELLE

OXFORD

UNIVERSITY PRESS

OXFORD
UNIVERSITY PRESS

Oxford University Press is a department of the University of Oxford.
It furthers the University's objective of excellence in research, scholarship,
and education by publishing worldwide.

Oxford   New York
Auckland   Cape Town   Dar es Salaam   Hong Kong   Karachi
Kuala Lumpur   Madrid   Melbourne   Mexico City   Nairobi
New Delhi   Shanghai   Taipei   Toronto

With offices in
Argentina   Austria   Brazil   Chile   Czech Republic   France   Greece
Guatemala   Hungary   Italy   Japan   Poland   Portugal   Singapore
South Korea   Switzerland   Thailand   Turkey   Ukraine   Vietnam

Oxford is a registered trademark of Oxford University Press in the UK and certain other countries.

Published in the United States of America by
Oxford University Press
198 Madison Avenue, New York, NY 10016

Library of Congress Cataloging-in-Publication Data
African American national biography / editors in chief Henry Louis Gates Jr., Evelyn Brooks Higginbotham. – 2nd ed.
p. cm.
Includes bibliographical references and index.
ISBN 978-0-19-999036-8 (volume 1; hdbk.); ISBN 978-0-19-999037-5 (volume 2; hdbk.); ISBN 978-0-19-999038-2 (volume 3; hdbk.);
ISBN 978-0-19-999039-9 (volume 4; hdbk.); ISBN 978-0-19-999040-5 (volume 5; hdbk.); ISBN 978-0-19-999041-2 (volume 6; hdbk.);
ISBN 978-0-19-999042-9 (volume 7; hdbk.); ISBN 978-0-19-999043-6 (volume 8; hdbk.); ISBN 978-0-19-999044-3 (volume 9; hdbk.);
ISBN 978-0-19-999045-0 (volume 10; hdbk.); ISBN 978-0-19-999046-7 (volume 11; hdbk.); ISBN 978-0-19-999047-4 (volume 12;
hdbk.); ISBN 978-0-19-992077-8 (12-volume set; hdbk.)
1. African Americans – Biography – Encyclopedias.   2. African Americans – History – Encyclopedias.
I. Gates, Henry Louis.   II. Higginbotham, Evelyn Brooks, 1945-
E185.96.A4466 2012
920'.009296073 – dc23
[B]
2011043281

1 3 5 7 9 8 6 4 2
Printed in the United States of America
on acid-free paper

African American National Biography

Taborn, Earl "Mickey" (21 July 1922–1996), baseball catcher, was born in Carrier Mills, Illinois, the eleventh of twelve children of Joe Dennis Taborn and Mary. A rural settlement in Saline County, Carrier Mills had a population of less than two thousand. Country life was conducive to outdoor activity, and Earl, with plenty of access to playmates, developed his baseball skills in a racially unrestricted climate. His parents were descended from residents of Lake View, a mixed race community where black, Indian, and white heritage were part of nearly everyone's family background. The founders had migrated out of southern states like North Carolina to escape legal restrictions and persecution of free blacks. They established the town after the War of 1812 and built a thriving unsegregated enclave in southern Illinois that was a stop on the Underground Railroad. As a consequence of his unique upbringing, Earl was not adapted to the proscriptions and parameters of Jim Crow society.

Taborn's uncles taught him how to play baseball, and he became so enthralled that he would not come into the house when his family called him for dinner. He began his career in the Negro National League as a catcher with the St. Louis Giants. In the tradition of MOSES FLEETWOOD WALKER, Taborn distinguished his abilities as a receiver. He spent several years stationed in the Philippines with the U.S. Army but left the military to pursue professional baseball. Tabor joined the Kansas City Monarchs in 1946, at the age of twenty-four. The franchise became the longest running in Negro league history.

Established in 1920, the Negro leagues provided a significant outlet for players and spectators. It was where many acclaimed sportsmen got their start. As America's quintessential pastime, however, baseball's segregated leagues were a heartbreak for many African American players who had demonstrated the skills and prowess to be contenders in the big leagues. Discrimination in American sports dimmed the prospects for national recognition of black professional athletes.

The 1940s were some of the most vibrant seasons for the Monarchs, a golden age that produced star players. The decade held several series victories, earning distinction as a dynastic era in which notables like LEROY "SATCHEL" PAIGE and JACKIE ROBINSON were part of its winning club. Taborn became a starting player in his first year and was Paige's catcher when thousands filled the stadium for a glimpse of their feats.

Taborn built his batting average from .205 in his initial season to .345 by 1948. Sports enthusiasts praised the strength of his arm and described his reach as accurate. It was a sign of promise for the young catcher, whose star seemed on the rise in photographs with his friend LIONEL HAMPTON, the famed musician, who was a Monarchs fan. Taborn was surrounded by players whose statistics and gamesmanship became legend in American baseball.

While Robinson broke the color barrier in 1947 as a shortstop with the Brooklyn Dodgers, not all major league teams quickly followed suit. The leagues gradually opened their doors with contract offers to a select number of black players. It meant, however, that only a few blacks obtained recognition. Taborn's years with the Monarchs earned him measured success, and he was picked up during the winter months by the International League. He played for the New York Yankees on a Newark farm team. It became a disappointment, however, when he realized that he was to be a relief player for white players, such as Yogi Berra, who might be injured.

While integration was gradual, the attention of black fans was redirected toward major league teams. As a result, opportunities available in the Negro leagues were diminished. Taborn returned to play for the Monarchs in 1951 but only stayed for a season before being drawn into a wider circuit. Mexico and the Caribbean offered greater exposure throughout the Western Hemisphere for black players. He joined the Mexican leagues and became a celebrity while playing for the Cuadron de la Muerto of Puerto Rico, where one umpire described him as the best catcher he had ever seen. He also played for teams in Veracruz and Panama and was the last player to come from the Negro leagues to Mexico. He encountered a completely different life from the second-class citizenship in America and did not return to the United States until he retired to San Antonio, Texas, in 1961. He died in San Antonio.

Taborn married Aurora Melendez after moving to Mexico City. They had two children. Taborn spent eleven years with Nuevo Laredo, where his batting average reached .314. In 1957 he hit twenty-seven home runs and garnered the record for the most in one year. He was also the lead slugger that year and earned the most home runs in one game in 1961. He was a showman, a charismatic player who satisfied the fans with his acrobatic moves, nearly throwing himself into the mesh as a testament to his efforts to win the game. Mexican baseball had never seen anyone with such batting capabilities and defensive power.

When it was reported that he was part Indian, Taborn was quickly nicknamed "Redskin Taborn" and "El Indio," and he was often mistaken for being Mexican. Because he rarely spoke of his life in the segregated leagues of the United States, his children had little knowledge of his success as a catcher or his African American heritage. His daughter, Rosemary, was often asked whether her father was the great Earl Taborn, which led to a discovery of a scrapbook of memorabilia preserved by one of her aunts. In 2003 Taborn was honored by the Negro Leagues Baseball Museum, which houses an autographed baseball and photos from his career.

FURTHER READING

Negro Leagues Baseball Museum, Earl Taborn Collection. http://www.nlbm.com/NS/ArticleDetail.cfm? ArticleID=17 (2004).

Riley, James A. *The Biographical Encyclopedia of the Negro Baseball Leagues* (2002).

R. ISET ANUAKAN

Takeall, Arthur Oliver (7 Jan. 1947–), ventriloquist, radio personality, and emcee, was the oldest child born to Bertha and Arthur Takeall in Annapolis, Maryland. His father worked at the Navy Experimental Station, and his mother was a homemaker and community activist. Takeall was a sickly child who stuttered and developed rheumatic fever in the seventh grade. To regain strength from his illness, he ran track at Wiley H. Bates High School, the area's all-black school. He also learned ventriloquism to cope with his stutter. Takeall continued to participate in a variety of sports throughout his life and learned karate from U.S. Marine Corps gunning sergeant Howard George. By the time he was seventeen, Takeall had a black belt and gave lessons to others at the nearby white school, Annapolis High School, in 1964. He also held a variety of jobs, including one as a cashier at Dairy Queen, which was an unusual task for a black boy in the 1960s since few blacks worked at the Dairy Queen at this time. People would come into the store often and watch him ring up orders and give customers change. After school, he had a radio program with the local station, WABW, which he got by gaining attention due to his ventriloquism. It was there that he worked with his sidekick, a Howdy Doody puppet that he painted black and called Little Brother. His name was sometimes shortened to Lil' Bro.

Takeall managed to beat the draft to the Vietnam War when in 1965 he joined the U.S. Air Force and became a security police officer. His primary task was to aid PATRICIA ROBERTS HARRIS, appointed by President Lyndon Johnson as ambassador to Luxembourg; she was the first black woman to serve as an ambassador. The job enabled him to wear civilian clothes and travel throughout Europe. Whenever he visited places, such as Cologne, Germany, or Great Britain, he brought Little Brother along and performed at ceremonies. During his time in the air force, his audience included Prince Philip of Great Britain, Ethiopian Emperor Haile Selassie, and Kwame Nkrumah, founder and first president of Ghana, at banquets, dinners, and ceremonies. Each time he ended one performance, Takeall was asked to visit another country and perform. In between shows, he maintained a television program, *Arthur Takeall and Friends*, which, naturally, featured Little Brother, at the Spangdahlem Air Force Base.

After serving five years in the air force and receiving an honorable medical discharge in February 1970, Takeall returned to the United States with a growing reputation as an entertainer. He moved to Knoxville, Tennessee, and was hired at radio station WJBE, which was owned by JAMES BROWN. Takeall began as the noon radio announcer and then advanced to work in several positions at the station: afternoon drive radio announcer, program director, and music director. His connections with associates in the industry, people he met in the service, and associates of Brown at the station only expanded his work as an emcee. Whenever acts came to the state to perform, Takeall would be asked to provide the opening act.

The job with Brown enabled Takeall to move on to several other radio stations, and he appeared in programs in Tennessee (WLOK, 1972–1973), Louisiana (WBOK, 1976–1977), Texas (KAPE, KIXY, 1970), and Washington, D.C. (WOOK, 1974). Takeall was selected as *Billboard* magazine's Radio Personality of the Year Award three times (KIXY, 1970; WJBE-AM, 1971; WBOK-AM, 1977) for his work at Brown's station and his jobs in Louisiana and Texas. While receiving one of his awards, Takeall attracted the attention of the owner of the Las Vegas, Nevada, station KVOV. Takeall was offered a job and he moved to Las Vegas in 1977.

By this time, Takeall had given Little Brother the moniker Scooter, after a young patient at St. Jude Hospital in Memphis. The boy had leukemia, and the staff often referred to him as a "bad motor scooter." Takeall kept the name as an honor to the patient and the hospital. While in Las Vegas, Takeall and Scooter took over the morning program on KVOV. One of their signature acts was waking up celebrities by calling their hotels early in the morning, which often produced humorous results. He remained at KVOV until 1979.

Takeall spent the 1980s traveling the country and performing with Scooter. He returned to New Orleans and was hired as an ambassador to the World's Fair in 1984. The job required additional travel so he could promote and help plan the event. It was in this same period that Brown was sentenced to six years in prison after police accused him of carrying an unlicensed firearm and assaulting a police officer, along with other offenses. Brown's imprisonment was an outrage for many celebrities,

and "Free James Brown" T-shirts were the latest fashion. In 1989, Takeall returned to Baltimore (he had previously worked at WSID in 1974) and visited disc jockey Charles "Chuck" Green, at WEBB, where they spoke about Brown's incarceration. At one point, Takeall believed the microphone was off and began playing a song called "You Got the Right One Baby, Uh-huh." Some of the radio audience called to say that the song should be on a record. Takeall later visited Brown in prison and performed for him and the other inmates. The show included the song.

It was that song that resulted in a long controversy between Takeall and PepsiCo, Inc., since he sang the song in 1989 and Pepsi created the commercial in 1990. Takeall said that the company used his song and lyrics verbatim in a series of Diet Pepsi commercials featuring singer RAY CHARLES. The company also licensed the song to Paramount Pictures and 20th Century Fox, and it appeared on the soundtracks of *Coneheads* and *Rookie of the Year*. Takeall sued the company in 1992, but a federal judge in Baltimore threw out the case. He appealed it all the way to the Supreme Court, which refused to hear it in 1994. Takeall retained a new attorney in 2006, who aimed to prove that Takeall had the rights to the entire twenty-three-word song that encompasses the sentence "you got the right one baby, uh-huh." The American Society of Composers, Authors and Publishers later froze royalties of the song to the writers who used it in the advertising campaign. Takeall owned the copyright to the song.

Although reluctant to discuss his private life, Takeall was a single father with three children. In 2007, he planned to travel to Africa for the Thirst for Water project, Playpumps Systems. This humanitarian effort places pumps similar to merry-go-rounds on the tops of wells in African villages to protect the water from getting infected from mosquitoes and other impurities.

FURTHER READING

Chiu, Donna. "Annapolis Ventriloquist Has a New Legal Battle," *The Capital*, 15 June 2006.
Johnson, Gary. "The Arthur Takeall Interview," *Black Men in America.com*. Available online at www.blackmeninamerica.com/reality.htm.

SHANTEÉ WOODARDS

Talbert, Naomi (3 Mar. 1843–?), prohibitionist, voting rights activist, civil rights activist, writer, and poet, was born Naomi Bowman in Michigan City,

Indiana, as one of three children of Elijah and Guilly Ann Bowman. The Bowmans were free blacks and natives of Ohio. Naomi was raised in Indiana with her parents and siblings. The segregated public schools in Michigan City would not admit black children, so her parents hired a private teacher. At a very early age, Naomi developed a talent for writing poetry. At the age of twelve, she was admitted to a previously all-white public school. There is some indication that when the white parents in the Michigan City community recognized her talents for writing poetry, they agreed to admit her to the public school. Unfortunately, after her mother's death in 1860 Naomi's father decided that further education would not be necessary for his daughters; and when she was seventeen, he ended her schooling.

In 1863 Naomi married William Talbert, a barber from Valparaiso, Indiana. The Talberts were originally from Indiana, but they moved from Valparaiso, Indiana, to Michigan City, Indiana, in order for Talbert to care for an ill sister. Five years later, she moved to Chicago with her father and the rest of her family. During this period Talbert lost her first-born son but celebrated the birth of her second son. In Chicago she and her husband had two more children. Talbert began her temperance work in Chicago with the International Organization of Good Templars (IOGT). The IOGT, founded in Utica, New York, in 1851, endorsed temperance through education and promotion of individual abstinence from drugs and alcohol. From 1869 to 1879 Talbert worked to achieve suffrage rights for women, wrote numerous articles on this subject, and lectured on behalf of women, Christianity, and temperance. Some of her writings were published in the *Chicago Tribune* and the *Dayton Journal*. She was a speaker at the Woman's Rights Convention in 1869 and was known for her candor in condemning racism and sexism. One of her poems entitled "Centennial Poem," published in 1876, stressed that women and blacks should take advantage of their freedom in order to improve their communities and the nation. After her husband became ill, she first worked as a hairdresser and then helped to organize and manage an orphanage for blacks where she eventually became a teacher to support her family. William Talbert died in 1877.

In 1879 Talbert moved with her children and her father to Columbus, Ohio, where she continued to work as a hairdresser. A few years later in 1881 she met and soon married Lewis Anderson, who was employed by a bank and was also a successful financier. When the family moved to Wichita, Kansas, her husband continued to work as a banker, which allowed Talbert to continue to focus her efforts on lobbying for women's rights; in addition, she continued to write poetry, lecture, and support the temperance movement. She opposed segregation even when other influential leaders in the black community, such as BOOKER T. WASHINGTON, believed that segregation was a way to ensure equality for blacks. Talbert actively campaigned against segregation. In Kansas, she promoted the efforts of the women's suffrage movement and the Women's Christian Temperance Union. In the 1880s Talbert discovered that an existing children's home in Wichita excluded black children, so she and other black women began working to establish a home for black orphans. By 1890 the orphanage that she helped to create was operating and receiving city and county stipends for support. In 1892 Talbert successfully lobbied with white suffragists for a suffrage referendum to extend the right to vote to women. She also worked for women's suffrage in California in 1895, but not much more was recorded regarding her life. Furthermore, there is no record of her death.

Talbert was well respected and praised by the educated women with whom she shared a passion for the advancement of women's rights and empowerment, including Susan B. Anthony. Early in her life she worked tirelessly to provide homes for black children. She most assuredly had the distinction of being a pioneer in defending children's rights and one of a long line of civil rights activists in the United States. She was also the first female civil rights activist.

FURTHER READING

Majors, Monroe A. *Noted Negro Women* (1893).
Smith, Jessie Carney, ed. *Notable Black American Women Book II* (1996).

GREER C. BOSWORTH

Talbot, Gerald "Jerry" Edgerton (28 Oct. 1931–),
activist, black history collector, and first elected black state legislator in Maine, was born in Bangor, Maine to Arvella (McIntyre) and Wilmot Edgerton Talbot. He is the oldest of their six children.

Talbot's mother was a caterer in Bangor and his father had a long career as head chef at the Bangor House, one of Maine's premier restaurants in the mid-1900s.

Gerald E. Talbot is an eighth-generation Mainer. His paternal ancestors migrated to Maine from

Bridgewater, Massachusetts, in the late eighteenth century, and at least one, Abraham Talbot, served in the American Revolutionary War. He owned a brickyard in China, Maine, where a family cemetery in the woods was uncovered in the 1970s.

Talbot's maternal ancestors have deep roots in New Brunswick, Canada, as did the majority of black families in Bangor. The migration from New Brunswick to Bangor began in the late nineteenth century and, along with black settlers from various Atlantic rim ports, produced a vibrant, visible black community, which began thinning out after World War II. Talbot's "Bangor, My Home Town," in the 2006 book *Maine's Visible Black History*, is the authoritative written description of Bangor's black community in its heyday, when he was growing up and known as "Timber." He wrote about the black families, their names and occupations, and the most influential black institution in Bangor—the Columbia Street Community Center (CSCC). During and after World War II, CSCC provided avenues of culture, education, and sports for their people who had been marginalized because of their color. Talbot and other blacks in Bangor credit CSCC and their families, most of whom owned their own homes, for their sense of self-worth and their success.

Talbot's resume is filled with a lifetime of achievements and numerous honors, including an Honorary Doctorate of Humane Letters from the University of Southern Maine (USM) in 1995; but he is proudest of his graduation from Bangor High School. A 2 March 1988 editorial in Brewer, Maine's, *The Register* focused on Talbot's loyalty to Bangor, thirty-five years after he had moved away, and his pivotal part in JESSE JACKSON's presidential campaign:

> Jackson has got to give Talbot credit for much of his success in Maine. Talbot, the kid that pulled himself up by the bootstraps, served in the Maine legislature and hasn't forgotten his roots or the friends he used to scuffle with in his boyhood.

Talbot moved to Portland, Maine, in 1953, served in the U.S. Army, and married Anita

Gerald "Jerry" Talbot, black historian and Maine politician, in a 2002 photo. (Doug Jones/*The Portland Press Herald*.)

Joan Cummings in 1956. Anita Talbot came from a long-standing black Portland family that worked for the railroads. She and Gerald had four daughters. "A minority in a minority," he laughs at himself. Talbot is known for his humor, fairness, tenacity, reconciliation skills, and storytelling.

After numerous occupations Talbot became a printing compositor for Guy Gannett Company in Portland, where he worked for twenty-five years. During that time he researched his family history, collected black history artifacts, and developed an active consciousness about racial discrimination and the disenfranchisement of many other groups of people in Maine, such as Native Americans, economically poor people, and gays and lesbians.

In 1964 he was elected president of the newly reformulated Portland chapter of the National Association for the Advancement of Colored People (NAACP), a year after his participation in the 1963 "March on Washington" when he heard and heeded Dr. MARTIN LUTHER KING JR.'s speech. In 1965 he participated in the Voter Registration Drive in Laurel, Mississippi, and in 1967 he led the Portland NAACP chapter in hosting the New England Regional NAACP in Portland. He was its vice president in 1971 and inducted into its New England Civil Rights Hall of Fame in 2009.

Talbot was catapulted into a Maine leadership role that took on Fair Housing and led to the formation of the Maine Human Rights Commission in 1971. He continued as president of the Portland NAACP intermittently until 1980.

In 1972 Talbot broke the "whites only" barrier in the Maine State Legislature and became its first elected black member. He served for six years in the House of Representatives, being elected three times for the two-year terms. Talbot educated the legislature about minorities, whether racial or low income. He was the first black to chair the legislature's Human Resources Committee. His signal legislation, passed in 1977, outlawed the use of offensive names, specifically derived from the word Negro, on maps and to designate geographic features and places. This landmark legislation has been a model for abolishing other offensive naming practices in Maine and throughout the country.

Talbot was appointed to the Maine State Board of Education by Governor Joseph E. Brennan from 1979 to 1984 and was elected by the board as its president in 1984. He has been on the governing boards of Maine Vocational Technical Institutes, the Edmund S. Muskie Institute of Public Affairs, and the University of New England. In the 1990s Talbot was an AARP Minority Affairs national spokesman and in the late 1990s he was chair of the Maine Advisory Committee to the U.S. Commission on Civil Rights.

In 1980 he established Black Education and Cultural History, Inc. (BEACH), which sponsored educational scholarships and workshops and conferences on racism and interracial marriages and adoptions. BEACH published "Twenty Years, Portland, Branch NAACP, 1964–84," and in 1992 it sponsored "A Tribute to Black Women of Maine" to honor ten outstanding women.

Talbot took his collection of black history all over Maine and into New Hampshire and spoke to student classes and community groups. Gerald and Anita Talbot donated his collection to USM in 1995. This extensive donation started the African American Collection of Maine and was the impetus for USM to establish a diversity center. In 2006 USM named an auditorium the Gerald E. Talbot Lecture Hall.

In 1999 he and H. H. Price formed Visible Black History, a partnership for producing educational materials on black history in Maine, including published articles, a web site (http://www.visibleblackhistory.com), and the first comprehensive book on the subject, *Maine's Visible Black History*, in 2006.

FURTHER READING

The Gerald E. Talbot Collection is housed in the African American Collection of Maine, Jean Byers Sampson Center for Diversity in Maine, University of Southern Maine, Portland, Maine.

Barry, William David. "Gerald Talbot, 67" in "The Ten Most Intriguing People in Maine," *Portland* (November 1998).

Hoose, Shoshana. "Proud Roots: Tracing the Talbot Family in Maine," *Maine Sunday Telegram* (17 & 24 February 1991).

Hoose, Shoshana, and Karine Odlin, producers of documentary video on Maine black history. *Anchor of the Soul* (1994).

Lee, Maureen Elgersman. *Black Bangor: African Americans in a Maine Community, 1880–1950* (2006).

Price, H. H., and Gerald E. Talbot. *Maine's Visible Black History: The First Chronicle of Its People* (2006).

H. H. PRICE

Talley, André Leon (16 Oct. 1948–), journalist, was born in Washington, D.C., the son of William Carroll Talley, a printing press operator at the U.S. Patent Office by day and a taxicab driver by night, and Alma Ruth Davis. In December 1948 Talley's parents took their infant son to the home of his maternal grandmother, Bennie Frances Davis, in Durham, North Carolina. The couple returned to the nation's capital, and Talley remained in Durham, where he was raised by his grandmother. Davis, who was born in 1898, cleaned dormitory rooms at Duke University each weekday until she was sixty-five and also took care of her mother, China Roberson, until the latter died in 1960. William and Alma Talley eventually divorced. Talley attended three segregated schools in Durham, Lyon Park Elementary, Whitted Junior High, and Hillside High. At Whitted, Talley especially enjoyed his French classes, where his teacher, Cynthia Smith, instilled a love of French language and culture in him. While attending Hillside, Talley worked as a student librarian. In addition to school and books, Talley's formative years centered around family, church, periodicals, and music. He cherished his home life with his grandmother, biannual trips to Washington with her to visit his parents and shop at the department stores, summers at his father's

home in Washington, and other relatives' visits to his grandmother's home during holidays and various family events. Talley, who was baptized when he was twelve or thirteen, attended church regularly with his grandmother. On Sundays, after church and dinner, he walked to Duke University, where he purchased the *New York Times* as well as the American and French editions of *Vogue* magazine. After perusing the periodicals, he clipped pictures from them and tacked them on each wall of a spare room that he referred to as his inner sanctum. The room reflected Talley's goal of pursuing a career as a fashion editor at a magazine. Inspired by the images of the African American models NAOMI SIMS and Pat Cleveland in the pages of *Vogue*, he realized that blacks could have careers in the fashion world. When he had money leftover after buying periodicals each week, he purchased music by Motown recording artists.

After graduating from Hillside High, Talley attended North Carolina Central University in Durham, and each summer of his undergraduate

André Leon Talley backstage at the W Lounge during Olympus New York Fashion Week, held in Bryant Park, New York City, 9 February 2005. (AP Images.)

career he worked in Washington, D.C., as a park ranger at the Lincoln Memorial and other sites. He planned to teach and majored in French. One of his professors was Irene Jackson, the mother of MAYNARD HOLBROOK JACKSON JR., Atlanta's first African American mayor. Talley heeded Irene Jackson's advice to apply to Brown University's graduate school and was awarded a full scholarship to pursue a Ph.D. in French Studies there after his graduation from North Carolina Central University in 1971. While matriculating at Brown, Talley participated in the university's student exchange program with the Rhode Island School of Design, completed at least one course there, and was a fashion and gossip columnist for the Rhode Island School of Design's newspaper. At Brown he wrote a thesis titled "North African Figures in Nineteenth Century French Painting and Prose" and earned a master's degree in 1973. Although Talley subsequently enrolled in doctoral courses, he abandoned academe for the fashion industry in New York.

Talley's entry into the world of fashion was via a volunteer position at the Metropolitan Museum of Art's Costume Institute, where his assistance in preparing the exhibit Romantic and Glamorous Hollywood Design impressed Diana Vreeland, director of the institute. In 1975 Talley worked temporarily as a receptionist at an animal shelter until Vreeland, who had served as Vogue's editor in chief from 1963 to 1971, recommended him for a job at Andy Warhol's magazine Interview. Talley, who had contributed occasional items to "Small Talk," Interview's fashion and society column, was hired as a typist and receptionist for the magazine, and he continued to contribute to the column. One month later he was promoted to Interview's fashion editor. In August 1975 he left Interview to work as an accessories marketing editor for Women's Wear Daily. Less than two years later he was appointed the publication's Paris fashion editor before becoming its Paris bureau chief. Talley's tenure at Vogue began in 1983, when he was hired as the magazine's fashion news director, a position he held until he was appointed Vogue's creative director in 1988, the same year that Anna Wintour became editor in chief at the magazine. Talley left Vogue in 1995 and lived in Paris until his 1998 return to Vogue as editor at large to create "Stylefax," a column later retitled "Life with André." Over the years Talley used his influence to advocate greater visibility for African American models on magazine covers and in fashion shows and to promote African American fashion designers.

The 1989 deaths of his grandmother and Vreeland, the two most influential individuals in Talley's life, led him to write his first book, A.L.T. (2003), his autobiographical tribute to the grandmother who raised him and the friend who mentored him. A.L.T. also pays homage to his father, who worked two jobs to help support his son and who died in 1993. Talley's father was the inspiration for A.L.T. 365+ (2005), which commemorates Talley's years as a prolific photographer and is a collection of his celebrity photographs.

Talley received the 2003 Council of Fashion Designers of America Eugenia Sheppard Award for Excellence in Fashion Journalism. In addition the Savannah College of Art and Design established the André Leon Talley Lifetime Achievement Award, and he served on the college's board of trustees. Talley was also a member of Abyssinian Baptist Church in Harlem and was recognized as Abyssinian's largest individual contributor.

After the 1970s Talley, a self-described raconteur, enjoyed extraordinary success as a print journalist. As an arbiter of style and a fashion icon, he became the most prominent African American in the fashion industry.

FURTHER READING

Talley, André Leon. A.L.T: A Memoir (2003).
"Andre Leon Talley," Current Biography Yearbook (2003).
Henderson, Ashyia N., ed. "André Leon Talley," Contemporary Black Biography, vol. 56 (2006).

LINDA M. CARTER

Tampa Red (1900/1904?–19 Mar. 1981), blues singer and guitarist, was born Hudson Woodbridge in Smithville, Georgia, the son of John Woodbridge and Elizabeth Whittaker. His parents died when he was a child, and he was raised by his maternal grandmother in Tampa, Florida, eventually taking her last name, Whittaker. Perhaps inspired by an older brother who played guitar, he learned his own guitar style early, favoring an open-E tuning—called "sebastapol"—and playing with a slide. Already proficient in his teens, he began playing whenever and wherever he could make money, first in Florida, then Mississippi, Arkansas, Missouri, and Illinois. By 1925, however, he had made his way to Chicago.

In Chicago he often worked the streets alone, dazzling passersby with his instrumental dexterity. Eventually he teamed up with the piano player THOMAS ANDREW DORSEY, known as "Georgia Tom." By that time, Whittaker also had a nom de blues, "Tampa Red." Piano-guitar duets were popular in the late 1920s and 1930s, epitomized by the collaboration between LEROY CARR and Scrapper Blackwell, but Tampa Red's slide guitar gave his duets with Georgia Tom a new and distinctive sound. After a brief association with Paramount Records and the vocalist MA RAINEY, Tampa Red and Georgia Tom jumped to the Vocalion label and hit the big time with a 1928 novelty song, "It's Tight Like That." The double-entendre tune took the country by storm, becoming one of the biggest hits of the late 1920s and early 1930s and creating a new pop genre dubbed "hokum." While the successful duo continued to collaborate on numerous recordings, Tampa Red also recorded solo as "Tampa Red the Guitar Wizard," ultimately participating on over eighty Vocalion issues. After a tour on the vaudeville circuit in 1928 and 1929, Tampa Red and Georgia Tom returned to work in Chicago, but their partnership ended around 1932 when Dorsey decided to pursue gospel music.

After Dorsey's defection, Tampa Red, until then a heavy drinker and ardent womanizer who was "married" perhaps a dozen times, settled down with a wife, Frances (maiden name unknown), who became his business manager and partner, providing stability for his career until her death. He also entered a two-decade association with RCA Victor's Bluebird label and Lester Melrose, Chicago's most influential blues A&R man. The Bluebird-RCA tenure, spanning from 1934 to 1953, proved as successful as the Vocalion years. With a style that was becoming more and more urbane, Tampa Red was one of the label's most prolific artists, especially in the 1930s and 1940s, working alone or with a pianist, and after 1936, with a larger group known as Tampa Red and Chicago Five. He continued to produce hits, including the 1942 hokum tunes "Let Me Play with Your Poodle" and "She Wants to Sell My Monkey."

Through the late 1930s and 1940s Tampa Red continuously worked the Chicago club circuit, sometimes solo, sometimes with other artists, among them the guitarists BIG BILL BROONZY and Willie B. James and the pianists Joshua Altheimer, Black Bob (Hudson), and Big Maceo. Starting in the late 1930s Tampa Red also had a nine-year job as the resident artist at a club just across the street from his South Side apartment. The apartment had become a blues landmark—a rehearsal hall, community kitchen, and gathering place for musicians, particularly newcomers from the South who needed an introduction to Chicago. The guitarist BIG JOE WILLIAMS went

so far as to claim that every blues artist who came to Chicago stayed with Tampa Red and Frances, or "Mrs. Tampa," as she was affectionately known. Even the settled artists like Broonzy, MEMPHIS MINNIE, JOHN LEE "SONNY BOY" WILLIAMSON, ROOSEVELT SYKES, LIL GREEN, ARTHUR CRUDUP, or WILLIE DIXON visited to socialize, audition, or rehearse. As Dixon portrayed it in his autobiography, "Lester Melrose would be drinking all the time and Tampa Red's wife would be cooking chicken and we'd be having a ball" (61).

Through the 1940s Tampa Red worked with the pianists BLIND JOHN DAVIS and Johnnie Jones, the bassist Ransom Knowling, and the drummer Odie Payne. In the late 1940s he became less active in club work but continued to record, even scoring a hit in 1949 with his composition "When Things Go Wrong with You (It Hurts Me Too)." His final two sessions for RCA Victor came in 1953 and included the harmonica players Sonny Boy Williamson No. 2 and WALTER HORTON and the guitarist Willie Lacy. These recordings were solidly in the 1950s Chicago electric mode, showing his ability to keep up with changing times (at least in the recording studio).

In 1954, after Frances died, a grieving Tampa Red began to drink excessively and was eventually hospitalized for an alcohol related nervous breakdown. He later recorded albums aimed at the blues-revival audience and performed in California in 1961, but alcohol-related tremors had affected his playing and he showed little interest in making a comeback. Although he was visited by his old music cronies and talked with various blues researchers, he spent the last years of his life in relative seclusion, first in the care of a companion, Effie Tolbert, then, after she died in 1974, in nursing homes. He died in Chicago's Central Nursing Home. He was inducted into the Blues Hall of Fame in Memphis the year he died.

For over a quarter century, Tampa Red was one of Chicago's most popular blues artists, cutting more records than any other artist of his era, with the possible exception of Big Bill Broonzy. Critics generally concurred that he was the finest slide guitarist of his time, possibly of all time, with an incredibly precise touch and pure tone. He was also one of the most influential, putting his stamp on the work of ELMORE JAMES and ROBERT NIGHTHAWK, among others. Moreover, he was a gifted songwriter whose best compositions—"When Things Go Wrong with You," "Anna Lou Blues," "Black Angel Blues," and "Love (Her) with a Feeling"—became standards. Although he recorded and performed for the African American market throughout his career, his compositions crossed racial and genre lines, even showing up in the repertoires of western swing artists like Bob Wills and Milton Brown.

Famous in his early days as the man with the gold guitar, playing an expensive National Tri-plate steel-body guitar, he was one of the first artists in Chicago to switch to an electric guitar, possibly as early as 1938. Finally, he was a friend to countless musicians who shared his table, his home, and his good will. As his friend and fishing partner Broonzy wrote in a 1964 autobiography, "There's only one Tampa Red and when he's dead, that's all, brother" (116).

FURTHER READING
Broonzy, William. *Big Bill Blues: Big Bill Broonzy's Story As Told to Yannick Bruynoghe* (1964).
Dixon, Willie, and Don Snowden. *I Am the Blues: The Willie Dixon Story* (1989).
Sheldon Harris. *Blues Who's Who: A Biographical Dictionary of Blues Singers* (1989).
This entry is taken from the *American National Biography* and is published here with the permission of the American Council of Learned Societies.

BILL MCCULLOCH AND
BARRY LEE PEARSON

Tandy, Vertner Woodson (17 May 1885–7 Nov. 1949), New York State's first registered African American architect and the most celebrated black architect in New York City during the Harlem Renaissance, was born Vertner Woodson Tandy in Lexington, Kentucky, the son of Emma Brice and Henry A. Tandy. Although his father was a very successful contractor, the young Tandy was more interested in the design of buildings.

In 1902, Tandy attended Tuskegee Institute in Alabama, where he studied architecture. Tuskegee first offered architectural courses in its mechanical industries department in 1892 following BOOKER T. WASHINGTON's recruitment of black MIT graduate ROBERT R. TAYLOR. Tandy received his certificate in architecture in 1905. He also served on the faculty before leaving. Tandy then relocated from Alabama to Ithaca, New York, where he attended Cornell University in the architecture program. In 1906, he and six friends (known today as the Seven Jewels) started the first black Greek letter college fraternity Alpha Phi Alpha. Tandy was also that organization's first treasurer and the designer of its fraternity pin. Throughout his life, he remained actively involved

in the operations and growth of the fraternity. In 1908, Tandy completed his architectural studies at Cornell and moved to New York City.

Black architectural firms were just coming into existence. Three black architectural firms, all established by former Tuskegee graduates, opened between 1901 and 1906 in other cities. Tandy began his practice in 1908 when he set up his office in New York City. In collaboration with George Washington Foster Jr., the second black architect to be licensed in New Jersey, the office of Tandy & Foster Architects was born. At the time that Tandy opened his office in what is now considered midtown Manhattan, the area was the home to thousands of black families, many living in substandard conditions. African Americans were looking to northern Manhattan for better housing. The move to Harlem was just beginning.

Founded in 1818, St. Philip's Church was one of the wealthiest black New York churches and had been the first black organization to purchase residential property in Harlem. St. Philip's hired Tandy & Foster Architects to design their new church in Harlem, which began construction in 1910. The church, a neo-Gothic styled structure on West 134th Street, is today a New York City landmark and on the New York State and National Register of Historical Places.

In 1912, Tandy married Sadie Hale Dorsette, a public school teacher who graduated from New York's Barnard and Columbia Teacher's College. They had one son, Vertner Tandy Jr. They were considered among the most prominent families who lived in Harlem's Striver's Row area.

In 1915 (after his collaboration with Foster had ended), Tandy transformed two existing rowhouses into MADAME C. J. WALKER's grand Harlem townhouse (since demolished). Walker, a wealthy black businesswoman who had made her fortune in hair care products, also had Tandy design a thirty-four-room mansion for her in Irvington-on-the-Hudson, New York. Built in 1917, the Villa le Waro Mansion was considered at the time America's grandest black-owned house. The mansion is also on the National Register of Historical Places. Tandy designed schools throughout the country, including Webster Hall at the Chandler Normal School, the school he attended as a child in Lexington, Kentucky.

Tandy was involved in various other aspects of Harlem life. A state regiment was formed in Harlem, making it the first black militia in the state. After the declaration of World War I, the Fifteenth Regiment became a part of the New York State

Villa Lewaro, the residence of famous black entrepreneur and millionaire Madame C.J. Walker. Designed by architect Vertner Woodson Tandy in 1918, the house was built in Irvington-on-Hudson, Westchester County, New York. (Library of Congress/ Historic American Buildings Survey, Prints and Photographs Division.)

National Guard as the only regiment with black officers (it later became the 369th Regiment). Tandy was the first African American to pass the commissioning exam and was made First Lieutenant. The unit was shipped out to France in 1917 and returned in 1919 as heroes.

As Harlem's premier architect, Tandy designed several of the most popular buildings of the period. In 1919, Tandy designed MAMIE SMITH's Garden of Joy, a large, open-air nightclub where its famous singer/owner regularly appeared (the site was razed in 1923 to make way for the Renaissance Ballroom). Tandy designed the Imperial Elk's Lodge built in 1924 at 150 West 129th Street. Meetings organized there led to the formation of A. PHILIP RANDOLPH's Brotherhood of Sleeping Car Porters.

Although Tandy worked with and hired white associates and draftsmen, he was an important mentor and employer of black talent. John L. Wilson, who was later licensed and started an architectural practice in Harlem, worked at Tandy's office from 1924 to 1926. Tandy also employed and mentored HILYARD ROBINSON, who went on to become a very prominent black architect in Washington, D.C. In 1935, Hilyard Robinson, who headed the planning team for Washington, D.C.'s, first large-scale, low-income housing project, Langston Terrace, invited Tandy to become a part of that team.

Tandy's volume of new building design work decreased dramatically during the Depression, with much of his work consisting of alterations to existing brownstones and small commercial buildings. In 1945, Tandy was one of the architects, along with architect Edwin Forbes and the architectural firm of Skidmore Owings Merrill, who designed the Abraham Lincoln Houses, a large low-income housing development built in Harlem.

Vertner Tandy died in 1949, before completion of the construction of his most modern design—the Ivy Delph Terrace Apartments at 19 Hamilton Terrace. This notable six-story apartment building was built for Dr. Delph and his wife, an African

American couple, who wanted to develop environmentally friendly housing for African American families. This Tandy building is also on the National Register of Historical Places.

Tandy was sixty-four years old at the time of his death. The funeral, which was held at St. Philip's Church, was followed by a three-volley salute by the New York National Guard.

FURTHER READING

Mitchell, Melvin L. *The Crisis of the African-American Architect: Conflicting Cultures of Architecture and (Black) Power* (2002).

Wesley, Charles H. *History of Alpha Phi Alpha: A Development in Negro College Life* (2000).

ROBERTA WASHINGTON

Tanner, Alethia (?–1864), grocer and community leader, was born Alethia Browning in the late eighteenth century in Maryland to parents whose names are unknown. No information is available about her early life. Referred to alternatively as Aletha, Lithe, Lethee, or, most commonly, Lethe, Browning grew up enslaved in southern Maryland and first appears in the historical record at the time of her manumission by Joseph Daugherty in Washington, D.C. In July 1810 Daugherty had paid Rachel Pratt of Prince George's County, Maryland, $275 for Browning, manumitting her four days later "for value received and other good causes" (Provine, 154). Subsequent histories refer to the $275 payment to Pratt as a deposit toward the sum of $1,400 that the whitewoman demanded in return for Browning's freedom. Browning made the payments herself with money earned through independent work in Washington, D.C.

Rachel Pratt, the mother of the Maryland governor and U.S. senator Thomas George Pratt, also owned Browning's two sisters, Laurana and Sophia Browning, their children, and grandchildren. Sophia Browning ran a market stand in Alexandria, Virginia. She saved over $400, enough money to purchase the freedom of her husband, George F. Bell, who was enslaved on a neighboring estate. Bell in turn purchased his wife's freedom for five dollars in 1809 and the couple worked over the next several years to free their remaining children from Pratt. In 1807 Bell and three other former slaves established the first school for black children in Washington.

Perhaps drawing inspiration from the success of her sister Sophia, Alethia Browning opened her own grocery stand in the District of Columbia while still enslaved by Pratt. The stand earned her the money necessary to purchase her own freedom. Situated on the periphery of the President's Park (later Lafayette Square), the stand's central location and proximity to the White House also allowed her to forge connections with the capital's elite. Tradition cites Thomas Jefferson as both a customer and sometime employer of Tanner during his tenure at the White House, and Senator Richard M. Johnson served as a witness for her manumission of her sister and nephews. Most importantly, the business allowed Browning to achieve the financial wherewithal needed to rescue over twenty people from enslavement.

At some point following her emancipation, Browning apparently married and took the surname Tanner. City directories from the 1860s listed her as the widow of Jeremiah, but no further information exists about her husband. It does not appear that she had any children.

Tanner began the process of emancipating her family about fifteen years after her own manumission. She began by purchasing the freedom of her older sister Laurana Browning Cook and her children and grandchildren. It took Tanner over a decade to complete the purchase of the entire Cook family. In 1826 she paid Rachel Pratt $1,450 for Laurana Cook and five of her children. Two years later she purchased the remaining Cook family, paying, according to some estimates, a total of approximately $5,300 for her sister, her ten children, and five grandchildren. Between 1845 and 1846 Tanner also procured the freedom of at least thirteen other individuals between the ages of one and forty, including a number of her neighbors, Lotty Riggs and her four children, Charlotte Davis, and John Butler, who became a prominent Methodist minister.

Washington's population of free blacks in the early nineteenth century was an unusually resilient and cohesive community that built businesses, churches, and schools in the developing city. Having grown from 2,549 in 1810 to 11,131 by 1860, the city's free black population far outpaced the number of slaves in the city. The opportunities available to Tanner in Washington allowed her to continue her efforts on behalf of her family in the years following their emancipation.

The Cooks in particular emerged as one of Washington's most successful and respected families. Tanner paid twelve and a half cents per month for her nephew JOHN FRANCIS COOK SR. to attend the Columbia Institute. In 1834 Cook assumed leadership of the school (later called Union Seminary), which eventually became the city's largest black school. Cook became a pioneering Washington, D.C., clergyman. After his death in 1855 Cook's sons continued the direction of the Union Seminary; one son, GEORGE F. T. COOK, eventually became superintendent of Colored Public Schools of Washington and Georgetown, a position he held from 1868 to 1900. JOHN FRANCIS COOK JR. became a prominent businessman and public official.

Tanner continued to operate her grocery until at least 1853, when she last appeared in the city directories under that occupation. A mainstay of her community, Tanner became a founding member of the Union Bethel Church (later the Metropolitan AME Church), a church organized by slaves and former slaves in Washington, and her involvement in African Methodism earned her reverence as "the mother of the Church." She and brother-in-law George Bell eventually rescued the church from foreclosure, providing personal backing to pay for the property when it was put up for auction.

At least as early as 1847 Tanner owned a frame house located near the White House on the corner of Fourteenth and H Streets, N.W., where by 1850 she resided with Henrietta Reed, listed in that year's census as an eleven-year-old mulatto. The 1860 census suggests that Reed probably remained with Tanner for an extended period—it lists an unnamed person between ages ten and twenty-four as a member of Tanner's household. This individual may be the same Henrietta who later married Tanner's nephew Thomas Cook.

Tanner composed a will on 15 May 1847. The document's shaky signature suggests that she could at the very least write her name. She bequeathed her house, along with her bed and bedding, to Thomas Cook. By the time of her death in 1864 she had outlived the two executors of her will, John Francis Cook Sr. and Francis Dutcher. Her grandnephew John F. Cook Jr. filed the will; he and his brother Joseph Tanner Cook inherited the remainder of Tanner's estate. Two years following Tanner's death, Washington's commissioner of education, Henry Bernard, remembered her in a report to the U.S. Congress. In addressing the state of African American education in the District of Columbia, Bernard hailed Tanner as a woman "whose force of character and philanthropy gave her remarkable prominence here and elsewhere among her race, who commanded the respect of all who knew her" (Bernard, *Report on Schools of the Colored Population*, House Ex. Doc 315, 41st Congress, 2nd Session (1869–70), 197).

FURTHER READING
The papers of the Cook family are held by the Moorland-Spingarn Research Center, Howard University, Washington, D.C.

Corrigan, Mary Beth. "The Ties That Bind: The Pursuit of Community and Freedom among Slaves and Free Blacks in the District of Columbia." In *Southern City, National Ambition*, ed. Howard Gillette (1995).

Green, Constance McLaughlin. *The Secret City: A History of Race Relations in the Nation's Capital* (1967).

Fitzpatrick, Sandra, and Maria R. Goodwin. *The Guide to Black Washington* (1990).

Wayman, Alexander. *Cyclopedia of African Methodism* (1882).

CARLA JONES

Tanner, Benjamin Tucker (25 Dec. 1835–15 Jan. 1923), African Methodist Episcopal (AME) bishop, was born in Pittsburgh, Pennsylvania, the son of Hugh S. Tanner and Isabel (maiden name unknown). Straitened circumstances forced him to support himself as a part-time barber while studying at Avery College in Allegheny City (now Pittsburgh), Pennsylvania, from 1852 to 1857. But in 1856 his life took a new direction when he converted to Methodism and received a license to preach. He trained at Allegheny and Western Theological Seminary for three years and in 1860 was ordained both deacon and elder in the AME Church. Unable to afford travel expenses to an appointment in Sacramento, California, he served instead as a substitute minister at a Presbyterian church in Washington, D.C. In 1858 he married Sarah Elizabeth Miller; they had seven children, the most famous of whom was HENRY OSSAWA TANNER, who became a painter of international renown.

During the Civil War, Tanner ministered to freedmen in the U.S. Navy. He founded the Alexander Mission on E Street in 1862, the same year he was accepted into the AME Baltimore Conference. Thereafter he was appointed minister to churches in Georgetown (1863–1866) and Baltimore (1866–1867). In 1867 he became principal of the AME school in Frederick, Maryland, and published his first book, *An Apology for African Methodism*, a study of AME beliefs and polity. In 1868 the General Conference made him its chief secretary and editor of its journal, the *Christian Recorder*. He labored for sixteen years in Washington, D.C., in that capacity, developing a large readership and building a distinguished literary career through terse, forceful writing. In 1884 he helped found and served as first editor of the *AME Church Review* quarterly.

In 1888 Tanner was elected bishop by the General Conference. During his first quadrennial assignment as bishop, he supervised AME activities in Canada, Bermuda, and the West Indies. Thereafter he resided primarily in the Northeast, working diligently among constituents in New England, New York, New Jersey, and eastern Pennsylvania. He urged members everywhere to remain loyal to the church because of the strength that it provided. African Americans had risen out of slavery, he reminded listeners, and they still faced a thousand forms of discrimination in their own day. In such conditions only Christian truth gave AME adherents true freedom; the church was God's instrument for producing good works that would endure. He encouraged members to see that the communion and love found within the church gave people the power to overcome human suffering and social ills. In this way he was an early advocate of black unity and self-help.

Tanner took interest in other denominations and in ways of cooperating with them. In 1901 he attended the Third Ecumenical Methodist Conference in London, England, and presented a paper titled "The Elements of Pulpit Eloquence." As early as 1892 he had begun working with other bishops in attempts to unite major black churches. In 1908 he participated in the first Tri-Council of Colored Methodist Bishops, a meeting of representatives from his own denomination, the AME Zion Church, and the Colored ME Church. This black counterpart to the National Council of Churches, founded the same year, allowed for much more cooperation in providing standard hymnals, catechisms, and other liturgical aids. Turner did not succeed in persuading the three groups to merge into a single ecclesiastical body, but he did heighten their commitment to better the social conditions of black citizens while simultaneously meeting their spiritual needs. In 1908 he retired on half pay, the first in his denomination to receive an Episcopal pension. After fifteen more years of occasional preaching and writing, he died in Philadelphia. Tanner's book-length publications include *The Negro's Origin; or, Is He Cursed of God?* (1869), *An Outline of Our History and Government for African Methodist Churchmen* (1884), *Theological Lectures* (1894), and *The Dispensations in the History of the Church, and the Interregnum* (2 vols., 1898, 1899).

FURTHER READING

Seraile, William. *Fire in His Heart: Bishop Benjamin Tucker Tanner and the A.M.E. Church* (1999)

Obituaries: *New York Times* and *Philadelphia Public Leader*, 16 Jan. 1923.

This entry is taken from the *American National Biography* and is published here with the permission of the American Council of Learned Societies.

HENRY WARNER BOWDEN

Tanner, Henry Ossawa (21 June 1859–25 May 1937), painter and draughtsman, was born in Pittsburgh, Pennsylvania, the son of BENJAMIN TUCKER TANNER, a bishop of the African Methodist Episcopal Church and editor of the *Christian Recorder*, and Sarah Miller. Tanner's parents were strong civil rights advocates; his middle name, Ossawa, was a tribute to the abolitionist John Brown of Osawatomie.

The Tanner family moved in 1868 to Philadelphia, where Henry saw an artist at work in Fairmont Park and "decided on the spot" to become one. His mother encouraged this ambition although his father apprenticed him in the flour business after he graduated valedictorian of the Roberts Vaux Consolidated School for Colored Students in 1877. The latter work proved too strenuous for Tanner, and he became ill. After a convalescence in the Adirondacks, near John Brown's farm, in 1879 he entered the Pennsylvania Academy of Fine Arts and studied under Thomas Eakins and Thomas Hovenden, his mentor. At the academy the illustrator Joseph Pennell and a group of his friends heaped racial abuse on Tanner, who would not be deterred from his goal, because the academy was "where I had every right to be."

Tanner's professional career began while he was still a student. He made his debut at the Pennsylvania Academy Annual Exhibition in 1880. During this period he specialized in seascape painting, such as *Hazy Morning at Narragansett* (c. 1880; Washington, D.C., private collection), while also rendering memories of his Adirondack sojourn as evinced by *Burnt Pines-Adirondacks* (c. 1880; Hampton University Museum). His tendency toward using overlapping shapes and diagonal lines to render recession into space was announced in these works and can be seen over the whole of Tanner's career. Also, the rich browns, blues, blue-greens, and mauves, with accents of bright red, in the palettes of these pictures remained constant in the artist's oeuvre.

During the mid-1880s Tanner decided to become an animal painter, because they were less numerous than marine painters. A superb example of this genre is *Lion Licking His Paw* (1886; Allentown Art Museum). His unlocated picture of an elk attacked by wolves, shown at the World's Industrial and Cotton Centennial Exhibition at New Orleans in 1884, prompted the Reverend WILLIAM J. SIMMONS to conclude in his book *Men of Mark* (1887): "His pictures take high rank.... [Do not] think he is patronized ... through the influence of his father, or because someone takes pity on him, trying to help a colored man to rise. No! It is merit" (185). In addition to easel paintings Tanner provided illustrations for the July 1882 issue of *Our Continent* and the 10 January 1888 issue of *Harper's Young People*.

In 1889 Tanner opened a photography studio in Atlanta, Georgia. After it failed, he taught drawing at Clark College in Atlanta, where he met Bishop and Mrs. Joseph Crane Hartzell, who arranged Tanner's first solo exhibition in Cincinnati in 1890 to help him raise funds for European study. Tanner set sail on 4 January 1891 for Rome, but after arriving in Paris, he decided to remain there and enrolled in the Académie Julian, where his teachers were Jean-Paul Laurens and Jean-Joseph Benjamin-Constant. Tanner was also influenced by the painter Arthur Fitzwilliam Tait, whose work Tanner had encountered while convalescing in the Adirondacks. He was affected by the works of the artists in the circle of Paul Gauguin at Brittany in the early 1890s and later by the art of Diego Velazquez and El Greco. Tanner did not, however, become an imitator of any of these artists' styles. Tanner made Paris and Trépied, France, his permanent homes for the remainder of his life, although he visited the United States periodically.

Tanner returned to the United States in 1893 and delivered a paper on the achievements of black painters and sculptors at the Congress on Africa held at the World's Columbian Exposition. In his own work he was motivated at this time to concentrate on sober, sympathetic depictions of African American life to offset a history of one-sided comic representations. *The Banjo Lesson* (1893; Hampton University Museum), in which an older man instructs a young lad, is the first painting that can be ascribed to Tanner's new efforts. It was inspired by the poem "A Banjo Song," which PAUL LAURENCE DUNBAR included in his 1892 *Oak and Ivy* collection. Stylistically, Tanner's like for multiple and conflicting light sources sparkle in *Banjo Lesson* and became a characteristic of his manner. He unveiled it at the Paris Salon—the prestigious French annual juried exhibition. The *Banjo Lesson*'s theme of age instructing youth recurs in

The Thankful Poor (1894; William H. and Camille O. Cosby Collection) and *The Young Sabot Maker* (1895; Washington, D.C., private collection), which conjures up images of Jesus in the carpentry shop of Joseph.

At the turn of the twentieth century Tanner was devoting himself almost exclusively to biblical scenes as a result of both his devout family background and economic opportunities provided by the subject. Tanner's art was also informed by his extensive travels to the Holy Land in 1897 and 1898–1899 and to North Africa in 1908 and 1912. Among his famous works depicting religious scenes are *Resurrection of Lazarus* (1896; Musée d'Orsay, Paris), which was bought by the French government; *Nicodemus Visiting Jesus* (1899; Pennsylvania Academy of the Fine Arts); *Mary* (1900; LaSalle University Art Museum); *Return of the Holy Women* (1904; Cedar Rapids Art Gallery); *Two Disciples at the Tomb* (1905–1906; Art Institute of Chicago); and *Christ at the Home of Lazarus* (c. 1912; unlocated). Almost all of Tanner's biblical themes are centered around ideas of birth and rebirth, both physically and spiritually. Devoted since childhood to equality for African Americans, Tanner chose these themes because they related to President Abraham Lincoln's Emancipation Proclamation, which promised freedom, or birth and rebirth, to black slaves. This approach was also consistent with Tanner's desire to render sympathetic depictions of African Americans.

Although Tanner made a relatively small number of portraits over his career, those he did paint were of individuals involved with equality and other humane concerns. Notable are the James Whistler–inspired *Portrait of the Artist's Mother* (1897; Riverdale, N.Y., private collection); the formal portrayal of his early supporter and secretary of the Freedman's Air and Southern Education Society, *Joseph Crane Hartzell* (1902; Hampton University Museum); the distinguished civil rights leader Rabbi Stephen Samuel Wise (c. 1909; unlocated); and the illustrious educator BOOKER T. WASHINGTON (1917; State Historical Society of Iowa). Stylistically, Tanner's portraits follow the patterns of his subject pictures; however, they are characterized by a very shallow recession into space or a certain flatness. On the other hand, there is a continued consistency of the rich brown, blue, blue-green, and mauve palette spiked with bright reds, while multiple light sources abound. These stylistic characteristics are particularly notable in genre scenes based on Tanner's visits to North

Africa, as can be seen in *Flight into Egypt: Palais de Justice, Tangier* (c. 1908; National Museum of American Art) and *Sunlight, Tangier* (c. 1912–1914; Milwaukee Art Museum).

Tanner's mature style, which began around 1914, is characterized stylistically by experiments with the thick build-up of enamel-like surfaces, as in one of his last paintings, *Return from the Crucifixion* (1936; Howard University Gallery of Art). During the early years of World War I, Tanner was so frustrated over the military situation that he was unable to create art. While his artistic production was in abeyance, Tanner was a major figure in the American Red Cross; he worked with convalescing soldiers while serving as assistant director of Farm and Garden Services. His artistic career was resumed on 11 November 1918, Armistice Day, when the American Expeditionary Force authorized Tanner's travel to make sketches of the war front, as represented in *Canteen at the Front* (1918; Washington, D.C., American Red Cross).

Tanner garnered ample recognition in the international art literature of his time from critics for periodicals such as *Revue de l'Art, Gazette des Beaux-Arts, International Studio, Fine Arts Journal*, and *Brush and Pencil*. One contemporary critic stated in 1911, "He makes his home continuously in Paris, where many claim that he is the greatest artist that America has produced" (E. J. Campbell, "Henry O. Tanner's Biblical Pictures," *Fine Arts Journal* 25 [Mar. 1911]: 166). In the final years of his career Tanner's work depicted a preponderance of good-shepherd themes, with which he expressed a strong sense that Jesus watches over his flock and that together man and God overcome evil. Tanner exhibited frequently on both sides of the Atlantic, and several medals from the French Salon jury made him exempt from the jurying process, or *hors concours*, in 1906. He was awarded a gold medal at the 1915 Panama-Pacific Exposition and the prestigious French Cross of the Legion of Honor in 1923. Tanner was elected full academician of the National Academy of Design in 1927.

Tanner's personal life was interwoven with his professional career. In 1899 he married Jessie Macauley Olssen, a white woman from San Francisco who frequently served as his model. They had one child. His wife died in 1925.

Henry O. Tanner was extremely proud of his race but at times lamented the humiliation and sorrow that being black caused him. Moreover, he was sad that he could not live freely in America, the country he loved. It would be impossible to imagine the succeeding generation of African American artists who contributed to the Harlem Renaissance without the example of Tanner's single-minded pursuit of artistic success and his subsequent international recognition. Tanner died in Paris and was buried at Sceaux, Hauts-de-Seine. The U.S. Postal Service issued a commemorative stamp in his honor in 1973.

FURTHER READING
Tanner's papers are in the Archives of American Art, Smithsonian Institution. Valuable information is also included in the Alexander papers at the archives of the University of Pennsylvania.
Mathews, Marcia M. *Henry Ossawa Tanner: American Artist* (1969).
Mosby, Dewey F. *Across Continents and Cultures: The Art and Life of Henry Ossawa Tanner* (1995).
Mosby, Dewey F. *Henry Ossawa Tanner* (1991).
Obituary: *New York Herald Tribune*, 26 May 1937.
This entry is taken from the *American National Biography* and is published here with the permission of the American Council of Learned Societies.

DEWEY FRANKLIN MOSBY

Tanner, Sarah Elizabeth (1840–2 Aug. 1914), founder, treasurer, vice president, and president of the Women's Parent Mite Missionary Society of the African Methodist Episcopal (AME) Church, sometimes known affectionately by her family as Sadie, was born Sarah E. Miller in Winchester, Virginia, where her parents were by state law considered the property of persons whose names are lost to history. Her life paralleled that of her husband, AME bishop BENJAMIN TUCKER TANNER, but reflected her own distinct service to church and community.

In 1843 her family escaped via the Underground Railroad, settling in Pittsburgh, Pennsylvania, where she attended day school and Allegheny Institute, established by Reverend Charles Avery in 1849 as a school for young Americans of African descent (see Brown, 1988, and Verdino-Sullwold, 1991). Benjamin T. Tanner, the freeborn son of a Pittsburgh river boatman, also attended Avery, working as a barber to pay his way, before going to Western Theological Seminary and entering the ministry. Her father, Jefferson Miller, died when she was sixteen; in order to help support her family, she left school and began work as a teacher.

She married the future Bishop Tanner on 19 August 1858, two years after he was licensed to preach by the AME church. The Methodist tradition of itinerant ministry kept the family moving from Pittsburgh, where their first children were born, to assignments in Washington, DC, Virginia, and Maryland, for the first ten years. They had nine children, of whom two died in infancy. The Tanners moved to Philadelphia in 1868, when Reverend Tanner was elected to edit the *Christian Recorder*, and moved in 1872 into the home where the family lived for the rest of their lives, which is now listed in the National Register of Historic Places.

The Women's Parent Mite Missionary Society (WPMMS) was organized in Philadelphia 8 May 1874, after planning meetings earlier in the year in Washington, DC. As editor of the *Christian Recorder* until 1884, of the *AME Church Review* 1884–1888, and after 1888 when he was elected bishop, Reverend Tanner visibly worked to inspire and encourage women to assist the church's evangelization. It was natural that his wife took an active role, and was named as one of thirty women on the Board of Managers. One of the first projects was raising money to support an AME missionary in Haiti—an assignment undertaken by Reverend CHARLES WESLEY MOSSELL.

Sarah E. Tanner served as a vice president of the society, 1883–1888; president, 1888–1892; vice president again, 1892–1895; and acting president, 1895–1899, a duty shared with Mrs. FANNY J. COPPIN, wife of Bishop L. J. COPPIN. In 1896 she was one of a committee of five from the national society who participated in organizing the New Jersey conference branch. She was called on to serve again, 1907–1911, as treasurer.

Tanner later wrote that WPMMS drew together local church units of women from the AME Church into one national organization, defining their relationship to established male governing authorities. One area of missionary work was Africa, referred to even in missionary deliberations of "colored" or African denominations in America as "the Dark Continent" (Keller, p. 95). The society sent a mission to Sierra Leone in 1888, led by SARAH GORHAM, and supported establishment of an AME church in South Africa.

Although her activity in civic women's organizations is less well documented, Tanner firmly advocated that clubwomen refute the common assumption that women are only interested in sensational news, fashion, and society columns, by focusing on study of "solid" authors recognized as examples of high culture. She authored several articles, including "Reading" (*Women's Era*, June 1895, 13),

"The Mite Society" (*Review*, 12 Jan. 1896, 378–382), and in the *Christian Recorder*, "To the Parent and Auxiliary Mite Missionary Societies" (12 Dec. 1878), "Mite Society" (26 Aug. 1880), and "Annual Meeting" (7 Dec. 1882).

In 1900, after her daughter Mary's husband, AARON ALBERT MOSSELL JR., left the family, Mary and her children came to live with the Tanners. Tanner resigned her position as treasurer of the missionary society on 25 January 1912, due to declining health, or (as she told the society's fifth Quadrennial Convention meeting in Chicago the following 9–13 November), "circumstances over which I had no control compelled me to resign" (Seraile, p. 186). After her death twenty months later, the *Christian Recorder* eulogized her as "distinguished for her great patience and devotion to her husband and her children," and as "an indulgent, loving, wise and Christian mother." *Recorder* editor Richard R. Wright Jr. in a separate editorial added that her "active outside life proved that the arduous duties of a mother do not necessarily mean the neglect of other things needful."

Her husband survived her by nine years. Among her distinguished children and grandchildren were Dr. HALLE TANNER JOHNSON, a medical doctor; Reverend Carl Tanner, an AME minister; HENRY OSSAWA TANNER, a world-renowned artist; and SADIE TANNER MOSSELL ALEXANDER, a civil rights lawyer. She was remembered in 1915 with the establishment of the Sarah E. Tanner Memorial Fund to provide support to widows and orphans of AME missionaries. In 1936 WPMMS merged with the Women's Home and Foreign Missionary Society, a separate AME body organized in 1893, to form the Women's Missionary Society; some local chapters of the WMS have been named in memory of Sarah E. Tanner.

FURTHER READING

Brown, Hallie Quinn. *Homespun Heroines and Other Women of Distinction* (1988).

Keller, Rosemary Skinner, and Rosemary Radford Ruether. *In Our Own Voices: Four Centuries of American Women's Religious Writing* (2000).

Seraile, William. *Fire in His Heart: Bishop Benjamin Tucker Tanner and the A.M.E. Church* (1998).

Verdino-Sullwold, Carla Maria. "Henry Ossawa Tanner: The Whole World Kin." *The Crisis,* June–July 1991, 18.

Wright, Richard R. *Centennial Encyclopaedia of the African Methodist Episcopal Church* (1916). Posted online by University of North Carolina's

"Documenting the South" project: http://docsouth.unc.edu/church/wright/wright.html.

CHARLES ROSENBERG

Tapscott, Horace (6 Apr. 1934–27 Feb. 1999), pianist, composer, orchestra leader, and teacher, was born Horace Elva Tapscott in Houston, Texas, the son of Mary Lou Malone, a stride pianist and tuba player. Tapscott never knew the identity of his father. At age nine Horace moved with his mother to Los Angeles, where they lived in a segregated black neighborhood near the city's black musicians' union, Local 767.

Tapscott began playing piano and trombone in elementary school, and in high school he met the legendary black music teacher Samuel Browne, who had a decisive impact on him as a musician and a human being. Browne taught music at Jefferson High School in Los Angeles and exerted a profound influence on the development of Tapscott and many of his peers. Through Browne and other older black musical mentors and teachers, like Lloyd Reese, Tapscott met and worked with other aspiring professional musicians in the community. These young black Los Angeles musicians and composers—a significant number of whom later became jazz legends, including ERIC DOLPHY, CHARLES MINGUS, DEXTER GORDON, SONNY CRISS, FRANK MORGAN, ADDISON FARMER, ART FARMER, and DON CHERRY—had all been exposed to Browne and Reese's insistence on high academic and technical standards and the importance of creating and sharing music with others. These values and a sense of pride in one's own cultural and social heritage rubbed off on Tapscott, who said his long-term association with Browne and his wide circle of gifted pupils left him with a sense that "music had a deeper meaning that related to people coming together." Tapscott never forgot that lesson, which became an integral part of his own life as an artist and a teacher.

While still in high school in the late 1940s, Tapscott began playing music with numerous jazz bands on Los Angeles's famed Central Avenue, the black Los Angeles equivalent of Harlem's 125th Street, where a thriving cultural and economic mecca of independent African American businesses, nightclubs, creative artists, and entertainment venues flourished. In 1952 Tapscott graduated from high school and joined the U.S. Air Force, where he continued to play trombone in the air force band and began to compose music. "All I had to do was write and perform with the orchestra,"

recalled Tapscott. "It allowed me to develop because I had a forum for my ideas, top quality people to carry them out." He began to seriously study the piano, a decision that played a major role in his life after the service. Upon returning to civilian life in 1956, Tapscott played with the GERALD WILSON Orchestra, a big band led by one of the West Coast's major jazz composers and bandleaders.

In 1958 Tapscott toured throughout the country with LIONEL HAMPTON's orchestra. However, Tapscott was disillusioned by the pervasive racism he found in the South during the tour as well as with the commercial aspects of big band playing. When the band returned to Hollywood in 1961, Tapscott decided to stay at home in Los Angeles and organize his own ensemble. Shortly after he left Hampton, Tapscott was involved in an automobile accident on his way to a job. He made it to the job but played with a split lip and missing teeth, which left him with a weakened embouchure. He soon abandoned the trombone altogether and made the piano his major instrument. Before long Tapscott developed an original style of his own, and he began to seriously pursue composing and arranging music.

In 1961 Tapscott founded a large ensemble, the Pan African People's Arkestra, which remained active for the rest of his life and continued after his death, producing several powerful works. Tapscott recruited many local musicians and other artists as part of a collective community-based organization he called the Union of God's Musicians and Artists Ascension (UGMAA), which was the larger umbrella organization of the Arkestra. This group's goal was to create and sustain self-determination in music and the other arts by channeling artistic activity in the community and developing a greater sense of cultural consciousness and self-respect. As a mentor and teacher to many younger musicians and artists, Tapscott was not only giving back but also seriously adhering to Browne's agreement that "he would teach me as long as I would agree to pass it along." Tapscott dedicated the rest of his life to creating and developing an infrastructure for musical and artistic creativity in the black Los Angeles community of Watts. After the August 1965 Watts riots, which were a response to ongoing problems of racism in Los Angeles, Tapscott's organization received official funding from government reform sources, which allowed an expansion of its activities.

Unable to attract the attention of local media and music critics, whom Tapscott saw as corrupt people who expected to be "wined and dined for their efforts on our behalf," he decided to forgo their help and rely on his own community-based efforts to promote his band and cultural organization. As he pointed out, the reason he first took music to the schools, churches, and streets was that he could not dictate terms to the record companies. Performing weekly for ten years at the Emmanuel Church of Christ in Los Angeles, Tapscott and his growing number of artists, students, and teachers built a formidable and lasting institution that helped many musicians and other artists develop careers and improve their lives. Throughout the 1960s and 1970s the Arkestra played hundreds of benefit concerts; taught workshops in music, dance, writing, multimedia, and the visual arts; supported independent black political and economic organizations; and provided free tuition to thousands of poor, young people who wished to develop their musical and other artistic talents.

Seldom venturing from Los Angeles and determined to keep alive both his big band and his vision of community cultural development and expression, Tapscott put his own recording career on hold for many years before making his 1969 debut album with the Arkestra. Finally, in the 1980s and 1990s Tapscott and his Arkestra toured Europe. Tapscott also began recording on his own, producing a major series of critically acclaimed albums in solo, trio, quartet, quintet, and orchestral formats until his death.

FURTHER READING
Tapscott, Horace. *Songs of the Unsung: The Musical and Social Journey of Horace Tapscott*, ed. Steven Isoardi (2001).
Obituaries: *New York Times*, 3 Mar. 1999; *London Independent* and *Los Angeles Times*, 6 Mar. 1999.

KOFI NATAMBU

Tarrant, Caesar (c. 1740–1797), patriot, was born into slavery, probably at Hampton, Virginia. The identity of his parents is unknown. In his early adulthood, Caesar was sold to Carter Tarrant upon the death of his master Robert Hundley. His purchase price exceeded the normal price for male slaves because Tarrant had a particular skill, that of a river pilot. Just how Tarrant acquired the skill is unclear. Typically, the Tidewater-area river pilot was white and passed the skill on to his son. In any case, Tarrant would eventually use this skill to parlay his freedom.

Sometime prior to the American Revolution, Tarrant married Lucy, the slave of a neighbor, John Rogers. This so-called broad marriage of slaves who resided apart from one another produced three children. Throughout his life, Tarrant longed for his family's freedom.

The American Revolution provided Tarrant with the chance to secure his own liberty. His knowledge of the waterways as a pilot could have been valuable to either side. John Murray, Lord Dunmore, the last royal governor of Virginia, promised in his 1775 Proclamation freedom to all runaway slaves who would join his "Ethiopian Regiment." Many African Americans decided to do just that. Indeed, many more African Americans actively supported the British than the patriots. Tarrant, however, for reasons that are not known, chose to support the patriot cause. This was fortunate for the patriots, as Tarrant quickly demonstrated his abilities. His skill induced the Virginia Navy Board to appoint him a pilot in the Virginia State Navy, one of seven such appointments. For three years Tarrant successfully piloted a number of vessels, enhancing his reputation as a skilled and valiant pilot.

Among the several ships Tarrant piloted was the tender *Patriot*. In 1777 a group of ships commanded by Commodore Richard Taylor encountered the British naval vessel *Lord Howe*. When it appeared that the British privateer would escape, Taylor personally took command of the *Patriot*, piloted by Tarrant. Tarrant skillfully maneuvered the faster ship, which succeeded in ramming the larger and better-armed British vessel. Fierce fighting resulted in numerous deaths and injuries on both sides, including Taylor, who was shot. Nevertheless, Tarrant's skill and bravery in the face of enemy fire earned him praise from his captain, who stated he had "behaved gallantly."

In addition to this engagement, Tarrant piloted the vessel when the Americans captured the British ship *Fanny*, which was attempting to bring supplies to British troops in Boston. Although the *Patriot* was later captured, no record indicates that Tarrant was on board at the time.

Following the Revolution, Tarrant returned to the status of slave despite the heroism he had displayed. His master Carter Tarrant continued to make money from his slave's important skills. When Carter Tarrant died in 1784, Caesar Tarrant was willed to Mary Tarrant, Carter Tarrant's wife. The will stipulated that Caesar Tarrant was to remain her slave for her natural life and, further, he was to be given to Francis Tarrant, their son, upon the death of Mary. If it had not been for the intervention of the Virginia General Assembly, Caesar Tarrant might not have been freed.

In 1789 the Virginia General Assembly moved to secure Tarrant's freedom. The reason for this action is not clear, though numerous possibilities exist. Other pilots who were his friends may have petitioned on his behalf, the navy board may have taken some action, or Tarrant may have petitioned. What is clear, however, is that Tarrant was finally free by 1789.

By the act of the assembly, "in consideration of which meritorious services it is judged expedient to purchase the freedom" of Tarrant, a representative contacted Mary Tarrant and expressed the assembly's intention to manumit Caesar Tarrant. After the purchase price was agreed upon, a certificate manumitting Caesar Tarrant was issued to Mary Tarrant. Having become a free man, Caesar Tarrant, infected with what BENJAMIN QUARLES termed blacks' "contagion of liberty," then worked to secure the freedom of his family.

At the time of Tarrant's manumission, his wife and children were held in bondage by John Rogers. In 1793 Rogers freed Lucy and their fifteen-month-old daughter Nancy. The other children, Sampson and Lydia, remained enslaved, presumably because of their high value. What prompted the manumissions is not clear. It is not known if Caesar Tarrant worked for Rogers, Tarrant raised the money through his own efforts, or Rogers felt some need to liberate the mother and young child. The "Reason for Manumission" expressed in the records of Elizabeth City County simply state that Lucy was the "wife of Caesar Tarrant" and Nancy was the "daughter of Caesar Tarrant." Payment of some specified amount or "faithful service," as indicated for others set free, were not listed as reasons for Lucy or Nancy's freedom.

With part of his family free, Tarrant purchased a lot in Hampton in a section where white river pilots lived. This further indicated how highly regarded Tarrant was among this closed brotherhood of river pilots. Indeed, these white river pilots petitioned the legislature in 1791 to include skilled black river pilots among those granted licenses. They more than likely thought of Tarrant as they fashioned this request.

Yet freedom proved ephemeral. Although Tarrant had the respect of his peers, was now a property holder, and apparently continued to pilot the rivers, he, like other free African Americans, could not fully enjoy the benefits of liberty. As an African American, he could not vote or hold public office; neither could he testify against any white person nor serve on a jury. Full citizenship was reserved for others; "freedom" for African Americans was limited. It has been argued that Hampton may have been something of an anomaly among southern communities as there appeared to be a strong "cordiality between" the races. Yet even there Tarrant's dream for his family went unrealized.

Tarrant died in Hampton, Virginia, only eight years after receiving his freedom, while his two older children remained in bondage. The thirst for freedom—Tarrant's legacy—was not abandoned by his descendants and heirs. His will specified that all his property be given to his wife and that upon her death the proceeds from the sale of that property be used to purchase his eldest daughter's freedom. Whatever remained was to be given to Tarrant's son, Sampson. In a concluding comment, Tarrant asked the county court to "see justice done my children."

After another twenty-five years, Lydia obtained her freedom. Prior to that, she was sold to a Norfolk resident for the sum of $250. When in 1822 her mother was able to purchase her freedom, Lydia herself left a child in bondage. The fate of Sampson is unclear, because his name disappears from the records. It is possible that he died still enslaved. What is clear, however, is that despite Tarrant's contributions to American freedom, he, like so many antebellum African Americans, was unable to secure justice for his children.

FURTHER READING

A few scattered references, such as manumission records, a deed to a lot purchased in Hampton, and Tarrant's will, are in the Elizabeth City County court records in the Virginia State Library in Richmond.

This entry is taken from the *American National Biography* and is published here with the permission of the American Council of Learned Societies.

MICHAEL E. HUCLES

Tarry, Ellen (26 Sept. 1906–23 Sept. 2008), author and Catholic activist, was born in Birmingham, Alabama, the first of three girls born to Robert Tarry, a barber, and Eula Meadows, a seamstress for wealthy white people in Birmingham. Tarry wrote in her autobiography, *The Third Door* (1955):

Anthropologists ... would probably have said that my father was a mulatto and my mother an octoroon. I do not know what scientific name they might have used to describe my two sisters and me. I do know a lot of unscientific names were used, but I was a young lady before I really understood. Mamy once laughingly said we were a 'duke's mixture'; to me, that seemed closer to the truth than anything else did.

Born into a warm, loving, and supportive family, Ellen only realized her complexion was an issue when she entered the segregated Birmingham Slater School. In elementary school, because of her light color, African American children called her names. Later, when she was a grown woman, white people called her insulting names and she witnessed southern-style police brutality toward African Americans. Tarry was raised a Methodist, but in 1921 she was sent to a Roman Catholic boarding school for African Americans. Saint Francis de Sales Institute in Rock Castle, Virginia, prepared her for college. A month before Ellen left for boarding school, her father suddenly died. She started school grieving over her father's death and resistant to the worship practices of the Roman Catholic Church. She had promised her father before he died that she would never become a Catholic, but gradually she warmed to the new faith. In 1923, after receiving permission from her mother, she converted. She remained a devout Catholic throughout her life. After her graduation in 1923, Tarry returned to Alabama and attended the Alabama State Normal school from 1923 to 1925 to prepare to teach. In the South being an African American and a Roman Catholic were both difficult.

Tarry accepted a teaching position in the Birmingham school system in 1925. She wrote in her autobiography that her school was "housed in half of one of a dozen or more wooden shacks separated from the main building.... Each structure housed two classes of forty to fifty pupils" (72). She wrote that it was "hard not to think about the red-brick building which housed the nearest elementary school for white children" (72). Wanting to provide her students with material about outstanding African Americans, she wrote a series of sketches to use in her classroom. Guillermo Talliferro, who edited the African American newspaper the *Birmingham Truth*, read her stories about prominent African Americans and hired her away from her teaching position. By 1929 she was writing a column, "Negroes of Note," that focused on African American accomplishments, such as the work of BOOKER T. WASHINGTON and JAMES WELDON JOHNSON, and discussed issues such as segregation. The white establishment saw her column as controversial, and one editorial she wrote about President

Herbert Hoover and Jim Crow so irritated Theodore Bilbo, then governor of Mississippi, that he read the entire article over the radio and suggested the writer should be burned. She feared for her own safety and the safety of her mother and sisters.

In August 1929 Tarry left for New York City with a plan to work a year, save money, and attend Columbia University Journalism School. She arrived in New York just two months before the October stock market crash. Unable to find a suitable job, for nearly five years she worked variously as an elevator operator, waitress, and night club attendant. She stopped telling interviewers that she was African American and in a few instances "passed" just to have a job to pay the rent, but even these jobs ended once her race was discovered. She wrote in her autobiography that she was not trying to pass; she just did not volunteer the information. She described her life during the Depression in Bernard Sternsher and Judith Sealander's *Women of Valor*: "We had to close our eyes and minds to so much" (189). During this period Tarry lived in a small apartment in the Sugar Hill section of Harlem, known during the Harlem Renaissance as a center of music clubs and the home of many prominent African Americans. In 1936 she visited Birmingham, and when she returned to New York City she moved away from Sugar Hill, returned to her contacts in the church, and became involved in the Roman Catholic outreach program centered around Friendship House, an interracial justice center in Harlem.

Tarry also met writers of the Harlem Renaissance, such as CLAUDE MCKAY, COUNTÉE CULLEN, LANGSTON HUGHES, and Johnson. By the end of 1936 she had accepted a position as a writer-researcher on the Federal Writers' Project gathering material for a history of African Americans in New York. She also won a scholarship to study with Lucy Sprague Mitchell, a child advocate in the 1920s and founder of the Writers' Laboratory and Bank Street College. The college, a leader in childhood education by the early twenty-first century, was founded to discover the best learning environments that enabled children to reach their full potentials. Tarry's participation in the Writers' Laboratory at Bank Street College provided her with the environment she needed to write. In December 1939 she published her first children's book, *Janie Belle*. The book featured African American main characters who were portrayed in a positive manner. In 1942 she met the Viking children's book editor May Massee, and Tarry became a Viking author. She persuaded Massee to use only African American illustrators for Tarry's stories about African American children. At the time this was a major breakthrough in children's books. While she wrote children's books, Tarry also worked at the *Amsterdam News* from 1942 to 1943.

In 1943 Tarry left New York to organize a Friendship House in the South Side of Chicago. In 1944 she returned to New York and was briefly married to a soldier. There is some mystery surrounding this marriage—she mentions it only briefly in her autobiography: "On the chain around my neck was a wedding ring. I had married the soldier named Patton in a secret civil ceremony. One week later I had discovered that the contract had not been made in good faith. No one shared my secret" (244). She had one daughter and continued to write books about famous blacks and stories featuring black children.

Tarry also held various positions for the Archdiocese of New York, including director of community relations for the Saint Charles (Bortreno) School and Community Center Fund. She helped to launch a campaign headed by an integrated leadership of Catholic, Protestant, and Jewish leaders to build a new Saint Charles School in Harlem. Tarry continued writing and worked in the civil rights movement in the 1950s; in 1963 she attended MARTIN LUTHER KING JR.'s March on Washington.

Tarry's autobiography, *The Third Door*, was published in 1955. *The New York Times* (4 Aug. 1992) reported that at a weeklong celebration of the world's black cultures in Atlanta, Georgia, Tarry received the Living Legend Award, given to those individuals who "represent the vitality and perseverance of African Cultural themes throughout the world." Ten of Tarry's children's books remained in print in the early twenty-first century. She died in New York City at the age of 101.

FURTHER READING

Tarry, Ellen. *The Third Door: The Autobiography of an American Negro Woman* (1955).

Houston, Helen. "Ellen Tarry," in *Notable Black American Women*, vol. 1, ed. Jessie Carney Smith (1992).

Sternsher, Bernard, and Judith Sealander, eds. *Women of Valor: The Struggle against the Great Depression as Told in Their Own Life Stories* (1990).

LINDA SPENCER

Tate, Claudia (14 Dec. 1946–29 July 2002), professor of English and African American studies, was born in Long Branch, New Jersey, to Harold N. Tate, an engineer, and Mary Austin Tate, a mathematician. Her parents received their degrees from North Carolina Central University in Durham. During World War II they came to Fort Monmouth, New Jersey, where her father served as an engineer in the army and her mother worked for the U.S. Department of Defense. Tate was an honor student at Rumson–Fair Haven Regional High School in New Jersey and received her bachelor's degree in English and American Literature from the University of Michigan, Ann Arbor in 1968.

Tate subsequently entered the graduate program in Harvard's English Department, where she was one of only a few black women. She received her Ph.D. in English and American Literature and Language in 1977. Tate started teaching at Howard University in Washington, DC, and joined George Washington University in 1989. In 2002, when she died of lung cancer at the age of fifty-five in Fair Haven, New Jersey, Tate had been a professor of English and African American studies at Princeton University for five years.

Tate was known for her unexpected approaches to literature. She looked at writers and themes not included in the canon. Before her first book publication, she examined the works of three writers, RICHARD WRIGHT, GAYL JONES, and NELLA LARSEN, in essay form. All three writers reappear in her later works. Her first book *Black Women Writers at Work* (1983), was a collection of interviews. It discusses writers not yet seriously considered in a scholarly context at that time, such as the Nobel Prize winner TONI MORRISON and ALICE WALKER. The publication is considered to have set new directions for the critical and theoretical discourse on African American women writers. Valerie Smith, a professor at Princeton and a colleague of Tate's, said this first work "set a new standard for the interview as a genre" (http://www.princeton.edu/pr/news/02/q3/0731-tate.htm).

In her second book, *Domestic Allegories of Political Desire: The Black Heroine's Text at the Turn of the Century* (1992), Tate focused her attention on domestic fiction of the post-Reconstruction era. A number of texts had thus far been neglected because they did not join the ranks of angry accusation against white political oppression. Writers such as PAULINE HOPKINS and KATHERINE DAVIS CHAPMAN TILLMAN had been dismissed as apolitical and overly concerned with conventional plots such as love and family. Tate was able to show the different perspectives of these writers' first readers and the following generations, thus emphasizing their works' great contribution to the contemporary discussion.

In her mid-career work Tate concentrated on psychoanalytical literary criticism and cultural studies. Her third book *Psychoanalysis and Black Novels: Desire and the Protocols of Race* (1998) looks at five novels with nonblack protagonists from the 1940s and 1950s. This was new territory at the time, and again these texts had largely been overlooked because of their occupation with personal rather than political issues. Her work convinced critics that black writers could move beyond the racial issues to which they had been confined for the longest time.

At the same time Tate reviewed the works of other scholars. Her reviews appeared in *Tulsa Studies in Women's Literature, American Quarterly, American Studies International, SIGNS, The New York Times Book Review*, and *African American Review*. She examined black women writers as well as themes of feminism, race, and drama.

Tate received many honors throughout her career. In 1979–1980 she was a fellow of the National Endowment for the Humanities. She received Andrew Mellon Incentive Awards in 1982–83 and 1983–84, and served as a distinguished visiting scholar at the University of Delaware and Rutgers University in 1986 and 1987. She belonged to the Modern Language Association and the American Studies Association and served on the editorial advisory boards of the *African American Review, American Literature*, the *American Quarterly*, and *SIGNS*. She was a fellow of the National Humanities Center in 1999–2000. In December 2001 the Princeton Program in African American Studies held a conference in her honor. It consisted of two panels, "Gender, Culture and Psychoanalysis" and "Narratives of Gender, Race and Nation." Colleagues from all over the United States attended the event and presented their papers on approaches to Tate's work.

When Tate fell ill in the summer of 2000, she had just completed a fellowship at the National Humanities Center in North Carolina and was working on her fourth book, in which she examined the black female figure in American film. She had schooled herself in film criticism. Unfortunately, the manuscript was never sufficiently developed for publication. Tate was survived by her two sons. In 2003 the *Journal of African American History* devoted an entire volume to Claudia Tate's legacy. Among the scholars who paid tribute were Nell Irvin Painter and Hazel Carby.

FURTHER READING
Painter, Nell Irvin. "Introduction: Claudia Tate and the Protocols of Black Literature and Scholarship," *Journal of African American History*, Winter 2003.
Obituary: *African American Review*, Winter 2002.

GRETA KÖHLER

Tate, Mary Lena Lewis (5 Jan. 1871–28 Dec. 1930), preacher, bishop, church founder, and administrator, was born Mary Lena Street in Vanleer, Dickson County, Tennessee. Mary Lena was the first of four girls born to Belfield Street and Nancy Hall. Both of her parents were born into slavery, Belfield around 1830 and Nancy around 1839. Belfield had two sons (Jeff and Felix) and Nancy had one son (Filmore) from previous marriages. After Emancipation, Belfield continued farming and marketing his produce and by-products in Vanleer, Cumberland Furnace, and Dickson, Tennessee. Belfield acquired considerable property in Dickson County. His property, as well as his agricultural and entrepreneurial skills, was passed on to his children. Nancy was an "ex-house girl" for the wealthy William Bell family, which operated the prestigious Cloverdale Academy at Cloverdale, Tennessee. Nancy readily availed herself of the educational experiences available in the Bell home, and thus gained a good grasp of mathematics and language fundamentals. These she passed on to her daughters in structured "at home" learning experiences. Her parents' backgrounds had a profound impact and relevance in the development and ministry of Mary Lena Lewis Tate, founder of the international religious organization known as the Church of the Living God, the Pillar and Ground of the Truth Inc. in 1903.

Perhaps the most important event in the development of the young Mary Lena Street was what has been called "post-slavery psychological liberation" (Lewis, 2005). Unlike west Tennessee, middle Tennessee was not a significant cotton producer. On the other hand it was very rich in iron ore, especially in the Highland Rim counties, including Dickson County. Montgomery Bell, the notorious iron mogul, developed a number of iron-producing furnaces in middle Tennessee. Bell owned a significant number of slaves, and others were hired out to his operations, sometimes on an annual basis. Workers at the furnaces, both black and white, were highly valued for their iron-fabricating skills and productivity. Generally they faired much better than their counterparts in other parts of the state. After the war many now-free blacks remained with the establishments as hired employees. The ambiance of the furnaces produced a cadre of independent-thinking, proud, skilled laborers, whose productivity was compensated in considerable workman benefits, including food and clothing, monetary allowances, and medical attention.

Mary Lena Street married David Lewis in 1888 and two sons were born to them in Vanleer, Walter Curtis and Felix Early, in 1890 and 1892, respectively. David Lewis and several of Mary Lena's half-brothers were employed at Cumberland Furnace. The onset of Mary Lena's spiritual unction began after the birth of her second son. Around 1895 the family relocated to the city of Dickson, her husband's hometown, and she joined the local Methodist church with him. During this time she felt her calling to preach the Gospel so strongly that she made it known to the pastor of the church, to which he emphatically replied, "Not in this church!" The Methodist pastor's negative reaction to her deeply felt calling to the ministry was to her an affront. The situation eventually brought about discord in the family and among her relatives. By 1898 her marriage to David Lewis was dissolved and she, along with her two sons, began her initial ministry.

Tate's early ministry was a reaction against the local influences of a rural Tennessee community, which she described as "filthy," and the local church membership, which seemed to ignore the situation. Thus was the beginning of her developing theology regarding "cleanliness" (later developed into the doctrine of True Holiness and Sanctification) and the biblical right of women to preach the Gospel.

Mary Lena's early audiences were in Dickson and Steel Springs, Tennessee, and nearby communities. She delivered her first "sermon" at Paris, Tennessee. In 1898 she gathered her followers into a group called the Do Rights. This group grew considerably and extended as far as Murfreesboro, Tennessee, and into the states of Georgia and Alabama, attracting a considerable following of some three hundred to five hundred adherents. Mary Lena's ministry carried her into Waycross, Georgia, Paducah, Kentucky, and Brooklyn, Illinois, preaching on the streets, in churches, and wherever she could find an audience. During this early ministry she was married to Elijah Estes. She traveled thousands of miles in mule-drawn wagons, decrepit automobiles, barges, and steamboats to places throughout the eastern United States. In 1903 she reorganized the Do Rights group into bands and restyled the organization as the "divinely inspired" Church of the Living God, the Pillar and Ground of the Truth as recorded in the Bible in First Timothy 3:15. In 1908, in Greenville, Alabama, Mary Lena Estes experienced the "outpouring of the Holy Spirit" upon herself. Afterward she began teaching her followers to receive the baptism of the Holy Ghost as recorded in the Book of Acts. In 1908 she called the first general assembly of the swiftly growing organization in Greenville and formally organized the church group. Over nine hundred people attended this conclave. She was ordained to the bishopric and selected as the first chief overseer by the elders present. Mary Lena married Robert T. Tate, a native of Fort Davis, Alabama, in 1916. From 1908 through 1918 the organization grew very rapidly and extensively. Mary Lena Lewis Tate extended her works throughout the southern, eastern, and midwestern United States. The organization experienced its first major split in 1929.

Mary Lena Lewis Tate succumbed to complications of gangrene and sugar diabetes in Philadelphia, Pennsylvania. She passed away on 28 December 1930 and was interred in Dickson County. After her death the organization separated into three other divisions. In 1969 her remains were relocated to a memorial gravesite in Greenwood Cemetery in Nashville, Tennessee. Today organizations that still remain loyal to the founding efforts of Mary Lena Lewis Tate are located in forty-eight of the fifty states of the United States and in a number of foreign countries.

FURTHER READING

Dupree, Sherry Sherrod. *Biographical Dictionary of African-American, Holiness-Pentecostals: 1880–1990* (1989).

Lewis, Meharry H. *Mary Lena Lewis Tate: V I S I O N !, A Biography* (2005).

Mendiola, Kelly Willis. *The Hand of a Woman: Four Holiness-Pentecostal Evangelists and American Culture, 1840–1930*, Ph.D. diss. (2002).

Payne, Wardell. *Directory of African American Religious Bodies* (1991).

MEHARRY H. LEWIS

Tate, Merze (6 Feb. 1905–27 June 1996), political scientist and educator, was born Vernie Merze Tate in Blanchard, Michigan, the daughter of Charles Tate, a farmer and businessman, and Myrtle Katora (Lett) Tate, both descendants of free blacks who had settled in Michigan under the Homestead Act of 1862. Tate had a sister, Thelma, who was ten years her senior, and a younger brother, Myrle K. The valedictorian and only African American member of her class at Blanchard High School,

Merze graduated after the tenth grade when the school burned down. To qualify for college admission she attended Battle Creek High School, where she won the Hinman Oratorical Contest. In 1927 Tate received a B.A. in Education from Western Michigan Teachers College (now Western Michigan University) in Kalamazoo, becoming the school's first African American woman graduate.

From 1925 to 1926 Tate taught elementary school at the Calvin Center School in Cassopolis, Michigan. Since professional employment in Michigan was limited by de facto segregation, she applied elsewhere for a high school teaching position. In 1927 she accepted a teaching position at the newly opened Crispus Attucks High School in Indianapolis, Indiana, which had an all-black student body, faculty, and administration. She taught there until 1932, concurrently earning an M.A.from Teachers College at Columbia University, which she completed in 1930. From 1932 to 1935 she studied international relations at Oxford University in England, earning the BLitt degree in 1935. Between 1931 and 1935 she also attended summer courses at the Geneva (Switzerland) School of International Studies and the University of Berlin. With the financial help of a Julius Rosenwald Fund Fellowship, Tate began doctoral studies at Radcliffe College in 1939. When she received her Ph.D. in 1941, she became the first African American woman to receive a Ph.D. in Government and International Relations. Tate later received five honorary degrees.

Following the employment pattern of other well-educated African Americans prior to desegregation, Tate was a teacher and administrator at several historically black institutions. She taught history and served as dean of women at Barber College in Concord, North Carolina, during 1935–1936 and chaired the social sciences division at Bennett College in Greensboro, North Carolina, from 1936 to 1941. She taught political science and served as dean of women at Morgan State College, from 1941 to 1942, and in 1942 she joined the faculty of Howard University. In 1948 Tate was one of three representatives from the United States to participate in a UNESCO seminar on the preparation of instructional materials on the United Nations and its related agencies for international use. Tate was a noted authority on diplomacy, disarmament, and the Pacific region. In 1942 the Bureau of International Research of Harvard University and Radcliffe College published her dissertation. Her first book, *The Disarmament Illusion: The Movement for a Limitation of Armaments to 1907*, was published in 1942. Her other books include *The United States and Armaments* (1948), *The United States and the Hawaiian Kingdom: A Political History* (1965), and *Hawaii: Reciprocity or Annexation* (1968). During 1950–1951, under the auspices of a Fulbright Fellowship from the U.S. State Department, Tate lectured in India and traveled extensively. Subsequent travel and research grants from the American Council of Learned Societies in 1959, the *Washington Evening Star* in 1960, and the Rockefeller Foundation in 1961, and a James M. Nabrit Jr. grant in 1962–1963 contributed to the publication of more than thirty articles in scholarly journals and two books on Hawaii, which earned her a reputation as a leading expert on Hawaii. In 1973 she published *Diplomacy in the Pacific: A Collection of Twenty-seven Articles on Diplomacy in the Pacific and Influence of the Sandwich (Hawaiian) Islands Missionaries*. In addition to Hawaii, Tate conducted research in Fiji, New Zealand, Australia, Great Britain, France, West Germany, and Africa.

Having spent more than fifty years as a well-regarded secondary and postsecondary teacher and thirty-five years at Howard University, Tate retired from Howard in 1977. Much honored for her scholarship, Tate received numerous awards throughout her career, including the National Urban League Achievement Award in 1948, the Radcliffe College Alumnae Achievement Award in 1979, and the Distinguished Alumnus Award from the American Association of State Colleges and Universities in 1981.

Tate's books continue to be required reading in college classrooms, and her presence is particularly felt through the Merze Tate Annual Seminar in Diplomatic History at Howard University, the Merze Tate Fellowship for the Mary Ingraham Bunting Institute at Radcliffe College, and the Merze Tate Scholarship at Western Michigan University. The Merze Tate Center for Research and School Reform at Western Michigan University studies the use of technology in teaching. Tate died of cardiac arrest in 1996 in Washington, D.C.

FURTHER READING
Harris, Joseph E. "Professor Merze Tate: A Profile—
    1905–1996," *Negro History Bulletin* (July–Dec. 1998).
Spacey, James G. "Black Women in Focus,"
    Philadelphia New Observer, 21 Dec. 1988.

                                JAYNE R. BEILKE

Tate, Thelma Horn (15 Sept. 1934–20 May 2005), academic and international librarian, educator, and scholar, was born Thelma Horn to Daniel Horn, a farmer and a minister, and Cora Ingram, a housewife. She was raised in the rural town of Coatopa, Alabama, with her brother Herman Horn and sister Mattie James (née Horn). Tate majored in history, education, and library science to earn her bachelor's degree from Alabama State University in Montgomery in 1957. She received a master's degree in Library Science from the University of Illinois–Urbana Champaign, in 1961. Thelma Horn Tate began her career in education with the Chicago Public Library system, where she directed a K-12 school library during the early days of the civil rights movement. She was head librarian at the Mississippi Valley State University in Itta Bena, Mississippi, before she joined the Rutgers University library system in New Brunswick, New Jersey, in 1970.

Early in her career at Rutgers, Thelma Horn met James Russell Tate, an administrator at Rutgers. They married and had two sons, Alaric and Greg, before James Tate died in 1970. At Rutgers, Thelma Tate served as a reference librarian at the Alexander Library on the main campus, as well as at the Mabel Smith Douglass Library on the Douglass College campus. Tate revitalized bibliographic instruction with the Rutgers student body, and developed the course "Shaping a Life," which taught freshman students all the components of adjusting to college life as well as how to effectively use the library on a research level. Always a champion of the underserved, Tate served the Rutgers libraries in many capacities during her career there, notably as the coordinator for services for patrons with disabilities and as chair of the Diversity Committee. She also assisted in developing Rutgers's library school internship program, where a three-year internship was offered to minority students to increase their representation in academic librarianship. She also served on university committees, such as the Puerto Rican Advisory Group and the Equal Opportunity Board.

Renowned internationally as a scholar in librarianship as applied to information technology, Tate presented many lectures and papers at conferences worldwide, and traveled to more than twenty-five countries, including, but not limited to, such places as Havana, Cuba; New Delhi, India; Bangkok, Thailand; Spain; and Israel. Tate particularly focused on outreach library services to countries in Africa. Tate spent time in Nigeria, Uganda, Zimbabwe, and South Africa. She helped set up libraries, bringing a satchel of reference books and demonstrating the uses of each book. She also assisted in designing two assessment projects to evaluate libraries in Kenya and Zimbabwe.

Considered an expert on mobile libraries, Tate traveled tirelessly, assisting resident groups in developing book delivery systems for communities that lacked money for vehicles and gasoline. Utilizing indigenous resources, Tate employed the use of donkeys, camels, and boats to deliver books to people. These innovative methods of book delivery services remained in use in Africa in the early twenty-first century. Tate wrote several books on mobile library services, including *Camel Library Services in Kenya, July 22–28, 2001: Report on the Assessment of Non-Motorized Mobile Libraries* (2002) and *The Donkey-Drawn Mobile Library Services in Zimbabwe, August 6–13, 2001: Report on the Assessment of Non-Motorized Mobile Libraries* (2002). These were published by the International Federation of Library Associations (IFLA), an organization in which Tate was actively involved. During various conferences and symposiums at Rutgers's libraries, Tate also escorted and assisted a continuous stream of international librarian speakers and guests, including a princess from Nigeria.

In recognition of her contributions, in 1999, Rutgers University appointed Tate as coordinator of Global Outreach Programs at the university, and in 2002, awarded her its Human Dignity Award. Throughout her career, Tate received accolades and awards from various areas of librarianship, served on committees and advocacy panels, and published an array of articles, books, and presentations related to the profession. Tate was a leader and member of various library organizations. Being especially active as a leader of IFLA, Thelma chaired committees within the organization, edited newsletters for its units, prepared presentations, moderated seminars and committee sessions, and wrote a compendium of articles, papers, and books. As a representative of IFLA, Tate networked with other organizations and universities throughout the world to connect them with international concerns of librarianship. Tate was also a trustee board member of the Global Literacy Project, Inc. (GLP), a nonprofit organization that sent books to countries throughout Africa, Asia, and the Caribbean. She was an active member of the American Library Association (ALA), where she led numerous committees and units, as well as maintained long-standing and active memberships with the ALA's Library Instruction Round Table (LIRT), the International Relations Round Table (IRRT), and the Black Caucus of the ALA (BCALA). Tate was also a member of the Alpha

Kappa Alpha sorority and held memberships with the Black Librarians Network, the New Jersey Library Association, the Association for the Study of Afro-American Life and History, and a local chapter of the Urban League. As the outreach librarian for Rutgers, Tate was the Jean E. Coleman Library Outreach Lecturer at the ALA Annual Conference in Toronto in 2003. She was also honored just five days before her death, receiving the Douglass Medal from Rutgers University's Douglass College.

Tate suffered a year-long battle with cancer before succumbing on 20 May 2005 in New Brunswick. The Global Literacy Project established the Thelma Tate Humanity Award to recognize the advocacy, activism, and service of community members who reflected Tate's commitment to service. The GLP also created the Annual Thelma Tate Lecture/Symposium, an academic colloquy that served as a professional development tool to explore global issues around literacy.

Thelma Tate's work in academia and as an advocate for rural and international librarianship has inspired a new generation of African American librarians to realize that the profession is multifaceted and more far-reaching than previously thought possible. Her work created a bridge between the African and African American cultures that will continue to evolve. Those who are passionate about equitable access to information, nationally and globally, will be able to look at the work of Thelma Tate and recognize the cultural value and necessity of librarianship.

FURTHER READING

Memorial Program: Voorhees Chapel, Rutgers University, 15 June 2005.

Ramsamy, Edward. "Thelma H. Tate—A Tribute," 20 May 2005.

Global Literacy Project. http://www.glpinc.org/ Graphics/structure%20graphics/Board%20Bios/ TRIBUTE-THELMA_TATE.pdf.

Obituary: *Home News Tribune Online, Obituaries.* http://www.ancestry.com, United States Obituary Collection.

VANESSA J. MORRIS

Tatum, Art (13 Oct. 1909–5 Nov. 1956), jazz pianist, was born in Toledo, Ohio, the son of a mechanic. The names of his parents are unknown. Tatum was born with cataracts in both eyes. Several operations partially restored vision in one eye. Not considering himself blind, Tatum identified colors and played cards. Information regarding Tatum's early musical life is sketchy. It is believed that he taught himself the hymns that his mother sang. In his teenage years he entered the Toledo School of Music and, with the help of glasses and the Braille method, learned to read music. On his own, Tatum studied piano rolls, phonograph recordings, radio broadcasts, and the work of various musicians. Tatum later acknowledged FATS WALLER and a radio pianist named Lee Sims as his principal musical influences. It was also in his teenage years in Toledo that Tatum began to perform in small cafes and at house-rent parties. One of his earliest career breaks came around his seventeenth birthday when he was hired to be the staff pianist for WSPD Radio in Toledo. His job responsibilities included a fifteen-minute solo spot that was eventually broadcast nationally. In 1932 Tatum became accompanist to the cabaret vocalist ADELAIDE HALL, best known for her wordless 1927 recording with DUKE ELLINGTON of "Creole Love Call." With Hall he traveled to New York City, astounding other pianists with his formidable technique. Tatum received invitations to gigs at cabarets and after-hours clubs and would, to the regret of the house pianist, ask to sit in with the band.

Art Tatum, jazz pianist, plays in the Vogue Room, New York City, c. 1947. (© William P. Gottlieb; www.jazzphotos.com.)

Tatum made his first Brunswick solo recordings while in New York City in 1933, including "Tea for Two" and "Tiger Rag." He worked in Cleveland in 1934–1935 and Chicago in 1935–1936, returning to New York City in 1937 for radio dates, club performances, and recordings for Decca, including his solo "Gone with the Wind"/"Stormy Weather" and his "Body and Soul" recording, which featured him as band leader. Tatum toured England in 1938 and from the late 1930s to the early 1940s made New York City his home, performing on tour in other cities, including Los Angeles. Tatum became, along with COLEMAN HAWKINS and BILLIE HOLIDAY, one of the largest draws on Fifty-second Street in New York City. He recorded as soloist for Decca on "Sweet Lorraine"/"Get Happy" and "Rosetta" in 1940 and again in 1941 as band leader, producing "Stompin' at the Savoy"/"Last Goodbye Blues." In 1943 Tatum organized a trio that included SLAM STEWART on bass and TINY GRIMES on guitar. When Grimes departed in 1944, Everett Barksdale stepped in. The trio, along with NAT KING COLE's trio, was one of the most influential in the early 1940s. Tatum recorded in 1944 as bandleader for World Jam Session ("I Got Rhythm"/"I Ain't Got Nobody") and for Comet ("Body and Soul") and played a concert at the Metropolitan Opera House. The year 1945 saw recordings as a sideman with BARNEY BIGARD on "Please Don't Talk about Me When I'm Gone" and "Blues for Art's Sake."

Tatum made a cameo appearance in the film *The Fabulous Dorseys* in 1947. He continued his extensive recording career with "Yesterdays" on the Just Jazz label and "Willow Weep for Me"/"Aunt Hagar's Blues" for Capitol in 1949 and the album *Art Tatum Piano Discoveries* in 1950.

Between December 1953 and January 1955 Tatum recorded more than one hundred piano solos in four sessions for Norman Granz, including *The Genius of Art Tatum* on the Clef label. The Granz association also featured several small group recordings with jazz greats such as Benny Carter (*The Art Tatum–Benny Carter–Louis Bellson Trio*, 1954) and ROY ELDRIDGE and BEN WEBSTER (*The Art Tatum–Ben Webster Quartet*, 1956), as well as *The Art Tatum Trio* (1956). He also recorded in 1955 as sideman with LIONEL HAMPTON on *Lionel Hampton and His Giants*.

Tatum is known for his impeccable technique, touch, sense of rhythm, command of harmony, and ability to improvise well beyond any of his contemporaries. He remained a perfectionist throughout his life, practicing scales and exercises tirelessly. The influence of Fats Waller is discernible in his early recordings. The 1933 Brunswick recordings reveal a distinct stride style in "Tea for Two" as well as what later became a stylistic trademark: arpeggios and crisp long runs in up-tempo pieces. Sudden interruption of phrases with new improvisational ideas is common as well. In all, Tatum made six recordings of "Tea for Two," a favorite of his as it featured modulation sections. His flare for reharmonization and chromaticism can also be heard in his recording of Duke Ellington's tune "Sophisticated Lady." His solo is permeated with chromaticism, chord substitutions, fluid high register runs, and double-time sections.

By the late 1930s Tatum was moving away from the stride style and forging a more personal improvisational style. Bitonal concepts can be heard in "Gone with the Wind" (1937), and blues elements can be heard in "Stormy Weather" (1937). In "Over the Rainbow" (1939) we hear his favorite rhythmic device (free-strict-free), clear crisp runs, temporary modulations, and reharmonization techniques. Tatum's knowledge of classical music is also apparent in his recordings of Antonín Dvořák's "Humoresque" and Jules Massenet's "Élégie," recordings geared to an audience that would be interested in jazz versions of classical material.

Tatum preferred ballads and popular song renditions, recording only twelve blues in his entire career. In "Wee Baby Blues," "Last Goodbye Blues," and "Battery Bounce" he was accompanied by a six-piece band (and by Joe Turner on two recordings). Tatum chose strong blues chord structures and tasteful and contextually appropriate improvisational ideas. He avoided chromatic and reharmonization concepts, staying within the context of traditional blues.

Tatum's growth as a soloist continued in the 1940s, as shown by longer and more continuous phrases, sometimes eight-, ten-, twelve-bar and longer phrases. His musical identity and style continued to evolve within the context of the trio performances. The influence of OSCAR PETERSON and his trio can be heard in Tatum's recording of "I've Got Rhythm" and "Flying Home." In both pieces he limits the use of stride concepts and creates long, linear lines more similar to the style of pianists Peterson, BUD POWELL, and BILLY TAYLOR.

In all, Tatum made more than six hundred recordings. His most mature playing can be heard on recordings he made for Capitol and Columbia in 1949 and on his solo recordings for Norman Granz, 1953–1955, on the Clef label. "Willow Weep for Me" remains a brilliant demonstration of the use of generic motivic ideas to create musical continuity. Each chorus has its own identity, he uses rhythmic contrast and blues concepts, and the rhythmic, harmonic, and improvisational ideas meld perfectly in the *aba* form. "Aunt Hagar's Blues," also on Capitol, is another example of some of his best recording.

The jazz critic André Hodeir's contemporary assertion that Tatum merely ornamented melodies with arpeggios and in the process destroyed rhythmic pulse was met with rebuttals. Marathon recording sessions, Tatum's poor health, his indulgences in food and alcohol, and his long hours led to a decline in his performances. Tatum's best playing remained in after-hours clubs. He died of uremia in Los Angeles, California. Tatum's influence can be heard in the performances of diverse stylists such as Bud Powell, Lennie Tristano, Billy Taylor, Chick Corea, and HERBIE HANCOCK.

FURTHER READING

Laubich, Arnold, and Ray Spencer. *Art Tatum: A Guide to His Recorded Music* (1982).

Lester, James. *Too Marvelous for Words: The Life and Genius of Art Tatum* (1994).

Schuller, Gunther. *The Swing Era: The Development of Jazz, 1930–1945* (1989).

This entry is taken from the *American National Biography* and is published here with the permission of the American Council of Learned Societies.

EDDIE S. MEADOWS

Tatum, Beverly (27 Sept. 1954–), college administrator, educator, and clinical psychologist, was born Beverly Daniel in Tallahassee, Florida, to Robert Daniel, who taught art at Florida Agricultural and Mechanical University, and Catherine Maxwell Daniel. Raised in Bridgewater, Massachusetts, Tatum is a fourth-generation college professor following in the footsteps of her paternal great-grandfather William Hazel, who was the first dean of Howard University's school of architecture; her paternal grandparents Victor and Constance Daniel, who led Maryland's Cardinal Gibbons Institute; and her father. Tatum earned a Bachelor of Arts degree in psychology from Wesleyan University in 1975, graduating magna cum laude. She also received a Master of Arts and Doctor of Philosophy degrees from the University of Michigan in 1976 and 1984, respectively. In 2000 Tatum earned a Master of Arts degree in Religious Studies from Hartford Seminary. While at the University of Michigan, she married Travis James Tatum, a professor of education, in July 1979, and two children were born to this union, Travis Jonathan and David Alexander.

Tatum has had a distinguished career as a psychologist, professor, and scholar. She served as a lecturer in the Black Studies Department at the University of California at Santa Barbara from 1982 to 1983 and later held professorships at Westfield State College from 1983 to 1989 and Mount Holyoke College from 1989 to 2002. At Mount Holyoke, she was a professor in the department of psychology and education and later, chair. In 1998, Mount Holyoke's board of trustees appointed Tatum as dean of the college and vice president for student affairs. After thirteen years of service, she was named Mount Holyoke's acting president for the 2002 spring semester.

Dr. Tatum has written numerous articles, book chapters, and books on gender and academic achievement, racial development in teens, and the impact of race on classroom dynamics. She published *Assimilation Blues: Black Families in a White Community* in 1987. In 1997 she wrote *Why Are All the Black Kids Sitting Together in the Cafeteria? And Other Conversations about Race*, which was named the 1998 Multicultural Book of the Year by the National Association of Multicultural Education. She is also the author of the 2007 work *Can We Talk about Race? And Other Conversations in an Era of School Resegregation*. In addition to her scholarship, Tatum worked in independent practice as a clinical psychologist from 1988 to 1998, conducting individual and group counseling on issues of diversity and multicultural organizational development.

On 19 April 2002, the Spelman College board of trustees appointed Tatum as the institution's ninth president and third African American female to head the historically black college for women. Located in Atlanta, Georgia, Spelman, a liberal arts college founded in 1881, has educated several generations of black women leaders including the author Pearl Cleage and Children's Defense Fund founder MARIAN WRIGHT EDELMAN. Tatum succeeded Spelman president and alumna Audrey Manley, who was also a former U.S. surgeon general.

After her appointment, Dr. Tatum remarked, "as the granddaughter of a Spelman woman [Constance Eleanor Hazel Daniel], I have been the beneficiary of its wonderful legacy of preparing black women for leadership, and I look forward to working with the faculty, staff, students, and alumnae to build on its long tradition of academic excellence and mission of empowerment and service."

She was formally installed as president in March 2003. Under Tatum's leadership, applications for admission to Spelman increased significantly, making it one of the most selective women's colleges in the United States. Tatum also worked to increase scholarships for students, created the Center for Leadership and Civic Engagement, and expanded the college's curriculum to include Chinese-language instruction.

Dr. Tatum is the recipient of numerous honorary degrees and in 2005 she was named the Brock Prize Laureate for her many contributions to the field of education. She has sat on many national boards including the Institute for International Education and the Carnegie Foundation for the Advancement of Teaching and is a former member of the President's Advisory Board for the White House Initiative on Historically Black Colleges and Universities under George W. Bush.

FURTHER READING

Spelman Messenger: The Alumnae Magazine of Spelman College (Winter/Spring 2003): 8–9.

"Tatum to Be Next Spelman President." *College Street Journal* [Mount Holyoke] (26 April 2002).

CRYSTAL R. SANDERS

Tatum, Goose (3 May 1921?–18 Jan. 1967), basketball entertainer, was born Reece Tatum in Union County, Arkansas, the son of a farmer who served as a traveling Methodist preacher on the weekends. Tatum admitted that the 1921 birth date was "an estimate," and claimed not to have a birth certificate. Some guessed that he was as much as ten years older.

Although gangly, Tatum was an athletic youth while growing up around the Arkansas towns of Calion and El Dorado. He got his nickname as a teenager when he leaped to catch a pass during a touch football game, prompting an onlooker to yell "look at that ol' Goose fly." He also played a little basketball, but his best sport was baseball, and after high school he took a job with a sawmill in the Ozarks that fielded a semiprofessional team.

The origins of Tatum's professional baseball career are unclear, but one story is that he hitchhiked 900 miles to Louisville, Kentucky, in 1939 for a tryout with a minor league team, the Black Caps. In 1941 he joined the Birmingham, Alabama, Black Barons of the Negro American League as a reserve first baseman, also playing outfield on occasion. While with the Black Barons he may have been briefly loaned to the Minneapolis-St. Paul Gophers of the fledgling Negro National League, a team owned by the founder and coach of the Harlem Globetrotters, Abe Saperstein. But Winfield Welsh, manager of the Black Barons and a friend of Saperstein's, was generally credited with seeing Tatum's basketball potential. When his team had a game rained out, the players organized a basketball game at a local gymnasium. It was soon apparent to Welsh that the six-foot-three-inch Tatum's unusually long arms (eighty-four inches from fingertip to fingertip) gave him an extra advantage in the sport, and the manager contacted Saperstein to see if he would be interested in Tatum for the Globetrotters.

Organized in Chicago in 1927, the Globetrotters had established themselves as one of the better professional teams in the country, winning what amounted to a national championship tournament in 1940. Tatum admitted that when he attended a tryout camp in 1942, "There were so many others who played better than me. Guess they left me on the squad because I wanted to play so badly" (Vecsey, 56). He signed with the Globetrotters that June, but continued to play baseball in the off-season for the rest of the decade. Saperstein arranged for Tatum to be traded to the Cincinnati Clowns in 1943, a baseball team that engaged in comedy routines similar to those of the Globetrotters. The franchise moved to Indianapolis in 1945–1946, and Tatum was the starting first baseman from 1946 to 1949. While he was not an outstanding player, he was selected to play in the Negro League East–West All-Star Game in 1947.

Tatum's basketball skills improved considerably during a 1942–1943 stint in the U.S. Army Air Corps. He played on a Lincoln, Nebraska, base team that featured several professionals, and in his free time he practiced the ballhandling skills that the Globetrotters had shown him. By the time he was discharged, Tatum was capable of holding his own as a member of a top professional team.

It was as an entertainer, however, that Tatum distinguished himself. In an effort both to boost attendance as they barnstormed across the country and to keep audiences interested as the team ran up the score against overmatched opponents, the Globetrotters had begun to supplement their performances with fancy ballhandling and with clowning. The latter element became more prominent when Tatum joined the team because he showed an unusual gift for comedy. "You laughed at Goose just looking at him," remembered teammate MARQUES OREOLE HAYNES. "A lot of people try to be funny," said Saperstein, "but they fall flat on their faces because they lack that sixth sense that tells a genius like Tatum precisely the time to punch across a particular caper" (Zinkoff, 140).

Tatum originated many of the routines that became Globetrotter staples. He would attach rubber bands to the basketball so it would come back to him as he shot a free throw, sneak over to the opposing team's huddle during a timeout and pretend to listen, or borrow a hat or purse from a member of the audience and then jump back on the court to catch a long pass and score. He worked at his craft, getting ideas from circus clowns and ice shows. Others were purely his inspiration, as when he convinced a baker in Marseilles, France, to create a loaf of bread in the shape of a basketball. During the game he deftly substituted the loaf and amazed spectators and players alike when he took a bite out of the "ball."

The Globetrotters finally began living up to their name in the early 1950s, touring Europe and other parts of the world with Tatum as the top attraction. His unusual appearance, infectious grin, and knack for physical comedy allowed him to charm audiences around the globe. His salary rose to a reported $65,000 a year, making him one of the best-paid athletes in any sport. But away from the court he was "moody, almost morose." "Dr. Jekyll and Mr. Hyde had nothing on Goose," said Haynes. He hated to travel and sometimes would disappear for a week or more. As Saperstein fined and ultimately suspended him, tension between the two grew, and in 1955 Tatum left to become co-owner of the Harlem Magicians, a squad formed by former teammate Haynes. Together they made over $1 million in two seasons before Tatum dissolved the partnership.

Tatum, who often carried thousands of dollars in a paper sack, did not handle financial matters well, and in 1959 he served ninety days in jail for failing to pay $118,000 in taxes. He was married three times, but his personality contributed to numerous domestic problems. Haynes remembered Goose's first wife, Nona, chasing Tatum through an arena with a gun, and Tatum dragging his third spouse, Naomi, out into fifteen-degree weather by the hair. They stayed together, however, and had two children, settling in El Paso, Texas.

In the 1960s Tatum formed the Harlem Road Kings, playing with them when health permitted. He missed much of one season because of a broken leg, and by the mid-1960s he had developed chronic liver problems. A fatal heart attack felled him at his El Paso home as he was preparing to fly to Dallas for a game. He died at Providence Hospital and was buried at Fort Bliss.

"No one will ever match him," said Haynes. "Goose was a genius," agreed Globetrotter teammate Leon Hillard. "He had a feeling for his audience, for the situation, that was unbelieveable. He could be so funny, we'd all be laughing right on the court" (Vecsey, 64). Tatum entertained millions and was a prime reason that the Harlem Globetrotters became the most popular sports team in the world.

FURTHER READING

"The Golden Goose Is Gone," *Sepia*, Mar. 1967.
Menville, Chuck. *The Harlem Globetrotters: Fifty Years of Fun and Games* (1978).
Smith, Marshall. "Basketball's Court Jester," *Life*, 9 Mar. 1953.
Vecsey, George. *Harlem Globetrotters* (1970).
Walker, Josh. *The Harlem Globetrotters* (1996).
Zinkoff, Dave, with Edgar Williams. *Around the World with the Harlem Globetrotters* (1953).
Obituary: *New York Times*, 19 Jan. 1967.
This entry is taken from the *American National Biography* and is published here with the permission of the American Council of Learned Societies.

KENNETH H. WILLIAMS

Tatum, Jack "Assassin" (Nov. 1948–July 2010), professional football player, was born John David Tatum in Crouse, North Carolina, to Lewis Tatum, a welder, and Annie Mae (Starr) Tatum, a housewife. His childhood was spent moving from city to city in New Jersey with his parents, including Paterson and Clifton. They settled down in Passaic, New Jersey, when Tatum was in the eighth grade.

During Tatum's sophomore year at Passaic High School, his physique generated inquiries into what sport he would like to play. Tatum was afraid of becoming a football player because he feared that he might hurt someone, but his father and uncle convinced him to try it. When Tatum joined the football team as a defense player, he was not allowed to practice tackling owing to Coach John Federici's fear that other players might be hurt. Tatum persuaded Federici to let him play offense, and Tatum's positions were running back, defensive back, and fullback. He began to receive college offers as early as his junior year, but Federici kept all recruiters away until Tatum's senior year, the year he was selected first team All-State and was named high school All-American. He graduated from high school in 1966. Tatum entertained offers from over three hundred university football teams, but he chose the Ohio State University's Buckeyes after he met Woody Hayes, the Buckeyes' celebrated head-coach.

Tatum joined the Buckeyes as a running back, but by the second semester of his freshman year, in 1967, he had been moved to defense. He led the defense for the next three years, During Tatum's years at OSU, the Buckeyes achieved a record of 27 wins and 2 losses, won the 1968 National, and played in two Rose Bowls (1968 and 1970). He was a two-time All-American (1969 and 1970) and had been named National Defensive Player of the Year (1970). Tatum graduated from OSU in May 1970 and was selected as the nineteenth pick in the first round of the 1971 National Football League (NFL) draft by the Oakland Raiders as a defensive back.

Three weeks later, Tatum signed a three-year, six-figure contract with a $50,000 bonus. Consequently a statement appeared in the press that the Oakland Raiders had hired the "assassin." The moniker stuck with Tatum the rest of his life. He played a total of ten seasons. In Tatum's nine years with the Raiders, he was voted to three consecutive Pro-Bowls (1973–1975) and was a member of one Super Bowl winning team (1977). Tatum was traded to the Houston Oilers in 1980, and he finished his football career with them. In his one year with the Oilers, he played all sixteen games and recorded a career high, seven interceptions.

Despite Tatum's success as a football player, he is often remembered in infamy because of one incident. On 12 August 1978, in a game between the Oakland Raiders and the New England Patriots, Tatum hit Darryl Stingley, a wide receiver for the Patriots. The hit broke Stingley's fourth and fifth vertebrae, leaving the receiver quadriplegic. Under NFL rules at the time, Tatum's hit was not a violation, and no penalty was called. Tatum claimed that he tried to visit Stingley at the hospital, but Stingley's family refused. Tatum said repeatedly that he had nothing to apologize about, while Stingley said that though Tatum did nothing wrong, he had forgiven him. The hit tainted Tatum's record as a great football player.

At the end of his football career, Tatum focused on his personal life and his charitable works. He established the "Jack Tatum Fund for Youthful Diabetes" to increase diabetes awareness and to finance diabetes research. The fund is a part of the Central Ohio Diabetes association, where Tatum worked for ten years. Jack Tatum met the woman who would become Denise Tatum in 1980, after his football career was over. They had three children. Tatum, a diabetic throughout his football career, underwent an amputation in February 2003 to remove several toes due to infection caused by diabetes. In March of the same year, the bottom half of his left leg was amputated due to a clogged artery. On 11 July 2003, Tatum underwent an operation to repair an abdominal aneurysm, to help open arterial blockages, and to facilitate blood flow to the legs. He died on 27 July 2010 in Oakland, California, from an apparent heart attack. He is survived by his wife, three children, and several grandchildren.

FURTHER READING
Tatum, Jack. *They Call Me Assassin* (1980).
Farmer, Sam. "Tatum Receives Support," *Los Angeles Times*, 12 Aug. 2003.
Schudel, Matt. "Jack Tatum Dies; Oakland Raiders 'Assassin' was 61," *Washington Post*, 28 Jul. 2010.

CHINWE MORAH

Taulbert, Clifton (19 Feb. 1945–), author, businessman, and inspirational speaker, was born Clifton LeMoure Taulbert in Glen Allan, Mississippi, the eldest child of Mary Esther Taulbert, a schoolteacher who later became a Head Start Center director, and Willie Jones, a Baptist preacher. Because his mother was unmarried at the time of his birth, Taulbert's great-grandparents, Joe and Pearl Young, raised him so his mother could continue her education. When his great-grandmother became too ill to care for him, Taulbert moved to live with his great-aunt, Mrs. Elna Peters Boose, or "Ma Ponk."

Taulbert's childhood memories included patronizing the black minstrel show, working with his uncle in an icehouse, and being the first black hired to work in the white-owned Hilton Food Store. Before graduating from high school, Taulbert worked the cash register in addition to his duties of stocking, cleaning, and delivering groceries. A bright and precocious child, Taulbert began his education at age four in a one-room schoolhouse whose one teacher provided instruction for students in grades one through eight. Because of Jim Crow laws, Taulbert traveled over fifty miles each way daily to all-black O'Bannon High School in Greenville, Mississippi, despite living within walking distance of the white high school in his hometown. In 1963 he graduated as valedictorian of his class and moved to St. Louis, Missouri, to live with his father's relatives. While there he became one of the first blacks hired to work at Jefferson Bank and Trust, which had vehemently refused to hire blacks for white-collar positions until after the St. Louis branch of the Congress of Racial Equality (CORE) picketed the bank for weeks. Hoping to move out of his entry-level position as a bank messenger, Taulbert began night classes at the St. Louis chapter of the American Institute of Banking, his first integrated school experience. He temporarily delayed his education as America's increased involvement in the Vietnam War influenced his decision to volunteer for service in the United States Air Force in an effort to avoid the draft and direct ground combat.

Taulbert served four years in the air force where he experienced his first integrated living conditions at Lackland Air Force Base (Texas), began writing his memoirs, learned to ski while at Dow Air Force Base in Bangor, Maine, and received a special assignment to serve with the prestigious Eighty-ninth Presidential Wing in Washington, D.C. Upon being honorably discharged on 18 August 1968, Taulbert moved to Tulsa, Oklahoma, and earned a bachelor's degree in History and Sociology in 1971 and a graduate banking degree from Southwest Graduate School of Banking at Southern Methodist University in Dallas, Texas. He worked as a banker, health-care administrator, and businessman. In 1985 he founded the Freemount Corporation, which is largely responsible for the national marketing and distribution of the Stairmaster Exercise System, and which was named after his great-great-grandparents' Mississippi Delta plantation that was sold without their knowledge at a tax auction. His success as a businessman afforded him the opportunity to polish and publish his memoirs

Once Upon a Time When We Were Colored (1989) recounted Taulbert's early life in Glen Allan and ended with his departure for St. Louis. His stories focused on everyday events—eighth-grade cotillions, hog killings, and quilting bees. In the sequel *The Last Train North* (1992), a Pulitzer Prize nominee, Taulbert paralleled the inequalities found in northern life with those of his hometown of Glen Allan. He watched as urban cities exploded with political and social activism. Moreover he learned that the North had not fulfilled its promises to southern black migrants, and that low-paying factory and domestic jobs replaced fieldwork. *Watching Our Crops Come In* (1999) completed his three-volume memoir. Taulbert recognized the irony between the fight for civil rights in America and the battle to spread democracy in the Vietnam delta. Because of his enlistment Taulbert was prevented from active participation in the struggle for civil rights and he watched silently from the sidelines as his sister was jailed in January 1968 during a protest at the University of Mississippi, six years after its first black student, JAMES MEREDITH, integrated the school. Despite his limited participation in the civil rights movement, Taulbert volunteered for Robert Kennedy's presidential campaign and was deeply affected by his assassination in June 1968.

Taulbert's writings earned him international acclaim, honors, and awards. He co-produced the award-winning film *Once Upon a Time When We Were Colored*, which was based on his first memoir; it won the 1997 Black Film Award at the Acapulco Black Film Festival and a 1997 Image Award. He also co-produced the award-winning documentary *The Era of Segregation: A Personal Perspective*, which won the Cine Golden Eagle Award (1993), a coveted prize for excellence in documentary and informational film, and the New York Film Festival's Silver Medal (1993). In 1996 he received a NAACP Image Award and was inducted into the Tulsa Hall of Fame. In 2003 Taulbert won the RICHARD WRIGHT Award of Literary Excellence. He also received an honorary doctorate from Oral Roberts University.

In addition to his memoirs Taulbert wrote *The Journey Home: A Father's Gift to His Son* (2002), the Little Cliff children's series, and *Eight Habits of the Heart: Embracing the Values That Build Strong Families and Communities* (1997), which launched his latest venture, the Building Community Institute, of which Taulbert served as president. In 1968 Taulbert moved to Tulsa, his adopted "hometown," with his wife Barbara Jackson, formerly of Eudora, Arkansas. They had two children, Marshall Danzy and the late Kathryn Anne, who succumbed to complications from sickle cell anemia.

LISA C. LAKES

Taylor, Alrutheus Ambush (1893–4 June 1954), historian and educator, was born in Washington, D.C., the son of Lewis Taylor and Lucy Johnson (occupations unknown). Educated in the Washington, D.C., public schools, Taylor entered the University of Michigan and received a B.A. in Mathematics in 1916. He taught English for one year at Tuskegee Institute and then worked with black migrants at both the national and the New York branch of the Urban League as a social worker from 1917 to 1918. In 1919 he accepted a position at West Virginia Collegiate Institute, where he taught mathematics, history, economics, and logic and began his long association with African American historian CARTER GODWIN WOODSON. That year he married Harriet Wilson; they had no children.

Taylor had been brought to the institute by JOHN WARREN DAVIS, its enterprising young black president, who was determined to improve the quality of the faculty and staff. In 1920 Davis hired Woodson, who soon befriended Taylor and encouraged his interest in history. Woodson published Taylor's first investigation, on Negro congressmen during Reconstruction, in the *Journal of Negro History* in 1922. At Woodson's suggestion, and under the auspices of the Association for the Study of Negro Life and History, which Woodson had founded in 1915, Taylor enrolled in the graduate degree program in history at Harvard University. Woodson had also received his doctorate from Harvard and studied under the same eminent historians, Edward Channing and Albert Bushnell Hart. Taylor also worked with social historian Arthur M. Schlesinger Sr., who further stimulated Taylor's interest in African American history. Woodson not only guided but also financed Taylor's studies for an M.A. and Ph.D. in American History, which were received from Harvard in 1923 and 1935, respectively.

In 1922 Taylor became the first young black scholar to join Woodson's research staff at the Association for the Study of Negro Life and History, where he served as a full-time investigator. His research on blacks in the Reconstruction of South Carolina after the Civil War was published in Woodson's journal in 1924 and brought out in book form the same year. Taylor continued his studies of southern Reconstruction, focusing on Virginia, and published an essay and monograph in 1926. In these works Taylor began to overturn the prevailing view of black ineptitude during Reconstruction by demonstrating that white racism, violence, and greed were largely responsible for the failure of political reform. He pointed to the many accomplishments and achievements of black politicians. Taylor's interpretation was largely echoed in W. E. B. DuBois's masterly interpretation, *Black Reconstruction* (1935), as well as in subsequent studies of the period. In 1938 Taylor published a historiographical essay in the *Journal of Negro History* on historians and their interpretations of Reconstruction that praised the work of DuBois but acknowledged that the work of black scholars had largely gone unnoticed.

In 1926 Taylor joined the faculty at Fisk University, where he served as professor of history and chairman of the department. A gifted and popular teacher, Taylor also was known for his administrative skills. He assumed additional administrative responsibilities as Dean of the College of Arts and Sciences from 1930 to 1951. Among his accomplishments was the admission of Fisk as a fully accredited institution in the Southern Association of American Universities; it was the first black school to obtain accreditation.

In the 1920s Taylor assisted Woodson with research and revisions for the textbook *The Negro in Our History* (1922) by providing surveys on former slaves, black Baptists, and the status of free blacks in the antebellum South. Using the manuscript census, Taylor assisted Woodson in the compilation of lists of free blacks who owned property, including slaves. In the 1940s he published a study of blacks in Tennessee (*The Negro in Tennessee 1865–1880* [1941]) and coauthored a study of community activities among black youth (*A Study of the Community Life of the Negro Youth* [1941]). Taylor retired from Fisk in 1951, but remained active in Nashville. He was a member of several local community organizations and served on the board of trustees of Nashville Kent College of Law. At his death, he left unfinished a history of Fisk University.

After his first wife's death in 1941, Taylor founded a scholarship at Fisk in her honor. He married Catherine Buchanan in 1943; they had no children. Taylor died in Nashville, Tennessee.

FURTHER READING

Taylor's papers are in the Fisk University Archives. Other correspondence can be found in the papers of his black contemporaries, especially Luther Porter Jackson, whose papers are housed at Virginia State University in Petersburg.

Goggin, Jacqueline. *Carter G. Woodson: A Life in Black History* (1993).

Meier, August, and Elliott Rudwick. *Black History and the Historical Profession, 1915–1980* (1986).

This entry is taken from the *American National Biography* and is published here with the permission of the American Council of Learned Societies.

JACQUELINE GOGGIN

Taylor, Anna Diggs (9 Dec. 1932–), lawyer, judge, and civil rights activist, was born Anna Katherine Johnston in Washington, D.C. Her parents sent her to private school because they felt it would be more challenging than the local schools, and in 1950 she graduated from the Northfield School for Girls in Massachusetts. She earned a B.A. in Economics from Barnard College in 1954 and three years later a law degree (LLB) from Yale. Unable to find employment with a private law firm due to racial and gender discrimination, she became a solicitor in the Department of Labor under J. Ernest Williams, the first African American to hold sub-cabinet rank (assistant, associate, or deputy secretary) in the federal government.

Taylor married the U.S. congressman Charles Diggs (D-Mich.) in 1960 and moved to Detroit. She served as a prosecutor for Wayne County (1961–1962) and assistant U.S. attorney for the Eastern District of Michigan (1965–1966). She spent the summer of 1964 in Mississippi with a National Lawyers Guild civil rights program that provided legal services to civil rights activists. In fact she arrived on the day three civil rights proponents disappeared and with other attorneys was confronted by a hostile crowd of whites when they went to the sheriff's office to inquire about those who had disappeared. She then served as legislative assistant and Detroit office manager (1967–1970) to her husband until they divorced in 1970. She married S. Martin Taylor in 1976.

Taylor became an associate (1970) and later a partner (1971) in the private law firm of Zwerdling, Maurer, Diggs, and Papp. Her specialty was labor law, and her clients included the United Auto Workers, the Registered Nurses' Association, and the American Federation of State, County, and Municipal Employees. Although her firm's clients were labor unions, she spent a substantial amount of her own time representing individuals in race, gender, and age discrimination lawsuits. She was retained by the Detroit city government in the landmark 1974 case *Detroit Boat Club and Detroit Yacht Club v. City of Detroit*. The city gave dollar-a-year land leases to the two clubs, yet neither had ever inducted a black member. In 1967 the Department of Parks and Recreation issued a rule requiring that private clubs on city land must take affirmative action to implement nondiscrimination in employment and membership, which the clubs challenged. The dispute was settled in 1975, when the clubs agreed to numerous procedures to allow for the induction of minorities and affirmative action in employment.

In 1975 Taylor returned to the public sector as supervising assistant corporation counsel in charge of the labor litigation section of the Law Department. In this capacity she oversaw the relationships of all departments of city government with over fifty public employee unions, labor negotiations, and civil rights litigation for the city.

Beyond her efforts on behalf of racial and gender equity, in the 1972 presidential election she cochaired Michigan Lawyers for Hubert Humphrey, and after the Democratic National Convention she cochaired Michigan Lawyers for George McGovern. She also served as cochair of the Lawyers Committee for COLEMAN YOUNG in Young's 1973 campaign for mayor of Detroit. She taught Labor Law in the Public Sector at Detroit's Wayne State University Law School in 1976.

Taylor made history on 17 May 1979, when President Jimmy Carter nominated her to be the first African American federal judge from the state of Michigan. Her nomination to the U.S. District Court for the Eastern District of Michigan was confirmed by the U.S. Senate on 31 October 1979. She served as chief judge from 1996 to 1998, which made her the chief administrative officer of that court. On 31 December 1998 Judge Taylor took "senior status," which is the equivalent of semi-retirement in that the judge in question still hears cases but with a reduced workload.

District courts are the trial courts in the federal judicial system. They have jurisdiction to preside over trials on virtually all categories of cases and controversies arising under federal law, civil as well as criminal. The system is organized geographically, so Taylor's jurisdiction involved cases arising only in the eastern part of Michigan. Although exclusively a labor lawyer for the first twenty years of her career, upon ascending to the bench, Taylor heard cases as diverse as hate crimes, civil rights violations, JESSE JACKSON's challenge to the rules of the Michigan Democratic Party, the constitutionality of a Christmas Nativity scene on public property, affirmative action, and discriminatory treatment of incarcerated Cuban nationals, to name just a few.

Taylor served in scores of professional, educational, and community associations. Some of the more prominent professional groups are Federal Judicial Center Committee on District Judge Education, District of Columbia Bar Association, Michigan Bar Association, Federal Bar Association, Detroit Bar Association, Wolverine Bar Association, National Lawyers Guild, Michigan Association of Black Judges, Women Judges Association, and National Bar Association. Her honors and awards similarly are impressive in quantity and quality: National Bar Association Women Lawyers' Division Award, Sojourner Truth Award of National Negro Business and Professional Women, Detroit and Wolverine Bar Association Bench-and-Bar Award, Detroit Urban League Achievement Award, International Institute Hall of Fame, Marygrove College Honorary Doctor of Laws, and Barnard College Alumna of the Year Award, again to name just a few.

FURTHER READING
Alexander, Susan, ed. "Anna Diggs Taylor," in *Almanac of the Federal Judiciary*, vol. 1 (2005).
U.S. Courts, the Federal Judiciary. U.S. District Courts. Available online at www.uscourts.gov/districtcourts.html.

GERARD S. GRYSKI

Taylor, Benjamin H. (1 July 1888–24 Jan. 1953), Negro Baseball Leagues' first baseman, pitcher, manager, and umpire, was born in Anderson, South Carolina. "Ben," as he was usually known, was the youngest of four baseball brothers who also included the famed manager C. I. TAYLOR, "Candy" Jim Taylor, and "Steel Arm" Johnny Taylor, and he became the premier Negro leagues first baseman during the first quarter of the twentieth century. Throughout his career Taylor was one of the most productive players offensively, ending with a .354 lifetime batting average. He was quick on ground balls and could make all the plays at first, making the other infielders look good by digging out low throws and making difficult plays with such ease that they appeared routine.

Taylor began his playing career in 1908 as a pitcher with the Birmingham Giants and recorded an impressive 22–3 win-loss record in 1909. Two years later, with the St. Louis Giants, he is credited with a 30–1 record. Although he continued pitching for several years afterward, it was with his bat and play at first base that he earned his greatest renown.

When his brother C. I. assumed the managerial reins of the West Baden, Indiana, Sprudels in 1910, Taylor moved with him. Playing as a combination pitcher and first baseman, his baseball acumen was beginning to attract the attention of baseball's top teams. During these formative seasons, he turned in some solid performances on the pitcher's mound, but he also continued his early hitting promise, registering a .379 average in 1912. Moving to Chicago in 1913, where he joined brothers Jim and Johnny, he played first base for RUBE FOSTER and his Chicago American Giants. However, Taylor gained his greatest fame while playing with the Indianapolis ABCs. He stepped into the cleanup slot, hit a robust .333, and remained in that batting slot as long as he was with the ABCs. In 1914 the left-handed Taylor batted .335 and fashioned a performance that earned

him most valuable player and led the team's surge to the championship.

Sandwiching a trip between the 1915 and 1916 seasons, Taylor made a sojourn to Cuba, where he left behind an impressive .500 batting average. He remained with the ABC's through 1918, leaving for a season with the New York Bacharach Giants in 1919 for his first endeavor into the managerial ranks. He returned to the ABCs in 1920 and continued to hit with authority. He compiled averages of .323, .407, and .358 in his last three seasons with the team (1920–1922). Following the death of his brother C. I. in 1922, Taylor managed the ABCs for a season before leaving the team in the spring of 1923 to travel east again. He assumed the responsibility of organizing the Washington Potomacs ball club and hired his brother Johnny as pitching coach.

Taylor was credited with hitting over .300 in fifteen of his first sixteen years in baseball, but with the managerial pressures to produce a winning team in 1924, he had what he considered his worst offensive year but still led his team in batting average (.314) and home runs (15). Although as manager he forged respectable personal statistics, the ball club had a disappointing season. When the Potomacs were disbanded, he joined forces with OSCAR CHARLESTON and the Harrisburg Giants in Pennsylvania for the 1925 season and hit for a .328 average as playing manager. From there Taylor moved to the Baltimore Black Sox, again as playing manager, replacing PETE HILL in midsummer 1926. The team suffered disciplinary problems, and Taylor's stay there was troubled. Almost immediately after his arrival, in an effort to instill some semblance of discipline, he dispatched the free-spirited slugger John Beckwith to Harrisburg in a trade. The following summer Taylor suffered cuts that required twenty stitches when he and several other Black Sox players were injured as a cement truck sideswiped their team automobile. Although past his prime and despite the hardships due to the club's poor record under Taylor's management (1926—23-36, 1927—36-30, 1928—the Eastern Colored League collapsed and Baltimore joined the American Negro League), he still stroked the ball for averages of .242, .307, and .336 during his three seasons in Baltimore.

Prior to the start of the 1929 season, in a trade of managers, Taylor was traded to the Atlantic City Bacharach Giants for Dick Lundy and signed what was thought to be the highest salary in black baseball. With the Bacharachs, at age forty-one, he still hit .322 to close both the decade and his playing career, finishing with a .334 lifetime batting average in black baseball. After his career as an active player ended, Taylor continued in baseball in various capacities. He umpired in both the East-West League in 1932 and the Negro National League in 1934. He also managed and coached with several teams at different levels of competition, including the Baltimore Suns in 1933, where he tutored BUCK LEONARD on the finer points of playing first base. Modest, easygoing, and soft-spoken, Taylor was a true gentleman who maintained a fair and professional demeanor, and he was an excellent teacher of young players.

After he retired, Taylor was an active businessman, acquiring the rights to print and distribute game programs and scorecards at Bugle Field, where the Baltimore Elite Giants played. In the latter years of his life, he operated a poolroom for a time. But he broke his left arm in a fall and, when it was not properly set, lost the arm to amputation. He died of pneumonia in Baltimore, Maryland. He was inducted into the National Baseball Hall of Fame in 2006.

FURTHER READING

Hogan, Lawrence D. *Shades of Glory: The Negro Leagues and the Story of African-American Baseball* (2006).

Lanctot, Neil. *Negro League Baseball: The Rise and Ruin of a Black Institution* (2004).

Riley, James A. *The Biographical Encyclopedia of the Negro Baseball Leagues* (1994).

LUKE NICHTER

Taylor, C. I. (20 Jan. 1875–23 Feb. 1922), baseball player, manager, and executive, was born Charles Isham Taylor in Anderson, South Carolina, the son of Isham B. Taylor, a Methodist minister, and his wife Adaline (maiden name unknown). Known throughout his life as C. I., he was the fifth of twelve children. He attended school in Anderson County, South Carolina, and later attended Clark College in Atlanta, where he lettered in baseball and was rated the best third baseman in the Atlanta Intercollegiate League. During the Spanish-American War Taylor served in Company H of the Tenth U.S. Cavalry.

Following the war Taylor began his illustrious eighteen-year managerial career in black professional baseball. He began as player-manager of the Birmingham Giants of Alabama in 1904. He played second base and managed the club until 1909. At different times throughout his six years in Birmingham he had three of his younger brothers, John, Jim, and Ben, playing for him. Each

of these brothers would have highly successful careers within Negro League baseball.

In 1910 Taylor moved his team to West Baden, Indiana, where he continued to manage and play second base. After four seasons with the West Baden Sprudels, Taylor purchased half interest in the Indianapolis ABCs baseball club in 1914. The ABCs were named for their original sponsors, the American Brewing Company. It was with the ABCs that Taylor gained his greatest fame.

During his years as manager of the ABCs Taylor built a team that was consistently a dominant force in black professional baseball. During the winter of 1915–1916 Taylor took his team to Cuba to barnstorm against the Cuban professional team, the first time an African American professional baseball club had traveled to the island. By 1916 Taylor had built a ball club that successfully challenged the perennial power of black professional baseball, the Chicago American Giants. At the conclusion of the 1916 season, Taylor's ABCs defeated the Chicago American Giants, five games to four, to become the "World's Colored Champions."

Taylor was instrumental in the creation of the first successful black baseball league, the Negro National League, which was formed on 13 February 1920 in Kansas City, Missouri. He had advocated the formation of an organized league since reading an 18 April 1914 article in the *Indianapolis Freeman* newspaper. The league consisted of eight black professional teams from the Midwest. Taylor became vice president of the league, an office he held until his death. He continued to take great pride in his own team, always making sure that they were one of the best dressed on and off the field. Taylor's Indianapolis ABCs hosted the inaugural Negro National League game on 2 May 1920, with the ABCs defeating the Chicago Giants 4-2 before a crowd of eight thousand. Within the organized league structure, Taylor's ABCs continued to play winning baseball.

Taylor was well known and respected in the black community of Indianapolis. He owned and operated a pocket billiard parlor that was reported by the *Indianapolis Freeman* to be the "finest and most elaborately equipped in the Middle West." It became the premier gathering place during winter months for baseball discussion and debate, known as the "Hot Stove League." Taylor was also active within the Masonic fraternity and attained the level of thirty-third-degree mason.

In 1922 Taylor fell ill with pneumonia and died in Indianapolis. He was survived by his wife, Olivia. They had no children.

FURTHER READING

Riley, James A. *The Biographical Encyclopedia of the Negro Baseball Leagues* (1994).

This entry is taken from the *American National Biography* and is published here with the permission of the American Council of Learned Societies.

TODD BOLTON

Taylor, Carol (27 Dec. 1931–), the first black flight attendant of either sex for a U.S. airline and an activist, was born Ruth Carol Taylor in Boston, Massachusetts, the older of two children of Ruth Irene Powell, a registered nurse, and William Edison Taylor, a barber and farmer, who lived in nearby Cambridge.

After several years in New York City, the family moved to a farm in Trumansburg, in upstate New York, where Taylor grew up. She attended Elmira College for Women in Elmira, New York, and New York University in New York City, became a registered nurse in 1955 upon graduation from the Bellevue Schools of Nursing at New York University, and practiced nursing for the next three years.

With the nation's airlines under pressure to break the color line, Taylor became one of about eight hundred "Negro girls" interviewed by Mohawk Airlines, a regional carrier based in Ithaca, New York, which she said wanted worldwide publicity. Being, as she later explained, "near-white enough with aquiline features, so-called" and having deliberately given safe answers to airline interviewers' questions, she made her initial flight as the "first Negro airline hostess" on 11 February 1958. The landmark was reported in *The New York Times*, the *New York Herald Tribune*, and *Time* magazine and on the cover of *Jet*. Bored by the job, she quit after six months, never having been invited to eat with the other crew members. Nonetheless, once Taylor broke the color barrier, other airlines gradually began adding black people to their flight crews. Fifty years later in 2008, Taylor's accomplishment was memorialized by the New York State Assembly.

In 1960 she married Rex Norman Legall and gave birth to a daughter, Cindy Legall. In 1969 she had a son, Laurence Legall Taylor, whose father was a colonel in the Barbados military, Laurence G. Quintyne, M.B.E. Her grandson, Tyler Legall, was born to her daughter in 1997. Taylor's husband died in 2008.

After spending about five years in Trinidad, London, and New York City, during which she covered the 1963 March on Washington for *Flamingo*, a British magazine with an Afro-Caribbean readership, Taylor settled in Barbados and lived there from 1964 to 1977. She was a community activist on consumer affairs and women's rights, among other issues.

Wanting a less insular life for her children, Taylor brought them to Brooklyn in 1977, where she remained for more than thirty years. As a widely known grassroots activist, she spoke, wrote commentaries for local black-owned newspapers, and attended innumerable demonstrations against police brutality and other injustices, even shaving her head once to call attention to her protest.

Calling herself a "blacktivist," she deployed neologisms and nontraditional spellings in articles, riffs, and jeremiads; on handmade signs; and during media interviews and speeches in order to raise public awareness that all people on earth are part of a single "hue-man" race descended from "beautiful blue-black" Africans—although, she said dryly, some people "are more rinsed-out than others." She firmly rejected "African American" as exclusionary and identified herself as "a black African." Varying her diction and enunciation from cultivated to rowdy, scatological, gleeful, or satiric at will, she advocated the word "colorism" as more accurate and incisive than "racism." She considered "race" a bogus concept and words like "biracial," "transracial," and "interracial" meaningless. Yet she said, "If you're not playing the race card, you're not playing with a full deck." In order "to agitate," she said that God is a black woman.

Taylor saw "untreated racism/colorism" as a rampant disease in the United States. In 1982 she decided that a racism quotient test, analogous to an IQ test, was needed. Collaborating with a psychologist, Mari P. Saunders, she developed what came to be called the Racism/Colorism Quotient Test (RQ). Its twenty multiple-choice questions were designed to reveal the extent of the test-taker's bias regarding workplace, neighborhood, and social situations. Then education and healing—"remedial ethnotherapy"—could follow in a nonthreatening, nonjudgmental vein.

In the same year Taylor and Saunders founded the Institute for "Interracial" Harmony, inserting the quotation marks later, to administer the test and offer diversity training in the public and private sectors. The Institute's motto was "Prejudice is learned. It can be unlearned." The RQ test could be taken, free of charge, at the Institute's website, http://www. racismtest.org. Test-takers received their scores and evaluations immediately, online.

When the RQ test was published in 1992 by *The Village Voice*, a local weekly newspaper, four thousand of its predominantly white, liberal readers submitted responses. A third of them, Taylor said, were "dysfunctional in their responses to color and cultural differences." She often wrote to journalists and to political, civic, educational, and religious leaders, urging that the RQ test be given to all police, judges, jurors, teachers, doctors, and others before they were allowed to make decisions affecting black people's lives.

After her teenaged son was mugged twice and then treated like a criminal when he sought help from the police, Taylor self-published *The Little Black Book: Black African Male Survival in America or Staying Alive and Well in an Institutionally Racist Society* (1985). The pocket-sized pamphlet contained about thirty rules and recommendations to protect young black men, whom Taylor considered an endangered group. By 2008 she said that more than two hundred thousand copies of *The Little Black Book* had been sold, often in bulk, at two dollars each. Taylor carried copies with her everywhere she went, wearing a sign on her clothing identifying herself as its author and selling single copies on sidewalks and buses. The pamphlet was also available from bookstores, schools, unions, libraries, and religious organizations and from http://www. littlcblackbook@juno.com.

While objecting to nationwide suppression of black voting, she herself refused to vote after the early 1980s, regarding the system as corrupt. She dismissed voting as "a major soporific for the control of the masses." Holding dual U.S. and Barbadian citizenship, she said, "I am a world citizen." She continued advancing her views on current affairs online at http://www.caroltaylorword.blogspot.com.

Her work was covered by *The New York Times*, *The Washington Post*, the New York *Amsterdam News*, *The Boston Globe*, *New York Newsday*, *Library Journal*, the Gannett newspaper group, and other news organizations.

Taylor's impassioned blactivism, visible in her raised, clenched fist or one-finger salute at demonstrations, was coupled with receptivity to strangers of all colors in her daily life. She welcomed conversations with them. When people recognized her and greeted her warmly, asking "How are you?" her usual reply was succinct. "At war," she said.

FURTHER READING
Gubert, Betty Kaplan, Miriam Sawyer, and Caroline M. Fannin. *Distinguished African Americans in Aviation and Space Science* (2001).

MARIE SHEAR

Taylor, Cecil Percival (15 Mar. 1929–), pianist and composer, was born in New York City, the son of Percy Clinton Taylor, a chef, and Almeida Ragland. Cecil grew up on Long Island where at home his father sang the blues and played records by LOUIS ARMSTRONG and ERROLL GARNER, among other jazz greats. His mother played violin and piano and started giving Cecil piano lessons when he was five; within a year he was playing Chopin. He also took tap-dance lessons and later studied with a timpanist and several other piano teachers, especially Charlotte Levy. The influence of Cecil's mother was clearly profound; she was a sophisticated woman who spoke French and German and introduced Cecil to Schopenhauer when he was ten. When she died, when Cecil was only twelve, he stopped practicing piano for a while, missing both her discipline and her personal support.

Taylor enrolled in the New England Conservatory of Music (NEC) in 1952, but he later had few fond memories of his experiences there. He was denied admission to the composition department, and he later referred to his teachers as clerks, a comment on their disdain for African American musical traditions. Taylor's most important early influences spanned the widest possible range. He studied classical composers like Stravinsky and Bartók but also jazz pianists and composers like Garner, Lennie Tristano, THELONIOUS MONK, HORACE SILVER, FATS WALLER, and above all DUKE ELLINGTON. For a short time he was even drawn to the dense tonal clusters of Dave Brubeck.

Taylor's earliest gigs were with the trumpeter HOT LIPS PAGE and the altoist JOHNNY HODGES in 1953, and he played regularly in Boston-area clubs during the early 1950s with musicians like GIGI GRYCE, Jaki Byard, Charlie Mariano, Serge Chaloff, and Richard Twardzik. After graduating from the NEC, Taylor lived briefly with his father in Queens, and in 1956 he recorded his first album, *Jazz Advance* (Blue Note), with Steve Lacy on alto sax, Buell Neidlinger on bass, and Dennis Charles on drums. Compared to what was to come, the music sounds almost straight-ahead, but Taylor was already moving beyond postbop forms to explore dynamic extremes, dissonances, and tone clusters. *Jazz Advance* gained Taylor some attention and led to a six-week appearance at the Five Spot, a local rhythm and blues club. Though the owner complained about the length of Taylor's sets, Taylor nevertheless filled the seats with fans and put the club on the jazz map. In 1957 he appeared at the Newport Jazz Festival, and in 1958 he appeared—to great critical acclaim—at the Great South Bay Jazz Festival. He then recorded a series of albums that solidified his status: *Looking Ahead* (1958), *Stereo Drive* (1958; later known as *Coltrane's Time*), and *Love for Sale* (1959). Though these albums contain both his own compositions and standards, Taylor's interpretation of even familiar tunes like "Love for Sale" was ironic and mocking.

By 1960 Taylor had left the bebop framework completely behind, firmly establishing his musical identity with a series of recordings for Candid Records: *The World of Cecil Taylor* (1960) and *Air, Jumpin' Punkins, New York City R&B*, and *Cell Walk for Celeste* (all 1961). The personnel fluctuated, but the saxophonists ARCHIE SHEPP and Steve Lacy, the trombonist Roswell Rudd, the bassist Neidlinger, and the drummers Charles and BILLY HIGGINS proved to be sympathetic interpreters of Taylor's evolving musical conception. During the summer of 1961 Taylor played a gig with Shepp and Charles at Raphael's in Greenwich Village, and one night a young alto saxophone player named JIMMY LYONS sat in. Taylor was so taken with Lyons's playing that he invited him to join the group for a performance at the Five Spot, initiating a creative relationship that was the most important in Taylor's life and that lasted until Lyons's death in 1986.

Already Taylor displayed in abundance his unique power, stamina, physical intensity, and percussive approach to the piano, together with the free use of dissonance and forays into atonalism, that won him critical acclaim but elicited disdain from more conservative critics and jazz fans. The renowned composer Gil Evans invited him to play three cuts on Evans's album *Into the Hot* with a group that included Shepp and Lyons, Sunny Murray on drums, and HENRY GRIMES on bass. In the fall of 1962 Taylor played a thirteen-week gig at the Take Three Club in Greenwich Village with Lyons and Murray, joined occasionally by Grimes. In 1962–1963 he led a trio on a seven-week tour of Denmark, joined by the saxophonist ALBERT AYLER; a live recording at Café Montmartre was later released as *Nefertiti, the Beautiful One Has Come*. This was true energy music, played at a blinding speed and with irresistible momentum that could also quite unexpectedly relax into a breathtakingly beautiful ballad tempo. As the writer Gary Giddins observed, it was also the first time that Taylor "realized he did not have to suit his improvisational impulses to a set rhythm and chords; he could, to the contrary, create a kinetic center and force time and harmony to accommodate him" (1998, 457).

And yet Taylor found relatively little steady work in the United States during the 1960s; periodically he found himself unemployed, working as a dishwasher, coffee shop deliveryman, and record salesman. He averaged one concert appearance a year and only sporadic nightclub jobs. Club owners regarded him as a financial liability; he might fill their seats, but he also insisted on a properly tuned piano, and patrons understood that his music demanded attentive listening, cutting into the profitable bar take. The music business in general liked him no better; his demands for quality pianos and decent studio conditions meant that he made no recordings from 1963 to 1965. And despite a passionate fan base, there were also hostile audiences unprepared for his listening demands. Taylor did play in the October Revolution in Jazz concert in New York in 1964, with the Jazz Composers Guild in 1964 and 1965, and at a five-week gig in 1965 at the Village Vanguard. And he recorded two of his most important recordings in 1966 for Blue Note: *Conquistador*, with Andrew Cyrille on drums, Bill Dixon on trumpet, Lyons, Grimes, and Alan Silva, and *Unit Structures*, also a sextet. In 1968 he also recorded with the Jazz Composers Orchestra, a large free-jazz group founded by the pianist and composer Carla Bley and the trumpeter Michael Mantler.

Taylor's growing popularity finally allowed him to make a living from his music by 1967, though a commercially oriented, nearsighted music business kept him out of the recording studio from 1962 to 1968. The turning point came in the early 1970s. In 1969 Taylor was appointed to a residency at the Fondation Maeght in Paris, with SAM RIVERS, Cyrille, and Lyons. He taught at the University of Wisconsin in 1970–1971, and from 1971 to 1973 he was, along with Cyrille and Lyons, an artist-in-residence at Antioch College; also in 1973 he was awarded a Guggenheim fellowship. Taylor's music continued to develop, and audiences seemed to relish the demands that this complex, energetic music placed on them, sitting in rapt attention through two-hour concerts. In 1973 he toured Japan, Europe, and the United States and began to release recordings at a rate that continued unabated even as he turned seventy. *The Spring of 2 Blue Jays*, released on his own label, Unit Core Records, in 1973, with Cyrille, Lyons, and Sirone on bass, is one of the best introductions to Taylor's music. Side one features one of his tour de force solo performances, side two his quartet, with Lyons, Cyrille, and Sirone on bass.

Silent Tongues (1974) is a solo concert from the Montreux Jazz Festival. *Dark unto Themselves*

(1976) is a powerful quintet performance. In 1977 Taylor joined MARY LOU WILLIAMS for a much-anticipated concert performance, an unusual meeting of disparate styles that did not quite jell. In 1978 Taylor released a series of acclaimed sextet recordings: *One Too Many Salty Swift and Not Goodbye* and *It Is in the Brewing Luminous* for HatHut and *Cecil Taylor Unit* and *3 Phasis* for New World Records. A meeting with the drummer MAX ROACH at Columbia University in 1979 was an unqualified success—two exploratory modernists meeting on equal terms. More unexpected were meetings at the White House, where after performances President Jimmy Carter asked Taylor if Horowitz knew about him, and Attorney General Griffin Bell followed him offstage and asked where he could find his records.

The 1980s found Taylor triumphant. His style began to embrace greater lyricism, and he began to introduce his solo performances with recitations of original poetry. He released three of his greatest solo recordings: *Fly! Fly! Fly! Fly! Fly!* (1980), *Garden* (1981), and *For Olim* (1986), a recording of particular beauty. During the mid-1980s he played regularly with Lyons, the former Coltrane drummer RASHIED ALI, the young bassist WILLIAM PARKER, and a variety of other sidemen, releasing powerfully impressive recordings like *Olu Iwa* (Soul Note, 1986), *Live in Bologna* (1986), and *Tzotzil/Mummers/Tzotzil* (1987).

But the highlight of Taylor's career came with a month-long festival in Berlin, a celebration of his music that also yielded thirteen compact discs of recordings on the German FMP label. These sessions embrace the entire breadth of Taylor's style, from his quietest moments to his most melodramatic and boisterous, but as Giddins notes, "they are weighted, controlled, intensified, leavened by the accountability of collaboration." There are two big-band sessions (the first in Taylor's recording history), trios, several duets with percussionists, and two wonderful solo performances, particularly *Erzulie Maketh Scent* (1988), "a long meditation on music as a magical force."

In 1991 Taylor was awarded a MacArthur Fellowship that gave him long-deserved financial independence. In 1990 and 1991 he produced a pair of solo recordings for FMP (*Double Holy House* and *Tree of Life*) that are among his most lyrical. In the late 1980s he established the Feel Trio, with Parker and the drummer Tony Oxley; this group, too, produced several critically praised recordings for FMP, notably *Looking* (1989) and *Celebrated Blazons*

(1990). There were also forays with new partners throughout the 1990s. *Qu'a: Live at the Irridium* (2 vols., 1998) was a quartet with Harri Sjostrom on soprano sax, Dominic Duval on bass, and Jackson Krall on drums (the latter two were frequent partners during the 1990s). Taylor recorded a lyrical duet with the violinist Mat Maneri at the Library of Congress in 1999 and a seven-part suite with the Italian Instabile Orchestra in 2000. Throughout the 1990s he performed frequently with dancers and ballet companies. In 2002, at the age of seventy-three, Taylor recorded one of his greatest solo albums in a concert at Willisau, Switzerland, a performance that showed no diminution of his powerful skills. Finally, in 2004 Taylor led a fifteen-piece band, the Cecil Taylor Orchestra Humaine, in a performance of a series of new compositions at New York's Iridium Jazz Club, suggesting yet another direction for the most prolific and creative of all modern jazz artists.

Well into his seventies Taylor was, to say the least, still a force unto himself. Deeply rooted in the blues and jazz traditions, a master of the techniques and concepts of European art music, he followed no muse but his own. His intellectual, emotional, and musical curiosity was boundless. In one typical day he listened to Chinese classical music, Duke Ellington, Victoria de los Angeles singing Purcell, a Brahms piano concerto, and LEONTYNE PRICE singing the last movement of Strauss's *Salome*. He practiced ten to twelve hours a day when preparing for concerts, working out the structures of his performances ahead of time and freeing himself to integrate his own inspired improvisations. Despite the demands that his playing placed on the audience, he always saw his playing as an extension of the jazz tradition, not a rejection of it. His constant reshaping of dynamics and rhythms, his interest in what he calls "the variety of pulses that exist in a given moment," are rooted in the playing of EARL HINES and ART TATUM. But above all Taylor placed his music in the expressive cultural and spiritual contexts of the African American tradition. "Playing is not a question of energy," he said. "It's spiritual transformation" (Balliett, 1996, 518). He wanted his audience to "feel what he feels," as Whitney Balliett noted. And as Taylor observed to Giddins, "To feel is perhaps the most terrifying thing in this society" (Giddins, 1981, 282).

FURTHER READING

Balliett, Whiney. *American Musicians II: Seventy-One Portraits in Jazz* (1996).

Giddins, Gary. *Riding on a Blue Note: Jazz and American Pop* (1981).

Giddins, Gary. *Visions of Jazz: The First Century* (1998).

Jost, Ekkehard. *Free Jazz* (1974).

Litweiler, John. *The Freedom Principle: Jazz after 1958* (1984).

Spellman, A.B. *Black Music: Four Lives* (1966).

RONALD P. DUFOUR

Taylor, Charles Henry James (21 Apr. 1856–25 May 1899), lawyer, journalist, and diplomat, was born in Perry County, Alabama, the son of a slave, Rufus Carson, and an unnamed slave mother. In 1869, after teaching himself to read and write, the youth ran away from his father's cotton farm to Savannah, Georgia, and took a new surname: Taylor.

An ambitious, gifted student, C. H. J. Taylor enrolled at Savannah's Beach Institute while delivering newspapers and working as a commission house messenger. Much of the higher education he later claimed, however, cannot be documented. No definitive records exist for his claimed enrollments at Oberlin College or the University of Michigan at Ann Arbor, though he may well have studied law at Wilberforce University. In 1877 he was admitted to the Indiana state bar and became a deputy district attorney, before arriving in Leavenworth, Kansas, in about 1880 (Smith, p. 494).

Taylor soon moved to Wyandotte County (Kansas City), there establishing a reputation for hard work and political independence as deputy city attorney from 1882 until 1887. Taylor traced his Democratic politics to his participation as a stump speaker in the violent 1876 South Carolina gubernatorial campaign of Wade Hampton, during which he later recalled being attacked by a mob and "crippled" (*New York Times*, 7 Dec. 1887); eight years later, Taylor avidly supported Grover Cleveland for president. In March 1887, President Cleveland appointed Taylor as U.S. minister resident and consul general in Liberia—at thirty, he was the youngest such nominee to date, perhaps the youngest ever. Confirmed by the Senate, he spent just four months in Monrovia, resigning for health reasons, and chronicled the adventure in his 1889 book, *Whites and Blacks*, with few good words for Liberia's climate or its political situation.

An active 1888 campaigner for Cleveland's reelection, Taylor participated in the Democratic Colored National Conference (*New York Times*, 27 July 1888). After practicing law briefly in Baltimore and Atlanta, where he edited the *Southern Appeal*, he returned to Kansas, losing legislative races in 1890 and 1892 as a Democrat-Populist candidate. Taylor edited Kansas City's *American Citizen* newspaper, trumpeting calls for blacks to jettison Republicanism, and led the 1893 fight to kill neighboring Missouri's proposed "Jim Crow" separate coach law. Yet even as Democratic leaders sent him out in 1891 to speak on behalf of Iowa candidates, black Republicans ridiculed and shunned Taylor and his wife Julia socially.

In late 1893, President Cleveland nominated Taylor as U.S. minister to Bolivia, the highest diplomatic post to that nation, but the Senate balked, citing opposition to Taylor among Bolivian officials (*New York Times*, 21 Dec. 1893). The next year, Cleveland named Taylor recorder of deeds for the District of Columbia, a traditional post for African Americans; the Senate eventually confirmed Taylor, but not without an adverse committee report and more political drama.

By 1894 Taylor also presided over the Negro National Democratic League, but his penchant for unorthodox actions and unpredictable remarks brought new enemies. An 1895 campaign to remove him as recorder for allegedly soliciting political contributions from public employees, led by W. CALVIN CHASE's *Washington Bee*, ended with Taylor's exoneration by the Civil Service Commission and his successful libel suit against Chase. Taylor resumed his Baltimore law practice, but soon returned to Atlanta to edit the *Appeal* and serve as dean of the law department at Morris Brown College.

Ill with heart trouble in early 1899, Taylor spent weeks in a "private room" at Johns Hopkins Hospital, insisting on paying $7 a week for the curtained-off end of a public ward, the only accommodations available for African Americans. His presence prompted an anecdote, decades later, from Connecticut Medical Society president Dr. Walter R. Steiner, who recalled Taylor's persistently sending for Steiner (whom Taylor introduced as "my doctor") to meet his every visitor.

His death soon afterward drew mixed reactions. An *Atlanta Constitution* columnist (28 May 1899) offered a backhanded assessment: "He was well known at home and abroad.... In his way, he did what he could for his country and his people." Except for HARRY CLAY SMITH's *Cleveland Gazette*, black journalists offered even fainter praise. But at Morris Brown's commencement, days later, Reverend H. T. Johnson of Philadelphia paid Taylor a rare "eloquent tribute," remembering "one of the ablest representatives of the Negro race" (*Atlanta Constitution*, 31 May 1899). His death was front-page news in the

Baltimore Sun (26 May 1899), which later reported his funeral in detail.

Even in death, Taylor remained controversial. Former President Cleveland, nettled by charges of having once invited Recorder Taylor to a White House luncheon, steadfastly denied it, provoking a well-publicized attack on Cleveland's veracity by a Kansas congressman (*New York Times*, 13 April 1904).

FURTHER READING

Smith, J. Clay, Jr. *Emancipation: The Making of the Black Lawyer, 1844–1944* (1993).

Steiner, Walter R. "President's Address: Reminiscences" (1935).

Woods, Randall B. "C. H. J. Taylor and the Movement for Black Political Independence," *Journal of Negro History*, Summer 1982.

Obituaries: *Washington Evening Star*, 26 May 1899; *Baltimore Sun*, 26 May 1899.

BENJAMIN R. JUSTESEN

Taylor, Council (3 July 1917–5 July 1999), anthropologist, was born Council Samuel Taylor in Brooklyn, New York, the son of Walter Knight Taylor and Odelle Grace Robinson Taylor. "Count," as his intimates called him, was dynamic, tall, a stylish dresser, and a great storyteller, using his deep voice for dramatic effect. Colleagues, students, and teachers remembered him adorned with a French beret, ascot, and an ornate walking stick.

Taylor passed as a white man during the 1940s. From 1942 to 1946 he served in the marines—well before President Harry Truman issued Executive Order 9981 to desegregate the U.S. Armed Forces— where he saw combat duty with the Air Delivery Squadron and Aviation Supply during World War II. A most striking feature of his biography is that as a gay, black man, Taylor served as a platoon sergeant in aviation supply in several locations in the South Pacific and near China during the war and received an honorable discharge in February of 1946. Following combat experience, he entered Yale University in 1947 at the age of 29. Bringing his war experiences to New Haven, he excelled in various academic endeavors and extracurricular activities. His awards and recognitions include Scholar of the House in anthropology, the Elihu William Brinkerhoff Jackson Memorial Scholarship, member of the Pierson Organization, president of Chi Delta Theta and the Aurelian Honor Society (Gilliam, 56). Besides studying anthropology, he was the president of the Elizabethan Club, in which

he met writers such as Mary McCarthy, William Penn Warren, and W. H. Auden. After receiving his bachelor's degree in 1950, Taylor entered Yale's Ph.D. program in anthropology. During graduate school he developed expertise in a variety of topics from racism to dance. In 1955 he received his Ph.D. in Anthropology, under the supervision of Sidney W. Mintz, for his dissertation "Color and Class: A Comparative Study of Jamaican Status Groups." This original research predated contemporary studies that analyze the relations between racism, racial classification, and class power. He showed how class standing influenced the way Jamaicans perceived skin color and race.

After receiving his doctorate, he served as book review editor for the *American Anthropologist* and became assistant professor of anthropology at the University of California, Los Angeles (UCLA). Despite writing a pathbreaking dissertation, Taylor published little. His main contributions to anthropology and education rested in the classroom and institution building. Gradually his interests took him in a more radical direction as he committed himself to politics in anthropology. He was a founding member of the Caucus of Black Anthropologists, which emerged from an experimental session on black curriculum in anthropology at the 1968 American Anthropological Association (AAA) meetings in Seattle, Washington. The caucus focused on expanding black curriculum in anthropology, increasing minority participation in AAA (students and professors), and drawing greater attention to African American contributions to anthropology and the social sciences in general. He was among the founding members, including JOHNETTA COLE, who transformed the caucus into the Association of Black Anthropologists, which the AAA officially recognized in 1974.

Taylor also distinguished himself as a teacher and mentor. He intrigued students by relating anthropological knowledge to modern politics—as one UCLA student of Taylor's popular anthropology course remembered, he used scientific jargon to describe a famous "witch-hunter," whom students learned at the end of the course was Joseph McCarthy. He was denied tenure at UCLA and then took positions at Northern Illinois University (1963–1964) and at California State University, Northridge (1964–1968) and as distinguished professor of anthropology at Morehouse College (1968–1969). In 1969 he moved to the State University of New York, Old Westbury, because the institution was experimenting with new pedagogical programs in response to the 1960s. In his second year at Old Westbury, Taylor played a key role in the college's administration and was the acting president in 1970; he mobilized the college around the ideas of student participation, internationalism, and interdisciplinary education. After returning to the faculty, he cofounded the interdisciplinary program Politics, Economics, and Society. Taylor distinguished himself as a teacher in the fields of African social anthropology, Caribbean ethnology, dance, and black politics in the United States. In 1981 the State University of New York Board of Trustees honored him as the Distinguished Teaching Professor. Upon retirement from Old Westbury, he taught Pan-African studies at California State University of Northridge from 1985 until 1992.

Though many people remember Count fondly, few knew him well. He was a private man and remained an inscrutable figure, his charm matched by his elusiveness. At the 1993 annual meetings for the AAA, he showcased his enigmatic character by speaking uncharacteristically frankly about his life. His former colleague Angela Gilliam organized a special session to celebrate his 75th birthday and honor him as a founding member and past president of the Association of Black Anthropologists. He stunned the crowded room of admirers by admitting that he had passed for white during his years as a student at Yale. He talked about how he and his boyhood friend Anatole Broyard, the famous essayist and editor for the *New York Times*, followed their mothers' advice about disconnecting themselves from black Americans. A Jamaican immigrant, his mother was class and race conscious and believed that Taylor would have the best opportunities in the United States if he passed for white. Years later many of the attendees talked about his public revelation and disagreed about the significance. Some argued that he was courageous in trying to push debates about racism in the academy in new directions.

FURTHER READING

Taylor, Council. "Color and Class: A Comparative Study of Jamaican Status Groups," Ph.D. diss., Yale University (1955).

Estes-Hicks, Onita. "Remembering Dr. Councill Samuel Taylor: In Memoriam," *Transforming Anthropology* (2000).

Gilliam, Angela. "Remembering Dr. Councill Samuel Taylor: Count Through the Years," *Transforming Anthropology* (2000).

Harrison, Ira E. "The Association of Black Anthropologists: A Brief History," *Anthropology Today* (1987).

Harrison, Ira E., and Faye V. Harrison, eds. *African-American Pioneers in Anthropology* (1999).

Obituary: *Anthropology News* (1999).

GEORGE BACA

Taylor, Eddie (29 Jan. 1923–25 Dec. 1985), blues singer and guitarist, was born in Benoit, Mississippi, the son of Joseph Taylor and Mamie Gaston, farmers. By his own account his parents separated when he was two, leaving his mother to raise three children while trying to eke out a living on a Mississippi Delta farm. When not helping out with farm chores, Taylor showed an early interest in music, possibly inspired by Elizabeth Douglas, a singer and guitarist later known as MEMPHIS MINNIE, who supposedly knew his mother and looked after him when he was still a child.

Starting around age seven or eight, Taylor began sneaking out to house parties to hear itinerant blues musicians such as CHARLIE PATTON, ROBERT JOHNSON, and BIG JOE WILLIAMS. Taylor recalled, "I used to go out at night to where they were playing. Sometimes they wouldn't let me in because I was too small. I would crawl under the house and lay there, listening to the music through the floor." Recognizing his interest, his mother bought him a guitar when he was thirteen, and he began teaching himself to play. He also tried to teach a younger friend, JIMMY REED. Taylor expanded his repertoire of songs and guitar techniques by traveling around the Delta to hear well-known musicians, claiming later in life that he learned to play mainly from Patton and Johnson, arguably the most storied characters in the Delta blues tradition.

By the late 1930s Taylor's family had moved a few miles to Stringtown, Mississippi, where he played the streets on Saturday nights, performing songs by Patton, PEETIE WHEATSTRAW, ARTHUR CRUDUP, and, for white patrons, Roy Acuff. He said he could earn more in tips on a Saturday than a field worker could make in a week.

In 1943 Taylor moved to Memphis and got a job driving a truck. He continued to work as a street musician, too, steadily expanding his network of musical acquaintances. He claimed to be one of the first Memphis blues musicians to play electric guitar, purchasing one in 1947, and he formed a band that included his brother Milton on drums and Joe Hill Louis on guitar and harmonica.

In 1949 Taylor moved to Chicago, reunited with his father, who had become a policeman, and got a job in the shipping department of a television plant. He also reunited with Jimmy Reed, occasionally working with his former boyhood friend in various bands around Chicago and in northern Indiana.

After a brief stint in the MUDDY WATERS band in 1953, Taylor launched a seventeen-year recording partnership with Reed, cutting eight sides for the new Vee Jay label in Gary, Indiana. Although Taylor was the superior instrumentalist, Reed was the featured artist and vocalist on those sides, one of which—"You Don't Have to Go!"—became a hit. Taylor returned to the Vee Jay label for sessions in January and December 1955, recording several sides of his own. The second session produced a classic Chicago blues single, "Big Town Playboy," backed by "Ride Em on Down," which supposedly sold 37,000 copies, providing Taylor with his only substantial hit and his nickname, "Playboy."

For the remainder of the 1950s Taylor was often on the road with Reed, playing primarily to young white audiences who found Reed's lazy boogies well suited to popular dance steps of the early rock and roll era. Back in Chicago, however, Taylor continued to play mainly for African American audiences, working with his own band at Pepper's Lounge on the South Side and backing such artists as ELMORE JAMES and JOHN LEE HOOKER at club appearances or recording sessions.

By the late 1950s and early 1960s Taylor's work with Reed became stressful and more erratic because of Reed's severe alcoholism. Taylor toured Europe with Reed in 1969 and continued to back his old partner on recordings through 1970, but he increasingly looked for opportunities elsewhere. He continued his work on Chicago's club scene, backing the guitarist Floyd Jones and the harmonica player Paul Butterfield, among others. In 1966 he teamed up with Jones, the pianist OTIS SPANN, the harmonica player WALTER HORTON, and the drummer Fred Below to record a documentary album on Testament, which was well received by critics. He toured Europe with the guitarist Jimmy Dawkins and the pianist ROOSEVELT SYKES in 1970 and also played the Ann Arbor Blues Festival that year.

A sought-after sideman, Taylor maintained a steady schedule of club, festival, and session work until he died in Chicago, survived by his wife, Lee Vera, and eight children. He was inducted into the Blues Foundation Hall of Fame in Memphis two years after his death.

Although Taylor never learned to read music, making his mark primarily as a sideman and session player, he was an important link in the evolution of American blues, connecting the acoustic innovations of the early Delta masters, the styles of the Beale Street musicians in Memphis, and the Chicago electric ensemble sound that flowered in the 1950s. As a master of the Mississippi-derived blues tradition, in which musicians accompanied each other by listening and blending in, Taylor was uncanny at making other musicians sound better when he played with them. Employing variations of the walking bass and boogie riffs he said he learned from Robert Johnson, Taylor contributed substantially to the recordings of such artists as Elmore James and John Lee Hooker. He is probably best remembered, however, for his years of recording with Jimmy Reed and his contribution to the so-called Jimmy Reed sound that made Reed the number one crossover artist of his era. But as Taylor himself put it, "What Jimmy Reed sound? It's my sound. I learned it on the guitar down in Mississippi." Although he had to support himself with menial day jobs most of his career, Taylor remained true to his musical calling. "This is all I know, nothing but guitar," he once said. "I don't even know how to shoot pool."

FURTHER READING

Harris, Sheldon. *Blues Who's Who: A Biographical Dictionary of Blues Singers* (1979, 1989).
Leadbitter, Mike, ed. *Nothing but the Blues* (1971).
Rowe, Mike. *Chicago Blues: The City and the Music* (1973; U.S. ed. 1975).
Obituary: *Living Blues* 72 (1986).
This entry is taken from the *American National Biography* and is published here with the permission of the American Council of Learned Societies.

BILL MCCULLOCH AND
BARRY LEE PEARSON

Taylor, Eva (22 Jan. 1895–31 Oct. 1977), vaudeville singer, was born Irene Gibbons in St. Louis, Missouri, the daughter of Frank Gibbons and Julia Evans. Her father died when she was fifteen months old and her mother had difficulty providing for her, and so her career in show business began as a toddler, dancing and singing with Josephine Gassman and her Pickaninnies, a vaudeville act headed by a former opera singer. In this capacity she toured America annually and also visited Hawaii, Australia, and New Zealand from around 1904 to 1906, Europe in 1906, and Australia again from 1914 to 1915.

Gibbons met the songwriter and publisher CLARENCE WILLIAMS while performing in Chicago. Married in New York in 1921, they had three children; their daughter Joy, using the stage name Irene

Williams, later became an actress and singer, touring in *Porgy and Bess*. Having grown too old for Gassman's act, Gibbons became a featured soloist in Harlem from 1921 to 1922 at the Lafayette Theater, where she took the stage name Eva Taylor. In 1922 she held a modest solo role in the pioneering African American musical comedy *Shuffle Along*. That same year she also toured with the variety show *Step on It*, appeared in the show *Queen o'Hearts* in New York City, and broadcast with Williams's trio on Vaughn De Leath's *Musical Program* on WEAF in New York City.

Later Taylor became a familiar voice on the radio. She explained, "I specialized in ballads, not blues. That and my diction qualified me for the white radio and records market. No one could tell on a record or a broadcast whether I was coloured or white" (Napoleon, 30). She recorded sessions for Columbia with the Charleston Chasers, a white jazz studio group, in June and September 1929. This in turn led to recordings with the bandleader Ben Selvin and then to a staff job at radio station WEAF. The pianist WILLIE "THE LION" SMITH added that Taylor "was known as 'The Dixie Nightingale' and for several years performed on sustaining programs from nine to nine-fifteen every morning over radio station WOR in New York. She made three hundred and fifty dollars per week and turned every cent of it over to Brother Clarence." Among these broadcasts were *Major Bowes Capitol Family Show*, *The Morning Glories Show*, *The Rise of the Goldbergs*, *The Eveready Hour*, *The Atwater Kent Hour* (all from 1929); *The General Motors Show* (1931); *The Kraft Music Hall* (1933); *The Rye-Crisp Show* (1935); and finally *The Sheep and Goat Club*, in which she made a guest appearance in August 1940 and did so well that she took over the character of Sister Clorinda Billup.

From around 1942 Taylor focused on entertaining at local hospitals. Later she reduced her activities further, singing only occasionally. Williams died in 1965, and in 1967 Taylor visited England. Mary Rust, her English hostess in 1967, wrote, "Everyone that has met her has fallen under her spell.... When Eva walks in, it is like the sun coming out." Taylor sang with the Sweet Peruna Jazz Band in Copenhagen in 1974, at the Overseas Press Club in New York in 1974 and 1975, and in Copenhagen and Stockholm in 1975 and 1976. She died in Mineola, New York.

Taylor is best remembered for Williams's Blue Five recordings in sessions of December 1924 and January 1925 with the cornetist LOUIS ARMSTRONG and the reed player SIDNEY BECHET among the instrumentalists. Her vaudeville-style performances include "Mandy, Make Up Your Mind" and "Cake-Walking Babies from Home." She sang with a rich tone, a fast vibrato, a (sometimes overly) precise articulation of lyrics, and a good feeling for jazz rhythm.

FURTHER READING

Dixon, Robert M. W., and John Godrich. *Recording the Blues* (1970).

Harris, Sheldon. *Blues Who's Who: A Biographical Dictionary of Blues Singers* (1979).

Smith, Willie "the Lion," with George Hoefer. *Music on My Mind* (1964; repr. 1975).

This entry is taken from the *American National Biography* and is published here with the permission of the American Council of Learned Societies.

BARRY KERNFELD

Taylor, Gardner Calvin (8 June 1918–), Baptist church minister and leader, was born in Baton Rouge, Louisiana, to Washington and Selena Taylor; his father was a minister of the Gospel. Both parents were literate and native to Louisiana, where his grandparents had been enslaved.

After earning an A.B. degree from Leland College in Baker, Louisiana, in 1937, Taylor enrolled at the Oberlin Graduate School of Theology, and was ordained a Baptist minister in 1939. Already serving as pastor of Bethany Baptist Church in Elyria, Ohio, from 1938 to 1941, he was awarded a Bachelor of Divinity degree from Oberlin in 1940. He married Laura Bell Scott, a Cleveland native and 1937 graduate of Oberlin, on 25 August 1941, accepting a call to Beulah Baptist Church in New Orleans from 1941 to 1943. He returned to Baton Rouge, serving as pastor of Mt. Zion Baptist Church, from 1943 to 1947.

In 1948 Taylor was called at age twenty-nine to Concord Baptist Church of Christ in Brooklyn, New York, where he served as pastor for forty-two years. Concord had just celebrated its centennial in 1947. Only five years later, he led the church through rebuilding after a fire that destroyed the Marcy Avenue edifice, which the church had acquired in 1939. A new building was completed 1 June 1956.

He arrived about the same time that the Brooklyn Dodgers brought JACKIE ROBINSON onto the team; Branch Rickey, the Dodgers general manager, who assembled a postwar team to obliterate the color barrier, sought Taylor's help in making sure Robinson was welcomed and succeeded. In retirement, Taylor recalled that time as "ambiguous," much less rigid than the south, with mobility on subways and buses, but residence strictly segregated by race, with no opportunities for African Americans in government jobs at all (Oliphant, *Praying for Gil Hodges*, pp. 54–55).

Actively involved in community development and the civil rights movement, Taylor insisted throughout his life that "the preacher has no warrant to speak to our social ills save in the light of God's judgment and God's grace" (Bond, p. 53, citing Taylor, *How Shall They Preach*, p. 84). Addressing a 1965 gathering of Baptists, he asked, "Is there a larger sin against God than to hold men responsible for the drudgery involved in building a community while denying to them the freedom of participating in that community?" (*Baptist Press*, 24 June 1965, p. 30).

Among the outreach ministries Concord developed during Dr. Taylor's tenure were the Concord Credit Union in 1950, the Concord Baptist

Gardner C. Taylor speaks at the Progressive National Baptist Convention on 10 August 2011 in Washington, D.C. (AP Images.)

Elementary School in 1960 (initially organized and overseen by Mrs. Laura Scott Taylor), a nursing home and rehabilitation center, and a seniors' residence. Taylor was elected in 1958 to the first of two terms as president of the Protestant Council of New York City, the first Baptist as well as the first African American to hold that position, and the same year was elected a member of the city board of education.

In 1960 Taylor was invited by over three hundred Baptist ministers, among them Rev. Martin Luther King Jr., to challenge incumbent Joseph H. Jackson for the presidency of the National Baptist Convention. Jackson and the majority of the board of directors had been lukewarm at best and often critical of the nonviolent civil disobedience movement of the Southern Christian Leadership Conference led by Rev. King. In a tumultuous series of events, Jackson was proposed by a nomination committee for re-election by acclamation. Taylor's supporters demanded a recorded roll call vote; officials loyal to Jackson declared the convention over, but delegates remained for a roll call vote, which favored Taylor. Jackson refused to step down, keeping control of the treasury and Convention property, backed by the board of directors. Taylor joined a movement to create the Progressive National Baptist Convention, organized in November 1961 at Zion Baptist Church in Cincinnati, by ministers seeking to build "a Democratic Convention Dedicated to Christian Objectives" (Avant, p. 25). In 1967 Taylor was chosen as president of the convention. The nature of his progressive Baptist theology is exemplified by the following quote, which appears in *How Shall They Preach*: "The great corporate issues of our society—poverty, pollution, the international violence of war, anarchy, race and the national priorities," Taylor argued, "are not primarily political matters; they are rooted profoundly in our attitude toward the God whose retainer the preacher is honored to be" (Bond, p. 55).

Taylor became known not only for his community involvement but also for the thoughtful passion of his preaching, which served as an example to many. He was a mentor to the civil rights leader and business executive Vernon Jordan, among others. His 1976 Lyman Beecher Lectures, published in 1977 as *How Shall They Preach*, drew together his sense of justice on earth and spiritual righteousness, in ringing oratory, exhorting that "if the undertaking does not have some sanctions beyond human reckoning, then it is indeed rash and audacious for one person to dare to stand up before or among other people and declare that he or she brings from the Eternal God, a message for those who listen that involves issues nothing less than those of life and death." Taylor's sermons and writing about preaching also include *The Scarlet Thread, Chariots Aflame, We Have This Ministry,* and *Words of Gardner Taylor.*

Taylor has been invited to teach in many colleges as an adjunct faculty member, including Harvard and Yale divinity schools. He received Honorary Doctor of Divinity degrees from Leland College, Colgate Rochester, and Benedict College, together with honorary degrees from Harvard Divinity School and Union Theological Seminary, an L.H.D. from Albright College, and three orders from the Republic of Liberia. Taylor retired from Concord in 1990, awarded by his congregation the title of Senior Pastor Emeritus. Taylor's wife of fifty-five years died in 1995 after being hit by a truck; he married Phillis Strong on 30 July 1996 and moved to Raleigh, North Carolina. In 2000 President Bill Clinton awarded Taylor the nation's highest civilian honor, the Presidential Medal of Freedom.

FURTHER READING

Taylor, Gardner C. *Black Churches of Brooklyn* (1996).

Taylor, Gardner C. *The Words of Gardner Taylor, Volumes 1–6.* (2007).

Avant, Albert A. *The Social Teachings of the Progressive National Baptist Convention, Inc. Since 1961* (2003).

Bond, Susan. *Contemporary African American Preaching: Diversity in Theory and Style* (2003).

CHARLES ROSENBERG

Taylor, George Edwin (4 Aug. 1857–23 Nov. 1925), labor activist, journalist, and presidential candidate, was born in Little Rock, Arkansas, the son of Bryant Taylor, a slave at the time of George's birth, and Amanda Hines, a free woman. George had twelve siblings. In 1861 his mother died in Alton, Illinois, where she had been cared for by a William Lovejoy. After the death of his mother, Taylor became homeless, drifting, never knowing where his next meal would come from, and losing contact with his brothers and sisters. On 8 May 1865 he alighted from the steamer *Hawkeye State* in the town of La Crosse, Wisconsin. He attended public schools for one year but then met Nathan Smith, a black man, who sheltered him and later adopted the young boy. In La Crosse, Taylor worked as a farmer with his new family. More important, for the first time he was in the midst of a black family that was free and self-sustaining. Learning to farm

meant that he could sustain himself economically. Farming was not, however, to be his life work. His adopted father enrolled him in Wayland Academy, a Baptist college in Beaver Dam, Wisconsin, but after three years Taylor left without a degree, lacking money and his health deteriorating.

After leaving school in 1880 Taylor obtained a job as a reporter for several newspapers, including the *Daily Republican and Leader* and the *Chicago Inter-Ocean.* He quickly distinguished himself as a reporter and writer and became associate editor of the *La Crosse Evening Star.* His work continued to excel, and he soon became editor in chief and part owner. On 15 October 1885 Taylor married Mary L. Hall in Prairie du Chien, Crawford County, Wisconsin. The next year he founded the *Wisconsin Labor Advocate,* a weekly paper that was affiliated with the Knights of Labor of western Wisconsin. He continued to work closely with the local labor movement, and as a result of his political skills, Frank Powell was elected mayor of La Crosse, placing local government in the hands of organized labor. At this point in his career as a political activist, Taylor had developed a clear anticapitalist perspective. Although he never called himself a socialist, he nevertheless opposed capital and even rent. But he did not just condemn capital, he also worked for the protection of labor. In 1887, for example, he was a delegate at the Wisconsin State Union Labor Party convention and served on the central committee of the Farmer and Workingmen's Party. His newspaper quickly became the organ of the Wisconsin Union Labor Party.

Taylor's skills quickly gained national attention through the labor movement. As a delegate from Wisconsin, he attended the convention of the United Labor Party in Cincinnati, Ohio, and delivered a speech that was well received by those in attendance. He had clearly outgrown La Crosse and on 1 January 1891 moved to Oskaloosa, Iowa, where hundreds of blacks had settled after leaving the South. In Iowa his political activities flourished. In 1892 he was elected an alternate delegate to the Republican National Convention. He had not only obtained recognition among national labor leaders but also more generally among African Americans. On 4 June 1892 he attended a national convention of blacks held in Chicago at the Washington Art Palace that formed the Colored People's National Protective Association and elected Taylor its president. The convention pledged to fight the election of Benjamin Harrison as president if he did not support their platform of racial inclusion and established a committee of prominent blacks to coordinate these efforts. The committee consisted of Taylor, FREDERICK DOUGLASS, and Charles M. Ferguson of Houston, Texas, a Texas delegate to the Republican National Convention in 1892. Their task was to lobby the Republican Committee on Resolutions for a statement of support for the constitutional rights of blacks. Since Harrison and the Republican Party would not support black constitutional rights, the committee urged that Harrison be rejected as a candidate. The convention ignored Taylor's committee's recommendations, the Republican Party nominated Harrison for president, and Taylor's group issued an "Appeal to the American Negro" for the creation of a separate political party. Douglass did not support this move since a year earlier President Harrison had appointed him minister-resident and consul-general to the Republic of Haiti.

By 1893 Taylor had returned to Oskaloosa and organized a new weekly called the *Negro Solicitor*, the most radical of any of his previous papers. He served as editor until 1900, when he sold the paper. He then worked at A. B. Little, a coal mining company, in Coalfield, Iowa, as superintendent of a plant. By 1901 he had returned to farming in Albia, Iowa, and he remained there until 1903, when he relocated to Ottumwa. But he never abandoned his involvement in national black politics. From 1900 to 1904 he served as president of the Negro National Democratic League and as justice of the peace in Monroe County, Iowa. Taylor, like many blacks, left the Republican Party and attempted to move the Democratic Party closer to a progressive (labor and black) agenda. The failure to influence the party resulted in Taylor and others leaving the Democratic Party in 1904 and forming the National Liberty Party in St. Louis, Missouri. In 1904 Taylor was the party's nominee for president of the United States. Ironically, at the time of his nomination by the black independent party, Taylor also served as chairman of the National Negro Democratic League, a Democratic Party affiliate. He also served as grand chancellor of the Knights of Pythias of Iowa and Supreme Chair of the Negro Supreme Lodge in Jacksonville, Florida, where he died in 1925.

FURTHER READING

Materials on Taylor are in the Area Research Center, Murphy Library, University of Wisconsin–La Crosse.

Walton, Hanes, Jr. *Black Political Parties* (1972).

Walton, Hanes, Jr. *Black Politics: A Theoretical and Structural Analysis* (1972).

ROBERT JOHNSON JR.

Taylor, Hound Dog (12 Apr. 1917–17 Dec. 1975), blues singer and guitarist, was born Theodore Roosevelt Taylor in Natchez, Mississippi, the son of Robert Taylor and Della Herron. Little is known about his family or his early life, except that he grew up in the Mississippi Delta around Tchula and Greenwood. Taylor later claimed he worked on a cotton farm, and spent only one day in school. He also claimed he was forced at gunpoint to leave home at age nine after an altercation with his stepfather.

Working various jobs around Tchula in the mid-1930s, Taylor taught himself to play guitar, learning mainly from watching other local musicians. Later he met the guitarist ELMORE JAMES, and the two often worked together in the late 1930s, teaming up with the harmonica player Aleck Miller—later known as SONNY BOY WILLIAMSON—the guitarist ROBERT JUNIOR LOCKWOOD, and others to play at Delta jooks, suppers, and dances. Taylor also played on an early broadcast of Miller's radio show, *King Biscuit Time*, on station KFFA in Helena, Arkansas. Initially, Taylor played in both standard tuning and in the open E tuning used by James, whose slide-guitar style he began to emulate. Later in his career he played exclusively in an open-key, bottleneck style.

In 1942, by Taylor's own account, he left the Delta and fled north to escape a lynch mob that came looking for him after hearing rumors of a tryst between Taylor and a married white woman. Arriving in Chicago, he got a steady job and began playing with other southern blues musicians in the Maxwell Street market district in his spare time. In the late 1940s he began receiving club bookings, but the pay was so poor that he kept working his day job. In 1950 or 1951 he married Fredda Horne, with whom he eventually had five children. He continued to moonlight as a musician through the 1950s, finally turning to music full time around 1957.

In 1958 Taylor met Brewer Phillips, a Mississippi-born guitarist who had worked in West Memphis in the 1940s with the pianist ROOSEVELT SYKES and other artists. Phillips claimed he met Taylor by coincidence after Taylor had stolen his guitar. Whatever the circumstances, the two teamed up with the drummer Levi Warren the next weekend and played at the Rock and Roll Club. Thus began a seventeen-year association that was marked by friendship, bitter fights, and great musical compatibility.

In a later interview with John Anthony Brisbin, Phillips accurately summed up the relationship: "I shot Hound Dog and Hound Dog shot me. We was good friends" (25).

Taylor's nickname in Mississippi had been Nitter. In Chicago he became known to fellow musicians as Hound Dog, a wry commentary on either his face or, as Taylor himself claimed later, his womanizing.

Taylor, Phillips, and Warren played together, off and on, into the 1960s, sometimes performing several clubs a night to boost their meager earnings. Warren left the group to tour with the pianist and vocalist Willie Mabon in the mid-1960s and was replaced by Ted Harvey, a Chicago native who had started out as a jazz drummer. The new trio became known as the House Rockers, a name that captured their raw, good-time boogie sound and the onstage clowning of Taylor and Phillips. Phillips and Harvey kept day jobs, but Taylor, essentially supported by Fredda, was out playing every night, whether he was paid or just sitting in with somebody else's group. Harvey recalled the unending schedule of low-paying club appearances: "Some of them we would walk in and play for nothing. Then the second time we'd go in there, they get a big bucket." Whether playing for tips or fifteen dollars, Taylor would generally drink twenty dollars worth of whiskey, playing marathon two-hour sets and cracking bad jokes between songs. The House Rockers, with their aggressive, chaotic sound, became a fixture on the club and festival circuits, even touring Europe in 1967, but their music was old fashioned by 1960s standards, and there was little interest in recording the group. Taylor's entire record output during the 1960s consisted of two singles—one for Bea & Baby, the other on Firma—both of which bombed.

In 1970 Taylor's club work attracted the interest of two avid blues fans, Wesley Race and Bruce Iglauer, who tried to interest the Delmark label in recording Taylor. Unsuccessful, Race and Iglauer collaborated on their own album project, releasing *Hound Dog Taylor and the House Rockers* in 1971. The album was an artistic success, breathing new life into Taylor's career and launching Alligator Records, which became a major label for electric blues through the 1980s. The album—and a follow-up in 1974—also helped introduce Taylor to the predominantly white blues-revival audience. He began to get bookings at major festivals, universities, and big blues/rock clubs from Ann Arbor to Seattle. For Taylor, the new audience represented a financial breakthrough, but it was short-lived. Years of whiskey and cigarettes and countless hours in smoke-filled bars had taken their toll. Taylor developed lung cancer and in 1975 entered Cook County Hospital, where he died.

Hound Dog Taylor and his House Rockers presented a musical paradox. As regulars in Chicago's African American clubs, they became an anachronism in the world of black soul music; at the same time, they were a perfect crossover vehicle for the white blues-revival audience. The sound was unsophisticated, frenzied, and down-home as the House Rockers blasted out blues and boogies with gusto and lots of laughter. Taylor's slide style and his use of cheap Japanese guitars gave him a singularly raw sound. He changed chords or took leads as the mood struck him, often causing Phillips to holler over the din to the drummer, "Don't let him get away, Ted." A musician who made up in energy whatever he might have lacked in artistry, Taylor was an unforgettable character.

FURTHER READING

Brisbin, John Anthony. "Let's Have Some Fun: Brewer Phillips Remembers Hound Dog Taylor," *Living Blues* 117 (Oct. 1994).

Harris, Sheldon. *Blues Who's Who: A Biographical Dictionary of Blues Singers* (1989).

O'Neal, Jim, and R. T. Cuniff. "Hound Dog Taylor," *Living Blues* 1, no. 4 (Winter 1970–1971).

Obituary: *Living Blues* 25 (Jan.–Feb. 1976).

This entry is taken from the *American National Biography* and is published here with the permission of the American Council of Learned Societies.

BARRY LEE PEARSON AND
BILL MCCULLOCH

Taylor, Koko (28 Sept. 1935–3 June 2009), blues singer and songwriter, was born Cora Walton in Bartlett, Tennessee, near Memphis, the daughter of Annie Mae and William Walton, sharecroppers. Nicknamed "Koko" because she loved chocolate, she and her two sisters sang gospel in the Baptist church. Koko and her three brothers preferred blues (though her father viewed blues unfavorably), which they heard on records and on the Memphis radio station WDIA. Unable to afford instruments, her brothers made their own and secretly played blues as Taylor sang. Her mother died in 1939, and her father died around 1947 or 1948, making Koko and her siblings orphans. Over the next few years she lived with various relatives. Leaving school in the sixth grade, Koko met the Memphis truck driver Robert "Pops" Taylor, who was twelve years her senior, and they migrated to Chicago's South

Side in 1953, marrying shortly thereafter. Koko Taylor found work as a domestic in an affluent North Shore suburb and Pops in a slaughterhouse. They had one daughter.

Taylor began performing publicly in the late 1950s, encouraged by Pops, who played guitar. They frequented blues clubs, where Taylor sat in with musicians, including MUDDY WATERS, HOWLIN' WOLF, BUDDY GUY, ELMORE JAMES, and JIMMY REED. She also performed at local schools and dances with Guy Wells and JUNIOR WELLS. Her singing impressed WILLIE DIXON, who was in the audience at a Sunday jam session in Big Bill Hill's Pepper's. He invited her to audition for Chess Records and produced her first two singles, "Honky Tonky" and "Like Heaven," for the independent label USA (1963). Taylor also sang lead vocals on "What Kind of Man Is This?" "Which'a Way to Go," and "I'm Looking for a Man" on *Chicago Blues: A Bonanza All Star Blues* (Spivey Records, 1963). Dixon recognized Taylor's gifts and chose songs (Taylor recorded nearly two dozen Dixon compositions) that could showcase her stage persona and powerful voice. In 1965 she recorded her first hit, Dixon's "Wang Dang Doodle," which

reached number 4 on the rhythm and blues charts. The success of "Wang Dang Doodle"—which became her signature song—launched Taylor's career, leading to both a tour with Waters, Reed, and BO DIDDLEY and regular club work. Dixon encouraged Taylor (a proficient blues guitarist) to write her own songs. Inspired by her husband, her first composition was "What Kind of Man Is This?" In 1969 Chess issued her first album, a collection of singles. During the 1970s Taylor's career expanded despite several setbacks. Leonard Chess died in 1969. Dixon produced two singles for his Yambo label (1970) and her last Chess album, *Basic Soul* (1971). In 1972 the label folded; Taylor did not record again for five years. Working regularly on weekends at North Side clubs, she was among the first generation of blues musicians to build a career performing for white audiences. Her appearance at the 1972 Ann Arbor Blues Festival prompted Taylor and Pops (who became her business manager) to form her own band, the Blues Machine, comprised of musicians dedicated to blues. The largest venue Taylor had played to date, the festival brought further exposure (Atlantic Records issued a live album) and led to a national tour and a new

Koko Taylor performs during the 2006 New Orleans Jazz and Heritage Festival in New Orleans on 5 May 2006. (AP Images.)

recording contract with Alligator Records. Taylor, the label's first woman, made her first Alligator recordings in 1974. Her Grammy-nominated *I Got What It Takes* (1975) included her own "Voodoo Woman." Taylor's next six Alligator albums either won or were nominated for awards. Her successful *The Earthshaker* (1978) featured "I'm a Woman" (cowritten with Ellas McDaniel (Bo Diddley). An answer to Water's "Mannish Boy," Taylor's song became a feminist anthem; its boasting lyrics asserted female independence and power.

Taylor continued to perform in Chicago's clubs and broadcast live over WOPA. Now recognized as the reigning "Queen of the Blues," by the 1980s she performed frequently in New York, including an appearance in July 1980 at the Kool Jazz Festival. That year Taylor won her first W. C. HANDY Award. After releasing *From the Heart of a Woman* (1981), Taylor took part in the Smithsonian Institution's February 1982 conference on the blues, which included the scholar STERLING BROWN and the blues artists Dixon and TAJ MAHAL. Two years later Taylor won her first Grammy for her contribution to the compilation *Blues Explosion*. In 1987 Taylor released *Live from Chicago: An Audience with the Queen*, which captured the energy and intensity of her stage performance. Tragedy struck on 4 February 1988, when Taylor and her band were involved in a near-fatal van accident near Knoxville. She broke her shoulder, collarbone, and four ribs and spent six months recuperating. Pops went into cardiac arrest; he never recovered and died on 22 March 1989. Taylor returned to the stage that summer at the Chicago Blues Festival and New York's Summerstage in Central Park. She released the Grammy-nominated *Jump for Joy* (1990). Taylor experienced another loss in 1992, when her friend and mentor Dixon died.

After releasing *Force of Nature* (1993), Taylor took a seven-year break from recording, though she continued to tour. In 1996 she married Hays Harris. In November 1999 she opened Koko Taylor's Celebrity Blues Club on the South Side of Chicago, near the old Chess Records building. Comanaged by her daughter, it showcased aspiring bands and female blues singers. Intended as a sister club to Buddy Guy's Legends (then a few blocks away), it closed to the public in November 2002.

Further artistic recognition came in 2000, when she was the subject of the Chicago PBS documentary *I Got What It Takes: The Life and Times of Koko Taylor*. She released one of her best albums, *Royal Blue*, featuring B. B. KING. In late January 2002 Taylor had another setback. After fainting at her nightclub, she underwent angioplasty. Forced to reduce her schedule because of poor health (high blood pressure and diabetes), she began to focus on her nonprofit Koko Taylor Celebrity Aid Foundation. In the summer of 2002 she returned to performing to headline the Chicago Blues Festival and won the W. C. Handy Blues Award for Best Traditional Female Artist that fall. In September 2004 she received one of the country's highest honors, a National Endowment for the Arts Heritage Fellowship, awarded for artistic excellence and contributions to cultural heritage, which included a $20,000 prize.

Considered one of the most important post–World War II female blues singers, Taylor began her career at a time when women were absent from blues. Regarded as one of the hardest-working blues performers, she appeared in major concert halls and festivals. A prolific songwriter, she recorded more than one hundred albums and penned several hundred songs. Taylor, like the earlier female blues artists MA RAINEY and BESSIE SMITH, stands as a feminist icon. Her classic "I'm a Woman" and songs in which she changes the gender of lyrics composed by males challenge prevailing female gender roles. Especially dedicated to mentoring female blues musicians, she remained committed to keeping the blues tradition alive.

Taylor won every major blues award, including *Billboard*'s Top Blues Album (*Royal Blue*) and a Grammy Award. From 1980 to 2006 she received twenty-three W. C. Handy Awards. She was inducted into both the Memphis Blues Hall of Fame (1999) and the Hollywood Blues Foundation Hall of Fame (1992). In 1993 Chicago mayor Richard M. Daley honored her with a Legend of the Year Award and declared 3 March Koko Taylor Day. In 2003 she received the R&B Foundation Pioneer Award. In June 2009 the "Queen of Chicago Blues" passed away in Chicago due to complications arising from gastrointestinal surgery. She continued to perform until a month before her death.

FURTHER READING

Aldin, Mary Katherine. "Koko Taylor: Down in the Bottom of That Chitlin' Bucket," *Living Blues* (July–Aug. 1993).

Aykroyd, Dan, and Ben Manilla. *Elwood's Blues: Interviews with the Blues Legends and Stars* (2004).

Frantz, Niles. "Koko Taylor: Forever the Queen of the Blues," *Blues Revue* (June 1998).

Hollis, Larry, and Eddie Ferguson. "Koko Taylor: Interview," *Cadence* (May 1984).

O'Neal, Amy. "Koko Taylor," *Living Blues* (Sept.–Oct. 1978).

DISCOGRAPHY

The Earthshaker (Alligator, 1978).

From the Heart of a Woman (Alligator, 1981).

I Got What It Takes (Alligator, 1975).

Koko Taylor (Chess, 1968).

Live from Chicago: An Audience with the Queen (Alligator, 1987).

Queen of the Blues (Alligator, 1985).

Obituary: *Chicago Tribune*, 3 June 2009.

GAYLE MURCHISON

Taylor, Lawrence (1959–), football player and actor, was born in Williamsburg, Virginia, the second oldest of the three children of Clarence Taylor, a shipyard worker, and Iris (maiden name unknown), a clerk and cashier. Growing up on the outskirts of town, separated from his closest neighbor by a divided highway, Lawrence had little contact with people outside of his family. The only place he regularly socialized was at school, where he was an average student with perfect attendance. The family lived modestly. Testing the household rules and trying to avoid his parents' discipline gave Lawrence events around which he built an identity. For example, when sent to the grocery store with a check for the family's monthly grocery bill, he purchased a large quantity of candy that he resold at school for a profit. This business venture continued for years and was so successful that he became known as the "Candy Man."

When Taylor was fifteen, he became involved in organized football for the first time, playing for the Williamsburg Jaycee football team. He was recruited by their coach, who first saw Taylor's athletic ability displayed on the baseball diamond. The main attraction of joining the team for Taylor was not football, however, but rather the team's annual trip to Pittsburgh. It was not until his sophomore year at Lafayette High School that Taylor was recruited to play for the school by the linebacker coach, Mel Jones. Jones convinced Taylor to "play with the big boys, 'cause they don't give scholarships in the recreational league" (Taylor, *LT over the Edge*, 14). He tried out for and made the varsity football team during his junior year. Playing a variety of positions, both offense and defense, Taylor found that he preferred to hit rather than be hit. After researching great linebackers, such as Ray Nitschke and Sam

Huff, he realized that "aside from being smart, a good linebacker was also a mean sonuvabitch" (Taylor, *LT, Living on the Edge*, 20). Lawrence was a bench player for the first half of his junior year until a game against Bethel High School, the best team in their district, in which he recorded his first sack and blocked a punt, which his team recovered for the game-winning touchdown. Taylor never returned to the bench again and became a regular in the local papers. Although he was named an All-State player on both offense and defense his senior year, he was not heavily recruited by colleges.

The two schools that offered him scholarships were the University of Richmond and the University of North Carolina. Taylor chose North Carolina, was red shirted his freshman year, played out of position his sophomore year, and did not become a football force to be reckoned with until his junior year, when he was named starting outside linebacker. As a starter, he had his first great game against North Carolina State, when he forced a fumble that led to his team's victory. Publicity poured in following the game. Taylor remained unstoppable for the rest of his college career, terrorizing opposing offenses with his speed and powerful tackling. He earned several nicknames while at college, including "Monster," "Godzilla," and "Filthy McNasty"; however, these were not solely based upon his football prowess. Along with several other players from the team, Taylor partied often, picked fights at local bars, and on one occasion scaled his six-story dormitory building to get to his room rather than take the stairs. In 1980, Taylor's senior year, he was named to the All-American and All-ACC teams and was ACC Player of the Year. While in college, Taylor met Linda Cooley, whom he married in 1982; they had three children. The couple divorced in 1996.

After excelling in college, Taylor was drafted second overall by the New York Giants in 1980. He was fortunate not only in his natural athletic ability but also that the Giants had some of the best defensive coaches in National Football League (NFL) history, particularly Bill Parcells and Bill Belichick. The Giants, with strong defensive play, went from winning four regular season games in 1980 to nine in 1981 and playing in the National Football Conference (NFC) championship game. Taylor was named rookie of the year and defensive player of the year and was selected for the first of his nine consecutive Pro Bowls. The next season was shortened by a strike, which provided Taylor with the free time to experiment with cocaine and develop a habit that continued during the 1983 season, in which the Giants won only three games. At the conclusion of the season the billionaire businessman Donald Trump contacted Taylor about playing in the U.S. Football League (USFL), a competing football league that Trump was trying to build. Taylor, making only $190,000 a year with the Giants, agreed to a contract with Trump for $4 million over five years with a $1 million signing bonus. When Taylor's agent told the Giants about this contract, they quickly moved to keep Taylor on their team. To retain the services of the best defensive player in the NFL, the Giants paid Taylor $6 million over six years and bought out the contract that Taylor had signed with Trump and the USFL.

The Giants steadily improved over the next three seasons, posting a winning record in each. In 1984 and 1985 the Giants advanced to the NFC championship game but lost. In 1986 Taylor had his best overall season with 20.5 sacks, helping to lead the Giants to a Super Bowl victory over John Elway and the Denver Broncos. Unfortunately, even as the team improved and Taylor excelled, he was beginning to use drugs more heavily. His cocaine habit was infamous and obvious by 1985, when he failed a urine test. Instead of seeking help, Taylor simply began to use a friend's urine to make it appear that he was clean. Also that year he made crack cocaine his drug of choice. After the 1985 season, confronted by his wife, family, and friends, Taylor entered a rehabilitation program and stayed clean for the 1986 season.

After achieving the ultimate football high of winning Super Bowl XXI and being named the league's most valuable player in 1986, Taylor once again began using cocaine. He failed his first official NFL drug test in 1987, but due to the NFL's three strikes rule, he was not disciplined for the infraction. With only fleeting bouts of sobriety, Taylor's drug use was further enabled by the players' strike and the use of replacement players.

In August 1988 Taylor failed a second drug test and was suspended for the first four games of the regular season. Now with two strikes, a third failed drug test would result in Taylor being banned from football for life. This fear was powerful enough to keep him from using cocaine until after he retired from football. In 1989 Taylor, who continued to drink heavily and run up large bar tabs, decided to open his own restaurant and nightclub. His two ventures were LT's, a restaurant and bar, and First and Ten, a strip club. While initially these ventures appeared successful, corrupt managers and business partners led to financial difficulties after Taylor retired from football.

During the 1990 season the Giants once again won the Super Bowl, beating the Buffalo Bills. After this victory head coach Parcells retired, and Belichick left to coach the Cleveland Browns. Under the direction of Coach Ray Handley the team went downhill, and Taylor suffered his first serious injury, tearing his Achilles tendon. Not wanting to leave the football field for the last time on a stretcher, he decided to return for a final season in 1993.

When Taylor retired at the end of that season, he had revolutionized the way outside linebacker was played, becoming the archetypical model for the modern linebacker. After his retirement, Taylor's motivation to remain drug-free vanished, and he dove back "into drugs like Greg Louganis diving into a pool" (Taylor, *LT over the Edge*, 166). Simultaneously he lost millions, claiming his partners and investors stole money from his restaurant and strip club. In trouble with the IRS, he was forced to declare bankruptcy in 1998. After two convictions for buying cocaine and one for failing to pay child support, Taylor was ordered into rehabilitation. However, it was not until 1998 and his bankruptcy that he began to take his rehabilitation seriously. The only bright spot of the mid-nineties for Taylor was when the Giants retired his number 56 in 1996.

After 1998 Taylor fought his addiction successfully and found work making celebrity appearances, acting, and as a television commentator and contestant on FX's *Toughman Show*, and he remarried in 2001. Taylor was inducted into the Football Hall of Fame in 1999 in recognition of his career as one of the fastest, hardest-hitting linebackers to ever play the game.

FURTHER READING

Taylor, Lawrence, with David Falkner. *LT, Living on the Edge* (1987).

Taylor, Lawrence, with Steve Serby. *LT over the Edge* (2003).

"Lawrence Taylor," Number 4, *Sporting News*, http://www.sportingnews.com/nfl/100/4.html.

Whitley, David. "L.T. Was Reckless, Magnificent," ESPN.com, http://espn.go.com/sportscentury/features/00016487.html.

JACOB ANDREW FREEDMAN

Taylor, Major (26 Nov. 1878–21 June 1932), bicyclist, was born Marshall Walter Taylor in Indianapolis, Indiana, one of eight children of Gilbert Taylor and

Saphronia Kelter, free blacks from Kentucky who moved to Indianapolis after the Civil War. Gilbert, a veteran of the Union army, became a coachman for a well-to-do white family, the Southards, whose son became Marshall's close friend. According to Taylor's autobiography, he spent his childhood years playing with upper-class white children and was able to have his own bicycle. In his teens Taylor found work in bicycle shops, where his phenomenal trick riding skills attracted crowds and caught the attention of shop owners. They outfitted him in a flashy uniform and nicknamed him "Major," a name that became his trademark for the rest of his life. When Taylor won his first race at age thirteen, Louis D. Munger, a bicycle manufacturer, saw his potential and took the lad under his wing. He remained Taylor's employer, guide, promoter, and confidante until he died in 1929.

Taylor's prime riding years came at a propitious time, coinciding with the development of the modern chain-driven safety bicycle and the pneumatic tire. With the cumbersome high-wheelers gone at last, cycling became the most popular sport in the nation, ahead of baseball, football, basketball, and boxing. The League of American Wheelmen had ten thousand members in 1890 and one hundred thousand eight years later. The winning cyclists of the day were feted and idolized by millions, but the professional side of cycling was "lily-white" until Taylor came along.

Indianapolis in the 1890s was segregated. Although Taylor had been spared much of the degradation of Jim Crow segregation in his early years, when he began to win racing prizes competing against white riders, he became the target of slurs and threats. In the fall of 1895 Munger and Taylor moved to Worcester, Massachusetts, where Munger established the Worcester Cycle Manufacturing Company and set about grooming Taylor for his spectacular career. Worcester had been a center of abolitionism before the Civil War, and memories of that liberal tradition remained. Taylor was permitted to join the YMCA, where he undertook an intensive bodybuilding program. Three years later, despite threats, boycotts, and prejudice, Taylor won the title of world champion in sprints. He became national champion in 1900 and the first black superstar. He may have made over seventy-five thousand dollars during his career.

Despite his brilliant statistics (seven world records in 1898 alone), Taylor lost many races because of unfair combinations. White riders used the "pocket" technique to block him from breaking away from the pack at the close of a race. His finishing kick was the most spectacular in the world, but he could not use it when he was jammed in by riders on sides and front. Without fully realizing what was happening, Taylor became a symbol of national significance. As the first black athlete to challenge whites successfully in a major professional sport, he became a celebrity, sometimes competing before paying crowds of ten thousand and more. Some whites found it unthinkable for a black man to dominate such an important and lucrative sport, and the League of American Wheelmen split on the race issue, largely because of Taylor.

Bicycle racing offered a variety of contests, ranging from the quarter-mile sprint to the 594-kilometer road race between Paris and Bordeaux. Taylor was a sprint man; in his prime he could beat anyone in the quarter-mile, half-mile, mile, and two-mile races. He once did the mile in one minute and thirty-one seconds from a standing start and in one minute and nineteen seconds from a flying start; both times were world records. Although he seldom entered the longer contests, he did win one seventy-five-mile road race.

The controversy over race that made Taylor the target of bigotry also made him the hottest item on the track. The more he was ganged up on and fouled, the more popular he became with the fans. More than one promoter had to swallow his misgivings and allow Taylor to compete, even though Taylor was not permitted to join either of the main cycling associations. Taylor's manager, William Brady, also managed the white heavyweight boxing champions Jim Corbett and Jim Jeffries.

In 1900 Taylor married Daisy Victoria Morris and purchased a nice house in the tony white neighborhood of Columbus Park. At first they encountered ugly hostility from some of the bigoted residents of the Worcestor community, but eventually most of his neighbors came to take pride in having a celebrity in their midst. He was a faithful member of John Street Baptist Church, he neither drank nor smoked, and he read his Bible every day. Unlike the flamboyant and controversial boxer JACK JOHNSON, Taylor was a model of propriety in the eyes of middle-class whites, and he became wildly popular in central Massachusetts. When the Worcester Coliseum velodrome was built in 1900, he was the main star on opening night and for months to come.

In 1901 Taylor sailed for Europe on a spectacularly successful tour of sixteen cities, during which he successively defeated the national champions of

Denmark, Germany, Belgium, England, and Italy, plus other noted racers. Despite his refusal to race on Sundays, he attracted huge crowds, who, even as he was trimming their national champions, cheered for *le nègre volant* ["the flying Negro"], as Robert Coquelle, a French writer and cycling promoter, had dubbed him. Taylor returned to Europe in 1902 and won forty races against the best riders the Europeans could muster. After a third triumphant tour in 1903, Coquelle and Paul Hamelle, in a monograph on Taylor, concluded that he was "the most extraordinary, the most versatile, the most colorful, the most popular cyclist, the champion around whom more legends had gathered than any other and whose life story most resembled a fairy tale" (quoted in Ritchie, 204).

Taylor toured Australia from 1902 to 1904, competing before huge crowds, breaking records, and winning plaudits for his distinctive fluid style, with very little movement of the upper body. After returning to Worcester, he retired from competition to spend more time with his wife and their daughter, Sydney. He became a familiar figure in downtown Worcester at the wheel of his French limousine. In 1907 Taylor was enticed back to Europe. Thirty pounds overweight, he underwent a grueling training schedule that got him back into shape. Despite a slow start, he logged some spectacular wins. He went back in 1908 and 1909, but by then his career was on the wane. He retired permanently from cycling in 1910.

Taylor's life after his retirement went downhill. Although he had been prudent with his money during his racing years, he had no other skills. He invested fifteen thousand dollars in a business venture that flopped. He tried to enter Worcester Polytechnic Institute to study engineering but was turned down, ostensibly because he had no high school degree. His health began to give way, and he may have had an enlarged heart from all those years of training. In the 1920s he came down with a painful case of shingles. With no steady income, he was forced to sell his wife's jewelry and other items that he had purchased in better times. Finally, he had to sell their cherished home, and the family moved into a modest apartment. His wife, who had come from an educated family, went to work as a seamstress. Gradually, she became estranged from Taylor, as did their daughter.

In December 1926 Harry Worcester Smith, a noted sportsman and Taylor's longtime friend, organized an appeal for the old champion. "No citizen who has ever lived in Worcester has made the worldwide fame enjoyed by Major Taylor," Smith wrote to the Worcester *Evening Gazette*. "The black man, racing against white for large purses, fighting combinations of race against race all over the world, wrote his name in flaming letters high in the sky of sportsmanship. None ever shone brighter." The appeal brought in twelve hundred dollars, which surely helped, although it probably was a terrible psychological blow to an intensely proud man to have to accept even that kind of charity.

Taylor's final energies went into his autobiography, published at his own expense as *The Fastest Bicycle Rider in the World: The Story of a Colored Boy's Indomitable Courage and Success against Great Odds* (1929). It is a long, rambling book, filled with details of individual races but not enough information about Major Taylor, the man. Ill and broke, Taylor went door to door selling his book. His wife left Worcester and went to New York; she never saw Taylor again. In 1930 he, too, left Worcester and headed for Chicago, his car filled with copies of his book. In Chicago he lived at the YMCA, from which he went forth every day to peddle his autobiography. He died in the charity ward of Cook County Hospital and was buried in the pauper's section of the Mount Glenwood Cemetery. The *Chicago Defender*, an African American newspaper, was the only one to note his death.

In 1948 a group of former bicycle racers and black athletes, with the financial help of Frank Schwinn, owner of the Schwinn Bicycle Company, had Taylor reburied in a more fitting place in the cemetery, with an appropriate plaque. But Major Taylor's best epitaph may be taken from the preface to his autobiography: "I am writing my memoirs, however, in the spirit calculated to solicit simple justice, equal rights, and a square deal for the posterity of my down-trodden but brave people, not only in athletic games and sports, but in every honorable game of human endeavor." In 2000, a century after he had become national champion, a campaign was begun in Worcester to raise $250,000 for a statue of Major Taylor, to be placed in front of the Worcester Public Library.

FURTHER READING

A collection of Major Taylor's papers, trophies, and memorabilia is housed at the Indiana State Museum in Indianapolis.

Taylor, Marshall W. *The Fastest Bicycle Rider in the World: The Story of a Colored Boy's Indomitable Courage and Success against Great Odds* (1929, repr. 1972).

Nye, Peter. *Hearts of Lions: The History of American Bicycle Racing* (1988).

Ritchie, Andrew. *Major Taylor: The Extraordinary Career of a Champion Bicycle Racer* (1988).

ALBERT B. SOUTHWICK

Taylor, Mildred D. (13 Sept. 1943–), author of books for young adults, was born Mildred Delois Taylor in Jackson, Mississippi, the younger of two daughters of Deletha Marie (Davis) and Wilbert Lee Taylor, a local trucker. Despite the family's deep ties to their homestead, Wilbert Taylor moved his family from Jackson to Toledo, Ohio, only three months after Mildred's birth in response to a racially motivated incident at his workplace and with the intention of raising his children in a climate free of bigotry. Taylor enjoyed growing up on Toledo's busy Dorr Street, where an extended family of cousins, aunts, and uncles packed the house to capacity, providing Taylor and her older sister Wilma with the same

Mildred Taylor argues that allowing nursing assistants to dispense routine medicine in nursing homes would hurt residents during a news conference at the Illinois State Capitol in Springfield, Illinois, 31 March 2005. (AP Images.)

kind of loving family network explored in Taylor's novels. Equally enjoyable were the frequent car trips to Mississippi to see extended family. These visits, punctuated by hours of rich storytelling sessions by her father and relatives, helped Taylor learn more about her ancestors, like her great-grandfather who was the son of a white Alabama plantation owner and a slave woman. The expansive oral tradition of these stories and her father's lively and animated delivery affected Taylor so deeply that by the time she was only nine or ten years old she had decided to become a writer.

When the Taylor family relocated to a large house in a newly integrated Toledo neighborhood, Taylor experienced the sudden shock of being a minority. In 1954 she was the only black student in her sixth-grade class. Taylor internalized her role as the "the only one" (Taylor, 273), driving herself to perfection in her schoolwork and behavior, believing that the repercussions of her actions would resonate far beyond herself. Taylor entered Toledo's Scott High School in 1957; even though the school was half white and half black, Taylor still felt marginalized because of her participation in the school's predominantly white college preparatory courses and the National Honor Society. As the "token black," Taylor was "always aware that all black people would be reflected in what [she] did, whether it was good or bad" (Taylor, 274). Taylor graduated from Scott High School in 1961 and enrolled in the University of Toledo with plans to travel to Ethiopia with the Peace Corps after graduation, a decision that she had made at sixteen after hearing a speech by John F. Kennedy. Determined to help their daughter make practical choices and convinced that she would lose interest in the Peace Corps, Taylor's parents encouraged her to major in teaching.

Armed with a major in English, a minor in history, and numerous creative-writing credits, Taylor sat for the Peace Corps entrance exam during her senior year of college. News of her acceptance created conflict in the Taylor household, where none of her many relatives except her sister believed that she should make the trip. Prayers and careful contemplation by Taylor's mother, as well as her father's chance meeting with a man who had benefited from American missionary services, helped dissolve her family's disapproval. Taylor left for Ethiopia in 1965. She fell in love with the people and the land so deeply that she considered permanent residency. Eventually, however, reminded of the American South and her family by the

Ethiopian sense of heritage, storytelling, and family cohesion, Taylor returned home in the summer of 1967. She spent the next year traveling and working for the Peace Corps until in 1968 she began graduate school at the University of Colorado. Deeply involved with a number of black student groups, Taylor worked steadily to develop black pride and increase the rights of black students across campus. After receiving an M.A. in Journalism in 1969, Taylor continued to develop initiatives for the black studies program while working as a study skills coordinator at the university.

The first turning point in Taylor's career came in the form of a rejection letter from an editor at *Life* magazine who, a few months after Taylor's graduation, had asked her to write an article but then rejected it as lacking the vigor that he had previously noted in her writing. Surprised and disappointed, Taylor returned to Ethiopia in the summer of 1970 to reevaluate her life goals. Soon thereafter she briefly returned to her job at the University of Colorado before moving to Los Angeles in 1971 to pursue her dream of becoming a writer.

Taylor met Errol Zea-Daly shortly after arriving in Los Angeles, and in 1972 the couple married. The following year, discouraged by countless literary rejections and her dwindling savings, Taylor was surprised to win a writing contest sponsored by the Council on Interracial Books for Children. Her manuscript, the story of a tree-cutting incident by money-hungry white men, appeared as *Song of the Trees* in the spring of 1975, the same year that Taylor and Zea-Daly divorced. In 1976 Taylor published *Roll of Thunder, Hear My Cry*, her best-known work. Featuring Cassie Logan, a black adolescent girl who was inspired in part by Taylor's sister and who reappears in several of Taylor's later books, the young adult novel won the prestigious Newbery Medal sponsored by the American Library Association in 1977.

Taylor's stories about personal pride and principle in the face of racism continue in the *Roll of Thunder* sequels, *Let the Circle Be Unbroken* (1981) and *The Road to Memphis* (1990), and in its prequel, *The Land* (2001). Taylor's other books include *The Friendship* (1987), *The Gold Cadillac* (1987), *Mississippi Bridge* (1990), and *The Well: David's Story* (1995).

Cassie does not narrate all of Taylor's books, and many of the novels take place in the mid-twentieth century or earlier. Each story focuses on the timeless theme of growth, tracing an individual's development. The books are filled with individuals making principled choices and provide a road map for young adults, helping them through the modern-day maze of racism, intolerance, and bigotry.

In 2003 Taylor, herself the mother of a daughter, won the inaugural NSK Neustadt Prize for Children's Literature, and in 2004 the governor of Mississippi declared 2 April 2004 Mildred D. Taylor Day.

FURTHER READING

Taylor, Mildred D. "Mildred D. Taylor," in *Something about the Author Autobiography Series*, vol. 5, ed. Adele Sarkissian (1988).

Crowe, Chris. *Presenting Mildred D. Taylor* (1999).

SYLVIA M. DESANTIS

Taylor, Preston (7 Nov. 1849–13 Apr. 1931), stonecutter, porter, educator, funeral director, and preacher, was born a slave in Shreveport, Louisiana, the son of Zed and Betty Taylor. When Preston was one year old, his parents moved to Lexington, Kentucky, where at age four young Preston heard a sermon in the First Baptist Church of Lexington and subsequently stated, "Some day I'll be a preacher" (Clement Richardson, *The National Cyclopedia of the Colored Race* [1919]). In 1864, at age fifteen Preston enlisted in Company G, 116th U.S. Infantry, as a drummer. He was present at the sieges of Richmond and Petersburg in Virginia, and at the surrender of Robert E. Lee. Taylor's regiment also served in Texas and New Orleans, Louisiana, before he exited the army on 17 January 1867 (Simmons, *Men of Mark*).

After serving in the military, Taylor became a stonecutter and was skillful at fashioning monuments and engraving marble. But racial tensions between white and black workers in marble yards forced him to abandon this lucrative trade. He consequently became a porter on the Louisville and Chattanooga Railroad, and over a four-year period he gained a reputation as "one of the best railroad men in the service" (Simmons, *Men of Mark*). After turning down a promotion to become assistant baggage master on the Louisville and Chattanooga Railroad, Taylor, knowing that white contractors preferred Irish labor, used his increasing influence in the Louisville community and negotiated for African Americans, and he helped blacks secure a contract to build the Big Sandy Railway from Mount Sterling, Kentucky, to Richmond, Virginia.

While in Mount Sterling, Taylor preached for the black Christian church of that community. The Disciples of Christ (or Christian Church) and

Churches of Christ owe their origins principally to two men, Barton W. Stone (1772–1844) and Alexander Campbell (1788–1866), who called for a return to what they perceived to be New Testament Christianity. This religious movement is sometimes referred to as the Restoration movement or the Stone-Campbell movement. While working as a Disciples of Christ preacher, from 1879 to 1884 Taylor edited the column "Our Colored Brethren" in the *Christian Standard*, a religious paper published by white Christians in Cincinnati, Ohio. This position established Taylor as an influential leader among African American Disciples. In 1885 Taylor received an appointment as the financial agent for the Christian Bible College in New Castle, Kentucky. The newly established school for black ministers in the Stone-Campbell movement ended abruptly owing to insufficient monetary support.

After the failure of the Christian Bible College, Taylor relocated to Nashville, Tennessee, to launch a series of business ventures. After working with M. S. Combs, Taylor became a funeral director and opened the Taylor Funeral Company in 1888. This business produced both caskets and jobs for the African American community, and it extolled Taylor as an influential leader among black Nashvillians. In addition to his mortuary business Taylor developed a beautiful burial site, Greenwood Site, for blacks in Nashville. Greenwood Cemetery was supplemented and complemented by Greenwood Park, an amusement park for the city's black residents. The park included "a club house, with restaurant and refreshment stand; a theatre, skating rink, roller coaster, shooting gallery, box ball, knife, cane and baby rack, merry-go-round, a zoo, and a base-ball park" (Richardson). Taylor married Georgia Gordon, a member of the internationally acclaimed Fisk Jubilee Singers.

The creation of Greenwood Cemetery and Greenwood Park marked Taylor as a potent leader in the African American community. Thus he used his influence to give economic stability to fellow black Nashvillians by providing jobs, by erecting a retirement home and orphanage, and by opening a bank. In 1904 Taylor collaborated with eight other black entrepreneurs to establish the One Cent Savings Bank & Trust Company. Such an enterprise made Taylor both influential and affluent. He also participated in the founding of Tennessee State Agriculture and Industrial State Normal College (later Tennessee State University) in 1909.

Even though Taylor oversaw impressive economic and educational pursuits, he was first and foremost a committed church leader. In 1886 he assumed leadership of the Gay Street Christian Church, first established in 1855 as an offshoot of the white Vine Street First Christian Church. In 1891, because of allegations of sexual impropriety, church leaders ousted Taylor, who then established a church in a doctor's building on Spruce Street. After Taylor's death this congregation merged into Gay-Lea Christian Church on Osage Street. In 1917 Taylor became president of the National Colored Christian Missionary Convention. In his first address he excoriated white Disciples of Christ for holding improper racial attitudes toward black people: "The attitude of our white brotherhood on the race question accounts largely for our smallness.... For if the white brother can include in his religious theory and practice the colored people as real brothers, he will have avoided the heresy of all heresies" (Cardwell). Over the next fourteen years Taylor continued to serve as president of the National Colored Missionary Convention. In his final address he stressed the importance of the preacher: "In all the ages the Minister has been God's leader of men; he has been the key man" (Todd Simmons, *Discipliana*). Taylor died in 1931 with a net worth of almost $500,000, making him one of the wealthiest men in Nashville.

FURTHER READING

Cardwell, Brenda Marie. "Three Concerns of Black Disciples from 1917 to 1969," master's thesis, Lexington Theological Seminary, Louisville, Kentucky (1981).

Henry, Kenneth E. "Unknown Prophets: Black Disciple Ministry in Historical Perspective," *Discipliana* 46 (Spring 1986).

Simmons, Todd W. "Preston Taylor: Seeker of Dignity for Black Disciples," *Discipliana* 60 (Winter 2000).

Simmons, William James. *Men of Mark: Eminent, Progressive, and Rising* (1887; repr. 1968).

EDWARD J. ROBINSON

Taylor, Prince (1755–1828), sailor, cooper, soldier, surveyor, farmer, and innkeeper, was born in Lunenburg, Worcester County, Massachusetts. Taylor's father was probably Prince Taylor (?–1804), a slave of John Taylor of Lunenburg. It is not known if the younger Prince Taylor was born a slave or free. In occupation and location, Taylor continually reinvented himself to cope with changing circumstances. He did not marry.

Taylor served as steward on the fourteen-gun brig *Diligent* under Captain Brown for five months in 1779 during the failed Penobscot expedition, America's greatest naval disaster until Pearl Harbor. In his 1818 Revolutionary War pension deposition, Taylor declared, "I am by trade a Saylor" (Revolutionary War Pension Application, Massachusetts service, dossier #S.42.463, National Archives). On 6 March 1781 he accepted the bounty paid by the town of Lunenburg to enlist in the Continental Army for the next three years. His enlistment record indicates that he was then twenty-six years old, five feet ten inches in height, "black" in complexion, and a cooper by trade. His Sixth Massachusetts Regiment served at West Point, New York, for the next two years. During his service, Taylor earned extra pay as a cooper in the Commissary Department, repairing casks and barrels. Taylor was discharged from Revolutionary War service on 23 December 1783 by the commander in chief, General Henry Knox. With his war service, Taylor won his freedom, if in fact he had been enslaved upon entering military service.

After the Revolution, Taylor became a pioneer, settling the northern frontier of New York. In 1786 he assisted Joseph Laurant, a French Canadian war veteran, locate and survey a five-hundred-acre land grant on Lake Champlain that was awarded to Laurant by the state of New York. Taylor was given 420 acres of the grant in payment for his surveying services, a transaction not recorded with the county clerk until 1799. By 1791 Taylor, then thirty-six years old, had purchased his own 250-acre farm for $2.50 an acre on a peninsula extending into the northern end of Lake George, near Fort Ticonderoga, the scene of endless conflict during both the French and Indian War and the Revolution. There on 1 June 1791 Secretary of State Thomas Jefferson and Congressman James Madison (both Virginia slave owners and future presidents) were surprised to encounter Taylor, a "free Negro ... [who] possesses a good farm ... which he cultivates with 6 white hirelings [indentured servants]." One can only imagine the concurrent reactions of their fellow visitors, Jefferson's slave James Hemings and Madison's manservant Matthew. "By his industry and good management [Taylor] turns [the farm] to good account," wrote Madison in his travel journal; this encounter with Taylor prompted Madison's most extended commentary during his summer tour of the lakes. Madison recorded that Taylor "is intelligent; reads writes & understands accounts, and is dextrous in his affairs.... He has no wife, and is said to be disinclined to marriage, nor any woman on his [Ticonderoga] farm" (Maguire, 20). In 1805

the traveler Elkanah Watson also noted the solitary farm at the north end of the lake: "Prince, a free son of Africa, holds one of the best [farms]. May heaven bless him If he deserves freedom" (70). A 1798 survey shows Taylor's house on lot thirty on Black Point. This is virtually the only arable land on the northeastern shore of the lake. The peninsula on which Taylor's farm was located was still called Black Point in the early twenty-first century and was prime real estate for vacation homes.

As the shores of Lake Champlain and Lake George were rapidly being settled, Taylor was a key figure in all manner of "founding" activities in the Ticonderoga vicinity. By 1808 Taylor and his co-commissioner of highways, Lodewick Shear, laid out and surveyed the first roads in the town of Putnam, New York, immediately south of Taylor's farm. A religious man, he was among the founding members of the Episcopal church in Ticonderoga in 1792. Seventeen years later, in 1809, he enrolled as an early congregant in the first Congregational church in Ticonderoga. In 1811 he swore an oath to serve as an overseer of highways in Putnam, Washington County, on a document that preserves his signature.

"Heritage tourism" took off apace at the beginning of the nineteenth century. Americans and Europeans delighted in the opportunity to view America's sublime and picturesque landscapes and the related historic sites along the corridor of the Hudson River, Lake George, and Lake Champlain, a route soon codified in print as the "Fashionable Tour" (1822) and the "Northern Tour" (1825). Taylor capitalized on the burgeoning tourist traffic. Around this time he apparently abandoned farming and turned to less physically strenuous work as Ticonderoga's first innkeeper. By 1808, now fifty-three years old, he had leased two lots at the outlet of Lake George (then called Alexandria, later part of Ticonderoga). In 1811 he opened a place of public entertainment at the start of the portage between Lake George and Lake Champlain. The following year he received a license from Essex County, making his the first sanctioned tavern in Ticonderoga. The county imposed restrictions: he could not "Keep a Disorderly inn or Tavern or Suffer or permit any Cock fighting gaming or Playing with Cards or Dice or Keep any billiard Table or other gaming Table of Shuffle board within the inn or Tavern by him to be Kept or within any out house yard [or structure] adjoining there unto" (County Clerk's Office, Essex County, New York, application for tavern license, 25 June 1812). Taylor developed a reputation that endured more than a generation as "a man of wit, of good parts, and withal of sincere piety, and few were the weddings or parties or festivals in town in which his art as cook, or waiter, and chief director of the eatables, was not brought into contribution" (Cook, 55).

But by 1818 Taylor, sixty-three years old, found himself in "reduced circumstances." He sought support from the country's first veterans' relief program. Taylor reported that he was "unable to perform manual Labour by means of age & two ruptures, which have been of long standing." He had no family nor relations to support him. When revised Revolutionary pension laws tightened eligibility in 1820, Taylor submitted the required inventory of his possessions as proof of his poverty: a handful of household furnishings, utensils, "old religious books," and "his necessary clothing & bedding" (Pension dossier #S.42.463). The total value was $69.43. Taylor thence forward received a Revolutionary War soldier's pension of $8 a month. He died in 1828. The Daughters of the American Revolution erected historical markers commemorating Taylor's farm site and his inn in 2005.

FURTHER READING

Taylor's application for a tavern license, 25 June 1812, is in the Essex County, New York, records; his signature is on the Oath of Overseers of Highways, 15 April 1811, in the Putnam, New York, records; and his application for assistance, is in Revolutionary War Pension and Bounty Land Applications: Massachusetts Service, dossier #S.42.463, National Archives.

Cook, Flavius J. *Home Sketches of Essex County: Ticonderoga* (1858).

Lape, Jane M. *Ticonderoga: Patches and Patterns from Its Past* (1969).

Maguire, J. Robert. *The Tour to the Northern Lakes of James Madison and Thomas Jefferson, May–June 1791* (1995).

Massachusetts, Office of the Secretary of State. *Massachusetts Soldiers and Sailors of the Revolutionary War*, vol. 15 (1896–1908).

Watson, Elkanah. "Journal of Remarks from Albany to Lake Champlain, Augt 1805," manuscript diary, box 3, journal E, New York State Library.

NICHOLAS WESTBROOK

Taylor, Robert Robinson (8 June 1868–13 Dec. 1942), the first academically trained African American architect and the first black graduate of the Massachusetts Institute of Technology (MIT), was born in Wilmington, North Carolina, to Emily Still and Henry Taylor, a literate slave who, given virtual freedom by his white father and master, prospered independently as a merchant, carpenter, and coastal trader. Little is known about Emily Still, other than that she was described as a "mulatto" and was ten years younger than her husband. Presaging the future career of his son, Henry Taylor also constructed a number of businesses and homes in Wilmington. Robert R. Taylor studied at Wilmington's Gregory Institute, an American Missionary Association school, where he was taught by white New Englanders who were ambitious for their charges. Though it is possible that the Gregory Institute's teachers pointed Taylor to MIT, the impetus might have come from other Wilmingtonians. A wealthy white boy who lived around the corner from the Taylor home graduated in engineering in 1885 and Francis Bacon, brother of the designer of the Lincoln Memorial, studied architecture at MIT. Taylor once said that he had wanted to earn a liberal arts degree at Lincoln University, the elite college for African American boys near Philadelphia, before gaining his technical education. Instead, he worked with his father as a builder for a year or two before entering MIT in the fall of 1888.

Taylor's MIT years were a success. He was at or near the top of his class and was awarded a scholarship for the final two years. While Taylor's own architecture class of about twelve was distinctly Yankee, his institute class would have been international. A wag wrote in *Technique 1890*, an MIT student yearbook, that "Sixty-seven percent [of one student class] were light-complexioned, thirty-three percent dark. Eleven percent wore eye glasses; one was color blind; and fifty percent thought they had mustaches" (58). Taylor would have been among that 50 percent as well as the darker 33 if he were a member of the class under review. Taylor's thesis design, two boards with a plan and elevation in ink and watercolor, was for a home for aged Civil War veterans from the North and South. Taylor received a bachelor's degree in Architecture from MIT in 1892. He corresponded with BOOKER T. WASHINGTON in the summer of 1892 while working as a "building mechanic" at a hotel at Oak Bluffs, on Martha's Vineyard. Taylor may have then gone to Cleveland, Ohio, to practice.

In November 1892 he arrived at Washington's Tuskegee Normal and Industrial Institute, which was established to serve the desperately poor former slaves in Alabama's rural hinterland. Taylor was to teach architectural and mechanical drawing for the trades students and to design buildings. His first Alabama completion was a frame industries building for a Tuskegee daughter school, Mt. Meigs, near Montgomery, and he probably drew the printed cottage plans that were given out to farmers attending conferences at the institute. Taylor's construction of brick buildings on campus began with Science Hall (later Thrasher) and continued through the 1890s with the chapel, the Oaks for Booker T. Washington, the vast boys trades building, and Huntington Hall girls' dormitory. He also designed many wooden structures, including a primary school, student and faculty housing, a hospital, and barns.

Teaching, however, was Taylor's heaviest task, since all industrial students had to draw everything they were to make. Every trade—steamfitting, plumbing, tailoring, tinsmithing, carriage building and wheelwrighting, masonry, and carpentry—started with plans and elevations because drawing promoted modern industrial processes, cognitive skills, and creativity. Drawing had a racial dimension even though it was also fundamental to white schools. Taylor wrote that drawing taught the executive thinking that slave artisans, supposedly working only under supervision, were thought to have lacked. Tuskegee's army of drawing students seems to have overwhelmed their teacher, contributing to his decision to return to Cleveland in 1899, a year after his marriage to Beatrice Rochon. The couple had four children prior to Beatrice Rochon's early death in 1906. Taylor married again in 1911 to Nellie Green Chestnut, a teacher. The couple had one child. In Cleveland Taylor worked for a white architect and on his own while keeping Tuskegee as a client. He designed the institute's girls' industries building Dorothy Hall, the Lincoln Gates, boys' and girls' bath houses, and the Huntington Memorial Academic Building.

In 1902 he returned to Tuskegee, but as director of industries, not as a teacher. He was now responsible for hundreds of students enrolled in a complicated curriculum that interlocked with the academic department, but that also produced marketable goods and services for the region. Students learned their trades through this practice, acquiring the knowledge that Washington hoped would counteract discrimination, as he believed that tolerance and even admiration would follow from white dependence on black skills.

Taylor's buildings from 1903 until Washington's death in 1915 included the brick Carnegie Library, Rockefeller Hall, four Emery dormitories, the Office Building, Douglass Hall, White Hall, Tantum Hall,

John A. Andrew Hospital, the Veterinary Hospital, and New Laundry (later the visitors' center). He also designed Carnegie libraries for black colleges in Salisbury, North Carolina, and Marshall, Texas. Taylor's buildings show sensitivity to site, scale, and the richly textured, multihued Tuskegee bricks. Windows of different shapes and sizes are placed as in syncopation. The massing is triadic—an emphasized center with subsidiary wings—but each building ingeniously differs from the others in how this is managed. The three libraries and several more Tuskegee buildings have large classical columns like those on county courthouses or white people's mansions. The architecture seems to deny the Jim Crow restrictions locking in all around it. Although Taylor did not design the largest building of the Washington era, the imperially scaled Tompkins Dining Hall, he was involved in every phase of the building's design and construction. After Washington's death Taylor formed an architectural partnership with Louis H. Persley (1890–1932), then the institute's drawing teacher. Together they designed buildings for the newly established College Department, a multipurpose structure at Selma University, and a Masonic temple and office building in Birmingham. The visual character of these large and technically more advanced works is less intimate or personal than the earlier ones.

As an institute officer after 1903, Taylor's off-campus responsibilities gradually increased along with a reputation for interracial tact. He might address the trustees in a New York meeting or meet with millionaire donors in their homes. In 1923, as ranking institute officer when Tuskegee's second principal, ROBERT RUSSA MOTON, was away, Taylor faced down the Ku Klux Klan as it drove past the campus. He was subsequently named vice principal although he continued his previous duties as department head as well as head of buildings and grounds. Taylor served on a politically sensitive committee that evaluated Red Cross refugee camps for black victims of the 1927 Mississippi River flood. In 1929 he went to Liberia to help found the Booker T. Washington Institute. There he assessed the country's agricultural and industrial potential, outlined a curriculum to serve it, advised on governance and staffing, sketched a campus plan, and designed a few buildings. Taylor capped the trip with a grand tour of Europe. That year Lincoln University awarded him an honorary doctorate.

In 1932 Taylor suffered a massive heart attack while visiting his son in Chicago. This son, Robert Rochon Taylor, was a housing activist; the high rise

Robert Taylor Homes, the nation's largest public housing project, would be named after him. Robert Robinson Taylor then retired from Tuskegee, returning to his native Wilmington so that his presence would not burden his successor. There he lived a gentleman's life with a townhouse, a waterside cottage, and a car and driver to travel between them. In retirement he worked to achieve racial fairness. He served as the first African American on the board of a black state college, Fayetteville State Teachers College, and along with Hugh MacRae, a white leader of the 1898 Wilmington coup d'état, lobbied the federal government for funding to establish a black farm community. In addition to advocating better civic amenities for Wilmington's African American population, he supported greater fairness in the federal government. In 1941, for example, he wrote to the director of the U.S. Civil Service Commission to request that federal job applications not require photographs.

In December 1942, while visiting family, Taylor died in the Tuskegee chapel that he had designed and which he considered his greatest architectural accomplishment. A month following his death the New Brooklyn Homes in Wilmington, North Carolina's first public housing project, was renamed the Robert R. Taylor Homes in his honor.

FURTHER READING

Papers related to Robert R. Taylor's life and career are housed at the Tuskegee Archives at the Tuskegee Institute in Alabama, which were closed as of 2007. Taylor's MIT thesis and other materials related to his undergraduate career are at the MIT Institute Archives & Special Collections, Cambridge, Massachusetts.

Weiss, Ellen. "Robert R. Taylor of Tuskegee: An Early Black American Architect," *ARRIS: Journal of the Southeast Chapter of the Society of Architectural Historians* 2 (1991): 3–19.

Williams, Clarence G. "From 'Tech' to Tuskegee: The Life of Robert Robinson Taylor, 1868–1942." http://libraries.mit.edu/archives/mithistory/blacks-at-mit/taylor.html.

Wilson, Dreck Spurlock. *African American Architects: A Biographical Dictionary, 1865–1945* (2004).

Obituaries: Chicago *Bee*, 17 Jan. 1943; *Journal and Guide* (Norfolk, Va.), 9 Jan. 1943.

ELLEN WEISS

Taylor, Susan (Susie) Baker King (6 Aug. 1848– 6 Oct. 1912), teacher and nurse during the Civil War, was born on the Isle of Wight, one of the Sea Islands off the coast of Georgia, the eldest of nine children of slaves Hagar Ann Reed and Raymond Baker. When Susie was 7 years of age, she and one of her brothers were allowed by their master to live in Savannah with their grandmother, Dolly Reed, a free person of color. Determined to see her grandchildren learn to read and write even though state law at the time prohibited the education of blacks, Reed found a way around the legislation; she sent the children to a secret school run by a friend. After two years, Susie attended another secret school, followed by private tutoring (also illegal). By the time she was 12, Susie was one of probably only a few slaves in Georgia who had command of written English.

Susie Baker King Taylor, in a fronstpiece image included with her 1902 book *Reminiscences of My Life in Camp with the 33d United States Colored Troops Late 1st S. C. Volunteers.* (Courtesy of Documenting the American South, the University of North Carolina at Chapel Hill Libraries.)

In early April 1862, a year after the Civil War began, Susie escaped to freedom, thanks to her uncle, who brought her with his family of seven to St. Catherines Island, off the Georgia coast. From there a federal gunboat transported them to St. Simons Island, within Union lines and far from their master's reach. As one of the only freed slaves who could read and write, 14-year-old Susie was soon asked by Union authorities to organize a school for the black children on the island. Supplied with two large boxes of books, she taught about 40 young-sters and a number of adults who came to her in the evening. Little did the young former slave real-ize that she was an educational pioneer: the first African American to teach openly in a school for people of color in the state of Georgia.

At age 15, Susie married Edward King, a sergeant in a newly formed black regiment, the 1st South Carolina Volunteers (later reorganized as the 33rd U.S. Colored Troops). For the remainder of the war she traveled with King and his regiment, initially serving as a laundress, but she soon became the soldiers' teacher. Yet with all her good works as an educator, it was actually as a nurse that Susie made her greatest contribution. As an African American caregiver, she was a rarity among Civil War nurses. Of the more than 5,000 women who served in that capacity during the conflict, most were white and middle class and were paid $12 per month; the majority worked in hospitals, far removed from the combat zone. Susie, however, was not paid for the three years of work she performed, and she traveled with the regiment and provided care to its members much closer to the battlefield. In so doing, she was most likely the first woman of color—and probably the youngest woman, white or black—to serve as a nurse on the front lines during the Civil War.

Soon after the war came to an end, Susie and her husband returned to Savannah. There she opened a school in her home for black children, teaching some 20 students and receiving as tuition a dollar per month from each of them. Edward King, a car-penter by trade, was unable to find work because of laws known as "black codes" that made it impossi-ble for African Americans to practice a skilled craft on their own. He eventually found employment as a longshoreman, unloading goods from vessels in Savannah's harbor.

Hoping to have a family, Susie was happy to dis-cover that she was pregnant. But her joy turned to sorrow when, only months before her delivery date, her husband suddenly died. Alone and without income (her students had left her to attend a free school built by the federally sponsored Freedmen's Bureau), she placed her newborn son with her mother and took work as a servant for a wealthy white family. Over the next decade or so, from the late 1860s to the late 1870s, Susie continued to serve as a domestic at different times for several families, one of which relocated to Boston, Massachusetts, and invited her to join them. Unable to bring her son, she left him in the care of her mother and headed north.

After working as a servant for several rich and influential families, in 1879 Susie married Russell Taylor, of whom little is known. Her marriage enabled the former nurse and teacher to pursue projects that she had set aside while trying to sur-vive as a single woman of color. In 1886 she helped to organize the Massachusetts chapter of the Women's Relief Corps. The organization was designed to pro-vide aid and comfort to the aging veterans (white and black) of the Union Army.

As Susie devoted her time and energies to help-ing those who had served, she herself suffered a per-sonal tragedy. In early February 1898 she received word from Shreveport, Louisiana, that her 31-year-old son, who was affiliated with a traveling theater company, was unwell. Arriving in Shreveport, Susie immediately went to her son's bedside. Finding him gravely ill, she wanted to take him to Boston and tried to purchase for him a ticket for a berth on a railroad sleeping car. Because he was black, no rail-road company in the South would sell her one. For Susie, the injustice was maddening. Her son, whose father had fought to preserve the Union, had been denied under that same Union a berth to carry him home to die, because he was black. He died several days after Taylor left for Boston.

In the years following her son's death, and as America entered the twentieth century, Susie won-dered whether the Civil War had been fought in vain. "All we ask for is 'equal justice,'" she wrote in her memoirs. "I hope the day is not far distant when the two races will reside in peace. ... I know I shall not live to see the day, but it will come" (*Reminiscences*, pp. 136–137, 141).

Susie Baker King Taylor died in 1912 at the age of 64.

FURTHER READING

Taylor, Susie King. *Reminiscences of my Life in Camp with the 33rd U.S. Colored Troops, Late 1st South Carolina Volunteers: A Black Woman's Civil War Memoirs*, ed. by Patricia W. Romero (1988).

Henig, Gerald S. "Pathfinders: Civil War Nurse," *American Legacy: The Magazine of African-American History & Culture* (Spring 2008).

Leonard, Elizabeth D. *All the Daring of the Soldier: Women of the Civil War Armies* (1999).

GERALD S. HENIG

Taylor, Susan Lillian (23 Jan. 1946–), author, editor, magazine publisher, and entrepreneur, was born in New York City to Lawrence Taylor and Violet (Weekes) Taylor. Taylor came from a long line of Caribbean-born entrepreneurs whose business acumen has a profound impact on her throughout her life. Her great-grandmother, Susan Braithwaite, was born in Barbados and owned both a soda business and a hot pepper sauce venture in the late nineteenth century, while her grandmother, Rhoda Weekes, had a tailor shop in

Susan L. Taylor arrives at the Annual NAACP Image Awards held at the Shrine Auditorium on 25 February 2006 in Los Angeles, California. (AP Images.)

Harlem and helped to build the family businesses of bars and liquor stores during the 1930s and for decades afterward. Taylor's own parents owned a liquor store together, as well as the first black-owned women's boutique in East Harlem.

Little is known of Taylor's childhood or early education, but in 1966, at age twenty, Taylor married William Bowles, a businessman and the owner of a local hair salon. In her early twenties Taylor worked as an actor with the Negro Ensemble Company, but she decided to transition to more steady employment after the birth of her daughter, Shana-Nequai, in 1969. Taylor's marriage ended suddenly, just six weeks after Shana's birth. A single mother living on her own, Taylor became a licensed cosmetologist. After conducting extensive research, she upheld family tradition by becoming a fourth-generation entrepreneur (her daughter would later also become an entrepreneur, as the owner of Custom Crowns, a Georgia-based beauty supply company). In 1970, at age twenty-four, Taylor created her own skin-care product line called Nequai Cosmetics. The company did well, and Taylor set up a distribution system to transport products from the Bronx to the Caribbean. Although Taylor's husband took control of Nequai Cosmetics following their legal separation that same year, her success led to new opportunities. She was invited to write beauty articles for the newly launched *Essence* magazine on a freelance basis.

In 1971 Taylor became the magazine's part-time beauty editor. The story of what happened to her next was one that she would repeat often to audiences across America and was a testimonial to the power of her faith. With no money for rent or car repairs, Taylor was rushed to an emergency room in the midst of an anxiety attack with severe chest pains. Walking home from the hospital later that evening she passed a church and wandered in, hearing the pastor deliver a message that would change her forever. The sermon was about living in faith. Immediately Taylor made a vow to change her attitude. She remained convinced for years afterward that it was this inner shift that brought outer transformation in her life.

Not long after this experience Taylor was offered a full-time job at *Essence* as beauty and fashion editor. In this capacity she made sure that readers saw images of black women who spanned the entire range of skin tones. Nor did she shy away from realistic body images, insisting on using models of average weight. Taylor's motto was, "Everyone is not a size nine, nor should she feel she has to be" (*New York Times*, 5 Apr. 1985). In 1981, with eleven years' experience at the magazine, Taylor was named editor-in-chief by the magazine's publisher, Ed Lewis. It was a controversial appointment, and several staffers were angered by the fact that Taylor had virtually no experience editing feature-length articles. Others were reportedly baffled by the fact that she got the job without having a college degree. Some quit, leaving the magazine in protest. But what Taylor brought to *Essence* went beyond formal training or a college education. In her monthly column, "In the Spirit," she wrote about her own insecurities, the pain of failed relationships, and the challenges of raising a daughter alone. She also shared her steadfast belief in the power of a God who is unconstrained by religious institutions or dogma. More than anything, Taylor did what no magazine editor had done before her: she spoke directly to the hearts, minds, and spirits of black women.

Taylor also threw her entrepreneurial spirit into the magazine, playing a key role in expanding its audience in print and broadcast media. In 1983 she was named host and executive producer of *Essence*, the first nationally syndicated African American magazine television show, which aired in sixty domestic markets and several Caribbean and African countries. In 1986 she became vice president of Essence Communications, Inc., and in 1987 she launched the Essence Awards show. In 1989 she was named senior vice president of Essence Communications, Inc. That year Taylor's personal life took a turn as well, when she married Khephra Burns, a writer and editor.

Having received an honorary doctorate from the nation's first black college, Lincoln University (others would follow from the University of Delaware, Spelman, Dillard, Stillman, and Bennett Colleges), Taylor remained driven to meet her own personal goal of an earned diploma and, in 1991, six years after she enrolled, she completed a bachelor's degree in Sociology from Fordham University in New York.

While her personal and professional victories appeared to be inspirational to *Essence* readers, mainstream publishers questioned whether or not her essays would appeal to a mass-market audience in book form. As editor Malaika Adero noted, they were confused by her frequent references to God in a book that was not purportedly about religion (*Black Issues Book Review*, Nov.–Dec. 2004). In fact Taylor had launched a whole new genre, one that Adero later termed "bibliotherapy." Her collection, *In the Spirit: The Inspirational Writings of Susan L. Taylor*, was published in 1993, by Amistad, a black-owned independent publisher.

Under Taylor's direction the *Essence* brand continued to expand. In 1994 she helped launch The Essence Music Festival, an annual event in New Orleans. With more than 200,000 attendees, it became one of the largest music festivals in the country. Two more books followed: *Lessons in Living* in 1995 and *Confirmation: The Spiritual Wisdom that Has Shaped Our Lives*, co-edited with her husband, in 1997. In 2000 Taylor stepped down from her position as editor-in-chief and became editorial director, a position responsible for the overall vision and image of the publication. In 2002 Taylor was inducted into the American Society of Magazine Editors' (ASME) Hall of Fame for her lifetime achievements. In 2005 *Essence* was sold to Time, Inc., a move that many lamented as the end of an era, and the final chapter for what had been a black-owned company. A poll conducted by blackenterprise.com found that 34 percent of respondents considered the move a "sell-out," compared to 14 percent who thought it made good business sense (*Black Enterprise*, March 2005). For more than three decades Taylor had embodied and defined the *Essence* brand, making it the most widely respected publication for black women in the world.

Taylor was an advocate for the poor and the disadvantaged, active on a wide range of issues while serving on boards for organizations such as Joint Center for Political and Economic Studies, Aid to Children of Imprisoned Mothers, Edwin Gould Services for Children and Families, Commission on Research in Black Education, The Future PAC, and Essence Cares.

KRISTAL BRENT ZOOK

Teage, Hilary (1805–21 May 1853), colonizationist, statesman, editor, and author of the Liberian Declaration of Independence, was born in Gooch-land County, Virginia, the son of Colin or Collin Teage (1785–1839), probably a slave on the plantation of Joshua Nicholson. His mother (name unknown) was probably also a slave in the Nicholson household. Details of Hilary Teage's early life are sketchy. Colin Teage was an artisan who made stable gear, a position above that of a field laborer but one that led to his separation from his family when he was sold in 1807 to the owners of a Richmond tack shop. Sometime in the next thirteen years, Colin Teage was licensed to preach in Baptist churches and saved enough money to purchase the freedom of his wife, son, and daughter in 1819 and 1820 and to reassemble his family. He bought land in Henrico County outside Richmond.

Ordained in 1820, Colin Teage was among the black Richmonders who discussed emigration to West Africa. In 1821 the Teage family sailed on the *Nautilus* for Freetown, Sierra Leone. In 1822 they and other émigrés (some had succumbed to malaria in Sierra Leone) moved to Cape Mesurado, Liberia. After another remove to Sierra Leone, the family resettled in Liberia in 1826.

It seems indisputable that Hilary Teage received substantial schooling as a young boy because his adult writings are literate and sophisticated, but nothing is known about his education. There was a charity school for blacks in Richmond organized by a white Baptist, William Crane, and it possible that Teage attended it. Teage became politically active in Liberia in the 1830s, and he invested in several trading and manufacturing businesses. He promoted self-rule for the American Liberian settlers (as opposed to the stewardship of the American Colonization Society). He collected and published official documents of the Liberian state as well as a history of the settlement. His peers elected him president of the Liberia Lyceum in 1845. The lyceum functioned for about five years after that. In 1835 he became editor and in 1849 owner of the *Liberia Herald*. He held a number of Liberian political offices, such as senator, attorney general, and secretary of state, from 1835 until his death. Following his father, he filled pulpits in several Baptist churches. The date of his marriage is not known, but his wife Eliza sailed to Liberia in 1820 at age seven, so a wedding in the 1830s seems likely. There is no record of the marriage producing children.

Trade between Liberia and the United States involved shipping finished products, such as tools, firearms, metalwares, tobacco, and preserved foodstuffs, to West Africa, while raw materials, such as palm oil, woods, groundnuts, and coffee beans, flowed to North America. The benefit of this trade to Liberia is unclear. It seems unlikely that it was profitable for the settlers, who tried without great success to promote their exports in Great Britain as well as the United States. Teage himself, despite his commercial efforts, seems to have made little headway in this trading system. He declared bankruptcy in 1846.

Colonization, as institutionalized in the American Colonization Society, was often dismissive and belittling of blacks. The American Liberian settlers and the indigenous peoples of Liberia were often at odds over use of land and labor as well as over prices of trade items. Teague charted a middle course in his writings. He was a civilizationist, believing that native people should be Christianized and brought into the orbit of Euro-American culture and economy. Yet he objected to practices such as appropriating land from native people without just recompense. He also criticized the remaining outposts of the slave trade in West Africa. His writings range from poetry to exhortations to African Americans to emigrate, to commentary on native culture, to paeans to hard work and sobriety, to state papers. The composition for which Teage is most renowned is the 1847 Liberian Declaration of Independence.

In the 1840s the leaders of the American Liberian settlers felt the need to end their dependency on the American Colonization Society and to forge a new republic. Before a constitution was written (in 1847), a declaration of independence was required. A constitutional convention charged Teage with its composition. He borrowed much from the 1776 American Declaration of Independence. The Liberian document in part reads:

A Declaration of Independence by the Representatives of the People of the Commonwealth of Liberia in Convention Assembled. July 16, 1847. We, the representatives of the people of the commonwealth of Liberia, in convention assembled, invested with the authority of forming a new government, relying upon the aid and protection of the Great Arbiter of human events, do hereby in the name and on behalf of the people of this commonwealth, publish and declare the said commonwealth a free, sovereign, and independent state, by the name and title of the Republic of Liberia. We recognize in all men certain inalienable rights; among these are life, liberty, and the right to acquire, possess, enjoy, and defend property. By the practice and consent of men in all ages, some system or form of government is proved to be necessary to exercise, enjoy, and secure their rights, and every people have a right to institute a government, and to choose and adopt that system, or form of it, which in their opinion will most effectively accomplish these objects, and secure their happiness, which does not interfere with the just rights of others (Huberich, vol. 1, 145).

The document was signed by twelve men, including Teage, who were convened for the constitutional convention in Monrovia. The convention wrote a constitution that included a bill of rights. Teage remained in public service for six more years, until an illness ended his life. He died in Monrovia, Liberia.

FURTHER READING

Beyan, Amos J. *The American Colonization Society and the Creation of the Liberian State: A Historical Perspective, 1822–1900* (1991).

Burrowes, Carl P. "Black Christian Republicans: Delegates to the 1847 Liberian Constitutional Convention," *Liberian Studies Journal* 14, no. 2 (1989): 64–89.

Huberich, Charles Henry. *The Political and Legislative History of Liberia* (1947).

JOHN SAILLANT

Teamoh, George (1818–c. 1883), slave, Virginia state senator, and diarist, was born into slavery in Norfolk, Virginia, the son of David Teamoh and Lavinia, slaves. He was raised in Portsmouth, and his parents perished during his early childhood. Teamoh portrayed his owners, Josiah and Jane Thomas, as humane in their treatment of him. Josiah Thomas, a carpenter, was employed at Gosport Naval Yard as a working-class artisan. While caring for Teamoh, the Thomases, in dire financial need, hired him out at age fourteen to Captain John Thompson's farm and brickyard, three miles north of Portsmouth. Thomas had gone from owning his own business to becoming an employee; his reversal of fortune affected not only himself and his spouse but their prized possession, Teamoh. This also significantly altered Teamoh's perception of reality as the young man was transformed from a comparatively benignly treated domestic servant to one subjected to a harsh industrial production regime supervised by a brutal overseer named Silverthorne.

The autodidact Teamoh left critical clues for later generations in a diary recovered from the Carter G. Woodson Collection of the Library of Congress by Teamoh's great-great-granddaughter, the literary scholar Rafia Zafar. In the diary Teamoh provides one of the missing links between the ages of orality and literacy in capturing the slave experience and tracing one man's passage to both freedom and power. In 1841 Teamoh, then twenty-three, married a woman named Sallie; they had one son and two daughters. Though still enslaved, Teamoh was a wage earner who practiced several skilled trades, ranging from caulking to running a newspaper press for the *Clay Banner* and the *Naval Intelligencer*, and he was not above doing day labor. In the complex arithmetic of the peculiar institution, however, Teamoh's spouse and children were not owned by the couple he regarded as his master and mistress, whose own financial straits prevented them from purchasing Teamoh's family.

This state of affairs had a dramatic impact upon the next stage of Teamoh's adult life. In 1853 he suffered the excruciating pain of witnessing his family members sold while he remained in the custody of the Thomases. Aware of his agitated state of mind following the sale, Teamoh's owners hired him out to a merchant cargo ship, the *Currituck*, which was bound for Germany and then New York. Teamoh fled from the ship, living for a time in New Bedford, Massachusetts, a place he called a "beacon of freedom." By the time he jumped ship, Teamoh had lost his oldest children, who were sold away in a Richmond market. Teamoh's wife and youngest daughter were bought by a Richmond man, who seems to have treated them kindly before he sold them to another owner, who impregnated Teamoh's youthful daughter.

From the summer of 1853 through early 1855, Teamoh lived and worked in New Bedford, a city well known for its antislavery activism and important free black community. Nevertheless, he still found galling racial prejudice there as he struggled as a day laborer and caulker, a trade FREDERICK DOUGLASS also once plied in the same city. In 1855 Teamoh relocated to Providence, Rhode Island, where he worked as a domestic servant before moving to Boston to be with two half brothers. In Boston, Teamoh associated with the city's dedicated antislavery community and was befriended and mentored by WILLIAM COOPER NELL, a close ally of William Lloyd Garrison, and the artisan Coffin Pitts, who taught Teamoh tailoring and laundering.

In 1865 Teamoh made his way back to Portsmouth after its occupation by Union troops. Two years later Teamoh's agitation for fairer wages for shipyard workers precipitated his election to the Reconstruction era Virginia State Constitutional Convention. This led to Teamoh's historic ascendance as Virginia's pioneer African American state senator. As Republicans organized in 1866 and 1867, he mobilized Portsmouth's black electorate under the Union League banner, becoming one of only three black delegates seated at the constitutional convention. From 1869 to 1871 Teamoh served in the state senate, where he supported formation of a labor union that included both blacks and whites at the Gosport Navy Yard. His role in improving labor conditions in the shipyards, organizing his party, framing the constitution, providing leadership in the city's African Methodist Episcopal Church, and fairly representing his constituents in the legislature all stand as lasting achievements during a challenging time.

By 1869, however, the brief window of democratic opportunity was closed in Virginia. Unsuccessfully resisting the resurgence of conservative white Democratic Party forces, Teamoh's Republicans succumbed to electoral defeats and factionalism in the 1871 poll. Moreover the loss of his political position coincided with a precipitous decline in his personal and financial fortunes. Suffering like many others in the depression of 1873, he experienced both health problems and economic ruin as the decade wore on, losing his home in 1881 due to default, just as segregationists were gaining the day. Teamoh, who remained a caulker for the rest of his life, disappears from view in 1883 after a forced sale of his property. Zafar reports that his wife was listed as a widow at her death on 2 September 1892. This suggests that Teamoh died between 1883 and 1892. The circumstances through which Teamoh coped with the vicissitudes of life, from slavery to freedom, the loss of his loved ones, and the rise and fall of the brief moment of democracy during Reconstruction, gave him a lasting place in the pantheon of leaders who struggled to bring Virginia back into the land of the free.

FURTHER READING

Teamoh, George. *God Made Man, Man Made the Slave: The Autobiography of George Teamoh*, eds. F. N. Boney, Richard L. Hume, and Rafia Zafar (1990).

Flanders, Alan. "Area's First Black State Senator Was Educated on the Job," *Virginian Pilot Ledger Star*, 3 July 2003.

Foner, Eric. *Freedom's Lawmakers* (1996).

Grover, Kathryn. "Fugitive Slave Traffic and the Maritime World of New Bedford," a Research Paper Prepared for New Bedford Whaling National Historical Park and the Boston Support Office of the National Park Service (1998).

DAVID H. ANTHONY III

Teer, Barbara Ann (18 June 1937–21 July 2008), performer, entrepreneur, and cultural leader, was born in east St. Louis, Illinois, to Fred L. and Lila B. Teer. Teer has been recognized for her exceptional talent as a dancer and actress, and most notably for founding the National Black Theatre, located in Harlem, New York, on historic 125th Street.

Teer was born into a family that was well known as both educators and community leaders. Her parents provided a nurturing home environment for her and her older sister Fredrica and they both went on to excel.

Teer graduated from Lincoln High School at age fifteen. She studied at Bennett College in Greensboro, North Carolina, Connecticut College, and the University of Wisconsin. She graduated magna cum laude with a bachelor's degree in Dance Education in 1957 from the University of Illinois at age nineteen. After graduating, Teer studied dance with Mary Wigman in Berlin and at Etienne Decroux in Paris. At the same time she appeared in festivals in Switzerland. She then relocated to New York City, where she pursued her career in entertainment. Teer danced under the tutelage of Alvin Nikolais at the Henry Street Playhouse, as well as with the ALVIN AILEY Dance Company in such notable locales as Brazil.

Teer made her first appearance on Broadway in 1961 in *Kwamina* as a dancer, and later received a Tony Award for this performance. She switched

Barbara Anne Teer, founder and CEO of the National Black Theatre, looks over the program at the start of the Manumission Day Celebration at St. Augustine's Episcopal Church in New York, 6 July 2003, in commemoration of the freeing of slaves in New York on 5 July 1827. (AP Images.)

her focus to theater after sustaining a knee injury in 1962. While studying acting with Sanford Meisner, Lee Strasberg, Paul Mann, Philip Burton, and Lloyd Richards, she taught dance at Wadleigh Junior High in Harlem.

In 1964 she appeared in *Home Movies*, for which she later won a Vernon Rice Drama Desk Award as best stage actress, as well as an Obie Award. She also performed in the made-for-television movie *Carol for Another Christmas*, for which she was credited as Barbara Ainteer. She also performed in Douglas Turner Ward's *Happy Ending* with the Negro Ensemble Company, a group she cofounded.

She joined the original cast of *Ward's Day of Absence* in 1966 for which she won another Obie, as well as the original version of Ron Milner's *Who's Got His Own*. Her television appearances included the *Ed Sullivan Show, Camera Three*, and *Kaleidoscope*. She had performed with PEARL BAILEY in Las Vegas, and DUKE ELLINGTON in Chicago.

By 1967 Teer had become disillusioned with the entertainment casting system. She had decided to wear her hair natural, and subsequently was not getting cast in any roles. The parts she was offered were those of maids, prostitutes, and exotics. She then fired her manager and agent, and took off for a six-month sabbatical back home in east St. Louis.

It was not long, however, before she returned to New York. When AMIRI BARAKA was arrested in Newark as part of the civil rights movement, Teer returned to produce and direct a benefit to raise funds for his release from prison. Teer subsequently directed *The Believers*, cowritten by Joseph Walker.

It was at this time that the National Black Theatre (NBT) was born. It originated in 1968 out of a Harlem loft called the East Wind that Barbara shared with Gylain Kain, an actor from the Last Poets. Teer identifies NBT's performance goals as to raise the level of consciousness, be political, educate, clarify issues, and entertain. James Hatch describes NBT's role as "a theatre which would embrace the dual heritage of being African and American by combining the elements of the black Pentecostal church with the ceremonial rites of the Yoruba from Nigeria."

While developing the theater, Teer continued to perform in films such as *Slaves* with OSSIE DAVIS in 1969, and *The Angel Levine* in 1970. Barbara co-wrote with Charlie L. Russell *A Revival: Change! Love! Organize!* in 1972, and wrote and directed *Soljourney into Truth*, which NBT produced in 1977. Her repertory company first performed *Soljourney* in Trinidad and Guyana, before traveling to Nigeria to showcase it at the international festival FESTAC.

Although the original loft burned down in 1983, Teer found funding to open a $10 million complex in November 1990. It was then that NBT also became the first revenue-generating black theater in the country. A list of the theater's productions includes *Revival* (1972), *Whirlwind* (1980), *Soul Fusion* (1982), *One Monkey Don't Stop No Show* (1984), *Legacy* (1987), *The Song of Sheba* (1991), *A Tribute to Lady Day* (2004), and *Yesterday Came Too Soon* (2005), a stage play based on the actress DOROTHY DANDRIDGE's life.

Teer was once married to New York–born comedian and actor GODFREY CAMBRIDGE. He passed away from heart failure in Los Angeles in November 1976. Her second marriage to Michael Adeyemi Lythcott was a union that produced a son, Michael F. "Omi" Lythcott, and a daughter, the actress Barbara A. "Sade" Lythcott.

Teer received an honorary doctorate of law degree from the University of Rochester in New York in 1994. The following year the University of Southern Illinois bestowed on her its honorary doctorate of humane letters degree. NBT related that "Dr. Barbara Ann Teer is a model of how the vision, talents and leadership of one person can inspire thousands of individuals and mobilize a community to reclaim and regain its ability to take care of its own" (National Black Theatre, 2). Teer's work celebrated the African presence in America through the National Black Theatre. She died in Harlem at the age of 71.

FURTHER READING

Bond, Melinda. "A Balancing Act," *Institute for Afro-Americans in Journalism Newsletter* (1991).

Jones, Martha. "National Black Theatre: Temple of Liberation for Black Nation in Harlem," *Theater* (Summer 1972).

National Black Theatre. "Brief Biographical Sketch: Dr. Barbara Ann Teer," National Black Theatre clip file (2005).

Thomas, Lundeana Marie. *Barbara Ann Teer and the National Black Theatre: Transformational Forces in Harlem* (1997).

MELINDA BOND SHREVE

Temple, Edward S. (20 Sept. 1927–), track-and-field coach, was born Edward Stanley Temple in Harrisburg, Pennsylvania, the only child of Christopher Richard Temple and Ruth Naomi. He primarily was raised by his grandparents and as a child frequently attended a Baptist church, where he regularly found trouble. Temple's parents decided to enroll him in music, and he maintained this interest as an adolescent. In 1942 he entered John Harris High School in Harrisburg. As an all-state athlete in football, basketball, and track and field, Temple was eager to compete at the college level. He intended to attend college in Pennsylvania at Cheney State Teachers College, Westchester College, or Pennsylvania State University, but Tom Harris, the track-and-field coach at Tennessee Agricultural and Industrial State College (Tennessee A&I; later Tennessee State University) in Nashville, had other plans. Harris, who also recruited Temple's rival Leroy Davis, another track-and-field star at John Harris High School, wanted both athletes to compete at the historically black university in Tennessee. In 1946 Temple and Davis graduated as two of six African Americans out of a class of two hundred at the public high school in Harrisburg, and both men enrolled at Tennessee A&I in the fall of that year.

As a college student, Temple accepted a work-aid scholarship, the common type of funding for track-and-field athletes before full athletic scholarships became the standard. On the track Temple posted competitive times of 9.7 and 21.5 in the 100- and 220-yard dashes, respectively, but he did not become a star athlete at the national level.

In May 1950 Temple graduated with a B.S. in Health and Physical Education, and two months later, on 22 July, he married his college sweetheart Charlie B. Law of Hartsville, Tennessee; they had two children. Charlie B., as she was commonly known, became the surrogate mother of Temple's Tigerbelles, the nickname for the Tennessee State University women's track-and-field team since 1953. Upon graduation, Temple found work in a number of fields. The president of Tennessee A&I, Walter S. Davis, hired Temple in 1950 to coach men's and women's track. While coaching, Temple also attended graduate school and worked in the campus post office with his wife. Temple also refereed local junior and senior high basketball games, where he discovered Wilma Rudolph, the famed track-and-field sprinter during the early 1960s. In 1952 Temple officially became the fourth head coach of the Tennessee State University women's track-and-field team, and he ran the program on an annual budget of $300.

After obtaining his M.S. in Health and Education with a minor in Social Science and Sociology in 1953, Temple fully embraced his coaching duties and

used CLEVE ABBOTT as a model to build a successful team. Abbott, a member of U.S. Track and Field Hall of Fame and coach of fourteen outdoor national championships at Tuskegee University, implemented a summer training program as a recruiting method to obtain young talent. Since many rural African American families in the 1950s could not afford to send their children to college, Temple's summer program gave black girls the chance to gain a college degree, become world-class athletes, and develop successful careers after college.

Temple's teams brimmed with talent. In 1948 the Tennessee State athlete Cynthia Thompson, a Jamaican sprinter, competed at the 1948 Summer Olympic Games, and in 1951 Jean Patton set a new American record in the 200-meter dash at the Pan-American Games in Buenos Aires, Argentina. Temple faced considerable financial difficulties and challenges as Tennessee State did not even have an official track. The only place to practice was a partial cinder track that dead-ended at a dump near the agricultural department's animal pens. Poor training conditions did not stop Temple from building a successful program, and in 1953 he recruited Mae Faggs. At the 1952 Olympic Games, Faggs and her fellow Tennessee State star Barbara Jones anchored the U.S. women's 400-meter relay team to a gold medal. Faggs and Jones became the first Tigerbelles to win Olympic medals under Temple's tutelage as coach. In 1955 Temple coached his team to victory in the first integrated Amateur Athletic Union (AAU) meet in Ponca City, Oklahoma. Temple continued to prepare his Tigerbelles to be Olympic champions, and by the 1956 Summer Olympic Games in Melbourne over half of his protégés were on the U.S. women's team (including Faggs, Margaret Matthews, Isabelle Daniels, Willye B. White, and Rudolph). His hard work was not in vain, and in 1960 the U.S. Olympic Committee (USOC) appointed him head coach of the women's team for the Summer Games in Rome. In 1964 the USOC again named Temple head coach, making him the first coach of consecutive teams in U.S. Olympic history. This coaching honor was bestowed upon him a third time for the 1980 Moscow Olympics, but the United States boycotted the event.

As a head coach, Temple also encouraged his Tigerbelles to excel academically. By the time of his retirement in 1994, thirty-nine of his forty Tigerbelles had completed their degrees, and about fifteen pursued graduate degrees. Also by 1993 his Tigerbelles had won thirty-four national championships, twenty-three Olympic medals, and over two dozen Pan-American Games medals, and they had set over twenty-eight indoor and sixteen outdoor world records. In addition eight of his Tigerbelles have been elected to the National Track and Field Hall of Fame. His contribution to sports and society is notable for creating spaces for young black women to be active leaders in the public during an era that often sought to keep them invisible and silent. Temple was inducted into the National Track and Field Hall of Fame in 1989 and also was selected to the Black Athletes Hall of Fame and the Tennessee Sports Hall of Fame, among others. He assisted the International Track and Field Committee, one of many organizations he served in the 1990s. In 1993 Tennessee State University began the Edward S. Temple Seminars, aimed at eliminating sexism in sports.

FURTHER READING
Temple, Ed, with B'Lou Carter. *Only the Pure in Heart Survive* (1980).
Lewis, Dwight. *A Will to Win* (1983).

JAMAL RATCHFORD

Temple, Lewis (1800–18 May 1854), blacksmith, abolitionist, and inventor, was born in Richmond, Virginia. Of his parents and formal education, nothing is known; according to one biographer, he was unable to sign his name. Sometime during the 1820s Temple migrated to the whaling town of New Bedford, Massachusetts, where in 1829 he married Mary Clark, a native of Maryland. In 1830 their first child, Lewis Jr., was born, followed by a daughter, Nancy, in 1832. Sometime later, a third child, Mary, was born; she died at age six.

What little is known about Temple suggests a resourceful and principled individual. Whether he escaped Virginia as a slave or left as a freedman is uncertain, but in any case he had a better life in Massachusetts than the one he would have led in Richmond, apparently finding work in New Bedford soon after his arrival. Town records indicate that by 1836 he had established his own whalecraft shop on one of the wharves that serviced ships. An active participant in local affairs, he paid the annual poll tax and was elected vice president of an antislavery organization, the New Bedford–Union Society, established in 1833. In 1847 the middle-aged Temple was arrested and charged with "rioting," after he and three other black men were accused of disrupting a "pro-slavery lecture." New Bedford was, in fact, home to a large African American community. As a prominent resident of the town, he almost certainly aided a number of runaway slaves, including FREDERICK DOUGLASS.

In 1848 Temple invented "Temple's Toggle," which historians of maritime technology have proclaimed as the most important innovation in whaling since the twelfth century. Whalers harvested their prey by first piercing the animal's body with a fluted (barbed) harpoon that was tied to a boat or floating drag. After a period of struggle, the hunters finished off the exhausted whale with a lance. Unfortunately for whalers, however, many whales dislodged traditional harpoons, which were forged from a single piece of iron. Temple's solution was a two-piece harpoon whose external appearance resembled the older, single-piece weapon. Once the Temple harpoon entered the whale, the animal's movements caused the fluted part to pivot on an axle by ninety degrees (i.e., "toggle"), thereby making all but impossible its removal through the surface wound. This simple idea dramatically increased the efficiency of whaling, and in a few years virtually all American harpoonists used the Temple toggle, continuing to do so into the 1950s.

Temple's role in the invention of the toggle harpoon was far more complex than this story suggests, however. European whale hunters had used similar harpoons centuries earlier, although they abandoned the device during the Middle Ages. The toggle subsequently survived in various forms among the Eskimos of Greenland. Curiously, European and American whalers knew of the Eskimo harpoons as early as 1654 but continued to employ single-piece irons. Two centuries later many, if not most, of the half dozen or more blacksmiths in New Bedford probably had heard of the Greenland technology, but Temple took the initiative of translating that knowledge into American form. The Temple toggle also owes its origins to the nearly unique ethnic diversity of the whaling industry. During the early nineteenth century American owners of whaling ships, largely because of the difficulty of recruiting local sailors, began signing on men who hailed from virtually every corner of the world. Although the proportion of African American sailors went into decline after 1830, it is nevertheless possible that Temple learned of Eskimo harpoons from an Eskimo seaman.

After inventing the toggle, Temple lived and worked in New Bedford for six years. Doubtless still active in an abolitionist movement electrified by the Fugitive Slave Act of 1850, he also signed a temperance petition addressed to the town's mayor in 1853. Regrettably, he never attempted to patent his invention, although he lived long enough to witness the whaling industry begin to adopt it almost universally. Nevertheless, he began to achieve a measure of prosperity, partly because he obtained a maintenance contract with the city government. In 1854 he hired a contractor himself, to build a large whalecraft shop.

Temple died under tragic circumstances. During an autumn evening in 1853 he tripped over a plank of wood that city workers had carelessly left behind at a sewer construction site. The injuries ruined him for physical labor and weakened his health. Although Temple petitioned the city for two thousand dollars in compensation, a favorable decision eluded him until ten days after his death, on 18 May 1854. Although the Common Council ordered the sum to be paid to his estate, for unknown reasons his heirs collected none of it.

FURTHER READING

Grover, Kathryn. *The Fugitive's Gibraltar: Escaping Slaves and Abolitionism in New Bedford, Massachusetts* (2001).

Haber, Louis. *Black Pioneers of Science and Invention* (1970).

Hayden, Robert C. *Eight Black American Inventors* (1972).

James, Portia P. *The Real McCoy: African American Invention and Innovation, 1619–1930* (1989).

Kaplan, Sidney. "Louis Temple and the Hunting of the Whale," *Negro History Bulletin* (Oct. 1953).

GARY L. FROST

Temple, Ruth Janetta (1 Nov. 1892–8 Feb. 1984), physician and community health educator, was born in Natchez, Mississippi, second of the six children of Amy Montague (Morton) Temple, an untrained nurse and state-licensed teacher, and Richard Jason Temple, the pastor of Natchez's First Baptist Church and the traveling secretary for a church association. Both parents sustained a warm, intellectually stimulating environment for their children and the constant flow of visitors of all races, religions, and incomes who came to their home. Amy Temple homeschooled the children to protect them from the indignities of segregated public education, and informally but skillfully tended sick community members. In girlhood Ruth Temple considered nursing, but decided on medicine after learning that there were women doctors.

In 1902 Temple's father died suddenly. The next day his widow delivered their last child, and Ruth tended the baby and her grief-paralyzed mother. Two years later, the family moved to Los Angeles, California, where Amy Temple, with six children

to raise and lacking a California teacher's license, found work as a practical nurse. Ruth cared for the younger children and attended Berendo Elementary School. At age thirteen she displayed her precocious healing ability when she successfully performed CPR on a young boy who almost drowned in an oil ditch. At some point during her youth she also drew her family into the Seventh-day Adventist Church because it emphasized health. After attending Los Angeles High School, she won a scholarship to San Fernando Academy, an Adventist boarding school, and graduated three years later.

During high school Temple pointedly addressed the Los Angeles Forum, a black men's leadership, discussion, and community action group, about male mistreatment of women. Afterwards T. W. Troy, a forum leader, persuaded the group to make her dream of medical school possible by paying her tuition. In 1913 Temple enrolled in what was then the College of Medical Evangelists at Loma Linda University. Temple became deeply impressed with *The Ministry of Healing* (1905) by Ellen White, the visionary and founder of Seventh-day Adventism. White advocated disease prevention through wholesome daily habits like a vegetarian diet and considered physicians responsible for basic health education. In 1918, Temple became Loma Linda's first black graduate and Los Angeles County's first black female doctor. Delilah L. Beasley identified her as "the first colored woman physician in the state" (*Negro Trail Blazers of California*, 94). There were only about sixty-five black female physicians practicing in the country at the time.

While conducting a part-time private practice in East Los Angeles, Temple distinguished herself as an obstetrical intern (1923–1928) with the Los Angeles City Maternity Service. In 1928 she married Otis Lawrence Banks, a real estate developer. So she could focus fully on her work, they chose not to have children. Outraged that thousands in the area lacked basic health care, yet unable to obtain funds for a licensed free clinic, the newlyweds purchased a bungalow at 4920 Central Avenue with their own money and transformed it into the Temple Health Institute. For two years, they lived in the building's old chicken coop.

In 1928, before Temple's move to the bungalow, a mother whose baby son had pneumonia fearfully refused the doctor's offer of hospital or in-home treatment. The mother explained that she loved her child and did not want him among strangers. The baby died soon afterwards. Temple later recalled: "I knew then what God wanted me to do ... [E] ven given the best health resources in the world, people had to be educated to use them" (*The Sun*, 12 Feb. 1984). The same year, as she launched her free clinic, Temple organized her first Health Study Clubs with children, parents, teachers, and anyone else who wanted to learn and teach others about basic matters like substance abuse, immunization, nutrition, and sex education.

In 1941 the Los Angeles City Health Department offered to pay Temple's expenses if she earned a Master of Public Health degree at Yale University. Her mentor there, the public health pioneer Charles-Edward Amory Winslow, defined health as "complete physical, mental, and social wellbeing, and not merely the absence of disease or infirmity." In 1948 the World Health Organization adopted his definition as its own. Temple spent two decades working as a Los Angeles City health official. She founded the Community Health Association in 1943 and Community Health Week the next year. She mobilized neighborhood associations, schools, PTAs, YWCAs, churches and synagogues, service agencies, and private medical practices to create and participate in Health Week events, study clubs, local health information centers, and block-to-block trainings. In the June 1958 *Journal of the American Medical Women's Association*, Temple explained the "ABCs" of the "citizen's basic health training" that was at the core of all these programs: "(A)cquiring Basic Health Knowledge, (B)ringing into Practice What Is Learned, (C)ommunicating [it] to Contacts" (241). Her training methods generated intense local, national, and global interest.

In 1959 Temple lost her husband of more than thirty years. In 1962 she retired as a paid city employee, but she remained active in planning Community Health Week and directed medical services for the Southern California Conference of Seventh-day Adventists. She belonged to the Women's University Club, the American Medical Association, the California Medical Association, the California Congress of Parents and Teachers, and Alpha Kappa Alpha. Her honors included Eleanor Roosevelt's Woman of the Month Award, a *Look* magazine Applause Award, International Women's Year honor from the worldwide Seventh-day Adventist Church (1975), Loma Linda Alumnus of the Year (1983), and community service commendations from two California governors—Edmund G. "Pat" Brown and Ronald Reagan—and four United States presidents—Kennedy, Nixon, Carter, and Reagan.

In a 1978 oral history interview, Temple revealed that she could work with almost anyone because she never completely agreed with any one group's agenda and thus was free to identify and emphasize areas of common ground. When asked about contemporary feminism, Temple said she surely believed in "women's liberty" but not necessarily all of "women's liberation" as customarily understood. She disagreed that there was a right to abortion, apart from situations like rape or risk to the woman's life, because the fetus was "a life" starting at "conception." She did strongly advocate contraception and long-term state support for parents and children involved in unplanned pregnancies (Schlesinger Library interview, 38–39).

Temple expressed satisfaction with her personal legacy, including her choice of nonparenthood. "With all of the babies I've delivered and both of my sister's children that I helped raise, why, I have all the children in the world" (*Los Angeles Times*, 11 Feb. 1984). At the age of eighty-six, she spoke to representatives of forty nations at a health conference in Africa, and the audience gave her a standing ovation. Months before her death at ninety-one, she radiated pride as the Los Angeles Health Department renamed its East Los Angeles clinic the Ruth Temple Health Center. As of 2007, low-income Angelinos could go there for services like family planning, immunizations, mammograms, and infectious disease testing and treatment. Temple's prevention-oriented, comprehensive approach to health reached millions in her own city and throughout the world.

FURTHER READING

The Department of Archives and Special Collections, Loma Linda University Libraries holds materials on Ruth Janetta Temple.

Arthur and Elizabeth Schlesinger Library on the History of Women in America. *Black Women Oral History Project, Volume 59: Interview with Ruth Janetta Temple, June 12, 1978* (1979).

Friesen, Gery P. "The Dr. Ruth Temple Health Center," *Loma Linda Alumni Journal* (Sept./Oct. 1983).

Gamble, Vanessa Northington. "Physicians," in *Black Women in America*, 2nd ed., ed. Darlene Clark Hine (2005).

Howard, T. R. M. "Negro in the Light of History," *The California Eagle* (29 Sept. 1933).

Obituaries: *Los Angeles Times*, 11 Feb. 1984; *The Sun*, 12 Feb. 1984.

MARY KRANE DERR

Terrell, Ernie (4 Apr. 1939–), WBA heavyweight boxing champion, entertainer, and businessman, was born in Belzoni, Mississippi, one of ten children of Lovick Terrell, a metal dipper, and Annie Terrell. Terrell's family moved to Chicago in 1953. As a teenager, Terrell discovered the Midwest Gym, on the corner of Madison and Hamelin streets near Garfield Park, and became interested in watching big-name professional fighters—men like Rocky Marciano, Kid Gavilan, SUGAR RAY ROBINSON—train. Observing great fighters sparked Terrell's desire to become a boxer, and while enrolled in Farragut High School, from which he would graduate in 1959, he began to enter amateur tournaments.

Terrell won the Chicago Golden Gloves tournament and later captured an intercity Golden Gloves championship. In 1957, while still in high school, Terrell turned professional. Also that year, while organizing a talent show to celebrate his high school graduation, Terrell purchased his first guitar. Along with his brothers J. C. and Lenon, and his sisters Velma and Jean (in 1970 Jean would replace DIANA Ross in the Motown singing group the Supremes), he formed a band called Ernie Terrell and the Heavyweights, with whom he would tour for thirteen years, playing clubs in cities including Miami and Las Vegas. In 1967 the band performed on the

hour-long ABC variety show *The Hollywood Palace*. After high school, Terrell attended Wright Junior College in Chicago.

As a professional, Terrell boxed on the Chicago circuit for the first four years of his career. Fighting as a heavyweight, he won twenty-three out of twenty-six fights before being knocked out in seven rounds by the contender Cleveland Williams on 3 April 1962, a defeat that he would avenge a year later. Around this time, Terrell was noticed by a New York manager, Julius Isaacson, who was believed to have connections with organized crime. With Isaacson as his manager, Terrell began to gain publicity and was matched against top fighters. He responded with impressive wins over the contender Zora Folley and the future light-heavyweight great BOB FOSTER, which put him in line for a bout with the highly ranked Eddie Machen on 3 March 1965 for the vacant World Boxing Association (WBA) heavyweight championship. The WBA championship had become available when the organization stripped MUHAMMAD ALI of the title for fighting a rematch against former champion SONNY LISTON, who had been dropped from the

Ernie Terrell (right) and World Heavyweight Champion Muhammad Ali stand face to face during the weigh-in for the heavyweight title fight in Houston, Texas, 6 February 1967. (AP Images.)

WBA's rankings after being arrested. Terrell won a unanimous decision over Machen and defended the title twice more over the next sixteen months but was not given much recognition by the press and the public as a heavyweight champion, since he still had not faced the undefeated Ali. Terrell and Ali met for the undisputed heavyweight title on 6 February 1967. The bout was characterized by an ugly buildup in which both fighters launched personal attacks on one another. Terrell told the press that Ali was not a good role model because he had refused to be drafted into the Vietnam War and was a member of the Nation of Islam, which Terrell asserted was a hateful organization that worsened race relations. He also refused to call Ali by his chosen name, instead repeatedly calling the champion by his birth name, Cassius Clay. Ali responded by questioning Terrell's commitment to black America and by vowing to destroy him when they met in the ring. The fight was no contest, as Ali brutalized Terrell over fifteen rounds, winning a unanimous decision. After Ali hit Terrell, he would ask the struck fighter, "What's my name?" Many fans found this unnecessary and believed that Ali had carried Terrell the full fifteen rounds to inflict as much damage to him as possible. Terrell suffered an eye injury during the bout, which he claimed was the result of Ali's fouling him, that required surgery. The defeat was so overwhelming that it essentially ended Terrell's career as an effective fighter.

Terrell fought eleven more times, winning seven, but a first-round knockout loss to Jeff Merritt in 1973 convinced him that his days as a boxer were finished. Terrell nonetheless thrived after that loss, having engineered a series of successful business ventures that left him financially secure. From his base on Chicago's South Side, Terrell worked as a music producer before turning his attention to promoting boxing in the Windy City. He did well in this regard and was responsible for a number of important fights in Chicago, including the 1979 welterweight championship bout between Pipino Cuevas and Ronnie Shields, and the 1981 middleweight title match between MARVIN HAGLER and Mustafa Hamsho. During this period, Terrell also patched up his relationship with Ali and promoted one of his exhibition fights. Terrell's most successful endeavor has been the Ernie Terrell Inc. Maintenance and Supply Company, founded in 1988, which hires out janitors for businesses and institutions. As of 2002, the corporation had four hundred and fifty employees and key government contracts with Chicago's Board of Education and Police Department.

FURTHER READING
Ashe, Arthur R., Jr. *A Hard Road to Glory: The African-American Athlete in Boxing* (1988).
Hauser, Thomas. *Muhammad Ali: His Life and Times* (1991).
Sammons, Jeffrey T. *Beyond the Ring: The Role of Boxing in American Society* (1988).

MICHAEL EZRA

Terrell, Mary Eliza Church (23 Sept. 1863–24 July 1954), educator and social activist, was born in Memphis, Tennessee, the daughter of Robert Reed Church, a businessman, and Louisa Ayres, a beautician and hair salon owner. Her father, a former slave, used his business acumen to become the first black millionaire in the South.

Mary's educational experiences reflected her privileged background. After completing her elementary education at the Antioch College laboratory

Mary Church Terrell, founder and the first president of the National Association of Colored Women, c. 1900. (Library of Congress.)

school in Yellow Springs, Ohio, she attended the Oberlin Academy (1875–1880) and Oberlin College (1880–1884), earning a B.A. with a concentration in Classical Languages. While at Oberlin College, she received many honors, including appointment as the freshman class poet, editor of the *Oberlin Review*, and member of the Aeolian Society. It was also at Oberlin that she encountered overt racism, which strengthened her resolve to excel.

After graduation Mary wanted to teach but was persuaded by her father not to work and, instead, to return to Memphis. He considered it inappropriate for a young woman of her social and economic standing to work for wages. A year later, however, against her father's wishes, she accepted a teaching position at Wilberforce College in Ohio. In 1887 she moved to Washington, D.C., and joined the faculty at the M Street Colored High School (later Dunbar High School). There she met her future husband, Robert Heberton Terrell, chairman of the language department, who later became a municipal judge in Washington.

In 1888 Mary reconciled with her father, who then financed her two years of study and travel in Europe. After much inner searching she decided to return to the United States, understanding that again her race, rather than her deeds, would influence her ability to achieve her goals.

Because Washington's school board would not employ married women, Mary, who had wed Robert Terrell in 1891, was forced to resign her position. Three of her children died in infancy, but one daughter survived, and in 1905 the couple adopted the daughter of Mary's half brother. Mary Terrell had already realized she could not be satisfied with performing only the domestic and social duties expected of a middle-class wife, however. In 1892, when she learned of the lynching of her childhood friend Thomas Moss, she, along with FREDERICK DOUGLASS, requested a personal appointment with President Benjamin Harrison to appeal for his public condemnation of lynching. Anticipating political repercussions, Harrison, as would many presidents succeeding him, refused to honor their appeal.

Moss's lynching in Memphis motivated Terrell to reevaluate her responsibilities as a black woman. She quickly emerged as a committed social activist. In 1892 she helped form the Colored Women's League in Washington. As a founder and the first president of a federation of such organizations, the National Association of Colored Women (NACW), 1896–1901, Terrell's influence extended throughout the nation. As leader of the NACW, an organization that encouraged the development of self-help and social service programs among black women, Terrell was recognized as a leading female spokesperson for African Americans. During her tenure as the NACW president, she addressed many interests and concerns affecting African Americans, and specifically black women, such as disenfranchisement, segregation in the public sector, economic inequities, and lynching.

Terrell incorporated data on the status of black women in many of her speeches. She earned a reputation as a dynamic speaker who over the course of thirty years addressed audiences throughout the United States and abroad. As a noted advocate for racial and gender equity, Terrell was invited to speak at the 1898 biennial session of the National American Woman Suffrage Association (NAWSA). Because her speech "The Progress and Problems of Colored Women" was highly praised, she was asked to address a much broader topic, "The Justice of Woman Suffrage," at the 1900 NAWSA biennial session. In spite of the efforts of some white suffragists to exclude black women from the movement, Terrell remained an active suffragist. Even after the ratification of the Nineteenth Amendment, she continued her efforts to ensure that black women would also benefit from the amendment's passage. In 1904, as the only African American delegate, Terrell spoke before the International Council of Women in Berlin. Her speech, given in German, received glowing accolades. Underlying Terrell's activism was a desire to empower black women as they worked toward inclusion and equity for all African Americans. In the introduction to her autobiography, she stated, "A white woman has only one handicap to overcome—a great one, true, her sex; a colored woman faces two—her sex and her race. A colored man has only one—that of race." Terrell consistently championed causes, programs, and organizations that sought the improvement of the quality of life for black women and, by extension, all African Americans. She was also very active in the national and international arenas of interracial cooperation. Terrell was extremely proud of her years of unpaid service on the Washington, D.C., Board of Education (1895–1901, 1906–1911). The first black woman in the United States to hold such a position, she wrote in her autobiography that she had attempted to "promote the welfare of the pupils, facilitate the work of the teachers and raise the standards."

Terrell was a member of many organizations, including the National Association for the

Advancement of Colored People (NAACP), for which she was a charter member of the national branch, and was an ardent worker for the Republican Party. While Terrell was president of the Women's Republican League of Washington, D.C., her organizing skills were recognized by the national party. In 1920 Republican Party officials appointed her director of work among black women in the East. She was reappointed to the same position in 1932.

To ensure that her voice was heard, Terrell became a prolific writer. She is credited with the writing of twenty-six articles and numerous poems and short stories. Her writings appeared in such journals and newspapers as *The North American Review, The Independent, The Crisis, The Journal of Negro History, The Nineteenth Century and After,* and the *Boston Herald.* Racism and its effects upon African Americans and the United States were often the theme of her writings. Her autobiography, *A Colored Woman in a White World,* highlighting her personal struggles against racism, was published in 1940.

During the 1940s and 1950s Terrell's national recognition was enhanced by her efforts to end segregation in the public accommodations of Washington, D.C. Often described as a militant activist during the years just before her death, Terrell joined those who advocated, for the times, more aggressive acts of protest and resistance—boycotts, picket lines, and sit-ins. The organized protest against the Thompson Restaurant in Washington resulted in the 1950 case of the *District of Columbia v. John Thompson,* though it was not until 1953 that segregation in eating facilities was ruled unconstitutional in the nation's capital, upholding 1872–1873 laws prohibiting discrimination against "respectable persons" in restaurants. The Supreme Court's validation of the old laws paved the way for desegregation of restaurants, hotels, and theaters in the District of Columbia.

Throughout her life Terrell's fortitude and vision inspired many to work for the advancement of African Americans. In the black woman's club movement, she motivated middle-class women to use their skills and resources to develop child-care centers, mothers' clubs, and kindergartens for those of lesser means. Convinced that rights for black women were inextricably tied to equal rights for the race, Terrell also promoted woman suffrage, adult education, and job training opportunities. After the death of her husband in 1925, she chose not to remarry. Until her death at her home in Highland Beach, Maryland, Terrell remained a staunch advocate for reform and progress.

FURTHER READING
Mary Church Terrell's papers are housed at the Library of Congress and the Moorland-Spingarn Research Center at Howard University. Significant references to her life's works are also included in various record groups at the Bethune Archives in Washington, D.C.
Terrell, Mary Church. *A Colored Woman in a White World* (1940).
Jones, Beverly. *Quest for Equality: The Life and Writings of Mary Eliza Church Terrell, 1863–1954* (1990)
Obituaries: *New York Times* and *Washington Post,* 29 July 1954.

This entry is taken from the *American National Biography* and is published here with the permission of the American Council of Learned Societies.

CYNTHIA NEVERDON-MORTON

Terrell, Robert Heberton (25 Nov. 1857–20 Dec. 1925), attorney and the first black federal judge in the United States, was born in Orange, Virginia, a freeborn son of the former slaves William Henry Harrison Terrell and Louisa Ann (Coleman) Terrell. During the administration of Ulysses S. Grant, the Terrell family moved to Washington, DC, where Harrison Terrell was a member of the White House domestic staff and Robert Terrell was educated in the city's public schools.

Robert Terrell went on to preparatory school at Lawrence Academy, Groton, Massachusetts, before graduating from Harvard University with a bachelor's degree in 1884—the third African American to do so, and the first to graduate cum laude from Harvard. While at Harvard, he supported himself as a clerk at the U.S. Customs House in Boston. Returning to Washington, he taught classes at the segregated Preparatory High School for Colored Youth (later called M Street High School, then Dunbar High School) from 1884 until 1889. In 1889 Terrell received a bachelor's degree in Law from the city's Howard University, and one year later, was awarded a master's degree in Law from that school, all the while working as a chief clerk at the U.S. Treasury Department.

Terrell again taught at M Street High School from 1890 to 1893. After being admitted to the District of Columbia bar in 1893, he established a Washington-based legal partnership with the former Mississippi congressman JOHN ROY LYNCH, which they dissolved in 1898, after Lynch was offered a permanent military commission in the U.S. Army by President McKinley. Terrell once again became principal of the city high school, a position he held until November 1901, when President Theodore Roosevelt appointed him as the first black justice of the peace in the District of Columbia. In 1910 President William Howard Taft named him to the city's municipal court, and until his death, Terrell was the nation's only black federal judge.

Although a Republican himself, he was periodically reappointed to the judgeship, including under the Democratic administration of Woodrow Wilson, and served as a municipal judge until his death. His rulings, subject to review by the District of Columbia Court of Appeals, were routinely upheld, with just five reversals in twenty-three years. Among the most notable of his decisions was one upholding the Ball Rent Act, enacted by Congress during World War I as an antiprofiteering measure, and opposed by landlords; after higher courts declared the act unconstitutional and overturned his ruling, the U.S. Supreme Court disagreed and reinstated his verdict.

Terrell's wife, MARY ELIZA CHURCH TERRELL (1863–1954)—Mollie to her friends—was among the best-known and most influential African American women and public speakers of her era. Daughter of the Memphis millionaire ROBERT REED CHURCH, she was a graduate of Oberlin College and the first woman appointed to the Washington, DC, school board. Married on 28 October 1891, in Memphis, the Terrells had four children, only one of whom lived to adulthood: Phyllis Church Langston.

Occupying the highest ranks of Washington's black aristocracy, the Terrells were among a select group of homeowners recruited by Charles Douglass for his Highland Beach development of summer cottages on the Chesapeake Bay, near Annapolis. There the social atmosphere was "easy and pleasant" for Terrell and other wealthy Washingtonians (Gatewood, p. 45).

In 1898 Terrell was elected vice president of the District of Columbia branch of the new National Afro-American Council, but resigned that position to serve as principal of the M Street High School. He was also a member of the National and Washington Bar Associations, the Masons, and Pi Sigma Phi fraternity. An officer and shareholder in the black-owned Capital Savings Bank, and a member of the Washington Board of Trade, he served for many years as chairman of the board of trustees of Lincoln Congregational Church, into which his own Park Temple congregation was merged.

An amateur historian, Terrell was the author of numerous pamphlets, including *The Negro in America since Emancipation*, *Negro Soldiers in All the Wars of America*, *The Negro of Today*, and *A Glance at the Past and Present of the Negro* (1903). Judge Terrell served on the Howard University law faculty, and during the wartime years of 1917 and 1918, was chairman of the Community Service for Colored People in Washington.

After suffering a series of strokes, Terrell died at his home in Washington at age sixty-eight. An evening law school named in his honor operated in Washington from 1931 until 1950. His collected papers are housed in the Library of Congress, Manuscript Division, Washington, DC, along with those of his wife.

FURTHER READING

Gatewood, Willard B. *Aristocrats of Color: The Black Elite, 1880–1920* (1990).
"Robert Heberton Terrell." In *National Cyclopedia of American Biography*, Volume 47 (1965).
Terrell, Mary Church. *A Colored Woman in a White World* (1940; reprint, 1970).

BENJAMIN R. JUSTESEN

Terrell, Sister O. M. (18 Aug. 1911–24 Feb. 2006), singer, guitarist, songwriter, and evangelist, was born Ola Mae Long in Atlanta, Georgia, to Mary Long, a laundress. Mother and daughter lived in racially segregated Atlanta's Summerhill district, just a few blocks from Decatur Street, Atlanta's black commercial and entertainment center.

In 1922, Ola Mae was put out to work as a cook and housekeeper in the home of Devereaux F. McClatchey, a Southern Bell Telephone executive. This was her first experience living outside the segregated Summerhill neighborhood. The following year she underwent a conversion experience at a revival held at the Fire Baptized Holiness Church, a Pentecostal denomination organized in Anderson, South Carolina, in 1898 and originally an integrated association.

The black members of the Fire Baptized Holiness Church, in response to increasingly strict enforcement of "Jim Crow" laws, in 1908 withdrew and formed the Colored Fire Baptized Holiness Church with about one thousand members in twenty-seven churches. Reverend William E. Fuller, one of the founding members of the original integrated association, was appointed general overseer of the new group and, by 1916, had moved the central offices from Greer, South Carolina, to Atlanta.

After her conversion, Ola Mae taught herself to play the guitar and began composing religious songs that she sang at the municipal market on Decatur Street. For the remainder of the 1920s she lived in Atlanta, attending church and working as a laundress or as a cook in white homes.

In the early 1930s, Ola Mae Long began an itinerant life of musical evangelism. Still affiliated with the Fire Baptized Holiness Church, she preached and sang on street corners and in churches in towns large and small in Georgia and South Carolina. She married Jim Robert Terrell and adopted her evangelistic name of Sister O. M. Terrell. They had a son, Robert, and separated at an unknown later date.

On 6 April 1936 two tornadoes struck Gainesville, Georgia, where Sister Terrell was living, killing 203 people. Sister Terrell wrote a ballad about the event the next day. The opening lines mark the time and place:

> April the sixth in nineteen and thirty-six
> A storm visit Gainesville,
> And left the people in a bad shape.

Sister Terrell took the song to a job printer and had "ballets" (a single broadside sheet of lyrics) printed. These she sold on the streets to the crowds attracted by her street corner singing. This fundraising tactic, along with singing in churches of various denominations for offerings, supported the evangelist during these years.

After World War II, Sister Terrell was rotating her residencies between Marion, Greenville, and Charleston, South Carolina. In was in the latter city that she came to the attention of the owners of WPAL radio. WPAL had begun as a country music station but could not successfully compete with several others in that format. No radio station was serving Charleston's large black population at the time and WPAL's white owners decided, in 1949, to abandon country music for a mix of gospel and rhythm and blues that would appeal to black listeners.

Elder Joyner, the programmer of WPAL's gospel music, introduced Sister Terrell to the station's owners. They were impressed enough to give her a weekly program in the summer of 1952. Playing her unusual slide-guitar style and singing fervently, Sister Terrell became an attraction on the airwaves of Charleston.

Eventually a demonstration recording of Sister Terrell was made using the station's studio facilities. When the disc was sent to Columbia Records in New York, the response was positive. Sister Terrell was asked to travel to Nashville to record at Columbia's studios. On 19 February 1953 she recorded six of her songs with the label's artist and repertoire director

Don Law supervising. Over the next year three double-sided discs were released. Unfortunately they were marketed as part of Columbia's Country/Western Series, most likely as a result of the recording location in Nashville. Sister Terrell was the only black Columbia artist among the bluegrass, western swing, and white quartets in the country/western record bins. Her records did not sell well, and her contract was canceled.

In November 1955 Sister Terrell moved back to Atlanta, living at various addresses near or on Decatur Street. She renewed her personal relationship with the Fire Baptized Holiness Church and Bishop Fuller and his family. Her activities through the 1960s and 1970s were more directly tied to church-sponsored programs than her earlier self-directed evangelism had been. She spent her middle and elder years in Atlanta, in neighborhoods she knew well from her earliest days. As a result, during the peak years of folk music's popularity, the mostly white promoters of folk music overlooked Sister Terrell. This was a time that brought many black folk artists to stages in Newport, New York, Berkeley, and Los Angeles, where mainstream America was exposed to these musicians. As with her Columbia Records association, Sister Terrell, through unfortunate circumstance, missed an opportunity to carry her art into popular culture.

It was in the 1990s that those outside her Holiness culture finally discovered Sister Terrell's music. In 1991 a series of four record album anthologies under the Columbia/Legacy rubric was issued. *News & the Blues: Telling It Like It Is*; *The Slide Guitar: Bottles, Knives & Steel, Vol.1*; *The Gospel Tradition: Roots & Branches, Vol.1*; and *Preachin' the Gospel: Holy Blues* made available all of Sister Terrell's recordings from 1953. One song, "God's Little Birds," was used in an off-Broadway play. Fans of American vernacular song knew Sister Terrell at last.

Ola Mae Terrell suffered a series of strokes even as her music was being disseminated. She spent her last years in a nursing home in Conyers, Georgia, where her church family gave her spiritual comfort. Small royalties from her recordings helped with her material needs.

FURTHER READING

Country Gospel. Compact Disc (2005). Contains all Sister Terrell's recordings.

Clark, Elmer T. *The Small Sects in America* (1949).

Nemerov, Bruce. "I'm a Holy Ghost Preacher: Bruce Nemerov Interviews Sister O. M. Terrell." *Blues & Rhythm* 141 (1999).

BRUCE NEMEROV

Terry, Clark (14 Dec. 1920–), jazz trumpeter, flugelhorn player, and vocalist, was born into a family of eleven children in St. Louis, Missouri. Nothing is known of his parents or Terry's earliest years, but by the time he was fourteen, Terry was accompanying his tuba player brother-in-law Cy MacField to rehearsals to listen, and during the Depression, Terry played a trumpet he made from a garden hose and a kerosene funnel until neighbors collected $12.50 for him to purchase a horn at a pawnshop. While attending Vashon High School, Terry learned to play the valve trombone and joined the Tom Powell Drum and Bugle Corps, where he learned to read music. He also played bugle in the school concert band. A self-taught musician who never had a formal music lesson, Terry practiced doodling vowels on the horn and learned circular breathing, enabling him to hold notes longer. In 1935 Terry fell under the influence of jazz star LOUIS ARMSTRONG and, after graduation, played on riverboats and band engagements with FATE MARABLE, a mentor of Armstrong's.

Terry left St. Louis at age sixteen to tour with Rubin and the Cherry and with other bands into the Illinois cities of Peoria, Danville, and Champaign. In 1942 he joined the navy at the North Chicago, Illinois, Great Lakes Naval Station, a pioneer in racial integration, with Terry being one of the first African Americans to report for boot camp. Because of his general interest in music and brass instruments in particular, Terry joined the marching, concert, and jazz bands at the Great Lakes Naval Training Station. Among others, he played there with GERALD WILSON.

In 1945 Terry was discharged and returned to St. Louis to play for a short time with percussionist and vibraphonist LIONEL HAMPTON. Then he joined trumpeter George Hudson's band, staying eighteen months, afterward playing commercial jazz with an orchestra led by saxophonist Charlie Ventura. He then had a short stint with Houston saxophonist Eddie "Cleanhead" Vinson, and in 1946 Terry became the first black member of Charlie Barnet's band in California. Terry joined bandleader-pianist COUNT BASIE in 1948 and from 1951 until 1959 was featured soloist for DUKE ELLINGTON's band. During the Ellington period, Terry had his greatest influence on the musical development of MILES DAVIS and Davis's former student QUINCY JONES. Terry also played with singers ELLA FITZGERALD, DINAH WASHINGTON, BILLIE HOLIDAY, SARAH VAUGHAN, RAY CHARLES, and Dianne Reeves (whom he discovered); with pianists OSCAR PETERSON and THELONIOUS MONK; with composer BILLY STRAYHORN; with tenor saxophonists BEN WEBSTER, DEXTER GORDON, COLEMAN HAWKINS, and Zoot Sims; with trumpeters DIZZY GILLESPIE and Jon Faddis; with vibraphonist MILT JACKSON; and with valve trombonist Bob Brookmeyer.

After returning from a 1960 European tour with Harold Arlen's *Free and Easy Show*, directed by Quincy Jones, Terry had become an internationally known, featured artist and the first African American musician on regular NBC payrolls with Doc Severinsen's *Tonight Show* Orchestra. When he was inducted into the Kansas City Jazz Hall of Fame, Johnny Carson presented him the award during the televised ceremony. During his tenure at the *Tonight Show*, Terry scored, sang, and recorded "Mumbles," a smash hit known by his nickname, based on a scat routine he had developed with his good-humored approach to music. In 1971 Terry started New York's jazz education unit, Jazzmobile, which emerged from the Harlem Youth Band, becoming "the world's busiest jazz clinician," according to the National Association of Jazz Educators. When *Tonight Show* moved to California in 1972, Terry stayed in New York and toured with *Jazz at the Philharmonic*, produced by Norman Granz.

A National Endowment for the Arts (NEA) Jazz Master and composer of more than 200 songs, Terry made more than 300 recordings, including those with his own small groups and his two big bands (Clark Terry's Big Bad Band and Clark Terry's Young Titans of Jazz), and with the Duke Ellington Orchestra, the Chicago Jazz Orchestra, the London Symphony Orchestra, the Dutch Metropole Orchestra, and with high school and college ensembles. He has performed at Carnegie Hall, Lincoln Center, New York's Town Hall, and jazz festivals on seven continents; he has toured with the Newport Jazz All Stars and Jazz at the Philharmonic; and he was a featured guest of Skitch Henderson's New York Pops Orchestra. In 1985 Terry was named an American Man of Music, joining renowned black vocal artist WILLIAM WARFIELD, composer Aaron Copland, and pianist Van Cliburn.

In 1991 Terry was inducted into the NEA Jazz Hall of Fame. In 1994 he was inducted into the Big Band and Jazz Hall of Fame. That same year he launched a four-year jazz degree program at the Clark Terry International Institute of Jazz Studies at Teikyo Westmar University in LeMars, Iowa. In 1996 he received a star on the St. Louis Walk of Fame. An author and educator, Terry has written three books: *Let's Talk Trumpet: From Legit to*

Jazz, Interpretation of the Jazz Language, and *Clark Terry's System of Circular Breathing for Woodwind and Brass Instruments*. He has received a Grammy Award, two Grammy certificates, three Grammy nominations, thirteen honorary doctorates, a German knighthood, and the French Order of Arts and Letters. As a jazz ambassador for U.S. State Department tours in the Middle East and Africa, Terry entertained seven presidents, and he hosted the Clark Terry Jazz Festivals on land and sea and jazz camps since 2000. In 2005 the Jazz Journalists Association named him "Trumpeter of the Year."

FURTHER READING

An interview with Terry from 15 September 1993 conducted by Jimmy Owens for the Louis Armstrong Jazz Oral History Project is available at the Schomburg Center for Research in Black Culture.

Cohodas, Nadine. *Queen: The Life and Music of Dinah Washington* (2004).

Gioia, Ted. *The History of Jazz* (1998).

Hinton, Milt and Clark Terry. *Seeing Jazz: Artists and Writers on Jazz* (1997).

Travis, Dempsey J.; introduction by Clark Terry. *Louis Armstrong Odyssey: From Jane Alley to America's Jazz Ambassador* (1997).

Yanow, Scott. *Bebop* (2000).

SUNNY NASH

Terry, Lucy (c. 1725–11 July 1821), first known African American poet, was born in Africa. The facts of her early years are not known with certainty. But, as best as can be determined, she was brought to New England about 1729 through the port of Boston by Barbados-based slave merchants. As the property of Samuel Terry, a Harvard-educated aspiring minister, she lived initially in Mendon, Massachusetts, west of Boston and perhaps in Union in northeast Connecticut. She was sold to Ebenezer Wells, a Deerfield, Massachusetts, merchant and tavern holder, sometime before 15 June 1735, which is the date of her baptism. Her baptism record notes her as "servant to Ebenezer Wells," as slaves were often euphemistically described in New England. Many Deerfield slave owners had their slaves baptized during the Great Awakening, and Terry's baptism proved the beginning of her lifelong religiosity. She was admitted to the fellowship of the Church of Deerfield (full communion) in 1744.

During Terry's first years in Deerfield, in western Massachusetts, the town enjoyed peace. However, with the outbreak of King George's War in 1744, Indian attacks again became a concern. On 25 August 1746, fifty Abenaki men, commanded by French officers, raided Deerfield's Bars area, a farmland meadow. Several Deerfield inhabitants were killed, wounded, or kidnapped, and Terry recounts this incident in her only known poem, "Bars Fight." Although written in 1746, it was not published until 20 November 1854 in the *Springfield [Massachusetts] Daily Republican*, as part of a profile of Deerfield. Terry composed this ballad of twenty-eight lines in a familiar singsong style, lending itself to easy memorization, and doubtless led to frequent recitation among Deerfield's population, for whom Indian abductions were a central part of local history. Dickson D. Bruce suggests in *The Origins of African American Literature* (31–32) that the poem is important not so much as literature as it is indicative of the storytelling role Terry created for herself in Deerfield's white society, and of her self-confident expressiveness. Sharon M. Harris, in *Executing Race: Early American Women's Narratives of Race, Society, and the Law* (150–181), sees the poem as satirical, when viewed in the context of a slave, who had been abducted from Africa as a child, writing of white townspeople being abducted into Indian captivity.

On 17 May 1756, Terry married ABIJAH PRINCE, a former slave from nearby Northfield, Massachusetts, who had gained his freedom five years earlier. At the time of their marriage, Terry was still enslaved to Wells. It is not known how Terry was freed, but it is reasonable to assume that Prince purchased her freedom not long after their marriage. They had six children: Caesar (14 Jan. 1757–6 Aug. 1835), Duruxa (1 June 1758–Sept. 1826), Drucilla (7 Aug. 1760–21 Nov. 1854), Festus (12 Dec. 1763–c. 1820), Tatnai (2 June 1765–7 May 1820), and Abijah Jr. (12 June 1769–c. 1793).

For the next twenty years or so they lived in Deerfield. Sometime in the mid-1760s, Abijah Prince acquired one hundred acres in Guilford, Vermont, and he, and perhaps the family, spent frequent periods there clearing the land and constructing a homestead. Around 1775, they left Deerfield for permanent resettlement on their Guilford farm. The following decade, however, would prove difficult because of the harassment instigated by a near neighbor, John Noyes, a man of some means and prominence, from Stonington, Connecticut. Abijah Prince employed the local court system to fight the encroachment and property damage that occurred, which included attacks on their children and destruction of their crops. But in June 1785, when the financial and personal strains became intolerable, Lucy Prince traveled to Norwich, Vermont, and appeared before the state's Governor and Council, which comprised the highest executive branch of state government to request protection. Her personal petition, which would have been noteworthy in those days for a woman, let alone a black woman, met with success, and it was the first documented instance of her eloquence and persuasiveness. Her accounts of the oppression and injuries they suffered from Noyes led Governor Thomas Chittenden to recommend to the Guilford town government that the Princes be protected until the matter be resolved in the courts, which it was soon after in favor of the Princes. She is also reputed to have argued, quoting extensively from the Bible, before the trustees of Williams College, in Williamstown, Massachusetts, in support of the admission of one of her sons. There is no record in the Williams College archives to substantiate this, however, although it is quite possible, considering that her husband had served in King George's War with Williams family members (including Ephraim Williams whose bequest led to the college's founding), and that she and Prince were personally acquainted with at least one Williams College trustee.

Following Abijah Prince's death in 1794, Prince and her grown children relocated to Sunderland, Vermont, where, by virtue of Abijah Prince's position as an original town proprietor, they should have had ownership of more than three hundred acres. Proprietorship of New England towns can be thought of as ownership of corporations: the proprietors jointly owned the land underlying the town, and they formed the town's governing body. Subject to provincial law, they made their own rules and decided how and when to divide up the jointly held town property and distribute it to themselves as individual owners. The governor approved the location of the township, and the list of its initial owners or proprietors. Prince discovered that certain questionable land transactions had occurred years before, primarily by the hands of an unscrupulous proprietor, effectively stripping them of the property on which they had hoped to settle.

This realization led to a series of court battles to recover the family's lost property from the current owner, Colonel Eli Brownson. Brownson, a financially prominent Revolutionary War hero with connections to the Ethan Allen family, had no part in the original and questionable transactions, his family having bought the properties later. These court cases would span seven years and reach the Vermont Supreme Court. As legend has it, her legal arguing, which went before the U.S. Supreme Court, was better than had been heard from any Vermont lawyer. There is no record of Prince employing professional legal representation, and considering her gift with words and her past success before the governor and council, she may likely have argued these cases herself. Unfortunately, most of the relevant Vermont court materials from this time were lost to fires, making it impossible to substantiate this. What is known, though, is that their case against Brownson reached the Vermont Supreme Court in June 1799, which decided in favor of the Princes, awarding them their rightful property. Soon after, however, Brownson initiated a countersuit, which reached the Vermont Supreme Court in 1804. The matter ultimately was decided in June 1804 by court-appointed referees, who ruled in favor of Prince and her sons. However, in a disappointment to her, a financial award was given them representing the value of the land, but the possession of the land was left with Brownson, recognizing his family's long "ownership" and land improvement. With the state courts seemingly no longer an option, and determined to remedy what she perceived to be an injustice, Prince took her case to the Sunderland town government. Again, her powers of persuasion were effective. In 1806, the town accepted the validity of her argument and purchased the two lots that were originally allocated to Abijah Prince. One was given outright to them, and one was held by the town in trust for them for their occupancy and use.

Prince and three of her children would spend the remainder of their lives on land she spent close to a decade legally battling for. Although remembered for her place in literary history, her determination in fighting for her rights was not unlike several other blacks of her time such as Belinda, but her eloquent persuasiveness decades before abolition, makes her unique in American history. She died in Sunderland, Vermont, her eulogy delivered by the mixed-race Congregational minister, author, and Revolutionary War veteran LEMUEL HAYNES. Her obituary, appearing in the *Vermont Gazette* on 14 August 1821, noted that "In this remarkable woman there was an assemblage of qualities rarely to be found among her sex. Her volubility was exceeded by none, and in general the fluency of her speech captivated all around her, and was not destitute of instruction and edification. All considered her a prodigy in conversation. She was much respected among her acquaintance."

FURTHER READING

Bruce, Dickson D., Jr. *The Origins of African American Literature* (2001).

Finkenbine, Roy E. "Belinda's Petition: Reparations for Slavery in Revolutionary Massachusetts." *The William and Mary Quarterly* (Jan. 2007).

Gerzina, Gretchen Holbrook. *Mr. and Mrs. Prince. How an Extraordinary Eighteenth-Century Family Moved Out of Slavery and into Legend* (2008).

Harris, Sharon M. *Executing Race: Early American Women's Narratives of Race, Society, and the Law* (2005).

ANTHONY GERZINA

Terry, Roger C. (13 Aug. 1921–11 June 2009), Tuskegee Airman who was court-martialed at Freeman Field, was born Roger Cecil Terry in Los Angeles, California, the son of Edith Frances (Ross) Terry and Joseph Roger Terry, a driller for Standard Oil. In 1920 Joseph Terry had secured employment in the oil fields in Venezuela, but before departing for Venezuela, he worked in the California oil fields where a drilling accident took the life of his partner. Fearing for her husband's life, Roger's mother decided that her husband should not continue as an oil driller and the family remained in California.

Terry attended elementary and high school in Compton, California, attended Compton Junior College, and graduated from the University of California at Los Angeles (UCLA) at the age of nineteen. At UCLA Terry played basketball, and he and JACKIE ROBINSON, the first African American to play in major league baseball, were the only two African Americans playing in the Pacific Coast Conference. After graduating from UCLA, Terry remained an extra semester to play basketball. An advertisement in the *Daily Bruin*, UCLA's campus newspaper, solicited males to join the air force, and Terry volunteered.

Terry passed the written examination in early 1942. The air force required that pilots be less than five feet nine inches and 160 pounds. Terry, at six feet two and a half inches and 175 pounds, did not qualify to be trained as a fighter pilot, but was contacted by James L. Plinton, a primary instructor at Tuskegee's Moton Field, who stated that if he came to Tuskegee, Alabama, they would teach him to fly and to be a flight instructor. Terry was excited about the prospect and left immediately for Tuskegee.

Terry completed flight training at Tuskegee and received both a private and a commercial pilot's license. Three weeks before work on his instructor's rating was to be completed, plans for the 477th Medium Bombardment Squadron were initiated. As bomber pilots had higher weight and height requirements than did fighter pilots, Terry was qualified and joined the 477th Bomb Group. In 1945 Terry was stationed at Godman Field, Kentucky. Godman Field had one officers' club, which was used by African American officers. The club was open to white officers, but they primarily used the officers' clubs at the adjacent base, Fort Knox.

When the unit transferred to Freeman Field in Seymour, Indiana, there were two officers' clubs. One club, furnished with a mess house, a guest-house, a fireplace, and a game room with tables, billiards, and table tennis, was designated for the sole use of white officers. The other club, lacking the same facilities, was designated for the use of the African American officers. To minimize the appearance of racism, white officers were designated as "supervisors" and given use of the well-furnished facility. African American officers were designated as "trainees" regardless of their professions, degrees, time in service, or combat records, and were relegated to the inferior officers' club. In April 1945 the African American officers attempted to enter the "white" club in small groups instead of en masse to avoid the appearance of a mutiny. Each officer was inspected for any improper uniform violations and sought entrance to the officers' club in small groups. Each group was turned away and was replaced by another group who also attempted to enter.

On 5 April 1945 Roger Terry, Lieutenant James Kennedy, and Flight Officer Oliver Goodall were detained at the entrance to the officers' club by First Lieutenant J. D. Rogers. Terry attempted to walk around Rogers, but Rogers physically blocked his path. Rogers charged that Terry pushed him aside to gain entrance to the club. Terry was arrested and charged with "offering violence against an officer and willfully disobeying a command from an officer." That night thirty-five other African American officers were arrested and forced to remain in quarters and were released only for meals. In total sixty-one African American officers were arrested, but Terry and Second Lieutenants Shirley Clinton and Marsden Thompson were held in isolation. Thompson, the first of the officers to enter the club, and Clinton, who was physically assaulted by Rogers, were charged with "willfully disobeying a lawful command from Lieutenant Rogers, their superior officer" (Warren, 170). Clinton and Thompson were restricted to quarters and the mess halls. Terry was held in solitary confinement at

Freeman Field for two weeks and was sent back to Godman Field for eighty days.

The court-martial trial of Thompson and Clinton was held on 24 June 1945. Both men were acquitted. Terry's trial was held on 3 July 1945 and he was acquitted of disobeying an order, but was convicted of jostling a superior officer. He was fined fifty dollars a month for three months. After his release Terry was branded a "troublemaker" and had difficulty being accepted by any base, including Godman Field and Tuskegee Army Air Field. He was eventually sent to Norton Field in San Bernardino, California, where he was the only African American on the base.

Upon being discharged, Terry enrolled in law school at UCLA. He attended the University of Southern California for a year and a half, but due to money constraints, he transferred to Southwestern University School of Law. He graduated from Southwestern in the top tenth of the class. Terry took the bar exam but, as a convicted felon, failed because of "moral turpitude." He worked as a detective with District Attorney S. Ernest Roll for eleven years. Terry married Anna Williston in 1949; the couple would have two sons, Mark and Jeffrey.

After Roll's death in 1956 Terry became a private detective and later worked as a probation officer for the Los Angeles County Probation Department. Terry retired from the Probation Department in 1984. Terry served as national president of Tuskegee Airmen, Inc. from 1993 to 1996. In 1995 the Tuskegee Airmen National Convention was held in Atlanta, Georgia. Then Secretary of the Army Rodney Coleman presented a pardon to each of the men arrested at Freeman Field. A special honor was paid to Roger Terry and his wife for all the injustices suffered as a consequence of the Freeman Field Mutiny.

Terry died from heart failure in Los Angeles at the age of 87.

FURTHER READING
Warren, James C. *The Tuskegee Airmen Mutiny at Freeman* (1995).
Obituary: *Los Angeles Times*, 14 June 2009.

LISA M. BRATTON

Terry, Sonny (24 Oct. 1911–12 Mar. 1986), blues harmonica player and vocalist, was born Sanders Terrell in Greensboro, North Carolina, the son of Ruben Terrell, a tenant farmer, and Mossiline Smith, a singer. Terry learned to play folk-blues harmonica from his father, who was an amateur musician. Two unrelated childhood injuries led to the loss of sight in both of his eyes. Not unlike other black, blind men at the time, Terry took up a musical career because he was unable to obtain other work. He began to travel to nearby cities, playing on street corners and begging for change. In Durham, he met another blind street musician, BLIND BOY FULLER, a talented singer and performer on the National steel guitar. The two began to perform together and in 1937 went to New York City to record for the American Record Company (ARC) label. A year later, jazz producer John Hammond invited Terry to perform at his legendary From Spirituals to Swing concert at Carnegie Hall.

From the beginning of his recording career, Terry had a unique and easily recognized style, melded from the field hollers of his youth, with a strong African influence. Unlike smoother performers like the popular DEFORD BAILEY, who specialized in elaborately worked out instrumentals, Terry favored improvising fills around the singer or guitarist he was accompanying, often hollering or "whoopin" in between the notes, so that his parts combined vocal and instrumental sounds. Terry's backwoods style was perfectly reflected in his solo pieces, such as a recreation of a fox chase, complete with the sounds of the barking dogs, running feet, and cornered prey.

After Fuller died of blood poisoning in 1941, Terry formed a partnership with a younger guitarist, BROWNIE MCGHEE, who was Fuller's protégé. The duo settled permanently in New York in 1942, at the beginning of the first folk-music revival. They befriended twelve-string guitar player LEAD BELLY, who was one of the stars of the revival, and began performing with him as well as with other folk revivalists including Pete Seeger and Woody Guthrie. Nightclub work led to Terry's first big break, a featured part in the 1947–1948 Broadway production of the musical *Finian's Rainbow*. The duo appeared together in the original production of Tennessee Williams's play *Cat on a Hot Tin Roof* a decade later.

Through the 1950s and 1960s, Brownie McGhee and Sonny Terry were well-loved performers on the folk-revival circuit and were regulars at popular folk festivals including those held in Newport and Philadelphia. They recorded for many revival labels, including Folkways and Prestige, and toured extensively through North America, Europe, and Australia. McGhee's relaxed style of singing and fairly simple guitar playing made their music much more accessible for urban audiences than some of the other traditional blues singers. Still, Terry maintained a distinctive style, combining nonverbal vocalizations with his energetic harmonica work.

In the late 1960s and 1970s, McGhee and Terry recorded with more elaborate instrumental backing, reflecting the influence of rock and pop productions; consequently, the recordings dropped somewhat in quality, because the two musicians often sounded uncomfortable playing in front of electric guitars and drums. Oddly, in the early 1980s, after playing together for forty years, the duo broke up because Terry felt that McGhee was getting too much attention from the critics and audience. He made one final solo album, backed by blues rocker Johnny Winter and electric bluesman Willie Dixon, along with drums, but soon advanced age and disease led him to stop performing and recording. Terry had a wife named Emma, whose maiden name is unknown, as is the date of their marriage. He died in Mineola, New York.

FURTHER READING

Glover, Tony. *The Blues Harp of Sonny Terry* (1975).
Obituary: *New York Times*, 12 Mar. 1986.
This entry is taken from the *American National Biography* and is published here with the permission of the American Council of Learned Societies.

RICHARD CARLIN

Tex, Joe (8 Aug. 1933–13 Aug. 1982), singer and songwriter, was born Joseph Arrington Jr. in Rogers, Texas. Arrington, a gifted singer from his youth, performed around his hometown for tips, and, as a high-school junior, he won amateur talent shows in Houston and at New York City's legendary Apollo Theater. After graduating from high school in 1951, Arrington, whose stage surname honored his home state and the white singing cowboy Tex Ritter, moved to New York, where he began touring the theater circuit that included the Apollo and Washington, D.C.'s Howard Theatre. He signed to King in 1954 Records, then riding the early success of Tex's idol, JAMES BROWN. (Tex's and Brown's respective stage shows bore an energetic similarity.) While Tex scored a few minor hits during his King tenure (including Coasters-style novelties like "Charlie Brown Got Expelled"), he achieved his first real success in 1961, after meeting Buddy Killen, a powerful Nashville song publisher and record producer, who had built the largest country-music publishing house, Tree, before expanding his interests into record production and distribution.

Seeing Tex perform in a Houston honky-tonk, where—according to Killen—the white owner had assumed Tex to be white, Killen was so immediately taken by Tex's blend of country and R&B that in 1962 he started Dial Records, an imprint specifically designed as the home for Joe Tex releases. While Killen eventually recorded a variety of other R&B and soul acts on the label, no Dial artist ever approached Tex's centrality either creatively or commercially. Killen and Tex found their groove (after some initial disappointments) when in 1965 the cagey producer took Tex to Fame Studios in Muscle Shoals, Alabama, then in the relative infancy of its prominence as a recording center. Working with an interracial group of musicians from Nashville, Texas, and Muscle Shoals, Tex cut "Hold What You've Got," a sparse, gospel-inflected ballad. Released in 1965, the record climbed to number 5 on the *Billboard* charts, marking the first southern R&B to gain such a high commercial plateau. For this reason, and because of the song's signature sound, many writers consider "Hold What You've Got" a defining moment in the development of southern soul.

The success of "Hold What You've Got" catapulted Tex to R&B stardom and to a position of success and acclaim that he held throughout the next decade. As soul music developed, Tex remained one of the genre's most popular and influential exponents. His early hits replicated the successful formula of his original hit, combining spare, churchy musical textures with lyrics (sometimes spoken) that warned of love's costs and consequences, like 1965's "One Monkey Don't Stop No Show." Tex also recorded up-tempo dance numbers such as the call-and-response-driven "Show Me" (1967), emotive love songs like the insistent "I Want To (Do Everything for You)" (1965), and even ballads that resembled both country recitations and gospel sermons, like "The Love You Save" (1966). Through these hits, Tex came to define the southern-based subgenre known as "country-soul," notable for its shared blues, gospel, and country influences. At his 1965 to 1970 peak, Tex was as popular as any southern soul star, and had a run of hits that competed even with Motown giants like the Four Tops or MARVIN GAYE. His prominence within R&B was symbolized by his involvement in the Soul Clan, a one-off soul "supergroup" with SOLOMON BURKE, Arthur Conley, Don Covay, and BEN E. KING that recorded the hit single "Soul Meeting"/"That's How I Feel" in Nashville in 1967.

In 1966 Tex converted to the Muslim faith and joined the Nation of Islam, reflecting the ongoing push in African American cultural politics towards nationalist philosophies. In 1972 he changed his off-stage name to Joseph Hazziez (though he kept the stage name Joe Tex). Tex's new name, religious conversion, and identification with the controversial Nation certainly reflected the prevailing winds of the time, but also spoke to what Buddy Killen (and southern-soul chronicler Peter Guralnick) described as Tex's long-held belief in independent black assertion. Even though his music was deeply interracial both in its foundations and execution, Tex himself was distrustful of any white person (besides Killen) on any significant level (Killen, 260).

The changes in his personal life were not directly reflected in the course of his career, as the hits continued through the end of the 1960s and into the next decade, during which time he continued producing the funky dance hits and heartfelt ballads of his early career. Particularly noteworthy in this regard are "Skinny Legs and All," a 1967 smash that re-created the spontaneous atmosphere of Tex's live shows within a humorous lyric based in the African American "dozens" tradition of playful insults, and the back-to-back hits "I Gotcha" and "You Said a Bad Word," which in 1972 brought Tex (and Killen) into the funk era, with a polyrhythmic beat underpinning Tex's playful, slightly ribald vocalization. During this period, Tex also cut *Soul Country* (1968), a covers album that made his country influences explicit; although the album became a minor hit, it received little radio airplay. In 1974, he left the music business to focus on his faith, but he returned to touring in 1975.

Tex's final moment in the spotlight came in 1977, when he and Killen (this time serving as cowriter, as well as producer) collaborated on "Ain't Gonna Bump No More (With No Big Fat Woman)." The track pointed to all of Tex's signature roles, of preacher, trickster, dance leader, and love balladeer, all within the context of a smoldering, disco rhythm track. Just as Tex had previously scored hits with songs that marked the arrival of southern soul and funk, with this song he now gestured to the latest musical phenomena dominating black airwaves and dance floors. The song reached the R&B Top 10, and crossed over to the Pop Top 40.

After the success of "Ain't Gonna Bump No More," Tex retreated from the spotlight, returning to his family and ranch in Navasota, Texas. He reunited with the Soul Clan in 1981, but rarely performed, and he recorded next to nothing in the last five years of his life. In 1982, Tex died of a heart attack. He left behind a legacy as one of soul's most consistently successful and admired performers, with a chameleon-like career that maps the development of southern soul, funk, and even disco within its many creative and commercial high points.

FURTHER READING

Guralnick, Peter. *Sweet Soul Music: Rhythm and Blues and the Southern Dream of Freedom* (1986).

Hoskyns, Barney. *Say It One Time for the Broken Hearted: Country-Soul in the American South* (1998).

Killen, Buddy with Tom Carter. *By the Seat of My Pants: My Life in Country Music* (1993).

CHARLES L. HUGHES

Tharpe, Rosetta (20 Mar. 1915–9 Oct. 1973), gospel singer and guitarist, was born Rosetta Nubin in Cotton Plant, Arkansas, the daughter of Willis Nubin and Katie Bell (maiden name unknown). Her parents were divorced when Tharpe was very young, and her mother, who sang in a local church choir, became a traveling missionary. By the time Rosetta was six, she had learned to play guitar and she and her mother had moved to Chicago. They began to make public appearances from a base at the 40th Street Church of God in Christ, with Rosetta billed as "Little Sister" because of her small stature. In the early 1930s she married Pastor Thorpe, an elder in the Holiness Church in Pittsburgh, Pennsylvania, and began touring in Florida in a trio with her mother and husband. After her separation from her husband, she retained his name as her professional name, changing one letter. They were appearing in Reverend Cohen's church in Miami in 1938 when Tharpe came to the attention of the management of Harlem's Cotton Club, where she later auditioned.

As a result, Tharpe was included in the *Cotton Club Parade of 1939*, in which, in the words of the *New York Times* (16 Oct. 1938), she led "an impious version of a Holy Roller meeting below the Mason and Dixon line." She made her first recordings on 31 October 1938 for Decca Records and the following month appeared at the Paramount Theater in New York with COUNT BASIE and his orchestra. On 23 December 1938 she was featured at Carnegie Hall in the first of John Hammond's "From Spirituals to Swing" concerts. At this time and up to the mid-1940s her repertoire mixed gospel and secular songs, and she became particularly noted for her song "I Want a Tall Skinny Papa."

During 1939 and early 1940 Tharpe continued to appear at the Cotton Club and also made theater appearances with CAB CALLOWAY and his orchestra in shows based on the Cotton Club Revue. A feature article in *Life* (28 Aug. 1939), titled "Sister Swings Same Songs in Church and Night Club," claimed Tharpe was singing on weekdays in the Cotton Club and on Sundays in the Church of God in Christ in Harlem. However, a letter from the pastor (*Life*, 23 Oct. 1937, 6) informed the editors that she was "no longer identified with, or renders service to, this or any other Assembly of the Church of God in Christ." She was featured again in the second "From Spirituals to Swing" concert in December 1939 and in late 1940 was presented in a "Spirituals to Swing" cabaret show at Cafe Society Downtown in New York.

In June 1941 Tharpe became a featured singer with LUCKY MILLINDER's orchestra and remained with him, with a few interruptions, until mid-1944. During this period she recorded both with the band and as a solo gospel performer and in August–September 1941 made three short films ("soundies") with Millinder's band for the Panoram video jukebox. In 1944–1945 she worked with the bands of DON REDMAN, FLETCHER HENDERSON, and Calloway, before rejoining Millinder for a southern tour in July–August 1945.

After this, Sister Tharpe returned to performing religious material exclusively, though she continued to appear in theaters and jazz venues. She was still recording for Decca Records, often accompanied by groups led by the blues pianist Sammy Price. Their "Strange Things Happening Every Day" (1944) was the first of several of her records to become a Top 10 hit in what were then the race record charts. In late 1946 Tharpe began appearing in concert and on record in duet with Marie Knight, a partnership that proved both commercially successful and artistically fruitful, and from about 1949 she began working again with her mother, with whom she recorded some powerful duets. In 1950 mother and daughter made two appearances at the Apollo Theater in Harlem, presenting "Spirituals in the Modern Manner." "God," said Sister Tharpe, "is as likely to be found at the Apollo as anywhere else; he doesn't stay at church all the time."

At some point in the 1940s Tharpe had been married to a man named Forrest Allen. On 3 July 1951 Tharpe married Russell Morrison, a former manager of the vocal group The Ink Spots, in a ceremony at Griffith Stadium in Washington, D.C., attended by twenty-five thousand guests and recorded for commercial issue. Morrison acted as his wife's manager for the remainder of her career. The partnership with Marie Knight ended in 1954 after they made

some secular recordings that attracted very unfavorable attention from church activists. Though Tharpe did not wish to continue with this experiment, she found that attitudes in the sanctified church had hardened since her previous return to the fold in the 1940s and that she was not readily reaccepted as a religious artist. Partly as a result, she began to make extensive tours of southern country churches, but from 1957 she also made frequent European tours, finding a renewed audience among jazz and blues enthusiasts. Back in the United States, she made appearances on the folk circuit, including the Newport Folk Festival. In 1969 she was featured in the French film *L'Aventure du Jazz*.

On 13 November 1970, while on a European tour, Tharpe suffered a stroke in Geneva, Switzerland, and was later hospitalized at Temple University Hospital, Philadelphia. After the amputation of a leg she made a sufficient recovery to resume touring briefly in 1972–1973 with the vocal group the Nightingales, but she succumbed to a second stroke. Tharpe died in Philadelphia, Pennsylvania.

Though the best-known performer in what has sometimes been dubbed the "Holy Blues" style, exemplified also by the work of Sister O. M. Terrell and Mary Deloatch, Tharpe belonged to a tradition widespread in the sanctified churches, most of whose representatives became known to nonreligious audiences, if at all, only through records. Her vibrant, highly emotional contralto, echoed by her swinging and inspired guitar playing, earned her a permanent place in the annals of African American music.

FURTHER READING

Dixon, Robert M. W., John Godrich, and Howard W. Rye. *Blues & Gospel Records, 1890–1943* (1997).

Hayes, Cedric J. *A Discography of Gospel Records, 1937–1971* (1973).

Hayes, Cedric J., and Robert Laughton. *Gospel Records, 1943–1969: A Black Music Discography* (1993).

Heilbut, Anthony. *The Gospel Sound* (1985).

This entry is taken from the *American National Biography* and is published here with the permission of the American Council of Learned Societies.

HOWARD RYE

Thierry, Camille (Oct. 1814–Apr. 1875), poet, was born in New Orleans, Louisiana, the son of a Frenchman from Bordeaux and his light-skinned black mistress. Little more is known about Thierry's birth and parentage. Though an American, Thierry spent most of his life in France, which he considered more enlightened and cultured than his native land; he also believed that in Europe he could escape prejudice against his African American heritage.

Thierry was well educated; he was initially tutored at home but went to a day school as an adolescent. As he prepared to sail to attend college in Paris, however, his father died, and Thierry was left with a healthy patrimony. He subsequently scrapped his plans for college and went into business in New Orleans. Although Thierry accumulated a small fortune, was considered one of the wealthiest African Americans in antebellum Louisiana, and was a member of the New Orleans Freedmen's Aid Association, he soon discovered that he was not cut out for the daily grind of the financial world. Thierry then spent several months ferrying between the United States and France, until 1855, when he decided to make France his permanent home, and he left his substantial holdings in America in the care of the agents Lafitte, Dufilho & Company. Although he spent several months frequenting salons and literary events and writing poetry in vibrant Paris, Thierry soon tired of the socialite's life and retreated to Bordeaux, where he lived quietly and in solitude. No longer burdened by financial cares or drudgery, nor distracted by Paris, Thierry was free to give himself entirely to his aesthetic interests.

Thierry became especially interested in poetry as a young man and began to write large amounts of verse in French. In 1843 his poem "Idées" was published in *L'album littéraire* of New Orleans. Thierry was one of the earliest and most prolific African American poets of Louisiana; his style was described by Rodolphe Desdunes as "elegant and graceful, with a natural mode of expression and a felicitous use of symbols." In 1845 Armand Lanusse selected fourteen of Thierry's poems for inclusion in his anthology *Les cenelles*, a collection of French poetry written by African American men; Lanusse chose for publication in the volume twice as many poems by Thierry as by any other poet. Thierry went on to publish a few more poems in 1850 in the *Orléanais*. Thierry's popularity and reputation are also evidenced in the words of Paul Trevigne, a critic for the *New Orleans Louisianian*, who wrote in the 25 December 1875 edition, "His poems are composed with peculiar care, and comprise all the various rhythms of French prosody. Some of them are to be classed among the finest poetical efforts of Louisiana's most gifted writers." But Thierry never felt completely free in the hierarchical Creole society, despite his wealth and

fame. Not until his move to Bordeaux did he feel unfettered enough to write poems not only about love and nature, but also about racial discrimination and prejudice.

Thierry suffered a major financial loss in 1873, when his agents went bankrupt and he lost both his rental income and his investment capital in their firm. He left Bordeaux to untangle the confusion of his business holdings, and he was persuaded to transfer the titles of all his real estate—including six houses—to his brokers, who had reincorporated. In exchange for a perpetual annuity of fifty dollars per month Thierry agreed to place his net worth of approximately forty-three thousand dollars into their hands. Thierry soon returned to Bordeaux, getting back to his true love, poetry, and he soon collected his scattered poems, some of which had already been printed in Louisiana. The poems were published at his own expense in 1874 as *Les vagabondes*. Although this small volume was highly acclaimed in Europe in Thierry's day, it was virtually unknown in the United States for several years and is now a very rare book. These poems showed the influence of Alphonse de Lamartine and Charles-Hubert Millevoye; they are carefully structured and graceful. The book centers on the lives of three Creole beggars whom Thierry remembered from his boyhood in New Orleans, and one of the most famous of the poems was "Mariquita La Calentura," which details the trials of a Spanish family.

Shortly after the publication of *Les vagabondes*, Thierry lost his annuity and was left destitute when Lafitte, Dufilho & Company failed again. The shock of the financial loss was immense, and Thierry died soon thereafter in Bordeaux. He had never married.

In the years after Thierry's death his verse remained popular in France and was frequently reprinted in the Creole press of Louisiana. Today most Americans know very little about Thierry, for his poems were published primarily in Louisiana periodicals, his verse is written entirely in French, and most of the few books containing his verse are rare and out of print. Few translators, critics, or biographers have focused on Thierry and his work beyond passing references. But despite his self-imposed exile and use of French-language verse, Thierry discussed American issues. As Desdunes notes, Thierry "understood the apathetic disposition of his people. He realized that a man such as he could count only upon himself in the battles of life." Thierry represented the tragedy of a divided nation;

though wealthy, talented, and sophisticated, Thierry could never achieve the promises of the American dream, and some of his most scathing stanzas depicted this angst. In one short poem, he wrote,

> I heard no voice speak to me,
> Not even the voice of a mother.
> I fought alone when the thunder roared ...
> I comforted myself!

In the antebellum South and during Reconstruction, Thierry voiced his pain and his disapproval of American racism through his verse, exhibiting courage and a subtle appeal for change in the face of racial hostility.

FURTHER READING

Thierry's poems and papers, including *Les vagabondes*, are at the New Orleans City Hall Archives and at the Howard Memorial Library.

Blassingame, John W. *Black New Orleans, 1860–1880* (1973).

Caulfeild, Ruby Van Allen. *The French Literature of Louisiana* (1929).

Desdunes, Rodolphe Lucien. *Nos hommes et notre histoire* (1911). Translated as *Our People and Our History: A Tribute to the Creole People of Color*, trans. Dorothea Olga McCants (1973).

Herrin, M. H. *The Creole Aristocracy: A Study of the Creole of Southern Louisiana* (1952).

Thierry, Camille. *Les vagabondes: Poésies américaines*, ed. and trans. Frans C. Amelinckx and May Rush Gwin Waggoner (2004). Bilingual edition.

This entry is taken from the *American National Biography* and is published here with the permission of the American Council of Learned Societies.

ANNE M. TURNER

Thomas, Alma (22 Sept. 1891–25 Feb. 1978), painter and educator, was born Alma Woodsey Thomas in Columbus, Georgia, the eldest of four daughters of John Harris Thomas, a businessman, and Amelia Cantey, a seamstress and dress designer. Perhaps because she was born with slight hearing and speech impediments, Alma gravitated toward the visual arts. Motivated by escalating racial violence that culminated in the nearby Atlanta riots of 1906, the Thomases moved to Washington, D.C., in 1907, settling into a house on Fifteenth Street that Alma lived in until she died. She attended the segregated Armstrong Manual Training High School, where she excelled in math and architectural drawing. After graduating in 1911, she entered the Miner Normal School, earning a teaching certificate in 1913. From 1915 to 1921 she taught arts and crafts at the Thomas Garrett Settlement House in Wilmington, Delaware.

Thomas enjoyed designing costumes for local productions in Wilmington, and in 1921 she enrolled at Howard University, intending to study costume design. Within a year, however, she had transferred to the newly established department of fine arts organized by James V. Herring. Under the tutelage of Herring and the sculptor May Howard Jackson, Thomas became the first graduate of the department when she received a B.S. in 1924. Thomas taught drawing briefly in Pennsylvania at the Cheyney Training School while awaiting a post in Washington. In February 1925 Thomas began teaching art at Shaw Junior High School, a segregated Washington public school. She remained there for the next thirty-five years.

Teaching allowed Thomas a life of social and economic freedom that was rare for unmarried women, especially African American women. She was a passionate, creative, and demanding teacher. Among other extracurricular activities, she organized the School Arts League, through which she arranged for trips to museums and lectures and opened the first art gallery in a Washington public school. Thomas spent the summers of 1930 through 1934 at Columbia University's Teachers College in New York, earning an M.A. degree in Education in 1934. Her master's thesis on marionettes led her back to New York the following summer to study with Tony Sarg, a well-known marionette maker and puppeteer. After her return to Washington, Thomas organized the Marionette Club, for which she made marionettes and presented shows for local African American children barred from attending whites-only performances.

During her summers in New York City, Thomas frequented the Harlem scene, as well as downtown New York art events such as the exhibition openings at Alfred Stieglitz's An American Place. Back in Washington she became increasingly active in the city's art community. In 1943 she cofounded, with Herring and Alonzo J. Aden, the Barnett Aden Gallery, Washington's first avant-garde venue and the first to show both black and white artists. Through her association with the gallery, Thomas met artists and curators and became part of the progressive art scene. In 1946 she joined the Little Paris Studio, a working group of local artists established by LOIS MAILOU JONES and Céline Tabary. The group, which met twice a week at Jones's house to encourage and critique each other's work, helped convince Thomas to return to school to study painting. In 1950 she began a decade of evening and weekend classes at American University, where she studied with Robert Gates, Joe Summerford, and Jacob Kainen. During this time her work was included in several local group art exhibitions, and in 1960 she was given her first solo show, Watercolors by Alma Thomas, at the Dupont Theater Art Gallery in Washington.

In 1960 at the age of sixty-nine Thomas retired from teaching and devoted herself to painting. She continued to work with children, coordinating art exhibitions and classes for the D.C. Commissioners Youth Council and educating local children at Uplift House and Beauty Club, a neighborhood program she founded. Thomas's independent spirit and creative curiosity were instrumental in forging this second career. Her intense focus on painting spurred eighteen years of imaginative experimentation and the evolution of a distinctly personal style.

Thomas's paintings from the 1950s are primarily figurative still lifes, influenced by cubism and post-impressionism. As the decade closed, however, she became increasingly interested in abstraction and abstract expressionism's emphasis on pure color, the flatness of the picture plane, and visible brush-strokes. Thomas's first abstract oils, including *Blue and Brown Still Life* (1958), *City Lights* (1959), *Red Abstraction* (1959), and *Yellow and Blue* (1959), resemble Hans Hoffman's compositions. By the early 1960s Thomas had switched to watercolors, which she found best suited her primary subjects, light and color. Later she asserted: "A world without color would seem dead. Color for me is life" (*New York Times*, 4 May 1972) and "light is the mother of all color" (*Washington Post*, 15 Apr. 1979).

Nature, in its every permutation, was Thomas's lifelong muse and subject. She spoke often about the trees, flowers, and animals in her life, of the changes in seasons, light, and weather, and of her memories of a bucolic childhood in Georgia, summer at her grandparents' plantation in Alabama, and afternoons at the arboretum in Washington. Whether inspired by the dappling of light, reflections in water, phenomena viewed through a microscope or telescope, or landscapes seen from above, Thomas's work renders anew the marvels of the natural world.

Following a debilitating arthritis attack in 1964 that left Thomas bedridden, JAMES PORTER proposed mounting a major retrospective of her work at the Howard University Art Gallery. Between the period

of her convalescence and the opening of the exhibition in 1966, Thomas had shifted to total abstraction, revealing the characteristics that became her signature style, rectangular shapes of intense colors organized in rows and patterns. A few months before her death, Thomas claimed that an epiphany bore the change in style: "I looked at the window.... Why the tree! The holly tree! I looked at the tree in the window and that became my inspiration. There are six patterns in there right now that I can see ... so that tree changed my whole career, my whole way of thinking" (*Washington Post*, 15 Apr. 1979). There were other influences as well, including Henri Matisse's collages and paper cutouts, which Thomas saw in New York in 1963; the increasingly conceptual approach to abstraction practiced by artists such as Mark Rothko and Helen Frankenthaler; and the work of the Washington Color School painters Kenneth Noland, Gene Davis, Morris Louis, Thomas Downing, and Howard Mehring, with whom she is most often associated.

Thomas certainly shared with the Washington Color School painters an interest in optical effects and geometry, and the primacy of color and her work show a particular debt to Kenneth Noland's color banded circles and Gene Davis's colored vertical stripes. But unlike the Washington group, who stained, or soaked paint into, their canvases to achieve a totally flat picture plane and used masking tape to attain a hard edge, Thomas applied paint in a hearty fashion that owned more to the early abstract expressionists and action painters. "Alma's stripes," as she called them, were consciously designed and executed (using large elastics stretched around the canvas as a guide), but they revealed the gestural mark of the artist. Thomas's work always maintained a tactile, handcrafted quality. Produced in her kitchen/studio, she used palette knife as often as a brush and often held canvases in her lap, turning it to reach unpainted corners, which provided an intimate relationship with each work.

Thomas fully developed her style with a series she called *Earth Paintings*, produced between 1968 and 1972. With titles like *Iris, Tulips, Jonquils, and Crocuses* (1969), *Wind Dancing With Spring Flowers* (1969), and *Earth Sermon—Beauty, Love, And Peace* (1971), these acrylic paintings have been likened to mosaics of tile or glass, quilts, cascading water, and kaleidoscopes. The hot colors, solar phenomena, aerial views, and optimism inspired by the space program stirred Thomas to create a second series during this period, called *Space Paintings*, which included her 1970 paintings *Launch Pad*, *Blast Off* and *Snoopy Sees a Sunrise* (1970).

In 1969 Thomas's work was exhibited at the White House and the residence of the mayor of Washington. Over the next few years her paintings were displayed internationally through the U.S. Department of State's ART in Embassies Program. She received solo shows at the Franz Bader Gallery in Washington in 1968 and at Fisk University in 1971. In 1972 Thomas and her work reached a broader audience through a retrospective exhibition at the Corcoran Gallery of Art, and the opening day was declared Alma Thomas Day in Washington, D.C. A few months later the Whitney Museum of American Art in New York mounted a small exhibition of her work, making her the first black woman to have a solo show at the influential museum. Thomas, at age eighty, was feted by the press, and positive reviews appeared in publications such as the *New York Times* and *Art International*. Thomas showed with ELIZABETH CATLETT, as well as with her friends LAURA WHEELER WARING and Lois Mailou Jones, in Baltimore in 1972, and she had a solo exhibition at New York's Martha Jackson Gallery in New York the following year.

Despite deteriorating eyesight and chronic arthritis, Thomas, who was only five feet tall, was painting ever-larger canvases, averaging six feet. Thomas's mature style demonstrates her sophisticated understanding of contemporary art. She was an avid reader of art books and magazines, and she kept abreast of current exhibitions. By 1972 she was reducing the number of colors used in her all-over paintings and was experimenting to produce optical effects. Her compositions became more complex, with the stripes and paint blocks loosening and with the modulations of color, particularly background colors, becoming more finely tuned. *Antares* (1972) is a study in red, and *Cherry Blossom Symphony* (1972) offers a sensory interpretation of the pink flower. As 1973 progressed, Thomas allowed her paint blocks to take on different shapes and increased the rhythm across the picture plane, qualities evident in *Fiery Sunset* and *Phantasmagoria*, both from 1973.

In 1974 Thomas tripped on a television cord and broke her hip. She was unable to work for almost two years, but in February 1976 she returned to painting. Over the next eight months she painted furiously, producing more than fifty canvases in preparation for a second show at the Martha Jackson Gallery. During this period her style progressed. Thomas referred to these paintings as her "hieroglyphs." And indeed they appear to be communicating in a mysterious language, interpreting the movement and sound of nature. The enhanced syncopation exuded by these late works is reflected in their titles: *Red Azaleas Singing and Dancing Rock and Roll Music*, *Scarlet Sage Dancing a Whirling Dervish*, and *Babbling Brook and Whistling Poplar Trees Symphony*, all from 1976.

In 1981, three years after her death, the National Museum of American Art in Washington (later the Smithsonian American Art Museum) held a retrospective exhibition of Thomas's paintings. Thomas's work can be found in more than thirty major museum collections, including the National Gallery of Art, the Art Institute of Chicago, the Whitney Museum of American Art, and the Metropolitan Museum of Art.

FURTHER READING

Thomas's papers are at the Archives of American Art, Smithsonian Institution, Washington, D.C.

Foresta, Merry A. *A Life in Art: Alma Thomas 1891–1978* (1981).

Wayne Museum of Art. *Alma W. Thomas: A Retrospective of the Paintings* (1998).

LISA E. RIVO

Thomas, Andre J. (15 Aug. 1952–), choral director, composer, arranger, and author was born Andre Jerome Thomas in Wichita, Kansas, the only son and first of three children born to Leva J. Thomas, a carpet cleaner, and the third child and only son of Willie Mae Caldwell, a coach cleaner. By age four Thomas's proclivity for music was evident. MAHALIA JACKSON and other gospel greats engaged his spirit and music took up permanent residence within his soul. His mother watched as the passion for music established itself within her son and as much as she may have hoped it to be fleeting, she accepted the inevitable and engaged a teacher for him. His teacher was a stern woman, demanding nothing less than flawlessness from her student. As he learned his first piece, she would rap him on the knuckles when he played it incorrectly. His mother found this method of reinforcement to be unacceptable, so the lessons ended. She informed her son that he needed to be satisfied with singing in the church choir and search out a different path in life.

As Thomas grew, music became an even more cherished companion. Ensuring that her son received a good education was imperative to Thomas's mother, so she sent him from a predominantly black school in the neighborhood to a public school on the other side of town. Although his sister taught there, he would be a one-man integration team within the student body. Being the only African America was daunting and the music room became his haven. It was there that he received his introduction into the world of choral music. Around that time the church that he attended was in search of a choir director. After deliberating they concluded that, rather than engage an outsider, they should have Thomas direct the choir. So at the age of fourteen he became their director, a decision that caused dissension amongst the ranks. Some felt that a fourteen-year-old had no business directing them and voiced that opinion. Thomas's mother caught wind of the grumblings and like the proverbial lioness protecting her cub she pounced, letting them know exactly what she thought. With only three rehearsals under their belt Thomas knew that he'd never gain the respect of his choir with "mama" fighting his battles, so one of his first official acts was banishing her from the choir. When Thomas's peers were finger popping to R&B, his heart and soul gravitated towards the classic standards. Choral music was what he knew; it fit him perfectly. It was who he was and who he was destined to be.

Upon entering Friends University in Wichita, Kansas, Thomas's musical aspirations soared as he glimpsed all that the musical world had to offer. While attending Friends University, Thomas was introduced to Jester Hairston (1901–2000, an educator, conductor, composer/arranger, and actor) who made a profound difference on Thomas's musical psyche. Hairston shed light on the importance of the African American contribution to the genre. Thomas intensified his melodic pursuit and joined the university's choir, The Singing Quakers. He also had the opportunity to flex his musical muscle when he was hired to play for musicians appearing at a musical festival in Wichita. This gave Thomas a deep sense of pride and solidified his desire to pursue his musical career. Thomas had had an appointment to the U.S. Air Force Academy, but decided to attend Friends University, intrigued by its choir.

Thomas earned his baccalaureate in music education in 1973 and began teaching. He earned his masters of music in piano performance from Northwestern University in 1976. In August 1978 he married Portia Russell and began work on his doctorate. Three years later he joined the University of Texas faculty and in January 1982 celebrated the birth of his son, Jordan. In the spring 1982 he received his doctorate of music in choral conducting from the University of Illinois. In 1984 Florida State University offered Thomas several positions,

and that autumn he became the Owen F. Sellers Professor of Music, Director of Choral Activities, and Professor of Choral Music Education. In 1985, he began conducting the University Choir. In December 1986 the Thomas family welcomed their daughter, Taylor. Thomas began serving as the Artistic Director of the Tallahassee Community Chorus in 1988.

Thomas has conducted choirs throughout the United States as well as in Europe, the Republic of China, the Philippines, Sweden, Australia, and in Vietnam (with the Florida State Choir). He has been a guest conductor of such notable orchestras and choirs as England's Birmingham Symphony Orchestra and Germany's Berlin Radio Choir. Thomas is a renowned lecturer, composer, and arranger bringing a soulful flavor to the traditional choral world. He boasts an extensive repertoire of music and along with two of his colleagues has produced two instructional videos *What They See Is What You Get* with Rodney Eichenberger (choral conductor), and *Body, Mind, Spirit, Voice* with Anton Armstrong (choral conductor). Furthermore Thomas has authored the book *Way Over In Beulah Lan': Understanding and Performing the Negro Spiritual* (2007) and article "Singing Black Gospel Music and Spirituals" (*Reformed Worship Magazine* no. 14, December 1989), and been a contributing author for *Composers On Composing for Choir* (June 2007). He is a past president of both the Florida American Choral Directors Association (ACDA) and the Southern Division of ACDA.

Thomas has been honored with the 1993 Florida State University's Award for Excellence in teaching; the 1995 Florida chapter of ACDA's Wayne Hugoboom Distinguished Service Award; and the 1996 Florida State University's Dr. Martin Luther King Jr. Distinguished Service Award.

Humble and unmoved by his own talents, Thomas doesn't boast of the magnitude of his contribution to this genre. He says "he's just being who he is, doing what he does." When Thomas entered this field, the African American choral conductor was almost a phenomenon, but today he stands shoulder to shoulder with many of his brothers and sisters. It was conductors like Andre Thomas, Jester Hairston, James DePriest, Anton E. Armstrong, Moses G. Hogan, Norma Raybon, and a minuscule company of their brethren that blazed the trail that has immersed them in a genre not traditionally thought their territory. But in the true tradition of their African ancestry Thomas (and the others) are just taking that which was passed down to them, putting their touch to it and passing it on to generations yet to come.

FURTHER READING

Thomas, Andre J. *Way Over In Beulah Lan':
Understanding and Performing the Negro Spiritual*
(2007-Heritage Music Press).

WEBSITES

Florida State University College of Music Faculty,
Andre J. Thomas, http://music.fsu.edu/thomas.htm.
Tallahassee Community Chorus, Florida's Premier
Community Chorus, Dr. Andre J Thomas, Artistic
Director, http://www.tcchorus.org/HTML%20
Background%20Chgs/MaroonDrThomasPage.htm.

DISCOGRAPHY

My Shepherd Will Supply (2008).
Songs From My Heart: Choral Music of André Thomas
(2004).

COMPOSITIONS AND ARRANGEMENTS

"Barbara Allen" (Heritage Music Press, 2005).
"Beautiful City" (Heritage Music Press, 2006).
"Go Down 'N the Valley and Pray" (Heritage Music
Press, 2007).
"I'm Gonna Sing" (Heritage Music Press/Lorenz
Publishing Company, 2005).
"I Will Sing Praises" (Choristers Guild/Lorenz
Publishing Company, 1996).
"John Saw Duh Numbuh" (Heritage Music Press/
Lorenz Publishing Company, 2001).
"Let Everything" (Laurel Press/Lorenz Publishing
Company, 2001).

JANELLE F. H. WINSTON

Thomas, Charles Leroy (17 Apr. 1920–15 Feb. 1980), U.S. Army officer and Medal of Honor recipient, was born in Birmingham, Alabama. Federal Census records indicate that he was likely the eldest son of Elie and Mary Thomas. In the 1930s the Thomas family subsequently moved northward, as many African American families did during the Depression Era in order to find greater prospects for employment, and settled in Detroit, Michigan. Here, Thomas's father worked at the Ford Motor Company's River Rouge plant, while Thomas gained a solid education. Said to have "a bookish interest in planes and electronics" (Cohen), Thomas graduated from Cass Technical High School in 1938, and subsequently worked for Ford Motor with his father. By 1942 Charles Thomas was enrolled at Wayne State University and majoring in mechanical engineering when he received notice that he was being drafted to serve in World War II.

Thomas began his military career on 20 January 1942 and was originally assigned to an infantry unit. However, with his advanced education and the promise he showed as a soldier in his first year of service, Charles Thomas was chosen as an officer candidate for one of the army's black units then being formed, and was subsequently commissioned as a second lieutenant in March 1943 and assigned to the 614th Tank Destroyer Battalion at Fort Hood, Texas. All of the men in the 614th were African American, excepting its commander and three senior officers. Of the 80 battalions in the army's Tank Destroyer Command during the war, only two were manned by African Americans. While at Fort Hood, Thomas underwent training with the rest of his fellow officers and enlisted men, developing unit cohesion and gaining valuable knowledge in the field of antitank operations, especially in the operation of the M3 halftrack vehicle and the towed 3-inch antitank gun. Unlike other tank destroyer units, the 614th was not equipped with any self-propelled antitank weapons, such as the M10 or the new M18 Hellcat. Very soon, not only would Charles Thomas demonstrate to the fullest his leadership skills, but his company would also make history.

The service of black soldiers, men like Charles Thomas, JOHN FOX, and RUBEN RIVERS, in World War II was important to America's overall war effort in manning combat and support units. However, their contributions also achieved an even higher level; not only did these men overcome the prejudice that confronted them in the armed forces at nearly every turn, but they also proved themselves to be good soldiers, the equal of their white counterparts. Indeed, time and again in America's early conflicts, the competency and heroism of black soldiers had to be continually proved. However, the service of black soldiers in World War II would largely put this issue to rest once and for all, though formal recognition for their heroism in the form of our nation's highest military award, the Medal of Honor, would be years in coming.

In September 1944, the men of the 614th were shipped overseas to Europe, and in October the unit was sent to France, where it saw its first action against the Siegfried Line while attached to the 3rd Cavalry. Several weeks later the 614th was attached to the 103rd Infantry Division and continued operations on the border between France and Germany. On 14 December 1944, elements of the 411th Infantry and Company C of the 614th Tank Destroyer Battalion were assigned to attack German positions in the French town of Climbach. Volunteering to lead the assault team, First Lieutenant Charles Thomas, riding in a M20 armored scout car, led the advance, hoping to draw the fire of enemy artillery fire so as to reveal their position. The German forces waited until the Americans had advanced deep into the valley before opening fire, quickly wrecking Thomas's scout car. Though wounded with glass and shrapnel fragments, Thomas responded by manning the car's .50 caliber machine gun and killed a number of German soldiers advancing on the American forces. Thomas was subsequently wounded again, this time in the chest, stomach, and legs, but continued to man his gun until his ammunition ran low. He then sought refuge under the wrecked scout car, and from here positioned the men of Company C and directed the fire of their antitank guns. The situation was dire, for if the company could not return fire, they soon would be wiped out. However, this was not to be; the men of the 614th were rallied by the continued leadership of their badly wounded lieutenant and got their guns into position and firing. Despite attempts to evacuate Thomas for medical treatment, he refused until his men were in position and an officer to replace him could be found. In the end, the town of Climbach was captured by the Americans, but were it not for Charles Thomas the outcome of the battle might not have been so favorable. In January 1945 Thomas was awarded the Distinguished Service Cross for his gallantry in action, the army's second highest award, and promoted to captain. His command in the 614th, Company C, was awarded the Distinguished Unit Citation, the first such award ever made to an African American unit.

Following his action in France, Charles Thomas never saw combat action again. He was eventually returned stateside for medical treatment at Percy Jones Hospital in Battle Creek, Michigan, and was discharged from the army in 1947, having attained the rank of major. He subsequently married Bertha Thompson in July 1949 and had two children, Linda and Michael. A quiet and unassuming man, Charles Thomas seldom spoke of his military service, even to his family, but did carry the scars from his battle wounds for the remainder of his life. He worked a variety of jobs, including that of a missile technician and an Internal Revenue Service computer programmer. Thomas even attended classes again at Wayne State University in the area of mechanical engineering. Charles Thomas

Charles Leroy Thomas, Purple Heart and posthumous Medal of Honor recipient (c. 1943). (United States Department of Defense.)

subsequently died from cancer and was buried at West Lawn Cemetery in Wayne, Michigan, a largely forgotten hero.

In 1992, over a decade after the death of Charles Thomas, the subject of the army's discriminatory practices when it came to the award of the Medal of Honor entered the public debate, and in response the government commissioned Shaw University in Raleigh, North Carolina, to study the issue. After a four-year study, a report was issued that identified ten men, Charles Thomas among them, all of whom were awarded the Distinguished Service Cross, but would have been awarded the Medal of Honor had it not been for their race. The army themselves investigated the findings, and, in Thomas's case, agreed. After Congress passed a special law that waived the statute of limitations regarding the award, President Bill Clinton presented the posthumous Medal of Honor to the family of Charles Thomas and six other African American soldiers, including RUBEN RIVERS, WILLEY JAMES, EDWARD CARTER JR., and GEORGE WATSON, on 13 January 1997 in a historic

White House ceremony. Charles Thomas's service to his country was forgotten no more.

FURTHER READING

Cohen, Warren. "Recognizing Valor: Profile of Charles Thomas, African-American World War II Hero." *Michigan History Magazine* (1997).

Converse, Elliot V., Daniel K. Gibran, John A. Cash, Robert K. Griffith, and Richard H. Kohn. *The Exclusion of Black Soldiers from the Medal of Honor in World War II* (2008).

Hanna, Charles W. *African American Recipients of the Medal of Honor* (2002).

GLENN ALLEN KNOBLOCK

Thomas, Clarence (23 June 1948–), U.S. Supreme Court justice, was born in Pin Point, Georgia, the son of M. C. Thomas, a maintenance worker, and Leola Anderson, a worker in a crab-and-oyster plant. Two years later M. C. Thomas moved to Philadelphia, Pennsylvania, leaving his young wife to look after Clarence, their eldest child, Emma Mae, and a son not yet born, who would be named Myers after his maternal grandfather, Myers Anderson. The family struggled. Like most of their neighbors, they lived in a one-room wooden shack with no indoor plumbing, and although Leola Thomas was renowned as the fastest crab-and-oyster packer in town, the meager wages she earned barely covered the needs of a family of four. To make ends meet, she worked extra hours as a domestic.

In 1954 Clarence Thomas entered the first grade at Pin Point's all-black Florence Public School, a few months after the U.S. Supreme Court's landmark school desegregation decision in *Brown v. Board of Education*. White resistance to change, however, ensured that the public schools of Georgia remained segregated throughout the 1950s. When the children were not in school or with their mother at work, Clarence and Myers had free rein to climb the palmettos, maples, and magnolias that towered over Pin Point and to scoop crabs from the banks of nearby marshes. Such idyllic memories may explain Thomas's later insistence that his family was not "poor" and that, unlike the inner cities of the 1980s, Pin Point offered a safe, peaceful, and "positive environment" in which to grow up (Greenya, 27). Yet Thomas left Pin Point at the age of seven, after their house burned down, and the family moved to a crowded tenement in Savannah. One year later, when Leola Thomas could no longer cope, Myers Anderson adopted his daughter's two sons and provided them with a far more positive environment for future success than their sister would enjoy. While Emma Mae returned to hard-scrabble Pin Point to live with an aunt, the boys lived in a comfortable six-room house with indoor plumbing and could depend on Anderson, a successful entrepreneur who ran a home-heating-oil business, to provide financial security. Her brothers might have argued, however, that Emma Mae did not have to endure the onerous tasks required of them by their grandfather, who worked from sunup to sundown and expected at least as much from Clarence and Myers. Though Thomas later praised his grandfather as the epitome of a hard-driven, self-made entrepreneur, his recollection of Myers Anderson in the early seventies was not quite so fond. He told friends at Yale Law School that if he or his brother even overslept, they were beaten.

Strict discipline was also the rule at the all-black Catholic parochial schools in which Anderson enrolled his grandsons, though the nuns at these institutions provided the Thomas boys with an academically rigorous education as well. Anderson, a Baptist, and his grandsons converted to Catholicism and was determined that Clarence enter the priesthood. At first, Thomas shared his grandfather's goal, and in 1964 he was one of the first two African Americans to enter the St. John Vianney Seminary outside Savannah. He excelled academically there and at the Immaculate Conception Seminary in Missouri, which he attended in 1967. But like many student pioneers of desegregation, he struggled socially. By 1968 the racist attitudes of his fellow seminarians convinced Thomas that there were "too many rednecks" at Immaculate Conception, and he abandoned his dream of becoming a priest, transferring to Holy Cross, a Jesuit college in Worcester, Massachusetts, that accepted him under its new affirmative action program.

At Holy Cross, Thomas flirted with the separatist ideas of the Black Power movement, but he was also the only black student on campus to oppose a planned separate dormitory for African Americans. However, when that dorm opened, he moved in, taking with him his white roommate. Thomas also volunteered at a Black Panther–run breakfast program for underprivileged children in Worcester, but he devoted most of his time to his studies, graduating ninth in his class and with honors in English. One day after graduation he married Kathy Ambush, a student at a nearby college, with whom he had one son, Jamal. The couple divorced ten years later.

Thomas's academic progress appears to some as a textbook example of affirmative action. Access to the superior facilities at Holy Cross, along with a dedication to hard work, gave Thomas the grades that enabled him, again under an affirmative action program, to enroll at Yale Law School. By the time he graduated from Yale in 1974, however, Thomas had begun to believe that such programs stigmatized their beneficiaries as less qualified than other students. Still, his first full-time job, as a lawyer working for John C. Danforth, the attorney general of Missouri, was also the consequence of a kind of affirmative action. Danforth, a Yale Law School graduate and a moderate Republican, had gone to his alma mater specifically to recruit a black attorney for his office.

Although he had been an ardent Democrat at Holy Cross and Yale, Thomas switched his allegiance to the Republican Party in the mid-1970s, in part because of the influence of THOMAS SOWELL, a conservative black economist who opposed federal welfare and affirmative action programs. Thomas's friendship with Jay Parker, a black Republican activist, also furthered his political ambitions. Parker, who notoriously had links to the apartheid regime in South Africa and Central American death squads, was also a confidante of Edwin Meese III, who ran the Republican transition team after Ronald Reagan won the 1980 presidential election. Meese asked Parker to oversee the transition at the Equal Employment Opportunity Commission (EEOC), and Parker recruited Thomas, then an aide to Danforth in the U.S. Senate, to assist him.

In 1981 President Reagan appointed Thomas to serve as the assistant secretary for civil rights in the Department of Education and nine months later nominated him to chair the EEOC, the federal agency responsible for enforcing the nation's civil rights laws. Thomas's eight-year tenure, the longest in the commission's history, was credited with improving the agency's efficiency and morale, although many in the civil rights community criticized him for trying to weaken or even end affirmative action. During Senate hearings on his reappointment as EEOC chief in 1986, however, Thomas stated his personal reservations about affirmative action but accepted that since the Supreme Court had ruled in favor of such programs, he would uphold such laws. Such pragmatism ensured that only two of the committee's fourteen senators opposed his reappointment.

Indeed, it was Thomas's increasingly outspoken speeches and law review articles, rather than his specific actions as EEOC chief, that earned him the enmity of civil rights leaders. In a well-publicized 1980 interview in the *Atlantic Monthly*, Thomas singled out his own sister to exemplify what he believed were the evils of welfare dependency, claiming that she "gets mad when the mailman is late with her welfare check." (Emma Mae Thomas has rejected this claim, arguing that she was, in fact, employed in a nursing home at the time of her brother's statement and that she had previously gone on welfare to look after their aunt, who had suffered a stroke.) Thomas also made headlines in 1984, when he complained to the *Washington Post* that civil rights leaders preferred to "bitch, bitch, bitch, moan and moan, whine and whine" to the media rather than work on the problems faced by black families. Such blunt critiques raised some hackles, from JESSE JACKSON, among others, but they did not prevent President George H. W. Bush from nominating Thomas to the U.S. Circuit Court of Appeals for the District of Columbia in 1989. Several months later the Senate Judiciary Committee voted thirteen to one to confirm his appointment.

President Bush's nomination of Thomas in 1991 to the U.S. Supreme Court proved much more controversial. Although the Bush administration made much of Thomas's personal journey from segregated Pin Point to the federal judiciary, civil rights groups highlighted the nominee's lack of judicial experience. The NAACP, which had not challenged Thomas's previous nominations, eventually opposed him, a major blow to the Bush administration, albeit one that was leavened by opinion polls suggesting that a significant minority of African Americans supported the nominee. Several prominent black businessmen, including JOHN JOHNSON, the publisher of *Ebony* magazine, declared their backing for Thomas, as did the poet MAYA ANGELOU. Like many who defended the nominee, Angelou did so despite her opposition to his record at the EEOC, in the belief that Thomas was "young enough to be won over" to the cause of affirmative action and the goals of the NAACP.

On the eve of the 10 September 1991 Senate hearings on the nomination, most political analysts predicted a tight vote but anticipated that Thomas would be approved. The senators—and the nation at large—could not, however, have anticipated the controversial allegations of Anita Hill, a former aide to Thomas at the Department of Education and the EEOC, who testified to the Senate Judiciary Committee that her boss had sexually harassed her on several occasions. Thomas denied Hill's allegation that he had tormented her with sexual innuendo and had persisted in his graphic descriptions of pornographic movies and boasts about his sexual prowess, even though she had asked him to desist. Indeed, in the glare of the massed ranks of the media and with millions watching on television, the nominee condemned the allegations as part of a cynical attempt to derail his nomination. Using a metaphor that angered many of his black critics but also earned him sympathy among some African Americans, Thomas claimed to be the victim of a "high-tech lynching for uppity blacks" who refused to toe the line with the liberal civil rights establishment.

Hill's allegations and Thomas's denials transformed the hearings. Republicans rallied around the nominee, although some partisans appeared even more interested in casting aspersions on Hill's character and credibility. The judge, for his part, believed that his political opponents and the media had maliciously intruded on his private life, and he resented press coverage that he thought was critical of Virginia Lamp Thomas, whom he had married in 1987 and who was white. Opinion polls

taken immediately after Hill's testimony indicated that a majority of both black and white Americans believed the judge, not Hill. Poll data suggesting that southern blacks were particularly supportive of Thomas also persuaded several previously uncommitted southern Democrats to vote for him. On 15 October enough of these Democrats voted for Thomas to secure his confirmation by fifty-two votes to forty-eight.

During the next few months, however, it became clear that the Hill-Thomas hearings had sparked a national debate on the issue of sexual harassment and that public opinion had turned in favor of believing Hill's allegations. The National Organization for Women and other feminist groups were already opposed to Thomas for his declared opposition to affirmative action and for speeches in which he opposed a woman's right to an abortion. The skeptical questioning of Hill by the all-white and all-male Judiciary Committee prompted these groups to mount a crusade against sexual harassment in the workforce and also encouraged several women to run for the U.S. Senate in 1992. One of them, CAROL MOSELEY BRAUN, became the

Justice Clarence Thomas, then Supreme Court nominee, testifies before the Senate Judiciary Committee on 12 October 1991 in Washington. Thomas was later confirmed as an associate justice of the Supreme Court on 15 October 1991. (AP Images.)

first African American woman and the first black Democrat elected to that chamber.

The consistently conservative cast of Justice Thomas's judicial opinions and votes disappointed those who believed that he would have a liberal change of heart once he was on the bench. Even so, in 2002 he received praise from some of his detractors for his efforts to end First Amendment protection of cross burning. On the whole, however, Thomas has proved to be no less determined in his conservative beliefs than his predecessor THURGOOD MARSHALL was in his liberal views. In affirmative action cases such as *Aderand Constructors v. Pena* (1995), Thomas voted with the majority to weaken federal guarantees that minority firms receive a portion of government contracts. Significantly, his opinion noted that his own grandfather had not needed racial preferences to obtain contracts for his fuel business. He was also in the majority in voting rights cases, such as *Shaw v. Reno* (1993), which weakened the use of race in determining the composition of congressional districts. Liberal civil rights advocates have expressed particular hostility to Thomas's position in cases involving the constitutional rights of criminal defendants, notably his dissent in *Hudson v. McMillan* (1992), in which he declared that the beating of a prisoner by his guards was neither cruel nor unusual punishment.

Justice Thomas and his fellow conservatives on the bench set aside their general disposition to favor states rights in the 2000 presidential election case of *Bush v. Gore*, overturning the Florida Supreme Court's opinion that the state should continue its recount of questionable ballot tallies. That decision gave George W. Bush the presidency and ensured an administration that, like Thomas, opposed affirmative action, favored the death penalty, and sought to limit abortion rights. During his bruising confirmation process in 1991, Thomas's views had appeared wildly radical to many commentators. A decade later those views had entered the mainstream of American politics.

Indeed, by the 20th anniversary of Thomas's appointment in 2011, some Supreme Court observers noted that Thomas had in many respects become the Court's intellectual focal point and leader. According to *The New Yorker's* Jeffrey Toobin, Thomas's continued refusal to participate in oral argument obscures for many the intellectual heft of his written opinions, which have been praised on both the left and the right. Akhil Reed Amar, a liberal Yale Law School professor, has compared Thomas to Justice Hugo Black, whose dissents on

issues of free speech in the 1930s and 1940s were viewed as quixotic, but which ultimately came to define the liberalism of the Warren Court in the 1950s and 1960s. Likewise, by 2011, Thomas's once lonely positions on the free speech rights of corporations, the right to bear arms, and the powers of the federal government had come to be joined by George W. Bush appointees Samuel Alito and Chief Justice John Roberts, as well as Thomas's fellow originalist, Antonin Scalia. In several important cases, notably in the 2010 *Citizens United* case that invalidated the McCain-Feingold Bipartisan Campaign Reform Act of 2002, even the moderate conservative, Anthony Kennedy, followed Thomas's claim that there is no difference, under the First Amendment, between an individual and a corporation, and that any limitations on campaign spending are thereby a restriction of First Amendment rights.

Thomas has remained a controversial figure. In 2010 the political activities of his wife on behalf of the right wing Tea Party and, in particular, her role in lobbying against the BARACK OBAMA administration's Affordable Care Act, prompted some critics to suggest he should recuse himself from any Supreme Court ruling involving that legislation. Thomas has given no indication that he should do so. In 2007, Thomas published an autobiography, *My Grandfather's Son: A Memoir*.

FURTHER READING

Greenya, John. *Silent Justice: The Clarence Thomas Story* (2001).

Mayer, Jane, and Jill Abramson. *Strange Justice: The Selling of Clarence Thomas* (1994).

Morrison, Toni, ed. *Racing Justice, En-gendering Power: Essays on Anita Hill, Clarence Thomas, and the Construction of Social Reality* (1992).

Thomas, Andrew Peyton. *Clarence Thomas: A Biography* (2001).

Toobin, Jeffrey. "Partners: Will Clarence and Virginia Thomas Succeed in Killing Obama's Health-care Plan?" *The New Yorker*, 29 Aug. 2011.

STEVEN J. NIVEN

Thomas, Cora Ann Pair (8 Sept. 1875–10 May 1952), principal, missionary, and mission superintendent, was born Cora Ann Pair in the village of Shotwell (later Knightsdale), Wake County, North Carolina, the second of twelve children of Harmon Pair, a minister. Her mother's name is unknown. She attended and completed the high school in Shotwell and then entered Shaw University in Raleigh, North Carolina.

Thomas graduated from Shaw in 1895 with a higher English diploma. In the nineteenth century, historically black colleges and universities provided students with an education from elementary to high school. The majority of the slaves who gained their freedom in 1865 were illiterate, and any school they attended would have had to begin with a basic education. Thomas received a higher English diploma, which meant she had majored in English and earned at least a high school diploma.

After graduation, Thomas served as principal of an orphanage in Oxford, North Carolina. Between 1904 and 1906 she took postgraduate courses in missionary training at the theological school of Fisk University in Nashville, Tennessee. In November 1908 she married William Henry Thomas, who had been born in Jamaica but came to the United States to complete his higher education. The couple met at Shaw University, where William Thomas earned his AB and BTh degrees. The month after their marriage, the Lott Carey Convention (LCC) sent the Thomases to work in Brewerville, fifteen miles from Monrovia, Liberia. Cora Thomas was sponsored by the Women's Baptist Missionary Convention of North Carolina.

A lack of financial resources limited the missionary activities of the LCC and the National Baptist Convention to West Africa. By 1915 the LCC had placed most of its American-born missionaries in Liberia. In that country the LCC built on the foundation that had been laid by James O. Hayes, the first missionary of the Baptist State Convention of North Carolina.

The Thomases arrived in Liberia early in 1909. Shortly after their arrival, William Thomas became a naturalized Liberian citizen, although Cora Thomas did not do so, probably because she still had family in the United States or because she planned to return to the United States when her missionary assignment ended. At Brewerville, William Thomas served as superintendent of the Lott Carey Mission and expanded the work of the LCC in Liberia. He also extended the work of the convention in Liberia into a pioneer area, that of journalism. For a while he operated the only printing press among black Baptists in Liberia. In 1909 he began publication of the *Watchman*, a monthly paper of the Brewerville station. A number of churches in Africa had printing presses to spread their message among the indigenous people.

Meanwhile Cora Thomas taught at the Lott Carey Mission School in Brewerville. Hundreds of boys and girls and young men and women attended the mission school. They graduated and went back into the community to work as teachers, ministers, and business and political leaders in Liberia.

William and Cora Thomas worked together at the Lott Carey Mission for thirty-three years with a few furloughs to the United States. During that time William Thomas served as superintendent of the mission and principal of the Baptist boarding high school as well as preacher and teacher at the Lott Carey Mission School in Brewerville. He died in Liberia on 4 September 1942 and was buried on the mission station. The couple had four sons, all born in Brewerville.

After her husband's death, Cora Thomas was appointed superintendent of the mission, succeeding her husband and continuing the work he had begun. She served in that capacity for four years. In 1946 she left Liberia because of failing health but returned to the country in November 1951 with the Lott Carey Pilgrimage Group. After a severe attack of malaria, she died in Brewerville, Liberia. She was buried on the Lott Carey Mission School campus next to her husband.

FURTHER READING

Boone, Clinton C. *Liberia as I Know It* (1929).

Fitts, Leroy. *Lott Carey: First Black Missionary to Africa* (1978).

Freeman, Edward A. *The Epoch of Negro Baptists and the Foreign Mission Board* (1953).

Martin, Sandy D. *Black Baptists and African Missions: The Origins of a Movement, 1880–1915* (1989).

Rux, Mattie E., and Mary M. Ransome. *Fifty Years of Pioneering in Christian Missions: History of the Woman's Auxiliary to the Lott Carey Baptist Foreign Mission Convention, 1900–1956* (n.d.).

SYLVIA M. JACOBS

Thomas, Edna Lewis (1886–22 July 1974), actress, was born in Lawrenceville, Virginia, but grew up, from the age of one, in Boston. No information about her parents is available. At the age of sixteen she married Lloyd Thomas, the owner of a custom tailoring business. It is not known when the couple left Boston, but by 1918 they were living in Harlem, where Edna Thomas performed in a benefit performance for Rosamond Johnson's music school at the Lafayette Theatre. The elegant Thomas, who looked much younger than her thirty-two years, was pursued by the Lafayette manager Lester Walton to become a member of the stock company. Despite her husband's objections, Thomas finally succumbed, making her professional debut in Frank Wilson's

Confidence at the Putnam Theatre in Brooklyn. Thomas quickly became a Lafayette favorite, appearing over the next several years in *Turn to the Right*, *The Two Orphans*, *Nothing But the Truth*, *Are You a Mason?*, *Within the Law*, *The Cat and the Canary*, and *Rain*. In 1923 she replaced EVELYN PREER in the Ethiopian Art Theatre's *Salome*. She also appeared in the Ethiopian Art Theatre's *Comedy of Errors* and *The Gold Front Stores*. The critic Theophilus Lewis recalled Thomas's "delightful gold digger" as a "moment of glory" in the theater (Black Theatre Scrapbook).

In 1925 Thomas portrayed Celie in Eugene O'Neill's *The Dreamy Kid*, a curtain-raiser to *The Emperor Jones* with PAUL ROBESON. In 1927 Thomas joined the cast of David Belasco's sensational *Lulu Belle*, for which the Boston-bred, light-complexioned Thomas had to "black up" and learn a southern dialect, which she accomplished by studying the dialect poems of PAUL LAURENCE DUNBAR. In 1928 Thomas performed *Why Women Cheat* and *In the Underworld* for the Alhambra Players. In the fall of that year Thomas replaced Marie Young as Clara in *Porgy*, traveling to London with the company. By this time Thomas was well established as one of the artistic and cultural leaders of the Harlem Renaissance, an intimate friend of LANGSTON HUGHES, A'LELIA WALKER, Carl Van Vechten, JAMES WELDON JOHNSON, Grace Nail Johnson, FREDI WASHINGTON, and Olivia Wyndham, who shared a home with Thomas and her husband.

In 1930 Thomas appeared as Dr. Bess on Carlton Moss's *Careless Love* radio program; in 1932 she was back on Broadway in *Ol' Man Satan*, playing Maggie (Mary Magdalene). The following year Thomas played Ella, a faithful, forgiving wife, opposite her friend Fredi Washington's temptress, Sulamai, in Hall Johnson's *Run Little Chillun*. Along with Washington, Thomas auditioned for the celebrated role of Peola, a black girl who passes for white, in the 1934 film *Imitation of Life*. Washington got the role, but the two friends shared the common dilemma of being black actors who did not look or sound black enough for unimaginative casting directors. As Thomas recalled, she was frequently dismissed as "too refined, too cultured, too white—when all the time every beat of my heart was Negro" (Thomas clippings file, Billy Rose Theatre Collection).

From 1934 to 1935 Thomas appeared in the Theatre Union's acclaimed and controversial *Stevedore*, a dramatization of labor and racial conflicts that Congress condemned as Communist propaganda. The producers and performers of *Stevedore* were interested in protesting racial and class injustices, and they gave benefit performances for the League of Struggle for Negro Rights, the Actors Fund, and the Scottsboro Defense Fund (aimed to help free the nine young men falsely accused of rape in Scottsboro, Alabama). In 1936 Thomas performed the role of Lady Macbeth in one of the era's most notable theatrical events, Orson Welles's *Macbeth* for the New York Negro Unit of the Federal Theatre Project (FTP). Set in Haiti and featuring an all-black cast, *Macbeth* was a sensation seen by more than one hundred thousand people, greatly admired by many, and discussed by everyone. Thomas was also generally applauded for her portrayal of Lavinia in the FTP's *Androcles and the Lion*.

In addition to performing, Thomas was an administrative assistant for the FTP, and in 1939 she was appointed acting head supervisor for all FTP Negro productions, replacing J. Augustus Smith in that capacity. After Congress dismantled the FTP in 1939, Thomas was instrumental in helping found a playwrights' company to carry on the momentum garnered by the Negro units of the FTP in fostering black artists. Thomas was on the board of directors of the Negro Playwrights Company, which produced Theodore Ward's *Big White Fog* in 1940 at the Lincoln Theatre. Thomas was also a founder and leader of the Negro Actors Guild, serving as a vice president from 1938 to 1939 and as acting executive secretary in 1941.

Thomas returned to Broadway in 1943 as Sukey, a runaway slave, in the long-running *Harriet*, with Helen Hayes. In 1945 Thomas took on another controversial role, as a southern woman desperate to protect her son in the antilynching drama *Strange Fruit*. From 1947 to 1950 Thomas portrayed the Mexican flower vendor in *A Streetcar Named Desire*, in the original Broadway production with Marlon Brando and Jessica Tandy, on tour with Anthony Quinn and Uta Hagen, and in the film version with Brando and Vivien Leigh. She also made guest appearances on television's *The Enforcer* and *Take a Giant Step*.

In the late 1960s Thomas lost the two people she loved most: her intimate friend Olivia died in 1967, and the following year Lloyd Thomas died. The three had lived together since at least the 1920s. Edna Thomas died in New York, of heart disease, six years later. In 1982 one of her FTP collaborators, the musician Leonard Paur, provided this assessment of her unique gifts: "There was about her a sense of quality and absolute total professionalism which permeated not only her performance, but affected the performance of everyone involved with her. She lifted her stage by reason of her own integrity and greatness" (Gill, 75).

FURTHER READING

A clippings file on Edna Thomas is available in the Billy Rose Theatre Collection, New York Library of the Performing Arts. Programs and clippings related to productions in which Thomas appeared may also be found in the Billy Rose Theatre Collection, as well as in the Black Theatre Scrapbook and Fredi Washington Papers, both at the Schomburg Center for Research in Black Culture, New York Public Library. Correspondence between Thomas and Carl Van Vechten, Grace Nail Johnson, and others is held in the James Weldon Johnson Collection, Yale Collection of American Literature, Beinecke Library.

Gill, Glenda E. *White Grease Paint on Black Performers: A Study of the Federal Theatre, 1935–39* (1988).

Obituaries: *New York Times*, 24 July 1974; *Variety*, 31 July 1974.

CHERYL BLACK

Thomas, Frank P. (13 May 1913–15 July 1974), journalist, civil rights advocate, and entrepreneur, was born Frank Pierce Thomas in Tuscaloosa, Alabama, the son of Franklin Thomas and Maggie Mabry. As a fireman for the Mobile and Ohio Railroad, his father earned a decent living for the family. The elder Thomas was a native of Barber County, Alabama, the home of the legendary segregationist governor George C. Wallace. Maggie Mabry Thomas was the daughter of former slaves who migrated to Tuscaloosa. The Thomases were progressive and taught their only child to be disciplined and to value education and hard work. Frank, who grew up in some of the most racially turbulent years in Alabama, used these values to become one of Mobile's most respected and accomplished black leaders.

Thomas's first love was writing, which he discovered as a young child. At the age of eight he hawked the *Birmingham Age Herald*. He later became an agent and circulation director for the *Herald* in Tuscaloosa. In high school Thomas honed his skills by working as a reporter and agent for the *Birmingham Reporter* and the *Tuscaloosa Warrior* and as a reporter and circulation supervisor for the *Tuscaloosa News*. After graduating from high school in Tuscaloosa during the late 1920s, Thomas attended Stillman College in Tuscaloosa for two years. While there, he edited the school's newspaper

and worked as a correspondent and circulation representative for the *Atlanta Daily World* and the *Birmingham World*.

In 1933 Thomas began working as editor of the *Tuscaloosa World*, a Scott Syndicate newspaper that also published the *Atlanta Daily World*. Thomas had a heart for civil rights and believed that, as a member of the media, he would have an outlet for his ideas. His blunt and uncompromising articles often antagonized whites and blacks. In 1933 he published articles supporting three black men who had been accused of murdering a white girl in Tuscaloosa. Deputy sheriffs dragged two of these men from their jail cell and shot them to death. Believing that the men were innocent, Thomas defended the murdered men in the *Tuscaloosa World*. As a result, a lynch mob forced him to flee to Montgomery.

In Montgomery, Thomas attended Alabama Teachers College and began writing for the weekly black newspaper the *Montgomery World*. Although Thomas earned a teacher's certificate at Alabama Teachers College in 1936, he did not earn a bachelor's degree because his interest was in journalism. In Montgomery he met Lancie Black, whom he married in December 1938. They had one daughter. Black was a Tuskegee College alumna with a degree in Economics. Eloquent and intellectually gifted, she had a lifelong impact on her husband.

From there the Thomases traveled to Birmingham, where Thomas became an editor for the *Birmingham World*. In 1942, during the booming wartime economy, Thomas moved his family to Mobile, where he launched the *Mobile Weekly Review*, a regional version of the *Tuscaloosa Review*. He worked briefly with Mobile's civil rights leaders, including JOHN L. LeFLORE, on issues of social inequity. Thomas believed that the military offered blacks more social and educational opportunities than civilian life did, and he enlisted in the U.S. Navy in late 1942. However, when a physical examination revealed an asthmatic condition, he received an honorable discharge and moved his family to Chicago for a short stint.

By the mid-1940s Thomas had returned to Tuscaloosa, and with his wife he started the *Alabama Citizen*. The *Citizen* quickly became a vocal opponent of racial injustice. Hard work and dedication soon allowed the Thomases to have offices in both Tuscaloosa and Selma, Alabama.

The early 1950s helped cement Thomas's legacy. First, he took journalism courses under the renowned professor and journalist Armistead Pride at Lincoln University in Jefferson County,

Missouri, and he also attended the Megenthaler Linotype School in New York, where he learned to be a linotype operator. Both proved invaluable in the next phase of his life. Second, his family and their paper were threatened after the Thomases accompanied AUTHERINE LUCY to the University of Alabama, where she was applying to the graduate program in 1952. When a mob arrived at the newspaper to demolish the machines and kill the staff, it was deterred by several hundred blacks armed with rifles, shotguns, knives, and baseball bats. Although violence forced the university to dismiss Lucy after attending classes only three days, their efforts led to Lucy becoming the first African American admitted to the university in 1956. The Lucy case would have a direct impact on the admission of VIVIAN MALONE and James Hood—the first African Americans to attend the university at the undergraduate level in 1963.

Thomas was a resident of Tuscaloosa from the mid-1940s to the early 1950s, but his earlier stay in Mobile endeared him to that city. As a result he commuted often to Mobile until he became a permanent resident in 1954. When Thomas returned in 1954, the *Mobile Review*, which he had started in 1942, had been taken over by the *Gulf Informer*, a subsidiary of the Mobile Press Forum Sun. However, that same year I.H. Rhone, editor of the *Gulf Informer*, died. Thomas became the editor of the *Informer* and changed its name to the *Mobile Beacon*, the moniker that it carried into the early twenty-first century. Thomas again joined forces with men like LeFlore, and the *Beacon* emerged as the voice of Mobile's civil rights movement. Through the *Mobile Beacon* the black community obtained the information it needed to comprehend and confront racism and racial inequality in Mobile. In 1964 the *Alabama Citizen* and the *Mobile Beacon* merged.

Thomas remained a central figure in the struggle for civil rights in Mobile until his death there in 1974. However, his legacy continued to grow. He was posthumously inducted into the Alabama Newspaper Hall of Honor at Auburn University in 1983, he was enshrined in the Black Press Gallery of Distinguished Newspaper Publishers at Howard University in 1988, and he was inducted into the Alabama Newspaper Hall of Honor at the University of Alabama in 1993. His commitment to human equality throughout the state but particularly in Mobile was integral to the success of the civil rights struggle in Alabama. His courage to stand against social injustice despite numerous threats against his life and his family and his remarkable passion and skill as a journalist made life better for all blacks in Alabama.

FURTHER READING

Melton McLaurin's Oral Interview Project, which includes a personal interview with Thomas, and the John LeFlore Papers, which include a detailed record of his leadership in the Mobile National Association for the Advancement of Colored People (NAACP) and personal interviews, are available at the University of South Alabama Archives in Mobile. Information on Thomas is in the Branch Files of the NAACP, Manuscript Division, Library of Congress, Washington, D.C.

TIMOTHY MARTIN BROUGHTON

Thomas, Franklin Augustine (27 May 1934–), attorney and philanthropic foundation president, was born in New York City to James Thomas, a laborer, and Viola (Atherley) Thomas, a housekeeper. Thomas grew up in the Bedford-Stuyvesant section of Brooklyn, the youngest of six children in a close-knit family of West Indies heritage. When Franklin was eleven years old, his father died, and his mother took a second job during World War II as a machinist to support the family. However, when the war ended and the soldiers returned home, many companies replaced the minorities and women they had hired with war veterans, and Thomas's mother lost her machinist position.

Despite the violent atmosphere in his neighborhood, Thomas was a well adjusted child socially and academically. He was a Boy Scout and an excellent student who maintained high course marks. By the time he entered Franklin J. Lane High School, he stood six feet four inches tall and was a natural basketball player. He played the star center position on his school team, and his teachers often referred to him as a leading example for other students. In his senior year of high school, Thomas was offered both sports and academic scholarships from several universities.

He accepted the academic scholarship from Columbia University and continued to play basketball in college, becoming the first African American to be captain of an Ivy League basketball team. In 1955 and 1956, he was voted the league's most valuable player. While attending Columbia, Thomas became involved with NAACP efforts to increase the enrollment of African Americans at the school. In 1956 he graduated with a bachelor's degree. He had also completed Reserve Officers Training

Corps (ROTC) training, which earned him a commission in the U.S. Air Force, where he served for four years. Thomas was a captain and eventually flew missions as a navigator with the Strategic Air Command. He left the air force in 1960 to attend Columbia Law School, and he graduated with an LLB degree in 1963 with moot court honors. He was admitted to the New York state bar in 1964.

From 1964 to 1965, Thomas served as an assistant U.S. attorney in New York and then worked as New York's deputy police commissioner for legal matters (and was the city's only African American deputy police commissioner) from 1965 until 1968. In 1967 U.S. Senator Robert F. Kennedy (D.-N.Y.), seeking a way to improve the living conditions in the Bedford-Stuyvesant neighborhood, created a nonprofit community development agency to raise and coordinate redevelopment funds. Thomas was recommended to Kennedy as a possible candidate to run the agency. Upon meeting with the young attorney, Kennedy was impressed and appointed Thomas as president and CEO of the new Bedford-Stuyvesant Restoration Corporation.

For the next ten years he worked to improve the Bedford-Stuyvesant community, successfully raising and managing $63 million for urban restoration. Under his direction, job training, financial opportunities, and community facilities were provided for residents. A 200,000-square-foot shopping complex was built, 400 brownstone buildings were restored, 120 neighborhood businesses were created or expanded, three new apartment complexes were built, a $21 million mortgage pool was created, and the Billie Holiday Theater was established. More than 7,000 residents were placed in jobs, and a major corporation, IBM, opened offices in the neighborhood. Thomas's urban redevelopment program became a model for many other community-based development programs across the country. His work earned him a national reputation, and he was offered, but declined, many job opportunities—including a cabinet position as the secretary of Housing and Urban Development under President Jimmy Carter. During his tenure at Bedford-Stuyvesant Restoration Corporation, Thomas served on the board of directors for many large, high-profile corporations like AT&T, CBS, Citibank, and the Cummins engine company.

In 1977 he left the Bedford-Stuyvesant Restoration Corporation and returned to the law. He held a private practice from 1977 to 1979, and headed New York's John Hay Whitney Foundation. Thomas served on the Ford Foundation board for two years beginning in 1978 and became its chief officer in 1980 following the retirement of McGeorge Bundy. The Ford Foundation was one of the largest philanthropic organizations in the country. When Thomas took over the foundation as chief officer, its assets had declined from $4 billion to $2.8 billion. Under his direction the organization was reorganized and redirected to focus on education, foreign policy, and immigration studies. He partnered the foundation with corporations to provide financial resources for urban renewal, human rights, and Third World development projects. By the time Thomas left the foundation in 1996, the Ford Foundation endowment had grown to $5.8 billion.

Thomas was named one of four "kingmakers" in corporate America by *Fortune* magazine (11 Aug. 2003). He also received many prestigious awards, including the Lyndon Baines Johnson Award (1974); the John Jay and Alexander Hamilton Awards (1983); the Columbia University Medal of Excellence (1976); and the Council on Foundation's Distinguished Grantmaker Award (1995). He also received honorary degrees from Yale University (1970), from Fordham University (1972), from the Pratt Institute (1974), from Pace University (1977), and from his alma mater, Columbia University (1979).

After leaving the Ford Foundation, Thomas served on the board of directors of many large companies, such as Lucent Technologies and PepsiCo, and he worked as a consultant for the TFF Study Group, a nonprofit organization dedicated to renewal and development in South Africa. Thomas chaired the September 11th Fund, which offered financial relief for the victims of 11 September 2001 terrorist attacks.

FURTHER READING
"Franklin A. Thomas," *Contemporary Black Biography*, vol. 49 (2005).
"Franklin A. Thomas," *Notable Black American Men* (1998).
Thomas, Franklin A. *Ford Foundation Report* (2005). www.fordfoundation.org.

ANGELA BLACK

Thomas, Irma (14 Feb. 1941–), singer and business owner, was born Irma Lee in Ponchatoula, Louisiana, the daughter of Percy Lee, a steel mill worker and longshoreman, and Vadar (maiden name unknown), an elevator operator. At the age of three, Irma moved to New Orleans with her parents, but when the time came for her to start first grade, she returned to the country to live with her aunt. When she was in fourth grade, she moved back to New Orleans to stay.

In New Orleans, Irma, whose other musical influences included singing in church and listening to records of her father's favorites, like PERCY MAYFIELD and MAHALIA JACKSON, soaked up the emerging rhythm and blues scene of the city. At age fourteen, however, her youth came to a sudden halt when she became pregnant. Her parents insisted that she marry the father of the child, Eugene Jones. Irma's mother cared for the child while Irma worked nights washing dishes at a restaurant. The marriage did not succeed. By the time she was eighteen Irma was living with Andrew Thomas, had three children, and was waiting tables at a club. She pestered the leader of the house band, the Untouchables, until he gave her a tryout in 1959. The club's owner fired her for not keeping an eye on the customers, but the Untouchables had a new female singer. Throughout the 1950s one of the typical patterns of New Orleans rhythm and blues music, in addition to relentless eclecticism and innovation (a constant in all the city's music scenes over time), was a piano-led band with a female lead singer. By 1960 she also had her own recording contract with Minit Records in New Orleans. Right before joining Minit, she put out her first hit, "(You Can Have My Husband, but Please) Don't Mess with My Man," with Ron, an even smaller local label. This single peaked at number 22 on the national rhythm and blues chart in the summer of 1959. However, music historians agree that the flip side of that almost risqué 45, "Set Me Free," was more effective at suggesting the depth of her talents. From 1961 to 1963, working with ALLEN TOUSSAINT as her producer in the Minit studios, Thomas recorded a string of powerful singles that showcased her smoky, evocative, accomplished vocal talents. These included standouts like "It's Raining" and "Too Soon to Know." None quite hit the heights of popularity that other African American female singers of her generation were achieving, but most were solid sellers in the southern rhythm and blues market. She was popular enough that Coca-Cola hired her to endorse its product in regional newspapers and magazines, making her one of the first African Americans hired by a large, white-owned corporation for that job.

In 1964 Thomas, who usually worked with songs from other writers, penned "Wish Someone Would Care." She had married Thomas in 1962 but was now in the process of a divorce again, and her record label had been bought by the larger

Irma Thomas, blues singer, during an interview at her home in New Orleans, Louisiana, 21 April 1989. (AP Images.)

company Liberty, which released the ballad she had just written and watched it rise to number 17 on the *Billboard* national charts. The B-side of that single was "Time Is on My Side," originally written by Jerry Rogovy for the jazz trombonist Kai Winding but now recorded with new lyrics written by Thomas. It became a huge hit, but not for Thomas. Instead, the British blues borrowers the Rolling Stones released their own note-for-note copy in 1964, and it became their first top-ten hit in the United States.

Meanwhile Thomas released a string of other mid-level hits in the mid-1960s. Much of the decade was also spent touring the college circuit, playing at hundreds of southern fraternity and sorority parties. After about 1965, however, changing popular music tastes limited the marketability of her recorded music. She moved to the famed blues label Chess in 1967, but her recordings for them at the Muscle Shoals studio in Alabama did not pay off. After they released a few underpromoted singles, she split with the label. Her stay with Atlantic, perhaps the premier soul music label, was also short and unsatisfying. She complained later that the producers there had been trying to make her sound like DIANA ROSS, whose trilling girl-group tones were about as different from Thomas's rich, bluesy voice as another set of rhythm and blues pipes could possibly be. In 1969, after Hurricane Camille wiped out many of the local clubs where Thomas played, she moved to Los Angeles, where she took a job selling auto parts. Although she played at various venues in California and released a couple of singles and one album, *In between Tears* (1973), with the local label Fungus, her career appeared to be on the decline.

Thomas moved back to New Orleans in 1976. The next year she married Emile Jackson. Her attempts to break back into the recording business were frustrating, but she continued to play locally. She also launched new sidelines, capitalizing on the title of her collection of 1960s hits, *Soul Queen of New Orleans* (Maison du Soul, 1977), by appearing in a number of local television commercials. Thomas also opened up a club called the Lion's Den in New Orleans. She released another album, *Safe with Me* (1980), with the label Maison du Soul, but that also floundered.

In 1986 Rounder Records approached Thomas about signing with them. She did so and revived her recording career. Her third album with Rounder, *Live! Simply the Best* (1990), won a Grammy nomination. She released a gospel album a few years later, and her other albums included a collaboration with the white blues singers Tracy Nelson and Marcia Ball and a collection of the songs of Dan Penn, who wrote or cowrote several 1960s soul music hits.

By 2006 Thomas had released ten albums of new recordings and one compilation with Rounder in twenty years. She continued to mix rhythm and blues and soul standards with new material. Her music defied categorization, as did her voice, which moved easily from up-tempo to ballads, from modern-sounding rhythm and blues smoothness to growling blues to shouting gospel praise. The title "Soul Queen of New Orleans," officially awarded to her by the mayor of the city in a 1989 ceremony, merely evoked the decade of her greatest hits—the 1960s—rather than describing her soul genre. She also made an effort to select mature material, suitable for a woman who looked young for a grandmother but who had seen and learned a lot in her life. This careful effort paid off with another Grammy nomination, this one for her collaboration with Ball and Nelson, *Sing It* (Rounder, 1998).

When Hurricane Katrina hit New Orleans at the end of August 2005, followed by the man-made disaster of the flood and the federal government's inept response to the resulting humanitarian crisis, Thomas was singing in Austin, Texas. Some months later, when she was finally able to reenter the city, she found her club devastated. Her return to the club makes a memorable scene in Robert Mugge's documentary *New Orleans Music in Exile* (2006). She had already selected most of the songs for her new album *After the Rain* (2006) before Katrina hit. But the recording of tracks like the blues classic "Another Man Done Gone" took on a new depth of meaning when she sang "Another man done gone / The water's at his door, he couldn't stay no more…. I didn't know his name, so many fled that day / Another man done gone." In 2007 *After the Rain* was awarded the Grammy for best blues album released in 2006.

FURTHER READING

Hannusch, Jeff. *I Hear You Knockin': The Sound of New Orleans Rhythm and Blues* (1985).

Ilva, Jyrki. "Irma Thomas: The Soul Queen of New Orleans." Available at www.helsinki.fi/~ilva/irma .html.

Sinclair, John. "An Audience with the Soul Queen of New Orleans," *Blues Access* (Spring 2000).

EDWARD E. BAPTIST

Thomas, Isiah Lord, III (30 April 1961–), professional basketball player, coach, and front-office executive, was born in Chicago, Illinois, the youngest of nine children of Isiah Thomas II, a plant foreman, and Mary Thomas, a civil servant. The family lived in a poor, high-crime neighborhood on the city's west side. Thomas's father lost his job at International Harvester, was forced to work as a janitor, and, when Thomas was three years old, left the family. His mother held the family together, attempting to insulate the children from drug abuse and violent crime, even to the point of once using a shotgun to scare off neighborhood gang members.

Growing up in such difficult circumstances under the protection of his older siblings, Thomas developed a veneer of smiling innocence that hid a street-smart inner toughness. Seeing the Harlem Globetrotters play basketball ignited a desire in the young Thomas to master the game himself. As a high school junior at St. Joseph's in Westchester, he led his team to an appearance in the 1978 Illinois state championship game. Thomas played on the undefeated U.S. gold medal-winning team, coached by Indiana

University's Bob Knight, at the 1979 Pan American Games held in Puerto Rico.

Entering Indiana as a freshman in the fall of 1979, Thomas stayed there only two years. As a freshman, he averaged almost fifteen points per game and was selected the following summer for the U.S. Olympic team that was ultimately unable to play because of the U.S. boycott of the 1980 Olympics held in Russia. Returning to Indiana that fall, Thomas led the Hoosiers to the 1981 National Collegiate Athletic Association title despite clashing frequently with the equally strong-willed Knight. Thomas elected not to return for his junior year and was selected by the Detroit Pistons as the second overall pick in the 1981 National Basketball Association (NBA) draft (he later patched up his relationship with Knight and completed his bachelor's degree in criminal justice at Indiana in 1987).

Thomas's thirteen-year tenure as a professional player, taken together with his subsequent career as coach and front-office executive, was characterized by dazzling highs and crushing lows. The Pistons were a dismal team in 1981–1982, Thomas's rookie year, posting a 21–61 record. Thomas established himself as the leader of the Pistons even as a roster of skilled and hard-nosed players, including Kelly Tripucka, Bill Laimbeer, Vinnie Johnson, Joe Dumars, Dennis Rodman, Rick Mahorn, and Adrian Dantley, was gradually built around him. Averaging more than twenty points per game from 1982–1983 to 1986–1987, Thomas gained universal respect around the NBA for his toughness and ability to finish games strongly. He also worked tirelessly to raise money for charities and to promote education, going so far as to personally pay the college tuition for dozens of students.

Isiah Thomas married Lynn Kendall, a teacher, in 1985. They had a daughter, Lauren, and a son, Joshua.

The Pistons, under head coach Chuck Daly, fought and scraped their way to the 1987 Eastern Conference finals, a brutally physical seven-game series against the celebrated Boston Celtics of Larry Bird, Robert Parish, and Kevin McHale that ended in a three-point Detroit loss in the decisive seventh game. Thomas and the Pistons reached the NBA finals in 1988, only to lose to the defending champion Los Angeles Lakers led by EARVIN "MAGIC" JOHNSON (despite Thomas's NBA playoff-record twenty-five points scored in a single quarter of game six). During the 1988–1989 season, the Pistons (now known to fans as the "Bad Boys") combined balanced team play with a notoriously aggressive,

physically intimidating style to record a 63–19 regular season and a four-game sweep of the Lakers in the finals for their first NBA championship. One year later, the Pistons became the sixth team in NBA history to win back-to-back titles by defeating the Portland Trailblazers. Thomas was named Most Valuable Player of the finals.

During the 1990–1991 season, with Thomas beginning to suffer a string of injuries and rival Michael Jordan reaching peak form, the Pistons were knocked off their NBA Eastern Conference pedestal by the Chicago Bulls. In Detroit's final home game of the 1993–1994 season, Thomas's playing career ended when he tore his Achilles tendon. His career statistics included 18,822 points, 9,061 assists, and 1,861 steals, each a Pistons team record.

The business-savvy Thomas gained administrative experience as president of the NBA Players Association from 1989 to 1994 and by investing in both American Speedy Printing Centers and OmniBanc Corp. He swiftly moved into a second basketball career by becoming head of basketball operations and part owner of the Toronto Raptors in 1995. After leaving that team in 1997, he worked for NBC as a basketball broadcaster and became owner of the professional, non-NBA-affiliated Continental Basketball Association (CBA) in 1999. Although honors for Thomas's playing career continued—in 1997 he was one of fifty players selected to the NBA's Fiftieth Anniversary All-Time Team and he was inducted into the Basketball Hall of Fame in 2000—his management, coaching, and business activities were less successful. The CBA folded in February 2001, with Thomas receiving widespread blame from fans, players, and coaches. Hired to coach the NBA's Indiana Pacers in 2000, Thomas was fired in 2003 when his old on-court foe Larry Bird took over as team president. After joining Madison Square Garden as president of basketball operations with authority over the New York Knicks, Thomas was an active but unsuccessful administrator, deemed a poor judge of talent as a result of lucrative deals given to mediocre players. In 2006 Thomas fired coach Larry Brown and took over coaching duties himself.

New York fans and sportswriters railed against Thomas as the Knicks failed to improve under his coaching. One of the lowest points of his career came on 2 October 2007 when a federal jury found that he had sexually harassed and verbally abused a former Knicks senior vice president of marketing. The jury assessed an $11.5 million judgment against Madison Square Garden, but Thomas escaped financial penalty. He was removed as president and coach of the Knicks in the spring of 2008. In October of that year, news outlets reported that Thomas had attempted suicide with an overdose of sleeping pills, a charge denied at first by Thomas but eventually confirmed during a televised interview on ESPN. On 15 April 2009, Thomas made a new start toward restoring his reputation when he was introduced as the men's basketball coach at Florida International University, a member of the largely unheralded Sun Belt Conference.

FURTHER READING

Challen, Paul. *From the Back Court to the Front Office: The Isiah Thomas Story* (2004).

DAVID BORSVOLD

Thomas, J. J. (25 Dec. 1888–3 Nov. 1963), grassroots organizer, architect, and minister, was born Jasper Jacob Thomas in Mobile County, Alabama, the youngest of three boys. Little is known about Thomas's mother; his father, whose name is not known, was a successful construction worker, a trade that quickly became one of Thomas's passions. Thomas married Mary Whisper in the early 1900s, and they had seven daughters. Thomas also had a son prior to this marriage, but there is no information about the details of this union.

Thomas traveled widely, visiting England and France. In Africa he learned about different architectural styles and cultural, social, and political organization. He admired and corresponded with MARCUS GARVEY, and in Mobile he publicly organized and supported black pride and self-sufficiency projects.

In 1948 Thomas was instrumental in both organizing and directing the strategy for defeating the Boswell Amendment, the most racially discriminatory voting law passed in Alabama since Reconstruction. The Boswell Amendment came on the heels of the *Smith v. Allwright* decision, in which the U.S. Supreme Court ruled the Democratic primary unconstitutional. The Democratic primary was based on a long history of political discrimination. After the Civil War, African Americans began entering the voting process in large numbers. To impede this process, southern Democrats tampered with voting laws to create what became known as the "all-white" Democratic primary. As an all-white party, the Democratic Party initiated measures such as the cumulative poll tax, literacy exams, and other means to disfranchise individuals they considered to be potentially dangerous to the status quo. They were politically conservative southern whites who wanted to create a political machine that would be accountable only to itself. The result of such a prejudicial selection process led to an all-white party that silenced the voice of blacks throughout the South. After the *Allwright* decision, blacks in other states in the South demanded similar legal action. However, conservative leaders enacted policies that either circumvented the abolition of the Democratic primary or established obstacles to African American suffrage. In 1945 Alabama's state legislators passed the Boswell Amendment, which required African Americans who intended to vote in an election to read, write, show understanding, and explain any portion of the U.S. Constitution to the satisfaction of the state's board of registrars. A year later Alabama abolished its Democratic primary but ratified the Boswell Amendment.

Thomas, whose motto was "a voteless people is a hopeless people," identified with frustrated black veterans who had served the United States in World War II but were denied the right to vote upon returning home. Already a member of the Mobile NAACP, Thomas organized the Negro Veteran Voters League (NVVL). By the latter part of the 1940s the activities of the league overshadowed the activities of the local and state NAACP on behalf of black enfranchisement. In 1948 Birmingham's NAACP, working with the Mobile NAACP, took action to repeal the Boswell Amendment. Under the leadership of Thomas, who believed that the Mobile chapter should have initiated the lawsuit, members of the NVVL filed a separate lawsuit (*Davis v. Schnell*), which was heard by the federal district court.

On 7 January 1949 three members of the Mobile federal court ruled that the Boswell Amendment was unconstitutional because it had been used by the Mobile Board of Registrars to prevent Alabama citizens from registering based on their lack of ability to read and comprehend the U.S. Constitution. *Davis v. Schnell* became the landmark case for voting rights in Alabama. The plaintiff successfully argued that the Mobile Board of Registrars violated African Americans' constitutional right to vote. After the defeat of the Boswell Amendment, Thomas organized other efforts to support black enfranchisement in Mobile.

Thomas was also a respected architect. In the early 1940s he designed the Thomas Building on Davis Avenue, the hub of black urbanity in Mobile. The Thomas Building symbolized the prosperity, pride, and culture of Mobile's African American community. As such it was a reflection of progress and independence for black Mobilians. The 2-story, 26-room building housed Thomas's office, a restaurant, a beauty shop, a television repair shop, and rooms for black visitors to Mobile. Also, because of his impeccable reputation in the trades, he was hired to supervise the construction of the Hillsdale Heights project, Mobile's largest housing community for blacks in the 1950s.

Thomas was a deeply religious man who believed that human progress could not happen without education and spiritual values. He was an ordained minister and an associate pastor of the Mount Zion Baptist Church in Mobile.

FURTHER READING

The McLaurin and John LeFlore Papers in the University of South Alabama Archives in Mobile and the Branch Files of the National Association for the Advancement of Colored People, Manuscript Division, Library of Congress, Washington, D.C., have information on Thomas and the Boswell Amendment.

Davis-Horton, Paulette. *The Avenue: The Place, the People, the Memories* (1991).

TIMOTHY MARTIN BROUGHTON

Thomas, Jack (25 Apr. 1924–12 Nov. 1987), World War II and Korean War soldier and Distinguished Service Cross recipient, was born in Dawson, Georgia, the son of the farmer William Thomas. By 1930 William Thomas was a widower and was living with his three young sons, Jack, William Jr., and Hillary, in the home of Millie Brown in Dawson. While still young boys, the Thomas brothers became orphans with the death of their father. Nothing further is known for certain of Jack Thomas's life prior to his joining the army during World War II.

On 4 March 1943, eighteen-year-old Jack Thomas was inducted into the U.S. Army and a week later gained his first taste of army life when he arrived at the Reception Center for new recruits at Fort Benning, Georgia. Shortly thereafter, Thomas was sent westward for further training, arriving at Wolters, Texas, on 23 March. Here, as part of the 66th Infantry Training Battalion, he underwent another week of training before being sent northward to Fort Dix, New Jersey, where he was assigned to the 522nd Quartermaster Truck Regiment on 4 July 1943, the 561st Quartermaster Service Battalion on 27 August, and then the 342nd Quartermaster Service Company on 20 September. Private Jack Thomas remained with this unit when it was shipped overseas on 2 December 1943 from New York, arriving in Scotland on 10 December. For the next thirteen months, Thomas served in his quartermaster unit in the U.K., helping to keep supplies for the Allied forces organized and on the move as operations for the D-Day invasion of Europe progressed from the planning stages to reality by 6 June 1944.

The service of African American soldiers in World War II, men like Jack Thomas, WILLY JAMES, and RUBEN RIVERS, was important to the overall war effort, but is often unheralded. While over one million African Americans served in the army during the war, only several thousand men were actually assigned to combat units and were deployed into battle. Indeed, most men, including Jack Thomas, were assigned to segregated service units, including transportation companies (such as the famed "Red Ball" truckers), quartermaster units, construction battalions, or field artillery regiments serving in secure areas. These units were important to the overall war effort, but it was galling to black soldiers and civic leaders alike that they were not allowed to actively fight for their country due to prevailing racial attitudes and stereotypes. The long-held view by many white senior commanders that as soldiers African Americans were inferior to their white counterparts would be proven wrong when men like Private Jack Thomas were finally given a chance to acquit themselves on the field of battle.

By March 1945 the war in Europe had been dragging on for over five years, while for the last thirteen months Private Jack Thomas had served with his quartermaster unit in England. We know nothing of his thoughts at the time; it is likely that Thomas, like many black soldiers, was anxious to play a greater part in the war than he had been allowed up to that time. Perhaps he was tired of the dreary English weather, or maybe he was fed up with how his fellow American soldiers treated him. While the English people treated the "Black Yanks" (their collective nickname for African American soldiers) very well and welcomed them into their homes, white soldiers were often difficult to deal with, creating an atmosphere that was reminiscent of the American South. Whatever the case may be, when the American army in the spring of 1945 sought black volunteers to serve as replacement soldiers in weary combat units, Jack Thomas was one of about two thousand volunteers accepted for this new role. On 12 March 1945 he was assigned to the Headquarters Company of the 60th Infantry Regiment, 9th Infantry Division, just days after the regiment had crossed the strategic bridge over the Rhine River at Remagen, Germany. Within two weeks, Private Thomas was assigned to Company G of the 60th Infantry Regiment and underwent quick training, earning his Combat Infantry Badge (CIB) on 5 April 1945. Thomas was subsequently assigned to Company E, and just four days after earning the CIB, he was leading a squad in action near the town of Harzgerode, tasked with knocking out an enemy tank that was blocking the American advance. Thomas, "skillfully directing the deployment and firing of his squad ... advanced upon the enemy position and hurled two hand grenades, wounding several hostile soldiers. When two of his men manning a rocket launcher were wounded he picked up the weapon and launched two rockets at the enemy, preventing them from manning the tank. This gallant soldier then picked up one of the rocket launching team who was seriously wounded and with utter disregard for the intense small arms and automatic weapon fire, carried his comrade to safety" (Award of Distinguished Service Cross— Thomas Service Records). Following this successful action, Private Thomas and the men of the 60th Infantry Regiment continued their fighting, mopping up the last remnants of German armed resistance in the area until Germany's final surrender in May 1945.

Though the war in Europe was over, Private Jack Thomas's actions in April had not gone unnoticed; the hard-fighting rookie was recommended for the Distinguished Service Cross (DSC) award by regimental officers for his valorous actions, a decoration second only to the Medal of Honor in the army. The recommendation was subsequently forwarded up the chain of command and initially, like most such recommendations for black soldiers, was denied. However, later research would show that this denial was overridden by none other than General George Patton. If ever a general knew a fighting soldier when he saw one, it was Patton. As a result, by General Order #255 on 18 September 1945, Private First Class Jack Thomas was awarded the DSC. He would be one of only nine African American soldiers to be so decorated during the war. No black soldier during the war was awarded the higher Medal of Honor.

Now promoted to corporal, Jack Thomas remained with the 60th Infantry for only six months, and by 22 August 1945 was serving in the headquarters company of the 350th Field Artillery Battery when he received the DSC. Thomas would subsequently remain in Europe and served in several supply units until his arrival back home in late January 1946. He would continue to serve in the army during the postwar years until his eventual retirement after twenty years service in 1963. During these years, Jack Thomas rose to the rank of staff sergeant and served overseas during the Korean War as part of the 574th and 50th Transportation Heavy Truck companies, but never again served as a combat infantryman.

After retiring from the army, Jack Thomas lived in Albany, Georgia, for many years, not far from his hometown of Dawson. He was married to Elizabeth Childs at an unknown date, probably before he retired, and had one known child, Jack Jr., but nothing further is known of his personal life. Upon his death, he was buried at the Main Post Cemetery at Fort Benning, Georgia, a location at which he had served for a number of years during his army career. While Jack Thomas has remained a largely forgotten figure, his name did come to the fore briefly in the late 1990s, when he was one of ten black soldiers that fought in World War II recommended as possible candidates for the Medal of Honor. Scholars at Shaw University in Raleigh, North Carolina, had been selected by the army to study its awards and decorations practices regarding African American soldiers during World War II, and Jack Thomas was among the nine men identified as DSC recipients whom the army might consider for the Medal of Honor. However, it was not to be; Jack Thomas was one of three men recommended who were subsequently dropped for Medal of Honor consideration without explanation.

FURTHER READING
The service record documents of Jack Thomas's Official Military Personnel File were consulted for this article, obtained via the Freedom of Information Act. The originals are held at the National Archives and Records Administration, St. Louis, Missouri.
Converse, Elliot V., Daniel K. Gibran, John A. Cash, Robert K. Griffith, and Richard H. Kohn. *The Exclusion of Black Soldiers from the Medal of Honor in World War II* (2008).

GLENN ALLEN KNOBLOCK

Thomas, James P. (1827–16 Dec. 1913), entrepreneur and adventurer, was born into slavery in Nashville, Tennessee, the son of a slave, Sally Thomas, and a prominent white jurist, John Catron. Catron, who ended his career as a U.S. Supreme Court justice, did nothing for his son. It was left to Sally Thomas to free him. By taking in laundry, she scraped together

$350 of the four hundred dollars demanded for his freedom. A sympathetic planter, Ephraim Foster, who knew of her fear that her spendthrift master would sell Thomas, lent her the balance. She repaid him, but in order to circumvent Tennessee law, which required newly manumitted slaves to leave the state or forfeit their freedom, Foster agreed to retain legal ownership of Thomas. Foster made it clear, however, that he did not consider Thomas his property.

As a child, Thomas helped his mother in her laundry and attended a school for free people of color in Nashville. Although technically a slave, Sally maintained her own home and business in the city and supported herself and her son. Thomas also gained valuable work experience. From a white physician he learned dentistry and bloodletting, and from an enslaved barber he learned the art of dressing hair and trimming beards. At nineteen he opened his own barbershop. He did well, and his clientele included some of the most distinguished citizens of Nashville.

James Thomas made two trips to the North as a personal attendant to wealthy planters. On the first trip he was still legally a slave, and he was continually being urged to seize his chance and escape. However, he had friends, family, and a thriving business back home. Moreover, after several encounters with the virulent racism of the "free" North, he had no wish to stay. Eventually, Thomas approached Ephraim Foster and asked to have his manumission papers filed in order to make his freedom a legal reality. Foster complied without hesitation. Then, relying on his reputation as a hardworking and trustworthy member of the community, and on the friendship of many in Nashville's white elite, Thomas petitioned the county court to be exempted from the law that would have forced him into exile. The court granted his request.

Despite his material success Thomas was restless, especially after the death of his mother in 1850. He had already been to New Orleans as a teenage slave, working his passage on a steamboat. In 1855 he returned as a freeman. In his memoirs he recalled vibrant antebellum New Orleans, its wealth, its mix of peoples and cultures, and its thriving slave market.

Once back in Nashville, Thomas was intrigued by news of the exploits of the filibuster (and Nashville native) William Walker in Nicaragua. After being defeated in a bid to establish an independent state in northern Mexico, Walker had invaded Nicaragua in 1855, declared himself president, and

sent out a call for volunteers to join the army that he was organizing to defend his new republic. With his nephew, John H. Rapier Jr., Thomas set off to join in what he imagined would be a great and glorious undertaking. Reflecting on his experiences many years later, he observed: "When I was going to Nicaragua people would ask, what are you going there for? I thought it strange to put that question to me when such grand opportunities were presented. ... But before I left [Nicaragua] I was asking myself what did I come here for? ... I did learn that there is a great deal in Immajination." Walker was happy to welcome the two African American freebooters, but Thomas's enthusiasm waned when he learned that Walker planned to reintroduce slavery into the territory that he controlled. Thomas and Rapier returned home, but Thomas remained in contact with Walker. Both Walker and his brother tried to persuade Thomas to go back to Nicaragua on a second foray.

Back in Nashville, Thomas did not stay put for long. His travels took him to Wisconsin, back to Tennessee, to Iowa, and then to Kansas. In 1857 he arrived in St. Louis. There he found work as a steward on a steamboat and as a barber at the elegant barbershop and baths operated by Henry Clamorgan. Henry's half brother, CYPRIAN CLAMORGAN, also befriended Thomas and included a sketch of him in his *Colored Aristocracy of St. Louis* (1858), describing the Tennessean as "a man of mark ... [whose] character, moral and intellectual, would do honor to the proudest white man in the land" (59).

His friendship with the Clamorgans brought James Thomas into contact with other members of St. Louis's affluent free black community. He soon began courting Antoinette Rutgers. Antoinette's father, Louis, was the son of the Dutch merchant Arend Rutgers by one of his slaves. Arend had transferred substantial amounts of real estate to Louis, and at Louis's death his inheritance passed to Antoinette, his only surviving child. Unfortunately for James Thomas, Louis Rutgers's redoubtable widow, Pelagie, rejected him as a suitor for her daughter. Thomas persisted, even converting to Catholicism and joining the congregation of St. Vincent de Paul, the church at which Pelagie and Antoinette worshipped. Unmoved, Pelagie continued to withhold her consent and did her best to induce Antoinette to marry into one of the city's established free families of color. Not until Pelagie Rutgers died could the couple marry. Their wedding, which took place at St. Vincent de Paul on 12 February 1868, was, by all accounts, an elegant affair.

With his own savings and his wife's inheritance, Thomas embarked on a career as a real estate broker. He acquired a large number of valuable properties and proved, as he had done in the past, that he was a shrewd and resourceful man of business. By 1870 he was the richest African American in Missouri. A report in the 6 July 1871 *New York Daily Tribune* put his wealth at a half million dollars. In their tastefully decorated home on Seventh Street in St. Louis, the Thomases lived comfortably, if unostentatiously.

In 1873, at the height of his prosperity, Thomas traveled to Europe as a gentleman of leisure. He was pleasantly surprised to discover that few Europeans shared the overt racist attitudes of white Americans. Once back in St. Louis he dissolved his partnership with Henry Clamorgan and opened his own establishment at the new Lindell Hotel. His place of business was described by one visitor as "the handsomest barbershop in the world" (*Cleveland Gazette*, 23 Oct. 1886). Profits from the barbershop and various rental properties were invested in yet more real estate. The Thomases gave generously to a wide range of religious and charitable causes. They also patronized African American artists, although their commissioning of a statue of the Virgin Mary at the Cross for Pelagie Rutgers's grave in Calvary Cemetery involved them in an ugly and protracted legal dispute with the sculptor EDMONIA LEWIS.

In 1877 the Thomases brought a new home in Alton, Illinois, and it was there that they raised their family. They had five children: James Louis Rutgers, Pelagie Sarah, Arend John, Joseph, and Anthony. By the late 1880s James Thomas began making plans to retire. However, he lost heavily in the Panic of 1893. His fortunes were just starting to recover when a tornado struck St. Louis, severely damaging much of his rental property. Then Antoinette Thomas's health began to fail. After a long and painful illness, she died in November 1897. Thomas mourned her as "the best of wives … the best woman in the world."

Antoinette Thomas's death was a financial as well as an emotional loss for her husband. The marriage settlement that the couple had been obliged to enter into under the terms of Pelagie Rutgers's will stipulated that Thomas would have no right to Antoinette's money if he outlived her. The family estate was already encumbered as a result of Thomas's earlier business setbacks. Now the house in Alton, along with its contents, had to be auctioned off to pay creditors.

James Thomas and his sons spent the months immediately after Antoinette Thomas's death and the sale of the family home with his daughter Pelagie and her husband in Chicago. Eventually, though, Thomas salvaged some of his property in St. Louis and returned to the city, boarding with one of his sons, Joseph, before settling into a small apartment at 616 Rutger Street (named, ironically, for Antoinette's Dutch grandfather).

Thomas had begun making notes for his autobiography while in Alton. Now he worked to organize his random jottings into a coherent memoir. The task occupied him on and off until his death. His narrative is a fascinating account of his rise from slave to wealthy freeman, his many adventures (and occasional misadventures), and his reflections on the nature of American society.

The last months of James Thomas's life were marked by illness, poverty, and bereavement. Two of his sons, Anthony and John, predeceased him. A third, Joseph, outlived him by less than a month. By the time of James Thomas's death, the Rutgers-Thomas estate had dwindled to almost nothing. Nevertheless, the attendance at his funeral, and the tributes paid to him in the St. Louis press, proved that he had not been entirely forgotten. After a funeral mass at St. Vincent de Paul, the church that had been his spiritual home for almost half a century, he was buried beside Antoinette in St. Louis's Calvary Cemetery.

FURTHER READING

Thomas, James. *From Tennessee Slave to St. Louis Entrepreneur: The Autobiography of James Thomas*, ed. Loren Schweninger (1984).

Clamorgan, Cyprian. *The Colored Aristocracy of St. Louis*, ed. Julie Winch (1999).

JULIE WINCH

Thomas, James Samuel (8 Apr. 1919–10 Oct. 2010), minister, was born in Orangeburg, South Carolina, to James Samuel and Dessie Veronica Thomas. His father was a Methodist minister, and he followed in his footsteps by becoming an ordained Methodist minister and later a bishop. Thomas Jr. graduated from Claflin College in Orangeburg, receiving a bachelor of arts degree in 1939. He went on to obtain a bachelor of divinity degree from Gammon Theological Seminary in Atlanta in 1943 and a master of divinity degree from Drew University in 1944. Cornell University awarded him a Ph.D. in Sociology in 1953.

While gaining his education, Thomas also became a Methodist minister in South Carolina. He was ordained a deacon in 1942 and was received as an elder in 1944. He married Ruth Naomi Wilson on 7 July 1945, and they had three daughters. He served several congregations as a young minister, but in 1948 he returned to Gammon to join the faculty as professor of rural church and director of fieldwork, a position that he held until 1953. He then became associate general secretary of the Methodist Church's board of education, and he held that position until elected a bishop in 1964.

While at the board of education, he was responsible for supervising the twelve historically black colleges supported by the Methodist Church. Most of these institutions were underfunded and facing considerable pressure to upgrade their facilities, faculties, and curriculum. Although some, like Clark College in Atlanta, received accreditation from the Southern Association of Schools and Colleges in 1957—the first year that historically black colleges were permitted full membership—others of these colleges struggled to receive full accreditation. Thomas developed financial support for these institutions within the annual conferences of the Central Jurisdiction, the all-black jurisdictional conference created when the Methodist Episcopal Church, the Methodist Protestant Church, and the Methodist Episcopal Church, South united in 1939.

During the period 1960–1964, the Central Jurisdiction appointed him to the Committee of Five, an ad hoc committee to advise the jurisdiction regarding desegregation proposals made by the Methodist Church's Commission of Thirty-Six, a church commission created to speed Methodist desegregation. Thomas headed the Committee of Five and worked closely with bishops of the Central Jurisdiction and JAMES P. BRAWLEY, president of Clark College and an influential lay leader in the Central Jurisdiction.

In March 1962 the Committee of Five organized a special meeting of leaders of the Central Jurisdiction in Cincinnati, Ohio. There the black Methodist leaders of the Methodist Church rejected the first set of proposals for desegregation coming from the Commission of Thirty-Six. After the Cincinnati meeting, the Committee of Five developed a plan to shift boundaries of annual conferences in the Central Jurisdiction so that no African American annual conference straddled the boundaries of regional jurisdictional conferences. Thomas also authored a proposal accepted by the 1964 General Conference to establish local advisory councils in each area of the South and Southwest so that Methodist leaders could desegregate all levels of the church, including church-related institutions such as colleges, hospitals, and homes.

Thomas's leadership in the Committee of Five paved the way to his election as a Methodist bishop by the Central Jurisdiction at its 1964 meeting. Because of the progress made through annual conference realignment, Thomas transferred into the North Central Jurisdiction and became bishop of the Iowa Annual Conference. He became the first African American Methodist bishop to preside over an annual conference that was almost entirely white in membership. At the time of his election he was the youngest person to be elected a bishop in the history of the Methodist Church. No major American church at that time had such a high-ranking African American supervising so many white members. Well over six feet tall and clearly an African American, Thomas was an unmistakable presence in Iowa, a state with a very low percentage of African Americans. Thomas served as bishop in Iowa for twelve years and then presided over the East Ohio Annual Conference for another twelve years.

At the 1972 General Conference of the United Methodist Church (Methodists became the United Methodist Church in 1968), Thomas presented the work of a commission that he chaired that revised the church's social principles. Among issues addressed for the first time was the issue of homosexuality. He delivered the Episcopal Address, the state of the church address written in conjunction with the entire Council of Bishops, at the 1976 General Conference. He also served a one year term as president of the Council of Bishops.

After retiring in 1988, Bishop Thomas taught at the Perkins School of Theology at Southern Methodist University, and more recently he served as bishop-in-residence at the Candler School of Theology at Emory University. In 1992 he wrote *Methodism's Racial Dilemma*. At the 2004 General Conference, which met in Pittsburgh, Pennsylvania, site also of the 1964 General Conference, he was given special recognition for his contribution to ending racism in the Methodist Church.

A person of dignity and grace, Bishop Thomas was an example of successful minority leadership in an organization that was largely white, both during the height of the civil rights movement and in the years since. He had the difficult task of interpreting African American anger and resentment regarding racism to a largely white audience in parts of the country where Jim Crow legislation never existed. At the same time he was committed to the Gospel as a message of good news for all persons, regardless of race and background. Through his personal life and his professional duties he wanted Methodists to see that their fellowship had just as much vitality and meaning in the second half of the twentieth century as it had in the early American republic. He died in 2010 at the age of 91.

FURTHER READING
Thomas, James S. *Methodism's Racial Dilemma* (1992).
Murray, Peter C. *Methodists and the Crucible of Race, 1930–1975* (2004).

PETER C. MURRAY

Thomas, Jesse O. (21 Dec. 1885–?1972), laborer, machine operator, carpenter, contractor, and administrator, was born in Pike County, Mississippi, the second oldest son of six children. Jesse attended a rural, one-room school that typically had seventy-five to one hundred students per teacher ranging across seven grade levels. Because teaching everyone at one time was impossible, students were given weekly assignments to learn and perform on each Friday for the community. As a young boy, Jesse had a knack for public speaking and looked forward to making speeches to the community.

Thomas's family lived comfortably despite the fact his mother was ill and often bedridden. While the family could not be considered wealthy, they always had more than enough to eat. Thomas had always believed that his family owned the land they worked on, but when they were suddenly evicted, he learned that his father was actually a sharecropper, not a landowner.

Thomas's family began sharecropping on a neighboring plantation in McComb, Mississippi. Shortly after they arrived in McComb, Jesse's mother died. The eviction and the death of his mother together had a powerful effect on Jesse. He refused to remain a sharecropper and leave himself susceptible to the same hardships and consequences his father accepted as a way of life. After his mother's funeral, he ran away to Natalbany, Louisiana, in hopes of finding a better way of life for himself and his family. Jesse was adamant that he would own the land that he and his family worked on to avoid ever being evicted from their home again. He was fourteen.

Whereas his hometown community of Pike County had a distinct social divide between the owners and the workers of the land, race was not a point of contention. The city of Natalbany was a different story. Whites were only 10 percent of the population, but they held all of the administrative and managerial occupations. This left the black population with the unskilled and semiskilled jobs. Undaunted, Thomas found employment his second day in Natalbany at the local sawmill. He was hired to work ten-hour days at nine cents an hour. Within the first year he had saved enough money to send a letter to his father with money and supplies. From that day until his father died, Thomas took responsibility for his family in McComb. He never missed a day of work, and after ten years of enduring the grueling work of hauling timber, he was promoted to a machine operator. With this promotion came a substantial increase in wages, but he was still not satisfied.

In 1906, at the age of twenty-one, Thomas was accepted at Tuskegee Institute (later Tuskegee University) in Alabama. In no time at all he became a prominent figure on campus and was elected president of his class. One of his first acts in that position was to convince the entire class to abandon an increasingly dangerous campus tradition. Every year the senior classmen would hold a "hazing" session for the junior classmen. Each year the hazing became more and more brutal. Thomas rallied the entire junior class together and as a whole decided to boycott the traditional initiation ritual. Later, when the students went on strike because of the food quantity and quality, Thomas organized a committee to mediate a contract with the college and the food service.

When he graduated, Thomas was recommended by BOOKER T. WASHINGTON to represent Tuskegee as first director. He was authorized to set up headquarters in Rochester, New York. Thomas raised more money in his first year than any other director. His passionate campaigning made it possible to educate many young black Americans in vocational areas and trades.

In 1912 Thomas became president of Voorhees Institute. On 1 August 1917 he married Nellie Ida Mitchell and the couple later had a daughter. During their first year of marriage two events occurred. First, both of Nellie's parents died. The newly married couple assumed responsibility for all of their siblings, both his and hers. Second, Thomas took a leave of absence from Voorhees to accept two positions, supervisor of Negro economics for the state of New York and examiner in charge of the U.S. employment services.

Thomas's campaign became employing educated black men in their trades and vocations. He found it ironic that the same individuals who contributed funds to educate blacks were less than agreeable to hiring these blacks after they finished their educations. Because of this paradox, Thomas resigned from the government to establish the southern office of the National Urban League in Atlanta, Georgia, in 1919. In the 1900s the National Urban League was responsible for successfully employing the largest number of trained black Americans in the country. Prior to the National Urban League, African Americans had to resort to unskilled or sharecropping jobs to earn a living.

In 1941 Thomas became senior promotional specialist for the U.S. Treasury. This position enabled him to educate the black community regarding buying bonds from the Treasury Department. He resigned from the Treasury Department in 1942 to be in the first group of African Americans to join the American Red Cross. On 1 May 1943 he was named special assistant to the director of domestic operations of the American Red Cross. Thomas helped break down racial barriers within the national headquarters, opening the way for black professionals to serve in the Red Cross.

In his autobiography he wrote that there were two guiding principles in his life. First, duty belongs to humans, while destiny belongs to God. Second, all people are created equal, but some become better than others through their actions and usefulness, not by birth. Thomas and his wife spent their lives traveling from state to state and to foreign countries promoting quality lives for blacks. Up until his death in 1972, Thomas remained a passionate activist for the rights of black Americans in the United States.

FURTHER READING

Thomas, Jesse O. *My Story in Black and White: The Autobiography of Jesse O. Thomas* (1967).
American Red Cross Museum. Available at www. redcross.org/museum/exhibits/aaexhibit_4.asp.

CHRISTINE SCHNEIDER

Thomas, Joe (24 July 1909–6 Aug. 1984), jazz trumpeter, was born Joseph Lewis Thomas in Webster Groves, Missouri. His parents' names are unknown. His father was a church deacon, and his mother sang in the church choir. By about age eight Thomas was playing cornet in church and in a band organized by a Mr. Sims and directed by P. B. (or P. G.) Langford (or Lankford), a multi-instrumentalist from whom he took lessons. He attended high school and then Lincoln University in Jefferson City, Missouri.

Thomas played for one night in the riverboat bandleader Charlie Creath's band. He then worked for several years with far lesser known bandleaders in St. Louis, the upper Midwest, and New Jersey before joining the pianist FLETCHER HENDERSON's big band from around March to May 1934. After working with the banjoist Ferman Tapp at Smalls' Paradise in Harlem in September 1934, Thomas joined the bassist Charlie Turner's big band at the Arcadia Ballroom. In mid-1935 the pianist FATS WALLER took over its leadership. Thomas rejoined Henderson from the summer of 1935 to September 1936.

Thomas played in the big bands of Willie Bryant in 1937 and the pianist CLAUDE HOPKINS in 1938–1939. In May 1939 he joined the saxophonist and arranger BENNY CARTER's big band for engagements at New York City's Savoy Ballroom, touring, and recordings. Excellent early examples of his clean and swinging mid-range trumpeting style may be heard on "When Lights Are Low" (1939) and "Sleep" (1940). This affiliation with Carter reportedly overlaps with Thomas's membership in the pianist JAMES P. JOHNSON's band from December 1939 to November 1940, but because Johnson suffered a stroke in August 1940, these dates are somewhat unreliable. During this period Thomas also led his own band with singer Babe Matthews, whom he married in the early 1940s.

In 1941 Thomas worked briefly with the pianist Joe Sullivan and participated in two fine studio sessions with the singer Joe Turner in the pianist ART TATUM's band, including "Rock Me Mama" and two takes each of "Lonesome Graveyard" and "Lucille" from the second session in June. In March 1942 he recorded and toured with Fats Waller's big band, and he worked with the pianist TEDDY WILSON's six-piece group at Café Society Uptown from August 1942 to October 1943.

At a recording session under ROY ELDRIDGE's leadership in January 1944, Thomas outplayed his fellow trumpeters Eldridge and Emmett Berry on versions of "Don't Be That Way" and "St. Louis Blues," in which he is the second trumpet soloist. Other notable recordings include "Through for the Night" with the drummer COZY COLE in February, "That's My Weakness Now" and "It's the Talk of the Town" with the saxophonist Pete Brown in July, and "Russian Lullaby" with the vibraphonist Red Norvo in October. From the latter part of the year into early 1945 Thomas was at the Onyx Club in the clarinetist BARNEY BIGARD's group, with which he also recorded. He recorded "Black Butterfly" and "Pocatello" as a leader in August 1946.

Around 1947 Thomas worked in the guitarist Eddie Condon's band, giving concerts at Town Hall and Carnegie Hall. He was with Cole again early in 1948 and with the tenor saxophonist Bud Freeman in the Chicago area in 1949. A published photograph, captioned 1950, shows Thomas performing with the reed player Eddie Barefield and the drummer BIG SID CATLETT, presumably also in Chicago soon before Catlett's death.

In 1952 Thomas played with the pianist WILLIE SMITH at the Central Plaza in New York. At some point during the 1950s he led a small group at the Village Vanguard. He was a member of Henderson's posthumous reunion band under the cornetist REX STEWART's direction for a concert in 1957 and subsequent albums in 1957 and 1958. He also recorded on clarinetist Tony Scott's album *Blues for "the Street"* in 1958.

During the 1960s Thomas toured northeastern cities, often in the company of the trombonist J. C. HIGGINBOTHAM. He freelanced with the clarinetist BUSTER BAILEY's sextet at an outdoor concert at the Museum of Modern Art in New York and on the recording of Hopkins's album *Let's Jam* in 1961. In 1964 he worked at Condon's club and performed at the Newport Jazz Festival. He worked with Hopkins again in 1966. Poor health and a serious operation limited Thomas's opportunities to perform during the 1970s, although he participated in a nostalgic concert with Carter at Carnegie Hall on 2 July 1972. He died in New York City. Thomas is one of the many trumpeters who carried on the lyrical (rather than the demonstrative) side of LOUIS ARMSTRONG's trumpeting.

FURTHER READING

Balliett, Whitney. *Dinosaurs in the Morning* (1962).
McCarthy, Albert J. "Joe Thomas," *Jazz Monthly* 9 (Aug. 1963).
Schuller, Gunther. *The Swing Era: The Development of Jazz, 1930–1945* (1989).
This entry is taken from the *American National Biography* and is published here with the permission of the American Council of Learned Societies.

BARRY KERNFELD

Thomas, John Curtis (3 March 1941–), Olympic high-jumper, athletic official, and businessman, was born in Boston, Massachusetts, to Curtis Thomas, a bus driver for the Massachusetts Bay Transportation Authority (MBTA), and Ida Kate (Shanks) Thomas. With his brother and sister, he grew up in Cambridge, Massachusetts, and attended Rindge Technical High

School. There he was a Boy Scout (Eagle Scout), on the newspaper, and captain of the track and tennis teams. Though initially unable to high-jump six feet, after his coach changed his style from the western roll (facing sideways) to the straddle (facing down), Thomas cleared 6 feet 8¼ inches and was named team captain and chosen for the national All-American High School Track Team, an honorary team of the best high school athletes, before graduating in 1958.

In the fall of 1958 he entered Boston University on an athletic scholarship. He was on the dean's list, captained the track team, and received a B.S. in Physical and Psychology Rehabilitation in 1963. He studied ballet at the Boston Conservatory of Music from 1962 to 1964, and he attended the Boston School of Accounting in 1969. His ballet training for "body control" in the high-jump and lifting of weights up to four hundred pounds were ahead of their times in training techniques (personal interview, 2005). Asked in early fan mail if he had problems "because of his race," he answered that he had not (Haley, 222).

Thomas dominated U.S. high-jumping during the early 1960s as U.S. record holder and the first man to jump 7 feet indoors (the first 7-foot jumper, Charles Dumas, cleared 7 feet ½-inch, or 2.15 meters, in the June 1956 Olympic trials). A consistent 7-foot jumper for a decade, the 6-foot 5½-inch, soft-spoken Thomas broke the U.S. high-jump records thirteen times with his loping straddle style. During college, he won seven Amateur Athletic Union (AAU), two National Collegiate Atheletic Association (NCAA), and six Intercolleagiate Amateur Athletic Association of America (IC4A) high-jump titles. He was on the U.S. Olympic team in 1960 and 1964, the U.S. national team from 1958 to 1968, and the U.S. Maccabiah team to Israel in 1961 and 1967.

As a seventeen-year-old Boston University freshman, Thomas set his first indoor world record at 6 feet 11 inches at Dartmouth College on 10 January 1959, and a week later at the Boston Knights of Columbus games he raised it to 6 feet 11¾ inches. A week later on 31 January, at the Millrose Games in New York, his first 7-foot jump was disallowed when an official failed to re-measure after the jump (*Current Biography*, 1960). On 14 February he made his first official 7-foot record at the New York City Athletic Games, and a week later he raised it again to 7 feet 1¼ inches at the Amateur Athletic Union (AAU) National Meet in New York.

A freak March 1959 accident when he was operating an elevator seriously injured his left jumping foot and almost ended his career. He dropped out of college for the semester while his foot healed after a series of operations. But back in school that September, he was jumping 7 feet again by January 1960, when he raised the indoor world record to 7 feet 1½ inches on 30 January. He increased the indoor record to 7 feet 2½ inches at the Chicago Daily News Relays on 11 March 1960. He began to set a series of outdoor world records on 30 April, when he jumped 7 feet 11 1/16 inches (2.17 meters) at the Penn Relays. Then on 21 May 1960, he improved the mark to 7 feet 1¾ inches at a meet at Briggs Field, near his house in Cambridge, and to 7 feet 2 inches (2.18 meters) at the AAU national championships in New York on 24 June 1960. On 1 July 1960 at the United States Olympic Trials at Stanford University, he set his final world record at a career-high 7 feet 3⅞ inches (officially, 7 feet 3¾ inches, or 2.22 meters).

Thomas, at nineteen years old, was the "cinch" for the gold medal at the 1960 Tokyo Olympics (*Sport*, Aug. 1961), but to the surprise of millions around the world, he finished third at 7 feet ¼ inches (2.14 meters) behind two obscure Russians (Robert Shavlakadze, gold, and the future world record holder, Valery Brumel, silver) at 7 feet 1 inch (2.16 meters), in what was then considered "one of the greatest upsets in history" (*World Week*, 5 Apr. 1961). In a series of eight duels between Thomas and Brumel in California, New York, and Moscow from 1961 to 1963, the Russian dominated the matches as "Thomas showed the world how a champion should lose" (*World Week*, 5 Apr. 1961). Thomas's single victory was at the February 1963 Los Angeles Times Indoor games at 7 feet ¼ inches (2.14 meters) when he won on fewer misses over an injured Brumel.

In the 1964 Tokyo Olympics, at the end of a grueling four-hour competition, Thomas tied Brumel's height at 7 feet 1⅞ inches (2.19 meters), which stands as a great comeback for the American jumper, who received the silver medal to Brumel's gold because of one more miss. The series of 1960s duels and Olympic contests embodied the cold war competition of the era. As Arthur Ashe noted, "It was always the U.S. versus Russia. Freedom versus Communism. Us versus them" (Ashe, 187). It did not prevent the friendship that grew between Thomas and Brumel, which led to a joint documentary on the high jump (Brumel would raise the world record to 7 feet, 5¾ inches, or 2.28 meters, in Moscow on 26 September 1962, before his career was disabled by a motorcycle accident in 1965; he died in 2003). Though Thomas never cleared higher

again than his 7 feet 2¾ inches indoors in 1964, and was sidelined during the 1965 indoor seasons for an operation, he jumped over 7 feet more than 190 times from 1959 through 1968. He was selected for the Boston University and Helms Foundations halls of fame in 1982, and the U.S. Track and Field and National Track and Field halls of fame in 1985.

Outside of athletics, Thomas held a variety of jobs. He was a corporate salesman in 1964–1966, a vocational counselor at Neighborhood Youth Corp in 1966–1967, the director of Hawthorne House Neighbor Center in 1972–1973, and a probation officer for the city of Boston in 1967–1972. He was an account executive for WCVB-TV, Channel 5, in 1973–1978; for General Motors Truck Division in 1978–1981; for New England Telephone in 1981–1982; and for AT&T in 1982–1985. He was self-employed from 1985 to 1994 with John Thomas Property Services. From 1969 to 1983, Thomas was assistant track coach at Boston University. In 1994, he became director of athletics at Roxbury Community College in Boston and a senior staff member of the nationally renowned Reggie Lewis Track & Field Center in Roxbury.

Thomas was made honorary sheriff of Middlesex County, Massachusetts, in 1959. He was a board member of the Boys Clubs of Boston, Boy Scouts of America, Cambridge YMCA, and Boston Athletic Association, and international director of Athletes United for Peace. He was also a member of the Massachusetts Governor's Council on Physical Fitness and U.S. President's Council on Physical Fitness, U.S. Olympic Committee advisory board, U.S. Information Services, and the NAACP. The John Thomas High-Jump is a featured field event at the annual Millrose Games in New York City.

John Curtis Thomas was the first man to break the 7-foot high-jump barrier consistently and was an inspiration to a generation of high-jumpers. He continued that leadership in athletics in the city of Boston. He was married and the father of four children.

FURTHER READING
Ashe, Arthur. *A Hard Road to Glory: A History of the African-American Athlete* (1988).
Current Biography, 1960.
Haley, Alex. "The Jumpingest Man on Earth," *Reader's Digest* (June 1960).
Jauss, Bill. "Nothing Political to Thomas' Leaps," *Chicago Daily News*, 5 Feb. 1964.
Masin, Herman. "Jumping for Joy," *World Week* (5 April 1961).

Jauss, Bill. "Thomas Eyes Relays Comeback," *Chicago Daily News*, 5 Feb. 1963.

Schaap, Dick. "John Thomas' Lonely Battle," *Sport* (Aug. 1961).

"Thomas Proud of His Legacy," *Newark Star Ledger*, 11 Jan. 1978.

RICHARD SOBEL

Thomas, John W. E. (1 May 1847–18 Dec. 1899), teacher, politician, and attorney, was born into slavery as John William Edinburgh Thomas in Montgomery, Alabama. His exact date of birth is not known, although the generally accepted date is 1 May 1847. He was the only child of Edinboro Thomas, a free African American who worked as a ship porter and hotel waiter, and Martha Thomas, a slave owned by Elizabeth L. and Dr. Lawrence A. McCleskey.

While Thomas was young, the McCleskey family relocated to Mobile, Alabama. Although Thomas was a slave, the McCleskey family provided him with an education. At the age of eight Thomas began teaching other blacks, often using a horse stall as a classroom. Edinboro Thomas tried to buy his son's freedom, but McCleskey would not sell him. In 1865 Thomas's father bought a small lot of land on the near South Side of Chicago, which became the site of the John Thomas residence.

Thomas married Maria Reynolds in 1864, and in the late 1860s they moved to Chicago with their infant daughter Hester. Thomas opened the first school for African Americans in Chicago in his own house. According to one newspaper, he would teach children during the day and teach the children's parents at night. Thomas and his wife also operated a grocery out of their home. The Great Chicago Fire of 1871 missed their home by only three blocks; however, in 1874 another large fire burned their home and neighborhood to the ground. Thomas rebuilt his house on the same piece of property.

Like most politically active African Americans of the time, Thomas was a Republican, and he became active in the Second Ward Republican Party organization. With his education, his involvement in the community, and his interest in politics, Thomas became a leader of Chicago's small African American community.

In 1876 Republicans nominated Thomas as one of their two candidates to run for three state representative positions in the Illinois Second Legislative District. The nomination came despite the fact that African Americans made up less than 2 percent of Chicago's population. The selection of an African American for the position caused some opposition. Several leading Republicans of the district sought to overturn Thomas's nomination, including Robert Todd Lincoln, the son of President Abraham Lincoln. Thomas remained as a Republican nominee and easily won one of the three seats in the legislature, making him the first African American to serve in that chamber.

In August 1878, as Thomas was preparing to seek renomination, his wife Maria died. In October 1878 the Republicans of his district did not renominate him for a second term and instead nominated two white candidates. This led to a threatened revolt from the party among the city's black voters, who thought that Thomas had been slighted. Thomas, however, worked hard to ensure that black citizens remained loyal to the Republican Party. During the next two years Thomas returned to teaching, studied law, and married Justine Latcher of Chicago. He was admitted to the bar in February 1880. That fall he again failed to receive a nomination to run for state representative. With no African American slated to run for any elective office in Chicago, African American voters again threatened to leave the Republican Party. Once again Thomas maintained his party loyalty and worked for the election of the Republican ticket. Shortly after November he moved to Washington, D.C., where he worked as a clerk in the U.S. Treasury.

In 1882 Thomas returned to Chicago, where he successfully sought the Republican nomination for the state legislature, defeating a large field of hopefuls that included three other African Americans. Thomas won the election, but despite his receiving a committee chairmanship, personal crises made the term a difficult one. In May 1883 his second wife died shortly after giving birth. Two weeks later their infant daughter also died.

That fall Thomas was a compromise choice to chair a statewide colored convention. Leading Illinois blacks called four colored conventions during the 1880s to discuss issues of concern to the race. Black leaders at the 1883 convention were deeply divided between those who wished to stay loyal to the Republican Party and those who felt that the race should become more politically independent. Thomas was able to prevent the convention from passing resolutions critical of the Republican Party. In 1885 Thomas again was a compromise choice to chair a state colored convention. Once again Thomas was able to keep the convention from endorsing anti-Republican resolutions.

In 1884 Thomas was reelected to a third term in the legislature. During this term he pushed through the state's first civil rights act, which banned discrimination in public places. The civil rights act became Thomas's legislative legacy. Thomas also served on the powerful judiciary committee and helped elect John A. Logan to the U.S. Senate in one of the most contested Senate races in Illinois history.

Despite his legislative record and party loyalty, Thomas was not renominated for the legislature in 1886, although he did ensure that an African American ally was nominated to succeed him. Thomas won election to one term as a township clerk in 1887, but he subsequently lost bids for nomination as county commissioner, city alderman, and state senator. In 1892 the Republican state convention selected him to run as a presidential elector. Thomas continued to be active in politics after 1892, but his elective career was finished. He practiced law throughout the 1890s, with his primary place of business being the police court at the Harrison Street Police Station, a dismal place described vividly in William T. Stead's famous muckraker book *If Christ Came to Chicago* (1893).

In 1887 Thomas married Crittie Marshall, and together they had six children, four of whom lived to be adults. Thomas passed away at his home. When he died, newspapers said that he was the wealthiest African American in the city of Chicago.

FURTHER READING

Joens, David A. "John W. E. Thomas and the Election of the First African American to the Illinois General Assembly." *Journal of the Illinois State Historical Society* 94 (Summer 2001): 200–216.

DAVID JOENS

Thomas, Lorenzo (31 Aug. 1944–4 July 2005), writer, poet, and educator, was born in the Republic of Panama, the son of Herbert Hamilton Thomas, a pharmacist and chemist, and Luzmilda (Gilling) Thomas, a community organizer. Thomas's family emigrated from Panama to New York City in 1948. Having spoken only Spanish until that time, Thomas was teased by other children for his poor English. The trauma of being derided for his lack of language skills led to Thomas's intense interest in learning to read and write English. He has cited his early attempts to master the language as the spark for his interest in poetry. In a 1981 interview, Thomas said, "I had to write the language down before talking" (Rowell, 19).

Thomas attended Queens College, where he earned his B.A. in 1967. He later did graduate study

and worked as a librarian at the Pratt Institute in Brooklyn. While at Queens College, Thomas became associated with the Umbra workshop, a gathering of mostly young black writers who met weekly to discuss each other's work. Members included ISHMAEL REED, David Henderson, Calvin Hernton, TOM DENT, Rolland Snellings (later Askia Muhammad Touré), and others.

Umbra met from 1962 to 1964 and during that time helped give its members a distinct voice within New York literary circles. Many Umbra poets read their works in a number of local coffeehouses and reading series. Members also produced the literary magazine *Umbra*, which lasted from 1963 to 1974. Some members of Umbra, including Thomas, later became key figures in the Black Arts Movement beginning in 1965. Thomas's writing appeared not only in *Umbra* but also in a number of other small-circulation magazines, such as *Angel Hair, C: A Journal of Poetry, Sum*, and *The Rivoli Review*. His first book, *A Visible Island*, was published by Adlib Press in 1967.

As for the other members, Thomas's association with Umbra helped foster his sense of black culture and identification with an African heritage, as well as providing him with a constructive environment in which to explore the use of poetry as a means of commenting on the social and political issues of the 1960s. Thomas's previous notions of "race consciousness" had developed earlier from his family. His father had been an avid reader of the *Chicago Defender* and other black periodicals, and members of Thomas's family shared an interest in news about blacks around the world. According to Thomas, "I was always keeping track of what was happening with Black people, of their doing excellent things, being the best in whatever field they were in" (Rowell, 20).

In 1968 Thomas joined the U.S. Navy and served as a communications adviser in Vietnam from 1971 to 1972. Returning to the United States, he worked briefly as a librarian at Pace College in New York. Thomas's second book, *Fit Music: California Songs, 1970*, was published in 1972 by Angel Hair Books. Described by Thomas as "one kind of poetic record of my Vietnam experience" (Waldman/Warsh, 604), the collection traced the arc of this experience in spare and ironic language.

Thomas's second publication with Angel Hair was his book-length poem *Dracula* (1973), which he had originally written in 1966. In this work Thomas used the imagery of the Dracula character, especially as seen through film adaptations, to comment on American culture. To Thomas the United States had become a place "whose heritage and biography was death."

In 1973 Thomas was invited to serve as writer-in-residence at Texas Southern University in Houston. After his year of residency, he decided to stay in Houston and became active in the local writing community. Thomas taught creative writing at the Black Arts Center in Houston (1974–1976) and worked with the Poetry-in-the-Schools programs in Texas, Oklahoma, Florida, Arkansas, and Georgia. His relocation to Texas helped foster in him an appreciation of southern black writers, and his interest in folk traditions, which grew out of his family and the multiethnic environment of New York, were expressed in his organization of blues festivals in Texas and his co-authorship with Louis Guida and Cheryl Cohen of *Blues Music in Arkansas* (1982).

The 1970s continued to be a productive period for Thomas's writing. The latter half of the decade saw the publication of *Framing the Sunrise* (1975), *Sound Science* (1978), and *Chances Are Few* (1979). *The Bathers* (1981) is a comprehensive collection bringing together Thomas's poems from New York and Texas, along with those dealing with his Vietnam experiences.

In 1984 Thomas joined the faculty of the University of Houston–Downtown as an adjunct lecturer and became a professor of English, teaching American literature and creative writing. Thomas lectured extensively and wrote numerous articles and scholarly works on African American literature. He edited *Sing the Sun Up* (1998), a collection of essays on teaching African American literature, and authored the well-received *Extraordinary Measures: Afrocentric Modernism and Twentieth-Century American Poetry* (2004).

Apart from his criticism, Thomas continued to write poetry. An expanded edition of *Chances Are Few* was published in 2003, while the following year saw the publication of *Dancing on Main Street*, Thomas's largest and most mature work, as well as the chapbook *Time Step: 5 Poems, 4 Seasons*.

Thomas died of emphysema on 4 July 2005. Throughout his career as both a poet and teacher, Lorenzo Thomas championed the importance of African American voices within the canon of American literature. From his early work with Umbra to his later critical studies of black writers, Thomas contributed his own voice to that canon, and helped showcase the importance of others writing in the African American tradition.

FURTHER READING

Dent, Tom. "Lorenzo Thomas," in *Dictionary of Literary Biography*, vol. 41 (1985).

Kane, Daniel. *All Poets Welcome: The Lower East Side Poetry Scene in the 1960s* (2003).

Pinson, Hermine. "An Interview with Lorenzo Thomas," *Callaloo* (Spring 1999).

Rowell, Charles H. "Between the Comedy of Matters and the Ritual Workings of Man: An Interview with Lorenzo Thomas," *Callaloo* (Feb.–Oct., 1981).

Waldman, Anne, and Warsh, Lewis, eds. *Angel Hair Sleeps with a Boy in My Head: The Angel Hair Anthology* (2001).

CHRISTOPHER HARTER

Thomas, Piri (30 Sept. 1928–17 Oct. 2011), autobiographer, poet, artist, and activist, was born John Peter Thomas in New York City's Harlem Hospital in 1928. His mother, Dolores Montañez, came to New York from Puerto Rico. His father, Juan Tomás de la Cruz, was a Cuban-born laborer who had also moved to the United States from Puerto Rico. Piri Thomas was the eldest of their four surviving children. "Piri" was a nickname given to him by his mother.

The Thomas family was very poor throughout his childhood. He spent his early years in poverty-stricken, ethnically diverse, Depression-era Harlem. When he was thirteen years old, his father hit the numbers and moved the family to Babylon, Long Island. The very dark-skinned Thomas suffered so much from racial discrimination and feelings of displacement in suburbia that he left his family, moved back to Harlem, and began living on the streets. It was at this point that young Piri became heavily involved in street gangs and crime, and he developed an addiction to heroin. In 1945 his beloved mother died of cancer. The emotional turmoil of losing her sent him further into illegal activity. In 1950 Thomas and two other men attempted to rob a nightclub in Greenwich Village; in the ensuing struggle with the police, an officer was shot. Thomas was convicted of attempted armed robbery and sentenced to prison at Sing Sing and Comstock for five to fifteen years. A former dropout, he earned his high school diploma while in prison. He also learned brick masonry and began exploring various religions, including studying with black Muslims. He was paroled in 1956 and began work as a youth counselor in Harlem, serving as a role model and confidante to young men in situations similar to his own.

While in prison, Thomas was introduced to JOHN OLIVER KILLENS's novel *Youngblood*. Inspired by Killens's story and style, Thomas decided to try his hand at writing and began penning an autobiography. (The original manuscript was later accidentally destroyed by his wife, and Thomas had to rewrite it.) After his release, he became friends with Killens, who invited him to join the Harlem Writers Guild, a group of writers that included such luminaries as Killens, PAULE MARSHALL, and JOHN HENRIK CLARKE. Thomas occasionally attended meetings of the guild from 1962 to 1965, reading his work and listening to other writers read their work. He was also encouraged by filmmaker Richard Leacock (who was doing a documentary on Thomas's community work) to complete the book he had begun writing in prison and to submit it to the editor Angus Cameron at the Alfred Knopf publishing house. After rewriting the book, he sent it to Cameron, and it was accepted.

In 1967 *Down These Mean Streets*, Thomas's first autobiography, was published to wide acclaim. Written in a unique, jazz-influenced lingo peppered with street slang and Spanglish, the stream-of-consciousness narrative chronicles his life as a poor youth in Spanish Harlem, and was one of the first to deal with the experiences of Puerto Ricans in New York City. Criticized by some for its explicitness, *Down These Mean Streets* openly exposes the realities of poverty in the inner city. The book follows Thomas from early childhood to life as a young gang member to his stint in prison and his battle to overcome drug addiction. Thomas is presented as a typical Harlem youth and attempts to explain the sociological and psychological issues faced by these young people as they attempt to navigate adolescence in a world fraught with dangers. He once described his thought process while writing *Down These Mean Streets* this way:

> I was writing for all of us who were living in that hell. I was not born a criminal from my mother's womb, none of us who had been into the so-called criminal activity had been born criminals from our mother's womb. We were all born very beautiful children, just like any other little babies, into a very criminal society of racism and bigotry and horror to the nth degree, not to leave out promises that very rarely, if ever, came to be (Stavans).

Down These Mean Streets is also notable for its exposure of racism and color consciousness in American culture, especially within the Latino community. As a dark-skinned, obviously African-descended Puerto Rican in a family of light-skinned, blue-eyed siblings, Thomas was subjected to taunting and often felt devalued, especially by his dark-skinned father. In *Down*

These Mean Streets he struggles with a search for a fixed identity, going back and forth between ethnic groups and attempting to locate the meaning of each identity, as he "felt both Puerto Rican and Black. ... And yet there was a little part in me that was white, too" (Binder). He even ventures into the American South in the 1940s with an African American friend to test his status; describing himself early in the journey as "a Puerto Rican trying to make Negro," he eventually comes to accept the reality of inescapable ethnic distinctions in the United States, declaring himself both Puerto Rican and black American. In his later work and in interviews, Thomas, highly interested in social justice and the eradication of racism, also stresses the need to look beyond what he considers artificially constructed social divisions based on skin color.

Savior, Savior, Hold My Hand, the follow-up to *Down These Mean Streets*, was published in 1972. It continues Thomas's story after his release from prison, as he joins the Pentecostal church, begins a family, deals with racism, and works as a youth counselor in 1960s Harlem. While working with young people, Thomas became the subject of two documentaries: Leacock's *Petey and Johnny* (1963) and *The World of Piri Thomas* (1968), produced by GORDON PARKS. In addition to his lifelong activism on behalf of urban children, Thomas retained a deep concern for those in the penal system. During the 1960s and 1970s, he volunteered in New York City's prison and drug rehabilitation programs and served as a staff associate with the Center for Urban Education. In 1974 *Seven Long Times* was published; it chronicles Thomas's years in prison and calls attention to the inadequacies of the American prison system.

Along with his ongoing community projects, Thomas began exploring modes of artistic expression other than autobiography. He began painting in the late 1960s and branched out into other written media; his play *The Golden Streets* was produced by the Puerto Rican Traveling Theatre in 1970. He also published a book for children (*Stories from El Barrio*, 1978) and two audio collections of "wordsongs": *Songs from the Street* (1994) and *No Mo' Barrio Blues* (1996). In 2002 Thomas was featured in another documentary, *Every Child Is Born a Poet: The Life and Work of Piri Thomas*. His first book, *Down These Mean Streets*, is considered Thomas's most outstanding and enduring work.

In 1958 Thomas married Daniela Calo; the couple had five children, Pedro, Ricardo, Sandra, Reyna, and Tanee. They eventually divorced, and he married Betty Gross in the 1970s. This second marriage lasted until Betty's death in 1985; it resulted in three children. Thomas later married Suzanne Dod.

Thomas was one of the first widely read authors who documented the experiences of Puerto Rican people in New York City. He differs from earlier writers like Jesús Colon in that his work primarily concerns Puerto Ricans born and reared on the U.S. mainland, instead of those who come to New York from the island. The protagonists of his books are intimately familiar with and connected to American culture and are deeply affected by its racism and class division. As he explained to an interviewer, as a black Puerto Rican from New York, he experienced a special kind of identity crisis: "I had no identity, I knew that I was not part of life in the U.S., and yet I never knew what Puerto Rico was about" (Binder).

He is considered one of the unofficial forefathers of the Nuyorican movement of the 1970s. (The Nuyoricans were a group of New York-based writers and artists of Puerto Rican descent including Miguel Algarín, Pedro Pietri, and Nicholasa Mohr.) Yet Thomas himself, while applauding the outpouring of artistic expression, personally denied being linked closely with the movement: "I never identified too much with Newyorican because I felt it kept me stereotyped to one place. … Hell, I didn't get rid of one slave master of the mind to get another slave master of the mind, not even if the master speaks my tongue" (Cintron). After the personal struggles he faced as a young man, Thomas was determined to not allow himself to be defined by any one identity, insisting that he is African American as well as Puerto Rican and refusing to let either identification cancel out the other: "I don't think I opted for it. I think the whole world believed me to be *un negrito*. And I looked in the mirror and I saw myself a *negrito*, but I also felt myself to be a Latin black, a fine, clean Latin black" (Hernandez).

Thomas died of pneumonia at his home in El Cerrito, California, on 17 October 2011.

FURTHER READING

Binder, Wolfgang. "An Interview with Piri Thomas," *Minority Voices: An Interdisciplinary Journal of Literature and the Arts* (Spring 1980).

Cintron, Humberto. "An Interview with Piri Thomas," *Forkroads: A Journal of Ethnic American Literature* (Fall 1995).

Hernandez, Carmen Dolores. "Piri Thomas," in *Puerto Rican Voices in English: Interviews With Writers* (1997).

Hernandez, Carmen Dolores. "'They Have Forced Us to Be Universal': Interview with Piri Thomas," *The Official Piri Thomas Website*. Available at www.cheverote.com/reviews/hernandezinterview.html.

Luis, William. "Black Latinos Speak: The Politics of Race in Piri Thomas's *Down These Mean Streets*," *Indiana Journal of Hispanic Literatures* (Spring 1998).

Luis, William. "Puerto Ricans in New York: *Memoirs of Bernardo Vega* and Piri Thomas's *Down These Mean Streets*," in *Dance Between Two Cultures: Latino Caribbean Literature Written in the United States* (1997).

Stavans, Ilan. "Race and Mercy: A Conversation with Piri Thomas," *Massachusetts Review: A Quarterly of Literature, the Arts, and Public Affairs* (Autumn 1996).

KRISTINA D. BOBO

Thomas, Rufus (26 Mar. 1917–15 Dec. 2001), singer, disc jockey, comedian, and dancer, was born in Cayce, Mississippi, to Rufus Thomas Sr., a sharecropper, and his wife Rachel. At age two Thomas came to Memphis with his parents and four older siblings. He proved his talents as a performer early on, appearing as a frog in a school play at age six and as a tap dancer in theater productions at Booker T. Washington High School. In tenth grade, he performed in blackface at his first minstrel show, the *Brown Brevities*. After one semester at Tennessee A&I University, Thomas decided to become a professional entertainer. He participated in a number of traveling entertainment troupes in the 1930s, including the Rabbit Foot Minstrels, the Georgia Dixon Traveling Show, and the Royal American Tent Shows.

In November 1940 Thomas married his high-school sweetheart, Cornelius Lorene Wilson. Their three children would become successful in the music world in their own right: soul singer Carla Thomas, keyboard player Marvell Thomas, and singer, music teacher, and songwriter Vaneese Thomas. In 1941 Thomas began working at a textile plant, which was a steady job he would hold until 1963. In the meantime, his entertaining career continued as part of the tap-dance and scat-singing outfit Rufus and Bones (with Robert Couch), on his own as the host of amateur shows at the Handy and Palace Theatres, and as a touring singer and dancer. In 1951 he began to work as a disc jockey at WDIA in Memphis, the first black radio station in the United States. His mentor was his former high school teacher Nat D. Williams, who also worked at WDIA as a disc jockey. As the host of talent shows in Beale Street clubs and also the host of the radio programs *Hoot 'n' Holler* and *Sepia Swing Club*, Thomas helped launch the careers of notable performers such as B. B. KING, Bobby Bland, Junior Parker, IKE TURNER, and Roscoe Gordon. Thomas would remain with WDIA until 1974 and return to the station in the early 1990s.

However, it was for his long and productive career as a recording artist that Thomas would win his most lasting fame. His recording career began in 1949 with "I'll Be a Good Boy" for the Star Talent label and continued with cuts for Chess and Meteor. In 1953 he recorded "Bear Cat," which was an answer song to WILLIE MAE THORNTON's massive hit "Hound Dog," for Sam Phillips's Sun Records. With its suggestive lyrics, the song made it to number three on the R&B charts and was Sun's first hit; but the song also led to a copyright-infringement lawsuit by the owner of Thornton's record label, Don Robey, which Sam Phillips lost and which seriously threatened the fledgling label. In the wake of Elvis Presley's success, Phillips's Sun Records began to favor white performers who would appeal to white audiences, which meant that Thomas would record only one more song for the label. He continued to perform in clubs and on the radio but recorded only sporadically throughout the rest of the 1950s.

Thomas had his biggest success while in his forties and fifties. In 1960 he recorded a duet with his seventeen-year-old daughter Carla for Satellite Records, which would later change its name to Stax. "Cause I Love You" was the first hit for Stax and the beginning of Carla Thomas's career as a soul singer. As a solo performer, Rufus Thomas recorded a number of dance hits for Stax, the most successful being "Walkin' the Dog" (1963). The song became a top-ten pop hit and was covered by the Rolling Stones on their first album. The stripped-down instrumentation and the gritty but humorous singing on Thomas's original stood in contrast to the suave pop singles issued by the Motown label at the time. In the following year, Thomas released "Can Your Monkey Do the Dog?" "Somebody Stole My Dog," and "Jump Back." Thomas's career peaked again in 1970 and 1971 with three dance singles on Stax that all made the R&B singles chart's top five: "Do the Funky Chicken," "(Do the) Push and Pull," and "The Breakdown." Backed by Booker T. and the MGs—or sometimes by the Bar-Kays—Thomas's songs for Stax featured a funky groove that put him in the company of other musical innovators such as JAMES BROWN and WILSON PICKETT. On stage, Thomas's outrageous wardrobe included pink shorts

Rufus Thomas checks out a guitar once used by rock 'n' roll pioneer Carl Perkins with Hard Rock Cafe president Jim Berk in Memphis, 28 May 1997. (AP Images.)

and a matching cape with white boots. Billed as "the World's Oldest Teenager," Thomas defied his age by singing, joking, and displaying impeccable footwork usually associated with performers thirty years younger than him. In 1972 Rufus Thomas appeared at the Wattstax festival at the Los Angeles Coliseum in front of a predominantly black audience of more than one hundred thousand. Envisioned as a "black Woodstock," Wattstax featured the majority of Stax's roster, including ISAAC HAYES, Carla Thomas, and the Bar-Kays, as well as the Reverend JESSE JACKSON, who delivered his famous "I am somebody" speech. Thomas incited the crowd to dance the Funky Chicken on the off-limits field in front of the stage and managed to direct them back to the stands afterward.

With the collapse of Stax in 1975, Thomas's career began to wane, but he continued to record for smaller labels. He tried rap music on *Rappin' Rufus* for the Ichiban label in 1984 and traditional blues on *That Woman Is Poison!* for Alligator in 1990. He appeared in such films as Jim Jarmusch's *Mystery Train* (1989), Robert Altman's *Cookie's Fortune* (1999), and numerous documentaries. In 1996 he was the coheadliner at the Olympic Games in Atlanta, along with the soul singer William Bell. In 1997 the city of Memphis renamed Hernando Street as Rufus Thomas Boulevard. Thomas received the Pioneer Award from the Rhythm and Blues Foundation in 1992 and was inducted into the Blues Hall of Fame in 2001. That same year, he died of heart failure in Memphis at age eighty-four.

Rufus Thomas was a pioneering black disc jockey and entertainer who provided two highly influential recording labels, Sun Records and Stax, with their first hit singles. Throughout the second half of the twentieth century, Thomas was one of the most illustrious figures of Memphis's lively music scene. Thomas's talents as a singer, dancer, and comedian had a lasting influence on later generations of blues, funk, and soul musicians.

FURTHER READING

Bowman, Rob. *Soulsville, U.S.A.: The Story of Stax Records* (1997).

Gordon, Robert. *It Came from Memphis* (1995).

Guralnick, Peter. *Sweet Soul Music* (1986).

Obituary: *New York Times*, 19 December 2001.

DISCOGRAPHY

Walking the Dog (Stax 24703).

That Woman Is Poison! (Alligator ALCD-4769).

The Best of Rufus Thomas: Do the Funky Somethin' (Rhino 72410).

ULRICH ADELT

Thomas, Sally (1787–10 Sept. 1850), emancipated slave and antebellum businesswoman, grew up on a tobacco plantation in Albemarle County, Virginia. Information about her parentage is scarce, but some reports suggest that Sally Thomas was of mixed racial heritage. She had two sons, John and Henry, apparently by John L. Thomas, who was the brother of her enslaver, Charles L. Thomas. Years later, she had a third son, JAMES P. THOMAS, whose father was Tennessee Supreme Court Chief Justice John Catron.

Following the death of her owners, Mr. and Mrs. Charles Thomas, the remaining members of the Thomas family, led by John L. Thomas, transported Sally Thomas—and about forty other servants of the family estate—to Nashville, Tennessee, in 1817. Charles Thomas's will stipulated that Sally and her two sons, John and Henry, remain together. She feared being sold separately from her sons and worried for the safety and well-being of John and Henry, as it was common practice for slave traders to divide family units if dividing them would increase profits. During the early 1820s Nashville showed signs of becoming a bustling, flourishing city that was rife with opportunities even for some blacks in urban areas. Accounts suggest that special allowances and privileges were granted to light-skinned blacks or those of mixed race. However, state laws forbade slaveholders from freeing servants.

Sally Thomas's Tennessee slaveholder, one of Charles Thomas's descendants, gave Sally either tacit or explicit freedom to work about town, and she was eventually able to rent her own house. However, since there was no formal deed of emancipation from the state, she was still considered an enslaved person.

The Thomas family allowed Sally to work outside the household and to save money, but she was required to pay them a portion of her meager earnings for such privileges. Thomas's determination to free her family from bondage meant long days working as a laundress in downtown Nashville. Her lifelong plan was to save enough money to purchase her own freedom and that of her sons. She washed, cleaned, and delivered the fancy garments, accoutrements, and fine linen of Nashville's well-to-do, impressing many of them with her excellent work and superior service.

Sally did not purchase manumission papers for John, her oldest son. Instead, she allowed him to take an apprenticeship with Richard Rapier, a riverbarge captain who earned a living by transporting groceries and other provisions to the city's residents along the western rivers. John (whose surname became Rapier) and Richard Rapier soon relocated the shipping business to Florence, Alabama. In Richard Rapier's will, he stipulated that his servant, John, would be emancipated upon his death. He even set aside one thousand dollars to purchase his emancipation from the Thomas family's estate. The executors of the will respected Rapier's wishes; and following his death in 1826 the Alabama General Assembly granted John his freedom.

In 1834 Sally's family was threatened when she learned that the Thomas estate was to be split up yet again among its remaining living heirs. John Martin, a distant kinsman of the Thomas family, inherited a portion of the Thomas estate, which included Sally and her third son, James. According to James's reminiscences, Martin was described as an affable but reckless man who would sell anything in his possession for money. Undoubtedly, this unsettling prospect solidified her resolve to ensure that James be protected from being sold or traded. At the time of the estate distribution, he was appraised at four hundred dollars—just short of Sally's total savings. She sought advice from influential Nashville lawyer, Ephriam H. Foster, who lent her the rest of the money to purchase James's freedom. She would eventually emancipate herself as well; but despite her valiant efforts, Tennessee law still required them both to obtain a manumission deed from the state. Upon emancipation, the freedman was required to leave the state because free blacks were not allowed to settle in Tennessee. Although James possessed manumission papers granted by his slaveholder, the state of Tennessee regarded him as an enslaved person, although he was gainfully employed as a Nashville barber.

As for Sally's son, Henry, this highly valuable and "likely" slave was appraised at a figure that far exceeded Sally's savings at the time of the estate distribution in 1834. She urged him to escape to Canada and freedom by traveling through Kentucky, Ohio, and New York. Henry's journey as a fugitive was not without its obstacles. At one point, he stole a boat and tried to row it over a waterfall with his wrists still chained. He managed to find someone who was willing to help him break free from the iron shackles, only to be arrested in Ohio. Henry then escaped from jail, made it to New York, and eventually settled in Canada.

James went on to become an affluent, literate, well-respected, and trusted local barber, free to move about the city and even abroad. He even accompanied Andrew Jackson Polk, a wealthy relative of President James Polk, on his travels to New York City and Europe. On 6 March 1851 James went before the Tennessee court system to make his case for freedom and to apply for an exception to reside in Tennessee. Supported by prominent attorney Foster, Thomas was found to be a productive, industrious, upstanding Tennessean, worthy of this special exception and the nine judges consequently granted his emancipation. James Thomas was allowed to reside in Tennessee and retain his thriving barbershop. His beloved mother had succumbed to the cholera epidemic only six months earlier; thus, James Thomas could not share this special triumph with a loved one. However, she and all three of her sons had become free before the Civil War.

Thomas is buried at the historic Nashville City Cemetery among the thousands of Tennessee citizens governors, mayors, some of the famous Fisk University Jubilee Singers, educators, and other former slaves. Thomas used her special status as black entrepreneur in the burgeoning antebellum city of Nashville, Tennessee, to purchase freedom for herself and her children.

FURTHER READING

Franklin, John Hope, and Loren Schweninger. *In Search of the Promised Land: A Slave Family in the Old South* (2006).

Schweninger, Loren. *James T. Rapier and Reconstruction* (1978).

MELANIE THOMAS

Thomas, Vivien Theodore (29 Aug. 1910–26 Nov. 1985), pioneering cardiovascular surgeon, was born in Lake Providence, Louisiana. In 1912, to avoid the frequent flooding of their river town home, his parents, William Maceo Thomas and Mary Eaton, moved their family to higher ground in Nashville,

Tennessee. William, a carpenter and contractor, and Mary, a seamstress, found plenty of work in the prosperous capital, and they were soon able to buy a plot of land and build a house.

Vivien, the youngest of four children, took advantage of Nashville's reputation as an educational center. There was an excellent public school system as well as several institutions of higher education—including one of only two medical schools in the nation that admitted qualified African Americans. He graduated from high school in 1929. As important to his education as the standard curriculum of languages, mathematics, history, and the sciences was the training he received in carpentry from his father. Studying in the morning and working afternoons and weekends, Thomas earned not only his diploma and craft skills but also a decent wage. He had planned to spend the money he saved from his carpentry work on college tuition. However, the Depression forced him to delay his education plans.

Thomas found a new job at Vanderbilt University in Dr. Alfred Blalock's laboratory. Blalock was researching experimental shock, particularly how muscle injuries cause low blood pressure. Working in this lab under Dr. Joseph Beard, Thomas developed his surgical skills and a deep enthusiasm for laboratory research. In 1930 the collapse of the bank that held all his savings dashed Thomas's hopes for a college education. Blalock persuaded an angry and resentful, and now broke, Vivien Thomas to continue at the lab and work toward a career in research. Over the next decade Thomas remained at the lab, developing his surgical skills until he became an integral member of the expanding laboratory team. In 1940 Blalock accepted an offer to become surgeon in chief and chairman of the Department of Surgery at Johns Hopkins University, and he invited Thomas to go to Baltimore with him. Weighing alternative job possibilities and new family responsibilities—he had married Clara Beatrice Flanders in 1933, and they had had two daughters by 1938—Thomas decided to accept Blalock's offer.

Thomas faced quite an adjustment in moving to Baltimore, including learning how to deal with racial tensions in the hospital. As the only African American scientific researcher at Hopkins, Thomas had to negotiate the prejudices of his colleagues and the hospital complex. His advanced surgical skills, Blalock's support, and the great latitude Blalock gave Thomas in laboratory matters helped him overcome his sensitivity to this situation.

Blalock's team, with Thomas conducting the bulk of the laboratory work, continued their investigation of surgical shock and cardiovascular surgery. In particular, they addressed a World War II phenomenon known as "crush syndrome," in which people who had been crushed under fallen debris suffered high blood pressure and went into shock. Although Thomas's work on this project had attracted the attention of the U.S. government, it was the part he played in researching "blue babies" that earned him his place in the history of medicine.

In 1943 Dr. Helen B. Taussig, a pediatric cardiologist and director of the Cardiac Clinic in the Harriet Lane Home for Invalid Children, approached Blalock concerning heart disease in children. She was especially interested in the problem of blue babies, in whom anatomical abnormalities of the heart result in an insufficient amount of oxygen in the blood, giving a bluish tint to the complexion.

Drawing on Taussig's extensive clinical and autopsy observations and her large collection of defective hearts, Thomas and Blalock organized a research protocol. Applying their shock work to this new problem, Thomas successfully re-created the heart defect in dogs. Reversing the procedure, he discovered that by rerouting an artery to send the blood through the lungs a second time he could increase the amount of oxygen in the bloodstream. All that remained was the daunting move to use their technique on a human patient. After training himself in Thomas's technique, Blalock preformed the first blue baby operation—with Thomas literally standing over his shoulder—on a very young girl named Eileen. It was a success, and her rapid recovery attracted the world's attention, drawing patients from around the nation and Europe. In 1950 the Blalock team administered the one-thousanth blue baby treatment.

A crucial member of the laboratory, Thomas did not receive public recognition for his research until much later. Only after twenty years did he find himself listed as a collaborator on a Blalock publication. Even though Blalock eventually persuaded the hospital to increase Thomas's substandard pay, Thomas was forced to supplement his income by selling medical supplies to Baltimore's African American physicians. Over the next three decades Thomas matured as a scientist and administrator as the laboratory expanded in size and scope. Under a series of laboratory directors and as collaborator with an even larger number of surgical research investigators and medical students, he made additional significant contributions to cardiac research.

After working in the background for nearly thirty years, Thomas finally began to receive the recognition he was due. In 1969 the physicians he had collaborated with since 1941 paid him the honor of commissioning his portrait. Still hanging in the Blalock Lobby of the Johns Hopkins Hospital next to Blalock's, it is a testament to Thomas's influence. In 1976 the University of Maryland at College Park awarded Thomas an honorary doctor of science degree. That same year the Johns Hopkins University presented him with an honorary doctor of law degree and appointed him to the faculty as Instructor of Surgery. He retired in 1979, and, after being ill for several months, died in Baltimore in 1985.

FURTHER READING

Thomas's papers are located at the Alan Mason Chesney Medical Archives of the Johns Hopkins Medical Institutions.

Thomas, Vivien. *Pioneering Research in Surgical Shock and Cardiovascular Surgery: Vivien Thomas and His Work with Alfred Blalock* (1985), republished as *Partners of the Heart: Vivien Thomas and His Work with Alfred Blalock: An Autobiography* (1997).

Harvey, A. McGehee. *Adventures in Medical Research: A Century of Discovery at Johns Hopkins* (1976).

Obituaries: *News American* and *Baltimore Sun*, 27 Nov. 1985.

LLOYD ACKERT

Thomas, William (12 Mar. 1931–10 Oct. 1980), actor, was born in Los Angeles, California, to Will Thomas, a janitor, and Mattie Thomas. He became famous at the age of three when he assumed the role of Buckwheat on the television series *Our Gang*.

In February 1934 Thomas was discovered at one of a series of auditions that *Our Gang* producer Hal Roach staged at the Lincoln Theatre in a predominately black section of Los Angeles to find a replacement for the show's previous African American characters, played first by Allen Clayton "Farina" Hoskins and then by MATTHEW BEARD. Thomas's character was modeled after Hoskins's; both wore ragged, oversized clothes, had kinky pigtailed hair, were of ambiguous gender, and used exaggerated facial expressions. These characteristics, and Buckwheat's stylized dialect, led to much criticism that his character, like Farina, perpetuated the "pickaninny" stereotype that originated in blackface minstrelsy. Thomas, however, insisted that Farina, Stymie, Buckwheat, and the show's other African American characters were always treated as equals to their white counterparts (Maltin and Bann, 268).

From 1934 to 1945 Thomas appeared in nearly one hundred *Our Gang* films, as well as a handful of projects not related to *Our Gang* or his Buckwheat character, including *Mokey* (1942), the Oscar-winning short *Heavenly Music* (1943), and the western *Colorado Pioneers* (1945). His film career ended by the fall of 1945, at which point he entered public school. Upon graduation from high school, he joined the army and served in the Korean War. Afterward he became a film laboratory technician with Technicolor in Hollywood, the career he remained in for the rest of his life. He married and had one son, William Thomas Jr., in 1950. Aside from a 1974 appearance on NBC's *The Tomorrow Show* with other *Our Gang* alumni, he did not make any further television or film appearances.

Despite Thomas's retirement from the screen, the character of Buckwheat remained in the public eye, with no fewer than six impostors claiming to have portrayed Buckwheat at one time or another. Matthew Beard's sister Carlene had in fact played the character of Buckwheat in one film, as had Willie Mac Walton-Taylor in three others. After Thomas's death at age forty-nine from a heart attack, several of his obituaries noted that he had been involved in a dispute with James E. Frazier, who claimed to have been the real Buckwheat. Ten years after Thomas's death, a man named Bill English appeared on the television show *20/20* claiming that he, and not Thomas, had been the real Buckwheat. After protests from friends and family, including his son and George "Spanky" McFarland, who played opposite Buckwheat in *Our Gang*, the news show issued a retraction, and the story's producer resigned.

William Thomas Jr. was similarly upset by EDDIE MURPHY's portrayal of an adult Buckwheat in a series of sketches on *Saturday Night Live* in the 1980s. The first sketch aired on the one-year anniversary of his father's death, a fact that Thomas found to be distasteful. He wrote a letter of protest to Dick Ebersol, the show's producer, who apologized publicly. Murphy, for his part, insisted that those who conflated Thomas the actor and Buckwheat the character were mistaken, and his portrayal of Buckwheat was no reflection on Thomas (Maltin and Bann, 268).

Thomas himself, though, was identified publicly with Buckwheat long after his film career ended, and his son perpetuated this identification both through licensing his father's image and by establishing the Buckwheat Memorial Scholarship at California State University, Northridge, the younger Thomas's alma mater, in 1992. That the scholarship is named for Buckwheat, rather than for the actor who played him, raised some eyebrows upon its inception and rekindled debate about the politics of race and representation that have long circulated around the character of Buckwheat. Some students and members of the press have claimed that naming the scholarship after Buckwheat perpetuates minstrel-derived stereotyped representations (Wallace). Its defenders, including William Thomas Jr., pointed to the pioneering work that the African American cast members of *Our Gang* did in opening up the television industry to black actors. The show's defenders also noted that *Our Gang* was integrated while the country was still subject to *de jure* segregation (Wallace).

Buckwheat, both as child actor and pop icon, suggested the complex transitions that popular representations of and by African Americans underwent from the minstrel stage and vaudeville to twentieth- and twenty-first-century mass media.

FURTHER READING

Maltin, Leonard, and Richard W. Bann. *The Little Rascals: The Life and Times of Our Gang* (1992).

Wallace, Amy. "Scholarship Keeps Controversial Image in the Spotlight," *Los Angeles Times*, 8 Nov. 1992.

Obituary: *Washington Post*, 12 Oct. 1980.

ERICH NUNN

Thomas, William Hannibal (4 May 1843–15 Nov. 1935), clergyman and author, was born in Pickaway County, Ohio, the son of a Virginia free black (name unknown) and Rebecca Fisher Thomas, an Ohio free black. None of Thomas's immediate ancestors had been slaves; he was descended from two generations of light-skinned African Americans. His light complexion and his status as a free black played a major role in Thomas's later assessment of his race.

During Thomas's formative years his family lived in Ohio, Indiana, and Michigan before returning to Ohio in 1857. Like other free blacks in the Old Northwest, they experienced second-class legal status and all manner of racial discrimination. Thomas's father reportedly helped fugitive slaves from the South make their way to freedom in Canada. As a teenager, Thomas performed farm labor, attended school briefly, and in 1859 broke the color barrier at Otterbein College in Westerville,

Ohio. His enrollment led to a race riot, and he soon left the school. Denied entrance to the Union army in 1861 because of his skin color, Thomas served as acting principal of Union Seminary Institute, a manual training school near Columbus, Ohio, established by the African Methodist Episcopal (AME) Church.

From September 1861 to July 1863 Thomas worked as a servant in two white army units, the 42nd and 95th Ohio Volunteer Infantry regiments. In September 1863 he enlisted in Ohio's first black regiment, the 127th Ohio Volunteer Infantry (renamed the Fifth U.S. Colored Troops), and was quickly appointed sergeant. Thomas served with distinction in several campaigns and was awarded a silver medal for bravery at New Market Heights, Virginia. Following the fall of North Carolina's Fort Fisher in February 1865, Thomas received a gunshot wound in his right arm that led to its amputation. He suffered from severe medical complications and pain from this wound for the remainder of his life.

After the war Thomas began a thirty-year career as a national correspondent for the *Christian Recorder*, the weekly newspaper of the AME Church. His articles provided him with a forum for a broad range of religious, social, and political commentary. Many of his contributions advocated church reform, including more systematic collection and disbursement of the church's money and better-educated clergy. During Reconstruction Thomas studied theology at Western Theological Seminary in Allegheny City, Pennsylvania, served as a financial agent for Wilberforce University in Ohio, and was appointed an AME pastor in the Monongahela, Pennsylvania, circuit. In 1867 he married Martha (maiden name unknown), a widow with two sons, and together they had one son. By 1878 Thomas had abandoned Martha and later lived with other women. Thomas's second wife, Zenette (maiden name unknown), died in 1906.

In 1871 Thomas moved to Rome, Georgia, as principal of a school administered by the Freedmen's Aid Society of the Methodist Episcopal Church. In 1872 he joined the faculty of Clark Theological Seminary in Atlanta. Thomas next moved to Newberry, South Carolina, where he practiced law, was appointed a trial justice, served as a colonel in the militia, and became active in Republican Party politics. In the contested 1876 campaign, Thomas was elected to the South Carolina legislature. He lost his seat, however, when Governor Wade Hampton and the "Bourbon" Democrats took office in 1877. Through his Republican connections Thomas received a diplomatic appointment in 1878 as U.S. consul to Saint Paul de Loanda in Portuguese Southwest Africa.

Over the next two decades Thomas moved to Boston and published widely, especially in the scholarly *A.M.E. Church Review*. In 1886 he launched a magazine, *The Negro*, that failed after two issues. In 1890 Thomas published a monograph, *Land and Education*, a work that urged blacks to improve themselves through prayer, high moral values, education, and land acquisition. This work summarized several reform proposals that Thomas espoused during the 1890s. During this decade, however, he grew increasingly despondent and became severely critical of his race. His pessimism appeared full-blown in 1901, when the Macmillan Company published his book *The American Negro*.

In this work Thomas distanced himself from members of his race, especially black women and black clergymen. Intolerant and hypercritical, he attacked blacks (but not those with light skin) as depraved, immoral, irresponsible, and destined to fail. Thomas looked to mixed-race individuals like himself as the future leaders of people of color. Though he had long advocated reforms among blacks and had "passed" as a white man earlier in his life, Thomas's radical attack on blacks (as differentiated from biracial African Americans) was unusual but not unprecedented. Few white critics in the age of Jim Crow assaulted blacks with as much crude venom as Thomas did in *The American Negro*.

The book received widespread national attention, appealing to white racists who cited it as sufficient evidence of the need to repeal the Fifteenth Amendment. *The American Negro* also served to rally many in the black community against Thomas—as someone whom they deemed to be a rank traitor in their midst. Race leaders, including BOOKER T. WASHINGTON, W. E. B. DUBOIS, and CHARLES W. CHESNUTT, mounted a sustained attack on Thomas and his book. Washington even sought to use his connections to suppress distribution of *The American Negro*. Critics in the black community branded Thomas a "black Judas." They charged him with hypocrisy and unearthed numerous indiscretions in Thomas's personal and professional life. Blacks in Memphis threatened to lynch Thomas if he ever ventured into their city.

After the publication of *The American Negro*, Thomas responded to his accusers in the popular literary magazine the *Critic*, defending his book as "a serious sociological study." In later years he published several articles about his life but never completed a proposed full-length autobiography. Thomas lived in obscurity in Everett, Massachusetts, until 1912, when he returned briefly to Rome, Georgia. From 1915 until his death he resided in Columbus, Ohio, working into his nineties as a janitor. Although Thomas received the opprobrium of black Americans after the publication of *The American Negro*, some nonetheless acknowledged the legitimacy of a few of his criticisms. His sharp and extreme statements, however, contributed less to the black reform tradition than to his sounding an alarm for blacks to pull together to combat enemies from both inside and outside the race.

FURTHER READING

Newby, Idus A. *Jim Crow's Defense: Anti-Negro Thought in America, 1900–1930* (1965).

Smith, John David. *"Black Judas": William Hannibal Thomas and "The American Negro"* (1999).

This entry is taken from the *American National Biography* and is published here with the permission of the American Council of Learned Societies.

JOHN DAVID SMITH

Thomas-Graham, Pamela (1963–), corporate executive, management consultant, attorney, and author, was born in Detroit, Michigan, to Marian Thomas, a social worker from Georgia whose maiden name is unknown, and Albert Thomas, an engineer from South Carolina. The younger of two children, Pamela's older brother, Vincent, became a lawyer and law school associate dean. She grew up with a mother who worked outside the home and a father who supported women developing themselves intellectually and professionally. Albert Thomas maintained the same expectations of performance for both Pamela and her brother. Both parents were strong believers in the principles of obtaining an education and applying oneself. The climate in the Thomas home also held civil rights leaders and lawyers in high esteem, which motivated Pamela and Vincent to dream of becoming lawyers in the tradition of THURGOOD MARSHALL. Pamela loved to read, and she excelled in her schoolwork. Her peers at Lutheran High School West in Detroit selected her as not only the "smartest" but also the "most likely to succeed." Additionally, she participated in the drama club and school choir.

The idea of Pamela attending Harvard University was never questioned in the Thomas household. A friend of the family who was a Harvard alumna began taking her to Harvard functions when she was only in the fifth grade, and from that time on she knew that was where she would continue her studies. While her mentor and parents believed that she would matriculate at Harvard, others were not in agreement. A high-school guidance counselor told her that such expectations were "unrealistic," Thomas recalled in a 2004 speech given at Harvard Law School and published in the following year's *Harvard Journal of Law and Gender* (available at http://www.law.harvard.edu/students/orgs/jlg/vol27/thomas-graham.php). The counselor told Thomas that it would be better if she did not apply and suffer the inevitable disappointment of rejection since no other Lutheran High West graduate had ever been accepted to Harvard. Such warnings only served to strengthen her resolve. Harvard accepted her and while there she was voted the student "showing the most promise." She went on to be elected to Phi Beta Kappa and to graduate magna cum laude with a B.A. in Economics in 1985. She was also presented the top honor that Harvard awards to a female graduate, the Captain Jonathan Fay Prize. Continuing her interest in law and economics, she continued to study at Harvard, earning both J.D. and MBA degrees in 1989. Never one to pass over an opportunity to seek new challenges, she served as editor of the *Harvard Law Review*. During her law school education she met Lawrence Otis Graham, another law school student, whom she would marry in February 1992.

Thomas-Graham took her legal and business training to McKinsey & Company, the largest management consulting firm in the world, and from 1989 to 1999 she worked closely with CEOs from Fortune 500 companies in McKinsey's media and entertainment practice. The consulting that she did with McKinsey allowed Thomas-Graham to refine her knowledge of developing growth strategies. Her no-nonsense business style meshed with working collegially to increase productivity and effectiveness. McKinsey & Company named her a partner when she was only thirty-two years old, making her the organization's first African American female partner. Thomas-Graham acknowledged that her life had been one of trailblazing as an African American woman and that she believed in turning the challenging role of "first" into an advantage and viewing it as an opportunity.

Consulting at McKinsey stimulated her entrepreneurial spirit, but Thomas-Graham felt ready to do more than guide others in the running of a company; she wanted to take on a company of her own in the role of president. In 1999 she met Jack Welch, then CEO of General Electric, which owned NBC, CNBC, and MSNBC. Their meeting was the first step toward thirty-six-year-old Thomas-Graham being hired as president and CEO of CNBC.com, the business network's new Web site. The late 1990s was a propitious time to take on a financial Web site, and with so many people focused on the financial news that CNBC.com provided, Thomas-Graham made the dot-com a force to be reckoned with.

In February 2001 she was tapped for president and chief operating officer of CNBC, and by July of the same year she was appointed the network's CEO. CNBC was a global leader in business news and financial market coverage and aired in more than 200 million homes around the world. Thomas-Graham's responsibilities included the network's programming, business development, and synergy enhancement between the television and Internet strategies of CNBC. CNBC had record profitability during the July 2001 to February 2005 tenure of Thomas-Graham. The network's audience possessed the highest income of any network on cable television, and it attracted a younger primetime audience with the programming changes that she instituted. Thomas-Graham directed the design and construction of CNBC's new global headquarters, a 350,000-square-foot complex in Englewood Cliffs, New Jersey. Such successes helped pave the way for her promotion to chairman of the network in February 2005.

Concurrent with her professional advancements, Thomas-Graham gave back to the community, a goal stressed in her parents' home. She was active with Girls Incorporated, a well-established organization that nurtured the talents of girls from low-income families, and encouraged them to succeed, despite their disadvantaged background. She also played a key role in bringing Mattel and *Working Woman* magazine together to create the Working Woman Barbie doll. She has also served on the boards of the New York City Opera, the American Red Cross of Greater New York, the Harvard Alumni Association, and others.

Her outstanding business performance and community service were recognized with her being named one of *Fortune* magazine's 50 Most Powerful Blacks in Business, *Television Week*'s 12 People to Watch, *Black Enterprise*'s Corporate Executive of the Year, *Ms.* magazine's 2003 Woman of the Year, and the 40 Under 40 list of rising young executives by *Crain's New York Business* plus many more.

Thomas-Graham balanced her professional career with her family life. She and her husband raised one son and a set of twins, one boy and one girl, in Westchester County, New York. Beginning in 1998, Thomas-Graham published her Ivy League Mystery series, featuring Nikki Chase, a Harvard economics professor. The books received critical acclaim, were published in Germany and Japan as well as in the United States, and have been optioned for a feature film by actor MORGAN FREEMAN.

Those who learned of the many undertakings of Pamela Thomas-Graham were baffled that one person could find enough hours in the day to accomplish all that she did. Her mother gave away her secret. Thomas-Graham only needed four hours of sleep to maintain her demanding lifestyle. She made a practice of rising at 4:00 A.M. to have time to devote to her writing before her children awoke.

FURTHER READING
Clark, Robyn D. "Excellence by the Graham," *Black Enterprise* (Sept. 2001).
Jenkins, Carol. "Pamela Thomas-Graham," *Ms.* (Winter 2003).
Norment, Lynn. "3 at the Top: Major Executives Tell How They Are Dealing with the Crisis," *Ebony* (Feb. 2002).

PAULETTE K. POLLEY-EDMUNDS

Thompkins, William H. (3 Oct. 1872–24 Sept. 1916), Spanish-American War veteran and Medal of Honor recipient, was born in Paterson, New Jersey, the son of the New York natives John and Angeline Thompkins (also spelled "Tompkins"). His father practiced the trade of a teamster, while his mother was a housekeeper. William attended public school in Paterson, where he learned to read and write and later became a teamster like his father. His skill in working with horses, perhaps fostered from an early age, proved valuable in his subsequent military service.

William Thompkins was working as a teamster in Cleveland, Ohio, when he enlisted in the U.S. Army on 2 August 1889 for a term of five years. He was assigned to the 9th Cavalry Regiment, one of four army units (two cavalry, two infantry) manned entirely by black enlisted soldiers, likely because of his horse-handling experience, and soon went westward with his regiment to serve on the western frontier. He gained his first combat experience as a participant in the Pine Ridge Campaign against the Sioux in South Dakota, the last major conflict of the Indian Wars. Private Thompkins's first term of enlistment expired in 1894 at Fort Robinson, Nebraska, but he quickly reenlisted in the army and remained a soldier for nearly the rest of his life.

When the Spanish-American War broke out in 1898, William Thompkins was serving with his regiment at Fort Robinson when it was called for service in Cuba. The men of the 9th and 10th Cavalry regiments subsequently journeyed to Tampa, Florida, in May 1898 and stayed there for several weeks until a portion of the men, about fifty in number, were embarked for a voyage to Cuba along with a number of Cuban troops and American volunteers aboard the transport *Florida* to perform a special mission, namely to make a landing and reinforce Cuban insurgents. The first attempt to make a landing by the American forces on 29 June at Cienfuegos was repulsed by the Spanish, so another attempt was made the next day, this time at the village of Tayabacao. This attack, too, was unsuccessful, and during the harried nighttime withdrawal several wounded men were left behind. A number of rescue attempts to save the wounded were subsequently made, but each failed. Finally, another rescue was planned using the black cavalrymen available, with Lieutenant George Ahern, a white officer, chosen to lead the effort. The enlisted men selected by the commander of the detachment, Lieutenant Carter Johnson, to make the rescue were William Thompkins, by now a sergeant; George Wanton, a fellow Paterson, New Jersey, native; Dennis Bell; and FITZ LEE. The five men departed from the transport *Florida* in a small boat under cover of darkness and made a successful landing. Despite heavy fire from the Spanish troops, who were alert for yet another rescue attempt, Thompkins and the rest of the men worked quickly to locate the wounded men and brought them safely off. When Lieutenant Johnson returned stateside in 1899, he recommended all four of his black cavalrymen for the Medal of Honor, which awards were quickly approved by June 1899. William Thompkins received his Medal of Honor while still in Cuba.

The service of men like William Thompkins and AUGUSTUS WALLEY, the "Buffalo Soldiers" of the 9th and 10th Cavalry regiments, is not only important for the heroic deeds they performed under fire to earn them the Medal of Honor, but also serves as a reminder of the overall valuable service performed by black soldiers under difficult circumstances in the American military during the late nineteenth century.

Following his service in Cuba, William Thompkins continued to serve in the army in a variety of posts stateside. He was later transferred to the all-black 25th Infantry Regiment and saw service at the Presidio in California and Fort Lawton in Seattle, Washington. Sergeant William Thompkins received his final discharge from the army at Schofield Barracks in Hawaii on 6 February 1910 and stayed in Hawaii for a time before returning stateside to California. Perhaps worn out by his years of rugged service, Thompkins died in San Francisco, California, at the age of forty-four, and was interred at the San Francisco National Cemetery, where a Medal of Honor headstone marks his final resting place.

FURTHER READING

Hanna, Charles W. *African American Recipients of the Medal of Honor* (2002).

Schubert, Frank N. *Black Valor: Buffalo Soldiers and the Medal of Honor, 1870–1898* (1997).

GLENN ALLEN KNOBLOCK

Thompson, Bennie Gordon (28 Jan. 1948–), U.S. congressman, was born in Bolton, Mississippi.

Thompson received a B.A. degree in Political Science from Tougaloo College in Jackson, Mississippi, in 1968 and a master's of science degree in Educational Administration from Jackson State University in Jackson, Mississippi, in 1972. He also matriculated at the University of Southern Mississippi, where he worked on a doctorate degree in Public Administration. His résumé includes teaching stints in the public school system in Mississippi as well as being an adjunct professor at Jackson State University.

Thompson was a member of Ashbury United Methodist Church in Bolton. He married the former London Johnson, and he and his wife had one daughter, BendaLonne.

Thompson first entered public service when he was elected alderman in his hometown of Bolton, Mississippi, in 1969. He served in this capacity until 1973. In that year he was recognized as the Politician of the Year by Jackson State University. Having established a credible record at the grassroots level, Thompson was elected Bolton's mayor in 1973 and held this office until 1979. As mayor, Thompson was instrumental in bringing the first rural doctor, fire engine, and trained volunteer fire department to the town. His ascent up the ladder of public service continued with his being elected a supervisor of Hinds County, District 2 in 1979, where he served for thirteen years (1980–1993).

In 1993 he was elected to U.S. House of Representatives, Second District of Mississippi. His election came as a result of a special election called to fill the vacancy created by the resignation of MIKE ESPY, who had been named Secretary of

Agriculture by President Bill Clinton. Because many of his constituents in his Mississippi Delta district were poor and illiterate, Thompson emerged as a vocal advocate for African Americans and the poor. In 1975 Thompson was one of the original plaintiffs in the Ayers desegregation case, which was aimed at addressing disparate funding of black and white institutions of higher education in Mississippi. Because of the importance of agriculture to the Second District, Thompson served on the U.S. House Agricultural Committee. Acting as a voice for disadvantaged communities, Thompson initiated legislation designed to address past discrimination of African American farmers as a result of unfair Department of Agriculture programs, for example, by proposing legislation designed to provide funding to the U.S. Department of Agriculture's office of Assistant Secretary for Civil Rights.

Thompson was also recognized by the National Black Nurses foundation for his support and advocacy of adequate health care for all citizens, regardless of socioeconomic status. A major hallmark of his career was when he received a presidential appointment to serve on the National Council on Health Planning and Development.

Outside of his Washington, D.C., duties, Thompson was also active in his home state. He was one of the founding members of the Mississippi Association of Black Mayors and the Mississippi Association of Black Supervisors. He served on the board of trustees of Tougaloo College, the board of directors of the Southern Regional Council, and the board of directors of the Housing Assistance Council.

FURTHER READING

Jeter, Lynne W. "Incumbent Ready for Second District Campaign (On The Record with Bennie Thompson)," *Mississippi Business Journal*, 22 Apr. 2002.

RICHARD T. MIDDLETON IV

Thompson, Charles Henry (19 July 1895–21 Jan. 1980), educator and psychologist, was born in Jackson, Mississippi. Both of his parents (Reverend Patrick Henry Thompson and Mrs. Sara Estelle [Byers] Thompson) taught at Jackson College. After completing his high school education at Wayland Academy in Virginia, he enrolled at Virginia Union University in Richmond, Virginia, in 1914 and earned his bachelor's degree in 1917. He received a second bachelor's degree from the University of Chicago in 1918. He was drafted into the army and was stationed at first at Camp Grant in Illinois. He

later served in France, rising to the rank of infantry personnel regimental sergeant major.

After his discharge he returned to the University of Chicago, where he earned his master's degree in 1920. From 1920 to 1921 he served as psychology instructor at Virginia Union University. He was director of instruction at the Alabama State Normal School from 1921. He received his doctorate in educational psychology, the first black to receive such a degree, from the University of Chicago in 1925. His dissertation research was on teacher curricula. He was an instructor in psychology and social science at Summer High School and Junior College in Kansas City, Kansas.

He came to Howard University in 1926. With the support of President MORDECAI JOHNSON he founded the *Journal of Negro Education* in 1932 and remained its editor-in-chief until 1963. The purpose of the journal was to document the conditions of Negro schools and to examine the consequences of segregated education. "Thompson's magazine now seized the torch that had been let fall when *The Crisis* lost its founder. The *Journal* was, to be sure, far less polemical than *The Crisis* had ever been, but it served a similar purpose: to inform, to arouse, to inspire" (Kluger, p. 168).

Thompson convinced many black scholars to contribute articles to the journal for free. A major theme that ran through these articles and Thompson's more than one hundred editorials was the inherent inequality of segregated schools. Thompson provided scholarly support for the work of THURGOOD MARSHALL and the NAACP Legal Fund's quest to overturn *Plessy v. Ferguson*, the Supreme Court's 1896 ruling in support of racial segregation. He served as an expert witness in cases challenging segregated schools, including *Sweatt v. Board of Regents of the University of Texas et al.* in 1946, *Sipuel v. Board of Regents of the University of Oklahoma* in 1948, and *McLaurin v. Oklahoma State Regents* in 1950. The psychologists KENNETH CLARK and MAMIE CLARK published an article in the *Journal* in 1950, which showed that the majority of black children between five and seven years of age colored a picture of a child (supposedly like themselves) in a color lighter than their own skin color. This study was included in the appendix to the brief submitted by social scientists in support of the plaintiff in the *Brown v. Board of Education of Topeka* in 1955.

During his forty years at the university Thompson held such positions as professor and chairman of the Department of Education, dean of the College of Liberal Arts, and dean of the Graduate School.

His accomplishments in these positions include the establishment of procedures to offer scholarships to promising high school students, the development of faculty tenure policies, the requirements for students to enter Howard's master's programs, and the beginning of doctoral programs at Howard.

During his career Thompson was an editorial consultant to the *Nation's Schools* from 1943 to 1950 and the *World Book Encyclopedia* from 1942 to 1962. He was a U.S. representative to UNESCO from 1946 to 1949. He was a fellow in the American Association for the Advancement of Science and a national board member of the NAACP. He was also a member of the National Education Association, the American Association for Higher Education, and the National Society for the Study of Education.

He retired as dean emeritus from Howard University in 1966. His wife Mae (Stewart) Thompson died in 1975. He died on 21 January 1980 in Hyattsville, Maryland. He is buried in Lincoln Memorial Cemetery in Suitland, Maryland.

FURTHER READING
Davis, Lenwood G., and Belinda S. Davis. "Charles H. Thompson: A Bibliography." *Journal of Negro Education* 50 (1981): 111–121.
Kluger, Richard. *Simple Justice: The History of Brown v. Board of Education and Black America's Struggle for Equality* (1980).
Obituary: *Washington Post*, 23 Jan. 1980.

STEPHEN A. TRUHON

Thompson, Clara Ann (1869–1949), poet and lecturer, was born in Rossmoyne, Ohio, the daughter of John Henry Thompson and Clara Jane Gray, former slaves. Other Thompson children included the poets PRISCILLA JANE THOMPSON and Aaron Belford Thompson. Thompson attended the Amity School and received private tutoring in Rossmoyne, near Cincinnati. A member of the Baptist church, the NAACP, and the YWCA, she taught briefly but devoted most of her time to her literary work. Thompson gave readings from her poetry, and she has been described as being a "fine elocutionist." Although in her second book of poetry, *A Garland of Poems* (1926), she remarks that her wish had been to be a novelist, Thompson's literary output consisted of two volumes of poetry. Thompson states that "the writing of poetry has been thrust upon me—I write it because I must." Never marrying, she lived with her sister and her older brother, Garland Yancey Thompson. Her first volume, *Songs from the Wayside* (1908), is dedicated to them.

A number of Thompson's poems are written in dialect. *Songs from the Wayside* contains several such poems, including "Uncle Rube's Defense," "Uncle Rube on the Race Problem," and "Uncle Rube to the Young People." In these poems the speaker, an elderly black man, offers sage advice on race relations in a light, folksy style. He tells whites that "de way to solve de [Negro] problum, / Is, to let de black man be." Other humorous poems in *Songs from the Wayside* include "The Old and the New," in which a woman refuses to stop making joyful noise in church; "Mrs. Johnson Objects," in which the speaker tells her children not to play with "po' white trash"; "The Easter Bonnet," in which a black woman learns not to hint "For the white-folks cast-off clothes"; and the eerily modern "The Christmas Rush," about last-minute shoppers.

Most of Thompson's poems, however, are religious in tone, including "His Answer," "The Easter Light," "The Skeptic," and "The Empty Tomb." There are also several elegies, including "To My Dead Brother," which seem to indicate that there was another Thompson brother besides Aaron and Garland. In both "If Thou Shouldst Return" and "She Sent Him Away," a woman regrets spurning a suitor, perhaps an indication that Thompson rejected an offer of marriage and later regretted her decision. Many of her poems are similar to those in the "Black Genteel School," later represented by such poets as COUNTÉE CULLEN and GEORGIA DOUGLAS JOHNSON. These writers tended to write on "universal" themes, with poems on racial topics usually emphasizing the positive and progressive.

A Garland of Poems is dedicated to Thompson's eldest brother (the title has an obvious pun on his name) and was published in Boston in 1926. It is similar in tone and scope to her first book. There is another Uncle Rube poem, "Uncle Rube on Church Quarrels," which, like LANGSTON HUGHES and ZORA NEALE HURSTON's 1930s play *Mule Bone*, pokes gentle fun at the squabbles between different religious denominations. There are a number of other dialect pieces in *A Garland of Poems*, including "Pap's Advice," "Goin' to Foot It All the Way," and "Aunt Mandy's Grandchildren." In "Showin' Off," the speaker exclaims, "Showin' off! dat's one fault children, / Dat's a-harmin' of de race." Also included in this volume are several elegies, such as "I Have Lived for This Hour," "Our Deceased Leader," and "Life and Death" (for BOOKER T. WASHINGTON). Religious poems abound, including "You'll have to Come Back to the Road," "Consecration," "Communion Prayer," and "Let Us Get Back to God."

A Garland of Poems contains two interesting poems about blacks involved in World War I. "Our Soldiers" concerns the black troops leaving Cincinnati to train for the war, and "Our Heroes" praises the black troops upon their return to the city. Among the other poems in the book is the lengthy "What Mean This Bleating of the Sheep," which was published separately in 1921 and reprinted in *A Garland of Poems*. In this poem Thompson chronicles America's history of racial discrimination and warns of God's retribution if such behavior does not cease. While proclaiming that America's "flag is trailing in the dust," the poem asks what has become of the country's "pledge of faith: 'In God We Trust?'"

In her foreword to *A Garland of Poems*, Thompson claims that in the poems "pertaining to my people, whom I love very dearly, … I have endeavored to present both sides [black and white] of the subject, knowing that no problem can be truly solved in any other way." Therefore, Thompson is willing to cast blame on blacks as well as whites. In "Our Side of the Race Problem," for example, she criticizes envy within the African American community.

Thompson later lived with a niece in Cincinnati and gave catechism instruction at St. Andrew's Episcopal Church, where she was a member. She died in her niece's home and was buried in an unmarked grave in the United American Cemetery in Cincinnati.

Clara Ann Thompson wrote several distinctive poems, including "Mrs. Johnson Objects," "His Answer," "What Mean This Bleating of the Sheep," and the Uncle Rube poems. Perhaps she sums up her status best in the poem "The Minor Key." Here the speaker longs for a poem that will last "Long after I have ceased to sing" but laments that "Alas!- this is the fate for me: / To ever sing in a minor key." Thompson may be a minor poet, but she sings in a voice that still has its own memorable sound.

FURTHER READING

Dabney, Wendell P. *Cincinnati's Colored Citizens, Historical, Sociological, and Biographical* (1926).

Roses, Lorraine Elena, and Ruth Elizabeth Randolph. *Harlem Renaissance and Beyond: Literary Biographies of 100 Black Women Writers, 1900–1945* (1990, 1997).

Obituary: *Cincinnati Enquirer*, 20 Mar. 1949.

This entry is taken from the *American National Biography* and is published here with the permission of the American Council of Learned Societies.

LOUIS J. PARASCANDOLA

Thompson, David (13 July 1954–), basketball player, was born David O'Neal Thompson in Boiling Springs, North Carolina, the eleventh child of Ida Gentry and Vellie Thompson. Vellie worked for the army surplus store and was fired without cause after nineteen years, one year short of pension eligibility. He then worked as a janitor. Vellie was also a deacon at the Maple Springs Baptist Church, where young David spent many hours singing in the choir. The Thompson family was deeply religious and lived off a dirt road in a three-bedroom, cinder block house with no indoor toilets.

At age five David received a basketball from his mother for Christmas. He began playing on a dirt court that he and his brother, Vellie Thompson Jr., constructed in a country field near their home outside Shelby. Playing for countless hours on the soft surface helped develop Thompson's extraordinary jumping abilities that later became an integral component of his legend. He first dunked a basketball as an eighth grader. Thompson also wore ankle weights during the day and targeted his leg muscles in an array of creative exercises. Thompson's older brother Vellie was his basketball mentor throughout his childhood. Together the two boys refined their skills on their homemade dirt court and in pickup games at Gardner-Webb College and Holly Oak Park.

North Carolina was strictly segregated during most of Thompson's youth, and he attended the all-black Green Bethel School until the ninth grade, when Shelby's Crest High School finally integrated. Standing six feet tall, Thompson played his first organized basketball for the Crest junior varsity in 1967. Unfortunately for Thompson, a ban on dunking in both high school and college was instituted that same year. He joined the varsity the following season and, under Coach Ed Peeler, became a North Carolina high school legend. Crest compiled a record of 54–15 during Thompson's tenure, and he was heavily recruited by major programs. His dream was to play in the Atlantic Coast Conference (ACC) like his basketball idol Charlie Scott.

Thompson, at six feet four inches, entered North Carolina State University in 1971. That fall his standing vertical jump of forty-two inches set a new mark and was widely publicized in the *Guinness*

Book of World Records. North Carolina State, under coach Norm Sloan, went undefeated (27–0) in 1972–1973 but was unable to participate in the National Collegiate Athletic Association (NCAA) tournament due to recruiting violations surrounding Thompson's signing. The following year North Carolina State went 30–1 and captured the national title, dethroning the University of California, Los Angeles (UCLA) Bruins. "David Thompson was the single greatest college player I ever played against," wrote UCLA's Hall of Fame center Bill Walton (Thompson, vii). Thompson was voted most valuable player (MVP) of the 1974 NCAA tournament.

The jumping and shooting (over 54 percent) exploits of Thompson continued to bring him national recognition. He was named ACC Player of the Year and first team All-American for three consecutive years (1973–1975). Thompson was the unanimous College Player of the Year in 1975. Plus he inspired a new generation of athletes that was amazed at his combination of fundamental basketball skills and explosive athleticism. Thompson is widely credited with popularizing the alley-oop play and later acquired the nickname "Skywalker."

Thompson was the first player selected in the 1975 National Basketball Association (NBA) draft but instead chose to sign with the Denver Nuggets of the rival American Basketball Association (ABA). He was the ABA's rookie of the year and the All-Star game MVP. At that same All-Star game, Thompson and JULIUS "DR. J" ERVING were the top competitors in the first slam dunk contest. Months later the league dissolved, and four ABA teams were welcomed into the NBA.

Thompson stayed with the Nuggets when the team joined the NBA and was voted first team All-NBA for two consecutive seasons. One memorable highlight occurred on the final day of the 1977–1978 season, when he scored an amazing seventy-three points in a game against Detroit. Hours later the San Antonio Spur's GEORGE GERVIN scored sixty-three and won the NBA scoring crown by the closest margin ever.

Thompson continued to be one of the most popular, influential, and prolific players in the country as his high-flying, above-the-rim style helped revolutionize modern basketball. In 1978 he re-signed with the Nuggets for $800,000 per year, the largest professional sports contract ever. He also received a lucrative shoe endorsement deal with Pony. Thompson was the MVP of the 1979 NBA All-Star game, making him the only player to be named MVP in both the ABA and the NBA. But a growing alcohol and drug problem began to hinder his effectiveness. After sustaining a knee injury at the New York City disco Studio 54 in March 1984, he never played in another NBA game. Over nine professional seasons (seven in Denver and two in Seattle), he averaged 22.7 points per game.

Thompson married Cathy Barrow on 31 January 1979; they had two daughters. Thompson's number 33 jersey was retired by the Denver Nuggets, and his number 44 was the first jersey retired by North Carolina State. A knee injury he obtained during the 1992 NBA Legends Game is believed to be the primary reason the league stopped that event during All-Star Weekend. Thompson was enshrined in the Naismith Basketball Hall of Fame in 1996.

Thompson eventually overcame his reliance on drugs and alcohol. He moved back to Shelby, North Carolina, and rededicated himself to Christianity. He began delivering motivational speeches and participated in "fantasy" basketball camps. His influence resonated long after he retired. "David Thompson was my inspiration," said the basketball legend MICHAEL JORDAN (*Skywalker*).

FURTHER READING

Hoffman, Anne Byrne. *Echoes from the Schoolyard* (1977).
Pluto, Terry. *Loose Balls*, repr. ed. (1990).
Skywalker (DVD) (2005).
Thompson, David, Sean Stormes, and Marshall Terrill. *Skywalker* (2003).

WAYNE FEDERMAN

Thompson, Eloise Bibb (28 June 1880–8 Jan. 1928), writer, was born Eloise Alberta Veronica Bibb in New Orleans, Louisiana, the daughter of Charles H. Bibb, a U.S. customs inspector, and Catherine Adele (maiden name unknown). Eloise's artistic talent manifested itself at an early age. Eloise was still a teenager when Boston's Monthly Review Press published her *Poems* in 1895. *Poems* features elegies such as "In Memoriam. FREDERICK DOUGLASS," romantic tales such as "A Tale of Italy," nature poems such as "Early Spring," and poems based on literary, biblical, and historical figures. The collection also features a poem titled "Tribute to the Sweet Bard of the Women's Club," dedicated to her fellow contemporary writer Alice Ruth Moore (ALICE DUNBAR-NELSON), who later married the poet PAUL LAURENCE DUNBAR.

Bibb's poetic style and subject matter are representative of African American female poetry of the nineteenth century. As Ann Allen Shockley notes, "Much of nineteenth-century black women's poetry was Victorian. They wrote eulogies, lyrical verses, and poems with themes of romance, family, religion, and nature" (117). *Poems* has received mixed reviews from other modern literary critics. Vernon Loggins notes that "little can be said [of *Poems*] except that the verse is neat and prim" (335). Although Joan R. Sherman praises the poems with figures drawn from the Bible, history, and literature—poems such as "Eliza in Uncle Tom's Cabin" and "Anne Boleyn"—for their lack of "excessive sentimental embroidery," Sherman notes that the poems on nature and the dedications to Douglass and Moore are "trite, weak verses" (206).

After the publication of *Poems*, Bibb studied at Oberlin Academy from 1899 to 1901, and then she returned to New Orleans to teach school. In 1903 she enrolled in Teachers' College at Howard University in Washington, D.C. A discrepancy exists regarding the date of her graduation from Howard University. According to an Oberlin alumni update form that she filled out in 1908, she graduated from Howard in January 1908. However, the Howard University Directory of Graduates lists her graduation year as 1907. In 1908 Bibb obtained a job in Washington, D.C., as head resident at the Colored Social Settlement, a position that she held for three years. Eloise Bibb married Noah Davis Thompson, a fellow devout Catholic and a prominent journalist, in 1911 in Chicago. When the two married, they were considered "well matched because of their common interest in religion, literature, and the advancement of the Negro in the United States" (Scally, 115). They did not have any children together, but Noah Thompson had one son with his first wife, who had died shortly after giving birth.

The couple moved to California in 1911. Noah Thompson worked in real estate and held positions at the *Evening Express*, the *Morning Tribune*, and the *Liberator*. Eloise Thompson worked as a special feature writer for the *Morning Sun* and the *Los Angeles Tribune* and contributed freelance articles to magazines, including *Out West* and *Tidings*, a Catholic publication for which she wrote an article titled "The Church and the Negro." Delilah L. Beasley, a contemporary of the Thompsons, praised Eloise Thompson's work, referring to "The Church and the Negro" and a poem titled "A Garland of Prayer" as "notable contributions" to *Tidings* (254).

Thompson also wrote plays. In 1915 the motion picture director Thomas Harper Ince purchased her first play, *A Reply to the Clansman*, which she wrote in response to *The Clansman*, the novel by Thomas Dixon on which D. W. Griffith based his notorious film masterpiece *Birth of a Nation* (1915). Thompson's play was never filmed because Ince ended his relationship with Triangle Film Corporation. Later Griffith became interested in filming her play, but he "faltered over what he called 'the formidable obstacles in the way of successful production' and at last, yielding to his advisers, decided not to produce it" (*Opportunity*, Feb. 1925, 63). Cecil De Mille viewed the play as "a sincere and equitable treatment of an important subject" (*Opportunity*, 63). Between 1920 and 1924 Thompson's plays *Caught*, *Africans*, and *Cooped Up* were staged in New York and California.

In addition to her playwriting in the 1920s, Thompson wrote short stories, two of which were published in *Opportunity*: "Mademoiselle 'Tasie—A Story" (Sept. 1925) and "Masks" (Oct. 1927). "Masks" was published nine months after the Thompsons relocated to New York City, where Noah Thompson had obtained a position with *Opportunity* as a business manager. "Mademoiselle 'Tasie—A Story" centers around a black woman with a light complexion who has fallen to a lower socioeconomic status after the Civil War; she weds someone, but her family disapproves of him because of his dark skin and his lack of refinement. "Masks" focuses on Julie, a black woman who marries a black man with a light complexion in an attempt to have a child who can pass for white. After giving birth, she is surprised to discover "that [the child's face] was identical with the one in the locket about her neck. It was the image of her chocolate-colored mother."

Thompson died of cancer a year after she moved to New York City. A memoriam in *Opportunity* in February 1928 notes both her achievements and her potential: "She wrote stories and plays and released a few of these which took rank promptly among the best work of our new writers" (37). Thompson's work serves as an important stage in the development of the African American literary tradition, linking the Victorian literature of the late nineteenth century to the flowering of musical, visual, and literary arts in the 1920s and 1930s period known as the Harlem Renaissance. With its foreign and historical settings, *Poems* exemplifies much of the romantic poetry by African American women of the late 1800s. In contrast Thompson's later short stories, such as "Mademoiselle 'Tasie—A Story" and "Masks," reflect a distinctive African American consciousness and a willingness to address the complex social, political, and racial issues of the era—a willingness that likewise marked the works of Thompson's contemporaries ZORA NEALE HURSTON, JESSIE REDMON FAUSET, and NELLA LARSEN.

FURTHER READING

Beasley, Delilah. *The Negro Trail Blazers of California* (1919; rpt. 1969).

Loggins, Vernon. *The Negro Author: His Development in America to 1900* (1964).

Scally, Mary Anthony. *Negro Catholic Writers, 1900–1943: A Bio-Bibliography* (1945).

Sherman, Joan. *Invisible Poets: Afro-Americans of the Nineteenth Century*, 2d ed. (1989).

Shockley, Ann Allen. *Afro-American Women Writers, 1746–1933: An Anthology and Critical Guide* (1988).

Obituary: *Oakland (California) Western Outlook*, 21 Jan. 1928.

This entry is taken from the *American National Biography* and is published here with the permission of the American Council of Learned Societies.

SHARON LYNETTE JONES

Thompson, Emeline (1822?–?), wrongly seized free woman, litigant in the case *Emeline, a free woman of color v. Jesse P. Bolls* (May 1847), was born around 1822 on the farm of John and Patsy Martin outside of Nashville, Tennessee, to a woman named Rhoda and an unknown father. Although there is little information about Emeline's early life, evidence suggests that she was never educated because the original petition filed much later by her attorney, Peter W. Gray, only displays a scratch for Thompson's signature. The nature and status of her employment with the Martins are unclear. After an unknown length of time Thompson traveled to Louisiana with a daughter of the Martins, Eliza, and Eliza's new husband, John Seip. While in Rapides Parish, Louisiana, Thompson gave birth to two boys, John and William; the father of one of the boys was an unidentified biracial slave of the Seips, and, according to testimony, this slave passed for the husband of Emeline. No other information concerning Thompson's time in Louisiana remains.

Sometime before 1846 Thompson journeyed to Texas, and on 20 December 1846 a white man by the name of Jesse P. Bolls claimed ownership of her. Thompson responded courageously by pursuing a redress of grievances by legal means—a legal avenue almost universally denied to African Americans in the antebellum South. The original legal petition in the case filed in the Eleventh District Court in Houston, Texas, by her attorney, Peter Gray, stated that Bolls "with force and arms assaulted your petitioner and then and there took, imposed, and restrained her and her children of their liberty, and held her & them in servitude from said day to the commencement of this suit against the laws of the land and will of the petitioner." Bolls countered this claim by asserting that his mother had purchased Thompson, and that, as her son, he was administrator of her estate.

Gray worked diligently to present the most convincing body of evidence on behalf of his client. Gray, a young attorney in Houston, was later to become a Texas state senator, member of the Confederate House of Representatives, district judge, and associate justice of the Texas Supreme Court. In an era in Texas when pretrial discovery was not the norm, Gray sent written interrogatories to various people well acquainted with Thompson who resided in Louisiana, Tennessee, and even Pennsylvania. The testimonies that seem to have garnered the most attention were those concerning the life of Thompson's mother, Rhoda. A few of the interrogatories corroborated the fact that Rhoda was brought as a slave to Philadelphia, Pennsylvania, in 1816 to reside there for eight months. The trip was apparently arranged by Donnelson Caffrey, her owner and the father of two of her children. Under the laws of Pennsylvania, Rhoda was emancipated by virtue of residency in the state for a period longer than six months. Although Thompson was not born until around 1822, Rhoda's free status was apparently conferred upon all her subsequent children, Thompson included.

An analysis of the laws and precedent governing the decision of the case, *Emeline, a free woman of color v. Jesse P. Bolls*, is a difficult undertaking both because of the incomplete court records and because of the changing status of Texas during this period. Within a relatively brief period of time Texas evolved from a Spanish colony to a Mexican state in 1821, from a Mexican state to an independent republic in 1836, and from a republic to a state of the United States in 1845. While the laws governing slavery changed during this period, what is clear is that during the early days of the republic free blacks were prohibited from living in Texas, unless they had resided there prior to independence from Mexico or had successfully petitioned the government for residence. In 1848 there were several laws in effect that would have prevented Thompson from entering or residing in Texas, and, as an African American, she was certainly not afforded the same legal rights as other residents of the state.

Thompson's case was tried before a jury that was composed of twelve white men, many of whom were slaveholders. The presiding judge, C. W. Buckley, owned a significant number of slaves in 1860 and owned at least a few at the time of Thompson's case, as did her own attorney, Peter Gray. It was this group of men that largely determined her legal fate. And yet, for reasons that are not readily apparent, the jury returned the verdict: "We, the Jury, find the Plaintiff and her children are and are to remain free, and we find damages in the amount of one dollar."

Interestingly, a related case was tried in Nashville, Tennessee, in April of 1844. The case, *Rhoda, George, Margaret, and Matilda v. Mrs. Patsy Martin*, upheld the freedom of several of Thompson's kin. While the exact relationship between this case and Thompson's cannot be determined, they both seemed to hinge upon the important testimonies that proved Rhoda to have spent time in Pennsylvania in 1816. Perhaps this case was cited as precedent in *Emeline, a free woman of color v. Jesse P. Bolls*, but no extant evidence proves such a relationship. A thorough search of the 1850 Texas census reveals no evidence of Thompson. She most likely left the state in which her freedom was so perilously upheld. There has been some speculation that she returned to Louisiana and took the last name of her sister, Lucy Thompson. Emeline Thompson's appearance in the historical record is brief but an indelible testimony to her courage and tenacity.

FURTHER READING

Muir, Andre Forest. "The Free Negro in Harris County Texas," *Southwestern Historical Quarterly* xlvi. 3 (Jan. 1943).

Pipkin, Michael W. "*Emeline, a free woman of color v. Jesse P. Bolls*: The Law of Freedom and Slavery in Antebellum Texas," M.A. thesis, Dartmouth College (2005).

MICHAEL W. PIPKIN

Thompson, Era Bell (10 Aug. 1906–30 Dec. 1986), author and editor, was born in Des Moines, Iowa, the daughter of Stewart C. Thompson and Mary Logan. In 1914 she moved with her family to Driscoll, North Dakota, where her father was a farmer and, from 1917 to 1921, a private messenger for Governor Lynn Frazier during legislative sessions. After moving to Bismarck in 1920, her father operated a secondhand store, and when he died in 1928, Era Thompson briefly operated the store to pay off his debts.

Thompson attended the University of North Dakota from 1925 until she was forced to drop out of college in 1927, owing to illness. She wrote for the campus newspaper and excelled in athletics, establishing five state and tying two national intercollegiate women's track records. In 1930, having won twenty-five dollars in a contest to name a bedspring ("King Koil"), she used the money to visit friends in Grand Forks, North Dakota. There she met the Reverend Robert E. O'Brian, a Methodist pastor, who later became president of Morningside College. Thompson moved with him and his family to Sioux City, Iowa. A recipient of a Wesleyan Service Guild Scholarship (1931), she graduated from Morningside College in 1933 with a B.A. in Social Science. While a student, she wrote humor and sports columns for the campus newspaper and won a sweater in athletics.

Thompson moved to Chicago in 1933 and found that the only jobs available were doing housework. "It didn't help to tell people I was a college graduate," she recalled. She moved from housework to the Illinois Occupational Survey to the Works Progress Administration, where she demonstrated her continued journalistic ambitions by publishing an in-house newspaper at a WPA job. Thompson did postgraduate study at the Northwestern University Medill School of Journalism in 1938 and 1940 while continuing to work at her WPA job. From 1942 to 1947 she was an interviewer with the U.S. and Illinois Employment Service. "After ten years' experience in Chicago, with and without jobs, it is a pleasure to be on the other side of the desk, on the giving side instead of the asking," she wrote at that time.

In 1945 she received a Newberry Library fellowship to write her autobiography. *American Daughter*, which emphasized her North Dakota childhood, was published in 1946 and reprinted in 1967 and 1986. Thompson wrote with warmth and good humor about her early life in a predominantly white state and about her eventual discovery of black history and culture. The book is positive and optimistic, characteristics the author maintained throughout her life. In the preface to the 1967 edition, Thompson wrote, "Usually an autobiography is written near the end of a long and distinguished career, but not taking any chances, I wrote mine first, then began to live."

Thompson joined the Johnson Publishing Company, in Chicago, as associate editor of *Negro Digest* in 1947; she served as co-managing editor of *Ebony* magazine from 1951 to 1964 and as international editor from 1964 until her death, although she was semiretired after 1970. While she was with

Ebony, she wrote more than forty bylined articles. Thompson traveled widely, visiting 124 countries on six continents. "I spend two or three months in a country before doing any writing about it, until I have had extensive interviews with hundreds of people and have the 'feel' of the country," she told a newspaper interviewer in 1966. *Africa, Land of My Father*, based on a tour of eighteen African countries, was published in 1954.

As an African American female journalist, Thompson was a pioneer. "I wanted to be a journalist," she told an interviewer in 1966. "There wasn't anyone to tell me there weren't any opportunities for a Negro in journalism, so I went ahead and prepared myself for that career." Herbert Nipson, with whom she worked as co-managing editor of *Ebony*, described her as "a very independent person who worked and fought for women's rights long before it became a national issue." A senior *Ebony* editor, LERONE BENNETT JR., said Thompson "opened the paths for women at the management level for journalists in this country."

Thompson also worked to foster greater understanding between the races and to break down the barriers of prejudice. She closed her autobiography optimistically, declaring, "The chasm is growing narrower. When it closes, my feet will rest on a united America." Although she saw the chasm widen at times, she remained confident for most of her life that, as she wrote in 1946, "most Americans are fair; that my people and your people can work together and live together in peace and happiness, if they but have the opportunity to know and understand each other." Her background gave her a unique perspective that she used to promote racial understanding. Her books and articles provided insight on racial attitudes in various societies. A two-part series on racial "amalgamation" in Brazil (1965) revealed the complexities of racial barriers in that country. *White on Black: The Views of Twenty-two White Americans on the Negro* (1963), which she coedited, traced the changes in attitude witnessed in *Ebony* over the period 1950–1963.

Thompson received two honorary degrees and the Distinguished Alumni Award from Morningside College (1974). Other honors included the Society of Midland Authors Patron Saints Award (1968) and the Theodore Roosevelt Roughrider Award bestowed by the state of North Dakota (1976). She was one of fifty black women featured in Women of Courage, an exhibit at the Chicago Public Library's Cultural Center in February 1986. She died at her home in Chicago. She had never married.

FURTHER READING
Thompson's papers are in the Carter G. Woodson Library, Chicago.
Thompson, Era Bell. *American Daughter* (1945, repr. 1986).
Anderson, Kathie Ryckman. "Era Bell Thompson: A North Dakota Daughter," *North Dakota History* 49 (Fall 1982).
Obituaries: *Chicago Tribune* and *Chicago Defender*, 31 Dec. 1986; *Chicago Sun-Times*, 1 Jan. 1987.
This entry is taken from the *American National Biography* and is published here with the permission of the American Council of Learned Societies.

GERALD G. NEWBORG

Thompson, Henry Curtis (Hank) (8 Dec. 1925–30 Sept. 1969), Negro League baseball player, first player to integrate the St. Louis Browns, and second player to integrate the American League, was born in Muskogee, Oklahoma, the son of Ollie Thompson, a railroad worker, and Iona Thompson, a cook and domestic. His parents separated when Hank was five or six, and he reacted by playing baseball constantly, even skipping school to do so. This practice caught up with him when, at age eleven, he was arrested for truancy and sent for six months to Gatesville Reform School near Dallas, Texas. It was here that Thompson played on his first organized team. Released after a year, Thompson lived for a brief period with his father and then went back to his mother, but he did not go to school. Instead, he hung out at the Texas League Dallas Steers ballpark, eventually getting the job of throwing batting practice and shagging flies. Here his ball-playing ability was noticed, and he was asked to play for a Negro semipro team in Dallas.

With World War II depleting Negro League ranks, Kansas City Monarchs owner B. C. Sorrell became interested in Thompson, who was too young to be drafted, and encouraged him to try out for the team in 1943. Seventeen years old, Thompson traveled alone from Dallas to New Orleans and made the team. There were some major stars on the Monarchs, including future Baseball Hall of Famer SATCHEL PAIGE, but it was also a team that played as hard off the field as on.

Thompson's baseball career was temporarily halted by World War II when he turned eighteen and was drafted into the army. He fought in the Battle of the Bulge and was mustered out of the army as a sergeant in June 1946, just in time to rejoin the Monarchs in the heat of a Negro League pennant race. The Monarchs won the pennant, but they lost the Negro League World Series to the Newark Eagles, led by future Hall of Famers LARRY DOBY and MONTE IRVIN. For Thompson, the season's highlight was a postseason barnstorming tour against a team of major league All-Stars led by future Hall of Famer Bob Feller. For seventeen days' work on the tour he earned $7,500, more than he had earned in an entire season with the Monarchs. Following this he went on to play winter ball in Cuba, where he met his future wife, Maria Quesada.

He returned to the Monarchs for the 1947 season, but baseball was changing. JACKIE ROBINSON became the first African American Major Leaguer in sixty-three years when he joined the Brooklyn Dodgers to open the season. And on 6 July, Larry Doby became the first-ever black American Leaguer when he joined the Cleveland Indians. Hank Thompson, meanwhile, was batting a sparkling .347, and the St. Louis Browns took notice. They purchased his contract and that of a teammate, Willard Brown. On 17 July 1947 Hank Thompson became the first African American to play for the St. Louis Browns; he went hitless and made an error in a 16–2 loss to the Philadelphia Athletics. Thompson's tenure with the Browns was short, only thirty-six days, during which he played second base and batted .257. Some of the other players displayed racism toward him, such as three players who refused to autograph baseballs with him in the locker room. When Thompson was released, he protested, pointing out that he was performing better than many other players, but to no avail.

Thompson went back to the Monarchs, but in the spring of 1948 he was arrested for murder when he shot an acquaintance in a beer garden. Released on bond, he went on to have another big year for the Monarchs, batting .375 with a slugging percentage of .633.

At the end of the season he and Monte Irvin were sold to the New York Giants. Placed at the Giants' minor league affiliate in Jersey City, Thompson hit .303 in fifty-five games with twelve home runs, and on 5 July 1949 he and Irvin were called up to the Giants and became the first African Americans to integrate that team (Irvin technically was the first to integrate the team by playing first in a 4–3 loss to Brooklyn on 8 July 1949). On this day he set more milestones, when he became the first African American to face an African American pitcher when he came up to bat against Don Newcombe, and the first African American to play in both the National and American Leagues. He had an excellent year for the Giants, batting .280 in seventy-five games. During the season he also married Maria Quesada; they had no children. In 1950, his first full season in the majors, he had another great year, batting .289 with ninety-one RBIs and setting the major league third baseman record (since broken) for double plays with forty-three. In 1951 he played in his first World Series, and when he joined WILLIE MAYS and Monte Irvin in the outfield, the trio became the first African American outfield in major league history. Thompson experienced racism on the Giants, however. He said that opposing players would say racist slurs and pitchers would throw knockdown pitches, aiming directly for his head.

Thompson had a nine-year major league career, including another World Series appearance in 1954. He also started drinking heavily, and quickly came undone in retirement. Having saved virtually no money from his playing career, Thompson became a bartender in Harlem and then went through a series of menial jobs. In late 1958 he was arrested for stealing a car; the next year he was convicted of spousal abuse and was divorced. In 1961 he robbed a liquor store and was arrested. Only the intervention of Giants owner Horace Stoneham and baseball's commissioner Ford Frick kept him out of prison. In 1963 he robbed another liquor store, this time in Houston, Texas, and was sentenced to ten years in prison, but he served only four. After his release in 1967, Thompson married Betty Thomas, moved to Fresno, California, and worked as a playground supervisor. They had no children. He died of a stroke in 1969.

Thompson was a deeply flawed racial pioneer, but an important one, and a very good ballplayer. His achievements have almost certainly been minimized because of his criminal record.

FURTHER READING

Thompson, Hank, with Arnold Hano. "How I Wrecked My Life—How I Hope to Save It," in *The Best of Sport 1946–1971*, ed. Al Silverman (1971).

Riley, James A. *The Biographical Encyclopedia of the Negro Baseball Leagues* (1994).

Obituary: *New York Times*, 2 Oct. 1969.

STEPHEN ESCHENBACH

Thompson, Holland (1839 or 1840–1887), waiter, storekeeper, and politician, was born near Montgomery, Alabama, to slave parents whose names are unknown. His parents had been brought to Alabama from South Carolina in the 1830s by their owner, William H. Taylor, who became a wealthy planter in Montgomery County. Taylor also owned Thompson but appears to have allowed him to hire out his time as a waiter at the Madison House hotel in Montgomery prior to the end of the Civil War. Thompson learned to read and write and probably enjoyed greater freedom than most slaves in Alabama, though as a slave, he was not allowed to marry legally. He did, however, have a common-law wife, Binah Yancey, who was born in 1842 in Alabama and was owned by William Lowndes Yancey, a prominent Alabama secessionist politician. Like her husband, Binah Yancey was able to read and write and enjoyed a relatively high social status within the slave community. Thompson and Yancey had a son, Holland Jr., in 1862 and married legally at the earliest opportunity to do so in August 1865. The couple had four more children.

Thompson's business and political career after Emancipation was remarkably similar to those of other slave artisans like WILLIAM BEVERLY NASH, also a waiter, who served in the South Carolina legislature during Reconstruction, and WILLIAM FINCH, a tailor elected to the Atlanta city council in 1870. Like Finch and Nash, Thompson had been able to save some of his earnings while a slave, and upon Emancipation he invested this money in property and in a small business that served as a springboard to political prominence. Yet even before he purchased a grocery store in Montgomery in 1866, Thompson attended a statewide black convention in Mobile in November 1865 where he urged his fellow African Americans to organize independently of whites. Throughout 1866 and 1867 he gave several speeches advocating measures likely to secure land for the freedmen, though he was adamantly opposed to land confiscation from South Carolina's former slaveholders. He also opposed the formation of black militia companies, believing that they frightened whites. Thompson nonetheless championed full political equality for black men—which also frightened whites in the Black Belt—and was a delegate to the Alabama Republican state convention in 1867, the same year that he was one of only a few blacks appointed to the state's Republican executive committee.

In February 1868 Thompson was elected to represent Montgomery in the Alabama House of Representatives, and he won reelection in 1870. His first term proved uneventful, but in his second term Thompson served on the important Finance, Capitol, and Corporations committees and actively participated in debates. He also became more radical in his political views. More often than not he was unsuccessful—for example, in his attempt to establish in Montgomery a county advocate to provide legal defense for the indigent. He also failed in an attempt to replace a tax on the ownership of dogs, which disproportionately affected poor farmers of both races, with a tax on diamond jewelry, which would have disproportionately affected the wealthy. The house adopted his amendment to a bill prohibiting racial discrimination on railroads in February 1870, but the measure was defeated in the senate. Perhaps Thompson's most notable success was the adoption of his resolution requiring that the American flag be flown at the capitol. While serving in the house, Thompson was also elected to four terms on the Montgomery city council from 1869 to 1877 and on the city's school board from 1870 to 1873. In both of these posts he enjoyed greater success than in the legislature. He helped establish a system of public schools, increased poor relief, raised the salaries of the city's street workers, and appointed African Americans to the Montgomery police force.

Even more than his business interests and close ties to whites, Thompson's political prominence during Reconstruction was a consequence of his leadership role in the black church. He had belonged to the black branch of Montgomery's First Baptist Church during slavery, and in May 1865 he was elected president of the First Colored Baptist Sabbath School. Exactly two years later seven hundred of Montgomery's black Baptists formalized their separation from the white Baptist church by laying the cornerstone of the First Colored Baptist Church. Much of the money for the new church had been raised by Thompson, one of four trustees, who also served as church clerk, superintendent of First Colored's Sunday school, and president of its missionary society. He also founded and organized Montgomery's Second Colored Baptist Church, later renamed the Dexter Avenue Baptist Church. Thompson was the most prominent nonminister in Baptist affairs in Alabama, serving as statewide superintendent of Baptist Sunday schools and as corresponding secretary of the state's Colored Baptist Missionary Convention between 1868 and 1872.

Thompson failed, however, to win the Republican Party's nomination for a seat in the U.S. Congress, losing out in 1872 to JAMES T. RAPIER. The freeborn Rapier was wealthier, better educated, more moderate in his politics, and more adept than Thompson in dealing with the various factions within the Alabama Republican Party. Rapier also had a strong political base in Montgomery's rural hinterland as well as in the city itself. Thompson might have expected to draw upon his support among Alabama Baptists, but during 1871 and 1872 he was involved in a series of public disputes with members of the American Missionary Association and the State Baptist Convention. His expulsion from the First Baptist Church in 1872 for allegedly misusing church funds was only temporary—he was reinstated and appointed treasurer the following year—but his reinstatement came too late to save his political career.

Thompson's personal affairs were also troubled after 1872. Two years after his wife died in childbirth in 1873, his eldest son, Holland Jr., died also. Thompson remarried, to a woman named Charlotte, in 1874; they had a son and a daughter, though both children died in infancy. The end of Reconstruction also coincided with a decline in Thompson's financial fortunes. According to the 1870 census, he owned real estate worth five hundred dollars and had personal property worth two hundred dollars; by the 1880s the value of his properties had declined to only forty dollars. He died from cancer in November 1887.

Although he was not among the first rank of southern black Reconstruction politicians, Thompson was, at least from 1865 to 1872, one of the most powerful black political and religious leaders in Alabama. Perhaps his greatest legacy was his founding of Montgomery's Dexter Avenue Baptist Church, whose pastors later included VERNON JOHNS and MARTIN LUTHER KING JR., men who, like Thompson, combined a deep spiritual faith with a passionate commitment to political action.

FURTHER READING

Bailey, Richard. *Neither Carpetbaggers Nor Scalawags: Black Officeholders during the Reconstruction of Alabama, 1867–1878* (1997).

Rabinowitz, Howard N., ed. "Holland Thompson and Black Political Participation in Montgomery, Alabama," in *Southern Black Leaders of the Reconstruction Era* (1982).

STEVEN J. NIVEN

Thompson, Jacob (fl. 1860s), cook and survivor of the 1864 Fort Pillow Massacre in Tennessee, was born a slave near Brown Mills, Virginia (later Pentress, West Virginia). Practically all that is known about him can be found in his testimony before a joint committee of the U.S. Congress about the Fort Pillow Massacre. He testified that he had been a slave of a man named Colonel Hardgrove in Virginia and had run away from him early in the Civil War; then he returned to his master for a short period, then ran away again. Thompson's indecision was not at all unusual among young male slaves during the Civil War. Union advances into Confederate territory emboldened many slaves to make their escape, just as Confederate counterattacks gave pause to would-be escapees. Whatever his hesitation, Thompson twice risked being captured by slave patrollers or taken by Confederate troops while making his way to the Union lines. He did not enlist in the army, but for the two years prior to April 1864 he served as a battlefield cook with the Fifteenth Illinois Cavalry, Company K. During that time his company saw battle at Pea Ridge, Arkansas, in March 1862; Perryville, Kentucky, in October 1862; and Stones River near Murfreesboro, Tennessee, in early January 1963.

In April 1864 Thompson was working as a cook in the hotel at Fort Pillow, Tennessee. The hotel was Confederate-built, but at the time it was a Union-controlled garrison overlooking the Mississippi River, fifty miles north of Memphis. At Fort Pillow, Major Lionel F. Booth commanded between 280 and 300 white native Tennessean Unionist troops and 305 African American soldiers, most of whom were members of the Sixth U.S. Colored Heavy Artillery (thirty-five of them were from the Second U.S. Colored Light Infantry). There may have been as many as seventy noncombatants at the garrison, including women, children, and support staff such as Thompson. In their successful assault on Fort Pillow on 12 April, however, Major General Nathan Bedford Forrest and his Confederate force of fifteen hundred men made few distinctions between civilian and soldier, but they did have a marked preference for killing black troops over white troops. Historians' estimates are that 64 percent of the black Union soldiers present at the fort were killed that day; but only 31 to 33 percent of white Union soldiers died. In total, almost exactly half of the Union soldiers at Fort Pillow were killed after being overwhelmed by Forrest's superior troop numbers, with a 50 percent death rate being extremely high for a Civil War skirmish. In the first flush of battle, Forrest believed that the Union death toll could have been as high as 71 percent, and some of his aides even suggested an 81 percent death rate.

The vast majority of casualties at Fort Pillow occurred after the Union forces surrendered. Forrest, like other Confederate commanders, promised to show traditional mercy to white troops but gave no quarter to black soldiers, who were viewed as slave rebels and "contraband" of war. This was most certainly the case at Fort Pillow, where just over half of the white Union soldiers were taken prisoner, but only one in six black Union soldiers were captured and left alive. The imbalance between the number of soldiers killed and wounded was also remarkable. During the Civil War there were generally seven soldiers wounded for every one soldier killed; but among African American troops at Fort Pillow, there were more than six combat deaths for every wounded survivor.

Thompson's testimony is just one of many from the Union side suggesting that Confederate racist motivations exacerbated the extraordinarily high death rate at Fort Pillow. Although Thompson was not an enlisted soldier, he found himself fighting for his life when a Confederate private shot him in the hand and then in the head as he raised his arms in surrender. The enemy soldiers then beat Thompson on the side of his head with the breech of their guns. Although he survived, Thompson watched as approximately fifty Union soldiers, white and black, were gunned down in cold blood, many of them begging for mercy. His claim that Confederate troops nailed four or five black sergeants and two white soldiers to logs and then set them on fire was confirmed by other witnesses. Given the significant efforts of some Forrest biographers to obscure the murderous role of the future Ku Klux Klan leader and blame the excessive force at Fort Pillow on undisciplined troops, Thompson also testified to having witnessed General Forrest giving orders following the surrender.

After testifying about his experiences at Fort Pillow at Mound City Federal Hospital in Illinois, Thompson disappears from the historical record. Given his injuries and the unsanitary conditions of many Civil War army hospitals, he may have been just as lucky to survive his stay at Mound City as he was to escape Fort Pillow alive. Confederate General James R. Chalmers believed that the events at Fort Pillow "taught the mongrel garrison of blacks and [white] renegades a lesson long to be remembered" (Fuchs, 79). But African Americans and their white pro-Union allies learned something quite different. In several of the battles that followed, vengeful Union troops refused to take Confederate prisoners. Both on the home front and on the front lines, "Remember Fort Pillow!" became a rallying cry, especially among African Americans determined to end slavery and, they hoped, the racism that made the bloody debacle at Fort Pillow possible.

FURTHER READING

Jacob Thompson's testimony on the Fort Pillow Massacre appears in U.S. Congress Joint Select Committee on the Conduct of the War. Reports on the Subcommittee on the "Fort PillowMassacre," 38th Congress, 1st Session, Report No. 65. Washington, D.C.: Government Printing Office, 1864.

Cimprich, John, and Robert C. Mainfort Jr. "The Fort Pillow Massacre: A Statistical Note," *Journal of American History* (1989).

Fuchs, Richard L. *An Unerring Fire: The Massacre at Fort Pillow* (1994).

STEVEN J. NIVEN

Thompson, John (1812–?), fugitive slave, memoirist, and sailor, was born into slavery on the Wagar plantation in southern Maryland, the son of two field slaves whose names remain unknown. Although there is little information about Thompson's life beyond his memoirs, his descriptions of his experiences in slavery as well as his adventures as a black seaman are important contributions to our knowledge of both those worlds.

John Thompson's recollections of his early years are vague at best. His realization that he was a slave came at age six, when he witnessed the sale of his oldest sister. Even at that early age, as Thompson recounted in his memoirs, he was engaged in backbreaking work in the corn, wheat, and tobacco fields of the Wagar plantations. Like many slave-narrative authors, including HARRIET JACOBS, HENRY BIBB, Solomon Northup, WILLIAM PARKER, SOLOMON BAYLEY, JAMES MARS, and WILLIAM GRIMES, Thompson stressed the arbitrary violence of daily life and the dehumanizing effects of slavery on both slave and master. His early memories are replete with acts of barbarism inflicted on the slave population by members of the Wagar family, both children and adults.

The most important event of Thompson's youth came when he was assigned to carry the lunches of two young members of the Wagar clan to school each morning. Thompson remarked to one of the children, Henry Ashton, that he wanted to learn to read. Young Ashton volunteered to give him lessons, despite Thompson's warnings that Ashton's uncle, John Wagar, would object. For the next two years Henry taught Thompson from his own reading and spelling books. They would often leave early for school and then take advantage of the cover offered by the wooded terrain in the region. By the time the lessons ended two years later, John Thompson had mastered the rudiments of reading and writing. Thompson remarked that his new skills changed his life by allowing him access to the teachings of the Holy Bible. But they also made him a subversive influence on the slave culture of the Old South. Later in his life, the skills that contributed to his religious awakening also led to his decision to flee to the North.

Central to Thompson's narrative are the role of religion in the slave quarters and the shifting attitudes of the planter class to the upsurge in slave religiosity. Planter society in southern Maryland, according to Thompson, was predominantly Catholic or Episcopalian. By the 1820s new denominations were organizing meetings and making inroads in the slave quarters. The Methodists and Baptists used their plainspoken theology, revival techniques, and democratic ecclesiastical structures to win many slave converts. Thompson was especially enamored of Methodism, about which he wrote in ecstatic terms. In those years, however, the fervor generated by the Methodist "meetings" caused great anxiety in the hearts and minds of slaveholders, though they were loath to outlaw the denominations outright. Laws and ordinances were passed to regulate the movement and gathering of slaves, especially on Sundays. To be outside the slave quarters after dark was punishable by flogging or worse. Thompson claimed that the Wagar family went so far as to purchase a slave whose main talent was playing the fiddle, believing that music and dancing were safer emotional outlets for the enthusiasm of the slaves.

Interestingly, there was a noticeable shift in the minds of those Maryland tidewater planters concerning the influence of religion among the slaves. By the middle 1830s planters financed the construction of churches and the formation of slave congregations. They also advocated the preaching of a theology of submission among slaves. Religion became yet another mechanism of social control in slave society. Thompson's writing demonstrates that those beliefs were a double-edged sword. Slaves were apt to interpret Christian teaching in ways that helped them to endure the hardships of slavery and to craft a worldview of resistance and hope. When he fled the South, Thompson was aided along the way by his own faith as well as by other people of faith who provided the informal network that facilitated his escape.

Thompson's faith was not the only aspect of his life that proved subversive to the slave system. As he grew older, his literacy became another source of trouble and the inadvertent cause of his own growing awareness of his debased station in life. He claimed that for years he secretly carried with him a newspaper article containing an 1830 speech by John Quincy Adams, which served as an inspiration to him while he was in bondage. When it was accidentally discovered that he possessed the ability to read and write, the news spread among local slaveholders like wildfire. Local constables and magistrates instructed slave patrols to pay special attention to Thompson. On two occasions he was arrested on fabricated charges of writing "passes" for escaped slaves. In fact, it was that charge to which Thompson attributed his own escape. When three of Thompson's slave acquaintances disappeared one evening, the local magistrate put a three-hundred-dollar bounty on his head, prompting Thompson to flee northward.

Thompson's narrative does not end when he gains his freedom. Within a year of crossing into Pennsylvania, he made his way first to Philadelphia, where he continued to hone his reading and writing skills in night school, and finally to New Bedford, Massachusetts. New Bedford was the center of the American whaling industry and home to an estimated seven hundred fugitive slaves and free blacks, including Lewis Temple, who established his own whalecraft shop in the 1830s. Many fugitive slaves found places on whaling crews, and Thompson, too, looked to whaling as an effective means of evading the slave catchers who had dogged his path. He persuaded a captain preparing for a long journey to take him on as a steward.

Thompson learned the basics of keeping a ship's mess from another fugitive slave in New Bedford. Even after it was discovered that he had misrepresented his skills, the captain took pity on him, loaned him a cookbook, and gave him a few cursory lessons in the preparation of breads and pastries. Thus began a two-year voyage that very nearly took the fugitive slave around the world. The *Milwood* sailed along the Outer Banks of Newfoundland, south along the coast of Africa, around the Cape of Good Hope to Madagascar, into the Indian Ocean, and as far as New Zealand before it returned to New Bedford. Thompson's memoir provides an in-depth description of nineteenth-century whaling practices. He was also a keen observer of the many peoples and cultures that he encountered along the way. He toured a mosque at prayer time and watched conflicts arising from a civil war in the Comoros islands. By the time of his return to the United States, Thompson was a tested seaman and cosmopolitan world traveler.

The scarcity of sources for Thompson's life is certainly frustrating to the historian, but the story he left behind is a treasure trove of information about both the Underground Railroad, made famous by HARRIET TUBMAN, and the "maritime underground railroad," which enabled seafaring fugitives like MOSES ROPER to escape to freedom.

FURTHER READING

Thompson, John. *The Life of John Thompson, A Fugitive Slave; Containing His History of 25 Years in Bondage, and His Providential Escape* (1856).

Cecelski, David S. "The Shores of Freedom: The Maritime Underground Railroad in North Carolina, 1800–1861," *North Carolina Historical Review* 71 (April 1994): 174–206.

Grover, Kathryn. *The Fugitive's Gibraltar: Escaping Slaves and Abolitionism in New Bedford, Massachusetts* (2001).

Mathews, Donald G. *Slavery and Methodism: A Chapter in American Morality, 1780–1845* (1965).

MARK ANDREW HUDDLE

Thompson, John E. W. (1855–6 Oct. 1918), physician and diplomat, was born in Brooklyn, New York, to parents whose names and occupations are unknown. In 1865 he moved with his parents to Providence, Rhode Island, and over the next eighteen years was educated at schools in Massachusetts, Connecticut, and Rhode Island. In 1883 he graduated from Yale Medical School with high honors and shortly thereafter married the well-educated daughter of a Yale University carpenter.

Thompson then spent eighteen months in Paris (1883–1884), further learning the latest medical techniques. He returned to the United States late in 1884 and established his residence and medical practice in New York City. Quickly becoming socially and professionally prominent, he was cited by contemporaries as an example of the possibilities of self-improvement open to African Americans who were afforded educational opportunities. He also gained a reputation within New York social circles for his proficiency in French and his knowledge of international law.

On 7 May 1885 Democratic U.S. president Grover Cleveland nominated Thompson as the minister resident and consul general to Haiti. The appointment included, by convention, the position of chargé d'affaires to the Dominican Republic. The outgoing Republican administration of Chester Arthur had nominated, and the Senate had confirmed, GEORGE WASHINGTON WILLIAMS for these positions, but the incoming Cleveland administration had withdrawn the nomination. Thompson, that rare black leader in the late century who had affiliations with the Democratic Party, then evinced interest in the position.

In addition to his Democratic Party allegiance, Thompson came with high recommendations from prominent leaders: Yale's President Noah Porter, the Catholic bishops of New York and Delaware, and the future New York City mayor Abram S. Hewitt—all declared Thompson the best-suited African American for the position. On 16 September 1885 the Senate confirmed Thompson as the minister to Haiti and chargé d'affaires to the Dominican Republic. He was, at age thirty, one of the youngest Americans to serve in those posts. He served in the positions until the end of the first Cleveland administration (1885–1889).

It was a period of civil war in Haiti between the supporters of François Légitime and Florvil Hyppolite, and Thompson helped to manage the U.S. policy of neutrality in the conflict. In particular, he worked closely with the U.S. secretary of state Thomas Bayard in dealing with issues of asylum, especially attempts by the partisans to use American ships for those purposes. Thompson understood the underlying social and political causes of the civil war and correctly estimated the likelihood that the conflict would not soon be resolved.

With the onset of the Republican administration of Benjamin Harrison, Thompson resigned his diplomatic post on 18 February 1889. Encouraged to retain Thompson for the sake of stability and continuity of American policy, and to alleviate fears for the future, Harrison kept him in Port-au-Prince with orders of strict neutrality. He remained there until 15 October 1889 and was succeeded by FREDERICK DOUGLASS. Thompson then ended his diplomatic career and returned to the United States with his wife and three-year-old son.

For the next twenty-four years, Thompson practiced medicine in New York City and was an active leader of the city's medical establishment (1889–1913). Notably, he served on the board of directors of McDonough Memorial Hospital, an institution founded to care for indigent New Yorkers, most of them African American. He was one of the hospital's corresponding secretaries and one of its managers, and served on its executive and nominating committees. In addition, he chaired the board of the Training School for Nurses and the Medical Board, and made financial contributions to the hospital. He was also a prominent leader of New York City's black Catholic community. A parishioner of Saint Benedict the Moor—the first black Catholic church in New York City and the first such church north of the Mason-Dixon line—he made financial gifts to the church even while he was serving in Haiti, and his involvement continued in the decades afterward.

After the presidential election of 1892 and the return of Democrat Grover Cleveland to office in 1893, Thompson looked again for a diplomatic posting, particularly France. But the president, a conservative "Bourbon Democrat" at best, judged that a black man could not be sent to represent the United States in a European country and instead offered Thompson the position of surgeon general at the Freedmen's Hospital in Washington. The hospital had been established during the Civil War and in the postbellum era became the teaching hospital for Howard University Medical School, even while it remained under federal control. Thompson, however, rejected the offer. In the period immediately following his failure to achieve a new diplomatic post, he was arrested and convicted for erratic behavior and disorderly conduct, although there is no evidence for the origin of such behavior.

Around 1913, Thompson moved to Bridgeport, Connecticut, where he practiced medicine until his death on 6 October 1918. On that day, Thomas Saloway, a patient who felt that Thompson's treatments had harmed his health rather than improved it, stabbed the doctor in the hallway of his office. Thompson died in an ambulance on the way to the hospital.

FURTHER READING

Materials on Thompson's tenure as minister to Haiti can be found in the Records of the Department of State, Dispatches from U.S. Ministers to Haiti, 1862–1906, M 82, rolls 20–23 (1885–1889); and in the Department of State, Diplomatic Instructions, Haiti and Santo Domingo, M 77, rolls 96 (1873–1888) and 97 (1888–1898). These are located in the National Archives, Washington, D.C.

"John E. W. Thompson." *National Cyclopedia of American Biography,* vol. 13 (1907).

Shelley, Thomas J. "Catholic Greenwich Village: Ethnic Geography and Religious Identity in New York City, 1880–1930," *The Catholic Historical Review* 89.1 (Jan. 2003).

Obituary: *New York Age,* 12 Oct. 1918.

KENNETH J. BLUME

Thompson, John Robert, Jr. (2 Sept. 1941–), college basketball coach, was born in Washington, D.C., to Anna Thompson, a housewife and cleaning woman, and John Robert Thompson, a laborer. Thompson grew up in a poor but loving family that was forced to relocate several times to various places in the D.C. area during Thompson's childhood. Although his parents were not able to give him many material goods, Thompson frequently cited that their ability to express love while instilling discipline was the greatest single influence on his basketball coaching success.

Following his graduation from Archbishop John Carroll High School in Washington, D.C., Thompson, who would eventually grow to six feet ten inches, accepted a basketball scholarship to Providence College. He helped to lead the team to the 1963 National Invitation Tournament (NIT) Championship and the school's first trip to the National Collegiate Athletic Association (NCAA) tournament in 1964. An All-American his senior year, Thompson graduated in 1964 as Providence College's leader in points, points per game average, and field goal percentage. He was also second in rebounds. From 1964 to 1966 he served as the legendary BILL RUSSELL's backup (and thereby acquired the nickname "The Caddy") on the Boston Celtics in the National Basketball Association (NBA) and helped the team capture two consecutive NBA championships. Thompson retired from the NBA in 1966 and took over as head coach of the D.C.-area Saint Anthony High School boys' basketball team. He proved to be an imposing presence on the sidelines, as he towered above officials, opposing coaches, and most players, while brandishing what would become his signature: a white towel over his shoulder. He also became a great teacher, leading the team to a 122–28 record before receiving an offer in 1972 to become the head coach of the Georgetown University men's basketball team, which had just completed a 3–23 season. By accepting the position, Thompson became just the seventh African American head basketball coach at a predominantly white university. He also served as an assistant coach on the U.S. Olympic gold medal team of 1976.

Thompson wanted his players to succeed off the court as well as on, so one of the first people he hired at Georgetown was Mary Fenlon, an ex-nun who had taught Latin and English in high school; he made her his "academic conscience." With Fenlon overseeing the players' academic progress, Thompson was free to focus on coaching. Their combined expertise, Thompson believed, would ensure that his players had all they needed to achieve excellence on every level. Just as he had at Saint Anthony, Thompson quickly made Georgetown a winning team, leading the team to the NCAA tournament in just his third season. Over the course of his twenty-seven-year career, Thompson led the Hoyas to 596 wins (thirty-first all-time among Division I coaches as of 25 August 2006) and coached twenty-six players who were selected in the NBA draft. (Eight of these players were chosen in the first round, and two—Patrick Ewing in 1985 and Allen Iverson in 1996—were chosen as the first pick overall.)

Thompson exerted his control over all aspects of the Georgetown basketball program, going so far as to close practices to the media and prohibit reporters from talking to his players. Thompson's supporters pointed to the program's success and to the exceptional graduation rate (97 percent for his career) of Thompson's four-year players. His detractors adopted the phrase "Hoya Paranoia" as a label for the coach's strict oversight. Thompson used the term to bolster the "us against the world" attitude within his program that helped its players and coaches bond together. Many in the media reported that Thompson often used racial divisiveness to further that attitude, and those reports exacerbated the controversy that occasionally surrounded Thompson. Other controversies arising during his tenure included star center Alonzo Mourning's involvement with a reputed D.C. drug dealer (and Hoya fan) Rayful Edmond III. This was a relationship that ended, according to many reports, when Thompson summoned Edmond to his Georgetown office and threatened to inflict bodily harm on him if he did not cease interacting with Mourning. Also controversial was Thompson's outspoken opposition to the NCAA's Proposition 48, which imposed eligibility requirements based predominantly on standardized tests. In Thompson's view, Proposition 48 discriminated against African American athletes, who were at a disadvantage when taking the "mainstream-oriented" Scholastic Aptitude Test. "Certain kids," he said at the time, "require individual assessment. Some urban schools cater to poor kids, low-income

kids, black and white. To put everybody on the same playing field is just crazy" (Fullinwider, "Academic Standards and the NCAA"). Another wave of controversy surrounded Thompson's decision, as head coach of the 1988 Olympic men's basketball team, to leave Danny Ferry off the roster. Ferry was a white player who would win the 1989 Naismith College Player-of-the-Year Award, but Thompson instead chose to include Mourning, a black high-school player (and Georgetown recruit).

In spite of these controversies, Thompson left the game as one of the most successful coaches in the history of college basketball. His teams appeared in three NCAA Final Fours (1982, 1984, 1985), and in 1984 he became the first African American coach to win a Division I NCAA Championship when Georgetown defeated the University of Houston by a score of 84–75. In 1985 Thompson also became the first African American to serve as president of the National Association of Basketball Coaches. In all, Thompson's teams played in fourteen straight NCAA tournaments from 1979 to 1992, made twenty-four consecutive postseason appearances (twenty NCAA, four NIT), and won seven Big East Tournament titles. He won many coach-of-the-year honors, including three from the Big East Conference (1980, 1987, 1992), and one each from the U.S. Basketball Writers Association (1984), the *Sporting News* (1984), the National Association of Basketball Coaches (1985), and United Press International (1987). He was also head coach of the U.S.'s last amateur Olympic basketball team, which captured the bronze medal in 1988.

Thompson resigned suddenly from his position at Georgetown University on 8 January 1999, during a press conference speech laced with profanity, citing the strains of marital problems. There was some speculation at the time, however, that Thompson was being pressured to resign. He was replaced by one of his assistants, Craig Esherick, who struggled to follow his former boss and was eventually replaced by Thompson's son, John Thompson III, who helped return the Georgetown University basketball program to a position of national prominence. Thompson's younger son, Ronnie, who served as an assistant coach under his father, was the head basketball coach at Ball State University. Thompson was inducted as a coach into the Naismith Memorial Basketball Hall of Fame in 1999.

After his retirement from coaching, Thompson worked as a commentator for NBA and college basketball games and hosted his own sports talk show, *The John Thompson Show*, on Sports Talk 980 (WTEM-AM) in Washington, D.C.

FURTHER READING
Baker, Paul. *John Thompson and Georgetown Basketball* (1992).
Platt, Larry. *Only the Strong Survive: The Odyssey of Allen Iverson* (2002).
Shapiro, Leonard. *Big Man on Campus: John Thompson and the Georgetown Hoyas* (1991).

DANIEL DONAGHY

Thompson, Joseph Pascal (20 Dec.? 1818–21 Dec. 1894), clergyman, physician, and abolitionist, was born in slavery in Winchester, Virginia. The names of his parents are unknown. Although the scant records of his early life differ on the details, most sources indicate that while still a "youth" he ran away from his master and found refuge with a kindly family in Williamsport, Pennsylvania. This household provided the moral and religious influences that shaped Thompson's commitment to physical and spiritual healing. In the evenings and winter months he attended common school, where he proved studious and ambitious. For a time he worked with a physician at Middletown Point (later Matawan), New Jersey.

Although he retained a lifelong interest in medicine, Thompson was resolved to become a minister. He studied theology privately with the Reverend Dr. Mills of Auburn Theological Seminary in Auburn, New York, and was licensed to preach in 1839. For several years he probably worked as an itinerant preacher. In 1846 he was ordained as a deacon in the African Methodist Episcopal (AME) Zion Church. In 1847 he was ordained as an elder and was appointed as minister to the AME Zion Church on Washington Street in Newburgh, New York; he lived nearby. Thompson strengthened the church's institutional foundations by arranging for its incorporation and paying off its debt within a few years. Thompson married Catherine Gilchrist of Williamsport, Pennsylvania; they had one daughter.

In 1853 the AME Zion Church sent Thompson to do missionary work in Halifax, Nova Scotia, Canada. In addition to spreading the gospel, he offered medical assistance to needy parishioners. He soon understood that the physical and spiritual needs of his people were closely related. To acquire formal training in medicine, Thompson enrolled at the Jefferson Medical School in Philadelphia, Pennysylvania, from which he was awarded an M.D. in 1858.

That same year Thompson returned to the AME Zion Church in Newburgh; as physician and minister, he became a respected community leader. Around this time, too, he became one of the chief superintendents of the Underground Railroad. Thompson's father-in-law, S. Gilchrist of Williamsport, would arrange for Thompson to meet with runaway slaves who had crossed into Pennsylvania. Thompson would take them to Harrisburg, Pennsylvania, and then, walking only at night, would lead them another 130 miles to the home of JERMAIN WESLEY LOGUEN in Syracuse, New York.

During watch-night services on New Year's Eve in 1860, a mob of whites attacked Thompson's church, shattering the door and otherwise desecrating the church. Thompson—who had acquired considerable standing in the entire community—managed to have the leaders of the mob arrested; they eventually were forced to pay one hundred dollars for repairs to the church.

Through his activities with the Underground Railroad, Thompson became acquainted with prominent abolitionists, including FREDERICK DOUGLASS. But though Douglass was opposed to the "back to Africa" movement, Thompson became intrigued by the views of HENRY HIGHLAND GARNET, a founder of the American Colonization Society in West Africa, which encouraged African American resettlement in Africa. Thompson supported Garnet's overall objectives but sought to ensure that on arriving there, African American emigrants would find in Africa a congenial and worthy Christian civilization. To that end he established the African Civilization Society; the year of its founding is unknown. "The providence of God most clearly indicates that the time has come for enlightened, liberal, systematic, earnest measures for civilizing Africa," Thompson declared at the annual meeting of the society in 1861. He called on his followers to extend their missionary activity and to encourage the extensive cultivation of cotton in Africa, which would provide the economic basis for an advanced civilization. Thompson called on members of the society to answer the call of Providence to return to Africa "as pioneers in an army of civilization—not as refugees from oppression, but as missionaries of social reform, equipped with industrial arts, with liberal education, with Christian faith." Thompson invoked the authority of Abraham Lincoln for this crusade; some sources indicate that Thompson advised top federal officials during the Civil War on policies toward the South.

Thompson held subsequent pastorates in New York City and in the Hudson Valley in upstate New York. In 1876 he was consecrated to the bishopric of the AME Zion church in Louisville, Kentucky. In 1878 he organized a conference in the Bahamas and in 1882 served as a delegate to the Methodist ecumenical council in London. Thompson died in Newburgh and was buried in the Union Colored Cemetery in New Windsor, New York.

Thompson was a remarkable man who acquired a solid reputation in two separate professions; he became a beloved community leader even as he addressed central issues of great importance to the nation. His African Civilization Society was shunted aside by the European colonization of Africa during the last half of the nineteenth century.

FURTHER READING

Hood, J. W. *One Hundred Years of the African Methodist Episcopal Zion Church* (1895).

Moore, John Jamison. *History of the A.M.E. Zion Church in America* (1884).

Nutt, John J. *Newburgh: Her Institutions, Industries, and Leading Citizens* (1891).

Walls, William Jacob. *The African Methodist Episcopal Zion Church: Reality of the Black Church* (1974).

This entry is taken from the *American National Biography* and is published here with the permission of the American Council of Learned Societies.

KEVIN BARRETT

Thompson, Mildred Jean (12 Mar. 1936–1 Sept. 2003), abstract artist, printmaker, and sculptor, was born in Jacksonville, Florida, the youngest of eight children of Ruth Voight, a schoolteacher, and Erlan Thompson, a pharmacist. As a little girl, she knew that she wanted to be an artist. Her earliest efforts were in photography, processing and developing prints in the darkroom that her father built for her. Thompson graduated from Old Stanton High School in 1953. Her father wanted her to attend Florida A&M, but she insisted on going to Howard University in Washington, D.C. Although she had spent many years painting, Thompson entered Howard without any formal training in art. At Howard she studied with JAMES A. PORTER, an artist and the author of the 1942 book *Modern Negro Art*, the definitive study of African American art in its time. Porter was influential in Thompson's development as an artist and was her mentor until his death in 1970.

Though talented, Thompson lacked confidence in her abilities during her first year at Howard. At Porter's suggestion, Thompson attended the Skowhegan School of Painting and Sculpture in Maine in the summer of 1956, her junior year. When Thompson returned to Howard in the fall, she was full of self-confidence gained from the discipline of painting on a daily basis. From 1953 to 1957 she attended Howard University, where she earned a bachelor of arts degree specializing in painting, art history, and art education. After Thompson's graduation, Porter was instrumental in her enrollment at the Brooklyn Museum School, where she received a Max Beckmann Scholarship to study painting, sculpture, and drawing. In an essay about her life, Thompson wrote, "I owe all of what I am to James Porter and his influence…. [H]e carried me."

Thompson wanted to study in Paris, but Porter recommended that she study in Germany, where he felt that the concentrated programs in graphic art, the disciplinary rigor, and the opportunity to study German Expressionism—already an influence on her work—would better serve her development. Thompson attended the Hochschule fur Bildende Kunst (Academy of Fine Art) in Hamburg, West Germany, from 1959 to 1961. During her first year she studied painting, drawing, lithography, and etching. In her second year Thompson mounted her first solo show at the Galerie Sander in Hamburg, where she received much praise and was given the prestigious Reemstma Stipendium (funded by a large German cigarette manufacturer well known for sponsoring artists), which covered all her expenses.

Just prior to her successful exhibition at Galerie Sander, Thompson sent Porter a collection of prints she had completed in Germany. Porter wrote her a few months later to inform her that Caresse Crosby had seen her work at an exhibition at Howard University and was impressed by her talent. Crosby, who had founded the Black Sun Press with her husband Harry Crosby, was a gallery dealer in New York as well as a patron of surrealism, modernism, and abstract art. Crosby invited Thompson to study at Castle of Rocca Sinibalda in Italy that summer at her expense.

In 1960 Thompson spent the summer in Italy, where she worked on watercolors and woodcuts. Academy students were encouraged to experiment and work with other art forms, so Thompson studied calligraphy, jewelry making, and textiles along with her usual coursework of painting, lithography, and etching. The techniques she learned while working in these different mediums were critical to her artistic development. In 1961 Thompson decided to move to New York City, confident that her work would be well received. But once there she met with a great deal of resistance, finding that gallery dealers were not interested in doing business with an African American artist.

In the fall of 1961 Thompson received the first of two fellowships to go to the MacDowell Colony in Peterborough, New Hampshire. She spent about six months there painting and drawing. Although the work progressed well, she remained dissatisfied. Thompson wanted the United States to be as receptive to her work as Europe had been. The racial tensions of the 1960s and the lack of acceptance and recognition became intolerable to her, and in 1962 she returned to Germany, where her work was well received. Primarily known for her vibrantly colored large abstract oil paintings, Thompson also made numerous black-and-white drawings, etchings, and prints. Her work reflected her interest in physics, psychology, spirituality, and music. She spent more than ten years in Germany in self-imposed exile, producing art in different mediums, including large-scale wooden sculptures, and working as a part-time art teacher at the Madchen Gymnasium in Duren, Germany.

Thompson, convinced by her family and friends that the United States was no longer the inhospitable place she had left more than a decade before, returned in 1974. That year she received grants and awards from the National Endowment for the Arts, the Florida State Arts Council, and the Tampa Arts Council for Arts Expansion and was voted one of the Outstanding Black Women in America by the Smithsonian Institution. For three years she was artist-in-residence for the city of Tampa and Hillsborough County, and from 1977 to 1978 she was artist-in-residence at Howard University. For the next seven years she worked as a documentary photographer with Marie-Genevieve Ripeau, a French film director who received a grant to do a documentary about the Cloisters Museum in New York. Upon completion of that project, Thompson worked with Ripeau on the full-length feature film *En l'absence du peintre* (In the absence of the painter), a film about the life of Paula Mondersohn-Becker, considered a founder of the German Expressionist movement and a companion of the poet Rainer Maria Rilke. Although Mondersohn-Becker was considered an Expressionist, her work comprised a personal style and vision that defied categorization. The film won first prize at the San Remo, Italy, film festival and the Beauborg Festival in France.

In the fall of 1985 Thompson accepted an artist-in-residence position at Spelman College, and she taught at other Georgia colleges, including Morris Brown College, Agnes Scott College, and the Atlanta College of Art. In addition to numerous public, private, and corporate collections, Thompson's work is exhibited in the Brooklyn Museum of Art, New York; the Museum of Modern Art, New York; the Howsch Museum, Duren, Germany; and the Smithsonian American Art Museum, Washington, D.C.

Thompson spent the remainder of her life with her partner of eighteen years, Donna Jackson, in Atlanta, Georgia. As a female African American abstract artist trained in the tradition of great master European artists, Thompson is of historical significance and a great inspiration for future generations of artists.

FURTHER READING

Thompson, Mildred. "Memoirs of an Artist," *Sage* 4, no. 1 (Spring 1987): 41–44.

Thompson, Mildred. "Sculptor Mildred Thompson's Experiences in Europe and the United States," *Black Art: An International Quarterly* 1, no. 3 (1977).

Obituary: Associated Press, 7 Sept. 2003.

KRYSTOFER A. MEADOWS

Thompson, Priscilla Jane (1871–1942), poet and lecturer, was born in Rossmoyne, Ohio, the daughter of John Henry Thompson and Clara Jane Gray, former slaves from Virginia. She was the sister of the poets CLARA ANN THOMPSON and Aaron Belford Thompson. Priscilla attended school in Rossmoyne, near Cincinnati, and was tutored privately. She considered a career in teaching, and her love of learning is evident in her poem "Lines to an Old School-House." However, ill health, perhaps tuberculosis, prevented her from pursuing this vocation. Instead Thompson devoted her energies to writing, publishing, and giving readings of her poetry. She also worked for her church, Zion Baptist, where she was a Sunday school teacher for many years. She never married but lived in Rossmoyne with her sister Clara and her brother Garland Yancey Thompson, who was a sculptor.

Thompson's first book of poems, *Ethiope Lays* (1900), is dedicated to Garland and describes him as "best beloved" and a "friend and warder." This book, like Thompson's second book, *Gleanings of Quiet Hours* (1907), was published and sold by the author. In the introduction to *Ethiope Lays*, Thompson says that she aims "as nearly as possible to picture the real side of my race bringing in the foreground, their patience, fortitude and forbearance, devoid of that undertone of sarcasm, generally courted." The poems deal with such themes as romantic love, death, religion, and race.

Many of Thompson's love poems in *Ethiope Lays* have a chivalric tone, such as "Knight of My Maiden Love," where the lover is described as "stalwart and manly." However, in other poems, including "Evelyn," "Alberta," and the humorous "An Unromantic Awakening," the love objects are women. Although it is impossible to establish Thompson's sexual orientation, several of her poems are intriguing precursors to the poems of the Harlem Renaissance poets Mae Virginia Cowdery and Gladys May Casely Hayford, who also wrote women-centered love poems.

A number of Thompson's poems concern religion, and several convey a simple beauty. Two of these poems, perhaps the best of the religious verse, use biblical inscriptions. In "The Vineyard of My Beloved" the reader is warned that God will cast out the "blighted vines" (sinners) from the vineyard. "David and Goliath" clearly links the plight of David and the Israelites with the condition of blacks.

Among the more notable poems in *Ethiope Lays* are the ones concerning race, which are in general more prominent in Priscilla Thompson's work than in that of her sister, Clara. A strong sense of the beauty and virtue of black women is apparent throughout *Ethiope Lays*. In what may be Thompson's finest poem, "The Muse's Favor," the speaker praises "The oft slighted, Afric maids" whose "pure and simple heart" and "beauty rare" make them "half divine." A number of her poems, including "A Southern Scene," "My Father's Story," "Freedom at McNealy's," and "The Old Freedman," deal with racial oppression. The speaker in "To a Little Colored Boy" offers to befriend the child whom she knows will suffer from discrimination. And in striking words, "Address to Ethiopia" pleads:

> Oh rise in union great and strong!
> Hold each black brother, dear;
> And form a nation of thine own,
> Despite thy tyrant's jeers!

In her introduction to *Gleanings of Quiet Hours*, Thompson says that the poems "are closely associated with a proscribed race" and that she attempts "to bring to light [the race's] real life and character." In this work not only does she repeat many of the

same themes as in *Ethiope Lays*, but several poems are simply reprinted. There are religious poems, love poems (including, again, some addressed to women), and several poems about race. Thompson addresses race in "The Husband's Return," which portrays an emancipated slave's return to his former home after the Civil War to claim his wife from a southern planter. These newer poems are distinguished, however, by more humor and by far greater use of dialect. Often, in fact, Thompson employs dialect for humorous purposes, as in "An Afternoon Gossip" and in the longest of her poems, "The Favorite Slave's Story," where she skillfully uses dialect for seventy-two stanzas.

Despite ill health, Thompson lived into her seventies. Records do not indicate her place of death, but most likely it was Rossmoyne. Although her themes do not always display great originality, she used a variety of rhyme patterns, used dialect well, and wrote passionately about black life. As Ann Allen Shockley notes, Thompson's "poems are 'gleanings' from the life of a small-town black woman poet who was ahead of her time, who envisioned and wrote of black women's splendor and the strength of her race." The more spirited of Thompson's poems, such as "Address to Ethiopia," "David and Goliath," "The Muse's Favor," and "The Favorite Slave's Story," still deserve an audience.

FURTHER READING

Sherman, Joan R., ed. *Collected Black Women's Poetry*, vol. 2 (1988).
Shockley, Ann Allen. *Afro-American Women Writers, 1746–1933: An Anthology and Critical Guide* (1988).

This entry is taken from the *American National Biography* and is published here with the permission of the American Council of Learned Societies.

LOUIS J. PARASCANDOLA AND
CAMILLE E. BEAZER

Thompson, Robert Louis (Bob)

Thompson, Robert Louis (Bob) (Jan. 1937–30 May 1966), abstract painter, figurative expressionist, and abstract expressionist, was born in Louisville, Kentucky, the son of Cecil D. Thompson, a self-educated, charming, and hardworking entrepreneur who was the only African American owner of a dry cleaning plant in Kentucky. His mother had a degree from Kentucky State Normal School and expected her three children to attend college, graduate, and pursue professional careers. Thompson's sisters received degrees from Fisk University and Meharry Medical College in

Nashville, Tennessee. After graduation from high school, Thompson received a full Reserve Officers' Training Corps (ROTC) scholarship and left Louisville to begin his premedical studies at Boston University in 1955. After a frustrating first year, Thompson withdrew because of his poor grades and lack of interest in the course work. Family members urged him to return home and to enroll in the University of Louisville to study art. He excelled as an art student and was awarded the Allan R. Hite Art Scholarship after the first semester and retained it for the length of his college career. He also took courses at the Art Center Association from the painters Mary Spencer Nay and Eugene Leake.

For a southern city, Louisville was relatively progressive in terms of race and culture, and Thompson was comfortable with his hometown's cosmopolitan arts and cultural scene. For him, race was not a barrier, and he moved in many of Louisville's arts circles. Though he was an avid jazz enthusiast, Thompson also appreciated the opera and symphony. His literary tastes were eclectic and included Dylan Thomas, T. S. Eliot, e. e. cummings, and LANGSTON HUGHES. In the 1950s, a group of young African American fine arts students at the university, including SAM GILLIAM, Robert Douglas, Ken Young, Bob-Carter, Eugenia Dunn, Fred Bond, and Thompson formed Gallery Enterprises. With its bohemian flair, Gallery Enterprises stretched the boundaries of Louisville's arts scene by experimenting with performance art and holding poetry readings and jam sessions featuring avant-garde jazz in integrated settings.

In the summer of 1958 Thompson traveled to Provincetown, Massachusetts, and on Cape Cod he studied at the Seong Moy School of Painting and Graphic Arts. This experience influenced him to move from abstract to more figurative painting style. After a solo exhibition at Arts in Louisville in February 1959, Thompson moved to New York City, settling on the Lower East Side. In New York he became a regular at the Five Spot, a popular jazz club. There he became friends with and painted portraits of the jazz greats of the era who performed at the club.

A year later, in 1960, he held another solo show, his first in New York, at the Delancey Street Museum. He also married Carol Plenda in 1960. In the spring, after Thompson received a grant, the couple left for Europe, with Paris as the first stop. One of the most significant things about this first trip to Europe was that Thompson was able to experience firsthand the European paintings that he had been studying for years. Thompson and his wife left Paris and moved on to the island of Ibiza, Spain. With support from a Whitney Opportunity Fellowship, Bob and Carol Thompson remained in Europe until 1963.

Upon his return to New York, Thompson began to exhibit more, both in solo and group exhibitions, and public and private collectors actively collected his work. In 1965 the Thompsons returned to Europe, traveling to Rome, where he painted and studied Italian Renaissance masterpieces, but Thompson's hard living, heroin addiction, and daredevil tendencies took their toll on his body. In March 1966 he had a gallbladder operation but did not give himself time to recuperate. Refusing to follow the doctor's orders, he neither slowed his pace nor rested, and he died in Rome of an apparent drug overdose. Thompson had lived exuberantly and died prematurely at the age of twenty-nine.

Thompson's life and his work were ardent and irrepressible. He created more than one thousand works in just seven years. Some of the works were very large, extending more than one hundred inches in width. While Thompson's art is not easily classified, his biographer Thelma Golden best summarizes it:

> He was a narrative painter, enamored of images, real and imagined, but equally enthralled by the freedom, the painterliness, and the aesthetic bravado of Abstract Expressionism, not to mention the unfettered palette of the German Expressionists. At his most developed, Thompson melded abstraction into his figuration. It was an inspired synthesis, the creation of style to serve his unique vision of a new contemporary art (Golden, 15).

FURTHER READING

Driskell, David C. *The Other Side of Color: African American Art in the Collection of Camille O. and William H. Cosby, Jr.* (2001).

Golden, Thelma. *Bob Thompson* (1998).

PAULETTE COLEMAN

Thompson, Ulysses "Slow Kid" (28 Aug. 1888–17 Mar. 1990), dancer and comedian, was born in Prescott, Arkansas, the son of George Thompson, whose father, Aaron Thompson, was a local white doctor. Thompson's mother, Hannah Pandora Driver, was six years older than his father and came from a large family that "populated that whole community," as Thompson would later recall (Helen Armstead-Johnson Collection). The four Driver brothers, including Thompson's maternal grandfather, owned their farms. Several of the Driver girls became schoolteachers in the area, and a Driver cousin of Thompson's was nominated for a bishopric in the 1960s.

Although his family was upwardly mobile, Thompson himself had only a rudimentary education; men in the family were expected to work as farmers and laborers. When Thompson was seven years of age, his mother died; after this tragic loss, life at home was not pleasant for Thompson. His father remarried repeatedly, and Thompson had numerous half brothers and sisters in addition to an older brother and sister by the same mother. After his mother's death, Thompson lived with a grandmother temporarily. He ran away from home sometime between the ages of twelve and fourteen; and over the next several years, he worked in a stave factory, a quarry, a mining camp, and a slaughterhouse. At sixteen years of age he served time on a chain gang in Mineola, Texas, after being caught riding atop a passenger train car. He was beaten while imprisoned, and after local whites burned his cell, he served the remainder of his sentence chained by his neck to a stake in a hayloft.

Around 1910 Thompson found work as a cook with the Mighty Hagg Circus, and then apprenticed in such troupes as the Gillie Medicine Show and Dr. Fuller's Louisiana Medicine Show. These were rough tent shows featuring "geeks" and "hootchiecootchie" girls, and performers in this particular show-business environment endured disagreeable living conditions and danger at the hands of rowdy locals. Thompson worked his way up to a better class of shows, and around 1915 he joined the Ringling Brothers Circus. By the end of that year he had joined Ralph Dunbar's Tennessee Ten as their dance director. In this show he met a young soubrette named FLORENCE MILLS, hiring her as a replacement for a girl who had left the show.

Through the teens Thompson toured widely on the African American vaudeville circuit. By the end of the decade he began to work the white vaudeville circuit as well, with the B. F. Keith organization. He married for the first time during this phase of his career, but little is known of his first wife, a dancer named Letitha Blackburn.

Thompson served in France as a "musician third class" during World War I. He is not known to have played an instrument, and probably served as a drum major and entertainer with his regiment, as did NOBLE SISSLE and other performers in the war. By war's end Thompson was proficient in several forms of show dancing, including the cakewalk and minstrel dances, the buck and wing, and tap. He

became best known for his specialty or "eccentric" dances. These ran the gamut from highly acrobatic "jumping" dances—a *New York Times* critic referred to him as "Jumpin' Jack" in 1921 ("Plantation Revue," 18 July 1822)—to a slow motion routine that earned him his lifelong nickname, "Slow Kid."

In 1920 Thompson joined the cast of a show called *Folly Town*, where he reencountered Mills, now an up-and-coming showgirl. Both joined the cast of the long-running musical *Shuffle Along*, with Mills replacing the star of the show, Gertrude Saunders. On the strength of their work in *Shuffle Along*, Mills and Thompson, now dancing partners, were hired by impresario Lew Leslie to perform in the floor show at his plantation restaurant. This show became so successful that Leslie moved it to Broadway as the *Plantation Revue* in 1922. In the same year, Thompson and Mills were married; it is not known what had become of Thompson's first wife.

Through the remainder of Mills's life, she and Thompson worked together, and he was frequently credited with putting her career ahead of his own. They traveled to England with *From Dover to Dixie* (a renamed version of the *Plantation Revue*) in 1923. In 1924 they were back in New York, in *From Dixie to Broadway*; 1925 found them again in London with Lew Leslie's *Blackbirds*, which also enjoyed a successful run in Paris. In 1927 the *Blackbirds* cast made a triumphant return to New York. However, Mills soon died of appendicitis, a tragedy which sent shock waves through the entertainment world. Her funeral was among the biggest New York had ever seen.

By 1930 Thompson's American career was waning, although he continued to work, playing the Howard Theatre in Washington, D.C., in 1929 and Harlem's Lafayette Theatre in 1931. He had never been a headliner during his joint career with Mills, taking a back seat to her and several other stars, including the dancer-comedian Johnny Hudgins; however, he had a stock of routines, songs, and jokes as well as dance numbers—some of these were his own creations, others were by such leading writers as Henry Creamer. In the wake of Mills's death, Thompson embarked on a series of tours in Europe, Asia, and the Pacific, now often as headliner. In 1933 he played the Garden Petits Champs in Constantinople (later Istanbul). On this same tour, he played Bucharest in Romania and Berlin in Germany, among other cities. In 1937 he was with George Sorlie's *Crispies and Crackers* tour of the South Pacific, including Hobart (in Tasmania), and stops throughout Australia. Two years later Thompson was with Teddy Weatherford's *Plantation Nights* show in Colombo, Ceylon (later Sri Lanka), and appeared at a Jewish Relief Charity Cocktail Dance in Bombay. Other Asian stops during this extended tour included Singapore, Manila, Surabaya, Penang, Rangoon, Saigon, and Shanghai.

Long after he ceased performing regularly, Thompson remained busy by attending to the Florence Mills estate. Initially there was a move to create a permanent memorial to her, and Thompson served as treasurer of the Florence Mills Theatrical Society from 1927 to 1929, but these efforts came to nothing. Thompson received a sizable payment from the Hollywood firm of Herzbrun & Chantry in 1943, granting them the right to develop a treatment of Mills's life and promising Thompson both an advisory role and the chance of an acting part in the piece. He also appears to have contributed to the Harlem portion of a guidebook to New York City and was paid a percentage by Grayson's Guides Company in 1950. In 1969 he was in contact with the playwright and theater historian Loften Mitchell about another attempt to create a musical about Mills's life.

In 1936 Thompson married his third wife, Dr. Sophronia Turner; she died two years later. In 1946 he married his fourth wife, Dr. Gertrude Curtis, the first African American female dentist in New York. Dr. Curtis died in 1973 at the age of ninety-three. Show business historians and chroniclers of African American culture sought Thompson out in his old age. Through the 1980s he also kept in touch with numerous correspondents, particularly show folk, in such far-flung locales as Australia. "Slow Kid" Thompson spent his last five years in a retirement home in Arkansas, where he was looked after by two nieces; he died there at the age of 101. As a veteran of World War I, Thompson was entitled to a veteran's burial and was interred at the Little Rock National Cemetery in Arkansas.

FURTHER READING

Thompson's papers are included, as are those of
   Florence Mills, in the Helen Armstead-Johnson
   Collection, Schomburg Center for Research in
   Black Culture, New York Public Library.
Obituary: *Arkansas Gazette*, 19 Mar. 1990.

ELLIOT HURWITT

Thompson, William H. (16 Aug. 1927–6 Aug. 1950), Korean War soldier and Medal of Honor recipient, was born in Brooklyn, New York. Little is known about his family background, except that he was raised by a single mother, Mary Henderson, and was a resident of Decatur Street in the Bronx for most of his youth. One account of Thompson's life states that he dropped out of school at an early age and spent his teen years hanging out on the streets of New York. Whatever the circumstances of his early life may have been, William Thompson would discover his calling upon reaching adulthood when he joined the military.

In October 1945 William Thompson enlisted in the U.S. Army in the Bronx for a three-year term; his reasons for joining the military are unknown. Perhaps he was inspired by the stories of wartime valor of World War II, whether in the newspapers, on the movie screen, or from local veterans returning home, or maybe he saw it as a way to gain meaningful employment. In his first few years of service after completing his initial training stateside, Private Thompson was stationed in Adak, Alaska. The duty in this cold-weather setting did not dampen Thompson's enthusiasm for military service; to the contrary, it was in Alaska that Thompson gained a reputation as a good soldier and a fine marksman. After he reenlisted in the army in 1948, he served in the 6th Infantry Division in Korea, which was performing occupation duty. When that regiment was sent back to the United States in January 1949, Thompson was transferred to the 24th Infantry Regiment for occupation duty in Japan and subsequent duty in Korea.

The unit in which William Thompson served during the Korean War was a segregated regiment manned by black enlisted personnel and junior officers and commanded by white senior officers. In fact, the 24th Infantry was one of the original all-black regiments in the army, created by Congress in 1866. Its continued existence as a segregated outfit in the immediate post–World War II years was a clear reminder that the army left much to be desired in its policies toward its African American soldiers. Even though President Truman had issued Executive Order 9981 in July 1948 ordering the desegregation of America's armed forces, the army was slow to comply, and would not do so until the Korean War was well under way.

The 24th Infantry regiment would see combat action during the first year of the Korean War, but the seeds of its demise had already been planted even before its arrival in Korea. The old notions from World War II lingered afterward in the military regarding the competence and intelligence of black soldiers. These feelings with regard to the men of the 24th were reinforced during their occupation duty in Japan, where they were stationed on an island and physically isolated from white regiments and suffered from false rumors about their competence and leadership. Thus, even before the men of the 24th Infantry were sent for combat duty in Korea, prejudice against the regiment ran high. While their performance as a unit in Korea would be judged adversely due to many factors, and remains controversial to this day, the actions of individual soldiers, men like William Thompson and CORNELIUS CHARLTON, would amply demonstrate that competence and courage were qualities that were not possessed by white soldiers alone.

The 24th Infantry Regiment arrived from Japan in late July 1950. Private First Class William Thompson served as a machine gunner in Company M, a heavy weapons unit. The 24th saw its first action at Yechon and achieved a small victory, and then was shifted to the area of Sangju. On the evening of 5–6 August 1950 elements of the 24th were operating near Haman, Korea, when they were attacked by a large contingent of North Korean troops and took heavy fire. Some companies immediately retreated in disorder rather than standing and fighting, but not all did. Elements of Company M, including Private Thompson, stood their ground and rallied around Second Lieutenant Herbert Wilson with two heavy machine guns as their main firepower. When one of these machine guns was knocked out by a grenade, the main defense of the group fell to Private Thompson and his machine gun. Though the subject of intense enemy fire, Thompson calmly maintained his position and blocked their advance with a withering fire.

When a lull in the fighting took place after the enemy sought cover, Lieutenant Wilson ordered a withdrawal to higher ground. However, Thompson refused to move and stayed in position; when Wilson made his way to Thompson, he found the private was badly wounded, but still maintaining his fire. During their talk, Thompson stated "that he knew he was dying and that he planned to stay where he was" (Hanna, p. 143). Despite efforts to forcibly remove Thompson, he would not go and urged his officers to leave and that his fire would cover them. Wilson reluctantly agreed and was one of the last men to see Thompson alive; the private's steady fire not only covered the withdrawal, but also killed many enemy soldiers in the process. When the area was recaptured by Company M a few days later, Private William Thompson was found by his machine gun, with numerous dead enemy soldiers

around him. He finally succumbed to wounds received from an exploding grenade.

For his actions at Haman, Korea, Private First Class William Thompson was awarded the Medal of Honor, which was presented to his mother Mary by General Omar Bradley on 21 June 1951. Thompson was buried at the Long Island National Cemetery, Farmingdale, New York. Less than a year after Thompson's death, in October 1951, the 24th Infantry Regiment was disbanded and the army effectively desegregated, its members dispersed among regiments that had formerly been all white. However, this move would prove to be a bitter irony for the memory of the first African American soldier to be awarded the Medal of Honor since the Spanish-American War. The 24th Infantry was not desegregated because of the excellent performance by soldiers like Thompson, but rather because of the lesser soldiers within the regiment. Within a short time after his death, the 24th would suffer from poor leadership and performance in combat at all levels. Though the unit would also have some success during this time, its highly publicized failures doomed the 24th and led to the army decision to disband the regiment.

FURTHER READING

Bowers, William T., William M. Hammond, and George L. MacGarrigle. *Black Soldier, White Army: The 24th Infantry in Korea* (1997).

Hanna, Charles W. *African American Recipients of the Medal of Honor* (2002).

GLENN ALLEN KNOBLOCK

Thompson, Willie (30 May 1935–), educator, was born William Mack Thompson in Hamilton, Georgia, the fifth of six children of Ocie Thompson, a tenant farmer, and Lizzie Pearl Thompson, a domestic worker. In 1950, at only age fifteen, Willie graduated after completing the eleventh grade at segregated Spencer High School. After a series of jobs, including pulp woodcutter, gardener, and busboy, he joined the Marine Corps in 1952.

Willie grew up learning from his mother, family, and teachers that you had to fight for your rights. His family had faced racism and oppression for generations, experiences that would shape Willie's character and sense of himself. His mother and grandmother had lived in communities that had witnessed lynchings and where the leaders of white mobs went unpunished and gained local fame for their crimes. Willie's brother, Horace, was injured at the age of eleven, while cutting wood for the house of the owner of the tenant farm where the family worked and lived. Horace almost died at the segregated hospital in Columbus, Georgia, but President Franklin Delano Roosevelt's doctor saved Horace's leg and life during the doctor's annual visit to Columbus from Warm Springs, where Roosevelt often spent time. Willie's father, Ocie, was killed when a train hit his car while he was crossing the tracks in 1943. The owner of the tenant farm where his family worked and lived evicted Lizzie when she refused to remove her oldest son, Joseph, from school to fill his father's place on the farm. The farm owner also forced Lizzie to sign over the death benefit check from an insurance company to him and gave her only some of the money. Lizzie later used the money to pay for Willie's sister, Pearline, to attend nursing school at Tuskegee Institute.

Willie's mother Lizzie then married Aldena McCotton, a friend of her dead husband. Willie believed that Lizzie's spirit and determination, along with the eviction and second marriage, rescued his family from poverty and deprivation. The family planted three acres of produce, and tended chickens, pigs, and a cow for milk and butter. Lizzie continued to take in washing and ironing, while Aldena worked as a farm laborer, yardman, and well digger.

Thompson's entire life was nurtured by his mother's fierce pride and determination to be treated as a first-class citizen. Frustrated by dead-end jobs and hoping to earn money for college through the GI Bill, Thompson volunteered with the Marines in 1952. Although President Harry Truman had ordered the desegregation of the U.S. military in 1948, the pace of compliance was slow, and was not completed until 1963. Due to continued de facto segregation, instead of the office job he had requested, Thompson was assigned to a job in the all-black Stewards Service Corps. As a steward, he had to serve food to officers who called Thompson and his fellow stewards "niggers." He accepted a demotion in order to be transferred to an integrated supply company where racism was less overt. In 1952, when Thompson started sending part of his paycheck from the military, Lizzie was able to buy two acres of land, but it was not until 1955, the year Thompson was discharged, that Thompson's checks enabled Lizzie to build a four-room house.

Thompson grew up in a family tradition that placed a high value on education. Lizzie, who only had a sixth grade education, made it a priority to keep her children in school and encourage them to go to college. Thompson's maternal great-grandfather, Lewis Hudson, a slave house servant born in Georgia, sent his youngest daughter Ethel to Spelman College in the late nineteenth century. Ethel was an inspiration to the family. She taught school and became a principal in Pine Mountain, Georgia. Thompson's maternal aunts, Mariah and Rossie, both became teachers, as did Rossie's daughter, Nettie Paul. Thompson spent summers in Cataula, Georgia, and attended school with his aunt Rossie and cousin Nettie Paul.

Thompson carried on the family tradition of higher education and teaching. After four years in the Marines, Thompson moved to Los Angeles to attend Los Angeles City College. Thompson's eldest cousin and his wife hosted Thompson while he attended City College, to help reduce costs. Thompson transferred to San Francisco State, where he was Vice President of the Student Committee on Political Education—a civil rights and peace group. He graduated in 1961 with a B.A. in education and social services. A scholarship from the National Institute of Mental Health allowed Thompson to enter social work school. In 1967, he received his MSW from University of California, Berkeley. In 1995, after 24 years of teaching, Thompson became Emeritus Professor of Sociology at City College of San Francisco.

After college, drawing on his family's history of oppression and fighting to protect their rights, Thompson was vice-president of the Los Angeles Congress of Racial Equality, helping recruit Freedom Riders. Thompson was deeply committed to struggles for social justice outside of the United States as well as within it. He also joined Accion in Caracas, Venezuela, where he helped fight poverty. He was a summer counselor for the Encampment for Citizenship in Puerto Rico in 1962, a camp that brought together young adults of different backgrounds. While at the Encampment, Thompson met its biggest supporter, Eleanor Roosevelt. He worked for the San Francisco chapter of the Urban League; wrote about the War on Poverty; worked for Glide Memorial Church in San Francisco as director of its United Fund for Social Change; and was the first black milk truck delivery driver working for Spreckles Creamery in 1964.

Thompson was driven by the principle that family solidarity and teaching others are part of giving back and supporting the struggles of people of color around the world. Thompson helped found the Bay Area Association of Black Social Workers. He worked with Kwanzaa Celebrants, and published a Kwanzaa Handbook. Thompson was a member of the Bay Area Anti-Apartheid Committee, and the

Haiti Action Committee. Thompson wrote numerous articles about Africans in the African diaspora. In his later years, he still actively supported international social and political struggles for African and Caribbean people. He enjoyed spending time with his son Kwame Nguvu Thompson and Kwame's wife Michelle, his grandchildren Keana and Kobe, and his Congolese godson, Willie James Ongagna, who is named after him. In the twenty-first century he remained committed to peace and social justice issues through his blog and Myspace page http://www.myspace.com/williemackthompson.

FURTHER READING

Black, Algernon D. *The Young Citizens: The Story of the Encampment for Citizenship* (1962).

Black, Allida, et al., eds. "Encampment for Citizenship," from The Eleanor Roosevelt Papers, *Teaching Eleanor Roosevelt* (2003).

Gray, Fred. *Bus Ride to Justice* (2002).

Ransby, Barbara. *Ella Baker and the Black Freedom Movement: A Radical Democratic Vision* (2003).

Rose, Thomas, and John Greenya. *Black Leaders: Then and Now* (1984).

San Francisco Bay View National Black Newspaper. http://www.sfbayview.com.

Weiss, Nancy J. *Whitney M. Young, Jr., and the Struggle For Civil Rights* (1989).

TOM ROSE

Thompson Patterson, Louise (9 Sept. 1901–27 Aug. 1999), cultural and political radical, activist, and feminist, was born Louise Alone Toles in Chicago, the daughter of William Toles, a bartender, and Lula Brown Toles. In 1904 Louise's parents separated, and in the next ten years she lived throughout the Northwest with her mother and her stepfather, William Thompson. Often the only black child in town, Louise was the target of vicious racial insults. In an effort to maintain her self-respect she strove to excel in school. In 1919 she enrolled at the University of California at Berkeley. There she attended a lecture by W. E. B. DuBois, a founder of the National Association for the Advancement of Colored People. "For the first time in my life," she recalled, "I was proud to be black." DuBois's talk prompted Thompson to dream of traveling to New York City and becoming involved in racial politics. In 1923, one of only a handful of black students, she graduated cum laude in economics.

With the encouragement of DuBois, Thompson took a position in 1925 at a dilapidated black college in Pine Bluff, Arkansas, and in 1927 at the Hampton Institute. But her support for a student strike against the school's racially conservative administration cost Thompson her job. In 1928 she took a position as a social worker with the National Urban League in New York City. But she soon became disillusioned with the profession's paternalism. She also became immersed in the Harlem Renaissance, working as the secretary to ZORA NEALE HURSTON and LANGSTON HUGHES. Hughes remained a lifelong friend. In 1928 Thompson married the novelist Wallace Thurman, but they separated after less than six months.

With the onset of the Depression, Thompson gravitated toward the left. In 1931 she founded the Harlem branch of the Friends of the Soviet Union, and Harlem intellectuals congregated at her apartment to discuss Marxism and the Soviet Union. In 1932 she was asked to organize a group of African Americans to travel to the Soviet Union and make a film about racial conditions in the United States. Thompson pulled together twenty-two black artists and writers, including Langston Hughes. The film was canceled after they arrived, making international headlines. Yet Thompson was deeply impressed with the Soviet Union, viewing it as a striking model for building a society committed to social equality. "Because of what I had seen in the Soviet Union," she recalled, "I ... was ready to make a change" (LTP Papers, 14 May 1987 interview, 22).

After she returned to Harlem, Thompson became widely known as "Madame Moscow" for her vocal support of the Soviet Union. Her critics included the African American journalist HENRY LEE MOON, who had been one of the cast members for the film. She was also attracted to the Communist movement because of its efforts to free the SCOTTSBORO BOYS, nine black adolescents who had been falsely accused and sentenced to death for raping two white women in Alabama. In 1933 she organized a successful Scottsboro march in Washington, D.C., and joined the Communist Party; in 1934 she joined the International Workers Order (IWO), a Communist-affiliated fraternal organization. By the end of the decade Thompson was elected IWO national secretary. In 1937 she attended the Paris World Congress against Racism and Fascism and observed the Spanish Civil War. In 1938 she cofounded with Hughes the short-lived Harlem Suitcase Theater, which produced the wildly popular *Don't You Want To Be Free?*

In 1940 Thompson married the Communist leader WILLIAM PATTERSON, and they moved to Chicago. Three years later she gave birth to a daughter. In the late 1940s she and Patterson, along with DuBois, ALPHEAUS HUNTON JR., and PAUL ROBESON, formed the Council of African Affairs, an organization dedicated to ending colonialism. By 1950 the Pattersons had returned to New York.

In 1951 Thompson Patterson, with the actor Beulah Richardson and the journalist CHARLOTTA BASS, founded the Sojourners for Truth and Justice, an all-black women's progressive civil rights organization. The group issued a call for African American women to join in a demonstration "to call upon our government to prove its loyalty to its fifteen million Negro citizens" (LTP Papers, box 15, folder 26). The stifling anti-Communist political atmosphere of the era partially contributed to the Sojourners' demise.

Louise and William Patterson fell victim to McCarthyism during the early 1950s. On 6 April 1951 Thompson Patterson was called to testify in *People of New York v. International Workers Order*, a New York State court case, because of her involvement with the IWO, which had been deemed a "subversive" organization. She invoked the Fifth Amendment but was not jailed. William Patterson, however, was jailed and lost his passport because of his political activities. Thompson Patterson organized national campaigns to free him and for the return of his passport, as well as those of DuBois and Robeson.

Although some African American activists broke their ties with the left, Thompson Patterson continued agitating for progressive causes. In the early 1960s she helped the noted historian Herbert Aptheker found the American Institute for Marxist Studies. In 1969 she returned to the Soviet Union, marveling at the tremendous changes that had taken place there. The Pattersons' New York apartment served as a place where many young black militants came to gain valuable political insight.

In the early 1970s Thompson Patterson headed the New York Committee to Free ANGELA DAVIS, the African American Communist who had been accused of involvement in the shooting death of a California judge in August 1970. After her husband's death in 1980, Thompson Patterson founded the William L. Patterson Foundation. In the late 1980s, with the assistance of the scholar Margaret Wilkerson, Thompson Patterson began writing her memoirs. She was discussed in numerous critically acclaimed studies of DuBois, Hughes, the Harlem Renaissance, and the black left, and she appeared in several documentaries. She also received many awards. By the mid-1990s Thompson Patterson's health declined; consequently her memoir was never completed. It would have been a fascinating account of an extraordinary African American woman who took part in many of the most significant social, political, and cultural movements in the United States and abroad during the twentieth century.

FURTHER READING
The main body of Thompson Patterson's papers can be found at the Special Collections Department, Robert W. Woodruff Library, Emory University, Atlanta, Georgia. Information can also be found about her in the Matt N. and Evelyn Graves Crawford Papers, Special Collections, Emory University; the Langston Hughes Papers, Beinecke Rare Book and Manuscript Library, Yale University, New Haven, Connecticut; and in the Communist Party USA Files, Library of Congress, Washington, D.C. The Tamiment Library at New York University contains audiotapes of Thompson Paterson's lengthy 1981 interview with Ruth Prago, which was part of the Oral History of the American Left (OHAL) project.

Kelley, Robin. "The Left," in *Black Women in America: An Historical Encyclopedia*, ed. Darlene Clark Hine (1994).

Massiah, Louis. *Louise Alone Thompson Patterson* (2002).

Naison, Mark. *Communists in Harlem during the Depression* (1983; repr. 2005).

Wilkerson, Margaret. "Excavating Our History: The Importance of Biographies of Women of Color," *Black American Literature Forum* 24, no. 1 (Spring 1990): 73–84.

Obituary: *Los Angeles Times*, 19 Sept. 1997.

This entry is taken from the *American National Biography* and is published here with the permission of the American Council of Learned Societies.

ERIK S. MCDUFFIE

Thoms, Adah Belle Samuels (12 Jan. 1870?–21 Feb. 1943), nurse and nurse administrator, was born in Richmond, Virginia, the daughter of Harry Samuels and Melvina (maiden name unknown). She attended public school in Richmond and taught there before deciding to pursue a career in nursing. In 1893 she moved to Harlem to study elocution and public speaking at the Cooper Union. After attending the Woman's Infirmary and School of Therapeutic Massage in New York City, Samuels received a diploma in 1900. She worked initially as a

Adah Belle Samuels Thoms was a charter member and later president of the National Association for Colored Graduate Nurses, an original inductee of the American Nurses Association Hall of Fame, and the author of *Pathfinders*, the first history of African American nurses. (Austin/Thompson Collection, from National Library of Medicine.)

private duty nurse in New York City before return ing south in 1902 to Raleigh, North Carolina, where she joined the nursing staff of St. Agnes Hospital. At some point she married a physician, Dr. Thoms, about whom little is known. He died shortly after they returned to New York in 1903.

After resettling in New York, Adah Thoms entered the newly organized school of nursing at Lincoln Hospital and Home. White women had founded the hospital in 1893 to provide health care to black New Yorkers, and the nursing school was opened in 1898. Thoms, in her second year at Lincoln, secured the position of head nurse on a surgical ward. She graduated in 1905, and Lincoln immediately hired her as a full-time operating room nurse and as the supervisor of the surgical division.

Possessed of keen social skills and a healthy regard for work, Thoms had a long and eventful career at Lincoln Hospital. In 1906 she became assistant superintendent of nurses, a position she held until her retirement eighteen years later. As assistant superintendent, she improved nursing training by launching, in 1913, a six-month post-graduate course for registered nurses. In 1917, just five years after the establishment of the National Organization for Public Health Nursing, she inaugurated a course in public health nursing.

Although Thoms was admired for her pioneering administrative work at Lincoln Hospital—few black women were accorded such opportunities—she left an even more important legacy as a result of her involvement in the successful struggle to professionalize black women nurses. In 1906 MARTHA MINERVA FRANKLIN, an 1897 graduate of the Woman's Hospital Training School for Nurses in Philadelphia, Pennsylvania, launched a bold initiative. She mailed more than 1,500 letters to black graduate nurses, hospitals, and nursing schools to gauge interest in forming a professional association of black nurses. She envisioned an organization that would challenge the exclusion of black nurses from membership in the American Nurses' Association while providing a space for them to meet and address their own need for employment registries, better jobs, advanced training, and greater access to supervisory positions within hospital hierarchies.

Thoms, as president of the Lincoln Hospital School of Nursing Alumnae Association, responded to Franklin by inviting her and interested nurses to meet in New York City as guests of the association. Thoms and the Lincoln association sponsored the August 1908 meeting of fifty-two nurses. Out of their deliberations emerged, in 1908, the National Association of Colored Graduate Nurses (NACGN), with twenty-six charter members. Franklin was elected president and was reelected to the same office in 1909. Thoms was named the treasurer. In 1916 she was elected president of the NACGN, a position she occupied until her retirement from Lincoln Hospital in 1923.

As one of the most prominent black nurses, Thoms became a staunch advocate for stronger educational programs in the black hospital nursing schools, and she advocated greater use of black nurses in public health work sponsored by public and private agencies. Indeed, throughout the last decade of her career, she became the model for black nurse involvement in a variety of community organizations and projects. In 1916 she collaborated with both the National Urban League and the National Association for the Advancement of Colored People in an attempt to improve conditions for black patients at local hospitals and for nursing students enrolled in the training schools.

America's entry into World War I created a great demand for nurses, and Thoms worked on many fronts to ensure that black nurses become a part of the war effort. When Congress declared war on Germany in April 1917, she rallied black nurses to enroll in the American Red Cross Nursing Service, which was the only way for them to enter the U.S. Army Nurse Corps. However, the black nurses who applied to the American Red Cross were rejected. Thoms, along with a number of African American leaders, protested the racial practices of the Red Cross and of the U.S. military. She met with policy-makers and wrote letters to Jane A. Delano, head of the American National Red Cross Nursing Service, protesting the exclusion of black nurses. Thoms was told in December 1917 that a limited number of black nurses would be allowed to enroll. The Red Cross accepted its first black nurse in July 1918. However, appointment to the Army Nurse Corps, with full rank and pay, did not come for black nurses until December 1918, too late for the war but just in time to help with the massive influenza epidemic.

Not content to sit and wait for the Red Cross and the U.S. military to recognize and accept black nurses, Thoms helped to establish a new order of black war nurses, the Blue Circle Nurses. The Circle for Negro War Relief hired black nurses to work in poor or rural black communities, teaching residents the importance of sanitation, a healthy diet, and appropriate clothing. In 1921 the assistant surgeon general of the army appointed Thoms to serve on the Woman's Advisory Council of Venereal Diseases of the U.S. Public Health Service.

After her retirement in 1923 Thoms married Henry Smith, who died months later. During the next few years Thoms concentrated her considerable energies on compiling statistical information about, and writing the history of, black nursing schools and their graduates. In 1929 she published the first book on black nursing, *Pathfinders: A History of the Progress of Colored Graduate Nurses.* Throughout the next decade she remained committed to the advancement of black women in the nursing profession and to the integration of the American Nurses' Association. She had a number of close professional relationships with white nurses. She objected to suggestions that nurses merge with black doctors in their National Medical Association. Ultimately, Thoms was a racial pragmatist. She believed that until integration was accomplished, black nurses had to support and strengthen their own organizations and institutions, creating their own paths to equality.

To celebrate her record of outstanding service to black nursing and her relentless efforts to improve conditions within a still-segregated health-care delivery system, the NACGN in 1936 named Thoms the first recipient of the Mary Mahoney Medal, founded in honor of the first black graduate nurse. Thoms's active involvement in the St. Mark's Methodist Episcopal Church and her work with the Hope Day Nursery, a unique day-care center for the black children of working mothers, were limited only by failing health because of heart disease and diabetes. During these later years her niece, Nannie Samuels, lived with her. Even after her death in New York City Thoms was recognized for her many contributions to her chosen profession. In 1976 she was inducted into the Nursing Hall of Fame. She was buried in Woodlawn Cemetery in New York under the surname Smith.

FURTHER READING

Davis, Althea T. "Adah Belle Samuels Thoms, 1870–1943," in *American Nursing: A Biographical Dictionary*, ed. Vern L. Bullough, et al. (1988).

Hine, Darlene Clark. *Black Women in White: Racial Conflict and Cooperation in the Nursing Profession, 1890–1950* (1989).

This entry is taken from the *American National Biography* and is published here with the permission of the American Council of Learned Societies.

DARLENE CLARK HINE

Thorburn, W. Garth (19 May 1928–12 Jan. 2010), foreign service official, was born in New York City to Wesley Orlando Thorburn and Amy Constantine, both of whom were Jamaican natives. His mother studied music at the Juilliard School of Music, and his father studied mechanical dentistry at Pennsylvania State University. Thorburn was the youngest of their three children. He lived in Jamaica for fifteen years and graduated from Wolmer's Boys School in 1945 before returning to the United States in 1946.

In 1947 Thorburn enrolled in Agricultural Economics and Extension Education, which prepared African American men for careers in segregated agricultural extension service offices in all of the ex-Confederate states as well as in the U.S. Department of Agriculture's Federal Extension Service, at Hampton Institute, Hampton, Virginia, earning a B.S. in 1951. When Thorburn moved from his northern urban birthplace to prepare for a career in agriculture extension, blacks employed in segregated agricultural extension service offices across the South had been professionalizing extension education for more than thirty years. They had defined professional standards, formed professional organizations (i.e., the National Negro County Agricultural Agent Association and the National Negro Home Demonstration Agent Association), and managed to protect their positions by becoming more involved in planning and management.

Thorburn enlisted in the army in 1952. He married Doris Boags while he served in the military during the Korean conflict. They had two children, Garth and Michele. In 1954, after Thorburn completed his tour of duty as a noncommissioned officer, he accepted a position with the USDA's Foreign Agricultural Service (FAS), which formed in 1953–1954 following reorganization of the USDA's Office of Foreign Relations. The FAS worked to identify and develop markets for U.S. agricultural surplus by collecting and disseminating market information; promoting sale of farm products abroad, particularly in friendly foreign countries; removing trade obstacles; and sharing technical expertise and other information with foreign countries to help them become better consumers. The FAS designated attachés to officially represent the United States on issues related to agricultural trade.

Between 1954 and 1956 Thorburn strengthened his credentials for such foreign service by taking graduate courses in Agricultural Economics at the University of Maryland, while stationed in Washington, D.C. Foreign posts prevented him from completing the degree. Other African Americans with extension experience likewise entered foreign service during this time, but Thorburn pursued a career, not just a temporary position, abroad. He became the first African American professional hired by the FAS. His language skills (Portuguese, Spanish, French, and English) and training in agricultural economics led to his appointment as third agricultural officer in the FAS attaché office in Paris, France, in 1956. In 1961 he was promoted to São Paulo, Brazil. In this position he ran one of three FAS offices in the country and maintained trade data on coffee, sisal, and cocoa among other agricultural commodities.

He gained additional experience with international commodities during two years with the Sugar and Tropical Products Division in Washington, D.C., before he began managing the USDA's FAS office in Bogotá, Colombia. Thorburn collected data on coffee, sugar, cocoa, and tea, all major international commodities with political as well as economic significance in world trade. His efforts, as a USDA official, to document coffee and cocoa production as the basis for trade quotas provided accurate data not available from producers or local marketers.

Foreign service represented a new outlet for rural reformers during the cold war era. Thorburn worked to collect accurate data to stabilize world trade in agricultural commodities, but changing U.S. foreign policy likewise made technical expertise in agriculture useful. African American agricultural extension agents likewise found themselves employable in foreign posts. U.S. officials justified the placement of minorities as technical experts in nations prone to communist influences because the experts could improve the living conditions for rural natives and thus help fight communism by providing viable alternatives. Several African nations, unstable politically because of the wave of decolonization sweeping the continent, and parts of the Middle East and Asia seemed appropriate geographic regions to station Americans of color because of their proximity to communist nations. U.S. officials also believed that by involving black experts in agriculture in the international reform effort, the citizens downtrodden by race bias could serve as proof to foreigners who criticized racist practices in the United States that the U.S. government took seriously its responsibility for eliminating race discrimination and improving race relations at home, and could be trusted to do so abroad.

The interest in sending technical experts abroad began with the Point Four Program, an international relief effort undertaken by the U.S. Department of State. President Harry S. Truman introduced the idea as the fourth point in his inauguration address on 20 January 1949. He indicated that the United States must boldly provide technical assistance to poor people in "underdeveloped areas" who suffer because of "primitive and stagnant" economies. Point Four sought African American extension agents for two-year stints as technical experts to facilitate rural reform, raise the nation's standard of living, and develop its economic resources.

Thorburn's service came at a high price to his personal safety and family security. He avoided a kidnapping attempt in Colombia, and he and his first wife divorced as he served as FAS attaché in Brazilia, Brazil, between 1972 and 1974. Between 1974 and 1976 Thorburn directed the Sugar and Tropical Products Division in Washington, D.C. He married Sylvia Regina Baratto Pinto in 1976 and they had two children, Stephanie and Natalie. In that same year he was transferred as agricultural attaché to Nigeria (covering Cameroon and Ghana as well). In 1980 his title changed, though he remained responsible for managing USDA Foreign Agricultural Service offices. That year he became agricultural counselor and was transferred to New Delhi, India (covering Nepal and Sri Lanka also). In 1987 he was transferred as agricultural counselor to Ankara, Turkey (covering Syria), where he served until he retired on 20 December 1990. Over his thirty-five-year career with the FAS, he served on four continents and negotiated trade agreements that affected the world.

African Americans engaged in foreign service experienced some freedoms denied them in the United States during the 1950s and 1960s. Even though technical experts and agricultural attachés such as Thorburn had to abide by U.S. government regulations while abroad, they faced less race bias. Furthermore, they believed that they made a difference in international development, and they remained committed to the service. Thorburn's son, W. Garth Thorburn II, followed his father's career path, entering USDA foreign service six months after his father retired. Thorburn II worked for four years in Washington, D.C., before assuming responsibilities as deputy director of the Agricultural Trade Office in Hong Kong. In 1998 he was appointed agricultural attaché of the Agricultural Trade Office in Kiev, Ukraine. He died in Sarasota, Florida, at the age of 81.

FURTHER READING

W. Garth Thorburn's oral history interview was collected as part of the Oral History Project, George P. Schultz National Foreign Affairs Training Center, the Association for Diplomatic Studies and Training, Arlington, Virginia.

Borstelmann, Thomas. *The Cold War and the Color Line: American Race Relations in the Global Arena* (2001).

Pinder, Frank E. *Pinder: From Little Acorns* (1986).

Plummer, Brenda Gayle. *Rising Wind: Black Americans and U.S. Foreign Affairs, 1935–1960* (1996).

Reid, Debra. *Reaping a Greater Harvest: African Americans, the Extension Service, and Rural Reform in Jim Crow Texas* (2007).

DEBRA A. REID

Thorne, Jack (1863?–14 Nov. 1941), newspaper correspondent and storyteller, was born David Bryant Fulton in Fayetteville, North Carolina, the son of Benjamin Fulton, a public carter, and Lavinia Robinson Thorne. The oldest of fourteen children of Hamlet and Amy Robinson, Lavinia grew up a slave in Robeson County, North Carolina, in the absence of her parents but under the "indulgence of her master" (Thorne, *Eagle Clippings*, 7), who taught her to read the Bible at a very young age. At fourteen Lavinia married Benjamin. Raising ten children, Benjamin and Lavinia settled in Wilmington, North Carolina, in 1867.

In 1887, after completing his education at the segregated Williston School and Gregory Normal Institute in Wilmington, Thorne moved to New York City but found it difficult to find meaningful employment. He obtained work in 1888 as a porter for the Pullman Palace Car Company, spending nine years at the job. In addition, he toiled "four years in a large music house" and "two years at odd jobs" (*Eagle Clippings*, 7).

He finally landed a job at the Central Branch of the Young Men's Christian Association of Brooklyn in 1901. Shortly after arrival in Brooklyn, Thorne earned sufficient funds to have his wife Virginia Moore Thorne join him. Employment remained tenuous for Thorne. He had to stay vigilant to the ruses of unethical employment agencies, particularly those that collected fees from several prospects for the same job. It was also common at the time for employers to pit African Americans against other workers for the political gain of the employers; Thorne's stint in 1892 as a strike-breaking stevedore for the Ward Steamship Company in New York was one of his most memorable examples (*Eagle Clippings*, 8–9). Thorne began writing shortly after he moved to New York. Alex Manly (1866–1944), the black editor of the *Wilmington Record*, asked him to write articles for his paper, and Thorne wrote about the economic, social, and political conditions of blacks he encountered during his travels as a porter. Thorne published these articles in 1892 in *Recollections of a Sleeping Car Porter*.

Though Thorne argued many unpopular and courageous positions in the *Wilmington Record*, a black-owned newspaper, and the *Brooklyn Eagle* on the perennial injustices to the poor, disenfranchised, and blacks, his lasting contributions to African American literature and culture are his short stories or sketches. For instance in *Recollections of a Sleeping Car Porter*—the first work to bear the pen name Jack Thorne—he drew on his experiences as a Pullman porter to introduce *Record* readers to character types ("cracker" or "poor white trash," the ruthless and servile "cap'n," the vapid and pontificating "colonel," the tragic mulatto, the trickster, the unknown bard, the outlaw, and the matriarch) that he would later hone in *Hanover, or the Persecution of the Lowly* (1900) and *Eagle Clippings* (1907).

A literary hybrid, *Hanover* on the surface is a graphic replay of the complex race and class tensions that intersected in 1898 to engender the Wilmington race riot. But on a deeper level, it is among the most poignant explications of the tenuous status of both black and white women in the American South. That it is dedicated to IDA B. WELLS, "the eminent heroine," should come as no surprise. Wells's stinging editorials in the *Memphis Free Speech* against racism and sexism, her personal rebellions against racism, and the loss of a teaching job due to white paranoia find analogues in *Hanover*. Moreover, Wells's racial insights and political views are vehemently recreated in *Hanover*: the Colonel, pompous, anachronistic, classist, and racist; Teck Pervis, duped "poor white trash"; Molly Pierrepont, redemptive octoroon; the Georgia white woman, unconditional paranoid defender of white womanhood; Amanda Pervis, benign, compassionate, vulnerable, "poor white trash"; Ben Hartright, racist, hypocrite, and adulterer indifferent to racial lines; Calvin Sauls, "Good Nigger" and racial traitor; and Reverend Selkirk, courageous black minister.

Eagle Clippings (1907) comprised mostly various installments of Thorne's column in the *Brooklyn Daily Eagle*. Its contents, he wrote in the book's introduction, "are the outpourings of a heart full of love for a maligned race and jealous of their wrongs." In his column, Thorne attacked race maligners such as black colonization advocate John Temple Graves; Thomas Dixon, author of *The Clansman*; and Anne Carter, a "woman correspondent" (*Eagle Clippings*, 44) to the *Brooklyn Eagle* (7 Sept. 1904) who castigated Thorne's *Eagle* columns: "From my point of view, I hardly think there is another paper aside from the 'yellows' that would permit such disgusting, anarchistic matter as you print about once a week from the pen of the Negro admirer, Jack Thorne. All papers without Negro blood on the staff put these dreadful, ignorant, ranting productions in the waste basket" (*Eagle Clippings*, 44).

At the end of what he called "this little book," Thorne demonstrated his mastery of African American character types. He laughed at the trickster porter who employed guile and humor to relieve an unsuspecting passenger of his whiskey. He included "Egypt's Ghost," a story of deception reminiscent of CHARLES WADDELL CHESNUTT, Poe, or Hawthorne. He also eulogized the poet PAUL LAURENCE DUNBAR as the unknown bard who "chose to sing that the skeptical might look behind the ebony exterior and see there the sweet, loving and forgiving heart." He lauded HENRY BERRY LOWERY, the black North Carolina outlaw who induced "awe and terror in North Carolina."

Though Thorne continued to write short stories, poetry, and essays after publishing *Eagle Clippings*, many were not published. However, *Poem to Abraham Lincoln* was published as a broadside in 1909. In addition, an eleven-page pamphlet from 1912, *A Plea for Social Justice*, reiterated his lifelong defense of the black woman. Thorne produced two other significant works during this period: "Mother of Mine; Ode to the Negro Woman" (1923) and "Race, Unification; How It May Be Accomplished" (1913), an essay outlining the process for realizing racial harmony and equality.

After the end of his first marriage, Thorne married Katie Gummer, also from Wilmington, in 1917. He died 14 November 1941 and was buried in Brooklyn. He never replicated the success garnered by his novel *Eagle Clippings*. Although he continued to write, he could not find a publisher. Thorne read his unpublished ode "Mother of Mine; Ode to the Negro Woman" to the Annual Convention of the New York Colored Women's Club in July 1923 (Andrews, 590). Little is known about his private and public life after that reading.

A friend once observed that Thorne was "an eccentric on the Race question." Another cautioned him, "Your pen is a venomous weapon. You are doubtless right; I admire your grit, but you might make it a trifle milder" (*Eagle Clippings*, 3). In his refusal to feed racial pabulum to friend or foe lies Thorne's significance and, despite their being rarely read a century later, the permanence of his newspaper columns.

FURTHER READING
Thorne, Jack. *Eagle Clippings* (1907).
Andrews, William. "Jack Thorne," in *Dictionary of American Negro Biography*, eds. Rayford W. Logan and Michael R. Winston (1982).
Cecelski, David S., and Timothy B. Tyson, eds. *Democracy Betrayed* (1998).
Gunning, Sandra. *Race, Rape, and Lynching: The Red Record of American Literature 1890–1912* (1996).

FLOYD OGBURN JR.

Thornton, Robert Ambrose (6 May 1902–7 Mar. 1982), physicist and university administrator, was born in Houston, Texas, to Frank Thornton, a laborer, and Mary Jane Sullivan, a midwife. Thornton graduated from Houston Colored High School, which reached only the eleventh grade, and later attended Los Angeles Polytechnic High School to earn credits in language and mathematics to satisfy college entrance requirements. Rejected for military service in the Army Corps of Engineers because of his race, he enrolled in the Case School of Applied Science in Cleveland, Ohio, but again was forced to change his plans when he was denied access to the school's racially segregated army training program. Upon entering Howard University in 1918, his perfect test scores in mathematics and science enabled him to attain a position as a student teacher. Thornton graduated from Howard with a bachelor's degree in Mathematics and Physics in 1922 and earned his master's degree in Physics at the Ohio State University in 1925.

On 4 June 1924 Thornton married Jessie Lea Bullock; they had no children. Thornton taught mathematics and physics at three historically black institutions: at Shaw University from 1922 to 1925, at Johnson C. Smith University from 1928 to 1929, and at Talladega College from 1929 to 1944. Upon leaving Talladega, he taught physics and was director of basic studies at the University of Puerto Rico from 1944 to 1947 before returning to class as a student himself to take a doctorate in physics and the philosophy of science, with a minor in mathematics, at the University of Minnesota. His dissertation, completed in 1947, was titled "Measurement, Concept Formation, and Principles of Simplicity: A Study in the Logic and Methodology of Physics."

More teaching and administrative assignments followed for Thornton after he received his doctorate. He began at the University of Chicago as an associate professor of physical sciences, and in 1950 he moved to Brandeis University to become an associate professor of physics. Three years later he returned to black institutions, first as a dean of instruction at Dillard University from 1953 to 1955, and then as the dean of the basic college at Fisk University from 1955 to 1956.

As a young man, Thornton was also an aspiring singer who gave recitals, auditioned to replace PAUL ROBESON in the Broadway hit musical comedy *Shuffle Along*, and fraternized with such talents as ROLAND HAYES and HENRY THACKER BURLEIGH. More significant, however, was his association with the Nobel laureate Albert Einstein. Thornton first saw Einstein at a lecture that the renowned theoretical physicist delivered in German in 1921 at the Belasco Theater in Washington, D.C., but he understood little that was said. In November 1944, while in the process of establishing a liberal arts program at the University of Puerto Rico, Thornton sent a letter to Einstein asking him to provide a brief synopsis of his views on the philosophy of science

and the scientific method that could serve as an underpinning of the program. Einstein graciously obliged and sent him a handwritten reply.

Einstein suggested to Thornton that knowledge of the history of science and the philosophy of physics plays a crucial role in establishing a scientist's independence and in mitigating prejudices. Einstein maintained in his reply that "this independence created by philosophical insight is—in my opinion—the mark of distinction between a mere artisan or specialist and a real seeker after truth" (Greene, 106). Einstein and Thornton's initial personal contact began nine years of correspondence and led to seven face-to-face meetings. In an interview with a reporter for the *Washington Post*, Thornton recalled his meetings with Einstein, one at Princeton University in which he tried to impress Einstein with his command of physics and mathematics. Einstein, who listened intently to what he had to say, cautioned Thornton: "Slow down, professor, I've always had trouble with math" (West). Thornton recalled:

I thought I was going to meet a godlike presence when I walked in his house. But he quickly dispelled that. He was casually dressed and calm, very down to earth. Years later when I saw him, I'd always formulate a problem. I wanted to know about his notations and his mathematical concepts. The conversations were always about some aspect of theory. I had been calling theories true and false. He corrected that. He told me that any theory is tentative…. He'd always say, "Do you have anything else to ask, professor?" (West).

The recipient of the Associated Students Faculty Award in 1959 and the California State College Teaching Award in 1968, Thornton repeatedly admitted that it was never his ambition to be a great scientist. Instead he strove to become what he called a "master teacher." Among his writings are three coauthored course texts on physics and articles on education, most notably "On the Analysis of Transfer of Training" in the *American Journal of Physics* in December 1951 and "Comments on Scientific Methodology" in the book *Teilhard de Chardin: In Quest of the Perfection of Man* (1973).

Thornton left the South in 1956 to teach at San Francisco State College (later San Francisco State University) and served as the dean of the school of natural sciences from 1963 to 1967. He moved across town to teach physics at the University of San Francisco from 1967 to 1977. Unwilling to retire and give up teaching and public service, he continued lecturing and serving on various local boards and committees, including the San Francisco Consortium of Colleges and Universities, the Senior Citizens Commission of San Francisco, and the advisory board of the Schools of the Sacred Heart. In 1976 Thornton began three years of teaching with the Fromm Institute for Continuing Education, and from 1980 to 1982 he was the much revered Distinguished Visiting Professor in the College of Physical Science, Engineering, and Technology at the University of the District of Columbia. Thornton's achievements as a leader in education—including his service on several high-profile statewide education panels and active membership in professional associations, fraternities, and civic groups—were recognized by the California State Senate with a commendation in 1978. In 1979 the University of San Francisco awarded Thornton an honorary doctorate in science. Illness prevented him from attending a ceremony held on 12 December 1981 at which the physical science building on the campus of San Francisco State University was dedicated as Robert A. Thornton Hall in honor of the university's first science dean and its first African American dean. Before his death from cancer in 1982 in his home in Fairfax, Virginia, Thornton had begun the task of editing transcripts of conversations and correspondence with Albert Einstein.

FURTHER READING

Greene, Robert Ewell. *Robert A. Thornton, Master Teacher: Scholar, Physicist, Humanist* (1988).

Sammons, Vivian O. *Blacks in Science and Medicine* (1989).

West, Hollie I. "A Life in Physics: Robert Thornton and the Einstein Connection," *Washington Post*, 30 May 1980.

ROBERT FIKES JR.

Thornton, Willie Mae (11 Dec. 1926–25 July 1984), blues singer known professionally as "Big Mama," was born in Montgomery, Alabama, the daughter of George W. Thornton, a minister, and Mattie (maiden name unknown). After her mother died in 1940, Thornton supported herself, becoming at age fourteen a member of Sammy Green's *Hot Harlem Revue*, an Atlanta variety show that toured southeastern cities. She sang, danced, played harmonica and drums, and performed comedy for the revue until 1948, when she quit over money. She had already developed a reputation for bluntness, blues shouting, heavy drinking, and cross-dressing.

Thornton next worked the club scene in Houston, Texas, where she was signed by Peacock Records owner DON D. ROBEY, who began to develop her talent—a turning point in her career. Robey selected her musical material, booked her personal appearances, and arranged for professional attention to the way she appeared onstage. "Partnership Blues," backed with "I'm All Fed Up," was her first Peacock single, released in 1951. The next year Robey arranged for Thornton to become a featured singer with the Johnny Otis Rhythm & Blues Caravan, which was well known in black communities all over the country. Thornton played in the North for the first time, impressing critics and audiences with her smoky, country-style blues shouting. *Cash Box* noted in 1952 that she was a 250-pound "show-stopper" of the Otis revue. When she appeared at Harlem's Apollo Theater, she so electrified the audience that the headliner never got to appear on the first show. "That's when they put my name in lights," Thornton remembered, when "Little" ESTHER PHILLIPS had to make room for "Big Mama" Thornton.

"Hound Dog," her fourth Peacock single, made Thornton famous nationally. She used a frenzied, aggressive shouting style in the simple blues song, composed and written by Jerry Leiber, Mike Stoller, and Johnny Otis and arranged primitively for bass, guitar, and drums. The rawness of the sound and the overt sexuality of the lyrics made "Hound Dog" an immediate hit in urban black America in 1953. The song was recorded by ten different artists (mostly country and western) before Elvis Presley's 1956 version. It was Thornton's only hit, though she never made any money on it.

Robey linked Thornton, now flush with success, with his biggest star, JOHNNY ACE, a heart ballad singer. The contrasting singing styles made an effective package, playing to enthusiastic audiences in every section of the country and culminating in a joint Apollo appearance in 1954. Ace and Thornton were, said the *New York Age-Defender*, the "reigning 'king and queen of blues.'" For Thornton, this period represented the pinnacle of her career, which all came crashing down at a Negro Christmas Dance in 1954, when Ace killed himself playing Russian roulette. According to Thornton, his last words were, "I'll show you that it won't shoot." With Ace's death, everything unraveled. Her records failed to hit the charts, and by 1957 Thornton was living in the San Francisco Bay area, without a recording contract. It is possible that her Peacock contract was simply not renewed, but she insisted she quit because the label had cheated her.

The late 1950s and early 1960s—a bad time to be a raw, female blues singer—were an inauspicious period for Thornton. She played clubs in northern California, sometimes as a drummer or harmonica player with a combo and sometimes as a singer, appearing on stage in skirts worn over men's trousers and work boots. The British rock invasion of 1964 created the climate for a blues revival, however, and older, traditional blues performers were in demand once again, this time by enthusiastic young, white audiences. Thornton played jazz festivals, folk festivals, and blues festivals in the United States and abroad.

Janis Joplin began to study Thornton's stage mannerisms at this point, emulating her sexual ambiguity and employing Thornton's composition "Ball and Chain" as her signature song. Flattering as that was, it represented one more instance of exploitation. Thornton had signed away the song's copyright years before and saw none of the royalties the song generated. Now there were two white artists who had risen to the top with her material: "Didn't get no money from them at all," Thorton complained. "Everybody livin' in a house but me. I'm just livin'." Thornton continued to perform and record throughout the 1970s. After Peacock, probably her best work was with Arhoolie Records, though she also recorded for Kent, Galaxy, Vanguard, Mercury, Pentagram, and other labels.

Her health deteriorated in the late 1970s, reportedly after a car crash, and those who saw her at the San Francisco Blues Festival in 1979 were shocked to see her so thin and frail. She still had her voice, however, and at the Newport Jazz Festival in 1980, dressed in a man's three-piece suit and straw hat, she stole the show. This was her last public appearance of note. She slipped into obscurity, suffering from cirrhosis caused by almost forty years of heavy drinking. She weighed only ninety-five pounds when she died of a heart attack at her Los Angeles boardinghouse residence. At her request, her funeral was conducted by the Reverend Johnny Otis. The Southern California Blues Society raised money to pay her burial expenses. Ben Windham called her career "a long and circular journey that went from rags to rags."

As one of the last traditional southern blues singers, Thornton's influences were clearly the classic blues singers of the 1920s and 1930s, particularly MA RAINEY and BESSIE SMITH, in both music and lifestyle. Thornton set the standard for the blues singer who left home early, according to Thulani Davis, and who "was not an outcast so much as a castout, a been-gone, a far-away, a woman with a will to be outside of society." Like her earlier counterparts, Thornton was personally aggressive, hard-drinking, sexually ambiguous, and outrageous on stage. Ma Rainey may have sung about "Going downtown to spread the news / State Street women wearing brogan shoes," but it was Big Mama Thornton who wore those brogans on stage during her entire career.

FURTHER READING

Davis, Thulani. "The Blues Talk Back," *Village Voice*, 9 July 1980.

Gart, Galen, and Roy C. Ames. *Duke/Peacock Records: An Illustrated History with Discography* (1990).

Harrison, Daphne Duval. *Black Pearls: Blues Queens of the 1920s* (1988).

Shaw, Arnold. *Honkers and Shouters: The Golden Years of Rhythm and Blues* (1978, 1986).

Windham, Ben. "Big Mama Thornton," *Alabama Heritage* (Fall 1987).

Obituaries: *Los Angeles Times* and *New York Times*, 28 July 1984; *Rolling Stone*, 13 Sept. 1984; *Living Blues*, Summer/Fall 1984.

This entry is taken from the *American National Biography* and is published here with the permission of the American Council of Learned Societies.

JAMES M. SALEM

Thorpe, Earlie Endris (9 Nov. 1924–30 Jan. 1989), historian, was born in Durham, North Carolina, the son of Eural Endris Thorpe, cotton and tobacco mill worker, and Vina (Dean) Thorpe. Thorpe's mother died before his fourth birthday. In 1932 Eural Thorpe married Bessie Love, who raised Eural's three children with Vina as well as Eural and Bessie's own three children. The Thorpes, who were Baptists, valued religion and education. Despite the limited family income all six children completed college.

Thorpe graduated from Durham's Hillside High School in 1942; he earned a scholarship to attend North Carolina College for Negroes (NCCN), the first state-supported liberal arts college for African Americans, founded in 1910 by JAMES E. SHEPARD. Thorpe attended NCCN for one year before he was drafted into the segregated U.S. Army during World War II. He served in the Ninety-second Infantry Division, initially assigned to Fort Huachuca, Arizona, where he was stationed until January 1944. Although he scored exceedingly well on the admission tests for Officers' Candidate School and Aviation Cadet School, like many

African Americans he was denied the opportunity to attend either school. After shipping overseas, Thorpe served with the Ninety-second Signal Corps behind the lines in Italy as a clerk-typist. After the war in Europe ended, Thorpe studied journalism and public speaking at the University of Florence.

Following his discharge from the army in 1946, Thorpe returned to Durham and married Martha Vivian Branch, a public school teacher and a graduate of Bennett College in Greensboro, North Carolina. The Thorpes had two daughters, Rita Harrington and Gloria Earl. Thorpe returned to NCCN, where he majored in history and studied under Joseph Taylor, JOHN HOPE FRANKLIN, and HELEN EDMONDS, the only three African Americans with PhDs in History in the state. Edmonds said of Thorpe that he was "perhaps, the most brilliant student of my career" (letter to author, 16 Dec. 1990). Thorpe completed his B.A. in History in 1948 and earned an M.A. in History from NCCN in 1949. With no Ph.D. program in history at NCCN—or for that matter at any black college in the nation—and with white colleges in the South refusing to admit black students to graduate or undergraduate studies, Edmonds advised Thorpe to apply to Ohio State University, where she had earned her own PhD, the first African American woman to do so. At Ohio State, Thorpe became the first black graduate assistant to teach a class in the history department. He earned his Ph.D. in 1953.

Unlike most black historians of his generation Thorpe focused his research on African American history. A prolific researcher and writer, Thorpe published twenty-three articles and nine books; many of his books were seminal. His first book, *Negro Historians in the United States* (1958), a revision of his dissertation, was the first work devoted to the writings of black historians. In 1971 he published a revision of this work as *Black Historians: A Critique*.

In 1961 Thorpe published another groundbreaking work, *The Mind of the Negro: An Intellectual History of Afro-Americans*. Based on a broad survey of black writings and speeches from the slavery era to the 1954 Supreme Court ruling in *Brown v. Board of Education*, Thorpe found that the "central theme" of black thought was African Americans' "quest for freedom and equality" (xi). In 2001 the historian Robert L. Harris Jr. observed that *Mind of the Negro* was "still the most comprehensive study of black thought in the United States" (Harris, 166).

Influenced by the emerging field of psychohistory, Thorpe sought to articulate a new, sweeping, psychoanalytically based interpretation of slavery. But before he could do so, in 1959 Stanley Elkins published *Slavery: A Problem in American Institutional and Intellectual Life*. Comparing chattel slavery to Nazi concentration camps, Elkins argued that because of the harsh nature of slavery, African Americans became Sambos, that is, docile accommodationists to the institution. In 1962 Thorpe published "Chattel Slavery and Concentration Camps" in the *Negro History Bulletin*, where he employed psychology to analyze slavery and authored the first critique by a historian rejecting Elkins's interpretation. Citing numerous examples of black resistance to slavery, Thorpe, who for years had sought to correct historical interpretations like Elkins's that devalued or dehumanized antebellum blacks, demonstrated that the Sambo personality was merely a façade that showed whites what they wanted to see. Moreover, Thorpe argued that the docile, lazy, and happy personality stereotype of the slave was promulgated by American slave owners as a psychological justification for the institution of slavery.

Interested in group psychohistory, Thorpe applied psychoanalytical theory to the history of slavery in the antebellum South and published *Eros and Freedom in Southern Life and Thought* (1967) and *The Old South: A Psychohistory* (1972). In *Eros and Freedom* Thorpe marshaled more evidence to undercut Elkins's concentration-camp analogy. Influenced by his goal of improving black-white relations in the turbulent 1960s, Thorpe sought to demonstrate that antebellum history was marked by affection between blacks and whites. By showing that there was affection between the races in the Old South, he hoped to reduce the animosity between the races and thus advance the goals of the civil rights movement.

In 1972 Thorpe published his most important work of psychohistory, *The Old South: A Psychohistory*, which refuted the key conclusion of *Eros and Freedom* of affection between master and slave. Influenced by the militancy of the Black Power movement and the emerging feminist movement, Thorpe now emphasized conflict between master and slave, slave resistance, and slave-master brutality.

Thorpe's works on psychohistory received mixed reviews. Many critics—notably historians who used a psychohistory paradigm—applauded him as a pioneer for applying psychoanalytic principles to the history of slavery. By contrast, most mainstream historians remained unconvinced by his interpretations.

A devoted teacher of history, Thorpe spent his entire career at historically black colleges and universities. He taught at Stowe Teacher's College in St. Louis, Missouri, from 1951 to 1952; Alabama A&M College in Normal from 1952 to 1955; Southern University in Baton Rouge, Louisiana, from 1955 to 1962; and North Carolina College (known after 1969 as North Carolina Central University) from 1962 to 1989, where he served as history department chair from 1963 to 1973. A dedicated teacher, Thorpe directed fifty-four master's theses, and sixteen of his students went on to earn PhDs.

During the late 1960s, amid the call for black studies, Thorpe brought the study of black history to historically white colleges and the general public. In 1968 he directed a weeklong workshop at Duke University for college teachers to prepare them to offer African American history courses. Indeed, Thorpe may have been the first African American to teach history at Duke University. Thorpe also lectured on black history for a thirty-minute television show called *Black Heritage*, which aired on 19 November 1968. In 1969 he helped design a thirty-credit-hour black studies major at North Carolina Central University. From 1971 to 1972 Thorpe taught black history at Harvard University, flying to Boston every Thursday morning and returning to Durham that night.

From 1979 to 1982 Thorpe served as president of the Association for the Study of Afro-American Life and History. In 1980 President Jimmy Carter declared February to be Afro-American History Month, with Thorpe present for the official signing of the declaration in Washington, D.C. Thorpe died in Durham, North Carolina, in 1989.

FURTHER READING

Earlie Thorpe's papers are housed in the Special Collections of William R. Perkins Library, Duke University, Durham, North Carolina.

Harris, Robert L., Jr. "African American Intellectual and Political Thought," in *The African American Experience: An Historiographical and Bibliographical Guide*, eds. Arvarh E. Strickland and Robert E. Weems (2001).

JERRY GERSHENHORN

Thrash, Dox (22 Mar. 1893–19 Apr. 1965), printmaker and co-developer of the carborundum mezzotint process, was born in Griffin, Georgia, the second of four children of Gus Thrash and Ophelia Thrash. Little is known about Thrash's father, and it is believed that his mother was a housekeeper and cook for a local family. Thrash left school after the fourth grade, seeking work to help support his family. In a letter to artist Jacob Kainen, dated 7 October 1948, Thrash stated, "After fifteen [I] began to travel through out [sic] the country doing odd jobs. My ambition to be an artist caused me to settle in Chicago." In 1911, at the age of eighteen, Thrash arrived in Chicago, Illinois. He obtained a job as an elevator operator for the American Bank Note Engraving Company and by 1914 had enrolled in night school at the Art Institute of Chicago. He attended classes part time for four years and then had another three years of full-time schooling for a total of seven years of formal training. Thrash eventually completed his studies at the Art Institute in 1923.

In 1917 Thrash enlisted in the U.S. Army to serve in World War I. He served with the 365th Infantry Regiment, 183rd Brigade, 92nd Division; this was an outfit composed of so-called buffalo soldiers. In June 1918, Thrash's infantry left Hoboken, New Jersey, for the port of Brest in France, where he was wounded, exposed to poison gas, and eventually suffered from shell shock. He celebrated the 1918 Armistice while recovering in a field hospital. Shortly thereafter, Thrash returned to Chicago to resume his studies at the Art Institute. After completing his training, Thrash traveled across the country from 1923 to 1925, working various odd jobs and studying with private tutors. Thrash made keen observations of African American life during his travels, and these memories would help him create the portraits of everyday black America for which he would become famous. He eventually settled in Philadelphia, Pennsylvania.

With the advent of President Franklin Delano Roosevelt's New Deal programs, African American artists throughout the country found themselves the beneficiaries of the Works Progress Administration (WPA) and Federal Arts Project (FAP). In 1937, Thrash was hired to supervise the Fine Print Workshop of the Philadelphia FAP. Thrash would ultimately supervise the Graphic Division for three years. It was through WPA/FAP that Thrash developed and matured as an artist and gained recognition for his paintings and murals. Thrash, however, realized that he had not perfected his etching techniques, although he had received training in the graphic arts.

The years 1930 to 1940 saw Thrash at his most prolific. He began studying at the Graphic Sketch Club in Philadelphia under the tutelage of aquatint artist Earl Horter. Thrash became one of Horter's best students and acquired an intimate knowledge of the aquatint techniques for which Horter became well known. Along with fellow artists Hubert Mesibov and Michael J. Gallagher, Thrash developed the carborundum mezzotint printmaking process in December 1937, a technique that would define the bulk of Thrash's work. Because "carborundum" was a trade name and could not be patented, Thrash labeled the newly discovered technique "carbograph" and later, "Opheliagraph," in tribute to his mother, Ophelia.

In 1940 Thrash married Edna McAllister after a four-year courtship; they had no children. Thrash's reputation in Philadelphia as a stellar printmaker continued to the end of his life. He continued to exhibit in Philadelphia through the munificence of organizations such as the Pyramid and Tra Clubs organizations dedicated to African American artists, and he also mentored young, up-and-coming black artists.

Some of his more notable exhibitions were the First Harmon Foundation Exhibit (1933), an exhibition of WPA artists' prints at the Philadelphia Museum of Art (1938), the New York World's Fair (1939), and a solo exhibition at the Smithsonian Institute in 1948. And although Thrash enjoyed a successful career as an artist almost from the outset, he maintained a position as a house painter with the Philadelphia Housing Authority from 1945 until his retirement in 1958. Thrash's works were held in the collections of the Baltimore Museum of Art, the Metropolitan Museum of Art, the Library of Congress, the Whitney Museum of Art, and Lincoln University. However, the largest and most comprehensive collection of Thrash's work could be found at the Philadelphia Museum of Art.

Thrash died at age seventy-two from a massive heart attack. He was buried in the U.S. National Cemetery in Beverly, New Jersey.

FURTHER READING

Ittmann, John. *Dox Thrash: An African American Master Printmaker Rediscovered* (2001).

Taha, Halima. *Collecting African American Art: Works on Paper and Canvas* (2000).

Thrash, Dox. *The History of My Life,* typescript (n.d.).

C. M. WINSTON

Thurman, Howard W. (18 Nov. 1899?–10 Apr. 1981), theologian and mystic, was born Howard Washington Thurman in Daytona, Florida, the second of three children of Saul Solomon Thurman, who laid railroad track, and Alice Ambrose, a domestic worker.

Most sources date his birth year as 1900; the most recent collection of his works gives 1899. Thurman was seven when his father died. Other than his mother, the most influential person upon Thurman's childhood was his grandmother, Nancy Ambrose, a former slave and midwife who helped raise Howard and his two sisters. Thurman remembered her as a devout and strong woman who bolstered the children's self-esteem by teaching them the lesson she had learned from a slave preacher years before, "Remember, you aren't slaves, you aren't niggers, you are God's children" (Thurman, 21).

Walking along the seashore as a child, Thurman had a mystical experience of the unity of all living things and of himself as bound up with nature. He regarded this experience as one of the defining moments of his life, a touchstone of integrity and stability.

Thurman began high school in 1915 at the Florida Baptist Academy in Jacksonville. He graduated as valedictorian of his class and qualified for a tuition scholarship to Morehouse College in Atlanta, which he entered in 1919. There he became friends with his debating coach, BENJAMIN MAYS, studied with E. Franklin Frazier, and majored in economics. The intellectual breadth and self-confident leadership of Morehouse president JOHN HOPE and dean Samuel Howard Archer left a lasting impression.

In his senior year, Thurman declined an invitation to teach at Morehouse and applied to Newton Theological Seminary in Massachusetts to study religion, only to learn that Newton did not admit black students. In 1923 Thurman entered Rochester Seminary in New York, living for the first time in a totally white world. His mentor at Rochester, George Cross, recognized Thurman's intellectual and spiritual gifts and urged him to devote himself to "the timeless issues of the human spirit" instead of becoming absorbed in the struggle for civil rights (Thurman, 60).

After graduating from Rochester in 1926, Thurman married Kate Kelley, a social worker, and moved to Oberlin, Ohio, to serve as pastor of Mt. Zion Baptist Church. In Oberlin, Thurman began to feel a connection between his own inner life of prayer and the needs of his congregants. His sermons became more reflective and meditative, less informational, as he sought to communicate on a deeper level. These explorations of the inner spirit attracted a steady stream of white visitors.

Thurman came across a small book, *Finding the Trail of Life* (1926), by the Quaker mystic Rufus Jones and immediately recognized a kindred spirit. Jones's emphasis on religious experience so impressed Thurman that he began a program of independent study at Haverford College in Philadelphia, where Jones taught Philosophy of Religion. He read the classics of Christian spirituality, participated in seminars and weekly conferences with Jones, and occasionally attended Quaker meetings. Thurman's childhood intuition of the unity of all being, his sensitivity to nature, and his growing conviction that spiritual experience is the ground of wholeness and community were confirmed by his courses in mysticism and by his personal encounters with Jones.

Returning south later that year, Thurman took up a joint position teaching religion at Morehouse and the Bible as literature at Spelman College, also in Atlanta. A series of talks on the spirituals allowed him to reflect upon the sources of African American spirituality and eventually resulted in *Deep River* (1945), one of his most important books. He enjoyed teaching but found his greatest satisfaction in spiritual counseling. In 1932 his wife Kate contracted tuberculosis and died. Grieving, and exhausted by his teaching and pastoral duties, Thurman sailed for Europe, seeking restoration and direction.

In 1932 MORDECAI JOHNSON, president of Howard University, appointed Thurman as a professor in the School of Religion. That same year, Thurman remarried. His wife, SUE BAILEY THURMAN, a collegiate secretary for the YWCA, was a graduate of Spelman. In 1935 Thurman and his wife accepted an invitation to travel to India on a goodwill visit sponsored by the Christian Student Movement and the International Committee of the YMCA-YWCA. The trip proved to be a catalyst for the vocations of both Thurmans.

In India the Thurmans had a three-hour conversation with Mohandas K. Gandhi, who questioned them about racial discrimination among American Christians and asked them to sing for him the slave spiritual "Were You There When They Crucified My Lord?" which he deeply admired because "it got at the universal human experience under the healing wings of suffering" (Thurman, 134). Attacked by a Hindu lawyer for his allegiance to Christianity, a religion that historically enslaved and oppressed dark-skinned peoples, Thurman responded by distinguishing the religion of Jesus, which supported the oppressed, from Christianity, which often supported discrimination and oppression. Elaborating this theme most fully in *Jesus and the Disinherited* (1949) and *The Luminous Darkness* (1965), Thurman claimed that Jesus, as a member of an oppressed and rejected minority,

identifies with the disinherited and offers to them the realization that they are of infinite value as children of God.

A daylong encounter with Kshiti Mohan Singh, a scholar of Hinduism, conversation with the poet Rabindranath Tagore, visits to Hindu temples, and a visionary experience at the Khyber Pass inspired Thurman to seek a religious fellowship that could transcend racial barriers by emphasizing the commonality of spiritual experience.

His appointment as dean of Rankin Chapel at Howard in 1936 increased Thurman's national reputation as a preacher and teacher of extraordinary talent. Experimenting with worship, he introduced dramatic tableaux and liturgical dance to the chapel's vespers service. In 1943 he received a letter from Alfred Fisk, a white Presbyterian minister and philosophy professor, seeking a black seminarian or young minister to fill a part-time position as co-pastor of an interracial congregation in San Francisco. Thurman interpreted Fisk's letter as a providential call. Risking financial security, he took leave from his position at Howard and moved to San Francisco with his wife and two daughters.

In 1944 Fisk and Thurman became cofounders and co-pastors of the Church for the Fellowship of All Peoples, a community integrated in both leadership and membership, and dedicated to the ideal that religious experience must unite rather than divide. Services at the church included meditation and reflective silence and celebrated the variety of cultures represented in the congregation. Church members pledged themselves to a statement of commitment, instead of a traditional creed. The congregation decided to forego denominational ties that might impose doctrinal limits on inclusiveness and chose not to locate in a black neighborhood to avoid becoming a black-only church. In *Footsteps of a Dream* (1959), an account of the origin of Fellowship Church, Thurman acknowledged that the logic of his position on interracial community required the eventual demise of the separate black church.

Supporters from around the nation (including Eleanor Roosevelt) joined a network of associate members to further the Fellowship ideal. In 1946 Fisk returned to full-time teaching and Thurman became the senior pastor of Fellowship Church. He traveled extensively, lecturing and preaching to support the church and to spread news of its vision of interracial and interfaith community. Books of sermons and meditations transmitted his ideas to a far larger reading public.

In 1953 Thurman left Fellowship Church to become dean of Marsh Chapel at Boston University. He continued to preach, lecture, and write on behalf of ecumenical and interracial cooperation, stressing his conviction that the search for community is embedded in the very fabric or structure of life itself. He retired in 1965. Returning to San Francisco, he continued to write and lecture, while he chaired the Howard Thurman Educational Trust, a charitable and educational foundation. Several of his most important works were published in these years, including *The Search for Common Ground* (1971) and his autobiography, *With Head and Heart* (1979). After his death in 1981, the trust continued to make available Thurman's books and taped sermons to a worldwide audience. Over one hundred Howard Thurman listening rooms located in the United States, Asia, Africa, and Europe enabled new generations to hear his voice.

Thurman's influence, although considerable, was more personal than institutional. The liberal character of his theology, which emphasized spiritual experience over church doctrine, and ecumenical fellowship over denominational tradition, limited the impact of his personal charisma upon institutional change. To those who criticized him for not leading a social movement, like a Gandhi or a MARTIN LUTHER KING JR., Thurman responded that he was not a movement man; that his gift was to articulate the truth of universal spiritual experience. He chose to lead by example and by offering counsel behind the scenes as a board member for the Fellowship of Reconciliation, the Congress of Racial Equality (CORE), and the National Association for the Advancement of Colored People (NAACP). WHITNEY YOUNG, VERNON JORDAN, LERONE BENNETT, NATHAN HUGGINS, and Martin Luther King Jr. were a few of the better-known individuals among many who said they were influenced by Thurman's life and words.

Most of Thurman's books have been reprinted, and a three-volume edition of his papers is due to publish in the early twenty-first century. Articles, dissertations, and monographs about his thoughts have appeared steadily since his death. The Howard Washington Thurman National Memorial is located at Morehouse and contains the remains of Howard and Sue Bailey Thurman.

FURTHER READING

Howard Thurman's papers are housed in the Department of Special Collections at Boston University. The Howard Thurman Papers Project is at Morehouse College.

Thurman, Howard. *With Head and Heart: The Autobiography of Howard Thurman* (1979).

Makechnie, George K. *Howard Thurman: His Enduring Dream* (1988).

Yates, Elizabeth. *Howard Thurman: Portrait of a Practical Dreamer* (1964).

ALBERT J. RABOTEAU

Thurman, Sue Bailey (3 Aug. 1903–25 Dec. 1996), author, editor, historian, musician, and advocate for interracial, intercultural, and international understanding, was the youngest of nine children born to the Reverend Isaac George Bailey and Susie E. (Ford) Bailey, of Pine Bluff, Arkansas. The Reverend Bailey founded a college preparatory academy for black students in Dermott, Arkansas, and had affiliations with the Arkansas Baptist Convention and the National Negro Business League. Susie E. Bailey was president of the Southeast District Baptist Women's Association and was active in women's clubs. Their daughter, Sue, graduated from Spelman Seminary in 1920 and in 1926 became the first black student to receive a bachelor of science degree in Music from Oberlin Conservatory.

Bailey joined the music department at Hampton Institute in Hampton, Virginia, following graduation. In 1928 she moved to Harlem and assumed the role of the YWCA's national secretary for Colleges of the South. Her parents' efforts influenced Bailey's social activism. She lectured throughout Europe and established the YWCA's first World Fellowship Committee, bridging relations between cultures at home and abroad. In 1932 she married the Morehouse graduate and famed theologian the Reverend HOWARD THURMAN. They relocated to Washington, D.C., where he joined the faculty at Howard University's School of Religion. The Reverend Thurman had a daughter from an earlier marriage that had ended with his first wife's death, and his union with Bailey Thurman produced another daughter. Bailey Thurman and her husband were of shared purpose. Under the framework of spiritual thought they brought diverse groups together and built community around social, educational, and activist programs.

One of Bailey Thurman's role models, and her husband's as well, was the early-twentieth-century black leader MARY MCLEOD BETHUNE. The founder of Bethune-Cookman College in Daytona Beach, Florida, and the National Council of Negro Women (NCNW), she inspired the young Howard

Thurman, who grew up in Daytona Beach witnessing Bethune's struggles to establish the college. Her unwavering faith and perseverance would be driving values for Bailey Thurman and her husband.

In 1939, four years after founding the NCNW, Bethune established an archives committee. She found the young activist Bailey Thurman a welcome addition and an eager proponent of the vital need to document and preserve black women's history. NCNW launched its first official publication, the *Aframerican Woman's Journal*, in 1940. The magazine was a vision of its editor, Bailey Thurman. She saw intrinsic worth in encouraging blacks, particularly women, to become aware of their heritage and the importance of its preservation. That foundation was set long before her NCNW days; she and her mother had supported numerous historical preservation endeavors. By encouraging her readers to search attics for documents, artifacts, and relics for the archives and a museum, she set in motion plans to establish the national archives at NCNW's national headquarters, also known as Council House. Though dreams of doing so did not come to fruition under Bailey Thurman's leadership, NCNW realized its goal of establishing the national archives in 1979 with the unveiling of the Mary McLeod Bethune Memorial Museum and National Archives for Black Women's History; there is no doubt, however, that Bailey Thurman's legacy was instrumental in this outcome. With the National Park Service now serving as the keeper of these treasured holdings and Council House, African American women will have a documented presence throughout history.

The United States needed the kind of change Bailey Thurman championed. The ill effects of racism, segregation, and other overt acts of discrimination were daunting. She confronted these issues proactively, often in partnership with her husband and guided by enlightened reflection. Yet when Bailey Thurman and her husband took a small delegation of African Americans on an eight-month pilgrimage to India in 1935, under the auspices of the YWCA-YMCA International Committee, they had misgivings. They struggled with how to represent the segregated American Christian church abroad in a country of brown-skinned people struggling for independence from Great Britain. The tour was life-changing, in large measure because of a three-hour conversation with Mohandas K. Gandhi that broadened their international political vision and commitment to inter-cultural understanding. In 1944 Bailey Thurman's

husband left Howard University, and they relocated to San Francisco, where he and a white co-pastor established the Church for the Fellowship of All Peoples, the first interracial, nondenominational church in the United States.

Like her husband, Bailey Thurman desired transformation, not only in the church but also in the broader community. Noting the swelling of the black population in San Francisco brought on by World War II, she began, once again, to document. Her published writings were about black pioneers in San Francisco's history, including the 1800s entrepreneur WILLIAM ALEXANDER LEIDESDORFF, who was in the maritime trade. She played a role in the naming of a street after him. She also established the NCNW's San Francisco chapter, developing the organization into a powerful base of social change for black women, their families, and communities.

In 1953 Bailey Thurman traveled to New England with her husband, where he became professor of spiritual resources and dean of Marsh Chapel at Boston University. He was the first black man to serve as dean of a traditional white university. Bailey Thurman saw an opportunity to present what was missing: documentation of African American history. In 1966 she founded the Museum of African American History, which is "dedicated to preserving, conserving, and interpreting the contributions of African Americans." Using historical examination, she chronicled the presence of African Americans in Boston and New England. She and her husband remained in Boston until 1968, when they returned to San Francisco, where they had established an educational foundation that supported African American young people. She continued that mission after her husband's death in 1981.

Sue Bailey Thurman died in San Francisco on Christmas Day in 1996. Though much of her life's work is linked with that of her husband, her noteworthy place in the annals of history, like that which she ensured for countless other African Americans, has not been forgotten.

FURTHER READING

Broussard, Albert S. *Black San Francisco: The Struggle for Racial Equality in the West, 1900–1954* (1993).

Collier-Thomas, Bettye. *Towards Black Feminism: The Creation of the Bethune Museum-Archives* (1986).

Fluker, Earl, and Catherine Tumber. *A Strange Freedom: The Best of Howard Thurman on Religious Experience and Public Life* (1998).

PATRICIA E. GREEN

Thurman, Wallace (16 Aug. 1902–21 Dec. 1934), Harlem Renaissance writer and editor, was born in Salt Lake City, Utah, the son of Oscar Thurman and Beulah Jackson. His father left the family while Wallace was young, and his mother remarried several times, possibly contributing to his lifelong feelings of insecurity. Thurman's lifetime struggle with ill health began as a child, and his fragile constitution and nervous disposition led him to become a voracious reader with literary aspirations. Thurman entered the University of Utah in 1919, but he quickly transferred to the University of Southern California, where he studied for entrance into medical school until 1923. After leaving college, Thurman worked in a post office to support himself while he wrote a column for a black newspaper and edited *Outlet* magazine. In the fall of 1925 Thurman journeyed to Harlem, where he worked for meals in various capacities for Theophilus Lewis, editor of *Looking Glass*, whose recommendation resulted in a position as managing editor for the *Messenger*. Thurman used his skills in the publishing industry to support his artistic endeavors, and he later moved to the white magazine *World Tomorrow* as circulation manager. Eventually he became editor in chief at the publishing firm of Macaulay Company.

Thurman's first priority, however, was always art, and his most noteworthy contribution to the Harlem Renaissance was his publication in 1926 of the short-lived magazine *Fire!!* Although *Fire!!* was shakily financed by contributions from its own editorial collective, its impact went beyond its meager circulation. Through the magazine, Thurman established himself as the galvanizing force behind the younger generation of Harlem Renaissance writers, such as ZORA NEALE HURSTON and LANGSTON HUGHES, who wished to be freed from what they perceived as the propagandistic motivations and thematic limitations advocated by older black critics such as W. E. B. DUBOIS and ALAIN LOCKE. These critics, as well as much of the black press, reacted negatively to the journal, claiming that its content was too lascivious and that the journal gloried in images of dissipated black working-class life instead of glorifying the respectable black middle classes. In the aftermath of the commercial failure of *Fire!!*, Thurman began another journal, *Harlem*, that was less controversial among critics and less confrontational with its readers. It specialized in short fiction and theater and book reviews and sought to provide its readers with a guide to Harlem's activities and attractions. This magazine also lasted one issue.

Despite his homosexuality Thurman married Louise Thompson in 1928, shortly before his 1929 theatrical success, *Harlem*. The couple had no children and later divorced. Cowritten with William Jourdan Rapp, *Harlem* dealt with the topic of southern transplants adjusting to life in the black urban metropolis. Based on Thurman's short story "Cordelia the Crude" in *Fire!!*, the play dealt with black urban realities such as male unemployment and it introduced white theatergoers to the Harlem rent parties and the numbers racket. It was to have been the first part of a trilogy, coauthored with Rapp, titled *Black Belt*. The second play in the trilogy, *Jeremiah the Magnificent*, dealt evenhandedly with the MARCUS GARVEY phenomenon, yet the play was never produced. The final play, *Black Cinderella*, explored intraracial prejudice but remained unfinished, possibly because the authors were discouraged by their inability to stage *Jeremiah the Magnificent* or to interest Hollywood in *Harlem*.

In 1929 Thurman published his first novel, *The Blacker the Berry*, to mixed reviews. The novel tells the story of Emma Lou Morgan, a dark-skinned black woman whose obsession with light skin (or internalized self-hatred) results repeatedly in personal misfortune. Thurman deftly investigated the many ironies of this situation, as middle-class Emma Lou's own prejudice against dark-skinned working-class blacks remains disconnected in her own mind from the unjust social snobbery that she encounters from the mulatto society whose social circle she covets. In 1932 Thurman published a satirical roman à clef, *The Infants of Spring*. This novel offered a somewhat grim prognosis for the lasting achievements of the Harlem Renaissance. Thurman portrayed the young black artists in the novel as hampered by the suffocating management of older black critics, the faddish attention of a white audience, and their own bloated egos. Thurman evinced concern for the fate of talented if untrained artists within a racially charged milieu that simultaneously inflated their accomplishments while circumscribing their significance. He also explored the difficulties inherent in trying to negotiate the opposite demands of art as racial propaganda and art as transcending race. In that same year, Thurman also released a muckraking novel, *The Interne*, cowritten with Abraham L. Furman, about unethical medical practices and the pressures of a medical bureaucracy on a young intern at a hospital where Thurman, ironically, died several years later.

In 1934 Thurman went to Hollywood to write scripts for an independent production company for $250 a week. He wrote scripts for two films, one of which, *Tomorrow's Children*, a serious social problem film dealing with state-mandated sterilization, survives today. Ill health cut short his tinseltown sojourn, and he returned to Harlem later that same year. Although warned about taxing himself, Thurman collapsed at a party and was admitted to City Hospital on Welfare Island. He was diagnosed with tuberculosis and gradually weakened until his death. The death of Thurman and fellow Harlem Renaissance writer RUDOLPH FISHER within days of each other marked for many the symbolic end of the Harlem Renaissance.

FURTHER READING

The majority of Thurman's papers are in the James Weldon Johnson Collection at the Beinecke Library, Yale University. Smaller collections of his letters are in the Moorland-Spingarn Research Center at Howard University and the William Jourdan Rapp Collection at the University of Oregon Library.

Bontemps, Arna. "Portrait of Wallace Thurman," in *The Harlem Renaissance Remembered*, ed. Bontemps (1972).

Lewis, David Levering. *When Harlem Was in Vogue* (1981).

Obituary: *New York Amsterdam News*, 29 Dec. 1934. This entry is taken from the *American National Biography* and is published here with the permission of the American Council of Learned Societies.

MICHAEL MAIWALD

Thurmond, Michael (4 Jan. 1953–), Georgia commissioner of labor, state representative, and lawyer, was born in Athens, Georgia, the youngest of nine children of Sidney and Vanilla Thurmond. His parents were sharecroppers.

Athens is home to the University of Georgia, which remained segregated until Thurmond was eight years old. Thurmond's home in rural Clarke County was a world away from the university. He recalled, "I was sixteen before we got an indoor bathroom" (author's interview with Thurmond, 2005). But his parents made education a priority. All the Thurmond children finished high school and four of them—including Michael—finished college.

Thurmond attended segregated schools until his senior year in high school, when the county schools consolidated in 1971. The black high school, Burney Harris, was slated for closure, not integration, and Thurmond led an unsuccessful protest against the closing. When the school board sought and won an injunction to stop the students from protesting, Thurmond was summoned to court. He later said the experience sharpened his interest in going to college. It also led to his selection to serve on a biracial student committee. Thurmond said it was the first time he had ever had any significant encounters with whites. That same year he and a white student were elected co-presidents of the student body. Although small and slender, Thurmond played high school football, where he earned the nickname "Mighty Mouse." He received his undergraduate degree from Paine College in Augusta, Georgia, in 1975 and a law degree from the University of South Carolina in 1978. He returned home, was married to Janice Mathis, and served a year as an assistant Athens city-attorney before starting a solo law practice. Thurmond also turned to journalism, starting a short-lived African American newspaper in his hometown and writing columns on black history for the white-owned Athens daily newspaper. Those columns were later collected in his first book, *A Story Untold: Black Men and Women in Athens History* (1978).

From an early age Thurmond wanted a career in politics. As a child, he had practiced his oratory behind his family's house, preaching to the trees. He saw his pursuit of a law degree as a step toward elected office. "Having grown up in what would be described as poverty, I wanted to make a difference," Thurmond said. "I wanted other people not to have to experience a life without the material things that many folks take for granted" (author's interview with Thurmond).

Thurmond's first forays into politics met with frustration. He made two unsuccessful attempts in 1982 and 1984 to unseat a white incumbent representing Athens in the Georgia General Assembly. Thurmond sued (and won) to have more black polling places and black registrars. Although he was criticized and even threatened as a result of the suit, it helped open the door to his success against the same incumbent in 1986. He also made the deliberate decision to build a black-white coalition. A Democrat, Thurmond became the first African American elected to the Georgia General Assembly from Clarke County since Reconstruction. At the time, he was also the only black member elected from a majority-white district.

In 1989 Thurmond divorced. He was married a second time in 1990 to Zola Fletcher, with whom he had a daughter. In the state legislature Thurmond

Michael Thurmond, Georgia Labor Commissioner and then Chairman of the Martin Luther King Holiday Commission, sits with Coretta Scott King, the wife of slain civil rights leader Martin Luther King, Jr., during an awards ceremony in Atlanta, 14 January 2000. (AP Images.)

pressed for tax relief for poor people. But not until 1991, when Governor Zell Miller needed a substitute for his own failing proposal to lift the sales tax on groceries, did Thurmond make progress. Miller adopted Thurmond's plan as a compromise, implementing an income tax credit for low-income Georgians.

Thurmond's gift for mixing powerful oratory with humor made him stand out in the 180-member House. He was elected chairman of the Legislative Black Caucus, a post he held from 1990 to 1992. In 1992 the legislature redrew Georgia's legislative and congressional districts. Under the guidelines then in place to interpret the Voting Rights Act, the white majority in the legislature conceded the imperative to make three of Georgia's eleven congressional districts majority black. Thurmond ran in the new Eleventh District, stretching from Atlanta's eastern edge to Augusta and south to Savannah. He

proposed a combination of tax breaks and innovative employment incentives to revitalize the impoverished region. But Thurmond finished fourth in a five-way primary race, which his House colleague, CYNTHIA MCKINNEY, won. Following his defeat, Thurmond returned to Athens and endured a spell of what he called "political exile." To console himself, and to reexamine his understanding of his home state, he began work on what would become his second book, *Freedom: An African-American History of Georgia, 1733–1865* (2001), a chronicle of resistance to slavery in Georgia.

Thurmond's exile came to an end in 1994 when Governor Miller appointed him head of the state Division of Family and Children's Services. Along with the appointment came a daunting mandate: implement the welfare reform ideas that were then gaining national ascendancy. Although Thurmond's friends viewed it as a political suicide mission, Thurmond took on the task. He developed the "Work First" program, which included an idea that he had voiced during his failed congressional campaign. Employers who hired welfare recipients were given the recipients' welfare payments to offset the cost of wages—a strong incentive to hire people on the welfare rolls. "We called it welfare reform without the meanness," Thurmond said (author's interview with Thurmond). The plan won generally positive reviews, and resulted in a fifty-thousand-person reduction in Georgia's welfare recipients.

Thurmond left the state agency in 1997 for a brief stint as a distinguished lecturer at the University of Georgia's Carl Vinson Institute of Government. But in 1998 he returned to politics, running in a statewide race for commissioner of labor. The commissioner oversees unemployment insurance, employment services, vocational rehabilitation, and a variety of other job-related functions. Finishing first in a three-way primary race, Thurmond bested a white opponent in a runoff election and then defeated a Republican in the general election. He became the first African American elected to a statewide office in Georgia without first having been appointed to fill a predecessor's unexpired term. Thurmond has pushed to bring more computerization to the department and make its services more accessible to citizens. Through the 1980s and 1990s and into the new millennium, an era that saw black voters and candidates gain clout in Georgia, Thurmond was among the most successful leaders of that trend.

FURTHER READING
Much of the information for this entry was collected during an interview with its subject on 20 Sept. 2005.
"Election '98: Georgia; Statewide Offices," *Atlanta Journal-Constitution*, 4 Nov. 1998.

DON SCHANCHE JR.

Thurston, T. W. (9 Apr. 1866–1956), educator, minister, industrialist, physician, was born Thomas Wellington Thurston Jr. in Moorefield, West Virginia, to Betty (Jones) Thurston and Thomas W. Thurston Sr., both of West Virginia. Thurston grew up in Moorefield and attended Romney High School before leaving to receive his theological education in New Jersey. According to an article featuring Thurston in *Who's Who of the Colored Race*, after high school, Thurston studied theology under Reverend J. A. Gayley of Princeton University.

Thurston married Julia Lacey of Washington, D.C., in 1890. The couple went on to raise eight children.

Thurston began his career as an educator. He moved from West Virginia to Fort Barnwell, North Carolina, and served as the principal of the Barnwell Normal and Farm Life School for Colored Youth. His work as an educator later intersected with his career in manufacturing with his pioneering work in the textile industry.

By 1895 Thurston made national news by becoming among the first African Americans involved in the rapidly developing textile industry. In this period, mills across the country hired African Americans in custodial positions and rarely allowed them any opportunities in skilled labor, including management. Thurston and the Ashley & Bailey Company, a white-owned textile firm based out of Paterson, New Jersey, were pioneers in desegregating the textile industry. From 1895 to 1899, Thurston managed the Five Points Silk Mill, located in Columbia, Pennsylvania, and owned by the Ashley & Bailey Company. The mills ran with a black labor force with Thurston as superintendent and Emanuel Epps as bookkeeper. Epps was the first African American graduate of Pennsylvania's Millersville Normal School in 1897. The mill did not last long, due to financial difficulties, but the company decided to try again, but this time in the South.

In 1899 Thurston scouted locations for the firm and opened up a new plant in Fayetteville, North Carolina. The company created the first white-owned and African American managed and operated silk textile factory in the South. Thurston developed a relationship between the African American community in Fayetteville and the company. He negotiated the agreement between the local school board and the company to build an industrial school for the employees and children of Ashley Heights, the African American neighborhood of Fayetteville and the site of the mill. The deal included the deeding of land that became part of what is now Fayetteville State University, the second oldest African American college in North Carolina.

Thurston gained a reputation for strict control within the mill complex. With the help of prominent local women such as Gertrude Hood, he managed four hundred employees, the majority of whom were women and children. The company's employees did the work that only white workers performed in other sites. They spun and wove cloth and darned and dyed materials. Thurston's success in managing garnered national attention. Publications from the

National Economic Association and *The Negro in Africa and America* featured Thurston and recognized his pioneering work in industry. Not only did he spearhead a movement to desegregate the booming Southern textile industry, he also aided figures such as Booker T. Washington in the creation of the National Negro Business League in 1900. The organization promoted the importance of business and industry in the black community, particularly in the South. In the two decades following the initial organization of the mill, firms across the South developed textile firms utilizing black-only labor. He also showcased the work of African American textile workers in Charleston, South Carolina's Inter-State and West Indian Exposition in 1901. He worked alongside national figures such as Booker T. Washington and local ministers and industrialists to display the talents and accomplishments of the workers employed at the Ashley & Bailey Company to emphasize the possibilities of black labor in textiles.

After almost fifteen years of success in Fayetteville, the Ashley & Bailey Company closed, selling off all of its assets including the site in Ashley Heights. After the company closed its doors, Thurston and his family continued to reside in Kinston, North Carolina, where he had managed another small silk mill. By the 1920 census, Thurston held a new career as a physician and continued to live with his wife and children. His wife Julia died in 1929 in Philadelphia. After her death, Thurston married his second wife, Ruby, and they continued to raise their family until his death in 1956. Reverend Thurston's funeral was held in the St. Peter's AME Zion Church in New Bern, North Carolina.

FURTHER READING

Mather, Frank Lincoln, ed. *Who's Who of the Colored Race: A General Biographical Dictionary of Men and Women of African Descent*, vol. 1 (1915).

Pullen-Burry, B. *Ethiopia in Exile: Jamaica Revisited* (1905).

Silva, Kathryn M. *Six Days Thou Shalt Labor: African Americans in the Southern Textile Industry* (2010).

Tillinghast, Joseph Alexander. *The Negro in Africa and America* (1903).

KATHRYN M. SILVA

Tiffany, Cyrus (?–?), a sailor during the War of 1812, served under Commodore Oliver Hazard Perry during the Battle of Lake Erie. Little is known about Tiffany before his service under Commodore Perry and nothing afterward. Federal Census records indicate that he was likely the man by the same name residing in Bristol, Massachusetts, in 1790. A free man, Tiffany possibly earned a living as a sailor during peacetime like many other African Americans living in coastal New England. He likely joined the navy out of necessity; the War of 1812, extremely unpopular in New England, virtually shut down merchant trade on the high seas, leaving thousands of sailors, black and white, unemployed. Perhaps motivated by a combination of patriotism and the need to make a living, many of these sailors subsequently enlisted in the navy or served on privately armed merchant ships to join in the fight against Great Britain. By early 1813 Cyrus Tiffany was a member of the navy, alternately listed as a seaman or musician, serving in a fleet of gunboats stationed at Newport, Rhode Island, under the command of then Master Commandant Perry. When Perry was transferred to a command in the Great Lakes theater of operations in February 1813, 150 of his men at Newport, including Tiffany and other black sailors such as NEWPORT HAZARD, Jesse Williams, HANNIBAL COLLINS, and ANTHONY WILLIAMS, volunteered to join his fledgling Lake Erie squadron. Little did these men know that they would take part in one of the most decisive and bloody battles fought during the War of 1812.

The action in which Cyrus Tiffany gained notice began in the early morning hours of 10 September 1813 when the American fleet, stationed on the western end of Lake Erie, spied the sail of a British ship on the horizon and sailed out of Put-In-Bay. The subsequent Battle of Lake Erie pitted a British fleet consisting of six ships, including the *Detroit* and *Queen Charlotte*, against a superior American force consisting of the twenty-gun brigs *Lawrence* and *Niagara* and seven other vessels. Commodore Perry's original plan assigned each of his vessels a specific place in the line of battle, with the most heavily gunned ships of his fleet, *Lawrence* and *Niagara*, designated to fight it out with the most heavily gunned ships of the British fleet, the *Detroit* and the seventeen-gun *Queen Charlotte*. However, while Perry sailed the *Lawrence* forward to engage the enemy, his commander in the *Niagara*, for reasons unknown to this day, lagged behind and failed to join the fight. As a result, Perry and the men of the *Lawrence*, Cyrus Tiffany included, endured the brunt of the British fleet's combined attack for two hours. Taking heavy fire at close range, the crew of the *Lawrence* sustained heavy casualties; the dead and wounded littering the deck and the ship left a terrible wreck topsides. The part Tiffany played

Cyrus Tiffany in the Battle of Lake Erie, 13 September 1813. Mural by Martyl Schweig, at the Recorder of Deeds building in Washington, D.C., built in 1943. (Library of Congress/Prints and Photographs Division.)

in this battle was of an interesting nature. One unnamed participant would later recall that "when the engagement approached, the Commodore … placed him on the berth deck with a musket & bayonet, with orders to charge upon any one attempting to skulk below. Shortly after the battle began the men fell so thick & fast that the Commodore observed the hatchway crowded with wounded, where passage below seemed to be obstructed. On going there he found them charged upon by 'old Tiffany', who swore they were a set of skulkers, and should not come below" (Altoff, p. 41). Such duty as that performed by Cyrus Tiffany may seem unusual today,

but in the days of the wooden sailing navy it was not at all unusual and officers often had to post guards to prevent scared crewmen from abandoning their posts and seeking shelter below decks in the heat of battle. Clearly, Perry had great faith in Tiffany's ability to help keep the men of the *Lawrence*, sailors and soldiers alike, at their posts. Interestingly, the same participant that describes Tiffany's actions in battle also states that the commodore wished to keep Tiffany out of danger as best as he could by assigning him this guard duty, a sign that Perry also held a personal regard for him. Despite the condition of the American flagship, the guns of the *Lawrence* had also inflicted considerable damage among the British ships and Perry was not willing to yield the fight. Deciding on a bold course of action, Perry turned over command of the *Lawrence* to a junior officer, boarded the ship's cutter along with four of his men, and was rowed under heavy fire back to the *Niagara*, which had yet to take part in the fight. Assuming command of a fresh ship with a full crew, Commodore Perry renewed his attack and soon gained the advantage with the now-battered British fleet. Although the *Niagara* took heavy fire, the tide of battle had turned and the British fleet eventually capitulated. In this one decisive battle the British were swept from control of Lake Erie, leaving American forces in control of Ohio and the area of the Old Northwest Territory.

The record of Cyrus Tiffany's service in the Battle of Lake Erie is an important reminder that African Americans were combatants in the War of 1812, a fact often overlooked because of a dearth of crew lists and other military records from the period. Although the names of many of these men have been lost to history, it was through their skilled and dedicated service that men like Tiffany were vital participants in the epic naval engagements of a conflict sometimes referred to as America's second war for independence.

Cyrus Tiffany, having gained the trust of Oliver Hazard Perry, stayed with the commodore after the battle, accompanying him to his new command, the frigate *Java* under construction at Baltimore, in July 1814 and made a subsequent cruise in that ship to the Mediterranean in 1815–1816. One account states that Tiffany was with Perry "to the day of his death" and that the commodore "always took the most humane care of him" (Altoff, p. 41). However, after Oliver Hazard Perry's untimely death aboard the USS *Nonsuch* during a diplomatic mission to Venezuela in August 1819, Cyrus Tiffany, too, disappears from the pages of history and the details of his subsequent service and life are unknown.

FURTHER READING

Altoff, Gerard T. *Amongst My Best Men: African Americans and the War of 1812* (1996).

GLENN ALLEN KNOBLOCK

Tiger, Dick. *See* Ihetu, Richard "Dick Tiger."

Til, Sonny (8 Aug. 1925–9 Dec. 1981), rhythm and blues singer, was born Earlington Carl Tilghman in Baltimore, Maryland, the son of Charles and Ella Tilghman. As Sonny Til, lead singer of the Orioles,

an early Rhythm and Blues group, he inspired an entire generation of black singers who then went on to take R&B and transform it into rock 'n' roll. In the late 1940s the Orioles were at the forefront of black popular music.

Earlington picked up the nickname "Sonny" from his favorite record as a child: Al Jolson's "Sonny Boy." From the start, Til knew he wanted to be an entertainer. "In my class book, I said I want to be a singer; I want to make it in show business" (author interview with Til, 1974).

After World War II, Sonny began singing in amateur shows. The Orioles (originally called the Vibra-Naires) came together in early 1948 at the amateur shows held in West Baltimore (mainly at the Avenue Café). Sonny knew baritone George Nelson from his neighborhood, bass Johnny Reed played with bands in the area, and tenor Alexander Sharp was another singer who entered the amateur shows. Sonny said, "We used to go out on the corner of the club at night and sing out there and the guys would throw us fifty cents, a dollar. That's how we started, as a street singing group" (author interview with Til, 1974). The fifth member of the group was guitarist/second tenor Tommy Gaither.

In April 1948 Sonny and the Vibra-Naires went to New York to appear on the *Arthur Godfrey Talent Scouts* radio show. The winner of this contest got to appear on Godfrey's extremely popular daytime radio show for a week. Because they did not come in first, the Vibra-Naires dejectedly went home. But what they did not realize was that they had made such a big hit (causing the show to receive many phone calls and telegrams) that Godfrey wanted them to appear on his show despite their loss. He sent a telegram to their manager, Deborah Chessler, and the Vibra-Naires appeared twice in May.

Through their manager, Sonny and the group got a recording contract with Jubilee Records. However, before they recorded, the name Vibra-Naires was replaced by the easier-to-spell Orioles (to honor the state bird of Maryland).

In July 1948 Sonny Til and the Orioles had their first session, at which they recorded the Deborah Chessler-written "It's Too Soon to Know." From the beginning, the Orioles concentrated on ballads, with Sonny as lead and George Nelson doing the second bridge. This was in deference to the Ink Spots' style of a "talking bass" on the bridge of a song.

In July 1948 "It's Too Soon to Know" was released. It started taking off almost immediately and by the time it had finished its seventeen-week run on the national R&B charts, it had risen to number one. More surprising is that it peaked at number thirteen on the mostly white Pop charts, something not many R&B songs did in those days. The song catapulted the Orioles to the top.

Although the Orioles are generally thought of as innovators, art does not exist in a vacuum. In turn, other artists influenced them. Sonny's idols were NAT "KING" COLE, the Cats and the Fiddle, the Ink Spots, the Mills Brothers, and Charles Brown.

The Orioles were a genuine phenomenon. The girls in the audiences reacted to Sonny in the same way girls had reacted to Frank Sinatra in the late 1930s and in the way they would later react to Elvis Presley. There was screaming, crying, and fainting in the theater. Sonny was handsome and acted the part of a true matinee idol.

What Sonny did was croon love ballads, holding the microphone stand in such a way that he seemed to be making love to it. His ballads sounded different from those of his contemporaries. The music was simpler; the arrangements were simpler; and the singing was sensual. When the boys in the audience saw the reaction of their girls to Sonny Til, many were inspired to start their own groups, just to get the same adulation. Thus, Sonny became the nucleus of the nascent R&B vocal group explosion.

With Sonny in the lead, the Orioles had hit after hit for the next five years: "(It's Gonna Be a) Lonely Christmas," "Tell Me So," "A Kiss and a Rose," "I Challenge Your Kiss," "Forgive and Forget," "What Are You Doing New Year's Eve," "Baby Please Don't Go," and their biggest, "Crying in the Chapel."

However, their success backfired on them. In the mid 1950s, the Orioles found that there were now so many groups around (working for less money) that bookings were getting scarce. If a promoter had $1000 to spend, he'd rather spend it on hiring several lesser-known acts than on just hiring the Orioles.

By early 1955 the once "High-Flying Orioles" were plummeting earthward; they'd fallen on hard times. After their biggest success, "Crying in the Chapel," it would logically be assumed that they would only get top-notch material. But the song was also their undoing because Jubilee Records reasoned that if something worked once, it would work again (and again and again and …). Therefore, the material they recorded began to take on a religious and quasi-religious tone. Sales and work fell off. Worse, in the middle of it all, the style of the Orioles changed dramatically; they were trying to keep up with the times (with the revolution that they themselves had started), but it is hard to tell just what it was that they were trying to change to, because the songs did not fit in with what was going on around them.

In mid-1955 the original Orioles disbanded and Sonny formed a new Orioles around a group called the Regals, who sang modern harmony. This fascinated him and he was eager to learn it. All the original Orioles' material was rearranged in modern harmony style, making their hits sound very different at shows, which didn't please their longtime fans.

They also left Jubilee and switched to Vee-Jay Records. The sound of the Vee-Jay Orioles is strange in comparison to that of the glory days on Jubilee. Indeed, it appears that Vee-Jay had no idea what to do with the Orioles at all. They were advertised as a pop group, but the sound wasn't R&B, it wasn't modern harmony, and it wasn't really pop. They lost their fan base without acquiring the burgeoning new teen market.

In June 1958 Sonny was signed as a soloist by Roulette Records, although he continued to appear with his Orioles. Most of the material from this period is only a shadow of his former sound.

In mid-1961 Sonny put together a new Orioles group that recorded for the CHARLIE PARKER label. Most of the songs recorded in this period were an attempt to recapture his earlier sound and there are some very worthwhile results. Sonny sang with various incarnations of the Orioles through the years (including one aggregation that alternated as an Ink Spots group).

During the final years of his life, Sonny was plagued with health problems. In 1980 diabetes caused him to have part of his left foot amputated. He spent his last year performing on crutches.

On 9 December 1981 Sonny Til passed away from a massive heart attack at the age of fifty-six in Washington, D.C.

The Orioles did not go unappreciated in their own time—they won all the awards and adulation the industry and their fans could give them. The Orioles, and especially Sonny Til, were the root influence of perhaps thousands of aspiring singers.

FURTHER READING

Goldberg, Marvin. Interview with Sonny Til. 14 Dec. 1974. Transcript is in the author's possession.

Goldberg, Marv. *The Orioles*, http://home.att.net/~marvy42/Orioles/orioles1.html.

Warner, Jay. *American Singing Groups: A History from 1940s to Today* (2006).

MARV GOLDBERG

Tildon, Toussaint Tourgee (15 Apr. 1893–22 July 1964), physician and psychiatrist, was born in Waxahachie, Texas, the son of John Wesley Tildon, a physician, and Margaret Hilburn. Tildon received a bachelor's degree from Lincoln University in Pennsylvania in 1912. He then studied pre-law at Harvard University for one year before entering medical school at Meharry Medical College in Nashville, Tennessee. He transferred to Harvard Medical School, earning an M.D. in 1923 and specializing in psychiatry and neurology.

At that time the Tuskegee Veterans Administration Hospital, aided by the National Medical Association, was recruiting qualified physicians to evaluate patients. Health care for African Americans was limited, and doctors at Tuskegee attempted to improve health care in the Deep South. Few black physicians practiced in Alabama, and blacks suffered injuries from work and diseases prevalent in the region. The establishment of a veterans' hospital at Tuskegee created the need for professional physicians and nurses who could treat the large percentage of psychiatric cases seen among World War I veterans.

Tildon was selected for a special training program in psychiatry and neurology at Boston University. With three other physicians, he prepared to join the neuropsychiatric department at the veterans' hospital. Tildon studied with Solomon Carter Fuller, a prominent black neurologist at Boston University.

Moving south in October 1923, Tildon was one of the first six African American doctors on staff at Tuskegee's veterans' hospital. Since the hospital's establishment, white physicians and personnel staffed the facility despite the demands of black leaders that qualified black physicians be placed in charge. In racially tense Macon County, local whites protested the hiring of black professionals, but Veterans Bureau director Frank T. Hines, who selected the new medical men, insisted that the black physicians commence service. Tildon began work as a junior medical officer in psychiatry. In 1924 he married Margaret Cecelia Greene; they had four children, including son Toussaint Tourgee Tildon Jr., who became the chief of thoracic and vascular surgical service and acting assistant chief of surgical service at the Tuskegee Veterans Administration Hospital.

Continuing his medical training with hospital director Eugene Heriot Dibble Jr., Tildon eventually became the clinical director of the neuropsychiatric department. Tildon served as a colonel in World War II. When Dibble resigned in July 1946, Tildon was named manager and director of the Tuskegee Veterans Administration Hospital. During his twelve-year directorship, he set high standards for the hospital. He achieved professional progress by securing accreditation for the hospital's residency program in medicine and dentistry; he also secured professional recognition for black physicians in the Tuskegee hospital as well as at other government hospitals and medical facilities.

After World War II the federal government decided to reorganize veterans' hospitals to accommodate the increased number of patients. Politicians and physicians acknowledged that more teaching programs were needed to prepare competent personnel. In January 1946 Congress created a graduate training program in the Veterans Administration, enabling physicians and dentists to complete residencies at veterans' hospitals.

The Tuskegee Veterans Administration Hospital cooperated with medical and dental schools at the University of Alabama and Emory University, in Atlanta. Tildon supported resident education in the Tuskegee Veterans Administration Hospital's Department of Medicine and Surgery. Residents could train in medicine, surgery, or dentistry.

Tildon concentrated on establishing fully accredited residency programs. He also was concerned with securing government medical positions for black physicians. The Veterans Administration and government hospitals offered black medical personnel access to secure and satisfying medical employment.

In addition to acting as a mentor to black physicians, Tildon pursued research on encephalitis in African American veterans. He also conducted experiments with syphilis and heart disease suffered simultaneously with tuberculosis. He published articles about these concerns in such periodicals as the *U.S. Veterans' Bureau Medical Bulletin*.

Tildon retired from the Tuskegee Veterans Administration Hospital on 31 January 1958. He and his wife remained in Tuskegee, where they were active in the African Methodist Episcopal Church. Tildon died in Tuskegee.

FURTHER READING
Daniel, Pete. "Black Power in the 1920s: The Case of Tuskegee Veterans Hospital," *Journal of Southern History* 36 (1970).
Morais, Herbert M. *The History of the Afro-American in Medicine* (1976).

Yancey, Asa G., Sr. "Tuskegee Veterans Administration Medical Center: Genesis and Opportunities It Provided in Surgery," in *A Century of Black Surgeons: The U.S.A. Experience*, ed. Claude H. Organ and Margaret M. Kosiba (1987).

Younge, S. L. "Toussaint Tourgee Tildon, Sr., M.D., 1893–1964," *Journal of the National Medical Association* 56 (Nov. 1964).

This entry is taken from the *American National Biography* and is published here with the permission of the American Council of Learned Societies.

ELIZABETH D. SCHAFER

Till, Emmett Louis (25 July 1941–28 Aug. 1955), lynching victim, was born near Chicago, the son of Louis Till, a soldier, and Mamie Elizabeth Carthan, a clerical worker. After completing the seventh grade in an all-black elementary school on the South Side of Chicago, "Bobo" Till was sent on vacation to the Mississippi Delta in late summer 1955. His hosts were his great-uncle, Moses Wright, a sharecropper, and Wright's wife, Elizabeth.

On the evening of 24 August, after a week of visiting, the fourteen-year-old Till joined seven other black teenagers for a trip to Money, a hamlet in Leflore County. There, he entered a store owned and operated by Roy Bryant, a twenty-four-year-old former soldier who was momentarily absent, and his wife, Carolyn Bryant, the twenty-one-year-old mother of their two sons. She was five feet tall and weighed 103 pounds. Witnesses disagreed about what happened next, but apparently a couple of the adolescents began taunting Till, daring the five-foot four-inch, 160-pound Chicagoan to ask Mrs. Bryant for a date. Rather than evade the challenge, he bought some bubble gum, then, according to Mrs. Bryant's testimony, he firmly squeezed her hand and asked: "How about a date, baby?" When she immediately withdrew from him, she claimed Till jumped between two counters to block her path, raised his hands, and held her waist, reassuring her, again according to testimony that she later gave in court: "Don't be afraid of me, baby. I ain't gonna hurt you. I been with white girls before." Mrs. Bryant also testified that he used "unprintable" words. It was then that one of Till's cousins rushed in and dragged him from the store, as Mrs. Bryant ran to get a pistol. As the group drove away, she testified, Till exclaimed, "Bye, baby," and "wolf-whistled" at her.

According to Roy Bryant, two days after the alleged incident, a black customer informed him of this breach of Jim Crow etiquette. Claiming later that his sense of honor had been violated, Bryant asked his half brother, J. W. "Big" Milam, a thirty-six-year-old veteran of World War II, to accompany him the next night to punish the northern visitor. Armed with pistols, Bryant and Milam drove in Milam's pickup truck to the Wrights' shack, abducted Till, and pistol-whipped him. Then, near Glendora, Till was forced to tie himself to a cotton gin fan that would weigh his body down just before he was murdered and dumped into the Tallahatchie River.

Although an indictment of whites for such a crime was very rare in Mississippi, all five lawyers practicing in the county seat of Sumner volunteered to represent the defendants pro bono, an offer that Bryant and Milam accepted. A month after the murder, perhaps seventy reporters from major newspapers and magazines covered their trial, at which the defendants were acquitted by a jury of their peers— twelve white men. Despite Mamie Till's wrenching testimony and Moses Wright's identification in court of the two abductors, the jurors needed little more than an hour to reach their decision, which sent shock waves of editorial criticism and black protests throughout the country as well as abroad. The crime and the exoneration later affected writers and musicians as important and diverse as novelists TONI MORRISON and JAMES BALDWIN (both of whom wrote plays about it), scenarist Rod Serling (who wrote a television drama), singer Bob Dylan (who wrote a song), and poet GWENDOLYN BROOKS (who wrote a ballad).

Because the victim was so young, because the infraction of the segregationist code seemed to outsiders so minor, and because the culprits were freed while the U.S. Department of Justice declined to intervene, the case exposed, like no other episode, the vulnerability of the region's blacks. The sense of black precariousness in the rural South helped to spur the civil rights movement. That assault against Jim Crow was facilitated when the intensity of the southern commitment to preserve its "way of life" was revealed. The brutality of Bryant and Milam and the communal support they commanded helped to erode the arrangement of white supremacy that they believed themselves to be reinforcing. Their crime made sense only in terms of a caste system that they took for granted, and yet paradoxically the murder was especially appalling because that system was already beginning to collapse. The intricate intermingling of tradition, race, and caste was entering a phase of decomposition, heightened by the growing realization of the anachronism of such violence during the cold war struggle for the support of the emerging Third World. Till's death became notorious because it intersected the antinomies of black and white, male and female, urban and rural, North and South, old and new, and native and stranger.

FURTHER READING

The papers of William Bradford Huie, the journalist who cracked the case by paying the acquitted defendants to recount their crime in *Look* magazine, are deposited at Ohio State University.

Huie, William Bradford. *Wolf Whistle* (1959).

Whitfield, Stephen J. *A Death in the Delta* (1988).

This entry is taken from the *American National Biography* and is published here with the permission of the American Council of Learned Societies.

STEPHEN J. WHITFIELD

Till, Hannah (1721–1825), who accompanied the Continental Army during the revolutionary war as a cook, was enslaved at birth, owned by four different men over half a century, and by the end of the war was a free woman, settling in Philadelphia and living to the age of 104.

One of the few contemporary written accounts is that of John Fanning Watson, who writes that his sister saw Till alive at the age of 104. Later published accounts say she died at 102. Her date of birth is not recorded, estimated only by subtracting the length of her life from the year she died.

Watson wrote that Till had told him her childhood name was Hannah Long Point—a name her father acquired for successful deer hunting at a place called Long Point. She was born in Kent County, Delaware, assigned by law as the property of John Brinkley, Esq. He sold her at the age of fifteen, and she was brought to Pennsylvania by an owner of record whose name is unknown. At age twenty-five she was sold to Parson Henderson of Northumberland, and at thirty-five to Parson John Mason, a Presbyterian minister in New York. She worked for Mason from the mid-1750s until the outbreak of the war for independence from the British Crown, through the period of the Stamp Act agitation, the Townshend Duties, and other grievances that led to open conflict with Britain. Sometime in 1776 or 1777, Mason agreed that she would cook for the officers of the Continental army, as part of General George Washington's "household."

Records early in the war refer to her as "negro Hannah" or "Hannah Mason." In 1777 General Washington's accounts show that she was a paid servant, and a portion of her wages were withheld to purchase her freedom for the sum of fifty-three pounds. Payment in pounds, the British currency, and that of some colonies, was "hard money," measured in gold or silver, while payment in dollars was printed "Continental" money, which rapidly lost value due to inflation.

Reverend Mason signed a receipt 19 December 1778 for thirty-two pounds New York currency in "full for my servant Hannah's wages who was in the service of His Excellency General Washington" (Loane, p. 107). Another of the rare documentary clues to her life is a receipt in George Washington's papers dated 23 June 1780 in Morristown, New Jersey. It records receipt of $86 for two months wages, signed "Hannah Till, her mark." By this time, she apparently was free, because she received her pay in full, directly (in dollars), and had adopted the surname of Till, probably at the time of her marriage.

Isaac Till, a skilled cook like his future wife, had also been loaned to General Washington, by a Captain John Johnson, in 1776. He benefited from a similar arrangement; of his seven pounds monthly pay, he kept forty shillings (two pounds), and eventually purchased his own freedom. Later writers created the legend that Washington lived in a tent during the winter at Valley Forge, out of solidarity with his freezing rank and file, and lived on the same meager rations. He and his staff occupied a stone house, albeit a small one, which Till remembered was quite crowded.

The kitchen supplies the Tills were given money to purchase, inventory, and prepare included cheese, oysters, partridges, onions, potatoes, cabbages, turnips, parsnips, eggs, veal, chicken, turkey, apples, hams, sirloin beef, mutton, loaf sugar, coffee, chocolates, cranberries, currants, and citrons. They were clearly skilled in culinary arts. Martha Washington joined her husband each winter, and supervised some of the kitchen work. Year round, a housekeeper named Elizabeth Thompson oversaw preparation of food for twenty-five to thirty people.

One of Till's later recollections was that when a shipment of hard gold or silver money, known as specie, arrived to pay the French army, the house used as army headquarters was so crowded that the money was stored in her pastry room, even as she continued to use the room in preparing meals.

Till was assigned for six months late in the war as cook for the Marquis de Lafayette, a French volunteer officer who initially served as Washington's aide-de-camp. From the memories Till related to Watson, it is likely that Till was assigned to cook for Lafayette in 1780 or 1781, when he had returned from a trip to France, and commanded the army shadowing British General Cornwallis as it moved across Virginia to Yorktown. This would have meant cooking high-quality cuisine, served on fine china, with ingredients packed and unpacked from military wagons, with a rapidly moving army, while the British repeatedly tried to capture the high profile commander for whom she cooked. The logistics alone would have been worthy of an officer's commission, not to mention the hazards such duty inevitably entailed.

The Tills settled in Philadelphia, and Hannah apparently outlived Isaac by a number of years. Near the end of her life, Hannah Till lived at 182 South Fourth Street in Philadelphia, a little below Pine Street. During Lafayette's tour of America in 1825, he was informed by John Fanning Watson where she was living in Philadelphia, and stopped to visit her. Later, when she was several months behind on her rent, she was informed that Lafayette had paid it. She died shortly thereafter.

FURTHER READING

Loane, Nancy K. *Following the Drum: Women at the Valley Forge Encampment* (2009).

Watson, John Fanning. *Annals of Philadelphia: Being a Collection of Memoirs, Anecdotes and Incidents of the City and Its Inhabitants* (1830).

CHARLES ROSENBERG

Till-Mobley, Mamie (23 Nov. 1921–6 Jan. 2003), mother of EMMETT LOUIS TILL, civil rights movement activist, and educator, was born Mamie Elizabeth Carthan in Hazelhurst, Mississippi. She was the only child of John and Alma Carthan, sharecroppers who left the South soon after she was born and settled in the town of Argo near Chicago. Mamie's mother, a matriarch in the Church of God in Christ, raised her according to very strict moral principles and encouraged her to excel in academics. Despite the support of her mother and a large network of relatives both in Argo and in Mississippi, Mamie's health was shaken by her parents' divorce in 1932. A child of the South who was raised in the vicinity of Chicago, Mamie maintained close ties with her birthplace; moreover, her urban environment encompassed both northern and southern influences.

In 1940 she married Louis Till, a native of Madrid, Missouri, and an amateur boxer. Louis impressed her during their courtship by breaking the rules of segregated seating in a local drugstore. A year later, the couple had a son, Emmett Louis Till (also known as Bobo), but by 1942 Louis and Mamie Till had separated. Louis joined the army and in 1945 was killed in Italy. The Department of Defense sent Till a note alluding to his "willful misconduct" and a silver ring engraved with the initials "LT" and the date "May 25, 1943." Till eventually passed this ring on to Emmett.

Suddenly deprived of both military spousal benefits and assistance in raising Emmett (when her mother remarried), Till moved to Detroit where she met her second husband, Lemorris "Pink" Bradley, whom she divorced in 1952. Back in Chicago, she took a job at the Social Security Administration, then at the U.S. Air Force Procurement Office. There she met Gene Mobley Jr. who became her third husband in 1957. Overburdened with her responsibilities as a single mother, Till was nevertheless aware of the effects of segregation in Chicago. However, she was not attuned to the heightened racial tensions in the South, especially in the wake of the 1954 *Brown vs. Board of Education* ruling against segregation in schools.

For instance, she hadn't known that Reverend George Lee and Lamar Smith, two African Americans engaged in registering voters, had been murdered in Mississippi during the summer of 1955. This tragic event had occurred just before she allowed fourteen-year-old Emmett to spend several weeks in the care of her uncle, Moses Wright, a sharecropper and preacher in the small town of Money, Mississippi. The details of the incident that occurred on 24 August 1955 at the local grocery store owned by a white couple, Roy and Carolyn Bryant, remain shrouded in uncertainty: Alone in the store with Carolyn, Emmett allegedly "wolf-whistled" at her. On 28 August, Roy Bryant and his half-brother, J. W. "Big" Milam, took Emmett at gunpoint from his great-uncle's home, beat him beyond recognition, shot him in the head, and dumped the corpse, weighted with a gin fan, into the Tallahatchie River. Found two days later, the body was identified by the engraved silver ring Emmett inherited from his father. Bryant and Milam, initially indicted, were soon acquitted of kidnapping and murder charges. Meanwhile, information was leaked to the press by the prosegregationist U.S. senator James Eastland that Emmett's father had been executed in Italy for the rape of two women and the murder of a third—an astonishing and belated revelation for Till-Mobley that illuminated a new father-son connection: "Maybe they both were lynched," she said (*Death of Innocence*, 204).

Despite her grief, she mustered the courage to demand that her son's body be shipped back to Chicago. Her subsequent decision to have an open-casket funeral so the world would see "just how twisted, how distorted, how terrifying race hatred could be" (*Death of Innocence*, 142) transformed her son's gruesome death into martyrdom and gained her recognition as a major crusader for the civil rights movement. Tens of thousands of people filed past Emmett's casket, protest rallies were organized in major U.S. cities and abroad, and New York Congressman ADAM CLAYTON POWELL called for an economic boycott of Mississippi products. The domestic and international press published photos of the young victim of white supremacy, which generated a global outcry. Upon her return from the trial in Sumner, Mississippi—an experience that could have endangered her life—Till-Mobley, now fully conscious of the systemic causes of her son's murder, embarked on a public-speaking series under the auspices of the National Association for the Advancement of Colored People (NAACP). She called her new political awareness "death of innocence" (*Death of Innocence*, 200).

Following a falling-out with the NAACP because of her request that she be paid for speaking engagements, Till-Mobley was ousted from the civil rights frontline. Because of her mother's apprehension, she did not connect with other prominent women in the civil rights movement, such as CORETTA SCOTT KING, ROSA PARKS, and MYRLIE EVERS-WILLIAMS, before the late 1980s. Instead, at thirty-three years of age, she went back to school, graduating cum laude from Chicago Teachers College in 1960. She then obtained a master's degree in Administration and Supervision from Chicago's Loyola University in 1975. She taught in Chicago elementary schools for twenty years, where she organized the Emmett Till Players, a student theater group that toured the country. In 1973 the Church of God in Christ bestowed upon her the honorific title of "Mother Mobley," by which she would become best known in her later years.

Till-Mobley continued to tell her son's tragic story relentlessly, tying in the theme of lynching with that of motherhood—though her public appearances were only on small circuits, until a new spur of public interest brought her back into the limelight. In 1976 a monument depicting Emmett Till with MARTIN LUTHER KING JR. was erected in Denver's City Park. In its opening segment, a PBS series called *Eyes on the Prize* (1987)

reassessed Emmett Till's murder as the spark of the civil rights movement. Additionally the Civil Rights Memorial in Montgomery, Alabama, founded in 1989, displayed Emmett's name prominently. Playwright David Barr requested Mamie's collaboration in writing the play *State of Mississippi vs. Emmett Till*, which was staged in 1999. Filmmakers Stanley Nelson and Keith Beauchamp produced groundbreaking documentaries on Till in 2003 and 2005, respectively; and along with the NAACP, they called for a reopening of Emmett Till's case, which had been Till-Mobley's lifelong wish.

Politically active until the end of her life, Till-Mobley fought against the death penalty, which she considered legal lynching, and unequivocally supported the cause of reparations, equating slavery with centuries of uncompensated violence. In 2002 she received an apology from Jackson City councilman Kenneth Stokes and a lifetime activism award from a Massachusetts senior citizen action group. Also in 2002 she completed her autobiography, *Death of Innocence*. She died in Chicago from kidney failure, but "with her boots on," as one of her relatives, Reverend Wheeler Parker, stated in his eulogy.

Till-Mobley's determination to turn her son's mutilated body into a weapon in the fight against racism placed her in a long tradition of African American women such as SOJOURNER TRUTH, IDA B. WELLS-BARNETT, and ANGELA DAVIS, whose political commitment advanced the cause of human rights and social justice. Till-Mobley's activism contributed to bringing U.S. racial relations under renewed scrutiny, and conversely, to making the United States more aware of the race dynamic in its domestic and international affairs. In 1958 the American decision to vote against Apartheid at the United Nations was indicative of changing American politics in the international arena.

FURTHER READING

Feldstein, Ruth. "'I Wanted the Whole World to See': Constructions of Motherhood in the Death of Emmett Till," in *Motherhood in Black and White. Race and Sex in American Liberalism, 1930–1965* (2000).

Pollack, Harriet, and Christopher Metress. *Emmett Till in Literary Memory and Imagination* (2008).

Till-Mobley, Mamie, and Christopher Benson. *Death of Innocence. The Story of the Hate Crime That Changed America* (2003).

SYLVIE KANDÉ

Tillman, Katherine Davis Chapman (19 Feb. 1870–?), poet, novelist, dramatist, and essayist, was born in Mound City, Illinois, to Laura and Charles Chapman, of whom little is known. After graduating from high school in Yankton, South Dakota, Chapman attended the State University of Louisville in Kentucky and Wilberforce University in Ohio. She began writing early and at eighteen published her first poem, "Memory" (1888), in the *The Christian Recorder*. She also published early stories in the periodical *Our Women and Children*, and poems and articles in the *Indiana Freeman*.

By 1894 Chapman had married George Tillman, an African Methodist Episcopal (AME) minister who had also attended Wilberforce University. Biographical information on the couple is very limited, and the exact date of their marriage remains unknown. Tillman's many subsequent poems, essays, and stories appeared in AME Church publications such as the *Christian Recorder* and the *A.M.E. Church Review*, as well as in other African American periodicals, including *Voice of the Negro*. She also wrote plays, which were published by the A.M.E. Book Concern. Tillman's works were written for readers who, like herself, were religious African Americans.

Tillman wrote during a particularly turbulent period in African American history. Black leaders such as BOOKER T. WASHINGTON, W. E. B. DuBois, and IDA WELLS-BARNETT were articulating a variety of responses to the urgent problems posed by lynching, segregation, and migration. Tillman's writing gave a religious and domestic emphasis to the prevailing political ideas. In novellas such as *Beryl Weston's Ambition: The Story of an Afro-American Girl's Life* (1893) and *Clancy Street* (1898), she told stories of African American women who were at once humble hard workers, aspiring professionals, and self-sacrificing Christian daughters, wives, and mothers striving for the good of their race. In essays such as "Afro-American Women and their Work" (1895), poems such as "The Negro" (1902), and plays such as *Fifty Years of Freedom, or From Cabin to Congress* (1910), Tillman narrated African American history and accomplishments and spoke of the power of Christianity to sustain oppressed people and overcome injustice.

Some of her writing also had a satirical edge. In "Bashy" (1902), a narrative poem about a dark-skinned prostitute, and "The Blue Vein Club" (1902), a brief satire of the exclusive clubs formed by light-skinned, middle-class blacks, she mocked and condemned intraracial prejudice. Her more gently humorous poem "When Mandy Combs Her Head" (1902) was a wry ballad that explored the relationship between black women and their hair.

Though the date of Tillman's death remains unknown, she continued to publish at least until 1922. For decades her writing was uncollected and out of print, but in 1991 Claudia Tate edited a one-volume edition of her work for Oxford University Press's historic Schomburg Library of Nineteenth-Century Black Women Writers Series. Tillman's writing is now available to readers interested in African American women, writing, religion, and politics in the late nineteenth and early twentieth centuries.

FURTHER READING
Dunnigan, Alice. "Early History of Negro Women in Journalism," *Negro History Bulletin* (1965).
Saunders, Kirsten. "Katherine Davis Chapman Tillman," in *African American Authors 1745–1945: A Bio-Bibliographical Critical Sourcebook*, ed. Emmanuel S. Nelson (2000).
Tate, Claudia. *Domestic Allegories of Political Desire: The Black Heroine's Text at the Turn of the Century* (1992).
Tate, Claudia. "Introduction," *The Works of Katherine Davis Chapman Tillman* (1991).

BRIALLEN HOPPER

Tillman, William (1834–?), seaman and Union hero during the Civil War, was born a free black in Milford, Delaware. Very little is known about his early life. In 1850, when William (nicknamed Billy) was sixteen, the Tillman family moved to Providence, Rhode Island. Within a year young Tillman struck out on his own and chose to become a seaman.

Like most African Americans engaged in the maritime trade during this period, Tillman was restricted to serving as a cook or steward, sometimes holding down both positions. Throughout most of the 1850s Tillman worked on the vessels owned by Jonas Smith and Company, located on Front Street in New York City. According to the recollection of Captain Lewis Davis, an employee of the company, Tillman sailed on ships active in the coastal trade, carrying cargo and passengers to Southern ports and returning with cotton, lumber, tobacco, and rice. There is no evidence that Tillman sailed beyond the South Atlantic coast, at least not until the summer of 1861, when he signed on to serve as a cook and steward for the *S. J. Waring*, a large freight-carrying sailing vessel (also known as a schooner), bound for Montevideo, Uruguay, and Buenos Aires, Argentina.

These were dangerous times for merchant ships. On 12 April 1861 rebel batteries had opened fire on Fort Sumter in Charleston, South Carolina, igniting civil war. To make up for its lack of a navy, the Confederate government had authorized privately owned vessels to seize Union ships.

When the *S. J. Waring* set sail from New York City on 4 July 1861 members of the crew were well aware of the danger posed by these so-called privateers on the high seas. The first few days out were uneventful. On Sunday morning, 7 July, however, the sailor on watch spotted a ship about a mile away. As it drew within shouting distance, it hoisted the Confederate colors. With its five cannons aimed pointblank at the *S. J. Waring*, there was no possibility of escaping this well-armed privateer, soon identified as the *Jefferson Davis*.

The captured schooner's crew was taken aboard the privateer except for a passenger (who inexplicably chose to stay), two seamen, and Tillman. A Confederate crew with orders to sail to Charleston soon joined them.

During the voyage Tillman learned that the rebel officers intended to sell him as a slave once the vessel arrived at its destination. Determined to protect his freedom, Tillman, with the help of one of the Union seaman, planned to take control of the ship. On the evening of 16 July Tillman's accomplice alerted him that the Confederate captain, first mate, and second mate had all fallen asleep. Seizing a hatchet, Tillman went into the captain's cabin and struck him over the head with his sharp-edged weapon. The two other Confederate officers suffered a similar fate. After the conspirators dumped the bodies overboard, Tillman took command of the vessel and set sail for New York City, where it arrived five days later.

The story of William Tillman and the *S. J. Waring* soon spread like a prairie fire—first over the city, then throughout the Union, into the Confederacy, and even across the Atlantic. Understandably the Union hero received a negative press in the rebel states, but everywhere else he was lionized for his valor and courage—"the splendid son of Africa," was how the *New York Herald* described him (22 July 1861).

Others were quick to point out that Tillman was responsible for producing the Union's first naval victory of the war. "[T]he nation," wrote Horace Greeley of the *New York Daily Tribune*, "was indebted to this black steward for the first vindication of its honor on the sea" (21 July 1861).

Nor was this the only consequence of Tillman's exploits. For several months prior FREDERICK DOUGLASS, the Union's most prominent African American spokesperson, had attempted to convince the government to enlist blacks in the army, but without success. The War Department and most members of Congress were of the opinion that men of color were inferior and not up to the task of soldiering. William Tillman's "brave heart and nerves of steel," Douglass argued, put to shame those who questioned the black man's capacity to fight for his country (*Douglass' Monthly*, August 1861). Though the Union Army would not budge on the issue until a year later, the Union Navy began enlisting African Americans as early as September 1861, spurred on perhaps in part by reports of Tillman's brave actions.

At twenty-seven, Billy Tillman had become an instant celebrity. Wherever the young man went in New York City, crowds of people followed him, anxious to shake his hand and wish him well. Despite a lack of formal education, Tillman appeared comfortable in the public limelight. Not only was he of sharp mind, but he had a charming physical presence as well. As a *New York Daily Tribune* reporter observed, the heroic seaman was "of medium height, rather strongly built, crisp hair," and "bears an expression of honesty, strong common sense, with touches of humor" (22 July 1861).

Tillman's financial well-being also took a turn for the better, or so it appeared. At first the insurance underwriters of the *S. J. Waring* and its cargo promised him a hefty cash reward, then reconsidered and refused to pay him a recovery fee. The case went to the district and appellate courts, both of which ruled that Tillman should receive an award of $7,000 (equivalent to nearly a half million dollars today).

It is not known if he ever received the money. After the appellate court handed down its decision in early 1862, William Tillman vanished from the historical radar screen. No verifiable evidence has turned up to document his later years.

Tillman's disappearance from the public record, however, should in no way diminish his valor and courage. Against significant odds he rose up to defend his freedom and to bring honor to his country. The late-nineteenth-century black spokesperson and educator BOOKER T. WASHINGTON declared that William Tillman "was as brave as a lion," and for this alone he deserves to be remembered (Washington, p. 283).

FURTHER READING

For primary source material, see "William Tillman, Cook," unpublished typescript, Edward H. Davis Papers, San Diego Historical Society; U. S. District Court for the Southern District of New York (Admiralty case file A16-369/377) and U. S. Circuit Court for the Southern District of New York in the Second Circuit (Court Error and Appeal case file 1-295), National Archives and Records Administration, Northeast Region, New York; *Harper's Weekly*, 3 August 1861; *New York Daily Tribune*, 21–23 July 1861; and *Douglass' Monthly* (August 1861).

Henig, Gerald S. "William Tillman: The Union's First Black Hero," *North & South* 10 (July 2007).

Jones, Steven W. "A Confederate Prize Crew Meets its Match in William Tillman," *Sea History* 93 (Summer 2000).

Quarles, Benjamin. *The Negro in the Civil War* (1953).

Washington, Booker T. *A New Negro for a New Century* (1900).

GERALD S. HENIG

Tilmon, Levin (1807–1863), pastor and community activist, was born in Caroline County, Maryland, to an unnamed father and Sidney Rotter, both slaves. After he was manumitted at a young age, Tilmon's mother (who was also manumitted) indentured him in or around 1815 to a farmer in Northern Delaware. Life as an indentured servant was not much better than life as a slave, and on multiple occasions Tilmon physically resisted cruel masters. Around 1824 Tilmon escaped on a vessel via the Delaware River to Philadelphia but was quickly recaptured and jailed. While in jail, Tilmon learned that his insolvent master planned to sell him out of state to a slave trader, which was considered kidnapping under Delaware state law. With the help of the community and through legal means, Tilmon was able to free himself from his master and finish the four remaining years of his indenture in Wilmington, Delaware, serving under masters of his own choosing.

But the master Tilmon ultimately chose was Jesus. In August 1829 Tilmon returned to Philadelphia, and then he moved on to Princeton and Trenton to attend and teach at boarding schools. In Trenton in the winter of 1830 Tilmon joined the African Methodist Episcopal (AME) Church. In the spring of 1831 he returned to Philadelphia. In early 1832 he married Isabella Lee; but just five weeks later she died. Thrown into despair, Tilmon turned to religion, experiencing a total conversion that changed the saddest hour of his life into what he eventually described as the happiest. Sometime in late 1832 or 1833 he remarried, and in 1834 he purchased a small estate in Camden, New Jersey, for his family. But Tilmon had heard the call: in the spring of 1836 he obtained his preacher's license from Bishop MORRIS BROWN of AME Bethel Church in Philadelphia. In July he embarked upon the New Jersey circuit, but financial hardships at home quickly grounded him. Beginning in the summer of 1837 he worked in the beer business for the next seven years, amassing enough money to leave his family comfortable and to enable him to return to "the more noble work" he felt God had in store for him (Tilmon).

From October 1844 to June 1845 Tilmon traveled hundreds of miles on Long Island and throughout New England, preaching to African American, white, and Native American audiences. At the AME Conference in New York City in June 1845, Tilmon became a deacon and officially joined the itinerancy. He was sent to Norwich, Connecticut, where he first showed himself to be an energetic church-builder and leader. He repeated that performance in Providence, Rhode Island, from 1846 to 1848. In 1848 Tilmon was sent to Rome, New York, which was a hotbed of increasingly political abolitionism. Tilmon became involved in an ambitious, but ultimately unsuccessful, scheme to form an African American settlement on the property of wealthy land magnate and radical white abolitionist Gerrit Smith in Florence, just northwest of Rome. FREDERICK DOUGLASS had initially thrown his support behind the scheme, but then he publicly withdrew upon hearing reports that the land was undesirable. This prompted Tilmon to chide Douglass in a personal letter.

Tilmon's growing confidence as a community activist in enterprises such as the Florence scheme seems to have coincided with and possibly caused his eventual estrangement from the AME Church. Sometime in 1850 Tilmon moved to New York City and organized an independent religious society, the First Colored American Congregational Methodist Society, incorporated in October 1852. Tilmon's church quickly became a model for and center of community activism for prominent African American leaders like Douglass and JAMES McCUNE SMITH. Particularly significant in the eyes of these two leaders was the church's Young Men's Literary Productive Society, which put on exhibitions that demonstrated African American skill in oratory and rhetoric and denounced slavery. When Douglass attended an exhibition during a New York City visit in May 1853, he was so impressed that he posed a question that must have been music to the marginalized Tilmon's ears: "Why will not the ministers of 'Zion' and 'Bethel' Church copy the very laudable example of Rev. L. Tilmon?" These were Tilmon's halcyon days.

In 1853 he published his autobiographical writings as well as a collection of sermons to which were appended a discourse on the necessity of black economic and educational initiatives and a brief series of "autobiographical sketches" of prominent African Americans. On 16 July 1854, while on her way to play the organ at Tilmon's church, Elizabeth Jennings suffered injuries when thrown from a streetcar by a conductor who refused her passage on the basis of her race. Tilmon quickly organized a meeting and introduced stern resolutions against such discrimination, which launched Jennings's successful lawsuit against the streetcar company, eventually earning her a $225 award and the right to ride. This legal victory received national attention and was a major coup in the early campaign against segregation. In early 1855 Douglass presented lectures at Tilmon's church, attracting large crowds—as did McCune Smith. At the same time, Tilmon formed the Colored American Grove Association, which purchased a six-acre plot of woodland at Rye Neck, New York, for the purpose of offering a "comfortable retreat for all respectable persons." Douglass and McCune Smith both spoke at the Grove's opening celebration in May 1855, and the cornerstone was soon laid for another Colored Congregational Methodist Church nearby.

Perhaps as a result of all these successes, the church that Tilmon had once been driven from seemed to want him back. On 23 December 1857 it was announced that Tilmon's First Colored American Congregational Methodist Church would unite with the AME Zion Church. But it seems Tilmon and his congregants had grown to savor their independence, for in May 1858 they tendered their resignation from the organization. Tilmon's last years seem to have been spent in ministerial duties for the religious society he had founded and in community activist projects such as opening an employment office. As one acquaintance wrote, Tilmon was "a man of decided energy and character, whose motto is, 'never to fail' in anything he undertakes." He died in 1863.

FURTHER READING

Tilmon, L. *Tilmon, Pastor of a Colored Congregational Methodist Church in the City of New York. Written by Himself* (1853).

Tilmon, L. *Brief Miscellaneous Narrative of the More Early Part of the Life of L.* (1853).

JARED WINSTON HICKMAN

Timmons, Bobby (19 Dec. 1935–1 Mar. 1974), jazz pianist and composer, was born Robert Henry Timmons in Philadelphia, Pennsylvania, the son of a minister. His parents' names are unknown. Bobby started playing the piano at age six, studying with his uncle. At some point during his childhood he was a church organist. This experience, and more generally his upbringing within the African American gospel church, would deeply affect his jazzmaking. Timmons also spent one year at Philadelphia's music academy.

Timmons came to New York in 1954. In February 1956 he joined the trumpeter Kenny Dorham's Jazz Prophets, modeled after the drummer ART BLAKEY's hard bop group, the Jazz Messengers. After working with the trumpeter Chet Baker from April 1956 to January 1957 Timmons joined the saxophonist SONNY STITT's group from February to August 1957. That same year, working as a sideman, he also recorded a number of albums with the trumpeter LEE MORGAN (such as *The Cooker*), the tenor saxophonist HANK MOBLEY, and the trombonist Curtis Fuller. From August 1957 to March 1958 Timmons was a member of the trumpeter Maynard Ferguson's big band.

Timmons's most important affiliation began in July 1958 when he joined Blakey's group. During this time Timmons wrote "Moanin'" for the album *Art Blakey with the Jazz Messengers*, which was recorded in October of that year. "Moanin'" became a modest hit in this version, and it reached a wider audience after the vocal group Lambert, Hendricks, and Ross recorded their rendition in 1959, with Jon Henricks's lyrics to Timmons's instrumental theme. Blakey's group toured Europe late in 1958, and while performing in Paris, the Jazz Messengers recorded the sound track to the 1959 film *Des femmes disparaissent*. Back in New York Timmons participated in the recording of one of Blakey's greatest albums, made live in April at the nightclub Birdland and released as *At the Jazz Corner of the World*. In the summer of 1959 in New York, Timmons contributed to the sound track of another French film, *Les liaisons dangereuses 1960*.

From October 1959 through February 1960 Timmons was a member of the alto saxophonist CANNONBALL ADDERLEY's quintet, to which he contributed the instrumental hits "This Here" (also known as "Dis Here") on *The Cannonball Adderley Quintet in San Francisco* (1959) and "Dat Dere" on *Them Dirty Blues* (1960). Timmons returned for another extended stay with Blakey from March 1960 to June 1961. Albums from this period include Morgan's *Leeway* (1960), Blakey's *The Freedom Rider* (1961) and *Jazz Messengers!* (1961), and Timmons's first albums as a leader.

Timmons's career declined rapidly because of his addiction to alcohol and drugs, although he led groups in New York and Washington and continued to record under his own name until 1966. In 1970 he participated in a jazz piano concert at Judson Hall in New York, also making a brief European tour with the trumpeter CLARK TERRY in July 1973, by which time he was already severely ill. He died in New York City of cirrhosis of the liver. He was survived by his wife Estelle and their son; her maiden name and the marriage date are unknown.

Timmons is remembered as a composer and pianist in the soul jazz style at a point when this offshoot of hard bop was popularized. His song "Moanin'" is one of the finest examples of how the harmonic structure and melodic flavor of African American gospel music might be brought into jazz. "This Here," built on a somewhat altered blues progression, additionally brings in the characteristic lilting 6/8 rhythmic feeling of some gospel songs, but its unsatisfying musical and emotional content falls on the cute and light side of soul jazz, as does the follow-up, "Dat Dere." In the 1960s performers such as Les McCann and Ramsey Lewis took up this aspect of Timmons's playing, which pointed away from jazz toward soul.

Timmons's hard bop piano playing is analogously colored by its soulful riff and its blues-oriented approach. It is also revealing of Timmons's melodic inclinations that on "Hi-Fly" from Adderley's San Francisco date, he quotes the opening phrase of 1944's popular "I'm Beginning to See the Light" not in the typical bop manner of a fleeting insertion but rather by presenting this little phrase as an arranged swing riff, stated three times.

As a consequence of his success, Timmons was pigeonholed as a soul jazz pianist. Such a limiting label evidently caused him considerable frustration. His improvisations on "I Hear a Rhapsody" and "You Don't Know What Love Is" from the *Jazz Messengers!* album are among many recorded examples of his ability also to play in a more abstract and restrained bop style.

FURTHER READING

Feather, Leonard. "Bobby Timmons," *Contemporary Keyboard* 6 (Aug. 1980).

Gardner, Barbara. "Timmons in a Tempest," *Down Beat* (24 Nov. 1960).

Obituaries: *New York Times*, 2 Mar. 1974; *Down Beat* (11 Apr. 1974).

This entry is taken from the *American National Biography* and is published here with the permission of the American Council of Learned Societies.

BARRY KERNFELD

Tindley, Charles Albert (7 July 1856–26 July 1933), Methodist minister, was born in Berlin, Maryland, the son of Charles and Ester, both slaves. He was self-educated. In 1885 he was examined for ministerial orders by the Delaware Annual Conference, a black Methodist Episcopal Conference. He was admitted on probation and assigned to the Cape May, New Jersey, church where he served for two years. In 1887 he was ordained deacon and transferred to the South Wilmington, Delaware, church. Subsequently he served as statistical secretary to Reverend Joseph R. Waters. Ordained an elder in the Delaware Conference in 1889, he was again transferred, this time to the Odessa, Delaware, charge. Between 1890 and 1900 Tindley served pastorates at Pocomoke and Pocomoke circuits in Maryland and at Fairmount and Wilmington in Delaware, where he served historic Ezion Methodist Church. In 1900 he was appointed presiding elder of the Wilmington District. Concurrent with his term of office as presiding elder, he became pastor at Bainbridge Street Methodist Church, Philadelphia, Pennsylvania, which he served for thirty-three years. He continued to obtain an education: he attended the Brandywine Institute Theological Course, and by correspondence he took the Greek course at Boston University School of Theology.

By 1906 Tindley's church had become the premier black congregation in Philadelphia. In his sermons and with his own musical compositions, Tindley strove to provide an atmosphere of warm fellowship among the members of the middle-class congregation. Between 1901 and 1916 he published "Songs of Paradise," writing the words for thirty-three songs and the music for sixteen. East Calvary Methodist Episcopal Church, as the Bainbridge Street Church was renamed, became a center and symbol of black culture and religion in Philadelphia. Tindley himself developed strong personal friendships with important political and social leaders, including John Wanamaker and Russell H. Conwell. Tindley frequently became involved in social issues, developing a feed-the-hungry program and opposing the proliferation of movie theaters in the city.

Returning from the Delaware Annual Conference in 1920, having been defeated in his bid to be elected to the Methodist episcopacy, Tindley began to make plans to construct a massive cathedral for his congregation of more than seven thousand. Guided by the advice of John Wanamaker, the financial campaign was a success, and the new building was completed by Thanksgiving 1924. Unfortunately, the first service held at the church was dimmed by the sudden death of Tindley's wife, Annie Daisy Henry, whom he had married in 1884 and with whom he had had six children.

Tindley's personal life soon took several more unhappy turns. His secret marriage to Jenny Cotton, a widow, in 1925 infuriated the eligible women in his church who, upon discovering that he was married, called in their loans on the building program. In addition, his adult children did not accept the marriage and rebelled against their stepmother. To make matters worse, he was charged with breach of promise to marry Alice MacDonald of Newark, New Jersey, with whom he was briefly acquainted. Although the charges were dropped, the seventy-year-old clergyman's reputation was besmirched and the church's fortunes suffered. In a desperate attempt to reduce the debt, the church invited the flamboyant evangelist G. Wilson Becton to conduct services at the temple, which he did for several months in 1930, regularly receiving "consecrated dime collections." Tindley objected to this intrusion and watched the quality of his ministry erode. In the end Becton was expelled from the temple, whereupon he took his Gospel Feast Party to a nearby boxing arena and competed with Tindley for the attentions of religiously minded black Philadelphians.

Nonetheless, at his death in Philadelphia, Tindley was still the undisputed leader of the Delaware Annual Conference. His temple—which later was renamed the Tindley Temple Methodist Episcopal Church in his honor—claimed ten thousand members, with a Sunday school of two thousand pupils and seventy-two teachers. In his last year of ministry alone he raised twenty-four thousand dollars for the conference benevolence program. Owing to his famous published sermon, *Heaven's Christmas Tree* (1915), and many published hymns and gospel songs, Tindley also was well remembered as the "Prince of Preachers." The official historian of the Delaware Annual Conference wrote of him that "his towering physique, his commanding voice, his matchless eloquence, his cogent reasoning, his inimitable style, and his unbounded faith, all combined to render him the most popular preacher of his time."

FURTHER READING
The church records of the Tindley Temple Methodist Episcopal Church in Philadelphia constitute a history of Tindley as a pastor. Other helpful materials can be found in the Eastern Pennsylvania Annual Conference Archives at St. George's United Methodist Church in Philadelphia.

Jones, Ralph H. *Charles Albert Tindley: Prince of Preachers* (1982).

Tindley, E. T. *The Prince of Preachers: The Remarkable Story of Charles Albert Tindley of Philadelphia, Pennsylvania* (1942).

Obituaries: *Philadelphia Tribune*, 27 July and 3 Aug. 1933.

This entry is taken from the *American National Biography* and is published here with the permission of the American Council of Learned Societies.

WILLIAM H. BRACKNEY

Tio, Lorenzo, Jr. (21 Apr. 1893–24 Dec. 1933), jazz musician, was born Lorenzo Anselmo Tio in New Orleans, Louisiana, the son of Augustin Lorenzo Tio, a clarinetist, and Alice Majeau. According to his younger brother, music came to Lorenzo naturally "as easily as drinking a glass of water." He began study of the clarinet with his father and an uncle, Louis "Papa" Tio, by about 1898. As his interest deepened, he practiced diligently, often playing scales for hours at a stretch. He also attended Catholic school and the black public schools as a child. His first professional experience came when he marched with his father's brass band in about 1903, after the family moved to Bay St. Louis, Mississippi.

The family had moved back to New Orleans by 1908, and Tio, whose ancestry included Spanish, French, and African American forebears, began to perform frequently in the musical scene of the so-called Creoles, or, more accurately, "Creoles of color," the sizable New Orleans population of persons with a mixed heritage such as his own, appearing often with both the Excelsior and Onward brass bands. He also played dance engagements with FREDDIE KEPPARD's Olympia Orchestra and later BUNK JOHNSON's Eagle Band. In 1914, after gaining prominence as a clarinet soloist in various bands in the dance halls of Storyville, Tio married Lillian Bocage, younger sister of the Creole cornetist Peter Bocage.

Although solidly trained in traditional musical techniques, such as sight-reading and sight-transposing, Tio was also interested in the emergent jazz style and on his own developed the ability to improvise fluently. This unusual combination of skills had helped him become the leading young clarinetist in the city by the early 1910s. Like his father and uncle, Tio also taught studio clarinet lessons throughout most of his musical career. Generally he adopted the same teaching procedures used by his elders, reflective of the Creole-of-color musical ideals and deriving from the European conservatory tradition. Tio's work as a teacher flowered in the second and third decades of the century, simultaneous with a steady rise in the popularity of jazz and the proliferation of ready venues for a large number of practitioners at both the professional and amateur levels.

Beginning clarinetists often undertook private lessons as a matter of course; the role of the instrument in early jazz as provider of ornamented melodies and counterlines called for a relatively high degree of technical facility, usually attainable only with directed study. Known as a demanding mentor, Tio was the teacher of a number of significant clarinet stylists, including Jimmy Noone, OMER SIMEON, BARNEY BIGARD, ALBERT NICHOLAS, and (briefly) SIDNEY BECHET. At least eleven of his other students also pursued successful careers as jazz musicians on a local or regional level.

Like many New Orleans musicians, Tio spent time in Chicago, going there in 1916 or 1917 with a quintet led by the cornetist MANUEL PEREZ. While in Chicago Tio also socialized and occasionally performed with Keppard and taught the young Simeon. Tio performed regularly with Perez's band at the popular Arsonia Cafe through 1917, but the next summer, after a period of freelancing, he and his wife returned to New Orleans, where their only child, a daughter, was soon born.

After brief stints with a band led by PAPA CELESTIN and another group, the Maple Leaf Orchestra, Tio joined a society-dance orchestra led by the violinist ARMAND JOHN PIRON. This ensemble was known for its ability to play in both the sweet and hot styles, and it performed regularly throughout the 1920s for white audiences, primarily at Tranchina's Restaurant on Lake Pontchartrain and at the New Orleans Country Club. The group also traveled twice to New York City, in 1923 and 1924, for engagements at the Cotton Club and the Roseland Ballroom.

In New York the Piron Orchestra made a series of recordings for Victor, Okeh, and Columbia. The thirteen surviving cuts from this effort—a good example being "Lou'siana Swing"—show Tio to have been an accomplished and articulate clarinetist with ample technique to execute fast, angular lines across all registers. The principal hot (improvising) soloist of the orchestra, Tio consistently employed the bright sound and fast vibrato characteristic of the early jazz style. The complete recordings of the Piron Orchestra are available as *Piron's New Orleans Orchestra*.

Sometime in 1926 Tio suffered a paralytic stroke and temporarily lost feeling on one side of his body. He recuperated at home and depended on income from private teaching. Within six months he was able to return to his position with Piron, although a few contemporaries felt that the stroke took a permanent toll on his technical abilities.

The Piron Orchestra split up in 1928, and after performing for a time in the French Quarter of New Orleans with Peter Bocage's Creole Serenaders, Tio moved his family to New York City. Joining the New York local of the musician's union in October 1930, he played with a variety of bands, including JELLY ROLL MORTON's. He also began to market a few original compositions and is said to have supplied sketches of dance melodies to Barney Bigard and DUKE ELLINGTON. By the early 1930s, however, the swing style had taken firm hold in New York and the expatriate New Orleans musicians, whose playing styles had matured two decades earlier, found employment increasingly scarce. Bechet, now Tio's friend, helped him land work, and by about 1932 both had joined the house band at the Nest in Harlem. This was Tio's last steady engagement; his health failed during the autumn of 1933, and he died of heart failure on Christmas Eve.

Tio remains one of the foremost clarinetists among the group of New Orleans musicians who contributed to the development of the jazz style. Known as a consummate performer and teacher to musicians across all of the city's cultural divisions, he worked with Freddie Keppard, Bunk Johnson, and Jelly Roll Morton, among others, during a twenty-five-year career that included extended stays in Chicago and New York. Moreover, through his dual role as performer and teacher Lorenzo Tio Jr. may be said to have done as much as anyone to help crystallize and disseminate the distinctive New Orleans clarinet sound of the 1910s and 1920s.

FURTHER READING

Bigard, Barney. *With Louis and the Duke: The Autobiography of a Jazz Clarinetist*, ed. Barry Martyn (1985).

Kinzer, Charles E. "The Tios of New Orleans and Their Pedagogical Influence on the Early Jazz Clarinet Style," *Black Music Research Journal*, vol. 16, no. 2 (Autumn 1996).

Suhor, Charles, and Dan Morgenstern. *Jazz in New Orleans* (2001).

Obituary: *Louisiana Weekly*, 13 Jan. 1934.

This entry is taken from the *American National Biography* and is published here with the permission of the American Council of Learned Societies.

CHARLES E. KINZER

Tobias, Channing Heggie (1 Feb. 1882–5 Nov. 1961), reformer and civil rights leader, was born in Augusta, Georgia, the son of Fair J. Robinson, a coachman, and Clara Belle (maiden name unknown), a domestic worker. Because both his parents had to live in their employers' homes, Tobias was raised by a friend of his mother. It is not known why he used a last name different from that of his parents.

Tobias later recalled that when he was ten years old, he heard a speech by the white president of Paine College. Inspired by the speaker's humanity and vision, the boy managed to attend Paine College Preparatory Academy from 1895 to 1898, and then enter Paine College. In 1900, still a student, he was ordained a minister of the Colored Methodist Episcopal Church. He graduated two years later and enrolled in Drew Theological Seminary in Madison, New Jersey, where he received a BD in 1905, followed three years later by a DD from the University of Pennsylvania. In 1908 he married a classmate from Paine, Mary C. Pritchard; they had two children.

The couple returned to Augusta, where Tobias taught biblical studies at Paine until 1911. Meanwhile, a gift from Julius Rosenwald, the president of Sears, Roebuck, had spurred the Young Men's Christian Association (YMCA) to build a network of centers for black youth. Since blacks were excluded from most existing Ys, this represented a significant expansion of the program. Tobias was one of three black international secretaries hired by the Y to oversee its "colored work." Twelve years later, when the National Council established a Colored Work Department, Tobias became its senior secretary. In this capacity he traveled throughout Europe, Africa, and the Far East giving lectures, observing, and representing the United States at international YMCA conferences.

Year after year at these conferences Tobias criticized the American Y for permitting racial discrimination within its own ranks and for ignoring "flagrant violations" of the Fourteenth and Fifteenth Amendments in the wider society. In 1936, for example, Tobias noted that the United States and South Africa were almost the only countries in the world that maintained segregated Ys. Various resolutions on racial justice were passed, but Tobias dismissed them as mere "expressions of conviction and hope," since they carried no requirements for action. His persistence on this matter is a tribute both to his own courage and to the Y's continuing willingness to retain a foreign representative who was such an outspoken critic.

Tobias believed that until true equality was achieved, blacks must hold on to the separate associations that they themselves administered, rather than accept subordinate status in white-controlled groups. For this reason he accepted his separate, racially defined department within the Y and repeatedly emphasized the importance of the network of black-controlled Ys across the country. "The Y is our source of refuge," he told one critic. Yet even as he spoke, the Depression was eroding the Y's funding; during the 1930s services for blacks were cut back with particular severity. Tobias lost half his staff, and between 1925 and 1934 the number of black Ys in the country fell from 179 to 50.

Despite his frustrations within the Y, Tobias was gaining recognition as a black leader. He served on the Commission on Interracial Cooperation from 1935 to 1942, which was organized to educate southern whites about the need for racial justice. He and other civil rights spokesmen also began consulting regularly with a group known informally as the Black Cabinet, composed of the forty or fifty blacks who held positions in President Franklin D. Roosevelt's administration. The members shared information, advocated the appointment of blacks to government positions, and exerted pressure when incidents of discrimination were reported. In addition, Tobias joined periodic delegations to the White House—usually representing larger groups such as the Urban League—to press for presidential action against racial discrimination. Roosevelt received his visitors with courtesy but acted on relatively few of their requests.

In 1941 Tobias joined the Committee on Negroes in Defense Industries and co-wrote their widely publicized manifesto, which asserted: "The time has come for the lasting repudiation of race as an influence in determining the policies of the Nation." During the war he served on the National Advisory Committee on Selective Service, as well as the Joint Army and Navy Committee on Welfare and Recreation. He also joined the board of the NAACP in 1943.

In 1946 Tobias became the first black director of the Phelps-Stokes Foundation, established to improve educational opportunities for blacks. That year he joined another delegation to the White House, to protest the wave of racial violence that had followed World War II. In response, the new president, Harry Truman, established the President's Commission on Civil Rights. Tobias was one of two blacks on the fifteen-person commission, which submitted its report in October 1947. Although Truman did not adopt the Commission's most sweeping recommendations against segregation, his civil rights message to Congress in January 1948 incorporated ten substantive proposals from the report and aroused great hostility among southern Democrats.

Tobias's wife died in 1949, and two years later he married Eva Arnold; they had no children. In 1951–1952 he served as alternate delegate to the Sixth General Assembly of the United Nations, then meeting in Paris. Upon retiring from Phelps-Stokes in 1953, Tobias accepted the chairmanship of the NAACP board. The following year he presided over the launching of a ten-year campaign against segregation, designed to culminate with the centenary of the Emancipation Proclamation in 1963; the campaign slogan was "Free by '63." Tobias retired in 1959 and died two years later in New York City.

In an era marked by pervasive and explicit discrimination, Tobias devoted his career to working for racial justice. When the NAACP won its historic case against school segregation in 1954, Tobias characteristically urged the organization to use "the spirit of give and take" in working out the implementation of its victory. This principle governed his career and indeed made it possible. Although his professional base was a white-dominated organization that itself tolerated segregation, Tobias survived by the strength of his talent and by blending his high ideals with pragmatism, his unyielding determination with, as he said, "calm reasonableness." He was an important member of the generation of black leaders whose courage and persistence set the stage for the civil rights victories of the 1960s.

FURTHER READING
Mjagkij, Nina. *Light in the Darkness: African-Americans and the YMCA, 1852–1946* (1994).
Murray, Pauli. *Song in a Weary Throat* (1987).
Obituary: *New York Times*, 6 Nov. 1961.
This entry is taken from the *American National Biography* and is published here with the permission of the American Council of Learned Societies.

SANDRA OPDYCKE

Todman, Terence (13 March 1926–), career diplomat and six-time U.S. ambassador, was born Terence Alphonso Todman in Saint Thomas, Virgin Islands, the son of Alphonse and Rachel Todman. Terence's father worked as a grocery clerk and occasionally as a stevedore, while his mother worked as a laundress and housemaid.

After graduating as the salutatorian from his high school in Saint Thomas, Todman began his college education at the Polytechnic Institute of Puerto Rico. Military service interrupted his education, however, and he spent four years in the U.S. Army. Following completion of his duties he returned to finish his bachelor's degree in Puerto Rico and then went on to Syracuse University, where he earned an M.A. in Public Administration in 1953.

By that time Todman had decided that he wished to pursue a career in diplomacy, and after passing the federal entry exams in 1952 he took a position with the Department of State. It did not augur well when Todman was told upon arriving that he did not sound American enough and that his Virgin Islands accent would prohibit him from any important diplomatic assignments. The more significant barrier to Todman's career, however, was his race. The Department of State had a long history of exclusion and segregation, so much so that the black press routinely referred to the department as the "lily-white club." Few African Americans were able to secure diplomatic positions, and when they did, they quickly found their opportunities for advancement extraordinarily limited.

Todman himself quickly discovered the limitations. When he was sent to the Foreign Service Institute in Virginia for his training, he found that the only nearby eating establishment barred African Americans. Todman made enough noise about the situation that the Department of State eventually leased part of the restaurant just to serve its employees—Todman included. As for his assignments, Todman also faced the old problem of limited opportunities. During his first years in the

Department of State he served in a variety of capacities: a position with South Asian Affairs where he worked primarily with India, some work with the United Nations Trusteeship Council Commission, and in 1957 his first overseas assignment, to New Delhi. He later spent time in Lebanon, where he received Arabic language training, and in 1964 he became deputy chief of mission in Togo.

But there were also deep frustrations. Despite his fluency in Spanish, Todman was told that Latin American assignments were off-limits for African Americans. And even with his Arabic language training, Todman soon found that the same rule applied to the Middle East. In each case Todman was told that the nations in these regions would take as an insult the appointment of a senior U.S. African American diplomat.

Like many African American diplomats, Todman spent much of his career in Africa. In 1969 he received his first appointment as a U.S. ambassador to the nation of Chad. Next was a tour as U.S. ambassador to Guinea. In 1975 after three years in Guinea, Todman looked forward to his next assignment with optimism. He had handled two very difficult postings with great skill, and he now pressed the Department of State for an assignment to the Middle East. Todman was frustrated when the department responded instead with offers of more posts in sub-Saharan Africa. To the surprise of his superiors Todman simply refused these offers and steadfastly demanded that he receive an assignment outside of Africa that would use his skills more fully.

The impasse was settled when the original nominee for the U.S. ambassadorship in Costa Rica was turned down by Congress. Todman reminded the department of his Spanish language skills, and in 1975 he was named U.S. ambassador to Costa Rica. This marked the first appointment of an African American as ambassador to a Latin American nation.

In Costa Rica, Todman faced situations both serious and absurd. The growing civil unrest in Nicaragua threatened to pour over into Costa Rica, and Todman had to work constantly to reassure the Costa Rican government that the United States would protect Costa Rica's sovereignty. Meanwhile Todman's tenure in Costa Rica coincided with the stay of the financier Robert Vesco, who had fled there to escape criminal charges in the United States. Despite Todman's being authorized only to keep the Department of State informed about Vesco's movements, Vesco took it into his head

that Todman was going to kidnap him and return him to the United States. Vesco's paranoia led to some farcical moments as he tried to avoid Todman in restaurants and other public places.

After his two years in Costa Rica, Todman's career changed dramatically in 1977 when the new administration of President Jimmy Carter selected Todman to serve as assistant secretary of state for inter-American affairs. When Todman accepted, he became the first African American to head one of the geographical divisions in the Department of State. His brief tenure was marked with some significant successes. He worked to establish closer relations with Cuba, and this led to the establishment of interest sections by each nation in the other's land. Todman also played a key role in organizing the public relations campaign for the contentious Panama Canal treaties.

His service as assistant secretary ended on an acrimonious note, however, soured by problems in Nicaragua, which faced the slow crumbling of the dictatorial regime of Anastasio Somoza and the challenge of the leftist Sandinista rebels. Though Todman was no supporter of the brutal Somoza regime, he also believed that many administration officials failed to recognize what he believed to be the Communist control of the Sandinista movement. When it became apparent that his opinions on the matter were in stark contrast to those of others in the Carter White House, he stepped down from the post in 1978 to become ambassador to Spain.

Prior to 1978 six other African Americans had served as ambassadors or ministers to European nations. None, however, had served in a major western European post such as Spain. Todman arrived in Spain at the height of anti-American tensions, and a Socialist government came to power while he was ambassador. Nevertheless Todman was able to assist in negotiating a very delicate treaty concerning the U.S. use of naval and air bases in Spain and worked with Spanish officials to gain that nation's entry into the NATO alliance. Todman remained in Spain for five years. In 1983 he was offered a number of different assignments and chose Denmark, partly because of its increasing importance in NATO discussions but also because his background as a native of the Virgin Islands (a colony of Denmark's until its sale to the United States in 1916) gave him a deep interest in Danish culture.

In 1989 Todman accepted his last ambassadorial assignment when he took a post in Argentina. Just a few days after his arrival the Argentine president announced his resignation and a new government took power. The political turmoil only added to Todman's difficulties as he tried to repair U.S.-Argentinian relations, which had been fraught with tension during the past decade. He was remarkably successful, assisting the Argentine government in acquiring several large loans and economic assistance grants. His efforts paid off when Argentina became the only Latin American nation to participate in the first Gulf War against Iraq.

By 1993 Todman had been with the Department of State for more than four decades and had served as U.S. ambassador to six different nations. He retired that year with the rank of career ambassador, one of only thirty or so individuals to gain that rank in U.S. history and the first African American to do so. In recognition of his tremendous career he was honored at a retirement ceremony held at Statuary Hall in the U.S. Capitol; he was the first government employee ever to receive such an honor.

Retirement for Todman did not mean an end to his activities. He became one of the leading figures in planning honors for the centenary of RALPH BUNCHE, one of America's best-known African American diplomats. In 2003 Todman was appointed by the Organization of American States to serve as its special envoy in Haiti. Todman's main jobs were to help the Haitians restore security and order as well as establish a political basis for democratic elections and a stable government. Despite three visits to Haiti to meet with the competing parties, Todman's mission ended in frustration when the political system continued to deteriorate throughout late 2003 and early 2004.

FURTHER READING
Krenn, Michael L. *Black Diplomacy: African Americans and the State Department, 1945–1969* (1999).
Miller, Jake C. *The Black Presence in American Foreign Affairs* (1978).

MICHAEL L. KRENN

Tolan, Eddie (29 Sept. 1909–31 Jan. 1967), track and field athlete and Olympian, known as "The Midnight Express," was born Thomas Edward Tolan in Denver, Colorado, the son of Edward Tolan and Alice (maiden name unknown). When Tolan was a youngster, his parents moved first to Salt Lake City, Utah, and then to Detroit, Michigan, in search of better employment opportunities. In Detroit he received his secondary education at Cass Technical High School. Tolan, who played quarterback on the football team and sprinted on the track team,

garnered national attention through his exceptional running ability. The highlight of his high school football career came in 1926, when the five foot seven, 140-pound speedster rushed for six touchdowns against rival Western High School. Although a subsequent knee injury limited his gridiron ability, Tolan in 1927 ran 100 yards in 9.8 seconds, establishing a Michigan state high school record.

Upon graduating from high school in 1927, Tolan received a football scholarship to the University of Michigan in Ann Arbor. Although his size prevented him from succeeding as a college football player, his running speed propelled him into the limelight as one of the nation's swiftest sprinters. He failed to qualify for the 1928 Olympic Games, but in 1929 he became the first runner to record a legitimate world record of 9.5 seconds in the 100-yard dash, in winning the Western (later Big Ten) Conference Championship. That year Tolan also won the 100- and 220-yard dashes in the Amateur Athletic Union (AAU) Championships. One of the first African American runners to compete extensively in Europe, he equaled the world record of 10.4 seconds for 100 meters twice in 1929. The following year Tolan defended his AAU title in the 100-yard dash, but he lost the 220-yard dash to his rival George Simpson of Ohio State University. In 1931 Tolan claimed Western Conference titles in the indoor 60-yard dash and the outdoor 100- and 220-yard dashes. Later that year he won the 220-yard dash in the AAU, the National Collegiate Athletic Association, and the Intercollegiate American Amateur Athletic Association championships. After graduating from the University of Michigan in 1931, Tolan coached track and taught health and physical education at West Virginia State College in Institute, West Virginia. He earned a spot on the U.S. Olympic Team in the 100 and 200 meters in 1932, finishing second in both events to RALPH HAROLD METCALFE of Marquette University. But in the 1932 Summer Olympic Games in Los Angeles, California, Tolan triumphed over Metcalfe in both events. Although both sprinters were timed in 10.3 seconds in the 100 meters, Tolan was declared the gold medal winner and new Olympic record holder after an examination of the photo finish revealed that his entire body had crossed the finish line ahead of Metcalfe's lean. In winning the gold medal in the 200 meters, Tolan set an Olympic record of 21.2 seconds and led an American sweep of the medals, as Simpson won the silver medal and Metcalfe

Eddie Tolan (center) stands with the other winners of the 200-meter track and field event at the Olympic Summer Games in Los Angeles, California, 3 August 1932. Tolan won the gold; George Simpson (left) the silver, and Ralph Metcalfe (right) the bronze. (AP Images.)

garnered the bronze medal. Tolan's performance, as well as Metcalfe's, inspired rising young African American track and field athletes such as JESSE OWENS and Eulace Peacock.

After the 1932 Olympics, Tolan wanted to study medicine, but the Great Depression thwarted his dreams of returning to school. He tried to capitalize on his athletic fame by joining the famed vaudeville act of BILL ROBINSON; however, their schedule of 103 shows, which would have earned $1,500 per week, was canceled after the first week. Jobless and broke, Tolan returned to Detroit and lived with his mother, who continued to support him and his siblings. In 1933 he began working as a file clerk at the Wayne County Register of Deeds Office, and in 1935 he returned to the track to capture the world professional sprinting championship in Australia. During World War II, Tolan worked in the stock control department of the Packard Motor Car

Company. Following the war, he owned and operated a gasoline filling station for about eight years. After selling his filling station and working briefly as a burial insurance salesman, Tolan returned to the education profession as a health and physical education teacher in the Detroit public school system in 1955. Tolan, who never married, died of kidney failure and a heart attack in Detroit.

Tolan was one of the most popular track and field athletes prior to World War II. With his thick black-rimmed spectacles taped solidly to his ears, he propelled his stubby frame down the track with incredibly fast leg action, delighting American and European audiences alike. Through his success in the 1932 Summer Olympics, Tolan followed in the tradition of University of Michigan alumni Archibald Hahn and Ralph Craig, who, respectively, accomplished the same feat in 1904 and 1912. As the first African American double Olympic gold medal sprinter, he belongs to a select group of twentieth-century dashmen who have legitimately claimed the title of "world's fastest human."

FURTHER READING

Ashe, Arthur. *A Hard Road to Glory—Track and Field: The African-American Athlete in Track and Field* (1993).

Baker, William J. *Jesse Owens: An American Life* (1986).

Quercetani, Roberto L. *A World History of Track and Field Athletics* (1964).

Obituaries: *New York Times* and *Detroit Free Press*, 1 Feb. 1967.

This entry is taken from the *American National Biography* and is published here with the permission of the American Council of Learned Societies.

ADAM R. HORNBUCKLE

Tolbert, Margaret Ellen Mayo (24 Nov. 1943–), chemist, was born Margaret Ellen Mayo in Suffolk, Virginia, the third child of J. Clifton Mayo, a landscape gardener who served in the army during World War II, and Martha Artis Mayo, a domestic worker. Margaret's parents separated while she was very young. During her early years she and her siblings became orphaned when her mother died, and her education suffered. The family was raised by neighbors in order to keep them together and then by their father's mother Fannie Mae Johnson Mayo. Her father died, and her grandmother became ill and could not care for the family. There was no room for Margaret when her siblings were placed with a relative. But early in school she realized that a good education was the way to success, and she thrived even though she had to work as a maid during high school to support herself. Margaret worked for the Simon A. Cook family as a maid and babysitter so they virtually adopted her. This family together with her high school teachers encouraged Mayo to think about college and made the college trips with her to talk to college officials. She enrolled in the Tuskegee Institute (later Tuskegee University) because it was of a historical black college that encouraged black students and because the Cooks had friends on the faculty. She supported herself at Tuskegee with the aid of a small scholarship, working odd jobs, and help from her friends including the Cooks. It was at Tuskegee that she decided to major in chemistry, a decision that shaped her future career path.

Mayo expanded her knowledge of chemistry by working on undergraduate research projects with Professor C. J. Smith and L. R. Koons at Tuskegee.

During the summers she conducted undergraduate research at Central State College in North Carolina and at Argonne National Labs. She graduated from Tuskegee in 1967 and enrolled in Wayne State University in Detroit, Michigan. She received an M.S. in Chemistry in 1968 and returned to Tuskegee as a professional technician in the laboratory, conducting research on the undergraduate research project that she had previously started. Mayo, during her undergraduate and graduate career, became interested in improving the science education of minorities; because of this and her excellent academic record, she was recruited into a doctoral program by Brown University and received a scholarship from the Southern Fellowship Fund to finance her doctorial studies. At Brown she worked with Professor John N. Fain on research to determine the biochemical reactions that take place in the liver, the topic of her Ph.D. dissertation that she completed in 1974. She continued this research later in Brussels, Belgium, at the International Institute of Cellular and Molecular Pathology. She also worked as a visiting professor at Brown which resulted in two major research reports on the biochemistry of the liver.

Mayo married and divorced twice and had one son. She married her first husband Lawson Boila Johnson of Monrovia, Liberia (West Africa), in 1969 and divorced him in 1972. They had one son in 1969. She married her second husband Dr. Henry Hudson Tolbert of Chicago, Illinois, in 1972 and they divorced in 1978. Her only child Lawson Kwia Tolbert was adopted by her second husband.

Mayo had two other academic positions before becoming the first female director of the Carver Research Foundation and associate provost for Tuskegee University. She was able during her eight years as director to place the foundation on a sound financial basis and to build a communications network to allow several institutions to work collaboratively on research projects and write grants proposals that were more likely to be funded with institutions of higher learning in West Africa and with three of the U.S. national laboratories.

Mayo accepted a sabbatical position in corporate planning with the British Petroleum Corporation, where she became the highest-ranking African American female. She was a member of the team that brought about the merger of British Petroleum and Standard Oil. It was while there that she started working in her spare time on science education programs for science museums. The National Science

Foundation (NSF) recruited her for a three-year term as program director for the Research Improvement in Minority Institutions program because of her demonstrated skill in science administration, and she became the first female to serve in such a capacity at the NSF. Mayo's other accomplishments included being the first African American female to become the director of the division of educational programs at Argonne National Laboratory and the first African American to serve as special assistant to the vice chairs of the presidential committee on education and technology of the federal coordinating council for science, engineering, and technology.

Mayo began her third career, in government, in 1996 when she became the director of New Brunswick Laboratory (NBL), in Argonne, Illinois. As director of NBL, she used her knowledge of analytical chemistry, her management skills, and her interpersonal skills to direct her staff, most of whom were chemists. Her responsibilities included a role in the overall thrust of the United States in global nuclear nonproliferation and domestic nuclear security.

In 2002 she decided to call on her expertise in educational outreach, especially for minorities, and accepted a full-time job with the NSF. She also provided leadership to the congressionally mandated Committee on Equal Opportunity in Science and Engineering as the executive secretary and NSF executive liaison to the committee. As the spokesperson for the NSF, she was the person who was instrumental in helping to change the way science was taught to underrepresented groups. She was thereby instrumental in helping to increase the numbers of minorities and women who chose science or science education as a profession.

FURTHER READING

Kessler, J. H., et al. *Distinguished African American Scientists of the Twentieth Century* (1996).

Warren, Wini. *Black Women Scientists in the United States* (1999).

JEANNETTE ELIZABETH BROWN

Tolliver, William (1951–1 Sept. 2000), painter and mixed-media artist, was born William Mack Tolliver in Vicksburg, Mississippi. He was the second oldest of fourteen children in an impoverished family of cotton pickers. Tolliver demonstrated an early interest in art. In first grade, he copied pictures from the newspaper comic strips. By the time he reached the third grade, he was copying elaborate illustrations of Old Testament narratives found

in a family Bible. Tolliver's father bragged about his son's drawing ability, but never actively encouraged it. In contrast, Tolliver's mother enjoyed drawing; and even after a tiring workday, she encouraged her children's creativity and curiosity. She held drawing contests with William and his older brother, and she introduced William to art books available at the public library. It is estimated that Tolliver read more than four thousand books, mostly on art, during his youth.

Tolliver never attended a formal art class, but he studied Old Master paintings, modernist art, photographs, books, and comic books. He learned anatomy and proportion by copying figure studies from books and by persuading family members to pose for him. As he matured, he researched art materials, media, and techniques. Tolliver appreciated Vincent van Gogh's mastery of color and light and his ability to convey emotion in his art. Tolliver also admired the Dutch artist's indifference to making money from the sale of his art. Seeing Picasso reproductions in books, Tolliver noticed that his own style was similar to that of the revered Spanish artist: "I knew my lines were like Picasso's but it wasn't until later I knew why."

In 1965 Tolliver dropped out of school in the ninth grade to help his mother support his younger siblings. He left Mississippi for Los Angeles, and lied about his age so he could join the Job Corps. There he studied carpentry and illustrated the program's newspaper. Tolliver was befriended by a Job Corps instructor and fellow painter who helped him with technique. Still, Tolliver could not afford basic art supplies. He purchased paint-by-number sets and painted pictures according to the provided instructions. In this way, he learned color theory and the basic rules of mixing paint.

After leaving the Job Corps, Tolliver moved to Milwaukee intending to find a job as a carpenter. In the meantime, the sixteen-year-old was a studio assistant for a sculptor and continued painting. Milwaukee was a turning point for Tolliver; it was there that he began meeting other artists who inspired him to place a higher value on his own art. Tolliver observed that "back home in Mississippi, while all of my friends were out partying, I was painting all through the night. I painted on pasteboard— and I didn't know about canvas back then, and wouldn't learn about it till I was twenty and walked into my first art supply store. I was in another world, imagining what it would be like to be van Gogh" (Preston, *Art Gallery International* Feb.–Mar. 1986). From Milwaukee, he moved to Chicago and after a brief stay he returned to Vicksburg and got a job as a carpenter. While working as a full-time carpenter, Tolliver continued to paint on nights and weekends.

In 1977 Tolliver married Vicksburg native Debrah Cattlin. In 1981 he relocated his family to Lafayette, Louisiana, believing he could make more money there because of the oil boom. He worked as a housepainter and paperhanger for two years in Lafayette. Things were going well for Tolliver and his family until 1983 when the oil boom abruptly ended, and he suddenly found himself out of work. With no job and no income, Tolliver and his family relied on unemployment benefits. While looking for work, he continued to paint as a way of staying positive in his difficult financial situation.

Tolliver had been painting most of his life and never viewed his art as a way of making money. He never attempted to sell his paintings because he could not imagine anyone buying art from a person with no formal education. He usually gave away his paintings to anyone who wanted them. However, in this critical financial period, his wife contacted the local art association in order to sell some of Tolliver's work. Two Tolliver paintings ended up at a museum known as the Art Center for Southwest Louisiana. There, Cattlin met Ms. Francis Love, the Art Center curator, who immediately recognized Tolliver's considerable talent. She purchased one of his paintings as soon as it was offered to her.

Love made it clear that she was interested in acquiring more of Tolliver's work, but she wanted to meet the artist first. Because of his shyness and lack of confidence in his ability and background, Tolliver at first ignored her request, but eventually they met. The meeting went well, and he was comfortable once they started talking about art. Love wanted Tolliver to take some paintings to Bob Crutchfield, owner of the Live Oak Gallery, immediately. Eight months later, Tolliver was still unemployed and his unemployment benefits had run out. He finally brought eight paintings to Crutchfield, who took all eight pieces and sold them within the week. Tolliver soon became an artistic and commercial success and was represented exclusively by the Live Oak Gallery for three years.

Though Tolliver had been a painter for most of his life, he came into his own as an artist and art entrepreneur in the 1980s. By this time, Tolliver was uncomfortable with the arrangement of galleries wanting long-term contracts with artists and a 50 to 60 percent commission. In the late 1980s Tolliver opened his own gallery in Lafayette. As the gallery owner and resident artist, he kept all the profits. In 1991 Tolliver and his family moved to Georgia and opened the first African American fine art gallery in Atlanta's Buckhead community.

Tolliver was a versatile artist who had an almost photographic ability to recall the past. Much of his art was influenced by the memories from his Mississippi childhood and all the dignified, hard-working people he had known. Figure studies, abstracts, portraits, landscapes, semi-abstracts, and human interest stories were all a part of his artistic repertoire. Tolliver was a prolific artist. In the first two years after he was discovered, more than four hundred of his oil paintings, pastels, watercolors, and woodcuts were sold. He worked eighteen-hour days every day of the week—an unrelenting schedule that he kept up for many years. When his wife and business manager died in 1999, it was a great loss to him. Grief, poor health, and the physical and emotional toll of his grueling work schedule all contributed to Tolliver's untimely death on 1 September 2000 at the age of forty-nine in Atlanta.

FURTHER READING

Lamar, Hal. "William Tolliver Self-Taught Painter," *Atlanta Tribune* (Aug. 2004).

Preston, Sandy. "William Tolliver," *Art Gallery International* (Feb.–Mar. 1986).

PAULETTE COLEMAN

Tolson, Melvin Beaunorus (6 Feb. 1900–29 Aug. 1966), poet, teacher, and essayist, was born in Moberly, Missouri, the son of Alonzo Tolson, an itinerant Methodist minister, and Lera Ann Hurt, a seamstress. Some sources list his year of birth as 1898. Although his father's occupation required frequent moves to various towns in Missouri, Iowa, and Kansas, young Tolson's childhood was a happy one, relatively unscathed by the various forms of racial prejudice that many African Americans faced during the early twentieth century. After a brief stint at Fisk University following his graduation from high school in 1918, Tolson enrolled in 1919 at Lincoln University in Pennsylvania, where he earned a bachelor of arts degree in Journalism and Theology in 1923. In 1922 he married Ruth Southall, and together they raised four children. Tolson in 1931 entered a graduate program in comparative literature at Columbia University, though he was not overly concerned with the formal aspects of applying for the degree; it was not until 1940 that he was finally awarded the master of arts degree.

In 1923, fresh from college and only twenty-three years old, Tolson accepted a position as instructor of English and speech at a small African American college in Marshall, Texas, thus beginning a brilliant teaching career that he would maintain with dedication and energy for more than forty years. Tolson distinguished himself at Wiley College by coaching the debate team to a ten-year winning streak that included victories over champion teams from Oxford University and the University of Southern California. According to Robert M. Farnsworth, his experiences with the debate teams, which included circumventing the color line in racially divided towns throughout the South and the Midwest, often found their way into his creative and journalistic writings, particularly his columns written for the *Washington Tribune* during the 1930s and 1940s.

Tolson remained at Wiley until 1947, when he accepted a position as professor of English and drama at Langston University in the small African American town of Langston, Oklahoma. Although his years with the celebrated debate teams from Texas had passed, he soon established a solid reputation within the Langston community as a respected teacher and, in 1954, as the town's mayor, an office to which he was reelected three times. The capstone of Tolson's teaching career came in 1965, the year he had planned to retire from Langston University. At sixty-five years of age he accepted the Avalon Chair in Humanities at Tuskegee Institute, an appointment arranged by a former student of Tolson's who now chaired the English department at Tuskegee.

While his long teaching career provided stability and a consistent income for Tolson's family, it was as a poet that Tolson made a significant contribution to American literature and history. Tolson had tinkered with poetry and painting as a child and had experimented with several literary genres in his early years at Wiley College, but his professional career as a poet began in earnest in the early 1930s with his work on a lengthy manuscript, "A Gallery of Harlem Portraits." Tolson was strongly influenced by Harlem Renaissance poets, including LANGSTON HUGHES, COUNTÉE CULLEN, and CLAUDE MCKAY, whose writings he had studied extensively while writing his master's thesis at Columbia. "A Gallery of Harlem Portraits" represents an early example of Tolson's conviction that the distinct cultural expressions of the African American community, particularly the blues, jazz, and gospel forms, provide a wealth of material from which the black poet can draw for inspiration.

Although his first book-length manuscript was praised in a 1938 *Current History* column by fellow writer V. F. Calverton, who lauded Tolson for "trying to do for the Negro what Edgar Lee Masters did for the middlewest white folk over two decades ago," "A Gallery of Harlem Portraits" was rejected by publishers (Farnsworth, 58). Determined to continue writing, however, Tolson gained national recognition with "Dark Symphony," a poem that blends a profound historical consciousness of the African American struggle against adversity with a defiant message aimed at oppressors throughout the world. "Dark Symphony" won first place in a national poetry contest in 1940 and was published in the *Atlantic Monthly* in 1941. Shortly after these initial successes, *Rendezvous with America*, another book-length collection of poems, was accepted by Dodd, Mead and Company. Published in 1944, *Rendezvous* reflected the complexity of the American experience in the context of World War II. While many of the poems allude to the ironies inherent in a racially divided nation that was fighting a war to rid the world of racial supremacy, the book as a whole is also a celebration of America's diversity: "America? / An international river with a legion of tributaries! / A magnificent cosmorama with myriad patterns and colors!" (*Rendezvous*, 5). Tolson's book elicited enthusiastic reviews and nearly unqualified praise from prominent African American writers such as RICHARD WRIGHT, who opined that "Tolson's poetic lines and images sing, affirm, reject, predict, and judge experience in America…. All history, from Genesis to Munich, is his domain" (Farnsworth, 95). Following the success of *Rendezvous*, in 1947 Tolson was named "poet laureate of Liberia" at a ceremony in Washington, D.C., and shortly thereafter began work on a poem to celebrate the Liberian centennial. The result was *Libretto for the Republic of Liberia* (1953), a book-length ode that revealed Tolson's broad knowledge of modernist poetry and world history. Although *Libretto* garnered some strong reviews and elicited comparisons with the works of modernists such as Ezra Pound and T. S. Eliot, it was *Harlem Gallery: Book I: The Curator*, released by Twayne Publishers in 1965, that marked the pinnacle of Tolson's poetic career. Tolson envisioned *Harlem Gallery* as a multivolume epic exploring the full experience of African Americans throughout history, but his goal was never realized; he died a year later at a hospital in Dallas, Texas. Nevertheless, the first volume of *Harlem Gallery*, with its innovative use of language and its synthesis of modernist poetics and African American musical forms, ensured Tolson a place among the highest ranks of American literary masters. In the words of one reviewer, "The book is 'Gibraltarian' in content and apogean in scope.... He has taken the language of America and the idiom of the world to fashion a heroic declaration of, about and for Negroes in America" (Farnsworth, 277).

In 2007, Academy Award-winning actor DENZEL WASHINGTON portrayed Tolson in the movie, *The Great Debaters*, thus bringing Tolson's remarkable story to a far broader audience than ever before.

FURTHER READING

Tolson's papers are in the Library of Congress.

Berube, Michael. *Marginal Forces/Cultural Centers: Tolson, Pynchon, and the Politics of the Canon* (1992).

Farnsworth, Robert M. *Melvin B. Tolson, 1898–1966: Plain Talk and Poetic Prophecy* (1984).

Farnsworth, Robert, ed. *Caviar and Cabbage: Selected Columns by Melvin B. Tolson from the Washington Tribune, 1937–1944* (1982).

Farnsworth, Robert, ed. *A Gallery of Harlem Portraits* (1979).

Werner, Craig Hansen. *Playing the Changes: From Afro-Modernism to the Jazz Impulse* (1994).

Obituary: *New York Times*, 30 Aug. 1966.

This entry is taken from the *American National Biography* and is published here with the permission of the American Council of Learned Societies.

CHRISTOPHER C. DE SANTIS

Tolton, Augustus (Apr. 1854–9 July 1897), Catholic priest, was born in Ralls County, Missouri, the son of Peter Paul Tolton and Martha Jane Chisley, both of whom were slaves. Augustus was born on Stephen Elliott's plantation in northeastern Missouri and was baptized at St. Peter's Catholic Church at Brush Creek, near Hannibal, Missouri, on 29 May 1854. In 1861, when he was seven years of age, his father escaped slavery and went to St. Louis, where he died. In 1863, in the midst of the Civil War, his mother also escaped plantation slave life, taking Augustus and three siblings across the Mississippi River to Quincy, Illinois, a city in a free state that had drawn numerous refugee slaves. In Quincy his mother enrolled him in a Catholic school where he received some elementary education. He felt drawn to the priesthood and was privately tutored from 1873 to 1878 in Latin, Greek, and German by various priests at St. Boniface Church in Quincy. Thereafter he attended the Franciscan Quincy College from

1878 to 1880. Because no Catholic seminary in the United States would educate him, he was sent to the Urban College in Rome, Italy, in 1880 to obtain his studies for the priesthood.

After ordination in 1886, just two years after JAMES AUGUSTINE HEALY became the first African American to be ordained a Catholic priest (in Paris), Tolton returned to the United States, celebrating masses before large Catholic congregations in Hoboken, New Jersey, St. Benedict the Moor in New York, and St. Boniface in Quincy, Illinois. Although he was enthusiastically welcomed as one of the first African American Catholic diocesan priests by black, Irish, and German Catholics in Quincy and throughout the country, he began to experience resistance from a few white clergy as soon as he became pastor, in 1886, of St. Joseph's Church, a Quincy parish composed primarily of African American Catholics. Because many whites came to his services, a few white clergy became angry and jealous of his success. During these years in Quincy, from 1886 to 1889, Tolton came to fear for his safety and gradually became discouraged because of the lack of support he received from priests and his own bishop, James Ryan. He also felt the loneliness of being one of the only African American priests in the country, particularly at a time when the priestly fraternity was a strong source of personal identity and support for the Catholic clergy. He asked to be transferred to another diocese and in 1889 was installed in the diocese of Chicago.

In Chicago he became pastor of St. Augustine's congregation, a small African American parish that held services in the basement of St. Mary's Church. From 1889 to 1893 he solicited funds and helped to build St. Monica's Church as the parish for African American Catholics. During this period, too, he participated in the first African American Catholic congresses held in Washington, D.C., Baltimore, Maryland, and Chicago, national conventions of lay and clerical African American Catholic leaders who were developing a national consciousness of solidarity within American Catholicism. Under the leadership of DANIEL RUDD, the editor of the first African American Catholic newspaper, the *American Catholic Tribune*, published in Springfield, Ohio, various participants in the congresses also articulated their grievances about their treatment in the church and in society in general. Tolton was not one of the protesters. His speech at the first congress in 1889 focused on the need for Catholic education and vocations to the priesthood among African American Catholics. After the first congress, Tolton returned to Chicago, continued his pastoral work, raised money for his parish building projects, and lectured in various parishes and cities across the country. Because of the demands on his time and his generally poor health, Tolton resigned as pastor of his parish in 1894. He died in Chicago of a stroke.

Tolton was an effective church leader who carried the responsibility of representing African American Catholics in the clerical leadership at a time when the weight of that responsibility was heavy. Some in the Catholic community thought that he was not aggressive enough in representing the grievances and causes of African Americans in the church, and others thought that he was too effective in attracting Catholics to parishes where he preached. As one of the first fully African American diocesan priests, he carried a burden of representing race in a predominantly white immigrant church, and his priesthood was judged not simply by the standards of common human strength and frailty, but by criteria that demanded more of him because of his race.

FURTHER READING

Davis, Cyprian. *The History of Black Catholics in the United States* (1990).

Foley, Albert S. *God's Men of Color: The Colored Catholic Priests of the United States, 1854–1954* (1955, 1969).

Hemesath, Caroline. *From Slave to Priest: A Biography of the Rev. Augustine Tolton (1854–1897), First Afro-American Priest of the United States* (1973).

Ochs, Stephen. *Desegregating the Altar* (1990).

This entry is taken from the *American National Biography* and is published here with the permission of the American Council of Learned Societies.

PATRICK W. CAREY

Tomlin, Mike (15 March 1972–), professional football coach, was born in Newport News, Virginia, the youngest of two sons born to Ed Tomlin and Julia Pettaway. Ed was himself a professional footballer (he played for the Baltimore Colts and in the Canadian Football League). He left the family when Mike was less than a year old, and Julia moved in with her parents, working in the city's shipyards to make ends meet. Eventually they were again able to afford a place of their own. They relocated to the Denbigh neighborhood, which is where Tomlin attended schools. When he was six, his mother married a postal worker named Leslie Copeland. Copeland was a former baseball player,

and he encouraged Tomlin's interest in athletics. It was an uncle, however, who signed him up for his first youth football league. Tomlin was hooked. He saw football as his way out of his hometown and a way to win bigger and better things for his life. He graduated from Denbigh High and matriculated at the College of William and Mary in 1990.

From 1991 to 1994 Tomlin was a starting wide receiver for the W&M Tribe football team. His career was impressive. He ended his tenure with 101 receptions and a striking 2,046 yards. He set William and Mary gridiron records for his 20.2 yards per catch average and for his twenty touchdown grabs. In 1994 he was named a first-team All-Yankee Conference selection. He graduated with a bachelor's in Sociology in 1995. A year later, he married Kiya Winston, whom he had met in college. The two went on to have two sons and a daughter.

After his time at William and Mary, Tomlin was hired by the Virginia Military Institute as

Mike Tomlin, coach of the Pittsburgh Steelers, surveys the Baltimore Ravens during the first half of an NFL football game on 14 December 2008 in Baltimore. (AP Images.)

wide-receivers coach. He remained there only for 1995 before bouncing from position to position over the next several seasons. He served as a defensive and special teams assistant at the University of Memphis in 1996. The years 1997 and 1998 saw him at Arkansas State University as a position coach. A year later, he was hired as a defensive backs coach at the University of Cincinnati. He remained there until 2000.

Tomlin at last came to the attention of the National Football League (NFL) in 2001, when he was hired as a position coach by the Tampa Bay Buccaneers. As the leader of a tough-minded group of pro-bowl backs (Ronde Barber and John Lynch among them), Tomlin began to build his résumé as a defensive coach to reckon with. It was also during his time with the Bucs that Tomlin learned the Tampa 2 defense (in a nutshell: a simple, speedy defensive alignment with four men at the line of scrimmage, three linebackers, two cornerbacks, and a pair of safeties. The Tampa 2 relies on the athleticism and situational adaptability of its players to a greater-than-normal degree). Long one of the worst teams in the NFL, the Bucs began to turn their game around with a crushing defense and defensive take-aways. When the team went to and won Super Bowl XXXVII (2005) against the Oakland Raiders, the Bucs defense returned a trio of interceptions for touchdowns.

In 2006 Tomlin took a step up in the ranks of coaches when he was hired away from Tampa Bay by the Minnesota Vikings and given the position of defensive coordinator. Often in the NFL, defensive coordinator is the step before head coach, but for Tomlin the gap was unusually short. He remained in Minnesota only one season. That off-season, a pair of head coaching spots came open—one in Miami and another in Pittsburgh—and Tomlin interviewed for them both. The Miami Dolphins was a franchise that had fallen on hard times and seemed to be trapped in an endless rebuilding effort. The Pittsburgh Steelers, however, were and remained one of the NFL's most successful and storied franchises. Their outgoing head coach, Bill Cower, was the longest-tenured head coach in the NFL at fifteen seasons, and the Steelers had recently won a world championship victory in Super Bowl XL. In the end, Tomlin won the Steelers job and was thrust onto the national stage as the leader of one of professional sports' most legendary teams. He was just thirty-four years old.

Tomlin was certainly helped by the fact that his age was not a disqualifier for the Pittsburgh franchise, which had a history of taking chances on young, relatively untested coaches. Moreover, the team's owner, Dan Rooney, was the founder of the NFL's so-called Rooney Rule, which obligated NFL teams to interview minority candidates for coaching and front-office positions, where they were historically underrepresented relative to the number of African Americans on the field of play. Tomlin was just the tenth black head coach in the history of the NFL. He was also just the third person hired to coach the Steelers since the 1969 season, an impressive fact in a professional sports league where the average coaching tenure is said to be between three and a half and four seasons (depending on the source).

Tomlin was taking over a football team that seemed always to right itself following disappointing seasons. Its defense was legendary, and at the moment of Tomlin's appearance seemed to be working at a level of very high performance. Tomlin had already established himself as an ego-free pragmatist, and here he showed those characteristics again. Rather than firing the existing coaches and installing his own, he made the somewhat unusual step of keeping the coaching staff mostly intact. The move paid off. Tomlin's inaugural season, 2007, saw the Steelers post a 10–6 regular season record and win the NFL's AFC North division to make the playoffs. Notably, Tomlin's Steelers continued to dominate on the defensive side of the football, finishing 2007 as the top-ranked overall unit.

The following season, 2008, saw the Steelers continue as before. The team again boasted the league's top-ranked defense and finished the regular season with an impressive 12–4 record, again winning the North. The Steelers met their division rival, the Baltimore Ravens, in the AFC title game and won 23–14 on the strength of four defensive takeaways. The win earned the Steelers their second Super Bowl appearance in four seasons, making them the franchise with the second-most championship appearances (7), behind the Dallas Cowboys (8).

On 1 February 2009 the Steelers met the underdog Arizona Cardinals in Super Bowl XLIII. The Steelers forced three turnovers, but the Cardinals played hard and kept the game close. Only in the end did a Pittsburgh quarterback sack (and forced fumble) on a Hail Mary pass from Arizona's Kurt Warner seal the victory for Pittsburgh. With that win, Tomlin became the youngest head coach in the history of the league to win a world championship. He was also the only Steelers head coach to win a national title in so short a time.

Tomlin continued to excel. His winning percentage put him firmly among the elite in NFL coaching history and his personal style—collected, calm, undemonstrative—made him a favorite among both fans and players. When the Steelers franchise was hit with controversy—as happened surrounding allegations of sexual assault against the Steelers' quarterback Ben Roethlisberger (and a resulting suspension in 2010)—Tomlin managed to guide his team through difficult times. The 2009 season saw the Steelers finish a respectable but quiet 9–7. The following season, however, they were back in the playoff hunt. They again finished 12–4 and won the AFC North Division. The Steelers defense was dominant. They finished second overall in yards allowed but first in sacks and points allowed. In the playoffs, they beat the rival Baltimore Ravens and the New York Jets, earning yet another Super Bowl appearance. Tomlin became the youngest head coach at thirty-eight to win two NFL conference titles.

Super Bowl XLV was held in Dallas, Texas, on 6 February 2011. The Steelers faced off against the surging Green Bay Packers in what became not only the most-watched Super Bowl in league history but also the most-watched program in American television history. A championship game boasting two such storied and long-lived sports franchises drew in some 111 million viewers (the number beat the viewership of Super Bowl XLIV). The game lived up to expectations, but in the end the Steelers fell short, losing 31–25 on the strength of Green Bay quarterback Aaron Rodgers' MVP performance under center.

Despite the difficulty of that defeat, and the continuing controversy surrounding his franchise quarterback, it seems certain that Tomlin will be ranked among the NFL coaching elite for the foreseeable future.

FURTHER READING

Finder, Chuck. "Mike Tomlin: A Man of His Word." *Pittsburgh Post-Gazette*, 22 July 2007.

Maccambridge, *Michael. America's Game: The Epic Story of How Pro Football Captured a Nation* (2004).

JASON PHILIP MILLER

Toomer, Jean (26 Dec. 1894–30 Mar. 1967), writer and philosopher, was born Nathan Pinchback Toomer in Washington, D.C., the only child of Nathan Toomer, a planter from North Carolina, and Nina Pinchback, the daughter of the Reconstruction-era senator P. B. S. PINCHBACK. Pinchback was biracial, and he could easily have passed for white. In fact, his sister urged him to do just that when she wrote, "I have nothing to do with negroes am *not* one of them. Take my advice *dear* brother and do the same" (Kerman and Eldridge, 19). Toomer's grandfather ignored that advice, went on to become, briefly, acting governor of Louisiana, and was elected to both the U.S. House of Representatives and the U.S. Senate, though he was denied entrance to both houses.

Toomer once said that it would be "libelous for anyone to refer to me as a colored man" (Rayford Logan, *Dictionary of American Negro Biography* [1982], 598), and he felt betrayed when ALAIN LOCKE included some of his writings in *The New Negro* (1925), a book showcasing emerging black artists of the Harlem Renaissance. Unraveling the paradox of his life and work goes to the heart of the problem of race in America: Who is black, what is black culture, and who has the power to make these decisions?

Abandoned by her husband in 1895, Nina took her son to live with her parents in their stately home in Washington, D.C. Pinchback did not want his grandson to keep either the name Nathan or the name Toomer because they belonged to his delinquent father; the family began calling him Eugene instead, after another relative. As an adult, Toomer chose the form Jean. He grew up in a neighborhood where most of the children were white, and he did not think of himself as being different until he was about nine years old, when he entered the Garnet School for colored children. Then, for the first time in his life, the pall of race separated him from those he thought were his natural associates. He did not apply himself or excel academically, though he maintained a sense of entitlement and superiority over his peers. In 1906 Nina married Archibald Combes, an insurance salesman, and the family moved to New York, where they lived in predominantly white neighborhoods in Brooklyn and then in New Rochelle. However, when Toomer's mother died three years later, he returned to Washington to live with his grandparents, who had moved to a more modest residence in an integrated section of town. In 1910 Toomer enrolled at the M Street High School, which he described as "an aristocracy—such as never existed before and perhaps never will exist again in America—mid-way between the white and negro worlds. For the first time I lived in a colored world" (Kerman and Eldridge, 47).

Toomer saw himself as a person who could travel freely in the black world, comprehend its meaning, and imbibe its melancholy beauty, but he never claimed that world as his own, and he resisted every attempt at being claimed by it. In fact, at every juncture at which he was given the chance to indicate his racial identity (on college applications, marriage licenses, and so on), he chose to identify himself as white. This was not merely a subconscious motivation; Toomer was quite aware of his chameleon-like ability to straddle the color line. He remarked that "viewed from the world of race distinctions, I take the color of whatever group I at the time am sojourning in" (Kerman and Eldridge, 96).

Toomer's early adult years were devoid of focus. Between 1914 and 1917 he enrolled at the University of Wisconsin, Massachusetts College of Agriculture, American College of Physical Training in Chicago, University of Chicago, New York University, and City College of New York. He attempted to join the military but was rejected because of poor eyesight. For a brief time he studied privately to become a musician. Between each fleeting ambition, Toomer worked a variety of jobs: drugstore clerk, assistant librarian, fitter in a New Jersey shipyard, and car salesman. Financially, Toomer relied on his grandfather's largesse and, later, on the generosity of various women in his life.

Although he did not thrive in formal academic settings, Toomer was a voracious reader. He delved into works on Eastern religion and politics and the writings of Walt Whitman, George Bernard Shaw, and Robert Frost. While living in Greenwich Village in 1918, Toomer began writing poetry and short stories in earnest. Waldo Frank, a close friend and mentor, nurtured his literary aspirations and encouraged him to refine his talent. Destitute and desperate to make a success of writing, Toomer returned to Washington, secluded himself in a room rented by his grandfather, and devoted himself to his new craft.

An auspicious break came in the fall of 1921, when Toomer learned from one of his grandfather's visitors that the all-black Sparta Agricultural and Industrial Institute in Georgia was in need of a temporary principal. Toomer secured the position and moved to the South, where he took in the sight of blacks toiling in the soil, the sound of spirituals sung in black churches, and the drama of black life in the segregated South. This experience was artistically stimulating for Toomer; it contrasted sharply with his limited encounters with the Negro elite in Washington, and it supplied the inspiration and much of the content for his literary masterpiece.

Cane (1923) is a montage of self-contained vignettes interspersed with poetry. Each of its elements could stand alone (and several were published separately), but they fit together to form a harmonious testament to a segment of black life in the twilight between slavery and freedom. Toomer's female characters, in particular, are imbued with an aesthetic beauty and pathos that makes each of their stories compelling. This slim volume had a monumental impact, opening up new avenues of expression for Negro artists trying to find an authentic voice. It demonstrated that black folk culture could be rendered in powerful prose of a sort not often found in polemical novels and with an integrity that was lacking in the "happy darky" caricatures popular at the time. Similarly, its mosaic structure encouraged greater experimentation with form and presentation. LANGSTON HUGHES and ZORA NEALE HURSTON were so moved by *Cane* that they drove to Sparta as if they might find there a wellspring of creativity. Yet Toomer had written this gem and walked away. A gold rush followed, as other artists eagerly mined the black experience, which until then had not been fully appreciated as a fruitful source for serious works of literature, music, and art.

When *Cane* appeared in 1923 to moderate reviews and sales among the white reading public but to enthusiastic praise in Negro publications, such as the *Crisis* and *Opportunity*, Toomer realized that a place was being set for him at the table of black writers, whereas he had hoped to be accepted as a writer without reference to race. Toomer was disappointed that Waldo Frank, whom he had asked to write the book's introduction, referred to him as a "Negro," and Toomer bluntly refused to assist his publisher in any marketing strategy that featured him as a premier black talent. However, his choice of subject matter emphasized the very connection to blackness that he had hoped to avoid. Despite the prodding of those who yearned for more works like *Cane*, Toomer devoted the next four decades to writing material that explored universal rather than racial topics. For the rest of his life, he threw himself into a world of mystics, spiritualists, and new age thinkers.

Toomer's spiritual journey ranged from Jungian psychology to Scientology. He consulted psychics, journeyed to India in search of enlightenment, and became a noted Quaker. Toomer was most captivated with the teachings of the Russian philosopher George Ivanovich Gurdjieff, who developed a system of beliefs and exercises by which one could achieve a higher consciousness he called "Unitism." In 1924 Toomer became an acolyte of this movement; he met the guru in New York and by 1929 had made several trips to France to study at Gurdjieff's Institute for Man's Harmonious Development. Back in the United States, Toomer became a teacher of Gurdjieffian metaphysics. In Harlem he attempted to recruit members of the black intelligentsia, such as AARON DOUGLAS, NELLA LARSEN, and ARNA BONTEMPS. While speaking at a Gurdjieff gathering in Chicago, Toomer met Margery Latimer, a wealthy white writer. The two were married in 1931. Margery died within the year while giving birth to Toomer's only child, Margery.

In addition to *Cane*, Toomer wrote three unpublished novels: "The Gallowerps" (1927), "Transatlantic" (1929), and "Caromb" (1932). None of these books features black protagonists, and they were all rejected by the publishers to whom they were sent. *Essentials* (1931), a collection of aphorisms, was privately printed. In 1934 Toomer married Marjorie Content, a photographer and the daughter of an affluent Wall Street executive. They settled in Doylestown County, Pennsylvania, where Toomer continued to write essays and fiction that embodied his philosophy. The closest Toomer ever came to writing about racial issues after *Cane* was in a discursive poem called "Blue Meridian," which appeared in *The New American Caravan* (1936). This poem articulates a fantastic vision of the amalgamation of different races into a new order of being represented by the "blue" man. Toomer's play *Balo* appeared in Alain Locke's *Plays of Negro Life* (1929), and some of his early essays and short stories were featured in *Dial*, the *Crisis, Broom*, and the *Little Review*.

After a series of geriatric illnesses, Toomer died in 1967 in a nursing home in Bucks County, Pennsylvania, at the age of seventy-seven and in virtual obscurity. In 1969 *Cane* was reissued and has become an indispensable work in the African American literary canon. ALICE WALKER wrote in her review of *The Wayward and the Seeking* (1982), a collection of Toomer's previously unpublished work, that "*Cane* was for Toomer a double 'swan song.' He meant it to memorialize a culture he thought was dying, whose folk spirit he considered beautiful, but he was also saying goodbye to the 'Negro' he felt dying in himself. *Cane* then is a parting gift, and no less precious because of that. I think Jean Toomer would want us to keep its beauty, but let him go" (*New York Times Book Review*, 13 July 1980).

FURTHER READING

The main body of Toomer's papers is located at the Beinecke Rare Book and Manuscript Library, Yale University, New Haven, Connecticut.

Jones, Robert B., ed. *Critical Essays on Jean Toomer* (1994).

Kerman, Cynthia, and Richard Eldridge. *The Lives of Jean Toomer: A Hunger for Wholeness* (1987).

McKay, Nellie Y. *Jean Toomer, Artist: A Study of His Literary Life and Work, 1894–1936* (1984).

Turner, Darwin T., ed. *The Wayward and the Seeking: A Collection of Writings by Jean Toomer* (1982).

SHOLOMO B. LEVY

Toote, Gloria E. A. (8 Nov. 1931–), lawyer, activist, and businesswoman, was born in New York City to Frederick A. Toote, a bishop in the African Orthodox Church, and Lillian Tooks. Lillian Tooks had been born in Macon, Georgia, and her family moved to Philadelphia, Pennsylvania, immediately after her birth. Frederick Toote, descended from a Bahamian family, was heavily involved in the activities of his Harlem community and had become a major player in MARCUS GARVEY's African Orthodox Church, which was hugely popular at the time, and in the "Back to Africa" movement. Lillian was a homemaker until her children (Gloria's younger sister, Frances, rounded out the household) were older, and she became an information officer for a New York City municipal department.

Toote was a gifted child whose intelligence seemed boundless. The post-Depression years in New York were quite harsh for most working class families. While the Toote family never went hungry, Gloria recalled the many times that, because of her parents' generosity to those even less fortunate, she and her sister had to go without. In one case, Bishop Toote had taken money intended to buy new penny loafers for Gloria and given the money to a young boy who, he felt, needed new shoes more than did his daughter.

After elementary school Toote attended Harriet Beecher Stowe Junior High School (later the Thurgood Marshall Academy) on St. Nicholas Avenue. In the 1940s there were only two high schools for black students in New York, and the Tootes believed the schools were inferior to the more numerous white schools. Gloria had expressed her desire to study medicine, so finding a proper preparatory environment was essential. School assignments were made strictly according to residence; thus, in order to get Gloria into a white high school, Lillian Toote got together with some friends and pretended that Gloria lived in a building nearer the school she would ultimately attend—George Washington High School, which was virtually all white. Henry Kissinger and HARRY BELAFONTE were among the school's alumni.

It was Toote's first exposure to white people and a terribly traumatic experience for her. There were the expected instances of outright hostility to her presence and the lack of encouragement from some teachers. But she persevered; she served in the cadets of the Civil Air Patrol and eventually rose to be the New York City commandant of cadets. She graduated from George Washington in 1949 and had planned to attend City College of New York to study for a medical career, but because her science training had been poor, she decided to major in advertising. Her father opposed her plan, however, and with the help of family friend ADAM CLAYTON POWELL JR., secured for his daughter a place at Howard University. She was one of the youngest students there but soon made friends with other students like herself—young, bright, and inclined to activism—including ANDREW YOUNG, Clarence Pendleton, and TONI MORRISON.

As a freshman, the brash young woman threw herself into college life. She wrote for the Howard *Hilltop*, the campus newspaper, and eventually had her own column, called "Toote's Tally." For spending money she worked the telephone switchboard, without her father's knowledge, and became even more well known on campus. She joined the Howard Players, the popular and internationally traveled drama troupe. When her drama coach lovingly referred to her as a "diamond in the rough," Toote took it as an affront. She then set about learning and performing every task, from acting to directing to staging, and to producing the group's plays herself.

With a schedule of activity that would seem a burden to any student, Toote was approached about becoming a law student, even though she had not yet finished at Howard. So, without getting an undergraduate degree, she enrolled in Howard's law school, where, in her first year, the faculty met and decided to kick her out. The environment was highly discriminatory toward women, and Toote was still quite young, but with the aid of an older student who taught her how to study, she began to receive straight A's. To pay for her education, she did research (discrimination kept her from arguing in moot-court competitions) and ended up working for CHARLES HAMILTON HOUSTON and THURGOOD MARSHALL as they prepared to argue

Brown v. Board of Education. As Howard School of Law's youngest student ever, she received her J.D. degree in 1954 at the age of twenty-three.

She began practicing law in New York in 1955 and took a job in the private sector with the prestigious law firm of Greenbaum, Wolff, and Ernst. After earning an LLM degree from Columbia in 1956, she went to work—partly as a test case for discrimination—at *Time* magazine, where she was on the national affairs staff.

During the 1960s she founded or was chief executive officer for several corporations, including her own Toote Town Publishing and Toote Music Recording. She wrote a syndicated newspaper column for the *Amsterdam News* and served as general counsel for the Coordinating Council of Negro Performers, where, in reaction to the television industry's discriminatory hiring policies, she helped organize the first national boycott of the industry by blacks. In 1971 she was appointed assistant director of ACTION, a volunteer service agency that included the Peace Corps. In 1972 she received a Steuben glass star from President Richard Nixon for excellence in public service, and in 1973 she was confirmed by the U.S. Senate to be assistant secretary of Housing and Urban Development. She resigned in 1975 after a dispute that she insisted put her in the position of making the fair housing laws a bad bargain for the poor. When California governor Ronald Reagan sought the GOP nomination for president, Toote seconded his nomination and so became one of the Republican National Committee's Surrogate Program's most popular and requested speakers. In 1983 President Reagan appointed Toote as vice chairman of the President's Advisory Council on Private Sector Initiatives, and the following year she was a member of the U.S. delegation to the United Nations Preparatory Body for the World Conference on the Status of Women, held in Vienna.

Toote was instrumental in getting black charities included in the payroll checkoffs for federal employees and was responsible for getting the first federal government contracts for the National Council of Negro Women and the National Bar Association. She was a founding member or a member of Executive Women in Government, the Republican Women Federal Forum, Citizens for the Republic, the New York City Council of Black Republicans, the National United Black Fund, the National Political Congress of Black Women (later the National Congress of Black Women), and the NYNEX consumer advisory council.

In the 1990s Toote became an active member of the Board of Overseers at the Hoover Institute, a conservative think tank at Stanford University. That experience, along with the many problems attendant with being vocal, a woman, and a black Republican, led to her disillusionment with many of the programs that she once held dear. She retired in 2003.

FURTHER READING

Anderson, Bernard E., et al. *The Fairmont Papers: Black Alternatives Conference, San Francisco, December 1980* (1981).

Meisling, Richard J. "The New Black Conservatives," *New York Times Sunday Magazine*, 4 Oct. 1981.

Sleet, Moneta, Jr. *Special Moments in African American History, 1955–1996* (1998).

Smith, J. Clay, Jr., ed. *Rebels in Law: Voices in History of Black Women Lawyers* (1998).

LUTHER BROWN JR.

Torriente, Cristobal (1895–1938), baseball player, was born in Cuba. Nothing is known about his family or childhood. Torriente joined the Cuban army at age seventeen and was assigned to an army baseball team in Havana. His baseball talent soon came to the attention of the promoter Tinti Molina, who signed the young man to play in the United States for the Cuban Stars against black and semi-professional teams.

When Torriente, who had black, tightly curled hair and a slightly dark complexion, came to the United States in 1913, he experienced the limited opportunities and daily indignities forced upon African Americans living in a racially segregated society. American baseball mirrored the rapid expansion of legal and de facto segregation that occurred in American more generally in the 1880s and 1890s. The color line in baseball was drawn in 1884 when MOSES FLEETWOOD WALKER became the last African American to don a major league uniform until JACKIE ROBINSON joined the Brooklyn Dodgers in 1947.

Racial segregation made it more difficult for black players to earn a livelihood than their white counterparts. Most games were played on the road and scheduled on short notice against local semi-professional black or white teams. It was not unusual for players to play two games in a day against different teams and in different locations. The baseball fields were rudimentary and usually without locker rooms. Since black ballplayers were not allowed to stay in white-owned hotels, blacks typically found a black-owned boardinghouse, stayed with a black family, or slept outside. Meals were often taken out through the back doors of restaurants because blacks were not allowed to be seated in white eateries. It was not unusual for teams to fold during the season. Profits were slim to none, so payrolls were kept to a minimum with small rosters, which meant that men often played even when they were injured and pitchers were expected to field another position when not on the mound. Low salaries meant that black ballplayers had either to play in winter leagues in Latin America or California or to hold off-season jobs.

The final indignity heaped upon black baseball players was scant records of their games, which denied them recognition by their contemporaries and succeeding generations. Press coverage was limited because of the racism of white-owned newspapers and the games' haphazard schedule. Baseball is celebrated mainly through statistics, and the dearth of newspaper coverage meant that many games, even when they were mentioned in the press, did not include box scores. The careers of black ballplayers during the segregation era lack the historical record of their white counterparts, so trying to analyze a specific player's career is difficult.

Following Torriente's first season with the Cuban Stars in the segregated world of black baseball, he returned to his homeland to play in the Cuban Winter League. During his rookie year with the Havana Reds he played the outfield and accumulated a modest .265 batting average. Torriente stood five feet nine inches tall and weighed a husky hundred and ninety pounds. His massive torso combined with strong arms and powerful wrists, which he adorned with bracelets, equipped this left-handed hitter to drive baseballs off and over outfield fences. Torriente was predominantly a pull hitter and also was a notorious bad-ball hitter with power to all fields. The speed of Torriente's slender legs enabled him to reach first base on bunt hits. He led the league in triples five times and in stolen bases three times. Center field was Torriente's primary defensive position. There his speed enabled him to cover considerable territory, and his powerful, accurate left arm kept base runners in check. On other occasions he played left field, right field, first base, third base, and pitcher.

Torriente continued to tour the United States with the Cuban Stars until 1918, with stints on the All Nations team in 1913 and 1916–1917. There is no statistical record for his years of playing unorganized baseball in America, but he established himself as a superstar in the Cuban Winter League, hitting .300 or more in ten of twelve years and hitting .350 or better in seven years. Torriente earned two batting titles and a career average of .351, the third highest ever among players in the Cuban Winter League.

During five seasons in Cuba, Torriente's teams faced touring teams of white major leaguers. In twenty-eight of these games he batted ninety times and accumulated a .311 batting average. In an especially memorable game on 4 November 1920 his Almendares Blues team faced off against manager John McGraw's New York Giants, which had signed Babe Ruth for the Cuban tour. In five trips to the plate Torriente hit three home runs off the pitcher George Kelley and a double off Ruth, who had been a star pitcher before converting to the outfield, ending the day with six runs batted in. Both Ruth and Torriente were born in 1895 and were left-handed sluggers with powerful upper bodies and slender legs. After this prodigious display of power Torriente became known as the Babe Ruth of Cuba.

Torriente's excellent defense made him a fixture in the Chicago American Giants center field from 1919 to 1925, moving OSCAR CHARLESTON, considered one of the finest center fielders ever in the Negro Leagues, to left field. The American Giants won championships in 1920, 1921, and 1922, with Torriente hitting .411, .338, and .342, respectively. Torriente won the batting title in 1923 with a .412 average and batted over .300 in nine of his eleven seasons in the Negro Leagues, finishing his career in the Negro Leagues with the Kansas City Monarchs in 1926 and the Detroit Stars in 1927–1928.

Age and alcoholism eroded his playing, which led Torriente to drift among black teams below the level of the Negro Leagues from 1929 to 1934. He died in New York City in 1938. His body was returned to his homeland where he was inducted into the Cuban Baseball Hall of Fame in 1939. Frank Frisch, a white hall of famer, claimed that Torriente was so good that "I'd like to whitewash him and bring him up" (Holway, *Blackball Stars*, 125). The baseball historian and statistician Bill James ranked Torriente as the best Negro League player for 1923 and tied for best with the hall of famer Oscar Charleston for 1917 through 1919. In a list that includes all the baseball players who ever played in the United States, James ranked Torriente sixty-seventh between Shoeless Joe Jackson and Hank Greenberg. The Society for American Baseball Research ranked Torriente twentieth on the list of the all-time best Negro League players.

FURTHER READING

Bjarkman, Peter C. *Baseball with a Latin Beat: A History of the Latin American Game* (1994).

Holway, John B. *Blackball Stars: Negro League Pioneers* (1988).

Holway, John B. *Black Diamonds: Life in the Negro Leagues from the Men Who Lived It* (1989).

James, Bill. *The New Bill James Historical Baseball Abstract* (2001).

McNeil, William F. *Baseball's Other All-Stars: The Greatest Players from the Negro Leagues, the Japanese Leagues, the Mexican League, and the Pre-1960 Winter Leagues in Cuba, Puerto Rico, and the Dominican Republic* (2000).

Rogosin, Donn. *Invisible Men: Life in Baseball's Negro Leagues* (1995).

PAUL A. FRISCH

Toussaint, Allen (14 Jan. 1938–), pianist, singer, songwriter, arranger, producer, community activist, and philanthropist, was born in "Gert Town" (also referenced as "Gehrke" and "Goit" Town), a small African American neighborhood enclave on the west side of New Orleans, Louisiana, to Naomi Neville. By age seven, Toussaint began to play the piano—an instrument perfectly suited for his future career as a composer and songwriter of different musical genres. His grandmother had purchased the piano for his sister, Joyce, so she could learn classical music. While his older brother Vincent played guitar, Toussaint took piano lessons from his sister. He also entered Xavier University's Junior School of Music for a short while. He combined his formal musical training with the ability to learn songs by ear, a skill acquired through listening to and learning songs on the radio. During his preteen years, Toussaint was exposed to and influenced by a range of musical styles, from country music to the blues of ALBERT AMMONS, Lloyd Glenn, and RAY CHARLES. He was especially fond of the distinctive New Orleans *junco* blues performed by his primary musical influences, PROFESSOR LONGHAIR and Tuts Washington.

At thirteen years of age, Toussaint began a professional career as a pianist in a three-piece house band at the Dew Drop Inn, a principal venue on the 1950s New Orleans club scene. Around this time, Toussaint and Little Snooks Eaglin formed the Flamingos, a band that covered hits by Charles, FATS DOMINO, the Midnighters, and Professor Longhair. In 1955, after a brief stint of performing with Earl King, Toussaint began touring with the commercially successful Shirley and Lee.

By 1957 DAVE BARTHOLOMEW, the noted New Orleans musician/producer/songwriter and scout for Imperial Records, was employing Toussaint as a session pianist on Fats Domino and Smiley Lewis recordings. Toussaint soon became a successful freelance musician, hiring out his talents to producers like Johnny Vincent, Joe Ruffino, and Bartholomew. During this period, he also demonstrated his acumen as a musical arranger. Al Silvers, president of Herald/Ember Records, encouraged him to take over the production of a floundering Lee Allen recording session. Toussaint organized the musicians and created four new songs, including what was to become Allen's immensely popular hit, "Walkin' with Mr. Lee."

In 1958 Toussaint took on full responsibilities for composing, arranging, and producing music for Danny Kesler and Murray Sporn. Ten instrumentals were recorded in two days and were then purchased by RCA, which then released the songs in a collection entitled *The Wild Sounds of New Orleans* by Al Tousan (a respelling of his name for commercial purposes). In 1959 John Banashak and Larry McKinley formed Minit Records as a subsidiary of Lew Chudd's Imperial label. By 1960 Toussaint had joined Minit to supervise recording sessions and write songs, many of which became popular R&B classics of the decade, including the following: "It's Raining" for IRMA THOMAS ("The Queen of the Blues"), "Fortune Teller" and "Lipstick Traces (on a Cigarette)" for Benny Spellman, "Mother-in-Law" for Ernie K-Doe (a song almost discarded by the critical Toussaint), "Ooh Poo Pah Doo" for Jessie Hill, and "Ya Ya" for Lee Dorsey.

Between 1960 and 1963 Toussaint became New Orleans' preeminent musical arranger and songwriter, occasionally crediting the hits he wrote to his mother. In 1963 Al Hirt popularized "Java," a Toussaint instrumental from the *Wild Sounds of New Orleans*, while Toussaint himself began a two-year stint in the U.S. Army. He was discharged in 1965, the same year Herb Albert popularized Toussaint's instrumental "Whipped Cream" (later the theme song for a popular television program, the *Dating Game*). Toussaint would soon partner with Marshall Sehorn to create Sansu Enterprises. His new recording and production company recorded artists such as Dorsey, Lou Johnson, Betty Harris, and Earl King. Toussaint wrote a number of the songs that Sansu's recording artists popularized: "Everything I Do Gonh Be Funky (from Now On)," "Get Out of My Life Woman," "Ride Your Pony," and "Working in a Coalmine." One of

Toussaint's most successful decisions involved hiring a band in 1966 that he would name the Meters (later they would become the Funky Meters), to become Sansu's house band. The Meters added a solid, original rhythmic sound to the studio and its recording sessions.

In addition to his managing responsibilities at Sansu, Toussaint continued to compose his own music throughout the 1970s, releasing *Toussaint* (on the Scepter label) in 1971, *Life, Love and Faith* (1972), *Southern Nights* (1975), and *Motion* (1978). During this period, Toussaint and Sehorn opened Sea-Saint Studio and recorded Dr. John and Labelle, artists who would come to define the "new" New Orleans sound. From the 1970s through the early years of the twenty-first century, countless R&B, country, and rock musicians and singers relied on Toussaint's arrangements, songwriting, and musical accompaniment, including the following luminaries: Chet Atkins, Joe Cocker, Elvis Costello, Devo, Glenn Campbell, Grateful Dead, ETTA JAMES, Jefferson Airplane, the Judds, Chaka Khan, ALBERT KING, Ramsey Lewis, Little Feat, the Oak Ridge Boys, Robert Palmer, the Pointer Sisters, Bonnie Raitt, OTIS REDDING, Boz Scaggs, Paul Simon, and Three Dog Night. Toussaint also engaged in Broadway and Off-Broadway musical theater productions, performing and aiding in the musical direction of *Staggerlee* (1986), composing lyrics and music for *William Christopher* (1991), and performing and contributing to the musical direction of *High Rollers Social Aid and Pleasure Club* (1991). In an effort to record and preserve the New Orleans musical sound, in 1996 Toussaint cofounded NYNO (New York, New Orleans) with Joshua Feigenbaum and recorded *Connected*, his first solo album since the 1970s.

Toussaint was recognized for his fundamental contributions to Louisiana and New Orleans culture, receiving the Louisiana Lifetime Achievement Award and the Big Easy Award for Entertainer of the Year. His influence on American music also garnered him further accolades. In 1998 the Rock and Roll Hall of Fame inducted him into its nonperformer pantheon, and the U.S. Postal Service placed his image on a commemorative envelope. Along with Aaron Neville, Toussaint formed New Orleans Artists Against Hunger and Homelessness to provide relief for the city's needy, following the devastation of Hurricane Katrina in 2005. Subsequently, Toussaint divided his time between performances in New York and New Orleans.

FURTHER READING

Berry, Jason, Jonathon Foose, and Tad Jones. *Up from the Cradle of Jazz: New Orleans Music Since World War II* (1986).

Fensterstock, Alison. "On Top of the Charts: Allen Toussaint is as sharp and prolific as ever," *Gambit Weekly*, 1 May 2007.

DISCOGRAPHY

The Allen Toussaint Collection (1991).
The Complete Warner Bros. Recordings (2005).
Connected (1996).
Finger Poppin' & Stompin' Feet (2002).
From a Whisper to a Scream (1995).
I Believe to My Soul (2005).
Life, Love and Faith (1972).
Motion (1978).
A New Orleans Christmas (1997).
The River in Reverse, with Elvis Costello (2006).
Southern Nights (1975).
A Taste of New Orleans (1999).
Toussaint (1971).
The Wild Sound of New Orleans (1958).
The Wild Sound of New Orleans: The Complete 'Tousan' Sessions (1994).

SEAN ELIAS

Toussaint, Pierre (1766–30 June 1853), hairdresser, businessman, and philanthropist, was born a slave in the French colony of Saint Domingue (later Haiti). The names of his parents are unknown. Little is known of his early life except that, like his mother and maternal grandmother, he spent his youth as a house slave on a plantation in the Artibonite Valley near the port of Saint Marc. In the library of the plantation owner, Pierre Bérard, young Toussaint discovered the works of classical French preachers such as Bossuet and Massillon. Apparently it was from his reading of these sermons, rather than from any contact with the notoriously corrupt local clergy, that Toussaint developed his deep devotion to the Catholic faith. The main source for information on Toussaint's life is his autobiography, *Memoir of Pierre Toussaint, Born a Slave in Saint Domingo*, which was published anonymously by Hannah Lee Sawyer, a contemporary admirer, in 1854 following his death.

In 1787, as political conditions on the island deteriorated, Jean-Jacques Bérard, who had inherited his father's estate, left Saint Domingue for New York, accompanied by his wife, Pierre Toussaint, and four other slaves. The following year Bérard died suddenly in Saint Domingue on a fruitless visit to recover his property. His death left his widow, Marie Elizabeth Bérard, penniless in New York City. However, Toussaint supported her as well as himself from his earnings as a hairdresser, one of the few occupations that were open to African Americans. Shortly before her death, on 2 July 1807, she and her second husband formally emancipated Toussaint in a ceremony at the French consulate in New York City.

Thereafter Toussaint established a lucrative business as a hairdresser for upper-class women. His customers included the Hamiltons, Schuylers, and Livingstons, the cream of New York society. "As a hairdresser for ladies he was unrivalled," wrote one prominent socialite, Hannah Lee Sawyer. "He was the fashionable coiffeur of the day." Thanks to his income from this occupation, as well as a frugal lifestyle and wise investments, Toussaint prospered and was able to buy his own house at 144 Franklin Street. In 1811 he purchased the freedom of his sister Rosalie as well as that of another refugee from Saint Domingue, Mary Rose Juliette, whom he married in St. Peter's Church on 5 August 1811.

Although Toussaint's occupation as a hairdresser was financially rewarding, it was physically demanding. He regularly spent sixteen hours each day traveling throughout the city to the homes of his wealthy customers. The most convenient form of transportation would have been the extensive network of horse-cars, but African Americans were barred from using them, one example of the widespread racial discrimination that he had to endure in antebellum New York. Moreover, as an African American in the largely Irish Catholic community, and as a Haitian Catholic in the largely Protestant black community, Toussaint belonged to a minuscule minority within each of these minority groups and was thus doubly disadvantaged. Culturally he remained a Frenchman throughout his life, using French in his prayers, correspondence, and reading of Scripture.

Within the Catholic community, even during his lifetime, Toussaint enjoyed the reputation of an exceptionally devout and charitable person. Every day he attended the 6:00 A.M. Mass in St. Peter's Church, where he was a pewholder for many years. He was also a benefactor of the Church of St. Vincent de Paul, New York's first French Catholic church, established in 1840. Perhaps his favorite charity was St. Patrick's Orphan Asylum, an institution that he often visited. Although his marriage was childless, Toussaint and his wife made it a practice to take into their home destitute black children and to care for them until they were able to fend for themselves.

Toussaint played no role in the abolitionist movement, which is not surprising in view of the anti-Catholic sentiments of many abolitionists. Although he was one of the few African Americans in New York City who could meet the property qualifications to vote, there is no indication that he ever cast a ballot. He was essentially a private peace-loving person who eschewed any political activity that might lead to violence, a legacy of his own personal experience of revolution in Saint Domingue. When someone asked him why he was not an abolitionist, he replied: "They have not seen blood flow as I have." Rather, he sought to bring relief to blacks and whites alike through personal charitable efforts and generous financial contributions. He died in New York City, and a funeral Mass was celebrated for him in St. Peter's Church. The pastor, Father William Quinn, eulogized him as a faithful parishioner for sixty-six years "who always had wise counsel for the rich [and] words of encouragement for the poor."

In 1990 Cardinal John O'Connor of New York introduced in Rome the cause of Pierre Toussaint's canonization. In 1997 the Holy See declared him "Venerable," the first step in the lengthy process of securing official church recognition of him as a saint. His body was placed in the crypt beneath St. Patrick's Cathedral.

FURTHER READING

Toussaint's papers are in the Manuscript Division of the New York Public Library.

Toussaint, Pierre. *Memoir of Pierre Toussaint, Born a Slave in Saint Domingo* (1854; repr. 1992).

Jones, Arthur. *Pierre Toussaint: A Biography* (2003).

Sheehan, Arthur, and Elizabeth Sheehan. *Pierre Toussaint: A Citizen of Old New York* (1955).

Tarry, Ellen. *The Other Toussaint: A Modern Biography of Pierre Toussaint: A Post-Revolutionary Black* (1981).

Tarry, Ellen. *Pierre Toussaint: Apostle of Old New York* (1998).

This entry is taken from the *American National Biography* and is published here with the permission of the American Council of Learned Societies.

THOMAS J. SHELLEY

Towns, Edolphus (21 July 1934–), educator, activist, ordained Baptist minister, and U.S. Congressman, was born in Chadburn, North Carolina, son of Versie B. Towns, a homemaker, and Dolphus Towns, a sharecropper. Towns had one brother, James, who passed away in 1984.

Towns's youth was spent in North Carolina, where he witnessed the continuing challenges faced by African Americans in the rural South. Wanting more for her son, Towns's mother encouraged his interest in education. In 1952 Towns graduated from West Side High School in Chadburn. He went on to attend North Carolina Agricultural and Technical State University in Greensboro, North Carolina, where he graduated in 1956 with a Bachelor in Sociology degree.

After college Towns enlisted in the U.S. Army. In 1958, after being discharged from the military, Towns moved to New York City and began a teaching career in the city public schools, Fordham University, and Medgar Evers College. Towns also pursued a career in hospital administration at Beth Israel Medical Center in New York. In 1960 Towns married Gwendolyn Forbes. They had two children, Darryl, a New York State Assembly member, and Deidra.

During the 1960s, with the backdrop of the civil rights movement, Towns began preaching. He was licensed by the United Holiness denomination. Although he did not have a church of his own, he was very active and emerged as one of a growing cadre of black ministers moving between the pulpit and politics.

Towns was a recognized community activist and became heavily involved in local politics. In 1972 he won election as the Democratic State committee man for the New York Fortieth Assembly District in Brooklyn. In 1976 Towns earned a Master's degree in Social Work from Adelphi University and was appointed Brooklyn Bureau President, the first African American to serve in that post.

In 1982 Towns sought election to the newly districted Eleventh District. The district, composed of areas in the eastern and northern parts of Brooklyn, was majority African American and Hispanic. After winning the primary with 50 percent of the vote, Towns went on to win the general election with 84 percent of the vote.

By 1987 Towns was one of five ordained ministers among the twenty-three black house members of Congress: Rep. WILLIAM GRAY of Philadelphia, Pennsylvania; Rep. WALTER FAUNTROY of Washington, D.C.; Rep. FLOYD FLAKE of Queens, New York; and Rep. JOHN LEWIS of Atlanta, Georgia. The ministers represented the growing influence of black congregations exercising political will and representing the legacy of the civil rights movement.

In Congress, Towns served on the Oversight and Government Reform Committee, the Public Works and Transportation Committee, the Human Resources and Intergovernmental Affairs Committee, and the House Select Committee on Narcotic Abuse and Control. In 1989 Towns joined the Energy and Commerce Committee. In 1997 Towns left the Works and Transportation Committee.

In 1991 Towns began serving as the chair of the Congressional Black Caucus (CBC). His participation in the CBC led Towns to champion many causes that affected black communities. In 1992, in the wake of the Los Angeles riots, Towns emerged as the voice of black congressional members and decried the verdict acquitting the white officers accused of beating motorist RODNEY KING as unjust.

As a result of the 1990 Census, Towns's Eleventh District faced redistricting that would lower the number of African Americans, but increase the number of Hispanics represented. The Census also reduced the number of seats New York had in Congress, and Towns's district was renamed the Tenth. Towns would win the Democratic primary and go on to win the general election by more than 85 percent of the vote.

In 1997 Towns was criticized for supporting Republican Rudy Giuliani for mayor of New York. Giuliani was viewed negatively by many African Americans and Hispanics in New York. Activist AL SHARPTON questioned Towns's ability to represent minority interests and considered launching an election challenge. Sharpton did not challenge Towns; however, local Democratic party leaders did support Towns's primary challenger, Barry Ford. Towns won the primary with more than 50 percent of the vote and would go on to win re-election by 85 percent or more of the general election vote.

In 2000 Towns supported Hillary Clinton in her New York senatorial campaign. Clinton was viewed as an outsider to New York politics, but had developed strong relationships in the black community. Her husband, Former President Bill Clinton, opened offices in New York City and had strong ties to Towns and other New York politicians.

In the aftermath of 11 September 2001, Towns became a vocal advocate for securing aid for New York and his Brooklyn community. Towns supported President George W. Bush in authorizing the military invasion of Afghanistan in 2001, but was a vocal opponent of the Iraq War, voting against the Authorization for Use of Military Force against Iraq Resolution of 2002.

In 2008 Towns's support of Hillary Clinton in the Democratic primaries was viewed as controversial. Clinton was running against Senator BARACK OBAMA of Illinois, a black candidate with significantly high popularity among African American voters. Towns and a number of other black politicians were placed in a difficult spot of supporting Clinton, a candidate with whom they had strong relationships (and whose husband enjoyed strong support among black politicians), or a newer politician with whom they were less familiar, but who was highly popular among their constituencies. Towns's decision to support Clinton was met with the criticism that he was out of touch with the will of his constituents. A September 2008 *New York Times* article cited that his support of Clinton, while his district supported Obama, led a large constituency of voters to express their dissatisfaction with him and fueled the campaign of challenger Kevin Powell. With Clinton's loss in the primary, Towns shifted his support to Obama in the general election, but questions remained about his suitability to represent the will of the district.

In 2009 Towns became chairman of the House Oversight and Government Reform Committee. From this position, he had the jurisdiction to investigate any federal program and any issue that has federal policy implications—a broad mandate that allowed him to address a wide range of issues including health care, consumer protection, public education, business development, and government reform. Towns easily won re-election in 2010, even as the Democratic Party lost control of the House. Although Towns had expected to be the ranking member on the House Oversight Committee, Democratic leader Nancy Pelosi and the White House maneuvered to replace Towns from that position, in the belief that he was not aggressive enough to face the new Republican chair of the Committee, Californian Representative Darrell Issa. In the 112th Congress, Towns served as the ranking member on the Oversight Committee's Subcommittee on Government Organization, Efficiency and Financial Management.

FURTHER READING
Booker, Simeon, "Black Ministers: A New Force in U.S. Politics", *Jet*, 2 Feb. 1987, Vol. 71, No. 19, pp. 14–16.
"Edolphus Towns," *Black Americans in Congress, 1870–1907* (2008).

"Towns, Edolphus," *Biographical Directory of the U.S. Congress, 1774–Present.*

MICHAELJULIUS IDANI

Townsend, Arthur Melvin (26 Oct. 1875–20 Apr. 1959), a physician, minister, educator, university president, and business executive who had a distinguished career of service in many areas during his lifetime. Townsend was born in Winchester, Tennessee, to the Reverend Doc Anderson and Emma A. (Singleton) Townsend, both of whom were educators. The elder Townsend was not only a minister but also a principal and director of the Franklin County Negro Elementary Schools. Townsend's mother was a schoolteacher in Shelbyville, Tennessee. Townsend was reared in Winchester and received his formal education there; in 1891, however, he moved to Nashville, Tennessee, and enrolled at Roger Williams University. During his student days in Nashville, Townsend became active in church affairs: he served as organist in several Nashville churches, conducted Sunday school classes, and organized missions to hospitals and jails. Later, he joined the Spruce Street Baptist Church, where he met his future wife, Willa Ann Hadley, a Nashville native. Townsend's church and missionary activities later served as a launching pad for a productive career with the African American Baptist denomination.

In 1898 he earned his AB from Roger Williams University and graduated with honors as valedictorian of his class. He then enrolled in Meharry Medical College, where he completed his pathology and pharmacology studies in 1902, again graduating with honors. Townsend began his medical practice in Nashville and served on the Meharry faculty until 1913. He also served as president of the Robert F. Boyd Medical Society and the State Medical Association. In 1910 the *Journal of the National Medical Association* published his research on pellagra in two volumes. Ten years later, Townsend became the first alumnus of Meharry to serve on its board of trustees, a service he rendered for thirty-six years.

Although he had a successful medical practice, Townsend's interest in denominational causes increased and he became active in the Tennessee Baptist Missionary and Educational Convention. As secretary, he directed its financial campaigns and helped secure the convention's financial foundation. In 1913, five years after the reestablishment of Roger Williams University on Whites Creek Pike in Nashville, Townsend responded to the call of African American Baptists in Tennessee and accepted the presidency of this institution. Driven by his esprit de corps and a commitment to his alma mater, Townsend gave up his lucrative medical practice and devoted himself to the task of heading the university, which he did until 1918. During his tenure, Townsend worked closely with his wife, a Fisk University graduate (they married on 11 June 1902), who served as director of the Roger Williams Singers. Under her direction, the Singers (in the spirit of the Fisk Jubilee Singers) toured Tennessee and the nation to raise funds for the university. Through their efforts, three buildings were constructed on the campus.

While serving as president of Roger Williams University, Townsend accepted the call to the ministry. From 1917 to 1957 he periodically pastored Spruce Street Baptist Church and twice led the congregation in two major rebuilding programs. In 1918 he resigned from the presidency of Roger Williams University to become pastor of the Metropolitan Baptist Church in Memphis, Tennessee. This was a pastorate he held for two years before becoming secretary of the National Baptist Convention, USA, Inc., Sunday School Publishing Board. In 1920 he accepted the secretary position of the Sunday School Publishing Board in Indianapolis, Indiana, and after returning to Nashville, he went to work improving the quality of materials, publications, and services to the constituency of the Publishing Board. As they had done during their tenure at Roger Williams University, the Townsends worked together to improve their organization. Willa Townsend, a hymnologist, songwriter, and music director, served as the Board's music committee chairperson. She compiled and edited the *Gospel Pearls* and *Spirituals Triumphant* songbooks. One of her most successful publishing ventures was the *Baptist Standard Hymnal.*

Within a year after Townsend assumed leadership, the number of employees increased, as he had worked diligently to improve services to the Board's constituency. Housed in rented quarters, the Publishing Board needed new facilities and authorized Townsend to purchase or construct a new building. The officers of the National Baptist Convention were aware of Townsend's successful track record in the business and financial affairs of this denomination as well as other organizations. Townsend recruited people to traverse the country and raise funds from three hundred of the Convention's churches, associations, and individuals. The fund-raising efforts were a success, and the

Board purchased the Commercial Hotel on Fourth Avenue and Charlotte. In antebellum Nashville, slave traders had gathered at the hotel to discuss the buying and selling of slaves and other goods and merchandise. Negotiations for the purchase of the hotel were completed on 21 June 1921, and a little over a year later the building was demolished and Townsend hired the African American architectural firm of McKissack and McKissack to design a new structure. T. C. Windham, also an African American, constructed the building, which was completed in August 1925. In April of the following year, the structure was dedicated to and named in honor of DR. ELIAS CAMP MORRIS, who served as president of the National Convention from 1895 to 1922.

Under Townsend's leadership, the mortgage on the Morris Memorial Building was paid off in less than twenty years. As in other endeavors, Willa Townsend assisted her husband and used her talents to organize a $200,000 bond campaign to help pay off the debt. Townsend continued to lead the Sunday School Publishing Board of the National Baptist Convention, USA, Inc., until his death in 1959. Townsend's activities extended beyond his medical and denominational interests and included many other facets. He served as cashier of Nashville's second African American bank, the People's Bank and Trust Company, and was involved in the International Sunday School Association, the North American Committee for the World Council of Christian Education, the Free and Accepted Masons, the Knights of Pythias, and the International Order of Odd Fellows. A thirty-third-degree Mason, Townsend was active in the fraternal organizations in Nashville and Tennessee. As Endowment Treasurer of the Masonic Grand Lodge of Tennessee, he was instrumental in the establishment of the Masonic Home for the Aged.

Preceded in death by his wife Willa Hadley Townsend (1880–1947), Townsend died at the age of eighty-three while preparing to go to his office. Four days later, his funeral services were held at Spruce Street Baptist Church where he was remembered by Mayor Ben West for his contributions to Nashville. Dr. Harold D. West, president of Meharry Medical College, remembered him as a distinguished educator, physician, and trustee. Architect Calvin L. McKissack memorialized him as a businessman and builder, and Reverend Lewis H. Woolfolk and DR. NANNIE H. BURROUGHS, president of the Women's Auxiliary of the National Baptist Convention, USA, Inc., honored Townsend's denominational influence. Townsend was survived by his son, Dr. Arthur M. Townsend Jr. and his grandchildren, Arthur M. Townsend III, William Madison Townsend, and Beverly Banks.

FURTHER READING
Some information in this article was taken from the funeral programs of Mrs. Willa Ann Hadley Townsend (30 May 1947) and Dr. Arthur Melvin Townsend (29 Apr. 1959) and the Arthur Melvin Townsend Historical Marker File, Tennessee Historical Commission, Nashville, Tennessee.
"Dr. and Mrs. A. M. Townsend Observe 40th Wedding Anniversary, June 11—at Historic Spruce Street Baptist Church," *National Baptist Voice*, 1 July 1942.
Lovett, Bobby L., and Linda T. Wynn. *Profiles of African Americans in Tennessee History* (1996).
Wynn, Linda T. *Journey to Our Past: A Guide to Historical Markers in Tennessee* (1999).

LINDA T. WYNN

Townsend, Jonas Holland (c. 1820–c. 1872), abolitionist leader and journalist, sometimes listed as James H. Townsend and sometimes as J. Holland Townsend, was probably born in New York or Pennsylvania. Nothing is known of his youth or parentage, although by the early 1840s he had established himself in the black community in Albany, New York. He participated in black conventions in Buffalo and Rochester in 1843 and supported HENRY HIGHLAND GARNET's radical "Address to the Slaves," which called on enslaved African Americans to rebel against their owners. Between 1845 and 1848 Townsend attended Waterville College (later Colby College), but contrary to most accounts, he did not receive a degree.

He instead returned to New York, where in 1849 he began publication of the short-lived journal *Hyperion*, which FREDERICK DOUGLASS favorably reviewed in the 3 August 1849 *North Star*. A correspondent for *Frederick Douglass's Paper* described him during this period in a 31 August 1855 remembrance as "a tall, sedate, prim, puritanical, intellectual looking young man. We soon took the starch out of him … and transformed him from an embryo country person to a regular New York business man." One of the first issues contained Townsend's "Address to the Colored People of the United States," which Douglass reprinted in the 10 August 1849 *North Star*. The address asserted that the blacks "need to take a broader view of our connection in the human world" and should see themselves as part of a broader "Africo-American family … united by a common bond of fraternity and interest." Within the month, though, Douglass reported that *Hyperion* had folded.

Townsend left New York in November 1849 on the *Hampden* with a group of blacks (including Newport F. Henry, former porter for the Tappan Brothers) planning to mine for gold in California. Although he seems to have had a brief stint as a gold miner, Townsend settled in San Francisco by the early 1850s and became increasingly active in the black community there. Working with figures such as William H. Newby, MIFFLIN WISTAR GIBBS, and PETER ANDERSON, he aided in the fight for black testimony rights and education. He served as a leader in the State Colored Conventions of 1855, 1856, and 1857. He also wrote for *Frederick Douglass's Paper*, helped found and edit the San Francisco *Mirror of the Times*, and was an integral part of the San Francisco Athenaeum Association.

By 1858, however, Townsend had returned to New York, where he was a member of the New York Suffrage Association and continued to be active in the black convention movement. In 1859, he edited *Frederick Douglass's Paper* during Douglass's European tour and wrote three pieces for the fledgling *Anglo-African Magazine*: One of these was on racism and education (which discussed California in some depth), and there were also a pair of polemics, "Our Duty in Conflict" and "The Policy that We Should Pursue." The latter suggested that blacks should "inscribe … on our banners in characters of living light, 'better die than suffer our liberties to be taken away'" (October 1859, 325). In 1863, along with PASCHAL BEVERLY RANDOLPH and other delegates to a convention held in Poughkeepsie, he helped to draft the "Manifesto of the Colored Citizens of the State of New York," which emphasized the importance of tying the Civil War to the causes of freedom and black equality.

There is not much known about the end of Townsend's life. During the first years of Reconstruction, he reportedly worked for the New York Customs House. He moved to Texas around 1870 and was active in the Republican Party. Various sources place him in Brazoria, Galveston, and Waco; he may actually be the black teacher listed as "James Townsend" in the 1870 U.S. Census of Waco. Although both his public and personal life was shrouded in obscurity, Townsend nonetheless made his mark on both U.S. coasts as a writer and activist.

FURTHER READING

Lapp, Rudolph. *Blacks in Gold Rush California* (1977).
Ripley, C. Peter, et al., eds. *Black Abolitionist Papers* (1991).

ERIC GARDNER

Townsend, Robert (6 Feb. 1957–), actor, comedian, movie director, producer, and writer, was born into a family living on the west side of Chicago. His mother raised the family alone. Growing up as the second of four children, Townsend had his sights set on a professional baseball career, but he was also interested in acting from an early age. He was selected to join the Experimental Black Actors Guild at the age of sixteen. He attended Illinois University and Hunter College, part of the City University of New York. While going to school in New Jersey, he took acting lessons in New York City from the noted teacher Stella Adler and acted in the Negro Ensemble Theater. Townsend's stage debut was in a 1979 New York production of *Take It from the Top*, starring RUBY DEE and directed by

Robert Townsend, stand-up comedian and actor, in Los Angeles, 8 June 1987. (AP Images.)

OSSIE DAVIS. He also studied acting with Milton Katselas at the Beverly Hills Playhouse.

Townsend honed his comedy skills in standup work at the Improv in New York City and the X-Bag Theater in Chicago. His first movie experience was as an uncredited extra in *Cooley High*, released in 1975. Townsend's first credited movie appearances were in *Willie and Phil* (a remake of the French classic *Jules et Jim*), directed by Paul Mazursky in 1980, and *A Soldier's Story*, directed by Norman Jewison in 1984. At this time he also appeared on television, most notably in a minor role in an episode of the hit comedy series *M*A*S*H* in 1982. Townsend's comedy skills were used on television specials including *Rodney Dangerfield: It's Not Easy Bein' Me* and *Uptown Comedy Express*. He also had minor roles in the films *Streets of Fire* (1984) and *American Flyers* (1985). Townsend's directing and writing talents were first noticed with the release of his first feature film, the independently produced *Hollywood Shuffle* (1987). Townsend played the main character, Bobby Taylor, who is attempting to break into the movie industry as an actor but finds a hard road, owing to racial stereotyping. The comedy also starred co-writer KEENEN IVORY WAYANS. *Hollywood Shuffle*, which was financed entirely by Townsend, is a satire that challenges many of the stereotypes of black Americans presented by Hollywood film from its first inception through the "blaxploitation" era of the 1970s. The comedy was both critically and financially successful. That same year, Townsend directed EDDIE MURPHY in a standup comedy performance released as *Eddie Murphy Raw*. Other movies followed, including an uncredited appearance in *I'm Gonna Git You, Sucka*, a parody of blaxploitation directed by Wayans in 1988.

On 15 September 1990, Townsend married Cheri Jones. The couple would have three children before divorcing on 9 August 2001, citing irreconcilable differences.

Townsend bought the Hollywood Professional School (later Tinsel Townsend Studios) in 1990 and cast himself in *The Five Heartbeats*, a movie he wrote and directed in 1991 in which he plays a vocalist in an African American singing group. Townsend's vocal talents helped make the soundtrack to the film a bestseller, and he toured the United States with the singing group, the Dells. He later introduced the group when they were inducted into the Rock and Roll Hall of Fame in Cleveland. Two years later his increased Hollywood stature was evident; in his movie *The Meteor Man*, Townsend was able to cast veteran actors in a big budget movie. Comedians and actors BILL COSBY, Marla Gibbs, Robert Guillaume, JAMES EARL JONES, and Don Cheadle joined Townsend in a story about a man who acquires superhuman strength after being struck by a meteor. Townsend appeared as the character Robert Peterson in the television comedy titled *The Parent 'Hood* from 1995 to 1999. Some critics called this series *The Cosby Show* of the 1990s.

Townsend's talents were in demand, and he worked steadily during the late 1990s, directing the film *B.A.P.S.* in 1997, directing and acting with LOU GOSSETT JR. in the Showtime movie *Love Songs* (1999), and directing the Disney television movie *Up, Up, and Away!* (2000). Townsend also hosted the syndicated weekly *Motown Live* in 1998. His direction of *10,000 Black Men Named George*, a film exploring the union organizing of railroad porters and the life of A. PHILIP RANDOLPH, earned him an NAACP Image Award.

Black Listed, released in 2003, saw Townsend moving from comedy into drama. Influenced by a number of vigilante films released during the late 1990s and early 2000s, including JOHN SINGLETON's *Shaft* (2001), Townsend's film has as its main character a lawyer who compiles a list of clients that he has seen escape the hand of justice. He mails this list to a friend, only to find that the friend has decided to take the law into his own hands and kill the people listed in the letter. Rather than approach the topic using parody or satire, his previous approaches to film and television narrative, Townsend (who wrote, directed, and starred in the film) focused on the issues of social justice in a dramatic manner.

In 2004 the MBC Network named Townsend as its president. In his new role as media executive, he set as a goal the development of programming and entertainment that reflected African Americans and their lives positively, with a focus on family entertainment for the Black Family Channel. The 2005 season began with the *Black College Talent Hour*, *Gospel Soul Search*, and *Urban Kids Block*. These shows were written to stress the importance of education and problem solving, and featured the importance of practice in achievement in the arts. As part of the goals of the shows, Townsend launched a nationwide search to discover African American talent across the United States.

Townsend was honored with two Cable Ace Awards for his television work and several NAACP Image Awards for his comedy specials. His films were recognized as major influences on a new generation of African American filmmakers that emerged in the 1990s. The short-lived Fox channel variety series *Townsend Television* (1993) and WB's comedy *The Parent 'Hood* helped establish both new networks as viable competition for the major television networks. Townsend was a longtime supporter of the United Negro College Fund (UNCF), appearing regularly as a guest artist on the UNCF's national television fund-raiser *An Evening of Stars*, and as a regular speaker on behalf of the organization.

FURTHER READING

Alexander, George. *Why We Make Movies: Black Filmmakers Talk about the Magic of Cinema* (2003).

Diawara, Manthia. *Black American Cinema* (1993).

George, Nelson. *Post-Soul Nation: The Explosive, Contradictory, Triumphant, and Tragic 1980s as Experienced by African Americans (Previously Known as Blacks and before That Negroes)* (2004).

Rocchio, Vincent F. *Reel Racism: Confronting Hollywood's Construction of Afro-American Culture* (2000).

Watkins, S. Craig. *Representing: Hip Hop Culture and the Production of Black Cinema* (1999).

PAMELA LEE GRAY

Townsend, Willard Saxby, Jr. (4 Dec. 1895–3 Feb. 1957), labor leader, was born in Cincinnati, Ohio, the son of Willard Townsend, a contractor, and Cora Beatrice Townsend. (His parents had the same last name because they were cousins.) After graduating from the local high school in 1912, Townsend worked for two years as a redcap at the Cincinnati railroad station. He joined the army in 1916, served in France during World War I, and later helped to organize the Cincinnati company of the Ohio National Guard. He studied chiropody at the Illinois School of Chiropody, practiced briefly, and then moved to Canada. After two years in the University of Toronto's premedicine program he transferred to the Royal College of Science in Toronto, where he graduated in 1924 with a degree in chemistry. Meanwhile he supported himself working as a redcap and dining-car waiter on the Canadian National Railways.

After teaching in Texas for several years, Townsend moved to Chicago in 1929 and the following year married Consuelo Mann. They had one son. Some years after Townsend's death, the singer ALBERTA HUNTER said that she had been married briefly to Townsend (presumably before he married Consuelo Mann), but nothing more is known about that union.

The Depression hit blacks with particular ferocity, and in 1932 Townsend went back to working as a redcap. Men in this occupation (predominantly African Americans) were paid hardly any wages at all; they were expected to survive on customers' tips. Determined to improve matters, Townsend began to explore the possibility of forming a union. He faced tremendous odds because redcaps had so few other work options in a racially segregated job market and because blacks' experience with discrimination in unions had made them distrustful of organized labor. But Townsend had the advantage of working in Chicago, a transportation hub, and he could profit from the example of another pioneering black union, the Brotherhood of Sleeping Car Porters (BSCP). After organizing redcaps in five Chicago train stations, Townsend convened a meeting in 1936 to talk about forming an international union. Within the year the men founded the Labor Auxiliary of Redcaps, which was affiliated with the American Federation of Labor (AFL); it became the International Brotherhood of Red Caps in 1938. Townsend was elected as its first president, and after beating down an insurgency the following year, he held the office the rest of his life.

Like the sleeping-car porters before them, the redcaps faced intense opposition from white railroad workers, who sought to exclude them from bargaining rights by claiming that, since redcaps worked mainly for tips, they were independent contractors rather than railroad employees. Learning from the BSCP's example, Townsend persuaded the Interstate Commerce Commission to rule in 1938 that the redcaps were employees, which enabled him to negotiate contracts for better pay and better working conditions. Townsend also began organizing train porters and Pullman laundry workers, and in 1940 the union was renamed the United Transport Service Employees (UTSE). Meanwhile Townsend fought another battle to make the railroads obey the minimum wage rules of the 1938 Fair Labor Standards Act.

In 1942 the UTSE affiliated with the Congress of Industrial Organizations (CIO). Townsend joined the CIO's executive council and was made a vice president, thus becoming the first African American to hold office in the national labor movement. He joined the CIO's Committee to Abolish Racial Discrimination and the following year served as its secretary. He also threw himself into a successful battle to have his members classified as "essential workers" during the war, and he continuously resisted efforts by the Railway Clerks Union to absorb his union.

During his career Townsend experienced frequent conflicts with other black activists. He competed with A. PHILIP RANDOLPH's BSCP for members. In addition, many critics maintained that the Committee to Abolish Racial Discrimination made little progress under his leadership. Black autoworkers were enraged when he appeared before the 1949 United Automobile Workers convention to endorse President Walter Reuther's decision not to name a black vice president; Townsend argued that to do so would represent "racism in reverse."

Despite these controversies, Townsend was active and influential in African American public affairs, earning a Race Relations Leadership Award from the Arthur Schomburg Collection of the New York Public Library in 1942 and serving as an officer or trustee of organizations such as the National Association for the Advancement of Colored People, the Hampton Institute, the National Urban League, and the American Council on Race Relations. After the race riots in Detroit during World War II, Townsend stated, "This violence flows from basic economic ills," and he called for improved opportunities in voting, education, housing, and jobs for African Americans. He played a significant role in Chicago politics, and he consulted frequently on race relations with Chicago's Urban League.

Townsend was a director of the American Labor Education Service, he lectured on industrial relations at Seabury Western Theological Seminary in Evanston, Illinois, and he represented the CIO at many international conferences. In 1947 he served on a World Federation of Trade Unions committee that studied working conditions in Japan, China, Korea, the Philippines, and the Malayan states. He strongly opposed Communist influence in the labor movement. Also in 1947 he went so far as to undermine an organizing drive among North Carolina tobacco workers by bringing a weak union into the running and denouncing the competing (and much stronger) union as a Communist front; frightened by Townsend's allegations but unwilling to join the union that he supported, the workers voted to have no union at all.

Late in his life Townsend began studying law through correspondence courses and night school; he received an LLB from Blackstone Law School in 1951. Four years later, when the AFL and CIO were reunited, Townsend became a vice president of the new AFL-CIO. By this time his union had entered a period of decline, largely because of the railroad industry's own hard times. At the time of Townsend's death in 1957, the membership was three thousand—down from twelve thousand in 1944. Townsend died of stomach and kidney problems in Chicago, and some years later his union was absorbed by his old rival, the Railway Clerks Union.

Townsend often failed to act with the militancy that his critics thought necessary, yet many of his contemporaries saw him as a realist, working for what he believed was achievable in the context of his time. It is the tension between these two perspectives, as much as Townsend's actual accomplishments, that makes the story of his life an illuminating chapter in the history of African American labor.

FURTHER READING

Foner, Philip S. *Organized Labor and the Black Worker, 1619–1973* (1974).

Foner, Philip S., and Ronald L. Lewis, eds. *Black Workers: A Documentary History from Colonial Times to the Present* (1989).

Logan, Rayford, ed. *What the Negro Wants* (1944).

Obituaries: *American Federationist*, Mar. 1957; *AFL-CIO News*, 9 Feb. 1957; *New York Times*, 5 Feb. 1957.

This entry is taken from the *American National Biography* and is published here with the permission of the American Council of Learned Societies.

SANDRA OPDYCKE

Traylor, Bill (1 Apr. 1856–23 Oct. 1949), slave, sharecropper, and artist, was born in Benton, Alabama, on the plantation of George Hartwell Traylor, from whom Bill acquired his surname. His parents' names and occupations are not known, but they were likely slaves on the Traylor plantation. Although Traylor recalled 1854 as his date of birth (he could not read or write), the 1900 U.S. Census for Lowndes County recorded his actual birth date as two years later.

After the Civil War, nine-year-old Bill continued to live and work on the Traylor plantation, eventually becoming a sharecropper. George Hartwell Traylor died in 1881, leaving the plantation to his son, Marion. On 13 August 1891 Bill married a woman named Lorisa (some sources refer to her as Laura). At the time of the 1900 U.S. Census, Traylor had fathered nine children: Pauline (1884), George (1885), Sallie (1887), Nutie (1887), Rubin (1892), Easter (1893), Alline (1895), Lillie (1896), and a child born around 1900. He may have fathered a total of twenty or more children during his lifetime.

Bill and Marion were nearly the same age and were friends until Marion Traylor died in 1908. Bill remained on the plantation until the death of Marion Traylor's widow, Annie, in 1934. Members of the Traylor family believe that Bill stayed on the plantation specifically to care for his friend's widow.

It is unclear where Traylor went after leaving the plantation. By the time he left, his wife and children had moved north, the family members being spread out among various cities. Perhaps Traylor visited certain members of his family, but he decided to remain independent and live apart from them. By 1936 he had settled in Montgomery, Alabama, a city of over seventy-two thousand people. In Montgomery, he was only thirty-five miles from his hometown of Benton, a village of approximately seven hundred residents. Traylor found work on road gangs and in a shoe repair factory until rheumatism forced him to quit. He tried selling pencils, and he also received money from a federal welfare program. Traylor, who stood six-feet-four-inches tall with a full beard and two canes, became a fixture in Montgomery's black community. He befriended the owner of the Ross Clayton Funeral Home and was allowed to spend his nights sleeping on the backroom floor among the caskets.

He spent his days on Montgomery's Monroe Avenue, relatively alone and unable to work. However, at the age of eighty-three he began to draw. For his canvas he used pieces of irregularly shaped cardboard, usually from a shirt package or discarded display cards. Traylor began his drawings by using a straight edge to outline geometric forms. Then he would shape these forms with a pencil and add shading or color, rarely erasing. One of his first drawings depicted a tidy row of rats, cups, and shoes. As he continued to draw, Traylor showed great skill in balancing elements and manipulating shapes through relative size and placement. In another early piece, *Blacksmith Shop* (1939)—inspired by the blacksmith shop located behind the fence where he spent his days—Traylor arranged a row of tools and seven lively characters, two of whom are shoeing a horse while another pair of figures appears to be fighting over a jug. Images of farm animals, alcohol, and fighting appeared in nearly all of Traylor's drawings in a style that has been compared to African, Haitian, and Egyptian art, as well as Neolithic cave paintings. However, it is highly unlikely that Traylor had ever seen the styles of art that his paintings drew comparisons to.

In the spring of 1939 a young white artist named Charles Shannon and a group of like-minded culturally active youths from Montgomery's white, upper-middle class founded the New South Cultural Center in Montgomery, which served as a bookstore, library, studio, and gallery. Shannon was a Montgomery native and had received formal art training from the Cleveland Art School. On weekends, Shannon paid regular visits to Monroe Avenue, the black district of Montgomery's downtown area, with his sketchpad. That June, within weeks of Traylor's first drawings, Shannon encountered Traylor while the former slave and sharecropper was busily drawing. Shannon was intrigued by the old man, and the two became friends. Traylor had complained of being "alone and unable to work…" and felt "stalemated" (Shannon, 88). But he told Shannon that his discovery of pencil and cardboard had given him a new means of expression. Shannon remarked how "images from his long life welled up like pure water from a deep, hidden spring, and it continued to flow for three years" (Shannon, 88). Between 1939 and 1942 Traylor produced between twelve hundred and fifteen hundred drawings.

As Traylor drew, seated on a porch or on the sidewalk, an audience would gather around him. Sometimes friends from farms outside the city would visit on shopping trips—leaving their newly purchased bags of flour and jugs of kerosene with him while they went out drinking. Someone who stopped by to watch Traylor work taught him to sign his name, which appears in a looping scrawl on many of his drawings. Once a work was complete, he would hang it from a loop of string along a nearby fence, looking to attract an audience rather than entice buyers. Because he liked to draw scenes and people that he encountered on Monroe Avenue (good examples are *Man Bent at Waist with Bottle* or *Dog Attacking Man Smoking*, both produced around 1940 or 1942—Traylor sometimes signed but never dated his work), a passerby might see his own caricature hanging on Traylor's fence.

Shannon and members of New South supported Traylor by bringing him paints, colored pencils, and regulation-size poster board. He enjoyed the paints and colored pencils, but preferred regular pencils, crayons, and charcoal on the irregularly shaped scraps of discarded cardboard he found or the paper he left next to his work area to weather. In 1940 Shannon and the New South group mounted approximately one hundred of Traylor's drawings for the exhibition *Bill Traylor—People's Artist*. In the exhibition catalog, Shannon placed Traylor among the most significant black artists in U.S. history. The local press took notice of the exhibition, with a 31 March 1940 headline in the *Montgomery Advertiser* that read "The Enigma of Uncle Bill Traylor. Born a Slave, Untutored In Art, His Paintings are Reminiscent Of Cave Pictures—And Picasso" (Helfenstein and Kurzmeyer, 174). Traylor briefly attended the exhibition, climbing two sets of stairs with Shannon's help, but he never acknowledged responsibility for the exhibited works and promptly returned to his sidewalk studio.

During World War II both Shannon and Traylor left Montgomery and did not return until 1946, when Traylor was around 90 years old. By this time, he had lost a leg to gangrene yet wanted to continue drawing at his street "studios" on the corner of Monroe Avenue and Lawrence Street; but local authorities refused to permit it. Instead, he moved in with one of his daughters, Sarah Howard, and continued to draw until his rheumatism worsened, and he was placed in the Fraternal Hospital, an all-black nursing home in Montgomery. Although some published sources give 1947 as the year of his death, he actually died in 1949 and was buried at St. Jude's Church in Montgomery.

Shannon and his wife, Eugenia Carter Shannon, maintained possession of the bulk of Traylor's works. With Abstract Expressionism dominating the art market, they had little hope of Traylor's art gaining popularity. Their collection was kept in obscurity until the 1970s, when the Shannons cataloged Traylor's drawings; and in 1979 they held a small show of Traylor's work at the R. H. Oosterom Gallery in New York. In 1982 thirty-six of his pieces appeared in *Black Folk Art in America 1930–1980*, an exhibition at the Corcoran Gallery of Art in Washington, D.C., which received high critical praise. In the early 1990s Traylor's heirs filed suit against Shannon to take possession of the unsold drawings. In 1993 the lawsuit was settled out of court. The discovery of Traylor's work by the established art world encouraged the acceptance of works by similar self-taught artists throughout the American South, such as William Edmonson and Sister Gertrude Morgan.

FURTHER READING

Helfenstein, Josef, and Roman Kurzmeyer. *Deep Blues: Bill Traylor 1854–1949* (1999).

Karlins, N. F. "Bill Traylor," *Raw Vision* (summer 1996).

Montgomery Museum of Fine Arts. *Lively Times and Exciting Events: The Drawings of Bill Traylor* (1993).

Shannon, Charles. "Bill Traylor's Triumph," *Art and Antiques* (Feb. 1988).

THOMAS R. WOLEJKO

Trelling, Ursula. *See* Anderson, Regina.

Trent, Alphonso (24 Aug. 1905–14 Oct. 1959), bandleader and pianist, was born in Fort Smith, Arkansas. His parents' names are unknown. His father was the principal of a high school. Trent took piano lessons from W. O. Wiley and studied at Shorter College in Little Rock after leading a band in Muskogee, Oklahoma, in the summer of 1923. In 1924 he was a member of the guitarist Eugene Crooke's Synco Six. Its leadership passed to Trent, though Crooke remained in the group. The trumpeter Terrence Holder joined Trent's five-piece band to tour around Arkansas and Oklahoma. In 1925 the then eight-piece band, including the virtuoso trombonist Snub Mosley, went to Dallas. Russell reports that Trent was "small, wiry, durable, even-tempered and, like BENNIE MOTEN, persuasive and politic" (Russell, 61).

On the strength of Trent's performance the manager of the Adolphus Hotel offered him a two-week engagement, with the band expanded to ten pieces. According to Holder, Trent's orchestra presented a varied repertory of light classics, jazz, and dance music, strictly for white audiences. Such was the reception that it stayed at the hotel for a year and a half, holding the best-paying job of any African American dance orchestra in the South and Midwest. Indeed, affluence became a part of the band's image, which found its expression in fancy uniforms and expensive automobiles. Nightly radio broadcasts from the Adolphus on station WFAA in Dallas spread its fame. It was the first African American band to broadcast regularly, and only the white band Coon Sanders' Nighthawks was better known in that region of the country.

Success brought a stability uncommon in jazz and dance music: a comparison between a photo from 1925 and a flyer from early 1927 shows only one change in personnel when the band returned for a residency at the Adolphus. The group had left the Adolphus late in 1926 to tour Texas, and the following year it toured the Midwest. Late in 1927 the violinist, singer, and master of ceremonies STUFF SMITH joined the band in Louisville, Kentucky, and he was a featured soloist on the orchestra's first recordings, made the next year. "Black and Blue Rhapsody" (1928) affords an opportunity to hear Trent's own playing in a brief chordal and rhythmic piano solo.

The trumpeter Peanuts Holland, who with Mosley and Smith is prominent on the band's recordings, worked intermittently with Trent from 1928 to 1930.

From 1928 to 1930 Trent continued touring, including residencies in Detroit, Cincinnati, Buffalo, and Pittsburgh, as well as on riverboat steamers. The band received an encouraging reception during a week's stay at the Savoy Ballroom in New York, Trent having brought it there at the urging of FLETCHER HENDERSON. Trent was fearful, however, of losing his fine sidemen to New York bandleaders and chose to move on to play at the Plantation Club in Cleveland in 1930, where ironically he lost the band's uniforms and its entire library of musical scores in a fire.

As the years went by, membership became increasingly unstable, and in 1932 Trent himself left to care for his parents in Fort Smith. The band continued into 1933 under other leaders, and its last recordings include among others the trumpeters Holland and Harry Sweets Edison, the trombonists Mosley and Gus Wilson (brother of the pianist TEDDY WILSON), the tenor saxophonist Hayes Pillars (reported to be the idol of COUNT BASIE's future star soloist Herschel Evans), but not Trent. From 1934 he toured the Southwest with new bands, one of which included the electric guitarist CHARLIE CHRISTIAN. Later he concentrated on managing real estate, but he continued to lead a quintet at least until 1958 in his hometown, where he died.

By reputation, throughout the mid- to late 1920s Trent's was undisputedly the best of the southwestern and midwestern big bands, rivaling those of Henderson and DUKE ELLINGTON, New York's finest. Unfortunately his small and undistinguished recorded legacy does not help us to understand why the group was held in such high esteem. The best of the orchestra's eight issued recordings—"Black and Blue Rhapsody," "After You've Gone" (1930), Gus Wilson's arrangement of "Clementine," and "I've Found a New Baby" (both from 1933 and both without Trent)—present merely a highly polished jazz ensemble that featured imaginative but not exceptionally outstanding soloists or arrangements. In terms of innovation and quality, these now-obscure recordings are vastly inferior not only to Henderson's and Ellington's best and widely available contemporary sides but also to several equally well-known recordings made during the same period by a southwestern rival, Moten. Indeed, apart from Mosley's telegraphic, high-speed trombone solos, unlike anyone else's of that period, it is difficult to understand on the strength of these discs what, if anything, was strikingly original in Trent's orchestra. Conceivably his rivals may have borrowed—via touring, the newly emerging radio networks, and the national dissemination of recording—and recorded some of Trent's ideas, perhaps acquired during the ongoing interchanges among musicians during the 1920s, but such a question is impossible to answer. Hence the high place of Trent's orchestra in the jazz pantheon depends more on reputation than sound.

FURTHER READING

Brown, Kenneth T. *Kansas City … And All That's Jazz* (1999).

Driggs, Franklin S. "Jazz in Kansas City and the Southwest," in *Jazz*, ed. Nat Hentoff and Albert J. McCarthy (1959).

Pearson, Nathan W., Jr. *Goin' to Kansas City* (1988).

Russell, Ross. *Jazz Style in Kansas City and the Southwest* (1971).

This entry is taken from the *American National Biography* and is published here with the permission of the American Council of Learned Societies.

BARRY KERNFELD

Trethewey, Natasha (1966–), author, was born in Gulfport, Mississippi, to Eric Trethewey, a poet and professor from Nova Scotia, and Gwendolyn Ann Turnbough, a social worker from Mississippi. Because her father was white and her mother African American, her parents had to leave the state to marry, as miscegenation was still illegal in Mississippi in 1966. The marriage ended in divorce before Natasha entered grade school. Natasha grew up living with her mother in Decatur, Georgia, during the school year and with her father in New Orleans, where he was working on a Ph.D. at Tulane, and her maternal grandmother in Mississippi during the summers. She was influenced by her father's vocation as poet—her stepmother, Katherine Soniat, was also a poet and a professor at Virginia Tech—and spent many hours in the library reading during her childhood. Some of the obstacles her parents faced as an interracial couple in Mississippi are reflected in a number of the poems in *Native Guard* (2006), which also contains a series of elegies for her mother, who died when Trethewey was nineteen years old.

After graduating from Redan High School, Trethewey received a B.A. from the University of Georgia, where she majored in English and Creative Writing. After college she spent a year and a half working as a Food Stamp caseworker in Augusta, Georgia, before beginning graduate school. She received an M.A. from Hollins University, before attending the University of Massachusetts, where she received an MFA in Poetry and the Distinguished Young Alumna Award. While in Massachusetts she became a member of the Darkroom Collective, a group of African American poets in Cambridge who met to read and discuss each other's work and to sponsor readings by African American poets.

Trethewey's first volume of poetry, *Domestic Work* (2000), was selected by RITA FRANCES DOVE as the winner of the first Cave Canem Poetry Prize in 1999, and was also awarded a 2001 Mississippi Institute of Arts and Letters Book Prize and the 2001 Lillian Smith Award for Poetry. Her second volume, *Bellocq's Ophelia* (2002), named a notable 2003 book by the American Library Association, was awarded the 2003 Mississippi Institute of Arts and Letters Book Prize and was a finalist for the Academy of American Poets' James Laughlin and Lenore Marshall prizes. Trethewey's poems have been selected for the 2000 and 2003 *Best American Poetry* volumes, and she received the Grolier Prize for her poem sequence "Storyville Diary." Trethewey received fellowships from the Guggenheim Foundation, the Rockefeller Foundation, and the National Endowment for the Arts, and was named a Bunting Fellow at the Radcliffe Institute for Advanced Study at Harvard University. Her third collection, *Native Guard*, met with critical acclaim upon its release in 2006.

Trethewey's poetry seeks out what she calls "subjugated narratives" in both personal and public histories. All three of her collections address the problems of memory, and what is present even in its absence from public record. Using photographs and monuments as stimuli for these meditations on history, Trethewey evokes living history that can never be entirely captured by the documentary. In a lengthy and illuminating interview, Charles Rowell, editor of *Callaloo*, described the aim of Trethewey's poetry as "inscriptive restoration." *Domestic Work*, her first volume, was inspired by historical photographs of African Americans she saw in the University of Massachusetts art gallery. The opening poem of this collection, "Woman in Process," juxtaposes two women at work—one who stopped to pose for the photograph and the other who kept moving, thus creating a blur in the image that suggests an ongoing life outside of the picture frame. Interspersed with the poems inspired by photographs are poems inspired by family stories, particularly those of her maternal great-grandmother and her Aunt Sugar, who resist "framing" much as the women in the opening poem do. In

a review of *Domestic Work*, poet KEVIN YOUNG pointed out what became Trethewey's approach to the personal and the public in future volumes as well: "Trethewey brilliantly discusses family not for its extremes or its small hurts, but rather for the small intimacies that symbolize larger sufferings of history, both personal and public." In her second volume, *Bellocq's Ophelia*, Trethewey seems to depart from the theme of family as she creates a persona based on a woman in E. J. Bellocq's now famous photographs of Storyville prostitutes. Yet Ophelia's mother and teacher form an audience for the series of letter poems that comprise the largest section of this volume. Trethewey said, "I was searching for a persona through whom I might investigate aspects of my own mixed-race experience growing up in the Deep South" (Rowell). The wallpaper in a number of Bellocq's photographs matches that of Ebony Hall, an establishment featuring light-skinned African American prostitutes, and Trethewey's Ophelia identifies herself as such. *Bellocq's Ophelia* includes poems from several different perspectives—the poet, the madam, the photographer—offering us a multi-dimensional portrait of Ophelia, but mostly we hear from Ophelia's perspective. Trethewey chronicles Ophelia's journey to New Orleans' Storyville, her adventures there as she takes on the work available to her, her acquaintance with the photographer and her various collaborations with him as model, as composer of scenes, and finally as a photographer in her own right. The closing section of the volume is Trethewey's Grolier award-winning sequence, "Storyville Diary."

Native Guard proves simultaneously to be her most public and private book. She began the book as a poetic monument to the unlauded Louisiana Native Guard, an African American regiment stationed at Ship Island, off the coast of Trethewey's hometown in Gulfport, Mississippi. While writing poems to reinscribe the legacy of these servicemen, it suddenly became clear to Trethewey that there was a more personal erasure she needed to commemorate. In 1985 her mother had been killed by Natasha's stepfather, whom she had recently divorced, but Natasha had never ordered a headstone for the grave because she did not know what surname to use. She began writing elegies for her mother, at first keeping them private, but gradually publishing them. Finally they found their place in the collection alongside a sonnet sequence in the voice of one of the Native Guards, and poems about Mississippi history as it impacted her family's life.

The effect of the whole is an eloquent integration of the personal and the historical, the legacy of an "un-daughter" to the home that refused to fully claim her.

Today Trethewey is Associate Professor of Creative Writing at Emory University. She has also taught at Auburn University, the University of North Carolina-Chapel Hill, and Duke University where she was the 2005–2006 Lehman Brady Joint Chair Professor of Documentary and American Studies. Her poetry displays both a spare elegance and a complete mastery of both formal and free verse techniques, ensuring that it will endure as art even as it makes a significant contribution to the ongoing conversation of African American artists with the subject of history. In 2007 Trethewey was at work on a memoir.

FURTHER READING

Trethewey's biography and archived materials at the Creative Writing Program at Emory University are at http://www.creativewriting.emory.edu/faculty/trethewey.html.

Petty, Jill. "An Interview with Natasha Trethewey," *Callaloo* 19.2 (1996): 364–375.

Rowell, Charles Henry. "Inscriptive Restorations: An Interview with Natasha Trethewey," *Callaloo* 27.4 (2004): 1022–1034.

Young, Kevin. Review of *Domestic Work*. *Ploughshares* (Winter 2000).

ANN HOSTETLER

Trévigne, Paul (c. 1824 31 Aug. 1907) educator, scholar, editor, and political activist, was born in New Orleans, Louisiana, to Paul Trévigne Sr., a free, prosperous Afro-Creole carpenter and a woman known only as a Découdreau. Tévigne grew up in circumstances and enjoyed opportunities unknown to most African Americans living in the antebellum South. Few details of his childhood and education are known, but by around 1848 Trévigne, along with about a dozen other Afro-Creole educators, founded the Institution Catholique des Orphelins Indigents, a private institution for free black children in New Orleans, better known as the Couvent School. Here Trévigne taught foreign languages and developed a reputation among his peers as an accomplished teacher and scholar. By the time Union forces captured New Orleans in 1862, Trévigne had spent over a decade honing his craft as a political thinker and essayist. He would put these skills to extensive use during the turbulent times of Reconstruction.

During the summer months of 1862 a group of Afro-Creole activists in New Orleans hired Trévigne to become the editor-in-chief of their newly organized French-language newspaper *L'Union*. Beginning with its first issue on 27 September 1862, the pages of *L'Union* reflected the strong egalitarian convictions of its editor and his backers. Under Trévigne's stewardship, the paper became the nation's most outspoken advocate of universal male suffrage and citizenship for not only elite people of color such as themselves but also the thousands of recently freed slaves. By mid-1863 *L'Union* had become the official organ of the Republican Party's universal suffrage faction in Louisiana and had become bilingual in an effort to reach out to English-speaking allies. Unfortunately, Trévigne's uncompromising editorial stance had created enemies within Unionist ranks. Financial troubles finally forced the biweekly, then triweekly *L'Union* to cease publication in July 1864. Soon afterward, however, fellow Creole of color and political activist DR. LOUIS CHARLES ROUDANEZ funded the launching of a successor called *La Tribune de la Nouvelle Orleans* and put Trévigne in charge.

As the *Tribune's* editor, Trévigne hoped to unite all people of color behind the banner of universal suffrage so that they might play a more important role in determining the shape of Louisiana's Reconstruction government. In late 1864 the Belgian scientist and political radical Jean-Charles Houzeau joined Trévigne at the Tribune as managing editor. For the next two years, this first black-owned daily newspaper flourished financially and enjoyed the peak of its editorial influence. Unfortunately for Trévigne and his cohort, more conservative elements of the Republican Party exploited old cultural and class-conscious antagonisms between "American" and francophone blacks. By 1867 both black and white "centrists" chose a white, Northern-born recent arrival by the name of Henry Clay Warmoth for its gubernatorial candidate over the far more radical leadership of the city's Afro-Creole community. With the Republican Party's printing contracts now diverted to the Warmoth-friendly *New Orleans Republican* and facing competition from a competing black newspaper, P. B. S. PINCHBACK's *Weekly Louisianan*, regular publication of the *Tribune* ceased in February of 1869, reappearing only sporadically throughout 1870.

Trévigne had managed, however, to repair his relationship with the Republican Party's white power structure to the extent that by 1871 he had secured a post in the counting room of the U.S. Custom

House. Two years later, he received an appointment as the chief clerk of New Orleans's third municipal police court. When the Republicans lost control of Louisiana in 1877, however, he returned to work in the custom house. The ability of Trévigne and many others like him to secure federal patronage jobs was significant because such employment enabled them to continue their political activism without fear of economic reprisal. As a result, the Federal Custom House on Canal Street in New Orleans became the hub of both post-1877 Republican political power in Louisiana and served as a base of operations for Afro-Creole activists like Trévigne who would spend the rest of the nineteenth century in a rear-guard action against those who sought to wear away the gains of Reconstruction.

In 1877 New Orleans' integrated schools became the first target of the new Democratic regime of Governor Francis T. Nicholls. As a lifelong educator, Trévigne felt particularly strong about fighting what he considered a key reversal for a race that had for so long been deprived of the benefits of citizenship. In 1878 he brought suit against the New Orleans school board, charging that public school segregation violated the Fourteenth Amendment to the U.S. Constitution. The Supreme Court of Louisiana, however, ruled against his action the following January. Though the Supreme Court dismissed Trévigne's suit more on legal procedure rather than on Constitutional principle, the new Louisiana Constitution of 1879 rendered further pursuit of the matter moot. In bargaining with white Democrats, the black political powerbroker Pinchback had engineered a deal in which he and other black and white Republican politicians would endorse segregated schools in exchange for a state-supported institution of higher learning for people of color—the proposed institution would ultimately become Southern University.

Trévigne also made significant contributions to the literary arts in New Orleans, with his poetry and prose appearing alongside his editorials in *L'Union* as well as in the *Tribune*. Perhaps his most significant publication came between 1875 and 1876 when he produced the "Centennial History of the Louisiana Negro," serialized, ironically, in Pinchback's *Louisianian*. Trévigne returned to newspaper work between 1892 and 1896 when he became both the literary editor and chief editor of the French-language portion of *The Crusader*, a newspaper founded and edited by Louis A. Martinet and the official organ of the *Comité des Citoyens*. The committee organized to fight for a variety of civil rights causes and sought to counteract the tightening grip of Jim Crow in Louisiana, eventually provoking Homer Plessy's ill-fated test case against the state's "Separate Car" law. Inspired by radical francophone intellectuals from both sides of the Atlantic and possessed of a sense of noblesse oblige, Trévigne used this position of privilege throughout his life in order to better the lives of fellow people of color. He died in a deeply segregated New Orleans in 1907.

FURTHER READING

Bell, Caryn Cossé. *Revolution, Romanticism, and the Afro-Creole Protest Tradition in Louisiana, 1718–1868* (1997).

Desdunes, Rodolphe Lucien. *Our People and Our History: Fifty Creole Portraits* (1973).

Houzeau, Jean-Charles. *My Passage at the New Orleans Tribune: A Memoir of the Civil War Era* (1984).

Rousséve, Charles Barthelemey. *The Negro in Louisiana: Aspects of His History and His Literature* (1937).

JUSTIN NYSTROM

Trigg, Frank J. (31 July 1850–20 Apr. 1933) educator, cofounder of the Afro-Virginian state teacher's association, and principal and president of historically black institutions of higher education, was born in slavery, in the governor's mansion in Richmond, Virginia, the son of S. Frank Trigg and Sarah Ann (maiden name unknown), members of Governor John B. Floyd's household staff. According to his obituary, Trigg received an early education in Richmond before returning with the household to Abingdon, Virginia. When the former governor joined the Confederacy, Trigg accompanied him to Tennessee where he served as his personal valet. In 1863 after returning to Abingdon, John Floyd died and Trigg became the property of Floyd's son-in-law.

Following a farming accident that cost Trigg his right arm, he decided he should continue his education and he entered Hampton Institute around 1870. Hampton Institute was founded by General Samuel Chapman Armstrong, a leading American advocate of industrial education, in 1868. His educational philosophy was based on the concept of "self-help" which he believed would allow rural blacks, in particular, to receive "training" in agriculture and industry to become self-reliant, self-sufficient contributors to the rebuilding of the south.

At Hampton Frank Trigg made the acquaintance of BOOKER T. WASHINGTON, arguably Hampton's best-known graduate, and Eleanor Preston Taylor, also from Abingdon, who would become Trigg's wife. Hampton made a lifelong impression on Trigg. In a 1921 letter he recounted interactions with the school's founder. He wrote that the "Armstrong days are a pleasant oasis in my memory...." He was very proud of this "old hallowed spot" and always kept his alma mater informed of his accomplishments, referring to himself as Hampton's "child." He graduated in 1873 and spent a year at Norwich Academy in Connecticut completing a secondary-level industrial-agricultural course of study.

Later as a teacher and administrator, Trigg often attended Hampton teacher and education conferences, recruited its graduates for positions at the institutions he led, and strove to assist teachers in continuing professional development. Though he believed in industrial and agricultural education, entrepreneurship, and self-sufficiency, he was foremost a teacher of teachers. Trigg trained students to be teachers and role models who valued the work and rural culture of their students by doing that same work themselves. After his time at Norwich, he returned to Abingdon in 1875 to begin his career as an educator in its public schools. He married Ellen Preston Taylor in 1879 and began a family that would eventually include eleven children. In 1880 the Trigg family moved to Lynchburg, in central Virginia, where they remained for the next twenty-two years.

In the first years of his sojourn in Lynchburg, Trigg taught African American students in the city's segregated public school system. In 1893, however, he was asked to become principal of the newly established Virginia Collegiate and Industrial Institute (VCII) also known as the "Morgan Annex" because it served as the preparatory school of what is now Morgan State University in Baltimore, Maryland. The VCII provided college preparatory course work, normal-school training, and industrial and agricultural education on the Hampton-Tuskegee model, as opposed to the classical model of institutions like Fisk, Atlanta, and Howard Universities which offered degree programs in Greek and Latin and the literary arts. A Methodist Episcopal institution of higher education for African Americans, VCII received start-up funding and the purchase of land for the Lynchburg campus from the city's black Jackson Street Methodist Episcopal Church, whose other important congregant was the journalist and Methodist educator, I. Garland Penn. It was Penn, at the 1889 Colored Methodist Episcopal Conference in Charlottesville, Virginia, who spoke of the need for a normal-school institution in Lynchburg. Trigg was an elder and Sunday school teacher at the Jackson Street church.

In addition to being principal of VCII, Trigg taught English and geography, and his wife taught courses in domestic arts. The enrollment and reputation of the school in Lynchburg and within the Methodist Episcopal denomination were increasing when he resigned, in 1895, to become Lynchburg's superintendent of black public education, responsible for twelve teachers and five hundred students. During the week, the students were housed at the Jackson Street Methodist Episcopal Church. In summer months, Trigg and other black educators from Virginia organized teacher institutes sponsored by the Peabody Education Fund.

Trigg was secretary of the 1882 committee that organized the first institute in Lynchburg, which met at his church. Jackson Street Church was an important black religious, educational, and cultural center in the city of Lynchburg. The city itself, 189 miles south of Washington, D.C., was an important intellectual center, which hosted Booker T. Washington, FREDERICK DOUGLASS, and the Association for the Study of Afro-American Life and History, and was the home of the Harlem Renaissance poet ANNE SPENCER. It was also home to the Baptist Virginia Seminary and College where the young poet STERLING BROWN taught for two years. Out of Virginia's Peabody Institute summer programs, conducted throughout the state, a statewide black teacher's association was formed in 1887 in Lynchburg, when it was again the Institute's host. The State Teacher's Association eventually became the Virginia Teacher's Association (VTA). Trigg was one of VTA's cofounders and its first vice president.

Trigg remained in Lynchburg until 1902 when he became principal of Princess Anne Academy, in Princess Anne, Maryland, another constituent school of Morgan College on the Eastern Shore. He arrived at an important juncture in the life of the institution, transforming its curriculum, which had been geared toward literature, to one that better reflected the needs of the rural environment, population, and economy of Somerset County, and the Booker T. Washington approach to industrial education. With the help of Hampton administrators, he secured a grant from the John F. Slater Fund to implement a teaching program that would ensure that graduates were well qualified to teach. This was also a time when Princess Anne Academy was adapting itself as Maryland's "1890" or black land-grant institution in the state.

While at Princess Anne Academy, Trigg increased the school's enrollment; with the raised agricultural output of local farmers, black and white, who benefited from the farm institutes the Academy sponsored, so were the employment opportunities raised for students and graduates who would later contribute to the economy of the county as farmers, tradesmen, and entrepreneurs. What he had done for teachers in Virginia, he did for those pursuing other occupations in the southeast. In an 1899 newspaper article, his philosophy of teaching is clear: "The race has for thirty years prepared its teachers for the public schools, in this way it has done well. Now it must undertake to prepare first class farmers, and artisans in both wood and iron." Of the surrounding community and county, Trigg said that it "has received new life from the influence going out from the Academy." Outreach and the establishment of good community relations were a priority. His curricular adjustments and consideration of the dynamics of the community were foundations upon which the evolving future state institution would build.

In 1910 Trigg returned to VCII as principal, remaining for six years. As at Princess Anne Academy, he made important capital improvements, and the normal-school curriculum earned state certification to facilitate placement of VCII graduates in teaching positions. He had left VCII by the time a fire, during the 1917 Christmas holidays, destroyed the Lynchburg campus which had undergone major renovations during his tenure. There was discussion about rebuilding but the current principal and students moved to Morgan's new Baltimore campus and were absorbed into the parent institution. Princess Anne Academy continued as a branch institution until the state of Maryland acquired it.

Trigg planned to retire in 1916, but instead was called to the presidency of Bennett College in Greensboro, North Carolina. At the time Bennett, also a Methodist institution, was coeducational. When Trigg finally retired in 1926, Bennett was in the process of becoming a black women's college. The campus had new buildings, a strengthened academic program, and a library to serve the city's black community. Trigg died in Lynchburg in 1933, a dedicated Methodist Episcopal churchman who had led three institutions that were, and are still, part of the historically black college and university movement. He spent his adult life increasing the ranks of black educators, farmers, and tradesmen, and supporting their career development while helping to improve the communities in which they lived. In recognition of his work, Frank Trigg was posthumously made an honorary doctor of laws in 1992 by the University of Maryland, Eastern Shore.

FURTHER READING

Trigg's papers are in the University of Maryland, Eastern Shore, Frederick Douglass Library.

Hytche, William P. *Polishing the Diamond: A History of The University of Maryland Eastern Shore* (2002).

Picott, J. Rupert. *History of the Virginia Teachers Association* (1979).

"'The Way Out': Views of Prof. Frank Trigg on The Negro Problem," The *Lynchburg News*, 22 Jan. 1899.

White, Jane Baber. "Lynchburg's Professor Frank Trigg: From Slave to College President," *Lynch's Ferry* (Spring/Summer, 2000).

Wilson, Edward N. *The History of Morgan State College: A Century of Purpose in Action, 1867–1967* (1976).

NANCY-ELIZABETH FITCH

Trotter, Geraldine Louise Pindell (3 Oct. 1872– 8 Oct. 1918), journalist, was born in Boston, Massachusetts, the daughter of a lawyer, Charles Edward Pindell, and his wife, Mary Frances Pindell. Her family was prominent in Boston's African American community, and her uncle William Pindell led the Boston public school integration struggle in the 1850s. She attended the Everett Grammar School, studied at a business college, and then worked for ten years as a bookkeeper and stenographer for the Eli Cooley Company. In his autobiography, W. E. B. DuBois, who courted her, recalled she was "a fine forthright woman, blonde, blue-eyed and fragile." The journalist Ray Stannard Baker remembered her as a vivacious, petite, and fair woman who could have passed for white.

On 27 June 1899, Geraldine, or "Deenie," Pindell married WILLIAM MONROE TROTTER, an 1895 Harvard College graduate from the Boston neighborhood of Hyde Park. He was also from one of Boston's elite African American families and worked as a real estate and mortgage broker in the city. The couple lived at 97 Sawyer Avenue in a middle-class white neighborhood on fashionable Jones Hill in the Dorchester area of Boston.

In November 1901 her husband became the founder and crusading publisher of the national weekly *Boston Guardian* newspaper (1901–1957). From the start, the *Guardian* was critical of BOOKER T. WASHINGTON, as were most African American leaders in Boston, and Washington's Tuskegee Machine relentlessly used other black newspapers across the nation to denounce the *Guardian* and its editor. After Trotter's partner, George W. Forbes, quit the newspaper in 1903, Deenie Trotter became associate editor with her husband, and remained in that position until her death. She was the office manager, edited the society columns, and wrote articles on fashion and household management to attract more female readers. They published the paper every Friday evening at 3 Tremont Row on the site of William Lloyd Garrison's *Liberator*; the location was a symbol of their progressive views and abolitionist heritage. Their friend W. E. B. DuBois, who founded the Niagara Movement with Trotter in 1905, recalled no other paper "that for sheer biting inventive and unswerving courage, ever quite equaled the *Boston Guardian* in its earlier days." He noted in *The Crisis* in June 1927 that Booker T. Washington and "his followers literally shriveled before it," although it was "often as unfair as it was inspired." DuBois also remembered that Deenie Trotter gave up the thought of children and was utterly devoted to her husband while working with him, even when, owing to financial losses from the *Guardian* endeavor, they lost their home in Dorchester. As Stephen Fox, the biographer of Trotter, reports, Mrs. Trotter protested mildly about her husband's late hours working at the *Guardian*, but after the Boston Riot in 1903, when Trotter spent a month in jail for disrupting Booker T. Washington's address at the Columbus Avenue African Methodist Episcopal Zion Church, Deenie Trotter quietly became his most important supporter and co-worker. The couple made great personal sacrifices in a lifetime devoted to inspiring African Americans to believe in themselves and to fight for justice and civil rights.

Despite her efforts at managing the *Guardian*, and those of Trotter's sister, Maude Trotter Steward, and their friends, Trotter's militant newspaper was often in financial jeopardy, as Trotter was an erratic businessman and inefficient accountant. The *Guardian*'s literary style also suffered from his hectic schedule and chronic overwork. Booker T. Washington, against whom the *Guardian* tirelessly campaigned, covertly frustrated the Trotters' efforts to promote militant civil rights and other liberal causes in their newspaper. Nevertheless, as one of only around two hundred African American newspapers in the United States at that time, the *Boston Guardian* had an influence far beyond its modest circulation. However, the Trotters resisted DuBois's

invitations to join the NAACP, which he founded in 1909, because they objected to the white leadership of this civil rights organization.

Geraldine Trotter paid another price for her husband's personal differences and philosophical conflicts with other activists. Many friends no longer visited or invited her to socialize. DuBois stopped visiting the Trotters with his wife and daughter each summer. Her friend, the lawyer ARCHIBALD GRIMKÉ, a former slave and the nephew of the white abolitionists Angeline and Sarah Grimke, dropped out of her social circle, as did George W. Forbes, an Amherst College graduate and librarian for the Boston Public Library, and she was also dropped by the radical black lawyer CLEMENT G. MORGAN and his family. The *Booker T. Washington Papers* reveal that Washington secretly kept track of Trotter, but in 1906 he hired, to investigate Mrs. Trotter, James R. Woods Jr., a Boston private detective, who reported that she worked at the *Guardian* office every day.

In addition to her work on the newspaper, Mrs. Trotter was active in St. Mary's Episcopal Church in Dorchester, Public School Association, Women's Anti-lynching Society, Equal Rights League, Boston Literary and Historical Association, and St. Monica's Home in Roxbury, which sheltered infirm and elderly black women. During World War I, through the Soldiers' Comfort Units, she assisted black soldiers of the 519th Engineers at nearby Fort Devens. At the ceremonies in Roxbury in 1905 to honor the centenary of William Lloyd Garrison's birth, she said, "That is the great lesson we Colored people should learn, those of us who have had the advantages of education, who have seen life in its broadest light, to be willing to sacrifice and … to do for our own down-trodden people all in our power … to make their cause our cause, their sufferings our suffering."

After Mrs. Trotter died of the flu, William and the *Guardian* began a gradual decline. However, Geraldine Pindell Trotter remains an unusual example of an African American woman who achieved a prominent position in U.S. journalism and politics. Together she and Monroe, as her husband was known to friends, demonstrated against a Boston theater showing the film *The Birth of a Nation* (1915) and resisted the accommodationist views of Booker T. Washington, Theodore Roosevelt, and Woodrow Wilson, which they found offensive and ineffective. After Mrs. Trotter died, DuBois told *The Crisis* readers that "she never hesitated or wavered, and she yielded every little temptation of home and dress and company and leisure for the narrow office and late hours and public life; yet through it all she shone clear and fine, and died as one whom death cannot conquer." For many years the *Guardian* editorial page bore her picture and a dedication "To My Fallen Comrade, Geraldine L. Trotter, My Loyal Wife."

She was survived by her mother and sister, and was buried in Fairview Cemetery in Hyde Park. The handsome Trotter home, which they were forced to leave in order to support the *Guardian*, is listed on the National Register of Historic Places. In 1969 a new Boston public school was named in honor of William, Geraldine, and Maude Trotter, the William Monroe Trotter School. The Trotter Institute, founded in 1984 at the University of Massachusetts in Boston, also honors the memory of the Trotters.

FURTHER READING

Baker, Ray Stannard. *Following the Color Line: American Negro Citizenship in the Progressive Era* (1964).

Du Bois, W. E. B. *The Autobiography of W. E. B. DuBois* (1968).

Fox, Stephen R. *The Guardian of Boston: William Monroe Trotter* (1970).

Harlan, Louis R, ed. *The Booker T. Washington Papers*, vol. 9:46 (1972–1989).

Winch, Julie. "Geraldine Pindell Trotter," *Trotter Institute Review* (Winter 1988).

Obituaries: *Boston Globe*, 11 Oct. 1918 and 13 Oct. 1918.

PETER C. HOLLORAN

Trotter, James Monroe (8 Nov. 1842–26 Feb. 1892), soldier, music historian, and government office-holder, was born to a slave woman named Letitia and her white owner, Richard S. Trotter, in Grand Gulf, Mississippi, near Vicksburg. After escape or manumission, Letitia settled with her children in the free city of Cincinnati around 1854. Trotter completed his secondary school education and attended the Albany Manual Labor University, near Hamilton, Ohio, where he majored in art and music. During his school vacations and summers he worked as a cabin boy on shipping boats running on the Ohio and Mississippi rivers. After graduating from Albany, Trotter taught school in Chillicothe, Ohio, until June 1863.

In that year, Negro regiments were created for the Union army, and he enlisted in Company K of the Fifty-fifth Regiment of the Massachusetts Volunteer Infantry. While in the army Trotter continued to teach, holding class sessions for his fellow soldiers encamped in Charleston, South Carolina.

Rising quickly through the ranks, he became a second lieutenant, though the War Department did not officially recognize the commissions of black officers. Trotter was also a leader in the movement for equal pay of black Union soldiers. Congress had established army pay grades for African Americans at the level of laborer only; there were no provisions for paying black infantrymen or officers. Trotter and thousands of other soldiers refused pay until Congress finally allowed equal pay for all Union soldiers.

After the war Trotter settled in Boston, where African Americans had already established successful communities and good schools in the wake of the city's abolitionist fervor. For his service to the Union army, Trotter was rewarded by Boston Republicans with a clerkship at the Boston post office, a good job with political importance and steady pay. In 1868 Trotter returned to Ohio to marry Virginia Isaacs, whom he had met before the war. Virginia and James settled in Hyde Park, Massachusetts, in the suburbs of Boston. Virginia gave birth to five children, though only three survived past infancy. WILLIAM MONROE TROTTER was born in 1872 at Virginia's parents' farm in Chillicothe, and Maude (1874) and Bessie (1883) were born in Hyde Park.

To some extent, it is as the father of William Monroe that Trotter is best known. William would become one of the most famous African American agitators of the early twentieth century. He edited the militant Boston newspaper the *Guardian* and helped to found the Niagara Movement with W. E. B. DuBois in 1905 and the National Association for the Advancement of Colored People (NAACP) in 1909.

James Trotter may also be considered the first African American historian of American music, having published in 1878 a 508-page volume entitled *Music and Some Highly Musical People*. Essentially a biographical compendium of black music in the United States, it was a respected source on American music well into the twentieth century. Selling thousands of copies, the book is said to have played a role in the musical development of another famous musician, the author and activist JAMES WELDON JOHNSON.

In addition to his musical career, Trotter was one of the earliest black political "Independents," as he liked to call himself, at a time when most African Americans were unfailingly loyal to the Republican Party. Disillusioned with the Republicans owing to President Rutherford B. Hayes's withdrawal of troops from the South, the official end of

Reconstruction, and to the promotion of a white man ahead of him at the Boston post office, Trotter began working for the Democratic Party. He became a nationally known leader of the black Democrats, beginning with the Massachusetts gubernatorial campaign of Benjamin F. Butler in 1883. Like other African Americans who voted Democratic in an age of extreme racism in the Republican Party, Trotter was most disturbed by the few political options for black voters and believed that fidelity to the Republicans was contributing to black disfranchisement in the increasingly solid South.

Trotter's work for the presidential campaign of Grover Cleveland resulted in his nomination for the office of recorder of deeds of the District of Columbia, a presidential appointment. This was a highly lucrative patronage position previously held by FREDERICK DOUGLASS. Trotter had been Cleveland's second choice for an African American as recorder, but racist senators had managed to block James C. Matthews's appointment. In response to loud outcries by African Americans at the possibility of a white man succeeding Douglass, Republican senator George F. Hoar of Massachusetts broke party ranks to support Trotter (the compromise candidate), and the Senate voted to confirm him in 1887.

Black response to the confirmation was ecstatic, and the recorder position brought Trotter both wealth and fame. It paid handsomely through commissions for deeds registered, and it was one of the highest-ranking federal government positions held by a black man at the time; however, it also made Trotter a target for attacks by African Americans angered by his defection from the Republican Party. W. CALVIN CHASE, editor of the black paper the *Washington Bee*, in particular made Washington an uncomfortable place for Trotter to live and work.

Trotter died at his home in Hyde Park at age fifty after a long battle with tuberculosis and the lingering effects of an attack of pneumonia suffered a few years earlier. Leaving behind a small fortune and a legacy of pride, agitation, and independence, Trotter laid the groundwork for the spirit of militancy that would come to fruition through his son, William, and the early-twentieth-century movements for African American civil rights.

FURTHER READING

Fox, Stephen R. *The Guardian of Boston: William Monroe Trotter* (1970).

Grossman, Lawrence. *The Democratic Party and the Negro: Northern and National Politics, 1868–1892* (1976).

Stevenson, Robert. "America's First Black Music Historian," *Journal of the American Musicological Society* 26.3 (Autumn, 1973).

ERIC S. YELLIN

Trotter, William Monroe (7 Apr. 1872–7 Apr. 1934), newspaper publisher and civil rights activist, was born in Chillicothe, Ohio, the son of James Monroe Trotter, a politician who served as recorder of deeds under President Grover Cleveland, and former slave Virginia Isaacs. In addition to his political career, Trotter's father was an abolitionist, a veteran of the 55th Massachusetts regiment, and an authority on African American music. Raised among Boston's black elite and steeped in the abolitionist tradition, Trotter entered Harvard University and made history as the institution's first African American elected to Phi Beta Kappa. After graduating magna cum laude and earning his master's degree from Harvard, Trotter returned to Boston to learn the real estate business. He founded his own firm in 1899, the same year that he married Boston aristocrat Geraldine Pindell.

A turning point in Trotter's life occurred in 1901 when discrimination in his real estate business and worsening racial conditions throughout the country, and especially in the South, led to his increased militancy. In response to his frustration with segregation, disenfranchisement, and violence against blacks, Trotter founded the *Boston Guardian*, a crusading weekly newspaper. Cofounder George Forbes soon left the paper in Trotter's able hands. The *Guardian* was an overnight success that boasted a circulation of 2,500 by its first birthday. As editor and publisher, Trotter was articulate, fearless, and defiant. The *Guardian* reestablished the black press as a force in the struggle for civil rights.

Trotter's great crusade in the pages of his newspaper was a vendetta against BOOKER T. WASHINGTON. Trotter opposed Washington's complacent optimism in the face of increasingly intolerable racial conditions. He also disagreed with Washington's emphasis on manual and industrial training for blacks, with its accompanying denigration of the classical education. Trotter's opposition to Washington forced white America to acknowledge that all of black America did not adhere to Washington's conciliatory and accommodationist views. Trotter's frustration with Washington reached its boiling point in July 1903. When Washington came to Boston for a public appearance, Trotter and some thirty associates heckled the orator and asked him several embarrassing questions. A free-for-all erupted into what became known as the Boston Riot. Washington supporters then pursued the case to its conclusion, resulting in Trotter's being fined fifty dollars and imprisoned for a month. Trotter thereafter assumed the mantle of martyr.

Trotter has been credited with leading a resurgence of the protest tradition among African Americans of the early twentieth century. In 1905 he joined W. E. B. DuBois in founding the Niagara Movement, an early civil rights organization and precursor of the National Association for the Advancement of Colored People (NAACP). Trotter helped to push DuBois away from research and into defiance as the avenue down which African Americans would secure equal rights. The tenacity and independence that served Trotter well as a journalist, however, hampered his work as a political leader. Personal quarrels with DuBois created an estrangement between the two leaders. Chief among their disagreements was Trotter's insistence that a national civil rights organization had to be led and financed exclusively by African Americans. In 1908 Trotter founded the National Equal Rights League, an all-black organization that advocated militant efforts to secure racial equality. Although Trotter participated in the founding of the NAACP a year later, he would not accept the white leadership and financial support underpinning the association. As the NAACP's influence swelled, the uncompromising Trotter became isolated on the left wing of black leadership.

One of Trotter's most fiery interchanges occurred at the White House. Trotter, a political independent, supported Woodrow Wilson for president in 1912. When Wilson approved increased segregation in federal office buildings, however, the new president lost Trotter's support. The radical black leader took a delegation to the White House in 1914 and engaged Wilson in a jaw-to-jaw argument. After nearly an hour, the president ordered the vitriolic Trotter out of his office.

Trotter moved the struggle for racial equality in the direction of mass mobilization. In 1915 he experimented with picket lines and demonstrations by orchestrating a nonviolent effort to ban D. W. Griffith's epic motion picture *Birth of a Nation*. Trotter's arrest did not prevent him from leading some one thousand marchers to the statehouse two days later, thereby creating one of the earliest protest marches by Americans of African descent.

In 1919 Trotter announced plans to attend the Versailles Peace Conference in an attempt to have a racial equality clause adopted in the treaty. When the U.S. government denied his request for a passport, the defiant Trotter secured a job as a ship's cook and sailed to France. Although his efforts at Versailles ultimately failed, they garnered worldwide publicity—and Wilson's wrath. Trotter continued to raise his voice through the *Guardian*, doing so only by sacrificing both his own and his wife's personal wealth to finance the newspaper.

After Geraldine Trotter died in the influenza epidemic of 1918, her husband grew ever more isolated. The economic downturn of the Depression proved too overwhelming for Trotter, and he lost his newspaper early in 1934. Trotter died later that year, apparently of suicide, when he plunged from the roof of a three-story building in Boston on his sixty-second birthday.

FURTHER READING

A small collection of Trotter's papers is at Boston University, and some Trotter correspondence is in the papers of W. E. B. DuBois at the University of Massachusetts, Amherst.

Fox, Stephen R. *The Guardian of Boston: William Monroe Trotter* (1970).

This entry is taken from the *American National Biography* and is published here with the permission of the American Council of Learned Societies.

RODGER STREITMATTER

Troupe, Quincy Thomas, Jr. (22 July 1939–), poet, journalist, educator, and author of seventeen books, was born in St. Louis, Missouri, to Dorothy Smith, a homemaker, and Quincy Thomas Troupe (later changed to Trouppe), a star catcher and manager in professional baseball's Negro Leagues. Troupe and his younger brother, Timothy, born a year after him, spent their earliest years in a home in which both parents loved poetry, music, and travel. Negro League stars such as SATCHEL PAIGE, MONTE IRVIN, and ROY CAMPANELLA, all friends of his father's, visited the family home. As a young boy, Troupe spent the winter months with his family in Cuba, Puerto Rico, and Mexico where his father earned money playing baseball.

When he was about eight years old, Troupe's parents divorced. He and Timothy moved with their mother to a much poorer section of St. Louis, where they lived in a six-room apartment located above a supermarket. The apartment they shared with Troupe's maternal grandmother, Leona Smith, and his uncle, Allen, was situated across the street from an infamous bar where many bloody brawls and stabbings occurred—some of which Troupe actually witnessed. His mother, who was a petite, fastidious, and fair-skinned woman, took a job as a clerk in a downtown department store to support the family. On Saturday mornings, she read poetry to her sons; this was a routine Troupe hated at the time but later regarded as a prelude to a lifelong love of literature. His mother married a blues bass player, China Brown, who was a regular in the house band at the famous Club Riviera, where the greatest black musicians of the time played. Visiting baseball stars were soon replaced by blues musicians such as BO DIDDLEY, MUDDY WATERS, ALBERT KING, and HOWLIN' WOLF as guests at the family dinner table.

As a young student, Troupe imagined that he might one day become a historian, even though his mother wanted him to be a lawyer. His father, who he continued to visit across town, wanted him to play professional baseball. When his mother became concerned about Quincy's constant fighting, she moved again—this time to a predominately white neighborhood. He became one of a handful of blacks in a school of more than two thousand students, and his home was the only one on the block occupied by a nonwhite family. The new teachers derided Troupe's speech as unrefined, and he had occasional scuffles with white, male students opposed to blacks attending the school. Measuring at over six feet tall, the lanky teenager discovered an aptitude for basketball. He played point guard on the Beaumont High School basketball team, and during his senior year the team won the Missouri state championship.

Shortly after high school, Troupe married his girlfriend, Marilyn Gooden, and the couple had one daughter, Antoinette. He then accepted both a basketball and baseball scholarship to Grambling College (later Grambling State University); but once there, he felt almost immediately alienated by the conservative mores of the small Louisiana town. He refused to attend the required Sunday Vespers every week, and he was prone to fighting. Grambling officials sent him home before the end of the first semester. Six months later, they allowed him to return; but when similar problems occurred, Troupe dropped out of school and entered the army in 1959. Back in Missouri, a politically well-connected uncle, James "Pal" Troupe, helped secure Troupe a spot on the U.S. All-Army basketball team in France a year later. While there, the French professional league team in Orleans recruited Troupe to join its team, and he went on to play basketball across Europe as the only American on the team. It was during these years abroad that Troupe began to write. A friend from a wealthy French family introduced Troupe to Jean Paul Sartre, a writer and philosopher with whom Troupe had previously been unfamiliar. During their conversation, Sartre suggested Troupe write poetry as a means of honing his writing skills. Troupe subsequently discovered that he loved the form of poetry and began to read, keep a journal, and study poets such as Pablo Neruda and T. S. Eliot.

After his stint in the army, Troupe returned to St. Louis in 1963, where he divorced Gooden. Seeing few appealing prospects for settling at home, he decided to move closer to his father, who by then had relocated to Los Angeles. He was joined in Los Angeles by Fanita Howard, a former girlfriend and aspiring lawyer from St. Louis. Their relationship rekindled, the couple soon had a daughter, Tymmie, and a son, Quincy Brandon, but did not marry. Troupe began studying journalism at Los Angeles City College in the mid-1960s, then moved to Watts where he became active in the Watts Writers Workshop. The group was founded by Budd Schulberg, a successful novelist, screenwriter, and son of a wealthy Hollywood producer, after 34 people died during the violent social upheaval in Watts in August 1965. Workshop members included the poets Ojenke and Eric Priestly. Troupe also met the poets JAYNE CORTEZ, Alprentice "Bunchy" Carter, the writer STANLEY CROUCH, and ELAINE BROWN. In this halcyon period of his life, Troupe mingled with musicians such as HORACE TAPSCOTT, ARTHUR BLYTHE, and SLY STONE; he also became friends with actor ROSCOE LEE BROWNE. Through Browne, Troupe met Marlon Brando. Impressed by Troupe, Brando introduced him to JAMES BALDWIN, who became a mentor and friend for many years.

In the late 1960s, Troupe began publishing poems in journals such as *Sumac*, *Mediterranean Review*, and finally, in *New Directions*, gaining national exposure. He began reading poetry on the college lecture circuit and eventually landed a teaching job at Ohio University in Athens, Ohio, in 1971. Troupe spent the next two decades teaching literature at the City University of New York's College of Staten Island. He published his first book of poems, *Embryo*, in 1971, which was noted for its jazz-influenced use of vernacular language. He also won a government travel grant that took him to Ghana, Nigeria, Senegal, Guinea, and the Ivory Coast. In 1975 he coedited *Giant Talk: An Anthology of Third World Writings* with Rainier Schulte. By this time,

Troupe had become identified with a small but influential group of black writers that included ISHMAEL REED, CECIL BROWN, Calvin Hernton, Jayne Cortez, and Eugene Redmond. Members of this group had been a part of the Black Arts movement of the late 1960s but had since distanced themselves from it as it became increasingly polemic and less focused on artistic craft. Three years later, Troupe published *Snake Back Solos*, a collection of poems for which he won his first American Book Award, and he collaborated with producer David L. Wolper on *The Inside Story of TV's Roots*. In 1978 Troupe met Margaret Diane Porter, an advertising account executive at the *New York Times*, from Glouster, Mississippi. In 1983 she bore him a second son, Porter Sylvanus, and the couple married in 1986.

During the next twenty years Troupe wrote more poetry, and he also published numerous articles on black music and culture in major publications. His insightful profile of MILES DAVIS for a 1985 issue of *Spin* magazine prompted Davis to invite Troupe to collaborate on *Miles: the Autobiography* (1989), now considered a key text on the musician's life. In 1989 Troupe's career and renown enjoyed a great upswing while his personal life was plagued with drama. It began in January when he appeared on the cover of *Poets and Writers*, introducing him to a large audience. Then, in the spring, Simon & Schuster released *James Baldwin: The Legacy*, a collection of essays edited by Troupe that was both acclaimed and widely publicized. Amidst all the acclaim, however, Troupe's eldest son, Quincy Brandon, an engineering student at the New York State University at Stony Brook, was falsely accused of raping a white, female student, throwing his family life into crisis. Police later dropped the charges against his son, but not before a hailstorm of media coverage. That fall, he was one of twelve American poets chosen to appear on *The Power of the Word*, an Emmy-winning PBS program hosted by Bill Moyers.

In 1990 Troupe returned to California. While teaching at the University of California, San Diego, he published a memoir, *Miles and Me*, about his friendship with Miles Davis; he also coproduced and wrote a seven-part radio program about Davis that won a Peabody Award. In 1999 he became a founding editor of *CODE* magazine, a fashion and lifestyle magazine financed by *Hustler* editor Larry Flynt that focused on men of color. After a few years, however, Troupe left the publication when he felt its editorial agenda was beginning to take a new direction that he found unappealing. In 2002 California Governor Gray Davis appointed Troupe to be that state's first official poet laureate. But a background check revealed that Troupe's résumé had listed a degree from Grambling, even though he left the school after one year. He resigned from the post and within a year he had retired from teaching.

Back in New York, Troupe's literary endeavors expanded to writing children's books, and he also began editing the quarterly arts journal *Black Renaissance/Renaissance Noire*. In 2006 Troupe cowrote *The Pursuit of Happyness* with self-made millionaire Chris Gardner, whose story would become the subject of a Hollywood movie starring WILL SMITH.

FURTHER READING
"Quincy Troupe: An Interview," *The American Poetry Review* (Mar./Apr. 2005).
"Quincy Troupe; Live from the Poetry Wars," *QBR: The Black Book Review*, 30 Apr. 2004.
Troupe, Quincy, *Miles and Me* (2000).

JODY BENJAMIN

Trouppe, Quincy Thomas (25 Dec. 1912–12 Aug. 1993), professional Negro League catcher and major league baseball talent scout, was born in Dublin, Georgia, to Mary and Charles, a sharecropper. Troupe was the youngest of ten children. The Troupe family joined the Great Migration of African Americans fleeing the South for greater opportunities in urban centers in the North. Following a difficult encounter with a white overseer, Troupe's father and two of his older brothers moved to St. Louis in order to find work and secure enough money to bring the rest of the family to Missouri. Troupe stayed behind with his mother and other siblings, and when Troupe was ten years old, his father sent money for train fare, and the family was reunited in St. Louis. The family soon settled in Compton Hill where Troupe attended Touissaint L'Overture Elementary School and Vashon High School in the 1920s.

Troupe competed on both his high school and American Legion teams as a pitcher and catcher and led both teams to all-black league championships. During this time Troupe became personally acquainted with members of the St. Louis Stars, a professional black baseball team. He soon began to train with the Stars and competed in exhibition games with the team. He benefited from the advice of established Negro League stars like JAMES "COOL PAPA" BELL, TED "DOUBLE DUTY" RADCLIFFE, and MULE SUTTLES. After a series of short stints with various professional and semiprofessional squads, Troupe joined the Stars in 1931 as a catcher.

From 1931 to 1933, Troupe bounced from team to team, trying to find a permanent position and a lucrative salary. During those transient years Troupe played for some of the finest teams in the Negro Leagues, including the Homestead Grays and the Kansas City Monarchs, and he became acquainted with such luminaries as SATCHEL PAIGE and SMOKY JOE WILLIAMS. Troupe also sporadically attended Lincoln University during the off-season. At the end of the 1933 season, Troupe joined the Bismarck, North Dakota, Cubs. He remained a member of the team for four seasons, from 1933 to 1936. An integrated club that boasted superior Negro League talent, including Paige, Radcliffe, HILTON SMITH, and Troupe, the Bismarck Churchills gained a great deal of attention after winning the prominent, national semipro tournament in Wichita in 1935. Numerous major league scouts witnessed the Bismarck team's victory and Troupe's contribution to their success, approaching Troupe and his team's owner about their futures.

A multitalented athlete, Troupe competed in other sports during the baseball off-season. In 1935 he played basketball in the winter, and during the 1936 off-season, he competed as an amateur prizefighter. Troupe's brief career as a boxer was extremely successful. Despite his lack of experience, he won the Golden Gloves heavyweight championship in 1936.

Increasingly disenchanted with the difficult lifestyle and extensive traveling of black baseball, Troupe briefly retired. His retirement lasted only one season, and he returned to the Negro Leagues as a member of the Indianapolis ABCs in 1938. Although he found satisfaction on the field, Troupe was increasingly frustrated by the Jim Crow policies he encountered during road trips, such as restaurants refusing to serve African Americans, segregated movie theaters, and discriminatory treatment by police officers. He found a solution to his dilemma in 1939, when he joined the Carta Blanca team in the Mexican League. Troupe spent six seasons in the Mexican League, and during his time in Mexico, he gained a great deal of acclaim and recorded a batting average in excess of .300 each season. During his stay in Mexico, Troupe became enamored with the Mexican pronunciation and spelling of his last name, and Troupe became Trouppe in 1946.

Trouppe returned to the United States and the Negro Leagues in 1944 as a player-manager for the Cleveland Buckeyes. His stint as manager with the Buckeyes resulted in two pennants for the club, due to his managerial skills and extraordinary hitting ability. In 1946 while with the Buckeyes, Trouppe also played a major role in integrating the Negro League, acquiring white pitcher Eddie Klep. Klep was the first white player to compete in the formerly all-black league. From 1948 to 1951, Trouppe served as a player-manager for teams in both the Negro and Mexican Leagues.

In 1952 Trouppe finally got the chance to play baseball at the major league level, an opportunity he had been hoping for since becoming a professional baseball player in 1931. The Cleveland Indians signed the thirty-nine-year-old Trouppe in 1952. His tenure as a major league player was short-lived, however. After a mere six games, the Indians reassigned him to the minor leagues, and he retired as a player at the conclusion of the 1952 season. His fielding was fine in the six games that he started, but he only had one hit in ten at bats. His age and the wear on his body were significant. He was valued for helping to advise young pitchers and after his short stint in the majors, the Indians decided he was more valuable working with young pitchers in the minors.

Although Trouppe did not meet great success as a major league player, he was able to stay involved in baseball. In 1953 he was hired as a major league scout for the St. Louis Cardinals. Once again, he encountered racial bigotry and found that the integration of baseball had significant limitations. During his first appointment as a talent scout, Trouppe heavily petitioned St. Louis officials on behalf of ERNIE BANKS and ROBERTO CLEMENTE. After his employers refused to sign Banks, Clemente, and other African American prospects that he recommended, Trouppe's own contract was terminated.

Trouppe had a significant impact on the players he managed and recruited. His passion and knowledge of the game improved the play of numerous black ballplayers. Trouppe also preserved a great deal of Negro League history, a history that for many years was ignored. His photographs, films, and autobiography have provided historians with a rare glimpse into black baseball and have allowed documentarians such as Ken Burns an opportunity to showcase an overlooked chapter in American history. As a player, manager, scout, and amateur historian, Trouppe championed the accomplishments and abilities of African Americans and fought against the racist policies of major league baseball.

FURTHER READING

Trouppe, Quincy. *20 Years Too Soon: Prelude to Major-League Integrated Baseball* (1995).

Peterson, Robert. *Only the Ball Was White: A History of Legendary Black Players and All-Black Professional Teams* (1984).

Rogosin, Donn. *Invisible Men: Life in Baseball's Negro Leagues* (1995).

SARAH L. TREMBANIS

Truth, Sojourner (c. 1799–26 Nov. 1883), abolitionist and women's rights advocate, was born in Hurley, Ulster County, New York, the daughter of James and Elizabeth Baumfree, who were slaves. Named Isabella by her parents, she took the name Sojourner Truth in 1843. As a child, Isabella belonged to a series of owners, the most memorable of whom were the John Dumont family of Esopus, Ulster County, to whom she belonged for approximately seventeen years and with whom she remained close until their migration to the West in

Sojourner Truth, looks at the Bible presented by the Baltimore African American community, with Abraham Lincoln in the Executive Mansion, Washington, D.C., 29 October 1864. Painting by R. D. Bayley. (Library of Congress.)

1849. About 1815 she married another of Dumont's slaves, Thomas, who was much older than she; they had five children. Isabella left Thomas in Ulster County after their emancipation under New York State law in 1827, but she did not marry again.

In the year before her emancipation, Isabella left her master Dumont of her own accord and went to work for the family of Isaac Van Wagenen in Hurley. When a member of Dumont's wife's family illegally sold Isabella's son into perpetual slavery in Alabama, she took another remarkable step for a slave: she went to court and sued successfully for her son's return. She also had a conversion experience, was born again, and joined the newly established Methodist church in Kingston, where she met a Miss Grear, with whom she migrated to New York City in 1828. In New York, Isabella worked in private households and attended both the predominantly white John Street Methodist Church and the African Methodist Episcopal Zion Church, where she briefly encountered three of her older siblings who had also migrated to New York City. She adhered to a series of unorthodox religious societies: the Methodist perfectionists led by James Latourette, the urban missionaries to prostitutes of the Magdalene Asylum, and the Sing Sing "kingdom" or commune of the prophet Matthias (Robert Matthews). The Latourettes introduced Isabella to the Magdalene Asylum, where she met Elijah Pierson, a wealthy Pearl Street merchant. While working in Pierson's household, she met Matthias in 1832. As the only black and one of two working-class members of Matthias's commune, she believed wholeheartedly in his eclectic mixture of spiritualism, millenarianism, personal anointment, temperance, and holistic health practices. She remained his follower until the commune's demise in 1835, following allegations of murder and sexual irregularity. After another of the commune's members charged her with attempted poisoning, she sued successfully for libel and cleared her name. There is no record of her activities between 1835 and 1843, when she did household work in New York City.

Isabella was deeply affected by the millenarian agitation associated with the prophesies of William Miller, who warned that the second coming of Christ would occur in 1843. In the midst of the economic hard times that followed the panic of 1837, she, too, sensed impending doom. On the first of June 1843, acting on the instructions of what she believed to be the Holy Spirit, Isabella changed her name to Sojourner Truth—which translates as "itinerant preacher"—and set out toward the east to preach the need to embrace Jesus. Traveling to Brooklyn, Long Island, Connecticut, and the Connecticut River Valley, she went from one Millerite camp meeting to another. By the end of the year the Millerites were facing their Great Disappointment, when the apocalypse did not occur, and Sojourner Truth looked for a place to spend the winter.

Truth settled in the Northampton Association, a utopian community dedicated to the cooperative manufacture of silk, located in what is now Florence, Massachusetts. The Northampton Association had been founded in 1842 by several idealists, including George Benson, brother-in-law of the leading white Boston abolitionist, William Lloyd Garrison. The tenor of the Northampton Association was quite liberal; blacks were allowed access, and deep convictions about antislavery and women's rights were taken for granted. Reformers such as Garrison, the black abolitionist FREDERICK DOUGLASS, and the British antislavery member of Parliament George Thompson visited the community. Truth made her first appearance at an antislavery meeting in New York City in 1845, while she was living at the Northampton Association. When the association collapsed in 1846 and its lands were subdivided and sold to satisfy creditors, she bought a house on Park Street, paying off the mortgage with proceeds from sales of *The Narrative of Sojourner Truth*, which she had dictated to Olive Gilbert and had published in Boston in 1850.

During the 1850s Truth supported herself through sales of the *Narrative* and other mementos to reform-minded audiences. Sometime around 1847 she uttered the words that were to become her most famous. Truth was in the audience at Faneuil Hall in Boston when Frederick Douglass, despairing that slavery could be abolished peaceably, began to advocate insurrection. Indicting his lack of faith in God's goodness, Truth stood up and asked, "Frederick, is God dead?" To evangelically attuned, nineteenth-century sensibilities, her trust was more appealing than his radicalism. She and Douglass both spoke at a women's rights convention in Worcester, Massachusetts, in 1850. She addressed a similar gathering of Ohio feminists in Akron in 1851, giving what today is her most famous speech. Demanding that poor and working women also be counted as women, Truth was later quoted as having posed the rhetorical question, "And ar'n't I a woman?" which would make her reputation among twentieth-century feminists.

Truth visited Harriet Beecher Stowe, author of *Uncle Tom's Cabin*, in 1852 or 1853. Stowe wrote a preface to a new edition of *The Narrative of Sojourner Truth* and took notes for the essay that most effectively publicized Truth during her lifetime. Stowe published her widely cited "Sojourner Truth, the Libyan Sibyl" in the April 1863 *Atlantic Monthly*; her title, "Libyan Sibyl," crops up in connection with Sojourner Truth throughout the rest of the century.

In 1856 Truth sold her house in Massachusetts and moved to Michigan, where she was close to her daughters and their families, abolitionist supporters, Quakers of various sorts, spiritualists, and relatives of her Rochester friends Amy Post and Isaac Post (including Frances Titus, who edited the 1875–1878 edition of the *Narrative*). Truth also may have been in contact with a branch of Millerites who, under Ellen White, became the Seventh Day Adventists. Although she spent most of her time in Michigan in the town of Battle Creek, Truth joined what was at least her third planned community: she bought a house in 1857 and lived for several years in Harmonia, a community of progressive Friends. She continued her lecture tours throughout the 1850s. In a small town in northern Indiana in 1858, she faced down critics who doubted that so forceful an abolitionist could be a woman, by baring her breast and shaming her antagonists. In 1867 she built a house big enough for her daughters and their families on College Street in Battle Creek, making her remarkable among blacks for her real estate holdings.

During the Civil War, Truth met President Abraham Lincoln in his office in 1864 and worked with volunteers assisting Southern black refugees. During her stay in Washington she went to court to appeal successfully for her rights for a third time, asking for the right to ride what had been Jim Crow streetcars. Realizing that charity was only a palliative, and appalled by the freedpeople's continuing poverty, Truth initiated an effort to find them jobs in and around Rochester, New York, and Battle Creek, Michigan, in 1867. When this task overwhelmed her, she conceived of a plan for resettling freedpeople on government lands in the West. Traveling through New England, the Northwest, and into Kansas in 1870 and 1871, she collected signatures on a petition to Congress, but Congress never allocated any land to African Americans in the West or the South. In 1879, after Truth had retired, a spontaneous migration to Kansas of black Exodusters from Texas, Louisiana, Mississippi, and Tennessee took tens of thousands out of the post-Reconstruction South in which they justifiably feared reenslavement. Truth was unable to return to Kansas in support of the Exodusters. She died in Battle Creek.

In the nineteenth century, this tall, dark-skinned, charismatic, illiterate wisewoman who dressed like a Quaker was best known as a Methodist-style itinerant preacher and religiously inspired supporter of women's rights and the abolition of slavery. A familiar figure in reform circles, she also advocated temperance and associated with spiritualists and water-cure enthusiasts. In her own day she presented herself as the quintessential slave woman. In modern times she has come to stand for the conjunction of race, class, and gender in American liberal reform and symbolizes the unintimidated, articulate black woman. Acutely intelligent although totally unschooled, Truth represents a type of inspired, naive witness that has long appealed to Americans suspicious of over-education.

FURTHER READING
The richest manuscript collection on Truth is the Family Papers of Isaac and Amy Post in the Library of the University of Rochester.

Truth, Sojourner. *Narrative of Sojourner Truth* (1884; repr. 1998).

Bernard, Jacqueline. *Journey toward Freedom: The Story of Sojourner Truth* (1967; repr. 1990).

Ortiz, Victoria *Sojourner Truth, a Self-Made Woman* (1974).

Painter, Nell Irvin. *Sojourner Truth: A Life, a Symbol* (1996).

This entry is taken from the *American National Biography* and is published here with the permission of the American Council of Learned Societies.

NELL IRVIN PAINTER

Tubman, Harriet (c. 1822–10 Mar. 1913), Underground Railroad conductor, abolitionist, spy and scout, and social reformer, was born Araminta Ross in Dorchester County on Maryland's Eastern Shore, one of nine children, to slave parents Harriet Green and Ben Ross. She took her mother's name, Harriet, around 1844. This was also about the time she married John Tubman, a free black of about thirty-two years in age. The couple had no children.

The black community in which Harriet grew up comprised a mix of free and slave, skilled and unskilled people who married one another and formed interconnected, extended families. Freedmen and slaves worked together in the fields, swamps, forests, and canals. Harriet's father worked as a skilled slave, cutting and hauling timber for his master, Anthony Thompson, a lumber supplier for the area's shipbuilding industry. A favorite of Thompson's, Ross eventually won his freedom in 1840 by a provision in Thompson's will that stipulated staggered emancipation dates for all his slaves. The other family members did not fare as well. The death of Thompson's wife in 1824 effected the first family separation, when Thompson's stepson Edward Brodess inherited Harriet Ross and her children. Under the new master the family fell upon particularly hard times. The distance between the two plantations dictated only infrequent family gatherings, while Brodess's practice of hiring out his slaves, even the younger ones, separated the children from one another and from their mother for long periods of time. Brodess, like other slaveholders with small landholdings, commonly hired out his excess slaves or sold them in the slave market to meet expenditures. Several of Harriet Tubman's siblings were sold outside the state, though her mother was successful in saving her youngest son. With

Harriet Tubman in 1911, probably at her home in Auburn, New York. During her long life, she was internationally acclaimed as an Underground Railroad operator, abolitionist, Civil War spy and nurse, suffragist, and humanitarian. (Library of Congress.)

threats and cunning she hid him in the woods for a month, thus thwarting his sale into Georgia.

As a child, Harriet Tubman was hired out to several masters, serving them in a variety of capacities. She worked as a house servant, cleaning house and tending children. She often encountered cruelty and beatings from her white mistresses. She was sent at a young age to trap muskrats in the marshland of Dorchester County, where she became ill from the cold and wet surroundings. In her teens she was hired out most often as a field hand. She drove oxen, carted wood, plowed, crushed flax, worked in timber gangs, and labored as hard as a man. One master to whom she was hired enjoyed displaying her physical strength to his neighbors.

From an early age Harriet made clear her unwillingness to comply with the slave system. At seven years old she hid from a slave mistress for five days after being threatened with a beating for taking a lump of sugar. An episode during her teen years shows her tenacity and foreshadows the work for which she became most well known. When a fellow slave was threatened with a beating for going to a village store without permission, Tubman was ordered to help tie him down. She refused to help, so the overseer grabbed a two-pound weight and hurled it at her. The object struck her in the head, leaving an injury that caused narcoleptic seizures throughout her life.

Before her own escape to freedom, Harriet and her siblings worried constantly about being sold into deep southern slavery. Three sisters had suffered this fate, and when her master's death in 1849 portended the same, she determined to run away. The sale of Tubman's niece, also named Harriet, and her niece's two-year-old daughter, Mary Ann, proved the signal event that pushed her and her brothers to set out for freedom. Tubman's husband, John, refused to join them. Her brothers became fearful not long into the journey and returned, bringing Harriet back as well. Two days later she set out alone. She was probably emboldened by stories of other fugitives. Indeed, Maryland led the southern states in the number of escaped slaves. Nor was the route of escape completely unfamiliar to her. While working on timber gangs, she had learned of a world beyond slavery. In this largely male workforce she heard about and made the acquaintance of free black stevedores and seamen along the eastern seaboard. As the story of MOSES ROPER has indicated, black seamen historically constituted an important source of information linking together southern and northern black communities.

Tubman fled Maryland on foot, walking through Delaware and into Pennsylvania, traveling at night and hiding or sleeping by day. In Philadelphia and Cape May, New Jersey, she worked as a cook, maid, and laundress. However, feeling alone in her freedom, Tubman determined to have the community of her family and friends around her and saved her earnings in order to return south and rescue others. Her reputation as a liberator began in 1850 when she saved her niece Kessiah and her two children from sale in Baltimore; a few months later she returned to free her youngest brother. During that same year, enactment of the Fugitive Slave Law necessitated extra precaution and made it more difficult to take escapees to Canada. In 1851 Tubman stole back into Maryland for her husband, only to discover that he had remarried. Despite her great disappointment, she continued her rescue work undaunted—determined "to do without him."

Around 1855 Tubman took up residence in St. Catherine's, Ontario, Canada, an area to which she delivered many others to freedom. While she resided there, the abolitionist John Brown, who called her "General," sought her out to recruit soldiers for and lead his planned slave insurrection, which collapsed with the failure of the famed attack on the federal arsenal at Harper's Ferry, West Virginia. Tubman apparently supported Brown's plan and spoke admirably of him throughout her life, though illness and a change in date prevented her participation in the raid. In 1857 Tubman accomplished the difficult feat of delivering her own elderly parents to Auburn, New York. Since they were too feeble to walk, Tubman managed her parents' travel to freedom by wagon. She settled them in a modest home on property she bought in Auburn with assistance from New York (and, later, U.S.) secretary of state William Seward. Tubman took up residence there in 1865.

Tubman made fourteen trips back to the Eastern Shore between 1849 and 1860. Recent scholarship reveals that she directly rescued seventy to eighty slaves, some of whom were family members, and indirectly freed about fifty others through instructions she provided. She preferred traveling in the winter months when the daylight was shorter, and she solicited free blacks in Maryland to remove postings of slave runaway advertisements. She wore a variety of disguises and carried a gun to avert trouble and to prevent being betrayed by those who became weary or fearful. Tubman would give them a choice: either go forward to freedom or die. She carried paregoric to sedate babies so their crying would not give them away. Her ability to travel undetected rested upon an elaborate communication system, along with numerous strategies and routes. Her intimate knowledge of various routes and trade networks, wooded areas and waterways, enhanced her surreptitious and daring escapes, but she was also aided by an array of underground operatives—slave and free, rich and poor, white and black—who provided "safe houses" along the way.

Black churches and abolitionist friends like Thomas Garrett, WILLIAM STILL, and Lucretia Mott provided the fugitives with housing, clothing, transportation, and other resources. Tubman herself gave the greatest credit for her success to divine guidance. As a woman of deep religious faith, she found inspiration, like many other enslaved African Americans, in a mixture of evangelical Protestantism and African American folk beliefs. Thus she spoke of charms, experienced spiritual visions, and attributed her ingenuity and daring success to divine handiwork. From her perspective, God's power made it possible for her to boast of never having lost a "passenger." Tubman's success in delivering people from bondage resulted in her being given the moniker "Moses" in her lifetime.

With the onset of the Civil War, Tubman threw herself into the war effort. She traveled to coastal South Carolina in May 1862 and set about nursing wounded soldiers, bondmen, and bondwomen. She also sought to help newly freed women become self-supporting by washing and cooking for the soldiers. Continuing to display ingenuity and sensitivity, Tubman relinquished the privilege of receiving army rations like whites when local blacks expressed suspicion of this. Instead, she supported herself by selling pies, cakes, and root beer she prepared in the evenings.

Tubman's nursing skills and herbal remedies became known and sought after; on one occasion an officer requested that she travel to Florida to attend to troops suffering from severe dysentery. Receiving notes and passes from army officials, she passed freely among Union forces by foot and federal transport. Tubman's plain appearance allowed her to move effortlessly among the slaves, thus making her a valuable scout and spy in Confederate territory. She obtained information about cotton storage, ammunition deposits, and the location of black communities useful to the success of Union campaigns. She particularly admired Colonel James Montgomery, who had fought side by side with John Brown in "Bleeding Kansas," and she worked closely with him in the recruitment of black soldiers at Port Royal, South Carolina. With Montgomery's permission, she led a spying expedition up the Combahee River. The mission resulted in the capture by Montgomery's troops of large caches of material resources and the freeing of 756 slaves.

An independent and practical thinker in regard to gender conventions, Tubman sought appropriate attire for her army work. In a letter to northern friends she commented on her preference for pants or bloomers, given the difficulty of wearing a dress on scouting expeditions, especially when running. After the war she took pride in having worn "pants" and having carried a musket and other military accoutrements, which she saved as souvenirs. During 1865 Tubman served as a nurse, treating black patients at the James River contraband hospital in Virginia; near the end of the war she became matron of the Colored Hospital at Fortress Monroe.

In 1869 the unconventional Tubman married Nelson Davis, a former Union soldier twenty years her junior, though she kept her first husband's name. Like FREDERICK DOUGLASS and SOJOURNER TRUTH, Tubman raised funds for herself and her causes by selling copies of her biography, which was written by Sara Bradford. For twenty-five years Tubman wrote to the federal government in pursuit of her right to a military pension. Colonel Thomas Wentworth Higginson and General Rufus Saxton were among those who intervened unsuccessfully to obtain a government pension for her service. Ironically, two years after her husband's death in 1888 she was finally awarded a pension, receiving compensation not for her own service in the war but for her status as the widow of a black veteran.

Tubman's postbellum work focused on racial uplift efforts for elderly and destitute blacks. Seeing the connection of racial and gender oppression, she worked primarily with black women's groups and black churches, although she did accept monetary gifts from white supporters. She was a delegate at the July 1896 meeting of the Federation of Afro-American Women in Washington, D.C. When asked to address the group, she called for assistance in providing homes for the aged. She worked primarily through her local congregation, Thompson Memorial African Methodist Episcopal (AME) Zion Church, and through the larger AME Zion denomination. In 1896 she was successful in purchasing twenty-five acres of land adjoining her home, on which she sought to build facilities for the indigent. Her meager resources delayed completion of the facility until 1903. In that year she deeded the property to AME Zion trustees. In 1911 Tubman herself entered the Harriet Tubman Home for Aged and Indigent Colored People. She died two years later.

Tubman was a well-known and much respected figure among abolitionists and women's rights advocates of her time. Frederick Douglass lauded her willingness to work without public praise. The suffragist pioneer and leader Susan B. Anthony expressed high regard for "this wonderful woman." The abolitionist William Still said she was unequaled in courage, shrewdness, and altruistic efforts to deliver others. The historian BENJAMIN QUARLES noted that "esteem for her was practically universal among blacks of her day, including high and low, young and old, male and female, and cutting across sectional lines." Later generations would continue to honor her. Formal federal recognition of Harriet Tubman as an enduring model of heroism and patriotism has included naming a ship after her in World War II, designating her home in Auburn a national historic landmark in 1974, and issuing a postage stamp bearing her image in 1978.

FURTHER READING

Bradford, Sara. *Scenes in the Life of Harriet Tubman* (1869).

Humez, Jean McMahon, ed. *Harriet Tubman: The Life and the Life Stories* (2003).

Larson, Kate Clifford. *Bound for the Promised Land: Harriet Tubman, Portrait of an American Hero* (2003).

Quarles, Benjamin. *Allies for Freedom and Blacks and John Brown* (1974).

Quarles, Benjamin. "Harriet Tubman's Unlikely Leadership" in *Black Leaders of the Nineteenth Century*, eds. Leon F. Litwack and August Meier (1988).

ROSETTA E. ROSS

Tucker, C. DeLores (4 Oct. 1927–12 Oct. 2005), secretary of the Commonwealth of Pennsylvania, women's and civil rights activist, and campaigner against misogynistic lyrics in rap music, was born Cynthia DeLores Nottage in Philadelphia, Pennsylvania, the tenth of eleven children of the Reverend Whitfield Nottage, a minister, and Captilda Gardiner, a businesswoman. Because Tucker's father, an immigrant from the Bahamas, did not accept a salary from the churches that employed him, it was left to Tucker's mother, whom Tucker later described as a "Christian feminist," to provide for the family (*Washington Post*, 13 Oct. 2005). She did so by

starting an employment agency for Southern black migrants to Philadelphia, running grocery stores, and investing in real estate. Tucker's socially conservative parents did not allow her or her siblings to listen to popular music, go to dances, or date before the age of twenty-one. Tucker spent much of her early life in rural Montgomery County and often was the only African American in her class. She graduated from Philadelphia Girls High School in 1946. In 1951 she married William J. Tucker, a real estate executive. The couple had no children.

As a young woman, she had hoped for a career in medicine, but a year-long illness put a stop to those plans. She attended Temple University, Pennsylvania State University, and the University of Pennsylvania's Wharton School but did not receive a degree from these institutions. Sometimes referred to as "Dr. Tucker," she received an honorary doctoral degree from Villa Maria College in Erie, Pennsylvania, in 1972, and another from Morris College in Sumter, South Carolina, in 1976.

Tucker's civil rights activities were numerous and pioneering. During World War II, at age sixteen, she protested the color bar at the Bellevue Stratford Hotel in Philadelphia. In 1951 she took part in her first political campaign, working to register African American voters in support of the Democratic mayoral candidate Joseph S. Clark. Long active in the National Association for the Advancement of Colored People (NAACP) as a fund-raiser, she in 1961 received the organization's Freedom Fund Award and in 1965 marched with MARTIN LUTHER KING JR. and others in Selma, Alabama. Tucker was a delegate to President Lyndon Johnson's historic White House Conference on Civil Rights that same year.

From grassroots civil rights campaigns Tucker moved into politics and began a tradition of firsts. In 1968 she became the first African American and the first woman to serve on the Philadelphia Zoning Board. In 1971 she became the first black secretary of state in the United States, serving the Commonwealth of Pennsylvania through 1977. At that point Governor Milton Shapp fired her because of her alleged illegal use of state employees to write speeches for which she was paid $66,000 in fees. Tucker denied the charges. During her tenure she created the state's first Commission on the Status of Women and pushed Pennsylvania to become one of the first states to pass the proposed equal rights amendment. As part of her responsibilities as secretary of the commonwealth, she instituted voter registration by mail and supported the reduction of the voting age from twenty-one to eighteen. In 1976 Tucker was the first black woman to serve as chair of the Credentials Committee for the Democratic National Convention. She ran unsuccessfully for political office on three occasions—for lieutenant governor of Pennsylvania in 1978, for the U.S. Senate in 1980, and for the U.S. House of Representatives in 1992. Tucker was a vital member of the Democratic National Committee, where she served on the executive committee from 1972 to 1976, chaired its Black Caucus from 1984 to 1995, and was a leading member of the party's women's caucus. She was also the first African American to serve as president of the National Federation of Democratic Women in 1977.

In 1984 Tucker created the National Political Congress of Black Women as a means for black women in the professional and political fields to legitimate their demands for places at the electoral table. She formed the Committee on Presidential Appointments, and every four years she convened the committee and personally contacted the president in office at the time to promote a lengthy list of black, female candidates for appointments. She publicly lobbied for President Bill Clinton's labor secretary Alexis M. Herman, presidential candidate and former U.S. senator CAROL E. MOSELEY BRAUN, President George W. Bush's secretary of state CONDOLEEZZA RICE, and former assistant secretary of housing and urban development Constance B. Newman. In 1986 Tucker founded and served as president of the Bethune–Du Bois Institute, Inc., to promote cultural development of black youth through scholarships and education. As its publisher, she launched *Vital Issues: The Journal of African American Speeches*, a quarterly journal that reprinted speeches by prominent African Americans on a variety of topics, including politics, culture, religion, health, law, and civil rights.

Tucker was known for her extraordinary humility when it came to public recognition. She politely declined accolades such as the Black Leadership Forum's Lamplighter Award. Nevertheless, the list is long. She was included in *Ebony* magazine's 100 Most Influential Black Americans from 1972 to 1977 and again in 2001, and 2002 she was one of its 100 Most Influential Black Organization Leaders; she was nominated for Woman of the Year by *Ladies Home Journal* in 1975 and 1976; and in 1996 *People* magazine listed her in its 25 Most Intriguing People. In 1982 she was awarded the NAACP THURGOOD MARSHALL Award. CORETTA SCOTT KING, founder of the Martin Luther King

Jr. Center for Nonviolence, awarded Tucker the Martin Luther King Jr. Distinguished Service Award. In 1990 Tucker received the Philadelphia Urban League WHITNEY YOUNG Award.

Tucker's dedicated civil rights activism and her crusade against misogynistic rap lyrics gained her more national attention in the last decades of her life. Her concern for black youth grew into concern for black women and black female youth. In 1996 U.S. senator (then first lady) Hilary Rodham Clinton acknowledged Tucker's deep concern for children in her book *It Takes a Village*. Although a lifelong Democrat, Tucker's aggressive stance against rap led to her partnering with conservative Republicans such as Bill Bennett (secretary of education under President Ronald Reagan), with whom she publicly condemned Time Warner. A member of the Alpha Kappa Alpha Sorority, Tucker publicly voiced concern that such lyrics and attitudes threatened the moral foundation of the black community. She picketed stores that sold rap music and bought stock in music labels such as Sony and Time Warner so she could attend shareholders' meetings, where she condemned the companies for supporting gangsta rap and encouraging pornography. An important member of the NAACP, she protested its decision to nominate the rapper TUPAC SHAKUR for one of its Image Awards. Her relationship with the actual rappers was antagonistic. Most criticized her views as blinkered and intolerant, and a few, including Shakur, directly attacked her in their lyrics. For this Tucker filed a slander suit against Shakur's estate, but the case, in which she demanded $10 million in damages, was later dismissed.

In the mid-1990s Tucker's pioneering efforts to stand against a popular cultural phenomenon led to *Redbook* magazine naming her best qualified to be ambassador to the United Nations (in conjunction with the National Women's Political Caucus). In 1997 the National Newspaper Publishers Association presented her with the 1997 Newsmaker of the Year Award.

Tucker died at the Suburban Woods Health Center in Norristown, Pennsylvania. At her funeral, attended by state and national political leaders, former vice President Al Gore lauded her as "a four-star general in the battle for righteousness" (*New York Times*, 6 Nov. 2005). On 25 April 2006 a state historical marker honoring Tucker was unveiled at the State Museum of Pennsylvania in Harrisburg by Governor Edward G. Rendell, the Pennsylvania Historical and Museum Commission, and her husband. The unveiling was the start of plans to rename the North Building adjacent to the Pennsylvania State Capitol Building in Harrisburg the Secretary C. Dolores Tucker Building.

FURTHER READING
Tucker's husband donated her personal papers, video tapes, photographs, and items of clothing to the Pennsylvania State Archives and State Museum.
Henderson, Ashyia N. "C. DeLores Tucker," *Contemporary Black Biography,* vol. 12.
Hine, Darlene Clark, ed. *Black Women in America: An Historical Encyclopedia* (1993).
Smith, Jessie Carney, ed. *Notable Black American Women* (Dec. 1991).
Obituaries: *Washington Post,* 13 Oct. 2005; *New York Times,* 6 Nov. 2005.

LINDA CHAVERS

Tucker, Lorenzo (28 June 1907–19 Aug. 1986), actor, was born in Philadelphia, Pennsylvania, the son of John Tucker, a laborer, and Virginia Lee. From early childhood, Lorenzo Tucker wanted to be in show business; as an adolescent, he would write and stage back-porch shows, casting himself and his friends as performers. His mother, however, wanted him to be a doctor, but he deliberately quit Temple University in 1926 and left home for Atlantic City, New Jersey, where he met a chorus girl from one of the black nightclubs. Together they formed a ballroom dance specialty act, and by the end of 1926 they were performing on the black vaudeville circuit.

Tucker rose quickly through the ranks of black show business. Within a year he was touring with blues legend BESSIE SMITH, and in 1927 he was signed as a movie actor by black film pioneer OSCAR MICHEAUX. Tucker's good looks and urbanity made him a minor star of black stage and screen, and in the next few years he appeared in vaudeville shows, Broadway plays, and a dozen feature films made with black casts for African American audiences, known as "race movies." Micheaux, the most important and prolific of the race filmmakers, dubbed Tucker the "Colored Valentino" for the sake of publicity. Tucker appeared in at least eight Micheaux films, the earliest, *When Men Betray,* in 1928. Following appearances in two more Micheaux silent films, *Wages of Sin* (1929) and *Easy Street* (1930), Tucker starred in *Veiled Aristocrats,* Micheaux's 1932 sound remake of his 1925 silent film, *The House behind the Cedars,* based on CHARLES CHESNUTT's novel about passing.

But Tucker's fame was short-lived. The Great Depression, the advent of sound film, and other factors threatened the viability of race films, and by 1933 Tucker had quit show business, married Katherine Godfrey, and moved to Long Island, where he built himself a business as a carpenter and a house painter. The lure of show business was too strong, however, and Tucker returned to New York City and to acting, appearing in the Micheaux films *Harlem after Midnight* (1934), *Temptation* (1935), and *Underworld* (1937).

In 1942 he was drafted and spent the next three years in Europe, gaining the rank of sergeant in the 847th Army Air Corps Aviation Battalion. Though not a member of Special Services, Tucker nevertheless produced numerous stage shows for the 847th during the war. In many he served as the master of ceremonies. Most of these shows were staged before integrated audiences.

After being discharged in 1946, Tucker returned to black show business and appeared in a few more black-cast films. By 1950, however, such films were no longer being made because Hollywood had begun integration, and he spent the next ten years acting in black theater companies touring the United States and Great Britain. In 1962 Tucker quit show business again, divorced, and married his second wife, Julia Garnett. That same year he was hired as the autopsy assistant to the chief medical examiner of New York City, Dr. Milton Helpern. In this capacity Tucker assisted in hundreds of autopsies, most notably that of MALCOLM X in 1965.

Tucker retired in 1973, and after the death of his second wife, he married Mildred Childs. That marriage soon ended in divorce, and by 1977 he had relocated to Los Angeles, where he began to audition for movie roles. But the entertainment industry had passed him by; he spent his final years in Hollywood documenting black theater and film history in general and his own career in particular. During his life Tucker amassed over six hundred pounds of black film memorabilia, which, as the Lorenzo Tucker Collection, is now housed in New York City at the Schomburg Center for Research in Black Culture. In 1983 he married his fourth wife, Paulina Segura. There were no children from any of his marriages. He died in Los Angeles.

FURTHER READING
Bowser, Pearl, Jane Gaines, and Charles Musser. *Oscar Micheaux and His Circle: African-American Filmmaking and Race Cinema of the Silent Era* (2001).

Grupenhoff, Richard. *The Black Valentino: The Stage and Screen Career of Lorenzo Tucker* (1988).

This entry is taken from the *American National Biography* and is published here with the permission of the American Council of Learned Societies.

RICHARD GRUPENHOFF

Tucker, Rosina (4 Nov. 1881–3 Mar. 1987), civil rights activist, was born Rosina Harvey in Northwest Washington, D.C., to Lee Roy and Henrietta Harvey. The daughter of former slaves, she said her parents never talked about those days. "Very few former slaves talked about it," she later said in the hour-long 1982 documentary *Miles of Smiles, Years of Struggle*, "I overheard them talking to each other, but they didn't discuss it with the children." Tucker's father taught himself how to read and always instilled the value of a good education in his nine children.

After graduating from M Street High School, Tucker married Reverend JAMES CORROTHERS on 2 December 1899. The two soon had one son, Henry Harvey Corrothers. The couple lived in New York for a while and then moved back to Washington, D.C., in 1904.

After her husband died in 1917, Tucker worked as a clerk for the U.S. government. On Thanksgiving Eve in 1918 she married Berthea Tucker, a Pullman porter. They moved to a house on Seventh Street in Washington, D.C. Her husband's low wages and long working hours without overtime pay impelled her to become involved in the railroad union for black Pullman workers known as the Brotherhood of Sleeping Car Porters (BSCP), which was founded in 1925 in Harlem by Ashley Totten and A. PHILIP RANDOLPH.

In the early days of the Brotherhood, the organizers often had to act in secret; thus, it was common for their wives to do the work. Tucker reveled in the work she did for the union and traveled widely, recruiting Brotherhood members at railroad centers all over the country. She was determined to change the harsh working conditions her husband and the other African American porters had to work under. Not only were all the Pullman workers called "George," by white passengers and railroad employees, but they had no job security. They could be fired simply for not smiling frequently or for not looking happy. At a time when Jim Crow laws were still prominent, she was blunt and spoke up when she saw injustice.

In 1931 Tucker organized the local Washington, D.C., ladies' auxiliary of the BSCP, which provided financial and emotional support for the members of the Brotherhood. Soon, to everyone's astonishment, the women had raised a large sum of money by hosting parties, dances, and dinners. Tucker enlisted her church to help families of the Brotherhood who were experiencing illnesses and other difficulties, including loss of employment.

Also in the early 1930s, because of her role in organizing the union, Tucker's husband lost his job, which put a strain on the family. Soon after her husband's firing, Tucker walked into the office of Berthea's boss, banged on the table, and demanded that he put her husband back to work. She insisted that she was responsible for her own actions and that her husband's job should not be affected. The next day, her husband was back working on the trains.

In 1937 the union's efforts paid off, largely because of Tucker's work. The Pullman Company recognized the union and signed a contract, which was the first official agreement between a large U.S. corporation and a black union. In September 1938 the union wives established the International Ladies' Auxiliary and Tucker became its secretary and treasurer. That same year Tucker chaired the Constitution and Rules Committee at the union's national convention in Chicago. In 1945 Tucker's only son died of heart disease. Devastated, Tucker continued her work, marching on Washington in 1963, again with the brotherhood, and helping to merge the BSCP with the Brotherhood of Railway and Airline Clerks in 1978.

Tucker received numerous awards such as the Candace Award for leadership from the National Coalition of 100 Black Women, and in 1983 she received a humanitarian award from the Leadership Conference on Civil Rights. She also worked diligently for the Fifteenth Street Presbyterian Church and was a member of that Washington congregation for more than sixty-five years, where everyone knew her as "Mother Tucker." Later in life, she toured across the country, giving lectures that recounted the history of the Brotherhood and the Ladies' Auxiliary.

In 1982, at one hundred years of age, Tucker narrated the PBS documentary *Miles of Smiles, Years of Struggle*. The film, which chronicled the story of the Pullman porters' struggle to form a union, argued that this struggle laid the foundation for the modern civil rights movement. "The importance of the Brotherhood was that it proved blacks could organize, and it gave all black people hope," said producer Paul Wagoner. "The civil rights movement would probably have happened without the Brotherhood. But it would have been more difficult." When she was 102 years old, Tucker appeared before Congressional committees to lobby for greater protection for senior citizens.

Tucker died in 1987 at age 105 in Washington, D.C.; she had lived in the same house since 1918. In an unpublished autobiography she had written in her nineties, she wrote the following: "Today is my day, as it is your day. Although I live far removed from the time when I was born, I do not feel that my heart should dwell in the past. It is in the future. While I live, let not my life be in vain. And when I depart, may there be remembrance of me and my life as I have lived it."

FURTHER READING

Carney Smith, Jessie. *Notable Black American Women* (1996).

Essence (May 1985).

Gray White, Deborah. *Too Heavy a Load: Black Women in Defense of Themselves* (1999).

Jet (Oct. 1984).

Salem, Dorothy, ed. *African American Women* (1993).

Obituary: *Washington Post*, 5 Mar. 1987.

CHESYA BURKE

Tucker, Snake Hips (1905–1937), dancer, was born Earl Tucker, probably in Maryland. The names and occupations of his parents are unknown, and little is known about his early life. What has been determined about his later career is owed to the efforts of jazz scholars Marshall Stearns and Joan Stearns. Tucker is said to have arrived in New York City as a child. By the mid-1920s he was dancing regularly at Connie's Inn, a Harlem nightclub that catered to whites. By that time Tucker had already begun to work out his signature dance style and had acquired the nickname "Snake Hips," the name of an old hip-grinding dance. He was also renowned for making women in the audience scream and swoon with his steamy, erotic movements, which were wholly original and utterly inimitable.

Erotic dances had been an element of dancing to jazz music from the beginning: the "Mooche" around the turn of the century, the "Grind," shimmy-and-shake dancing, and others. But Tucker's act was in a class by itself, and it took eroticism in dancing to a level that has never been surpassed. It was a pelvic-grinding performance of his own invention that always enthralled, no matter how many times it was seen. Tucker's routine has been described in detail by many, including Marshall

and Jean Stearns, Mura Dehn, DUKE ELLINGTON, and LANGSTON HUGHES. He would dress in a silk blouse and tight black bell-bottom pants, with a tassel dangling from an ornate belt buckle. The first glimpse of his sharp and threatening appearance usually sufficed to quiet an audience. "Tucker had at the same time a disengaged and a menacing air, like a sleeping volcano," write the Stearns, who saw Tucker in action, "which seemed to give audiences the feeling that he was a cobra and they were mice." He would glide forward, rocking his hips in progressively greater motions, the tassel describing progressively greater circles, until his whole body was in motion. Tucker used his feet "merely for propulsion," wrote Hughes, "since his body did all the rest."

In the late 1920s Tucker began an association with Duke Ellington that would last the rest of his life. Ellington served as a kind of father figure and protector for Tucker, a brash, hot-tempered, and often violent partygoer and playboy who was usually armed with a razor. Ellington also found him a perfect stage accompaniment to his "jungle-style jazz," along with the usual shake-and-shimmy dancers. When Ellington opened at the Cotton Club on 4 December 1927, Tucker was a prominent part of the show, dancing to "East St. Louis Toodle-Oo." Later Ellington composed the "Snake Hips" dance, which he recorded in the summer of 1929, especially for Tucker; "Rockin' in Rhythm," too, was composed with Tucker in mind.

Tucker appeared in the musical *Blackbirds of 1928*, which opened at the Liberty Theatre on 9 May 1928 and which included BILL "BOJANGLES" ROBINSON. Critics described Tucker's performance as everything from astounding to scandalous. The most remarkable extant footage of Tucker is found in the two-reel film *Crazy House* (1931; not to be confused with a 1943 film with the same name). The action takes place in an asylum, and at one point the camera pans over to discover Tucker, playing an inmate, doing his stunning trademark dance in a long segment. Tucker also appears briefly in *Symphony in Black: A Rhapsody of Negro Life* (1935), a one-reel short subject devoted to Ellington. Tucker is doubtless also in the background of a number of other short subjects of the era.

Tucker was one of the few truly erotic stage performers and one of the few African American dancers of the 1920s and 1930s to achieve a measure of success without doing tap. Many performers drew from Tucker, including Albert Minns, Clifton Webb, and Elvis Presley. The so-called dirty dancing moves of the 1990s were but distant echoes of Tucker's sensuous, erotic performances. Tucker eventually grew ill from "internal ailments" (syphilis) and died in New York. Duke Ellington paid his hospital bills.

FURTHER READING
Hughes, Langston. *Black Magic* (1967).
Stearns, Marshall, and Jean Stearns. *Jazz Dance* (1968; repr. 1994).
This entry is taken from the *American National Biography* and is published here with the permission of the American Council of Learned Societies.

ROBERT P. CREASE

Tunnell, Emlen (29 Mar. 1925–22 July 1975), football player and coach, was born in Bryn Mawr, Pennsylvania, the son of Elzie Tunnell and Catherine Adams. Raised by his mother, a housekeeper, he was a star athlete in basketball and football at Radnor (Pennsylvania) High School. Upon graduating from high school in 1942, he attended the University of Toledo. In 1943 Tunnell played on the Toledo basketball team that advanced to the finals of the National Invitation Tournament in New York City before losing to St. John's University. During his single varsity football season at Toledo, Tunnell suffered a broken neck. After a period of recovery he joined the U.S. Coast Guard in 1944. In 1946, following his release from the service, he enrolled at the University of Iowa. Playing in both offensive and defensive backfields, Tunnell had a successful season with the Hawkeyes but was forced to sit out his senior year owing to eye surgery. When he graduated in 1948, Tunnell had a year of college football eligibility remaining; he decided instead to play professional football.

In the summer of 1948 Tunnell hitchhiked from his Garrett Hill, Pennsylvania, home to New York City seeking a tryout with the New York Giants of the National Football League (NFL). "I was just about to forget it and go home," he later recalled, "when I got a ride from a West Indian guy in a banana truck who took me all the way to the Lincoln Tunnel. And when I saw Tim Mara, the owner of the Giants then, he told me, 'Since you had the guts to come in and ask for a tryout, we'll give you one.'" Tunnell was signed by the Giants and became the first African American to play for the team. He fit in well on a team composed of about one-third southern players because of his genial personality, but he had a difficult time on the field during his rookie season. Juggled between offense and defense by Giants head coach Steve Owen, Tunnell suffered a loss of confidence and made a number of mistakes during games. As a result, he became one of the targets of disgruntled Giants fans, who booed substandard performances during a disappointing 4-8 season.

Tunnell's play improved as he was moved permanently to defensive back and punt returner toward the end of his rookie season; he continued to improve for the next several years. In an era when defensive backs were generally small, Tunnell, at 6'1" and around 200 pounds, was the first of a new breed of defensive backfield specialists who were both large and fast. In 1950 he became the key to the Giants' famed "umbrella" defense, which dropped two linemen off the usual six-man defensive line of scrimmage for added pass protection, and he was recognized as one of the league's outstanding defensive players. During his fourteen years in the NFL, Tunnell was named to the league's all-pro team four times and played in seven Pro Bowl games. In 1952 he gained a record 924 yards returning punts, kickoffs, and interceptions, thirty yards more than the total gained by the league's leading running back, Dan Towler of the Los Angeles Rams. The following year Tunnell contributed 819 yards on defense, better than all NFL ball carriers except two. When Owen was asked why he didn't use Tunnell on offense, the Giants coach replied, "What, and lose all those yards on defense?"

During his years with the Giants, Tunnell earned the nickname "Emlen the Gremlin" because of his ability to intercept opponents' passes. Over his career he intercepted a then-record seventy-nine passes and returned them for 1,282 yards. He also returned 258 punts for a total of 2,209 yards. Convinced that he was losing the speed required for a defensive back, the Giants released Tunnell in 1959, and he was signed by Vince Lombardi, a former Giants coach, who had been appointed head coach of the Green Bay Packers. During his three years with Green Bay, from 1959 to 1961, Tunnell helped stabilize the defensive backfield. "He meant a lot to the Packers then," Lombardi said. "He was a pastor, a cheerleader, and a coach as well as a player." Tunnell was a member of two NFL championship teams: the 1956 New York Giants and the 1961 Green Bay Packers. In 1962 Tunnell married Patricia Dawkins; they had no children. That same year he became a scout for the Giants, and from 1965 to 1973 he was a Giants assistant coach, making him the NFL's first African American assistant coach. He became the club's assistant director of professional personnel in 1974. During those years Tunnell was frustrated by the failure of NFL teams to hire black head coaches or more black management executives.

Among his many honors, Tunnell was selected as a member of the Professional Football Hall of Fame in 1967. He was the first African American so honored and the first player selected strictly for his defensive ability. In 1969 he was selected to the NFL's fiftieth anniversary all-time team. Tunnell died of a heart attack in Pleasantville, New York.

FURTHER READING

Tunnell, Emlen, with William Gleason. *Footsteps of a Giant* (1966).

Eskenazi, Gerald. *There Were Giants in Those Days* (1976).

Gottehrer, Barry. *The Giants of New York: A History of Professional Football's Most Fabulous Dynasty* (1963).

Smith, Don. *New York Giants* (1960).

Obituary: *New York Times*, 24 July 1975.

This entry is taken from the *American National Biography* and is published here with the permission of the American Council of Learned Societies.

JOHN M. CARROLL

Ture, Kwame. *See* Carmichael, Stokely.

Tureaud, Alexander Pierre (26 Feb. 1899–22 Jan. 1972), civil rights attorney, was born in New Orleans, Louisiana, the son of Louis Tureaud, a carpenter, and Eugenie Dejan. Tureaud's early childhood memories were warm and pleasant. He lived in an integrated neighborhood of African Americans, Italians, Filipinos, and Irish; the children played together in the streets and in one another's homes. Although New Orleans had few public schools for African American children in the early twentieth century, Tureaud was fortunate in that two were located in the downtown section where he resided. After completing the seven grades at Bayou Road School, he transferred to THOMY LAFON's public school for one additional grade.

As a boy, Tureaud was keenly aware of the racial segregation that characterized life in the city. The public parks, benches, and other public facilities had "for white only" signs on them at one time or another. His first direct experience with racial discrimination occurred when he worked in a small general store operated by two white women, who fired him after they discovered that he was African American. Tureaud was often mistaken for white because of his French, Spanish, and Indian ancestry.

In 1916 Tureaud decided, to the dismay of his family, to leave New Orleans. Even though he had acquired an elementary education, his prospects in the city were no better than those of young blacks who had not attended school. Moreover he had become thoroughly disgusted with the thought of a lifelong career as a cement finisher, the job he had held regularly during summer school breaks. When a friend told him that a labor recruiter was in the vicinity offering employment in Chicago, along with free transportation, Tureaud lied about his age in order to be eligible to go. Aged seventeen at the time, he told the agent he was twenty-one. That year he became one of the thousands of African Americans who took part in the "Great Migration" to urban centers of the North. Tureaud did not learn until much later that he and many others who were recruited were to be used as strikebreakers in the Chicago railroad yards. The opportunity to get away from southern segregation was lure enough for him and the trainload of others who left for Chicago.

Upon arrival he and the other migrants were taken to the railroad yards to begin the work of putting down roadbeds. Fearing for his safety, he left the railyard after less than three months, shortly securing work in a foundry as helper to a form maker. He soon left that job after being hospitalized for a back injury.

Although Chicago was quite an experience for Tureaud, it was not his final destination. He had long wanted to go to New York City, so he went there and lived for a while with his brother. He found that African Americans in both cities vigorously protested racial discrimination and other injustices. They filed lawsuits against hotels, restaurants, and theaters that refused to serve them. Influenced by these activities, he decided to pursue a legal career.

Tureaud moved to Washington, D.C., where he completed high school at Dunbar and Armstrong high schools in 1920. From 1920 to 1922 he studied law privately under a Professor Hart. After completing his secondary education, and with good letters of recommendation, Tureaud entered Howard Law School in Washington in 1922 and received the bachelor of laws degree with honors in 1925. During this time he had worked as a stock salesman for the Mutual Housing Company, which owned and operated several large apartment houses for African Americans in Washington, and as a library assistant for a while for the U.S. Justice Department. At commencement he was awarded a set of law books valued at five hundred dollars for making the highest grade in legal research. He passed the District of Columbia bar examination immediately following graduation. In 1926, after a brief period of practicing law in Washington, Tureaud returned to New Orleans. Immediately after his return to New Orleans, he accepted the job of cashier in the office of Comptroller of Customs. He remained at the customhouse until his resignation in 1941. In 1931 he married Lucille Dejoie, a graduate of Howard University's pharmacy school; they had six children. While it is clear that he was a registered Republican in the early 1930s, almost nothing is known of his activities in the party. Sometime during the early 1940s he changed his affiliation and became a Democrat.

Tureaud was admitted to the Louisiana bar in 1927. At the time there were only four African American attorneys in the state. He held the distinction of being the sole black lawyer practicing regularly in the state from 1937 to 1947. Tureaud's long association with the New Orleans branch of the NAACP began in 1927. After spearheading the ouster of the old guard leadership from the local branch, Tureaud helped to make the NAACP a symbol of progressive action and full equality for African Americans throughout Louisiana. Tureaud did not have a law firm and practiced alone. Among the numerous civil rights suits he filed were several that equalized salaries for public school teachers throughout the state (e.g., *Joseph P. McKelpin v. Orleans Parish School Board* [1941] and *Eula Mae Lee v. Jefferson Parish School Board* [1943]) and that permitted African American students to attend Louisiana State University's professional schools as well as the undergraduate and graduate schools (e.g., *Roy Wilson v. Board of Supervisors of Louisiana State University* [1950] and *Viola Johnson v. Board of Supervisors of Louisiana State University* [1956]).

One of his more difficult cases was the suit filed to integrate public schools in New Orleans in 1952. A decade-long struggle, from 1952 through 1962, *Bush v. Orleans Parish School Board* consumed thousands of hours of lawyers' and judges' time and was in and out of the courts twenty-four times. Tureaud's suits to integrate parks, playgrounds, and public facilities were all filed prior to passage of the Civil Rights Act of 1964.

Tureaud's legal work did not prevent him from active participation in state politics. He waged an unsuccessful campaign for a seat in the U.S. House of Representatives in 1958. Although he lost, his candidacy was a milestone, for it showed that an African American in the South could run for national office.

Identifying with all things Catholic, Tureaud was a lector in the Corpus Christi Church and regularly attended the Sunday morning Mass. In 1964 he went to Rome and while there was granted an audience with Pope Paul VI.

Tulane University inducted Tureaud into the Order of the Coif in 1971. He retired the same year to devote his remaining years to writing his autobiography and collecting and preserving historical documents relating to the history of African Americans in Louisiana, but a diagnosis of cancer prevented any real beginning of these projects. Although he was probably the most active civil rights lawyer in the state, he was not a wealthy man when he died in New Orleans. Much of his civil rights litigation was done on a voluntary basis.

Other honors were bestowed after Tureaud's death. The city of New Orleans named a street and building after him. Louisiana State University in Baton Rouge dedicated the A. P. Tureaud Hall in 1990.

FURTHER READING

Tureaud's papers are in Amistad Research Center, Tulane University.

Logsdon, Joseph. "Oral History of Alexander P. Tureaud Sr.," in Archives Department, University of New Orleans.

Worthy, Barbara A. "The Travail and Triumph of a Southern Black Civil Rights Lawyer: The Legal Career of Alexander P. Tureaud, 1899–1972," Ph.D. diss., Tulane University, 1984.

This entry is taken from the *American National Biography* and is published here with the permission of the American Council of Learned Societies.

BARBARA A. WORTHY

Turner, Benjamin Sterling (17 Mar. 1825–21 Mar. 1894), Reconstruction politician, was born a slave near Weldon, Halifax County, North Carolina. His parents' names are unknown. He was owned by Elizabeth Turner, a widow, who took the five-year-old Turner with her when, in 1830, she moved to Dallas County in Alabama's rich cotton-producing and slave-dense Black Belt. He grew up in Dallas County and in Selma, on the Alabama River.

When Turner was twenty, his owner sold him to Major W. H. Gee, her stepdaughter's husband, to pay off debts. Turner was intelligent and industrious, and an overseer once found him with a spelling book and threatened to whip him if he repeated the offense. The powerfully built Turner was placed in charge of Gee House, his new owner's hotel in Selma. Although state law prohibited the education of slaves, Gee's children ignored the statute and taught Turner to read and write. He honed his skills further by studying newspapers. When Gee died, his brother James T. Gee became Turner's owner, and Turner was placed in charge of James Gee's Saint James Hotel. Permitted to hire out his time, Turner operated a livery stable and a wood yard, and he became respected among both blacks and whites. He was an affluent man by 1860. At some point Turner married a black woman named Independence, but a white man purchased her for his mistress. The incident allegedly embittered Turner to the point that he renounced ever marrying again. In any event the 1870 federal census for Dallas County lists a Benjamin S. Turner, and beneath his name lists that of Osceola, a nine-year-old "mulatto" boy.

Benjamin S. Turner, first African American from Alabama elected to the national House of Representatives, c. 1870. (Library of Congress/Brady-Handy Photograph Collection.)

When the Civil War began, Turner bought two hundred dollars' worth of Confederate bonds. Throughout the conflict Selma was an important manufacturing and ordnance center for the Confederacy, and Turner continued his own business affairs. He also looked after the operations of his owner, who was absent serving with Confederate military forces. In spring 1865 the Union general James H. Wilson's cavalry forces swept through Alabama, capturing Selma and burning two-thirds of the city. Turner's properties were lost in the general destruction. He later sought reimbursement of eight thousand dollars from the Southern Claims Commission. It is not clear how much if any compensation he received, but Turner went to work and soon prospered as a general merchant.

After the war, concerned about the welfare of his race, Turner put up his own money to establish a school for black children in Selma. His efforts urging former slaves to make work contracts helped establish a peaceful return to order and earned him the respect of the white community.

After the Reconstruction Acts of 1867, Turner was appointed county tax collector with biracial approval. He resigned after a year and, running as an Independent, was elected city councilman. He and another former bondsman were Selma's first black city councilmen. When the town began paying them, Turner resigned, because he believed that in such destitute times a city official should serve without compensation. During the presidential election in 1868, when conservative Democrats failed to promise voting rights for blacks, Turner helped deliver the town and county to the victorious Ulysses S. Grant.

Turner recouped economically to the point that in 1870 he had personal property worth ten thousand dollars. He was nominated for Congress in that year with the aid of newly enfranchised blacks and native white Republicans, known derisively as "scalawags." His moderate political philosophy cost him the financial support of the First District's northern-born Republicans, the "carpetbaggers." Undeterred, Turner sold a horse to raise campaign funds, and, running on a platform of "Universal Suffrage and Universal Amnesty," he was easily elected. The district had a majority of black voters; in Dallas County alone blacks outnumbered whites 32,152 to 8,522. Turner was the first African American elected from Alabama to the U.S. House of Representatives.

In the House, Turner was appointed to the Committee on Invalid Pensions and impressed his congressional colleagues with his political ability and judgment. Besides his general work with the committee, Turner introduced three bills that provided pensions for individual Union army veterans, one of them a black man. During his term Turner established himself by both deed and word to be the antithesis of a Radical Republican. He introduced five bills to remove the Fourteenth Amendment's political disabilities from eight white Alabamians. Seeking aid for Selma, which was still rebuilding, Turner failed to obtain federal money for repairs to a war-damaged Episcopal church.

Turner's tenure was marked by three main attempts, all unsuccessful, to improve the economy of Alabama and the South. Denied floor time for supporting speeches, he had his remarks placed in the appendix of the *Congressional Globe*. The neophyte congressman strongly opposed the cotton tax imposed by Congress. In effect from 1866 to 1888, the tax was justified as a means of having the South pay a part of the war costs. For years southern states unsuccessfully petitioned Congress to refund the money. Turner presented a memorial from the Mobile Board of Trade asking for reimbursement, and he introduced his own bill to return the cotton tax to the southern states. He argued that the law was unconstitutional, favored foreign competitors over Americans, and hurt small farmers, both black and white, as well as landowners, merchants, and manufacturers.

Turner also failed to obtain passage of a bill appropriating $200,000 in federal money to construct in Selma a public building to be used primarily as a customhouse, post office, and revenue office. The Committee on Public Buildings and Grounds gave no serious attention to the bill.

Turner's most significant bill authorized U.S. land commissioners to purchase private lands sold at public auction, subdivide the acreage, and sell it to landless citizens living in the immediate vicinity. The property would be sold in tracts of 160 acres or as much less as the purchaser desired, and the buyer would pay 10 percent down and 10 percent annually. Turner intended "the landless and poor people of our country" to benefit, especially blacks. Calling the bill an act of justice made compelling by dire need, he asked priority of passage over various laws providing federal relief to foreigners. The bill never got past the Committee on Public Lands.

Turner returned to Selma and was renominated by the Republicans in the First District. His conservative course in Congress and nonpartisan patronage appointments provoked a challenge from Philip Joseph, black editor of the *Mobile Watchman*, who ran as an Independent. Joseph's action split both the black vote and the vote of white Republicans, and resulted in the election of Frederick G. Bromberg, a native white who ran for both the Democrats and the newly formed Liberal Republicans. After his defeat, Turner retired from seeking elective office.

The crippling economic depression of the 1870s forced Turner into bankruptcy, and he turned in desperation to farming. Actually, he owned more land—three hundred acres in Dallas County—than most whites owned. Though not a candidate himself, Turner sustained his interest in politics. He served three times on the state Republican Executive Committee through 1880, he was a delegate at large to the Republican National Convention in 1880, and he was a Republican presidential elector in 1880. After that, he withdrew from political affairs to concentrate on farming. Hard economic times continued, and he died in poverty on his farm near Selma.

In 1985 black and white committees working together in Selma succeeded in erecting a monument over Turner's grave. A white man, Jeremiah Denton, Alabama's first Republican U.S. senator since Reconstruction, delivered the memorial address at the ceremony.

FURTHER READING

Bailey, Richard. *Neither Carpetbaggers nor Scalawags: Black Officeholders during the Reconstruction of Alabama 1867–1878* (1991).

Christopher, Maurine. *America's Black Congressmen* (1971).

Schweninger, Loren. *Black Property Owners in the South, 1790–1915* (1990).

Seip, Terry L. *The South Returns to Congress: Men, Economic Measures, and Intersectional Relationships, 1868–1879* (1983).

Wiggins, Sarah Woolfolk. *The Scalawag in Alabama Politics, 1865–1881* (1977).

Obituary: *Huntsville* (Alabama) *Gazette*, 31 Mar. 1894.

This entry is taken from the *American National Biography* and is published here with the permission of the American Council of Learned Societies.

WILLIAM W. ROGERS

Turner, Benner C. (30 Oct. 1905–29 Jan. 1988), attorney, and college president was born Benner Creswill Turner in Columbus, Georgia, to Dr. Edwin J. Turner and Lila Mae Benner. His father was a respected medical doctor and community leader.

As a child, Turner excelled in the Columbus public school system. Wanting his son to have the best education and a pipeline to Harvard Law School, Dr. Turner sent young Turner to Phillips Academy in Andover, Massachusetts, in 1919. During his four years at Phillips Academy, Turner excelled athletically and academically. He was a member of the varsity wrestling team where he was noted for wrestling "remarkably well" (Phillips Academy's *Pot Pourri*, 1923). Turner was also well known and respected for his academic excellence. One year he was voted "class grind" (the hardest worker) by his classmates. During the spring of 1923, Turner graduated from the Classical Department at Phillips Academy with honors. By all accounts he was received well by his classmates and teachers despite being the only African American at the school. He was one of eighteen inductees into the Honorary Scholarship Society, cum laude. In addition, Turner was recognized for being the top graduating member in Latin composition.

In the fall of 1923 Turner entered Harvard College, where he pursued an A.B. in Economics and was a member of the freshmen wrestling team. Turner graduated in the spring of 1927 and was admitted into Harvard Law School for the fall. There were very few blacks at Harvard Law School in the pre–World War II era; Turner and his colleagues CHARLES HAMILTON HOUSTON (1923), WILLIAM

Benner C. Turner, president of South Carolina State College. (The SC State Historical Collections and Archives Department, Miller F. Whittaker Library, South Carolina State University, Orangeburg, SC.)

HASTIE (1932), and RAYMOND PACE ALEXANDER (1923) constituted a small cohort. Turner finished law school in 1930, earning an LL.B. degree. He finished 267th out of 411 in his law school class.

After graduation, Turner passed the Pennsylvania Bar exam and served as an associate for the Raymond Pace Alexander law firm in Philadelphia, Pennsylvania, the most prestigious black law firm in the nation. Like Turner, Alexander was a Harvard Law School graduate (1923). Turner worked primarily in labor-related and criminal cases associated with civil rights issues. His father's illness and untimely death in 1932 unexpectedly brought him back to Columbus, Georgia, to take care of his mother and to establish his law practice (a promise he had made to his father).

In an attempt to establish his law practice (1932–1942), Turner repeatedly took the Georgia Bar exam, which he failed. It was later determined that his exams were routinely thrown away because he was an African American. While attempting to pass the bar examination, Turner worked in real estate and tax service. In 1934 he married a close family acquaintance Julia Allen (whose father was the former Lincoln University president Benjamin Allen) and would have two children (Elizabeth Anne and Benner II) years later. In 1942 Turner accepted a position as a law professor and law librarian at the newly created Law School of the North Carolina College for Negroes (later North Carolina Central University) in Durham.

In 1947 the state of South Carolina created a segregated law school on the campus of South Carolina State College (State College) in Orangeburg. Turner was selected as its dean. On 14 November 1949, State College president Miller C. Whittaker died. Turner along with several faculty, administrators, and local school leaders were interviewed to succeed Whittaker. On 2 August 1950, Turner was selected to be the fourth president of State College. Selected by an all-white board along with the approval of then Governor J. Storm Thurmond, Turner was described as "an outstanding and highly qualified man.... We want nothing less than a man of ability, character and with a correct understanding of the American way of life, especially here in South Carolina" (Burke and Hine, p. 46).

Throughout his tenure (1950–1967), Turner constantly met with disapproval from the college community due to his handling of the civil rights activities on and off campus as well as for his compliance with the board of trustees. His expulsion of student government association president Fred

Moore and fourteen other students and termination of the contracts of six faculty members precipitated a six-day class strike and boycott of the college cafeteria (as part of an economic strike against the segregationist Orangeburg mayor Robert Jennings's Coca-Cola franchise and bakery business). Turner understood and believed in civil rights; however, as president of an African American public institution in the segregated South, he chose to comply with the racial status quo in order to advance the college. Ultimately his handling of the constant student unrest overshadowed his competence as an effective administrator, in which he improved the academic programs, physical plant, and faculty quality.

When Turner retired, he and his wife left Orangeburg and lived briefly in Jefferson City, Missouri, near the campus of the historically black Lincoln University. In February 1968, Turner's fears of students becoming victims of violence had come to fruition when three students were fatally shot by officers of South Carolina Highway Patrol (which would become known as the Orangeburg Massacre). Wanting to move away from the college campus and be near their children in the New England area, the Turners settled in Somersworth, New Hampshire. Turner lived out the rest of his days quietly, indulging his passion of reading and being active in a local church. Turner succumbed to heart disease and died essentially in obscurity. While his legacy has been tarnished by the student unrest during his administration, his life reflects the travails of African American college presidents during the mid-twentieth century.

FURTHER READING

Boyce, T. "I Am Leaving and Not Looking Back: The Life of Benner C. Turner." Ph.D. diss., Ohio University, 2009.

Burke, William L., and Hine, William C. "The South Carolina State College Law School: Its Roots, Creation, and Legacy." In *Matthew J. Perry: The Man, His Times, and His Legacy*, edited by W. Lewis Burke and Belinda F. Gergel, 17–61 (2004).

Grose, Philip. *South Carolina on the Brink: Robert McNair and the Politics of Civil Rights* (2006).

Hine, William C. "Civil Rights and Campus Wrongs: South Carolina State College Student Protest, 1955–1968." *South Carolina Historical Magazine* 4, no. 97 (1996): 310–331.

Hine, William C. "South Carolina's Challenge to Civil Rights: The Case of South Carolina State College, 1945–1954." *Agriculture and Human Values* (1992): 38–50.

TRAVIS D. BOYCE

Turner, Big Joe (18 May 1911–24 Nov. 1985), jazz, blues, and early rock-and-roll singer, was born Joseph Vernon Turner Jr. in Kansas City, Missouri, the son of Joseph Turner Sr. and Georgie Harrington, of whom virtually nothing else is known. After his father died in a railroad accident when Joe was four years old, he and his sister were raised by their mother and maternal grandmother. Joe Turner, who grew up singing in church choirs and on street corners and whose large frame belied his young age, began performing in Kansas City nightclubs while in his teens. His deep, roaring voice quickly attracted notice and garnered him a regular spot at several clubs. While doubling as a bartender and singer at Kansas City's Sunset Cafe in the early 1930s, Turner met the boogie piano player PETE JOHNSON, with whom he would collaborate over the next thirty years, producing some of Turner's most renowned recordings. Their club performances soon attracted the attention of the talent scout and record producer John Hammond, who in 1936 brought the pair to New York to perform and record.

In December 1938 Turner and Johnson played at Carnegie Hall in the "Spirituals to Swing" concert, sharing a bill with the blues and jazz luminaries BIG BILL BROONZY, SONNY TERRY, and COUNT BASIE. This celebrated show helped launch a national boogie-woogie craze. With their burgeoning success Turner and Johnson secured steady work at Manhattan's Café Society, where they performed songs that remained in Turner's repertoire for the rest of his career. The rollicking "Roll 'Em Pete," which they recorded for the Vocalian label at the close of 1938, became one of Turner's signature tunes and featured Johnson's thundering piano accompaniment. In 1940 Turner moved to the Decca label, recording with Johnson "Piney Brown Blues" and, backed by WILLIE "THE LION" SMITH, the jazz-tinged "Careless Love." After 1941 Turner's association with Johnson began to wane, although the pair periodically worked together throughout the 1940s and 1950s.

During World War II Turner settled in Los Angeles, where he quickly became a fixture on the West Coast jazz and blues circuits. In 1945 he married Lou Willie Turner, who died in 1972. From 1945 to 1947 Turner recorded for National Records, releasing in 1947 "My Gal's a Jockey," his first popular radio hit. Also that year, under the pseudonym Big Vernon, he cut the salacious "Around the Clock" for the Stag label. By the end of the 1940s almost all of the major West Coast labels featured at least one Turner record, as he switched in rapid succession from National to Stag, Aladdin, RPM, Downbeat/Swing Time, MGM, Freedom, and Specialty, and finally to Imperial Records in 1950 where he teamed with a young FATS DOMINO on "Still in the Dark."

By the early 1950s Turner's career appeared to be on the decline; demand for him to perform and record decreased. In an effort to energize his career he moved back to New York in 1950. Filling in for Jimmy Risling as the front man for Count Basie's group, Turner drew wide praise and was offered a recording contract by the Atlantic Records heads Herb Abramson and Ahmet Ertegun. In April 1951 Turner initiated his Atlantic work with the mournful "Chains of Love," which catapulted him back on to the rhythm and blues charts. Thus began Turner's most prolific period, during which he released a string of hits including "Sweet Sixteen," "Chill Is On," and "Don't You Cry." In 1953 he landed his first chart-topping hit, the stomping "Honey Hush." At the end of the year he went to Chicago, teaming up with the blues guitarist ELMORE JAMES on the risqué number "T.V. Mama."

The prolific Atlantic staff songwriter Jesse Stone penned the 1954 smash hit "Shake, Rattle, and Roll," a pioneering rock-and-roll song and Turner's second number 1 record. Turner's version offered a thinly veiled sexual metaphor. Sanitized versions of the song would prove even more popular—in part because radio stations were more willing to play them—when covered by white recording stars such as Bill Haley and the Comets and, later, Elvis Presley.

Now forty-three years old, Turner had become a bona fide star. His subsequent work, including "Flip, Flop, and Fly" and "Morning, Noon, and Night," all employed the same rhythmic formula as "Shake, Rattle, and Roll." In the mid-1950s he made several appearances on the television variety program *Showtime at the Apollo*, performing "Shake, Rattle, and Roll," and he also sang it in a Hollywood film of the same name. In 1956 he released "Corinna, Corinna," another hit record, and followed this with "Rock a While." As younger artists began to dominate the rock-and-roll charts, at Atlantic's behest Turner began recording more jazz-oriented material aimed at adult audiences. Critics later hailed his 1956 sessions in which he reunited with Pete Johnson, but at the time the public's interests had moved on, and Turner's career began to decline once more. In 1959 his association with Atlantic came to an end.

In the 1960s Turner made few recordings, despite a resurgence of public interest in seasoned jazz and blues performers—a revival that brought many of his contemporaries back into the spotlight. Turner, however, produced nothing that remotely approached a hit record. His only notable sessions were made in Mexico City in 1966, backed by his longtime admirers Bill Haley and the Comets. But these, too, failed to produce a hit, and Turner spent the decade in relative obscurity. By the early 1970s, though, his career picked up again, and he began recording for Norman Ganz's jazz label Pablo Records. These were essentially jam sessions, and the resulting records featured Turner's famous roaring vocals, accompanied by lengthy jazz solos.

By the 1980s Turner had suffered a stroke and contracted diabetes, yet he continued to record, singing on the 1983 compilation *Roomful of Blues*. He also performed in clubs around the country, frequently appearing on stage sitting in a chair, his enormous size and declining health forcing him to remain seated as his band played. Critics, though, claimed that Turner's voice still commanded the respect of fans, and he toured extensively until just before his death in November 1985. Pete Johnson sang at his funeral, and he, too, passed away the following spring.

Known as the Boss of the Blues, Big Joe Turner's reputation largely rests on his more accessible songs such as "Shake, Rattle, and Roll," yet his impeccable timing, confident persona, and powerful voice could fill a concert hall and delight audiences. His ability to excel in a wide range of vocal styles, from soulful crooning to joyous shouting, remains his lasting legacy.

FURTHER READING

Belz, Carl. *The Story of Rock* (1969).

Guralnik, Peter. *Lost Highway: Journeys and Arrivals of American Musicians* (1979).

Tosches, Nick. *The Unsung Heroes of Rock n' Roll: The Birth of Rock in the Wild Years before Elvis* (1999).

DISCOGRAPHY

Boss of the Blues (Atlantic 8812).

Classic Hits, 1938–1952 (JSP B00008LJHG).

The Very Best of Big Joe Turner (Rhino 72968).

BRENTON E. RIFFEL

Turner, Charles Henry (3 Feb. 1867–14 Feb. 1923), biologist and educator, was born in Cincinnati, Ohio, the son of Thomas Turner, a church custodian, and Adeline Campbell, a nurse. Although neither parent had attended college, Thomas Turner would eventually earn a reputation as "a well-read man, a keen thinker, and a master of debate [who] surrounded himself with several hundred choice books." Both parents, but especially the father, imparted a love of learning to young Charles. After graduating valedictorian of his high school class in Cincinnati, he proceeded to the University of Cincinnati, where he earned a B.S. in 1891 and an M.S. in 1892. His goal was to teach science and ultimately to head a technological or agricultural school for African Americans. As an undergraduate, he came under the influence of Clarence Luther Herrick, a professor of biology at Cincinnati and pioneer in the field of psychobiology. When Herrick established the *Journal of Comparative Neurology* in 1891, Turner became a regular contributor; he published eight research articles and at least six abstracts in the journal between 1891 and 1901. Text and illustrations from his undergraduate thesis, "Morphology of the Avian Brain," appeared in the inaugural volume.

Turner's first teaching appointments were at the Governor Street School in Evansville, Indiana (1888–1889), and for a brief period subsequently (1889) as a substitute in the Cincinnati public schools. In 1891 he was appointed to an assistantship in the biological laboratory at the University of Cincinnati, a position he held for two years. Anxious, as he put it, to "get to work among my own people," he wrote to BOOKER T. WASHINGTON in April 1893 requesting notification of any openings at black colleges. Later that year he became professor of biology and head of the department of science and agriculture at the all-black Clark University in Atlanta, Georgia. His tenure at Clark (1893–1905) was followed by posts at other black schools: principal of College Hill High School, Cleveland, Tennessee (1906); professor of biology and chemistry at Haines Normal and Industrial Institute, Augusta, Georgia (1907–1908); and instructor in biology at Sumner High School, St. Louis, Missouri (1908–1923). Sumner, founded in 1875, was highly regarded for the caliber of its faculty, which at one time had included EDWARD BOUCHET, the first African American to receive a Ph.D. (in Physics from Yale, 1876).

In 1907 Turner earned his Ph.D. in Zoology (magna cum laude) at the University of Chicago. At Chicago he worked under the eminent zoologists Charles Otis Whitman, Charles Manning Child, and Frank Rattray Lillie. He was one of the earliest black Americans to earn a doctorate in the biological sciences (Alfred O. Coffin had earned one at Illinois Wesleyan University in 1889). Turner's doctoral thesis, a study of the "homing" mechanism in ants, marked a watershed in his scientific research. Earlier, his work had followed classic morphological lines—that is, examination of an organism's form and structure by means of microscopic observation in the laboratory. Following his time at Chicago, his work became more behavioral, focusing on animals in the field, in their natural habitat. His goal was to continue developing insights into elusive problems of neurology and comparative psychology—problems first introduced to him by Herrick at Cincinnati.

While teaching in St. Louis, Turner established himself as an authority on insect behavior. He was the first to fully describe a unique movement—a pattern of gyration—that certain species of ant go through when returning to their nests. This movement came to be widely known, in the scientific literature, as "Turner's circling." Turner also showed that ant movement is influenced by landmarks and light, that bees respond to color and pattern as well as odor, that wasps and burrowing bees may memorize landmarks adjacent to their nests, that ant lions lie motionless for prolonged periods out of an involuntary response to external stimuli ("terror paralysis") rather than as a self-concealment or camouflage reflex, that certain insects can hear and distinguish pitch, and that cockroaches learn by trial and error (but forget quickly). The innovative experimental techniques and ingenious devices that Turner developed to carry out his work were admired and often emulated by other scientists. His reputation for accuracy and thoroughness resulted in several invitations to contribute annual literature reviews on insect behavior, vertebrate and invertebrate behavior, tropisms, and other topics to *Psychological Bulletin* and *Journal of Animal Behavior*. Turner's seminal work, "The Homing of Ants: An Experimental Study of Ant Behavior," is in *The Journal of Comparative Neurology and Psychology* 17 (Sept. 1907): 367–434. His longest work, coauthored with C. L. Herrick, is *Synopsis of the Entomostraca of Minnesota; With Descriptions of Related Species Comparing All Known Forms from the United States, Included in the Orders Copepoda, Cladocera, Ostrocada* (1895). In all, he published over fifty scientific articles (with at least three others appearing posthumously). His work appeared in major journals, such as *Science, American Naturalist*, and *Biological Bulletin*.

Turner's research was carried out with his own resources and in his spare time. The focus of his professional life was teaching. At Sumner he inspired in his students a curiosity about the natural world that outlasted their high school years. Also active in black civic organizations, Turner served as a director of the Colored Branch, St. Louis YMCA. He wrote occasional papers on racial issues for *The Southwestern Christian Advocate* and other publications. One article, "Will the Education of the Negro Solve the Race Problem?" in *Twentieth Century Negro Literature*, ed. D. W. Culp (1902), supported W. E. B. DuBois's contention (in opposition to BOOKER T. WASHINGTON) that college or university education—not industrial training—was the best way to stimulate prosperity for blacks and to promote interracial harmony. Drawing on his work as a biologist, Turner compared human and animal "societies." He theorized, for example, that "animals are prejudiced against animals unlike themselves, and the more unlike they are the greater the prejudice," but that with humans "dissimilarity of minds is a more potent factor in causing prejudice than unlikeness of physiognomy." He advanced this theory in support of his argument for equal educational opportunity, irrespective of race.

Turner was a member of the Entomological Society of America, the Academy of Science of Illinois, and the Academy of Science of St. Louis. He held elective office in the latter organization, serving terms as secretary of the entomology section and as council member. He was twice married, first (in 1888) to Leontine Troy of Cincinnati (she died in 1894) and later to Lillian Porter of Augusta, Georgia. Following his death in Chicago, a school for the physically handicapped—the Charles H. Turner School in St. Louis—was built in his memory.

FURTHER READING

A few Turner letters survive in the Herrick papers (part of the Neurology Collections), Department of Special Collections, Kenneth Spencer Research Library, University of Kansas.

Haines, D. E. "The Contributors to Volume 1 (1891) of *The Journal of Comparative Neurology*: C. L. Herrick, C. H. Turner, H. R. Pemberton, B. G. Wilder, F. W. Langdon, C. J. Herrick, C. von Kupffer, O. S. Strong, T. B. Stowell," *Journal of Comparative Neurology* 314 (1991): 9–23.

Hayden, Robert C. "Charles Henry Turner," *Seven Black American Scientists* (1970): 68–91.

Transactions of the Academy of Sciences of St. Louis 24 (Dec. 1923), a special memorial issue in Turner's honor.

This entry is taken from the *American National Biography* and is published here with the permission of the American Council of Learned Societies.

KENNETH R. MANNING

Turner, Darwin T. (7 May 1931–11 Feb. 1991), literary critic, educator, poet, was born Darwin Theodore Troy Turner in Cincinnati, Ohio, to Darwin Romanes Turner, a pharmacist, and Laura Knight, a teacher. His grandfather, CHARLES H. TURNER, was the first African American psychologist. A gifted and precocious student, Turner enrolled in the University of Cincinnati at the age of thirteen. By 1949, when Turner was eighteen, he had received his bachelor's degree with Phi Beta Kappa honors and a master's degree in English and American Drama. That same year, he married Edna Bonner. He taught English at Clark College in Atlanta from 1949 to 1951 and at Morgan State College in Baltimore from 1952 to 1957, while earning his Ph.D. in English from the University of Chicago in 1956. From 1957 to 1970 Turner held teaching and administrative positions at Florida A&M, North Carolina Agricultural and Technical State University, and the University of Michigan. Turner and Bonner divorced in 1961, and he married Maggie Jean Lewis, a teacher, in 1968. Turner settled in at the University of Iowa in Iowa City, where he became chair of the Afro-American studies department in 1972 and in 1981 was named the University of Iowa Foundation Distinguished Professor of English.

Turner's numerous publications and awards include a collection of poetry, *Katharsis* (1964), a book on Nathaniel Hawthorne's *The Scarlet Letter* (1967), and *In a Minor Chord: Three Afro-American Writers and Their Search for Identity* (1971). One of the first major studies of African American writers, *In a Minor Chord* examines the work of JEAN TOOMER, COUNTÉE CULLEN, and ZORA NEALE HURSTON. Turner published introductions and new editions to the works of PAUL LAURENCE DUNBAR, CHARLES CHESNUTT, as well as Hurston, Cullen, and Toomer, at a time when many of their writings were out of print. He compiled and edited more than a dozen collections of African American literature and edited a well-regarded compilation of the autobiographical writings of Toomer, *The Wayward and the Seeking: A Collection of Writings by Jean Toomer* (1980). He also coedited *The Art of the Slave Narrative: Original Essays in Criticism and Theory* (1982) and wrote an afterword to Haki R. Madhubuti's *Earthquakes and Sun Rise Missions* (1982). He contributed numerous articles on literary criticism and pedagogic studies to academic journals and anthologies of African American literature, and he received dozens of awards and honors over the course of his teaching and writing career. His poetry was published in several anthologies.

In reviewing his work on Toomer, TONI MORRISON praised Turner as "a scholar of fastidiousness and perception" (1). Friend and colleague Joe Weixlmann asserted that "Darwin Turner was a giant. His contributions to the study of African-American culture will long remain with us, and with those of generations to come," also remarking on "the intensity with which [he] approached his professional life" (8–9). In 1965, while chair of the English Department at North Carolina A&T, Turner delivered an incisive address on the teaching of composition in traditionally black colleges and universities, and his remarks were deemed "the most important statements ever made about college composition by an African American" (Gilyard, 634). A true pioneer in education, Turner produced a comprehensive treatise on modes of inclusion of African American studies in the college curriculum in 1970 in "The Teaching of Afro-American Literature," published in *College English*, a publication widely read by teachers of college-level literature. Turner was instrumental in the establishment of the Division on Black American Literature and Culture of the Modern Language Association, overcoming years of resistance within that organization toward African American studies. A tireless writer, teacher, and conference attendee, Turner's shaping of the study of African American literature and culture is evident in virtually all African American studies programs. He died of a heart attack in 1991 in Iowa City, leaving behind his wife and three children.

FURTHER READING

Darwin T(heodore Troy) Turner. *Contemporary Authors Online* (2007).

Gilyard, Keith. "African American Contributions to Composition Studies," *College Composition and Communication* (June 1999).

Morrison, Toni. "Jean Toomer's Art of Darkness," *Washington Post Book World* (July 1980).

Weixlmann, Joe. "A Tribute to Darwin T. Turner (1931–1991)," *Black American Literature Forum* (1991).

ALICE KNOX EATON

Turner, David J. (Oct. 1874?–23 Nov. 1932), pharmacist, bank owner, and mayor of an African American community, was born David Johnson Turner, the fifth of twelve children, to Moses and Lucy (Lulu) Turner in Cass County, Texas. During his teen years, the Turners joined the steady stream of African Americans who left Texas and other Southern states for the Oklahoma and Indian Territories. Many black migrants were attracted to Indian Territory, which was divided up among the Cherokee, Chickasaw, Choctaw, Creek, and Seminole Indians, known as the Five Civilized Tribes. Moses and Lulu Turner rented a farm in the Seminole Nation, Indian Territory, where David Turner and his younger siblings came of age.

In 1895, Turner wed Minnie, also a child of Texas migrants, and the young couple began raising their own family on a rented farm near Turner's parents. Within a few years, however, Turner moved his family to Earlsboro, Oklahoma Territory, where he changed his occupation from farming to business. By 1904, Turner had developed a reputation as an excellent businessman and attracted the attention of THOMAS HAYNES, cofounder of Boley, an all-black town in the nearby Creek Nation. Haynes invited Turner to move to Boley—established in 1903—to help build the new town. Accepting the challenge, David and Minnie Turner and their four children, Callie, David Jr., Lonnie, and Willie, moved by covered wagon. In December 1904, after taking courses for a pharmacy license, Turner opened Boley's first drug store. The fully stocked store also featured an ice cream parlor and the town's first telephone. In addition, Turner installed a vault in the store that was used to safeguard money and other valuable belongings of townspeople. He also sold life insurance policies and co-owned a real estate company that sold land to black migrants seeking to live in what grew to become America's largest all-black town. His later business investments included an ice plant, a brickyard, a lumberyard, a telephone company, and a newspaper. On 4 March 1905, Turner and other members of the Boley Business Men's League organized the Farmers and Merchants Bank of Boley. The bank, one of the first in Oklahoma to be owned and operated by African Americans, was incorporated in 1906. Over the years, Turner held various positions in the bank and by 1918 became its president, maintaining this position for the remainder of his life.

Turner was also heavily involved in local and county politics during the territorial period and after Oklahoma gained statehood in 1907. Within Boley, he was often a member of city council and was elected mayor at least two times. Initially, Turner was a member of the Republican Party and represented the town's Republican majority at countywide Republican conventions. When Oklahoma blacks were disfranchised in 1910, Turner was one of the first in the state to challenge the validity of the grandfather clause in the state courts. However, in 1912, when it became clear that the fight against the grandfather clause would be protracted and that victory was uncertain, Turner was among the group of African Americans who decided to join the Democratic Party in hopes of ensuring that the town maintained access to people in power. After the grandfather clause was overturned in 1915, he successfully sued the county to have Boley redistricted and to replace the town's voting booths, which were removed during disfranchisement. In 1920, Turner was appointed to the Oklahoma Commission on Interracial Cooperation by Governor J. B. A. Robertson.

In the mid-1920s, when a rash of bank robberies plagued the state, Turner helped establish a gun club among bank owners in his county. The members of this interracial club practiced shooting in order to protect themselves from bank robbers. Ironically, Turner died seven years later defending his bank against an infamous gang which had been committing bank robberies all over Kansas and Oklahoma. On 23 November 1932, three members of the Charles "Pretty Boy" Floyd gang drove into Boley intent on robbing Turner's bank. They entered the building, drew their weapons, and demanded that Turner empty the cash drawers. Defying this order, Turner instead set off the bank's alarm, which caused armed Boley citizens to rush toward the bank. Inside, the gang's leader, Charles Birdwell, responded to the alarm by fatally shooting Turner. An employee hiding in the bank vault returned fire and mortally wounded Turner's killer. As the two surviving gang members attempted to escape, they were confronted by an armed group of defenders outside the bank who shot one of them down and took the other, who dropped his weapons and surrendered, into custody until the sheriff arrived. Turner's funeral was attended by an estimated five thousand people of all races. Survived by his second wife, California Taylor Turner, he was buried in the old Boley city cemetery.

FURTHER READING
Crockett, Norman. *The Black Towns* (1979).
Washington, Booker T. "Boley, A Negro Town in the West," *Outlook*, 4 Jan. 1908.

MELISSA NICOLE STUCKEY

Turner, Henry McNeal (1 Feb. 1834–8 May 1915), African Methodist Episcopal (AME) Church bishop and emigrationist, was born in Newberry, South Carolina, the son of Hardy Turner and Sarah Greer, free African Americans. Sarah made great efforts to obtain an education for her son, despite the state prohibition against teaching African Americans to read. In 1848, after Turner's father died and his mother remarried, he was hired as a janitor by lawyers in Abbeville, South Carolina. Recognizing Turner's intelligence, they helped him to master many subjects, including arithmetic, astronomy, geography, history, law, and theology.

From 1848 to 1851 Turner attended numerous camp meetings conducted by Methodist evangelists and underwent a powerful conversion experience. He soon joined the Methodist Episcopal Church, South, probably in 1849, and determined to undertake a ministerial career. He was licensed to preach in 1853. Subsequently, he traveled throughout the South, holding huge audiences of blacks and whites spellbound with his fluid oratory and mastery of a wide range of subjects. In 1858 he traveled to St. Louis, where he was ordained as a minister of the African Methodist Episcopal Church, then the largest black denomination.

Turner married four times and was widowed three times. In 1856 he married Eliza Ann Peacher; they had fourteen children. Each of his subsequent marriages, in 1893 to Martha DeWitt, in 1900 to Harriet Wayman, and in 1907 to Laura Lemon, was childless.

From 1858 to 1863 Turner pastored AME churches in Baltimore and Washington, D.C. He continued his education, studying Latin, Greek, and Hebrew with various ministers and auditing medical classes at Johns Hopkins University. He won renown as a powerful evangelist, producing many converts during revivals. He also became involved in many social and political activities. He helped to raise money both for Wilberforce University in Ohio, founded by the AME Church's DANIEL ALEXANDER PAYNE in 1863, and for the assistance of contrabands, the fleeing slaves who sought refuge behind federal army lines. He befriended numerous members of Congress, including Representative Thaddeus Stevens and Senator Charles Sumner.

After President Abraham Lincoln's 1863 Emancipation Proclamation authorized the enlistment of African Americans in the Union army, Turner was instrumental in organizing the First U.S. Colored Troops, a regiment he subsequently joined as chaplain. Despite being incapacitated for several months by a bout of smallpox, Turner participated in nine battles, including those at Petersburg, Virginia, and Fort Fisher, North Carolina. He helped teach many soldiers in his regiment to read and held numerous revivals during lulls in the fighting.

In the fall of 1865 Turner was reassigned to a regiment in Atlanta, but he soon resigned his army commission to spend all of his time organizing the AME Church in Georgia. He settled in Macon, where he pastored the congregation that had recently joined the AME Church. He also served as the presiding elder for all AME churches in the state. His most difficult task was finding pastors for the churches that joined the denomination, since there were few literate black ministers. Turner solved this difficulty by encouraging ordinary African Americans to serve as ministers, often approaching strangers with the question, "Can you preach?" He also served as a prominent revivalist, converting thousands during protracted meetings.

In 1867 Turner turned to politics, helping to organize Union Leagues and the Republican Party in his state and serving as a delegate to the state constitutional convention in Atlanta. He was elected to the Georgia state legislature in 1868. Soon, however, he and twenty-three other African American legislators were expelled on account of their race—but only after Turner delivered a brilliant speech denouncing the expulsions. With the help of the U.S. senator Charles Sumner, he obtained an appointment as postmaster in Macon. He quickly came under unrelenting persecution by the white citizens of Macon and had to resign after being accused of passing bad currency and associating with a prostitute. In 1870 Turner and the other African American legislators reclaimed their seats in the Georgia legislature by order of Congress and served the remainder of their terms. He was subsequently defeated in his bid for reelection in the fall of 1870 in a disorderly election marked by considerable Democratic fraud and Ku Klux Klan violence.

Turner then retreated to Savannah, where he pastored an AME Church and compiled a new denominational hymnbook. He also served as a detective for the U.S. customs house. Elected manager of the AME publishing house in 1876, Turner moved to Philadelphia, Pennsylvania. He supported Rutherford B. Hayes for president and later visited him in Washington but criticized Hayes for removing federal troops from the South and for failing to appoint an African American to his cabinet.

Turner was long attracted to the notion of African Americans returning to Africa to "civilize" and Christianize the continent. As a result of the political repression and economic hardship suffered by many African Americans, he became a more vigorous advocate of this idea, even gaining election as an honorary vice president of the emigrationist American Colonization Society in 1876.

Turner was elected a bishop in the AME Church in 1880 and moved to Atlanta, where he continued to champion many reform causes. He denounced the U.S. Supreme Court when, in 1883, it voided much of the Civil Rights Act of 1875, declaring that the decision made it more urgent for African Americans to return to Africa. In 1885 he was the first bishop in his denomination to ordain a woman, Sarah Ann Hughes, to the ministry, but her ordination was overturned by the church two years later. His energetic advocacy of Prohibition won black support for an 1885 city ordinance banning the sale of whiskey. He evangelized vigorously on behalf of the AME Church throughout the southern and western states, helping to transform it from a small denomination based mostly in the North into a truly national denomination.

Turner visited Liberia and Sierra Leone in 1891, 1893, and 1895. His most successful trip was to South Africa in 1898, where he joined the Ethiopian church led by Mangena Mokone into union with the AME Church. Turner also intensified his efforts on behalf of African emigrationism during this decade. He edited and published two monthly newspapers, *The Voice of Missions* (1893–1900) and *The Voice of the People* (1901–1904), to disseminate his views on African missions and emigration. He inspired the formation of an International Migration Society, which arranged for two shiploads of emigrants to sail to Liberia in 1895 and 1896, but complaints from the ill-cared-for emigrants prevented him from promoting any more such voyages.

Turner articulated a theology strongly based on affirming blackness and defending civil rights. He stated that "a man must believe he is somebody before he is acknowledged as somebody.... Respect black." He called for learned black scholars to retranslate the Bible in order to make it "wholly acceptable and in keeping with the higher conceptions of the black man." Protesting the idolatry of whiteness in American Christian theology, Turner declared, "God is a Negro."

After suffering a stroke in 1899, Turner lost some of his enormous vitality. As the state of Georgia prepared to disenfranchise African Americans in

1906, he stated, "Hell is an improvement on the United States where the Negro is concerned." After he commented that "to the Negro in this country, the American flag is a dirty and contemptible rag," some white Georgians wrote President Theodore Roosevelt in an unsuccessful effort to have Turner charged with treason. The embittered Turner stated that he hoped to die outside of the United States because of its denial of human rights to African Americans, and, in fact, he died in Windsor, Ontario, while traveling on church business.

Turner's significance is multifaceted and far-reaching. His black theology and political activism paved the way for twentieth-century civil rights and black nationalist movements. His African emigrationism constituted a pointed challenge to the nation's retreat from civil rights in the post-Reconstruction era. Turner, however, devoted most of his time to his church work, not to politics, and he played a large part in making the AME Church the strongest and most influential organization controlled entirely by African Americans in the latter half of the nineteenth century.

FURTHER READING

A small but fascinating collection of Turner's papers, including a Civil War diary and numerous photographs, can be found at Howard University.

Angell, Stephen W. *Bishop Henry McNeal Turner and African American Religion in the South* (1992).

Redkey, Edwin. *Black Exodus: Black Nationalist and Back-to-Africa Movements, 1890–1910* (1969).

Redkey, Edwin. *Respect Black: The Writings and Speeches of Henry McNeal Turner* (1971).

This entry is taken from the *American National Biography* and is published here with the permission of the American Council of Learned Societies.

STEPHEN W. ANGELL

Turner, Ike (5 Nov. 1931–12 Dec. 2007), rhythm and blues, rock, and soul pianist, guitarist, vocalist, and composer, was born Ike Wister Turner in Clarksdale, Mississippi, to Izear Luster Turner and Beatrice Cushenberry. Both Creoles, Izear preached at the local Baptist church, while Cushenberry worked as a seamstress and raised Ike and his older sister Lee Ethel. When Turner was five or six, Izear was brutally murdered by a gang of white men who suspected him of sleeping with a white woman. With his father dead, Turner had to help support the family, and regularly devised small-scale schemes to bring in money. Beatrice remarried, and Turner's

rocky relationship with his new stepfather led to his running away from home several times.

It was also around the age of seven that Turner got his first exposure to his region's rich musical tradition. Inspired by local boogie-woogie luminary Pinetop Perkins, Turner convinced his mother to buy him a piano. By the time he reached high school, he was a competent pianist who, on the side, bootlegged whiskey and deejayed at the city's major radio station. The latter allowed him to absorb all the new music flowing into Clarksdale, including Turner's personal favorite, country. The teenaged Ike backed up bluesman ROBERT NIGHTHAWK and led his own group, the Kings of Rhythm, playing marathon gigs in the area's rough-and-tumble juke joints.

Turner's big break came in 1951, when B.B. KING recommended the Kings of Rhythm to Sam Phillips of Sun Studios. On the way to Memphis, Turner and his bandmates devised "Rocket 88," a furious, barreling car-based novelty tune. Mistakenly credited to the band's saxophonist, Jackie Brenston, and his nonexistent Delta Cats, the tune is often cited as the birth of rock 'n' roll and, due to an accident that befell sideman Willie Kizart's equipment in transit, the first example of intentionally distorted guitar

Ike Turner sings an R&B duet with Tina Turner. (AP Images.)

on record. Released nationally on Chess, "Rocket 88" eventually topped the charts; however, it led to a schism within the Rhythm Kings over whether Turner or Brenston was indeed the real star. Without Brenston and a few other defectors, Turner and the Kings relocated to Memphis and recorded with the likes of HOWLIN' WOLF and ELMORE JAMES. During this time Turner was also employed as a talent scout by Modern Records. In 1956 Turner and the Kings, whose leader now focused on guitar, took a gig in East St. Louis, Illinois. This would remain his base of operations until the early sixties, but the tireless (and demanding) Turner made sure that the Kings spent much of the year touring. He also found time to record for a variety of labels, including Flair and Federal, sometimes under aliases that shielded him from contract violations. That same year a young Tennessean vocalist named Anna Mae Bullock joined the Kings; her impassioned singing immediately became a central part of Turner's outfit, and she became one of Turner's many women. By 1958 they were married and had a son, Ike Jr.; by 1960, when she first recorded with Turner, she was known as TINA TURNER. The Kings cut "A Fool in Love" for Sue, which ended up being Turner's biggest hit since "Rocket 88." The band was renamed the Ike and Tina Revue, with Tina's formidable talents marking a new, more modern direction for the group.

The Ike and Tina Revue became one of the chitlin circuit's most incendiary acts, and Turner both satisfied and stoked the demand through nearly nonstop touring. A string of strong singles, including "I Idolize You," "Poor Fool," and "It's Gonna Work Out Fine," immediately followed "A Fool in Love" (1960), but by the mid-sixties the Revue had become primarily known as a live act. Ike's darker side also emerged during this time as he began using cocaine heavily, pushing his relationship with Tina into volatile, abusive territory. Unfairly or not he is now perhaps most well known for these two unfortunate tendencies, a reputation only bolstered by Tina's 1987 autobiography I, Tina and the 1993 film version What's Love Got to Do With It.

Despite the Revue's having stagnated somewhat, Tina was clearly a born star. In 1966 the eccentric Phil Spector proposed to produce an Ike and Tina album that featured far more Tina than Ike. In fact the title track of River Deep, Mountain High, which Spector considered his crowning achievement, included nothing from Ike. Three years later when the Revue was asked to open for the Rolling Stones and gain access to a wider audience, Tina's hypersexual stage presence, dynamic vocals, and sheer charisma were the undisputed main attraction. Taking a cue from their new fan base, the Revue began covering rock hits, such as "Come Together," "Proud Mary," and "I Want to Take You Higher," proving that the increasingly drug-addled Ike still had a hustle or two left in him. By 1975, however, Ike's personal problems and Tina's unwillingness to suffer under his thumb reached a critical mass; she abruptly left him during a 1975 tour, and the intimidation with which he responded only confirmed the "irreconcilable differences" cited in their 1976 divorce papers.

With Tina's departure Turner lost his muse, his longtime companion, and, most important, the key to his income. His attempts at a solo career floundered, his state-of-the-art Los Angeles home recording studio burnt down, and his drug abuse quickly spiraled out of control. Turner was arrested repeatedly for drug-related offenses, and due to imprisonment was unable to attend his (and Tina's) 1991 induction into the Rock and Roll Hall of Fame. The film release of What's Love Got to Do With It marked an absolute low point in the public's view of him, but after several failed comeback attempts, he went back to his blues roots to record 2001's acclaimed Here and Now. Coupled with his 1999 autobiography, Takin' Back My Name, it went a long way toward reminding audiences of his unique talent. Turner may be forever known as Tina's tormentor, but as her mentor—and, more importantly, as one of the post-war era's most influential musical figures—he deserves to also be recognized for his tremendous accomplishments. He died in San Marcos, California, at the age of 76.

FURTHER READING

Turner, Ike. Takin' Back My Name: The Confessions of Ike Turner (1999).

Collis, John. Ike Turner: King of Rhythm (2003).

DISCOGRAPHY

A Black Man's Soul (Pompeii SD-6003).

I Like Ike! The Best of Ike Turner (Rhino R2 71819).

The Kings of Rhythm Featuring Ike Turner: The Sun Sessions (Universal/Varese Sarabande 066232).

NATHANIEL FRIEDMAN

Turner, Jack (1840?–19 Aug. 1882), political activist, Republican party organizer, and lynching victim, was born a slave in Alabama. His parents' names are unknown. He lived on the Choctaw County farm of Beloved Love Turner, from whom he acquired his surname after emancipation. Jack Turner had no formal education but was described as articulate, perceptive, and courageous, with a commanding physical presence. He married Chloe (maiden name unknown) in the late 1860s, and they had four children. He remained in Choctaw County after being freed, working as a farm laborer around Mount Sterling and Tuscahoma.

After the Civil War, Turner became active in Reconstruction politics in Choctaw County. He was one of the organizers in 1867 of the county Republican Party, which was composed of local blacks and a few whites, including Turner's former owner. Turner took an active role in helping former slaves make the transition from slavery to freedom. He felt that freedom could best be expressed through voting, and he emerged as a leader of local blacks in the 1870s.

In the summer of 1874 Turner and other blacks organized a major political effort to gain statewide support for Republican candidates. They also supported independent candidates at the local level. The meetings held by Turner and the others were kept secret because of the hostility directed toward Republicans and blacks by the white Democrats. Turner and one of his cohorts sent a letter to the governor outlining the assaults and threats directed toward black families merely for exercising their rights to life and property.

Turner increased his political participation in the late 1870s and early 1880s. He supported Greenback and Republican coalitions that achieved a modicum of success against the Democrats in Choctaw County. An editorial in the *Choctaw County News* (10 Nov. 1880) expressed displeasure with Turner's activities, asserting that Turner and others would have to be taught that they could not assume political power over white men in the county; they would be taught a lesson through "severe measures" if gentle ones did not work.

Turner played a major role in organizing meetings, publicizing speaking engagements, and urging blacks to vote in the 1882 elections. Once again he supported a coalition of Greenbackers and Republicans in the election. White Democrats were upset when the coalition nearly defeated them in Choctaw County, and Turner was blamed.

While engaged in political activities, Turner worked as a tenant farmer. He did not wish to continue earning a living in this manner, so he worked hard to expand his operation and holdings. He often borrowed money against his crops and livestock. Two of Turner's benefactors were Seth Smith Mellen, principal of Mount Sterling Academy, and

Beloved Turner. He became relatively prosperous and in 1881 purchased from Mellen eighty acres of land between Mount Sterling and Tuscahoma Landing. Turner had the property deeded jointly to Chloe and his children.

Because Turner played such an active and visible role in Reconstruction political activities in Choctaw County, he became a target of political terrorism and legal harassment. He was often in and out of court on various charges, from gambling and assault to disturbing females by fighting near a place of public worship. Found innocent of some charges and guilty of others, he usually was fined from five dollars to twenty dollars, remaining in jail when he could not raise the money. Often, however, Beloved Turner and Seth Mellen served as his guarantors.

Turner, along with nineteen others, was once charged with participating in a "lynching" because they allegedly whipped someone who had divulged information from one of the secret meetings that Turner and his political cohorts held. All had agreed to this form of punishment before participating in the meetings. Turner pleaded guilty and was fined five hundred dollars. He could not pay the fine and remained in jail. Eventually Beloved Turner and others arranged for his release, but Turner was kept under surveillance.

After the 1882 elections, in which the success of the Greenback and Republican coalition humiliated local Democrats, Turner became the target of heightened resentment. Shortly after the election a package of fraudulent letters was "found" that revealed Turner as leader of a well-orchestrated plot to massacre all the white people of Choctaw County. Turner and six others were arrested and jailed in Butler, the county seat. Despite efforts at coercion, all the men denied the charges, except for one, who confessed to a plot after being beaten and tortured.

As word of the alleged conspiracy spread, a crowd converged on the jail with demands that Turner be hanged. The solicitor for the case proposed that a committee be organized to have the handwriting on the letters compared to that of Turner, who could barely read and write. The crowd that had gathered outside the jail voted to defeat the proposal. Then they selected a chairman and secretary; a motion was placed before the crowd (called a "committee of safety of the whole people") as to whether or not Turner should be hanged. The *Butler Courier* (30 Aug. 1882) reported that the vote was 998 to 2 in favor of hanging.

The chairman declared Turner guilty and pronounced the death sentence. Turner was taken from the jail by the mob, over the objections of the sheriff, and carried off to the courthouse square to be hanged. Turner is said to have "moved with quiet, unbowed dignity from the jail" (Rogers and Ward, *August Reckoning*, 100). He was asked if he had any final words. Turner restated his innocence, asked for his wife, and requested that his body be decently buried at the Saint John's Methodist Church cemetery in Mount Sterling. When efforts to quickly locate Chloe failed, Turner was hanged. The alleged conspiracy was created through forged documents in an effort to remove Turner as a political force in Choctaw County. All charges against the six other "conspirators" were dropped, and the case was dismissed on 24 October 1887.

FURTHER READING

Rogers, William Warren, and Robert David Ward.
    *August Reckoning: Jack Turner and Racism in Post–
    Civil War Alabama* (1973, 2004).
Rogers, William Warren, and Robert David Ward.
    "'Jack Turnerism': A Political Phenomenon
    of the Deep South," *Journal of Negro History* 57
    (Oct. 1972).
This entry is taken from the *American National
Biography* and is published here with the
permission of the American Council of Learned
Societies.

MAMIE E. LOCKE

Turner, James Milton (22 Aug. 1839?–1 Nov. 1915), educator and diplomat, was born a slave in St. Louis County, Missouri, the son of John Turner, a free black farrier, and Hannah, the slave of Aaron and Theodosia Young, formerly of Kentucky. Mother and son were freed by Theodosia Young on 12 March 1844. Educated in clandestinely operated schools in St. Louis in defiance of Missouri law, Turner was sent by his parents to preparatory school at Oberlin College in Ohio during the mid-1850s. He remained there for no more than two years and returned to St. Louis during the late 1850s. He worked as a porter until the outbreak of the Civil War, when he joined the war effort as a personal valet to Colonel Madison Miller, a Union officer.

Turner began his public career in 1865 when he became a member of the Missouri Equal Rights League, an organization formed to advocate the passage of the Thirteenth Amendment, the extension of the franchise for all adult black males, and educational opportunities for freedmen. He emerged as a leader of the group, serving as its secretary and speaking on behalf of its causes.

In 1868 Turner was hired by the Kansas City school board to teach in that city's black public school. The next year he taught briefly at a black school in Boonville, a Missouri River town with a large population of southerners and their descendants. Turner's advocacy of educational opportunities for blacks as secretary of the Missouri Equal Rights League, combined with his role as a teacher, identified him as a leading spokesman for black education in the state. In 1869 F. A. Seely, an agent for the Washington-based Freedmen's Bureau, hired Turner to investigate the condition of black education in Missouri and to promote the establishment of schools for blacks in the state.

For the next seven months Turner worked as an employee of the Freedmen's Bureau and as an unpaid agent of the State Department of Education. Virtually everywhere that he went Turner encountered hostility and, on occasion, the threat of violence. In spite of threats and what he termed the "meanness" of southern sympathizers, Turner pressed on. In his final report to Seely, written in late February 1870, Turner noted that he had "caused directly and indirectly the erection of seven or eight schoolhouses and opened thirty-two schools in various parts of the State."

One of the biggest obstacles to establishing schools for blacks, in addition to the pervasive racism in Missouri, was the shortage of black teachers. In January 1870, in an attempt to remedy this problem, Turner called a convention in the capital, Jefferson City, to urge the Radical Republicans—who had supported the emancipation of slaves—to provide state support for Lincoln Institute, a subscription school for blacks in Jefferson City. (Subscription schools were private schools that students paid a fee to attend.) As a result of Turner's efforts, the Missouri General Assembly appropriated five thousand dollars annually in state aid to Lincoln Institute. The school, which later became known as Lincoln University, was the major supplier of black teachers in Missouri for the next century.

Later in 1870 Turner was courted by the state's Radical Republicans, who found themselves at odds with the liberal faction of their party, primarily over the reenfranchisement of rebel sympathizers in the state. Turner's active campaigning for the Missouri Radicals in the 1870 election, combined with a Radical defeat at the polls, forced him to turn to the national Republican Party for patronage.

In March 1871 President Ulysses S. Grant appointed Turner minister resident and consul general for the United States to the republic of Liberia, making Turner the first African American to hold that position. Liberia, which was an important source of coffee for the United States, had been founded in the early 1820s by African American freedmen with the assistance of the American Colonization Society. Although Turner left for Liberia with enthusiasm and high hopes at having attained such an "exalted position," his Liberian experience was largely a disappointment. He thought the native Africans to be a "barbaric people" and the American blacks who had migrated there to be ineffective in self-government. He witnessed a coup in 1871 when the Whig president Edward James Royce was driven from power and assassinated by supporters of former president Joseph J. Roberts, a Republican. In 1875 Turner prevailed on the U.S. government to send a man-of-war to put down a rebellion of Grebo tribesmen against the American Liberians, expressing the hope that this "experiment of an African republic" could be saved. An American ship was sent, and the rebellion was suppressed.

Turner resigned his diplomatic position and left Africa for good in May 1878. He returned to a post-Reconstruction America that was much less solicitous of blacks than the America of 1871 had been. He sought the Republican nomination for a congressional seat from Missouri's Third District in the fall of 1878 but failed to gain serious support at the party's convention. Meanwhile he had become aware of the plight of black "Exodusters," whose flight from the post-Reconstruction South had landed many of them in St. Louis, destitute and without any prospects. He helped organize a moderately successful relief effort on behalf of the migrants. In 1879 Turner created the Colored Emigration Aid Association through which he hoped to settle Exodusters in Kansas and in Indian Territory.

While in Indian Territory, exploring the possibility of establishing black colonies, Turner became aware of the plight of the black former slaves of the Cherokee Indians. The controversy centered on whether the former slaves had a right to share in monetary grants made to the Cherokee Nation by the federal government in return for land cessions. Acting as an attorney for the Cherokee freedmen, Turner—in spite of his lack of legal training and of his never having been admitted to the bar—succeeded in getting Congress to pass the Cherokee

Freedmen's Act in 1888, which authorized the payment of seventy-five thousand dollars to 3,881 Cherokee freedmen, to be divided equally among them. Turner continued to work for the remainder of his life as an attorney on behalf of Cherokee freedmen, with varying degrees of success, in an effort to increase the number entitled to a share of money from land cessions. He also worked successfully to guarantee Cherokee freedmen a claim to future land cessions. He was unsuccessful, however, in his attempts to help Choctaw and Chickasaw freedmen gain land from their respective tribes.

The difficulty that he experienced in getting the Cherokee Freedmen's Act passed, combined with his growing frustration and disillusionment with white racism, embittered Turner and caused him first to abandon the Republican Party in favor of the Democrats and later to abandon politics altogether. Indeed, much of the latter half of his life was spent trying to recapture the prestige and influence that he had experienced during the Reconstruction era. His activities among black Missouri Masons during 1890–1910 brought him only little solace, and he died a frustrated man in Ardmore, Oklahoma, as a result of injuries sustained in a railroad tank car explosion.

Turner was arguably Missouri's greatest post–Civil War black leader, although his leadership abilities were restricted by intransigent white racism and his own often caustic criticism of the black masses. He shared much of his long life with Ella DeBurton, whom he married in 1867. After her death in 1907, Turner took Ella Brooks as his common law wife.

FURTHER READING

Materials related to Turner's career as a Freedmen's Bureau agent and as a U.S. minister and consul general to Liberia, along with materials related to his efforts on behalf of the Cherokee freedmen, are in the National Archives.

Kremer, Gary R. *James Milton Turner and the Promise of America: The Public Life of a Post–Civil War Black Leader* (1991).

Obituaries: *Washington Bee* and *Kansas City Sun*, 15 Nov. 1915.

This entry is taken from the *American National Biography* and is published here with the permission of the American Council of Learned Societies.

GARY R. KREMER

Turner, John Patrick (1 Nov. 1885–14 Sept. 1958), physician, author, hospital administrator, civic and organizational leader, and humanitarian, was born in Raleigh, North Carolina, the elder son of Jesse E. Turner, a chef, and Jennie Edwards Turner. The Turner family migrated during Turner's youth to New York City, where he continued his education in the city's public schools. Turner received his preliminary college education in the College of the City of New York and then enrolled in the Leonard Medical School of Shaw University at age seventeen (Cobb, p. 160). Shaw University, a historically black institution in Raleigh, North Carolina, was founded in 1865 by Reverend Henry Tupper under the auspices of the American Baptist Home Mission Society in an effort to educate the freedmen after the Civil War. Reverend Tupper was acutely aware that in addition to educating the head, heart, and hands, it was critical to train practitioners who could assist in alleviating the health disparities prevalent among blacks. With the approval of the school's trustees and a donation from Tupper's brother-in-law Judson Wade Leonard, students began to take preliminary courses for entry into the medical school in the early 1880s. Fully functional by 1882, the Leonard Medical School, which closed in 1918, became the first medical school in North Carolina to enroll blacks. Turner received his M.D. from the institution in 1906.

Upon graduating from Leonard Medical School, Dr. Turner moved to Philadelphia, where he became a resident physician at the Frederick Douglass Memorial Hospital and Training School. His affiliation with this institution would span more than a half-century. The hospital was founded in 1895 by Dr. NATHAN F. MOSSELL, the first black to graduate from the medical school of the University of Pennsylvania. Mossell, who also later served as president of the National Medical Association, recognized the need for an institution that would allow black physicians to practice their surgical skills, provide opportunities for internships, and increase access to quality health care. Dr. Turner served for a number of years as chief surgeon and as president of the staff. Two of the outstanding black physicians who served their surgical residencies under Turner were Dr. Frederick Douglass Stubbs and Dr. Clarence Sumner Greene Sr. Stubbs went on to become Turner's first son-in-law and a pioneering thoracic surgeon. Greene became the first formally trained black neurosurgeon and the first black diplomat of the American Board of Neurological Surgery. In 1948 Douglass merged with Mercy Hospital, another black-run hospital in Philadelphia, to form Mercy-Douglass Hospital. Dr. Turner later served in leadership positions at Mercy-Douglass as well.

After making Philadelphia his home, Dr. Turner immersed himself in the social, religious, civic, and medical activities of his community. His deportment, compassion, and medical skills quickly earned the young physician broad-based biracial support and respect. In 1908 Dr. Turner wed Marion C. Harris, and to this union one daughter was born.

At that time black Philadelphians lacked representation on several key boards and agencies in the city. With petitions from leaders of the black community, endorsements from the president of the State Board of Medical Examiners, and several noted medical professors in the city, Turner passed a Civil Service Examination and became the first black appointed as a medical inspector for the city's public schools in 1912 (*The Pittsburgh Courier*, 2 Mar. 1912). Dr. Turner's impact as an inspector became obvious when he successfully treated a ringworm outbreak at a school under his jurisdiction. This experience later provided him the impetus to write *Ringworm and Its Successful Treatment*, published by F. A. Davis Publishing Company in 1921.

Dr. Turner's innate leadership abilities also became apparent at the local, regional, and national levels in both medical and civic organizations. Due to the exclusionary practices of the mainstream medical associations—particularly in the South—black medical, dental, and pharmacy practitioners found it necessary to form parallel organizations. As a result the National Medical Association (NMA) was organized at the Cotton States and International Exposition in 1895 in Atlanta, Georgia. Dr. Turner was voted president-elect at the NMA's 1919 annual meeting in Newark, New Jersey, and ascended to its presidency at the close of the NMA's 1920 annual meeting in Atlanta (*Journal of the National Medical Association*, 12(4) [1920]: p. 39). During his tenure as president of the NMA, Dr. Turner also cofounded the Pennsylvania State Medical, Dental, and Pharmaceutical Association. In the early 1920s Dr. Turner completed postgraduate courses in surgery, internal medicine, and contagious diseases at the University of Pennsylvania, Jefferson Medical College, and Philadelphia General Hospital (Cobb, p. 160).

Dr. Turner again made history in 1931 by becoming the first black to be appointed a police surgeon in Philadelphia after earning the highest score among the applicants for the position on the Civil Service Examination (Kenney, p. 149). During his long tenure as a police surgeon, Dr. Turner sought and developed innovative techniques in identifying and treating narcotic and alcohol addictions.

Dr. Turner's service as a medical inspector for the public schools provided him with an unparalleled view into the health and socioeconomic challenges affecting the students' productivity. This experience proved to be advantageous when Dr. Turner became the first black appointed to the Philadelphia Board of Education in 1935 by a board of judges (*Baltimore Afro-American*, 15 June 1935, p. 13).

In addition to his appointed positions, Dr. Turner served on many civic boards and belonged to many organizations. He served on the YMCA's local and national committees and as a trustee of Shaw University, Cheyney State College, and the Allen AME Church. In honor of his public service Dr. Turner was awarded an LL.D. degree by his alma mater, Shaw University, in 1934 (*Philadelphia Tribune*, 24 May 1934). He was a 33rd-degree Mason and a member of both Alpha Boule of Sigma Pi Phi and Kappa Alpha Psi fraternities. Dr. Turner was also a member of the American Medical Association in addition to the National Medical Association and several local, county, and statewide medical organizations. At his retirement Dr. Turner was made president-emeritus of Mercy-Douglass Hospital's staff.

Dr. Turner died of cancer at age seventy-two at the private hospital of his second son-in-law in Detroit, Michigan. In recognition of his contributions and achievements, a Philadelphia middle school is named in his honor. Few in life contribute as extensively to their communities as Dr. Turner. His deportment, professionalism, rare leadership abilities, and altruistic dedication to uplifting his fellow humans warrant for him a place as one of the greatest community leaders of the twentieth century.

FURTHER READING

Cobb, W. Montague. "John Patrick Turner M.D. 1885–1958." *Journal of the National Medical Association* 51, no. 2 (1959): 160–161.

Kenney, John A. "John P. Turner, M.D., L.L.D." *Journal of the National Medical Association* 35, no. 4 (1943): 148–149.

Obituaries: *New York Amsterdam News*, 20 Sept. 1958; *Philadelphia Tribune*, 16 Sept. 1958.

ELVATRICE PARKER BELSCHES

Turner, Lorenzo Dow (21 Aug. 1890–10 Feb. 1972), linguist and cultural historian, was born in Elizabeth City, North Carolina. His father, Rooks Turner, earned a bachelor's degree from Howard University, then founded a school that later became the site of a state university. His mother, Elizabeth, was educated in the public schools of the state. Two of his brothers studied medicine and law. His family background provided inspiration for his great academic success.

Turner earned three academic degrees, contributed to American linguistic research in methodology and publications, founded and edited a newspaper, served as professor and administrative head at universities, founded journals, studied West African languages and participated in a Peace Corps project. He received a B.A. in English in 1914 from Howard University (in Washington, D.C.), an M.A. in English in 1917 from Harvard University, and a Ph.D. in English in 1926 from the University of Chicago. His dissertation, *Anti-Slavery Sentiment in American Literature Prior to 1865*, was published in 1929 by the Association for the Study of Negro Life and History in Washington, D.C. He also studied at the School of Oriental and African Studies of the University of London. There he studied the characteristics of Kimbundu, Kongo, Yoruba, Ifik, Ewe, Two, Fante, Hausa, Mende, Ga, and Wolof. Later, as a Research Fellow at Yale University, he also studied Umbundu.

He taught at Howard University from 1917 to 1928; and during his last eight years, he served as head of the English Department. After leaving Howard, he founded and edited the *Washington Sun* newspaper, which closed after one year. Then from 1929 to 1946 he served as head of the English Department at Fisk University in Nashville, where he designed the curriculum for the African Studies Program and assisted with preparation of a textbook, *Readings from Negro Authors for Schools and Colleges*. In 1946 he began teaching at Roosevelt University in Chicago, where he served as chairman of the African Studies Program and cofounded the Peace Corps training program that prepared volunteers for service in Africa. Turner retired from Roosevelt in 1967.

Turner is best known as the father of Gullah studies. That interest began in 1929 when he was teaching a summer class at South Carolina State College (later University) and first heard Gullah speech. Established scholars thought of Gullah as a form of substandard English. Turner suspected that the language was strongly influenced by African languages. Over the next twenty years, he interviewed Gullah speakers in coastal South Carolina and Georgia and made detailed notes on their language. The result of this project was the classic book *Africanisms in the Gullah Dialect* (1949), which immediately modified established academic thinking. *Africanisms* was the first detailed description of Gullah, and it remained the major book on Gullah, though a number of dissertations on this dialect have since been completed. Not only did Turner's study provide convincing evidence that African languages have influenced American English, but also helped make pidgin and creole studies an important discipline, and it paved the way for the systematic study of black English in the United States. So convincing was Turner's description of the origin, development, and structure of Gullah that his thesis—that Gullah is strongly influenced by African languages—was immediately accepted. Later, he also collected data on Louisiana Creoles (during summers when he was teaching at Alcorn College) and conducted linguistic research in Brazil for a year. His research in Brazil was prompted by his knowledge that many Africans had been enslaved there. Much of the data he collected there was not published during his lifetime, though he did publish a few articles based on his research in Brazil. Turner's research also served to promote research methodology in dialect geography and Creole linguistics.

Turner's interest in Gullah had been encouraged by his mentor, CARTER G. WOODSON, and through grants from the Association of Negro Life and History. His interests were also fostered by his association, beginning in the early 1920s, with others active in American linguistics as it developed, partly from American anthropology. Early associates included the staff of the Linguistic Atlas of the United States and Canada—Hans Kurath and others—and such scholars as Edward Sapir, Leonard Bloomfield, and anthropologist Melville Herskovits, who was also a relativist, understanding that all cultures produce individual cultural and art forms. He met these individuals partly as a result of attending a linguistics summer institute in 1930.

In 1931, he became the first black member of the Linguistic Society of America, long the premier linguistics organization in the United States. He later joined both the International Phonetic Association and the American Dialect Society.

Turner joined American linguistic socities as they were founded, and he was successful in obtaining grant funding from the American Council of Learned Societies for his early research. His first professional presentation on Gullah was to members of the American Dialect Society on 31 December 1932.

Turner continued research and publication, publishing in such diverse fields as linguistics, jazz, Zulu culture, Western education in Africa, and African American literature. He prepared works on the Krio language for Peace Corps volunteers and continued to inspire and encourage young scholars as he taught at various black universities during the summers.

FURTHER READING

Turner, Lorenzo Dow. *Africanisms in the Gullah Dialect* (1949).

Turner, Lorenzo Dow. "Some Contacts of Brazilian Ex-slaves with Nigeria, West Africa," *Journal of Negro History* (1942).

Turner, Lorenzo Dow. *Anti-Slavery Sentiment in American Literature Prior to 1865* (1929).

Wade-Lewis, Margaret. *Lorenzo Dow Turner: Father of Gullah Studies* (2007).

BETHANY K. DUMAS

Turner, Mary (?–19 May 1918), lynching victim, lived in Brooks County, Georgia, with her husband, Hayes Turner. The death of Turner's husband and her own lynching were tied to a crime against a white Brooks County planter and his wife. It was a horrid case of mistaken identity that led to the murder of both Mary and Hayes Turner.

On 16 May 1918 Hampton Smith, a farm owner, was murdered and his wife was beaten and left for dead. Smith's wife survived and later claimed the crime was perpetrated by three black men, whom she identified as Will Head, Eugene Rice, and Sidney Johnson. The men had allegedly entered the Smith home, stolen a rifle, and shot both Smith and his wife. The motive was believed to be tied to a gambling debt.

In a typical reactionary gesture of the times, angry whites aimed to avenge Smith's death and his wife's wounding. A white mob found Head right away, and after he allegedly confessed to the crime, he was hung from a tree near Troupeville, four miles from Valdosta. In his confession, Head reportedly implicated both Rice and Johnson in the crimes. Soon, the group found and hanged Rice. However, Johnson continued to evade them.

On 18 May 1918 Hayes Turner, Mary Turner's husband, was found and mistaken for Johnson; he was also hanged by the mob. Angry at the death of her husband and also eight months pregnant, Turner according to the *Atlanta Journal-Constitution* had "made unwise comments" (16 May 1918) about the execution of her husband. Demanding justice and rightly outraged, she vowed to obtain warrants for the arrest of his killers, seeking the help of federal authorities.

The Atlanta paper went on to report that "the people in their indignant mood took exceptions to her remarks, as well as her attitude, and without waiting for night fall … [found her] about sixteen miles north of Valdosta." At Folsom's Bridge over the Little River the group hanged Turner upside down by her feet, doused her with gasoline, and set her on fire. While she burned, her belly was cut open. A news reporter on the scene wrote, "Out tumbled the prematurely born child. Two feeble cries it gave—and received for the answer the heel of a stalwart man, as life was ground out of the tiny form." Turner's body was then riddled with bullets.

The *Atlanta Journal-Constitution* reported that Hampton Smith's gold watch had been found on Turner's body and that the plot to kill the Smiths had been conceived in her house—though the paper later admitted that these were simply speculations. Within a week, the Smiths' confessed murderer, Johnson, was found in a house in Valdosta, reported an article in *The Crisis* written by WALTER WHITE. A posse led by the police chief surrounded the house, as Johnson was said to be armed. According to later reports, the group exchanged gunfire until Johnson ran out of ammunition. When the shooting ended, the police chief had been injured, and Johnson was found dead of a gunshot wound. His body was taken out and mutilated.

Little else is known about Turner's life before she died in 1918 at Folsom's Bridge over the Little River. After her lynching, more than five hundred African Americans left the Valdosta area, leaving hundreds of acres of untilled land behind them.

FURTHER READING

Apel, Dora. *Imagery of Lynching: Black Men, White Women, and the Mob,* 25 Oct. 2004.

White, Walter. "The Lynchings of May, 1918 in Brooks and Lowndes Counties, Georgia: An Investigation," *The Crisis* (1918).

"Woman Lynched By Brooks Co. Mob," *Atlanta Journal-Constitution,* 17–24 May 1918.

CHESYA BURKE

Turner, Nat (2 Oct. 1800?–11 Nov. 1831), abolitionist and rebel, was born on the Virginia plantation of Benjamin Turner, the child of an enslaved woman named Nancy; the name of his father, also a slave, has not been recorded. Little is known about either parent. Family tradition holds that Nancy landed in Norfolk in 1795, the slave of a refugee fleeing the revolt in Saint Domingue (Haiti). Evidence indicates that after being purchased by Turner, Nancy was used as a domestic servant. Later in life, Nat Turner insisted that his father ran away when Nat was still a boy.

Early on, blacks and whites alike came to regard Nat as unusually gifted. Upon being given a book, the boy quickly learned how to read, "a source of wonder to all in the neighborhood." As a devout Methodist, Benjamin Turner was not only aware of Nat's literacy, he even encouraged him to read the Bible, as did his paternal grandmother, Old Bridget, who Nat later said was "very religious, and to whom I was much attached." Even assuming that some of what Turner later told the attorney Thomas R. Gray was exaggerated bravado—or that the white lawyer's editorial hand helped shape the pamphlet published as *The Confessions of Nat Turner*—there is little reason to doubt his assertion that he spent every possible childhood moment "either in prayer" or in reading books purchased for white children on nearby Southampton County farms and estates (Tragle, 306–307).

Aware of his unique abilities, young Nat "wrapped [himself] in mystery." When not doing light work in the fields, he kept to himself and "studiously avoided mixing in society." Unlike other enslaved boys, he neither played practical pranks on others nor touched liquor. Told by both his mother and grandmother that he was "intended for some great purpose," the unusually serious child devoted his limited leisure moments to "fasting and prayer." As was later said of FREDERICK DOUGLASS, whites spoke of Nat as being too clever to be raised in bondage, and Benjamin Turner once remarked that the boy "would never be of service to anyone as a slave" (Tragle, 307–308). In 1809 Benjamin Turner's oldest son, Samuel, purchased 360 acres two miles away. Nancy, Nat, Old Bridget, and five other slaves were loaned to Samuel to help him establish his cotton plantation, a move that became permanent the following year, when Benjamin died during a typhoid epidemic. It may have been at this point that Nat adopted the surname of Turner as a way of linking himself to his ancestral home, rather than as an act of homage to the deceased Benjamin Turner. Although the evidence for a spouse is circumstantial, the Richmond *Constitutional Whig* later reported that Turner married a young slave woman; this may have been a woman called Cherry, who was sold to Giles Reese when Samuel died and his estate was liquidated in 1822. Turner was sold to Thomas Moore for four hundred dollars, an indication that he was regarded as a prime field hand. Despite being short of stature and a little knock-kneed, Turner's shoulders were broad and well muscled from more than a decade of hard labor.

Embittered by the forced separation from his wife, Turner turned to fasting and prayer. He avoided large spiritual gatherings on Sundays, but at night in the quarters he willingly described what he had discovered during his solitary readings of the Bible. Sometime in 1825, while working in the fields, Turner had his first vision. "I saw white spirits and black spirits engaged in battle," he later recalled, "and the sun was darkened—the thunder rolled in the Heavens, and blood flowed in streams" (Tragle, 308). Certain that he was ordained to bring about Judgment Day, Turner began to conduct religious services at Barnes's Church near the North Carolina border. Most whites scoffed, but at least one man, Etheldred T. Brantley, an alcoholic overseer on a nearby plantation, asked Turner to baptize him before an interracial crowd at Pearson's Mill Pond.

On 12 May 1828 Turner experienced his most epochal vision to date. "I heard a loud noise in the heavens," he remembered, "and the Spirit instantly appeared to me." The voice instructed Turner to take up the "yoke" of Christ, "for the time was fast approaching when the first should be last and the last should be first" (Tragle, 310). Warned not to act until given a further sign by God, Turner was instructed to continue teaching but not to breathe a word of his plans to his family or friends.

Several months later Thomas Moore died, and Turner became the property of Thomas's nine-year-old son, Putnam. When the boy's mother married Joseph Travis, a local wheelwright, Turner and the other sixteen slaves on the Moore plantation found themselves under the supervision of yet another new master. When an eclipse of the sun took place in February 1831, Turner concluded that the time was near to act. He recruited four trusted lieutenants: Hark Travis, Nelson Williams, Henry Porter, and Sam Francis. Turner had known Hark Travis for years, as he was also a slave on the Moore plantation and now under the supervision of Joseph Travis. The five initially established 4 July as the date of the uprising, but Turner fell ill, perhaps as the result of fasting, and the target day passed. Since evidence exists that Turner was merely part of a much larger, two-state revolt, it is also possible that he was waiting for bondsmen across the border to rise first.

Turner's precise goals remain unclear. He may have planned to establish a maroon colony within the nearby Dismal Swamp, or the black evangelical may have preferred to leave the next step in his plan to God's will. But once the town of Jerusalem was within the grasp of his army, he could either fortify the hamlet and wait for word of the rising to spread across the countryside or retreat into the swamp and establish a guerrilla base in the interior. According to the *Norfolk Herald* (26 Sept. 1831), Turner later confessed that he planned to conquer "the county of Southampton [just] as the white people did in the revolution."

The rebels began around 2:00 A.M. on Monday, 22 August. Turner struck the first blow but failed to kill Joseph Travis with his hatchet. Hark finished the work, and killed the four other whites in the house, including the Travis baby in its cradle. By noon the slave army had grown to roughly seventy armed and mounted men. They had sacked fifteen houses and killed sixty whites; Turner killed one young woman, Margaret Whitehead. As they neared Jerusalem, a column of eighteen volunteers attacked the insurgents. Turner's men waded into the group, but the tide turned when reinforcements arrived. During the fighting, six of Turner's men were wounded, and several others, too drunk to continue, abandoned the army and made their way back to the quarters. By Tuesday only twenty rebels remained. In hopes of bolstering their numbers, Turner rode for the plantation of Dr. Simon Blunt, who owned sixty bondspeople. Understanding that the revolt had failed, Blunt's slaves cast their lots with the winning side. When they attacked the rebels with clubs and pitchforks, Turner's demoralized army collapsed. Among those badly wounded was Hark Travis, who survived only to be hanged on 9 September.

For more than a month Turner hid in a crude dugout beneath a pile of fence rails near Cabin Pond and the Reese farm, although if his wife aided him, there is no evidence of it. On Sunday, 30 October, as he worked to arrange the camouflage around his hiding place, Turner was accidentally discovered by Benjamin Phipps, a farmer who happened by on the way to a neighbor's. Turner was tried on 5 November by Virginia's special courts of *oyer and terminer*, segregated tribunals reserved for slave crimes; the accused man faced a series of justices rather than a judge, and no appeal was allowed except to the governor, John Floyd. The court quickly found Turner guilty, valued him at $375, and sentenced him to hang on 11 November. According to local tradition, Turner sold his body to a local doctor and used the money to buy ginger cakes as a last meal; aged residents of Southampton later confirmed to Drewry that whites "skinned [him] and made grease of the flesh" (98–102). Turner was thirty-one years old. Altogether, sixty-six men were tried. Twenty-one rebels, including Turner, were hanged, and another sixteen were transported outside the region.

Shocked by the rebellion, the Virginia legislature debated the prospect of gradual emancipation during the winter session of 1831–1832. Governor John Floyd endorsed manumission as the only way to avoid further violence, and assemblyman Thomas Jefferson Randolph submitted a plan for colonization of freed slaves based upon his grandfather's famous scheme. But in January the House of Delegates voted down the report calling for immediate emancipation and colonization by a vote of 85 to 73. Black Virginians, however, remembered Turner more fondly. As one twentieth-century resident of Southampton County put it, Nat was "God's man. He was a man for war, and for legal rights, and for freedom."

The conventional view that Turner was mentally unstable began to form immediately after his death. Southampton authorities refused to dignify his theology with the term "religion" and instead insisted that his desire to be free was "instigated by the wildest superstition and fanaticism" (*Norfolk Herald*, 4 Nov. 1831). At the height of the Jim Crow era, area whites still spoke of seeing Turner's skull, which was retained as a curiosity. Most described it as abnormal. The publication of William Styron's 1968 Pulitzer Prize–winning novel, *The Confessions of Nat Turner*, only contributed to the modern characterization of the slave leader as a dangerously irrational rebel. But rural Americans in the antebellum years would have had an equally difficult time understanding the rationalist tone of Styron's modern world. During the Jacksonian era, many Americans, white and black, devoutly believed that the end of time was near and that Christ would soon return to rule his earthly kingdom. To that extent, Turner was well within the popular millenarian religious tradition of the period and was hardly abnormal for his time.

FURTHER READING
Drewry, William S. *The Southampton Insurrection* (1900).

Greenberg, Kenneth, ed. *The Confessions of Nat Turner and Related Documents* (1996).
Greenberg, Kenneth, ed. *Nat Turner: A Slave Rebellion in History and Memory* (2003).
Oates, Stephen B. *The Fires of Jubilee: Nat Turner's Fierce Rebellion* (1975).
Tragle, Henry I., ed. *The Southampton Slave Revolt of 1831: A Compilation of Source Material* (1971).
DOUGLAS R. EGERTON

Turner, Thomas Wyatt (16 Mar. 1877–21 Apr. 1978), educator and civil rights advocate, was born in Hughesville, Maryland, the son of Eli Turner and Linnie Gross, farmers. The fifth of nine children born into a family of black Catholic sharecroppers, Turner spent eight years in the racially segregated public schools of Hughes County before entering an Episcopalian school for African Americans at Charlotte Hall in adjacent St. Mary's County. In his two years at Charlotte Hall (1892–1894), Turner fell under the sway of two missionary educators who persuaded him that learning was next to godliness and that teaching was a noble profession. From 1895 to 1901 he attended Howard University in Washington, D.C. (the first two years in preparatory school), receiving an AB in Biology in 1901. After teaching at Tuskegee Institute in 1901–1902, he taught in a Baltimore, Maryland, high school for the next decade. While there, Turner earned an M.A. at Howard in 1905. In 1907 he married Laura Miller of Hampton, Virginia. He next pursued doctoral work at the University of Rochester, Johns Hopkins University, Columbia University, and Cornell University, completing a Ph.D. at Cornell in 1921. In 1913 Turner accepted a position as professor of biology at Howard University, a position that he held until 1924. His next assignment took him to Hampton Institute, from which he retired in 1945.

Although Turner was a successful educator and an authority on plant nutrition and diseases who was listed in *American Men of Science*, his historical significance derives primarily from his civil rights work in the Roman Catholic Church in the United States. Growing up in the post-Reconstruction South, Turner acquired a strong aversion to racial discrimination and segregation. In 1910 he became the secretary of the charter branch of the National Association for the Advancement of Colored People (NAACP) in Baltimore. Later, in Washington, D.C., Turner headed up the first membership drive for the local branch of the NAACP. In 1913 Turner sent a letter to Cardinal James Gibbons in Baltimore, appealing to him (without success) to protest President Woodrow Wilson's segregation of federal agencies.

Discovering that discrimination against blacks also pervaded Catholic institutions, especially schools above the elementary level, Turner loudly registered his complaints in the Paulist *Missionary* in 1915 and 1916. It was World War I, however, that spurred Turner to form a black Catholic protest organization. After learning that the Knights of Columbus and the National Catholic War Council, the two major agencies concerned with assisting Catholic servicemen, excluded blacks, Turner and some of his friends formed the Committee of Fifteen. By the end of the war, the committee had set forth an agenda that included the securing of equal educational, economic, and spiritual opportunity for black Catholics and the elevation of their status in the Catholic Church. After the war, Turner's committee bombarded American bishops with protest letters against racism in the church, calling for the integration of the Catholic University of America and the formation of a black clergy (there were only five black priests in the United States in 1925). Well in advance of most white Catholic liberals, Turner classified racism as a sin, and he urged the Catholic hierarchy to denounce this sin "as the paramount evil of the age" (Turner to the Reverend E. R. Dyer, 18 Oct. 1919, Turner papers).

Despite the efforts of the Committee of Fifteen, the Catholic Church grew more racially reactionary as thousands of blacks left the South for northern cities that were increasingly dominated by white Catholics. In response to the worsening racial situation, in December 1924 Turner founded the Federated Colored Catholics (FCC). Although Turner stressed racial solidarity and black leadership, he welcomed the support of the white clergy. Subsequently, two Jesuits, John LaFarge and William M. Markoe, assumed major roles in the early development of the FCC. LaFarge, a quiet, Harvard-educated patrician from Newport, Rhode Island, used his growing influence as an editor of the New York Jesuit weekly, *America*, to champion the FCC. In 1929 Markoe, a younger and more militant Jesuit who was the pastor of a citywide black parish in St. Louis, offered his parish journal, the *Chronicle*, to serve as the official mouthpiece of the FCC. With the help of these talented and resourceful Jesuits, the black federation grew in size and importance, claiming to represent 100,000 black American Catholics by 1932.

From the start, however, LaFarge and Markoe conspired to reorient the FCC. As interracialists, both priests criticized the federation for being too racially conscious. Moreover, LaFarge, who was a gradualist, a paternalist, and an ecclesiastical conservative, wanted to change the FCC from a racial protest group to one devoted to Catholic Action, meaning that the lay organization would be under clerical control and that the FCC would shift its focus away from the divisive factor of race to the unifying and universal mission of the church. In addition, Markoe aspired to be the Moses of black Catholic deliverance, and he apparently believed this ambition was threatened by Turner's insistence on black leadership.

At the FCC convention in New York City in 1932, LaFarge and Markoe essentially hijacked the organization from Turner and his allies. The interracialists renamed the federation the National Catholic Federation for the Promotion of Better Race Relations and expunged references to "Negro" and "colored" from its constitution. After the convention, Markoe changed the name of the *Chronicle* to the *Interracial Review* and engineered a rump session of the federation's executive committee that ousted Turner from the presidency. In the heated debate that followed, LaFarge and Markoe charged Turner with being anticlerical, separatist, and even un-Catholic. The power that Turner allowed LaFarge and Markoe to garner in the FCC refutes the charge of anticlericalism, and Turner's lifelong fight against segregation renders the charge of separatism unpersuasive. Racial solidarity was for Turner a means of combating racism, never an end in itself. The debate between the Jesuits and Turner was really about clericalism versus lay power, about white gradualism versus black urgency for racial justice.

The federation's split retarded black Catholic leadership for a generation, but the FCC's efforts nonetheless bore some fruit. Correspondence between the FCC and the American hierarchy came to the attention of the Vatican, and Rome pressured American bishops to increase the black clergy and to treat blacks more fairly. Ironically, LaFarge quickly abandoned the reconstituted black federation and founded the Catholic Interracial Council of New York in 1934, a turning point in Catholic race relations that made the New York Jesuit the foremost Catholic spokesman for black rights over the next quarter century.

Although Turner kept the original FCC alive until 1952, it declined rapidly after 1932. After fading back into the relative obscurity of academia, Turner married Louise Wright of Goldsboro, North

Carolina, in 1936. His first marriage had ended with his wife's death in 1928. No children resulted from either marriage.

Turner lived well into the Black Power era and became a symbol for the rise of a racially conscious and proud African American Catholicism, a phenomenon applauded and institutionalized by the more pluralistic, post–Vatican II church. In 1976 the retired professor, now completely blind, presented the first Dr. Thomas Wyatt Turner Award on behalf of the black secretariat of the archdiocese of Washington, D.C., and the delegates at the sixth and seventh National Black Catholic Congresses in 1987 and 1992 reverently invoked Turner's name. A man finally honored in his time, Turner died in Washington, D.C., at the age of 101.

FURTHER READING

The Turner papers, which include his unpublished memoirs, are in the Moorland-Spingarn Research Center at Howard University in Washington, D.C.

Davis, Cyprian. *The History of Black Catholics in the United States* (1990).

McGreevy, John T. *Parish Boundaries: The Catholic Encounter with Race in the Twentieth-Century Urban North* (1996).

Nickels, Marilyn Wenzke. *Black Catholic Protest and the Federated Colored Catholics, 1917–1933* (1988).

Nickels, Marilyn Wenzke. "Thomas Wyatt Turner and the Federated Colored Catholics," *U.S. Catholic Historian* 7 (Spring/Summer 1988): 215–232.

Ochs, Stephen J. *Desegregating the Altar: The Josephites and the Struggle for Black Priests, 1871–1960* (1990).

Southern, David W. *John LaFarge and the Limits of Catholic Interracialism, 1911–1963* (1996).

Obituary: *Washington Post*, 23 Apr. 1978.

This entry is taken from the *American National Biography* and is published here with the permission of the American Council of Learned Societies.

DAVID W. SOUTHERN

Turner, Tina (26 Nov. 1939–), R&B, soul, and rock 'n' roll singer, was born Anna Mae Bullock in Brownsville, Tennessee, a small town about seventy-five miles north of Memphis. She grew up in nearby Nutbush with her older sister Alline and her parents, Floyd Richard (who went by the name "Richard") and Zelma Bullock. Her African American father was the supervisor at a white-owned farm, and her mother, who was part Cherokee, took care of the children. Soon after the attack on Pearl Harbor, Richard found work in a defense plant in Knoxville while Zelma worked as a waitress and a housekeeper, leaving their daughters to be cared for by relatives for two years. As the war drew to a close, the family reunited. They moved around western Tennessee, making a meager living by farming. Anna Mae attended school, helped pick cotton, strawberries, and other crops, and began singing in the church choir. Through it all, she dreamed of getting away from rural Tennessee and her parents' tumultuous, unhappy marriage. In 1949 her mother left Nutbush and the family to settle in St. Louis. Three years later, her father, who had remarried, moved to Detroit. Anna Mae and Alline stayed behind with a cousin, anguished by their abandonment. Just as difficult for Anna Mae was her sister's move to St. Louis soon after their father's departure.

Lonely and determined to get out of Nutbush, at age sixteen Anna Mae Bullock followed her mother and sister to the city, and it was there her life changed. In 1956 she discovered rock 'n' roll music at the Manhattan Club in St. Louis, where she first saw a band called the Kings of Rhythm, led by the charismatic IKE TURNER. After repeated pleas, she began singing with the band regularly, wowing audiences with her powerful voice and commanding, sensual stage presence. In 1958 she graduated from high school and on 20 August gave birth to a son, Raymond Craig. The father, saxophonist Raymond Hill, promptly left the band and St. Louis altogether. That year Ike transformed Anna Mae Bullock into Tina Turner, and she became a centerpiece of the band's live shows. In 1960 Ike and Tina enjoyed their first recording success with "A Fool in Love." The couple also had a child together, Ronald Renelle, born on 27 October of that year. More hit singles followed, such as "I Idolize You" (1960) and "It's Gonna Work Out Fine" (1961). Ike, the creative—and controlling—mastermind behind the music, changed his band's name to the Ike and Tina Turner Revue, and he added three backup singers known as the Ikettes.

The act became a smash, touring widely and recording prolifically. In 1962 Ike relocated the band to Los Angeles, home to a vibrant pop music scene, and then he and Tina rushed off to Tijuana for an impromptu wedding. (Tina would discover later that her marriage to Ike was illegal, as Ike had never divorced his previous wife.) Their record company, the New York-based Sue Records, released two of their albums that year, *It's Gonna Work Out Fine* and *Don't Play Me Cheap*. Ike and Tina spent the next few years touring exhaustively.

Their marriage was by all accounts not a happy one, given Ike's habitual infidelities and his alleged drug-fueled violence against Tina. But musically, she was poised for a breakthrough that would transform her into a star in her own right. In 1966, without Ike, she recorded the magisterial "River Deep, Mountain High" with acclaimed producer Phil Spector. It reached the top ten in the United States and became a huge hit in Britain, where the Ike and Tina Turner Revue opened for the Rolling Stones that fall. Their greatest commercial success came with the electrifying cover of Creedence Clearwater Revival's "Proud Mary," which reached number four on the American pop charts in 1971 and received the Grammy Award for Best R&B performance by a duo or group. Two years later, they scored another major hit with a backhanded ode to Tina's small-town roots, with the rollicking "Nutbush City Limits."

While the music was more popular than ever, Tina Turner's marriage to Ike was becoming unbearable. As she detailed later in her best-selling memoir, her husband was more than domineering—he was physically violent, mentally abusive, and prone to unpredictable fits of rage (all of which were exacerbated by his addiction to cocaine). On the evening of 4 July 1976, as the Revue prepared to take the stage for a bicentennial celebration in Dallas, Texas, Turner walked away from Ike, the band, and her contract. Her own personal independence day led to trying times, however, as she struggled with a solo recording career, releasing several unsuccessful albums in the late 1970s and grappling with repaying concert promoters who had lost money on the canceled Ike and Tina Turner Revue tour. On the bright side for Tina, however, her divorce became final in 1978.

Turner's musical comeback started in 1982 with the release of "Let's Stay Together," the AL GREEN hit from a decade earlier. As was true for most of her career to that point, her songs and solo tours were more popular in Europe and Britain than in the United States. She did, however, win another Grammy Award, this time for best female R&B performance. But Turner's triumphant return— and the point that she eclipsed her previous fame— came with her dazzling masterpiece, *Private Dancer* (1984), an album that ran the gamut from old-school soul ("Let's Stay Together") and swaggering rock 'n' roll ("Better Be Good to Me"), to the lush wistfulness of the title track and the world-wise strut of the runaway hit "What's Love Got To Do With It?" The album won four Grammy Awards,

and Turner launched a massive worldwide tour. She even became a hit with the MTV generation, as her videos played constantly throughout 1985 and her duet with Mick Jagger was the highlight of the global Live Aid concert, as the duo performed a scorching rendition of the Rolling Stones' classic, "It's Only Rock 'n' Roll." (Their iconic performance subsequently landed them on the cover of *Life* magazine.) Turner enjoyed several more hits in the 1980s, including a 1985 duet with Bryan Adams entitled "It's Only Love," 1985's "We Don't Need Another Hero (Thunderdome)" from the film *Mad Max Beyond Thunderdome*, and "Typical Male" off the 1986 album *Break Every Rule*, which was her multiplatinum follow-up to *Private Dancer*.

While Turner toured the world, performing with musical luminaries such as Jagger, Robert Cray, Phil Collins, and Eric Clapton, her autobiography, *I, Tina*, was published in 1986. Coauthored by music critic Kurt Loder, the book bristled with revelations about her abusive marriage to Ike (charges that he steadfastly denied). In 1993 the memoir was adapted for the screen, and audiences flocked to *What's Love Got to Do With It*, with Oscar-nominated performances by ANGELA BASSETT and LAURENCE FISHBURNE as Tina and Ike, respectively. Turner herself appeared in movies and television shows throughout her career, mostly as herself, singing. But she also had acting roles in *Tommy* (1975), *Mad Max Beyond Thunderdome* (1983), and *Last Action Hero* (1983).

The hit records and sold-out tours continued (though the latter became less frequent), as Turner scored top-ten hits with "The Best" (1989) and "I Don't Wanna Fight" (1993), and lesser hits such as the cover of John's "The Bitch is Back" (1993) and the theme from the James Bond film *GoldenEye* (1995). But in 2000, just beyond her sixtieth birthday, she announced that she would stop touring. She decided on a more selective schedule of individual performances and events, as well as more free time with her longtime partner, record executive Erwin Bach, the man she had lived with since 1986. (The couple owned houses in Nice, France, and Zurich, Switzerland.) In 1991 Ike and Tina Turner were inducted into the Rock and Roll Hall of Fame. Tina received a star on the Hollywood Walk of Fame in 1986 and was a Kennedy Center honoree in 2005. Turner was a major voice in the early decades of rock 'n' roll and a dynamic performer who overcame countless obstacles. By the end of the twentieth century, she had become rock 'n' roll's grand dame—and perhaps its most legendary survivor.

FURTHER READING

Turner, Ike. *Takin' Back My Name: The Confessions of Ike Turner* (1999).

Turner, Tina. *I, Tina* (1986).

STACY BRAUKMAN

Turner, William V. (c. 1821–?), educator, civil rights activist, and politician, was born in Virginia during the antebellum period, but his most important endeavors were carried out in post–Civil War Alabama. In 1865, while Alabama lawmakers designed oppressive black codes to control the political, occupational, and educational conduct of freedmen, Turner founded a school for former slaves at Wetumpka in Elmore County. During the next year, resistance abounded among local whites bitter about the Confederate defeat and the newly legislated status of free blacks. Because of white opposition and a scarcity of funds, Turner was forced to entrust the school to the Freedmen's Bureau. Turner regretted the decision, but he knew that he could not jeopardize his family by continuing to serve as headmaster. Students and sponsors could bring him joy, he had explained, but they could not keep his family from starving.

In addition to being an educator and administrator, Turner was a crusader for justice, an agent of the Republican-leaning *Mobile Nationalist*, an excellent orator, and a politician. After being physically assaulted by a white justice of the peace in 1866, Turner filed charges against the Democratic official. Turner was aware that this action might enrage many whites, especially Democrats, but he was not afraid of a backlash. In fact, Turner later reported similar violations against blacks to the Freedmen's Bureau and other local, state, and federal officials.

Turner's education advocacy and public stances against injustice helped to launch a political career that spanned the entirety of Alabama's Reconstruction period. In May 1867 he attended the Second Black (Colored Freedmen's) Convention that was held at St. Louis Street Church in Mobile. The convention attracted black Republicans from at least thirteen counties. Delegates agreed that Alabama's destiny was in Republicans' hands and that the Republican Party's destiny was in black people's hands. This idea conflicted with the views of some white Alabamians, who believed that black Republicans had been frustrated by certain white members' insistence on keeping blacks powerless and that the blacks wanted to create a separate party (as did Henry M. Turner and a number of

other black Georgians). The *New Orleans Tribune* helped dispel this myth when it revealed the main reason the colored convention was called in the first place—to secure harmonious relations with white Republicans.

During the convention, William Turner and other delegates called for the formation of an integrated public school system, requested relief programs for elderly and homeless people, and praised the Freedmen's Bureau for its work on behalf of black Alabamians. The delegates also asked the federal government to end the abuses carried out by former slave owners and federal soldiers, and they drafted a resolution proclaiming each delegate a member of the national Republican Party and thus eligible for any privilege that membership or federal law afforded them. In one of the strongest political pronouncements that any group of black Alabamians had ever made, Turner and his associates called these inalienable rights that any respectful citizen should have been able to enjoy without having to worry about being physically or verbally assaulted. Specifically, the delegates desired the same rights that white men enjoyed—for example, holding office, being jurors, riding public conveyances, and sitting at public tables and places of amusement alongside other law-abiding citizens. By 1868 Turner had begun to doubt the effectiveness of radical forms of Reconstruction. He believed that white Republicans could not resolve the countless economic, political, and social issues that black people faced; he also believed that most white Democrats were racists. In the Alabama House of Representatives, where Turner sat from 1868 to 1870, and during several meetings of the executive committee of the Alabama Republican party, Turner argued that only blacks themselves could determine their fate.

Turner emphasized black self-help in January 1871 when U.S. Congressmen JAMES THOMAS RAPIER, Turner himself, and at least fifty other influential black men organized the Alabama Negro Labor Union (ANLU) or Convention. In time the ANLU became one of the strongest black federations of labor in the South, and Turner was one of its most important agents. Doubtful that white employers would ever pay black workers a just wage, Turner supported an emigration scheme that, if carried out, would have relocated willing black Alabamians to Kansas.

In June 1872 Turner was chosen to represent Alabama at the national Republican convention in Philadelphia, Pennsylvania. Two years later he attended an Equal Rights Association (ERA) convention in Montgomery, Alabama. Turner became one of the ERA's most articulate spokespersons, and he agreed that Charles Sumner's civil rights bill should be supported and that black Republicans should have more power within the state Republican Party; but Turner was less certain about integration. He was particularly concerned about forcing integration on the people who lived in the Tennessee Valley, which was predominantly white.

Turner's disillusionment with white Republicans and the practicality of complete social equality by 1874—the year that ultraconservative Democratic rule was restored permanently in Alabama—reflected a wider concern among black Alabamians. At the outset of Reconstruction, Turner had been optimistic about the future of freedmen, shamelessly thanking God, Abraham Lincoln, and the Republican Party for ending slavery. However, white attempts to control every aspect of black life had caused Turner and other leading blacks to take largely separatist stances by the time Alabama was restored, or redeemed, in 1874. Although Turner never left the Republican fold, he did continue to criticize white Alabama Republicans for ignoring the concerns of black Alabamians and for relegating black members to minor positions within the state party.

FURTHER READING

Bailey, Richard. *Neither Carpetbaggers nor Scalawags: Black Officeholders in the Reconstruction of Alabama, 1867–1878* (1995).

Fitzgerald, Michael. *The Union League Movement in the Deep South: Politics and Agricultural Change During Reconstruction* (1989).

Foner, Eric. *Freedom's Lawmakers: A Directory of Black Officeholders During Reconstruction* (1996).

Foner, Philip S., and Ronald L. Lewis. *Black Workers: A Documentary History from Colonial Times to the Present* (1989).

Kolchin, Peter. *First Freedom: The Responses of Alabama's Blacks to Emancipation and Reconstruction* (1972).

BERTIS ENGLISH

Turpeau, David Dewitt (8 Nov. 1873–13 Feb. 1947), minister and politician, was born in Saint Martinville, Louisiana, to Michael Turpeau and Isabelle Hill Turpeau. The Turpeaus were Roman Catholics, as were many in that part of Louisiana, before the elder Turpeau was drawn to the Methodist Episcopal Church. Young Turpeau attended the elementary school in Saint Martinville before leaving his family and the intimacy of his hometown to enter Gilbert Academy High School in Baldwin. One of his instructors, Frank Dakin, found Turpeau to be academically gifted, and he became an important mentor who guided Turpeau's academic career.

Initially, Dakin envisioned Turpeau as one who would pursue a career in the field of architecture. Dakin believed that Turpeau would have greater opportunities for advancement in the North, so he facilitated his admission to Mount Kisco High School in New York. The Dakin family in Mount Kisco was well connected to the Methodist Episcopal Church and would bring Turpeau into their community of Christian believers. He joined the church in 1894, and after graduating from high school in 1896, he entered Bennett College in Greensboro, North Carolina. The college was founded by the Methodist Episcopal Church in 1873 and stopped accepting male students in 1926. Turpeau completed his bachelor of science degree in 1899.

Still pursuing a career in a scientific field, it was not until after he graduated that the providence of God nudged him closer to the ministry. In his autobiography *Up from the Cane Brakes*, Turpeau describes how during his train ride home he met the Reverend C. M. Chase (of the Delaware Conference) who convinced the young graduate that he, Turpeau, had a higher calling. Shortly thereafter, Turpeau was appointed a supply pastor in Sing Sing (now Ossining), New York. There he preached his first sermon to eight people in the basement of a house at the corner of Broadway and Acquadock streets. He recalled, "My first collection was two dollars. I was inducted into the Methodist ministry, being made a local preacher and given a change all in one breath" (Turpeau, *Cane Breaks*, 34). While pasturing the Sing Sing church, he attended the Christina and Missionary Alliance School at Nyack, New York.

In 1900 he matriculated at Drew Theological Seminary in Madison, New Jersey. During his tenure at Drew he joined the Delaware Conference and was appointed to the John Wesley Methodist Episcopal Church in New Haven, Connecticut. In his third year of ministry he was assigned to John Wesley Church in New Haven, when his three sisters introduced him to Ila Marshall through correspondence. Turpeau's intellectual and spiritual world continued to expand as he took several classes at

Yale University's Divinity School. He also received two other appointments while in the Delaware Conference; those appointments were in Hudson, New York, and Orange, New Jersey. Because of his sisters' persistence, he courted Marshall through correspondence, and they were married on 3 November 1901. The nuptials were performed by the Reverend I. L. Thomas, pastor of Asberry Methodist Episcopal Church in Washington, D.C. The newlyweds had never met in person prior to their wedding, so to identify each other in Washington, D.C., they both agreed to wear a red rose on their lapels. Their union produced eight children, including LEONTINE TURPEAU CURRENT KELLY, who rose to prominence in the Methodist Episcopal Church by becoming the first African American female bishop of any major denomination.

By transferring to the Washington Conference, Turpeau became the pastor of several area Methodist churches in Rockville, Maryland. He also served in Ames Church in Baltimore, Maryland, and Mount Zion in Georgetown, Washington, D.C. While in Washington, he served concurrently as the superintendent of the Colored Department, Anti-Saloon League of Maryland from 1912 to 1915. He also served as ex-superintendent of the Washington Conference of the Methodist Episcopal Church, 1920 to 1925. In 1924 he was called to Pennsylvania as the pastor of Pittsburgh Warren Church, where he remained for three years. In 1927 Turpeau was assigned to the Lexington Conference to serve as pastor to Calvary Methodist Episcopal Church in Cincinnati, Ohio. He stayed in Ohio for the remainder of his ministerial career, serving the Calvary Church for nine years. In 1936 he was elected district superintendent of the Cincinnati-Lexington circuit, an office he held for sixteen years.

While in Ohio, Turpeau became involved in politics, and in 1938 he was elected to the Ohio General Assembly as one of the representatives from Hamilton County. He would remain involved in Ohio political life for more than five terms in the house of representatives of the 97th General Assembly of Ohio. During his tenure he served on the finance and the welfare committees. Turpeau was not only active in politics—throughout his life he was a member of the Young Men's Christian Association, the NAACP, the Masons, the Odd Fellows, the Elks, and the Good Samaritans.

In 1942 he retired from the active ministry and devoted himself full-time to political life. As a member of two major committees, he was able to promote good legislation for all citizens of Ohio. In essence, Turpeau's ministerial and political careers maintained a tradition of African American vigilance within the Methodist Church. He sought to concern himself with the current affairs of the day and to speak to issues that affected the lives and livelihoods of his parishioners. The accountability of adults, in Turpeau's mind, had more to do with the future than the present. As he wrote, "Let us remember we must live for unborn generations and the only way to be a contributor to the coming children of the race is to leave something behind that will tell the story better than any words can tell them" (*Mount Zion Herald*).

FURTHER READING

Turpeau, David D. *Up from the Cane Breaks* (self-published autobiography).

Beason, Harriet. "Church Historian," *Mount Zion Methodist Episcopal Historical Journal* (1916–1920; unpublished).

The Central Christian Advocate, 22 May 1947.

Current, Angella. *Breaking Barriers: An African American Family and the Methodist Story* (2001).

"Four-and-Twenty Elder Rally," *Mount Zion Herald*, 26 May 1918.

Turpeau, D. Rossman. "The Turpeaus: A Family Odyssey," *Cincinnati Post*, 27 Feb. 1988.

IDA E. JONES

Turpin, Tom (1873–13 Aug. 1922), ragtime pianist, composer, and bar owner, was born Thomas Milton J. Turpin in Savannah, Georgia, the son of John L. "Jack" Turpin, a bar owner and amateur wrestler, and Lulu Waters. The Turpin family was prominent in Savannah's African American community, but by 1880 they had relocated to St. Louis, Missouri, where John Turpin opened the Silver Dollar Saloon. Young Tom began playing piano at an early age and was employed at one of the best-known bars in the city, the Castle Club, by the early 1890s. By 1893 he had opened his own saloon, which eventually became known as the Rosebud Bar, with Turpin grandly proclaiming himself "President of the Rosebud Club." The bar became a meeting place for local pianists, including Louis Chauvin.

Along with his brother Charles, Turpin performed locally at the bar and in tent shows. The duo became successful entertainment entrepreneurs, sponsoring ragtime piano contests, managing the local BOOKER T. WASHINGTON Theater (from about 1910), a key venue sponsoring black entertainment, and running the Jazzland Dance Hall. The brothers ran a number of legitimate and not-so-legitimate businesses, including pool halls, bars, and private clubs, and were purported to be involved with illegal gambling. Charles also became one of the first black members of the St. Louis police force, no doubt to keep their businesses protected from the intrusion of the law.

Tom Turpin is generally credited as the first African American to have a ragtime composition published. His "Harlem Rag" (1897) predated SCOTT JOPLIN's "Maple Leaf Rag" by two years. Like most of Turpin's compositions, "Harlem Rag" combines elements of folk rags with the more sophisticated improvisations of flashy city-based pianists like Turpin himself. The opening theme—a busy, melodically intricate, "finger busting" section—is typical of Turpin's showman-like compositions that were designed to impress an audience from the get-go.

Turpin published a handful of other compositions through 1905 that show increasing sophistication but are still much simpler in style than those of his contemporary Joplin. He remained more interested in effect than in achieving subtle gradations of color or tone; thus his pieces were well loved by flashy players like the ragtime banjoist Vess L. Ossmann, who made popular recordings of Turpin's "Ragtime Nightmare" (1900) and "Buffalo Rag" (1904).

For some reason Turpin's publishing activities then ceased, although he registered for copyright three further pieces that apparently are lost, and was said to be still performing and winning prizes as a ragtime pianist as late as 1916. He is believed to have written material for revues at the Booker T. Washington Theater as well as additional solo pieces, but none of this material has surfaced. He became increasingly involved in managing his family's extensive business holdings, which were far more lucrative to him than any publishing could be. Turpin, who weighed over three hundred pounds, died of illnesses related to his weight in St. Louis.

FURTHER READING

Blesh, Rudi, and Harriet Janis. *They All Played Ragtime*, 4th ed. (1971).

Jasen, Dave, and Trebor Jay Tichenor. *Rags and Ragtime: A Musical History* (1978).

This entry is taken from the *American National Biography* and is published here with the permission of the American Council of Learned Societies.

RICHARD CARLIN

Turpin, Waters Edward (9 Apr. 1910–19 Nov. 1968), writer and educator, was born in Oxford, Maryland, on the Chesapeake Bay's Eastern Shore. He was the only child of Simon and Mary Rebecca Waters Turpin. At age three he lost his father, yet his maternal grandfather, Captain Thomas Lambert Waters, told him several stories about enslaved and free blacks and made him feel strongly connected to his heritage. Captain Waters, of free black descent, operated his own fishing and ferry boats. His daughter Rebecca had hoped for an education, but her mother's sudden death in 1908 left her with the responsibility of caring for her nine siblings. She was married to Simon Turpin only a few years before becoming widowed. She briefly remarried, to a Mr. Henry, but was soon widowed again. She worked as a domestic, determined to secure for her son the educational opportunities she herself had lost.

From 1916 to 1922, Waters Turpin attended public elementary school in Oxford. After moving to New Jersey with his mother, he attended Burlington County Elementary School and Summit High School. During the early 1920s, Rebecca Henry worked as a domestic for the famous novelist Edna Ferber. In 1924, Henry sent her son to Baltimore's Morgan Academy, the college preparatory school associated with historically black Morgan State College (later University). There he became deeply interested in literature. During school breaks, he worked for his grandfather or helped with parties at Ferber's house. Ferber gave him access to her library.

Turpin earned his high school diploma in 1927 and enrolled as an English major at Morgan State. Recognizing that novels did not record black lives the same way Ferber's documented white lives, he decided to help close this literary gap, even as he prepared to become an educator. Ferber encouraged his writing. With Turpin as editor-in-chief, a group of literary-minded students, including his wife-to-be, Jean Fisher, started and published their work in the *Morgan Newsletter*. Turpin began planning a multigenerational novel about black lives on Maryland's Eastern Shore. He graduated from Morgan in 1931 with a B.A. in English.

Turpin earned his M.A. at Columbia University in 1932 while working fulltime in a Harlem delicatessen and writing his novel. He was then hired as a Works Progress Administration welfare investigator. He published short stories and poetry in the *Morgan College Bulletin*. Wanting to make ends meet and still write, he sought a teaching post. In

1935, he began to teach English and coach football at Storer College in Harpers Ferry, West Virginia. In June 1936, he wed Jean Fisher. They had a son, John Edward, and a daughter, Rosalie Rebecca (married surname: Belcher). Jean Turpin remained in Baltimore teaching at Morgan; they visited on weekends. In 1937, Harper and Row published Turpin's first novel, *These Low Grounds*, which presented an intergenerational black "saga of achievement" and established his "quest for cultural and racial mythos and effort to unveil the epic structure of hitherto neglected figures of his racial past" (Hollis, *These Low Grounds*, p. 41). The book was favorably reviewed by the NAACP's magazine *Crisis*.

During the summer of 1937, Waters and Jean Turpin drove to Chicago and conducted extensive research for his next planned novel, a family saga about the Great Migration of African Americans from the South to that city during the late 1910s. Harper and Row rejected the manuscript of *O Canaan!*, but Doubleday Doran published it in 1939. This novel, too, received good reviews but sold few copies. Turpin was repeatedly rejected for a Guggenheim Fellowship. He felt torn between his literary gifts and ambitions and his interests and talents in the more economically feasible occupation of teaching. By the time *O Canaan!* was published, he had left Storer and returned to Columbia for two years of doctoral studies.

In 1940, Turpin became an assistant professor of English at Lincoln University in Chester County, Pennsylvania. In March 1941, he was awarded a Julius Rosenwald Creative Writing Fellowship, allowing him a year's leave of absence to research and write full-time on a novel about slavery from the vantage point of slaves. He continued work on this book after his return to teaching. Among his students at Lincoln were the poet Bruce Wright and Kwame Nkrumah, the future president of an independent Ghana. Turpin was drafted into the military in 1944 and for the next year taught adult literacy classes at the Great Lakes Naval Station. Afterwards, he remained at Lincoln until the summer of 1950, when Nick Aaron Ford, head of Morgan's English department, invited him to teach there full-time, as Jean Turpin had already been doing for some time.

At Morgan, Turpin was well known and loved as a charismatic teacher of composition and literature and assistant drama director. He produced and directed two of his own plays on campus, *Let the Day Perish* (1950) and *St. Michael's Dawn* (1956), about the life of FREDERICK DOUGLASS. *Let the Day*

Perish was also produced on several other college campuses. In 1957, Turpin published *The Rootless*, his novel about slaves in eighteenth century Maryland. For two years, he headed the Division of the Humanities at Morgan. In 1960, he finally earned his Ed.D. at Columbia. In 1962, he recorded a forty-part television lecture series. Turpin and Ford also collaborated on two education books.

At age 58, Turpin died in Baltimore during an operation for abdominal cancer. He left behind a number of unpublished literary works, some complete, some not. More than a thousand people attended his memorial service. Most of them knew him better as an educator than as a groundbreaking writer. It was not until roughly a decade later that black studies conferences began to pay serious attention to Turpin's literary works. Burney Hollis considered Turpin a "forerunner of ALEX HALEY's *Roots* … who set out with the noble intention of giving Afro-Americans the cultural mythos and heroes which they, until *Roots*, did not have" (*These Low Grounds*, pp. 366–367). The fine arts center that opened at Morgan in 2001 included a theater named after Turpin. Unfortunately, as of 2009, Turpin's published novels all remained out of print.

FURTHER READING

Hollis, Burney James (ed.). *Swords upon This Hill: Preserving the Literary Tradition of Black Colleges and Universities: Papers from the Ford-Turpin Symposium on Afro-American Literature* (1984).

Hollis, Burney James. *These Low Grounds of Sin and Sorrow: The Life and Work of Waters Edward Turpin* (University of Pennsylvania Ph.D. thesis, 1978).

Reid, Margaret Ann. "Waters Turpin," In William L. Andrews, Frances Smith Foster, and Trudier Harris-Lopez, ed. *The Concise Oxford Companion to African American Literature* (2001).

MARY KRANE DERR

Turrentine, Stanley William (5 Apr. 1934–12 Sept. 2000), jazz tenor saxophonist, was born in Pittsburgh, Pennsylvania, the son of Thomas Turrentine Sr., a construction worker who earlier had played tenor saxophone and clarinet in the Savoy Sultans. His mother, Rosetta (maiden name unknown), was a pianist. As a child, Turrentine played piano by ear. At thirteen he took up cello but secretly learned to play his father's tenor sax when he was supposed to be practicing cello. Turrentine's love for the instrument and his potential talent were immediately apparent, and his father bought him a tenor sax and gave him strict instructions. He was to stand in a corner, projecting the saxophone's sound back toward himself, and play nothing but sustained tones, gradually working his way through the instrument's highest and lowest registers until he was satisfied with the tone quality of every note. This foundation yielded a gorgeous overall instrumental timbre, top to bottom, and on some notes a distinctive and immediately identifiable whooping sound that became in effect Turrentine's musical signature. Over the next few years he practiced with his father and went with his father to hear renowned jazz musicians at the jam sessions then flourishing in Pittsburgh. Music at the family's church was of little interest to Turrentine, but their home was situated next to a Sanctified church, with instruments blaring through open doors. Late in life he recalled that this raw form of African American gospel music was another strong influence on the development of his soulful playing.

Having begun to help support the family by playing locally, Turrentine at sixteen quit Pittsburgh's Schenley High School to join the guitarist LOWELL FULSON's rhythm and blues band, which for a time included RAY CHARLES on piano. Around 1952 Turrentine spent a period in Cleveland, where he played with the jazz pianist and arranger TADD DAMERON. Early in 1953 Turrentine replaced JOHN COLTRANE in the rhythm and blues band led by the alto saxophonist EARL BOSTIC, working alongside his older brother, the trumpeter Tommy Turrentine. Serving in the U.S. Army from 1956 to 1958, Turrentine was a member of the 158th Army Band. In March 1959, a few months after his discharge, he rejoined Tommy as a member of the drummer MAX ROACH's group, with which he recorded several albums and in March 1960 toured Europe. In the 1950s Turrentine married, and his first daughter was born. The relationship ended when, while they were living in Philadelphia, Pennsylvania, his wife suggested that he give up playing and apply for a job at the post office. Further details are unknown.

On 25 April 1960 Turrentine first made his mark in jazz as a soloist on the Blue Note label with a lengthy session under the leadership of the organist Jimmy Smith, issued on the albums *Midnight Blue* and *Back at the Chicken Shack*. In June of that year Turrentine began recording for Blue Note as a leader. There followed numerous such dates under his own name, including the albums *Up at Minton's* and *Z. T's Blues* (both from 1961); further sessions with Smith, including *Prayer Meetin'* (1963); a similar affiliation with the organist SHIRLEY SCOTT that yielded, among others, the albums *Dearly Beloved*

(1961) and *A Chip off the Old Block* (1963); and various LPs as a sideman under the leadership of such jazz musicians as the trumpeter Dizzy Reece; the pianists Duke Jordan, Horace Parlan, Duke Pearson, and HORACE SILVER; the drummer Art Taylor; the saxophonist IKE QUEBEC; and the guitarist KENNY BURRELL. Turrentine's solo on MA RAINEY's classic tune "See See Rider" from Quebec's album *Easy Living*, recorded in January 1962, exemplifies the blues roots of his style.

The emergence of the Hammond organ as a popular jazz instrument in the 1950s opened up the possibility of achieving a full-voiced sound with only three instruments, saxophone, organ, and drums, when the organist was of Smith's or Scott's stature and able to supply not only chords and melody but also bass lines in lieu of a bassist. In this economical manner, as a member of a soul-jazz trio with Scott, Turrentine toured African American nightclubs in the South, the so-called chitlin' circuit. Many such clubs had their own Hammond organs, thus relieving the musicians of the need to cart around these cumbersome, heavy instruments.

"Mr. T," as he was affectionately known, began playing with Scott in 1960, and the following year they married. They had three daughters. The oldest, Lisa, recalled the happiness of their home. The family lived, she said, the "Cosby life" before there was a *Cosby Show*. In summers they toured together, everyone packing into the car and heading to the parents' jobs. But in 1971, perhaps owing to the pull of successful individual careers, Turrentine and Scott separated. If their separation was due to personal animosity, they certainly kept a tight lid on it. Both were remembered time and again as among the most gracious, humble, and approachable people in the world of jazz. They subsequently divorced, and by 1975 Turrentine had married Rhita. Her maiden name and other details of this third marriage are unknown.

Like so many of his colleagues, Turrentine had no knowledge of the intricacies of recording contracts, licensing, royalties, and song publishing, and he entered into disadvantageous agreements with Blue Note. Unlike so many others, he was given a second chance when in the 1970s he taught himself the rudiments of musical finance while scoring huge successes with several recordings, beginning with the title track of his album *Sugar* (1970) and a version of Coltrane's tune "Impressions" from that same album. Each rendition anticipated a widely accessible blend of jazz and rhythm and blues that came to be known a quarter-century later as "smooth jazz." In 1974, on the title track of his album *Pieces of Dreams*, Turrentine's bluesy rendering of the melody was accompanied by a jazz group playing in a restrained bossa nova style and was fleshed out by an orchestra featuring French horns, strings, and harp. In this manner and in other ways, including the placement of his characteristic playing into a disco setting, Turrentine reached into the realm of "easy-listening" music.

In the mid-1980s, when the Blue Note label was reactivated, Turrentine resumed a soul-jazz style. He recorded the album *Straight Ahead* in November 1984 and toured in small groups of his own or in reunions with Smith and Burrell.

Turrentine suffered from high blood pressure, and in the late 1980s he experienced a pulmonary edema that put him into a coma for twenty-eight hours. Since the mid-1960s Turrentine had been living in New Jersey, just across the river from Manhattan. In an effort to lessen the stress in his life, he moved to a quieter place, Kensington, Maryland, and then settled in Fort Washington, Maryland. In the early 1990s he made two new soul-jazz albums, including *More Than a Mood* (1992). Turrentine toured extensively throughout the decade.

On 10 September 2000, before the last night of a week-long engagement at the Blue Note club, Turrentine suffered a stroke at a Manhattan hotel. Hospitalized in New York City, he died two days later. He was survived by his fourth wife Judith; her maiden name and the marriage date are unknown. Turrentine was the stepfather to her son.

FURTHER READING

James, Michael. "Introducing Stanley Turrentine," *Jazz Monthly* 7 (July 1961).

Nolan, Herb. "Dues on Top of Dues: Stanley Turrentine," *Down Beat* 5 (1975).

Obituary: *New York Times*, 14 Sept. 2000.

DISCOGRAPHY

Butler, Hunt. *The Stanley Turrentine Collection* (1997).

This entry is taken from the *American National Biography* and is published here with the permission of the American Council of Learned Societies.

BARRY KERNFELD

Twiggs, Leo (13 Feb. 1934–), educator and artist, was born Leo Franklin Twiggs in Saint Stephen, South Carolina, the eldest of six boys and one girl born to Frank Twiggs, a millworker from Greenwood, Mississippi, and Bertha Lee Meyers, from Saint Stephen. Though neither of Twiggs's parents had reached high school, they both encouraged him to pursue an education.

In 1950, when Twiggs was sixteen, his father died of cancer. Despite the tragic loss, his mother Bertha encouraged him to finish high school. To help sustain the family Twiggs took an after-school job doing janitorial work at the Star Theater in Saint Stephen, owned and managed by Wilder Funk. There Twiggs learned from the theater's white projectionist how to operate the projection equipment and control the lighting. When the projectionist quit, Twiggs acquired the job full time.

Twiggs graduated in 1952 as valedictorian of his high school class. As a graduation gift, Funk and his wife gave Twiggs a set of oil paints and a trunk. The paints were his first set, and with them he painted a replica of the theater's facade for Mrs. Funk. Twiggs's display of his artistic talent here, and throughout his community, captured the attention of the pastor of a local white Baptist church, who took Twiggs to see the Reverend Roy O. McClain of the First Baptist church in Orangeburg. McClain, in turn, phoned the president of Claflin College, a historically black college with a United Methodist affiliation, in nearby Orangeburg, South Carolina. The phone call led to a meeting between Twiggs and the Claflin president, and soon after Twiggs registered at Claflin.

Twiggs found his coursework as enjoyable as his work as a projectionist, especially his study of art with Arthur Rose. Rose, a native of Charleston, South Carolina, was a painter, sculptor, and head of the art department at Claflin. "Being under Arthur Rose at Claflin was the best thing that happened to me…. while he had his ideas about art he did not want me to paint as he did," Twiggs recalled (Fax, 335). With Rose, Twiggs took his first train ride, to Florida A&M University in Tallahassee, Florida, where he met such eminent black artists as Samella Lewis and Hale Woodruff. Twiggs graduated summa cum laude with a bachelor of arts degree in Art from Claflin College in 1956.

Upon graduation Twiggs completed a year of military service in Arizona and New Jersey. While stationed in New Jersey, he went to New York City and visited its museums and art galleries for the first time. Once discharged from the military Twiggs began teaching art at Lincoln High School in Sumter, South Carolina. His art students won awards in and out of the state. During the summers Twiggs pursued further study in art at both the Art Institute of Chicago and New York University. At

New York University, Twiggs studied under Hale Woodruff, who introduced him to abstract expressionism. Twiggs received his master of arts in Art Education from New York University in 1964 and returned to his teaching job in Sumter.

Twiggs met Rosa Johnson in Sumter and they married in 1961. The Twiggses were expecting the first of their three children when Twiggs accepted an offer to teach art at South Carolina State-College in Orangeburg. A few years later, the college's president, Benner C. Turner, informed Twiggs of federal money available for graduate study at the University of Georgia. Twiggs took the offer, and in 1970 completed his doctorate in art education and art criticism from the University of Georgia. He was the first African American to do so at Georgia and the only doctoral student in art at the university to be accepted into Phi Kappa Phi, the national honor society. His dissertation, "The Effects of Teaching a Method of Art Criticism on the Aesthetic Responses of Cultural Disadvantaged Junior High School Students," presented his discovery that his "students could make art, [but] few of them knew how to look at it and to understand what they were looking at" (Fax, 341). Twiggs returned to South Carolina State College and began expanding the art program, and in 1980 he established the I. P. Stanback Museum and Planetarium on the campus. The college was the only black school in the state that had both a museum and planetarium. Twiggs served as its director and chair of the art department from that year on.

Twiggs also managed to function as a practicing artist. His unique works, self-described as "batik paintings," were inspired by the ancient Egyptian technique in which designs are applied to a fabric with hot wax, and then the fabric is then dipped into a dye solution. Through this media, Twiggs explored various themes based on his experiences and childhood in the South. In a series of paintings titled *Commemorations*, Twiggs explores the relationships between the Confederate flag and the heritage of Americans and African Americans in the South. In his *We Have Known Rivers*, based on the poem *The Negro Speaks of Rivers* by Langston Hughes, Twiggs addressed the cultural dispersal of the black diaspora. His *East Wind Suite*, also called *Hugo Series*, focused on the destructive results of Hurricane Hugo in 1989, including the displacement of people in Charleston, South Carolina, and surrounding areas. In 2002 Twiggs was selected to create an ornament for the White House Christmas tree. Later works explored the southern blues.

In 1998 Twiggs retired from his teaching and administrative duties at South Carolina State University and was named professor emeritus in 2000. He was awarded an honorary doctorate of humanities degree from Claflin University, his alma mater, in 2003, and became the Distinguished Artist-in-Residence there. He has had more than sixty solo exhibitions and his works are in public and private collections nationally and internationally and were selected by the U.S. State Department to hang in American embassies in Italy, Togo, and Bangladesh.

FURTHER READING

Atkinson, Edward J., ed. *Black Dimensions in Contemporary American Art* (1971).

Cederholm, Theresa D. *Afro-American Artists: A Bio-bibliographical Dictionary* (1973).

Fax, Elton C. *Black Artists of the New Generation* (1977).

Lewis, Samella S., and Ruth G. Waddy. *Black Artists on Art*, vol. 2 (1971).

DAMOND L. HOWARD

Twilight, Alexander Lucius (26 Sept. 1795–19 June 1857), educator, minister, and legislator, was born in Corinth, Vermont, the son of Ichabod Twilight, a free African American farmer who served with the Second New Hampshire Regiment during the Revolutionary War, and Mary Twilight (whose maiden name is now unknown). Some historians believe that the name "Twilight" might have been chosen as an apt description of Ichabod Twilight's racial identity, which was somewhere between white and black—although legally he was black. Mary was probably also of mixed race, but she could have been a white woman who was described as "colored" in Corinth town records because she was married to a black man. Ichabod and Mary had started their family in Plattsburgh, New York, before moving first to Bradford, Vermont, in 1792 and then to Corinth in 1795, where they became the first black settlers in the township. Alexander was the third of their six children. Vermont had entered the union as the first free state in 1791, and fewer than 600 black people lived within its borders. Although the state prohibited slavery, racial attitudes in Vermont reflected the prejudices of the surrounding states, but the tiny size of the black population made discriminatory laws unnecessary.

The federal census of 1800 lists the members of the Twilight family in a racial category separate from white or slave called, "All other free persons, except Indians not taxed." Yet as an adult, Alexander

Twilight is found in the census of 1840 under "Free White Persons," along with his older brother Aaron. Similarly, Twilight's younger brother, Asaph, is described as "white" on his marriage certificate. Photographs and contemporaneous accounts that describe Twilight as "swarthy" or "bronzed" are sufficiently ambiguous in racial terms to suggest that he may have been able to pass for white, or he simply may not have called attention to his racial status when it was not already known.

In 1803 Ichabod Twilight deeded his farm to Aaron and left the family, presumably to find income elsewhere. The family was in such desperate financial straits that Mary was forced to contract Alexander, who was then eight, as an indentured servant until the age of twenty-one to Mr. William Bowen, whose property abutted the Twilight farm. Indentured servants were similar to slaves with three important exceptions: their terms of service were fixed; they had greater legal protection from the most severe forms of corporal punishment; and there was no racial stigma attached to the practice (indeed most indentured servants were white). Nonetheless Twilight managed to acquire a rudimentary education and was able to buy, or possibly he was given, his last year of service. In 1815 he enrolled at the Orange County Grammar School in Randolph, Vermont. He studied there for six years and completed the secondary curriculum and the equivalent of several college-level courses.

In 1821, at the age of twenty-three, Twilight enrolled at Middlebury College in Vermont as a third year student because of his advanced studies at Randolph. Four years after its founding in 1800, Middlebury had awarded an honorary master's degree to LEMUEL HAYNES, who may have been the first black clergyman in the United States ordained by a mainstream denomination. Twilight completed an academic curriculum that focused on Greek, Hebrew, and theology, and he became the first known African American to earn a college degree when he graduated in 1823. Two other black students graduated from New England colleges shortly thereafter: Ernest Jones from Amherst College in 1826 and JOHN BROWN RUSSWURM from Bowdoin College in 1826. It may have been serendipitous that Middlebury College awarded the first honorary and earned degrees to African Americans, for by the 1830s the college seems to have adopted a policy of racial exclusion—the graduation of the black nationalist Martin Freeman, the college's salutatorian in 1849, being a notable exception to this unwritten exclusionary rule.

After leaving Middlebury, Twilight found his first teaching position at a small school in Peru, New York. There he met a white woman, Mercy Ladd Merrill, who came from a family of some means and whose two surnames imply that she was a widow. They were married in 1826 and the following year, in addition to teaching, Twilight received his license to preach from the Champlain Presbytery in Plattsburgh, New York. For the rest of his life Twilight worked both as a teacher and as a preacher, often simultaneously. At his next teaching post in Vergennes, Vermont, he taught during the week, and on Sundays he walked to Waltham or Ferrisburgh to preach, alternating between congregations because neither could afford the services of a full-time minister.

In 1829 Twilight became the principal of the Orleans County Grammar School in Brownington, Vermont, in a region of the state known as the Northeast Kingdom, situated on a major stagecoach route between Boston and Quebec. At first he and Mercy lived in a small cottage near the school, but within a few years Twilight was inexplicably able to purchase a sixty-acre farm adjacent to the school, build a comfortable home, and speculate in frequent real-estate ventures. He was also ordained by the independent-minded Congregational Church soon after arriving in Brownington and became the local pastor there as well.

Under Twilight's watchful guidance the school's membership grew so rapidly that the number of students wishing to attend exceeded its capacity for local housing. The school board refused to build a dormitory despite Twilight's fervent urging; thus in 1834 he undertook that task as a personal mission. Portus and Carlos Baxter sold him a plot of land for one dollar on the condition that the site be used exclusively for the dormitory. Twilight temporarily resigned from the ministry in order to devote himself to the construction of a structure unprecedented in Vermont. Four stories tall, with sixty-five glass windows, dining facilities, classrooms, and meeting spaces, the dormitory was the first public building made of granite in the state. How Twilight financed this project remains a mystery. His precise building methods continue to engender architectural debate, and there are many humorous but apocryphal stories that concern the dormitory that Twilight named Athenian Hall in 1836, but that has come to be known as "The Stone Boarding House."

At times more than one hundred students, 30 percent of them women, attended the school, which produced many distinguished graduates, including James Strong, who later became president of Carleton College in Northfield, Minnesota. The students lived by a rigorous schedule. Each of the four terms lasted twelve weeks; students were expected to study ten hours a day, with only four weeks' vacation; and Sunday chapel service, led by Twilight, was mandatory. Although he seems to have been an altogether strict disciplinarian, Twilight was apparently a complicated individual. On one hand, some newspaper reports recalled his "four-foot-long strap ... to make potent in the cultivation of obedience and reverence in us boys" (Mosher, 84), but on the other hand, Twilight was known to inhale nitrous oxide (laughing gas) with his students for levity and relaxation.

Soon after the last stone was set in place on Athenian Hall, the state legislature began to consider a resolution to share revenue between Twilight's school and a new grammar school elsewhere in Orleans County. In an effort to avert this pending budget cut, Twilight took the bold step of running for the state legislature. He won, and when he took office in October 1836, representing the hamlet of Brownington, Twilight became the first African American to serve in a state legislature in the United States. Though he was appointed to the committee on education, he was frustrated by the triviality of many of the tasks that consumed his time. His voting record indicates that he was fiscally conservative, voting against a number of tax and salary increases. Surprisingly Twilight did not take advantage of his position as the nation's only black lawmaker to speak out against the horrors of slavery, and there is no indication that he worked with abolitionists in the state who helped escaping slaves flee to Canada. However his experience as an indentured servant may have influenced his support for a bill that would have abolished the practice of imprisoning people who could not pay their debts. That bill failed to pass, and Twilight could not prevent the legislature from dividing funds among his school and others, rather than increasing the education budget. Thus Twilight decided not to run for re-election in 1837.

For the next ten years Twilight fought with the trustees of the Browning Academy because they accused him of refusing to hire female teachers and charged him with the unlikely offense of relaxing the rules on compulsory church attendance. Twilight resigned or was fired in 1847 after eighteen years of service. Twilight and his wife moved to Canada, where he tried to start a school in Shipton (now Richmond, Quebec) called Twilight's Academy. After two years he moved to Hatley, Canada, near the Vermont border and taught at the Charleston Academy for three years. Meanwhile the Browning Academy suffered in Twilight's absence, and in 1852 the trustees invited him to return as headmaster. He accepting, saying, "This is the home of my choice, and here with the blessing of God I will devote myself to the interest of education" (Hahn, 48).

Twilight suffered a stroke in 1855, and when he died in 1857, he was buried at the Brownington Congregational Church within sight of Athenian Hall. Brownington Academy closed in 1859, and Mercy Twilight sold the hall in 1865. In 1918 the Orleans County Natural and Civil Historical Society, which Twilight had helped to found, purchased the property and has since operated it as an historic site. The possibility that Twilight's racial identity was not always evident does not diminish his accomplishments; rather, it illustrates the complexity and absurdity of the racial situation with which he had to contend.

FURTHER READING
A small but valuable collection of documents relating to Twilight's life can be found in the Alexander Twilight Collection at Middlebury College. Some of Twilight's papers, his restored home, and a great deal of memorabilia can be found at the Old Stone House Museum in Brownington, Vermont.

Hahn, Michael T. *Alexander Twilight: Vermont's African-American Pioneer* (1998).

Mosher, Howard Frank. "Alexander Twilight," *Vermont Life* (Autumn 1996).

Mosher, Howard Frank. *A Stranger in the Kingdom* (1989).

Nesbitt, Leroy, Jr. "The First African American to Be Awarded an Honorary Degree," *Journal of Blacks in Higher Education* (No. 8).

SHOLOMO B. LEVY

Tye, Colonel (c.1753–Sept. 1780), Loyalist guerrilla leader during the American Revolution, originally known as Titus, was the slave of John Corlis in Shrewsbury, Monmouth County, New Jersey. Titus was cruelly treated by his master and was often whipped for the most trivial offenses. Though John Corlis was a Quaker, as a slaveholder, he practiced few of the faith's pacifist beliefs. Even among Quakers that did hold slaves, Corlis proved abusive. Not only did he frequently whip Titus, he refused to teach him to read and write, he likely offered no religious instruction, and he refused to free him at age twenty-one, practices normally followed by slave-owning Quakers.

Given Titus's lowly status, it is therefore not surprising that he would have escaped from his master at the first opportunity. In November 1775, perhaps around the time of his twenty-first birthday, Titus ran away. Corlis placed an ad for his runaway slave on 8 November 1775, describing him as "near 6ft" in height and "not very black" (PBS, 1) and offered a £3 reward for his return. Titus would later return to Monmouth County, but in a far different manner than his former master could ever imagine.

After his escape, Titus made his way to Virginia to join Lord Dunmore's Ethiopian Regiment, an army unit composed largely of former slaves who received a promise of freedom upon joining. This regiment was raised by the royal governor of Virginia, John Murray, earl of Dunmore. Lord Dunmore had conceived the idea to raise a regiment of slaves in early 1775 with the realization that such a move would prove doubly useful; the slaves would not only be valuable as soldiers and laborers, but their flight from local plantations would raise havoc among the rebel planters. On 7 November 1775, Lord Dunmore made a formal proclamation declaring martial law in Virginia and stating that "I do hereby further declare all indented [*sic*] servants, Negroes, or others, (appertaining to Rebels,) free, that are willing and able to bear arms, they joining His Majesty's Troops" (Quarles, 19).

The proclamation, and its official publication a week later, caused great consternation in Virginia and coincided with Titus's bid for freedom in New Jersey. There can be little doubt that he soon heard of the proclamation while on the run and decided to join the British. Titus, now calling himself Tye, joined Lord Dunmore's Ethiopian Regiment and became a captain and "pride" of the regiment (PBS, 1). He was one of approximately three hundred slaves to join the regiment, in which each member was armed with his own musket and ammunition and outfitted in a splendid uniform with the words *Liberty to Slaves* emblazoned on his chest.

Though Captain Tye's activities with Lord Dunmore's Regiment are unknown, they were certainly short-lived. The unit had its first fight in mid-November 1775, on the Elizabeth River at Kemp's Landing, defeating a group of Patriot militiamen and capturing their commanding officers. However, on 9 December, Dunmore's regiment, which also included three hundred British regulars, suffered a defeat at Great Bridge at the hands of Woodford's Second Virginia Regiment. Thus defeated, Dunmore

retreated to Norfolk, spiked his cannon, and abandoned the city, never to return. As for the black men of his regiment, they were placed aboard Dunmore's ships for evacuation and transportation, where a smallpox epidemic reduced their numbers considerably. In August 1776, Dunmore's ships left Virginia waters for good; some headed southward, while others, like the one that surely carried Tye, sailed to British-held New York.

From 1776 to June 1778, the activities of Tye are unknown. However, he gained stature while fighting for the British during the Battle of Monmouth when he captured a local militia captain. The former slave subsequently became the leader of a small group of black Loyalists, the Black Brigade, who conducted raids in Monmouth County and his former hometown of Shrewsbury. Tye knew the area's geography well and conducted guerrilla raids against patriot homes, as well as those of slave masters and their friends, no doubt motivated in part by the cruel treatment he had once received. Bestowed with an honorary title of respect by the British, and well paid for his efforts, Colonel Tye soon became a skilled guerrilla leader who struck fear into the hearts of New Jersey Patriots.

In late 1779, his Black Brigade joined the renowned Queen's Rangers and conducted raids outside New York City to gather food and supplies. In June 1780, Colonel Tye led incursions into Monmouth County against local Patriots and solidified his reputation as a soldier; on 9 June he and his men captured and executed Joseph Murray, a local militia leader himself known for executing captured Loyalists. Three days later, he captured local militia leader Barnes Smock and twelve of his men and destroyed their cannons. Colonel Tye's Black Brigade continued their activities through the summer of 1780 in New Jersey, capturing local militiamen and raiding the area with impunity, suffering few casualties among their own members.

Colonel Tye's fortunes in war ran out in September 1780 when he attacked the home of Patriot Captain Josiah Huddy, who was hated for his executions of Loyalists. Huddy held off Colonel Tye's Black Brigade for several hours before escaping after his house was set ablaze. During the skirmish, Colonel Tye was shot in the wrist, and days later this seemingly minor wound turned into a fatal case of tetanus. Huddy would survive until his capture and eventual execution by the British in 1782.

The spectacular career of Colonel Tye serves as a reminder of the forgotten African Americans who served on both sides of the American Revolution—but especially those such as Tye, who served on the losing side of this war. More importantly, he serves as a reminder of the great "paradox," as historian Benjamin Quarles once remarked, that faced blacks, both free and slave, during the War for Independence. Those African Americans who fought for the British, Quarles reminded us, sought the same liberty that had moved Patrick Henry, John Hancock, and George Washington to seek American independence (Quarles, 32).

FURTHER READING

Kaplan, Sidney, and Emma Nogrady Kaplan. *The Black Presence in the Era of the American Revolution 1770–1800* (1989).

Public Broadcasting System (PBS). *Africans in America, Part 2, Colonel Tye, 1763–1780.* Available online at http://www.pbs.org/wgbh/aia/part2/2p52. html.

Quarles, Benjamin. *The Negro in the American Revolution* (1961).

GLENN ALLEN KNOBLOCK

Tyers, William H. (27 Mar. 1876–18 Apr. 1924), composer and bandleader, was born William H. Tyers, probably in Richmond, Virginia, although there are contradictory reports that he came from the West Indies or South America. The Tyers family had moved to New York by 1888, where William attended public school and studied music privately. He was in Hamburg in 1896, studying orchestration and working as librarian to a concert organization to support himself. Tyers returned to New York with a superior musical education for the time, and he was soon employed arranging music for the major white music publishers of the city, among the first African Americans to find such work. As of 1899 he worked primarily for the firm of Joseph W. Stern, an important publisher of piano rags and other African American music.

Tyers enjoyed a successful career as a dance orchestra leader during the craze for ragtime dances in New York. His association with JAMES REESE EUROPE's Clef Club dated from the organization's founding in 1910. When Europe left to found the rival Tempo Club in 1914, Tyers went with him. His "Tempo Club March" became the theme song of the joint Europe-Tyers organization, which also featured FORD T. DABNEY among its defectors from the Clef Club. Too old to join the American expeditionary forces in World War I, Tyers stayed behind, continuing his work as a leading bandleader. During the regular winter seasons of 1918–1923 he was in residence at the Strand Roof Garden. For those five summers he led the dance band at the Cave Grill, Mount Washington Hotel, in the Bretton Woods resort in New Hampshire.

While Tyers was well known in his own time as a bandleader, his work as a composer is of more lasting importance. He seems to have written virtually no songs, confining himself instead to instrumentals, many of them with exotic titles, a popular fad in his day. The best-known of these were "Maori: A Samoan Dance" (1908) and "Panama" (1911). There is no discernible trace of either New Zealand or Samoa in "Maori," but it is a charming piece of Latin-flavored dance music, as are many of Tyers's other works. These included "Trocha: A Cuban Dance," "Admiration," "Call of the Woods," "Soliloquy," "Mele Hula," "Flames and Fancies," "Dance of the Philippines," "La Mariposa," "La Fiancée," "Love's Contentment," "Barnyard Shuffle," "Aunt Mandy's Wedding," "Troopers Review," "Summer Moon," "Brazilian Butterfly," and "The Clarinet Polka." All of his known works appear to have been composed between 1896 and 1914. Most were issued by major New York publishers.

Tyers was an unusually sophisticated craftsman for a popular music composer of his generation, and the quality of his work is often outstanding. Few of his compositions are known today outside a small circle of specialists in ragtime-era music. However, those available on recording show an assured composer from the start. "Sambo: A Characteristic Two Step March" (1896) is among the earliest compositions in the ragtime style that would soon dominate American popular music. "Smyrna: A Turkish Serenade" (c. 1910) has nothing specifically Turkish about it but has a certain generic pop-music charm. It displays the same attention to structure as the better waltzes of Strauss, marches of Sousa, or piano rags of SCOTT JOPLIN. More clearly modeled on the European salon music of the day is his "Meno D'Amour," a light classical work from 1906 that Tyers labeled an "Intermezzo." Critics of the day sometimes compared such pieces favorably with the light fare coming out of the European capitals in the early years of the twentieth century, and with good reason.

The most famous pieces by Tyers, "Maori" and "Panama," are sufficiently fine to rank as standards, and both pieces held such status for years, even decades after their first appearance. Among the many later performers to feature Tyers's music were DUKE ELLINGTON, FLETCHER HENDERSON,

Luis Russell, and Tommy Dorsey. Tyers was featured in a striking photographic portrait accompanying a brief profile of him in the magazine *The Crisis* in 1912. Although he was little remembered by the beginning of the twenty-first century except by aficionados of ragtime-era music, he was one of the finest musical craftsmen of his era and a seminal figure in the development of African American music.

FURTHER READING

Fletcher, Tom. *100 Years of the Negro in Show Business* (1954).

Peress, Maurice. "Tyers, William H.," *International Dictionary of Black Composers* (1999).

ELLIOTT S. HURWITT

Tyler, Ralph Waldo (18 Mar. 1860?–2 June 1921), newspaperman and federal officeholder, was born in Columbus, Ohio, the son of James S. Tyler, a shopkeeper active in Republican Party politics, and Maria McAfee. Tyler attended public schools in Columbus and studied for one year in Baldwin, Missouri. As a teenager and young man, he worked as a coal shoveler, a teacher, a clerk for the Baltimore and Ohio Railroad, and a letter carrier. In 1888 he began a seventeen-year association with the *Columbus Dispatch*, a Republican daily newspaper, which provided a comfortable living for Tyler, his wife, and his three children.

After working his way up through the ranks of the *Dispatch* staff from janitor to stenographer and reporter to manager's assistant, Tyler attained the prestigious position of personal secretary to the publisher. One of only a few African American journalists employed by a white-owned daily newspaper, Tyler was able to afford a home in an affluent white neighborhood. Through his journalistic work, which included freelancing for black weekly newspapers, he also became involved in party politics, reporting on legislation that concerned black Ohioans. In 1896 he covered the Republican National Convention in St. Louis. During that convention Tyler became aligned with the influential Ohio Republican senator Mark Hanna through his friendship with George A. Myers, a black Cleveland politico who had been corresponding with Tyler since 1893.

During the 1890s Tyler pointedly declined to seek political office, believing that southern black leaders who did so compromised their ability to agitate for racial interests. After the turn of the century, he changed his mind and began seeking a federal appointment. His principal strategy was to befriend BOOKER T. WASHINGTON, President Theodore Roosevelt's sole adviser on black federal appointments. Tyler left the *Dispatch* in 1905 when it came under new ownership, and he briefly worked for the *Ohio State Journal* of Columbus before accepting a federal appointment as auditor of the U.S. Navy Department. For the next six years he drew a reported annual salary of four thousand dollars while overseeing 115 employees and all Navy Department purchases.

Some black leaders, including Myers, criticized Tyler for taking the job; they were angry about Roosevelt's decision in 1906 to dismiss three companies of black soldiers without fully investigating the charges that they had attacked white civilians in Brownsville, Texas. In his new position Tyler became a staunch defender of Washington and an apologist for the Brownsville decision. At Washington's suggestion Tyler wrote an editorial for the *New York Age*, labeling critics of Washington and Roosevelt "human ghouls, worthless parasites who represent nothing save selfish avarice" (Meier, 229). Tyler retained his post under President William H. Taft, for whom he campaigned in 1908 and later advised on federal appointments. Tyler lost his job after President Woodrow Wilson took office in 1913, but he again found employment through his alliance with Washington, this time as national organizer for the National Negro Business League. In that position he wrote syndicated columns on conditions in the South and on the migration of African Americans to the North. In 1916 Tyler also made an unsuccessful foray into electoral politics, garnering thirty thousand votes for Ohio delegate at large to the Republican National Convention.

Tyler made his biggest mark as a journalist during World War I. After serving most of the war as secretary of the National Colored Soldiers' Comfort Committee in Washington, D.C., he was selected as a government-sponsored war correspondent for all the black press. A group of black editors had demanded in June 1918 that their own reporter be sent to the war zone. Tyler's appointment was announced on 16 September, but his dispatches, which had to be cleared through both the Committee on Public Information and the military, did not begin appearing in black newspapers until just before the 11 November armistice.

For the most part Tyler's reports focused on the heroism of black soldiers in battle. "I was thrilled, and inspired by the enthusiasm of our men, and their eagerness to get into battle," he wrote, praising their "grim determination to maintain the race's traditional fighting reputation" (Scott, 291–292). Assigned to General John J. Pershing's staff, Tyler faced close scrutiny. Military censors warned him not to write any more reports like his exposé of discrimination against black soldiers in the YMCA. Accordingly, many of Tyler's dispatches, including his erroneous disavowal of rumors of wholesale demotions of black officers, seemed to serve the government's purpose of maintaining the morale of African Americans.

Yet Tyler did manage to slip past the censors a report that appeared in the 4 January 1919 *Cleveland Gazette* and other black newspapers. In this report Tyler revealed that white American officers had told the French command to treat black soldiers as an "inferior race." The revelation contributed to a widespread feeling of disillusionment among African Americans after the war.

On his return to the United States in 1919, Tyler spoke to audiences in northern cities about the black war record and filed a successful race-discrimination lawsuit against an Ohio restaurateur who denied him service. He worked as editor of two more newspapers—the *Cleveland Advocate*, a black weekly, and the *Columbus Ohio State Monitor*—before his death from apoplexy at his home in Columbus, Ohio.

Historians have judged Tyler a "shrewd politician whose main loyalty was to his own political career" (Harlan and Smock, vol. 6, 338, no. 1) and a "ruthless practitioner of *realpolitik*" (Gerber, 349). Although self-interest may have been Tyler's first motive, he never fully abandoned his early devotion to race advancement and solidarity. His dispatches from France reflect a pride in his fellow African Americans and concern for their plight, and he attempted to report truthfully in spite of government pressures that he soft-pedal the problems that he saw. The *Baltimore Afro-American* eulogized on 10 June 1921 that Tyler's report on the army memorandum to the French command "made Mr. Tyler known and respected from one end of the country to the other" among African Americans.

FURTHER READING

Some of Tyler's letters are in the George A. Myers Papers at the Ohio Historical Society, Columbus, Ohio.

Gerber, David A. *Black Ohio and the Color Line, 1860–1915* (1976).

Harlan, Louis R., and Raymond W. Smock, eds. *The Booker T. Washington Papers* (1977).

Meier, August. *Negro Thought in America, 1880–1915: Racial Ideologies in the Age of Booker T. Washington* (1963).

Scott, Emmett J. *Scott's Official History of the American Negro in the World War* (1919).

Obituary: *Baltimore Afro-American*, 10 June 1921.

This entry is taken from the *American National Biography* and is published here with the permission of the American Council of Learned Societies.

WILLIAM JORDAN

Tyler, Willie (8 Sept. 1940–), ventriloquist partnered by Lester, was born Willie Tyler in River Falls, Alabama, one of ten children (three sisters and six brothers) of James Otis Tyler and Georgia Tyler. His father worked at a Ford Motor Company plant just outside of Detroit. His mother stayed home to raise the children. Seeking better economic opportunities, the family moved to Detroit, Michigan, while Tyler was young. He grew up on Adelaide Street around the city's Hastings Street neighborhood.

Tyler became interested in ventriloquism at the age of ten when he saw an advertisement for the Maher Home Study Ventriloquism Course on the back of a magazine. With the help of a teacher, he signed up for ventriloquism lessons. Between delivering newspapers, Tyler began performing at clubs, variety shows, and talent contests in Detroit, Michigan. At the age of thirteen, a teacher helped Tyler purchase his first ventriloquist dummy out of a catalog. Once the dummy arrived, Tyler painted it brown to make it appear African American and called it Lester, after a kid he knew at school. The duo became known as Willie Tyler & Lester.

While in high school, Tyler performed in a variety of amateur shows in Detroit. After high school, at the age of seventeen, Tyler enlisted in the Air Force, where he spent the next four years. He was assigned to a Special Services Unit, as an entertainment specialist, which allowed him to perform at military bases throughout the states and in other countries and to enhance his skills as a ventriloquist. While in the Air Force, Tyler purchased a second, larger Lester for military variety shows. Because Tyler was doing stage shows, this Lester was big enough for audiences to see better.

Tyler finished his tour of duty with the Air Force when he was twenty-two years old. Making a living as a ventriloquist was tough for Tyler after his return home from the Air Force. He began working clubs and resorts around Detroit and performing during the summer at the Idlewild Resort in Northern

Michigan. During one of his performances at Idlewild a relative of BERRY GORDY saw Tyler's act and informed the executives at Motown of what he had seen. In 1964 Motown signed Tyler as a recording artist and he began to gain fame as the opening act for many Motown Stars. During the summer of 1964 Tyler also met his future wife, Elaine Horne, a dancer with the Arthur Braggs Revue. The couple married and had two sons.

Tyler began traveling as an emcee for the Motortown Revue (concert tours sponsored by Motown) and toured with then-unknown groups such as the Supremes, the Temptations, Little STEVIE WONDER, GLADYS KNIGHT and the Pips, the Spinners, the Four Tops, and others. The Motown revue traveled to New York, where Tyler landed on *The Merv Griffin Show* on 17 July 1968. In the early 1970s Tyler was making appearances in Las Vegas, where he worked with artists such as SAMMY DAVIS, JR., LOU RAWLS, LENA HORNE, Dolly Parton, Tom Jones, and Crystal Gayle. During this time he also appeared on *The Mike Douglas Show*, 1 June 1972, and *The Flip Wilson Show*, 21 October 1971.

In 1978 Tyler transitioned into dramatic film when he appeared as Virgil, a paraplegic in the Academy Award-winning movie *Coming Home*, with Jane Fonda and Jon Voight. Tyler played a ventriloquist, but had to use a Vietnamese-looking dummy for the movie, rather than Lester, his normal sidekick. Tyler continued to perform throughout the 1980s, appearing mostly as himself on television shows such as *The White Shadow*, *Powerhouse*, *What's Happening Now*, *Lou Rawls Parade of Stars*, and *Motown Returns to the Apollo*. In 1987 he and Lester appeared as a presenter on the *First Annual Soul Train Music Awards*.

Tyler continued to be in demand in the 1990s and kept busy performing and appearing on television shows such as *The Parent Hood*, *Pacific Blue*, and *In The House*. He also continued to travel and perform in clubs and other venues with Lester and was the recipient of a lifetime achievement award at the Las Vegas Ventriloquist Festival in June 2000. For Willie Tyler, performing as a ventriloquist has been his only job. He truly can say that show business is his life.

FURTHER READING

"An Odd Couple: Success Comes to Willie Tyler and Lester." *Ebony*, Oct. 1981.

Christian, Margena A. "Where Are Willie Tyler & Lester?" *Jet*, 21 April 2008.

Gelt, Gary. "Willie Tyler & Lester: Ventriloquist Finds Home, Sweet Home." *Los Angeles Times*, 7 Dec. 1980.

Kaz, Ed. "The Rare Motown Vinyl of Willie Tyler." *Discoveries*, June 2006.

West, Julius. "Lester's No Dummy: Says the Willie Tyler Family." *Black Family*, Sept.–Oct. 1982.

CHARLIE TOMLINSON

Tyner, McCoy (11 Dec. 1938–), jazz pianist, composer, and bandleader, was born Alfred McCoy Tyner in Philadelphia, Pennsylvania, the oldest son of Jarvis Tyner and Beatrice Stephenson, a beauty salon owner. When he was thirteen and attending Sulzberger Junior High School, Tyner's mother offered him the choice of formal music lessons: either voice or piano. Tyner received piano lessons at the Philadelphia Music Center for three and a half years. Even though he discontinued his formal piano lessons to enroll at West Philadelphia School of Music to study choir, he continued practicing on several neighbors' pianos after school. When Tyner was fourteen, his mother bought him his first piano, a Spinet, with hairdressing earnings that she had saved for over a year. The piano was set up in her beauty shop so Tyner could rehearse while his mother fixed her customers' hair.

By the time he was fifteen, Tyner had put together a seven-piece rhythm and blues band made up of classmates and neighborhood friends. It was around this time that Tyner met an influential group of young Philadelphia musicians who eventually became legendary jazz innovators, pianists BUD POWELL, his brother Richie Powell (also a pianist who was playing in MAX ROACH and CLIFFORD BROWN's band at the time), trumpeter LEE MORGAN, saxophonist ARCHIE SHEPP, and bassist Regie Workman. Powell became a major influence on Tyner, along with one of the legendary founders of the bebop jazz movement, pianist THELONIOUS MONK.

Tyner credited Powell and Monk for influencing his use of space and dexterity on the piano, particularly Monk's unique, harmonic concept, but Tyner continued to develop his own harmonic concept. It was around this time, while he was playing gigs around Philadelphia, that he first met a young saxophonist by the name of JOHN COLTRANE. Tyner began playing at various local jazz clubs and dance halls with trumpeter Calvin Massey's band, and while playing a gig at a local Philadelphia club called the Red Rooster, Tyner re-met Coltrane, who later became a central figure in Tyner's life.

At the time, Coltrane was gaining notoriety himself as a member of MILES DAVIS's band. The two developed a rapport, and Coltrane told Tyner that he was on the verge of forming his own band and wanted to include Tyner.

Coltrane was apparently so impressed with Tyner that he recorded a composition written by Tyner, which became the title track for his 1958 Prestige album, *The Believer*. By the time Tyner began attending the Granoff School of Music, he was taking piano gigs in other cities during his high school summer breaks. Tyner even played piano for a dance school and was exposed to various forms of music, including European classical and African music. With a steady stream of regular gigs where he could practice his skills, Tyner developed an explosively percussive left hand that set him apart from other pianists.

In 1959, Tyner was offered his first big break when he was approached by saxophonist Benny Golson to perform at the Jazz Workshop, a small but legendary club in San Francisco. Upon returning, Golson made it known that he wanted to form a band with Tyner in it, and Golson and trumpeter Art Farmer helped Tyner move to New York. Golson and Farmer formed the band, Art Farmer/Benny Golson Jazztet, and recorded their debut album, *Meet the Jazztet*, in 1960. But later that same year, Coltrane approached Tyner again, this time announcing that he had left the Miles Davis Quintet and wanted Tyner to be a member of his newly formed quartet.

The John Coltrane Quartet, which consisted of Coltrane on soprano and tenor sax, Tyner on piano, Jimmy Garrison on bass (originally Steve Davis on bass for the *My Favorite Things* recording on the Atlantic label), and Elvin Jones on drums, became known as one of the most influential bands in jazz history because of their dynamic musical chemistry. The Coltrane Quartet was touted as reinventing the sound of various folk classics such as "My Favorite Things," "Greensleeves," and "Inch Worm," infused with Coltrane's explosive range of chords on the horn backed by a world-class rhythm section. Tyner's sound was challenging to the usual harmonic structures and allowed him to be creative with a distinct rhythmic charge. His style was notable for being able to move "inside" the harmony with the right hand and "outside" the harmony with the left.

Tyner toured with the Coltrane Quartet almost nonstop around the world between 1961 and 1965 and recorded a number of classic albums including *My*

Favorite Things (Atlantic, 1960), *Live at the Village Vanguard* (Impulse, 1961), *Ballads* (Impulse, 1962), *Crescent* (Impulse, 1964), *A Love Supreme* (Impulse, 1964), and *The John Coltrane Quartet Plays* (Impulse, 1965). It was during this time that Tyner (who had converted to the Sunni Muslim religion and had even changed his name to Sulaiman Saud when he was eighteen) sought a deeper spiritual odyssey through his music. Both he and Coltrane became heavily influenced by African and East Asian musical elements and incorporated quartal and quintal harmonies and pentatonic scales into their music. Tyner was a founder of the new sound in jazz that went beyond the standard harmonic structures and delved into a modal structure.

In 1965, Tyner left the Coltrane Quartet to explore a solo career. From 1967 to 1970, he released a series of major post-bop albums on the Blue Note label, beginning with *The Real McCoy* (1967), *Tender Moments* (1967), *Time for Tyner* (1968), *Expansions* (1968), *Cosmos* (1969), and *Extensions* (1970). During this time, many jazz artists began experimenting with electronic instruments to create fusion jazz, and although Tyner stayed with the acoustic sound of the piano, he gained further critical acclaim by not straying toward fusion or the free jazz sound inspired by ORNETTE COLEMAN. His 1972 album, *Sahara* (Milestone/OJC), was innovative and textured with the rich sounds and rhythms of Africa. It received two Grammy nominations and was named Record of the Year in the Downbeat Critics Poll. He was named Pianist of the Year in the Downbeat Critics Poll four years in a row, from 1974 to 1977. In 1988, he received his first Grammy Award for a jazz compilation album titled *Blues for Coltrane—A Tribute to John Coltrane*, under the category Best Jazz Instrumental Performance, Group, which featured Tyner with several other heavyweight jazz artists including David Murray, PHARAOH SANDERS, Cecil McBee, and ROY HAYNES.

In the early 1990s, Tyner began expanding his range of musicianship by revisiting his early teen years as a bandleader, and he arranged his modal harmonies to accommodate a big band. In 1992, the McCoy Tyner Big Band won a Grammy Award for Best Large Jazz Ensemble Performance for *The Turning Point* (1991, Verve) and again in 1994 for *Journey* (1993, Verve). In 1995, Tyner received another Grammy Award for his quartet album, *Infinity* (1995, Impulse!).

In the 2000s, Tyner continued to tour regularly throughout the United States, Europe, and Japan, in addition to composing and arranging music for his fourteen-piece big band. In 2002, he received the Jazz Masters Award from the National Endowment for the Arts, a major achievement for a remarkable musical career. In 2005, he received an honorary doctorate of music from the Berklee College of Music.

FURTHER READING

Cabell, Arphelia K. Telephone interview with McCoy Tyner, 12 Feb. 2006.

Gioia, Ted. *The History of Jazz* (1997).

Lyons, Len. *The Great Jazz Pianists: Speaking of Their Lives and Music* (1983).

National Public Radio (Sonja Williams, Producer). *Jazz Profiles from NPR. McCoy Tyner: The Pianist* (2006).

ARPHELIA K. CABELL

Tynes, George W. (1908?–1982), Wilberforce graduate, All-American football player, animal husbandry specialist, and African American expatriate in the USSR, was born in Roanoke, Virginia. His parents' names are unknown, although one source noted that his father was a pastor. Tynes's family history was a mix of African American and Native American. One source cites his Native American heritage as Seneca, and another suggests he was a Dakota. Whatever his Native American heritage, as a man of African ancestry, Tynes was no less hampered by Jim Crow restrictions. He nonetheless earned a degree in Agricultural Education at Wilberforce in 1929 and had achieved some notoriety for his prowess on the football field. Under the name "Whirlwind" Tynes, he was also listed on the Pittsburgh *Courier* All-American football team in that same year. Despite these achievements, he was unable to find work in his chosen field, and in the early 1930s, was cited as having taught in a school in Baltimore and then, later, working as a longshoreman in New York. He was still struggling to make ends meet when he joined a team of eleven agricultural specialists recruited with the aid of Tuskegee agricultural scientist GEORGE WASHINGTON CARVER to help modernize the Soviet agricultural system in 1931.

Confronted by the Great Depression, even college-educated African Americans like Tynes found themselves unable to put their skills to work. Thus, when Tynes and his group left the United States that fall, most were driven not by a clear political objective but rather a desire for self-fulfillment and the opportunity to contribute to building a new kind of society. The fact that they were being welcomed—despite the color of their skin—was equally alluring. While few expected that they would remain a long time in the Soviet Union, many did renew their contracts several times before finally returning to the United States. Two of the group, who had begun families in the USSR, when confronted by the prospect of returning to American Jim Crow, chose instead to tie their futures to the Soviet experiment. OLIVER GOLDEN was one, and George Tynes was the other. When Tynes learned of the agricultural specialist program, he was immediately enthusiastic at the prospect and signed up on the spot. Little did he know when he and the group left in the fall of 1931, that he was making a choice that would affect the rest of his life. Tynes would never permanently return to the United States.

The African American group of agricultural specialists, made up of research chemists, irrigation specialists, agronomists, engineers, and animal husbandry specialists, was initially posted to Uzbekistan in Soviet Central Asia, where their charge was to revamp the Soviet cotton industry. One of the legacies of their work there was to produce a new strain of cotton by crossing seeds from the American South with indigenous Uzbek ones. The resulting hybrid brought in a variety that matured much more rapidly.

After the first three years on the Uzbek cotton collective farm, the Soviet Ministry of Agriculture dispersed the agricultural specialists to projects in other regions in the country. These specialists were there not only to work, but also to train farmers in these various locales. The specialists were sent to these different sites for two-year periods. This provided them time to help design and establish agricultural systems and procedures for which they were responsible, train local farmers and technicians to use the new techniques, and see some results of their efforts. Tynes, who had married a Ukrainian woman, Maria, in the interim, was appointed a "Zoo Technician" (Zoo was likely short for Zoological). He and his growing family were then posted to collective farms around the USSR: in the Cossack region, the Crimea, Soviet Georgia, the Ukraine, and Estonia. He and his wife had four children, three of whom survived into adulthood: Vyacheslav, Emilia (also written as Amelia), and Ruben. As of 2004, Vyacheslav was a journalist, Emilia was a science teacher and head of a support foundation for mixed-race children in Russia, and Ruben was a construction engineer. Tynes returned to the United States for a brief visit in

1936. Disappointed with the lack of change in race relations and economic opportunities, he decided that he would have better luck with the Soviet experiment. He returned to his wife and first child in 1936 and, within three years, officially took up Soviet citizenship.

Tynes's skills were in such high demand that when he was drafted for service in World War II, he was personally charged with the responsibility to supply the troops with duck meat. Thus, he and his family continued to live on farms throughout the War, ironically providing them with access to food from their farms, when many others had to contend with rationing during that difficult time.

After World War II, Tynes was appointed to a new Experimental Fish and Duck Farm on the outskirts of Moscow, where he remained until the early 1970s. Being posted to a factory or project in or near Moscow was considered the highest of praise in the Soviet system. Furthermore, the fact that this special project was designed with Tynes in mind demonstrated the Soviet appreciation of his long-standing contributions to the country. Throughout the 1950s and until his retirement, Tynes's home and farm proved to be a stable attraction for the African American expatriate community in Moscow, many of whom would regularly find their way out to the farm. A 1959 African American visitor to Moscow, William B. Davis, was taken out there on a visit. An impressed Davis noted of Tynes, "The Tynes family lies in a rural section on the outskirts of Moscow. They are more fortunate than most Russians.... George is the technical director of a game reserve. He is considered the leading authority on fish and ducks in the Soviet Union today and is able to provide his family with all the duck and fish they can eat" (p. 66).

Tynes brought significant innovations to the raising of ducks and other poultry and was recognized by the Soviet government for his contributions to the health and diet of a whole nation. Tynes was officially celebrated for his achievements when he received three medals from the All-Union Agricultural Exhibition for his work in duck culture. And, in the mid-1950s, Robert Robinson, another African American expatriate, noted that Tynes's work made it possible for the Soviet poultry exhibit to win first prize in an international fair in Belgium (Robinson, p. 324).

In the 1960s, in the spirit of Khrushchev's "peaceful co-existence," new opportunities came that allowed Tynes to pay another visit to the United States. Over the next twenty years, family members in the United States sponsored a few more trips to the country of his birth. His last visit was in 1980. When Tynes died in 1982, he was the oldest surviving member of the African American expatriate community that had migrated to the Soviet Union in the 1930s.

FURTHER READING

Blakely, Allison. *Russia and the Negro: Blacks in Russian History and Thought* (1986).
Davis, William B. "How Negroes Live in Russia," *Ebony*, Jan. 1960.
Robinson, Robert. *Black on Red: My 44 Years in the Soviet Union* (1988).

JOY GLEASON CAREW

Tyson, Cicely (19 Dec. 1933–), actress and model, was born in Harlem, New York, to William and Theodosia Tyson, immigrants from the Caribbean island of Nevis. Little is known of her parents' occupations, but her mother immersed the family in the Episcopalian and Baptist churches, where Cicely was involved in Bible study, singing, and playing the organ. The church became the center of her social life and the place where she developed her talents for theater and which served as her introduction to entertainment and performance, since Cicely obeyed her mother's strict codes on proper Christian behavior, avoiding secular activities such as going to the movies.

Tyson entered the workforce as a secretary for the Red Cross after graduating from Charles Evans Hughes High School. When encouraged by her hairdresser, Walter Johnson, to showcase his hairstyles, she embarked on a modeling career. Tyson attended the Barbara Walters School for modeling and was able to support herself through her fashion work. She also took acting classes at New York University and joined workshops that taught her techniques for stage, film, and television.

As the civil rights movement put a new spotlight on the issues of African Americans, Tyson was recruited by *Ebony* magazine to model on its pages. Fashion editor Freda DeKnight helped catapult Tyson's career to new heights, Tyson becoming a recognizable face in the fashion world. During this period, however, she questioned whether she could afford the luxury of just being a model without being politically engaged. Tyson's acting career began in theater in 1957 when she appeared in *Dark of the Moon*. Her off-Broadway performances introduced her to figures like JAMES EARL JONES, ISABEL SANFORD, and ALVIN AILEY, and she was twice awarded the Vernon Rice Award, for her role as Mavis in *Moon on a Rainbow Shawl* and for her part as Virtue in Jean Genet's play *The Blacks*. The New York production of Genet's play ran for two years, and Tyson captured the attention of the actor George C. Scott, who cast her in the televised series *East Side/West Side* (1963–1964). She was one of the first African American women to have a regular part in broadcast television. It was not her first time before television cameras, however, having made her debut in the PAULE MARSHALL drama *Brown Girl, Brownstones* in 1960.

During the next seven years Tyson appeared in BILL COSBY's television series *I Spy* and in daytime dramas. The paucity of acceptable dramatic roles for African Americans concerned her enough to begin refusing some offers, which led to a gap in her film career. Tyson also remained involved in theater, appearing in off-Broadway hits, such as

Cicely Tyson with her Emmy statuettes at the annual Emmy Awards presentation in Los Angeles, 28 May 1974. Tyson won best actress of the year and best lead actress in a television drama for her role in *The Autobiography of Miss Jane Pittman*. (AP Images.)

Trumpets of the Lord (1963) and *To Be Young, Gifted, and Black* (1969). At the end of the sixties she made her entrance into feature film as Portia in *The Heart Is a Lonely Hunter*. Her next role was playing opposite PAUL WINFIELD in *Sounder* (1972), a depiction of southern black life set in rural Louisiana during the 1930s. Her critically acclaimed portrayal of Rebecca Morgan, the strong and loving wife of a sharecropper, led to a National Society of Film Critics Award, and an Oscar nomination for best actress. Tyson recalled that this film was so successful because there were so few movies for black families to see. Furthermore it stood as a model for the public to re-imagine African Americans as human beings rather than as caricatures. When a white journalist reportedly admitted feeling discomfort over the idea that black families behaved a lot like his own, Tyson saw her work having an impact on prejudice.

Two years later Tyson captivated television viewers with her performance in the movie *The Autobiography of Miss Jane Pittman*. As the title character grew to 110 years of age, the film provided audiences with a compact, yet thought-provoking, presentation of American history from slavery to the civil rights movement. Tyson's onscreen transformation in age and demeanor signaled one of her greatest achievements and earned her two Emmy awards, becoming the first African American woman to win for outstanding lead performance.

Many impressive roles in television followed, including her performance as the mother of Kunta Kinte in *Roots* (1977), which earned her another Emmy nomination, and the part of CORETTA SCOTT KING in *King* (1978). With more than fifty-five films to her credit, Tyson presented the diverse stories of black America to American audiences. Her versatility continued to expand throughout the 1970s, from hosting "Sears Mystery Theater," a CBS radio program, to co-founding the Dance Theatre of Harlem with ARTHUR MITCHELL.

In 1981 Tyson married jazz musician MILES DAVIS. ANDREW YOUNG, then mayor of Atlanta, officiated at the nuptials, while Bill Cosby, who hosted the ceremony at his home, was best man. The couple divorced eight years later.

Tyson continued to make a mark in the entertainment industry, collaborating with celebrities like OPRAH WINFREY—with whom she co-starred in *The Women of Brewster Place* (1989)—on films that salute black women's lives. She also served as a mentor to young black actors, such as Kimberly

Elise, with whom she starred in *Diary of a Mad Black Woman* (2005).

Among the numerous organizations that paid tribute to Cicely Tyson are the Congress on Racial Equality (CORE), the National Council of Negro Women, and the Black Filmmakers Hall of Fame. Tyson had both a school of performing arts and a day named in her honor in Chicago. She held honorary doctorate degrees from Loyola Marymount, Atlanta, Lincoln, and Pepperdine Universities, and has been named Woman of the Year four times by the National Association for the Advancement of Colored People (NAACP). In 2010 Tyson was honored by the NAACP as its 95th Spingarn Medalist.

FURTHER READING

Bogle, Donald. *Blacks in American Films and Television: An Encyclopedia* (1988).

Hine, Darlene Clark, ed. *Facts on File: Black Women in America; Theatre Arts and Entertainment* (1997).

Smith, Jessie Carney, ed. *Notable Black American Women* (1992).

R. ISET ANUAKAN

Tyson, Michael Gerard (30 June 1966–), boxer, was born in Brooklyn, New York's Bedford-Stuyvesant section, the third child to Lorna Smith Tyson. Tyson's father, James Kirkpatrick, left the family in 1968, and Lorna Tyson soon moved to Brownsville, New York. Arrested for various crimes by the age of ten, in 1979 Tyson entered the Tryon School for Boys in Johnstown, New York. Bobby Stewart, a Tryon staff member, recognized Tyson's athletic potential and introduced him to the notable boxing trainer Constantine "Cus" D'Amato. Tyson quickly impressed the trainer, and on 30 June 1980 he was released from Tryon and placed in D'Amato's custody. While living with D'Amato in Catskill, New York, Tyson trained rigorously and studied the fight-film library maintained by cofounder of Big Fights, Inc., Jim Jacobs. Never dedicated to his education, Tyson was expelled from Catskill High School in 1982 after several allegations of harassing female students and a physical altercation with a male teacher.

Tyson did not complete high school. However, after a short twenty-five-bout amateur boxing career, he quickly graduated to the ranks of professional boxing in 1985—despite being left off the 1984 U.S. Olympic boxing team. When D'Amato died in November 1985, Tyson had already participated in thirteen professional bouts, winning each one by knockout. Despite the loss of his mentor,

Tyson continued his rise to boxing prominence with Jacobs as manager and Kevin Rooney as his trainer.

On 22 November 1986 Tyson's knockout victory over World Boxing Commission champion Trevor Berbick (the WBC being one of the three most commonly recognized sanctioning organizations in boxing) made Tyson the youngest heavyweight champion in the history of boxing. Moreover the carefully contrived image of Tyson as a poor black youth rescued and fashioned into a boxing champion by a benevolent white trainer made him one of the most popular athletes in the United States. But after becoming champion, his popular image began to erode. Tyson faced assault charges in 1987 and 1988, and the negative publicity garnered by those incidents increased during Tyson's year-long (1988–1989) marriage to television actress Robin Givens. Their marriage culminated in a *20/20* interview with Barbara Walters, in which a sedated Tyson stood beside a tearful Givens as she accused him of spousal abuse. Tyson would never regain the positive image associated with his early career.

Beginning in 1988 Tyson forged a close relationship with notorious boxing promoter DON KING and would subsequently fire Rooney and comanager Bill Cayton; Jim Jacobs succumbed to a secret battle with leukemia in January 1989. Tyson replaced his former training staff of Rooney, Cayton, and Jacobs with friend Rory Holloway and failed entertainer John Horne. This new entourage drastically reshaped Tyson's image. No longer was he an unfortunate child saved by white philanthropy and shaped by white suburban New York. Tyson's personality became racially antagonistic, and he would often credit his boxing success to his poor and violent upbringing. He became known as "Iron Mike" and "The Baddest Man on the Planet," and the champion began to put a soundtrack to his dramatic ring entrances: a rap song by Public Enemy that fittingly repeated the phrase "Don't believe the hype."

At the same time, Tyson's training regimen declined and his skills deteriorated. In Tokyo on 11 February 1990, he was upset by James "Buster" Douglas and lost his title to the forty-two-to-one underdog. A hasty attempt to regain his championship was cut short by a July 1991 date-rape accusation in Indianapolis. During the subsequent trial, Tyson's negative image was used as a defense strategy by his council, who sought to prove that when the accuser accepted an invitation for a late-night rendezvous with Tyson, she was implicitly consenting to sex. The strategy failed, and in March 1992 Tyson was sentenced to six years in prison. Tyson's conviction came only months after William Kennedy Smith was acquitted of a similar charge. This court decision created a perception of racial bias in the American judicial system that was exacerbated one month later, when the Los Angeles Police Department officers accused of beating RODNEY KING were acquitted and the streets of Los Angeles erupted in riots.

After serving three years, Tyson reemerged in 1995 with yet another new image—this time as a well-read Muslim convert. But "Team Tyson"— Holloway, Horne, and other affiliates of Don King Productions—also projected the same racially antagonistic attitude. Tyson's first opponent after his release was Peter McNeeley, an unproven Bostonian with a fabricated record whose only marketable asset was that his whiteness contrasted with Tyson's urban ghetto image. That bout lasted just eighty-nine seconds before McNeely's corner threw in the towel, forfeiting the match.

Tyson's comeback continued through 1996, when he regained the WBC championship from Frank Bruno in March. On 7 September Tyson successfully defended his title against Bruce Seldon in a terrible mismatch that became overshadowed by the infamous incident that took place after the bout: the fatal drive-by shooting of rap legend TUPAC SHAKUR on the Las Vegas strip. Tyson soon adopted Shakur's song "Ambitionz Az a Ridah" for his ring-entrance anthem as a demonstration of his ties to the hip-hop style known as "Gangsta Rap."

In November 1996 Tyson's undefeated comeback was upset by twenty-five-to-one underdog EVANDER HOLYFIELD. A rematch was set for the following June. In the interim, Tyson married medical student Monica Turner in 1997. During

Michael Tyson (left) fights Francois Botha of South Africa in the heavyweight bout at the MGM Grand Hotel & Casino in Las Vegas, Nevada, 16 January 1999. (AP Images.)

his second bout with Holyfield, Tyson's thug image became reality: a frustrated and bloodied Tyson bit both ears of his opponent, tearing away flesh and spitting cartilage onto the canvas. Tyson was disqualified from the bout, fined $3 million, and had his boxing license revoked.

When Tyson regained his license in 1999, he fought only once before assault charges stemming from a road-rage incident resulted in a one-year prison sentence. After his release, Tyson demonstrated similar tendencies in January 2002 when he started a brawl at a press conference promoting his upcoming WBC and International Boxing Federation title fight against Lennox Lewis. In June Lewis knocked Tyson out in the eighth round. That same year, Tyson and his wife Monica were divorced.

Though he received over $17 million for the Lewis match, adding to his career earnings of over $300 million, Tyson filed for bankruptcy in 2003. Increasing debt forced Tyson into sporadic matches against largely unknown challengers, but they did not generate enough profit to satisfy his creditors. In 2006 Tyson signed a contract with PRIDE Fighting Championships, a Japan-based mixed-martial arts organization desperate for a popular American competitor to make their product marketable in the United States. However, Tyson was arrested for drug possession and driving under the influence, and subsequently checked into a rehabilitation center before he could appear in a mixed-martial arts match.

FURTHER READING

Berger, Phil. *Blood Season: Mike Tyson and the World of Boxing* (1989).

Hoffer, Richard. *A Savage Business: The Comeback and Comedown of Mike Tyson* (1998).

O'Connor, Daniel, ed. *Iron Mike: A Mike Tyson Reader* (2002).

Roberts, Randy, and J. Gregory Garrison. *Heavy Justice: The State of Indiana v. Michael G. Tyson* (1994).

ANDREW SMITH

Tyson, Neil deGrasse (5 Oct. 1958–), noted astrophysicist, astronomer, and writer, was born in New York City, second of three children born to Cyril deGrasse Tyson, a former commissioner for human resources for the mayor of New York City, and Sunchita Tyson, a gerontologist. Tyson grew up in New York City, attending the Bronx High School of Science. His interest in science, particularly astronomy, began early; when he was nine years old, he saw his first magnified view of the moon through a pair of binoculars. Receiving a telescope for his twelfth birthday only furthered his already intense fascination with the universe. Tyson also took regular trips to the Hayden Planetarium and benefited from the classes offered there. When he was fourteen years old, he participated in an astronomy camp held in the Mojave Desert. These experiences gave Tyson enough expertise in the field of astronomy to begin giving lectures on the subject when he was fifteen years old, In fact, he was well known enough in the field by his high school graduation in 1976 that the famed astronomer Carl Sagan attempted to recruit Tyson to attend Cornell University where Sagan was teaching at the time. Tyson chose to attend Harvard University instead, seeing it as the educational birthplace of so many important scientists who had come before him.

Majoring in physics at Harvard, Tyson also joined both the rowing team and the wrestling team. In 1980 he graduated from Harvard with a B.A. in Physics. From there he went to the University of Texas at Austin where he began his graduate work in the field of astronomy, and in 1983 he earned a master's degree in Astronomy. He began a doctoral program at the University of Texas but in 1988 decided to return home to New York and finish his doctorate at Columbia University. In 1988 Tyson married Alice Young, a computer programmer and they had two children together. He also began his writing career around this time, and in 1989 he published his first book, *Merlin's Tour of the Universe: A Skywatcher's Guide to Everything from Mars and Quasars to Comets, Planets, Blue Moons, and Werewolves*. The book took the form of a series of common questions about the cosmos, with Tyson providing answers in easy-to-understand prose that was grounded in scientific fact. This book marked the beginning of his career in science communication, in which he would take complex scientific research and present the material in a form easily palatable to general audiences without being condescending. Many observers noted that Tyson seemed to fill the void left behind by the 1996 passing of Sagan—another gifted and passionate communicator. Tyson graduated from Columbia in 1991 with a Ph.D. in Astrophysics. He became a Visiting Research Scientist in Astrophysics at Princeton University, and in 1994 he published another science book for a general audience, *Universe Down to Earth*. Just two years later, in 1996, he became the first recipient of the Frederick P. Rose Directorship of the Hayden Planetarium in New York City, making him the youngest director of that planetarium in its history.

In 1998 Tyson published a sequel to his first book titled *Just Visiting This Planet: Merlin Answers More Questions about Everything Under the Sun, Moon, and Stars*. A year later he began writing the "Universe" column for *Natural History* magazine. In one 2002 column he noted an urban cosmological event that he named "Manhattan-henge." This was an event where the setting sun aligns perfectly with the Manhattan streetscape for two days out of the year, a cosmological experience that has grown in popularity since he first announced it. His writing and publishing career continued to flourish, and in 2000 he published, along with coauthors Charles Liu and Robert Irion, *One Universe: At Home in the Cosmos*, which won the American Institute of Physics' Science Writing Award for 2001.

Tyson himself won an award in 2000—though one of a less scientific nature. In that year, *People* magazine included him in its annual "Sexiest Man Alive" issue—he was proclaimed the "Sexiest Astrophysicist Alive." Though *People's* attention may have been flattering, the other honors he received the next year were perhaps more meaningful. In 2001 Tyson received a Medal of Excellence from Columbia University. The International Astronomical Union named an asteroid in his honor for his service to the "public's appreciation of the universe." Also in 2001 President George W. Bush appointed him to serve on the twelve-member commission to determine the future of the U.S.'s aerospace industry. That commission delivered its final report in 2002 offering ideas about the future viability of space exploration and transportation. Additionally, Tyson published two American Museum of Natural History books: *Cosmic Horizons: Astronomy at the Cutting Edge* (2001) and *City of Stars: A New Yorker's Guide to the Cosmos* (2002). In 2004 Tyson was appointed by President Bush to serve on another commission, this one being the nine-member team behind the Implementation of United States Space Exploration Policy, which many informally dubbed "Moon, Mars, and Beyond." That same year Tyson served as host for the four-part *Origins* mini-series as part of *Nova* on PBS, having coauthored the show's companion book, *Origins: Fourteen Billion Years of Cosmic Evolution*, with the California astronomer and writer Donald Goldsmith. Tyson also published *The Sky Is Not the Limit: Adventures of an Urban Astrophysicist* in 2004, which was a partial memoir.

In 2006 Tyson took on the job of hosting the PBS television series *NOVA Science Now* during the fall season. Also that year, the head of the National Aeronautics and Space Agency (NASA) appointed Tyson to serve on its crucial advisory committee, which guided the agency in its ongoing struggle to fit its vision within budgetary restrictions. He was awarded the Public Service Medal, NASA's most distinguished civilian medal, for his work with the agency. In 2007 he continued his prolific ways as a writer by publishing a collection of essays titled *Death by Black Hole: And Other Cosmic Quandaries*. He also wrote the foreword to Edward Belbruno's *Fly Me to the Moon: An Insider's Guide to the New Science of Space Travel* (2007) and served as vice president of the Planetary Society's board of directors for three years before becoming the board's chairman. He was a Fellow for the New York Academy of Sciences, a board member of the American Astronomical Society, a member of the International Planetarium Society, and received many honorary degrees for his many accomplishments in the fields of science and astronomy. In 2009 Tyson published *The Pluto Files: The Rise and Fall of America's Favorite Planet* (2009), in which he explained the history of Pluto's official demotion from the status of planet to "dwarf planet," by the International Astronomical Union, a change that was led by Tyson's study of the issue. It was announced in 2011 that Tyson would host a major television sequel to Carl Sagan's *Cosmos* series, to be aired in 2013.

FURTHER READING

Briggs, Jimmie L. "Looking Up: Astrophysicist Neil deGrasse Tyson," *Crisis* (May–June 2006).

Gray, Geoffrey. "Astrognostications: Forget Your Astrologer—Astrophysicist Neil deGrasse Tyson Is Here to Predict the End of the World," *New York* (Dec. 2006).

Shomaker, William. "Neil deGrasse Tyson," *Astronomy* (Mar. 2005).

Wagner, Cynthia, G. "Learning to Look Up: A Scientist Is Teaching the World to See the Universe," *Futurist* (Nov.–Dec. 2004).

AMY SPARKS KOLKER

Tyus, Wyomia (29 August 1945–), track-and-field athlete and the first individual to win gold medals in the same event in consecutive Olympiads, was born in Griffin, Georgia, to Willie Tyus, a dairy farmer, and Marie. The only girl and the youngest of four children, Wyomia Tyus was encouraged by her father to compete in sports, much to the chagrin of her mother, who felt that competing in sports was inappropriate for a young woman. Tyus began her athletic career as a basketball player in high school, but she soon switched sports when an athletic educator felt that her abilities would be better served in track-and-field competition. Initially Tyus had little success. She struggled in the high jump before switching her focus and developing her talents as a runner.

EDWARD STANLEY TEMPLE, the famed coach of Tennessee State University, discovered Tyus at the 1961 Georgia High School State Track Championship. Impressed with her drive and determination, Temple invited her to attend his summer track-and-field camp in Nashville. Under his tutelage, Tyus set a new American record in 1962 for the 100-yard dash at the girls' Amateur Athletic Union (AAU) championships. That same year she became a consensus All-American in the 50-, 75-, and 100-yard dashes—the first ever of either gender to hold such an honor for all three events in the same year. In 1963 she won the girls' 100-yard dash for a second time and competed in her first AAU senior meet, finishing second behind her soon-to-be teammate, EDITH MCGUIRE of the Tennessee State Tigerbelles.

Despite the absence of athletic scholarships, Tyus enrolled at Tennessee State in the fall of 1963. There she continued to train and hone her talents. However, her college career had an inauspicious beginning. The following July, during the AAU national outdoor championships in Hanford, California, Tyus finished in a four-way tie for first with a time of 11.5 seconds alongside her teammate McGuire, the former Tigerbelle Willye White, and the future Olympic hurdler Rosie Bonds of Riverside, California. During the Olympic trials in August, Tyus finished tied for third and barely made the Olympic team.

Tyus's performance at the 1964 Olympiad in Tokyo was her most impressive yet. During the preliminaries she tied a world record in the 100-yard dash with a time of 11.2 seconds. The following day in the finals her time was 11.4 seconds, good enough to win the gold medal. She finished more than 2 yards ahead of her closest competitor, adversary, and teammate McGuire, who, prior to the Olympics, was projected by *Track and Field News* to win the event. With fellow American Marilyn White finishing fourth, this was the closest the U.S. women's team got to sweeping an Olympic event. Tyus also competed in the 400-meter team

relay, in which she finished second and captured the silver medal.

To challenge the assertions made by the Soviet Union about the Americans' unequal treatment of blacks, the State Department sponsored a number of goodwill tours that featured black athletes as spokespersons. In 1966 Tyus and McGuire were part of the excursion that traveled to Massawa, Ethiopia, where they met with a number of schoolteachers and reporters and about one hundred children to demonstrate the rudiments of competitive running, such as starting, baton passing, and other fundamental elements of the sport.

In 1967, during the trials for the Pan-American games, Tyus finished in a disappointing three-way tie for third in the 100-yard dash and failed to qualify for the finals. However, she did finish tied for second in the 200-yard dash, and when the games began on July 29 in Winnipeg, Canada, she won the gold medal in the 200-yard dash and surpassed her qualifying time by almost a full second.

During the 1968 Mexico City Olympic Games, there was racial tension in the air as several African American athletes threatened to boycott the games. The boycott never materialized, but two sprinters, the bronze medalist John Carlos and the gold medalist TOMMIE SMITH, were suspended from the U.S. track team for raising their black-gloved fists in the air and removing their shoes on the victory stand in protest against racial injustice in the United States. For Tyus the 1968 games were extremely emotional in both a personal and a professional sense. She was facing a 100-meter field that was one of the most competitive ever assembled, with five world record holders competing in the event. And much to her frustration, Tyus broke the 100-meter world record in one heat, but the record was voided because officials decided she had been aided by strong winds. In the final heat she was charged with a false start. Eventually, however, she curbed her emotions and sailed to victory in the final race.

At twenty-three years of age, Tyus became the first person in Olympic history to successfully defend the 100-meter dash in consecutive Olympiads and set a world record in the process. This was a feat not duplicated until some twenty years later by CARL LEWIS. Tyus also competed on the 400-meter relay team, which captured the gold medal and set a new world record with a time of 42.8 seconds. After the competition, Tyus and the relay team dedicated their medals to Carlos and Smith.

In 1969 Tyus married, moved to Los Angeles, and retired from amateur athletics. However, four years later, after the birth of her daughter, she was once again running in national competitions. The International Track Association, formed in 1973, began a professional tour in which Tyus participated. The tour debuted in Pocatello, Idaho, drawing about ten thousand spectators before traveling to other cities, such as Portland, Oregon, Los Angeles, San Francisco, Oklahoma City, Albuquerque, and New York. Tyus won eight of eighteen races that year, and in 1974 she won twenty-three races—nearly every contest she competed in. She set a tour record in the 60-yard dash with a time of 6.7 seconds but was paid a mere $600 for her efforts.

Tyus then coached high school track and was a founding member of the Women's Sports Foundation. She was inducted into the Georgia Sports Hall of Fame in 1976, the National Track-and-Field Hall of Fame in 1980, and the International Women's Sports Hall of Fame in 1981.

FURTHER READING

Davis, D. Michael. *Black American Women in Olympic Track and Field* (1992).

Layden, Joe. *Women in Sports* (1997).

Tricard, Mead Louise. *American Women's Track and Field* (1996).

ARTHUR BANTON

Tzomes, C. A. "Pete" (30 Dec. 1944–), U.S. Naval officer and submarine commander, was born Chancellor Peter Tzomes in Williamsport, Pennsylvania, the son of James and Charlotte (Hill) Tzomes. Pete first thought about joining the navy when he was in eighth grade. A senior midshipman visited his school as part of the naval academy's program to attract future candidates and showed a fifteen-minute movie about the U.S. Naval Academy and the navy. Tzomes recalled, "I saw it and was impressed. A couple of weeks later I went to my guidance counselor and told him that that's what I wanted to do. … He told me that Negroes couldn't go to the Academy. … I didn't understand why he told me this. … After all, they didn't say anything about that in the movie they showed us" (interview, 9 Mar. 2007). Undaunted, Tzomes kept the idea of attending the naval academy firmly in mind—an idea made even more attractive by the television show *Men of Annapolis*. Tzomes later applied to his congressman for a nomination to attend the academy. After a short period of study at the State University of New York at Oneonta, Tzomes was accepted to the naval academy in 1963. And upon taking a written exam, he qualified as a second alternate.

As a member of the graduating class of 1967, Tzomes' plebe year at Annapolis was harsh, mainly because of his skin color. Academically, Tzomes achieved high marks, but fellow midshipmen proved to be hostile. As Tzomes remembered:

There were less [*sic*] than ten blacks among 4,000 midshipmen and only two in my class. … We were targets for the upper-classmen and heard the word "nigger" an average of five to ten times a day. The town of Annapolis itself was segregated, but those in our group, all the African Americans, we stuck together and had our own network. That's how I made it through. Luckily, in my plebe year my "Firstie," the 1st class midshipman in charge of me, had respect for us and could identify with our situation because he, too, was black. I'm light skinned, and he didn't know I was black during our initial encounter and asked me how it felt to have him as a leader. … I just kind of chuckled and said, "I'm black, too, sir" (interview, 9 Mar. 2007).

Support for Tzomes and his fellow black midshipman also came from the Annapolis community. The most important source of support was Lilly May Chase, a black woman who lived just outside the academy gates and in whose home they were always welcome. In Chase they found a welcoming and mothering figure to help them through their four years at Annapolis.

Upon graduation, Ensign Tzomes chose submarine duty and was accepted after an interview with the legendary Admiral Hyman Rickover, during which Tzomes was "thrown out of his office" (interview, 9 Mar. 2007) for not telling the hard-nosed admiral what he wanted to hear. However, Tzomes prevailed, and upon completing a year of nuclear-power training, he joined the crew of the *U.S.S. Will Rogers* (Blue crew) in February 1969. As the only black officer on the submarine and one of just a small number of black officers in the entire navy, Tzomes was subjected to discrimination from the very beginning of his service. His commanding officer, before giving him one particular assignment, made him take a written exam. This was not a requirement for white junior officers, but Tzomes persevered and was aided by "a black steward, SD1 Willie Wells, who looked out for me, helped cheer me up after a bad day … and made himself available to me socially in off-crew times" (interview, 9 Mar. 2007). Joining the crew of the submarine *Pintado* in December 1970, he met with similar racial prejudice, and Tzomes was mentored by a "black radioman, a chief, who took me under his wings" (interview, 9 Mar. 2007). Interestingly, his commanding officers on his first boats were fair enough, and race was never an issue in the wardroom, the officer's area of a submarine. However, some enlisted men had problems with taking orders from a black officer. With more patience than most people could muster, Tzomes told his men to look at the lieutenant stripes on his uniform and not at the color of his skin. From 1973 to 1976 he served on the submarine *Drum* as engineering officer and despite being unnecessarily questioned again about his qualifications—presumably because of his race—he helped the troubled boat pass its nuclear power exam with flying colors. Because of this performance, Tzomes soon gained the reputation as the best nuclear engineer in the U.S. Pacific fleet.

From 1976 to 1979 Tzomes served on the Nuclear Propulsion Examining Board of the U.S. Pacific fleet and gained an outstanding reputation under close scrutiny for his work there. After a rewarding and successful tour as executive officer on the submarine *Cavalla* from late 1979 to 1982, Commander Tzomes made history in May 1983 when he was named commander of the fast-attack submarine *U.S.S. Houston*; he had become the first African American to command a submarine. After leaving the *Houston* in May 1986, Tzomes would serve shore duty in a number of important billets, including a tour as commanding officer of the Recruit Training Command, Great Lakes. He retired from the U.S. Navy in July 1994 having attained the rank of captain. The importance of Tzomes's service in the U.S. Navy is self-evident. Not only was he a pioneer who paved the way for subsequent black officers, such as future admirals Anthony Watson and MELVIN WILLIAMS JR., but he also improved conditions for all African Americans serving in the U.S. Navy during the racially turbulent era of the late 1960s and early 1970s. He was part of a group of black officers in 1970 that presented Admiral Elmo Zumwalt's famed Z-Gram 66 to the Pentagon, a document that addressed the range of racial discrimination found in the navy and the ways in which such problems might be alleviated. Noting that this presentation "was not well received," Tzomes and others joined the forward-thinking Zumwalt in advocating for equal opportunity housing, the participation of minority wives in ombudsman groups, and the availability of ethnic products and services in navy exchange facilities.

Tzomes's success was also due in large part to the way he approached his unique status as the only African American in the naval crews he served. He stated that because it was his shipmates' first time being exposed to a black officer, it was his duty to make the experience positive. Tzomes also achieved success because he set high standards for himself and was determined not to squander the opportunity of being the first black submarine commander in the history of the U.S. Navy.

Tzomes remained active in the nuclear power field as an "emergency preparedness" manager for Exelon Corporation in Illinois. He had a son, Chancellor A. Tzomes II, as well as one granddaughter. He was the inaugural member of a group known as the Centennial 7, the first seven black submarine commanders in the submarine force's first one-hundred years from 1900 to 2000. Through this organization, Tzomes met periodically with those who followed in his footsteps, and the meetings prompted much reflection and remembrance. Despite the traumatic racial injustices he was subject to early in his naval career, Tzomes was not embittered by these experiences; in fact, he was deservedly content with all that he had accomplished.

FURTHER READING

This article is largely based on the author's interview with Captain Pete Tzomes on 9 Mar. 2007 and subsequent e-mail exchanges.

Knoblock, Glenn A. *Black Submariners in the United States Navy, 1940–1975* (2005).

Martin, C. Sunny. *Who's Who in Black Chicago—Inaugural Edition* (2006).

GLENN ALLEN KNOBLOCK

Uggams, Leslie (25 May 1943–), actress and singer, was born in New York City, to elevator operator and maintenance worker Harold C. Uggams and waitress Juanita Smith Uggams, and raised in the Washington Heights section of the city. She inherited her performing talents from her father, a singer with the Hall Johnson Choir, and her mother, a chorus dancer.

Uggams made her acting debut at age six in 1950, appearing as ETHEL WATERS's niece on the television series *Beulah*. She also made appearances on other TV programs, including *Your Show of Shows, The Milton Berle Show, The Arthur Godfrey Show*, and numerous children's shows. Her talent earned the seven-year-old a regular spot at Harlem's Apollo Theater as an opening attraction for LOUIS ARMSTRONG, ELLA FITZGERALD, and DINAH WASHINGTON.

A student at the New York Professional Children's School, Uggams was a teen contestant and singer on the CBS television series *Name That Tune*. Her performance so impressed Mitch Miller of Columbia Records that he offered her a recording contract and made her a regular on the first prerecorded television music program, *Sing Along with Mitch*. She made her feature film debut in 1960 as the offscreen singer whose voice accompanies the opening scenes of MGM's *Inherit the Wind* (1960), a film about the 1920s Scopes "monkey trial" in Tennessee; she sings "(Give Me That) Old Time Religion."

While a student at Juilliard, which she attended from 1961 to 1963, Uggams released her first of ten albums for Columbia, which featured her first hit single, "Morgan." She parlayed her extensive performance expertise into landing the lead in the stage musical *Hallelujah, Baby!*—a part originally written for LENA HORNE—which earned Uggams the 1968 Tony Award for best actress in a Broadway musical comedy.

On the basis of her singing and acting talent, Uggams became the first black female performer since Hazel Scott in the 1950s to host her own TV series, the 1969 CBS-sponsored *The Leslie Uggams Show*. Perhaps the television role for which she is best remembered, however, is her portrayal of Kizzy in the 1977 miniseries based on ALEX HALEY's *Roots*, which earned her the Critic's Choice Award for best supporting actress in 1978 and her first Emmy nomination for best leading actress. A primary role in the 1979 miniseries *Backstairs at the White House*, an Emmy-winning position as co-host of a 1983 nighttime audience-participation series dubbed *Fantasy*, and a turn as Rose Keefer in the daytime drama *All My Children* in 1996 rounded out Uggams's regular television appearances.

A tireless stage celebrity, Uggams continued to perform for concert and theater audiences. In 2005 she starred with JAMES EARL JONES in a production of *On Golden Pond* at New York's Cort Theater. Offstage, she was a founding member of the BRAVO Chapter/City of Hope, a charitable organization that investigates and treats blood-related diseases; she has served as a board member of the ALVIN AILEY American Dance Theater and a member of TADA!, the children's musical theater.

FURTHER READING

Graham, Lawrence Otis. *A Member of the Club: Reflections of Life in a Racially Polarized World* (1996).

Marmorstein, Gary. *The Label: The Story of Columbia Records* (2007).

ROXANNE Y. SCHWAB

Uncle Jack (1746?–6 Apr. 1843), preacher, teacher, and ex-slave, was born in Africa. Kidnapped and brought to America at age seven, the man later referred to alternately as "Uncle Jack" and "the African Preacher" was sold into slavery and resided in Nottoway County, Virginia. Very little is known of his early life, family, and exact place of origin before 1753 when he was purchased on the docks of the James River by a man named Stewart. He grew into manhood in Nottoway County, performing various plantation labors. At the age of forty, he encountered several missionaries who traveled throughout Virginia. They introduced him to tenets of the Bible, coaxing him in what would become his greatest vocation and earn him the title of "African Preacher." Christianity's essential ideas of grace, salvation, and the resurrected life inspired him out of the despair and bleak condition of slavery.

Jack hungered to learn more, and petitioned the children of his owner to teach him to read the Bible, paying his "tuition" with nuts and fruits. Literacy laws made it extremely difficult and dangerous to get any education, and whites who tutored blacks in reading could be fined and flogged as punishment. Once Jack became literate and familiar with the Bible, he succeeded in converting the owner's youngest son to the faith. As Jack became immersed in the study and articulation of the gospel, he earned a reputation as a gifted, sought-after speaker. He joined the local Baptist church and was officially ordained. Traveling as far as thirty miles to minister in adjacent communities, the African Preacher was granted a rare level of free mobility that few slaves enjoyed. After the death of his master, he purchased his own freedom, paid for with contributions from friends. Upon Uncle Jack's manumission, he bought land with donations from his flock, married, and lived in humble comfort, ministering to both blacks and whites.

Much of his religious teaching was illustrated through the use of nature motifs. Drawing upon what locals knew best, Jack made references to trees and tobacco leaves integral to his sermons. Changing seasons were the means to understanding death, regeneration, resurrection, and conversion. Holding two of the most esteemed positions among his brethren—that of being elderly and African-born—he was a beloved leader of the black community. The African Preacher visited the sick, officiated at funerals, and evoked greater authority on matters of justice than slave owners or overseers. Jack was noted for preferring substance over style in worship and was averse to boisterous or noisy prayer-making. He chided his congregation to love the Word without the fuss of loud confusion, and heed the rich insights in Christ's work. Willing to engage the doubtful gambler and the self-assured sinner, Jack's exchanges with others demonstrated the musing of a theologian. He was not inclined to provide forceful answers but rather employed rhetorical dialogues intent on leading the inquisitive to their own righteous, satisfying conclusion. An itinerant preacher, Jack had occasions to meet a variety of well-educated scholars, doctors, judges, and statesmen. Between 1825 and 1836, a Presbyterian minister and author conducted interviews with Jack, and collected testimonials to document his importance to the community. Reflections from his admirers emphasize the impact of his piety and mental acuity. Through this collection of letters and obituaries written by local Virginians, a portrait emerges of a spiritual leader who bridged two racially divided worlds.

Among the glowing reports of Jack's decidedly gentle nature and pious principles were those from local whites who attested to his profound influence in their community. Jack had had occasion to engage the ear of Reverend John Blair Smith, college president Hampden Sidney, and Reverend Archibald Anderson, a scholar from Princeton. They credited him with infusing their society with precious enlightened values. Jack's articulate command of speech was noted by his interviewer and biographer William S. White, as well as the editor of the *Virginia Literary and Evangelical Magazine*, Dr. James Rice. These men were particularly impressed that a semiliterate man of foreign birth with no formal university training spoke in a manner familiar to them and without dialect. Whites were struck with the wisdom and practical insights he brought to biblical passages, and regarded his life as especially noteworthy. They interceded with legal support when his property rights were threatened. His ability to procure respect, endorsements, and assistance from a privileged class was a notable achievement in an era when white suspicions of slave revolts were rampant. Uprisings in Virginia, like that led by NAT TURNER in 1831, incurred strong and sometimes lethal reprisals.

The African Preacher's persona may have worked to quell the fears of whites and reduced tensions between the races. Testimonies of his nonthreatening demeanor suggest that he authored an early form of accommodation—the style of influence perfected at the end of the nineteenth century by leaders like BOOKER T. WASHINGTON who generated white philanthropic support for Tuskegee Institute in Alabama. Jack, as an unusual figure of the early nineteenth century, produced a change in consciousness, specifically in reverencing values of kindness, moral behavior, and offering comfort to his community. As a Christian ambassador, he was also one of few blacks permitted into whites' inner circles where powerful lawmakers, politicians, and doctors received his counsel. Because Jack was well liked by some wealthy and powerful whites his advice was welcomed and trusted. He was revered by many who loved and cared for him as he grew to nearly one hundred years of age. He died in 1843, in Nottoway.

FURTHER READING

White, William S. *The African Preacher: An Authentic Narrative* (1849). Available at http://docsouth.unc.edu/white/menu.html.

R. ISET ANUAKAN

Uncles, Charles Randolph (6 Nov. 1859–20 July 1933), Roman Catholic priest and educator, was the first African American ordained to the priesthood in the United States. Uncles was born in Baltimore, Maryland, to Lorenzo and Anna Marie (Buchanan) Uncles, both of whom had been born free. His father worked for the Baltimore and Ohio Railroad as a machinist. Though the Oblate Sisters of Providence in Baltimore had educated his mother, Anna Marie Buchanan, the family did not become Catholics until the founding of Saint Francis Xavier Church, Baltimore, in 1864, the first American Catholic parish organized for blacks. Consequently, Charles was not baptized until 2 April 1875 at the age of sixteen. After receiving lessons at a small, private school for blacks in Baltimore, Uncles attended secondary school in Baltimore and in 1878 enrolled in the Baltimore Normal School for Teachers. He taught in the county's public schools from 1880 to 1883, and at a height of six feet two inches, Uncles was described as a handsome and imposing young man.

As a member of Saint Francis Xavier Church, Uncles became acquainted with the Mill Hill Josephites, an order of priests founded in England and dedicated to missionary work among blacks. Against his parents' wishes, he decided to join the Mill Hill order and commenced studies for the priesthood. Though the Mill Hill fathers were dedicated to black ministry, none of the members of that order were of African ancestry, and consequently, because of his race, Uncles was unsure whether he would be accepted into the order. The Reverend John Slattery, a Mill Hill father, supported Uncles and suggested that he apply to a Canadian seminary where other black seminarians had been admitted. Uncles was approved to study for the Mill Hill Josephites and was sent to Saint Hyacinth's College in Quebec, Canada, in the fall of 1883, where he graduated with honors five years later.

Returning to the United States in 1888, Uncles was sent to the newly opened Mill Hill school at Saint Joseph's Seminary in Baltimore. When he decided that he wanted to attend classes at the nearby Saint Mary's Seminary, the seminary superiors put Uncles's admission to a vote by the student body. The result was unanimous: Uncles would be granted entrance to Saint Mary's Seminary.

At the conclusion of his studies, James Cardinal Gibbons, archbishop of Baltimore, ordained Uncles a priest on 19 December 1891 in the cathedral at Baltimore. Uncles's ordination was the occasion of two important firsts: the first black priest of the Mill Hill order and the first black priest ordained in the United States. Other African Americans, such as AUGUSTUS TOLTON and SHERWOOD HEALY, had been ordained priests in Europe and returned to the United States to minister.

Uncles celebrated his first Mass as a priest in Saint Francis Xavier, the church in which he had received communion for the first time and had been confirmed as a Catholic. Two years after Uncles's ordination, the American branch of the Mill Hill fathers separated from its parent order, retaining the name Saint Joseph's Society of the Sacred Heart but known popularly in America as the Josephites. Uncles was one of the original five priests who founded the Josephite order in America in 1893, taking the letters *SSJ* after his name to mark his affiliation with the community.

Immediately following his ordination, Uncles was sent to teach at the Josephites' preparatory seminary, Epiphany Apostolic College, a high school and college first located in Walbrook near Baltimore and later in Newburgh, New York. By placing him in one of their educational institutions, Uncles's Josephite superiors hoped to spare him the trials he may have faced as a priest serving in a parish.

Well prepared for life as an academic, Uncles was fluent in Greek, Latin, and French. He was popular among his students, who affectionately called him "Daddy Uncles," and he taught courses in Latin, Greek, and English for more than four decades. Despite Uncles's ability as a seminary instructor, his religious superiors hoped that he would travel widely, promoting the cause of the Catholic mission to blacks. But after traveling to the southern United States as part of two mission bands, Uncles, bitter from his experience of racism and segregation, opted to return to Epiphany College, away from the public eye.

Though Uncles's religious superior, the Reverend John Slattery, had supported him through his seminary training and through ordination, he began to doubt Uncles's suitability for priesthood. He believed Uncles to be too independent, prideful, inattentive to his religious duties, and, still worse, unable to live as a celibate. Slattery became particularly disturbed when in 1900 a white religious sister working at Epiphany College accused Uncles of making advances toward her. The claim was never substantiated, and the woman was transferred away from Epiphany, yet the incident marred Uncles's reputation. A second incident a year later resulted in a warrant for Uncles's arrest, though the warrant was later retracted and the alleged criminal activity was unproved.

After these incidents, Uncles, who remained an instructor at the school, rarely left the grounds except to celebrate Mass at nearby black Catholic parishes. Uncles died at Epiphany Apostolic College in Newburgh, New York, and his death left the American Josephite order without any African American members for the first time in its history. It was not until eight years later that another African American was ordained a priest for the Josephites.

FURTHER READING

Archival material detailing the history of the Josephites and the life of the Reverend Charles Uncles, SSJ, can be found at the Josephite Archives, Baltimore, Maryland.

Davis, Cyprian. *The History of Black Catholics in the United States* (1990).

Foley, Albert. *God's Men of Color: The Colored Catholic Priests of the United States, 1854–1954* (1955).

Ochs, Stephen J. *Desegregating the Altar: The Josephites and the Struggle for Black Priests, 1871–1960* (1990).

Obituary: *New York Times*, 22 July 1933.

DAVID J. ENDRES

Unseld, Westley Sissel (14 Mar. 1946–), basketball player, executive, and coach, was born in Louisville, Kentucky, to Charles D. Unseld, a blue-collar worker, and Cornelia D. Unseld, a school cafeteria worker. The Unselds had seven children of their own and two adopted boys. In 1963 the National Conference of Christians and Jews honored the family with its brotherhood award for rebuilding a local recreation center damaged by a fire. The seed of community service was planted early in Wes Unseld's life and remained important to him. Athletic ability in the Unseld family was not limited to Wes. His brother George played basketball at the University of Kansas from 1962 to 1964. Wes credited Carl Wright, his freshman high school coach, with fueling his interest in basketball. Wright developed Wes's basketball skills in daily one-on-one contests.

At Seneca High in Louisville, Unseld played football and won the state championship in the discus throw. He also led his school to consecutive Kentucky state titles in 1962 and 1963. Although he had several hundred scholarship offers, Unseld chose Louisville because it would be easier for his father, who had suffered a heart attack, to watch him play. A six-foot-seven-inch center, Unseld was unusually short for that position, but at two hundred and forty-five pounds, he had enough bulk to compensate. In three years of varsity competition, Unseld averaged 20.5 points per game and 18.9 rebounds. During Unseld's college career, Louisville made two NCAA tournament appearances and one to the National Invitational Tournament at New York's Madison Square Garden. Unseld was named to the All-Missouri Conference team three times, from 1966 to 1968, and earned All-American honors twice, in 1967 and 1968.

Following his senior year, Unseld was caught in a bidding war between the NBA's Baltimore Bullets and the American Basketball Association's (ABA) Kentucky Colonels. Wes's father did not appreciate the tactics used by the Colonels, so Wes signed with Baltimore. The Bullets had never had a winning season, but with Gus Johnson, Earl Monroe, Kevin Loughery, and Jack Marin they did have the nucleus for a successful franchise. With Unseld providing stability at the center position, the Bullets improved to an impressive 57-25, the best record in the NBA's

Eastern Conference. Unseld averaged 13.8 points, pulled down 1491 rebounds, and demonstrated an uncanny ability to start the Bullets fast break with accurate outlet passes. The season's only disappointment came in the first round of the playoffs when the Bullets were swept in four games by the New York Knicks. After his first season, the NBA named Unseld Most Valuable Player and Rookie of the Year. Before Unseld, only WILT CHAMBERLAIN had won this double honor.

The 1968–69 season marked the beginning of Baltimore's intense rivalry with the New York Knicks. Coached by William "Red" Holzman, the Knicks featured WILLIS REED, WALT FRAZIER, Dave DeBusschere, Bill Bradley, and Dick Barnett. Between 1969 and 1974 the Knicks and Bullets met six consecutive times in the NBA Eastern Conference playoffs with the Knicks prevailing five times. The lone Baltimore triumph was in 1971 when the Bullets won the seventh game of the Eastern Conference finals 93-91, at Madison Square Garden. In the 1971 NBA finals, the Bullets were swept in four straight games by the Milwaukee Bucks led by KAREEM ABDUL-JABBAR and OSCAR ROBERTSON.

After the 1973–74 season, the Bullets moved to Washington, D.C. In 1975 the team made their second trip to the NBA finals against the Golden State Warriors. Although Baltimore had extensively restructured its roster, Unseld was still a key player. The other starters were Kevin Porter, Elvin Hayes, Phil Chenier, and Mike Riordan. Although every game was close, the Warriors, led by Rick Barry, won in four straight games.

In 1977 Unseld's Bullets acquired Bobby Dandridge, one of the game's best small forwards, and in mid-season the team also got Charles Johnson, an excellent guard. In 1978 the Bullets made their third trip to the NBA finals; this time they faced the Seattle Supersonics. Seattle had three outstanding guards, Dennis Johnson, Gus Williams, and Fred Brown. Its frontline included Paul Silas, Marvin Webster, and Jack Sikma. In the championship series, Unseld's performance was superb. After the Bullets lost the first game, Washington tied the series at one game apiece, as Unseld pulled down fifteen rebounds, dished out five assists, and set key picks that freed up teammates for open shots. After four more exciting games, the two teams met in Seattle for the seventh and deciding game. The Bullets survived 105-99, and Unseld, who played the entire series with knee pain, won MVP honors. The same two teams met in the championship the following year, but Seattle won that series four games to one.

After the 1980–81 season, Unseld retired from basketball. In thirteen seasons he scored 10,625 points (averaging 10.8 points per game) and snared 12,769 rebounds (averaging fourteen rebounds per game). Often playing on bad knees, Unseld had been the heart of a franchise that posted ten winning seasons and made twelve play-off appearances.

Off the court, in 1975 Unseld received the first Walter Kennedy Citizenship Award. Between 1969 and 1974, he was on the board of directors of Kernan Hospital in Baltimore, where he also volunteered to help children who needed orthopedic and plastic surgery care. In 1988 he helped to finance the Unseld School.

Over the years, Unseld had established a close relationship with Bullets' owner Abe Pollin. In 1981 Pollin made Unseld vice president of marketing, sales, and community relations. In 1988 Pollin made Unseld the Bullets' head coach, a position he held for seven seasons. That same year, Unseld was inducted into the Naismith Memorial Basketball Hall of Fame. Although Unseld was respected for motivating his team to play hard, he enjoyed only one winning season and compiled a 202–345 record. After he resigned in 1994, Abe Pollin made him the team's vice president and general manager in 1996, a position he held until the end of the 2003–2004 season. In 1996 a panel selected by the NBA elected Unseld to the list of the top fifty players in NBA history.

Unseld's accomplishments were not limited to the basketball court. In addition to his Walter Kennedy citizenship award, Unseld also played an instrumental role in providing financial assistance to help his wife Connie Martin Unseld realize her dream of creating a school devoted to early childhood education. The couple had two children, Wes Jr. and Kimberly. As a player, coach, executive, and citizen, Wes Unseld set high standards and earned the respect of his peers.

FURTHER READING

Naismith Memorial Basketball Hall of Fame. Wes Unseld Letter File.

Sutton, William A. "Westley Sissel Unseld, 'Wes,'" in *Basketball: A Biographical Dictionary*, ed. David L. Porter (2005).

DOLPH GRUNDMAN

Unthank, DeNorval (14 Dec. 1899–20 Sep. 1977), physician, community leader, and civil rights activist, was born in Allentown, Pennsylvania, the son of Albion Unthank, a cook for the railroad company, and Elizabeth (Sherman), a housewife.

Unthank earned a bachelor of arts degree at the University of Michigan and received his medical degree from Howard University. In 1929, he was recruited to Portland, Oregon, to serve as the one physician for the segregated African American community. As with most black citizens across the country, African Americans in Oregon were limited to the lowest-paying jobs. Employers in Portland followed a longstanding unwritten agreement by which only the railroad or hotels hired black workers. On the eve of World War II, an industrial survey showed that 98 percent of the employed black population worked in some capacity for the Union Pacific Railway or at the railroad terminus near downtown Portland ("Urban League Report—Race Relations in Portland, Oregon" (July 1968)). A few black women found work as domestics in homes and businesses, but all African Americans understood that no jobs were available for them in such areas as industry or retail.

When Unthank arrived in Portland, he moved his family into a modest all-white neighborhood. He immediately encountered strong neighborhood opposition, and vandals destroyed his property and stoned the house, breaking a window. Neighborhood representatives even offered him from $700 to $1,500 to move out. He did not give into these threats, however, and from that moment, despite an extremely busy medical practice, Unthank placed himself very much in the center of the protest against racial discrimination in Portland.

Portland city leaders manipulated local politics for their own purposes, disregarding the city's need for public services, and showed little interest in social problems—especially racial equality. At just under two thousand, the black community comprised less than 1 percent of the city's total population. There were sundown curfews and all black adults had to account for their presence at any time with a job verification. Bill Berry of the Urban League later stated that "no city outside the deep South had the suppression or the compression that Portland has in housing and employment" (*Oregonian*, 1 January 1956).

Throughout the 1930s, Unthank was Portland's only medical option for African Americans. Segregation barriers, customary in the city, kept some services, such as health care, in the black community. Black families could not receive treatment in local hospitals—house calls were necessary, and Unthank made himself available day and night. He was a dedicated physician and a friend to any minority group in the city. He not only served African Americans, he served Asians, Hispanics, Eastern Europeans, and whites.

Unthank was Portland's most notable and visible opponent of segregation and discrimination. In 1940, he was elected as head of the Advisory Council, an African American organization that hoped to pressure local leaders into providing equal access to economic opportunities related to war industry jobs. The council documented incidents of discrimination in the workplace around Portland, and expectations were raised further in 1941 when President Franklin Delano Roosevelt signed Executive Order 8802 and established the Fair Employment Practices Committee. This order forbade private employers holding government contracts from discriminating based on race, color, or national origin.

Unthank and the Advisory Council specifically targeted Portland's boilermaker and machinist unions as examples of the "systematic program of racial discrimination" (*Oregonian*, 2 December 1941) that excluded black workers from war industry jobs. After a battle of some eighteen months, the boilermaker's union reluctantly liberalized its policies on race, but that did not mean the end of discrimination. In 1942, an *Oregonian* headline read, "New Negro Migrants Worry City," referring to fewer than two hundred black workers who had recently arrived. The mayor, Earl Riley, stated that the city would not tolerate "undesirables" and that "Portland can absorb only a minimum of Negroes without upsetting the city's regular life" (*Oregonian*, 23 September 1942). "We Cater to White Trade Only" signs appeared in business windows, much to the dismay of Unthank and other African American leaders. Local protests in Portland were the subject of editorials and articles from black newspapers across the nation and eventually brought in support and political pressure from the NAACP.

The industrial and labor expansion of World War II created opportunities that African Americans throughout the United States seized upon to push for economic equality. The prospect of high wages in defense industry jobs in Portland persuaded several thousand African Americans to migrate west, and the black population of Portland rose to approximately 23,000. When efforts to limit black wartime employment were not entirely successful, Portland politicians and businessmen manipulated the housing market to ensure racial segregation. Through de facto segregation, they limited migrant blacks to housing in the most run-down area of the city or in hastily built federal public housing outside the city limits. At the end of the war, the lack of jobs and housing compelled a majority of these newcomers to leave the area. Nevertheless, the wartime migration of African Americans boosted what had been a nearly invisible black population of Portland to nearly ten thousand. To keep up with demand, in 1943 Unthank recruited an additional African American physician, Robert Joyner Jr., to serve his growing medical practice.

During World War II, Unthank served as president of the local NAACP chapter and championed resistance against racial barriers in employment and housing. Against the odds, he applied for membership to Portland's City Club and became its first black member in 1943. He encouraged the club to undertake and publish a significant 1945 study called "The Negro in Portland," which cited numerous examples of racism and discrimination that existed in the city, and opened the eyes of many citizens who had previously overlooked these practices. Unthank was also a co-founder of a Portland chapter of the Urban League—an organization that successfully fought for improvements in housing and employment for the black community. As more and more citizens, both black and white, voiced their support for change, a shift in popular opinion led to the passing of Oregon's 1953 Civil Rights Bill, which among many issues, overturned a law banning interracial marriages in the state.

Unthank was married and had four children. His dedication to his patients, to his community, and to racial equality made him an important figure in the history of the state of Oregon and especially the city of Portland. In 1958, the Oregon Medical Society named him Doctor of the Year. In recognition of his service to civil rights, grateful citizens pressed the city to dedicate DeNorval Unthank Park in North Portland in his honor in 1969. He was the recipient of several awards, including the distinguished citizenship award from the University of Oregon in 1971 and a similar award from Concordia College in 1975. Unthank's importance to the community and historical legacy were reflected in the large crowd of black and white mourners at his funeral in Portland, Oregon.

FURTHER READING
Pearson, Rudy. "African Americans in Portland, Oregon, 1940–1950: Work and Living Conditions—A Social History," Ph.D. diss., Washington State University (1996). http://www.blackpast.org http://www.ohs.org.

RUDY PEARSON

Upshaw, Eugene Thurman, Jr. (15 Aug. 1945–20 Aug. 2008), professional football player and union leader, was born in Robstown, Texas, to Eugene Upshaw, an oil field worker, and Cora (Riley) Upshaw, a domestic worker. As a boy, Upshaw honed his ability to endure unfavorable conditions while picking cotton in the fields surrounding Robstown. The harsh and sometimes brutal experience of working in the unforgiving Texas heat taught Upshaw lessons in humility and toughness. He learned early the value of a solid work ethic, while earning the extra money that his family could not afford to do without. The eldest of three sons, Upshaw was the example for his younger siblings, who often followed his lead and even in his footsteps: his younger brother Marvin Upshaw was a first-round draft pick of the Cleveland Browns in 1968.

Considered a stellar athlete at Robstown High School, where he showed promise in sports such as baseball, football, and track and field for the school team, the Cotton Pickers, Upshaw did not receive any offers for college scholarships. Instead, the self-starter walked onto the Texas A&I University (now Texas A&M University–Kingsville) football team in 1963 after enrolling in fall courses. After one week of practice, Upshaw impressed the coaching staff enough to earn his scholarship.

In 1967, after four years at Texas A&I, playing offensive tackle, center, and end, Upshaw, a six-foot-five-inch, 265-pound senior, was selected to the first team of the Lone Star Conference and the National Association of Intercollegiate Athletics (NAIA) All-America team. In addition, he won several coaches' awards for his outstanding play and leadership. A fierce competitor, as well as an extremely hard worker, Upshaw showed the professional scouts of organized football his skill and tenacity through his dominant play in both the 1967 Senior Bowl and Coaches' All-American Bowl. By all accounts, Upshaw was recognized by scouts as having the perfect combination of size, speed, tenacity, and intellect that could change a game. These unique qualities made him the perfect first-round draft pick for an upstart American Football League (AFL) club, the Oakland Raiders, in the first National Football League (NFL)–AFL draft in 1967. Seeking to challenge the division rival, the

Kansas City Chiefs, the Raiders saw Upshaw as an answer to the line play of All-Pro defensive linemen Ernie Ladd and JUNIUS "BUCK" BUCHANAN. This same year, Upshaw divorced his first wife, Jimmye Hill, with whom he had a son, Eugene. Upshaw received his bachelor of science degree in Secondary Education from Texas A&I University in 1968.

Battling in the "trenches" alongside Raider teammates such as perennial All-Pro offensive tackle ART SHELL JR., later to become the second African American head coach in professional football and the future head coach of the Raiders, Upshaw's efforts would help the Raiders organization establish its history of winning and its commitment to excellence. From 1967 to 1982, the Raiders made eleven playoff appearances (1967–1970, 1972–1977, 1980) and won three AFL and American Football Conference (AFC) championships and two Super Bowls (1976 and 1980). Upshaw was recognized as the only player in the history of the NFL to have started on teams participating in the football championships of the two professional leagues in three different decades, and the Raiders succeeded in winning Super Bowls XI and XV. Over a fifteen-year career, Upshaw, the ten-time Raider captain, started and played in 207 regular-season and in 24 post-season games, and he achieved numerous honors and distinctions during his tenure, including the AFC Lineman of the Year (1973, 1974, and 1977) and the NFL's Lineman of the Year (1977). He also made six consecutive Pro Bowl appearances from 1973 to 1978.

As a player, Upshaw served for seven years (1970–1976) as either an alternate or a player representative for the professional football players' labor union, the National Football League Players' Association (NFLPA), bringing the concerns of his Raider teammates to the attention of the players' association. Understanding the value of his and his fellow players' labor as significant to the success of the National Football League, Upshaw worked to ensure that the NFL would treat the players with fairness for their part in making the game popular. In 1976 he was voted to the NFLPA Executive Committee and four years later became the union president. In 1980 Upshaw's efforts as a voice for fairness in the sports industry, his leadership on the football field, and his service to both a local and national community were rewarded with the prestigious Byron "Whizzer" White Humanitarian Award from the NFLPA. Named after the former NFL player and Supreme Court justice of the United States, the award signifies the commitment to community, education, and achievement, to which all professional football players should aspire. In 1982 Upshaw, the consummate community servant and leader, was honored by the American Federation of Labor and Congress of Industrial Organizations (AFL-CIO) with its A. PHILIP RANDOLPH Award for his leadership. During the players' strike in 1983, Upshaw took part in the negotiations that provided the necessary revisions to the Collective Bargaining Agreement (CBA) between the NFLPA and the NFL that helped resume play after an eight-week stoppage of work.

In 1983 Upshaw succeeded the Players' Association's first executive director, Ed Garvey, eventually negotiating the extensions of the CBA in 1996, 1998, and 2001. Upshaw was married a second time, in 1986, to Teresa Buich, with whom he had two sons, Justin and Daniel.

By 1993 Upshaw was named to *Sporting News* magazine's one hundred most powerful people in sports list. Over his tenure with NFLPA, the professional, unflappable, and learned Upshaw was able to increase the trust, enthusiasm, and faith in the purpose of the NFLPA to secure the past, present, and future concerns and interests of professional football players. His vision for the organization went beyond the playing field and competed directly with the owners and vendors who marketed the marquee players of the league. During his career Upshaw used his celebrity status, time, and personal resources to assist organizations such as the March of Dimes and the Salvation Army in their efforts to change the lives of children. He also supported causes that worked to research and discover new ways to treat diseases such as sickle cell anemia and cystic fibrosis. Upshaw and the NFLPA recognized that the players wanted to take their helmets off and be seen and represented as individuals. As a result, in 1994 the NFLPA introduced the for-profit entity Players, Inc., which provides opportunities for players to take advantage of their individually unique marketability to create relationships with businesses and charitable organizations.

In 1987 Upshaw was inducted into the Pro Football Hall of Fame—the first player to play guard exclusively throughout his entire professional career to be so honored. In 1994 he was named to the NFL 75th Anniversary All-Time Team, and the AFL-NFL 25-Year All-Star Team. Upshaw's achievements as a player and executive are many, and he is admired by those who value his lifelong commitment to excellence. In 2004, based on his demonstrated leadership qualities of integrity, compassion, and perseverance, the Manheim Touchdown Club of Manheim, Pennsylvania, named a football award after Upshaw for the outstanding Division II Lineman of the Year. In 2007 Upshaw began his twenty-fourth year as Executive Director of the NFLPA, which promised to be as challenging as the previous years in which he served to represent the interests of the players. He died suddenly from pancreatic cancer at his home near Lake Tahoe, California, in 2008. He was 63.

FURTHER READING

Porter, David, ed. *African American Sports Greats: A Biographical Dictionary* (1995).

Wagaman, Michael. *The Unofficial Oakland Raiders Book of Lists* (2002).

Wiggins, David, ed. *African Americans in Sports* (2004).

PELLOM MCDANIELS III

Vails, Nelson (13 Oct. 1960–), Olympic cyclist, was born in Harlem, New York City, the youngest of the ten children of Robert Vails, a hospital orderly, and Louise Barnwell, a nurse. Nelson grew up in the Martin Luther King Towers housing project near Central Park. His childhood cycling experience was typical: a new bicycle for Christmas and days spent riding with friends. He received his first ten-speed racing bike from his older brother Ronnie, who formerly raced bicycles. In 1976 Vails began to ride recreationally in Central Park, a popular venue for area cyclists. He soon joined on rides with the Century Road Club, a bicycle racing club operating out of Central Park. The inexperienced but persistent Vails drew attention from club members, including Avalos York, an inveterate teacher of young cyclists, who mentored Vails and introduced to him the proper techniques of competitive bicycle riding.

In 1978 Vails began to compete and win in local Harlem races, and he became a regular participant in Century Road Club training rides. His apparent talent, powerful build, and outgoing personality caught the attention of the don of New York City cycling, Fred Mengoni. Mengoni showed Vails how to dress and act like a bike racer and was instrumental in shepherding Vails into the wider world of competitive cycling in the tri-state area. After graduating from Haaron High School in 1978, Vails began to work as a bicycle messenger in Manhattan, eight to ten hours a day, rain or shine. "Being a messenger always kept me in great shape. I'd work weekdays, train at night, and race on the weekends. It really helped my bike handling. Because

of it I never overreact when someone hooks me in a sprint" (Drake, 66). In homage to this stage of his career, Vails made a cameo appearance in the role of "Messenger in Maroon Beret" in Thomas Donnelly's *Quicksilver* (1986), a film about a bike messenger. The four hundred dollars to six hundred dollars a week that Vails made as a bike messenger kept him in racing gear and helped him support two daughters, Shanequa and Imani, whom he had fathered by the age of sixteen with Sharon McCrimmon. In 1981, Nelson and Sharon married; they divorced in 1985.

Along with a blossoming road-racing career, Vails began to compete in track events at the Kissena Velodrome on Long Island and at the Trexlertown Velodrome in northeastern Pennsylvania. His powerful, compact build and fearless demeanor made him a natural for track racing, a sport that features bicycles with no brakes and only one directly driven gear. Among the close-knit fraternity of track riders, Vails became known as "the Cheetah" because of his hugely muscular thighs and lightning-quick acceleration. Of all the track events, Vails excelled at the matched sprint, the track's glamour event, a 1000-meter high-speed chess match on wheels. Only the last 200 meters are timed, so the bulk of the race unfolds as a strategic battle of wits, the two riders stalking each other up and down the banked oval of the track, feinting quick bursts of speed, but mostly vying for position. The rear rider has the tactical advantage, so each rider tries to keep the other in front by riding slowly; sometimes one or both come to a complete halt. As the riders approach the 200-meter mark, all the strategic bobbing and weaving gives way to a brute display of power when one rider jumps and the other responds in an explosive sprint to the finish line. The strongest rider usually wins, but among equally matched riders, the rear rider enjoys the advantage of the front's slipstream and, if he times his move right, can slip around the front rider before the finish. The best sprinters today can cover 200 meters in a little over 10 seconds, which translates to a top speed better than 45 mph.

Vails became the New York State sprint champion in 1980, which qualified him to compete in the U.S. National Track Championships in San Diego, California. He arrived at the nationals as a relative unknown, but he quickly proved that he belonged. He failed to qualify for the quarterfinals, but his speed was unmatched. He set the quickest 200-meter time at 11.5 seconds, which earned him a spot on the United States national team in 1982 and an invitation to attend the new Olympic training camp in Colorado Springs, Colorado, that the United States Cycling Federation (USCF), the governing body of American bicycle racing, had opened to ready a team for the 1984 Olympics in Los Angeles.

After the bicycle craze of the late nineteenth and early twentieth centuries, when the public flocked to watch track racing in major American cities and at the portable wooden tracks that toured the county fair circuit, the sport lost much of its audience. The public took to automobiles, and young athletes who might have followed in the tracks of such cycling heroes as world champion sprinter Major Taylor instead looked to team sports and motorized racing. American bicycle racing dwindled to an amateur sport; any rider wanting a career had to go to Europe. But starting in the 1960s the sport began to revive in America, and by the late 1970s a critical mass of talented cyclists was beginning to compete successfully at the world level. The USCF worked to better the sport by establishing the Olympic training camp and hiring a hard-nosed, Polish-born coach named Eddie Borysewicz to mold the domestic talent into a formidable Olympic team. Vails moved to Colorado Springs to live and train at the compound; he was one of two cyclists to earn a spot to compete in the Olympic matched sprints. He and teammate Mark Gorski made it to the Olympic finals, where Gorski edged Vails for the gold medal, with Vails earning the silver.

Vails's Olympic success brought him both press coverage and lucrative opportunities like product endorsements. He made a good story: black kid from Harlem strikes Olympic silver. But his success also brought its share of distractions and temptations, and much of the press coverage focused on Vails enjoying the good life. He made no excuses for parlaying his Olympic success into a good lifestyle. "It was my time. I sold a lot of products; I made a lot of money," he says, pausing before adding, "and I made a lot of other people money." What the press didn't see, he insists, was his continued dedication to the sport. "Everyone saw Nelson at the party with a beer in his hand," he related, "but no one was around at six the next morning when I was awake checking my pulse getting ready to go on another training ride" (personal interview with subject, 2004).

Vails continued to ride well. At the 1985 World Championships in Bolzano, Italy, he won a gold medal in the track tandem event. Vails, his tandem partner Les Barczewski, and the future three-time Tour de France winner Greg LeMond were the only American riders to win medals at the World Championships that year. Vails failed to medal at the 1986 event, but his continued success at the national level earned him an invitation back to Colorado Springs to try out for the 1988 Olympic team. He got beaten in the sprint semifinals by Mark Gorski, his nemesis in 1984. With only an outside chance of making the team, he announced that he had a professional contract waiting for him and was going to turn pro.

Turning pro in cycling requires competing outside of the United States; there is more money, better competition, and better organization in Europe and Japan. For the professional track rider, the main event in Europe is the Six-Day circuit. Six-Day races are popular indoor track events staged on indoor wooden board tracks throughout Europe from October through March. They feature sixteen two-rider teams racing each night for six days in races called madisons, named after Madison Square Garden in New York City, where they began in the 1890s. Between madisons, race promoters stage exhibition events like matched sprints and the flying 200 meters, in which each rider approaches a timed 200 meter stretch of track with a flying start. From 1988 to 1995, Vails competed on the Six-Day circuit in these speciality events, setting many track records in the flying 200 meters.

Vails's success on the European track circuit led to an invitation to Japan in 1990 to compete in an event called Keirin. Keirin is a professional track-racing circuit that tours Japan every spring with great fanfare. It is a much-anticipated event that features 2,025-meter, multi-lap races among nine riders on which spectators wager. "It's just like horse racing," notes Vails. "We're like jockeys, but on bikes." With a slate of ten races a day over a three-day period, Keirin can be very lucrative for a good rider; Vails sometimes made up to $3,500 in one race. After his first Keirin season, Vails earned enough money to buy a house in Indianapolis, Indiana. Vails had moved to Indianapolis in 1988 with his second wife, Susan Shevlot, to be near the Major Taylor Velodrome, a world-class venue where he and many of the national team riders lived and trained during the off-season. Vails fathered his third child with Susan in 1992, a daughter named McKenzie. His marriage to Susan lasted until 1995.

Vails did well enough in Europe and on the pro circuit in the United States over the next four seasons to be invited back to ride Keirin each year. That was an honor bestowed to only a select few non-Japanese riders. "You just don't go over to Japan to ride Keirin," says Vails. "You have to be invited." Scouts attend European races to assess Keirin talent; Vails was first spotted in France during the 1990 professional world championships.

In 1995 Vails retired from racing, moved to Colorado Springs, and assumed a variety of non-cycling jobs, including sales and promotions in the sportswear industry and as a gate agent and flight attendant for SkyWest Airlines. Vails fathered his fourth child and first son, Trevor, with girlfriend Mary Quinn in 1998. Though he continued to ride recreationally, he claimed that his efforts to remain in the sport as a coach or instructor at the national team level were met with indifference by the USCF.

Nelson Vails's career is often compared with America's other famous black bicycle racer, Major Taylor. Both competed in a sport in which the participants and spectators are largely white; both were stars on the track and notable personalities off. But in contrast to Taylor's experiences with racial prejudice at the turn of the twentieth century, both in society at large and especially in competition, Vails claims he never felt singled out because of his race.

If Vails escaped racial prejudice, he didn't escape the fate of most American sports heroes: fleeting celebrity. Many in the cycling press predicted great things for Vails after the 1984 Olympics; his personal charm and good looks were a winning combination that just might vault him into the sports-marketing big leagues. But after a string of product endorsements directed mostly at the sport of cycling, a few stints as color commentator for televised bike races

on CBS and ESPN, and marketing a line of beach shorts under the Quicksilver name, Vails's celebrity faded in spite of his continued racing success. His relative obscurity reflects the tendency of the American public to be indifferent to the sport of cycling and to many of its heroes.

FURTHER READING
Unless otherwise cited, quotations in this essay are taken from a personal interview of Vails conducted by the author in 2004.
Drake, Geoff. "Nelson Vails On: Riding in Traffic," *Bicycling* (Dec. 1991).
Gorski, Mark. "Mark Gorski's Olympic Journal," *Bicycle Guide* (Autumn 1984).
Martin, Scott. "The Heroes of '84: What Happened to the Olympic Medal Winners Who Elevated American Cycling from Obscurity?" *Bicycling* (Jan. 1996).

DOUGLAS FLEMING ROOSA

Vaird, Lauretha (4 Aug. 1952–2 Jan. 1996), police officer, was born in Philadelphia, Pennsylvania, the only daughter of five children of Melvin Vaird, a street vendor of janitorial supplies, and Laura Vaird, a homemaker. Lauretha Vaird was the family's eldest child, and the tough-yet-compassionate guidance she provided at home would later prove to be an asset in her law-enforcement career. Her brother Levin described her as "the shining star of the family.... She helped raise us, and straightened us out when we got in trouble or didn't do what we were supposed to do" (telephone interview with Levin Vaird, 20 March 2007).

Before joining the police force, Vaird was a teacher's assistant in the Philadelphia's public-school system, working at Pickett Middle School and the Kinsey School from 1977 to 1985. In 1985 she applied for a job as a police officer, subsequently passing all the required exams and completing a rigorous training course at the Philadelphia Police Academy.

Vaird joined the Philadelphia Police Department in one of the most challenging periods in its history. The department had hired its first black officer in 1881 and its first female officers by the 1950s. By the late 1960s African American officers had become an important part of the force. Although the hiring of black officers became more prevalent by the 1970s, discrimination existed within the force itself, and was further manifested by the manner in which white officers dealt with Philadelphia's black citizens. Black officers found it difficult to gain the respect of white precinct sergeants and were often assigned duties well below their qualifications; while on the streets it was not uncommon for white officers, when arriving on the scene of a crime, to give precedence to the statements of white witnesses, and at times ignore completely statements by black witnesses (Rashid, 1).

By the late 1970s and throughout much of the 1980s, the Philadelphia Police Department's racial issues came to a head, and its relations with Philadelphia's black population suffered. The department's reputation was damaged primarily because of a series of incidents involving the radical MOVE group, a small organization whose members, mainly African Americans, were both armed and vocal in expressing their radical ideology, which included a back-to-nature ideal, and was essentially anarchist, anti-government, and anti-technology. The first confrontation with the group came in 1978, resulting in the death of a police officer and the subsequent arrest of nine MOVE members. The city became further polarized after the murder of Police Officer Daniel Faulkner on 9 December 1981. MOVE member MUMIA ABU-JAMAL was arrested for the murder and his subsequent conviction and death sentence would spark a firestorm of controversy that remained unresolved more than twenty-five years after the event. Matters with MOVE came to a head on 13 May 1985, during the administration of the city's first black mayor, W. WILSON GOODE. On that day police confronted MOVE at their Osage Avenue complex, dropping explosives by helicopter on the building's rooftop and starting a fire that destroyed more than sixty houses in an entire city block. When the fight ended, eleven MOVE members, including five children, had been killed, and a rift opened between the police and the city's African American community that would take years to ameliorate.

It was not long after this event that Lauretha Vaird decided to join the force. In 1986 Vaird became an officer of the law and was assigned badge number 5897 as one of Philadelphia's "finest." Unfortunately, few details of her career are available; fellow police officer Myra Jones said Vaird "was like the mother of us all" (*Jet*, 29 Jan. 1996, 1), while an anonymous fellow police officer later stated that Vaird "was the officer that was standing in the rain handling an auto accident, the officer that helped resolve family disturbances during the holidays, the officer who told kids to stay away from drugs and drove sick persons to the hospital.

She was the officer who helped children cross the street to go to school, that officer you saw sitting in a parking lot on patrol during a midnight shift.... Everyone knew Officer Vaird, she was the image of a true Police Officer and I am proud to say I knew her and worked with her" (Reflections, Officer Down Memorial Page). Lauretha Vaird's brother Levin recalled that "when people were arrested [Lauretha] would talk to them, sometimes right through the cell bars, and would counsel them and try to set them straight and get them help if they needed it" (telephone interview with Levin Vaird, 20 March 2007).

By New Year's Day 1996 Vaird was an experienced officer with nine years of service working out of the Twenty-fifth Precinct headquarters on Front and Westmoreland Streets. One day later, she was called by silent alarm to a bank robbery in progress at the PNC Bank branch in Feltonville and was the first officer to enter the bank. She was shot in the abdomen by a man who was hiding behind the door. She died within hours. Three suspects were eventually caught and tried for the crime; one, Christopher Roney, was sentenced to death.

Vaird was the first Philadelphia female police officer to die while attempting to prevent a crime. A communicant of the Mount Airy Church of God and Christ, she was given a hero's funeral and was buried in Ivy Hill Cemetery. Vaird was either divorced or never married; she was survived by two sons, Michael Cesar Vaird and Steven Vaird. In May 2007 the Boy's and Girl's Club in the Feltonville neighborhood of Philadelphia where she gave her life in the line of duty was renamed in her honor, and a local scholarship was established in her name in 2007.

FURTHER READING

Personal details about Lauretha Vaird's life were provided courtesy of her brother, Levin Vaird, in a telephone interview conducted on 20 March 2007.

Officer Down Memorial Page. "Lauretha Vaird, Reflections," http://www.odmp.org/reflections.php?oid= 14699.

Rashid, Nazia. *The Searches and Struggles of a Black Man in the 1960's.* http://www.newarkmetro.rutgers.edu/essays/displayphp?id=96.

Obituary: "Fellow Officers, Family, Friends Mourn Slain Philadelphia Police Officer Lauretha Vaird, Killed in the Line of Duty-Obituary," *Jet*, 29 Jan. 1996.

GLENN ALLEN KNOBLOCK

Valentine, Kid Thomas (3 Feb. 1896–16 June 1987), jazz trumpet player, was born Thomas Valentine in Reserve, Louisiana, the son of Peter Ferdinand "Pete" Valentine, an early jazz trumpet player, and Sarah (maiden name unknown). Pete Valentine had been a member of the Pickwick Brass Band, which played mostly for dances and other occasions in the Saint John the Baptist parish hall. Pete was proficient on most of the brass instruments in the band and also served as keeper of the instruments for the group, so Thomas had an opportunity to learn to play several instruments. By age ten Thomas was playing the valve trombone, but he switched to the cornet as his preferred instrument. In addition to performing with his father in the Pickwick Brass Band, Thomas also performed with Edmond, Robert, and Edward Hall, members of a well-known musical family in the area. By 1915 Thomas had formed a band called the Niles, named for the medicine sold by a local druggist who booked the band, and he was playing in several other bands around the New Orleans area.

Around 1923 Valentine moved to Algiers, a suburb of New Orleans. There he played with Elton Theodore's band at the Beleville Gardens, a dance pavilion for whites in Gretna, and at several New Orleans clubs. Theodore had been a banjo player in the Pickwick Band in Reserve, and after he migrated to Gretna to form his own band, Valentine joined him there. In Algiers, Valentine also studied with Manuel Manetta, a leading local music teacher, and after a few years Valentine became the leader of Theodore's band. Valentine worked with Jack Carey's band for less than a year and then, around 1926, formed his own band, the Algiers Stompers, to play in the dance halls and hotels in New Orleans. By this time Valentine had developed a unique jazz style characterized by a rough, guttural tone, raucous rhythmic punctuations of repeated notes, a full vibrato, and the use of various mutes and plungers—an exciting "stomp" style that earned him a devoted audience.

By 1936 Valentine began playing in Marrero at the Moulin Rouge Club, and he developed a strong relationship with Specks Rodriguez, who owned the club and several other dance halls in New Orleans. The Algiers Stompers performed as the house band at the Moulin Rouge for more than twenty years. In 1951 Valentine made his first recordings using local musicians, including Emile Barnes on clarinet and Harrison Barnes on trombone. Then he began recording with the Algiers Stompers and by 1954 had issued many popular recordings.

The rehearsals of Valentine's band often drew crowds of admirers, as did the frequent after-hours jam sessions of the local musicians that followed the rehearsals. In addition, Larry Borenstein hired Valentine and other musicians to perform at his art gallery in the late 1950s. These venues led to the idea of establishing a public forum featuring jazz, and Borenstein opened Preservation Hall in New Orleans in 1961. In 1963 Valentine and the clarinetist GEORGE LEWIS took the Preservation Hall band on tour throughout the United States. The band, with different personnel and under the leadership of Valentine and Lewis, also toured Japan in 1964 and 1965 and Europe in 1967. They performed at the Newport Jazz Festival in 1970, then toured throughout Japan, Australia, Canada, and Europe in 1971. In 1979 a tour of the Soviet Union was arranged by the U.S. State Department's Cultural Presentation Division. The band played in Tbilisi, Donetsk, Moscow, and Leningrad to enthusiastic audiences.

Though the personnel often changed, the band always remained true to its New Orleans roots and was known alternately as the Algiers Stompers or the Preservation Hall Jazz Band, according to its performing venue. After a crippling bout with the flu in 1984, Valentine found it difficult to continue playing, and his career waned. He died in New Orleans after a series of illnesses. His wife, Maggie Fleming Valentine, died in 1982. They had two daughters and two sons.

Valentine developed a robust roughhouse style of trumpet playing that featured extreme contrasts, from exciting blasts of musical force to poignant and subtle emotional renderings of gospel tunes, always delivered with a harsh, untempered tone. His style contrasted with the polished playing of the influential LOUIS ARMSTRONG, but like Armstrong, Valentine was a strong, disciplined, and inspiring leader. Valentine's best recordings include the LP albums *Kid Thomas' Algiers Stompers* (1951), *Kid Thomas at the Moulin Rouge* (1956), *Kid Thomas at Kohlman's Tavern* (1968), and *Kid Thomas 1981* (1981).

FURTHER READING

De Vore, Charles. "The True New Orleans Sound of Kid Thomas Valentine," *Mississippi Rag* 1, no. 4 (1974).

Obituaries: *Jazz Journal International* (Sept. 1987); *New York Times*, 19 June 1987; *New Orleans Times-Picayune*, 18 June 1987.

This entry is taken fr`om the *American National Biography* and is published here with the permission of the American Council of Learned Societies.

STEPHEN M. FRY

Van Engle, Dorothy (14 Aug. 1916–10 May 2004), actress, seamstress, and model, was born Donessa Dorothy Van Engle in the Harlem neighborhood of New York City to Fred Van Engle, a tailor, and Mynita Duncan. Her mother was born in Massachusetts to Willis and Mabelle Duncan, with whom the family lived at the time of Van Engle's birth. Her father, Fred Van Engle, was born on the island of Saint Kitts and worked as a tailor.

Van Engle was born during the Harlem Renaissance and lived in the same apartment building as the boxer JACK JOHNSON and the actress LENA HORNE, with whom she was friends. The Harlem Renaissance represented a creative boom and a period of recognition for African Americans in music, art, literature, politics, dance, theater, and business for those from and living in Harlem, considered the cultural haven for African Americans. In her Harlem neighborhood Van Engle mingled with celebrities and entertainment executives. Her raw talent, combined with these circumstances, led to her eventual career in entertainment.

Van Engle's beauty led her to an early career in modeling, most notably showcasing clothing and hairstyles in newspaper advertisements. The ads ran during the 1930s and early 1940s, and they were most often for hairpiece and hair-extension products designed for women with thinning or short hair. Ironically, Van Engle had naturally long hair that required no growth aid but that made for attractive photographs for companies advertising the use of their products. During this time Van Engle also worked as a seamstress, perhaps to supplement her modeling income.

Van Engle's stepfather, Arville "Snoopie" Harris, was the key to her future success. Harris was a talented musician who played the saxophone and clarinet. He worked with various musicians of the day, including CLARENCE WILLIAMS, Jack Butler, LeRoy Smith, CLAUDE HOPKINS, Maurice Rocco, and, most notably, CAB CALLOWAY. While playing saxophone in Cab Calloway's band, Harris mixed with many other well-established entertainers and entertainment executives. One of those acquaintances was OSCAR MICHEAUX, one of the few black independent filmmakers of the era. Produced under the Micheaux Book and Film Corporation, the director's "race films" contained messages with distinct racial undertones, geared toward eradicating the stereotypical depiction of African Americans in cinema. The characters in his productions often played educated and complicated characters who addressed contemporary themes.

Van Engle, a talented, intelligent, and distinguished actress, played an integral part in many Micheaux productions. She appeared in several of his movies during the 1930s and 1940s, including *Harlem after Midnight* (1934) and *Murder in Harlem* (1935), a murder mystery and love story in which she portrayed the character Claudia Vance. Van Engle also appeared in *Swing!* (1938) and *God's Stepchildren* (1938) for Micheaux. In addition to acting, Van Engle was personally responsible for sewing her costumes and was regarded as an accomplished actress and seamstress at the same time. Van Engle is still thought of as one of the most talented and beautiful black actresses of her time.

Near the end of her brief acting career, in approximately 1940, Van Engle met and married Herbert Hollon, a Harlem building superintendent. Shortly afterward she left the film business to raise a family. The Hollons had two sons, Herbert Jr. and Marc. Her husband, Herbert Sr., died in 1992. Van Engle lived in Port Charlotte, Florida (dates unknown). She worked for the Port Charlotte library before moving to Ocala, Florida, where she lived until her death in 2004.

FURTHER READING

Obituaries: *Jet Magazine*, 31 May 2004; *Daily Variety*, 8 June 2004; *New York Times* News Service, 14 May 2004.

NANCY T. ROBINSON

Van Horne, Mahlon (5 Mar. 1840–25 May 1910), clergyman, legislator, and diplomat, was born in Princeton, New Jersey, the oldest surviving child of Mathias and Diana (Oakham) Van Horne. He was educated in the Princeton schools, before enrolling in 1859 at Pennsylvania's Ashmun Collegiate Institute for Colored Youth (renamed Lincoln University in 1866), studying theology, education, Greek, Hebrew, and Latin. In 1868 he became one of the first six students to receive a bachelor's degree from Lincoln University, where he also pursued graduate studies beginning in 1871.

While still a student, Van Horne was married in 1862 to Rachel Ann Huston of Princeton, New Jersey. The couple had four children: daughters Florence V. (Miller) and Louisa S. A., and sons Mahlon H. and Mathias Alonzo Van Horne (Mathias was educated at Howard University and later became Rhode Island's first African American dentist). After being ordained as a minister in 1866, Reverend Van Horne accepted a temporary position in 1867 as principal of the Zion Presbyterian Church School (later the Wallingford School) for black students in Charleston, South Carolina, where he lived for about a year (Clarke, p. 308). After completing his studies at Lincoln University, Van Horne was next appointed to a vacant pastorate in 1868 at the interracial Union Congregational Church in Newport, Rhode Island, where he and his growing family remained for more than a quarter of a century.

A popular figure in Newport and a stalwart Republican, Van Horne became the first African American member of the Newport school committee in the early 1870s, though reportedly in exchange for supporting a Democratic mayoral candidate (Armstead, p. 123). Van Horne served on the school committee for two decades. He also supervised construction of a new church building in 1871, after the old Union Church burned and was demolished.

In March 1883 Van Horne became a ward member of Newport's City Republican Committee. Two years later, he became the first African American elected to the Rhode Island General Assembly, representing Newport in Providence as a Republican for three consecutive terms. He also remained active in Newport civic affairs, fighting tirelessly for civil equality for the city's black residents, and supporting the integration of Newport's public schools, along with his friend and colleague, the businessman and civil rights leader GEORGE T. DOWNING. In 1891 Van Horne was named Newport's most popular minister; he was also active in the Masons, as well as in African American mutual aid societies.

In 1897 a group of influential Rhode Islanders—reportedly including the Republican state committee chairman, state legislators, the attorney general, and five justices of the state supreme court—recommended Van Horne for appointment to federal office by President William McKinley. McKinley agreed, selecting Van Horne as the U.S. consul for Saint Thomas in the Danish West Indies, later to become the U.S. Virgin Islands.

Van Horne and his family lived for the next five years in Charlotte Amalie, the Danish colonial capital, where he won a devoted following among local residents. The American Protective League even petitioned Congress for Van Horne's appointment as territorial governor of the island group, in the event of its proposed purchase by the United States.

In January 1903, however, Van Horne's record was stained by federal charges of incompetence and neglect of duties, involving the alleged mishandling of unspecified sums of money entrusted to the consul's office. Despite pleas by local businessmen and officials for his reappointment, President Theodore Roosevelt decided to remove Van Horne from the post on 31 July 1903. He was replaced as U.S. consul by another African American, CHRISTOPHER H. PAYNE of West Virginia, a minister and lawyer who served until the Virgin Islands were finally acquired by the United States in 1917.

After leaving Saint Thomas, the Reverend Van Horne continued to take a strong interest in Caribbean affairs and remained in the West Indies until his death. He served as a church worker and missionary in Graceland, Antigua. His wife Rachel died there in 1907, as did Van Horne three years later, at age seventy. Both were buried on the island.

Upon his death, Van Horne was described by his hometown newspaper as "a man of excellent education and of great natural intelligence." The *Newport Mercury* (25 June 1910) also praised him as being "in every way one of the leading citizens of Newport" and "one of the leading colored citizens of the state."

FURTHER READING
Armstead, Myra Beth Young. *"Lord, Please Don't Take Me in August": African Americans in Newport and Saratoga Springs, 1870–1930* (1999).
Clarke, Erskine. *Our Southern Zion: A History of Calvinism in the South Carolina Low Country, 1690–1990* (1996).
Obituary: *Newport Mercury*, 25 June 1910.
BENJAMIN R. JUSTESEN

Van Peebles, Melvin (21 Aug. 1932–) filmmaker, writer, and entrepreneur, was born Melvin Peebles in Chicago, Illinois, to Marion Peebles, a tailor. His mother's name is unknown. Melvin graduated from Township High School in Phoenix, Illinois, in 1949 and spent a year at West Virginia State College before transferring to Ohio Wesleyan University in Delaware, Ohio. After graduating with a B.A. in English in 1953, he spent three years in the U.S. Air Force, during which time he met and married Maria Marx. In 1956 they had their first child, Mario, and moved to San Francisco, where Melvin found work as a cable car grip man, an experience he turned

Melvin Van Peebles, filmmaker, writer, activist, and entrepreneur, in 1998. (AP Images.)

into a book, *The Big Heart* (1957). In 1957, with no training or experience, Peebles wrote and directed three short films, *A King, Sunlight,* and *Three Pick Up Men for Herrick.*

Frustrated with the limited financial opportunities available to artists in America, the Peebleses, who now had a second child, Maggan, moved to the Netherlands in 1959. Peebles added "Van" to his surname and began acting with the Dutch National Theater. His marriage, meanwhile, was failing and Maria and the children returned to the United States. Van Peebles moved to Paris, where he scraped together a living doing odd jobs. In 1963 he made another short film, *Cinq cent balles,* and began writing fiction, motivated in large part by a desire to qualify for a union director's card. In 1964 he published his first novel, *Un Ours pour le F.B.I.* (A Bear for the F.B.I. [1968]), and then *Un Américain en Enfer* (An American in Hell), which was released in 1976 as *The True American: A Folk Fable.* A collection of short stories, *Le Chinois du XIV* (1966), and two novellas, *La Permission* (The Leave, 1967), about the repercussions of a brief affair between an African American soldier and a white French woman, and *La Fête à Harlem* (1967), quickly followed. In 1967 Van Peebles adapted *La Permission* into the feature

film, *Story of a Three-Day Pass.* The film premiered at the San Francisco Film Festival, where it won the critics' choice award and landed him a three-picture deal with Columbia Pictures. His first studio film, *Watermelon Man* (1970), a satire about a middle-class white man who wakes up one morning to discover he has become black, proved a mild commercial success.

In late 1970 Van Peebles left Columbia Pictures and invested his talents, $100,000 of his own money, and $50,000 borrowed from his friend BILL COSBY in *Sweet Sweetback's Baadasssss Song* (1970). Van Peebles produced, directed, wrote, edited, scored, and starred in this film, which follows Sweet Sweetback, a sex-show performer on the run in Los Angeles after attacking two white police officers who were beating a young black man. Sweetback was a new kind of black protagonist—an outlaw hero, stoic, urban, sexually powerful, and a skilled street fighter. Unlike other black antiheroes, Sweetback escapes punishment or death in the film.

Like pioneering filmmaker OSCAR MICHEAUX before him, Van Peebles used black actors and crew and marketed the film primarily to black audiences. Like Micheaux, he courted controversy and parlayed threats of censorship into an aggressive marketing campaign. He dedicated the film to "All the Brothers and Sisters Who Have Had Enough of The Man" and ending it with an on-screen warning: "Watch Out. A baad asssss nigger is coming back to collect some dues." When the film received an X rating, Van Peebles used the tag line "rated X by an all-white jury" on print ads and t-shirts. To everyone's surprise, the $500,000 film that had opened in only two theaters grossed $10 million by the end of the year, temporarily toppling *Love Story* from the number one spot at the box office. As Van Peebles told *The New York Times*, "It made five million [dollars] before three white people had seen it."

Sweetback arrived at a moment of tremendous social and political upheaval, with the nation in turmoil from nearly a decade of assassinations (President John F. Kennedy, MEDGAR EVERS, MALCOLM X, MARTIN LUTHER KING JR., and Senator Robert F. Kennedy), racial violence, the escalation of war in Southeast Asia, and a growing antiwar movement at home. Hollywood films were changing quickly too, with the graphic violence of *Bonnie and Clyde* (1967) and *The Wild Bunch* (1969) and iconoclastic films for a new generation, including *The Graduate* (1967), *Easy Rider* (1967), and *Midnight Cowboy* (1967). Van Peebles became a key figure among such American independent filmmakers as John Cassavetes, GORDON PARKS SR., and OSSIE DAVIS. *Sweetback* rejected the politics and social conventions of the black bourgeoisie epitomized by SIDNEY POITIER both on and off screen, insisting instead on an equation of blackness with the ghetto. The film was revolutionary in its insider point of view and its raw, confrontational depiction of class and racial tensions, sex, and violence. *Sweetback's* unique—and much copied—visual aesthetic employed montage, fast-paced editing, jump cuts, multiple exposures, split screens, and written text.

The film unquestionably resonated with black audiences. *Sweetback* "is based on a reality that is Black," wrote African American critic Clayton Riley. "We may not want him to exist, but he does" (*New York Times*, 25 July 1971). HUEY NEWTON lauded the film, and the Black Panthers reputedly made *Sweetback* mandatory viewing. Dueling opinions about the film appeared in both the black and white press. For many, Sweetback proved a corrective to the established Hollywood images of African American men as powerless buffoons or desexualized martyrs. For others, Sweetback seemed an incarnation of the familiar stereotype of the black man as a violent sexual predator. Moviegoers flocked to theaters despite criticism from the NAACP, CORE, and SCLC, complaints from some black nationalists that the film lacked direct political articulation, and concerns from women's groups about Van Peebles's depiction of women. *Sweetback*—along with Gordon Parks's *Shaft*, released only a few months later—inaugurated a spate of imitators targeted directly at black urban audiences. These "blaxploitation films," fifty or sixty of which were made by Hollywood studios in the first half of the 1970s, were characterized by black casts, urban settings, low production values, and an emphasis on violence, sex, and style, but without the overt politics of Van Peebles's film.

In the fall of 1971, with *Sweetback* still playing in many theaters, Van Peebles turned to Broadway with *Ain't Supposed to Die a Natural Death*, adapted from his 1968 LP *Brer Soul*, a jazz-soul-beat poetry fusion. The black-cast musical netted seven Tony Award nominations and ran for 325 performances. Late in the 1971–1972 theater season, Van Peebles mounted a second Broadway musical, *Don't Play Us Cheap*, adapted from *La Fête à Harlem*. This comedy about Satan's helpers dispatched to break up a house party was nominated for a Tony, and in 1973 Van Peebles directed a film adaptation.

Van Peebles's skillful marketing of his soundtrack for *Sweetback* helped open the door to the independent release of film soundtracks. In addition to soundtracks of his films and musicals, Van Peebles produced several other albums in the 1970s, including *As Serious as a Heart Attack* (1971) and *What the … You Mean I Can't Sing* (1974).

After writing the screenplay for the Warner Brothers film *Greased Lightning* (1977), about NASCAR champion WENDELL SCOTT, starring RICHARD PRYOR, Van Peebles started writing for television, penning the TV movie *Just an Old Sweet Song* (1976) and the mini-series *Sophisticated Gents* (1981). He returned to Broadway in 1980 with *Reggae*, and in 1982 he wrote, composed, directed, and starred in *Waltz of the Stork*, a thinly veiled autobiographical musical comedy. In 1983 he wrote and directed *Champeeen!*, a theatrical biography of BESSIE SMITH.

Van Peebles then began another, seemingly unlikely, career as a trader on the New York Stock Exchange. In 1986 he turned his eighteen months on Wall Street into a book, *Bold Money: A New Way to Play the Options Market*.

Van Peebles returned to acting with brief film and television appearances, including *LA Law* (1986), *Jaws: The Revenge* (1987), *Boomerang (1992)*, *Homicide: Life on the Street* (1997), and *The Shining*

(1997), and he won an Emmy Award for his script for the TV movie *The Day They Came to Arrest the Book* (1987). He collaborated with his son Mario on the critical and commercial failure *Identity Crisis* (1989), which Mario wrote and Van Peebles directed. Their book, *No Identity Crisis: A Father and Son's Own Story of Working Together* (1990), was slightly better received. Van Peebles appeared in the Mario-directed projects *Love Kills* (1998), *Gang in Blue* (1996), and *Posse* (1993), and in 1995 he wrote and Mario directed the universally panned film *Panther*. In the 1990s Van Peebles released several albums, including *The Melvin Van Peebles Collection* (1999) and *Ghetto Gothic* (1995), and in 1998 he toured with his cabaret show, *Roadkill Wid' Brer Soul*. In 2000 he wrote, directed, and scored the French-language film *Le Conte du Ventre Plein* (Bellyful).

Van Peebles's impact on film, music, debates about black aesthetics and politics, and especially on the next generation of black filmmakers is unassailable. His appearance as himself in SPIKE LEE's film *Do the Right Thing* (1989) expressed the younger filmmaker's debt. Van Peebles is characteristically blustery about his place in the history of African American cinema: "I'm not the father of Black modern cinema," he explained to George Alexander, "I'm the father of American independent film." Van Peebles has always been his own best salesman, discussing *Sweetback* in both Isaac Julien's blaxploitation documentary *Baadasssss Cinema* (2002) and Spike Lee's documentary *Jim Brown All American* (2002). In 1998 Van Peebles wrote and directed his own narrative on African American film history, *Classified X*. He proved his ability to laugh at himself, though, by playing a character named Sweetback in *The Hebrew Hammer* (2002), a Jewish spoof of blaxploitation films.

In 2003 Van Peebles's career came full circle when his son Mario directed and starred as his father in *How to Get the Man's Foot Outta Your Asss!*, a docudrama based on Van Peebles's book *The Making of Sweet Sweetback's Baadasssss Song* (1971, reprinted 1994). In 2008 Van Peebles directed and starred in *Confessions of a Ex-Doofus-Itchy Footed Mutha*, a film adaptation of *Waltz of the Stork*.

FURTHER READING

Alexander, George. *Why We Make Movies: Black Filmmakers Talk about the Magic of Cinema* (2003).

Guerrero, Ed. *Framing Blackness: The African American Image in Film* (1993).

Tate, Greg. "The MVP of Black Cinema," *Village Voice*, 13 January 2006.

LISA E. RIVO

Van Rensselaer, Thomas (c. 1800–c. 1850), abolitionist, civil rights activist, and journalist, was born a slave and spent the early years of his life in bondage in the Mohawk Valley near Albany, New York. His master was probably a member of Albany's wealthy Van Rensselaer family. He ran away from slavery in 1819 and, although his master circulated handbills and sent slave catchers as far as Canada to recover him, he eluded recapture. Eight years later he became legally free when slavery was finally abolished in New York State. In 1837 he visited and reconciled with his master, prompting the antislavery press to label him "a modern Onesimus," a biblical reference to Philemon 10:16.

While residing in Princeton, New Jersey, in the early 1830s, Van Rensselaer became attracted to the emerging antislavery movement. He settled in New York City by mid-decade, married, joined an independent black church, and established a restaurant that operated on temperance principles. It became a popular local eatery, and he supported himself and his family through this business over the next two decades. He also became prominent in black community affairs, supervising a Sabbath school, serving on the board of the Phoenixonian Literary Society, and helping to found New York's Society for the Promotion of Education among Colored Children. But his greatest achievements came in his antislavery and civil rights work.

He became a devoted follower of the antislavery leader William Lloyd Garrison and adopted his nonresistance philosophy, which eschewed political involvement. He was a founder and vice president of the United Anti-Slavery Society of the City of New York and represented that organization at annual meetings of the American Anti-Slavery Society (AASS). He spoke at anti-colonization meetings and presided at First of August celebrations of the end of slavery in the British Empire. A subscription agent for and contributor to Garrison's *Liberator*, he published letters and editorials in many other antislavery and African American journals. He often hosted visiting antislavery speakers at his home. Like many free blacks in the North, he regularly faced racial discrimination and was denied admittance to theaters, restaurants, hotels, and public resorts. On one occasion he was forced to spend the night on the deck of a steamboat after having paid for first-class accommodations. Van Rensselaer challenged such treatment in print and publicly attacked officials such as the city recorder Richard Riker, who had labeled blacks a criminal people. On another occasion, when the abolitionist Lewis Tappan unsuccessfully tried to have him appointed to an office in the city's Free Church, he sparred with the popular evangelist Charles G. Finney, who openly criticized the effort. In the latter part of the 1830s he challenged the federal fugitive slave law and served as a member of the executive committee of the New York Committee of Vigilance, which aided and protected hundreds of runaway slaves in the city.

After the American antislavery movement divided over the question of political involvement and other matters in 1840, Van Rensselaer sought to heal the breach, attempting to rally New York blacks behind Garrison while seeking to maintain good relations with political abolitionists. He published an open letter "to Colored Abolitionists" in the New York–based *Colored American*, calling for an end to the discord. But his opposition to antislavery political organizations, in particular the nascent Liberty Party, brought harsh personal attacks about racial discrimination at his restaurant, backsliding on temperance, and playing billiards on the Sabbath. So too did his editorial in the *Colored American*, which described his own race as a "proslavery and priest-ridden people" (*Colored American*, 29 May 1841). Eventually he established the Manhattan Anti-Slavery Society to sustain local Garrisonians. One of the few New York blacks to remain in the American Anti-Slavery Society, he served from 1840 to 1843 on the organization's executive committee. He continued to speak and preside at antislavery meetings and condemned the Mexican War. Ultimately concern about racial discrimination trumped his opposition to politics and in 1846 he joined the campaign for equal suffrage in New York State. He also represented local blacks at race conventions, including the 1847 National Convention of Colored People at Troy, New York, where he urged African American leaders to establish an independent bank for the race. Named to a committee to address the best means for abolishing slavery and racial prejudice in the United States, he and his colleagues called on members of their race to "*agitate!* AGITATE! AGITATE!!! till our rights are restored and our Brethren are redeemed from their Cruel chains" (Bell, *1847*, 14).

In January 1847, after more than a decade as a contributor to the antislavery press, Van Rensselaer joined Willis Hodges, a free black from Virginia, in establishing the *Ram's Horn*, a New York–based antislavery weekly. Initiated in response to racist editorials in the city's white newspapers, it may have been the most militant black newspaper of the antebellum period. It openly called for slave rebellion. The radical abolitionist John Brown supported the paper financially and contributed several essays, including "Sambo's Mistakes," a biting commentary on the alleged lack of militancy among northern free blacks. Hodges edited the journal for more than a year while, as business manager, Van Rensselaer raised funds and recruited subscriptions to keep the paper afloat. At one point the paper reached 2,500 subscribers. In early 1848 he bought Hodges's interest in the paper, assumed the mantle of editorship, and sustained it for a few months at his own expense. Although regular publication ended in July, he announced that he was moving it to Toronto, Canada. That apparently never took place, but a few scattered issues were published in late 1849 in Philadelphia, Pennsylvania.

Van Rensselaer was already quite aged when the *Ram's Horn* ended publication. FREDERICK DOUGLASS observed that he had "become hoary in the cause of freedom" (*North Star*, 11 Feb. 1848). Even so, he remained engaged in public life. Convinced that the emergence of the Free Soil Party offered a political opportunity for antislavery advocates to sway public policy, he abandoned nonresistance and backed the Free Soil presidential candidate Martin Van Buren in the election of 1848. He even wrote to Van Buren, offering his assistance in organizing African American support for the Free Soil ticket. This brought sharp criticism from Gerrit Smith and other political abolitionists in the Liberty Party. Van Rensselaer later participated in public protests against the Fugitive Slave Act of 1850. As the nation careened toward civil war, he spoke against disunion at annual meetings of the AASS.

In spite of his activism and his reputation as a restaurateur, Van Rensselaer's personal life remains an enigma. He is not listed in the U.S. census nor in most other public records. He disappeared from public life in 1855 and died sometime during the following decade. In the late nineteenth century, a pioneering historian of the African American press remembered him as an "undaunted advocate of the equal rights" of his race (Penn, 65).

FURTHER READING

Bell, Howard Holman, ed. *Minutes of the Proceedings of the National Negro Conventions, 1830–1864* (1969).

Hodges, Willis Augustus. *Free Man of Color: The Autobiography of Willis Augustus Hodges*, ed. Willard B. Gatewood (1982).

Penn, I. Garland. *The Afro-American Press and Its Editors* (1891).

Ripley, C. Peter, et al., eds. *The Black Abolitionist Papers, 1830–1865*, 5 vols. (1985–1992).

ROY E. FINKENBINE

Vanderpool, Jacob (fl. 1851), businessman, saloon owner, victim of exclusion code, was one of the few African Americans living in nineteenth-century Oregon. He also has the distinction of being the only person in the territory of Oregon to have been found guilty of the crime of being black and to have been expelled from his home. Nothing is known about his family or childhood and the only official recorded trace of his history still extant is a legal case mentioned in a local newspaper in Salem, Oregon, and in the transcript of his trial. His name did not appear in the 1850 Oregon Census.

The forces of racism common in the eastern United States followed settlers on their journey to the Pacific coast. Vanderpool is almost totally invisible in Oregon's recorded history. Except for the work of Elizabeth McLagan, his name scarcely appears in modern histories of African Americans or in histories of the western United States. Although the antebellum population of African Americans west of the Mississippi was very small, the laws controlling their behavior, limiting their enfranchisement, and preventing their immigration were severe and almost universal. Vanderpool fell victim to an exclusion code that had been put into law by the Oregon territorial government in 1849. The territorial legislature of Oregon enacted its first exclusion code in 1844 but repealed it in 1845 due to questions about enforcement; in 1849 an exclusion code was passed and maintained within the territorial laws. Voting and other civil rights were denied to Asians, Hawaiians, as well as to blacks and (explicitly) mulattos. The first exclusion code (on which the 1849 codes were modeled) included the following clauses:

> That when any free negro or mulatto shall have come to Oregon, he (or she as the case may be), if of the age of eighteen or upward, shall remove from and leave the country within the term of two years for males and three years for females from the passage of this act, and that if any free negro or mulatto shall here after come to Oregon, if of the age aforesaid, he or she shall quit and

leave the country within the term of two years for males and three years for females from his or her arrival in the country. (McLagen, 185)

On 20 August 1851 Vanderpool was arrested on suspicion of violating Oregon's exclusion code. Why Vanderpool was chosen from the tiny black population of fifty-four people recorded in Oregon's 1850 Census is not known. In fact, from court records it is known that he was a successful and seemingly prosperous business owner in Salem. Vanderpool was found guilty of residing in the Oregon Territory in violation of the exclusion code; after this decision was made, Vanderpool does not appear in Oregon's records. What happened to him, his family (if he had one), and his property is not known. While Vanderpool's case is intriguing, it is also significant as an example of the racial antipathies that existed in the American West and the legal and extralegal methods employed to maintain uniform whiteness. Racially biased exclusion was a national issue by the 1850s with Bleeding Kansas one example of the political and philosophical debate about the place of black people (slave or free) in the new Western territories and states. In the east, the focus of exclusion laws was on colonization and elimination of free black populations that already existed in these areas (there were laws that required freed slaves to leave the state in which he or she resided); in the west, the emphasis was on preempting the migration of black people, free or enslaved, into the "new" territories.

The exclusion of people on the basis of race was not limited to those of African descent, as is clear from Oregon's Constitution, which was ratified in 1859. The following passage from Article II, Section 6 of Oregon's official governing document explicitly states: "No Negro, Chinaman, or Mulatto shall have the right of suffrage." Even more revealing is that this section was not repealed until 28 June 1927. Many western states attempted to exclude Asians, Pacific Islanders, and blacks well into the twentieth century. The original inhabitants of Oregon (and the rest of the American West) did not fare any better. Almost from the beginning of Caucasian-Native American interactions (often through warfare), white settlers saw the indigenous peoples as an economic and political threat. The exclusion of blacks, mulattos, Asians, and all other nonwhite peoples was predicated on the "problems" that these people of color were seen to represent. And with the rampant racial prejudice stemming from the Atlantic states, there was an almost countrywide exclusion of non-Europeans. Although some of these (successful) efforts at legally implementing white privilege are well known and often included in school curricula, the early and significant case of Jacob Vanderpool is a rarely told tale.

FURTHER READING

Douthit, Nathan. *Uncertain Encounters: Indians and Whites at Peace and War in Southern Oregon 1820s–1860s* (2002).

McLagan, Elizabeth. *A Peculiar Paradise: A History of Blacks in Oregon, 1788–1940* (1980).

Taylor, Quintard. *In Search of the Racial Frontier: African Americans in the American West 1528–1990* (1998). http://bluebook.state.or.us/state/constitution/OGConstitution/ORConstitution/OriginalHeading. htm http://www.endoftheoregontrail.org/slavery.html.

TIMOTHY J. MCMILLAN

James Vanderzee Vanderzee's portrait "Wedding Day, Harlem, 1926." (Library of Congress.)

VanDerZee, James Augustus Joseph (29 June 1886–15 May 1983), photographer and entrepreneur, was born in Lenox, Massachusetts, the second of six children of John VanDerZee and Susan Elizabeth Egberts. Part of a working-class African American community that provided services to wealthy summer residents, the VanDerZees (sometimes written Van Der Zee or Van DerZee) and their large extended family operated a laundry and bakery and worked at local luxury hotels. James played the violin and piano and enjoyed a bucolic childhood riding bicycles, swimming, skiing, and ice fishing with his siblings and cousins. He received his first camera from a mail-order catalogue just before his fourteenth birthday and taught himself how to take and develop photographs using his family as subjects. He left school that same year and began work as a hotel waiter. In 1905 he and his brother Walter moved to New York City.

James was working as an elevator operator when he met a seamstress, Kate Brown. They married when Kate became pregnant, and a daughter, Rachel, was born in 1907. A year later a son, Emile, was born but died within a year. (Rachel died of peritonitis in 1927.) In addition to a series of service jobs, VanDerZee worked sporadically as a musician. In 1911 he landed his first photography-related job at a portrait studio located in the largest department store in Newark, New Jersey. Although he was hired as a darkroom assistant, he quickly advanced to photographer when patrons began asking for "the colored fellow." The following year VanDerZee's sister Jennie invited him to set up a small studio in the Toussaint Conservatory of Art, a school she had established in her Harlem brownstone. Convinced that he could make a living as a photographer, VanDerZee wanted to open his own studio, but Kate was opposed to the venture. This fundamental disagreement contributed to the couple's divorce in 1917.

VanDerZee found a better companion and collaborator in Gaynella Greenlee, a woman of German and Spanish descent who, after marrying VanDerZee in 1917, claimed to be a light-skinned African American. That same year the couple opened the Guarantee Photo Studio, later the GGG Photo Studio, on West 135th Street, next door to the Harlem branch of the New York Public Library. This was the first of four studio sites VanDerZee would rent over the next twenty-five years. With his inventive window displays and strong word of mouth within the burgeoning African American community, VanDerZee quickly established himself as Harlem's preeminent photographer.

By the early 1920s VanDerZee had developed a distinct style of portrait photography that emphasized narrative, mood, and the uniqueness of each image. Harlem's African American citizens—couples, families, co-workers, and even family pets—had their portraits taken by VanDerZee. With a nod to Victorian photographers, he employed a range of props, including fashionable clothes and exotic costumes, and elaborate backdrops (many of which he painted himself) featuring landscapes or architectural elements. Although they appear natural and effortless, VanDerZee's portraits were deliberately constructed compositions, with sitters posed in complex and artful arrangements. "I posed everyone according to their type and personality, and therefore almost every picture was different" (McGhee). VanDerZee made every sitter look and feel like a celebrity, even mimicking popular media images on occasion. In VanDerZee's photographs, sitters appear sophisticated, urbane, and self-aware, and Harlem emerges as a prosperous, healthy, and diverse community. Another characteristic of VanDerZee's portrait work was his creative manipulation of prints and negatives, which included retouching, double printing, and hand painting images. In addition to improving sitters' imperfections, retouching and hand painting added dramatic and narrative details, like tinted roses or a wisp of smoke rising from an abandoned cigarette. VanDerZee often employed double printing—at times using as many as three or four negatives to make a print—to introduce theatrical storytelling elements into his portraits.

Such attention to detail was commercial as well as artistic. VanDerZee never forgot that photography was essentially a commercial venture and that making his patrons happy and his images one of a kind helped business. He regularly took on trade work, creating calendars and advertisements and, in later years, photographing autopsies for insurance companies and identification cards for taxi drivers. But portraits, of both the living and the dead, were VanDerZee's bread and butter. Funerary photography, a practice begun in the nineteenth century and popular in some communities through the mid-twentieth century, was a major part of his business. VanDerZee's daily visits to funeral parlors culminated in his book *Harlem Book of the Dead* (1978). Harlemites of every background hired VanDerZee to document their weddings, baptisms, graduations, and businesses with portraits and on-site photographs. Organizations as diverse as the Monte Carlo Sporting Club, Les Modernes Bridge Club, the New York Black Yankees, the Renaissance Big Five basketball team, MADAME C. J. WALKER's Beauty Salon, the Dark Tower Literary Salon, and the Black Cross Nurses commissioned VanDerZee portraits. Today these photographs serve as an invaluable and unique visual record of African American life during Harlem's heyday.

In the 1920s and 1930s and into the 1940s VanDerZee photographed the African American leaders living and working in Harlem, including the entertainment and literary luminaries of the Harlem Renaissance: BILL "BOJANGLES" ROBINSON, JELLY ROLL MORTON, and COUNTÉE CULLEN; the boxing legends JACK JOHNSON and JOE LOUIS; and the political, business, and religious leaders ADAM CLAYTON POWELL SR. and ADAM CLAYTON POWELL JR., A'LELIA WALKER, FATHER DIVINE, and DADDY GRACE. In a move that anticipated the birth of photojournalism, VanDerZee took to documenting street life and events when he was hired by Marcus Garvey to create photographic public relations material for the Universal Negro Improvement Association (UNIA) in 1924. VanDerZee produced several thousand prints of UNIA parades, rallies, and the fourth international convention, including many of the most reproduced images of Garvey.

Unlike many of its competitors, VanDerZee's studio remained profitable throughout the Depression. After World War II, however, business steadily declined, the result of the popularity of portable cameras, changing aesthetic styles, and the broader financial decline of Harlem as middle-class blacks moved away from the area. In 1945 the VanDerZees purchased the house they had been renting on Lenox Avenue, but by 1948 they had taken out a second mortgage and by the mid-1960s were facing foreclosure. Fighting for his economic survival, VanDerZee worked primarily as a photographic restorer.

The reevaluation of VanDerZee's place in photographic history began with *Harlem on My Mind*, a groundbreaking and controversial 1969 exhibition at the Metropolitan Museum of Art. After being "discovered" by the photo researcher Reginald McGhee, VanDerZee became the single largest contributor to the exhibition, which drew seventy-seven thousand visitors in its first week. Unfortunately, the exhibition's success arrived too late to help the cash-strapped couple, and the VanDerZees were evicted from their Lenox Avenue house the day after the exhibition closed. Gaynella suffered a nervous breakdown as a result and remained an invalid until her death in 1976.

Hoping to resurrect his finances, VanDerZee established the James VanDerZee Institute in June 1969. With McGhee as project director, the institute published several monographs and organized nationwide exhibitions showcasing VanDerZee's photographs alongside work by young African American photographers. In the early 1970s VanDerZee became a minor celebrity, appearing on television, in film, and as the subject of numerous articles. Meanwhile, he found himself living in a tiny Harlem apartment and relying on his Social Security payments, having received little financial support from the VanDerZee Institute. Several benefactors helped VanDerZee in fundraising and in his attempts to wrest control of his photographic collection from the VanDerZee Institute, which in 1977 moved to the Metropolitan Museum of Art.

In 1978 the majority of his photographic materials held by the Metropolitan was transferred to the Studio Museum in Harlem, and in 1981 VanDerZee, who had saved almost every negative he had ever made, sued the museum for ownership of fifty thousand prints and negatives. The dispute was finally settled a year after VanDerZee's death, when a New York court divided the collection between the VanDerZee estate, the VanDerZee Institute, and the Studio Museum.

In 1978 VanDerZee married Donna Mussenden, a gallery director thirty years his junior who physically and spiritually rejuvenated the ninety-two-year-old photographer. Encouraged by Mussenden, VanDerZee returned to portrait photography, and in the early 1980s photographed such prominent African Americans as BILL COSBY, MILES DAVIS, EUBIE BLAKE, MUHAMMAD ALI, OSSIE DAVIS, RUBY DEE, JEAN-MICHEL BASQUIAT, and ROMARE BEARDEN.

James VanDerZee died in 1983, just shy of his ninety-seventh birthday, on the same day he received an honorary doctorate from Howard University. Although he was omitted from Beaumont Newhall's 1982 seminal volume *The History of Photography*, VanDerZee was honored in 2002 by the U.S. Postal Service with a postage stamp bearing his image.

VanDerZee's photographs chronicle African American life between the wars. His images of such landmarks as the Hotel Theresa and the Manhattan Temple Bible Club Lunchroom and of the ordinary drugstores, beauty salons, pool halls, synagogues, and churches of Harlem record the unprecedented migration of black Americans from the South to the North and from rural to urban living. His portraits offer a human-scale account of the New Negro and the Harlem Renaissance and of race pride and self-determination. Documenting the vitality and diversity of African American life, Van DerZee's photographs countered existing popular images of African Americans, which historically rendered black Americans invisible or degenerate. Here, instead, are images testifying to the artistic, commercial, and political richness of the African American community.

FURTHER READING
Haskins, James. *Van DerZee: The Picture Takin' Man* (1991).
McGhee, Reginald. *The World of James Van DerZee: A Visual Record of Black Americans* (1969).
Willis, Deborah. *VanDerZee: Photographer 1886–1983* (1993).
Obituary: *New York Times*, 16 May 1983.

LISA E. RIVO

Vandross, Luther (20 Apr. 1951–1 July 2005), singer, songwriter, and music producer, was born Luther Ronzoni Vandross in New York City, the youngest of four children born to Luther Vandross Sr., an upholsterer, and Mary Ida Vandross, a nurse. The seventh month of Mrs. Vandross's fourth pregnancy became fraught with peril when she was diagnosed with a ruptured appendix, and doctors were uncertain whether she and her unborn baby would survive. Mr. Vandross was asked to choose which life should be saved; fortunately, however, this potentially traumatic decision was not needed, as his wife survived and gave birth to Luther Jr., a healthy baby boy. As early as age three Vandross, who was nicknamed "Ronnie," exhibited an affinity for music. He became interested in the piano, and in 1956 began taking piano lessons. However, his piano instruction was brief because he hid when the piano teacher arrived at the Vandross's apartment. Also in 1956 Vandross's sister, Patricia, joined a doo-wop group, the Crests, and five-year-old Ronnie would disrupt the group's rehearsals in his parents' living room. The Crests recorded several singles, but Vandross's sister left the group before they recorded the hit single "Sixteen Candles." In 1964 Vandross attended a concert at Brooklyn's Fox Theatre in which Dionne Warwick sang "Anyone Who Had a Heart." At that moment Vandross realized that he wanted to mesmerize others the way Warwick captivated him.

While a student at William Howard Taft High School, Vandross formed a singing group, Shades of Jade, with classmates Carlos Alomar, Robin Clark, Anthony Hinton, Diane Sumler, and Fonzi Thornton. The sextet became members of the Apollo Theater's performing youth group Listen, My Brother, and Vandross and the other members occasionally served as the opening act

Luther Vandross accepts his award for favorite soul or R&B male artist at the 29th American Music Awards in Los Angeles, 9 January 2002. (AP Images.)

for headliners at the theater. The group recorded "Listen, My Brother" with "Only Love Can Make a Better World" on the flip side, and they appeared on several of the earliest episodes of *Sesame Street*, the children's show that debuted in 1969. That same year Vandross graduated from high school and matriculated as a liberal arts major at Western Michigan University, where he was the only African American student in his dormitory. At the end of his second semester, Vandross dropped out of college and began pursuing a career in the music industry.

During the 1970s Vandross became increasingly involved in the music world, yet he remained mostly unknown to the general public. In 1972 he wrote "Everybody Rejoice (A Brand New Day)," which was featured in both the 1975 Broadway production of *The Wiz* (an adaptation of *The Wizard of Oz*) and in the 1978 film version starring DIANA ROSS and MICHAEL JACKSON. Delores Hall's album *Hall-Mark* (1973) contained two songs written by Vandross including their duet, "Who's Gonna Make It Easier for Me?" Two years later "Fascination," a song Vandross wrote with David Bowie, was included on Bowie's *Young Americans* album—an album on which Vandross sang backup vocals and did vocal arrangements. During the remaining years of the 1970s Vandross provided either background vocals or vocal arrangements (or both) on at least forty-one albums by such artists as David Bowie, STEPHANIE MILLS, Judy Collins, Bette Midler, Chic, Ringo Starr, ROBERTA FLACK, QUINCY JONES, Barbra Streisand, and Cher. He also sang lead (or shared lead) vocals on approximately nine additional albums. Vandross was the opening

act and backup singer for Bowie's *Young Americans Tour* in 1974, and in 1975 he was a concert backup singer for Midler and Flack. He then formed a group named Luther, and in 1976 and 1977 produced the group's two albums that contained songs written by him. By the end of the decade Vandross's voice was heard by millions; he had become successful singing advertising jingles for a variety of companies such as NBC, AT&T, and Burger King.

In the 1980s and 1990s Vandross produced songs and albums for ARETHA FRANKLIN, DIONNE WARWICK, TEDDY PENDERGRASS, GREGORY HINES, Whitney Houston, and others; he also continued to write songs, sing background vocals, and do vocal arrangements for other artists. However, Vandross had to curtail his work for other singers as his recording career escalated. Vandross sang lead on two hit singles (the title track and "Searching") from Change's 1980 *The Glow of Love* album. The next year *Never Too Much* heralded Vandross's recording debut as a solo artist. The album, produced by Vandross, was certified platinum and catapulted him to R&B superstardom. From 1982 through 2003, eighteen more Vandross albums (including four compilations of hits, a Christmas album, and *Live 2003 at Radio City Music Hall*) were released, and most of these recordings reached platinum status. With the release of the 1989 single "Here and Now," Vandross received even greater recognition as a crossover artist. During his legendary career, Vandross garnered American Music Awards, Soul Train Awards, NAACP Image Awards, and Grammy Awards.

Of Vandross's eight Grammys, four were awarded for his 2003 album *Dance With My Father*, including two for the title song, which won for "Best Male R&B Vocal Performance" and "Song of the Year." The title song is Vandross's tribute to his father, who suffered a diabetic coma and died in 1959. Diabetes also claimed the lives of Vandross's brother and sister, Charles and Patricia, in 1992 and 1993, respectively. In 1999 Vandross's last surviving sibling, Ann, died; her death was attributed to asthma.

In April 2003 Vandross, who struggled with diabetes, hypertension, and weight problems, suffered a stroke and became comatose. His hospital room filled up with cards and letters from his fans, and at least ten thousand people e-mailed messages to him. Vandross's condition worsened after he contracted meningitis and pneumonia. On April 23 Aretha Franklin and JESSE JACKSON led a national prayer vigil for Vandross. He regained consciousness and was transferred to a rehabilitation center in June 2003. In February 2004 he appeared via videotape on the Grammy Awards and sang the opening lines from "Power of Love," his 1991 Grammy-winning hit; a few months later, in May, OPRAH WINFREY's visit with Vandross at the rehabilitation center was broadcast on her television show. However, Vandross never fully recovered from the stroke. He died at the John F. Kennedy Medical Center in Edison, New Jersey.

Luther Vandross, quintessential vocalist and acclaimed songwriter, was among the most commercially and critically successful R&B artists of the 1980s and 1990s. He dominated the R&B landscape in the postdisco and rap eras and helped define R&B's "quiet storm" subgenre.

FURTHER READING

"Luther Vandross," In *Contemporary Black Biography* (2004).

"Luther Vandross," In *Contemporary Musicians* (2004).

Seymour, Craig. *Luther: The Life and Longing of Luther Vandross* (2004).

Obituaries: *New York Times*, 2 July 2005; *Washington Post*, 2 July 2005.

LINDA M. CARTER

VanDuvall, Ernestine Caroline (16 Feb. 1921–25 May 2004), professional cook, singer, and entrepreneur, was born Ernestine Caroline Williams in Nicodemus, Kansas, the seventh of thirteen children of Charles and Elizabeth Williams. The members of the Williams family were descendants of Tom Johnson, a former slave of Vice President Richard M. Johnson of Georgetown, Kentucky. In 1877 the Johnson family migrated and settled in the historic all–African American town of Nicodemus. The tradition of cooks in the Johnson and Williams families dates back to days of slave kitchens, when Vice President Johnson hosted a large barbecue for the French general the Marquis de Lafayette in 1824. His slaves prepared over fifteen hundred pounds of barbecue meat for the event.

Ernestine grew up assisting her mother in the kitchen and learned to cook pies in a wood-burning stove. Her favorite pie to make (as well as to eat) was lemon meringue. The recipe for her lemon meringue pie and other recipes had been passed down for generations; however, Ernestine learned to add her own twist to these dishes.

At the age of nine Ernestine began working for a local restaurateur named Julia Lee. It was at Julia Lee's Café that Ernestine learned how to cook and

to serve the public. Lee taught her how to prepare and fry chickens, make desserts, assist in the preparation of other dishes, clean and iron the linens, set the tables, and dress and decorate the dessert and candy cabinets. Ernestine's favorite job was to sit on an orange crate and peel potatoes. During this time Ernestine became affectionately known as "Chub" because she had always been a chubby girl. However, she once told a customer not to call her Chub while she was working at Julia Lee's Café but to refer to her as Ernestine.

Ernestine was a quick learner and a hard worker, but she did have vices. Lemon drops were her weakness, and she could not resist the urge to suck the sugar off them before they were put in the display cabinet. In Nicodemus many people, adults and children alike, did not know that lemon drops came coated with sugar until Ernestine finally told them when she was older.

During her late teens and early twenties Ernestine and four of her sisters began a singing group called the Williams Sisters. They sang gospel music and played piano all across the state of Kansas, and they frequently traveled to Nebraska and Colorado. After singing off and on together for over forty years, the sisters finally recorded an album in the 1980s.

In Phillipsburg, Kansas, on 22 December 1947 twenty-six-year-old Ernestine married Phillip VanDuvall, also of Nicodemus. They never had children; however, Ernestine helped to rear Phillip's four children from a previous marriage. After they were married, Ernestine moved to Phillip's farm and raised chickens and turkeys for sale. In the years that followed she visited family and friends in Denver, Colorado, and occasionally worked as a cook and maid for several prominent Jewish families.

In the early 1950s, after the death of Ernestine VanDuvall's mother, she and Phillip visited one of his sons then living in Los Angeles. This was their first trip to California, and both loved it so much, they decided to move to Pasadena. Phillip secured a job with the city of Pasadena as a maintenance worker, and Ernestine began doing what she did best, which was cook. They purchased a modest home with a large kitchen, and she began to prepare meals and deliver them to workers at the local car washes. She also began a catering service, offering her home-cooked food to the general public. During this time she catered personal parties for the famous Walt Disney, founder and creator of the Walt Disney Company. Her business grew until she finally opened a small restaurant on Fair Oaks Avenue called Ernestine's Bar-B-Q. She sold not only barbecue but offered an entire "soul food" menu. She hired her two nieces Cheryl and Angela Bates, whom she trained and employed until they graduated from high school.

In the early 1970s Ernestine and Phillip VanDuvall returned to Nicodemus. They purchased a building and began renovating it for a restaurant. In November 1975 the restaurant was finished, and Phillip returned to California to bring back their remaining furnishings. On the return trip he died in a car accident. Although devastated and grief-stricken, Ernestine was determined to move forward and open the restaurant. In the spring of 1975 she opened Ernestine's Bar-B-Q on Highway 24. She catered parties and special events and served many businesses in the area. People came from all over the state to Ernestine's Bar-B-Q, where they ate her famous barbecue and wiped their hands on signature paper towels instead of napkins. She entertained guests by playing the piano and singing gospel and blues songs. Often she had the whole restaurant singing and playing along. Senator Robert Dole of Kansas, among other political leaders, ate at Ernestine's Bar-B-Q before she closed the restaurant in 1985. After closing the restaurant, the aging VanDuvall returned to California.

Pasadena had changed since the VanDuvalls had lived there, and things were not the same for Ernestine without Phillip. After two years in California, she was still depressed and yearning for home, so she returned to Nicodemus in 1987. In 1995 many of her family members and former customers convinced VanDuvall to reopen her restaurant. She did just that in a trailer on the land where she had grown up. She took her nephew Terry Jukes under her tutelage, and they worked together serving barbecue meals. She also began catering for her niece and former cook Angela Bates, who had returned to Nicodemus and opened a tour business. After horse-drawn wagon tours around Nicodemus, tourists were fed VanDuvall's barbecue. Once again, her name and demands for her barbecue were echoed across the state. To say "Nicodemus" was to say "Ernestine's Bar-B-Q."

In 2002 Bates opened an Ernestine's Bar-B-Q in Bogue, five miles from Nicodemus, and in 2003 she opened an Ernestine's Bar-B-Q in Nicodemus. VanDuvall's health was failing, and she had to be admitted to a nursing home. Although she had recently returned from a stay in the hospital, she was determined to be at the grand opening of the second Ernestine's Bar-B-Q restaurant. Also around this time the first annual Nicodemus Jazz and Blues Festival was sponsored by VanDuvall and Bates. Although VanDuvall did make it to the opening, she was confined to a wheelchair and only stayed for a couple of hours. During her brief appearance she greeted customers and sang one of her favorite blues songs, "I Hate to See That Evening Sun Go Down," to a crowd of over four hundred people.

VanDuvall died of kidney failure a year later, leaving a long and proud legacy for the succeeding generation. Before her passing, she saw her barbecue sauce professionally bottled. Ernestine's Bar-B-Q sauce was available for purchase in most stores across Kansas. VanDuvall was buried in the historic Nicodemus cemetery one mile north of the town. With her culinary talents, she left her mark in the pages of Kansas history and in the annals of the western United States.

FURTHER READING

Bates, Angela. *Ernestine's Bar-B-Q Cookbook and Autobiography* (2000).
Obituary: *Hill City Times*, June 2004.

ANGELA BATES

Vann, Robert L. (27 Aug. 1879–24 Oct. 1940), journalist, lawyer, and activist, was born Robert Lee Vann in Hertford County, North Carolina, the son of Lucy Peoples, who cooked for the Albert Vann family, and an unidentified father. His mother named him following a custom from slavery times, giving the last name of her employer to her children. The paternity of Vann, according to his major biographer Andrew L. Buni, is uncertain. It is thought that his father was Joseph Hall, a field worker, but there are no birth records to this effect. There is the possibility that his father was white but not the Vann that his mother worked for.

Vann spent his childhood on the Vann and Askew farms. He entered the Waters Training School in Winston, North Carolina, at age sixteen. In 1901 he enrolled in Virginia Union University in Richmond. After two years Vann moved to Pittsburgh and entered Western University of Pennsylvania (later the University of Pittsburgh), where he was the only African American and wrote for the student newspaper, the *Courant*. Upon graduating in 1906, he entered Western's law school and subsequently passed the Pennsylvania bar examination in 1909. When he set up practice in 1910, Vann was one of only five black attorneys in Pittsburgh. Business was so scarce that he postponed his wedding to

Jessie Matthews by one day in order to take a client to pay the preacher's fee. The marriage took place on 11 February 1910.

Vann soon found himself involved with a fledgling black newspaper, the *Pittsburgh Courier*; using his legal expertise, he had the paper incorporated and became its treasurer. In the fall of 1910 he became the *Courier*'s editor while continuing his law practice. Vann also became involved in Pittsburgh politics and was a leader in calling for civil rights laws and improvements in housing and municipal services. In 1917 he was named fourth assistant city solicitor as a result of his successful opposition to Pittsburgh's political machine in the mayoral election. Vann was also a member of the Committee of One Hundred, a group of black leaders who opposed the United States' entry into World War I.

The 1920s saw Vann making the *Pittsburgh Courier* profitable by focusing on important issues in the black community. He was a firm believer in the uplift ideology of BOOKER T. WASHINGTON and often lauded that black leader's movement in his paper. Though Vann tried several other business ventures without success, one of his most ambitious was a glossy photographic magazine on issues of interest to African Americans, the *Competitor*. Started in 1920, it ran only eighteen months. In the 1930s Vann went on to make the *Pittsburgh Courier* the largest and most popular black newspaper in the country by enlarging the sports section—the paper liked to take credit for "discovering" and promoting the boxer JOE LOUIS—and by sending a reporter to cover the Italian invasion of Ethiopia.

Robert L. Vann's political activity was on the rise through the 1930s. In a speech in Cleveland on 11 September 1933, as the Great Depression ravaged black America, Vann called upon African Americans to turn "their pictures of Lincoln to the wall" and vote for the Democratic Party. By 1936, as Vann had hoped, blacks did move to the Democratic column en masse and would remain there for the rest of the twentieth century. Vann served briefly in Washington, D.C., as a special adviser to the attorney general and on a Commerce Department advisory committee, but his effect on New Deal policies and the Black Cabinet was minimal, and he subsequently returned to Pittsburgh in 1935.

Vann served the remainder of his years fighting for civil rights, especially in the armed forces, and encouraging blacks to make their voting power "liquid" by supporting only those who would give them the fairest economic deal. Vann's health had always been precarious, and in 1940 he died in the Shadyside Hospital, Pittsburgh, after battling cancer.

FURTHER READING
Buni, Andrew L. *Robert L. Vann of the Pittsburgh Courier: Politics and Black Journalism* (1974).

CHARLES PETE T. BANNER-HALEY

Varick, James (1750–22 July 1827), Methodist leader, clergyman, and race advocate, was born near Newburgh in Orange County, New York, the son of Richard Varick. The name of his mother, who was a slave, is unknown. The family later relocated to New York City. With few educational opportunities for African American children growing up in New York City at the time, Varick by some means acquired very solid learning. Around 1790 Varick married Aurelia Jones; they had three girls and four boys. While he worked as a shoemaker and tobacco cutter and conducted school in his home and church, the ministry was clearly his first love. Having embraced Christianity in the historic John Street Methodist Church, Varick served as an exhorter and later received a preacher's license. Racial proscription in the Methodist Episcopal Church during the latter part of the 1700s and early 1800s prevented Varick, ordained a deacon in 1806, from receiving full elder's orders until 1822.

Varick emerged as a major religious leader in New York. The Methodist Episcopal Church, like other mainly white denominations in postrevolutionary America, gradually but clearly abandoned a previous stance toward African American members that was more firmly antislavery and less discriminatory than was to be the case in later years. As a result, a number of black Methodists withdrew from white-controlled congregations to form separate racial churches, some of which eventually united to form independent black denominations by the 1820s. As early as 1796 Varick led a number of African Americans out of the John Street Church and formed a separate black congregation, which in 1800 entered its first building and in 1801 incorporated as the African Methodist Episcopal Church in New York. It was commonly known as Zion Church. Because of legal maneuvering involving the incorporation agreement and the persistent efforts of white ministers to have access to the Zion pulpit, the congregation continued to struggle to attain true autonomy within the Methodist Episcopal Church. Efforts to effect some type of self-governing status under the general rubric of the predominantly white denomination ultimately failed. The Methodist Episcopal Church officials in the New York area were unwilling to depart from normal denominational polity and governance, insisting that the leadership of the church should be selected by the general body.

Varick also helped to organize the John Wesley Church in New Haven, Connecticut, which later connected with Zion and other bodies to form an independent black denomination. The African Methodist Episcopal Zion Church (AMEZ) emerged between 1820 and 1824 under the leadership of Varick and others. Unwilling to remain under the governance of the Methodist Episcopal Church, Varick and his colleagues equally objected to joining the African Methodist Episcopal Church (AME), formed in 1816 and headed by Bishop RICHARD ALLEN (1760–1831) of Philadelphia, Pennsylvania. Apparently, they found Allen's methods too autocratic and were alienated by the AME's attempt to "invade" Zion's domain by establishing congregations and seeking to win over churches to the AME in the New York City area. Varick was elected and consecrated the connection's first superintendent in 1822; he was reelected in 1824 and held the post until his death in 1827. The connection did not affix "Zion" as a part of its official church title until 1848, a move to distinguish it from its major competitor, the older AME. Denominating their chief officer as "superintendent" (although later they employed the terms "bishop" and "superintendent" interchangeably) and having him stand for election every four years, Varick and these Zionites clearly sought to differentiate themselves from the governance of both the Methodist Episcopal and the African Methodist Episcopal churches, including the goal of making provision for greater rights for the laity. Zionites in later decades, under attack from other Methodist bodies for not having an "authentic" episcopacy, began to use the term "bishop" more frequently and, perhaps for this and other reasons, eventually began electing these officers for life terms in 1880.

Varick tirelessly labored on behalf of racial freedom and advancement. In 1808 he delivered the thanksgiving sermon in a celebration in the Zion Church marking the federal government's prohibition of the importation of slaves. He also played a prominent role in William Hamilton's New York African Society for Mutual Relief, organized in 1808. Quite possibly Varick played a role in establishing the first African American masonic lodge in New York State, the Lodge of Freemasonry, or African Lodge, begun in 1812. The Methodist leader also served as one of the first vice presidents of the New York African Bible Society, founded in 1817 and later affiliated with the American Bible Society. Varick joined a group of religious and business leaders in supporting a petition to secure voting rights for blacks at the state constitutional convention held in 1821. The group's effort met with some success. After much discussion the convention approved a limited extension of suffrage conditioned by property ownership, the payment of taxes, and age.

He fought strenuously against the effort of the American Colonization Society (formed in 1816–1817) to repatriate blacks in Africa, joining with others to establish the African Wilberforce Benevolent Society of New York and other organizations to secure racial justice. Varick, along with black leaders such as PETER WILLIAMS JR. and Richard Allen, was instrumental in helping JOHN BROWN RUSSWURM and SAMUEL CORNISH publish in March 1827 the first black newspaper, *Freedom's Journal*, which operated for one year out of the Zion Church. Bishop Varick died in New York several months after the emergence of this newspaper and eighteen days after Independence Day 1827, the deadline set by the state of New York for all of its enslaved residents to attain their freedom. While he has been neglected in scholarly circles, Varick stands in history as one of the major leaders of American religion and independent black Christianity, as well as a testimony to the key role that African American church leaders played in effecting political and economic freedom for the entire race.

FURTHER READING
Walls. William J. *The African Methodist Episcopal Zion Church: Reality of the Black Church* (1974).
This entry is taken from the *American National Biography* and is published here with the permission of the American Council of Learned Societies.

SANDY DWAYNE MARTIN

Vashon, George Boyer (25 July 1824–5 Oct. 1878), educator, writer, and lawyer, was born in Carlisle, Pennsylvania, the son of John B. Vashon, a freeborn African American master barber, and Anne Smith. In 1829 the family moved to Pittsburgh, Pennsylvania, where John Vashon headed a number of self-help efforts in the African American community, including the establishment of a school for black children. Young George Vashon attended this school and later attended public schools in the city. In 1838 he and his classmates established the earliest Juvenile Anti-Slavery Society west of the Alleghenies. Two years later Vashon enrolled at Oberlin College in Ohio, which was one of a few colleges in the United States that then admitted black students. As a college student, he gave orations and participated in the literary society. During the winter term of 1843 Vashon taught school at Chillicothe, Ohio, instructing JOHN MERCER LANGSTON, who became the first African American congressman from Virginia. Returning to college, Vashon graduated with a bachelor's degree in 1844; he was the first black graduate of Oberlin.

After graduation Vashon returned to Pittsburgh, where he worked as a law clerk under Judge Walter Forward and contributed to MARTIN ROBINSON DELANY's African American newspaper, *The Mystery*. In 1847 Vashon completed his law studies and applied for admission to the Pennsylvania bar, but his application was rejected on racial grounds. Disillusioned, he made plans to emigrate to Haiti. While on his way there, however, he stopped in New York City, where in January 1848 he gained admittance to the bar. It is believed that he was the first black admitted to legal practice in New York State. Vashon then refocused his attention on Haiti, sailing there in February 1848. He became the Haitian correspondent for FREDERICK DOUGLASS's newspaper, *The North Star*. Finding the political situation in Haiti in turmoil, Vashon decided to teach at academies in Port-au-Prince and at Collège Faustin, the major Haitian educational institution.

Vashon returned to the United States in 1850. Finding his admittance to the bar blocked again in Pennsylvania, he moved to Syracuse, New York, and entered private law practice. There he participated in antislavery actions and in the Liberty Party. In 1853 he joined Douglass, his own father, and others in calling for the Colored National Convention, which was held in Rochester, New York, in July. Vashon also penned and published an epic poem, "Vincent Ogé," that same year. In 1854 Vashon joined the faculty at New York Central College in McGrawville, New York, as professor of mathematics and belles lettres. Three years later, financial difficulties at the college forced him to resign and return to Pittsburgh, where he became principal teacher at a black public school. While in Pittsburgh, in 1859 he married Susan Paul Smith (SUSAN PAUL VASHON), an assistant teacher at the school; they had seven children.

In late 1863 Vashon became president of Avery College in Alleghany City, Pennsylvania, serving in that capacity until 1867. He remained active in the black convention movement. In 1865 he attended the National Equal Rights League meeting in Cleveland, Ohio, and was elected its corresponding secretary. That same year he was involved with the Pennsylvania Equal Rights League Convention as a speaker and corresponding secretary.

Vashon again sought admission to the Pennsylvania bar in 1867. However, the bar's delay in deciding the matter forced him to apply for several government posts in Washington, D.C., in late 1867. He was appointed as an assistant in the Solicitor's Office of the Freedmen's Bureau, where he served as counsel for freedmen appearing before magistrates' courts. Concurrently he was placed in charge of the night school at Howard University, becoming that institution's first black faculty member, but lack of tuition fees forced the closing of the night school the following year. Vashon went on to work in a variety of positions with the Interior and Treasury departments until the fall of 1873. He simultaneously worked as a teacher examiner for the black schools in the District of Columbia and served on the boards of trustees for various black schools in the district. He contributed essays, poems, and translations to the national black weekly newspaper, *New Era*. Vashon participated in the 1869 National Convention of Colored Men, held in the District of Columbia. In September 1873 Vashon became professor of mathematics at Alcorn University (later Alcorn State University) in Lorman, Mississippi, a position that he retained until his death there of yellow fever.

Vashon's contributions as an early African American educator are significant because of his teaching at several institutions of higher education and because of his administration of secondary and postsecondary institutions. Equally important was, from the 1840s until his death, his participation in the black convention movement as a writer, speaker, and officer. His substantial literary output—essays, poems, and position papers, published in the black press—emphasized the general themes of moral improvement, education, and self-help.

FURTHER READING

Vashon's papers are in the Oberlin College Archives, Oberlin, Ohio.

Dyson, Walter. *Howard University ... A History 1867–1940* (1941).

Hanchett, Catherine M. "George Boyer Vashon, 1824–1878: Black Educator, Poet, Fighter for Equal Rights," *Western Pennsylvania Historical Magazine* 68 (1985).

Sherman, Joan R. *Invisible Poets* (1974).

Smith, J. Clay. *Emancipation: The Making of the Black Lawyer* (1994).

This entry is taken from the *American National Biography* and is published here with the permission of the American Council of Learned Societies.

FRANK R. LEVSTIK

Vashon, Susan Paul Smith (19 Sept. 1838–27 Nov. 1912), educator and activist, was born Susan Paul Smith, the daughter of Elijah Smith, a musician, and Anne Paul Smith, in Boston, Massachusetts. Though her father attained some fame for his music, it was her mother's family that placed her in Boston's black elite. Anne Paul Smith was the daughter of the Reverend THOMAS PAUL, founder of the Joy Street Church and an antislavery activist.

Elijah Smith was relatively absent from his daughter's life—in part because of his touring activities as a musician. The biographer Emma Gossett, writing in HALLIE Q. BROWN's *Homespun Heroines*, claimed that he gave a command performance for Queen Victoria in 1850. Anne Paul Smith died young, so Catherine Waterhouse Paul, the widow of Rev. Thomas Paul (who died in 1831), took her granddaughter in, and this meant that Susan Paul Smith was raised in one of the centers of American black activism. One of her uncles (also named Thomas) had apprenticed to the prominent white abolitionist William Lloyd Garrison and had then become a teacher in the community. One of her aunts, SUSAN PAUL, also taught and was active in a range of reform efforts, including the Massachusetts Anti-Slavery Society, the Boston Female Anti-Slavery Society, and the New England Temperance Society of People of Color. During her childhood, Smith undoubtedly saw figures ranging from WILLIAM COOPER NELL to LEONARD GRIMES as they associated with members of her family and participated with them in antislavery events.

Because she witnessed her family's struggles for African American rights, she would have understood the need to participate in this struggle herself. The late 1840s and early 1850s saw intensifying black protest—often led by William Cooper Nell—against Boston's segregated schools. Such protest may explain her family's choice in schools. Smith spent perhaps three years at a female seminary in Somerville, Massachusetts. Smith was reported to be the only African American in her class as well as the class valedictorian. She completed her education in 1854, and, probably because her grandmother had died, she moved to Pittsburgh, where her father had apparently settled.

In Pittsburgh Smith obtained a teaching post in the small, segregated African American school system. Her principal, GEORGE BOYER VASHON, had already built a reputation among northern free blacks. Vashon was fourteen years her senior and had also been born into a family of activists; he became Oberlin College's first African American graduate in 1844. In addition to writing for abolitionist newspapers and contributing fragments of a long poem, "Vincent Oge," to the 1854 volume of *Autographs for Freedom*, Vashon had taught at various schools in Haiti and Pittsburgh as well as at New York Central College. While some biographers of George Vashon date Smith and Vashon's marriage as late as 1859, Hallie Brown reports that the two were married on 17 February 1857. Regardless, by September of 1859 they had their first child, John Boyer Vashon, and Susan Vashon had left the classroom.

She did not leave activism, however. Both George Vashon and his father were involved in the Underground Railroad, and Vashon would have naturally provided aid. Further, Vashon nursed wounded soldiers throughout the Civil War—even as her family grew with the births of sons Frank and George in 1860 and 1861, respectively. The Vashons would have a total of seven children, though only four—the three sons and a daughter, Emma, born in 1867—would survive childhood.

The final years of the war, with their massive exodus of fugitive and former slaves, saw some of Susan Vashon's most important activist work. In 1864 and 1865 she organized a series of bazaars for sanitary relief that raised several thousand dollars to aid newly freed blacks in Pittsburgh and beyond. Building from their abolitionist roots, the Vashons turned their full energies to gaining civil rights for the now greatly expanded free black community. George, who had become president of Pittsburgh's Avery College in 1863, moved the family to Washington, D.C., where he took a post in the Freedmen's Bureau Solicitor's Office and helped found Howard University. Susan Vashon returned to teaching in 1872 in Washington's segregated public schools, and she later became principal of the Thaddeus Stevens School. Reconstruction in Washington, D.C., was a rich time for the Vashons.

Both were recognized as important educators, the family socialized with some of the finest minds of the time, and they saw many opportunities for African Americans. In addition to his work with the faculty at Howard, Vashon became active with the *New National Era* and seems to have befriended the African American writer FRANK J. WEBB. In 1874 George Vashon accepted a teaching post at the newly founded Alcorn University in Rodney, Mississippi, and while the family seems to have been close-knit, it is not clear whether Susan Vashon and the children accompanied him. He died there of yellow fever in 1878.

Vashon continued to work in the Washington, D.C., public schools. She was at Stevens School until 1880, when she seems to have, in essence, retired. Her three sons were grown, and at least two—John and Frank—had become teachers, the former in St. Louis and the latter in Washington, D.C. Undoubtedly John Vashon's successes in St. Louis proved a lure, and Susan Vashon, along with Frank and Emma, moved there in 1882. A niece, Georgiana Colder, who had lived with the Vashons since before 1880, accompanied the family to St. Louis. Over the next few decades she would stay with the Vashons and serve as Vashon's companion. At times during this period, other relatives—including, for a long period, her unmarried son John—joined Susan Vashon's home.

In St. Louis Vashon began a second career of sorts, that of club organizer. While she remained as active in the church as she had always been (in St. Louis she was a member of All Saints Episcopal Church), she also founded a Book Lover's Club, a Mother's Club, the St. Louis Women's Federation, the Informal Dames, and, most notable, both the St. Louis Association of Colored Women's Clubs and the Missouri Association of Colored Women's Clubs. In 1902 she was elected president of the Missouri Federation of Colored Women's Clubs, an arm of the National Association of Colored Women's Clubs (NACWC). A fellow former Bostonian, JOSEPHINE ST. PIERRE RUFFIN, only four years her junior, had been active in founding the NACWC, and Vashon's connections to the Boston and Washington black elite—in addition to her own formidable talents—probably empowered her work in St. Louis. In 1904, during the St. Louis World's Fair, she brought the NACWC there for its national convention.

By the early twentieth century, the Vashons were firmly established in St. Louis's black community. Susan Paul Vashon became one of the community's matriarchs, and all of her children attained both social status and economic security. John taught and worked as a principal in the St. Louis public schools until his death in 1924; in 1887 he was instrumental in establishing the St. Louis Young Men's Christian Association for Colored Men. His—and his family's—contribution to St. Louis education was recognized when the city opened Vashon High School after his death. George worked as a clerk in the city government, and Frank worked as a postal clerk. Emma was among the first graduates of Sumner High School, St. Louis's original black secondary school, and she taught for a time before marrying Andrew Jackson Gossin, a teacher.

Gossett noted that Vashon had a "puritanic cast" and was always firstly "a mother, profoundly so," who "directed the lives of her children with the personal guidance and watchful care of tenderest love and wisest admonition" (134). Though generally remembered for her relief work in the Civil War, Susan Paul Smith Vashon was a lifelong advocate of African American civil rights and education.

FURTHER READING
Information about Vashon can be found in the archival material at the Missouri Historical Society (Newspaper Morgue Files) and the Western Historical Manuscript Collection, University of Missouri at St. Louis, as well as from various U.S. censuses and city directories.
Gossett, Emma. "Susan Paul Vashon," in *Homespun Heroines and Other Women of Distinction*, ed. Hallie Q. Brown (1926).
Horton, James, and Lois Horton. *Black Bostonians: Family Life and Community Struggle in the Antebellum North* (1979).
Piersen, William D. "Susan Paul Vashon," in *Notable Black American Women*, ed. Jessie Carney Smith (1992).

ERIC GARDNER

Vaughan, Sarah (27 Mar. 1924–3 Apr. 1990), jazz singer, was born Sarah Lois Vaughan in Newark, New Jersey, to Asbury Vaughan, a carpenter, and Ada Vaughan, a laundress. Her father, who played guitar for pleasure, and her mother, who sang in the choir of the local Mount Zion Baptist Church, gave their only daughter piano lessons from the age of seven. Before her teens Vaughan was playing organ in church and singing in the choir. In 1942, on a dare from a friend, she took the subway into Harlem and entered the Apollo Theatre's legendary Wednesday-night amateur contest. She won the

Sarah Vaughn sings at the Café Society in New York City, c. August 1946. (© William P. Gottlieb; www.jazzphotos.com.)

ten-dollar first prize and a week-long spot there as an opening act.

That engagement launched a singer who would soon develop a voice of operatic splendor and an imagination to match. Embraced early on by the pioneers of bebop, "The Divine One," as she was called, absorbed their innovations and applied them lavishly to the Great American Songbook. Gunther Schuller, the Pulitzer Prize–winning classical conductor and scholar, called Vaughan the greatest vocal artist of the twentieth century: "Hers is a perfect instrument, attached to a musician of superb instincts" (Liska, 19). Unlike her peer CARMEN MCRAE, Vaughan was no probing interpreter of words. She communicated drama through sound, wallowing in a seemingly endless range of textures. In one drawn-out note she could change timbres repeatedly, from dulcet to husky, or make a feathery leap from bass to soprano.

After hearing her sing at the Apollo, crooner BILLY ECKSTINE, a reigning black heartthrob of the day, took her to meet his boss, the pianist and bandleader EARL "FATHA" HINES. Soon Vaughan was sharing the bandstand with Eckstine, as well as bebop pioneers CHARLIE PARKER and DIZZY GILLESPIE, who were in Hines's band. "I thought Bird and Diz were the end," said Vaughan. "Horns always influenced me more than voices" (Gold, 13). But she borrowed a lot from Eckstine, whose voluptuous swoops and overripe vibrato turned up in Vaughan's singing. In the summer of 1944 Eckstine left Hines to form a groundbreaking bebop orchestra and took Vaughan with him. She made her first recording, "I'll Wait and Pray," with the band on 5 December 1944. Thereafter she recorded for several small bop labels. But it was clear to George Treadwell, a handsome trumpeter with whom she shared a bill in 1946, that Vaughan's voice had commercial potential. After a brief courtship, they wed on 17 September of that year. Treadwell became her manager, investing thousands of dollars on a makeover for his wife, including a nose job, teeth straightening, and gowns.

Also in 1946, a glamorized Vaughan joined a new label, Musicraft. In 1947 her luscious cover version of Doris Day's hit "It's Magic" climbed to number 11. The next year she surpassed NAT KING COLE's "Nature Boy," reaching number 9. Every year from 1947 through 1952 she won *Down Beat*'s poll as best female jazz singer; through 1959 she had twenty-six Top Forty singles.

Vaughan's straddling of jukebox pop and modern jazz tended to frustrate both worlds. She went on the defense. "I'm not a jazz singer, I'm a singer," she said, while naming a wide range of favorite colleagues, from MAHALIA JACKSON to Polly Bergen (Liska, 21). In a fruitful relationship with Columbia from 1949 to 1953, Vaughan recorded show tunes, saccharin torch songs like "My Tormented Heart," and a now-classic LP with MILES DAVIS.

In 1954 she signed a dual contract with a pop label, Mercury, and its jazz subsidiary, EmArcy. Among the jazz milestones she created is *Sarah Vaughan*, a 1954 small-group album that teamed her with a bebop wunderkind, trumpeter CLIFFORD BROWN. Vaughan gained a new trademark in 1958 when she recorded "Misty," the ERROLL GARNER–Johnny Burke ballad, with a twinkly, sugar-dusted arrangement credited to QUINCY JONES. Her commercial stature rose as she recorded a series of kitschy hits, notably "Broken-Hearted Melody" (1959), a country-pop ditty with a heavy backbeat and a male chorus singing "doomp-do-doomp" behind her. "God, I hated it," she said later. "It's the corniest thing I ever did" (Liska, 21). Yet it reached number 7 and lifted her into a glamorous rank of white supper clubs. Vaughan even appeared in a 1960 gangster film, *Murder Inc.*

Also in 1960 Vaughan accepted a lucrative offer from Roulette, a gangster-run rock and jazz label. Through 1963 she created some of her best-loved work at Roulette: late-night jazz with guitar and bass (*After Hours* and *Sarah+2*) and sessions with the Benny Carter and COUNT BASIE orchestras. But she also made a series of string-laden ballad discs, and jazz purists continued to attack her. The grumbling rose during her second stint at Mercury, from 1963 to 1967. Vaughan later claimed that she quit the label, citing various grievances: she hated the pop material, the records were not promoted, and she was not getting royalties. She did not record again until 1971.

Vaughan's luck with men was not much better. Having divorced Treadwell in 1956—she claimed that all he had done for her had been for himself—Vaughan had taken on a new husband-manager in 1959: Clyde "C. B." Atkins, a former professional football player who now owned a Chicago taxi fleet. In 1961 the couple adopted a child, Deborah (now Paris Vaughan, an actress). Divorcing the violent Atkins in the 1960s, Vaughan found he had left her in heavy debt to the Internal Revenue Service. From 1970 through 1977 she had a more pleasant relationship with Marshall Fisher, a restaurateur who became her manager. But when asked in an interview about the men in her life, an angry Vaughan threatened to "throw up" (O'Connor, 96).

Vaughan's career gained new life when she signed with Mainstream, a jazz label run by Bob Shad, her producer at EmArcy. She made more blatant pop albums, along with *Live in Japan*, a double LP of Vaughan singing the standards she loved with a first-rate trio, and *Sarah Vaughan with Michel Legrand*, a sumptuous orchestral collaboration with the celebrated French composer-arranger. For the rest of her life Vaughan was a touring machine, second only to ELLA FITZGERALD as a living legend of vocal jazz. No longer did she record fluff. From 1977 through 1982 she made a series of uncompromising jazz albums for the Pablo label. These included *Send in the Clowns* (1982), Vaughan's third LP with the Count Basie Orchestra. The title song, from Stephen Sondheim's *A Little Night Music*, was her key showstopper of later years. Singing the lament of an actress who has triumphed onstage but not in love, the shy and private Vaughan gave a rare flash of autobiography. She delivered the song as a slow, emotional aria, lingering on the words, "Sure of my lines / No one is there." Returning to Columbia, she recorded the Grammy Award–winning *Gershwin*

Live (1982), a symphonic program she performed for years.

By now Vaughan had ended another marriage, to trumpeter Waymon Reed. Though sixteen years her junior, he died of cancer in 1983. Vaughan herself had smoked, drunk, and snorted cocaine for decades, with little audible damage. Her 1987 album, *Brazilian Romance*, proved this. But in 1989, soon after she won a Grammy for lifetime achievement, Vaughan was diagnosed with lung cancer. That October she returned to the Blue Note jazz club, her New York headquarters of the 1980s, for what would be her final performances. On 3 April 1990, one week after turning sixty-six, she died at her home in Hidden Hills, a Los Angeles suburb.

All of Vaughan's Mercury recordings are available in four box sets; her Roulette sides are gathered in *The Complete Roulette Sarah Vaughan Studio Sessions* (Mosaic). In 1991 the Public Broadcasting System aired a television documentary on Vaughan, *The Divine One*, as part of its *American Masters* series. In 2002 singer Dianne Reeves won a Grammy for her tribute album to Vaughan, *The Calling*. Reeves explained: "I'd never heard a voice like that, that was so rich and deep and beautiful, just sang all over the place. I thought, 'You mean, there are *those* kinds of possibilities?'" (Interview with author, 2000).

FURTHER READING
Dahl, Linda. *Stormy Weather: The Music and Lives of a Century of Jazzwomen* (Limelight Editions, 1996).
Gardner, Barbara. *Down Beat*, 2 Mar. 1961.
Gavin, James. Liner note essay for *The Complete Roulette Sarah Vaughan Studio Sessions* (Mosaic Records 8-CD set).
Gold, Don. *Down Beat*, 30 May 1957.
Liska, A. James. *Down Beat*, May 1982.
Mackin, Tom. "Newark's Divine Sarah." *Newark Sunday News*, 10 Nov. 1968.
O'Connor, Rory. *New York Woman*, Apr. 1988.
"Queen for a Year." *Metronome*, Feb. 1951.
Obituary: *New York Times*, 5 Apr. 1990.

JAMES GAVIN

Veale, Charles (?–1872), Civil War soldier and Medal of Honor winner, was born in Portsmouth, Virginia. While most of the details of his life are unknown, the beginning of the Civil War almost surely found him a slave, and in all likelihood he was one of thousands of Virginia slaves that sought their freedom by fleeing to the Union Army lines. One of the greatest challenges for President Lincoln and the War Department at the Civil War's outset was how to handle the flood of runaway slaves from the South that continually flowed through Union lines. Although the federal government remained committed to upholding slavery in the border states (Maryland, Kentucky, and Missouri), the War Department did not wish to return slaves to masters who might be using them to aid the Confederacy. Moreover, the Fugitive Slave Law remained in effect and soldiers were compelled to return escaping slaves to "loyal" masters. Many Union generals even pledged to suppress any slave insurrections.

Thus, for Charles Veale and countless other slaves in Virginia, their hero might have been a lawyer from Massachusetts, General Benjamin F. Butler, in charge of the Department of Virginia. When three escaped slaves made their way to Fortress Monroe in May 1861, they were brought before Butler; he listened to their tale of escape, and immediately ordered that they be fed and put to work within the fort. Incredibly, the next day a Confederate Army major visited the fort under a flag of truce and demanded the return of the slaves, citing Butler's legal obligations under the Fugitive Slave Law. In a rather humorous exchange, Butler replied that Virginia had seceded, and therefore he had no duty to enforce the laws of a foreign country. However, if the slaves' owners were willing to come to Fortress Monroe and take an oath of allegiance to the United States, then the slaves would be returned. Benjamin Quarles's book *The Negro in the Civil War* vividly describes the effect that Fortress Monroe had on escaped slaves: "The news of Butler's action quickly became known to the slaves in the vicinity of the fortress… A thousand calls went out… The joyful word was whispered that the time was at hand for the downtrodden 'to come up out of Egypt.' And forthwith there was a concerted effort to reach 'freedom fort'" (Quarles, 60). It may be that one of these "downtrodden" slaves was Charles Veale.

By September 1864 Veale was a private in the Fourth United States Colored Troop (USCT), originally formed in June 1863 by Colonel William Birney, son of the famed abolitionist James G. Birney, in Baltimore, Maryland. As was customary, agents were sent out to recruit soldiers for the regiment; perhaps Veale was one of these early recruits, along with Christian Fleetwood and Alfred Hilton. In September 1863 the regiment was sent south to Fortress Monroe (most likely where Veale enlisted) and received further training and more recruits.

Veale and his fellow soldiers in the Fourth USCT would see limited action in the Tidewater area as a part of several operations. The regiment was then assigned to Butler's Army of the James in late May 1864 and placed on the front lines opposite Petersburg, near Richmond. The regiment saw heavy action on 15 June 1864 as they stormed Petersburg Heights, capturing enemy ordnance.

In late September of 1864 the men of the Fourth USCT were stationed on the southern end of the Union line, opposite Confederate fortifications around Richmond at New Market Heights. In the early morning hours of September 29, Veale and his fellow soldiers in Company D and men from other USCT regiments were given the signal to attack Fort Harrison, one of four key forts in the Confederate line. The fighting on that day and the day after was fierce and would result in over five thousand Union casualties. Only one Union objective would be accomplished: Fort Harrison would be taken by the Union's black soldiers. Veale and the men of the Fourth USCT were involved in the fiercest fighting during the battle for the fort; and when the colors of Company D were in peril, Charles Veale, according to the official records of the U.S. Government Printing Office, acted in the following manner: "After two bearers of the regimental colors had been shot down, seized it close to the enemy lines and bore it through the remainder of the action" (United States Government Printing Office, 169). Bearing the regimental colors was a prestigious responsibility in battle during the Civil War; not only were these flags a source of fighting inspiration to a company or regiment, but they were also used by company officers as a rallying point for their men. Veale's valorous actions in carrying the colors after two men had previously been shot down were a tangible contribution, one of many that day by black troops, as they helped the Fourth USCT capture Fort Harrison. Less than two weeks later, General Butler would recognize many of his black soldiers for their heroic deeds at New Market Heights. Of Charles Veale he would state, "He has a medal for gallantry and will have the warrant of a color sergeant" (U.S. Government Printing Office, Official Records, 169). On 6 April 1865 Sergeant Charles Veale (his name was spelled "Veal" in his regimental records) was given the Medal of Honor, one of fourteen black soldiers to be so honored for their actions at New Market Heights. Following this epic battle, little is known about Veale's life. As a color sergeant, the could have taken part in the subsequent actions of the Fourth USCT regiments as in two expeditions to capture Fort Fisher, the capture of Wilmington, North Carolina, or in the surrender of Johnston's Army. He was mustered out of army service in late 1865.

Veale returned to his native Virginia after the Civil War, but nothing is known of his possible family ties. His surname and its variant were uncommon among African Americans in Virginia at the time; perhaps he was married to Sarah Veal, identified in the 1870 Federal Census as a fifty-year-old seamstress employed at the Howard Grove Insane Asylum in Richmond. Possibly because of his advanced age at enlistment, or perhaps due to the rigors of war, he died in 1872 in unknown circumstances. His final resting place can be found in the Hampton National Cemetery in Hampton, Virginia, with his grave marked by a Medal of Honor headstone.

FURTHER READING
Quarles, Benjamin. *The Negro in the Civil War* (1989).
United States Government Printing Office. *The War of the Rebellion: A Compilation of the Official Records of the Union and Confederate Armies* (1893).

GLENN ALLEN KNOBLOCK

Vedrine, Soliny (8 July 1943–), church planter, religious leader, and educator, was born to Elenise Zama Vedrine, a housewife, and Sauveur Vedrine, a tailor, in L'Asile, Haiti. Vedrine, the second of seven children, received his early education in L'Asile and later completed law school in Port-au-Prince, the capital of Haiti. In 1967 Vedrine, who had joined the Baptist church in 1955, immigrated to Texas in order to pursue theological studies at Dallas Theological Seminary. Vedrine chose this nondenominational seminary because of its emphasis on Biblical languages and its evangelical theology. Four years later he was awarded the ThM. In 1972 Vedrine married Emmeline Fougy, a social worker, with whom he had five children. He initially intended to return to Haiti after seminary, but his plan was curtailed when he was unable to raise funds to go back home. After preaching in New York City, he was much encouraged by two Haitian Christians who helped him discern that his field of ministry should be the Haitian community of Boston. In the early 1970s, Haitian immigrants were pouring into Boston, which encouraged ambitious ministers to open new churches for those compatriots.

In 1973 Vedrine opened the Boston Missionary Baptist Church, the second Haitian Baptist church in Boston. Besides these two Baptist churches, there was only a Seventh Day Adventist congregation serving the spiritual needs of the Haitian Protestants. At first Vedrine found little support from the established churches. He made numerous phone calls to most of the city's churches, but only one white pastor cared enough to welcome him. Nevertheless, after visiting several families, Vedrine opened his new congregation in a building used by an American church. In 1974 he affiliated his congregation with the Baptist General Conference (BGC), a predominantly white group, and with financial assistance from the BGC he erected a new church building in 1991—at the cost of a million dollars—that accommodated his five-hundred-member congregation.

As the first Haitian minister to join the BGC, Vedrine encouraged more than twenty Haitian congregations in Massachusetts, Rhode Island, Connecticut, New York, New Jersey, the Bahamas, and Haiti to affiliate with this Baptist body. In addition to the Boston Missionary Baptist Church, Vedrine also planted three other Haitian congregations in Massachusetts, Rhode Island, and Connecticut. In turn Vedrine encouraged the congregations he had planted to also birth four other churches in Rhode Island and Connecticut. Beginning in 1985 he led the BGC Haitian Pastors Fellowship, which he founded as a forum for ministers to learn about the denomination and mutually support each other. But Vedrine's influence was destined to grow beyond the confines of the Boston Missionary Baptist Church and the BGC.

In 1983 Vedrine was invited to teach at the Center for Urban Ministerial Education (CUME), the Boston extension of Gordon-Conwell Theological Seminary. CUME is a program intended for those doing inner-city work and offers certificates and graduate degrees in various areas of ministry and theology. CUME also provides course offerings in Spanish, (Brazilian) Portuguese, and Haitian Creole/French in order to better serve these ethnic communities. During his long and continuing service to CUME, Vedrine taught courses in Old Testament and New Testament studies, church history, and missions.

Vedrine encouraged dozens of Haitian pastors, ministers, and laypeople to secure theological training at CUME. For many years the only trained Haitian ministers working in the United States were those who had been to seminary in Haiti. Many Haitians who entered the ministry in America did so without formal training. By encouraging Haitians to be trained in ministry, Vedrine contributed to the quality of Christian service that the next generation of Haitian church leaders could provide in New England and beyond. He also recruited several Haitian faculty members for CUME, and by doing so he allowed them to secure their early start in advanced theological education.

Vedrine also influenced Haitian Protestantism through his work at Emmanuel Gospel Center (EGC), also based in Boston. Founded in 1938, the EGC is a Christian organization that seeks to understand and nurture the vitality of urban churches and communities. In November 1985 Vedrine joined the EGC as minister-at-large to the Haitian community. Six years later Vedrine founded the Fellowship of Haitian Evangelical Pastors of New England, of which he was the first president. In 1993 the pastors' fellowship held its first annual crusade, which drew more than two thousand people. Through the EGC, Vedrine provided much-needed Christian literature in French and Haitian Creole to the more than seventy Haitian churches that dot the Greater Boston area. In bringing Baptist, Pentecostal, and other Protestant Haitians together, Vedrine was instrumental in increasing the level of ecumenism among Haitian Protestant churches, some of which are still struggling with the sectarianism instilled by foreign missionaries back in Haiti.

In 1994 Vedrine became concerned about the plight of forty thousand compatriots living in the Bahamas. He was instrumental in gathering nineteen pastors in that country to network on evangelism and social ministries. Two years later he spearheaded the first annual Haitian Bahamas Crusade, which attracted three thousand participants. In addition to evangelism, the Bahamas crusades include workshops for youth, women, and pastors, as well as health clinics. Similar crusades were held in August 2005, 2006, and 2007 in La Romana, Dominican Republic. Vedrine's work outside the United States led EGC to change his job title to Director of Haitian Ministries International. Vedrine serves as mentor to Haitian ministers in the United States, Haiti, the Dominican Republic, and the Bahamas and truly enjoys an international ministry. In 1998 Vedrine engineered Vision Globale du Protestantisme dans le Milieu Haitien (Global Vision of Haitian Protestantism), a series of international conferences with Haitian ministers and theologians, also supported by the EGC. Vision Globale met three times in Florida: in Miami (1998), West Palm Beach (2003), and Pompano Beach (2007).

Through Vision Globale, Vedrine's contacts greatly expanded in Haiti, which led him to be part of a special group to meet with the Haitian head of state, President Boniface Alexandre, and some cabinet members in March 2004. Through Vision Globale, Vedrine was the pioneer Haitian church leader to create an intellectual forum where Protestant leaders living in Haiti and those living overseas freely interact. Vedrine's achievements led Atlantic College and Seminary (Nassau, Bahamas) and the Université Jean Price Mars (Port-au-Prince, Haiti) to award him honorary doctorates in 2002 and 2003, respectively. Vedrine's work significantly contributed to the development of Christianity within the Haitian diaspora.

FURTHER READING

Inside EGC, the bimonthly newsletter of the EGC, frequently provides information on Soliny Vedrine's activities. For some important biographical information, see the issues of October–November 2003 and September–October 2004. Newsletters are available at www.egc.org.

DAVID MICHEL

Veney, Bethany (1812?– ?), slave-narrative author, was born Berthena in Luray, Virginia, the daughter of an enslaved woman whose name is unknown and an unknown father. Commonly called Betty and later published under the first name Bethany, Veney grew up a slave in the rural Blue Ridge Mountains. Her first owner, the farmer James Fletcher, apparently held much of Veney's extended family, including her mother, five siblings, grandmother, and uncle. At age nine, following Fletcher's death, Veney and her sister Matilda—their mother had already died—fell under the ownership of Fletcher's oldest daughter Lucy. An unmarried woman, Lucy soon moved in with her sister and brother-in-law, a blacksmith named David Kibbler (sometimes spelled Kibler). Veney spent the remainder of her childhood in Kibbler's household.

Veney considered Lucy Fletcher a kind mistress, who, while abhorrent of slavery, felt powerless to free Veney and her siblings. Kibbler, on the other hand, was "a man of most violent temper, ready to fight anything or anybody who resisted his authority" and who subjected her to frequent physical abuse (Veney, 12). Veney also fiercely clashed with Kibbler over her religious conversion, inspired by visits to revival meetings at a nearby schoolhouse. Kibbler initially sought to prevent Veney's participation in these meetings, confining her in a neighbor's house, but later gave in to her determination. Her commitment to Christianity persisted throughout her life and colored her later reflections on slavery and freedom.

Lucy Fletcher periodically, and perhaps halfheartedly, promised Veney eventual freedom provided she behaved well and never married. Skeptical of her mistress's promises, Veney nevertheless consented to marry a man named Jerry, a long-held acquaintance enslaved on an estate seven miles from Kibbler's. Veney's religious devotion demanded that the ceremony be performed by a minister, though she remained cognizant of the threat of future separation. "I did not want [the minister] to make us promise that we would always be true to each other forsaking all others, as the white people do in their marriage service," she later wrote, "because I knew that at any time our masters could compel us to break such a promise" (Veney, 18). This premonition proved true less than a year later, when Jerry was imprisoned due to his owner's debts and, despite a failed attempt to run away, was later auctioned off to a slave trader who transported him to the southern market.

The devastating loss of her husband and the subsequent birth of a daughter, Charlotte, marked a turning point in Veney's perspectives on her enslavement. Most profoundly she feared a precarious future for her child, despairing "that a master's word can at any moment take [Charlotte] from her embrace" and the "almost certain doom … to minister to the unbridled lust of the slaveowner" (Veney, 26). Henceforth, unable to bear Kibbler's continued abuse and determined to seek a better life for herself and her child, Veney successfully persuaded Fletcher to sell Charlotte and her to a neighboring family, Mr. and Mrs. John Prince (sometimes spelled Printz). Veney and her daughter lived happily with the Princes for several years until, for reasons that remain unclear, she was sold without Charlotte to David McCoy (sometimes spelled McKay), the same slave trader who had purchased her husband. McCoy transported Veney to the slave auction in Richmond, hoping to capitalize on her reputation as a "faithful, hard-working woman" (Veney, 28). But Veney successfully thwarted her sale by cleverly feigning physical weakness and ill temper on the auction block. Unable to secure an acceptable offer, McCoy returned her to Luray and took her into his own household. He allowed Veney to take on outside work, and she earned money as a washerwoman, housecleaner, and field hand. While working as a

cook for a group of free black laborers, she met her second husband, Frank Veney, but the marriage did not last long. After the birth of a son, Joe, Veney agreed to pay McCoy twenty dollars per year to live independently. She moved with her son into a small rented house, finding permanent employment as a housekeeper for two northern miners, J. Butterworth and G. J. Adams. In December 1858 Adams purchased Veney and Joe—with the explicit purpose of freeing them—for $775 from the financially ailing McCoy. When the outbreak of the Civil War forced the miners to flee Virginia, Veney and her son went with them. Veney arrived in Providence, Rhode Island, a free woman, marveling that she now "had the same right to myself that any other woman had" (Veney, 31).

Veney settled comfortably into life in New England but soon tragically lost her son to illness. Shortly thereafter she followed Adams to Worcester, Massachusetts, where she remained until her death. With the end of the war, Veney returned to Virginia to retrieve her remaining family, which included her grown daughter Charlotte, and Charlotte's husband and child. While in Luray, Veney also visited her three previous owners, Kibbler, Prince, and McCoy, and while happy to be among "old familiar faces," she could also not "forget to be grateful for my escape from a system under which I had suffered so much" (Veney, 39). She returned to Worcester with sixteen family members in tow, all of whom settled permanently in the community. Veney herself had purchased a small home of her own. She became a prominent member of the Methodist church, where she may have been persuaded by members of the congregation to record her life story. At the age of seventy-four Veney related her life experiences in the form of a slave narrative. Dictated aloud, presumably to an M.W.G. of East Greenwich, Rhode Island, who composed the volume's preface, the narrative was published in Worcester in 1889 with endorsing statements from Rev. V. A. Cooper of Boston's Home for Little Wanderers and Rev. Erastus Spaulding of Millbury, Massachusetts, who claimed to have known the author for twenty-five years.

Veney's autobiography—with its themes of resilience and integrity in the face of adversity, the disruption of family relationships and the struggle for security, and the importance of a commitment to Christian ideals—fit into the typical mold of nineteenth-century slave narratives and sought not only to reveal the injustices of racial slavery to white audiences but also to ensure that the memory of its impact would not fade with the passage of time. The author of the volume's introduction, the Methodist bishop Willard Francis Mallalieu, imparted a hagiographic aura upon Veney's narrative, hailing the author as a "saintly, enduring spirit" who lived a "pure and spotless life" (Veney, introduction). Indeed through her narrative—which provides the only known facts of her life—Veney emerged as an individual who maintained her dignity and spirit despite the obstacles imposed by slavery.

FURTHER READING

Veney, Bethany. *The Narrative of Bethany Veney, a Slave Woman*, in *Collected Black Women's Narratives*, Schomburg Library of Nineteenth-Century Black Women Writers (1988). Available online at http://digital.nypl.org/schomburg/writers_aa19/.

CARLA JONES

Vereen, Ben (10 Oct. 1946–), actor, singer, and performer, was born Benjamin Augustus Middleton, the son of Essie Middleton, in Laurinburg, North Carolina. His father's name is not known. He was later adopted by James Vereen, who worked in a paint factory, and Pauline Vereen (maiden name unknown), a laborer, and raised in Miami, Florida, with their eight other children. Ben Vereen believed for most of his childhood that he had been born in Miami, Florida, to his adoptive parents. Pauline Vereen took on work as a costumer for concerts and theater performances after the family relocated to the Bedford-Stuyvesant area of Brooklyn, New York, when Ben was still quite young. Under her influence, Vereen trained as a dancer and singer, hopeful of a life on the stage and away from the want that afflicted the family. It was his grandmother, however, who insisted on an upbringing in the church for the young man, and it was at church that he first began to sing and perform publicly.

His talent did not go unnoticed. He attended local schools, but his skills came to the attention of a middle-school principal who urged him to apply to Manhattan's prestigious High School for the Performing Arts. Vereen complied and—reportedly having never heard of the school—auditioned and was accepted for the 1961 academic year. At the school, he studied under George Balanchine and Martha Graham, among other luminaries. He graduated in 1965 but was unable to find work as a performer. Dispirited, he enrolled in the Pentecostal Theological Seminary at Manhattan, but remained there only a few months before dropping out. A short time later, he was able to pick up

work in various summer stock companies and local dance troupes. In the late 1960s, while applying for a passport, he learned that he was adopted. He eventually arranged to meet his birth family, only to learn that his mother had died more than twenty years earlier.

The year 1966 proved a turning point, both professionally and personally. He married Andrea Townsley, and together the couple would have a son before divorcing. Vereen attended an open audition for a revival of the musical *Sweet Charity*, to be directed by Bob Fosse. Fosse recognized Vereen's talent, selected him as part of the cast, and took him under his wing, refining his dancing technique and becoming something of an artistic father figure for the young performer. The revival of the musical was successful enough that a feature-film version was produced, with Vereen reprising his role and starring alongside SAMMY DAVIS JR., who, like Fosse, became something of a mentor and for whom Vereen sometimes served as understudy. In 1971 Vereen played the part of Judas in Andrew Lloyd Webber's "rock opera" *Jesus Christ Superstar*. A year later, he was working with Fosse again in *Pippen*. That role won him a Tony Award for Best Actor in a Musical. In 1975 he shared a stage with Barbra Streisand in *Funny Lady*. Meanwhile, Vereen's celebrity was such that he began to make forays into television, gaining a wider viewing audience.

In 1975 he was offered his own variety show by the National Broadcasting Company (NBC), *Ben Vereen ... Comin' at Ya*, but the program was short lived with only handful of episodes produced. A year later, he made a guest appearance on Jim Henson's *Muppet Show*. In 1976 he married Nancy Bruner, and would have two daughters with her. In 1977 he played the role of Chicken George in the classic television miniseries *Roots*, a part for which he received both critical acclaim and an Emmy nomination. Two years later he appeared in Bob Fosse's film *All That Jazz*.

By the early 1980s Vereen had become a familiar enough presence that he was cast opposite Jeff Goldblum in the mystery/comedy series *Tenspeed and Brownshoe* on the ABC television network in 1980. The series lasted only a few episodes, though Vereen nevertheless became a somewhat familiar presence on broadcast television, making numerous appearances on a wide variety of programs throughout the 1980s and 1990s. Among them was *The Jesse Owens Story* (1984), *Webster* (1984–1985), *The Fresh Prince of Bel-Air* (1994), and *Star Trek:*

The Next Generation (1994), in the last playing the father of the character played by the regular cast member LEVAR BURTON.

Vereen's life, however, was not free of tragedy and controversy. The pressures of his public life led him to become addicted to cocaine, and he spent time in and out of rehab. In 1981 he appeared at the inauguration of the incoming president Ronald Reagan, but his performance in blackface raised widespread dismay and outrage. The letters pages of *Ebony* Magazine, for example, included many letters criticizing his inaugural appearance as "shameful," "demeaning," and "degrading." One irate correspondent even wrote that Vereen "ought to be tarred and feathered for the egotistical, insensitive, stereotypical niggeration of [himself] and all Black people" (*Ebony*, April 1981, p. 16). In 1986 one of Vereen's teenaged daughters was killed in an automobile accident on the New Jersey Turnpike. Vereen spiraled into a depression, and his abuse of cocaine grew worse. Fearing for his life, his family staged an intervention, and Vereen at last entered rehab and beat his addiction.

Much of his subsequent career was spent as a public educator on the dangers to young people of drug use. He founded the Celebrities for a Drug-Free America and began speaking around the country and raising money for awareness. He also resumed his performing career, appearing on stage and television. The year 1992, however, brought another setback. Vereen was involved in an auto accident, apparently having fallen asleep at the wheel, but was unharmed. The next day, though, he was walking near his home in Malibu when he was hit by a neighbor's car and thrown ninety feet. He survived but underwent a long and painful regimen of physical therapy. In 1993 he mounted a comeback on stage with *Jelly's Last Jam*. He went on to appear in productions of *Chicago* (1999), *Fosse* (2001), and *Wicked* (2005–2006), among numerous others.

While continuing to pursue a career in film and on stage, Vereen continued also to engage in a number of civic-minded works, antidrug advocacy, and (after being diagnosed with Type 2 diabetes in 2007) diabetes awareness campaigns.

FURTHER READING

Bordman, Gerald. *American Musical Theatre: A Chronicle* (2001).

Woll, Allen. *Black Musical Theatre: From Coontown to Dreamgirls* (1989).

JASON PHILIP MILLER

Verrett, Shirley (31 May 1931–5 Nov. 2010), opera singer and concert recitalist, the second of six children born to Leon and Elvira Verrett in New Orleans. Her parents were converts to Seventh-Day Adventism, and they maintained a fairly restrictive religious environment. Her father served as her first voice teacher. In 1943, to escape overt racism in the South, the family moved to Oxnard, California. In 1948 Verrett won a preliminary round of the Atwater Kent Vocal Competition. Celebrated baritone John Charles Thomas heard her performance, and he offered her the opportunity to study voice with the celebrated soprano Lotte Lehman at the Music Academy of the West. Verrett refused the offer. The following year she attended the Seventh-Day Adventist Oakwood College in Huntsville, Alabama, but Verrett completed only one semester before returning to California.

In 1951 Verrett married James Carter, a real estate broker and sheriff's deputy. She then sold real estate for several years in the San Fernando Valley. In 1955 she began formal training in voice. She studied spirituals and German lieder with celebrated choral conductor Hall Johnson and auditioned for Arthur Godfrey's TV show, *Talent Scouts*. While in New York for the show's taping, Verrett auditioned for Juilliard voice teacher Marion Freschl, who persuaded her to enroll at Juilliard. During her first semester, she tied for first place in the MARIAN ANDERSON Voice Competition. Although her Adventism affiliation made her initially resistant to a career in opera, Verrett's viewing of Maria Callas in a 1956 performance of Bellini's *Norma* pushed her in that direction. In 1957 she appeared in productions of *The Rape of Lucretia* and *Lost in the Stars*. In 1958 Verrett starred in a production of the latter work staged by the New York City Opera and won the Walter S. Naumburg Award. The following year she ended her marriage to Carter.

In 1959 Leopold Stokowski invited Verrett to sing with the Houston Symphony Orchestra. He later withdrew the offer when the symphony board refused to accept a black soloist. She eventually performed with Stokowski for the more prestigious Philadelphia Orchestra, an engagement that catapulted her to national prominence. Verrett made her European opera debut in *Rasputin's Todt* in Cologne and also participated in her first commercial recording: Beethoven's Ninth Symphony with Josef Krips conducting the London Symphony.

Verrett married Louis Lomonaco in 1963. That year she debuted as Carmen with the Bolshoi Opera (the first African American singer to perform with the company) and also sang several recitals throughout the Soviet Union. In 1964 Verrett signed an exclusive contract with RCA and recorded several operas and concerts for the label. Between 1966 and 1968 Verrett sang the mezzo leads in several European opera houses, including Covent Garden (*Un Ballo in Maschera, Aida*, and *Don Carlo*), and the Teatro Comunale in Florence (*Maria Stuarda*). Verrett made her New York Metropolitan Opera debut in October 1968, singing the lead in *Carmen* and as Eboli in *Don Carlo*. Verrett added substantial weight to her operatic repertory over the next few years, both in Europe and in the United States, including the following roles: Didon in *Les Troyens* (Rome), Amneris and Leonora in *Aida* and *La Favorita* (in Dallas), Dalila in *Samson et Dalila* (La Scala), and Azucena in *Il Trovatore* (Covent Garden).

During the 1970s Verrett reached the pinnacle of her career and would be recognized as one of the concert world's leading vocal artists. After a two-year absence from singing in New York, Verrett returned to the Met and made operatic history by singing in both the roles of Cassandra and Didon in Berlioz's *Les Troyens* in a single performance. This feat further boosted her career and international stature.

In 1974 Verrett scored another major triumph at the Met when she sang in the part of Neocle opposite Beverly Sills in *L'Assedio di Corinto*. The following year she had yet another major success at La Scala Opera House by singing in the part of Lady Macbeth (a performance televised throughout Europe); she came to define that role for future sopranos. She returned to the Met in the spring of 1976 to sing in the role of Adalgisa in Bellini's *Norma*, but she took over the title role during the Met tour. Adalgisa, her favorite operatic heroine, became another signature role for her. Verrett continued to add other soprano roles to her repertory, including Madame Lidoine in *The Dialogues of the Carmelites*, Amelia in *Un Ballo in Maschera*, and the title role in Puccini's *Tosca*.

Verrett solidified her place in the dramatic soprano pantheon by performing *Norma* in Europe, *Tosca* on PBS Live from the Met, and she eventually sang the roles of Aida and Desdemona (from *Otello*) in Boston. During the 1980s she continued to make news. In a concert at Carnegie Hall celebrating the eighty-fifth birthday of Marian Anderson, she sang jointly with one-time rival GRACE BUMBRY. Between 1983 and 1986 Verrett resided in France and sang in several roles for the Paris Opera, including Sinaide in Rossini's *Mose*, Iphigénie in Gluck's *Iphigénie en*

Tauride, the title role in *Alceste*, and the title role in Cherubini's *Médée*. In 1984 Verrett debuted at the Verona Opera as Tosca. That same year, the French government recognized her artistic achievements by presenting her with the Commandeur des Arts et des Lettres. In 1987 Verrett suffered the most serious crisis of her career: in Rome, she lost her voice prior to a scheduled performance in the role of Lady Macbeth. She went onstage and attempted to "speak" the role. Audience jeers forced her to withdraw before the conclusion of the act.

After returning to the United States with her family in 1987, Verrett debuted with the Chicago Opera as Azucena. By the 1990s Verrett was becoming less active as an opera singer, but she did add another opera role to her extensive repertory. She sang the part of Santuzza in Mascagni's *Cavalleria Rusticana*, which was staged for her in Siena. Verrett also made her big-screen debut with a speaking role in the film *Maggio Musicale*, which was released in Europe. In 1992 she made her final operatic appearances, playing the role of Leonora in *La Favorita* in Seville and Madrid. Afterward, she continued as an active recitalist.

In 1996 Verrett accepted a voice professorship at the University of Michigan and was eventually endowed as the university's James Earl Jones Distinguished Professor of Voice. In 1999 her singing voice appeared on the soundtrack of the Academy Award–winning Italian movie *La Vita e Bella*. She was the recipient of many awards for her recordings and received many honorary doctorates from many schools, including Northeastern University, Holy Cross College, and Virginia Commonwealth University. Her autobiography, *I Never Walked Alone: The Autobiography of an American Singer*, published by John Wiley & Sons, was released in 2003. Verrett's performances and recordings won her international fame and recognition as one of the leading singers in the post–Marian Anderson generation of African American classical vocalists. She died in Ann Arbor, Michigan, at the age of 79.

FURTHER READING

Shirley Verrett, *I Never Walked Alone: The Autobiography of an American Singer* (2003).

CHRISTOPHER BROOKS

Vesey, Denmark (c. 1767–2 July 1822), mariner, carpenter, abolitionist, was born either in Africa or the Caribbean and probably grew up as a slave on the Danish colony of St. Thomas, which is now a part of the U.S. Virgin Islands. When Denmark was about fourteen years old, the slave trader Captain Joseph Vesey purchased him to sell on the slave market in Saint Domingue (Haiti). The identity of Denmark Vesey's parents and his name at birth are unknown, but Joseph Vesey gave him the name "Telemaque." He became "Denmark Vesey" in 1800, after he purchased his freedom from lottery winnings. Vesey's family life is difficult to reconstruct. He had at least three wives and several children, including three boys—Sandy, Polydore, and Robert—and a girl, Charlotte. His first and second wives, Beck and Polly, and their children lived as slaves. His third wife, Susan, was a free woman of color.

Not suitable for sale in Haiti, Telemaque became Captain Vesey's slave and "cabin boy" and moved with him to Charleston, South Carolina, in 1783. In Charleston Vesey labored as an urban slave for nearly seventeen years. As a chandler's man and a multilingual laborer who could read and write in English and French, Denmark Vesey conducted business for his owner's trade company. He was part of a large, diverse, and stratified urban black community that outnumbered the local white population. The occupations of black Charlestonians, a mixture of slave and free persons, varied; the population included artisans, domestics, agriculturalists, and other skilled and unskilled laborers. African Americans took advantage of the city's illicit trade network as they struggled to make a living in a challenging environment, where they faced white oppression and intraracial economic competition.

In 1799, at age thirty-three, Vesey purchased his freedom, joining just over 3,100 other people of color who made up Charleston's community of free blacks. State regulations made life for free persons of color semiautonomous at best. Free blacks had white patrons and paid annual "freedom" taxes, which left them vulnerable to white control as they labored in a city determined to limit their earning potential, social standing, and political power. South Carolina slaveholders hired out laborers for the Charleston market, thus creating economic tensions among free and enslaved black laborers. Divisions mounted as distinctions were drawn between blacks and those who were of mixed race. In this complex society Vesey apprenticed under established craftsmen and became a well-known and respected carpenter. Marginalized from the free community of light-skinned blacks, Vesey readily identified with rural and urban slaves who lived an arduous life that he remembered all too well.

At the turn of the century Vesey joined a growing number of southern blacks and converted to Christianity. After a short-term membership in a segregated congregation of the Second Presbyterian Church, he became a Methodist. Inspired by RICHARD ALLEN's movement in Philadelphia, Pennsylvania, Charleston's black Methodist population, which outnumbered whites of the same faith, established their own church. By 1818 the African Methodist Church had become the centerpiece for black religious congregation and supported political and economic activism. Influenced by Old Testament teachings, Vesey grew increasingly critical of slavery and commonly spoke against the institution. He compared the African American plight to that of the Israelites and joined America's rising antislavery fervor by arguing that white slaveholders denied blacks rights that were sanctioned by God. These debates inspired a grand scheme of resistance to South Carolina's aged slavery institution.

It is not known how long Vesey planned his resistance movement. Some modern scholars and primary-source accounts maintain that his plot was detailed and well organized, and that Vesey discussed the plan at length with a small group of trusted lieutenants. His accused co-conspirators, Peter Poyas, Rolla Bennett, Monday Gell, and Jack Pritchard, were all members of the African Methodist Church. The movement sought the assassination of South Carolina's governor and Charleston's mayor, and the rebels planned to take the militia arsenal, burn the city, and slaughter white citizens. They believed that blacks from the countryside and city would join the uprising as it grew, culminating in a mass exodus to Haiti, where President Jean-Pierre Boyer had encouraged free-black American immigration. A series of confessions exposed the conspiracy and led to the arrest of 128 black men. Thirty-five of those arrested were hanged, and 40 were transported for their roles as co-conspirators in the revolt. Based on confessions and testimonies, South Carolina's courts named Vesey the chief organizer of the revolt and sentenced him to execution. He was hanged on 2 July 1822.

Vesey became a martyr for the American antislavery movement and a symbol for black resistance following his alleged role as mastermind of the 1822 insurrection. His life, the revolt, and his death have raised questions about nineteenth-century race relations and black resistance. Historians still debate whether the 1822 events in Charleston represented a failed, however expertly designed, uprising or whether the alleged Vesey rebellion occurred only in the minds of whites, and was fueled by rumors and deep-rooted white fears of slave resistance. The question remains: Was Denmark Vesey falsely accused because he was a literate and outspoken free black who used his thorough knowledge of Christianity to challenge American slavery? Or did he take this spirit of protest a step further, to plan what would have been, prior to NAT TURNER's rebellion in 1830, the largest slave revolt in U.S. history?

FURTHER READING

Egerton, Douglas R. *He Shall Go Out Free: The Lives of Denmark Vesey* (1999).

Lofton, John. *Denmark Vesey's Revolt: The Slave Plot That Lit a Fuse to Fort Sumter* (1983).

Pearson, Edward A. *Designs against Charleston: The Trial Record of the Denmark Vesey Slave Conspiracy of 1822* (1999).

Robertson, David. *Denmark Vesey: The Buried Story of America's Largest Slave Rebellion and the Man Who Led It* (1999).

TIWANNA M. SIMPSON

Vick, Harold (3 Apr. 1936–13 Nov. 1987), jazz and soul tenor saxophonist, was born Harold Edward Vick in Rocky Mount, North Carolina, to Alice (maiden name unknown). Other details about his parents, including the name of his father, are unknown. Vick took piano lessons at age eight for a few months but without serious interest. He began clarinet lessons at age twelve, and the following year he was given a good instrument by his uncle, the renowned jazz clarinetist and tenor saxophonist PRINCE ROBINSON. Two or three years later Vick began playing tenor saxophone while continuing his clarinet studies with Charles Woods at BOOKER T. WASHINGTON High School in Rocky Mount. During this period he was raised by his grandparents.

Vick studied sociology and psychology and played on the varsity basketball team at Howard University while working mainly in rhythm and blues bands. During his third year at Howard he commenced what amounted to a jazz apprenticeship, playing for two years at the Howard Theater in the pit orchestra under the direction of Rick Henderson, a former member of DUKE ELLINGTON's big band. Vick graduated with a degree in psychology in 1958.

Vick subsequently toured with the rhythm and blues bands of Red Prysock, Paul Williams (accompanying the singer RUTH BROWN), Lloyd Price, and KING CURTIS. From 1960 to 1964 he was a member of the organist Jack McDuff's soul-jazz group, with which he recorded regularly. In 1963 he made his first album as a leader, *Steppin' Out*. He also played in the mid-1960s with the organists Larry Young, Jimmy McGriff, Big John Patton, including the album *Along Came John* (1963), Wild Bill Davis, and Groove Holmes. He worked with the pianist Walter Bishop Jr. occasionally from 1964 through the remainder of the decade.

On the strength of a performance with the trumpeter DONALD BYRD at Carnegie Hall, Vick was given a recording contract for three albums, including *The Caribbean Suite* and *Straight Up*, both from 1966, when he also recorded with the pianist Duke Pearson. During this period he also held affiliations with the drummer PHILLY JOE JONES, the trumpeter HOWARD MCGHEE, the singer and pianist RAY CHARLES, and the Apollo Theater house band under Reuben Phillips. Vick led his own quintet, including the trumpeter WOODY SHAW and Bishop, around 1967. In that year he also performed in two plays, *The Coach with the Six Insides* and *The Lusitanian Bogey*. He was a member of the trumpeter DIZZY GILLESPIE's big band at the Newport Jazz Festival in 1968.

By the mid-1960s Vick also played other saxophones and several types of flutes and clarinets; he toured Europe as a woodwind player with the Negro Ensemble Company in 1969. Returning home, he lectured in public schools. Vick then worked in soul bands accompanying the saxophonist King Curtis and the singer ARETHA FRANKLIN. From 1971 to 1973 he was also a member of the drummer JACK DEJOHNETTE's fusion group Compost, making an LP of that name in 1972.

In April 1974 Vick suffered a massive heart attack, but he recovered quickly and resumed playing in August. Returning to work in soul-jazz organ groups, he joined that of SHIRLEY SCOTT, touring Europe, recording her album *One for Me* and his own *Don't Look Back* in November 1974, and remaining with Scott until at least 1976. Vick then worked as a studio musician and a jazz freelancer; in this capacity he joined McGriff for recording sessions in December 1980 and January 1981. He appeared in the movies *Stardust Memories* (1980), *The Cotton Club* (1984), and *School Daze* (1988), this last directed by SPIKE LEE. Vick died of a heart attack in New York City. He was survived by a daughter; details of his marriage are unknown.

Not an innovator, Vick was among those tenor saxophone soloists of his generation who moved back and forth comfortably over the hazy boundary between jazz and African American popular music. He was comfortable with the speed and headiness required to improvise melodies over bebop-derived chord progressions but also could play in a soulful, tuneful blues- and gospel-influenced manner.

FURTHER READING

Gardner, Mark. "Harold Vick," *Jazz Monthly*, no. 171 (1969).

Tomkins, Les. "Harold Vick," *Crescendo International* 14 (1975).

Obituary: *New York Times*, 17 Nov. 1987.

This entry is taken from the *American National Biography* and is published here with the permission of the American Council of Learned Societies.

BARRY KERNFELD

Vick, Samuel Hynes (1 Apr. 1863–8 July 1946), teacher, businessman, banker, Republican Party activist, and longtime U.S. postmaster of Wilson, North Carolina, was born a slave near Castalia in Nash County, North Carolina, during the Civil War. The oldest son of five children born to carpenter Daniel Vick and Fannie (Blount) Vick, Samuel received his early education at Wilson Academy in Wilson, where the Vick family moved shortly after the war's end in 1865.

A gifted student, Vick excelled at his studies, and in 1880 he was admitted to Lincoln University (then the Ashmun Institute, after Jehudi Ashmun, leader of 1820s Liberia) in Pennsylvania, from which he received both a bachelor's and a master's degree in 1884. While his father helped finance his education, Vick insisted on paying as much of his own expenses as possible by teaching school during summer vacations. His philosophy of pragmatic independence guided his life thereafter.

As one of the state's first large towns to implement a public graded school system in the 1880s, Wilson operated racially segregated schools for its children. Following graduation, Vick returned home to become teacher and principal at Wilson's public graded school for African Americans, a position he held for four years. He also quickly became active in local Republican Party circles. Following Benjamin Harrison's inauguration as U.S. president, Vick was nominated by U.S. representative HENRY PLUMMER CHEATHAM of the so-called Black Second—the third African American Republican to represent that predominantly black

district in Congress—as postmaster of the Wilson post office, with its lucrative annual salary of $1,500, one of the state's highest.

Despite grumblings by leading Democrats in largely white Wilson about political payoffs, Vick was confirmed by the U.S. Senate in September 1889 and served for nearly five years. His prudent management of the Wilson post office brought Vick grudging praise from the town's white community, unlike less fortunate black appointees at other post offices across the "Black Second" congressional district, some of whom were removed for alleged mismanagement of funds. His selection of younger brother William as postal clerk, mildly controversial at first, proved to be a sensible choice. After Vick's eventual replacement as postmaster in February 1894, he remained so influential locally that he was appointed in 1895 to the Wilson County board of education, on which he served until 1899.

Vick was married on 10 May 1893 to Annie Mariah Washington of Wilson, a graduate of Scotia Seminary. The Vick family eventually included four daughters (Annie Monte, Doris, Elba Louise, and Irma) and four sons (Samuel, Jr., Daniel Lionel, Robert Elliott, and the youngest, George White Vick).

His active role in Republican politics continued unabated, and he regularly attended national conventions, either as adviser or state delegate, from 1896 until 1916. Following the election of William McKinley as U.S. president in 1896, Vick emerged as the leading contender for reappointment as Wilson postmaster. In early 1898, U.S. representative GEORGE HENRY WHITE (R-North Carolina), who was also African American and Cheatham's brother-in-law, nominated Vick for the post, and local Democrats, impressed with Vick's earlier record, posed no objection. After his Senate confirmation in May 1898, Vick was among more than three dozen black postmasters whose appointments were secured by White during his first term, with active support by Republican U.S. senator Jeter C. Pritchard (Pritchard was white; his alliance with White was party-, not race-, based).

White and Vick also became personal friends. Vick's prowess as a real estate investor and businessman made him a natural investor in Whitesboro, the New Jersey land development company White unveiled in late 1901, after leaving Congress. After North Carolina voted to disenfranchise the majority of its black voters by constitutional amendment in 1900, the utopian town—constructed on 2,000 acres of a former slave plantation in Cape May County—was intended as a sanctuary for African Americans fleeing southern political oppression and Jim Crow segregation. Vick became the first president of the George H. White Land and Improvement Company, joining investors PAUL LAURENCE DUNBAR, Wiley H. Bates, and IDA GIBBS HUNT and HARRIET GIBBS MARSHALL, daughters of longtime diplomat MIFFLIN W. GIBBS. The new town grew only sporadically, and although it never achieved the prosperity for which its founders hoped, its healthful climate and congenial atmosphere made it a favored location for summer visitors, including Vick, who visited the site for years. Its streets still retain the names of Vick, White, Dunbar, and other founders.

Despite new political restrictions Vick chose to remain for the rest of his life in Wilson, where his real estate portfolio included the town's first movie theater for African Americans, the Orange Hotel, and the Wilson Commercial Bank, which he helped found and served as president. An active elder in the Calvary Presbyterian congregation, he served as superintendent of the Sunday school and as a delegate to church synods. In fraternal affairs Vick was both an active Freemason and an Odd Fellow, serving as Grand Master and Grand Secretary of the state society.

By early 1903 the political climate had changed significantly, depriving Vick of strong support in the restructured Republican Party, whose southern wing was now dominated by Senator Pritchard's "lily white" faction. Seeking to revive his fading chances for reelection by the Democratic legislature, Pritchard prevailed upon President Theodore Roosevelt to replace Vick as Wilson's postmaster, despite an outstanding record, with a white Democrat. Roosevelt named Vick's replacement in March 1903, and soon appointed ex-Senator Pritchard to the federal bench.

Vick, having now served as postmaster for almost a decade, took the loss in stride, concentrating on business interests and becoming a Wilson County notary public in 1905. Active in the National Negro Business League, Vick attended its national meeting as a state delegate in 1913. He continued to attend Republican national conventions, last serving as a state delegate in 1916 in Chicago, along with George White, an alternate delegate from his adopted Pennsylvania.

Although Vick retired from active participation in business and farming interests in the early 1930s, his national reputation continued to grow.

For nearly two decades, beginning in 1927, he was listed in editions of *Who's Who in Colored America*. Vick Elementary School in Wilson is named in his honor. He died at age eighty-three in Wilson.

FURTHER READING

Anderson, Eric. *Race and Politics in North Carolina, 1872–1901: The Black Second* (1981).

Kenzer, Robert. *Enterprising Southerners: Black Economic Success in North Carolina, 1865–1915* (1997).

Obituary: Raleigh (N.C.) *News and Observer*, 10 July 1946.

BENJAMIN R. JUSTESEN

Virgil, Osvaldo José (17 May 1933–), baseball player, was born Osvaldo José (Pichardo) Virgil in Monte Cristi, Dominican Republic. After Rafael Trujillo came to power, his family left for Puerto Rico, and then moved to the Bronx when "Ozzie" Virgil was fourteen. Though he failed to make the team at DeWitt Clinton High School, he played competitive sandlot baseball in the Bronx and Brooklyn. After graduating in 1950, Virgil enlisted in the U.S. Marine Corps Reserves, and was stationed at Camp LeJeune, North Carolina, where he played baseball with the corps team. Following his army service, Virgil was signed following a postwar tryout with the New York Giants, under the advice of the former Negro League owner Alex Pompez.

Virgil made his professional debut with St. Cloud of the Northern League in 1953, and had his breakout year with Dallas of the Texas League two years later, slugging seventeen home runs and earning an All-Star berth for the Double-A league. When he debuted with the Giants in September 1956, Virgil became the first Dominican player in Major League Baseball, before being sent back down to Triple-A Minneapolis, a level below the majors. He spent 1957 with the big league club; though he made the Sporting News All-Rookie team, he was regarded as a good fielder but poor batter.

In January 1958 Virgil was traded to the Detroit Tigers, the second-to-last team to integrate. The Tigers were under intense community pressure to bring up a player of color for their big-league squad, even drawing organized boycotts from black groups. Though the team's front office insisted it wasn't caving to pressure, Virgil was recalled from the minors that spring, and became the first Tiger player of color on 6 June 1958. Eleven days later, he made his debut at Detroit's Briggs Stadium to a standing ovation, and went 5-for-5 with a double.

Osvaldo José "Ozzie" Virgil in an undated file photo. (AP Images.)

Despite breaking the team's color line, Virgil wasn't fully accepted by some in the African American community as a "true representative." He himself insisted that "it made no difference ... that he became the team's first Negro player." Because of the attention paid to his skin color, Virgil's nationality was glossed over during his early playing years: as the first Dominican ballplayer, Virgil later became honored in a country that would yield a wealth of talent, including Sammy Sosa, PEDRO MARTINEZ, Albert Pujols, JUAN MARICHAL, and Felipe Alou and his brothers.

In 1959 Detroit assigned the versatile Virgil back to the minors to train at other positions. While in the Triple-A Charleston affiliate for the Tigers, Virgil saw action at every spot in the field except pitcher, and became the very definition of a utility player. After playing part of 1960 and 1961 with Detroit, the Tigers shipped him to the Kansas City Athletics. Virgil spent parts of the next four seasons with the systems of the Athletics, Baltimore Orioles, Washington Senators, Milwaukee Braves, and Pittsburgh Pirates, before spending his last years with the Giants.

Virgil remained with the Giants following his playing career, serving as a third-base and bullpen coach through 1972, before becoming a roving scout in Mexico, South America, and the Caribbean. Following his tenure with San Francisco, Virgil became a coach for the Montreal Expos, San Diego Padres, and Seattle Mariners.

Virgil had five children, one of whom, Ozzie Jr., became a two-time All-Star catcher for the Philadelphia Phillies, Atlanta Braves, and Toronto Blue Jays through the 1980s. In December 2006, to celebrate the fiftieth anniversary of his Major League debut, the Dominican Republic named an airport after Virgil.

FURTHER READING
Anderson, William M. "Ozzie Virgil Breaks the Color Barrier with the Detroit Tigers." *Michigan History Magazine* 81, no. 6. Nov./Dec. 1997.
Briley, Ron. "In the Tradition of Jackie Robinson: Ozzie Virgil and the Integration of the Detroit Tigers." *The Cooperstown Symposium on Baseball and American Culture*, 2002.

ADAM W. GREEN

Vivian, Cordy Tindell (C. T.) (30 July 1924–), minister, civil rights activist and organizer, was born to Robert Cordy and Euzetta Tindell Vivian in Howard County, Missouri. C.T. Vivian grew up in Illinois and attended Western Illinois University where he received a bachelor's degree in history in 1948. He began his career at the Carver Community Center in Peoria, Illinois, where he helped desegregate local restaurants. It was also in Peoria that Vivian met Octavia Geans; they were married in 1953 and would have seven children. Not long thereafter, Vivian was called to enter the ministry and moved to Nashville, Tennessee, to attend American Baptist Theological Seminary in 1955.

In Nashville, Reverend Vivian took a job as an editor for National Baptist Convention USA, Inc., where his outspoken demeanor and progressive vision often set him at odds with the rest of the editorial board. Vivian took over the pastorate of First Community Church and published a small newspaper called the *Nashville News-Star*. In Nashville he found a group of like-minded ministerial peers who strongly believed that an activism rooted in faith and love could help solve many of the problems facing African Americans living under Jim Crow in the twentieth century. Kelly Miller Smith of First Baptist Church was perhaps the best known and most influential of these leaders, and MARTIN LUTHER KING JR. asked Smith to form a Nashville affiliate of the Southern Christian Leadership Conference (SCLC). As the first vice president of direct action for the Nashville Christian Leadership Conference, or NCLC, Vivian had a strong influence on the burgeoning civil rights movement in Nashville. Vivian quickly built a reputation as a passionate advocate, a gifted strategist, and a fiery orator. When JAMES LAWSON arrived in Nashville in 1958, Vivian and Smith had built the foundations of a strong network between African American congregations and student groups.

Vivian, Smith, and Lawson held regular workshops in nonviolence as they sought to galvanize the Nashville Student Movement. Future SNCC (Student Non-Violent Coordinating Committee) and SCLC members DIANE NASH, JAMES BEVEL, Bernard Lafayette, and JOHN LEWIS all got their start in the movement as students in Nashville. Slightly older than the other students, Vivian combined selfless bravery with the leadership of an active minister. On 12 February 1960 the Nashville students began sit-in demonstrations at downtown lunch counters. As the demonstrations expanded into a full-fledged boycott of downtown stores, Nashville Mayor Ben West held meetings with local clergy. Tall and adamant, Vivian often took the lead in articulating the goals of the movement at these meetings.

On 19 April 1960 the home of Z. Alexander Looby, the attorney representing the students, was bombed. Under the guidance of Vivian, Smith, and Lawson, the students quickly organized a silent march from First Baptist Church to City Hall. Three to four thousand participants joined the demonstration, with Vivian, Nash, Lawson, and Lafayette at the head of the column. Mayor Ben West met the marchers on the steps of City Hall, where Vivian read a prepared statement chastising West for his failure to support desegregation. Diane Nash followed Vivian's statement by asking West if he thought segregation was morally acceptable. Mayor West then conceded that he did find segregation immoral and pledged to use his office to end this practice in downtown stores. The steadfastness, dedication, and success garnered by the Nashville Movement led King to characterize it as "the best organized and most disciplined in the Southland" (Fairclough, 60).

Like other veterans of Nashville, Vivian took his activism on the road, joining the Freedom Rides after violence stalled their progress in Alabama. Originally conceived by the Congress of Racial Equality (CORE), the Freedom Rides were intended to test the desegregation of interstate travel mandated by the Supreme Court in *Boynton v. Virginia* (1960) by traveling throughout the South and nonviolently integrating public facilities like bus stations and restrooms. Vivian joined the freedom riders in Montgomery, Alabama, on 24 May 1961 and rode the lead bus into Mississippi, where he was jailed with the rest of the riders. When he moved to Chattanooga in 1961, he continued to advise the NCLC, and in 1963 he served as the Tennessee Chairman for the March on Washington. That same year Vivian joined King's SCLC staff as Director of Affiliates. As part of the SCLC executive board, Vivian traveled throughout the country, performing reconnaissance and making contacts to prepare for upcoming direct-action programs.

Vivian organized the SCLC's foray into Selma, Alabama, where the reverend was at his most visible and outspoken. On 25 February 1965 Vivian led twenty-five demonstrators to the Dallas County Courthouse to protest a restrictive voter-registration policy. Finding the door barred by Sheriff Jim Clark, Vivian delivered an impromptu speech comparing Clark's policing to the oppressiveness of Hitler. As Clark turned to walk away, Vivian exclaimed, "You can turn your back on me, but you can't turn your back on justice" (Halberstam, 502). Clark wheeled and punched Vivian in the mouth, sprawling him backward on the steps. Police arrested Vivian, but the incident earned national media attention, further exposing the brutality of the Deep South's law enforcement tactics against blacks. Once released, Vivian helped organize a nighttime march in nearby Marion, Alabama. State troopers disrupted the demonstration, killing young demonstrator JIMMY LEE JACKSON. Vivian's powerful rhetoric and symbolic organization, as well as the subsequent violence of Alabama police, kept demonstrators motivated, earned sympathetic national attention, and provided the SCLC with substantial political leverage.

Vivian's creative use of nonviolence also influenced SCLC involvement in Chicago and St. Augustine, Florida, where he staged "wade-ins" to secure the integration of public beaches. Vivian left the SCLC in 1966 to work for Chicago's Urban Training Center. While living in Chicago, Vivian worked on programs to train other ministers for social activism, and he led efforts to integrate construction labor unions. In 1969 Vivian authored *Black Power and the American Myth*, one of the first comprehensive accounts of the civil rights movement. Vivian remained committed to social justice, founding the National Anti-Klan Network (Center for Democratic Renewal) in 1979 and the Black Action Strategies and Information Center (BASIC). He received honorary doctorate degrees from the New School for Social Research (1984) and Western Illinois University (1987). Throughout his life, Reverend Vivian pursued nonviolence as a complete philosophy—to motivate others and agitate for change.

FURTHER READING

Fairclough, Adam. *To Redeem the Soul of America: The Southern Christian Leadership Conference and Martin Luther King Jr.* (1987).

Halberstam, David. *The Children* (1998).

Selby, Earl, and Miriam Selby. *Odyssey: Journey through Black America* (1971).

W. BRIAN PIPER

Vodery, William Henry Bennett ("Will") (8 Oct. 1884–18 Nov. 1951), American composer, arranger, orchestrator, lyricist, and musical director, was born in Philadelphia, Pennsylvania, to William Henry Bennett and Selina (Buthanna) Vodery. His father, originally from Baltimore, Maryland, was a minister and a graduate of Lincoln University (1883); he continued graduate studies at the Theological Department of the College and later taught classes there. In September 1884 Vodery's father died unexpectedly; his mother later remarried.

Vodery's mother came from a musical background, and he was exposed to music as a young child. He studied the piano and violin while in the public schools of Philadelphia and graduated in 1902 from Central High School. His music education was supplemented with study of harmony and counterpoint, and private composition lessons at the University of Pennsylvania with Professor Hugh A. Clarke (1839–1928). A notable musical figure (composer, conductor, and writer on harmony and counterpoint), Clarke was also the founder of the university's Music Department. Vodery may have audited some of his classes even though he was not a matriculated student and did not graduate from the university.

Vodery worked as a librarian for the Philadelphia Orchestra and began to make a splash, attracting attention for his talents. For example, in 1903 the nineteen-year-old Vodery had his first three songs published in Philadelphia: "Boyhood Days," "Cause Her Dear Face on Me to Beam," and "My Country I Love Thee." The New Yorkers William A. Riley and J. F. Mastin supplied the lyrics. Among those to take note of Vodery's talent was Professor Louis Koemmennich, a noted instructor at the University of Berlin and assistant to Walter Damrosch. With the help and patronage of the Broadway performer Marquita Nicholai, Vodery studied piano, violin, orchestration, and arranging at the University of Berlin with Koemmennich. It was Koemmennich who was responsible for cultivating and nurturing Vodery's talent and skills as an arranger and orchestrator.

Vodery's mother and stepfather had a boarding house, and black vaudeville performers often roomed there. These entertainers were some of Vodery's earliest encounters with black musical theater, which greatly influenced him. During his young teenage years, Vodery had the opportunity to arrange music professionally for many black vaudeville acts in Philadelphia. These included the vaudeville team of GEORGE WALKER and BERT WILLIAMS, who discovered Vodery's talents and passion for musical theater and his art of arranging. They encouraged him to relocate to vaudeville in New York City.

Vodery relocated to New York City in 1904 and worked as a novice arranger and bandleader for numerous vaudeville performers. He directed *A Trip to Africa*, which later toured in Chicago. The following year, in 1905, Vodery became an arranger for Charles K. Harris Publishing Company in Chicago and a librarian for the Chicago Symphony Orchestra. He received lessons in harmony, orchestration, and conducting with Frederick Stock, the music director of the Chicago Symphony Orchestra. Vodery gained valuable experience arranging classical music. For example, he arranged Wagner's *Parsifal* for the conductor and Broadway producer Henry W. Savage. Vodery also composed works for the Chicago performance of *The Man from Bam* by Joseph Jordan and taught classes at Charles K. Harris's Chicago Music House.

By 1907 Vodery was back in New York City working as a professional musician; performing, composing, conducting, and arranging music for performers such as the vaudeville teams of George Walker and Bert Williams, and Murphy and Francis. He was also involved with theatrical productions such as *Abysinnia* (1906); *The Time, the Place, and the Girl* (1907); *The Oyster Man* (1907); *Bandana Land* (1908); *Dr. Beans from Boston* (1910); *Down in Dixie Minstrels* (1910); *My Friend from Dixie* (1911); and *The Blackville Corporation* (1911). Due to his talents and notoriety, in 1910 Vodery was asked to conduct a dance orchestra at the opening of the Howard Theater in Washington, D.C. Also that year, he conducted a minstrel show that was funded by the Colored Vaudeville Benevolent Association.

From 1913 to 1919, Vodery was the arranger in New York City for the Ziegfeld Follies. His close friendship with Bert Williams was a plus in helping him obtain that position. Williams, who had appeared with the Ziegfeld Follies, lavished much praise on him and promoted his talents. Vodery was also the conductor of the dance orchestra of the Coconut Grove of the Century Roof Garden in New York City. From 1913 to 1918, he composed songs for the Ziegfeld Follies and black theater and worked with such noted lyricists as Henry Creamer, Alex Rogers, Jean Havez, and his close friend Bert Williams. These included "I Was Certainly Going Some" (1913), "The Darktown Poker Club" (1914), "The Lee Family" (1916), and "When I Return" (1918). He also made arrangements for Bert Williams's "Hard Times," "Never Mo," and "Purpostus" (1915), and composed "Two Months in the Old Mill" (1919). Other works composed by him included "The Carolina Romp" (1913), "Carolina Fox Trot" (1914), "The Midnight Frolic Glide" (1915), and "Doraldina's Indian Dance" (1917).

Vodery became friends with George Gershwin in 1917. He provided orchestration advice when Gershwin was composing his Concerto in F and offered suggestions on breaking into the musical comedy arena. Vodery even helped Gershwin find work at Fox's City Theatre. Gershwin later asked him to orchestrate his opera Blue Monday and Show Girl.

With the outbreak of World War I, Vodery served as the bandmaster of the 807th Pioneers Infantry Regiment in France (1918–1919). He performed for such dignitaries as the president of France. By 1919 Vodery was in Chaumont France at the Bandmaster's School. He was the only black out of 42 selected from 163 bandmasters from around the United States to attend the school. A score of 80 percent was required on the entrance exam, and Vodery scored 98 percent, the highest of the 163 applicants. Vodery was so proficient in harmony and instrumentation that he did not have to take any classes in these subjects. In fact, he was selected by his instrumentation instructor, the pianist Robert Casadesus, as assistant instructor and taught instrumentation to a class of forty men. Vodery studied conducting with André Coplet, director of the Paris Symphony Orchestra, and Albert Stoessel, conductor of the St. Louis Symphony. He scored a perfect score of 100 percent on the finals and won a scholarship to study at the famed Paris Conservatory. But he decided to return to the 807th Pioneers Infantry Regiment.

Vodery returned to New York, working with the Ziegfeld Follies until 1932 and also in black theater. He gained much prominence as an arranger, composer, and conductor. For example, he was the arranger of EUBIE BLAKE's and NOBLE SISSLE's "Shuffle Along" and "Under the Bamboo Tree"

(1921). The following year, in 1922, he directed George Gershwin's opera Blue Monday. Vodery formed and conducted his Plantation Orchestra from 1922 to 1927. This orchestra performed in the United States and Europe with performers such as PAUL ROBESON, FLORENCE MILLS, and JOSEPHINE BAKER of the Lew Leslie revues. Vodery even offered an arranging position with this orchestra to the composer and oboist WILLIAM GRANT STILL.

Vodery's works during this time included songs with lyrics by Henry Creamer: "E-Gypsy Ann" for the show How Come (1923); and "Dusky Love" for Keep Shufflin'" (1928). He later worked as orchestrator, arranger, and director of Dover Street to Dixie and toured with Lew Leslie's Blackbirds production (1927). He was the choral director of Show Boat (1927–1929) at the Ziegfeld Theatre. The performers included the Will Vodery Jubilee Singers and JULES BLEDSOE.

Vodery was also the film composer and arranger for Fox Films in Hollywood (1929–1933) and produced Hills of Old New Hampshire and All for You. His other activities included musical director of the Will Vodery Jubilee Singers' performance in Strike Me Pink (1933); composer and consultant for the Century of Progress International Exposition in Chicago (1933–1934); musical supervisor and arranger for the Cotton Club Parade revues (1936–1940); composer and consultant for the New York World's Fair (1939) and the Golden Gate International Exposition, San Francisco (1939–1940). In 1945 Oscar Hammerstein asked Vodery to coach the singers in the revival of Show Boat, which was performed at the Ziegfeld Theatre (1946–1947).

Among Vodery's later works were the patriotic songs "N.A.G.A. Marching Chorus" (1941) and "The Unknown Soldier Lives Again" (1942); "Dearest Memories" (1943); "When Eden Was a Garden" (1944); "Jig Walk" (1945); "Tell Me What It's All About" (1947); "I.B.P.O.E. of W. March Song" (1949); and "Messed Up in Love" (1950). Vodery's final years were spent at 419 West 141st Street in Harlem's Hamilton Heights. He died at age sixty-seven in Manhattan on 18 November 1951, leaving his wife, Rosanne, and two sons, Will H. Vodery Jr. and Harry Vodery. In 1955 some of his manuscripts and papers were given to Carl Van Vechten by his wife. These are now housed at Yale University as part of the James Weldon Johnson Collection.

Vodery was more prolific as an arranger than as a composer; the majority of his compositions were songs. Described by DUKE ELLINGTON as "handsome, debonair, and always in gentlemanly attire," Vodery is celebrated as an outstanding and eminent vaudeville and Broadway dance and musical theater composer, musician, and arranger. Producers, performers, and publishers requested him, and his talents were recognized and well rewarded by many, including by the press. He influenced many, including Duke Ellington, whom he mentored. Vodery's harmonization, compositions, arrangements, orchestration, and his style of mixing jazz with nineteenth-century European classical music scoring were inspiring.

FURTHER READING

Southern, Eileen. *Biographical Dictionary of African-American and African Musicians* (1981).

Tucker, Mark. "In Search of Will Vodery." *Black Music Research Journal*, Spring 1996.

"Vodery, William Louis." In *International Dictionary of Black Composers* (1999).

BARBARA BONOUS-SMIT

Vogelsang, Peter (21 Aug. 1815–4 Apr. 1887), soldier, was born in New York City. The chief sources of information about his life and career are the official papers of the Fifty-fourth Massachusetts Volunteer Infantry Regiment and the regimental history, *A Brave Black Regiment*, written by Luis F. Emilio, a white officer of the regiment in which Vogelsang served from April 1863 until August 1865.

Among those helping with the recruitment effort was FREDERICK DOUGLASS, whose two sons joined the ranks of the Fifty-fourth, and Francis G. Shaw, a prominent New England abolitionist and father of Colonel Robert Gould Shaw, the regiment's white commanding officer. The elder Shaw recruited Vogelsang, a druggist and dry goods clerk in Brooklyn, who needed no special pleading to join up. A married man, Vogelsang was forty-seven years old, the oldest soldier in the Fifty-fourth Massachusetts, when he was mustered into service on 17 April 1863. His age and experience had their benefits; Vogelsang exercised an almost paternal influence on the soldiers of the Fifty-fourth. His peacetime work of stocking goods and filling orders also made him a natural for the post of regimental quartermaster sergeant, which he assumed in November 1863, after serving as first sergeant of Company H. On 24 April 1863—soon after the Fifty-fourth had gone for training at Camp Meigs in Readville, Massachusetts—Colonel Shaw already had words of praise for his father's special recruit: "Dear Father, I ought to have written you long ago,

that your man Vogelsang was accepted and is a sergeant in one of the new Companies. He is very efficient" (Shaw, 325).

Vogelsang did not engage in formal combat, however, until July 1863, when the regiment was sent to participate in one of the Union army's many assaults on Charleston, South Carolina. Characteristically, at first the regiment was not assigned to the main assault against Battery Wagner, a formidable earthen fort on Morris Island, to the east of the city. Instead the Fifty-fourth was sent to James Island, on the west side of Charleston Harbor. Its role was to try to divert the Confederates so that the main event might prove successful. (No direct assault on Battery Wagner would succeed, however. It was finally abandoned by the Confederates after a prolonged siege.)

On 15 July the regiment disembarked from the steamer *Chasseur* onto James Island. Here its men would serve for the first time with white troops (of the Tenth Connecticut). The Fifty-fourth was ordered to form a picket line, and early on the morning of 16 July it was attacked by six companies of the Twenty-fifth South Carolina Regiment. The attack must have been sudden because Sergeant Vogelsang, "who had a post at a palmetto-tree," later recalled that "in a moment one hundred Rebels were swarming around him" (Emilio, 58). Undaunted, Vogelsang led the men of Company H to their left to join forces with others of the regiment. With the improved numbers now at his disposal, he led the troops forward, taking a musket from a dead Confederate as he advanced. But the tide soon turned, and the Twenty-fifth South Carolina forced the picket line back. In the heat of the skirmish, Vogelsang and eight other men of Company H tried to escape across a creek. Several of the men were killed as they crossed, and seeing the futility of his attempted escape, Vogelsang turned to the pursuing Confederates, indicating his willingness to surrender. At that, a Confederate officer shot him in the chest. Sergeant Vogelsang suffered a severe injury and might well have been captured or killed, except that reinforcements finally pushed forward with the help of heavy guns onboard the federal steamers *John Adams* and *Mayflower*. The Confederates were forced to fall back as the Union troops advanced to reclaim their original battle lines. That Vogelsang was wounded trying to surrender points up one of the uglier facts of this often-ugly war: Confederate soldiers were so incensed by seeing African Americans in uniform that they would offer no quarter. It would happen again and again, as it did infamously at Fort Pillow in April 1864 and at the Battle of the Crater in July of that same year. Long after the incident on James Island, Vogelsang recalled that some of the men of the Fifty-fourth who tried to surrender were first tied up and then shot or bayoneted to death by Confederate troops (Yacovone, 248).

However, the bravery of men like Peter Vogelsang changed the minds of many white soldiers who fought for the Union, including those in command positions, such as Major General Alfred H. Terry, one of the divisional commanders of the Department of the South. Following the James Island skirmish, Terry told Colonel Shaw that he was "exceedingly pleased with the conduct of your regiment" (quoted in Yacovone, 40). As a result, the Fifty-fourth Massachusetts was given its most famous opportunity, the assault on Battery Wagner two days later, on 18 July. Remarkably, despite his injury, Sergeant Vogelsang took part in this action. Though members of the Fifty-fourth managed to breach the walls of the fort, without reinforcements they could not take the stronghold or disable the big guns that threatened approaches by both land and sea. Finally the regiment was forced to withdraw, having suffered heavy casualties, including the death of Colonel Shaw. Afterward Shaw was buried in a mass grave along with his fallen soldiers; this was meant as an affront, both to Shaw's memory and to the federal government for its policy of arming African Americans.

The efficiency and bravery of black troops did not impress everyone who wore the blue, and it certainly did not suggest economic parity for these worthy men. Edwin M. Stanton, the secretary of war, refused African Americans the standard thirteen dollars a month paid to white federal soldiers. Instead, African American troops were to be paid three dollars less. In protest the Fifty-fourth Massachusetts served for eighteen months without pay, supported by Colonel Shaw, who himself refused pay. After Shaw's death, however, Brigade Commander Colonel James Montgomery, a notorious Kansas jayhawker with whom Shaw had often sparred, "repudiated the regiment's demand for equal pay and derided the men as savages" and as a "race of slaves." "He berated them with scurrilous insults especially the obnoxious charge that light complexions exposed some men as the offspring of interracial 'rascality.'" Small wonder that Sergeant Vogelsang "never forgot the anguish he felt, especially because of Montgomery's slurs concerning skin color" (Yacovone, 272–273). Congress did not enact legislation guaranteeing equal pay for black and white soldiers until June 1864. Under the same act the men of the Fifty-fourth Regiment received back pay retroactive to the beginning of their service.

Despite this belated recognition of the contribution of black troops, the entrenched racism of the U.S. military was evident in its reluctance to commission black officers. Indeed it was not until January 1865, eleven months after the Fifty-fourth Massachusetts distinguished itself at the Battle of Olustee in northern Florida, that the War Department agreed to promote Sergeant STEPHEN A. SWAILS to the rank of second lieutenant, making him the first African American in a regular combat unit to become a commissioned officer. Further commissions would have to wait until the war was over, including a richly deserved second lieutenancy for Peter Vogelsang. This, too, was turned down by the War Department in May 1865. However, with more lobbying in Washington by Massachusetts governor John A. Andrew, Vogelsang was finally commissioned—now as first lieutenant—in June. He was also named regimental quartermaster and served in this capacity until he was mustered out of the service on 20 August 1865.

Vogelsang returned to New York after the war and worked as a clerk in a customs office until his death. The year before he died, he was interviewed by Luis F. Emilio. Vogelsang's comments were included in Emilio's regimental history, a good, forthright source of information about the Fifty-fourth and its heroic men, probably the most celebrated of the 180,000 African Americans who served during the Civil War.

FURTHER READING

Cox, Clinton. *Undying Glory: The Story of the Massachusetts 54th Regiment* (1991).

Emilio, Luis F. *A Brave Black Regiment: History of the Fifty-Fourth Regiment of Massachusetts Volunteer Infantry, 1863–1865* (1995).

Shaw, Robert Gould. *Blue-Eyed Child of Fortune: The Civil War Letters of Colonel Robert Gould Shaw*, ed. Russell Duncan (1992).

Yacovone, Donald, ed. *A Voice of Thunder: The Civil War Letters of George E. Stephens* (1997).

LEE PASSARELLA

Voorhis, Robert (c. 1769– ?), slave, sailor, and hermit, was born in Princeton, New Jersey. His parents' names are unknown. His mother was a slave, and he was told that his father was a white Englishman. He had one sister, who was three years older than he. When Voorhis was four years old, he was given to his master's daughter upon her marriage to John Voorhis, a German-born plantation owner. He moved to Georgetown in the District of Columbia and never saw his mother or sister again.

At the age of fourteen or fifteen, Voorhis was apprenticed to a shoemaker. Demonstrating little proficiency in his trade, he returned to his master's plantation, where he worked as a gardener until he was nineteen. At this time, he met Alley Pennington, an orphaned slave from Cecil County, Maryland, who promised to marry him, provided he secured his freedom. Voorhis convinced James Bevens, a supposed friend, to purchase him from his master for fifty pounds. Bevens agreed to destroy the bill of sale once Voorhis had repaid him the full amount. Voorhis subsequently married Pennington, and they had two children.

Three years into the marriage, Voorhis had repaid Bevens a substantial portion of the fifty pounds, but he had neglected to request or keep any receipts of payment. While Voorhis was with his family one evening, Bevens seized him and told him he was to be sold farther south. Late in the night Voorhis was forced aboard a schooner bound for Charleston, South Carolina, where he was sold at a slave auction. Before being taken away, he was allowed a few hours to wander unguarded through the city. Taking advantage of this opportunity, he surreptitiously boarded a sloop bound for Philadelphia, Pennsylvania, and concealed himself among the cargo.

Voorhis managed to reach Philadelphia without being discovered. Once ashore, he approached the Quakers for aid, in the meantime passing himself off as a freeman. His guise was uncovered, however, and Voorhis was imprisoned and then returned to his owner in Charleston. He was again sold at auction, this time to Peter Fersue, a wealthy doctor.

For eighteen months Voorhis worked as Fersue's house servant before attempting another escape, this time stowing himself aboard a brig bound for Boston. Deprived of food and water for almost five days, he finally revealed himself to the ship's crew. The captain was a Quaker and treated Voorhis with kindness, lending him money on their arrival in Boston and cautioning him to avoid certain areas of the city.

Voorhis traveled to Salem, Massachusetts, where he was recruited to work as a sailor on a ship headed to India. In the next several years Voorhis undertook several more voyages to Europe and to India. Having given up hope of reuniting with his first wife, he remarried and had another child. He continued to take extended voyages abroad and eventually separated from his second wife.

Twenty years after he had first left, Voorhis returned to Georgetown to search for his first wife and their two children. He learned that John Voorhis and his wife were dead and that Bevins had moved west. All Voorhis could learn about his own family was that his wife had reportedly killed herself and that his children had died soon after. Distraught, Voorhis retired to Rhode Island. He built a hut near Providence, where he resided in solitude except for an occasional trip into town. To the townspeople, he became known as Robert the Hermit.

Voorhis dictated the narrative of his life to Henry Trumbull, and it was published as *The Life and Adventures of Robert, the Hermit of Massachusetts, Who Has Lived Fourteen Years in a Cave, Secluded from Human Society ...* in 1829. At the time of the narrative's publication, Voorhis was described as about sixty years old, with a long black beard and tattered clothes. He lived an austere life, cultivating a small piece of land and feeding the cattle that grazed near his hut.

As a fugitive slave, former sailor, and hermit, Voorhis embodied many Romantic ideals, among them the rejection of authority, the desire for adventure, and the glorification of the solitary or rural life. Voorhis was considered a "strange and mysterious being" by his neighbors, and his narrative is partly written to rectify mistaken notions that Voorhis was paying penance for some sin or crime. The victim rather than the perpetrator of violence, Voorhis is depicted as a man of extraordinary character and spiritual fortitude, whose experiences of slavery transformed him into a local sage and mystic.

FURTHER READING

Voorhis, Robert. *The Life and Adventures of Robert, the Hermit of Massachusetts, Who Has Lived Fourteen Years in a Cave, Secluded from Human Society ...* (1829).

Andrews, William L. *To Tell a Free Story: The First Century of Afro-American Autobiography, 1760–1865* (1986).

Foster, Frances Smith. *Witnessing Slavery* (1979).

Starling, Marion. *The Slave Narrative* (1982).

JULIA LEE

Vroman, Mary Elizabeth (1923?–29 Apr. 1967), writer, novelist, screenwriter, and schoolteacher, was born in Buffalo, New York. Her father, Charles Cunningham, was an interior designer. Her mother was a teacher. At age three, Mary left Buffalo to live with an aunt in Antigua, in the British West Indies. She attended elementary and high school there. She received her bachelor's degree from Alabama State Teachers College, where she majored in elementary education and social studies. Following the career path of three generations of women on her mother's side of the family, Vroman became a schoolteacher after graduating from college.

Along with teaching, Vroman wrote short stories and fiction for both adults and adolescents. Her first short story, "See How They Run," published by the *Ladies' Home Journal* in 1951, was an immediate literary success. Acclaimed for its humanitarian quality, the story won the Christopher Award in 1952 for inspirational magazine writing. It was later made into the film *Bright Road* (1953), starring DOROTHY DANDRIDGE and HARRY BELAFONTE. Vroman, invited to Hollywood to serve as technical adviser to the film, assisted in the adaptation of the original story and had the distinction of being the first black woman admitted to the Screen Writers Guild.

Drawing on her experiences as a teacher in rural Alabama, Vroman realistically portrayed the plight of poor black students growing up in the rural South. Jane Richards, the novice third-grade teacher in "See How They Run," sees potential in her students despite their impoverished surroundings. Because of Jane's faith and perseverance, C.T., an underachiever, is motivated to work harder in order to be promoted to the next grade. Symbolic of the blind mice who have their tails cut off in the nursery rhyme, and from which the story took its title, Jane's students face a life of stunted hopes and expectations. As the title implies, however, these children are able to run from and overcome this fate when they are shown compassion and understanding. Although Vroman depicted the hardships of black children living in a segregated and racist environment, she insisted that she was not a protest writer. Rather, she wrote to portray the dignity and resilience of the children who lived under impoverished conditions. Vroman married Dr. Oliver M. Harper, a dentist, on 27 November 1963.

Vroman also wrote two novels and a book of nonfiction. Her first published novel, *Esther* (1963), depicts the difficult social conditions faced by African Americans, especially black women, in a small, rural, southern town. The protagonist, Esther Kennedy, fulfills her dream of becoming a nurse, overcoming the town's bigotry and her own unfortunate circumstances. *Shaped to Its Purpose* (1965), her second book, is a history of the first fifty years of the Delta Sigma Theta, a sorority of college-trained, professional black women founded in 1913 on the campus of Howard University. Vroman was a member of this sorority.

Harlem Summer (1967), her third book, was written for young adults. In this coming-of-age story, sixteen-year-old John Brown gains self-knowledge and a positive awareness of his black identity during a summer visit to Harlem. John experiences the multifaceted life of Harlem, which contrasts greatly with life in his Alabama home. Urban violence and poverty, race relations, black pride, "Garveyism," storefront religion, and attitudes of northern blacks toward southern blacks as well as toward blacks from the Caribbean are themes that Vroman explored in an accessible manner for young adult readers.

After the initial success of "See How They Run," Vroman continued to write and teach in Alabama and later in Chicago and New York City. She contributed short stories, poetry, and nonfiction to *Ladies' Home Journal*, *Freedomways*, and *National Education Association Journal*. She taught in Alabama, Illinois, and New York public schools for more than twenty years, and served as the music and art coordinator for the New York City Board of Education.

Vroman died in Brooklyn, New York, following complications from surgery.

FURTHER READING

Bachner, Saul. "Black Literature: The Junior Novel in the Classroom—Harlem Summer," *Negro American Literature Forum* 7 (Spring 1973).

Bachner, Saul. "Writing School Marm: Alabama Teacher Finds Literary Movie Success with First Short Story," *Ebony* (July 1952).

Obituary: *New York Times*, 30 Apr. 1967.

LINDA BOWLES-ADARKWA

Waddles, Mother (7 Oct. 1912–12 July 2001), philanthropist and ordained Pentecostal minister, was born Charleszetta Lina Campbell in St. Louis, Missouri. She was the eldest of seven children born to Henry Campbell, a barber, and Ella (Brown) Campbell. Charleszetta grew up in poverty, hardship, and emotional turmoil. Her father passed away while she was still young, and her mother lost four children before they reached adulthood. To help support her family, Charleszetta left school at age twelve to work in a myriad occupations, washing windows, cooking, selling food, and working as a housemaid. Married at the age of fourteen, Waddles was a widow by nineteen and remarried by twenty-one. She and her husband moved to Detroit. After two marriages and nine children, she met and married Payton Waddles, a Ford Motor Company employee.

Affectionately known as "Mother," Waddles was a soulful, spiritual woman who aimed to transform the lives of the discouraged and poor with small acts of kindness, advice, and practical gifts. Her life's work as a humanitarian began with canned-food distribution from her own basement in Detroit. In the 1950s she cooked, cleaned, and served warm hearty food to the homeless and needy for thirty-five cents a meal. She added small details to each meal—clean tablecloths and fresh flowers—that gave the meals' recipients a sense of dignity. Her aromatic cooking drew a crowd, both wealthy and poor, some generous patrons subsidizing the meals of others by paying greater sums. Hence Mother Waddles touched a wide base, forming community and drawing together groups of people through her love for food, helping, and giving. Throughout the years she served as a beacon of reprieve for those in need, providing counseling and empathy.

These small works attracted volunteers and eventually Mother Waddles's dream of serving the poor on a large scale grew into an international operation of giving. The Perpetual Help Mission, Mother Waddles's organization, eventually served thousands by offering material resources, compassion, practical and spiritual advice, learning opportunities such as job training and adult education classes, and emergency services. The stated mandate of Mother Waddles's organization was "to promote the kind of compassion and understanding that draws out inner strength in the human character, creates the pride of self worth to our communities and turns our eyes towards uplifting others less fortunate" (www.motherwaddles.com).

Mother Waddles stood apart from other philanthropists not only because of the personal connection she shared with the needy, but also because she always ensured that the recipient of service would maintain self-respect. "You can't give people pride, but you can provide the kind of understanding that makes people look to their inner strengths and find their own sense of pride," Waddles observed to *Reader's Digest* in 1972 (quoted in *New York Times* obituary, 12 July 2001). Mother Waddles was known nationally and internationally for her lifelong devotion to working with the poor, dejected, and socially isolated. Her work as an altruist, however, was neither motivated by recognition nor measurable by the awards she received (over 300). Mother Waddles's work as an efficient administrator, devoted activist, BBQ cook, and religious leader coalesced around her service and devotion to what she viewed as her own mission in life: to serve God by performing pragmatic works for others.

To promote her mission, Mother Waddles wrote and produced a number of texts, including *The Mother Waddles Soul Food Cookbook* (1970); *Mother and the Way She Waddles* (1985), an autobiography; and *Attributes and Attitudes*, an evangelical piece. Her life story was also preserved on tape as part of the Black Women Oral History Project. A 1969 twenty-two-minute film, *Mother Waddles*, and a 1990 PBS documentary, *Ya Done Good*, also chronicled her life and work.

Waddles died at the age of eighty-eight in Detroit, Michigan, but her work continued through the missions she generated in urban areas in the United States and abroad in Ghana, West Africa. The Mother Waddles Lots of Love Car Donation Program, which she started in Detroit, continued to generate funding for her programs. Remembered and honored posthumously, Mother Waddles represented community leadership. Michigan congressman JOHN CONYERS JR. named her one of three Detroit matriarchs, along with ROSA PARKS and the honorable Erma Henderson. "Mother Waddles' death," Conyers noted, "in many respects, marks the end of an historic era in Detroit during which a triumvirate of Matriarchs has provided an indelible imprint of majestic motherhood on the city, the state, the nation and the world" (Conyers, 2001).

FURTHER READING

Conyers, John, Jr. "Congressman Conyers Pays Homage to the Life and Legacy of Mother Waddles," press release (2001). Available online at http://www.house.gov/conyers/pr071301.htm

Cooks, Helen. "Mother Waddles," *Notable Black American Women* (1992).

Hine, Darlene Clark, ed. *Black Women in America: An Historical Encyclopedia* (1993).

"Mother Waddles," *Contemporary Black Biography* (2005).

Smith, Jessie Carney, ed. *Epic Lives: One Hundred Black Women Who Made a Difference* (1993).

Obituary: *New York Times*, 12 July 2001.

MICHELLE MADSEN CAMACHO

Waddy, Harriet West (20 June 1904–21 Feb. 1999), military officer, was born in Kansas City, Missouri. Waddy was raised by her maternal grandmother after the death of her mother; her father raised her only sibling, a brother, separately. Waddy had no further contact with her father but did occasionally correspond with her brother. When she was fourteen years old, Waddy wrote a letter to her grandmother that read, "I intend to make something of myself."

In 1920 Waddy attended Kansas State College of Agriculture and Applied Science in Manhattan, Kansas, for at least two years, earning a degree in secretarial skills. Waddy was married during this time, but it was quickly annulled for unknown reasons. In the 1930s she moved to Chicago and worked as a secretary to the director of medical services at Provident Hospital. It was there that she met the orthopedic surgeon John Chenault; Waddy and Chenault were married on 4 November 1933.

While in Chicago, the couple lived in the Bronzeville district located south of the city and home to many members of the black professional class. In 1936 their marriage ended and Chenault accepted a Rockefeller Scholarship to continue his studies at Iowa University, in Des Moines, Iowa. That same year Waddy resigned her position at the hospital and moved to Washington, D.C. where she worked for MARY MCLEOD BETHUNE at the National Youth Administration (NYA) and for Oveta Culp Hobby, the director of the newly formed Women's Army Auxiliary Corps (WAAC). It was in D.C. that she met her third husband, Charles West, who was a captain in the U.S. Army Medical Corps. They married in 1938 and lived in Washington, D.C., until the United States entered World War II, at which time West was transferred to Fort Huachuca, Arizona, and Waddy moved to Des Moines, Iowa, for WAAC training.

Based on Bethune's recommendation, Waddy was in the first group of women trained to become WAAC officers and was one of thirty-nine African American women selected for this distinction. Like many women who joined the WAAC, Waddy was patriotic and wanted to help end the war; she believed the best way to do this was to free a man to fight. Former General Jeanne Holm reflected that the women in the program did not have the "remotest idea that they were embarking upon a road that would eventually lead to permanent integration of women in the U.S. armed forces."

Unlike black male soldiers, who were under the command of white officers, black WAACs were commanded by black officers. Sociologist Brenda Moore wrote that for the first time in American history, women in general, and African American women in particular, were being trained for leadership positions in an auxiliary of an exclusively male institution. West was at the forefront of this paradigm shift.

Racial discrimination influenced the assignments for most black WAACs once they were commissioned—although, according to CHARITY ADAMS EARLEY, a member of the first graduating class, this was not the case with Waddy. Earley wrote in her autobiography, *One Woman's Army* (1989), that Waddy's assignment to WAAC headquarters in Washington, D. C., was predetermined and probably the result of her prewar affiliation with Bethune. At WAAC headquarters, one of Waddy's first duties was to serve as an army representative at recruiting offices around the country, often ceremoniously signing up a particular city's first recruit.

With a promotion to major, Waddy became the first African American WAAC to receive this rank, and she began investigating numerous reports of discrimination. In late 1943 Waddy graduated from Adjutant General School and was assigned to oversee the army's casualty branch, where she was in charge of fifty civilian typists—both black and white.

At the end of the war, Waddy and her husband, Charles, divorced. In 1949 she was assigned to Kitzingen basic training facility in Germany where she worked as the assistant post inspector. It was here that she met and married her fourth and final husband, Major Edward P. Waddy.

In 1959 Waddy left active duty as a lieutenant colonel, making her the highest-ranking African American female officer. She remained in the army reserves until 1969, while simultaneously working a civilian job for the Federal Aviation Administration in Los Angeles, California. Afterward, she and her husband moved to Portland, Oregon. She died in 1999 in Las Vegas, Nevada, after several years of suffering from Alzheimer's disease.

FURTHER READING

Harriet West Waddy's personal papers are at the Women's Army Museum, Fort Lee, Virginia.

African American Mosaic Chicago: Destination for the Great Migration. Library of Congress Resource Guide for the Study of Black History and Culture.

Earley, Charity Adams. *One Woman's Army: A Black Officer Remembers the WAC* (1989).

Holm, Jeanne. *Women in the Military: An Unfinished Revolution* (1993).

Moore, Brenda. *To Serve My Country, To Serve My Race: The Story of the Only African American WACs Stationed Overseas During World War II* (1996).

KELLI CARDENAS WALSH

Waddy, Joseph C. (26 May 1911–1 Aug. 1978), lawyer and judge, was born in Louisa County, Virginia. The names of his parents are unknown. The son of a railway worker, Waddy moved with his family to Alexandria, Virginia, in 1918 and then to Washington, D.C., where he graduated from Dunbar High School. Waddy used a cash award and scholarship that he won in a national oratorical contest to support his attendance at Lincoln University in Pennsylvania. After graduating with honors from Lincoln in 1935, Waddy attended Howard Law School in Washington, D.C., from which he graduated in 1938, first in his class. After graduation Waddy went to work for CHARLES HAMILTON HOUSTON, former dean of Howard Law School. At first Waddy worked for Houston without pay, supporting himself by working as an elevator operator, but Houston soon insisted that Waddy give up his nonlegal work and join Houston's practice. Waddy married Elizabeth Hardy Gregg in 1941; they had one son.

Waddy believed that lawyers ought to be what Houston called "social engineers," using their training to advance the interests of African Americans as a group. From 1940 to 1944 he assisted Houston in representing African American railway workers, primarily through the Association of Colored Railway Trainmen and Locomotive Firemen. The principal railway unions excluded African Americans from membership and often negotiated collective-bargaining agreements that gave preferences to white workers. Houston and Waddy developed a series of cases challenging these agreements as violations of federal labor law and of the Constitution. Eventually the cases reached the U.S. Supreme Court. In *Steele v. Louisville and Nashville Railroad* (1944) the Court agreed with Houston and Waddy that federal labor law required unions to represent the interests of African Americans fairly in collective bargaining, even if they excluded the African Americans from membership.

About the time that the *Steele* case reached the Supreme Court, Waddy entered the army, where he served as a sergeant for two years. On returning to Washington he rejoined Houston's firm. Waddy continued to represent railway workers after Houston's death in 1950. In 1952 and 1957 Waddy argued and won two sequels to the *Steele* case, *Brotherhood of Railway Trainmen v. Howard* (1952) and *Conley v. Gibson* (1957). In addition, he built a general civil and criminal practice, representing mostly African American clients in their ordinary business and family dealings. Waddy became one of Washington's leading African American lawyers. His law firm represented the defendant in *Mallory v. United States* (1957), an important Supreme Court case that foreshadowed the Warren court's later expansion of the rights of criminal defendants. The *Mallory* decision required federal prosecutors to bring defendants before magistrates promptly, making it more difficult for the prosecutors to extract confessions from defendants who might not understand the significance of talking with the police.

In 1962, in part to stabilize his income, Waddy accepted an appointment from President John F. Kennedy as a judge in the domestic relations branch of the District of Columbia municipal court. Five years later President Lyndon Johnson appointed Waddy to the federal district court in Washington. As a federal judge Waddy wrote a number of major decisions. One led to substantial changes in the educational arrangements for handicapped children in District of Columbia schools. Waddy drew on his experience as a domestic relations judge when *Mills v. Board of Education* (1972) held that the Constitution and federal law required the school board to provide an appropriate education for mentally retarded or physically handicapped children. Prior to this decision many such children had simply been excluded from the school system. Judge Waddy's decision required the school board to establish special education programs. Three years later, when he concluded that the board had failed to comply with this decision, Waddy held city officials in contempt of court. In 1977 he approved their special education plans.

Waddy was a careful but unexciting jurist. When he saw what he regarded as lawless behavior, he responded strongly. Reacting to police misconduct during antiwar demonstrations from 1969 to 1971, Judge Waddy entered a far-reaching order directing the city's police department to develop a comprehensive-manual outlining its policies for arrests during demonstrations. The court of appeals, however, reversed his order.

In addition, in 1973 Waddy wrote an important opinion establishing that members of Congress had standing to challenge executive decisions that effectively undermined the votes that they had cast in Congress. *Kennedy v. Sampson* (1974) was brought by Senator Edward Kennedy to challenge President Richard Nixon's decision not to sign a bill that would authorize assistance to medical schools and hospitals for establishing family practice programs. Instead of vetoing the bill and submitting it for an override, Nixon withheld his signature. This so-called pocket veto took place during Congress's five-day Christmas recess. Waddy held that it was unconstitutional to use a pocket veto during such a short recess.

Waddy lived with his family in a middle-class neighborhood of Washington, D.C. He resigned from the bench the day before he died in Washington.

FURTHER READING

Senate Committee on the Judiciary. *Hearing on Nomination of Joseph C. Waddy To Be District Judge*, 90th Cong., 1st sess., 2 Feb. 1967.

Obituary: *Washington Post*, 2 Aug. 1978.

This entry is taken from the *American National Biography* and is published here with the permission of the American Council of Learned Societies.

MARK TUSHNET

Wade-Gayles, Gloria (1 July 1938–), civil rights activist, educator, poet, literary critic, scholar, and writer, was born Gloria Jean Wade in Memphis, Tennessee, the older of two daughters born to Robert Wade, a gifted storyteller and Pullman porter, and Bertha Reese Willett. Though raised in the segregated South, Wade found a source of pride, courage, and comfort in the insulated African American community. Her mother, a former high-school valedictorian, understood the power of knowledge. The Wade home was replete with books on a variety of subjects. Bertha Wade would often engage her daughters on a range of topics, from politics to theology. Determined that her children succeed, she encouraged her daughters to academically excel in spite of a segregated school system. Like Bertha Reese Willett, Robert Wade stressed the importance of education. Though the pair were never married and separated when Wade was a young child, she—along with her sister—would visit their father in Chicago each summer. Robert Wade would take the girls to the University of Chicago, which was closed at that time to African Americans, to expose them to the idea and importance of higher education. As a teenager Wade, with her older sister Faye, worked at the Georgia Theatre in Memphis. When business was slow, the two girls would either study with or tutor the white owner's son and daughter. When the proprietor insisted that the young Wade girls refer to his children as "mister" and "miss," the Wade girls were insulted and wanted to leave, but their mother, recognizing how few jobs were available, did not let her daughters quit.

Wade was an exceptional student. Upon graduation from high school in 1955, the young scholar received a full academic scholarship to LeMoyne College, then the only college in Memphis that accepted African Americans. Initially majoring in math, Wade soon shifted to literature and writing. Four years later she earned a B.A. in English. After graduating cum laude, she began working on a master's degree in American literature at Boston University as a Woodrow Wilson fellow. Noting that Boston was vehemently racist, she became an active member of the Boston Committee On Racial Equality, organizing demonstrations and preparing pamphlets. Alongside Joseph Gayles, whom she met in 1959 and would later marry, Wade became an active participant in the civil rights movement. An integrationist, she also joined the Unitarian Church in Boston and the Congress for Racial Equality. In 1963, after receiving her master's degree, she returned to Georgia with her husband to teach at Atlanta's Spelman College, a historically black college for women. The pair divorced the next year. Her activism, however, continued.

Her nonviolent civil rights work in Atlanta led to multiple arrests and her ultimate dismissal from Spelman. She then spent the summer of 1964 teaching and registering voters in Mississippi as a member of the Confederation of Freedom Organizations. The following fall, while teaching at Howard University in Washington, D.C., Wade married Joseph Gayles. In 1967 the two moved to San Jose, California, where they started a family. They would have two children, Jonathan and Monica. In 1969 they returned to Atlanta as professors at the Atlanta University Center. Though estranged for some time before, Joseph Gayles and Gloria Wade-Gayles officially separated in 1992.

After earning her Ph.D. in American Studies from Emory University in 1981, Wade-Gayles returned to Spelman College as a full professor of English and Women's Studies in 1983. Throughout her teaching career she chose to remain at historically black institutions. In addition to her faculty appointment at Spelman, Wade-Gayles has taught at Morehouse College, Tougaloo College, and Bennett College. Between 1997 and 2000, she taught at Dillard College, where she held the RosaMary Eminent Scholar's Chair in Humanities and Fine Arts.

Wade-Gayles has received fellowships from Danforth (1974) and the National Endowment for the Humanities (1975). From 1987–1988, she received a United Negro College Fund Mellon Research Grant and, in 1991, was named Georgia Professor of the Year by the Council for Advancement and Support of Education. She was also a research

fellow at the W. E. B. DuBois Institute of Harvard University in 1990 and a recipient of the Presidential Award for Scholarship from Spelman College. She received the Emory Medal for outstanding scholarship and service (1994), the LeMoyne-Owen DuBois Scholar's Award, and the Malcolm X Award for Community Service in Atlanta. In 2001 Wade-Gayles founded Spelman's Independent Scholars Oral History Project, interviews with Southern African American women by Spelman students.

In 1984 Wade-Gayles's first book, *No Crystal Stair: Visions of Race and Sex in Black Women's Fiction 1946–1976*, was released. Borrowing its title from a Langston Hughes poem, *No Crystal Stair* presents essays about the works of influential writers, such as GWENDOLYN BROOKS, TONI MORRISON, and ALICE WALKER. *Anointed to Fly*, a collection of her poems, was published in 1991. Her critically acclaimed 1993 memoir, *Pushed Back to Strength*, documented Wade-Gayles's experiences, from living in a housing project within a segregated city to the emotional effect of sharing a jail cell with a woman accused of murder. Wade-Gayles published another autobiographical collection, *Rooted Against the Wind: Personal Essays* in 1996. She also edited a number of anthologies, including *My Soul Is a Witness: African American Women's Spirituality* (1995), *Father Songs: Testimonies by African-American Sons and Daughters* (1997), and *In Praise of Our Teachers: A Multicultural Tribute to Those who Inspired Us* (2003). She has written extensively on African American women and spirituality and African American women in fiction. Wade-Gayles continues to be passionate about activism, knowledge, and instruction—passions she attributes to her mother's "love for learning, her passion for ideas and her uncompromising humility."

FURTHER READING
Wade-Gayles, Gloria. *Pushed Back to Strength: A Black Woman's Journey Home* (1993).
Wade-Gayles, Gloria. *Rooted Against the Wind: Personal Essays* (1996).
Nelson, Emmanuel S., ed. *African-American Autobiographers: A Sourcebook* (2002).
NICOLE SEALEY

Wagoner, Henry O. (27 Feb. 1816–27 Jan. 1901), abolitionist, entrepreneur, journalist, and politician, was born free in Hagerstown, Maryland. His mother had been a slave, and his father was a white man of German descent whose last name was spelled Waggoner. Henry was taught the alphabet at the age of five by his paternal grandmother, and furthered his education in part through sporadic attendance at a school in nearby Franklin County, Pennsylvania, but primarily through dedicated self-study. His early life was spent in agricultural labor around Hagerstown, but at the age of twenty-two Wagoner set out on his own, sojourning briefly to Baltimore, then Cincinnati and Dayton, Ohio, and onto New Orleans and St. Louis, before settling in Galena, Illinois, in April 1839.

In Galena Wagoner learned the craft of typesetting at a small newspaper where he worked as a compositor into the early 1840s, accumulating a modest holding in real estate in the process. There he became acquainted with the lawyer and future congressman and diplomat Elihu B. Washburne, to whom Wagoner sold his property to help finance his move to Chatham, Canada West (later Ontario), in late 1843. Wagoner worked for the *Chatham Journal* newspaper and also taught school for black children. In 1844 he married an Indiana-born African American woman several years his junior, named Susan. The couple had a daughter, Marcellina, who was born in Canada around 1846. By 1847 Wagoner had relocated his new family to Chicago, where he remained until 1860.

In Chicago he engaged in various business enterprises, including barbering and the operation of a small mill, and continued to invest in real estate on a small scale. Wagoner also worked on the *Western Citizen*, an abolitionist newspaper, and took an active role in local underground railroad activities. During the 1850s he became well acquainted with the abolitionists FREDERICK DOUGLASS and John Brown, and was for a time the Chicago correspondent for Douglass's Rochester, New York, weekly, *Frederick Douglass' Paper*. Wagoner's family continued to grow with the births of a daughter Lucilla around 1847, a son Henry O. Wagoner Jr. around 1851, and a daughter Adella (or Adelina) around 1853. Wagoner may have had two other children while in Chicago who died prior to 1858.

After his mill was destroyed by fire in 1860 Wagoner temporarily left his family to make a new start in Colorado (at that time still a part of Kansas Territory), where the 1859 Pike's Peak gold rush was enticing many easterners to seek their fortunes. One of these was another black entrepreneur, his former neighbor from Chicago, Barney Ford, who was born in Virginia in 1822. He and Ford established themselves as barbers in the recently founded community of Mountain (or Montana) City, which would be renamed Denver upon the

creation of the Colorado Territory in 1861. With the onset of the Civil War Wagoner moved back to Chicago, where he assisted with the provisioning of U.S. troops. When black enlistment began after the 1863 Emancipation Proclamation, he played an active role in recruiting troops for black regiments in Illinois and Massachusetts, and among the self-liberated "contrabands" flocking to Union lines along the southern Mississippi River.

By late 1865 Wagoner and his family had moved back to Denver, where he would make his home for the remainder of his life. Wagoner became one of the most prosperous, influential, and respected African Americans in Colorado. By the time his wife, Susan, had passed away in 1870 Wagoner was a restaurant owner with real estate valued at more than six thousand dollars. He resided at that time with three of his surviving children, Adelina, Henry Jr., and Marcellina, along with Marcellina's husband, Robert L. Moss, and their young children, Ella and Robert Moss. Wagoner worked through the late 1860s and 1870s with other black activists in Colorado, including BARNEY LAUNCELOT FORD, Edward J. Sanderlin, and WILLIAM JEFFERSON HARDIN, to pursue full and equal rights for the state's African Americans. When Frederick Douglass's sons Lewis and Frederick Jr. moved to the state in the 1870s, Wagoner joined them in establishing an evening school in his home to instruct black adults in the principles of American government. In 1876 he was appointed head of the clerks in the state legislature, and in 1880 he became the first African American to serve as deputy sheriff of Arapaho County, responsible for serving legal papers and acting as bailiff in the district court. While holding this position he also served as an election judge in Denver's Ninth District. During the 1880s Wagoner continued to live with his daughters Adelina and the now-widowed Marcellina, while he augmented his income by barbering. His overall wealth during the mid-1880s was estimated at about twenty thousand dollars.

Wagoner remained active in both civic and professional life. When he died of natural causes at the age of eighty-four he was working as compositor for a local newspaper. At that time Wagoner was still living with his eldest child, Marcellina, now remarried to Robert Beatty, whose job as janitor at the state capitol may well have been secured through his father-in-law's connections. Also living in the household was his old friend, seventy-eight-year-old Barney Ford, who had continued his activism as he attained some prominence through his ownership of Denver's Inter-Ocean Hotel, built in 1874. Wagoner's longstanding activism in the areas of black voting and educational rights in Colorado, his relationships with key figures of the day, and his successes in business made him a well-known and respected figure among both blacks and whites in the growing city of Denver. He was one of the black pioneers of the post-emancipation western United States.

FURTHER READING

Berwanger, Eugene. *The Frontier against Slavery: Western Anti-Negro Prejudice and the Slavery Extension Controversy* (1969).

Taylor, Quintard. *In Search of the Racial Frontier: African Americans in the West, 1528–1990* (1999).

MITCH KACHUN

Waits, Freddie (27 Apr. 1943–18 Nov. 1989), jazz and soul music drummer, was born Frederick Douglas Waits in Jackson, Mississippi, the son of Lillie B. Weathers. His father's name is unknown. Waits played drums as a child and studied flute and drums at Lanier High School. At age sixteen, in the summer before his senior year, he toured with the Upsetters, accompanying the rhythm and blues musician Little Willie John. In this setting he first performed in New York City at Smalls' Paradise.

At Jackson State College, Waits majored in music, with flute as his primary instrument. While in college he played in bands that accompanied the rhythm and blues musicians PERCY MAYFIELD, IVORY JOE HUNTER, and SAM COOKE on tour, and SONNY BOY WILLIAMSON, JOHN LEE HOOKER, and MEMPHIS SLIM in their visits to Jackson. From about 1962 to 1963, traveling back and forth between Jackson and Detroit, where his stepmother lived, Waits worked as a house drummer for the emerging Motown label. He accompanied the Temptations, Martha Reeves and the Vandellas, the Supremes, and Little STEVIE WONDER. Owing to the absence of detailed discographical research into Motown Records, it is impossible to determine on which of the seminal hit records Waits might be drumming; he is mentioned on only one such disk, Wonder's first hit from 1963, "Fingertips."

In Detroit, Waits doubled as a jazz drummer in a group with the bassist Cecil McBee and the pianist Kirk Lightsey; the saxophonist Bennie Maupin also played with the group at times. After a Motown tour with SMOKEY ROBINSON, Reeves, MARVIN GAYE, and Wonder, Waits joined the saxophonist Paul Winter's group, twice touring Brazil. Waits then settled in New York, where initially he shared a loft with Maupin. At some point, probably during the Motown tour or after coming to New York, Waits performed with Choker Campbell's band at the Apollo Theater in Harlem. He also studied informally with Charlie Persip, then house drummer at the Apollo, and with Jo Jones.

Over the next decade Waits was extremely active, mainly in jazz. He worked with the trombonist Curtis Fuller, the trumpeter Donald Byrd—with whom he recorded in 1966—the trumpeter Kenny Dorham, the pianist Cedar Walton, the trumpeter GERALD WILSON's big band, and the singers Damita Jo and BETTY CARTER. Waits was a member of SONNY ROLLINS's trio in June 1966, and that same year he recorded with the pianist RAY BRYANT, whose rather bland album, *Lonesome Traveler*, exemplifies the sort of rhythmic patterns that Waits might have used in Motown sessions.

From 1966 to 1967 Waits was a member of the pianist Sir Roland Hanna's New York Jazz Sextet. From 1967 to 1970 Waits worked with the pianist MCCOY TYNER, with whom he made several recordings, including *Expansions* (1968). Around this time Waits married Haima (maiden name unknown); they had two sons. While with Tyner, who scuffled for work during these dark years of jazz, Waits also toured the United States and Europe—Europe in 1968 with the singer ELLA FITZGERALD. He worked on and off with the trumpeter Freddie Hubbard for three years. Fleeting associations during this period include work with the pianist Walter Bishop, with the singer JOE WILLIAMS, and with the saxophonist GARY BARTZ, as well as albums with the pianist Joe Zawinul in 1967, with the saxophonist JOHNNY HODGES in 1968, with the pianist ANDREW HILL—with whom he recorded *Grass Roots* in 1968, and another session in 1969—with the guitarist KENNY BURRELL in 1969, and with the saxophonist PHAROAH SANDERS in 1969.

By the 1970s Waits was sometimes known as Dahoud rather than as Freddie. Early in the decade Waits worked with the trumpeter LEE MORGAN's band, recording in 1971. Around this time he also held brief jobs with the flutist Hubert Laws; with the singers LENA HORNE, Dee Dee Bridgewater, CARMEN MCRAE, and Nancy Wilson; and with the saxophonist JIMMY HEATH. Most significantly, in 1971 he joined MAX ROACH's ensemble M'Boom Re: Percussion. Waits also accompanied the pianist Billy Taylor intermittently from 1971 to 1975 in various engagements, including television appearances.

In 1972 Waits was a member of the bassist Richard Davis's quintet for the making of the free jazz album *Epistrophy and Now's the Time*, which begins with a substantial drum solo by Waits. In and around 1973 Waits accompanied Fitzgerald at the Newport Jazz Festival and made the first of several European tours with M'Boom Re: Percussion. He also served as musical director for the PBS television series *Soul*, accompanying, among others, the singers AL GREEN and GLADYS KNIGHT; and he was the drummer both for the saxophonist James Moody's hard bop album *Feelin' It Together* and for Marvin Gaye's huge soul hit "Let's Get It On."

In the following year, 1974, Waits's multifaceted activities included touring Europe and Africa with the DUKE ELLINGTON orchestra under Mercer Ellington, contributing to Maupin's album *The Jewel in the Lotus* and to the reed player Bobby Jones's album *Hill Country Suite*, and performing with the Dixieland trumpeter Bobby Hackett at the Newport Jazz Festival. Waits also worked again with Nancy Wilson and embarked on a European tour with Hanna and the New York Jazz Quartet, which performed at the Laren International Jazz Festival in the Netherlands. In 1975, in addition to continuing work with Taylor, Waits rejoined Ellington, performing with the New York Jazz Repertory Company, with the saxophonists Jimmy Heath and Stan Getz and the drummer Grady Tate, at a time when Tate was presenting himself as a singer.

From the mid-1960s Waits had participated in the activities of the Jazzmobile, which supported jazz performance and education in Harlem. Working at times in association with the Jazz Interactions workshop and the New School for Social Research, Waits also gave concerts and taught in prisons, schools, and colleges. By 1976 these activities had led Waits to a formal position as a member of the music faculty at the Livingston College music department at Rutgers, the state university of New Jersey.

Waits continued, however, to pursue an active performance career, recording again with Fuller in 1978. In 1979 he formed Colloquium III with the percussionists BILLY HART and Horacee Arnold, recording the album *M'Boom Re: Percussion*, on which Waits plays various orchestral, African, Latin, and jazz percussion instruments as a participant in the group's pan-stylistic manner. In 1980 he also recorded the album BILL DIXON *in Italy* and another session with Hill, which produced *Strange Serenade*.

Waits's wife died from heart problems in about 1984. He remained active with M'Boom Re: Percussion, with whom he recorded the album *Collage* that same year. Waits was a member of the drummer Jack DeJohnette's trio when the leader worked as a pianist, recording *The Jack DeJohnette Piano Album* with the group in 1985. In 1987 Waits recorded again with Hanna's trio, in addition to performing in the pianist CECIL TAYLOR's quintet. From 1987 to 1989 he was a member, with the bassist Buster Williams, of the pianist Stanley Cowell's trio We Three, and he was also a member of Trio Transition with the pianist Mulgrew Miller and the bassist Reggie Workman. Both of these trios toured Japan and made recordings, including two CDs: *We Three* (1987) and *Trio Transition with Special Guest Oliver Lake* (1988). In 1989 Waits returned to Europe with M'Boom Re: Percussion and also with the vibraphonist Jay Hoggard, with whom he recorded. Waits died of pneumonia and renal failure in New York City.

For any listener familiar with their mid-1970s work, mentioning Richard Davis and Marvin Gaye, M'Boom Re: Percussion and Bobby Hackett, or Gladys Knight and Mercer Ellington in the same breath may seem disconcerting. Yet Waits was comfortable, accomplished, and stylistically adaptable in working with all of them. Never an innovator, he was nonetheless quite possibly the most eclectically talented professional percussionist of his century.

FURTHER READING

Feather, Leonard, and Ira Gitler. *The Encyclopedia of Jazz in the Seventies* (1976).

Potter, Jeff. "Life Experience: Frederick Waits," *Modern Drummer* 14 (Feb. 1990).

Primack, Bret. "Drummers Colloquium III: Multiple Percussionists Horacee Arnold, Billy Hart, Freddie Waits," *Down Beat* (Nov. 1979).

Obituary: *New York Times*, 22 Nov. 1989.

This entry is taken from the *American National Biography* and is published here with the permission of the American Council of Learned Societies.

BARRY KERNFELD

Walcott, Bess Bolden (4 Nov. 1886–18 Apr. 1988), educator and civil rights leader, was born Bess Bolden in Xenia, Ohio, the daughter of William Pinkney Bolden and Fannie Abigail Bizzell. No other information is available about her family. She graduated from Oberlin College in Ohio in 1908. BOOKER T. WASHINGTON, the founder of Tuskegee Institute in Alabama, recruited her to help organize the library at the school. Over the next fifty-three years Bolden held a number of positions at Tuskegee, including librarian, teacher, administrator, and museum curator.

Founded in 1881, Tuskegee Institute provided blacks a variety of educational opportunities at a time when most educational institutions admitted only whites. At first the school taught vocational and agricultural skills to enable blacks to earn a living. In the 1920s the school shifted from teaching vocational skills to academics and became an accredited institute of higher learning. While working at Tuskegee, Bolden also taught literature and started the publication *Tuskegee Messenger*, for which she wrote numerous unsigned articles. In 1911 she married William Holbrook Walcott; they had four children before the marriage ended in divorce in 1947.

In 1935 Bess Walcott was appointed director of the Public Relations Office at Tuskegee. She served in that capacity through 1946 and publicized the training of and subsequent feats of the Tuskegee Airmen. In 1941, with the onset of World War II, the U.S. War Department formed the black Ninety-ninth Pursuit Squadron. This unit of African Americans was trained at the Moton Field and Tuskegee Army Air Field in Tuskegee, Alabama, to fly single-engine and later multiengine bombers. The program expanded throughout World War II and involved a total of 992 African American pilots who flew 1,578 missions and in combat destroyed 261 enemy planes. The pilots won over 850 Distinguished Service Medals.

Walcott also organized an American Red Cross chapter at Tuskegee in 1918 and served the Red Cross in some capacity until 1951. She became the first black female to become an acting field director for the American Red Cross (1941–1942) at a time when prejudice prevented most blacks from serving in administrative positions in both public nonprofits and private business corporations. After the war she was reappointed acting field director (1946–1947), and she helped returning veterans and trained Red Cross volunteers. In 1951 Walcott became the curator of the Carver Museum. A colleague and friend of GEORGE WASHINGTON CARVER, Walcott gathered historic materials about Carver and Tuskegee, including Carver's correspondence and artwork. She also worked with the National Park Service's restoration of Washington's home, "the Oaks," located at Tuskegee. Her work led to Tuskegee's recognition by the federal government as a national historic site. Tuskegee University, the Carver Museum, and the Oaks were incorporated into the National Park Service and drew thousands of visitors yearly. Walcott retired from Tuskegee in 1961 at the age of seventy-five.

In 1962 Walcott was elected national vice president of the Women's International League for Peace and Freedom (WILPF), an international women's organization with branches in some fifty countries and one hundred branches in the United States. The organization was founded in 1919, evolving from the World War I pacifist organization the Women's Peace Party. The main goals of WILPF were disarmament, racial justice, and women's rights. Walcott made significant contributions in the area of racial justice. During the civil rights movement of the 1960s, Walcott served as national co-chairperson of the WILPF's Civil Rights Committee. She traveled throughout the South and talked with community leaders working to integrate public schools. Walcott often traveled to hot spots and worked to resolve differences among various groups working for integration. In December 1960, having seen media reports about efforts to integrate the New Orleans public schools, she traveled to New Orleans and concluded that there were "other things" not reported in the media that were blocking integration efforts. She wrote to the national secretary of the IWLPF on 29 December 1960 that, "The only way to get to these 'other things' was to come to New Orleans and talk to people representing widely separated interest groups." She found that the many "widely separated interest groups" working for integration were not communicating with each other and lacked unity of action. She set about to resolve the problem.

As a participant and a cute observer of the civil rights movement, Walcott's reports to the WILPF Civil Rights Committee provided valuable insights into the communities she visited and the actions people took for integration. Walcott's report to the WILFPF in 1961, for example, describes the picketing, sit-ins, kneel-ins, swim-ins, jailings, beatings, and burnings of Freedom Riders' buses and the voter registration work black and white civil rights workers did. She encouraged WILPF members to form Operation Appreciation to write to southerners working for integration in the South but, as she added in one of her reports, to convey appreciation in a sealed letter, not a postcard. Walcott continued working for black causes and from November 1964 to June 1965 was in Liberia as a consultant for the Tubman Center of African Culture at Cape Mount. Liberian President V. S. Tubman presented her with a citation and decoration in May 1965.

Walcott lived to be 101 years old and died on 18 April 1988 in Alabama. In 2003 she was inducted into the Alabama Women's Hall of Fame, an integrated state museum.

FURTHER READING

The Oberlin College Archives, Oberlin, Ohio, have documents relating to Walcott; her WILPF letters, papers, and reports are in the Swarthmore College Peace Collection, Swarthmore, Pennsylvania.

Alabama Women's Hall of Fame, "Bess Bolden Walcott (1886–1988)," http://www.awhf.org/walcott.html.

LINDA SPENCER

Walcott, Derek (23 June 1930–), poet, playwright, and literary and cultural critic, was born Derek Alton Walcott in the town of Castries on the Caribbean island of St. Lucia, then a British colony. It had experienced very slow Anglicization since its acquisition from the French after the Napoleonic wars. His parents, Warwick Walcott and Alix (maiden name unknown), were Methodists in a mostly Roman Catholic society. His mother was a schoolteacher and seamstress and, for many years, headmistress of the Methodist Infant School. She enjoyed acting and reciting. Walcott's father, an avid watercolorist and civil servant, died in 1931, leaving his wife to raise young Derek, his twin brother (Roderick Alton), and his sister (Pamela), who was two years older. Derek Walcott grew up in a house filled with books and other indications of the intellectual and artistic interests of his parents. After completing elementary school under the watchful eye of his mother, he won a scholarship to secondary school at St. Mary's College in Castries in 1941. Finishing in 1947, he taught at that institution until 1950. During these early years, perhaps the single most significant influence that shaped Walcott's path as a developing poet was his sense that he should follow in his father's artistic footsteps.

When he was only fourteen years old, Walcott announced his vocational intentions by publishing his first poem, "The Voice of St. Lucia," in the local newspaper. The poem dealt with learning about God through nature rather than through the church. In effect, Walcott challenged Roman Catholic supremacy in St. Lucia. When a local priest took up the challenge and replied in verse to accuse Walcott of blasphemy, it was clear to Walcott that he must be on the right track to have excited such a response, although he was also shocked.

By nineteen years of age Walcott had self-published two books of poetry: *25 Poems* (1948), which was released quickly in a second edition, and *Epitaph for the Young: A Poem in XII Cantos* (1949). He did not have the money to publish the first collection, but somehow his mother found enough to help him, and the book was finally

Derek Walcott, winner of the Nobel Prize in Literature, at a press conference in Charlottesville, Virginia, 8 October 1992. (AP Images.)

printed in Trinidad. Walcott sold copies in St. Lucia to friends and recovered the printing costs. One of the poems ("A City's Death by Fire") in that first volume captured the severe trauma and the multilayered significance of the destruction by fire on 19–20 June 1948 of a large part of Castries, a few days before Walcott's eighteenth birthday. In 1950, after cofounding (with Maurice Mason) the St. Lucia Arts Guild, he left St. Lucia for Jamaica on a scholarship to study for a bachelor's degree in French, Spanish, and Latin at the recently established (1948) University College of the West Indies (later University of the West Indies).

Walcott's inclination to pursue the writing of poetry and drama professionally appears to have been well established. In 1951 another collection of his work, *Poems*, was privately printed in the Caribbean. Walcott's first three books of poems can be said to belong to this apprentice period, when he was influenced by the contexts of life in St. Lucia, including learning to paint under the guidance of his father's friend Harold Simmons, and by his exposure to the work of such poets as Stephen Spender, W. H. Auden, Louis MacNeice, T. S. Eliot, Ezra

Pound, William Butler Yeats, Gerard Manley Hopkins, Dylan Thomas, John Crowe Ransom, and Robert Lowell. Walcott's early poetry depended heavily on the English literary tradition.

In 1953 Walcott moved to Trinidad, and, having earned the B.A. degree, he taught for a few years in Grenada, St. Lucia, and Jamaica. In 1953 he also married Faye A. Moyston, with whom he had a son, Peter, but the couple divorced in 1954. In 1957 he received the Jamaica Drama Festival Prize for his play *Drums and Colors*, and in 1958 he was commissioned to compose an epic pageant in celebration of the first time the West Indian Federal Parliament would meet. His success with that project earned him a Rockefeller grant to study the American Theater in New York City, and during that time he began work on one of his notable plays, *Dream on Monkey Mountain*, based upon reflections about St. Lucia, the Caribbean search for identity, and related concerns. An important stage in Walcott's career came in 1959, when he became founder-director of the Little Carib Theatre Workshop (later the Trinidad Theatre Workshop), in Port of Spain.

It is generally understood that his breakthrough as a mature poet came with the publication of his collection *In a Green Night* in 1962, and since then he has published several impressive collections, including *Selected Poems* (1964), *The Castaway and Other Poems* (1965), *Another Life* (1973), *Sea Grapes* (1976), *The Fortunate Traveler* (1981), *Omeros* (1990), *The Bounty* (1997), and *Tiepolo's Hand* (2000), as well as plays and essays. In 1962 he married Margaret Maillard, with whom he had two daughters, Elizabeth and Anna; the couple later divorced. His 2004 collection, *The Prodigal*, partly inspired by the death of his twin brother, Roderick, features the narrator informing Walcott that this "will be your last book."

Since the 1980s Walcott has combined university teaching in the United States, primarily at Boston University, with his artistic endeavors, maintaining a steady pace of creative productivity. In 1976 he married Norline Metivier, but this marriage ended in divorce in 1993. He won a prestigious John D. and Catherine T. MacArthur Foundation grant in 1981 and, in 1992, the Nobel Prize for Literature. His Nobel address, *Antilles: Fragment of Epic Memory*, was published in 1993. By 2007 Walcott divided his time between St. Lucia (where he has his home), the Caribbean, and the United States, where he continued to lecture in literature and creative writing. Walcott was appointed Professor of Poetry at the University of Essex in England in 2009. Two years later, he was awarded the TS Eliot Poetry prize, for

his collection, *White Egrets*. The prize is awarded annually for the best new collection of poems published in the United Kingdom or Ireland.

FURTHER READING

Walcott, Derek. "Leaving School—VIII," *The London Magazine* (Sept. 1965).
Als, Hilton. "The Islander," *New Yorker* (9 February 2004).
Baer, William, ed. *Conversations with Derek Walcott* (1996).
Burnett, Paula. *Derek Walcott: Politics and Poetics* (2001).
King, Bruce. *Derek Walcott: A Carribean Life* (2000)
Thieme, John. *Derek Walcott* (1999).

DAVID BARRY GASPAR

Walcott, Jersey Joe (31 Jan. 1914–25 Feb. 1994), professional heavyweight boxer, was born Arnold Raymond Cream in Merchantville, New Jersey, one of ten children of Joseph Arnold Cream and Ella Edna. His father was said to come from the West Indies and worked as a laborer. The extent of Walcott's formal education is unknown. At age sixteen he began his boxing career as a middleweight under the tutelage of former lightweight boxer Jack Blackburn. Arnold took the name of JOE WALCOTT, a favorite of his father's and the first African American to hold the welterweight title. He added "Jersey" to his new name for regional identification. In 1932 he married Lydia Talton; the couple had six children.

After struggling for many years as a sparring mate to JOE LOUIS and others, Walcott announced his retirement in 1941. By 1945 he was enticed by the financier Felix Bochicchio and the manager Joe Webster to rejoin the fight game. On 2 August 1945 he met Joe Balsi, the second ranking heavyweight, in nearby Camden, New Jersey. Although an underdog, Walcott won a decision over Balsi, which vaulted him to immediate recognition. In 1946 Walcott faced Jimmy Bivins, who had won twenty-five out of his last twenty-six fights and was a top contender for the heavyweight crown. After Walcott defeated Bivins, his win-loss record went to 25-2, earning him star appeal among the boxing public. At this time sportswriters and fans demanded a championship fight with Joe Louis. After Walcott defeated the notoriously tough Joey Maxim, Louis would no longer ignore him. After a seventeen-year wait Walcott earned a shot at the title. On 5 December 1947, in Madison Square Garden before 18,194 fans, he lost a controversial decision to the Brown Bomber. Although Walcott was a tremendous 10-1 underdog,

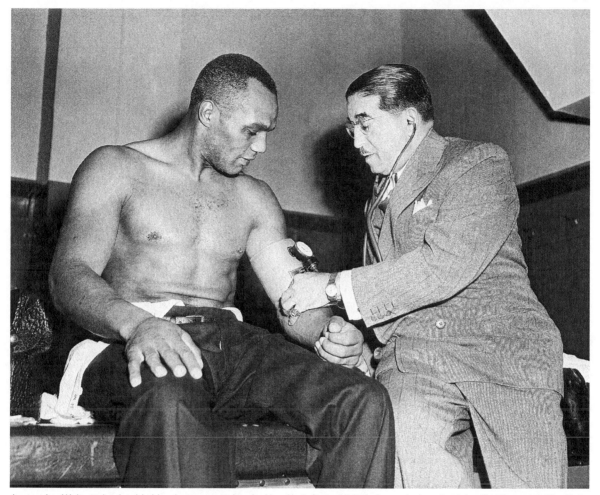

Jersey Joe Walcott, having his blood pressure taken by New York State Athletic Commission physician Dr. Vincent J. Nardiello (right), before his fight with heavyweight champion Joe Louis at Madison Square Garden in New York, 5 December 1947. (AP Images.)

he knocked Louis down in the first round (with Louis up at the count of two) and again in the fourth round (with Louis up at the count of seven). Winning the fight on points, Walcott decided to coast during the fourteenth and fifteenth rounds. The referee Ruby Goldstein scored the fight in favor of Walcott, but the two judges Marty Monroe and Frank Forbes scored it 9-6 and 8-6-1, respectively, for Louis. Walcott thus became only the third man to last fifteen rounds with Louis, with the Welsh fighter Tommy Farr and the Chilean Arturo Godoy being the first two. Total gate receipts for the fight were $216,477, eclipsing the twenty-year record of $201,465 established in 1927, when Jack Dempsey fought Jim Maloney. Walcott earned a purse of about $25,000, the largest of his career at the time. Six months later, in a rematch on 25 June 1948, Louis knocked out Walcott in the

eleventh round before a packed Yankee Stadium crowd of 42,657 fans.

The highlight of Walcott's boxing career came on 18 July 1951. Again an underdog at 6-1, Walcott had previously lost twice to EZZARD CHARLES, who was defending his crown for the ninth time. At the age of thirty-seven, Walcott knocked out Charles in the seventh round of a fifteen-round fight at Forbes Field in Pittsburgh, Pennsylvania. He thus became the oldest man to capture the heavyweight title, in his fifth championship opportunity; the previous oldest champion, Bob Fitzsimmons, was thirty-five in 1897 when he knocked out James Corbett in fourteen rounds in Carson City, Nevada. A crowd of 28,272 paid $245,004 to see the history-making event. The champion Charles received $99,564 for his effort, while Walcott took home $49,782. After the fight his wife Lydia said, "I never saw a man more determined to win."

Walcott successfully defended the title against Charles on 5 June 1952, in Philadelphia, Pennsylvania, taking a fifteen-round decision. He held the crown until 23 September 1952, when he met Rocky Marciano in Philadelphia. In a fight billed as "the best heavyweight championship fight since Jack Dempsey and Luis Angel Firpo," Marciano rallied from being behind on points to knock out the aging champ in the thirteenth round. Walcott's championship title came late in life and was short-lived.

From 1930 to 1953 Walcott had sixty-nine professional fights. He won fifty matches, thirty by knockout. The former heavyweight champion Gene Tunney recalled that Walcott "boxed well, cutely if not classically, and he had a strong punch in either hand." Walcott later became the New Jersey State Athletic Commissioner, and in 1969 he was inducted into the National Boxing Hall of Fame in Canastota, New York.

In later years Walcott served as a county sheriff in Camden, New Jersey. Perhaps Walcott will be best remembered for refereeing the controversial fight between MUHAMMAD ALI and SONNY LISTON in Lewiston, Maine, a small mill town near the New England coast. The rematch between Ali and Liston was held in a high school hockey rink, where only 2,434 patrons came to witness the bout. Historians have viewed the fight as either a great heavyweight match or the most disgraceful affair in title-fight history. In the opening round, Ali connected with a punch to Liston's jaw, which few fight fans saw, sending Liston to the canvas. A startled Walcott belatedly started his countdown. Liston rose within a few seconds, but ringside reporters shouted that Liston was indeed down for a ten-count. Yielding to media pressure, Walcott declared Ali the winner by knockout, and the champ retained his title.

Walcott died at Our Lady of Lourdes Medical Center in Camden, New Jersey. According to his nephew Richard Cream, Walcott died from complications from diabetes. He died without seeing GEORGE FOREMAN take his unique place in boxing history. On 5 November 1994, a forty-five-year-old Foreman knocked out Michael Moorer in the tenth round in Las Vegas, Nevada, wiping Walcott's name from the record book as the world's oldest heavyweight champion.

FURTHER READING
Ashe, Arthur R. *A Hard Road to Glory* (1988).
Carpenter, Harry. *Boxing: An Illustrated History* (1975).

This entry is taken from the *American National Biography* and is published here with the permission of the American Council of Learned Societies.

LARRY LESTER

Walcott, Joe (13 Mar. 1873–4 Oct. 1935), professional boxer, was born in Barbados, British West Indies. Facts about his parents, his education, and his early years are unknown. After coming to the United States in 1887, he worked as a cook, waiter, and elevator operator in Boston and became an amateur boxer and wrestler. Although unusually short (5 feet 1.5 inches) and almost always at a disadvantage to opponents in reach, he enjoyed immediate success because of his unusual upper-body strength, quickness, and agility. He joined a touring troupe of boxers and wrestlers under the management of Tom O'Rourke, meeting all comers in either sport. By 1893 Walcott was a recognized professional boxer in the lightweight division.

Walcott soon grew into a welterweight, winning nearly all of his fights. On 1 March 1895 he boxed a draw in a nontitle battle with the world champion, Mysterious Billy Smith, becoming a contender for the title. Walcott then twice reduced his weight to box the lightweight George "Kid" Lavigne, their second bout being for the world lightweight championship on 29 October 1897. The weight reduction may have affected Walcott, who weakened in the late rounds each time, thus losing two of the most memorable fights of the 1890s.

In 1898 Walcott lost a world welterweight title fight to Smith. Despite outstanding victories over Smith in a rematch and over much heavier opponents, including Dan Creedon, Joe Choynski, George Gardner, and Young Peter Jackson, it was not until 15 December 1901 that Walcott finally won the title by knocking out James "Rube" Ferns in five rounds at Fort Erie, Ontario. By that time Walcott, who was managed by O'Rourke throughout his career, had earned a reputation as a "giant killer" and acquired the nickname "Barbados Demon."

After successful title defenses against Tommy West and Billy Woods and many additional successes in nontitle fights, Walcott boxed the Dixie Kid (Aaron Brown) for the welterweight title on 29 April 1904 in San Francisco. Walcott thrashed his opponent until, without apparent cause, he was disqualified in the twentieth and final round. It soon became known that the referee had bet on Dixie Kid, and although technically having lost his title, Walcott continued to receive recognition as champion.

On 17 October 1904 in Boston, Walcott accidentally shot himself through the right hand. The same bullet killed his close friend and fellow boxer Nelson Hall. Not until July 1906 did Walcott box again, and soon afterward he lost his claim to the welterweight title as a result of two defeats by Billy "Honey" Mellody. In the second Mellody fight Walcott suffered a broken left arm. After these injuries he continued to box until 1911, but he was no longer a contender.

The boxing writer Charles Mathison described Walcott as "a stumpy negro, black as coal, standing but an inch and a half above five feet, [with a] round chubby face and head that sat close to his shoulders, without an observable connecting neck [and] rather a good natured expression on his features and a pair of small, twinkling black eyes." In ring style he was an extremely aggressive, two-fisted fighter who was always willing to exchange hard blows with opponents, even much bigger ones. However, when occasion required, he could box cleverly. Often he had to push himself up to his toes to land blows to the chins of taller opponents.

Walcott engaged in many other exciting fights, especially his draws with JOE GANS, SAM LANGFORD, and Jack O'Brien. His most memorable series of fights were with Kid Carter, Smith, and West. On several occasions he suffered unexpected losses. In 1900, in a fight with West in New York City, Walcott quit after eleven rounds, although well ahead, claiming an injured arm. Afterward no injury was found, and O'Rourke claimed that Walcott was coerced by threats from gamblers. Walcott also withdrew after fighting three rounds with Frank Childs in 1902, although he was ahead, again claiming an arm injury.

Walcott owned a large home and lived well during his championship days, but following his retirement from the ring he quickly descended into poverty. He worked as a porter, as a janitor, and at odd jobs. Little is known of his personal life except that he was married to Sally Dugan in 1894. In 1932 he was hospitalized and afterward lived with a sister in Philadelphia. He died after being struck by a car while hitchhiking without identification near Dalton, Ohio, on 10 October 1935 and was buried there. Walcott was inducted into the International Boxing Hall of Fame in 1991.

FURTHER READING

Fleischer, Nathaniel S. *Black Dynamite*, vol. 3, *The Three Colored Aces: The Story of George Dixon, Joe Gans, and Joe Walcott, and Several Contemporaries* (1938).

Goldman, Herbert G., ed. *The Ring Record Book and Boxing Encyclopedia* (1986–1987).

This entry is taken from the *American National Biography* and is published here with the permission of the American Council of Learned Societies.

LUCKETT V. DAVIS

Walden, Austin Thomas (12 Apr. 1885–2 July 1965), civil rights attorney and judge, was born in Fort Valley, Georgia, the son of Jeff Walden and Jennie Tomlin, former slaves. Walden earned a B.A. at Fort Valley Industrial School in 1902 and an M.A. at Atlanta University in 1907. He entered law school at the University of Michigan, where he received several prizes in oratory and an LLB in 1911.

Walden practiced law in Macon, Georgia, from 1912 until he entered the U.S. Army for service in World War I. He commanded Company I of the 365th Infantry in France and was a trial judge advocate in the Ninety-second Division. Walden returned from the war to marry Mary Ellen Denny, a Baltimore public-school teacher, in 1918; they had two children.

In 1919 Walden was commissioned a captain in the Officers Reserve Corps and moved his legal practice from Macon to Atlanta. His general practice in Atlanta prospered, but he became noted for his role in civil rights cases. In the 1930s, for example, Walden represented John Downer, an African American who was indicted, tried, convicted, and sentenced to death for rape in Macon after being rescued from a lynch mob by Georgia national guardsmen under the command of Major Elbert Tuttle. Walden and Tuttle, a white attorney who later served on the U.S. Court of Appeals for the Fifth Circuit, won a new trial for Downer with a writ of habeas corpus appeal to the Fifth Circuit court. Downer was retried and executed, despite evidence that he was a scapegoat. Yet Walden and Tuttle had sustained the principle that a defendant has a right to trial free of mob influence.

In the 1940s Walden led a six-year battle to win pay equity for African American schoolteachers in Georgia and a longer struggle to force county voter registrars to admit African American voters to Democratic Party primaries in the state. In litigation beginning in 1948, he was the lead attorney for Horace Ward's unsuccessful effort to win admission to the University of Georgia Law School in *Ward v. Regents of the University System of Georgia*. Later in the decade Walden was the lead attorney in suits to desegregate Atlanta's city buses and public schools. In 1961 he was the lead negotiator in discussions that led to the peaceful desegregation of lunch counters in Atlanta. He also helped to prosecute cases against Blackshirts and Ku Klux Klansmen who sought to obstruct the exercise of black voting rights.

Walden held many responsible positions. He was a founder and first president of the Gate City Bar Association in Atlanta, a founder and first co-chairman of the Atlanta Negro Voters League, chairman of the executive board of both the Atlanta Urban League and the Butler Street Young Men's Christian Association, chairman of the trustee board of Wheat Street Baptist Church, member of the board of directors of Citizens Trust Bank, president of the alumni association of Atlanta University, and counsel of the National Baptist Convention. He was a national vice president of the National Association for the Advancement of Colored People, a member of its national legal committee for forty years, and a president and member of the executive board of the Atlanta branch.

In politics Walden was a Republican until 1940, when he switched to the Democratic Party. After organizing the Atlanta Negro Voters League in 1949, he led the city's black voters into a coalition with its white elite to dominate the city's politics and to negotiate concessions from its white leadership for the next two decades. Walden campaigned for the Democratic Party's presidential candidates: Harry Truman in 1948, Adlai Stevenson in 1952 and 1956, and John F. Kennedy in 1960. In 1962 he was elected to the state Democratic Party's executive committee. A year later Walden retired from private legal practice, and President Kennedy appointed him to the American Battle Monuments Commission.

In 1964 Georgia Governor Carl E. Sanders appointed Walden a delegate to the Democratic National Convention, and Atlanta mayor Ivan Allen appointed him an alternate judge in the city's municipal court. Walden was the first African American to sit on the bench in Georgia. In 1964 he received an outstanding achievement award from the University of Michigan. "As he built up a successful practice," said the university's tribute, "he also involved himself deeply with the drive of his race for equal rights under the law, … became the beloved elder statesman of the Negro Community in Atlanta and … won the confidence of the city as a whole." He died in Atlanta.

FURTHER READING
Walden's papers are at the Atlanta Historical Society.
Dorsey, Allison. *To Build Our Lives Together: Community Formation in Black Atlanta, 1875–1906* (2004).

Harmon, David Andrew. *Beneath the Image of the Civil Rights Movement and Race Relations: Atlanta, GA 1946–1981* (1996).
Hornsby, Alton, Jr. "The Negro in Atlanta Politics, 1961–1973," *Atlanta Historical Bulletin* 21 (Spring 1977).
Obituaries: *Atlanta Daily World*, 3–8 July 1965; *Atlanta Constitution*, 3 July 1965; *Atlanta Journal*, 3 July 1965; *New York Times*, 3 July 1965.
This entry is taken from the *American National Biography* and is published here with the permission of the American Council of Learned Societies.

RALPH E. LUKER

Waldron, J. Milton (19 May 1863–20 Nov. 1931), Baptist minister and civil rights activist, was born John Milton Waldron in Lynchburg, Virginia. Waldron's early education was in the public schools of Louis and Amherst counties in Virginia. For college preparatory training, he attended the Richmond Institute (later Virginia Union University). Waldron attended Lincoln University in Pennsylvania and the Newton Theological Seminary in Massachusetts. Shortly after completing his seminary work in 1890, he moved to Washington, D.C., to serve as pastor of the small but distinguished Berean Baptist Church. In April 1892 he married Martha N. Mathews, a teacher in the D.C. public school system. They were married by the notable scholar and minister ALEXANDER CRUMMELL at his St. Luke's Episcopal Church.

Shortly after their wedding the Waldrons moved to Jacksonville, Florida, where Milton became minister of the Bethel Baptist Institutional Church. Waldron was largely responsible for the church's permanent incorporation in 1894 and the construction of its first major building in 1895. He also became a key community figure by establishing the church's many social programs, including a kindergarten, a community center, and a night school. While in Jacksonville, Martha worked for the industrial school and the home for boys at Bethel, which the Waldrons modeled on General Samuel C. Armstrong's Hampton Normal and Agricultural Institute.

In 1901 Waldron helped establish the Afro-American Industrial and Benefit Association, later the Afro-American Life Insurance Company. One of the first of its kind in the Deep South, the association sold health insurance and burial benefits policies and provided the only bank for African Americans in Jacksonville. In addition to his work with the Bethel Church, Waldron published the weekly magazine the *Florida Evangelist* between 1896 and 1902 and was involved with boycotts protesting Jim Crow rules on Jacksonville's streetcars.

In December 1906 Waldron was called to Washington, D.C., to take up the pastorate at the Shiloh Baptist Church. Shiloh had been the scene of much controversy and disagreement between congregants and their pastor, J. Anderson Taylor, and Waldron was hired to bring peace and distinction to the church. He took over the church officially in June 1907. As he had done in Jacksonville, Waldron greatly expanded Shiloh's services and prestige, establishing alley improvement committees and day care centers.

Increasingly uneasy with the ideas and policies of BOOKER T. WASHINGTON and his political machine, Waldron moved in a more activist direction. In 1905 he became treasurer of the Niagara Movement led by W. E. B. DuBois. His growing political independence led, in 1908, to his involvement with the founding of the National Negro American Political League. The League, which included the well-known activist WILLIAM MONROE TROTTER, organized a bolt of black voters from the Republican Party and Tuskegee's political organization. Few black voters left the Republican Party in 1908, but Waldron's campaign helped lay the groundwork for a more famous move of African Americans to the Democratic Party in 1912. That year, many black leaders, including Waldron, DuBois, and Trotter, supported Woodrow Wilson's presidential candidacy, leading an unprecedented one hundred thousand African Americans to cast their votes for the Democrat.

In 1913 Waldron became president of the Washington chapter of the NAACP. The local chapter was founded in part to protest the Wilson administration's segregation of the civil service and its failure to appoint African Americans to public office positions. After a battle among Waldron, D.C. branch members led by ARCHIBALD GRIMKÉ, and the main NAACP board in New York, Waldron was ousted from the presidency, allegedly for his continued support of Wilson and the Democrats.

With the entrance of the United States into World War I in 1917, Waldron worked to earn equal treatment of black soldiers in the nation's military services. He chaired the Committee of 100, a group of leading Washington citizens that pushed the Wilson administration into establishing a training camp for black officers. The camp was finally established in Des Moines, Iowa, in June 1917. Waldron also renewed his letter-writing campaign to Wilson (begun in 1913 to protest the president's segregation policies), asking the president to earn black support for the war effort through the equal treatment of African American soldiers.

After the war Waldron focused on improving black life in Washington. In the 1920s he served as president of the Alley Improvement Association. The association was dedicated to improving living conditions for those who made their homes in small shelters built in the alleyways behind the District's townhouses. He also worked hard to turn Shiloh into a leading institution among African Americans in the District. During his twenty-two-year pastorate he more than doubled the congregation. In 1924 Waldron moved the church to Ninth and P streets in the northwest quarter of the city. After a number of fires and the resulting financial strains on the church, he was forced by stress and declining health to resign his ministry in December 1929. He died at his home on V Street at the age of sixty-eight, leaving behind a legacy of church institutional building and progressive civil rights activism.

FURTHER READING

Crooks, James B. *Jacksonville after the Fire, 1901–1919: A New South City* (1991).

Lewis, David Levering. *W. E. B. DuBois: Biography of a Race, 1868–1919* (1993).

Moore, Jacqueline. *Leading the Race: The Transformation of the Black Elite in the Nation's Capital, 1880–1920* (1999).

Woodson, Carter G. *The History of the Negro Church* (1972).

Obituary: *Washington Evening Star*, 20 Nov. 1931.

ERIC S. YELLIN

Walker, A'Lelia (6 June 1885–17 Aug. 1931), heiress, businesswoman, patron of the arts, and Harlem Renaissance hostess, was born Lelia McWilliams in Vicksburg, Mississippi, the only child of Moses McWilliams and Sarah Breedlove McWilliams, who later was known as MADAM C. J. WALKER, the influential early-twentieth-century entrepreneur, philanthropist, and political activist. Almost nothing is known about Moses, who died around 1887. Although some sources say he was lynched, there is no credible documentation to support that claim. After his death, Lelia moved with her mother to St. Louis, where three of her Breedlove uncles worked as barbers.

The McWilliamses' transition to the unfamiliar, fast-paced city was made easier by the kindness of middle-class black women who were members of

St. Paul African Methodist Episcopal Church, and whose participation in the National Association of Colored Women (NACW) made them sensitive to the needs of such newcomers. In March 1890, while Sarah worked as a washerwoman, Maggie Rector— the matron of the St. Louis Colored Orphans' Home and an NACW member—enrolled Lelia at Dessalines Elementary School. Despite her mother's best efforts to create a stable life in ragtime-era St. Louis, Lelia's school attendance was inconsistent— nearly perfect some years, but sporadic in others— depending upon the whims of Lelia's abusive and alcoholic stepfather, John Davis, whom her mother married in 1894 and from whom she separated around 1903. Although Sarah and Lelia were sometimes on the verge of homelessness, Sarah managed to save enough money from her wages as a laundress to send Lelia to Knoxville College in 1902. Around the same time, Sarah began to experiment with hair-care product formulas to address severe dandruff and other scalp ailments that were causing her to go bald.

During the summer of 1906, Lelia joined her mother and new stepfather, Charles Joseph Walker, in Denver, where her mother had established the Madam C. J. Walker Manufacturing Company. As one of the company's first employees, Walker learned beauty culture—a method of hairdressing and "cultivating" healthy scalps—and her mother's "hair growing" process, which promoted hygiene, frequent shampooing, and the application of a sulfur-based ointment to heal the scalp disease that was so rampant at the time. That fall, as Madam Walker and her husband traveled throughout the southern and eastern United States, Lelia assumed control of the mail-order and manufacturing operation in Denver. When her mother established a temporary headquarters and the first Lelia College of Beauty Culture in Pittsburgh in 1908, Walker moved east as one of the company's first traveling sales agents. In early 1910, after her mother opened a permanent facility in Indianapolis, Walker took over the management of the Pittsburgh beauty school and sales agents' supply station.

Although Walker never was adopted formally by her stepfather, she substituted his surname for her own in order to make clear her connection to the family business. When she married John Robinson in 1909, however, she became known as Lelia Walker Robinson. While visiting Indianapolis in 1911, Walker (who had no biological children) was introduced by her mother to 12-year-old Fairy Mae Bryant, whose hip-length hair made her an ideal model for Madam Walker's scalp treatment demonstrations. In October 1912—with the promise to Bryant's family that she would receive formal education and business training—Walker legally adopted her through the court system in Pittsburgh, where they lived at the time.

In 1913, as Harlem was emerging as the cultural, political, and social mecca of black America, Robinson persuaded her mother to establish a Walker Company branch office on 136th Street near Lenox Avenue. In an exquisite limestone and brick, Georgian-style townhouse designed by architect and Alpha Phi Alpha founder Vertner Woodson Tandy, Robinson oversaw the six-week Lelia College training course and managed the company's northeastern sales territory. During World War I, in line with her mother's support of black troops, she hosted fund-raisers at her Harlem townhouse and volunteered as an ambulance driver for parades and formal occasions honoring the soldiers in the Colored Women's Motor Corps.

Upon her mother's death on 25 May 1919, Robinson became president of the Walker Company, inheriting much of her mother's real estate, including Villa Lewaro, the mansion in Irvington-on-Hudson, New York. Twelve days later on her 34th birthday, she married Dr. Wiley Wilson, a graduate of Howard University's Medical School. They divorced in 1925. Already a seasoned traveler—having visited Central America, the Caribbean, and Hawaii—Robinson crossed the Atlantic Ocean in November 1921 for a five-month excursion to Europe, Africa, and the Middle East. After attending the coronation of Pope Pius XI in Rome, she visited the Egyptian pyramids and Addis Ababa, Ethiopia, where she is said to have been the first American to have met Ethiopian Empress Waizeru Zauditu.

In 1922, for reasons that are not entirely clear, Lelia changed her name to A'Lelia. In May 1926, she married Dr. James Arthur Kennedy, a Chicago psychiatrist, who later was a physician at the Tuskegee, Alabama, Veterans Hospital. They divorced in 1931.

She is best remembered as the hostess of the Dark Tower, the salon on the top floor of her 136th Street townhouse that opened in October 1927 and served as a magnet for Harlem Renaissance writers, artists, actors, and musicians. Robinson's guest lists—for her Dark Tower soirees and the more intimate gatherings at her 80 Edgecombe Avenue pied-à-terre— were quite diverse, ranging from composer and pianist EUBIE BLAKE, author ZORA NEALE HURSTON, dancer FLORENCE MILLS, and actor PAUL ROBESON to downtown white writers Carl Van Vechten, Witter

Bynner, Muriel Draper, and Max Ewing, and an array of African and European royalty. Sculptors Augusta Savage and Richmond Barthé and photographer Berenice Abbott were among the artists for whom she modeled. Poet Langston Hughes, who was a frequent visitor, called her "the joy goddess of Harlem's 1920s" (Hughes, 245).

Walker, who had long suffered from hypertension, died of a stroke in a guest cottage in the resort community of Long Branch, New Jersey, after attending a friend's birthday celebration. Just as Walker's parties had been grand, so was her funeral, as more than eleven thousand people filed past her silver, orchid-filled casket. With Reverend Adam Clayton Powell Sr. presiding, Daytona Normal and Industrial Institute founder Mary McLeod Bethune eulogized her friend's daughter. In most obituaries, Walker inevitably was compared to her mother. One black newspaper harshly called her "happy, hapless life" a "tragedy" because her personal achievements as an entrepreneur paled alongside those of her precedent-setting mother (*New York News and Harlem Home Journal*, 22 Aug. 1931). But Hughes mourned the loss, likening her death to "the end of the gay times of the New Negro era in Harlem" (Hughes, 247). Many have blamed Walker for the financial demise of the Walker Company, but severely declining sales during the first years of the Great Depression, the upkeep of Villa Lewaro, and the Walker trustees' decision to build a million-dollar Indianapolis headquarters in 1927 had more actual impact on the company's fiscal health than Walker's admittedly extravagant spending. (Nevertheless, the company survived until the mid-1980s.)

During her lifetime A'Lelia Walker Robinson had indeed lived in the shadow of her more accomplished mother, with whom she had a loving but complicated relationship. While she may have lacked her mother's fortitude and perseverance, she inherited her flair for dramatic promotion and her expansive vision. Whereas Madam Walker influenced the commerce and politics of her era, A'Lelia Walker set the tone for the social and cultural aura of hers, in many ways creating the role of black American heiress.

FURTHER READING

A'Lelia Walker's correspondence is housed at the Indiana Historical Society in Indianapolis. Additional letters, legal documents, photographs, clothing, and other items are in the private collection of A'Lelia Bundles, Walker's great-granddaughter, in Washington, D.C.

Bundles, A'Lelia. *On Her Own Ground: The Life and Times of Madam C. J. Walker* (2001).

Hughes, Langston. *The Big Sea* (1944).

Lewis, David Levering. *When Harlem Was in Vogue* (1981).

A'LELIA BUNDLES

Walker, Aida Overton (14 Feb. 1880–11 Oct. 1914), singer, dancer, choreographer, and actress, was born Aida Wilmore Overton in New York City, the second child of Moses Overton, a waiter, and Pauline Whitfield Overton; both of her parents were originally from Richmond, Virginia. Overton became interested in singing and dancing while still a child. As a teenager she left school for the stage, a move her mother opposed. A tall, graceful young woman, Overton possessed a rich mezzo-soprano voice. In 1897 she joined the touring production of Black Patti's Troubadours, the famed troupe headed by Madame Sissieretta Jones. Overton appeared in two comedy sketches and received program credit.

In New York the following year Overton took part in a modeling session for a National Tobacco cigarette advertisement; there she met vaudeville comedians George Walker and Bert Williams. Overton and Walker posed in a cakewalk strut; the dance, developed by blacks in the prewar South, had recently become a national craze. Like Overton, Walker was an elegant and talented performer. Their professional and personal ties developed simultaneously. Soon after their initial meeting, they began to perform at well-attended cakewalk exhibitions held in New York music halls, where they established themselves as experts in the era's most fashionable dance. Overton was interviewed by the white press and invited to high-society gatherings, where she was paid to give cakewalk lessons. A complex figure, Walker was an ardent race man and an astute businessman who was also known for his love of fine-tailored clothes, parties, and women. His lifestyle remained unchanged after he and Overton married in 1899. Walker, a tireless promoter, saw to it that the wedding announcement also served as a publicity piece for the newly formed Williams and Walker Company.

Overton Walker was a prominent member of the troupe from its inception in 1898, and performed in all seven Williams and Walker ragtime musical shows: *Senegambian Carnival* (1898), *A Lucky Coon* (1899), *The Policy Players* (1899), *Sons of Ham* (1900), *In Dahomey* (1902), *Abyssinia* (1905), and *Bandanna Land* (1907). The first two enjoyed only moderate success. In *The Policy*

Players a mistaken identity plot was introduced that, once further developed and combined with an improved musical score, made *Sons of Ham* a hit. Like the company's future shows, this one was constructed along a loose, farcical plotline, and featured Williams and Walker's popular comedy routines. The Walkers' spectacular cakewalk was another strong draw. Like any other black musical troupe at the time, the company was compelled to present purely comedic, often self-mocking work (including "coon songs") and to avoid serious love scenes, characters, or themes. As an artist, Overton Walker resented these limitations. Nonetheless, the shows proved extremely popular with audiences both black and white.

In addition to presenting some of the famous comedy routines of the time, Williams and Walker productions showcased two newly emerging, distinctively African American art forms, ragtime music and pre-jazz dance. Overton Walker, never limited to her role as George Walker's dancing partner, played an increasingly large part in performing and developing the company's songs and dances. She appeared in several sketches in *The Policy Players*; when the company staged *Sons of Ham*, many critics saw in her the makings of a star comedian. Although others found that she failed to fully utilize her vocal power, by the end of the tour she had made the comic songs "Miss Hannah from Savannah" and "I Want to Be an Actor Lady" into the hits of the show. Both remained favorites throughout her career.

As she developed as a singer Overton Walker became equally known for her rendering of sultry torch songs that made the most of the rich, throbbing undertones of her voice. She also garnered acclaim as an accomplished and versatile dancer. To an upbeat, comic song she brought the fast-paced steps of the pre-tap style, buck and wing. When performing a number such as "Why Adam Sinned," her movements astonished the audience with their sensuousness and sheer fluidity; descriptions suggest a version of the shake, a black dance of the 1910s and 1920s. Beginning with *Sons of Ham*, Overton Walker received program credit as the choreographer and she became the first African American woman widely recognized in this role. Her well-rehearsed dancers were consistently praised for the seemingly effortless grace with which they executed complex and innovative steps. As an artist Overton Walker's goal was to present the "characteristics and natural tendencies in our people," which, she affirmed, "make just as

beautiful studies for the stage as to be found in the make-up of any other race, and perhaps far better" (quoted in Newman, 66).

The company's third show, *In Dahomey*, was noted for its high quality dance, especially in the company numbers, which critics deemed integral to the production's overall success. *In Dahomey* was Williams and Walker's most successful show, and it decisively established their preeminence among black musical troupes. In 1903 the company took *In Dahomey* to England, where they played a royal command performance and eight months of sold-out shows at London's Shaftesbury Theatre. The company's next show, *Abyssinia* (1905), was notable for its complex musical score (largely composed by WILL MARION COOK), lavish sets, and a large cast that included several animals. *Bandanna Land* (1907), more successful than *Abyssinia*, was the company's final production. George Walker, suffering from paresis, retired in January 1908. For the remainder of the tour, in addition to performing her own numbers, Overton Walker dressed in her husband's famously stylish clothes and rendered his song and dance numbers. After *Bandanna Land* closed, she and Williams considered undertaking future projects but failed to come to terms. In 1908 she performed in *The Red Moon*, a BOB COLE and JOHN ROSAMUND JOHNSON production billed as "a sensation in red and black." In 1910 she appeared in the cast of S. H. DUDLEY's *His Honor, the Barber*, and afterward retired briefly to care for her husband. Following his death in January 1911, Overton Walker toured vaudeville, performing songs and dances from the Williams and Walker shows.

Aida Overton Walker's most prominent solo appearance, and her last truly sensational role, came in 1912, when Broadway impresario William Hammerstein invited her to Broadway's Victoria Theatre, one of the country's premier vaudeville houses, to revive her performance of Salome, a character that had been faddishly popular several years before in venues ranging from the opera to the burlesque (where it was known as the "Dance of the Seven Veils"). Overton Walker's rendering of the dance had been incorporated into the *Bandanna Land* tour after George Walker's retirement. In that production, her Salome was followed by Bert Williams's send-up, in which he draped himself in gauze, his attention focused on a watermelon. The Hammerstein production, by contrast, was elaborately staged and ran a full nine minutes. Accompaniment was provided by a thirty-six piece orchestra playing music composed by JAMES REESE

EUROPE. Overton Walker, clad in shimmering costume, descended a flight of stairs, approaching her goal with characteristic languid grace.

During the last two years of her career she performed in several charity benefits in the black community, and she developed dances for younger African American women. Her health was in decline, however, and her stage appearances became increasingly rare. In September of 1914 she retired, suffering from what some sources referred to as a kidney complaint and others as a nervous breakdown. She died in New York City a month later.

Overton Walker's passing was widely mourned. Nearly a generation elapsed before African American women such as FLORENCE MILLS, ETHEL WATERS, and ADELAIDE HALL emerged as comparable talents. Mills, the most prominent of these, cited Overton Walker as a great influence on her own work. As the first notable African American woman choreographer, an acclaimed dancer, and a popular singer, Aida Overton Walker possessed a range of talents rivaled by few of her contemporaries.

FURTHER READING

Charters, Ann. *Nobody: The Story of Bert Williams* (1970).

Newman, Richard. *Words Like Freedom* (1996).

Sampson, George T. *The Ghost Walks* (1988).

Stearns, Marshall, and Jean Stearns. *Jazz Dance* (1964).

"Walker, Aida Overton," in *Notable Black American Women*, ed. Jessie Carney Smith (1996).

JOANNA WOOL

Walker, Albertina (29 Aug. 1929–8 Oct. 2010), gospel singer, was born in Chicago, Illinois, the youngest of nine children to Camilla Walker and Reuben Walker, a Works Progress Administration (WPA) worker. Greatly influenced by her mother's choral singing at West Point Baptist Church, Walker started singing at the age of three, and by four she was a member of the West Point children's choir. Coming of age in the midst of Chicago's growing hotbed of early gospel music, Walker absorbed the styles of the rising stars that would visit her church—ROBERTA MARTIN, Professor Frye, SALLIE MARTIN, and MAHALIA JACKSON. Jackson soon took Walker on as a protégé, and the young singer closely observed the inner workings of the developing gospel music circuit.

Noting that the key to success was to gain exposure on radio broadcasts, Walker began appearing on local gospel radio programs with West Point Baptist Church's group, the Pete Williams Singers. By the mid-1940s, the teenage Walker was touring with the prestigious Robert Anderson Singers, and her distinct contralto was already attracting attention. Anderson had been a highlighted performer with the Roberta Martin Singers, and he coached Walker on the important details of stage performance. The singer's husky, supple vocals served to anchor the group, and after several years they had amassed a loyal following.

In 1951 Robert Anderson retired, but his record producers were eager to retain Walker as a solo performer. Accustomed to being onstage with a group, Walker balked at the prospect of singing alone. She quickly organized the other Robert Anderson singers, Ora Lee Hopkins, Elyse Yancey, and Nellie Grace Daniels, to sing background for her. She dubbed her new group the Caravans.

In the beginning it was Walker who performed most of the group's solos, with the others providing intricate harmonies and tight rhythm. The purity of Walker's voice and her singular style made the Caravans stand out from all the other female gospel groups at the time, but by 1953, they had emerged as a powerful ensemble of soloists. With the addition of the house-wrecking vocals of Bessie Griffin, the group claimed their place as a groundbreaking force in gospel music. Establishing new territory with their arrangements and vocal style, their recordings of songs such as "Too Close to Heaven" and the traditional spiritual "All Night, All Day" showcased the Caravans' exceptional ability to blend ethereal harmonies with forceful, alternating leads.

By 1956 the Caravans were the undisputed queens of gospel, and Walker revealed an uncanny ability to recruit powerhouse performers such as Griffin, Dolores Washington, Dorothy Norwood, Inez Andrews, and SHIRLEY CAESAR. Walker guided each new member into the spotlight, and as one member would leave, she would be replaced by another, with talents as stunning as the preceding member. JAMES CLEVELAND came onboard as a keyboardist/arranger, and the group closed out the decade on the same rarified level as Walker's mentor, MAHALIA JACKSON.

The Caravans gained many honors, from ARETHA FRANKLIN's riveting cover of their "Mary, Don't You Weep," to the admiration and acknowledgement of contemporaries such as RAY CHARLES, to appearing with Jackson at Carnegie Hall in the early 1960s. Despite the reverence paid them and the hard work they put in, touring the country in a solitary Cadillac and performing in venues that included high school auditoriums, churches, and Madison Square Garden, the group earned a meager living.

At the time record companies did not foresee the money that could be made with gospel music. "We really sang for the Lord, we weren't making a lot of money," Walker said. "When Walter Hawkins broke with 'Oh Happy Day,' [in 1968] things changed. There was a lot more money available" (Cummings-Yeates, 7). As members began leaving to form solo careers or to get married, Walker disbanded the Caravans in the late 1960s. She took the opportunity to get married herself in 1968, to Leslie Reynolds. In the late 1980s Leslie Reynolds died; Walker married Rico Brooks in 1991.

Faced once again with the challenge of performing alone, Walker triumphantly recorded her first solo album, *God Is Love* in 1975. The record signaled the beginning of her impressive solo career, which includes more than sixty albums recorded from the 1970s through the 1990s. She sang such memorable hits as "Please Be Patient with Me," "Joy Will Come in the Morning," and "I'm Still Here."

The 1990s represented another turning point for Walker, now widely considered the "Queen of Gospel." After ten Grammy nominations, the singer finally won in 1994, with *Songs of the Church: Live in Memphis*, in the Best Traditional Soul Gospel Album category. Later that year, she joined singers from various genres, Thelma Houston, CeCe Peniston, Phoebe Snow, and Lois Walden to form the contemporary gospel group Sisters of Glory. They appeared at Woodstock 1994 and before the pope at the Vatican II concert. In 1995 they released *Good News in Hard Times*, an album of gospel standards. It was Walker's singular brand of gospel, however, that garnered her a Dove Award in 1997 for Traditional Gospel Album of the Year, for her solo album, *Let's Go Back: Live in Chicago*.

Albertina Walker's influence on gospel music touched many levels. She was famous for singing "behind" the beat, a traditional gospel technique of which she was one of the few remaining masters. As the founder of the Caravans, she helped highlight the careers of more gospel greats than any other group in the history of gospel music. Graced with a low, soulful voice, her performances displayed a range that soared beyond the merely beautiful to reach the sublime. Her musical legacy reflects the early foundations of gospel music, with its tightly woven harmonies and deeply spiritual inflections. At the same time, Walker's music reached into the future as it continued to influence contemporary gospel singers, such as Yolanda Adams, with her vocal style and dynamic arrangements. She died in Chicago at the age of 81.

FURTHER READING
Boyer, Horace Clarence. *How Sweet the Sound: The Golden Age of Gospel* (1995).
Cummings-Yeates, Rosalind. "Her Highness of Gospel: Albertina Walker," *N'digo* (2 Sept. 2004).
Darden, Bob. *People Get Ready! A New History of Black Gospel Music* (2004).
Walker, Lewis Newton, Jr. "The Struggles and Attempts to Establish Branch Autonomy and Hegemony: A History of the District of Columbia Branch National Association for the Advancement of Colored People, 1912–1942," Ph.D. diss., University of Delaware (1979).

ROSALIND CUMMINGS-YEATES

Walker, Alice Malsenior (9 Feb. 1944–), writer, activist, and educator, was born in Eatonton, Georgia, the youngest daughter of Willie Lee and Minnie Lou Grant Walker, who were sharecroppers. As the youngest of eight children growing up in the South, Walker experienced her share of familial and racial tension but also a good deal of closeness between, particularly, the female members of her family, whose talents and achievements she celebrates in her novels, poems, and essays. When she was eight years old, her brother shot her in the eye with a BB gun while they were playing cowboys and Indians, causing an injury that, despite later corrective surgery, scarred her for life. The incident led Walker into the first of several recurrent episodes of self-reflection and isolation, which, although desperately difficult, often resulted in the reassertion of her artistic voice.

A gifted child, Walker graduated from her high school as its valedictorian in 1961 and was awarded a scholarship to Spelman College in Atlanta. After two years she transferred to Sarah Lawrence College in New York, traveled to Africa in the summer of 1964, and graduated a year later. Her passage through adolescence and young adulthood was, like her childhood, not without its problems. Talented and idealistic but also a troubled young woman, Walker returned from Africa pregnant, though not by choice. Depression and suicidal feelings marked her final year at Sarah Lawrence. Once she had made the difficult decision to have an abortion, writing provided a refuge from self-destruction. The fruits of this period, poems later published in *Once* in 1968 and the short story "To Hell with Dying" (1967), ripened under the encouragement of the poets Muriel Rukeyser and LANGSTON HUGHES.

After college Walker went to work for the New York City welfare department. In 1967 she married the white Jewish civil rights lawyer Mel Leventhal, and the couple moved to the South to settle in Jackson, Mississippi. Both were active in civil rights—Walker canvassed for voter registration in her native Georgia and acted as a black history consultant for Head Start in Mississippi, while her husband worked for the movement as a lawyer. At the same time Walker kept on writing—at times professionally, as writer in residence at Tougaloo and Jackson State colleges, but mostly in her scarce spare time, which became scarcer still after the birth of her only child, Rebecca, on 17 November 1969.

Life in the South was not easy at this time and under these conditions. Walker wrote much later, in "Breaking Chains and Encouraging Life" (1980), published in the essay collection *In Search of Our Mothers' Gardens: Womanist Prose* (1983), about the censure she received from reviewers, not for her work but for her "lifestyle," meaning her interracial marriage. In 2000 she also published a memoir of the early years of her marriage, "To My Young Husband" in *The Way Forward Is with a Broken Heart*. Her daughter Rebecca Leventhal Walker, later still, published her own memoirs of growing up as a child of mixed descent in *Black, White and Jewish. Autobiography of a Shifting Self* (2001). At the time, however, the opinions of black critics and southern whites were minor concerns compared with Walker's intensely felt commitment to an interracial movement for civil rights, black and white together in nonviolent action under the leadership of men like MARTIN LUTHER KING JR. His death in 1968 disturbed her as much as his appearance on national TV had once excited and motivated her to join the movement, as she wrote in her tribute to him, "Choice," in *In Search of Our Mothers' Gardens*.

Domestic violence and abuse, witnessed in her youth in the South, were the major themes of her very early work, such as the award-winning short story collection *In Love and Trouble* (1973), and the novel *The Third Life of Grange Copeland* (1970). But civil rights inspired the next phase of Walker's writing. Besides several essays in *In Search of Our Mothers' Gardens*, her experiences in the civil rights movement also inspired the novel *Meridian* (1976) and some of the more critical stories in the collection *You Can't Keep a Good Woman Down* (1982), where Walker took issue with black nationalism.

The early to mid-1970s was a productive period for Walker—the poetry collection *Revolutionary Petunias* (1973) won the Lillian Smith Award—but the

stress of living in a tumultuous period in the South's history, and of balancing work with family life took their toll. Walker's marriage to Leventhal was dissolved in 1977. Walker then turned her attention to teaching and writing, accepting a position at Wellesley College in New England, where she designed and taught the first-ever course in black women's writing. By this time she had made a major discovery: that there existed a tradition of black women writers and artists who had found ways of expressing themselves creatively and making their presences felt in the world. She had discovered the artistry of black women like her mother and her ancestor May Poole, of indomitable spirit, who had created gardens and handed their stories down through the generations. She had discovered, notably, the writer and anthropologist ZORA NEALE HURSTON, who, like Walker, came from the South a stranger to metropolitan academe but who, while enrolled at Barnard College in New York, kept the faith with her people and was not ashamed to celebrate their creativity and wisdom.

The result of this discovery was the pathbreaking anthology *I Love Myself When I Am Laughing: A Zora Neale Huston Reader* (1979). Hurston, who had experienced some success but was forgotten by the time she reached middle age, had a profound influence on Walker. Certainly, the concept of "womanism," for which Walker has become renowned and which is often taken to mean, too simply, "black feminism," owes much to Hurston's example as a sassy, serious, sometimes outrageous but, most of all, independent-minded and proud black woman. She was a feminist before feminism was invented, like Shug in *The Color Purple* (1983).

Written in northern California, where Walker had moved in 1977 to devote herself full time to her art, with the support of Guggenheim and National Endowment for the Arts fellowships, *The Color Purple* was a turning point in Walker's career. Perhaps a radical change in living conditions made this possible: Walker was living in rural Mendocino County with her daughter and her new partner, Robert Allen. In the persona of Celie, an abused and downtrodden southern black woman who rises to her own spiritual and literal fortune through the love of Shug, a jazz singer, and a reunion with her long-lost sister, Nettie, the voice of the artist emerged fully developed in a Hurston-inspired everyday language that was both simple and poetic.

The Color Purple was a runaway success; it won the Pulitzer Prize and the National Book Award in 1983, but it also caused a good deal of controversy, especially after the film version, directed by Steven Spielberg,

Alice Walker, the first black woman to win the Pulitzer Prize for fiction for her book *The Color Purple*, 18 April 1983. (AP Images.)

came out in 1985. The main source of offense in the novel was Walker's depiction of lesbianism in the relationship between Shug and Celie; in the film it was the portrayal of black men as either child molesters (Albert) or buffoons (Harpo) that attracted virulent criticism. Because the tone of such criticism was often hateful, Walker revisited, after another of those periods of self-reflection and isolation, the debate around *The Color Purple* in the memoir *The Same River Twice: Honoring the Difficult* (1996). She commemorated in this volume the pain that criticism of *The Color Purple* had caused her, at a time when she was also suffering from Lyme disease and having relationship problems with Robert Allen.

Once again difficult times eventually produced new work, however, and in *The Temple of My Familiar* (1989) sexuality or, more accurately, sensuality and loving relationships—whether between lovers, within extended families, or in creation at large—were a major theme. Easily the longest and most challenging of Walker's novels, *The Temple of My Familiar* took the whole of world history and the kinship of humans with the natural world as its subject. Many of Walker's paganist beliefs found their expression here, as did her increasing awareness of her own bisexuality. This, and Allen's alcoholism, eventually led to a breakup in 1990; from then on Walker was mostly in relationships with women.

More than most writers, Alice Walker used her life in her creative work, often for didactic purposes. Typical is the incident of her brother shooting her in the eye with a BB gun. Walker often recounted this story to explain how, in apparently innocent children's games, boys learn the early scripts of masculinity: to inflict pain on those smaller and weaker than themselves, something that later in life may lead them to domestic violence. She also harked back to the memory of her "patriarchal wound" as a connection, through identification and trauma, with women in Africa who have to suffer female genital mutilation, often at a very young age. In the 1992 film documentary *Warrior Marks*, directed by Pratibha Parmar, Walker told her own story of the injury while filming young girls who were about to be mutilated. In the accompanying book *Warrior Marks: Female Genital Mutilation and the Sexual Blinding of Women* (1993) and in the novel *Possessing the Secret of Joy* (1992), Walker sought to educate the world about the crime of female genital mutilation. Departing from fiction writers' custom, she even ended her novel with an afterword, "To the Reader," in which she gave statistics on this practice and a list for further reading.

Besides being a writer who used her own life in her creative work, Walker thus was also an activist and an educator. She taught at a number of universities, including Berkeley and Yale, but it is as an informal educator, an elder or grandmother, that she came to style herself in the later works. Her womanist, environmentalist, and paganist credo was made most explicit in *Anything We Love Can Be Saved: A Writers' Activism* (1997), a book of essays and open letters on a range of issues, from wearing dreadlocks to the boycott of Cuba. The relation between the political and the personal, always a trademark of Walker's writing, remained paramount also in the pamphlet *Sent by Earth: A Message from the Grandmother Spirit after the Attacks on the World Trade Center and Pentagon* (2001).

The death of both her parents (her father in 1973 and her mother in 1993) and a brother (1996) caused Walker to reevaluate her relationship with her family. In *Anything We Love Can Be Saved* she wrote about the spiritual journey to make peace with her father and brothers at last. But the great love remained her mother; an essay titled "My Mother's Blue Bowl" concludes the collection in tribute.

This same theme of family relations—their difficulty and the eventual forgiveness that leads to reconciliation—suffused *By the Light of My Father's Smile* (1998), a novel that is a meditation on a writer's life and death. Walker's fascination with the mortality of art and artists dated back at least to her discovery of Zora Neale Hurston, whose premature death in obscurity Walker took in the late 1970s to be a cautionary tale about how little African American artists were valued. It seemed, however, that by the twenty-first century the Californian, bisexual, pagan, womanist Alice Walker not only was confident in her role as writer and medium but also was recognized worldwide as an elder and spiritual guide for generations to come.

Walker's work has continued with the 2006 publication of a collection of essays about social activism, *We Are the Ones We've Been Waiting For: Inner Light in a Time of Darkness*, which was later adopted as one of BARACK OBAMA's campaign slogans in the 2008 presidential race. She has continued to highlight human rights abuses, and in 2010 published *Overcoming Speechlessness: A Poet Encounters the Horror in Rwanda, Eastern Congo, and Palestine/Israel*, an extended essay on her visits to Central Africa and the Gaza Strip. In 2011 Walker published a mediation on her experiences raising chickens on her farm in northern California, *The Chicken Chronicles: Sitting with the Angels Who Have Returned with My Memories: Glorious, Rufus, Gertrude Stein, Splendor, Hortensia, Agnes of God, Tho Gladyoos, & Babe. A Memoir.*

FURTHER READING

Walker, Alice. *Anything We Love Can Be Saved: A Writer's Activism* (1997).

Walker, Alice. *The Same River Twice: Honoring the Difficult* (1996).

Walker, Alice. *In Search of Our Mothers' Gardens: Womanist Prose* (1983).

Walker, Alice. *The Way Forward Is with a Broken Heart* (2000).

O'Brien, John. "Alice Walker: An Interview" in *Alice Walker: Critical Perspectives Past and Present*, eds. Henry Louis Gates Jr. and K. A. Appiah (1993): 326–346.

Wilson, Sharon. "A Conversation with Alice Walker" in *Alice Walker: Critical Perspectives Past and Present*, eds. Henry Louis Gates Jr. and K. A. Appiah (1993): 319–325.

White, Evelyn C. *Alice Walker: A Life* (2004).

MARIA LAURET

Walker, Arthur Bertram Cuthbert, Jr. (24 Aug. 1936–29 Apr. 2001), astrophysicist and university administrator, was born in Cleveland, Ohio, the son of Arthur Bertram Cuthbert Walker Sr., a lawyer, and Hilda Forte, a social worker. At age five his family moved to New York City. Thanks to his mother, who recognized the boy's fondness for science and repeatedly intervened to prevent teachers from discouraging him, Walker enrolled in the Bronx High School of Science, where his interest in chemistry and physics heightened. In 1957 he graduated with honors in physics from the Case Institute of Technology (later Case Western Reserve University) in Cleveland, Ohio. He was elected to Tau Beta Pi, an engineering honor society, in 1955, and to Sigma Xi, a scientific research society, in 1960. At the University of Illinois at Urbana-Champaign, with the aid of fellowships and a research assistantship, Walker earned his master's degree in 1958 and a doctorate in Nuclear Physics in 1962, with a dissertation titled "Photomeson Production from Neutrons Bound in Helium and Deuterium."

Upon completing graduate studies, he entered the U.S. Air Force as a first lieutenant and worked at the Air Force Weapons Laboratory in New Mexico developing instrumentation for an experiment to measure the Van Allen belt radiation—protons and electrons trapped in the earth's magnetic field that can be hazardous to satellites traveling into outer space. From 1965 to 1974 Walker was a research scientist employed by the Space Physics Laboratory (SPL) of the Aerospace Corporation. Along with his collaborator H. R. Rugge, he directed the company's Space Astronomy Project and conducted groundbreaking experiments focusing on the earth's upper atmosphere. These projects included ground-based and space-based observations of the sun's corona, solar activity, and solar X-ray emissions measured by high-resolution X-ray spectroscopy and imaging, employing both grazing and normal-incidence X-ray optical systems that he later applied to astronomical observations and to biological materials.

Walker's pioneering work at the SPL attracted the-attention of scientists at Stanford University, and he joined its physics department in 1974. He directed the student observatory and taught popular courses in physics and astronomy. One of his projects resulted in the first soft X-ray image of the sun. A world-renowned expert in extreme ultraviolet (EUV) astronomy—important because the sun's radiation affects the chemistry of the earth's upper atmosphere and ozone layer—he produced an EUV image of the sun and solar corona that was heralded on the front page of the 30 September 1988 issue of *Science* magazine. When the image was shown at a session of the American Astronomical Society the audience erupted in applause.

Working with the National Aeronautics and Space Administration (NASA) in 1991, Walker and his colleagues Troy W. Barbee and R. B. Hoover were responsible for deploying fifteen specially designed telescopes with synthetic, multilayer mirrors via the multispectral solar telescope array (MSSTA) launched by a rocket at the White Sands Missile Range in 1991. In a subsequent launch nineteen similar telescopes were sent to an altitude of 230 kilometers to observe the sun's ultraviolet and soft X-rays. Using NASA's AXAF (Chandra) X-ray Observatory, the Hobby Eberly Telescope, and the Stanford Synchrotron Radiation Laboratory, in the late 1990s Walker led a group of scientists investigating phenomena related to the clustering of galaxies, the intergalactic gas, stellar chromospheres and coronae, supernova remnants, and the interstellar medium.

Constantly adapting new technologies to assist him in developing improved X-ray astronomical instrumentation, Walker was highly respected by fellow scientists and students, who valued him as a mentor. One of his better-known doctoral students at Stanford was Sally Ride, the nation's first female astronaut, whose dissertation he supervised and who collaborated with him in developing the first comprehensive model to demonstrate interaction of the interstellar gas and X-rays.

Gentlemanly and soft-spoken, Walker also did much to encourage African Americans to advance their studies in science. Seven of his eighteen doctoral students were from underrepresented groups. While at Stanford, Walker, who was associate dean of graduate studies from 1976 to 1980, saw the number of black physics graduate students increase to the point where Stanford in the 1980s and 1990s produced more blacks with doctorates in physics than did any other university in the nation. This increase was attributable in large part to Walker's actively recruiting and advising the black students, as well as finding sympathetic faculty to assist him in mentoring and training these students. Outside of the physics department Walker was a longtime member of the university's African and Afro-American Studies Advisory Committee and served as president of an informal black faculty organization that he dubbed the Banneker Group.

One of the high points in Walker's career was his appointment by President Ronald Reagan to the commission that investigated the tragic explosion of the space shuttle *Challenger* in 1986. Serving alongside Walker on the Rogers Commission were the former astronauts Neil Armstrong and Sally Ride, the Nobel laureate Richard Feynman, and the former U.S. secretary of state William Rogers. Walker's chairmanship of this commission was undoubtedly the most prominent among a number of academic and government consultative and investigative assignments.

In 1996, as chairman of the American Universities for Research in Astronomy (AURA) Scientific Advisory Committee, more commonly known as the Walker Committee, Walker facilitated the establishment of this country's only national solar observatory, the Sacramento Peak Solar Observatory. Walker was also chairman of NASA's Advanced Solar Observatory Science Working Group and of the National Science Foundation's Astronomy Advisory Group, and he was summoned to testify on science policy matters before several committees of the U.S. Congress. On 15 September 2000 a meeting was held at Stanford to pay tribute to Walker's life and accomplishments.

A month after attending the annual meeting of the National Conference of Black Physics Students, Walker died of cancer at his home in Stanford, California. He was survived by his wife, Virginia T. Walker; his daughter, Heather M. M. Walker; and his stepsons, Nigel D. Gibbs and Eric D. Gibbs. As a fitting memorial, *Black Enterprise* magazine in partnership with the National Society of Black Physicists founded the Arthur B. C. Walker Scholarship to aid promising college juniors and seniors majoring in physics.

FURTHER READING

Levy, Dawn. "Art Walker: 'Favorite Sun' of Solar Physics," *Stanford Report*, 4 Oct. 2000.

Spangenburg, Ray, and Kit Moser. *African Americans in Science, Math, and Invention* (2003).

Obituary: *New York Times*, 9 May 2001.

ROBERT FIKES JR.

Walker, Charles Thomas (5 Feb. 1858–29 July 1921), clergyman, civic leader, was born on the outskirts of Augusta, Georgia, in the small, rural community of Hephzibah. He was the youngest of eleven children born to Thomas and Hannah Walker. Thomas, a coachman for a prominent white planter and legislator, died a day before his son's birth. Walker's mother, a nurse and house servant, died eight years later. After her death, Walker moved among relatives and eventually worked as a field hand on the farm of his uncle, Reverend Nathan Walker, who served as pastor of the Franklin Covenant Baptist Church in Hephzibah. Charles joined that church in June 1873, and like other men in his family, he underwent ordination into the ministry four years later. Hannah taught her son his first Bible lessons and encouraged his love of reading and writing. After two summers of study at a Freedmen's Bureau school, Walker enrolled at the Augusta Baptist Institute in 1874 and took literary and theological courses. The school, which later moved and became Atlanta Baptist Seminary, was renamed Morehouse College in 1913. Although Augusta Baptist awarded no formal degrees or diplomas to its early graduates, Walker later received honorary doctorates from the State University in Louisville, Kentucky, in 1890 and from Atlanta Baptist in 1902.

While enrolled at Augusta Institute, Walker assumed pastorate duties in several rural churches, including his family's church, Franklin Covenant. While teaching classes at the church in the summer of 1879, Walker married Violet Franklin, a young woman from the area. The couple had four children. Less than a year after the marriage, the Walkers moved to LaGrange, Georgia, where Charles took charge of the First Baptist Colored Church as pastor. After a successful three-year tenure, Walker returned to Augusta and accepted an invitation from members of Central Baptist Church to replace their recently ousted pastor. Despite Walker's great gifts as a preacher, bitter feuds among church members jeopardized his future. By the spring of 1884 the situation at Central Baptist proved untenable and the congregation splintered into two separate churches. On 21 August 1885 Walker and three hundred parishioners established Beulah Baptist Church, later changing the name to Tabernacle. Within a few years, Tabernacle grew to become one of the largest black congregations in the South, and Walker emerged as one of the most influential African American religious figures in the country.

Following a successful five-week revival in Kansas City in 1892, Walker enjoyed national acclaim as a minister and passionate speaker and as a conservative black leader. Standing five feet six inches, Walker's small stature and boyish looks led many admirers to call him the "boy preacher." Often placards announcing his speaking engagements described him as "the Colored John the Baptist" or "the Black Spurgeon"—after the pastor of London's Metropolitan Tabernacle Church, Charles Haddon Spurgeon, who was thought to be the

greatest evangelist of his time (Floyd). In BOOKER T. WASHINGTON's *My Larger Education*, the Tuskegee leader noted that he did "not know of any man, white or black, who is a more fascinating speaker either in private conversation or on the public platform" (Washington, 231). In the summer of 1899 Walker's reputation attracted the attention of members of the Mt. Olivet Baptist Church in New York City, who sought a charismatic pastor to lead a congregation rife with internal divisions. To the dismay of Augusta parishioners, Walker stepped down from his position at Tabernacle. Not long after Walker's arrival to the San Juan District of New York, his phenomenal preaching attracted overflow crowds. He expanded Mt. Olivet's membership three-fold, conducted public lectures and revivals throughout the region, published collections of sermons and addresses, and led a committee to investigate the city's August 1900 race riot. One of his most significant accomplishments was the creation of a colored branch of the YMCA, located at 132 West Fifty-third Street.

At the end of 1901 Walker crafted an agreement that allowed him to resume his role as "nominal pastor" of Tabernacle, while still leading the Mt. Olivet congregation (Floyd, 123). While Walker lived in New York, Augusta educator SILAS XAVIER FLOYD published a laudatory biography entitled *Life of Charles T. Walker, D. D.: The Black Spurgeon*. The volume, recounting Walker's climb from slavery to the pinnacle of clerical power, included excerpts from a number of the minister's published pamphlets and essays: "A Colored Man Abroad or What I Saw and Heard in Europe and the Holy Land" (1891), "Truth From Another Angle on the Negro Question" (1900), "Colored Men for the Twentieth Century" (1900), "An Appeal to Caesar: Sermon on the Race Question" (1900), and "Reply to Hannibal Thomas" (1901).

Walker returned to Augusta in 1904. While working as a church pastor and traveling evangelist, he held numerous leadership roles. In 1880 he proposed the establishment of the Walker Baptist Institute and remained the school's financial agent for several decades. Four years later, he joined RICHARD R. WRIGHT SR., the principal of Augusta's Ware High School, in founding the *Augusta Sentinel* newspaper. During the Spanish-American War, President William McKinley appointed Walker to serve as the chaplain for an all-black volunteer infantry unit serving in Cuba.

In January 1904 he participated in a Carnegie Hall forum called to broker a truce between the competing positions of W. E. B. DuBois and Washington. Washington and Walker were quite close and shared similar beliefs. Washington made sure that Walker was among the invited participants at the 1904 conference. During major "race gatherings" in Georgia, Washington often dispatched Walker who then sent back reports of developments and discussions. Additionally, Walker remained active in the local and state Republican Party and held leadership roles in the National Baptist Convention and the Missionary Baptist Convention of Georgia. While an advocate of social reform and race progress, Walker adopted a gradualist posture and moderate tone throughout his public discourse. As he voiced outrage at white animus and violence that crippled black communities during the World War I era, he encouraged African Americans to support the military effort. Despite his own stint in New York City, he remained solidly opposed to schemes promoting migration to northern communities. Even as he worked to build a reputable YMCA chapter in Augusta, he remained far removed from the activities of the NAACP or the National Urban League in the community.

During the last two decades of Walker's life, he embarked on an aggressive fund-raising campaign to build a new sanctuary that permitted Tabernacle to expand its ministries to include literacy promotion, youth development, and training in home economics and industrial arts. While most of the resources for construction came from church members, Walker's extraordinary success as a pastor drew support from many white admirers, including John D. Rockefeller, whose contributions to Tabernacle's coffers further solidified the minister's national reputation. Ultimately Walker's extensive travels and his hectic schedule took a toll on his health. In 1919 the minister's exhilarating career slowed down as he worked in vain to recover from a stroke. He died in Augusta in the summer of 1921 and is buried on the grounds of the towering institutional church he built only a few blocks from his home. A local school and the central artery in Augusta's once-thriving black business district are named after Walker.

FURTHER READING

Bacote, Samuel William, ed. *Who's Who Among the Colored Baptists of the United States* (1913).

Caldwell, A. B., ed. "Charles Thomas Walker," in *History of the American Negro and His Institutions* (1917).

Floyd, Silas Xavier. *Life of Charles T. Walker, D. D.* (1902).

Washington, Booker T. *My Larger Education* (1911).

BOBBY J. DONALDSON

Walker, David (1796?–6 Aug. 1830), radical abolitionist and political writer, was born in Wilmington, North Carolina, the son probably of a free black woman and possibly of a slave father. Almost nothing is known about either parent; only a little more is known about Walker's years in the South. Walker was born in a town where by 1800 African Americans predominated demographically over whites by more than two to one. Their influence on the town and the region was profound. Most labor—skilled or unskilled—was performed by black slaves who were the foundation of the region's key industries: naval stores production, lumbering, rice cultivation, building construction, and shipping. The Methodist church in Wilmington was largely the creation of the local black faithful. The skill and resourcefulness of the African Americans amid their enslavement deeply impressed Walker.

Sometime between 1815 and 1820 Walker left Wilmington and made the short journey south to Charleston, South Carolina. He probably decided to move because free blacks composed a much higher percentage of the black population in Charleston than in Wilmington, had far greater economic opportunity there, and had created a number of social and benevolent organizations to serve their needs. How Walker was employed in Charleston is not known. By 1817 a number of the town's black religious leaders formed one of the first branches of the new African Methodist Episcopal church, founded in Philadelphia in 1816 by RICHARD ALLEN. Walker was probably exposed to this particular congregation and began then his deep devotion to Allen and his example of racial and religious courage. Walker must also have known of the relentless white efforts to close the church and the bitterness that these attempts engendered in many of its devout members. By 1821 these increasing attacks helped provoke several members to begin plotting a revolt against slavery in the region. This complicated plot—named after the free black carpenter who orchestrated it, DENMARK VESEY—coordinated slaves and free blacks in the city with slaves in the surrounding rice parishes to set fire to key points in the city, seize weapons caches, and murder whites indiscriminately in the confusion on a predetermined night in June 1822. However, the conspiracy was revealed very late by an informer, and all the principals were soon arrested, summarily tried, and hanged. Walker was in Charleston at least as late as 1821 and probably for this series of dramatic events in 1822 as well. This may have influenced his later efforts to link black empowerment and resistance in the South with religion.

By 1825 Walker had settled in Boston, Massachusetts, and had opened a used-clothing store near the city's wharves. In 1826 he entered the social life of the black community more fully, marrying a local woman, Eliza Butler, in February and in July becoming initiated into Prince Hall Masonry at African Lodge No. 459, North America's first black Masonic lodge. Membership in this order gave Walker immediate access to most of black Boston's prominent men, and he soon became a leading political force in the community. He also affiliated with a local black Methodist congregation whose minister, Samuel Snowden, was a fiery preacher and an impassioned antislavery activist. They developed a very close friendship. In 1827 Walker championed the United States' first black newspaper, *Freedom's Journal*, and was its principal agent in Boston. Along with his fellow lodge brothers he helped organize and police several parades, or "African Celebrations," in the heart of Boston's African American community, the heavily black-settled north slope of Beacon Hill. Walker spoke at one celebration honoring the visit of an African prince, IBRAHIMA ABD AL-RAHMAN, recently emancipated in the South. He also played a key role in creating the Massachusetts General Colored Association, formed no later than 1828 and one of the first avowedly black political organizations in the country. In December of that year Walker articulated its essential position: "[T]he primary object of this institution is to unite the colored population, so far, through the United States ... and not [withhold] anything which may have the least tendency to meliorate *our* miserable condition." By early 1829, a recent inductee into the tiny club of black homeowners in Boston and his community's leading political voice, Walker prepared to undertake his greatest challenge.

On 28 September 1829 Walker published the first edition of the work for which he is best known, *Appeal to the Colored Citizens of the World*, one of the most influential black political documents of the nineteenth century. Displaying a vehemence and outrage unprecedented among African American authors of the time, Walker's *Appeal* decried in vivid and personal terms the uniquely savage, un-Christian treatment blacks suffered in the United States, especially as slaves:

All I ask is, for a candid and careful perusal of ... my Appeal, where the world may see that we, the Blacks or Coloured People, are treated more cruel by the white Christians of America,

than devils themselves ever treated a set of men, women and children on this earth (i).

By depriving African Americans of secular education, the word of God, civil liberties, and any position of social responsibility, white Americans forced blacks closer and closer to the life of brutes." Indeed the most "insupportable insult" that whites hurled at blacks—expressed the most fully, Walker charged, in Thomas Jefferson's *Notes on the State of Virginia*—was that "they were not of the human family" but descended originally "from the tribes of *Monkeys* or *Orang-Outangs*." Walker feared the profound demoralization such pervasive attitudes would have on African Americans and intended the *Appeal* to be a clarion to them of their worth as humans, their noble history in Africa, and God's special love for them. Walker's *Appeal* challenged African Americans to uplift and organize themselves and cast off this oppression that, he proclaimed, God found an intolerable provocation and sinful for them to endure any longer: "[Y]our full glory and happiness ... under Heaven, shall never be fully consummated, but with the *entire emancipation of your enslaved brethren all over the world*" (29).

By late 1829 and throughout 1830 Walker terrified white southern authorities with novel efforts to circulate his pamphlet on their turf. Relying on black and white mariners to introduce the booklet into key southern ports, and sometimes using the mail, Walker sought especially to enlist the support of educated and evangelical black leaders in these towns in reaching out to the local black masses and rallying them to the message of the *Appeal*. His plan, while never fully formulated or enacted, nevertheless bespoke one of the boldest and most extensive visions of slave empowerment and rebellion ever conceived in antebellum America. Although officials in the South had stemmed the circulation of his book by late 1830, fear of his and his associates' further subversions continued to trouble them into 1831. Several states reacted by strengthening their laws against slave literacy, the circulation of antislavery matter, and contact between transient black seamen and local black residents in ports.

Walker's work remained an inspiration for many young African Americans who, by the early 1830s, were becoming much more assertive in their calls for an end to slavery and racial discrimination. The young black activist MARIA W. STEWART summarized black Boston's reverence for him in 1831 when she referred to him in a speech as "the most noble, fearless, and undaunted David Walker." Although rumors circulated widely that Walker's death in Boston was caused by poisoning from a southern assassin, his death certificate stated the cause as consumption, the same disease from which his infant daughter Lydia Ann had died a few days earlier. David Walker was probably the father of EDWIN GARRISON WALKER, who in 1861 became one of the first blacks admitted to the Massachusetts bar and who earned similar distinction when elected to the Massachusetts legislature in 1866. By the 1890s he had gained national prominence as the president of the Colored National League.

FURTHER READING

Aptheker, Herbert. *"One Continual Cry": David Walker's "Appeal to the Colored Citizens of the World" (1829–1830)—Its Setting and Its Meaning* (1965).

Hinks, Peter P. *To Awaken My Afflicted Brethren: David Walker and the Problem of Antebellum Slave Resistance* (1996).

This entry is taken from the *American National Biography* and is published here with the permission of the American Council of Learned Societies.

PETER P. HINKS

Walker, Edwin G. (1831?–13 Jan. 1901), leather worker, lawyer, and politician, was born Edward Garrison Walker in Boston to DAVID WALKER, a radical abolitionist and writer, and Eliza Butler, whose occupation is unknown. Although sometimes referred to as Edward G. Walker and E. G. Walker, he most commonly appears in the historical record as Edwin G. Walker. There is some dispute as to his date of birth, which one obituary gives as 26 September 1835, five years after David's death. Most sources suggest, however, that Edwin was, indeed, the son of the author of *Appeal to the Colored Citizens of the World* (1829), probably born several months after David's death in Boston in August 1830. His middle name may have been given in honor of the white abolitionist William Lloyd Garrison, who founded the abolitionist newspaper the *Liberator* in Boston in January 1831, inspired in part by Walker's *Appeal*.

After attending the Boston public schools, Walker served his apprenticeship as a leather worker, eventually opening his own shop and employing fifteen workers. He was also active in Boston's abolitionist movement, which his father had helped found in the early 1830s and which had grown dramatically by 1851, the year that Walker, along with LEWIS HAYDEN and ROBERT MORRIS, would help free the fugitive slave SHADRACH MINKINS from federal custody. Around this time, Walker became interested in the law, informally at first, through reading Blackstone's *Commentaries* and other legal texts, and later studying in the law offices of John Q. A. Griffin and Charles A. Tweed in nearby Charlestown. After passing the bar exam in 1861 and joining Boston's first generation of African American lawyers, Walker established his own law practice and soon was earning around three thousand dollars a year, enough to give up his leatherworking business. His practice catered primarily to members of the city's large Roman Catholic Irish population, whom he greatly admired for their ability to overcome the prejudice they first met as immigrants to Boston.

Once established as a lawyer, Walker turned to politics, joining the Republican Party, the natural home for most Boston abolitionists and African Americans. A compelling public speaker, he was, in the words of author William Ferris, an "orator of imposing and dignified physique" and "a bold asserter of Negro manhood" who, like his father, inspired a generation of black New Englanders (Ferris, *The African Abroad; or His Evolution in Western Civilization*, 1913, 767–768). In 1866 Walker ran for public office for the first time, winning the Ward Three seat in the Massachusetts General Court, the state legislature. That there were only three African American registered voters in the entire ward testified to Walker's skill in reaching across the color line, as well as to the strength of postwar white Bostonian radicalism. His victory was also assisted by divisions among his Republican and Democratic opponents. Several hours after Walker's victory in Ward Three, another African American, CHARLES L. MITCHELL, was elected to the General Court from Boston's Sixth Ward; most histories credit both Mitchell and Walker as being the first African Americans elected to an American state legislature.

Walker's period in elective office was, however, brief. Having fallen out with the Republican Party, he failed to gain their endorsement for a second one-year term in 1867. After 1867, he switched his allegiance to the Democratic Party, the traditional home of Boston's Irish Americans. Black Bostonians would not join the Democratic cause in large numbers until the New Deal era, but until that time Walker, in the late nineteenth century, and editor WILLIAM MONROE TROTTER, in the early 1900s, established a foothold for African Americans in that party. Walker's political independence earned him the friendship and support of Benjamin Butler, a Union general and Reconstruction-era radical Republican congressman who in 1882 reverted to the Democratic Party of his youth and won election as governor of Massachusetts. In 1883, in gratitude for his many years of support, Butler nominated Walker three times for a judgeship on the Charlestown District Court, but Republicans in the legislature blocked his appointment each time. The judgeship, which was the first awarded to an African American in Massachusetts, went instead to GEORGE L. RUFFIN, the first black graduate of Harvard Law School and a more loyal Republican than Walker.

Soured on mainstream party politics by this failure, in the late 1880s and 1890s Walker became more interested in more radical political movements. He believed that African Americans could learn much from Irish Americans' success in attaining full citizenship through political action and displayed photographs of Irish nationalist leaders on his office wall. Other African Americans in Boston, including Ruffin and Hayden, openly supported the cause of Irish independence from the British Empire, but few were as stalwart as Walker, who took the secret oath of the Fenian Brotherhood, a forerunner of the Irish Republican Army. Walker's emerging black national consciousness drew not only on his own father's writings but also on the militant example of Irish nationalists, forerunners of the Irish Republican Army, who in the 1880s waged a dynamite-bombing campaign against British targets. Speaking in April 1886 at a Boston meeting to protest a spate of racial attacks on blacks in Mississippi, he thundered, "If it is necessary that the colored people resort to the mode of modern warfare which [the Irish] adopted, let us do it" (Betts, 252). At the same meeting Walker denounced the systematic murder of eight thousand African Americans since the end of the Civil War, by lynch mobs and others, decrying that "no man has been punished" for those crimes (Betts, 252). The failure of the authorities to investigate these matters led Walker, along with Rhode Island activist GEORGE T. DOWNING, to establish the Colored National League in 1886. Walker, the Colored National League's first president, was also nominated for president of the United States in 1896 on a Negro Party ticket, but it is unclear whether he actually ran for that office.

Walker died in Boston in 1901. He is generally remembered as a pioneering lawyer and as the first African American elected to a state legislature. Arguably his greatest legacy, however, is his radical internationalism, which foreshadowed that of another black New Englander, W. E. B. DuBois, and his creative fusion of African American and Irish American political traditions.

FURTHER READING
There are some materials on Edwin G. Walker in the Burrill File, kept in the Special Collections Department of the Massachusetts State House Library in Boston.

Betts, John R. "The Negro and the New England Conscience in the Days of John Boyle O'Reilly," *Journal of Negro History* 51.4 (Oct. 1966).

Hopkins, Pauline E. "Edwin Garrison Walker," *The Colored American Magazine* 2 (March 1901).

Horton, James O., and Lois E. Horton. *Black Bostonians: Family Life and Community Struggle in the Antebellum North* (1979).

Obituary: *Boston Globe*, Jan. 1901.

STEVEN J. NIVEN

Walker, George Theophilus (27 June 1922–), composer, pianist, and college professor, was born in Washington, D.C., to West Indian–American parents. His father immigrated to Philadelphia and studied at Temple University Medical School before beginning a career as a physician. His mother, Rosa King, gave him his first piano lessons when he was five. A child prodigy, Walker graduated from Paul Laurence Dunbar High School in Washington, D.C., at the age of fourteen, the same year he offered his first public recital. In 1937 he accepted a scholarship to Oberlin College, where he studied piano under David Moyer and organ under Arthur Poister. He quickly impressed his professors and became the Oberlin Graduate School of Theology's organist in 1939. He graduated in 1941 at the age of eighteen with the highest honors in his class and aspired to a career as a concert pianist. He attended graduate school in Philadelphia at the Curtis Institute, where he studied with concert pianist Rudolf Serkin and Rosario Scalero, who had taught the great composers Gian-Carlo Menotti and Samuel Barber. Walker quickly stood out at Curtis, displaying an ability to write a wide range of compositions, including choral works, masses, organ pieces, cantatas, and sonatas.

Walker's musical career was full of trailblazing achievements. In the fall of 1945, at a time when racial discrimination severely limited the number of venues in which African American classical musicians could perform, he became the first black pianist to appear onstage at New York's Town Hall Auditorium. Two weeks later, after winning the Philadelphia Youth Auditions, he became the first black instrumentalist to perform with the Philadelphia Orchestra when he played Rachmaninoff's Third Piano Concerto. In 1946 Walker received an invitation to perform the Second

Piano Concerto of Brahms with the Baltimore Symphony. That same year, he wrote *String Quartet no. 1*. The second movement of that piece, *Lyric for Strings*, which he dedicated to his grandmother, aired frequently on the radio and remains one of his most popular works. Still, Walker grew angry and frustrated—eventually developing an ulcer—as he watched some of his white classmates receive many more opportunities to perform in prestigious venues and established international reputations. He signed with National Concert Artists (NCA) in 1950, becoming the first African American classical musician to receive representation by a major management firm. NCA helped secure some performances for Walker, but the firm was honest in telling him that his race made it more difficult for them to book him. Although he would eventually play and earn rave reviews in cities throughout Europe and the United States, Walker seriously doubted whether he would be able to earn a living as a performer during this period. In 1953, while performing in Europe, Walker abandoned his career as a concert pianist and returned to the United States to consider what else he could do with his life.

After consulting with his parents, Walker began to work on a career in teaching music. He taught for a year at Dillard University in New Orleans before enrolling in the Eastman School of Music's Ph.D. program in Rochester, New York, where he was delighted to find ample opportunities to compose and hear classical music. In 1956 he became the first African American to receive a doctorate from Eastman (where he also earned an Artist's Diploma in Piano) and in 1957, in addition to becoming the first composer to win a John Hay Whitney Fellowship, he left on a Fulbright Fellowship to study for two years in France with Nadia Boulanger, who had instructed some of the United States' most important twentieth-century composers. After finishing his Fulbright in 1959, he set out on another tour of Europe, playing highly anticipated concerts in Italy, Holland, and France.

Walker continued his teaching career in 1960 when he joined the faculty of the Dalcroze School of Music, part of the Juilliard School in New York City. A year later, he left for Smith College, where he taught from 1961 to 1968 and became the school's first African American faculty member to receive tenure. During his time at Smith, Walker began to see how he could fuse all of his various musical influences into his own unique style. He worked to de-emphasize, but not dismiss, the presence of African American musical forms, such as spirituals and the blues, in his work. At the same time, he strove to keep his music contemporary, displaying the influence of schools ranging from serialism to neoclassicism.

Walker served as visiting professor at the University of Colorado from 1968 to 1969 and finally as chairman of the music department at Rutgers University, where he taught from 1969 until his retirement in 1992. While at Rutgers, he also worked at Johns Hopkins University's Peabody Institute from 1975 to 1978 and at the University of Delaware for the 1975–1976 academic year, when he served as the school's first minority chair.

Over the course of his career, Walker published more than ninety works, and his compositions were performed by most of the world's leading orchestras and conductors. He received two Guggenheim Fellowships, two Rockefeller Fellowships, an American Academy of Arts and Letters Award, the Harvey Gaul Prize, MacDowell, Yaddo, and Bennington Composer Conference Fellowships, and numerous other awards. In addition, his work was commissioned by organizations such as the New York Philharmonic, the Cleveland Orchestra, the Boston Symphony, the Eastman School of Music, and the Kennedy Center for the Performing Arts. Walker also recorded for dozens of important record labels, including CBA, Desto, Orion, Mercury, and Albany Records. In 1996 he became the first African American to win the Pulitzer Prize while alive, which he received for his work *Lilacs for Voice and Orchestra*, which was commissioned as a tribute to the great African American classical vocalist ROLAND HAYES and was first performed by the Boston Symphony. To commemorate his lifetime contributions to American classical music, Washington, D.C., mayor MARION SHEPILOV BARRY JR. proclaimed 17 June 1997 as George Theophilus Walker Day in that city. Walker was elected to the American Academy of Arts and Letters in 1999 and in April of 2000 was inducted into the American Classical Music Hall of Fame. In addition, he received two Alumni Awards from the Eastman School of Music and the University Medal from the University of Rochester (1996) and honorary doctorates from Bloomfield College (1996), Curtis Institute of Music (1996), Lafayette College (1982), Montclair State University (1996), Oberlin College (1983), and Spelman College (2001).

FURTHER READING

Floyd, Samuel A., Jr. *The Power of Black Music: Interpreting Its History from Africa to the United States* (1996).

Randel, Don Michael, ed. *The Harvard Concise Dictionary of Music and Musicians* (2002).

Southern, Ellen. *The Music of Black Americans: A History* (1997).

DANIEL DONAGHY

Walker, George W. *See* Williams, Bert and George Walker.

Walker, Hazel Mountain (16 Feb. 1889–16 May 1980), educator, was born in Warren, Ohio, the daughter of Charles and Alice (Bronson) Mountain. Little information seems to be available about her family life or early upbringing. Presumably, she attended schools around Warren and matriculated at the Cleveland Normal Training School sometime around 1905 or 1906, intent on pursuing a life as an educator. She went on to Western Reserve University (later Case Western) and from there graduated in 1909 with a master's degree in education.

That same year, 1909, Walker found a job teaching at Cleveland's Mayflower Elementary. This was a time of change for urban schools in many parts of the country, particularly the North. The African American population of Cleveland's schools was growing quickly, but many of the students came from households with parents who could not read or write. Immigrant populations were growing also, and many of Walker's students were English learners. Adding to these challenges was the often-poor physical condition of Cleveland's black schools or the limited availability of materials and resources. Walker remained at Mayflower until 1936.

More remarkable, perhaps, were her extracurricular activities. She served as tutor for children caught up in the juvenile justice system. Many of these, it seems, were new arrivals to Cleveland and the city's schools who were finding the transition to a compulsory education a rocky one and had fallen afoul of local authorities. Walker threw herself into the task of making certain that they made the adjustment to school life without falling too far behind their peers. Meanwhile, usually during the summers, she attended Baldwin-Wallace College in pursuit of a law degree. She did this, it is said, in response to a belief widely held in certain quarters of society that black women could not become attorneys. Walker announced that she had no intention of leaving the field of education for that of law, but rather only wished to prove the naysayers wrong and attain a law degree. This she did in 1919, passing the Ohio bar in the same year.

In 1922 Hazel married George Herbert Walker. He died in 1956, and the couple had no children. Around the early twenties, she also spent some time acting in one of Cleveland's new African American Theaters, and she is often cited as the source of its name, Karamu House (the name is Swahili for something like "joyful place"). LANGSTON HUGHES was among its most prominent alumni. In 1936 Walker left Mayflower Elementary and was made principal of Rutherford B. Hayes Elementary. As such, she became one of the city's first black principals and the first black woman principal. She remained in that position until 1954, at which time she accepted the same role at a third elementary school, George Washington Carver. She remained at Carver until her retirement four years later. In 1961 she was asked to sit on her state's Board of Education. She did so for two years, at which point she left the city and relocated to Massachusetts, where she met and married yet another Walker, Joseph R. The couple had no children. By the time of her death in 1980, she had returned to the city that she had spent her professional life serving.

Hazel Mountain Walker is an example of the extraordinary-ordinary, a life full of activity and courage and a drive to serve the greater good; she was one of a kind and too often gets overlooked in our broader examination of historical movements and the people who drive them.

FURTHER READING

Ballard, Allen. *The Education of Black Folk: The Afro-American Struggle for Knowledge in White America* (1973).

JASON PHILIP MILLER

Walker, Herschel Junior (3 Mar. 1962), football player, was the fifth of seven children born to Willis Walker, a tenant farmer and factory worker, and Christine Walker, a housewife and seamstress, in the rural town of Wrightsville, Georgia. Raised in a strongly religious family, Walker didn't show interest in sports in his early years. As a slightly overweight child with a speech impediment, Walker was more interested in reading and writing poetry. When he was twelve years old, he began an intense workout regimen that he maintained for the next four decades, as he became a star football running back, and excelled in other athletic pursuits.

Walker ran track and played basketball and football for Johnson County High School. Along with leading his football team to their first state championship his senior year, 1980, the All-American running back also won the first Dial Award, a trophy given to the nation's outstanding scholar-athlete. After graduating in 1980, Walker attended the University of Georgia on a football scholarship.

He was an immediate sensation, setting an NCAA freshman rushing record, finishing third in the Heisman Trophy voting, and helping the school go undefeated and win the National Championship in the Sugar Bowl. In 1982 he became the first junior to win the Heisman Trophy, beating out future National Football League Hall-of-Famers John Elway and ERIC DICKERSON.

Despite an impressive academic record, Walker decided to turn professional following his junior year. With the NFL barred from drafting juniors, Walker joined the newly formed United States Football League, the brainchild of American businessmen who sought to capitalize on football's popularity by scheduling professional games during the spring and summer, the NFL's offseason. The New Jersey Generals signed Walker to a lucrative deal above the league salary cap, accomplished by issuing a "personal services" contract. Walker became the USFL's first superstar, leading the league with 1,812 rushing yards in the inaugural season. In 1985 Walker took home the USFL MVP award, running for a record 2,411 yards, the highest mark in any professional league.

Amid rumors that the USFL was in financial straits, the Dallas Cowboys gambled and selected Walker in the fifth round of the 1985 draft. When the upstart league folded in July 1986, Walker joined Tony Dorsett in the Cowboys' backfield. In his first NFL game, he rushed for two touchdowns against the New York Giants, and finished the season with twelve. Walker was named to the Pro Bowl in 1987, when he led the NFL in total rushing and receiving yards, and again in 1988.

Midway through the 1989 season, the Cowboys traded their star running back to the Minnesota Vikings in the biggest trade in NFL history. With Walker the focal point of the transaction, six players and twelve draft picks switched hands in what became a notable disaster for Minnesota, and one of the building blocks for the Cowboy dynasty.

Walker debuted well with the Vikings on 15 October 1989, when he ran for 148 yards against the Green Bay Packers after just two and a half hours of practice with his new team. But the rest of his tenure in Minnesota came under heavy criticism, as the Vikings faltered in the standings and Walker failed to record a 1,000-yard rushing season. His rights were bought by the Philadelphia Eagles before the 1992 season, then the Giants, and finally, the Cowboys again, where Walker played two final seasons as a backup and kick returner. Though Walker finished second all-time in total yardage with 18,168 (8,225 rushing) when he retired, his twelve-year career was considered something of a letdown, considering how stellar his collegiate achievements had been.

Walker's other interests were quite successful, if unusual for a football player. He completed his degree in criminal justice from the University of Georgia after his first season in the USFL; he performed one night in April 1988 with the Fort Worth Ballet, in an attempt by the institution to raise interest among younger fans; and he was recruited to be on the 1992 U.S. Olympic two-man bobsledding team, in which he and his partner placed seventh in Alberta.

After he retired from football in 1997, Walker started and ran a food services company, Renaissance Man International. In 2001 Walker and his wife, Cindy DeAngelis, divorced after nineteen years of marriage. The two had a son, Christian, in 2000.

In 2008 Walker revealed that he had long suffered from Dissociative Identity Disorder, a mental condition that resulted in numerous personalities. Along with his inability to remember certain life events, Walker explained that DID had led him to a suicide attempt and occasional aggressive behavior toward his ex-wife.

Continuing to utilize his athletic abilities, Walker became a professional mixed martial arts fighter in 2009, signing with a San José–based team and training with the American Kickboxing Academy. Earlier in 2009, Walker appeared on Donald Trump's reality television show, *The Apprentice*.

FURTHER READING

Walker, Herschel, with Gary Brozek and Charlene Maxfield. *Breaking Free* (2008).
Kirkpatrick, Curry. "More than Georgia's on His Mind." *Sports Illustrated*, 31 Aug. 1981.
Lieber, Jill. "I Am Not a Dog." *Sports Illustrated*, 12 Nov. 1990.
Prugh, Jeff. *Herschel Walker* (1983).

ADAM W. GREEN

Walker, Jimmie (25 June 1947–), actor and comedian, was born James Walker Carter in Bronx, New York. He was raised in a government housing project community and grew up in the impoverished streets of the South Bronx. Walker had dreams of becoming a professional basketball player and spent most of his time on the basketball court. Disillusioned with academia and his prospects for a career in athletics, he dropped out of high school and began working various odd jobs, including as a vendor at

Yankee Stadium, home to the New York Yankees baseball team. Fortunately, his luck changed, and Walker landed full-time employment with Grand Union Market, making deliveries for a humble wage. During this period Walker was ignited with an unfamiliar, yet welcomed, desire to complete his secondary education despite a grueling work schedule. He made arrangements, in 1966, to end his work shift early during the week so that he might attend night classes at Theodore Roosevelt High School in New York City. Walker was a student in the federally funded Search for Education, Evaluation, and Knowledge (SEEK) program for high school drop-outs at Roosevelt. He struggled with English grammar; however, in Oral Interpretation class he began to excel in writing. Upon delivering a written assignment to an amused classroom of his peers, Walker was taken by one classmate as a comedian; at that moment he realized he was funny and had potential for a career in comedy.

Walker successfully completed SEEK and enrolled at RCA Technical Institute to study radio engineering. Within a year he had earned a license and landed a position as a part-time engineer at WRVR, a small local radio station; shortly thereafter, he relocated to the larger WMCA, where he earned a much higher salary. Unbeknownst to Walker his career path would take yet another turn when a mutual friend introduced him to The Last Poets, a popular group of Black Nationalist musicians and poets who were in need of an opening act. Walker successfully auditioned and opened for The Last Poets on New Year's Eve, his career as comedian had begun. Walker maintained his position at WMCA yet toured with The Last Poets for eighteen months. Rapidly achieving notoriety, in 1969 he was sharing the stage with notable comics like Steve Landesberg, Bette Midler, and David Brenner, with whom he formed a coalition. With the help of Brenner, Walker became a regular at Budd Friedman's world-famous Improv Comedy Club in New York. At the same time he was an MC at the internationally renowned Apollo Theater— the youngest in the Apollo's long and rich history of MCs and entertainers. When Walker's comedic cohorts Brenner, Landesberg, and Midler were scheduled for The Jack Parr Show, they insisted that Walker be scheduled to appear with them. He was an instant success and was immediately invited to Los Angeles for a guest appearance on Dan Rowan's Laugh-In. Walker appeared again on The Jack Parr Show and contracted with CBS to engage the studio audience each week prior to the live recording of the sitcom Carlucci's Department. Subsequently, he began headlining at popular comedy clubs across the nation and resigned from his long held position at WMCA.

In 1972 Walker was approached by a casting director for Norman Lear, the writer and producer of the popular 1970s sitcoms All in the Family, Sanford and Son, and The Jeffersons. He was offered a role in Lear's latest sitcom endeavor, Good Times, about a black family struggling day to day in a Chicago housing project. Walker accepted, and in 1974 television audiences were introduced to him as J.J. Evans, the tall, skinny, vain, wise-cracking oldest son of James and Florida Evans, portrayed by the actors James Amos and Esther Rolle. The upcoming actors Bern Nadette Stanis and Ralph Carter portrayed the roles of his younger siblings Thelma and Michael, with whom he was always in a dispute; Janet Jackson became a central character, Penny, in seasons five and six. Created by Eric Monte, the writer and producer of Cooley High, and the actor Michael Evans, Good Times was a television first, having situated an impoverished black family as central to the program. Despite the seemingly cheerless theme of Good Times, it was a comedy with Walker's character as the primary source of humor. The program was widely successful and ran for six seasons from February 1974 to August 1979. Walker was widely recognized for his portrayal of J.J. Evans; in 1975 and 1976 Walker was nominated for a Golden Globe Award as Best Supporting Actor, Television; and in 2006 he won Nickelodeon's TV Land Impact Award along with other cast members from the sitcom. J.J. was popular for exclaiming, DY-NO-MITE! an expression that became associated with Walker himself. Years later he was unable to escape the persona of J.J. by adoring fans.

In 1975, Walker released his first stand-up comedy album, Dyn-O-Mite; that same year he appeared as the boxer Bootney Farnsworth in the BILL COSBY and SIDNEY POITIER comedy Let's Do It Again. He later earned roles in the short-lived sitcoms B.A.D. Cats and Bustin' Loose. Walker has made a career since Good Times of appearances in B-List satirical movies and roles type-cast as J.J. and J.J.-like characters. The popular late-night talk-show hosts Jay Leno and David Letterman were writers for Walker during the early years of his career in stand-up comedy; together he has made over twenty-five television appearances on their shows.

In February 1980 Walker married the actress Jerelyn Fields, the sister of the actress Kim Fields.

FURTHER READING

Campbell, Sean. *The Sitcoms of Norman Lear* (2006).

Littleton, Darryl J. *Black Comedians on Black Comedy: How African-Americans Taught Us to Laugh* (2006).

Neal, Mark Anthony. *Soul Babies: Black Popular Culture and the Post Soul Aesthetic* (2002).

SAFIYA DALILAH HOSKINS

Walker, Kara (26 Nov. 1969–), artist, was born in Stockton, California, to Gwen and Larry Walker, an artist and emeritus professor of art at Georgia State University. The youngest of three children in the family, Walker grew up in an artistically stimulating environment. Her father was chairman of the art department at the University of the Pacific, where her mother, in the School of Pharmacy, also worked, and Larry Walker enrolled his daughter at a very young age in children's art classes that he had organized for young people. Both parents encouraged her artistic and creative interests.

As a result of court-ordered busing in the 1970s, she first attended the predominantly white Kennedy Elementary School in north Stockton, then in second grade was bused to the more racially diverse King Elementary School in south Stockton, and then in third grade again bused to Kennedy Elementary, which by then had become more integrated.

Walker was thirteen years old when she was transplanted from the West Coast to the Deep South, and first exposed to the popular Confederate kitsch, racist memorabilia, and sexual fetishes distinctive of southern mythology that are invoked and refigured in much of her artistic work. The family moved from Stockton to Stone Mountain, Georgia, when her father was hired as the director of the School of Art and Design at Georgia State University. He served in that capacity from 1983 to 1993 and then continued his position as professor in the school through 2001, when he retired.

Walker matriculated at the Atlanta College of Art in 1987 and received her bachelor's degree in Painting and Printmaking in 1991. Mostly interested in abstract painting as an undergraduate, she began more experimental work with other genres as a graduate student at the Rhode Island School of Design, in Providence, Rhode Island, where she received her MFA in 1994. While still a graduate student she exhibited *Swan Song* at Atlanta College of Art in 1991. This early work reflected the eclectic influence of pulp fiction, cartoons, pornography, romance novels, and pop collectibles. It was at the Rhode Island School of Design that she developed her signature use of linocut, lithography, silkscreen, and etching. Her installations of life-size, black paper cutout silhouettes depicting provocative "plantation scenes" almost immediately made Walker the subject of political and artistic debate. The first solo showings in the early 1990s of her aesthetically stunning murals, including a one-artist exhibition at the Sol Koffler Gallery in Providence, Rhode Island, in 1994, offered views of the antebellum era, complete with racialized scenes of bestiality, pedophilia, incest, defecation, and sadomasochistic complicity.

In 1996 Walker married Klaus Burgel, a goldsmith and sculptor, in Providence. The couple had one daughter, Octavia.

Walker's work in the early to mid-1990s became famous both for her strikingly creative revival and revision of the silhouette form—more commonly associated with nineteenth-century "genteel" portraiture commissioned by middle-class aspirants—and for the political controversy surrounding her invocation of historical stereotypes. The contrasts between the polite form and provocative content, along with Walker's explicit desire to explore what she sees as a still-thriving American investment in racial fantasies, past and present, has garnered her both praise and criticism. One of her most vocal early critics included the Los Angeles artist BETYE SAAR, who insisted that Walker was, for all intents and purposes, merely recirculating and reinforcing the most vulgar racial and sexual stereotypes about African Americans. Yet others point out that the stereotypes of the "mammy," the "uncle," the sexually rapacious "house negress," and the atavistic "pickaninny" that emerge in Walker's art do so as ironic and iconographic comments on race relations, as a burlesque rather than an endorsement of stereotyping. To some extent this debate rehearses and extends those that took place in the first half of the twentieth century among African American artists, writers, and intellectuals about how the "New Negro" should be most appropriately and politically effectively represented.

Walker notes in interviews that her refiguring of such historically disturbing and psychically compelling images, far from indulging white racist appetites for stereotypes, is in part an attempt to plumb these images' subtler, almost incantatory, resonance in the contemporary moment. Against their white backdrop, Walker's black silhouettes deepen to three-dimensionality, suggesting a limitless field of fantasy and projection. The seductive hold and taboo pleasure that certain racial images have on the national psyche for whites and blacks are very much the subject of Walker's art and aesthetic; she asks, for example, in the exhibition catalog to the 1997 Renaissance Society show in Chicago, "How can this image contain for you all the secrets of the re-enactment of history in the arena of Desire?" This address to viewers, the attempt to engage viewers in meaningful, if often uncomfortable, forms of self-reflection, has been representative of much of Walker's work.

She continued to have solo exhibitions nearly every year during the 1990s (and sometimes more than one a year), including Look Away! Look Away! Look Away! at the Center for Curatorial Studies at Bard College (1995); two exhibitions at Wooster Gardens, New York: The High and Soft Laughter of Nigger Wenches at Night (1995) and From the Bowels to the Bosom (1996); Upon My Masters—An Outline, at the San Francisco Museum of Modern Art (1997); a show titled Presenting Negro Scenes, at the Carpenter Center, Harvard University (1998); Why I Like White Boys, An Illustrated Novel by Kara E. Walker, Negress at the Centre d'Art Contemporain in Geneva, Switzerland (1999); and The Emancipation Approximation at the Tel Aviv Museum of Art in 2001. In 2002 Walker represented the United States at the twenty-fifth São Paulo Biennale and also showed at the Kunstverein in Hannover, Germany, the Sammlung Deutsche Bank in Berlin, and in other European cities. In the summer and fall of 2003, Walker's "Excavated from the Black Heart of a Negress" was on exhibit at the Studio Museum in Harlem, New York. Moving Pictures was exhibited at the Solomon R. Guggenheim Museum and Guggenheim Museum Bilbao (2002 and 2003).

In 1997 Walker became the youngest recipient in history to receive the prestigious Catharine T. MacArthur Foundation Achievement Award, granting her the financial freedom to continue her creative endeavors. Walker's work in the late-1998 exhibition at New York's Wooster Gardens signaled a shift in form, moving from black and white silhouette to experimentation with collage and gouache drawings washed with coffee, and to some extent, a shift in focus, moving from an examination of negative black stereotyping to a critique of black boosterism, of simplistic celebrations of racial "uplift" and pride.

In 2002, the family moved to New York, where Walker accepted a position as officer of professional practice and associate professor in the School of Arts at Columbia University. In 2004, she received further prestigious recognition by being honored with the Lucelia Artist Award from the Smithsonian American Art Museum, which is given to exceptional artists under the age of fifty.

Walker's work has remained concerned with representations of African American identity and history, even as she continued to experiment with different media, including film. In 2005, she created a nearly sixteen-minute black-and-white DVD with audio, 8 Possible Beginnings or: The Creation of African-America, a Moving Picture by Kara E. Walker.

FURTHER READING

The Brent Sikkema Gallery in New York holds most of Kara Walker's work not on exhibition or in private collections.

Reid-Pharr, Robert. Kara Walker: Pictures From Another Time (2002).

Shaw, Gwendolyn Dubois. Seeing the Unspeakable: The Art of Kara Walker (2000).

MICHELE ELAM

Walker, Madam C. J. (23 Dec. 1867–25 May 1919), entrepreneur, philanthropist, and political activist, was born Sarah Breedlove in Delta (Madison Parish), Louisiana, the fifth of six children of Minerva to Anderson and Owen Breedlove Sr., sharecroppers and former slaves.

Orphaned at seven years old, she had almost no formal education during her early life. Around 1878—when racial violence was at its most virulent in her rural Louisiana parish—she moved with her elder sister, Louvenia Breedlove Powell, across the Mississippi River to Vicksburg. At fourteen Sarah married Moses McWilliams, about whom almost nothing is known, to escape what she called the "cruelty" of her brother-in-law Jesse Powell. Around 1887 when the McWilliamses' daughter Lelia, later known as A'LELIA WALKER, was two years old, Moses died. Although some sources say he was lynched, there is no credible documentation to justify such a claim.

To support herself and her daughter, Sarah McWilliams moved to St. Louis, Missouri, where her three older brothers had become barbers after joining the Exodusters, a millenarian movement of black Louisianans and Mississippians who had fled to Missouri, Kansas, and Nebraska in 1879 and 1880. For most of the next decade and a half, McWilliams worked as a washerwoman, struggling to educate her daughter in the city's segregated public schools. In 1894 she married John Davis, but his drinking, abuse, and philandering led to their separation around 1903. Her saving grace during this period was membership at St. Paul African Methodist Episcopal Church, whose middle-class club women and community workers lived by the words "Lifting As We Climb," the motto of the National Association of Colored Women (NACW), to which many of them belonged. Perhaps more than anyone, Jessie Batts Robinson—a teacher and wife of local newspaper publisher, C. K. Robinson—encouraged Sarah to seek more education as a way to better her life and helped her develop a vision of herself as something other than an illiterate laundress.

In 1903 as St. Louis prepared for the 1904 World's Fair, Davis supplemented her income by working as a sales agent for ANNIE TURNBO POPE MALONE, whose newly created Poro Company manufactured hair-care products for black women. Like many women of her era, Davis already had experimented with home remedies and other commercially available ointments in an effort to cure baldness and scalp disease that were caused by poor hygiene, stress, inadequate nutrition, and damaging hair-care treatments.

With $1.50 in savings, the thirty-seven-year-old Davis moved in July 1905 to Denver, Colorado, where she joined her widowed sister-in-law and four nieces and worked briefly as a Poro agent selling Malone's "Wonderful Hair Grower." In January 1906 she married Charles Joseph Walker, a St. Louis newspaper agent and promoter who had followed her from St. Louis to Denver. Adopting a custom practiced by many businesswomen of the era, she added the title "Madam" to her name, then began marketing a line of hair-care products as "Madam C. J. Walker." Despite Malone's later assertion that Walker had stolen her formula, Walker insisted that the ingredients for her own "hair grower" had been revealed to her in a dream by an African man. She also is said to have received assistance in developing her sulfur-based ointment—a centuries old cure for skin and scalp disease—from a Denver pharmacist, E. L. Scholtz, for whom she worked as a cook during her first few months in Colorado.

The myth that Walker invented the "hot comb," a steel, hair-straightening implement, persists, but is not true. Heated metal styling tools seem first to have gained popularity in France in the early 1870s when Marcel Grateau introduced curling irons—and the Marcel Wave—to European women. Similar devices probably were developed independently in

Advertisement for Madam C.J. Walker's line of cold creams and hair and complexion products, 17 January 1920. (Library of Congress.)

the United States. Acutely aware of the debate about whether black women should alter the appearance of their natural hair texture, Walker insisted that her ointments were conditioners, scalp treatments, and grooming aids rather than hair straighteners. Nevertheless, she and her sales agents were responsible for popularizing the use of the hot comb in America. Even as large numbers of black women have adopted natural hairstyles since the black pride and black power movements of the 1960s, the majority still straighten their hair with chemicals or heat. In September 1906 when Walker and her husband embarked upon an eighteen-month trip to promote her products and train new sales agents, the American hair-care and cosmetics industry was in its infancy. Settling briefly in Pittsburgh from 1908 to 1910, Walker opened her first Lelia College, where she trained "hair culturists" in the Walker System of hair care. In 1910 the Walkers moved to Indianapolis, then the nation's largest inland manufacturing center, to take advantage of its railways and highway system for their largely mail-order business. Walker quickly became involved in the city's civic activities, contributing $1,000 to the fund of a new black Young Men's Christian Association (YMCA) building. That gift, which was the largest such donation ever received from a black woman by the YMCA, launched Walker's reputation as a philanthropist and increased her visibility in the national black press.

In the midst of Walker's growing success, irreconcilable personal and business differences with her husband resulted in divorce in 1912, though she retained his name until her death. The next year her daughter A'Lelia persuaded Walker to purchase a Harlem townhouse on 136th Street near Lenox Avenue as a residence and East Coast business headquarters. In 1916 Walker joined A'Lelia in New York in order to become more directly involved in Harlem's burgeoning political and cultural activities and entrusted the day-to-day management of her Indianapolis manufacturing operation to her attorney, Freeman B. Ransom, and factory forewoman, Alice Kelly. From 1912 to 1918 Walker crisscrossed the United States, giving stereopticon slide lectures at black religious, business, fraternal, and civic gatherings. In 1913 she traveled to Jamaica, Cuba, Haiti, Costa Rica, and the Panama Canal Zone to cultivate the lucrative, untapped international market.

As an entrepreneur Walker stressed economic independence for women. "The girls and women of our race must not be afraid to take hold of business endeavor and … wring success out of a number of business opportunities that lie at their very doors," she told National Negro Business League convention delegates in 1913 (Bundles, 152). By 1916 the Walker Company claimed 20,000 agents in the United States, Central America, and the Caribbean. "Walker," according to historian Davarian Baldwin, "marketed beauty culture as a way out of servitude for black women" (Baldwin, 71). Walker supported her agents by advertising in dozens of black newspapers throughout the United States. Among the earliest advertisers in W. E. B. DuBois's *The Crisis* and A. Philip Randolph's *The Messenger*, she was credited by more than one publisher with helping to keep black newspapers afloat. In 1917, to foster cooperation among her agents and to protect them from competitors, Walker created the Madam C. J. Walker Hair Culturists Union of America, a national organization of sales agents and beauticians. That same year she organized the first federation of black hair-care and cosmetics manufacturers.

In July 1917 after the east St. Louis, Illinois, riot left at least thirty-nine African Americans dead, Walker joined the planning committee of the Negro Silent Protest Parade, where ten thousand New Yorkers marched silently down Fifth Avenue to protest lynching and racial violence. Heartened by the show of solidarity, Walker, along with James Weldon Johnson, realtor John E. Nail, and other Harlem leaders traveled to Washington, D.C., to present a petition to President Woodrow Wilson urging him to support legislation to make lynching a federal crime. Later that month at the first annual Walker Hair Culturists Union convention, Walker urged the delegates to "protest until the American sense of justice is so aroused that such affairs as the east St. Louis riot be forever impossible" (Bundles, 212).

When the United States entered World War I in the spring of 1917, Walker was among those, like DuBois and Johnson, who, with reservations and caveats, encouraged African Americans to cooperate with the nation's war effort. In support of black soldiers, Walker visited several segregated training camps, urged her sales agents to spearhead local war-bond drives, and became a leader in the Circle for Negro War Relief.

At the official opening of Villa Lewaro, her Irvington-on-Hudson, New York, estate in August 1918, she honored Emmett J. Scott, the former private secretary to Booker T. Washington and special assistant to the Secretary of War in Charge of Negro Affairs. She thought of Villa Lewaro—designed by architect and Alpha Phi Alpha founder Vertner Woodson Tandy, named by opera singer Enrico Caruso, and located near the home of industrialists Jay Gould and John D. Rockefeller—as a symbol to inspire other African Americans and as a venue to convene summits of race leaders.

Realizing that her wealth gave her visibility and credibility, Walker became increasingly outspoken on political issues. In early 1918 she was the keynote speaker at several National Association for the Advancement of Colored People (NAACP) fundraisers throughout the Midwest and East for the group's antilynching campaign. That summer she was honored at the NACW's convention in Denver for having made the largest individual monetary contribution to purchase and restore Cedar Hill, Frederick Douglass's Anacostia, Washington, D.C., home. After the end of World War I, she supported several efforts by African Americans to participate in the Versailles Peace Conference, including Marcus Garvey's International League of Darker Peoples. Although those initiatives were thwarted by the Wilson administration's denial of passports, Walker remained concerned about the rights of Africans and helped support DuBois's first Pan-African Congress in Paris in 1919. Walker's plans for a Liberian industrial training school for girls never materialized.

During the spring of 1919 Walker's long battle with hypertension began to exact its final toll. On Easter Sunday while in St. Louis to introduce a new line of products, she became so ill in the home of her friend, Jessie Robinson, that she was rushed back to Villa Lewaro in a private train car. Upon arrival she directed her attorney to donate $5,000 to the NAACP's anti-lynching campaign. During the last month of her life, Walker revamped her will, bequeathing thousands of dollars to black schools, organizations, individuals, and institutions, including MARY McLEOD BETHUNE's Daytona Normal and Industrial School for Girls, LUCY LANEY's Haines Institute, CHARLOTTE HAWKINS BROWN's Palmer Memorial Institute, Washington's Tuskegee Institute, and numerous orphanages, retirement homes, YWCAs, and YMCAs in cities where she had lived. When Walker died at Villa Lewaro, she was widely considered as the wealthiest black woman in America and reputed to be among the first self-made American women millionaires. At the time of her death, Walker's estate was valued at $600,000 to $700,000, the equivalent of $6 million to $7 million in 2007 dollars. The estimated value of her company, based on annual gross receipts in 1919, easily could have been set at $1.5 million. A'Lelia Walker, who later would become a central figure of the Harlem Renaissance of the 1920s, succeeded her mother as president of the Madam C. J. Walker Manufacturing Company.

Walker's significance lies as much in her innovative, and sometimes controversial, hair-care system as it does in her advocacy of black women's economic independence and her creation of business opportunities during a time when most working black women were employed as servants and sharecroppers. Her entrepreneurial strategies and organizational skills revolutionized what has become a multibillion-dollar international hair-care and cosmetics industry. She was a trailblazer of black philanthropy, using her wealth and influence to leverage social, political, and economic rights for women and African Americans. In 1998 Walker became the twenty-first African American to be featured in the U.S. Postal Service's Black Heritage Series. Her tangible legacy is best exemplified by two National Historic Landmarks—the Madam Walker Theatre Center, a cultural arts facility in Indianapolis, and Villa Lewaro, her Westchester County, New York, mansion—as well as by the many entrepreneurial awards that bear her name and the museum exhibits in which she is featured.

FURTHER READING

Madam Walker's papers are housed at the Indiana Historical Society in Indianapolis, Indiana. Additional documents, photographs, and memorabilia are part of the A'Lelia Bundles/ Madam Walker Family Collection in Washington, D.C. Other items are on view at the Madam Walker Theatre Center in Indianapolis.

Baldwin, Davarian. *Chicago's New Negroes: Modernity, the Great Migration, and Black Urban Life* (2007).

Bundles, A'Lelia. *On Her Own Ground: The Life and Times of Madam C. J. Walker* (2001).

Peiss, Kathy. *Hope in a Jar: The Making of America's Beauty Culture* (1998).

Rooks, Noliwe M. *Hair-Raising: Beauty, Culture, and African American Women* (1996).

A'LELIA BUNDLES

Walker, Maggie Lena (15 July 1864–15 Dec. 1934), civil rights and women's rights activist, community leader, and the first black woman to found and become president of a chartered bank in America, was born in Richmond, Virginia, to Elizabeth "Lizzie" Draper, a former slave, and Eccles Cuthbert, a white writer. Unwed at the time of Maggie's birth, Lizzie Draper worked as an assistant cook in the home of Elizabeth Van Lew, an ardent abolitionist and Union spy. In 1869 Lizzie married William Mitchell, a former slave, who worked as Van Lew's butler and later as the headwaiter at the posh St. Charles Hotel. A son, Johnny, was born shortly after the family's move to downtown Richmond. In 1878 William was robbed and murdered, leaving Lizzie and her two young children without savings, insurance benefits, or financial support, circumstances that informed Maggie's adult work on behalf of the economic status of black women. Lizzie, with Maggie's help, supported her family as a laundress. "I was not born with a silver spoon in mouth," Maggie stated later, "but instead, with a clothes basket almost upon my head." Maggie concluded her education in Richmond's segregated public schools with a call for racial justice. In 1883 at age fifteen, she organized one of the country's first African American school strikes when she led her nine high school classmates in protesting the disparity between black and white graduation ceremonies. Maggie taught school until her 1886 marriage to Armstead Walker Jr., a building contractor. Together they had three sons: Russell Eccles Talmadge, Armstead Mitchell, who died at the age of seven months, and Melvin DeWitt.

When she was fourteen Walker had joined the Grand United Order of Saint Luke, a fraternal organization founded by a former slave, Mary Prout, in Baltimore in 1867. The order, like many of the African American mutual benefit societies of its time, offered services that were generally unavailable to blacks through white agencies, including insurance policies, access to health care, and help with burials. In 1895 Walker formed the juvenile branch of the order and two years later was elected secretary of the endowment department. In 1899, having served in many positions during the previous ten years, Walker was elected right worthy grand secretary-treasurer, the order's top post.

When Walker's tenure as director began, the order was near financial ruin. Undeterred, she changed the organization's name to the Independent Order of Saint Luke (IOSL) and moved its headquarters to Richmond. In an effort to better inform the community the IOSL served, in 1902 Walker established and edited a weekly newspaper, the *Saint Luke Herald*. Through the *Herald*, which by 1925 had six thousand subscribers, Walker condemned segregation, lynching, and the lack of equal educational opportunities for black children. In 1903 Walker negotiated and supervised the construction of a four-story brick headquarters for the organization.

Walker became the first woman bank president in the United States when she founded the Saint Luke Penny Savings Bank in 1903. The black-owned bank, which had several women board members, recognized the unique situation and often limited resources of Richmond's blacks and its women in particular. Many of the bank's first customers were washerwomen (including Walker's mother) and children who were encouraged to "turn [their] pennies into dollars." The bank's slogan, "Bring It All Back Home," encapsulated the role the bank played in securing economic self-determination for the African American community. The bank's special commitment to the "small depositor" included a strong emphasis on financing black home ownership, and by 1920 it had helped purchase more than six hundred homes. Walker's leadership saw the bank through name changes, alterations in federal banking laws, and the merging of the Saint Luke Bank with the two remaining black banks in Richmond in 1930. The resulting Consolidated Bank and Trust Co. remains open, located across the street from its original site in Richmond. It is the oldest continuously black-owned bank in the United States.

Around the turn of the century, discrimination and hostility toward blacks increased. Segregation was concretized in every facet of life, and American

Maggie Lena Walker, a teacher and activist who worked to create businesses that would provide employment for African Americans, became the first African American female bank president. (Austin/Thompson Collection, by permission of National Park Service.)

blacks were systematically removed from political and civil positions of power. Walker's decision in 1905 to open the Saint Luke Emporium, a black-owned department store, signaled yet another attempt at establishing a self-reliant black community. The store, which sold goods at cheaper prices than were available to blacks in white-owned stores, closed in 1912 as a result of organized opposition from Richmond's white merchants. Walker's other projects, however, continued to thrive. Under her leadership, the IOSL grew from 3,500 members in 1899 to over 100,000 members from twenty-two states by 1925.

Walker led vigorous women's suffrage and voter registration campaigns. In the 1920 elections, 80 percent of Richmond's eligible black voters were women. The increased political voice of Richmond's black women was one factor in the formation of the Virginia Black-Lily Republican Party. As a protest against attempts by the "Lily-White" (all-white) wing of the Republican Party to expel blacks from party leadership positions, the Black-Lily Party ran all-black slates of state and national candidates, including Walker herself, who ran for state superintendent in 1921.

A tireless leader and activist, Walker cofounded both the Richmond branch of the NAACP and the Colored Women's Council of Richmond, which, along with other philanthropic projects, raised money for JANIE PORTER BARRETT's Virginia Industrial School for Colored Girls, one of two schools that Walker directed. She served on the board of the Richmond Urban League and as a member of its interracial commission, as a trustee of the Hartshorn College at Virginia Union University, and as a member of the Virginia State Federation of Colored Women, the Negro Organization Society of Virginia, and the International Council of Women of the Darker Races. Nationally, Walker sat on the executive committees of the NAACP and the National Association of Colored Women and worked as vice president of the National Association of Colored Women.

Walker was remarkable in her unwavering focus on the importance of entrepreneurship within the black community and, in particular, on the economic lives of black women. She promoted the employment of women outside domestic service, as well as broader racial self-empowerment and "buy black" programs. Black women must rely on and credit each other, she insisted. They must "band themselves together, organize, ... put their mites together, put their hands and their brains together and make work and business for themselves" (quoted in Brown, 271). The facts of her own life had taught Walker that black women must be given the skills and resources to support themselves. To this end, she worked on behalf of the National Association of Wage Earners, a women's organization that worked to expand economic opportunities for black women. In 1898 Walker played a key role in establishing the Woman's Union, a female insurance company whose motto was "The Hand That Rocks the Cradle Rules the World."

Walker artfully articulated the unique and complex position of black women. "Who is as helpless as the Negro woman?" she asked. "Who is so circumscribed and hemmed in, in the race of life, in the struggle for bread, meat and clothing as the Negro woman?" (quoted in Brown, 272). She understood that white women's expanding roles might limit opportunities for black women. She was also keenly aware of the criticism voiced by many within the black community that, by organizing, black women were staging an assault on the sanctity of the home. In word and action Walker showed that bettering the political and economic life of all African Americans necessitated tying race consciousness to the equality of women, with black men supporting the broadening of opportunities for black women.

Amid all her success, Walker endured great tragedy. In 1915 Walker's husband was accidentally shot and killed on the back porch of their house by their eldest son, Russell, who mistook his father for a burglar. Russell, who was tried and acquitted twice, never fully recovered from the incident and died in 1923. Despite confinement to a wheelchair in 1928 and other health problems resulting from diabetes and a 1907 fall that broke her kneecap, Walker remained active until her death from diabetic gangrene in 1934. In 1978 the U.S. Department of the Interior designated Walker's Richmond home a National Historic Site.

FURTHER READING

Walker's unpublished papers are available at the Maggie L. Walker National Historic Site, Richmond, Virginia.

Brawley, Benjamin. *Negro Builders and Heroes* (1937).

Brown, Elsa Barkley. "Womanist Consciousness: Maggie Lena Walker and the Independent Order of Saint Luke" in *Unequal Sisters: A Multi-Cultural Reader in U.S. Women's History*, ed. Vicki L. Ruiz (1994).

Dabney, Wendell P. *Maggie L. Walker and the I.O. of St. Luke: The Woman and Her Work* (1927).

LISA E. RIVO

Walker, Margaret (7 July 1915–30 Nov. 1998), poet and novelist, was born Margaret Abigail Walker in Birmingham, Alabama, the daughter of Sigismund Walker, a Methodist minister and college professor, and Marion Dozier Walker, a music teacher. A studious and sensitive child, Walker was encouraged to write by her parents, who inspired in her a love of books and music. She was also fascinated by her grandmother's stories of slave life in rural Georgia, and she began writing daily, both prose and poetry, at the age of eleven. Her parents moved to Louisiana to accept teaching positions at New Orleans College (later Dillard University). Walker graduated from Gilbert Academy in 1930 and matriculated at New Orleans College, but, on the advice of the poet LANGSTON HUGHES, her parents decided to send her north to study. In 1932 Walker transferred from New Orleans College to Northwestern University in Evanston, Illinois, from which she received an AB degree in 1935. During her time at Northwestern, she met the African American activist and editor W. E. B. DuBois, whose magazine *The Crisis* carried her first published poem in May 1934.

After graduating, Walker worked for the Federal Writers' Project in Chicago under the Works Progress Administration (WPA) and came to know such literary figures as RICHARD WRIGHT, with whom she collaborated closely as a member of the South Side Writers Group. She returned to school at the University of Iowa, where in 1937 she wrote the poem "For My People," which earned her national acclaim and became the title piece in a collection of twenty-six poems that were accepted as her master's thesis in creative writing in 1940. The next year she returned to the South to become an English instructor at Livingstone College in Salisbury, North Carolina. Her volume *For My People* appeared with an introduction by Stephen Vincent Benét. The collection won the Yale Series of Younger Poets Award, making her the first African American to be so honored. In 1942–1943 she taught English at West Virginia State College in Institute. In 1943 she married Firnist James Alexander, an interior decorator; they had four children. *For My People* contains three sections written in different styles but bound together by the theme of the southern black experience and the directness of their diction. The title poem in the first part is written in long, flowing lines of free verse that suggested Walt Whitman or Carl Sandburg to many reviewers and prompted Benét to describe the poem as containing "a controlled intensity of emotion and a language that … has something of the surge of biblical poetry" (Walker, 5). A second section is devoted to rhyming dialect ballads celebrating such traditional black characters as JOHN HENRY and STAGOLEE. Like blues songs, they draw on folk tradition and earned the critical comment that they reflected the influence of Langston Hughes or were, as Louis Untermeyer wrote, "like Paul Laurence Dunbar turned sour" (Walker, 371). The six sonnets that constitute the third section were praised for their formal skill but dismissed by some critics as lacking

Margaret Walker, accepting the Mississippi Arts Commission's Lifetime Achievement Award in Jackson, Mississippi, 8 April 1992. (AP Images.)

the intensity of the title poem. Although the critical response to the volume was mixed, the poem "For My People" placed Walker firmly in the tradition of social protest as an activist of unusual emotional depth and passion.

Walker returned to Livingstone for two years as a professor in 1945, and in 1949 she moved to Jackson, Mississippi, where she served as professor of English at Jackson State College until her retirement in 1979. During her tenure there she created and directed the Institute for the Study of the History, Life, and Culture of Black People and originated the Phillis Wheatley Poetry Festival. In 1965 she earned a Ph.D. from the University of Iowa, and the next year she published her only novel, *Jubilee*, which had been her doctoral dissertation. *Jubilee* is a realistic story of a slave family set before, during, and after the Civil War, based on the tales her grandmother had told her. It traces the life of the daughter of a white plantation owner and a slave, relating the oppression of her early life as a slave and the alienation of her postwar life cut off from the social structure she had known. Deeply researched over a period of thirty years, the novel was meticulous in its details of black folklore and culture and was generally well received, selling some three million copies in eleven languages during her lifetime. Some sources, however, criticized it for perpetuating the romantic myths of the nineteenth-century South from a black point of view and compared it to Margaret Mitchell's 1936 novel *Gone with the Wind*. In 1972 Walker defended her work vigorously, publishing *How I Wrote "Jubilee,"* a pamphlet describing its composition and the research that went into it. ALEX HALEY published his best-selling historical novel *Roots*, employing a similar oral style, in 1977; Walker in 1988 charged him with plagiarism. "There was nothing verbatim," she admitted, "but there were at least a hundred pages of out-standing similarities" (quoted in Milloy, 35). Although another writer did successfully charge Haley with plagiarism, Walker lost the case in court.

Three other collections of new poems—*Ballad of the Free* (1966), *Prophets for a New Day* (1970), and *October Journey* (1973)—appeared, all brief collections striking the same note of racial pride as her earlier volume, and in 1989 the University of Georgia Press published *This Is My Century: New and Collected Poems*. In 1974 she collaborated on *A Poetic Equation: Conversations between Nikki Giovanni and Margaret Walker*, discussing the experience of African American women poets. Her critical essays written between 1932 and 1992 were collected under the title *On Being Female, Black, and Free* in 1997. Her only effort at biography, *Richard Wright: Daemonic Genius*, appeared in 1987. Largely based on personal contact with her subject, it received a warm response in the literary community. Although long retired from teaching, Walker continued to be active as professor emerita, directing the institute she had founded in the 1960s. She died of breast cancer at her daughter's home in Chicago.

Despite her modest output, Margaret Walker made a substantial contribution to the literature of African American social protest, and the rolling cadences of "For My People" provide an enduring voice for her people.

FURTHER READING

Walker, Margaret. *For My People* (1942).
Barksdale, Richard K. "Margaret Walker: Folk Orature and Historical Prophecy," in *Black American Poets between Worlds, 1940–1960*, ed. R. Baxter Miller (1986).
Collier, Eugenia. "Fields Watered with Blood: Myth and Ritual in the Poetry of Margaret Walker," in *Black Women Writers (1950–1980): A Critical Evaluation*, ed. Mari Evans (1984).

This entry is taken from the *American National Biography* and is published here with the permission of the American Council of Learned Societies.

DENNIS WEPMAN

Walker, Moses Fleetwood (7 Oct. 1857–11 May 1924), baseball player and writer, was born in Mount Pleasant, Ohio, the son of Moses Walker, a minister and physician, and Caroline O'Harra. He grew up in Steubenville, Ohio, and in 1879 enrolled in historically integrated Oberlin College after two years in the school's preparatory program. The catcher on Oberlin's first varsity baseball team in 1881, Walker was the first African American to play white intercollegiate baseball. In 1882 and 1883 Walker played baseball and attended law school at the University of Michigan. Though an acclaimed ballplayer at both schools, he graduated from neither.

"Fleet," as he was popularly known, began his professional baseball career in 1883 with the Toledo Blue Stockings of the Northwestern League. In 1884, when the league champions joined the major league American Association, Walker became the first black major leaguer in history. His younger brother Welday "Weldy" Wilberforce Walker signed with Toledo in July 1884 and became the second black in the majors. The team folded after the season, and Walker, who was not signed by another major league club despite hitting .263, returned to the minors in 1885 with Cleveland of the Western League. The franchise disbanded in midseason, and he moved to Waterbury, Connecticut, in the Eastern League for the rest of 1885 and all of the 1886 season. Walker batted only .209 but advanced the next season to Newark, New Jersey, of the International League, probably because the manager of the Little Giants, Charley Hackett, who had managed Walker at Waterbury, wanted the poised, veteran catcher to work with a talented but temperamental young black pitcher, GEORGE WASHINGTON STOVEY. The unprecedented African American battery was a success: Walker hit .264 and Stovey posted a 35-14 record, setting the all-time league mark for wins in a season.

Walker's baseball career was affected by growing racial antipathy and segregation in the United States. One of seven blacks in the league in 1887, he was frequently subjected to racist taunts and even threats from fans, especially in Louisville, Kentucky, and Richmond, Virginia, as well as insults from the press. Racial tensions came to a head on 14 July when Cap Anson, who in 1883 had threatened to cancel an exhibition game between Chicago and Toledo if Walker played, refused to allow his White Stockings to play an exhibition against Newark unless Walker and Stovey were barred. Anson succeeded in banishing the black battery from the field, and, perhaps not coincidentally, the league's directors that same day voted to "approve of no more contracts with colored men." The drawing of the color line had immediate consequences. Only three blacks remained in the International League in 1888, two of them with Charley Hackett's Syracuse Stars, Walker and pitcher Bob Higgins. Higgins compiled a 20-7 record in leading the team to the league championship, and Walker, who batted only .170, was again humiliated by Anson by being banned from a postseason exhibition game with Chicago on 27 September. Walker returned to Syracuse in 1889 as the only black player in the league, but he was released in August after batting a mere .216 and defensively ranking next to last among the circuit's twenty-one catchers. The baseball career of the last black player in the major leagues until JACKIE ROBINSON joined the Brooklyn Dodgers in 1947 ended in 1890 after an unsuccessful effort to join Terre Haute, Indiana, of the Western Association.

Walker's baseball career was undistinguished and abbreviated not because of racial discrimination but because he was a mediocre player. Although praised for his strong throwing arm and speed on the bases, he was an erratic fielder and only a fair hitter, posting a career .226 batting average. His career might have ended in 1886 had not Hackett considered his experience and maturity valuable in the development of young black pitchers. Unlike his brother Welday, a political activist who publicly attacked the mounting racial discrimination in baseball, Moses Walker suffered in silence so as not to jeopardize his career, and he rejected the option of playing on all-black teams. If his education, gentlemanly demeanor, and thoroughly middle-class values earned him numerous defenders and protected him from the more degrading manifestations of racism, those same qualities apparently made the insults and indignities the more hurtful to him.

Walker's life remained troubled after his playing days were over. In the spring of 1891 he stabbed a man to death in a drunken fight outside a bar in Syracuse and was charged with second-degree murder. Found not guilty by reason of self-defense, he returned to Steubenville, where he worked as a railroad clerk and assisted his brother in operating a hotel known as a center of gambling and other "unsavory" activities. Alcohol and the "numbers"

game became conspicuous in his life. His wife, Arabella Taylor, whom he had married in 1881 and with whom he had three children, died in 1895. He married Ednah Jane Mason in 1898 (they had no children) and in December of that year was convicted of mail fraud and sentenced to a year in jail. Shortly after his release he moved to Cadiz, Ohio, and opened a combination opera house and movie theater. He faced constant struggles as a black entrepreneur in a white economic world; he never derived any financial benefit from several important patents in motion picture reel technology because he failed to follow up on the patents with potential manufacturers.

Race was the defining element in Walker's life. Born to mixed-race parents, his relatively light complexion eased his entry into white society, including professional baseball. Although gravitating more to white than black communities, Walker, who wed two mixed-race women, nonetheless remained a "black outsider" in the eyes of racist white America. Confused and tormented by a racially "divided heart," he at various times expressed mixed feelings of racial pride and hatred toward Caucasians, African Americans, and even those of mixed heritage like himself. Walker's lingering bitterness over past racial indignities and his personal and economic misfortune, along with his brother's increasingly militant political views, found expression in the advocacy of black nationalism and African repatriation nearly a decade before MARCUS GARVEY's popular Universal Negro Improvement Association movement. In 1908 Walker wrote a forty-seven-page booklet, *Our Home Colony: A Treatise on the Past, Present, and Future of the Negro Race in America.* An angry, simplistic polemic, it included Walker's viewpoint that the years after Emancipation in 1863 comprised the "colonial period" of African American history, a time when "the American [white] people were in no way prepared to accept the Negro with full equality of civil and political rights." Walker contended that the black man could never become "a full man or a fit citizen of this Republic" and that "nothing but failure and disappointment" awaited blacks in America because racial equality "is contrary to everything in the nature of man." In so doing, he rejected the then popular self-help and accommodationist theories of BOOKER T. WASHINGTON and argued that "the only practical and permanent solution of the present and future race troubles in the United States is entire separation by emigration of the Negro from America." That same year Walker and his brother opened an office for Liberian emigration in Steubenville and published a short-lived newspaper, *The Equator*. But Afrocentrism proved to be more a momentary venting of frustration than a considered ideology for Walker, who had been raised in a racially tolerant section of Ohio and educated in white schools. He continued to live and work in predominantly white communities, just as he had persisted in playing for predominately white baseball teams. Around 1922 Walker, who had fallen on hard times after the death of his second wife, moved to Cleveland, where he died.

FURTHER READING

Zang, David W. *Fleet Walker's Divided Heart: The Life of Baseball's First Black Major Leaguer* (1995).

Obituaries: *Steubenville Herald-Star*, 13 May 1924; *Cleveland Gazette*, 17 May 1924.

This entry is taken from the *American National Biography* and is published here with the permission of the American Council of Learned Societies.

LARRY R. GERLACH

Walker, Quok (1753–c. 1812) slave, farm laborer, plaintiff in a civil suit, and freedman, was purchased as an infant in 1754 along with his mother and father, Dinah (b. c. 1735) and Mingo (b. c. 1734), by James Caldwell of Rutland District, Worcester County, Massachusetts. As a freedman, Walker married Elizabeth Harvey in 1786. The date of his death is unknown; an 1812 public record in Barre, Massachusetts (part of Rutland District that was incorporated separately in 1774 and renamed in 1776), refers to Walker as deceased. Prince Walker (c. 1762–1858), another freed slave who lived nearby, may have been Quok Walker's brother.

Sometime in Walker's youth Caldwell promised him his freedom, to be granted when he was in his mid-twenties. However, Caldwell died intestate when Walker was a minor. Caldwell's widow, Isabell, inherited at least some members of the Walker family, and, according to court testimony later given by Walker, she reiterated the promise of manumission, designating the age of twenty-one as the point at which Walker would be free. After she remarried, her new husband Nathaniel Jennison assumed ownership of Walker. Isabell died in 1773, and Nathaniel refused to honor his wife's promise to Walker.

In 1780 the new Massachusetts constitution, inspired by the patriot cause in the War of Independence, was ratified. It included a declaration of human rights that stated, "All men are born free & equal, & have certain natural, essential & inalienable rights. Among which may be reckoned the right of enjoying & defending their lives & liberties." Walker may or may not have known about this statement of rights in 1781, but in that year he made a decision that would result in a judicial opinion about whether the Massachusetts constitution barred slaveholding. Walker fled Jennison, seeking refuge and employment with John Caldwell and Seth Caldwell, younger brothers of the man who had bought the Walker family in 1754. Jennison searched for Walker, and when he found the enslaved man working on the Caldwells' farm, he beat Walker and then confined him against his will. Jennison claimed surprise when local public opinion turned against him and he publicly asserted his right of ownership.

In short order, a series of suits and appeals followed, pitting Walker as well as the Caldwells against Jennison. In the Inferior Court of Common Pleas, Walker, represented by Levi Lincoln, filed a civil suit against Jennison claiming assault and battery and claiming that he was a free man when Jennison attacked and kidnapped him (*Walker v. Jennison*). Walker prevailed in his suit, and in 1781 he gained recognition of his freedom as well as monetary compensation. Meanwhile, Jennison sued the Caldwells for allegedly enticing Walker away from him and causing him to lose the black man's labor (*Jennison v. Caldwell*), and he initially prevailed. On appeal the Caldwell brothers hired Lincoln, who took the opportunity to launch an argument inspired by religion and notions of higher law against the institution of slavery itself.

Yet ultimately the approach of the courts referred most directly to the state constitution, not to higher law arguments that slavery violated divine will. The most significant court pronouncement arising from Walker's action resolved the case of *Commonwealth v. Jennison*, a criminal case in which the defendant was charged with assault in his seizure of Walker from the Caldwell farm in 1781. In 1783 Chief Justice John D. Cushing of the Massachusetts Supreme Judicial Court opined that the 1780 Constitution unambiguously outlawed slaveholding. His instructions to the jury included the statement that:

our Constitution of Government, by which the people of this Commonwealth have solemnly bound themselves, sets out with declaring that all men are born free and equal—and that every subject is entitled to liberty, and to have it guarded by the laws, as well as life and property—and in short is totally repugnant to the idea of being born slaves. This being the case, I think the idea of slavery is inconsistent with our own conduct and Constitution; and there can be no such thing as perpetual servitude of a rational creature, unless his liberty is forfeited by some criminal conduct or given up by personal consent or contract.

Jennison was fined forty shillings, but no record of the jury's reasoning or its response to the judge's instructions survives. Some slaves remained in Massachusetts after 1783, and no further provision of the state constitution outlawed slavery, but Walker's self-liberation and Cushing's instructions signaled the death of slavery in Massachusetts.

Walker was one of a number of African Americans of the Revolutionary years and the early republic who used legal means, such as suits and petitions, to undermine the slave system. We can also understand Walker as part of a larger movement in which New Englanders rejected slavery. Vermont prohibited slavery in its 1777 constitution. Connecticut and Rhode Island enacted gradual emancipation laws in the 1780s. New Hampshire made a Declaration of Rights in 1783 that was soon interpreted as antislavery. Massachusetts saw several challenges to slavery similar to that of Walker, and while some men, women, and children remained enslaved in the state the outcome of the Walker cases made it clear that slave owners no longer had the protection of the law.

FURTHER READING

Melish, Joanne Pope. *Disowning Slavery: Gradual Emancipation and "Race" in New England, 1780–1860* (1998).
Wiecek, William M. *The Sources of Antislavery Constitutionalism in America, 1760–1848* (1977).
Zilversmit, Arthur. *The First Emancipation: The Abolition of Slavery in the North* (1967).

JOHN DANIEL SAILLANT

Walker, Ruth "Rudy" and Frederick "Fredy" Walker (31 Aug. 1891–after 1928) and (9 Nov. 1893–May 1977), known as The Walkers, song and dance entertainers and actors, were both born in Chicago. It appears that at some time in 1902 the two juvenile dancers, brother and sister, traveled to Europe in the company of their mother, Ella Walker, herself an artist, born in Chicago in 1860 or 1864, according to her own conflicting statements. That they traveled with their own mother is mentioned in June 1903 and again in the winter 1904/1904 in Vienna, December

1906 in Stockholm, in November 1907 in Berlin, and again in February 1908 in Copenhagen. Billed as "Les Enfants Nègres," their presentations of the cakewalk dance attracted a lot of attention at the Nouveau Cirque at Paris and paved the way for a long career in Europe. They became so popular that they inspired a composer, a sculptor, and a movie film director, as well as cartoonists. Their portraits appear on many postcards; in fact, they might well have been the most often photographed black entertainers of the period. The cards show them in various dance poses—sometimes together and sometimes solo. Mostly they wear tall, calf-length socks and white dance shoes. The boy wore a white dance costume or gymnast's suit with a black sash, whereas the girl wore a short skirt.

It was presumably the French Pathé company that produced a short film featuring the cake walk performances by both black and white artists on the stage of the Nouveau Cirque. All the artists that can be seen in the film also had a series of postcards devoted to them. They are "Les enfants nègres," with ten postcards in series 142 (by early 1904 motifs of the original French series 142 were marketed in the United States by Franz Huld, Publisher, New York, in their series III "Cake Walk—Negro Dance"), "Les Soeurs Pérès" from Spain (postcard series 143), "Les Nègres" from the United States (series 144), and "The Elks", also from the United States (postcard series 145). Charles Gregory also had his own series of postcards, but he is not identified by name and the cards simply state "Nègre Joyeux."

This massive invasion of eccentric cake walk dancers started the "The Parisian Cakewalk Craze" (Whiting), so vividly remembered by Jean Cocteau: "They danced: skinny, crooked, their … knees higher than their thrust-out chins …. wrenching their gestures from themselves…. They reared, they kicked, they broke themselves in two, three, four. (…) The delirious public was on its feet stamping. Never has a trendy spectacle composed of saltpeter, not even the first jazz music accompanying the dances of Gaby Deslys at the Casino de Paris, never has a spectacle been comparable to this apparation" (*Negroes of the Theater*, p. 27; quoted in Gordon, pp. 336–337). The show purported to represent scenes from the life of American blacks. The first, set in an American bar, included a billiard match between the famous clowns Footit and Chocolate, a pickpocketing dog, a boxing match, and a cock fight, all interspersed with songs, dances, and jigs. The second scene, the hit of the evening, was a cakewalk contest danced in a forest clearing. The third, a "fête sur l'eau," took advantage of the Cirque's novelty attraction: a stage that could be flooded like a swimming pool. The conclusion was an extended song-and-dance number "dans un mouvement endiablé" ("Soirée parisienne," *Le Gaulois*, 28 Oct. 1902).

Whereas the other artists involved disappeared from memory, the likeness of Rudy and Fredy Walker appeared on the cover of the 1903 sheet music for "Joyeux nègres (Jolly negroes)," a cake-walk dedicated to John Philipp Sousa. (Sousa had directed the official orchestra at Paris during the 1900 World Exhibition.) The cover artwork is signed by L. Lucien Faure, a lithographer and graphic designer who otherwise had specialized in posters; in this case, at least, it is obvious that he was inspired by a motif of series 142 of the postcards. The composer of this cake walk, the earliest ever published by a Frenchman, was Rodolphe Berger. A further set of postcards was soon issued as giveaways by a French journal, *Le Sans-.Souci* in 1904, and in that year yet another set of cards were marketed, on which the Walkers demonstrated "Le Trans-Atlantic. Nouvelle Danse américaine au Nouveau Cirque"—the novelty of the cakewalk had worn off with regular patrons of the Nouveau Cirque and a new dance had to be introduced and new costumes tailored. The "Enfents Nègres" moved from Paris to Belgium, perhaps also the Netherlands, and back to France. In publicity they are henceforth referred to by their first names and variations thereof: Fred, Fredi, Fredy, or Rudy, Ruddy, Rudi, Roudy, and Ruth, respectively, and on one occasion Pandy & Fredy. A reviewer at Antwerp, Belgium, noted that they sang as well as danced. If they briefly returned to the United States, as they later stated in a passport application, they left no trace on passenger lists and resurfaced in Scandinavia in 1906 ("The outstanding act in Scala's December program was two negro children, Rudy and Fredy, who tap danced and flirted with great vigor and humour and a quite adult agility. They caused extreme joy, because they are curious and natural at one and the same time," *Politiken*, Copenhagen, 2 Dec. 1906), from where they continued to Germany, back to Scandinavia, and on to the Netherlands and other countries, including Hungary, Bohemia, Austria, France, Switzerland, and Russia. It must have been during their 1908 sojourn in Austria that Rudy and Fredy inspired sculptor Carl Kauba to cast a pair of painted bronze sculptures that are both simply titled "Cake Walk." The boy has white shirt, pants, shoes, and socks and red sash belt, holding a stick with long ribbons attached in his lower hand; the girl has white hat, dress, shoes, and socks and red choker and sash belt, with a fan on a long loop around her neck. Like the lithographer L. Lucien Faure before him, Kauba was clearly inspired by the 1903 postcards of "Les enfants nègres."

At the outbreak of World War I they toured Russia. Their whereabouts during the following years remains undocumented. (The Ruth Walker who was a featured revue star at Berlin's prestigious Grosses Schauspielhaus, in the company of both African American and top German entertainment stars, was a different person: "Ruth Walker the beautiful negress, slim as a young sapling, is not so versatile, but she knows how to stun her audience by virtuoso body movements between her waist and thigh. The little negro dancer Snow Ball, whom we already know from the Wintergarten, also steps very well and takes effect by being so tiny. The dance steps performed by Billie Collins have been coached by the great Brooks" [*Der Tanz*, 1928, p. 23].)

The two little children who had arrived in Europe in 1902 chose to pursue their career there and, for some three decades, impressed their audiences. Starting as cake-walking "pickaninnies" (although never advertised thus), they learned to sing and play musical instruments. They matured to head the bill even when performing in the company of top-rate continental artists. Although captured on film, they unfortunately did not make any sound recordings. We do not know when they retired, but Fred's death can be traced through his social security number: he passed away in May 1977 at age eighty-three. His last residence was Chicago.

FURTHER READING

Antréas, E. "*Le Joyeux Nègre (The Happy Coon): Cake Walk and Two Step, avec théorie par Charles Grégory du Nouveau-Cirque et de Parisiana, Professeur de Cake Walk, Conforme au Cake Walk dansé par Charles Grégory dans la Grande Pantomime Américaine Nautique Joyeux Nègres*" (1903).

Gordon, Rae Beth. "Natural Rhythm: La Parisienne Dances with Darwin: 1875–1910," *Modernism/modernity*, Vol. 10, No. 4, Nov. 2003.

Lotz, Rainer E. "Rudy & Fredy—'Les enfants nègres'—in Europe," *Doctor Jazz Magazine*, Vol. 44, No. 192, Mar. 2006, pp. 9–23.

Whiting, Steven Moore. *Satie the Bohemian—From Cabaret to Concert Hall* (1999).

RAINER E. LOTZ

Walker, T-Bone (28 May 1910–16 Mar. 1975), guitarist and singer, was born Aaron Thibeaux Walker in Linden, Texas, the son of Rance Walker and Movelia

Jimerson, musicians. In 1912 Walker moved to the Oak Cliff section of Dallas, where he later worked as a "lead-boy" for BLIND LEMON JEFFERSON. His talent as a singer and dancer emerged in his youth, and he made his first guitar from a cigar box, nails, and wire. At fifteen he danced on the same program with BILL ROBINSON, and for the next decade he played the guitar and banjo with Lawson Brooks's band. Around 1928 he toured with blues singer IDA COX, and in 1929 he won an amateur contest on a show that featured CAB CALLOWAY. In 1933 Walker met and played with the guitarist CHARLIE CHRISTIAN, who replaced him in Brooks's band when Walker left the following year. In 1934 Walker performed with the legendary blues singer MA RAINEY in Fort Worth. In 1935 he married Vida Lee, with whom he had three children. His first child had been born several years earlier, and subsequently Walker was the father of several children with several women. That same year he moved to Los Angeles.

During the late 1930s and early 1940s Walker performed successfully at clubs in Southern California: Little Harlem Club, Trocadero, and the Plantation. Beginning in 1939 he toured with LES HITE's Cotton Club Orchestra, first in the Midwest, and then in New York City. Earlier Walker had made a few records under the pseudonym "Oak Cliff T-Bone, the Cab Calloway of the South," in 1929 and then with Les Hite in 1940. His career as a recording star, however, began in earnest in 1942 with a series of recordings with Freddie Slack and His Orchestra.

During the war years Walker recorded for Capitol Records while touring army bases and starring at the Rhumboogie Club in Chicago. At this time he developed an ulcer that plagued him for the next fifteen years. He exacerbated his condition with a lifestyle of late nights, high-stakes gambling, and heavy drinking. In 1946 Walker formed his own band and went on the road, working one-nighters. The records made during the late 1940s were among his best, helping Walker achieve the height of his popularity.

Two recordings from 1947—"I Know Your Wig Is Gone," in the thirty-two-measure structure of American popular song, and "Call It Stormy Monday," in the twelve-measure blues structure—contain many of the musical characteristics that account for Walker's fame and influence. Perhaps most important is the variety of rhythms employed by Walker both as singer and guitarist. The beat, always swinging in fast numbers like "Wig," is subdivided in many ways. Sometimes Walker would almost recite or declaim the text, approximating the rhythms of ordinary speech. Other times he would employ phrasing and accentuation in a more strictly metrical and musical fashion. In a single piece, he would even modulate from the rhythms of speech to those of strict meter and back again. The boogie-woogie or shuffle rhythm, evident in "Tell Me What's the Reason" (1951), became a hallmark of Walker's later up-tempo recordings. Also evident on these recordings is the variety of tonal color Walker was capable of producing with the electric guitar and, to a lesser extent, with his voice. Within the limited context of ensemble blues, Walker's use of augmented triads and embellishing chromatic harmonies was advanced. Many of his recordings also contain jazz instrumentation.

Walker's voice sounded dry and smoky, and he relied on the recitative vocal inflections that characterize blues singing. He was at his best when expressing the cool, suave stance of the injured party. Less successful were Walker's numerous recordings of slow blues. In these he often resorted to musical formulas and clichés, and his voice rarely imparted the sincerity needed to make these songs persuasive. "Call It Stormy Monday" (1947), his most famous recording, is an outstanding exception.

The appearance of counterfeit recordings attested to Walker's success and popularity. In 1948 Black & White Records reported a counterfeit of "I Want a Little Girl," and in 1950 Imperial reported a counterfeit of "The Hustle Is On." In 1955 Walker began recording for Atlantic Records, the burgeoning independent label devoted to rhythm and blues, an idiom that depended directly on Walker's musical success for its own existence. But at this time Walker's career began a slow, steady decline until his death. He disbanded his group and had an operation for his ulcer. Four years later Walker was treated for a heart attack. In 1960 COUNT BASIE hired him, but apparently Walker in his own estimation did not fit in very well with the band. He said: "I wasn't drinking any more than the rest, but somehow I felt my act had fallen kind of flat. That's what *I* thought. I got to feeling real bad." Part way through the tour, Walker quit the band. He said: "I got me a break. And blew it to hell!" (Dance, 139).

Coinciding with the blues revival that took place first in Europe and then in the United States, Walker appeared in "Rhythm and Blues U.S.A.," a show featuring several blues musicians that toured Western Europe in 1962. This was the first of Walker's many appearances in blues festivals and tours. He continued to record—often in conjunction with these tours. In 1970 his "Good Feelin'" won the Grammy Award from the National Academy of Recording Arts and Sciences for the best ethnic recording.

In June 1974 Walker made his last public performance at the Nixon Theater in Pittsburgh. Later that year he was hospitalized in Los Angeles for bronchial pneumonia and then entered a convalescent hospital before his death there. A memorial concert in his honor was given at the Musicians' Union Auditorium in Los Angeles on 5 May 1975. The proceeds were used to help defray the cost of Walker's hospitalization.

Walker led a full but often sad life, which included impoverished beginnings, wide acclaim and financial reward, addictions to gambling and alcohol, and a protracted demise as a performer because of physical ailments. He is considered by many to be the father of modern electric blues, synthesizing the country sound of Blind Lemon Jefferson, the polished city sound of LEROY CARR, the visual display of a dancer and an acrobat, and the technological development of the electric guitar. Indeed, he was a pioneer electric blues guitarist. The dissemination of blues around the world and the subsequent universal popularity of Mississippi blues musicians such as B. B. KING were largely dependent on Walker's establishment of electric blues as a popular idiom in the post–World War II African American community. King, as well as nearly every other blues musician since the 1950s, readily acknowledged their indebtedness to Walker.

FURTHER READING

Dance, Helen Oakley. *Stormy Monday: The T-Bone Walker Story* (1987).

Shaw, Arnold. *Honkers and Shouters: The Golden Years of Rhythm & Blues* (1978).

DISCOGRAPHY

The Complete Recordings of T-Bone Walker 1940–1954, no. 130.

This entry is taken from the *American National Biography* and is published here with the permission of the American Council of Learned Societies.

ANDRÉ BARBERA

Walker, Weldy (27 Jul. 1860?–23 Nov. 1937), baseball player and activist, was born Welday Wilberforce Walker in Steubenville, Ohio. He was the fifth of six children born to Moses W. Walker, a physician and minister. He was reared, along with the rest of his siblings, by Caroline (O'Harra) Walker, but Weldy's death certificate lists his mother as Maria Simpson.

This information was supplied to the coroner by Walker's nephew Thomas Gibson, who in the early 1920s claimed not to know Weldy's mother's identity. It is unclear whether the change in Gibson's information evidences newfound knowledge, a disclosed Walker family secret, or fiction. Walker's first name likely paid homage to the local pioneer Alexander Welday (although when and why Walker changed its spelling is unknown), and his middle name likely honored the English abolitionist William Wilberforce.

Steubenville, where Walker would spend most of his life, was a racially progressive town known for its participation in the abolitionist movement and the Underground Railroad. In the early 1870s Steubenville High School was integrated just in time for Walker to attend. In 1881 Walker followed his brother Fleet—he would often follow Fleet throughout his life—to nearby Oberlin College, located in Oberlin, Ohio. Oberlin, unlike many other colleges at the time, embraced physical as well as mental exertion, and earlier that year the school had fielded its first varsity intercollegiate baseball team. Baseball's popularity had grown during the Civil War, and the sport was a prominent activity in Steubenville, where Walker and his brothers learned to play. Oberlin's team had already featured an African American first baseman, so there was little resistance when Fleet and Weldy Walker took the field. That spring the Oberlin Yeomen played five games, including one against the University of Michigan, whose players were sufficiently impressed to offer the Walker brothers and a teammate a spot on their team. In 1882 the Walker brothers joined the Neshannocks ball club of New Castle, Pennsylvania, fifty-five miles north of Pittsburgh. Though the Neshannocks was ostensibly an amateur team, Fleet and his Oberlin teammate Harlan Burket received payment for their play, and it is likely that Weldy, its second baseman, did as well.

In September 1882 the Walkers left the Neshannocks to attend the University of Michigan. Weldy Walker enrolled in the homeopathic medical school, hoping to follow in the footsteps of his father, the first African American physician in Steubenville and one of the first in Ohio. Michigan was one of the few remaining universities to offer homeopathic studies, a medical approach that emphasized treatment through close doctor-patient relationships and limited medication. Walker continued his studies for two years while playing catcher for the Michigan baseball squad.

At that point Walker entered baseball history as one of the only three African Americans, along with the first, his brother Fleet, to play major league baseball prior to 1947. In 1884 Walker joined the Toledo ball club where his brother had been playing since the previous summer. Fleet's presence that season caused controversy when the legendary Chicago White Stockings player and manager Cap Anson reluctantly declared, "We'll play this here game, but won't play never no more with the nigger in" (*Toledo Blade*, 11 Aug. 1883). Given his clout as the head of a world champion ball club, Anson was able in time to establish a ban on African American ballplayers throughout the major leagues that would last through nearly half of the next century. Before the ban took effect Weldy Walker debuted on 15 July with Toledo, which had been accepted that year into the American Association. Recruited to supplement the team, whose players had suffered a rash of injuries, he played five games in the outfield for Toledo, collecting four hits and scoring one run in eighteen at-bats. In October Fleet was released by Toledo, and Weldy went with him. He continued to play with some low-level professional teams, including one all-black team from Pittsburgh that presaged future Negro League ventures, but essentially Walker's baseball career was over.

After his baseball days, Walker pursued a more stable line of work. He purchased and operated the Delmonico Dining Rooms restaurant in Mingo, Ohio, near Steubenville, in October 1884. Six months later he sold his business to help Fleet run a theater cum opera house in Cleveland called the Le Grande House. In 1899, after Fleet's release from jail for a conviction of federal mail robbery, the brothers acquired the Union Hotel in Steubenville, Weldy serving as clerk and Fleet as proprietor.

Like his baseball career, much of Walker's life post-baseball featured bold attempts at exposing bigotry and encouraging integration. In 1884, when roller-skating rinks were becoming popular, Walker and a friend, Hannibal Lyons, attempted to integrate Steubenville's two rinks. The proprietor objected, saying, "You are colored and you can't skate" (Baseball Hall of Fame Library file). Walker and Lyons in turn filed a lawsuit against the proprietor. The judge sided with them in principle, awarding both men fifteen dollars in damages, but refused to order integration of the rinks. For their objections, Walker and Lyons were lambasted in the *Steubenville Gazette* and *Ohio Press* as rabble-rousers. Walker was not deterred from activism, though, as evidenced by a March 1888 letter to the nationally circulated *Sporting Life*.

Anticipating an Ohio State League ban on African American baseball players, he wrote:

> The law is a disgrace to the present age … and casts derision at the laws of Ohio—the voice of the people—that say all men are equal…. There should be some broader cause—such as want of ability, behavior, and intelligence—for barring a player than his color. It is for these reasons and because I think ability and intelligence should be recognized first and last—at all times and by everyone—I ask the question again, why was the "law permitting colored men to sign [baseball contracts] repealed (*Sporting Life*, 14 Mar. 1888).

In 1897 he attempted to organize African Americans by helping to form the Negro Protective Party (NPP). Despite support from Democrats hoping to fragment Republicans, the NPP failed to reach state ballots and soon disbanded.

In 1908 Fleet and Weldy Walker began efforts to lead African Americans to Africa, by force if necessary, proclaiming that whites and blacks were demonstrably incapable of coexisting in America. They began a newspaper called the *Equator*, for which Weldy served as local editor. That year they also published "Our Home Colony: The Past, Present, and Future of the Negro Race in America," a forty-eight-page argument for return to Africa written by Fleet. It was Fleet and Weldy's intention to engineer the mass exodus; Weldy in fact listed his occupation at the time as "General Agent for 'Our Home Colony' and Liberian Emigration" (Baseball Hall of Fame file). Yet just as their literature was being published, negative reports were coming back from Liberia on the progress of similar efforts. The Walkers never transported a passenger to Africa. It is a matter of speculation whether commitment to the cause or financial interests drove their efforts.

Walker continued to live at the Union Hotel in Steubenville for the remainder of his life, along with Fleet's oldest son, Thomas, and daughter Jeanette. While retaining his hotel duties for much of this time, Weldy Walker worked as a bootlegger during Prohibition. He never married nor fathered children, and he died of influenza at seventy-eight. Weldy Walker often followed his older brother, and he will always be remembered as an afterthought to Fleet's achievements. Yet he suffered many of the same abuses, and he provided comparable, if not more notable, examples of courage in the pursuit of justice.

FURTHER READING
National Baseball Hall of Fame Library file, Weldy
　　Walker, Cooperstown, N.Y.

Thorn, John, and Pete Palmer, eds. *Total Baseball* (1989).

Zang, David W. *Fleet Walker's Divided Heart: The Life of Baseball's First Black Major Leaguer* (1995).

CHRISTOPHER DEVINE

Walker, William (c. 1819–c. 1892), farmer, was born a slave in Southampton County, Virginia. Almost nothing is known of his parents, who were also slaves. Until his nineteenth or twentieth birthday he belonged to a Dr. Seaman, who also owned his mother and father. In August 1841 Walker's master sold him to Natt Blake and General Downs, who kept him and six hundred other slaves in a slave pen in Petersburg, Virginia, pending transportation to cotton farms in the Deep South. After penning the slaves for six weeks amid "echoes and groans," Blake and Downs marched them aboard the *Pellican*, which immediately sailed to New Orleans, Walker never seeing or hearing from his parents again (Gaines, 10).

The *Pellican*, "a floating carcass on the sea," held six hundred slaves like cattle among toxic air and cholera. It reached New Orleans six weeks after departing Petersburg, losing thirty-six of its human cargo before breaching the Straits of Florida. Once the slaves were in New Orleans, new slaveholders imprisoned them again. Walker was imprisoned for three months until the overseer Dick Fallon purchased him and four other slaves for Ed Purgoo, who governed his plantation from his home in Paris, France (Gaines, 11–13).

Purgoo's surrogate, Fallon, proved a brutal taskmaster, eager to live up to his nickname, "the Negro tamer." The Purgoo Plantation enslaved five hundred blacks to cultivate eleven thousand acres, five hundred of which grew cotton. Fallon's heartless murder of an infant slave with a whip so enraged Walker that he attempted to escape to Canada through Mississippi. But his freedom proved fleeting; Fallon captured him within two months and punished him with 125 lashes.

However, the Purgoo Plantation soon fell victim to a violent cyclone, which devastated trees, livestock, crops, and other property, and killed forty slaves. This natural disaster set the stage for Fallon's and Purgoo's demise. While observing an oncoming storm from his veranda, Fallon was struck dead by lightning. Soon thereafter Purgoo declared bankruptcy, sold his plantation to John Lynden and William Perry, and sailed for Paris.

Because of Walker's penchant for freedom, Lynden and Perry immediately sold him to Stephen Cary, a Missouri planter. In January 1849 Cary took Williams to his plantation, located about two miles from the Missouri River. That he considered Cary a "kind and humane master" might explain Walker's seemingly easy flight to Illinois and then to freedom in Windsor, Ontario, on 8 August 1859. Walker found day work in Detroit in October 1859 with the Honorable John J. Bagley and later labored on James F. Joy's farm about four miles northwest of Detroit. After two years Walker purchased ten acres from John Holmes.

With the Emancipation Proclamation and Robert E. Lee's surrender as backdrop, Walker prospered in hopes of finding his parents and inviting them to live with him. Unfortunately, however, his property adjoined twenty acres rented by Dick Sholtz. Given to jealousy, anger, and indolence, Sholtz destroyed forty-eight of Walker's chickens because Walker had rejected Sholtz's offer to purchase ten turkeys. Sholtz also abused his wife, Susan, frequently. One night she fled to Walker's house to escape physical abuse. In a drunken rage, Sholtz tracked her to Walker's house, accused them of adultery, and charged at Walker with a club. Walker seized his gun, fired, and killed Sholtz in self-defense. He wanted to declare self-defense and "let justice take its course." Unfortunately, a neighbor convinced Mrs. Sholtz and Walker that their only hope lay in concealing the body. When it was discovered a week later, the Wayne County prosecutor persuaded a jury that Sholtz's murder had been premeditated (Gaines, 14–66).

The jury returned a verdict of murder in the first degree. In December 1866 the judge sentenced Walker, Mrs. Sholtz, and the neighbor to life in Jackson State Prison in Michigan. Prison records indicate that Walker was received on 22 December 1866 and list his occupation as farmer. Christmas Day 1866 marked the beginning of twenty-four years of solitary confinement for Walker. It also began his Herculean struggle with the prison contract system, which exacted convict labor under brutal conditions for minimal or no wages. In fact, Walker found the system analogous to slavery: "Contract labor in Jackson prison is, by far, a worse system of slavery than ever existed on Southern soil" (Gaines, 75). Walker railed against unethical politicians, abusive guards, deplorable living conditions, malicious wardens, and the causal relationship between lack of education and recidivism.

On 24 December 1892 Walker finally left Jackson Prison, receiving an "absolute pardon." Ironically, he left behind "a colored prisoner, the author of this book" (Gaines, 206). Like FREDERICK DOUGLASS and other slave narrators, Walker employed the power of allegory (with Fallon and Purgoo) to concretize the evils of slavery. But he also went one step further: he reminded us that incarceration and contracting (like sharecropping) supplanted slavery, and that education is the only way to realize freedom.

FURTHER READING
Gaines, Thomas S. *Buried Alive (Behind Prison Walls) for a Quarter of a Century: Life of William Walker* (2003).

FLOYD OGBURN JR.

Walker, William Otis (19 Sept. 1896–29 Oct. 1981), newspaper publisher, was born in Selma, Alabama, the son of Alexander Walker, the owner of a café, and Annie Lee Jones. He went to Ohio to attend Wilberforce University, where he majored in business education and graduated in 1916. After a two-year stint at the Pullman Company, for which he was a porter, and Westinghouse in Pittsburgh, he returned to Ohio to take courses at Oberlin Business College, earning a degree in 1918. The next year he married Theresa Irmgard Brooks; they had no children.

After graduation Walker worked briefly with the Pittsburgh Urban League. He then joined the *Pittsburgh Courier*, the African American newspaper published by ROBERT LEE VANN, where he soon became city editor. A year later Walker joined the *Norfolk* (Virginia) *Journal and Guide*, a black newspaper published by P. B. Young, serving as city editor until he left in 1921 to co-establish the *Washington* (D.C.) *Tribune*. He remained at the *Tribune* for nine years as managing editor but quit because of bickering between the heirs of the paper's other cofounders. Walker spent the next two years as advertising manager of the Fair Department Store, the first integrated department store in the country. He later became manager of its Baltimore store.

In 1932 Walker moved to Cleveland to take over the floundering *Call and Post*, a black weekly that had resulted from the merger of the *Call*, founded in 1918, and the *Post*, founded in 1926. Walker's vision for the paper prevailed despite its large debt, inconsistent distribution, and inadequate facilities. He drew on his business and journalistic experiences to build a staff skilled in printing technology, news gathering, and news writing. Within a few years the paper claimed that it was distributed into every black home in the Cleveland metropolitan area, and it had state-of-the-art printing and photographic facilities.

Walker aligned himself with the local Republican Party and used the *Call and Post* to promote the Republican candidate for the 1932 mayoral race. The paper's endorsements resulted in Walker obtaining financial backing from his Republican colleagues, and the money was used to purchase mechanical equipment for the paper. The paper's former stockholders eventually reneged on their promise to pay operating deficits or to pay Walker's accumulating back salary. Thus in 1940 Walker and one of his political colleagues, Lawrence Payne, took over the paper, forming the P. W. Publishing Company. Walker became the sole owner after Payne's death in 1959.

Walker was an active journalist and publisher who aggressively championed black civil rights. He founded in 1935 the Future Outlook League, an organization that fought for the employment of African Americans in Cleveland stores and utility companies. Using the pages of the *Call and Post*, in 1935 the organization popularized the slogan, "Don't spend money where you can't work." As a result Ohio Bell, Woolworth's, and numerous other businesses began hiring blacks. This notion of boycotting places that discriminated later became a successful strategy of the civil rights movement of the 1950s and 1960s.

The *Call and Post* also led in the coverage of national events involving blacks. Walker was the first black journalist to interview the jailed SCOTTSBORO BOYS, nine young black men falsely accused in 1931 of raping two white women in Alabama. He used the *Call and Post* to crusade and to raise money for their defense. They were eventually freed. The *Call and Post* was also the first African American paper to provide action photos of the JOE LOUIS–Max Schmeling fight in 1938.

Known as the "Dean of Black Journalists," Walker was a leader in unifying the nation's black newspapers in their efforts to promote the welfare of African Americans. As a founding member of the National Newspaper Publishers Association (NNPA), Walker joined other black newspaper publishers in crusading for nondiscriminatory treatment of black soldiers during World War II. This unified front encouraged the racial integration of the armed forces in 1948. In 1945 Walker was among three black publishers selected by President Franklin D. Roosevelt to tour military bases in Europe and to report on the treatment and conditions of black soldiers. In 1958, as NNPA president, Walker called a Summit Meeting of Negro Leaders in Washington, D.C., to assess the civil rights conditions of blacks. Some three hundred black leaders attended the summit, which included a speech by President Dwight Eisenhower. Walker had divorced his first wife in 1955, and that year he married Naomi Russell, with whom he also had no children.

Walker also sought political office and was elected to three terms (1940–1941, 1942–1943, 1944–1945) on the Cleveland City Council. In 1963 the governor appointed him director of the Department of Industrial Relations, making Walker the first black cabinet officer in Ohio.

Although an avowed Republican, Walker actively endorsed the mayoral and congressional candidacies of the black Democrats CARL STOKES and LOUIS STOKES. The 1967 election of Carl Stokes in Cleveland was considered a major accomplishment because he was the first black elected mayor of a major American city. The *Call and Post* played a key role in this effort with editorials urging blacks to register to vote and challenging whites to put aside their bigotry. The paper also worked actively with several civil rights organizations to register people to vote. The paper, with the same zeal, endorsed the successful congressional candidacy of Stokes's brother Louis Stokes in 1968.

In more than sixty years with the black press, Walker won awards honoring his journalistic accomplishments, including one for his "Down the Big Road" columns, which contained both personal and political commentary. The *Call and Post*, under his tutelage, was also recognized for its excellence and leadership in black journalism. It was one of the first black papers certified by the Audit Bureau of Circulations, which ensures that circulation figures are accurate and legitimate, and wholly printed within in its own shop. Furthermore, during a time when African American newspapers were declining in circulation and revenue, the *Call and Post* was expanding. By the time of Walker's death, the *Call and Post* had expanded to satellite editions serving Cleveland, Cincinnati, Dayton, Columbus, and Akron, Ohio. Although its circulation, which was 26,670 at Walker's death, was larger than that of other prominent black newspapers, such as the *Chicago Defender*, it positioned itself as an Ohio paper rather than as a national one. Walker devoted some sixty to eighty hours a week to the *Call and Post* until he died there in his office, an octogenarian.

FURTHER READING

Walker's papers are at the Moorland-Spingarn Research Center, Howard University, Washington, D.C.

Davis, Russell H. *Black Americans in Cleveland from George Peake to Carl B. Stokes, 1796–1969* (1972).

Moore, Leonard N. *Carl B. Stokes and the Rise of Black Political Power* (2002).

Ross, Felicia G. Jones. "Mobilizing the Masses: The *Cleveland Call and Post* and the Scottsboro Incident," *Journal of Negro History* 84, no. 1 (Winter 1999).

Obituaries: *Cleveland Call and Post*, 7 Nov. 1981; *Cleveland Plain Dealer*, 30 Oct. 1981.

This entry is taken from the *American National Biography* and is published here with the permission of the American Council of Learned Societies.

FELICIA G. JONES ROSS

Walker, Wyatt Tee (16 Aug. 1929–), minister and civil rights activist, was born in Brockton, Massachusetts, the son John Wise Walker, a minister, and Eleanora Springer Walker. He attended Virginia Union University in Richmond, Virginia, graduating in 1950 with a bachelor of science degree in physics and chemistry. Shortly thereafter, acting on the advice of Dr. SAMUEL DEWITT PROCTOR, he changed his career focus from the sciences and entered Virginia Union University's School of Theology, over which Dr. Proctor was the dean, attaining a master's of divinity degree in 1953. He would earn his Doctorate in Theology from the Colgate-Rochester Divinity School in 1975 and later go on to additional graduate study at the University of Ife (Nigeria) and the University of Ghana.

On 24 December 1951 he married Theresa Ann Edwards, herself a graduate of Virginia Union University and of Howard University. She was later to be involved in civil rights protests in Petersburg, Virginia, the freedom rides, and the Birmingham campaign. The Walkers had three sons, Wyatt Tee Walker Jr., Robert Charles Walker, and Earl Maurice Walker; and a daughter, Ann Patrice Powell.

From 1952 until 1960 Walker served as pastor of Gillfield Baptist Church in Petersburg, Virginia, and almost immediately became involved in the civil rights movement, taking positions as branch president of the NAACP in Petersburg, member of the board for the Virginia Southern Christian Leadership Conference (SCLC), and state director of the Congress of Racial Equality (CORE). His closest mentor at this time was the redoubtable pastor VERNON JOHNS, who had left Dexter Avenue Baptist Church in Montgomery, Alabama (he was succeeded by Dr. MARTIN LUTHER KING JR.), to run a small grocery store in Petersburg. By 1958, employing the model of Dr. King's Montgomery Improvement Association, Walker had organized the Petersburg Improvement Association, which soon gained a reputation as the most effective and active of the neighborhood rights associations that sprang up in the late 1950s. On 1 January 1959 Walker put together Virginia's first substantial civil rights march, the Pilgrimage of Prayer, from what was then the Mosque Theater to the state capitol in Richmond, where the demonstrators registered their protest against Virginia's "Massive Resistance" policies against the federally ordered implementation of school desegregation, particularly the mandated school closures in several districts. Walker led the Petersburg Improvement Association in a sit-in to desegregate the Petersburg Public Library, which resulted in his being briefly imprisoned on the charge of violating Virginia law on segregation.

Impressed by the organization of the Petersburg Improvement Association, King asked Walker to take the position of SCLC executive director, in place of the interim director ELLA BAKER. King furthermore named Walker as his first chief of staff. He took up his new duties in August 1960. Walker's tenure in this position, 1960–1964, spanned the most eventful years in the SCLC's history. It was to be both a high point and a controversial period in his life. He organized an efficient bureaucratic structure that saw SCLC through the height of the civil rights campaign, but drew criticism for what was perceived in some quarters as his autocratic leadership style. In terms of financial management and growth, the change was phenomenal. When Walker began in 1960, he oversaw a staff of five and administered a forty-thousand-dollar budget; by 1964 his staff had grown to more than one hundred and the budget was approximately $1 million. Walker's methods of operation were highly structured, organized, and followed a precise chain of command, something that irked some of the younger activists. King's parting assessment, however, depicted him as a "sound and imaginative administrator." Walker was involved at the strategic, organizational level in the 1961 Freedom Rides as well as the 1961–1962 Albany campaign. He was undoubtedly the chief architect of the Birmingham campaign in 1963, coordinating the nonviolent protests to the minutest detail. Both he and his wife were brutally beaten by police officers during the subsequent riots. In July 1964 he resigned as chief of staff and executive director of the SCLC and was succeeded by ANDREW YOUNG.

From 1964 to 1967 Walker served as a marketing specialist at the Negro Heritage Library. He returned to the ministry, becoming interim pastor of the Abyssinian Baptist Church in New York City from 1965 to 1966. In 1967 he was called to the Canaan Baptist Church in Harlem and remained there throughout the rest of his ministerial career. In 1967 New York Governor Nelson A. Rockefeller asked him to serve as special urban affairs adviser to the governor's office, a post he held for ten years. That same year, his alma mater, Virginia Union University, conferred upon him the doctorate in humane letters, and he would subsequently serve on that institution's board of trustees. From 1975 to 1985 he served on the board of directors for the Freedom National Bank and was elected as chair on three separate occasions. As longtime chair of the Central Harlem Development Group, he has been actively involved in providing neighborhood housing. He accompanied the Reverend JESSE JACKSON to Syria in 1984 to negotiate the release of Lieutenant Robert O. Goodman Jr.—an incident that was recounted in his book *Road to Damascus* (1985). Walker was close to Jackson and was for many years a staunch supporter of Jackson's political campaigns, even serving as special assistant for his SCLC colleague on the Rainbow PUSH Coalition. But in 2001 he broke with Jackson over what he considered Jackson's lack of repentance concerning revealed sexual irregularities in his personal life. Walker became deeply involved in the World Council of Churches, becoming world commissioner for its Program to Combat Racism. In 1996 he was named president of the American Committee on Africa, and in 2001 chaired the Reverend AL SHARPTON's National Action Network.

Walker was a widely published scholar and was considered one of the nation's foremost authorities on African American church music. His published works include *The Black Church Looks at the Bicentennial: A Minority Report*; *Somebody's Calling My Name: Black Sacred Music and Social Change*; *China Diary*; *The Soul of Black Worship: A Trilogy—Preaching, Praying, Singing*; *Road to Damascus: A Journey of Faith*; *Spirits That Dwell in Deep Woods: The Prayer and Praise Hymns of the Black Religious Experience* (1987 to 1991; in three volumes); *Occasional Papers of a Revolutionary* (1980–1990; partially autobiographical); *Gospel in the Land of the Rising Sun*; *The Kaidanren Papers of Tokyo*; *The King of Love: My Days with Martin Luther King, Jr.*; *The African American Church and Economic Development*; *Afrocentrism and Christian Faith* (1993); *Soweto Diary: The Free Elections in South Africa*; *A Prophet from Harlem Speaks: Sermons and Essays*; and *Millennium End Papers: The Walker File '98–99*. His videos include *Confessions of an Ex-Crossmaker* and *The Music Tree*.

FURTHER READING

Dr. Walker's papers while he was executive director of the SCLC are in the King Library and Archive at the Martin Luther King Jr. Center for Nonviolent Social Change in Atlanta, Georgia (*Papers of the Southern Christian Leadership Conference*: Subgroup II, Section III). The Wyatt Tee Walker Archives and Museum is being planned for the Canaan Baptist Church in Harlem.

Walker, Wyatt Tee. *Occasional Papers of a Revolutionary* (1992).

Branch, Taylor. *Parting the Waters: America in the King Years, 1954–63* (1988).

Branch, Taylor. *Pillar of Fire: America in the King Years, 1963–65* (1998).

Morris, Aldon D. *The Origins of the Civil Rights Movement: Black Communities Organizing for Change* (1986).

RAYMOND PIERRE HYLTON

Wall, Fannie Franklin (1860?–14 Apr. 1944), clubwoman, children's home founder, and community activist, was born in Gallatin, Tennessee. Although she was one of the most prominent African American women in the San Francisco Bay Area in the first half of the twentieth century, very little is known about her early life and education.

Wall came to California with her husband, U.S. Army sergeant Archy H. Wall, when he was transferred from Silver City, New Mexico, to the Presidio army base in San Francisco during the Spanish-American War. Upon Archy's retirement from the army in 1900, the Walls settled in Oakland, California. They had three children: Lillian, Florence, and Clifton. Archy died in 1931 and was buried in the historic San Francisco National Cemetery. Upon her death, Wall was interred in the same grave.

Wall was a major figure in the black women's club movement in California. Black women's clubs flourished in the late nineteenth century. Club members were generally middle-class women who believed it was their duty to help the less privileged, especially children and women, in the black community. In California, as in other places, African American club women established institutions to care for orphans and the aged, provided day care services for children of working parents, established scholarships and libraries, and promoted voter education and civil rights. The black women's club movement emerged nationally in 1896 when the National Association of Colored Women (NACW) was founded to unite the efforts of individual clubs.

Fannie Wall was known throughout California for her work in the Northern Federation of Colored Women's Clubs, an association of Bay Area clubs organized by Elizabeth Brown in 1913. The Federation affiliated with the NACW in the same year. Wall succeeded Brown as president of the Northern Federation in 1914. She subsequently served multiple terms as president and treasurer of the organization.

In her tenure as president, she traveled extensively throughout the state, fostering alliances among club women. Among her other affiliations, Wall was active in the Urban League, the NAACP, the Mothers' Charity Club, the Arts and Industrial Club of Oakland, and the Sisters of the Mysterious Ten. She also established and served as chair of the Spanish-American War Auxiliary.

Her activities in the women's club movement on both the local and national levels brought her into the company of outstanding women of the era. When the Fourteenth Biennial Session of NACW convened in Oakland from 30 July to 6 August 1926, MARY McLEOD BETHUNE and her secretary were houseguests of Wall. Archie Williams, who was Wall's grandson and a gold medalist in the four-hundred-meter track event at the 1936 Olympics in Germany, recalled that Bethune had been a close friend of his grandmother and often stayed with the family when visiting the San Francisco Bay Area.

Committed to improving the quality of life for African Americans in the Oakland area, Wall frequently lobbied members of the white establishment, most notably long-term Oakland mayor John L. Davie, who served in office from 1895 to 1897 and from 1915 to 1931. Respected in both the black and white communities, she used her influence to promote better relations between the races.

Wall's most enduring legacy, however, was the orphanage and childcare center she helped to establish in Oakland. When the Northern Federation of Colored Women's Clubs incorporated in 1914, the first project it undertook was to found an orphanage and daycare facility for black children who were not being served by local charities and public agencies. Under the leadership of Wall and financial secretary Hettie Tilghman, the Federation successfully raised the funds needed to purchase a building for $1,200. Located at 1215 Peralta Street in west Oakland, the Northern Federation Home and Day Nursery opened on 10 November 1918. The facility served as an orphanage for children between the ages of five and fourteen and a day care center for children of working parents. Wall was the home's first president and administrator. She ran the charity on a daily basis for several years after its establishment as well. It was later renamed the Fannie Wall Children's Home and Day Nursery as a tribute to Wall's pioneering endeavors and leadership.

The Fannie Wall Home received financial support from various sources. Its three major sources of funding over the years included income from the sale of a home donated by former board member Josephine Hutton in 1919, support from the Community Chest from 1923 until 1958, and a bequest from the estate of author Theodore Dreiser in 1959, which provided a yearly income of $3,000. The home also sponsored benefits, charity balls, dinners, musicals, and rummage sales to raise money. Local black women's clubs and other community organizations also supported the home through donations and gifts.

The Victorian building on Peralta Street served as the Fannie Wall Home until 1928, when a larger house was purchased at 815 Linden Street. In 1941 the club women of the Northern Federation relinquished control of the charity to an independent corporation. During the following decades, the institution faced many challenges, including lack of money for building maintenance, scrutiny from social service agencies regarding the facility's management, and the push of massive urban renewal initiatives. In 1962 the Oakland Redevelopment Agency purchased and razed the Linden Street building in order to make way for the Acorn Redevelopment Project. Regrouping in 1964, the board of directors purchased another building at 647 Fifty-fifth Street, the present site of the home. During the 1960s and 1970s, the home's operations were suspended at various times. The orphanage program was eventually discontinued, and during the late 1970s the home operated as a childcare center and was later leased to Oakland's Head Start program. Although the Fannie Wall Home board of directors eventually relinquished control over the day care center, it became involved in other community enrichment programs. The Fannie Wall Home began sponsoring a scholarship program and an annual award of approximately $25,000 in scholarship money to college students in the Oakland area. As a testament to the life and legacy of Fannie Wall, above the entrance of the building on Fifty-fifth Street is the inscription "Fannie Wall Children's Home."

FURTHER READING
Information on Fannie Franklin Wall and the Fannie Wall Children's Home can be found in the archives of the Oakland Public Library's African American Museum and Library and in the History Room, Main Library, also at the Oakland Public Library.

Beasley, Delilah L. *Negro Trail Blazers of California* (1911; repr. 1969).
Davis, Elizabeth Lindsay. *Lifting As They Climb* (1933).
Hausler, Donald. "The Fannie Wall Children's Home," *Oakland Heritage Alliance News* (Summer 1986).
Irvin, Dona L. "Fannie Franklin Wall," in *Notable Black American Women, Book II* (1992).
Jackson, George F. *Black Women Makers of History, a Portrait* (1975).
Williams, Archie F. *The Joy of Flying: Olympic Gold, Air Force Colonel, and Teacher* (1993).
LINDA BOWLES-ADARKWA

Wallace, Charles (12 Aug. 1932–5 June 1986), businessman and government contractor, was born in Heanes City, Florida, the adopted son of David Wallace, a sharecropper, and Lonar Wallace. During the Great Depression the Wallaces moved to Georgia. Little is known of his early life except that Charles hated sharecropping, which he termed "sophisticated slavery" (*Black Enterprise*, Nov. 1976). During the Korean War, Wallace joined the U.S. Army and then returned to New York City, where he washed taxis and earned a high school diploma. In the late 1950s and 1960s, he carefully saved his earnings, opened two laundromats and a liquor store, and bought an oil truck to deliver home heating fuel. In 1971 Wallace married Juanita Wilson, and they reared four children.

During the presidential race of 1968 the Democratic and Republican candidates embraced the concept of "black capitalism": federal support for "socially and economically disadvantaged" business owners (in practice, racial minorities). President Richard M. Nixon distributed "black capitalism" aid through the Small Business Administration (SBA) and government contracting agencies. Nixon's "black capitalist" rhetoric inspired Wallace, who planned to create the biggest black business in the United States. Beginning in 1969 the SBA extended loans to expand Wallace's fuel oil business. Section 8(a) of the Small Business Act further authorized the SBA to "set aside" contracts for "disadvantaged" business owners. With assistance from the SBA and additional loans from Chase Manhattan Bank, Wallace & Wallace Fuel Oil Company expanded from one truck to nineteen and employed one hundred workers.

Wallace & Wallace's fantastic growth in revenue came through persistent political lobbying. Wallace allied himself with key congressmen, cajoled every president from Nixon to Ronald Reagan, and employed a dozen lobbyists to ensure media publicity and a continued flow of government contracts for fuel oil delivery. By 1977 the *New York Times* reported that the "ex-sharecropper" had received $30 million in 8(a) contracts to become one of the nation's "wealthiest black men" (23 Feb. 1977). From 1969 to 1977 the SBA considered Wallace a success symbol for its "black capitalism" initiative.

Wallace's grand ambition was to build the first black-owned oil refinery. The project attracted widespread media attention, from petroleum trade journals to national magazines and major newspapers. In 1971 the visionary entrepreneur established a separate Wallace & Wallace Chemical & Oil Corporation (WWCO) to manage refinery construction. The project garnered the support of the mayor of Tuskegee, Alabama, Johnny Ford, and the former segregationist Governor George Wallace. Charles Wallace pitched the impractical location (200 miles inland) as a job-creator for one of the nation's poorest counties. The state of Alabama issued a $40 million bond improving Mobile docks to import oil and also approved construction of a 200-mile pipeline to Tuskegee. Wallace chose the location partly for public relations: He promised to build a museum to honor the Tuskegee Army Air Corps of World War II, the famous all-black aviation unit. When complete, the $650 million project would have made WWCO the largest African American business.

Wallace's grandiose plans began crumbling in 1978, when Congress investigated the fraud and abuse associated with the Section 8(a) program. Meanwhile, Wallace's truck drivers went on strike, which led to the loss of a city school contract. Legal troubles added to Wallace's woes. By diverting SBA funds to his refinery project, Wallace ran afoul of agency regulations. The U.S. Justice Department investigated, and the SBA froze his bank accounts, thus forcing the company to lay off one-third of its employees. An anonymous SBA official stated, "it was a case of throwing good money after bad" (*Washington Star*, 7 Feb. 1979). In 1981 the SBA sued when Wallace defaulted on $11 million in loans; Wallace countersued unsuccessfully for $750 million, alleging a racist conspiracy against him by the government. An out-of-court settlement forced Wallace to repay debt, liquidate assets, and lose access to 8(a) contracts. The downsized company struggled in the 1980s. Still dreaming of his uncompleted refinery, Wallace died of cancer in 1986 in White Plains, New York. His wife continued to operate Wallace & Wallace Fuel Oil, a very small company with two employees. In 2004 she sold the business to family friends.

As he told the *Washington Post*, Wallace was "a product of the SBA"; his rise and fall illustrated the problems with the Section 8(a) program (11 Dec. 1977). It encouraged small business owners to expand beyond their ability to manage large government contracts profitably. Bureaucrats proved inept at developing small businesses into large ones that could survive in a competitive marketplace. In a June 1992 retrospective, *Black Enterprise* drew the moral that "building a business on government contracts can be rough going." Nevertheless, for a time, as the *Washington Post* noted, Wallace was a "fascinating" "Horatio Alger" success symbol for "black capitalism" (6 May 1978).

FURTHER READING

Asbury, Edith Evans. "Ex-Sharecropper Rising to One of Wealthiest Black Men," *New York Times*, 23 Feb. 1977.

De Witt, Karen. "S.B.A. Success Story, Rewritten," *New York Times*, 28 May 1978.

Knight, Jerry. "Fighting Hard for a Dream," *Washington Post*, 11 Dec. 1977.

Reynolds, Rhonda. "Where Are They Now?" *Black Enterprise* (June 1992).

Obituary: *Black Enterprise* (Sept. 1986).

JONATHAN J. BEAN

Wallace, Christopher. *See* Notorious B. I. G.

Wallace, Coley (1927–30 Jan. 2005), boxer and actor, was born in Jacksonville, Florida. His parents' names are unknown, and little is known about Wallace's early life. He first found work as a baggage handler for a railroad in Florida. At the suggestion of some of his friends who noted Wallace's size and strength, he left his home state in his late teens for New York City, where he hoped to establish himself as a heavyweight boxer.

Wallace progressed quickly as an amateur and entered the 1948 Golden Gloves tournament with an undefeated record. It was during this tournament that Wallace had his most famous fight. In the first round, he was matched against the winner of the New England Golden Gloves tourney, a rough and crude fighter named Rocky Marciano. Had Marciano not gone on to become the only undefeated heavyweight champion in the history of boxing, the fight might have been of little interest to future generations. Instead, the fight reached nearly mythic proportions over time. Wallace's *New York*

Times obituary (1 Feb. 2005) claimed that Marciano was knocked out in the fight and that it was his only loss as an amateur. These claims were unfounded, however. Marciano never suffered a knockout as either an amateur or professional, although he did lose several fights before turning professional—including this first fight with Wallace, which was won by decision, although even this was disputed by Marciano and some ringside observers at the time. One famous sportswriter recalled Wallace's knocking Marciano down at least twice and winning easily. Other reporters, and Marciano himself, remembered the fight differently, and claimed that Marciano was "robbed" by an unfair decision. In any case, Wallace went on to win the Golden Gloves heavyweight championship and was considered the last man to ever beat Rocky Marciano.

Wallace began his professional boxing career soon after this fight, but he was never able to match his amateur success. This was partly the result of what some of his friends and trainers referred to as his lack of a "killer instinct" in the ring. Some of it also undoubtedly had to do with the man who came to serve as Wallace's manager, "Blinky" Palermo. Palermo was a Philadelphia-based mobster who, together with Frankie Carbo (who was suspected in the 1947 murder of fellow gangster Bugsy Siegel), managed to control a large portion of championship boxing in the late 1940s and 1950s. Wallace was not Palermo's only boxer; he "managed" a number of fighters, including several world champions such as Ike Williams and SONNY LISTON. Wallace, who was just starting out, felt he had little choice in the matter: Palermo promised big fights and big paydays through his "connections." Instead, according to Wallace, Palermo stole part of his earnings, matched him too soon against quality fighters, and, in one case, even drugged Wallace to ensure his defeat.

Wallace eventually put together a respectable fight record of twenty wins and seven losses and even entered the ranks of the top ten heavyweights for a short period in the early 1950s. In his two biggest fights, however, Wallace came up short. In 1952, he fought Jimmy Bivins, another black fighter who never got a chance at the heavyweight title. Bivins dominated the fight and knocked Wallace out in the ninth round. One year later Wallace was matched with boxing veteran and former world champion EZZARD CHARLES. Wallace would later claim that this fight was marred because Palermo drugged him. Charles prevailed in a ten-round knockout.

Following his retirement from boxing shortly after the loss to Charles, Wallace found his most gainful employment as a bouncer for the legendary Savoy Ballroom in New York City. The owner of the establishment, a longtime fight fan, employed several former fighters including Herbert "Whitey" White, who organized the famous ballroom dancing group, the "Whitey Lindy Hoppers." According to those who remember Wallace at the Savoy, he usually handled problems with his charm and humor rather than his fists. He worked as a bouncer at a variety of other venues as well; he was working at the Audubon Ballroom the evening in February 1965 when MALCOLM X was assassinated.

The loss to Charles effectively ended Wallace's days as a heavyweight contender. But in 1953 another opportunity presented itself. A film biography of former heavyweight champion JOE LOUIS was being planned in Hollywood. The director, Robert Gordon, auditioned hundreds of young men before taking a look at Wallace. Wallace did bear an unusual resemblance to the great fighter and, unlike many of the others trying out for the role, actually knew how to box. Despite his lack of acting experience, Wallace was selected for the part. The 1953 movie *The Joe Louis Story* mixed old fight films featuring the real Louis and scenes—in and out of the ring—with Wallace portraying the slugger. The film received lukewarm reviews, with most comments on Wallace's performance focusing on his uncanny likeness to Louis.

His career in films continued sporadically after 1953. He played a small role in a 1957 sunken treasure adventure called *Carib Gold*. It was not until 1980 that he again appeared on screen, once again playing Louis, in the Academy Award–winning film *Raging Bull*. In 1989, he played in his last film, *Rooftops*, in a tiny role.

His role in boxing was not completely forgotten, however. In 1974 he was invited as one of boxing's notables to attend the classic "Rumble in the Jungle" in Zaire between MUHAMMAD ALI and GEORGE FOREMAN. Coley Wallace died in New York City at the age of seventy-seven from heart failure. He was survived by his wife, Pearlie-May, and a daughter, Pat.

FURTHER READING

Cassidy, Robert, Jr. *Ten-Count for Max Schmeling and Coley Wallace*. Available online at http://www.thesweetscience.com/boxing-article/1662/ten-count-max-schmeling-coley-wallace.

Tosches, Nick. *The Devil and Sonny Liston* (2000).

Obituaries: *New York Times*, 1 Feb. 2005; *Ring Magazine*, June 2005.

MICHAEL L. KRENN

Wallace, Daniel Webster (15 Sept. 1860–28 Mar. 1939), cattleman sometimes known as "80 John," was born near Inez in Victoria County, Texas, to Mary Wallace, a slave. Mary was born in Virginia, lived in Missouri, and was sold to Mary O'Daniels of Texas. Little is known of Mary's other children born in Missouri or of Daniel's father. Neither Webster's birth nor his young life distinguished him from other slave children born in that region of the state. Webster, as he was then known, spent his earliest days performing menial chores and graduated to field work by the time he reached adolescence. However, chopping cotton never was his preferred activity, and he looked forward to a day when he could become a cowboy.

Wallace began his cowboy career as a teenager in the mid-1870s on a cattle drive from Victoria to Coleman County. While Wallace was a tenderfoot, he carried out his responsibilities and finished the trail drive, convinced that he had made the right decision. The fifteen silver dollars he received further convinced him that he would continue in this lucrative occupation. It was not long before he signed on with Sam Gholson. Gholson, an early pioneer rancher and Indian fighter, provided Wallace the opportunity to perfect his skills as a cowhand. During his short tenure with Gholson, Wallace learned to work cattle on the open range, locate strays, identify cows by their markings, and work roundups. Wallace also became a competent wrangler and horse breaker. He started working for John Nunn, a cattleman who ran the NUNN cattle outfit, where Wallace broadened his experience with cattle, long drives, cowboy life, Indians, and death. Often work was solitary and for weeks or months at a stretch he would see no one. A cowboy who became sick or injured had little available help or treatment; he recuperated on his own or died. The main responsibility of cowboys was to deliver the herd to its designated location. Indians looking for horses and cattle sometimes crossed the path of cowhands on the trail, and in southwestern Texas the Comanche were known not only to steal livestock but also to torture those they encountered. In some cases where cowboys were outnumbered, the use of deception rather than bravado proved the wisest course of action. Wallace learned this lesson firsthand when a young cowboy bolted from a hiding place and was killed.

Wallace decided to change work environments and rode nearly four hundred miles to join the Clay Mann outfit in Taylor County, Texas. Mann had holdings in Mitchell, Kent, and Coleman Counties in Texas; in several counties in New Mexico; and in Chihuahua, Mexico. Wallace's experiences were deepened by the many trips that he made with Mann to his various ranches. This area of the western frontier was marked by violence where each man was his own law and protection. Outlaws made this region their home, Indian raids were common, and many of the working cowboys were killers. To address the lawlessness, communities formed vigilance committees that dispensed a rough range justice at the end of a rope until legal institutions were established. Facing the dangers and adventures of long cattle drives helped shape Wallace. He saw the vices that separated cowboys from their money at the end of the drive, and decided that this would not be his fate. When Mann relocated his operations to the area of present-day Colorado City, Texas, Wallace accompanied the herd that would provide him with a new name in cattle country. Mann branded his cows with a large "80" that stretched across their side. It was this 80 brand that changed Wallace's name for most of those who knew him to "80 John." He continued to work for Mann and established his reputation as a number-one cowboy and as a confidant who could be trusted with any discreet assignment. His close relation with Mann allowed him to receive a portion of his wages in cash and reserve a portion for the purchase of cattle. In several years, Wallace acquired and homesteaded a couple of sections of land near Loraine in Mitchell County, Texas.

Wallace decided at age twenty-five that his future required something that had eluded him up until this time: an education. He attended a school for blacks in Navarro County and was enrolled in second grade. While Wallace gained rudimentary literacy skills, his most significant accomplishment was finding Laura Dee Owens, who was finishing high school. Wallace convinced Owens that she should become his bride rather than pursuing the teaching career she had planned. Wallace and Owens traveled to west Texas and took up residence on one of Mann's ranches. After Mann's death, Wallace continued to work for Mann's wife, but always with an eye toward becoming a cattleman himself. His providence, acquisition of cattle, and good decision making were the essential qualities in what was a difficult and trying business. Droughts, economic downturns, bad winters, cattle thieves, and Indian raids were just a few of the problems Wallace faced. His wife proved a key factor in making a success of ranching. Her positive disposition and ability to endure trying circumstances provided a foundation upon which all else was built. Wallace also developed friendly relations with cattlemen with large holdings and bankers who were essential in making the necessary adjustments in difficult times. At a time when most cowboys traveled over the land like tumbleweeds and most cattlemen went bankrupt, Wallace developed a debt-free ranch holding of 8,820 acres over eleven square miles. He raised three daughters and one son and developed a reputation for hospitality, friendship, and a good business sense. It was these attributes that made him one of most respected men in west Texas. He died on 28 Mar. 1939, after having achieved what few others of any color had done.

FURTHER READING

Branch, Hettye Wallace. *The Story of "80 John"* (1960).

Crane, R. C. "D.W. Wallace ('80 John'), A Negro Cattleman on the Texas Frontier," *West Texas Historical Association Year Book 28* (Oct. 1952).

Earnest, Martha, and Melvin Sance. "Daniel Webster Wallace," *The Handbook of Texas Online*, www.tsha. utexas.edu/handbook/online/articles/WW/fwaah. html (2002).

Hales, Douglas. "Black Cowboy: Daniel Webster '80 John' Wallace," in *The Cowboy Way*, ed. Paul H. Carlson (2000).

Roach, Joyce Gibson. "Daniel Webster Wallace: A West Texas Cattleman," in *Black Cowboys of Texas*, ed. Sara R. Massey (2000).

MICHAEL N. SEARLES

Wallace, Sippie (1 Nov. 1898 1 Nov. 1986), blues singer, was born Beulah Thomas in Houston, Texas, the daughter of George Thomas Sr. and Fanny Bradley. Her nickname, "Sippie," derived from her twelve siblings, perhaps because of a childhood lisp. Her parents, like most Houston blacks in this era, may have worked as laborers or domestics. Her father was a deacon at the Shiloh Baptist Church, and the family was very religious. Sippie spent her preteen years playing piano and singing in the family church. Her older sister Lillie and older brother George Jr. encouraged her musical interest, and though her mother disapproved, she began to learn popular music.

Sippie attended school up to the seventh grade but left home by age fifteen to join her brother George, an aspiring pianist and composer, in New Orleans. There she married Frank Seals in 1914; their union lasted three years. Although both of her parents had died, Sippie returned to Houston in 1918 to live with her siblings. Still aspiring to sing professionally, she hoped to get a job with a road show on the black Theatre Owners' Booking Association circuit (TOBA). Her first job on the vaudeville circuit was that of a maid for a female snake dancer, Madame Dante, who was traveling Texas cities and towns. During these travels, she began singing casually with small bands for dances and picnics. Eventually she began working as a vocalist and was billed as "the Texas Nightingale." During this period she met and married Houstonian Matt Wallace, who for a time served as her manager and sometime emcee.

By the early 1920s Wallace's brother George was an established composer and publisher, working on the recording staff of W. W. Kimball Company's music-roll division as well as directing his own orchestra in Chicago. Wallace and her husband, her younger brother Hersal (a talented pianist), and her niece Hociel (also a blues singer) arrived in Chicago in 1923. During the same year Wallace was offered a recording contract with Okeh records.

Wallace's first recorded songs, "Shorty George" and her own composition, "Up the Country Blues," sold well and made her a blues star. Okeh records' promotion of Wallace as a recording artist in 1924 and 1925 made her much in demand as a performing artist, and she became a regular headliner on the TOBA circuit. In all, she recorded forty sides for the Okeh record label between 1923 and 1927, among them "Special Delivery Blues" with LOUIS ARMSTRONG on cornet. She also recorded with the noted cornetist KING OLIVER and the clarinetist SIDNEY BECHET. At least half of the recorded song material for Okeh records was composed by either Wallace or her brothers George and Hersal. In the mid-1920s Wallace, her husband, brothers, and niece moved from Chicago to settle on Detroit's East Side.

Although Wallace worked with other pianists, such as CLARENCE WILLIAMS and Eddie Heywood, her favorite accompanist was her teenaged brother Hersal. The death of Hersal from food poisoning in 1926 at age sixteen deeply affected Wallace. In 1928 her brother George was run down by a streetcar in Chicago and killed. Wallace had depended on both of her musical brothers to guide her musically as well as collaborate on song material. Their deaths may explain Wallace's failure to record for two years in the late 1920s.

In 1929 Wallace was put under contract with RCA/Victor records. She recorded four sides, yet only two were issued—"I'm a Mighty Tight Woman" and "You Gonna Need My Help." She had recorded her composition "Mighty Tight Woman" with Hersal on piano first for Okeh in 1926. On the RCA recording Wallace played piano as well as sang and was accompanied by Natty Dominique on cornet, HONORE DUTREY on trombone, and JOHNNY DODDS on clarinet.

By 1932 Wallace's career had faded. Not only were her composer brothers gone but the recording industry and popular music had also changed with the onset of the Great Depression. Songwriters were no longer writing blues with the same tempo, style, or rhythmic feel. Her husband and family church became her primary interests. In Detroit Wallace devoted her talent to the Leland Baptist Church, where she sang, played organ, and wrote religious hymns. Her husband died in 1936. In the 1940s Wallace became the guardian of her niece Hociel's three orphaned daughters.

Occasionally, she performed her blues repertoire in Detroit, sometimes accompanying herself on piano. In 1945 she released "Bedroom Blues" on Mercury Records. Although her performance was excellent, the record did not sell well, and Wallace slipped back into obscurity. She recorded "Fine Arts" in 1959 on the Detroit label, but it also was not successful. In 1966 old friend and fellow blues singer VICTORIA SPIVEY encouraged Wallace to come out of "retirement" and try performing in the folk-blues festivals that were becoming popular around the country. The pair worked together successfully on the folk and blues circuit. At sixty-eight years of age Wallace performed in Europe to a young, enthusiastic crowd and recorded on the Storyville label in Copenhagen, with ROOSEVELT SYKES and LITTLE BROTHER MONTGOMERY sharing piano duties. The 1966 recordings were essentially remakes of her old blues classics, and though Wallace lacked the upper range and vocal agility that she had when she was younger, these recordings helped bring her renewed popularity. Inspired by Wallace's own composition "Women Be Wise," included in the Storyville recordings, the American singer Bonnie Raitt helped stimulate interest among younger audiences in Wallace's vocal blues delivery.

In 1970 Wallace and Spivey recorded old blues standards that were issued on Spivey's own record label as *Sippie Wallace and Victoria Spivey*. Sometime that year Wallace became weak and supposedly had a mild stroke. However, neither this nor the beginnings of crippling arthritis deterred her from performing. In 1977, at age seventy-nine, Wallace performed in Lincoln Center's Avery Fisher Hall, still singing the blues.

In 1980 Wallace retired from her church job, but audience demand kept her performing. She made appearances on local and national television, and Detroit honored her with a "Sippie Wallace Day," which featured a blues concert. She also appeared at the 1980 and 1981 Kool Jazz Festivals. Wallace made her last recording in 1983 for Atlantic Records, titled *Sippie*, on which Raitt played slide guitar. The album was nominated for a 1983 Grammy Award, and in 1984 it won a W. C. HANDY Award for best blues album. Wallace continued to perform, accepting engagements at blues concerts in Germany and Denmark in 1986. Later that year Wallace died in Detroit.

As a young singer in the 1920s, Wallace possessed a lyrical quality and pleasant vibrato rather than the "growling" quality of some other notable female blues singers. Wallace sang from the heart and wrote songs from her life experiences; her vocal delivery captured audiences with its sincerity. She could sing and project in a bold and brassy way, but a sweet lilting quality could be detected in her early recordings. Sippie summed up her art by saying, "The Blues ain't nothin' but a message—it's when a woman tells a man that he done her wrong."

FURTHER READING

Bourgeois, Anna Strong. *Blueswomen: Profiles of 37 Early Performers, With an Anthology of Lyrics, 1920–1945* (1996).

Harrison, Daphne Duval. *Black Pearls, Blues Queens of the 1920s* (1988, 1990).

DISCOGRAPHY

O'Neal, Jim. "Sippie Wallace Discography," *Goldmine* (Nov. 1982).

This entry is taken from the *American National Biography* and is published here with the permission of the American Council of Learned Societies.

JAN SHAPIRO

Wallace, William "Onikwa" (15 Nov. 1938–1 Oct. 2008), photographer and film producer, was born in Chicago, Illinois, to William Howard Wallace, a chef and musician, and Margaret Shannon Wallace, a real estate broker. William was the younger of the couple's two children; his older sister, Jacquelyn, was born 9 August 1936. William attended Chicago's public schools, graduating from Betsy Ross Elementary in 1951 and Central YMCA High in 1955.

Wallace's uncle gave him a camera on his tenth birthday, triggering his fascination with photographic images. With money he earned from his paper route, Wallace bought his first developing kit the following year. Three years later his family moved to a new apartment, and their landlord, Anthony Haywood, was an accomplished freelance photographer with his own darkroom. Noticing Wallace's interest in the medium, Haywood took him under his tutelage. Guided by Haywood, Wallace developed the fundamental technical skills that prepared him for a career in photography. Drawn early to Chicago's vibrant music scene, specifically jazz and blues performances, he practiced by taking photos of classmates and friends who were aspiring musicians, shooting them routinely as they worked on arrangements during rehearsal sessions. He drew from these early lessons in later years when he photographed professional performers in clubs and other locations.

In 1958 Wallace married Johnnie Mae Dixon. They had two sons, William Howard Wallace III, born 30 January 1959, and Steven Craig Wallace, born 20 June 1961. Wallace was drafted into the army in 1959 and was stationed in Germany while the Berlin Wall was under construction. He served as an army intelligence specialist and was a regular contributor to the military newspaper *Stars and Stripes* and to the post information office. Honorably discharged in 1962 having completed his term of duty, he set up a professional photography practice, working from a small studio on Chicago's South Side. There he shot everything from portraits to commercial goods, doing photography for advertising campaigns for such local clients as Memphis Light, Gas and Water, WDIA-Radio, and grocers Hogue and Knott, and national companies including the Shaw Group, Lustrasilk, and Ultra Glow.

Wallace became increasingly interested in documentary subjects over the next five years, and by 1967 he was dividing his attention between making portraits of prominent jazz musicians and capturing the range of era-defining activities, especially those related to the civil rights movement. Involved in the movement as both a participant and an observer, Wallace documented firsthand such historic events as the JAMES MEREDITH March Against Fear in Mississippi in 1966 and the numerous demonstrations, rallies, and gatherings organized by the Student Nonviolent Coordinating Committee under the leadership of STOKELY CARMICHAEL. Wallace also was a regular contributor to the Nation of Islam's weekly newspaper *Mohammed Speaks*.

In the late 1960s the Poor People's Corporation in Mississippi formed Southern Media, an organization created to teach filmmaking to African Americans in an effort to increase their numbers in the industry. The program was launched under the leadership of Gere Martin, director of design at the San Francisco Art Institute. After moving to Jackson, Mississippi, to take part in the program, Wallace established a second residence in New York City so that he could also study filmmaking at the National Educational Television Minority Training Program.

Returning to Chicago in 1970, Wallace became the staff photographer for the African American weekly the *Chicago Defender*, a post he held for four years. During this period he also worked as a freelance documentary and feature filmmaker. The quality and significance of Wallace's work resulted in his receiving several notable awards, including the Best News Photograph of 1972 that he received for a pair of untitled photographs, one of a mother seated in a tight huddle with her five children around a small stove trying to stay warm and the second of a young teenage male being arrested for shoplifting as a group of kids watch. Both photographs were for the *Chicago Defender* and the award was presented by the National Newspaper Publisher's Association and the MARTIN LUTHER KING JR. Award from the National Association of Black Journalists.

Wallace took a position at MALCOLM X College in Chicago in 1974, where he spearheaded the development of state-of-the-art multimedia learning modules for a broad spectrum of subjects, notably reading and science—modules that could be tailored to meet individual student needs. His development team included graphic artists, writers, and academics.

Three years later Wallace moved to Memphis, Tennessee, to become the circulation manager and photographer for the *Tri-State Defender*. Subsequently he worked two and half years as a cameraman for WHBQ-13 in Memphis before taking the job as co-producer and cameraman for *Dateline Memphis*, a weekly public affairs program on WREG-TV. He wrote feature segments, shot film footage, and edited each show. Over the next five years Wallace successfully balanced the demands of weekly television production with those of being a freelance studio photographer, completing advertising and public relations work for the Shaw Group and Memphis's WDIA radio.

In 1984 Wallace returned to Chicago to establish his own business, BW Productions, a small film and television production company and photography studio in the city's Wicker Park neighborhood.

He secured jobs shooting stills for the DuSable Museum in Chicago, the McDonald's Corporation, Kraft Foods, the Independence Bank of Chicago, and others. At the same time, he continued to produce fine art photographs and participated in traveling group exhibitions mounted at the DuSable Museum, the Eastman Kodak Corporation in Rochester, New York, the Museum of Science and Industry in Chicago, and the Kenkeleba Gallery in New York. One year after returning to his hometown of Chicago to establish a full-time business, Wallace and Johnnie Mae divorced.

Cook County, Illinois, commissioned Wallace in 1988 to create a documentary photography portfolio of the day-to-day workings of the Public Defender's Office, from the courtroom to the county jail. The body of work produced was subsequently exhibited in every county courthouse in the state and constituted Wallace's first one-person show. In 1989 his work was included in a group exhibition organized by the Smithsonian Institution's Anacostia Museum in Washington, D.C., that traveled to more than fifteen venues across the United States. His work was also presented in group shows at the Ascension Gallery in Washington, D.C., at the Art Institute of Chicago, at the Graystone International Jazz Museum in Detroit, and at the first-ever Jazz McDonald's restaurant in Detroit.

Maintaining a professional interest in video, film, and television production, Wallace secured assignments that took him to war-torn Liberia in West Africa, the Navajo reservations and pueblos of America's Southwest, resettled Hmong communities in Minnesota, and the temple of a Vodun priestess in New Orleans. In addition he produced corporate films for the BP Amoco Oil Company and created a feature-length documentary on kickboxing called *Iron Thunder* (originally released as *Contemporary Gladiator*). He also worked with director Euzhan Palcy on the feature film *Wings Against The Wind*, the story of black female aviator BESSIE COLEMAN, in 1999.

Over a forty-year period, his photographs appeared in the *Chicago Defender*, *Globe*, *Commercial Appeal*, *Indigo*, and *Jam Sessions* newspapers and in *Ebony*, *People*, *Savoy*, *Jet*, *Women's Wear Daily*, *Home Furnishings Daily*, and other magazines. In addition he was producer and cameraman for *Catch the Spirit*, a weekly program for the United Methodist Church, and worked for several PBS television productions, including *Proudly We Serve: The Men of the U.S.S. Mason*, for the U.S. Navy Memorial and Destroyer Escort Historical

Foundation; *Yanks in Ireland*, a documentary about American soldiers in Ireland; *The Life and Times of Harold Washington*; and *Marriage—Just a Piece of Paper*. He also directed *Images of Life, Vision of Hope* for United Methodist Communications, served as the director and cameraman for the recording artist Charles Fambro's *River 2001*, and was cameraman for *Crucifixion* for the Lutheran Choir of Chicago.

In 2005 the Creative Arts Foundation in Chicago mounted an exhibition of Wallace's photographs. His images of MILES DAVIS, SUN RA, and PHAROAH SANDERS were among the photographs in the group exhibition Original Acts: Photographs of African American Performers in the Paul R. Jones Collection that traveled to four U.S. cities between 2002 and 2004. His photographs are in the permanent collections of the Schomburg Center for Research in Black Culture in New York and of the Paul R. Jones Collection at the University of Delaware. He died in 2008.

FURTHER READING

Amaki, Amalia. *Original Acts: Photographs of African American Performers* (2002).

Amaki, Amalia, ed. *A Century of African American Art: The Paul R. Jones Collection* (2004).

AMALIA K. AMAKI

Waller, Fats (12 May 1904–15 Dec. 1943), pianist, organist, singer, and composer, was born Thomas Wright Waller in New York City, the fourth of five surviving children of Edward Waller and Adeline (maiden name unknown). Edward was a Baptist lay minister, and one of young Thomas's earliest musical experiences was playing harmonium for his father's street-corner sermons. Thomas's mother was deeply involved in music as well, and the family acquired a piano around 1910. Although Waller had formal musical instruction during his formative years, he was largely self-taught and indulged in a lot of musical experimentation. Thomas's development as a jazz pianist really began in 1920, when, upon the death of his mother, he moved in with the family of the pianist Russell Brooks and then with the Harlem stride piano master James Price Johnson. Like his pianist contemporaries, Waller had learned some aspects of ragtime and jazz style from studying the player piano rolls of masters such as Johnson. Now his instructional experience consisted of sitting at one piano while Johnson sat at another. Johnson's earliest impression of Waller was that he "played with fervor" but that "he didn't have any swing then" (Peck, 20). At the time, young Thomas was playing quite a bit of organ and had not developed the propulsive and difficult stride left hand required of the jazz piano style of the day. Long hours of practice, association with Johnson and other stride masters, and formal studies with the pianist Leopold Godowsky and the composer Carl Bohm at Juilliard honed Waller's skills.

By 1922 Waller had embarked on a busy career cutting piano rolls and playing theater organ at the Lincoln and Lafayette theaters. In that same year he made his debut solo recording for the Okeh label with "Muscle Shoals Blues" and "Birmingham Blues." He also began accompanying a number of vaudeville blues singers, including Sara Martin and ALBERTA HUNTER. In 1923, through an association with the New Orleans songwriter CLARENCE WILLIAMS, Waller launched his own songwriting career with the publication and recording of "Wild Cat Blues."

In the mid-1920s many of Waller's instrumental compositions were recorded by the prominent FLETCHER HENDERSON orchestra, including "Henderson Stomp," which featured a brief sixteen-bar solo by Waller as guest pianist that demonstrated his muscular technique and innovative ascending parallel tenths in his left hand. Henderson also recorded Waller's "Stealin' Apples" and an overblown parody of the Paul Whiteman Orchestra called "Whiteman Stomp." During this time Waller began his association with the lyricists Spencer Williams and ANDY RAZAF. With Razaf, Waller wrote his most enduring songs, those included in the musicals *Keep Shufflin'* (1928) and *Hot Chocolates* (1929). *Hot Chocolates*, which premiered at Connie's Inn in Harlem, moved to Broadway within a month. "Ain't Misbehavin'," a song from that show, was a signature vehicle for CAB CALLOWAY and was largely responsible for propelling the singing career of LOUIS ARMSTRONG.

Waller became a star entertainer in his own right. His large physical dimensions—which earned him the nickname "Fats"—his wit, and his extroverted personality made him a comic favorite to millions. While many fans and critics saw Waller as a mere buffoon, they failed to grasp the true genius of his humorous presentation. Often given uninspired hack songs to record, Waller transformed the material into successful performance vehicles that simultaneously offered veiled, biting commentary. Through his musical and comic ingenuity, he chided pompous, high-brow society in the song "Lounging at the Waldorf" and tainted the glib romantic sentiment of Billy Mayhew's "It's a Sin to Tell a Lie" by modifying the lyric to "If you break my heart, I'll break your jaw, and then I'll die." Much like the interlocutors of minstrelsy, he used pompous, complex word replacements, such as "your pedal extremities are colossal" in place of "your feet's too big." Waller was also able to diffuse overt racist expressions in songs like "Darktown Strutters' Ball" by referring to it as "Sepia Town."

Waller had a long-running relationship with Victor Records dating back to 1926 and had an exclusive contract with them by 1934. He recorded prolifically with his own ensembles, Fats Waller and His Rhythm, and costarred with and accompanied other artists. In addition to an exhausting and ultimately fatal road tour schedule, he had his own regular radio program on WOR in New York (1931) and WLW in Cincinnati (1932–1934). He made four "soundies," song-length music videos on film that were shown in nickelodeon arcades, and appeared in three full-length films, *King of Burlesque* (1935), *Hooray for Love* (1935), and *Stormy Weather* (1943), costarring LENA HORNE, BILL "BOJANGLES" ROBINSON, KATHERINE DUNHAM, the Nicholas Brothers, and EDDIE "ROCHESTER" ANDERSON.

Fats Waller's ultimate contribution to music was as a pianist. Behind the comic exterior was an uncompromising and deeply gifted keyboard artist. His most sublime piano performances were recorded in a series beginning in 1929 that included "Handful of Keys," "Smashing Thirds," and "Numb Fumblin'." These pieces continued the two-fisted, swinging, and virtuoso solo style developed by James P. Johnson and others, but they also showcased Waller's own innovations, such as a graceful melodic sense and gliding walking tenths in the left hand that presaged modern swing. His influence can be heard in almost all the swing pianists who followed him, including COUNT BASIE. Waller had a love and deep knowledge of classical music, especially Bach, and in 1928 he was the soloist premiering in JAMES P. JOHNSON's *Yamekraw*, a concert work for piano and orchestra performed at Carnegie Hall. In London in 1939 Waller ventured into longer compositional forms with his *London Suite*, which was orchestrated and recorded by the Ted Heath Orchestra in 1950. Waller continued to record jazz, blues, and popular songs on his beloved pipe organ and was the first prominent artist to showcase the new Hammond electric organ in the 1930s.

In 1943 Waller's overweight condition and indulgences in food, tobacco, and liquor, combined with the exhausting pace of his career and several personal crises, including an alimony liability to Edith Hatchett, his wife of 1920–1923, that dogged him all his adult life, finally caught up with him. On a train returning to the East Coast from Hollywood after filming *Stormy Weather*, Waller died in his sleep somewhere around Kansas City. He was thirty-nine years old.

FURTHER READING

Hadlock, Richard. *Jazz Masters of the Twenties* (1965; repr. 1988).

Kirkeby, Ed. *Ain't Misbehavin': The Story of Fats Waller* (1966; repr. 1988).

Machlin, Paul S. *Stride: The Music of Fats Waller* (1985)

Peck, Seymour. "The Dean of Jazz Pianists," *PM*, 27 Apr. 1945: 20.

Shipton, Alyn. *Fats Waller: The Cheerful Little Earful* (2002).

Waller, Maurice, and Anthony Calabrese. *Fats Waller* (1977).

DISCOGRAPHY

Posnak, Paul, comp. *The Great Piano Solos 1929–1941* (1998).

"Thomas Wright 'Fats' Waller" in *Performances in Transcription 1927–1943*, comp. Paul S. Machlin, Music of the United States of America series, vol. 10 (2001).

DAVID JOYNER

Waller, John Louis (12 Jan. 1853–13 Oct. 1907), politician and foreign service officer, was born in New Madrid County, Missouri, the son of Anthony Waller and Maria (maiden name unknown), household slaves of Marcus S. Sherwood. Early in the Civil War, Union troops relocated Waller's family to Inka, Iowa, where his father was able to acquire a small farm. However, they lived in such poverty that his father hired John out to a local farmer at the age of twelve to help support the family. To John's good fortune, his employer encouraged literacy and allowed him to begin formal education in a rural schoolhouse in 1863. With the aid of citizens in nearby Toledo, Iowa, he was then able to gain admission to the local high school in 1867, graduating around 1870. At about this time he began to support himself by working as a barber, a trade he was also to pursue intermittently in later years when necessary. He married Amelia Lewis (date unknown); they divorced in 1876.

Waller enrolled at Cornell College in Mount Vernon, Iowa, in 1871 but had to abandon his studies again to help his family. In 1874 Waller began legal studies through the encouragement of Judge N. M. Hubbard of Cedar Rapids, who gave Waller free access to his personal library. In 1877 Waller was admitted to the Iowa bar and in 1878 to the Kansas bar, among the first of his race in both instances.

Seeking to assume leadership of the blacks who were then migrating to Kansas from the South in what was called "the great exodus of 1879 to 1892," Waller spent the next decade in Leavenworth, Lawrence, Topeka, and Kansas City, Kansas. He practiced law when the rare clients for a black lawyer appeared, became active in politics, and published two newspapers that promoted the cause of civil rights for blacks and furthered colonization schemes for frontier areas in Kansas, Oklahoma, Nebraska, and other western states. In 1879 Waller married Susan T. D. Bray, a widow with two children; they had four more children. In 1882 he and his wife began publishing a weekly newspaper, the *Western Recorder*, which lasted almost three years. His second newspaper venture was the *American Citizen*, launched in 1888 in Topeka with his cousin Anthony Morton and his brother L. J. Waller, who was managing editor.

Aware of the access to privilege that the Republican Party afforded selected African Americans in this era, by 1880 Waller had become a member of the Douglas County Republican central committee and of the Kansas state central committee. In 1883 he was elected to the Lawrence Board of Education. In the late 1880s he became a noted orator and a leading Republican campaigner, helping to ensure that the black vote, numbering some ten thousand at the time, would remain behind Republican candidates. As additional rewards, he was elected assistant sergeant at arms in the state house of representatives in 1887, was chosen as a Republican elector for Kansas in 1888, and was chosen as deputy county attorney in Topeka, Kansas, in 1889. However, his unsuccessful bid for election as state auditor at the Republican convention in 1890 convinced him that his prospects for further political advancement in the state were doubtful. He sold his interest in the *American Citizen* and concentrated his ambitions abroad.

At the time of his application to President Benjamin Harrison for a Foreign Service consular post in 1889, Waller was supported by all of the state's leading Republican organizations, the governor, and the Republican congressmen. Despite this, he failed to obtain one of the more prestigious posts. He was appointed instead as consul to Tamatave, Madagascar, where he served from February 1891 to January 1894. Remaining there afterward, he became embroiled in a bizarre international incident that resulted in his suffering eleven months of solitary confinement in a French prison. The French government, which was in the process of seizing control of Madagascar from 1894 to 1896, charged Waller through its military court of violating French postal regulations and transmitting military intelligence to the Malagasy, as the indigenous people of Madagascar are known, through one of his letters to his wife that detailed the conduct of the French forces as they took the island. His trial resulted in a sentence of twenty years of solitary confinement, for which he was transported to France.

The underlying purpose of France's action against Waller appears to have been to establish a basis for refusing to recognize a large land concession he had gained through close ties he had established with the reigning Malagasy government during his service. Waller had planned to exploit the 225 square miles he claimed, worth millions in rubber, mahogany, teak, and agricultural products, by leasing it out to establish an African American colony. The French invasion, however, discouraged potential investors. Among the attorneys who worked for Waller's release was the famous black educator and diplomat JOHN M. LANGSTON. Waller's release came only after resolutions from both houses of the U.S. Congress and vigorous activity on the part of the State Department. A condition of Waller's release from prison was that the U.S. government would not pursue his claims for any type of redress. His subsequent private appeals to the French government proved fruitless.

Returning to Kansas, Waller resumed his law practice and involvement in politics and also served as editor in chief of the *American Citizen* in 1896 and 1897. Responding to the Spanish-American War, in 1898 he helped organize Company C of the Twenty-third Kansas Volunteer Infantry Regiment, of which he was elected captain. He commanded it through its training and service in Cuba in 1898. After receiving an honorable discharge in 1899 in the United States, he returned to Cuba briefly to investigate its potential for his resettlement ideas. In July 1899 he published a letter through the Associated Press calling for emigration of three million blacks from the southern United States to Cuba, Puerto Rico, and the Philippines. For this purpose he proposed that Congress appropriate twenty million dollars to be repaid through duties on exports once the emigrants were settled and productive. Later the same year he announced formation of the Afro-American Cuban Emigration Society. Waller viewed emigration as the best solution to the racial problem in the United States and the best hope for economic prosperity for African Americans. Without emigration of part of the black population to alleviate white fears of being overwhelmed, he wrote, blacks would either be annihilated as the American Indians had or become amalgamated with whites, which he believed unfeasible. After all of his emigration projects failed, the repeated frustration of his own ambitions, and the lack of recognition of the contribution of black troops in the Spanish-American War, Waller became disillusioned with the Republican Party and supported the Democrat William Jennings Bryan in 1900. Waller died of pneumonia in Mamaroneck, New York.

FURTHER READING

Woods, Randall Bennett. *A Black Odyssey: John Lewis Waller and the Promise of American Life, 1878–1900* (1981).

This entry is taken from the *American National Biography* and is published here with the permission of the American Council of Learned Societies.

ALLISON BLAKELY

Waller, Odell (17 Feb. 1917–2 July 1942), sharecropper and laborer, was born Odell Jones in Pittsylvania County, Virginia, the son of Dollie Jones and a father whose name is not known. Shortly after Odell was born, his mother requested that her oldest sister, Annie, and her husband, Willis Waller, become his adoptive parents. After marrying Carl G. Harris, Dollie moved to Logan, West Virginia, leaving her sister and brother-in-law to raise the child. Initially the Wallers owned a twenty-five-acre farm near Gretna, Virginia, and co-owned a wheat binder, which they occasionally allowed other farmers to use. Because Odell had to help the Wallers farm, he withdrew from high school at age sixteen, completing only the third year.

While land ownership assigned the Wallers an economic status more secure than that of many of their neighbors—black and white—the Depression years engendered endless toil and struggle. When Willis Waller died in April 1938, Annie could not pay his debts, thereby causing mortgage foreclosure and the reduction to tenant status for herself and Odell. In January 1939 Annie and Odell became sharecroppers for Oscar Davis, a forty-six-year-old white tenant farmer beset with myriad misfortunes, including marital problems, pride, racial bias, and economic deprivation. That same month Waller married a woman named Mollie, whose maiden name is not known.

When Annie and Odell Waller began share-cropping for Davis, they lived in a shanty on his property. In exchange for working the corn, wheat, and tobacco crops, Davis promised them half of the tobacco crop and one-fourth of the corn and wheat. In January 1940, however, the Agricultural Adjustment Administration (AAA) dramatically reduced Davis's tobacco acreage allotment, motivating Davis to pocket the AAA reduction-acreage money and to make draconian cuts in the Wallers' tobacco shares. Although they pleaded for more tobacco acreage, Davis resisted their pleas, forcing Waller to work as a laborer for an electric contractor in Baltimore, Maryland, from April to July 1940.

In Waller's absence Annie and Mollie remained in Davis's shanty and worked the crops, including their own vegetable garden. In addition, Annie agreed to care for Davis's ailing mother for $2.50 per week. When Annie requested pay after three weeks of care, Davis reneged and also rejected Annie's compromise of a half sack of fertilizer in place of the money. Angered and frustrated, Annie refused to work tobacco, but Davis responded by having Annie and Mollie evicted, allowing them to tend only their vegetable garden. Nonetheless, the eviction did not usurp Annie's rights to her shares of the crops. In fact, Davis used Annie's wheat binder to harvest the wheat crop, but he balked when she requested her share.

The news of Davis's obstinacy brought Waller back to Pittsylvania County. On 15 July 1940, Waller and three other companions, including Annie, drove to Oscar Davis's house in hopes of reclaiming the Wallers' share of wheat. Within minutes of arrival, Waller requested his share of the wheat, drew a handgun from his pocket, fatally wounded Davis, and fled via Halifax County, Virginia, and New Jersey to Columbus, Ohio, where on 2 August 1940 he was extradited to the Chatham jail in Pittsylvania County. On 16 September the grand jury indicted Waller for murder, and his trial was scheduled to begin three days later.

The Odell Waller trial, like the SCOTTSBORO BOYS trial, which intersected it, reexposed the polarization, pain, and complexity of class, racial, religious, power, privilege, gender, and political issues in the South. And like the Scottsboro Boys, Odell Waller, one of thousands of impoverished black men, would become a symbol, metaphor, and martyr for causes beyond his grasp and life.

During the trial Waller's defense argued that fear and self-defense motivated the shooting, while Davis's family and the prosecution claimed premeditated murder, although witnesses on both sides presented inconsistent testimonies. Waller's first attorney, Thomas H. Stone, a Virginian, argued vehemently that Waller did not have a jury of his peers, since the jury consisted of all whites who had paid poll taxes, voted, and employed sharecroppers. Stone contended that payment of poll taxes seemed a prerequisite to voting and to jury duty, thus systematically excluding people in Waller's class from the political process and making them vulnerable to a class of persons without empathy for sharecroppers, since, in general, sharecroppers were too poor to pay poll taxes. Stone argued further for a change in venue, sensing that Jim Crow laws and attitudes in Pittsylvania County would render the trial a mockery.

To no one's surprise, presiding judge James Turner Clement quickly rejected all defense arguments. Stone's interjection of a rumor that Clement had been overheard predicting a guilty verdict for Waller did not endear him to the judge. Perhaps even more compromising was Stone's nebulous affiliation with the Revolutionary Workers League (RWL) and the Workers Defense League (WDL). The former was falsely connected to communism but given to vitriolic language, and the latter was sincerely engaged in raising funds for and defending Waller. The trial concluded in less than a day; the case went to jury in September 1940, and the jury returned in under an hour with a verdict of guilty on first-degree murder charges and a recommendation of a death sentence. Judge Clement sentenced Waller to die in the electric chair in Richmond on 27 December 1940.

The black community and the WDL expressed dismay and astonishment at the verdict and sentence, but no WDL member conveyed more consternation than PAULI MURRAY, the black activist, feminist, lawyer, priest, and poet. At the request of the WDL, Murray, joined by Annie Waller, traveled the country, eliciting funds for legal fees and informing the public about the travesty of justice manifested by the Waller case. No one disputed that Waller had killed Davis, but many denied that the act had been premeditated and deserved death. In fact, many deep-thinking citizens—black and white—perceived both Waller and Davis as victims of poverty and class war. Murray took the Waller case to Dr. LEON A. RANSOM of the Howard University law school and to THURGOOD MARSHALL at the national office of the NAACP. While they provided moral support and advice, they could not offer money, as the NAACP had already extended support to four young black men who had been accused of raping a white waitress.

Because of Murray's diligence and commitment, the WDL managed to garner sufficient legal fees to win a 4 March 1941 stay of execution from Virginia Governor James H. Price, creating time to pursue a writ of error from the Virginia Supreme Court of Appeals. With Murray's assistance, the attorney John F. Finerty, a member of the WDL's National Executive Board, navigated the complex frustrations of negative court decisions, stays of execution, resentences, reprieves, and denials of petitions to commute Waller's sentence to life in prison.

In spite of thousands of letters from prominent citizens, such as First Lady Eleanor Roosevelt, President Franklin Roosevelt, Pearl Buck, and A. PHILIP RANDOLPH, Odell Waller died in the electric chair in the state prison in Richmond, Virginia, at 8:30 a.m. on Thursday, 2 July 1942. His wife, Mollie, did not attend his funeral. A. Philip Randolph had planned a massive protest march in New York City, but barely five hundred protesters emerged.

Waller's death may have led to the U.S. Supreme Court's striking down of the Virginia poll tax in *Harper v. Virginia Board of Elections* (1966), ironically invoking the same arguments mounted by the attorneys Stone and Finerty twenty-four years earlier in Waller's defense. Yet there may be subtler significance to Waller's brief life and brutal death. In his dying statement, he wrote eloquently and profoundly: "[H]ave you ever thought Some people are alowed a chance over & over again then there ar others are alowed little chance some no chance at all when a fellow accident falls don't get one him with both feet help him up and when he see another ditch he will walk around it and advise others of the place so they can seen it" (Sherman, 190).

FURTHER READING

Murray, Pauli. *Pauli Murray: The Autobiography of a Black Activist, Feminist, Lawyer, Priest, and Poet* (1987).

Sherman, Richard B. *The Case of Odell Waller and Virginia Justice, 1940–1942* (1992).

FLOYD OGBURN JR.

Walley, Augustus (10 Mar. 1856–9 Apr. 1938), former slave, Buffalo Soldier, and Medal of Honor recipient, was born in Reisterstown, Maryland. Nothing is known of his family or early life. Walley worked as a general laborer and handyman before enlisting in the U.S. Army. He was shipped west and ordered to join Troop I of the Ninth U.S. Cavalry Regiment in 1878. Private Walley quickly established himself as a reliable and trustworthy soldier, as well as an impressive marksman. He would distinguish himself in the last of the Apache Wars during the 1880s when he became one of twenty-three black soldiers to receive the Medal of Honor for his service in the Indian Wars.

In July 1881 the Apache Indian warrior Nana led the remnants of the legendary Victorio's band of Apache fighters on a campaign to oust white settlers from eastern New Mexico. In a series of raids on the Texas and New Mexico border, Nana's raiders killed nearly a dozen civilians and absconded with or destroyed a substantial number of horses and cattle. Company I, Ninth Cavalry, was stationed at Fort Craig, New Mexico, when they were ordered into the field in pursuit of Nana. While they were encamped near the Cuchillo Negro Mountains on 16 August 1881, a Mexican rancher stumbled into their camp and reported that a group of Apache Indians had attacked his ranch and killed his wife and children. Lieutenant George Burnett quickly organized a detachment of fifteen soldiers, including Walley, to pursue the band of Indians. Reaching the abandoned ranch a few hours later Burnett and his detachment buried the mutilated bodies of the rancher's wife and three children. They picked up a few Mexican ranch hands who volunteered to form a posse to assist in the pursuit of the Apache. Burnett once again set out in pursuit of the raiders, who were headed for cover in the Cuchillo mountain range. However, instead of fleeing high into the mountains, the Indians carefully prepared an ambush along Cuchillo Negro Creek. Sensing a trap Burnett broke his small command into three sections with himself leading a few soldiers in the center and the Mexican posse on the left. His right wing was led by a veteran first sergeant named Moses Williams. As the three detachments approached Cuchillo Negro Creek the Indians opened fire from long range, pinning down Burnett's command under a hail of bullets. Instead of a handful of raiders the men of the Ninth Cavalry found themselves facing some forty to sixty veterans of the Victorio campaign. Burnett ordered his detachment to withdraw and link up with the rest of Company I, but in the confusion and noise four soldiers failed to hear the command. The raiders saw their opportunity to wipe out these unfortunate troopers and moved to cut them off. Two of the soldiers were seriously wounded and unable to move as a result of the heavy fire from the warriors. Recognizing the peril of these men Burnett gathered two volunteers, Williams and Walley, and charged forward to assist the trapped men. Walley rode through a hail of bullets to the most forward wounded man and dismounted. He dragged, pulled, and pushed the wounded soldier onto his horse before jumping on to steady the soldier and riding back to the positions held by Company I. Miraculously Walley was unhurt.

In recognition of Walley's bravery and coolness under fire Burnett recommended him for the Medal of Honor. Two other black soldiers were also recommended for commendation for their actions in the foothills of the Cuchillo Mountains. On 1 October 1890, Walley received the Medal of Honor.

Walley continued his exemplary service in the army and reenlisted several times with the Ninth and Tenth U.S. Cavalry. He rose steadily in rank, and in 1898 was ordered to Cuba with the Tenth as a first sergeant. Walley soon found himself once again in heavy combat. Shortly after the Tenth Cavalry and other army units in the expeditionary forces landed in Cuba, they were ordered to move toward the city of Santiago. The first significant battle of the campaign (that also featured the famous assault on San Juan Hill) was the Battle of Las Guasimas, Cuba, which took place 24 June 1898. The First U.S. Cavalry took heavier fire than had been anticipated from Spanish Regulars, well entrenched and heavily armed, and the regiment quickly found itself pinned down. The Tenth was ordered up in support and while under fire a Major Bell was twice severely wounded. As he had done in 1881 Walley charged forward in a brave and selfless attempt to save a wounded comrade. He and another officer were able to drag Bell to safety. In after-battle reports Walley was highly praised by the officers present, who commended his coolness under fire, bravery, and ability to make quick decisions.

Walley continued to serve with the Tenth Cavalry Buffalo Soldiers during the Cuban occupation before his regiment was reassigned to the Philippines for combat against the insurgents. He served in the Philippines occupation for nearly three years before returning to the United States and retirement from Company E, Tenth U.S. Cavalry Regiment, in 1907. Walley's distinguished military career spanned twenty-nine years. Perhaps missing the West of his early military service, Walley spent several years in Montana supplementing his retirement by working odd jobs. In May 1918 Augustus Walley volunteered for active duty to support his country during World War I. Deemed too old for active military service Walley was instead assigned to support work as a first sergeant in the Sanitary Corps at Camp Beauregard, Louisiana. He served for nearly a year before again retiring in March 1919. This time Walley returned home to Baltimore, Maryland, where he lived quietly until his death at the age of eighty-two.

FURTHER READING

Information regarding Walley's service is available from the Records of the Adjutant General's Office, United States Regular Army Returns, Ninth Cavalry, 1881–1883 (Record Group 94). National Archives and Records Administration Building, Washington D.C.

Kenner, Charles L. *Buffalo Soldiers and Officers of the Ninth Cavalry, 1867–1898* (1999).

Leckie, William H., and Shirley A Leckie. *The Buffalo Soldiers: A Narrative of the Black Cavalry in the West* (2003).

Schubert, Frank N. *Black Valor: Buffalo Soldiers and the Medal of Honor, 1870–1898* (1997).

Trask, David. *The War With Spain in 1898* (1997).

MICHAEL F. KNIGHT

Walls, Jesse (1791–c. 1870), a sailor who fought in the War of 1812, was a participant in the decisive Battle of Lake Erie, serving under Commodore Oliver Hazard Perry. Walls, his last name also given as "Wall" in some accounts, was a native of Pennsylvania and probably freeborn, but nothing is known of his early life. He may have been a resident of Erie, Pennsylvania, when the War of 1812 began, and his military service commenced by 1813.

Although Jesse Walls's military service is not recorded in any official records, the documents for this time period, such as ship's crew and prize lists, are far from complete; indeed, it is this lack of documentation that has often served to obscure the role that African Americans played in the War of 1812, a conflict often described as America's second war for independence. In fact, black soldiers and sailors, men like Walls, JOHN DAVIS, HANNIBAL COLLINS, and CYRUS TIFFANY, were extremely important in manning naval and privately armed ships, composing anywhere from 10 to 20 percent of their crews. Many black sailors served on regular merchant ships prior to the war and were vital to America's maritime commerce. When the war broke out, commerce on the high seas ground to a halt and many sailors, black and white alike, were soon unemployed. As a result, many of these men, surely motivated by a combination of patriotism and economic necessity, sought to join in the fight against Great Britain.

Whether Jesse Walls was a sailor by trade or perhaps was a soldier in a local militia unit that volunteered for sea duty is unknown, but by August 1813 he was a fifer on the twenty-gun brig *Niagara*. This vessel, along with the flagship *Lawrence*, was one of the mainstays of Commodore Perry's newly formed Lake Erie squadron and was built and launched at Erie, Pennsylvania, in the spring of 1813. Walls may have been a local recruit for the *Niagara*, but it is also possible that he was part of several drafts of men, sailors and soldiers alike, sent to man Perry's fledgling fleet. Interestingly, when Perry first took over the Lake Erie command, he found his force undermanned and begged for more men from his superior in overall command of naval operations on the Great Lakes, Isaac Chauncey. After much wrangling and delay, Chauncey finally sent Perry 150 men from his Lake Ontario fleet. Perry quickly, and inaccurately as it turned out, judged these reinforcements to be of poor caliber, complaining to Chauncey that they "are a motley set, blacks, Soldiers, and boys," although Chauncey staunchly defended his actions, stating that some of the blacks in his squadron "are amongst my best men" (Altoff, pp. 36–37). Jesse Walls and his fellow sailors would soon prove their worth in battle by achieving one of the most important American victories in the entire war.

The Battle of Lake Erie took place on 10 September 1813 when Commodore Oliver Hazard Perry and his fleet sailed out of Put-In-Bay to confront an experienced British squadron. Perry led in his flagship *Lawrence*, while the *Niagara*, with Jesse Walls aboard, was supposed to sail next in line according to the commodore's battle plan. One can easily imagine that Walls, as a fifer, may have been busy piping a martial tune to inspire the brig's crew in the looming battle. However, the action did not proceed as Perry had planned, and the *Niagara*'s captain, whether out of cowardice or a misunderstanding of orders is unclear, held his ship back and it was the *Lawrence* that bore the brunt of the battle for two hours. After that time Perry's flagship was a wreck and had suffered severe casualties; the outcome of the battle was in the balance. Clearly the *Lawrence* could not continue the fight, so Perry boldly transferred his command to the *Niagara* while under heavy fire and sailed forth once more to battle the British fleet. Might Jesse Walls have even piped the commodore aboard, as was the naval custom of the day? In any event, the men of the *Niagara*, now led by the indomitable Perry, were equal to the task facing them, and although they endured heavy fire they succeeded in turning what looked to be a sure defeat into a stunning victory. When the battle was finally over, Perry's fleet had captured virtually the entire enemy fleet and by doing so swept the British from control of Lake Erie and the surrounding area.

After the War of 1812 the details of Jesse Walls's life are sparse. He likely resided in the Erie, Pennsylvania, area, although he is not listed in census records, and perhaps worked as a sailor. In the 1850 Federal Census Walls is listed as a resident of Erie's East Ward (as was fellow veteran JAMES BROWN) and living with his wife Almira and sons Luke (born 1835) and Isaac (born 1838). Luke Walls's occupation is listed as that of a sailor, no doubt inspired in part by his father's service, whereas Jesse Walls worked as a laborer. Walls subsequently came to the attention of historians of the Battle of Lake Erie when he attended the dedication ceremony of a statue of Oliver Hazard Perry at Cleveland, Ohio, in 1860 and is noted in one popular historical account of the War of 1812. Walls's name is also found on list of survivors of the battle compiled in 1882, which notes his death in Erie at an unknown date.

FURTHER READING

Altoff, Gerard T. *Amongst My Best Men: African-Americans and the War of 1812* (1996).

Lossing, Benson J. *The Pictorial Field-Book of the War of 1812* (1868).

GLENN ALLEN KNOBLOCK

Walls, Josiah Thomas (30 Dec. 1842 – 15 May 1905), Reconstruction politician and U.S. congressman, was born near Winchester, Virginia. His parents' names are unknown and Walls's public statements regarding his parents' status during slavery are contradictory. Quite possibly he was born the slave of Dr. John Walls, a Winchester physician, but his dark skin casts doubt on the premise that Dr. Walls was also his father.

In 1861 Josiah Walls was kidnapped by Confederate artillerymen and put to work as a servant. He was freed by Union troops during the battle of Yorktown in May 1862 and sent to Harrisburg, Pennsylvania, where he attended school for a year, his only known formal education. In July 1863 he enlisted in the Third Infantry Regiment, U.S. Colored Troops (USCT), and took part in that unit's siege of Batteries Wagner and Gregg near Charleston, South Carolina. After their fall, his unit was stationed in northern Florida. In June 1864 Walls was transferred to the Thirty-fifth Regiment,

USCT, in Picolata, Florida, where he served as a first sergeant and instructor of artillery.

When Walls left the army in October 1865, he settled in nearby Alachua County, finding work first as a lumberer and later as a teacher at the Freedmen's Bureau School in Archer. In 1868 he bought an 80-acre farm in Newnansville. In 1873 Walls embarked on three business ventures. He bought at a low price a former cotton plantation of almost 1,200 acres that had been confiscated from a Confederate general, on which he began raising oranges and tomatoes; he was admitted to the Florida bar (legal training was not a prerequisite for admission in this frontier state) and, with two other black lawyers, opened a law firm in Gainesville; and he purchased the *Gainesville New Era*. In his first editorial, Walls promised to promote "every legitimate and judicious effort to develop the resources of the county" and that the "wants and needs of the people of color will receive special attention." Walls's political career began in 1867, when he attended the state Republican convention as a delegate. In 1868 he served as delegate to the state constitutional convention and was elected to the lower house of the Florida legislature. The next year he was one of five freedmen elected to the twenty-four-member state senate. In 1870 he was elected to the state's lone seat in the U.S. House of Representatives in spite of the removal of voting restrictions from most whites and the intimidation tactics employed by white terrorists to keep blacks from the polls. His white Conservative Party opponent contested the results of this election and eventually was declared the winner by a slender margin, but not before Walls had served in the House for almost two years. In 1872 Walls was renominated and returned to Washington, and during the 1873 recess he served as mayor of Gainesville. He was reelected to Congress in 1874 and served for over a year before the results of this election also were overturned in April 1876. Denied his party's nomination that year by Republicans eager to gain support from white voters, Walls successfully ran for state senator, a position he held until his retirement from public life in 1879. He then returned to his farm in Alachua County, which by now included more than 1,500 acres and a sawmill. He attempted two political comebacks—first in 1884 when he ran for Congress as an independent and then in 1890 when he ran for state senator—but was decisively defeated both times. Despite these defeats, he continued to play a major part in state and local politics through his activities on the Alachua County Commission and School Board as well as important

Josiah Thomas Walls, U.S. Congressman from Florida, photographed between 1860 and 1875. (Library of Congress.)

posts on county and state GOP executive committees. He also served as a brigadier general in the Florida militia.

Walls was one of only fourteen blacks to serve in the House during Reconstruction. He was not a gifted orator and usually read his speeches from a prepared text. He made up for his lack of eloquence by working ceaselessly for the interests of his constituents. He introduced bills to fund the construction of a railroad from the Georgia border to Key West and to improve Florida's rivers and harbors. He also sponsored acts to build customhouses, courthouses, and post offices and to create seven new postal routes in Florida; to protect the state's infant fruit industry from foreign imports in the tariff of 1872; and to secure a land grant for a state agricultural college.

Walls spoke out persuasively in favor of a national education fund financed by the sale of federal public lands to augment state-supported public education, because he believed that "education is the panacea for all our social evils, injustices, and oppressions." By improving public education in the South, Walls hoped to provide black children with the means of advancement while providing poor white children with opportunities to overcome nascent racial prejudice. He was particularly criticized by some of his supporters when he introduced a bill to lift the Fourteenth Amendment's restrictions on former prominent Florida Confederates (despite the fact that the bill was a quid pro quo rider to a civil rights bill) and again when he appointed to the naval academy the son of an ex-governor who was outspokenly opposed to black participation in politics and government. These moves, however, were consistent with his decision to "secure equal civil and political rights to all" and should not be interpreted as an attempt by Walls to curry white favor. He incurred the wrath of many white Republicans when at a southern black convention in 1871 he called on the GOP to nominate JOHN MERCER LANGSTON, the black orator and political leader, for vice president in 1872.

Walls was married twice. In 1864, while stationed at Picolata, he married Helen Fergueson, with whom he had his only child. When Helen Walls died in 1885, he married her cousin Ella Angeline Gass. After a frost ruined his crops in 1895, Walls moved to Tallahassee, where he became director of the farm at Florida Normal College, a position he held until his death there.

Walls was a political pragmatist who believed that whites and blacks must share power, and he worked for this ideal on the national, state, and local levels. Much of his political success can be attributed to the conciliatory stance he took toward white involvement in Reconstruction government, while at the same time quietly insisting on a major role in that government for blacks.

FURTHER READING

Klingman, Peter D. *Josiah Walls: Florida's Black Congressman of Reconstruction* (1976)

Richardson, Joe M. *The Negro in the Reconstruction of Florida, 1865–1877* (1965)

This entry is taken from the *American National Biography* and is published here with the permission of the American Council of Learned Societies.

CHARLES W. CAREY JR.

Walls, William Jacob (8 May 1885–23 Apr. 1975), African Methodist Episcopal Zion (AMEZ) bishop, civic leader, and author, was born in Chimney Rock, Rutherford County, North Carolina, the son of Hattie Edgerton and Edward Walls. His father died when Walls was only eight years old, leaving Hattie Walls, with the help of relatives and friends, to support and provide sufficient education for Walls and his three younger sisters. In 1899, at age fourteen, he entered the ministry. He was licensed to preach at the Hopkins Chapel AMEZ Church in Asheville,

North Carolina, and began as an evangelist. He was ordained as a deacon in 1903 and received full ministerial, or elder, orders in 1905. After attending Allen Industrial School in Asheville, he transferred to the AMEZ-supported Livingstone College in Salisbury, North Carolina, where he received a B.A. in 1908. Five years later he received a bachelor of divinity degree from the denomination's Hood Theological Seminary. During 1921–1922 he studied philosophy and journalism at Columbia University. While in New York City, Walls also studied the Bible at Union Theological Seminary, which was located near the university; twenty years later, in 1941, he attained an M.A. in Christian Education from the University of Chicago Divinity School.

From 1890 to 1905 Walls served as an evangelist, preaching throughout the nation. After 1905 he pastored churches in North Carolina and Kentucky. His pastorates in North Carolina were churches on the Cedar Grove Circuit in Cleveland from 1905 to 1907; Miller's Chapel, churches on the Sandy Ridge Circuit, and Moore's Chapel in Lincolnton from 1908 to 1910; and Soldier's Memorial, where he constructed a new church building, in Salisbury from 1910 to 1913. For the next seven years, from 1913 to 1920, Walls assumed the charge of the historic Broadway Temple AMEZ Church in Louisville, Kentucky, assisting the congregation to construct a new building in 1915. While pastoring in Louisville, Walls had the privilege of hosting the General Conference of the AMEZ in 1916, when the denomination first set an age limit for its bishops. This new rule effectively forced two sitting bishops into retirement, including Cicero Richardson Harris, who had assisted in Walls's ordination as an elder.

After serving as a chaplain in World War I, Walls won his denomination's election to the editorship of the official weekly news organ, the *Star of Zion*, in 1920. He tripled the circulation of the newspaper, placed it on a par with other major religious media, and lent his editorial voice in support of equal representation for the laity in the General Conference. After one term as editor he became the forty-second AMEZ bishop on 20 May 1924, serving actively in that capacity for forty-four years. In 1960 and 1964, before his permanent retirement from the active bishopric in 1968, his denomination recalled Walls from retirement for necessary episcopal service. Late in life Bishop Walls, at the age of seventy-one, entered his first and only marriage, to Dorothy L. Jordan, in 1956.

Walls was actively involved in ecumenical concerns within Methodism and Christianity in general, both before and after his elevation to the episcopacy. Among other things, he served as a delegate to the General Conference of the Methodist Episcopal Church, South, in 1918, to the General Conference of the Methodist Episcopal Church in 1928, and to the Ecumenical Methodist Conference during the 1921 to 1971 period. His involvement in non-Methodist ecumenical endeavors included the appointment of the president and war secretary to the American Clergyman's Commission to occupied Europe in 1947, the American Bible Society, the National Council of Churches, the World Council of Churches, the World Christian Education and Sunday School Convention, the United International Christian Endeavor Society, and the World Sunday School Association. Walls was a firm supporter of civil and human rights, and he was actively involved in the NAACP, the National Negro Business League, and Operation Breadbasket. As early as 1925 Walls staged a three-hour sit-in to protest waiters' refusal to serve him at the Union Railroad Terminal in Washington, D.C., because he would not remove himself to segregated seating. His civic and social activities included Phi Beta Sigma and Odd Fellow and Masonic memberships.

A member of the American Academy of Political Science, Walls was also a scholar, particularly on matters relating to race and the history of his denomination. Walls on one occasion wrote that he had particular interest in ancient, modern, and American history, especially the history of the AMEZ Church. He firmly believed that Christianity and the church were central as vehicles for blacks in Africa and the diaspora to attain full freedom, a viewpoint clearly reflected in his classic denominational history. He is best known for this massive and comprehensive work, *The African Methodist Episcopal Zion Church: Reality of the Black Church* (1974), which outlines AMEZ's involvement in issues of social justice from its earliest origins to the present. This work was compiled after his retirement from the episcopacy in 1968 and was commissioned by the General Conference, which appointed Walls the connectional historiographer and charged him with the responsibility of producing a comprehensive history of the AMEZ. Among other works, he authored *J. C. Price: Educator and Race Leader* (1943), about JOSEPH CHARLES PRICE, and a number of pamphlets, including *Pastorates and Reminiscences* and HARRIET TUBMAN. Walls contributed immensely to institutionalizing even further his concern for the history of the AMEZ Church and the African American people when

in the early 1960s he and his wife donated land to Hood Theological Seminary to be used as the site for a denominational archive. The building, the Walls Heritage Center, was dedicated in 1965. An indefatigable laborer on behalf of the AMEZ Church and Christianity, a civic leader, and an author, Walls left a profound legacy.

FURTHER READING

Walls's papers are at the Walls Heritage Center, Livingstone College, Salisbury, North Carolina.
Bradley, David Henry, Sr. *A History of the AME Zion Church, pt. 2, 1872–1968* (1970).
This entry is taken from the *American National Biography* and is published here with the permission of the American Council of Learned Societies.

SANDY DWAYNE MARTIN

Walrond, Eric (1898–1966), journalist and short-story writer, was born in Georgetown, Guyana, to a Guyanese father and a Barbadian mother who disappointed her landowning father by marrying below her class. Walrond lived in English- and Spanish-speaking Barbados with his parents until 1906, when his father deserted the family and his mother returned to her father's settlement near Black Rock in Barbados. Walrond's mother took her son to Panama in 1910, in a futile attempt to find her husband, who she thought had gone there to find employment in the newly opened construction of the Panama Canal. Walrond and his mother remained in Panama, settling in Colón, where Walrond's education in Spanish, first in public schools and then from 1913 to 1916 with private tutors, supplemented his earlier British schooling in Barbados and would form the rich understanding of Spanish culture he would later bring to his short stories.

Walrond's first job was as a clerk for the Health Department of the Canal Commission at Cristobal. He began work at the region's most important newspaper, the *Panama Star and Herald*, in 1916, where he filled the roles of general reporter, court reporter, and sportswriter at the paper. In 1918 Walrond emigrated to the United States, heading for New York City at the beginning of the explosively creative Harlem Renaissance. During the 1920s, Harlem became a national and international magnet for African Americans. The migration of southern blacks to the North continued, fueled by the increasing violence and narrowing opportunities in the South, and the lure of jobs, better education, and milder racism in the North. The next decade, which Walrond would spend in Harlem, would gain him recognition as one of the important writers of the Harlem Renaissance period.

Upon his arrival, Walrond intended to work at one of the many Harlem newspapers. When his attempts to find a position were unsuccessful, he decided to pursue his education. He studied for three years (1922 to 1924) at City College of New York and then from 1924 to 1926 he took creative writing courses at Columbia University. During these years, he worked odd jobs to support himself. Although his secretarial training helped him secure employment, his job searches brought him into contact with racism and discrimination on a scale he had not previously known in Panama and Barbados. These experiences would form the basis of much of his early writing. "On Being Black," his first story published in the United States, appeared in the *New Republic* in 1922, and it effectively re-creates the humiliations he experienced in his daily life in New York. It was in 1921 that Walrond reentered the world of journalism, when he became editor and co-owner of the black weekly the *Brooklyn and Long Island Informer*. His attraction to the vision of MARCUS GARVEY led him to leave that paper in 1923 to join Garvey's *Negro World* as associate editor. Walrond saw Garvey as the kind of political leader needed to combat the profound racism he had found in the United States.

Although he would become disaffected with Garvey, leaving him and the Universal Negro Improvement Association (UNIA) in 1925, during his three years with the UNIA Walrond wrote several articles on African American life for a number of periodicals and journals. He critiqued African American leaders BOOKER T. WASHINGTON, W. E. B. DuBOIS, and Garvey in "The New Negro Faces America" and examined migration in "The Negro Exodus from the South" (both in *Current History*, 1923). He explored Harlem in "The Black City" (the *Messenger*, 1924) and considered Garvey's popular appeal in a 1925 article in the *Independent*, titled "Imperator Africanus, Marcus Garvey: Menace or Promise?" When National Urban League leader and editor CHARLES S. JOHNSON invited him to leave *Negro World* and join him at *Opportunity*, Walrond's focus would move from journalism to fiction. The Urban League's periodical had been started in 1923 to provide more of a focus on cultural life than the NAACP's *Crisis*. It would initiate the literary contests that would not only encourage young talent like LANGSTON HUGHES, COUNTÉE CULLEN, and CLAUDE MCKAY but would also bring to Harlem budding writers such as HELENE JOHNSON, DOROTHY WEST, and ZORA NEALE HURSTON.

Walrond had already written and published short stories before he joined *Opportunity* in 1925 as business manager. In 1923, for example, four short stories had found their way into print: "Miss Kenny's Marriage," in September's *The Smart Set*, and "On Being a Domestic," "The Stone Rebounds," and "Cynthia Goes to the Prom"—all in *Opportunity*, respectively in August, September, and November. These early stories show Walrond's experimentation with realistic style and urban settings. The stories written between 1924 and 1927 are much more impressionistic and often treat life in the Caribbean; these are the works for which Walrond is remembered. In 1925, ALAIN LOCKE included Walrond's short story "The Palm Porch" in his landmark publication *The New Negro*. In 1926, the publication of *Tropic Death*, Walrond's collection of ten short stories, earned Walrond recognition as a master short-story writer and a central place in the Harlem Renaissance. In these ten stories, all set in the American tropics, he creates a lush natural world into which the aims of colonialism intrude, leaving its inhabitants culturally disoriented. The style, full of imagery, reveals Walrond's modernist, avant-garde approach, reminiscent of JEAN TOOMER's *Cane* and the poetry of ANGELINA WELD GRIMKÉ. Prominent Harlem Renaissance leaders and editors W. E. B. DuBois, CHARLES S. JOHNSON, JESSIE FAUSET, and Alain Locke celebrated Walrond's talent.

The information available on Walrond's life after he left Harlem in 1928 is quite sketchy. Following the success of *Tropic Death*, publishers Boni & Liveright gave him a contract for a book on the French involvement with the Panama Canal project. He continued to work at *Opportunity* until 1927 but published little. In 1928, Walrond was awarded both a John Simon Guggenheim Memorial Foundation Award and a Zona Gale scholarship at the University of Wisconsin. He left the United States permanently in 1928, book contract in hand, to conduct research in the Caribbean. With an extension of the Guggenheim grant, Walrond traveled through Europe, working on his manuscript, tentatively titled "The Big Ditch." Walrond lived for a considerable time in France as part of the African American community in Paris until 1931, sharing a studio with poet Countée Cullen. While in Europe, Walrond published a number of shorter pieces—articles and short stories in both Spanish and French magazines as well as in *The Black Man*, a Garveyite magazine, in 1932. After he made a short visit to his parents in Brooklyn in 1931, Walrond returned to France, to a small village outside Avignon. He lived the rest of his life in France and England, generally disappearing from the public eye. His book on the Panama Canal would remain unfinished.

When Walrond died in 1966 in London, England, he left behind questions about his personal life. It is known that he was twice married and had three daughters, Jean, Dorothy, and Lucille, but details about the identities of his wives and about marriage and birth dates are unknown. Walrond survives in WALLACE THURMAN's satirical novel about the Harlem Renaissance, *Infants of the Spring*, as the character Cedric Williams, "one of three Negroes writing who actually had something to say, and also some concrete idea of style." Indeed, his short fiction combines an impressionistic style with a keen, critical journalistic eye to bring a lush, yet bleak, Caribbean environment to vivid life. Walrond's voice speaks to the wide reach of the New Negro Renaissance from its center in Harlem out into the world.

FURTHER READING

Lewis, David Levering. *When Harlem Was in Vogue* (1981).

Parascandola, Louis J., ed. *Winds Can Wake Up the Dead: An Eric Walrond Reader* (1998).

MARY ANNE BOELCSKEVY

Walters, Alexander (1 Aug. 1858–2 Feb. 1917), African Methodist Episcopal Zion (AMEZ) bishop and social reformer, was born in Bardstown, Kentucky, the son of Henry Walters and Harriet Mathers, both of whom were slaves. He joined Bardstown's AMEZ Church in 1870 and studied in private schools there from 1866 to 1871, when he left to work in Louisville as a waiter. Walters completed his formal education in 1875, graduating as valedictorian of his Bardstown school. During a year as a waiter in Indianapolis, he studied theology with an AME pastor, was licensed to preach, and, in 1877, was appointed pastor of a newly organized AMEZ Church in the city. In 1877 Walters married Katie Knox, with whom he had five children. After she died in 1896 Walters married Emeline Virginia Bird; they had one child. When his second wife died in 1902 he married Lelia Coleman of Bardstown; they had no children.

Walters rose rapidly in the ranks of AMEZ pastors. He moved from appointments in Corydon, Cloverport, and Louisville, Kentucky, to San Francisco, California, and Chattanooga and Knoxville, Tennessee. Walters was first elected a delegate to his denomination's general conference in 1884, and in 1888 he became pastor of the prestigious Mother AMEZ Church in New York City. A year later he attended the World's Sunday School Convention in London, England, as a delegate of his denomination and was appointed general agent of its Book Concern. In 1892, at age thirty-four, Walters was elected to the episcopacy of the AMEZ Church. He is among the youngest men ever elevated to that denomination's office of bishops.

Walters was an active advocate for his race. In 1889 he and the journalist T. THOMAS FORTUNE called a meeting in Chicago, which organized the National Afro-American League to represent the interests of African Americans to the nation. It foundered in the depression of 1893, but five years later Walters persuaded Fortune to convene a meeting in Rochester, New York, to reorganize the league as the National Afro-American Council. Fortune presided at the meeting, but the conferees elected Walters as its president. When the council reconvened in Washington, D.C., later that year, a radical northern faction attacked BOOKER T. WASHINGTON and President William McKinley's administration for not defending the rights of the race. Walters's mediating address insisted that there could be no peace until black people were accorded equal rights but allowed that it would take time before that happened. He endorsed both industrial and higher education for his people and said literacy and property qualifications for the franchise were acceptable, if they were applied equally across racial lines. In short, said Walters, "Let us improve our morals, educate ourselves, work, agitate, and wait on the Lord."

Walters's interest in Africa took him to the London Pan-African Conference organized by Henry Sylvester Williams in 1900. Walters presided at the conference and was elected president of the Pan-African Association to promote unity among peoples of the African diaspora. From 1904 to 1908 he served as the nonresident AMEZ bishop of Africa. In 1910 he traveled to West Africa to reorganize his denomination's Cape Coast, West Gold Coast, and Liberia conferences. A year later Walters visited AMEZ congregations in Jamaica and Demerara. Because of responsibilities at home, he declined President Woodrow Wilson's offer to appoint him the U.S. minister to Liberia in 1915.

When W. E. B. DuBois broke with Booker T. Washington to organize black radicals for the civil rights struggle, he counted Walters as "leaning toward

Washington." By 1908, however, Walters was allied with DuBois and had joined the Washington, D.C., branch of the Niagara Movement. In January 1909 Walters, Mary White Ovington, Oswald Garrison Villard, William English Walling, and others discussed the need for a national biracial organization to defend the civil rights of African Americans. Their Call for a National Conference on the Negro outlined their grievances and summoned "believers in democracy" to a "discussion of present evils, the voicing of protests, and the renewal of the struggle for civil and political liberty." The conference chose Walters to serve on its Committee of Forty on permanent organization. When the second conference confirmed the Committee of Forty's recommendations, the National Association for the Advancement of Colored People (NAACP) was founded. Walters was chosen to serve on its national committee.

By 1908 Walters was convinced that the singular loyalty of his people to the Republican Party was no longer justified. After becoming a Democrat, he was named president of the National Colored Democratic League. In a personal letter to Walters during the presidential campaign of 1912, Democratic nominee Wilson assured him of "my earnest wish to see justice done" to African American citizens "in every matter, and not mere grudging justice, but justice executed with liberality and cordial good feeling." With that assurance, Walters campaigned vigorously for Wilson's election. He experienced a deep sense of betrayal when the Wilson administration appointed few African Americans to federal office and pursued a policy of racial resegregation throughout the government.

At the time of his death in New York, Walters was an officer of the Federal Council of Churches of Christ in America and of the United Society of Christian Endeavor and a trustee of both Howard University and Livingstone College. A tall, handsome man of light brown complexion, Walters had a commanding presence and was a gifted orator. His personal piety and liberal evangelical Christianity placed him among the foremost African American churchmen of his era.

FURTHER READING

Walters, Alexander. *My Life and Work* (1917).

Luker, Ralph E. *The Social Gospel in Black and White* (1991).

Mathurin, Owen C. *Henry Sylvester Williams and the Origins of the Pan-African Movement* (1976).

Walls, William Jacob. *The African Methodist Episcopal Zion Church* (1974).

This entry is taken from the *American National Biography* and is published here with the permission of the American Council of Learned Societies.

RALPH E. LUKER

Wamba, Philippe Enoc (3 June 1971–11 Sept. 2002), writer and editor, was born in Pomona, California, the son of Ernest Wamba dia Wamba, a professor of economic history, and Elaine Brown, a French teacher. His parents, who had met at the University of Western Michigan and married in 1966, had a bicultural marriage; Ernest had grown up in what is now the Democratic Republic of Congo (formerly the Belgian Congo, then Zaire), while Elaine was an African American from the Midwest, the daughter of a social worker and a research chemist. In his memoir, *Kinship: A Family's Journey in Africa and America* (1999), Philippe Wamba writes that by the time he was born his parents' marriage "was no longer an experiment in cross-cultural understanding" (*Kinship*, 45). Still, the rich complexities of life as an African and an African American were the source and the impetus of Wamba's own literary work.

Wamba's early childhood was spent mostly in the Boston area, where his father was on the faculty of Brandeis University, and where his older brother, Remy, died of leukemia in 1979. The following year, Wamba's father was offered a position teaching history at the University of Dar es Salaam in Tanzania, which he accepted. The family moved to the East African coastal city in 1980. There, Philippe later wrote, local children taunted him and his two younger brothers as *wazungu*, a Swahili word for outsider, non-African, even white, because the Wamba boys' American clothing and sneakers marked them as foreigners. It was at this point, Wamba writes, that he began to wonder about the sometimes painful stereotypes Africans and African Americans believe about each other, as well as the cultural commonalities and shared heritage.

In 1981 the family planned to travel to Zaire for the Christmas holiday; it was to be the first opportunity for the three Wamba sons to see their father's homeland and meet his family (the oldest son, Remy, had lived in Zaire as an infant, when their father was teaching at the university there). Ernest Wamba dia Wamba left for Zaire a week ahead of the rest of the family, because his vacation at the university began earlier than theirs did; when mother and sons arrived at the airport in Kinshasa, they were informed that he had been arrested by the Zairean regime of the dictator Mobutu Sese Seko. After five weeks in prison, where he was beaten and questioned about his writings and anti-Mobutu activism, the elder Wamba was detained in Kinshasa under a form of house arrest for a year. After two happy years in Tanzania, Wamba writes, his father's arrest and brutal treatment made him feel betrayed: "Africa was not a mystical, magical, and beautiful place, as I had thought; instead it was a place inhabited by evil and dangerous men—black men, at that—who had imprisoned and beaten my father and easily could have chosen to kill him. My naïve romance with Africa was over" (*Kinship*, 16).

In 1987 Wamba graduated from the International School of Tanganyika and left Tanzania to continue his studies in America. He attended the Armand Hammer United World College, a preparatory school for international students interested in history and world affairs, located in Montezuma, New Mexico. There he found an intimate, nurturing community where students commiserated about both the school's academic rigor and their own introduction or reintroduction to American racism (weekly shopping trips to nearby Las Vegas, New Mexico, featured regular verbal assaults from small-town whites and Latinos). Trips with an American cousin to Los Angeles shopping malls during vacations cemented Wamba's perceptions of the strange interplay between African and American black popular culture, where "Africa medallions and red-black-and-green beaded necklaces were favored fashion accessories" but also where his cousin's American friends, learning that he was from Africa, spoke to him as if he were "a deaf child" (*Kinship*, 213).

In 1989 Wamba entered Harvard College, where he elected the History and Literature concentration and wrote its first-ever senior thesis on African and African American studies. During his time at Harvard, Wamba writes in *Kinship*, he struggled to feel a part of some of the campus' black organizations, where racial solidarity could be forged around shameful American news events (for example, the Rodney King beating and Boston's notorious Charles Stuart murder case), but where, he often felt, African American students displayed a painful indifference to African issues. He found a home, he writes, in the Harvard African Students Association (HASA), with members who, like him, had both African and American ancestry and experiences.

After graduating with honors from Harvard in 1993, Wamba entered the Columbia University Graduate School of Journalism in New York, earning his master's degree in 1994. He worked in publishing as an editor at Frommer's, where he worked on travel books, and began writing *Kinship*. Essays on race, history, and personal experience appeared in the anthologies *Giant Steps: The New Generation of African American Writers* (2000, edited by his friend KEVIN YOUNG) and *Half and Half: Writers on Growing up Biracial and Bicultural* (1998). Wamba's work also appeared in publications such as *Transition* magazine, the *Daily News* in Dar es Salaam, and the *Weekly Journal* in London.

In the late 1990s Wamba's father became involved in Congolese politics as a freedom fighter seeking to establish a democratic government when the country's new leader, Laurent Kabila, emerged as yet another dictator after his overthrow of the Mobutu regime in 1997. Leading an armed faction called the Rally for Congolese Democracy, the elder Wamba left behind academia for a much harsher, more dangerous path, leading his son to worry not only for his safety for but the continent's future. The temptation to return was strong; he ends *Kinship* with an epilogue saying, "I sense it's time to go back home" (*Kinship*, 348).

It would be another three years before he got the opportunity. In 1999, the year *Kinship* was published, Wamba returned to Cambridge to helm Africana.com, an online venture initiated by Harvard's African American Studies chairman HENRY LOUIS GATES JR. The Web site was initially launched to promote a print and CD-ROM encyclopedia of the same name (Wamba had worked on an early prototype of the project), but under Wamba's leadership it evolved into a full-fledged online magazine. Devoted to exploring news and culture from all corners of the African diaspora, Africana.com featured reviews of books, movies, and music; columns on politics, culture, and lifestyle issues; and links to new stories from international sources.

Despite a decade spent living in the United States, Wamba's African identity was never far from him. "I'll dream in Swahili one night and English the next," he said in a 2000 interview in the *Boston Globe* (10 December 2000). In 2002 he received a fellowship from the Alicia Patterson Foundation to write a series of articles on African youth movements. Resigning his post at Africana.com, Wamba returned to Africa in April 2002, settling in Johannesburg with his fiancée, Marang Setshwaelo, and began his travels documenting the continent's hope. He died in a car accident in Kenya, where he had recently spoken with poor teenagers in the Nairobi slums. He was just thirty-one years old. Wamba was buried in Tanzania and was memorialized both there and in Cambridge, where Gates was among the speakers, saying that "Philippe lived on no man's hyphen." After his death, HASA formed an organization in Wamba's memory devoted to improving road safety in Africa, and the Department of African and African American Studies at Harvard endowed a prize in his name.

FURTHER READING

Kennedy, Randy. "His Father Is a Rebel Leader …," *New York Times*, 29 Aug. 1999.

Tuttle, Kate. "Tribute: Author, Editor, Activist Philippe Wamba, 1971–2002," *Black Issues Book Review* (1-Jan. 2003).

KATE TUTTLE

Ward, Aida (11 Feb. 1900–23 June 1984), singer and musical theater performer, was born Aida Mae Ward in Washington, D.C. Some sources give her birth year as 1903, but U.S. census records and passenger ship manifests say 1900. Her parents were Harry J. Ward and Susie D. Irving Ward. They married around 1899. Susie Irving Ward was born in Virginia around August 1880. Harry Ward was born March 1874 or 1875 in Cuba. He immigrated to the United States in 1880 or 1895 and became a naturalized citizen and a barber. Without naming the charges, the 1900 census lists him as a prisoner in D.C.'s United States Jail. It also records him as residing with his wife and daughter in the lodging house of his mother in law, Minnie Irving. Around 1902 Aida's brother Irving C. Ward was born. In 1910 Susie was working as a laundress and still living with her two children in her mother's lodging house. The 1910 census records Susie as married for eleven years, yet her husband is not listed as a member of the household. By 1930 she was married to South Carolina–born Simpson Wallace, a clerk in the Department of Commerce. As Susie Wallace she was known for supporting local charities and clubs.

Whatever difficulties her family may have experienced, Aida Ward graduated from M Street School (later Dunbar High School), where MARY CHURCH TERRELL and ANNA JULIA COOPER had taught. She also received voice instruction from the prominent classical singer LILLIAN EVANTI. Ward gave her first, and critically acclaimed, public concert at the Second Baptist Church, one of D.C.'s oldest black congregations.

By 1920 Ward had married Walter E. Gist and was living in New York City with him and their son Jerome, born there January 5, 1918. Walter Gist, born around 1894, worked as a dining car waiter. He apparently came from a South Carolina family transplanted to Buffalo, New York. During the early 1920s the couple separated. Aida Ward returned to D.C. and persuaded the initially skeptical Raymond Murray, owner of the Dunbar Theatre, that she deserved a chance as in-house pianist and organist. By 1923 she was back in New York City to pursue her musical career there. Walter Gist died in Buffalo around 1926. In 1929 Aida Ward publicly declared her engagement to Malcolm Thomas, who had worked with and befriended her at the Dunbar. It is uncertain whether they ever had a wedding. Ward briefly married, then divorced, a man named Edward Chavers. By 1936 Ward was married to Anderson Gilmer, a prosperous Detroit, Michigan, mortician who opened a business in New York City.

Aida Ward quickly succeeded in the black New York music scene. In 1923 she landed bit parts in the *Frolics* and sang with DUKE ELLINGTON and his band at the Hollywood Café, at Forty-Ninth and Broadway. The next year Lew Leslie, one of the first white producers to work with African Americans, hired her for the FLORENCE MILLS feature *Dixie to Broadway* and for later, acclaimed versions of the show in Paris and London. He also employed her at Harlem's Cotton Club, where she became legendary for outrageous pranks as well as for her musical talent. The young Dorothy Fields wrote three songs for a revue that debuted 4 December 1927. The opening night audience included Fields's collaborator James Mc Hugh, her whole family, including her parents, and notorious gossip columnist Walter Winchell, a family friend. As Fields later recounted, Ward did not sing the anticipated lyrics, but instead "belted out three of the most shocking, ribald, bawdy, dirtiest songs anyone had ever heard in the 1920s. I looked at McHugh, McHugh looked at me, my father didn't look at my mother; my brothers and sister looked down at their plates; and nobody dared look at Walter Winchell. My father said, 'You didn't learn those words home.' I said, 'I didn't write those words'" (Winer, p. 28).

Ward appeared in Leslie's *Blackbirds* revues with Mills starting in 1926. When Mills died suddenly, Ward served as her honorary pallbearer and filled in her role in *Blackbirds of 1928*. With this revue, Ward had a hit song, "I Can't Give You Anything But Love, Baby," which was penned, ironically, by Dorothy Fields. She starred in the enduring Broadway engagement of *Blackbirds* and continued to perform at the Cotton Club, Connie's Inn, and other venues throughout Harlem, sometimes with Duke Ellington or CAB

CALLOWAY. She had hits in 1931 with "Between the Devil and the Deep Blue Sea" and in 1932 with "I've Got the World on a String." Ward was one of the featured performers on the inaugural night of Harlem's Apollo Theater on 26 January 1934. The same year, she took the stage at Broadway's Beacon Theater with the white comedians Gracie Allen and George Burns, Jack Benny, and Milton Berle. During the 1930s and 1940s she frequently sang on the radio. Ward prospered financially as an entertainer, enough to buy a large house for her mother and grandmother in D.C. and to live with Anderson Gilmer in a comfortable apartment at 80 Saint Nicholas Place.

Soon after the end of World War II, Aida Ward left show business altogether to run a nursing home in Washington, D.C. She lived roughly half her life after the end of her musical career. A year after her son Jerome's passing, Aida Ward experienced a fatal bout of respiratory disease at age eighty-four. Her last residence was Capitol Heights, Prince Georges, Maryland. By then few remembered her as the vibrant contributor she was to the musical theater of the Harlem Renaissance and to the early days of radio. Yet she left behind a legacy of songs that many Americans of all races still knew and loved at the beginning of the twenty-first century, although frequently without remembering the dynamic performer who first introduced them to the public.

FURTHER READING

A sketch of Aida Ward as she appeared in *Blackbirds of 1928* can be found in the Robert Benney Collection of Original Drawings, *T-VIM 1984-005, Billy Rose Theatre Division, The New York Public Library for the Performing Arts.

Salamone, Frank A., and Cary D. Wintz. "Aida Ward," in *Encyclopedia of the Harlem Renaissance*, ed. Cary D. Wintz and Paul Finkelman (2004).

Smith, Jessie Carney. "Aida Ward," in *Notable Black American Women Book Two*, ed. Jessie Carney Smith (1996).

Winer, Deborah Grace. *On the Sunny Side of the Street: The Life and Lyrics of Dorothy Fields* (1997).

Obituaries: *Jet*, 16 July 1984;
Variety, 11 July 1984;
The Black Perspective in Music, Autumn 1984.

MARY KRANE DERR

Ward, Calvin Edouard (19 Apr. 1925–), concert organist, music theorist, and music educator, was born in Atlanta, Georgia, and was the second child and first son of seven children. Ward's mother, Effie Elizabeth Crawford Ward, a 1917 graduate of

Spelman College in the dressmaking department, was an instructor of sewing at the Evening School, Atlanta Board of Education. His father, Jefferson Sigman Ward, a graduate of the Haynes Institute, Augusta, Georgia, was a World War I veteran and a businessman. Both parents had Native American and black ancestry (his mother had Cherokee and black, his father Choctaw and black). They were active in community, cultural, social, religious, and political organizations.

In the Ward family home was a player piano, and music was a part of family life. Displaying musical abilities, the young Edouard Ward was able to memorize tunes at age two. The family's religious activities brought Ward into contact with classical music and hymns. By age four he had memorized many of the melodies he heard, playing them with his right hand on the player piano. Enrolled at age four in the kindergarten of the Atlanta University Laboratory Elementary School for gifted children, also known as the Oglethorpe School, he attracted his teacher's attention when he played the hymn "Just as I Am" in thirds on the classroom toy piano. The music teacher strongly urged that he begin formal music lessons in September 1930, when he entered the first grade. Within a year after Ward began formal lessons, he was playing complete sonatas and by the age of ten was accompanying the church choir and performing throughout the city.

Upon graduating from high school, Ward matriculated at Morehouse College, majoring in piano. His studies were interrupted by service in the U.S. Army (1946–1948), in which he reached the rank of sergeant chaplain's assistant. Following military service he resumed his music studies, at Northwestern University, where he earned the bachelor of music degree in 1949 and the master of music degree in 1950, both degrees in pipe organ. From 1950 to 1951 he taught at Florida A&M University, where he was also the university organist.

He received a Fulbright Fellowship in 1951, with which he studied organ at the Staats-Akademie für Musik in Vienna. In 1955 he earned a Ph.D. in Pipe Organ and Musical Research from Vienna's Universität Wien. On his return to the United States he taught at Southern University in Baton Rouge, Louisiana, from 1957 to 1958, and from 1959 to 1961 was chair of the Department of Music and Fine Arts at South Carolina State College.

On 11 October 1962 Ward married the Dutch-born Adriana Wilhelmina de Graaf at the Scots Church in Rotterdam, the Netherlands. The marriage ended in divorce in 1976; there were no children. In 1964 Ward accepted a position at New York's Kingsborough Community College, where he remained for two years before transferring to Tuskegee Institute to conduct the choir and chair the Department of Music from 1968 to 1972. He welcomed the opportunity to be part of the historic Tuskegee Institute, since its music department was basically patterned after that of Fisk University, the home of the Fisk Jubilee Singers. He valued Tuskegee's mission to educate teachers for service in southern rural schools and felt that, with his strong musical background, he could make an impression. From 1972 to 1977 he taught music theory, applied organ, and African American classical music at Johns Hopkins's Peabody Conservatory of Music. He later taught as an adjunct at the University of Maryland at Baltimore and at Coppin State College.

In 1986 Ward became the first participant in the Fulbright program of visiting professors to both lecture and perform. He was also the first African American visiting professor and co-conductor of the choir at the State Conservatory of Music in Vilnius, Lithuania, as well as the first American to make known the classical tradition of African American music in the former Soviet Union, being the first American guest conductor/lecturer of the Ave Sol Choir at the State Conservatory of Music in Riga, Latvia. The highlight of Ward's musical career came in 1986 when he became the first American organist to perform on the world-renowned pipe organ (built by Walcha Company of Stuttgart, Germany) in the Dome Cathedral in Riga, where its construction began in the early 1200s.

In 1979 Ward, who had also studied extensively the development of African music, was a guest lecturer at Cuttington University College in the Republic of Liberia and was a Phelps-Stokes African American Exchange Scholar at Kenyatta University College in Kenya. His hard work on the organ took him to the St. Petersburg State Conservatoire in Russia in the spring of 1986 as well as to St. John's Theological College in New South Wales, Australia, in the spring of 1990. In 1998 he accompanied the Street Theatre Dance Ensemble on piano in concerts at the Island Center for the Performing Arts, St. Croix, Virgin Islands.

In 1991 Ward retired from his work as a music specialist with the Trenton public school system, where for five years he administered music activities for the system and conducted vocal music workshops for teachers and students. Ward continued to perform on the organ and lecture about the life and musical contributions of SCOTT JOPLIN and

WILL MARION COOK, among others. He was also a tireless mentor and nurturer of young musicians and artist on the East Coast of the United States.

FURTHER READING

Much of the information for this entry was gathered during a series of interviews with its subject on 20 Apr. 2005, 1 May 2005, and 2 Mar. 2007. An oral history interview with Ward can be found at the Maryland Historical Society, Library of Maryland History, Oral History Collections OH 8251–8300 (document OH. 8293).

Agnew, Lorraine. "A Senior Scoop," *Courier-Post*, 22 Jan. 2007.

OTIS D. ALEXANDER

Ward, Clara (21 Apr. 1924–16 Jan. 1973), gospel singer and songwriter, was born Clara Mae Ward in Philadelphia, Pennsylvania, the last of three children of George Ward, a factory worker, and Gertrude Mae Walla Azalee Murphy Ward, a domestic worker. Her parents were farmers who left Anderson, South Carolina, in 1920 in search of the better job opportunities that were available to black people in the North. All of her family sang in the choir at Ebenezer Baptist Church, although at home on one occasion mischievous relatives reportedly encouraged young Clara to belt out the popular THOMAS A. DORSEY tune "Tight Like That," which was written when the legendary gospel composer was still a bluesman and long before the enthusiastic Clara was capable of understanding its meaning. Her musical tastes would later become fixed on old Negro spirituals, and she became a pioneer in creating modern gospel, but her desire to sing and perform never changed or abated.

Much of Clara's childhood was spent during the Depression, when frequent evictions kept her family in a perpetual state of motion and numerous school changes disrupted her education and made it difficult to make lasting friendships other than with her older sister Willarene (called Willa). The girls were often left in the care of relatives in Philadelphia or South Carolina, and for a period of years they were molested by an older cousin whose abuse did not come to light until Willa reached puberty. The girls' mother was a stern disciplinarian; her daughters loved her, but they feared her violent temper and resented her overbearing nature. While toiling over a tub of hot water in 1931, GERTRUDE MAE WARD claimed to have heard the voice of God telling her to "leave this place and go sing the gospel" (Boyer, 105). In 1934, she included

Willa and Clara in her divine mission, and the trio, first known as the Consecrated Gospel Singers, gained a local reputation as the Ward Singers.

Clara initially played the piano while lending vocal support to the group. After kidney and goiter operations, however, Gertrude Ward was forced to focus on business arrangements and yielded the demanding solos to her younger daughter. In this role, the sweet, melodious, and powerful voice that emanated from her slender frame began to distinguish her from the many soloists commonly found in church choirs. She had the good fortune of learning from Dorsey and SALLIE MARTIN, the reigning "Queen of Gospel," when the team visited Philadelphia with their pianist, DINAH WASHINGTON. Clara gained an appreciation for gospel music as an emerging American art form from Dorsey, and she gained the confidence to start writing her own material. From Martin she learned how to refine her unique sound without losing the characteristics, such as shouting, phrasing, and movement, that kept her music firmly rooted in the African American worship tradition. Throughout the late 1930s and early 1940s the group worked a network of church concerts. They made very little money, but the girls missed so much school in order to make bookings that they both dropped out. In 1941 Clara eloped and married Richard Bowman, of whom nothing is known. Gertrude Ward never approved of the marriage and insisted that Clara maintain a hectic schedule despite a difficult pregnancy. At the age of eighteen Clara lost the child, and her marriage ended in divorce shortly thereafter.

In 1943 the Ward Singers traveled to Chicago to attend the National Baptist Convention, which showcased the best gospel performers in the nation. MAHALIA JACKSON, Clara's chief rival in the decades to come, was then a beautician and a family friend who styled the Wards' hair before their performance, and she allegedly advised the group that because of the racist attitudes in the industry that they would make more money if they had a white agent. The Ward Singers won the hearts of the convention audience and drew the attention of record companies. After their performance, Willa and Clara went to a gay and lesbian party, where Clara acknowledged to her sister that she had been involved in some lesbian activity. When a surprised Willa asked for details, Clara said, "There's not a lot to tell. When you get real close just close your eyes tight and put your mind on somebody you really like a lot" (Ward-Royster, 69).

Their live performances were sensational, but the Ward Singers did not achieve great recording success with Savoy Records until 1949, when Clara developed a brilliant arrangement of "Surely God is Able," by W. HERBERT BREWSTER. She created a call-and-response between herself and the equally dynamic MARION WILLIAMS, whose rousing Pentecostal energy combined with a vocal range that could both pierce the highest soprano registers and descend into a resonant moan, hum, or preacher's whoop. Clara would call out with a stirring "Surely," and Marion would reply with a countrified "Showly" that provided a perfect counterpoint to their styles. They would continue in this antiphonal manner, repeating the same words with the variation and improvisation of jazz musicians. It became the first gospel record to sell over a million copies and became an instant classic that defined and secured a place for Clara and the Ward Singers in the annals of gospel history.

During the 1950s the Famous Ward Singers became the most popular gospel group in America. Previously gospel had been dominated by male quartets like the Dixie Hummingbirds, the Mighty Clouds of Joy, and the Soul Stirrers. Female stars like SISTER ROSETTA THARPE and WILLIE MAE FORD SMITH were essentially soloists. Not only did the Ward Singers introduce new harmonic structures, they accentuated the fact that they were women by replacing the standard choir robes with glamorous—though not excessively revealing—gowns, flashy jewelry, and fashionable wigs. With this new image and with their mink coats and limousines, the Ward Singers became as provocative as they were popular. In 1953 Clara started the Wards House of Music, which distributed many of the more than five hundred songs that she would eventually write or arrange, including "Prince of Peace," "Come In the Prayer Room," "Packing Up," and their other gold records, "How I Got Over" and "Move on Up." The Ward Singers headlined at the Apollo Theater, sold out Carnegie Hall, and in 1957, brought gospel to the Newport (Rhode Island) Jazz Festival. Even Elvis Presley wanted to record a gospel number with the group after singing a cappella with Clara Ward during a rehearsal for the *Ed Sullivan Show*. Throughout the United States and through their European tours, Clara helped to introduce gospel to millions.

In 1958 the group experienced its greatest loss when Marion Williams left to start a group called the Stars of Faith, along with four other members of the Ward Singers who were equally dissatisfied with the parsimonious financial arrangements dictated by Clara's controlling mother. Sometime later Willa would also branch out to form the Willa Ward Singers. The success that each group achieved separately never equaled that which they had enjoyed together. Clara continued to record and perform, but a forty-week engagement with a Las Vegas casino offended even some of her staunchest gospel supporters, such as JAMES CLEVELAND, who refused to sing at such establishments. For a time Clara was seen as the "bad girl" of gospel, but this did not keep her from stumping for John F. Kennedy during the 1960 presidential campaign or from performing at President Lyndon Johnson's inaugural gala. On Broadway she played Birdie Lee in LANGSTON HUGHES's religious satire *Tambourines to Glory*, and she performed benefit concerts in Vietnam for American soldiers. Back in the United States Clara and her mother moved to California, where they purchased a church that they renamed "The Gertrude Ward Miracle Temple for All People."

At the age of forty-three Clara, who was rarely allowed a vacation, suffered a debilitating stroke. The Reverend C. L. FRANKLIN, whom Willa described as Clara's "one and only heart, soul, and flesh real romance" (Ward-Royster, 100), rushed to her side. He was a widower, and his daughter, ARETHA FRANKLIN, dreamed of one day singing like Clara. After a short convalescence Clara resumed her demanding schedule for several years until she died of a fatal aneurysm in 1973. She was posthumously entered into the Gospel Music Hall of Fame in 1985. Clara had the voice, the look, and the opportunity to cross over into pop or rhythm and blues music; what she lacked was the desire: her heart was in gospel, the music that nourished her soul.

FURTHER READING

Boyer, Horace Clarence, and Lloyd Yearwood. *How Sweet the Sound: The Golden Age of Gospel* (1995).

Broughton, Viv. *Too Close to Heaven: The Illustrated History of Gospel Music* (1996).

Ward-Royster, Willa. *How I Got Over: Clara Ward and the World-Famous Ward Singers* (1997).

Obituaries: *Washington Post*, 21 January 1973; *Philadelphia Inquirer*, 22 April 1973.

SHOLOMO B. LEVY

Ward, Gertrude Mae (19 Apr. 1901–27 Nov. 1981), gospel singer and group leader, was born Gertrude Willa Azalee Murphy near Anderson, South Carolina, the eleventh of twelve children born to David and Hannah Murphy, both being farmers and Baptists. Gertrude completed eighth grade and,

like millions of African Americans, moved north. In 1920 she settled in Philadelphia, Pennsylvania, and married George Ward, with whom she had two daughters, Willa(rene) and Clara Mae, born in 1922 and 1924 respectively. In Philadelphia, Gertrude did domestic work while her husband joined an iron company, where he remained for forty-two years. The Ward family soon joined Ebenezer Baptist Church at Tenth Street and Girard Avenue and would remain active there for years. Both Ward and her husband joined the senior choir. In 1931 Ward claimed to hear the voice of God telling her, "Go sing my Gospel."

Ward aggressively pursued a singing ministry. She familiarized herself with gospel music through CHARLES ALBERT TINDLEY (1851–1933), a black pastor living in town and a gospel musician. Though Ward had been singing for years, she held her first anniversary concert in 1934. For that anniversary she brought in THOMAS DORSEY and SALLIE MARTIN as special guests and for the first time presented her singing daughters to the public. Ward was first soprano, Willa second soprano, and Clara sang alto. As the Wards faced a larger public, they adopted various names: the Consecrated Gospel Singers, the Ward Trio, Gertrude Ward and Daughters, the Ward Singers, and the Famous Ward Singers. In the early 1930s the Ward Singers were still singing for freewill offerings and sang throughout New Jersey, Pennsylvania, and Delaware. Later they toured the South as well as northern states.

Ward, with her soft voice, was the star of the group as the young girls first taught themselves how to play the piano and later picked up vocal music in elementary school. In time Willa took private lessons to sharpen her skills. Soon Willa and Clara were providing piano accompaniment to their own singing. In 1934 the Ward Singers, with Ward as manager, was the only steady female gospel group in existence.

Because the family struggled financially, Gertrude gave voice lessons for fifty cents an hour and managed the Taylor Brothers, a male singing group, to make ends meet. She later underwent a goiter operation that damaged her beautiful voice. This forced her to hire Elizabeth Staples as her replacement while she restricted her activities to acting as promoter and manager, and gradually several other female singers were added to the group. Ward took her group to Chicago in 1943 to perform at the annual session of the National Baptist Convention (NBC), an event that had often advanced performers' careers, such as that of Dorsey. The sensation the Ward Singers generated in Chicago opened numerous outlets for performance and provided them with a busy schedule of revivals and concerts within the NBC circuit. In time they moved into non-Baptist circles.

From 1940 to 1945 the Ward Singers inspired the creation and evolution of other female groups, such as the Sallie Martin Singers, the Original Gospel Harmonettes, Angelic Gospel Singers, and the Davis Sisters. After World War II, Ward hired Henrietta Waddy and MARION WILLIAMS as singers. Clara then relinquished the role of lead singer to Williams, a member of the Church of God in Christ, whose stellar soprano assured the national success of the Ward Singers.

In 1947 the Ward Singers began recording, and this may be when Ward added "Mae" to her business name. The record *Surely God Is Able*, with Marion as lead singer, was the first million-selling album ever produced by a gospel group and secured the Ward Singers a place in music history. It earned the Wards little money but exposed them to a national audience. In 1949 the Ward Singers had won so much fame that they drew fourteen thousand people at a concert in Washington, D.C. In 1950 they debuted at New York's Carnegie Hall. The following year Ward formed the Clara Ward Specials, which performed concurrently with the Ward Singers. Three years later, following the lead of such African American gospel musicians as Dorsey, Theodore R. Frye, and Martin, Ward founded her own gospel publishing company, Ward's House of Music.

The Wards were responsible for many firsts in the gospel singing industry. They exchanged their traditional choir robes for sequined evening gowns, wore jewelry and wigs, and traveled in Cadillacs. They were the first gospel group to sing at New York's Apollo Theater (1956), the Newport (Rhode Island) Jazz Festival (1957), and the Los Angeles Paramount Theater (1958). So far the Wards had performed mostly before black people; this changed in 1958 when they started performing on national television shows. However, they remained in touch with their roots by singing, at the urging of MARTIN LUTHER KING JR., for civil rights rallies and fund-raisers. By the late 1950s they had released fifty albums and toured Japan and Europe.

In 1958 the group plunged into decline when five members, including Williams, left after Ward failed to reimburse them for hotel expenses. Soon Willa left to form her own group. From the late 1950s to the late 1960s the Ward Singers' financial standing became so insecure that they performed in casinos and clubs. Still, they found time to sing for the presidential campaigns of both John Fitzgerald Kennedy and Lyndon B. Johnson. In 1960 large groups of blacks switched from the Republican to Democratic Party because they appreciated the support that presidential candidate Kennedy gave to King's wife when the black leader was in jail in a Georgia state prison.

In the 1960s Ward's husband died, and she and Clara later moved to California. An ordained evangelist since 1964, Ward opened the Gertrude Ward Miracle Temple for All People in Los Angeles. But from the mid-1960s things grew even more difficult for the Ward Singers. In 1965 Ward's House of Music closed and Clara died in early 1973. The loss of Clara sounded the death knell for the Ward Singers. Without Clara, Ward was unable to generate a steady income, and she lost both her house and the church. She moved back to Philadelphia, where she organized a male version of the Ward Singers, but it failed to catch on. She entered into a romantic relationship with Rudy Scott, her former driver, and briefly cohabited with him until she left to return to Los Angeles, where she died. Ward remains unequaled as founder and promoter of a female group that claimed a divine vocation, moved from obscurity into stardom, redefined gospel music showmanship, and enriched the black music repertoire.

FURTHER READING

Boyer, Horace Clarence, and Lloyd Yearwood. *How Sweet the Sound: The Golden Age of Gospel* (1995).

Ward-Royster, Willa. *How I Got Over: Clara Ward and the World-Famous Ward Singers* (1997).

DAVID MICHEL

Ward, Horace Taliaferro (29 July 1927–), activist, lawyer, politician, and judge, was born in LaGrange, Georgia, to Minnie Ward, a domestic worker. Horace Taliaferro Ward began his formal education at the age of nine, and graduated as valedictorian of East Depot High School in 1946. Ward then obtained his bachelor's degree from Morehouse University in 1949, and his master's degree from Atlanta University in 1950. Ward married Ruth LeFlore on 9 June 1956.

In 1950 Ward sought to further his education and challenge the all-white status of Georgia's flagship state university in Athens, the University of Georgia, by applying to the university's law school. The University of Georgia, like other Southern universities, steadfastly refused to admit African

American applicants. However, the National Association for the Advancement of Colored People (NAACP) worked to break down barriers for blacks to Southern higher education by using the court system.

After university officials rejected his application to the law school, Ward and his attorneys filed a lawsuit against the university in June 1952. He was assisted in his efforts by the Atlanta lawyer A. T. Walden and the national NAACP lawyers THURGOOD MARSHALL and ROBERT L. CARTER. During this period, the university and Georgia state politicians enacted measures in an attempt to keep the University of Georgia segregated. These included offering Ward a scholarship to attend a university out of state, and cutting off state funding to any institution if even one black applicant were admitted. In 1953, just as his lawsuit was about to be heard in front of a judge, Ward was drafted to fight in the Korean War, after having a hernia removed and being placed on the active duty list.

Undeterred, Ward continued with his lawsuit after he completed his tour of duty in 1955, now assisted by the local attorney Donald Hollowell and the national NAACP attorney CONSTANCE BAKER MOTLEY. However, once the lawsuit went to trial, Ward admitted during his testimony that he had accepted a place at Northwestern University in Chicago to study law. In February 1957, on the basis that Ward's divulgence made his application to the University of Georgia irrelevant, a federal judge dismissed Ward's case, and the university remained segregated until 1961.

Ward graduated from Northwestern University in 1959, and established himself as a preeminent lawyer in Hollowell's Atlanta law firm, which was primarily concerned with civil rights cases. Ward helped Hollowell appeal MARTIN LUTHER KING JR.'s hard labor sentence at Reidsville prison for a minor traffic offense in 1960. Along with NAACP lawyer Constance Baker Motley, and the Atlanta lawyers VERNON JORDAN and Hollowell, Ward was part of HAMILTON HOLMES and Charlayne Hunter's (later CHARLAYNE HUNTER-GAULT) legal team in the case against the University of Georgia, which would eventually lead to the desegregation of the university in 1961. Ward later joined Clarence Jones (chief counsel of the Ghandi Foundation, a part of the Southern Christian Leadership Counsel), William Kunsler (American Civil Liberties Union), and local counsel C. B. KING JR., to represent Martin Luther King Jr. and other African American leaders during the Albany, Georgia, protests in 1962.

In 1964 Ward won a state senate seat in Fulton County, to become only the second African American Democrat, after Leroy T. Johnson, to serve in the Georgia state senate. Ward was elected to the seat an additional four times: in 1966, 1968, 1970, and 1972. In 1968 Ward served as a delegate for Georgia to the tumultuous Democratic National Convention in Chicago. In 1969 he was appointed deputy city attorney of Atlanta, and in 1971 Ward was selected as assistant Fulton County attorney. Until 1970 he continued to work on civil rights cases in Hollowell's old law firm.

Governor Jimmy Carter appointed Ward to the Fulton County Civil Court in 1974, making Ward the first black to serve as a trial court judge in Georgia. Ward suffered personal tragedy when his wife of almost twenty years, Ruth, was killed in 1976 in their home by a neighbor. In 1977 Governor George Busbee nominated Ward to the Fulton County Superior Court. In 1979 Ward was appointed by then President Jimmy Carter, and confirmed by the U.S. Senate, to the U.S. District Court for the Northern District of Georgia, the first African American judge to serve on the federal bench in Georgia. He presided over a range of cases, but one of the most significant was a lawsuit against the University of Georgia by the former professor Jan Kemp, who sued the university for terminating her employment when she protested the academic policy for unqualified student athletes. The jury found University of Georgia officials guilty of unfair dismissal of Kemp, though Ward scaled back damages awarded by the jury from $2.3 million to $1.08 million. In 1994 Ward went on senior status for his judgeship.

FURTHER READING

Dyer, Thomas. *The Bicentennial History of the University of Georgia* (1985).
Pratt, Robert. *We Shall Not Be Moved: The Desegregation of the University of Georgia* (2005).
Wallenstein, Peter, ed. *Higher Education and the Civil Rights Movement: White Supremacy, Black Southerners, and College Campuses* (2009).

KRISTAL L. ENTER

Ward, Samuel Ringgold (17 Oct. 1817–c. 1866), abolitionist and newspaper editor, was born on the eastern shore of Maryland, the son of William Ward and Anne (maiden name unknown), slaves. In 1820 Ward and his parents escaped to Greenwich, New Jersey, and six years later settled in New York City. There Ward attended the African Free School, sponsored by the New York Manumission Society. He then clerked for two years in the law offices of DAVID RUGGLES and Thomas L. Jennings, African American reformers. Ward later recalled in his autobiography that he was "initiated … into the antislavery fraternity" after being wrongly imprisoned in 1834 on the charge of inciting a riot at Chatham Street Chapel, where African Americans were conducting an antislavery meeting.

Ward moved to Newark, New Jersey, in 1835 and taught school there until 1839. In 1838 he married Emily E. Reynolds of New York City; they had four children. The family moved in 1839 to Poughkeepsie, New York, where Ward taught at the Colored Lancastrian School. Licensed to preach by the New York Congregational Association in 1839, he held two pastorates in upstate New York, one an all-white congregation in the village of South Butler, Wayne County (1841 to 1843), and one in Cortland Village (1846 to 1851). He was apparently well received, for he said of the South Butler congregation, "The mere accident of the colour of the preacher was to them a matter of small consideration."

Ward was an eloquent orator and staunch advocate of African American rights. He made his debut as a lecturer in 1839 as an agent of the New York State Anti-Slavery Society. The American Anti-Slavery Society hired him as a traveling lecturer in 1840. A man of imposing physical presence, over six feet tall and weighing more than two hundred pounds, Ward made an excellent platform speaker. He condemned northern antiblack prejudice as well as southern slavery and developed an antislavery theology based on his interpretation of the life and mission of Jesus. Advertisements hailed Ward as "the Black Daniel Webster," and the *New York Tribune* called him "the ablest and most eloquent black man alive."

After the split within William Lloyd Garrison's American Anti-Slavery Society in 1840, Ward joined the newly formed American and Foreign Anti-Slavery Society, believing that slavery must be attacked with political weapons as well as with moral suasion. He became a lecturer for the Liberty Party in upstate New York around 1841 and was appointed a vice president of the American Missionary Association. The right of African Americans to vote became one of his most persistent themes. He also lectured on land reform and temperance. Unlike the prominent black abolitionist FREDERICK DOUGLASS, Ward endorsed the Liberty Party position that the U.S. Constitution

could be used to argue the abolitionist case. In 1848 he participated in the founding of the Free Soil Party, much to the displeasure of some of his former allies in the Liberty Party who believed that the Free Soil movement yoked political antislavery with forces hostile to the complete emancipation of African Americans from slavery in the South and racism in the North.

In addition to his powerful antislavery oratory, Ward contributed to reform efforts by writing for and editing several newspapers. He wrote editorials for the *True American* in Cortland for a short period, purchasing it in 1847. The paper was merged with Stephen A. Myer's *Albany Northern Star and Freeman's Advocate* in 1849 and renamed the *Impartial Citizen*. Beginning publication in Syracuse as a semimonthly sheet on 14 February 1849, Ward's paper was converted into a weekly organ of the Liberty Party that June. It ceased publication in Syracuse on 19 June 1850 but resumed the next month in Boston. Ward struggled to keep the paper afloat until October 1851, when he declared bankruptcy.

While in Boston, Ward delivered an impassioned denunciation of the Fugitive Slave Act of 1850 in a speech at Faneuil Hall. He put his own freedom at risk in 1851 by participating with other members of the Syracuse Vigilance Committee in the rescue of William "Jerry" McHenry from federal officers acting under the Fugitive Slave Act. To avoid arrest and prosecution for his part in the rescue, Ward took his family to the Buxton settlement in Canada West (later Ontario). During the next two years he promoted international support of the American abolitionist movement as an antislavery agent in Canada, and in 1853 he founded the *Provincial Freeman* as a voice of the Canadian African American community. That winter Ward went on a six-week, 565-mile tour of southwestern Canada West, later reporting, "Our tour satisfied us abundantly that the colored people of Canada are progressing more rapidly than our people in the States—that the liberty enjoyed here makes different men of those once crushed and dispirited in the land of chains."

The Anti-Slavery Society of Canada sent Ward to the British Isles in 1853 to solicit financial support for fugitive slave communities in Canada. His two and a half years in Great Britain were successful ones; he was well received by British audiences at his lectures against slavery and in behalf of the free produce movement. Ward published his autobiographical narrative, *Autobiography of a Fugitive*

Negro: His Anti-Slavery Labours in the United States, Canada and England, in 1855.

Possibly because of defaulting on a loan, Ward and his family sailed for Jamaica in the West Indies in 1855. He served a small Baptist congregation in Kingston until 1860 and was involved in local politics. In 1860 he began farming fifty acres of land in St. George Parish, which had been given to him while he was in England. In 1866 he wrote *Reflections on the Gordon Rebellion*, an examination of Jamaica's revolutionary leader, George William Gordon.

Ward died in Jamaica, poverty-stricken and far from central New York, where he had first established himself as a compelling and courageous opponent of slavery. Frederick Douglass wrote of Ward: "As an orator and thinker he was vastly superior, I thought, to any of us, and being perfectly black and of unmixed African descent, the splendors of his intellect went directly to the glory of race. In depth of thought, fluency of speech, readiness of wit, logical exactness, and general intelligence, Samuel R. Ward has left no successor among the colored men amongst us, and it was a sad day for our cause when he was laid low in the soil of a foreign country."

FURTHER READING

Burke, Ronald K. "The Anti-Slavery Activities of Samuel Ringgold Ward in New York State," *Afro-Americans in New York Life and History* 2 (1978).

Ripley, C. Peter, et al. *The Black Abolitionist Papers, 1830–1865* (5 vols., 1985–1992).

This entry is taken from the *American National Biography* and is published here with the permission of the American Council of Learned Societies.

MILTON C. SERNETT

Ward, T. M. D. (28 Sept. 1823–10 June 1894), African Methodist Episcopal (AME) minister, was born Thomas Myer[s] Decatur Ward in Hanover, Pennsylvania, to parents whose names are unknown. They had moved from Maryland a few months before his birth. A few sources claim that he was a nephew of SAMUEL RINGGOLD WARD; if so, this would make him the grandson of former slaves William and Anne Harper Ward. In 1838, he joined the AME Church, and in 1842 he helped found the AME Church in Wilkes-Barre. In 1843 he moved to Philadelphia, attended a Quaker night school, and began preaching in earnest.

After being admitted on trial to the New York Conference in 1846, he was ordained as a deacon in 1847 and as an elder in 1849; at some point in the late 1840s, already being praised for his eloquence and education, he shifted to the New England Conference, where he worked with DANIEL PAYNE and served as conference secretary in 1852. Bishop WILLIAM PAUL QUINN assigned him to serve as a missionary to California, and he traveled to San Francisco aboard the *Star of the West* in April and May of 1854.

As the AME Church's sole official representative, Ward quickly became a leader among the nascent AME community in California—especially northern California. He took over the factionalized St. Cyprian's AME Church (later Bethel AME) in San Francisco, united the church in fund-raising, paid off a looming debt, and oversaw the purchase of a large brick church in June 1862. He became a major presence among San Francisco African Americans, and, in 1857, he married Mary (maiden name unknown), a fugitive slave from Maryland who had come to California in 1855 and was working in the home of Indian agent General Edward Fitzgerald Beale. The couple does not seem to have had children, though a Rachel Smith, listed as an "adopted daughter," was living with them in 1880.

Aided by California activists with strong AME ties like BARNEY FLETCHER, Darius Stokes, Jabez Campbell, and JEREMIAH BURKE SANDERSON (whom he helped recruit from New Bedford for AME work in the West), Ward crisscrossed the state founding churches, organizing revivals, and advancing church goals. Such work naturally led him to political activism, and he represented San Francisco at the early California Colored Conventions of the 1850s, was elected to office at the 1863 convention held in San Francisco, and fought continuously for black civil rights—especially rights regarding court testimony and education. Later, he would work tirelessly for black male suffrage and serve as an agent and advocate for both the *Pacific Appeal* and the San Francisco *Elevator*.

He regularly communicated with AME officials in the East, attended the AME General Conference meetings throughout the 1860s, wrote letters that were published in the *Christian Recorder*, and gradually broadened his charge to include work with churches in Nevada and Colorado. By 1860, he had succeeded in achieving fuller recognition for California congregations, and he was instrumental in establishing the California Conference (sometimes referred to as the Pacific Coast Conference) of the AME Church in 1865. In part because of his efforts, his eloquence, and his careful politicking within the church hierarchy, he was elected in 1868 as one of the bishops of the AME Church. As the presiding bishop for the Pacific Coast, he had the daunting responsibility of overseeing churches from California to British Columbia. Bishop Payne preached his ordination sermon on 25 May, and James A. Shorter and John M. Brown were made bishops alongside him. When he returned to visit San Francisco in August 1873 and again in August 1880, he was treated as a hero in the black community.

After an appointment in 1872 leading the Georgia Conference (Georgia, Alabama, Florida, and Mississippi), Ward led conferences throughout the South and Southwest. He was integral to the founding of the Indian Mission Conference of the AME Church in 1879—an outreach effort to Native Americans—and to fund-raising to build a new church at Muskogee when the AME chapel there was burned down by arsonists in early 1885. He also continued to write, including a series of articles on the West for the *Christian Recorder* in the 1880s and early 1890s, poetry that was published in the *Recorder* and the *AME Review*, and, of course, sermons. Known throughout the church as "old man eloquent," he was especially active in educational efforts. His active support of Wilberforce University helped lead to an honorary doctor of divinity degree, and he helped found Shorter College in Arkansas in 1885.

Among his greatest educational efforts, though, was his work with Western University (now defunct) in Quindaro, Wyandotte County, Kansas. Begun as a school for free blacks in 1857 by Eben Blatchley, Western became a key AME outpost in the West in the 1880s and 1890s. Ward led the school's transition into the AME fold and headed the Board of Trustees for several years; his contributions were recognized when the university named its first permanent building Ward Hall. Though his various charges kept him traveling throughout the South and West, he maintained a home in the Washington, D.C., area throughout this period. His wife lived there until her death on 4 January 1883. He married a second time, to Rachel Ann Smith of Baltimore, who was several years his junior, on 11 June 1884.

He remained active in the AME Church until his death while in Jacksonville, Florida, on church work. His funeral and burial were held in Washington, D.C.; five AME bishops participated in the services. Ward became the namesake of Washington's Ward Memorial AME Church.

Massive in physique with a "sonorous" voice of "deep and rich tones," Ward once quipped that "the only positions I have filled have been those of a plowboy and a Methodist preacher" (Smith, 194). Given his enormous labors in establishing the AME Church in the West, it is no wonder that his colleague BENJAMIN W. ARNETT picked up on such language in his "Centennial Address on the Mission of Methodism to the Extremes of Society," delivered in 1884 at Wilberforce, calling Ward "the man that planted the banner of African Methodism and Christianity on the Rocky Mountains, and sowed the seed on the Sierra Nevadas" (18).

FURTHER READING

Beasley, Delilah. *The Negro Trail Blazers of California* (1919).

Payne, Daniel Alexander. *History of the African Methodist Episcopal Church* (1891).

Payne, Daniel Alexander. *Recollections of Seventy Years* (1888).

Smith, Charles Spencer. *History of the African Methodist Episcopal Church* (1922).

Obituaries: *Christian Recorder*, 14 June 1894 and 28 June 1894.

ERIC GARDNER

Ward, Theodore (Ted) (15 Sept. 1902–8 May 1983), dramatist and author of more than thirty plays about black life in America, was born James Theodore Ward in Thibodaux, Louisiana, the sixth of eleven children born to John Everett Ward Sr. and Louisa Mamie Pierre. John, who was born a slave in 1859, was the local black schoolmaster. He also sold books and patent medicines to supplement his income and was an early associate of BOOKER T. WASHINGTON. During slavery, John's mother had secretly learned to read and write, and as punishment her right hand was cut off at the wrist. She may have taught John to read and write, and he probably attended school during Reconstruction. As a young girl, Louisa saw her father murdered during the Thibodaux massacre of 1887 for joining the Knights of Labor.

Ward grew up in a loving but strict religious fundamentalist home where secular music and entertainment were forbidden. As a young boy Ward wrote a little play that his father threw onto the fire, damning it as the "work of the Devil." His mother's death in 1916 signaled the breakup of his family, and Ward went to New Orleans. There, he worked odd jobs in and around the white hotels until he and a cousin decided to go north, boarding a freight train and riding the rails as boy hoboes. Ward ended up in Chicago, where the antilynching crusader IDA B. WELLS BARNETT found him a job and a place to stay.

Later he resumed his travels, crisscrossing the country for more than ten years, visiting cities such as St. Louis, Kansas City, Seattle, Butte, Montana, and San Francisco and working as a bellhop, bootblack, barbershop porter, gambler, and stevedore. A lifelong autodidact, Ward, whose formal education had ended in Louisiana, once found a collection of the Harvard Classics in an employer's cellar. He read each day until he completed them all.

Ward's odyssey ended in Salt Lake City, Utah, where he was jailed for several months for selling bootleg gin. Ward, who was taught by his father, was an excellent writer. Bored in jail, he entered a short story in a magazine contest and won first prize. Gail Martin, editor of the *Deseret News* and a part-time instructor at the University of Utah Extension program, read it and went to visit him. They became friends, and Martin encouraged him to apply for a new writing fellowship established at the Univeristy of Wisconsin by Zona Gale, the first American woman dramatist awarded a Pulitzer Prize, which she won for her play *Miss Lulu Bett* (1920). Ward won the fellowship, becoming the first and, the following year, the second Zona Gale Fellow. At Wisconsin, Ward studied logic, rhetoric, and philosophy. Well known on campus as a writer and speaker, Ward also hosted a local radio program, reading poetry and essays. On weekends in Chicago, Ward, the handsome possessor of both a natural acting ability and a mesmerizing speaking voice, read poetry and acted out dramatic excerpts from works by writers such as JAMES WELDON JOHNSON and COUNTÉE CULLEN to audiences at black women's civic organizations. One evening, after seeing a poorly scripted agitprop production written by one of his classmates, a John Reed club member, Ward decided to write an antieviction skit, after which he recalled for the first time since his childhood the play his father had thrown on the fire.

In 1934, after two years at Wisconsin, Ward left Madison and found a Works Progress Administration (WPA) job teaching writing in Chicago. He taught dramatics and writing at the Lincoln Center and at the Countée Cullen Library. He worked there until he formally joined the Federal Theatre Project in 1937. In 1936, he entered another contest, winning second prize for *Sick 'n Tiahd*, a one-act play about fed up sharecroppers. A meeting with the first-prize winner RICHARD WRIGHT led Ward to provide his classroom for meetings of the South Side Writers Workshop, later known as the nucleus of the Chicago Renaissance (1932–1950). The group included GWENDOLYN BROOKS, MARGARET WALKER, Willard Motley, FRANK MARSHALL DAVIS, Arna Bontemps, Ruth Attaway, Alice Browning, Fern Gayden (the last two were later the editors of *Negro Story* magazine 1944–1946), sculptor Marion Perkins, and artists Bernard Goss and his wife, Margaret Taylor Goss. Later, MARGARET TAYLOR GOSS BURROUGHS and the dancer and anthropologist KATHERINE DUNHAM became close associates. LANGSTON HUGHES and Owen Dodson were essential participants.

Ward joined Chicago's Negro Unit of the WPA Federal Theatre Project, where he wrote his seminal work *Big White Fog* (1937). Directed by Kay Ewing, the play examines and exposes the lives of a middle-class black family whose aspirations are subsumed within the "fog" of American racism. The Federal Theatre national director Hallie Flanagan praised the play, saying, "*Big White Fog* was important because it dealt with a racial problem by a member of the Negro race" (Flanagan, 143). Expectations of racial conflict among mixed audiences proved groundless, and the play enjoyed an extended run (7 April 1938 through late May 1938) at the Great Northern Theatre in the Loop.

Like all the WPA's black units, the Chicago Negro unit was headed by a white director, Harry Minturn, assisted by SHIRLEY GRAHAM (later the wife of W. E. B. DuBois). After almost two months, the popular play was summarily moved to a faraway high school auditorium to make room for Graham's production of *Little Black Sambo*. *Big White Fog* closed on 30 May 1938 after only a few additional performances. Years later Ward recalled receiving Graham's apology for this devastating decision. *Even the Dead Arise* (1938), a powerful antilynching piece, and *The Falcon of Adawa* (1938), about Ethiopia's emporor Haile Selassie, were followed by *Skin Deep* (1939) and an adaptation for the stage of Wright's short story *Bright and Morning Star* (1939).

The end of the WPA stranded Ward and the rest of the *Swing Mikado* cast. The *Swing Mikado* was a traveling production of the Negro Unit. After *Big White Fog*, Ward joined the troupe. Just before the WPA was disbanded, they traveled as a group to New York, where Ward decided to remain and, with Hughes, PAUL ROBESON, Loften Mitchell, George Norford, THEODORE BROWNE, Powell Lindsay, and ALAIN LOCKE, formed the Negro Playwrights Company. Robeson headlined a gala fund-raiser at Harlem's famed Renaissance Ballroom, where black stars performed for a packed audience, enabling the company to stage *Big White Fog*, starring CANADA LEE as Victor Mason, at the Lincoln Theatre in 1940. The play suffered rejection by both middle-class blacks and downtown theatergoers, forcing the company to shut its doors after only a few weeks. Hughes called *Big White Fog* "the greatest, most encompassing play on Negro life that has ever been written. If it isn't liked by people, it is because they are not ready for it, not because it isn't a great play" (*Chicago Defender*, June 1940).

In 1940 Ward married Mary Sangigian, an Armenian American activist and a student of sculptor AUGUSTA SAVAGE. The couple had two daughters before they divorced in 1967.

Just Before Day, about two segregated World War II combat units that circumstances stranded together in the South Pacific, and *Deliver the Goods*, a war bond fund-raiser, appeared in 1942. During this period, Ward joined a group of writers, including Edmund Henefeld, David Shivitz (who later became attorneys), and Nicholas Biel, who called themselves the Associated Playwrights. The writers were located at the old Henry Street Playhouse (later Woody King's New Federal Theater) where Ward began work on his Reconstruction-era tragedy, *Our Lan'*. All the playwrights benefited from a workshop conducted by Professor Kenneth Thorpe Rowe, of the University of Michigan, who is also credited with helping Arthur Miller, Betty Smith, Lawrence Kasdan and Robert McKee. Rowe later used *Our Lan'* as an example of flawless playwriting in his textbook, *A Theater in Your Head*.

In 1947 director Eddie Dowling and producer Louis Singer brought the play from its successful run at Henry Street to Broadway's Royale Theatre in a Theatre Guild production that starred the soprano Muriel Smith and basso William Vesey. In the play, which featured Julie Hayden as the northern schoolmarm, newly freed blacks occupy and cultivate land seized on their behalf from former slaveholders by Union General William T. Sherman only to face eviction when the planters return to claim it. Ward's play won two National Theatre Conference fellowships (1946 and 1947) as well as a 1947 Theatre Guild Award. Ward was named the 1947 Schomburg Collection Negro of the Year, part of the New York Public Library system. Over Ward's strenuous objections, *Our Lan'*, which had been enthusiastically reviewed at Henry Street by the *New York Times* drama critic Brooks Atkinson, was substantially altered by the Broadway producers to conform to their stereotypical assumptions about audience expectations concerning "authentic" black life. After Atkinson gave the Broadway production a bad review, the play closed after only forty-two performances, embittering Ward for a second time. In 1948, Ward won a John Simon Guggenheim Foundation fellowship, which enabled him to complete *John Brown* (1949). Gene Frankel directed a Peoples Theatre production of the play at the Eldridge Street Theatre in Greenwich Village, with young actors Lee Marvin and Rod Steiger cast as Brown's sons. In 1951, the play was staged at the Skyloft Theatre in Chicago with *Whole Hog or Nothin'* (1949) and *Throwback* (1951).

The advent of the McCarthy era brought both ostracism and economic hardship to Ward, Robeson, Hughes, Lee, and hundreds of other creative artists from New York to Hollywood. Notwithstanding the political repression that threatened his career, Ward continued writing. He completed his prescient antidrug play *The Daubers* (1953) and the folk operas *Madison* (1956), based on FREDERICK DOUGLASS's story "The Heroic Slave" (1852), and *The Bell and the Light* (1954) with composer Irving Schlein. He wrote *Big Money* (1961), a musical comedy, with music by Frank Fields.

In the mid-1960s Ward returned to Chicago to head the Louis Theatre and School of Drama at the South Side Center for the Performing Arts, known as Ted Ward's Southside Center, where he taught acting and playwriting and staged *Candle in the Wind* (1966). During the 1970s Ward spent a year as playwright in residence at the University of Massachusetts at Amherst and another at the New Orleans Free Southern Theatre with support from the Rockefeller Brothers Foundation. In 1975 Ward received the second annual AUDELCO award as its Outstanding Pioneer of Black Theatre. Theodore Ward Day in Chicago was officially proclaimed on 23 April 1977. Each year Chicago's Goodman Theatre awards a playwriting competition prize named for the author. To the end of his life Ward continued writing, revising much of his earlier work, and resisting most efforts to anthologize his plays. Ward died of cancer in Chicago at age 80. Although much of his work is still virtually unknown to modern audiences, Ward's pioneering contribution to the development of twentieth-century black theater continues to generate widespread interest in this important body of work.

FURTHER READING

Abramson, Doris A. *Negro Playwrights in the American Theatre, 1925–1959* (1969).

Flanagan, Hallie. *Arena: The History of the Federal Theatre* (1940).

Fraden, Rena. *Blueprints for a Black Federal Theatre, 1935–1939* (1994).

Hatch, James V., and Ted Shine, eds. *Black Theatre U.S.A.* (1974).

Hughes, Langston. *Chicago Defender*, June 1940.

Kleibert, Stephen. *The Thibodaux Massacre of 1887.* Available online at www.dougriddle.com/essays/sk20021220.html.

Mitchell, Loften. *Black Drama: The Story of the American Negro in the Theatre* (1967).

Rodrigue, John C. *Reconstruction in the Cane Field: From Slavery to Free Labor in Louisiana's Sugar Parishes, 1862–1880* (2001)

Rowe, Kenneth Thorpe. *A Theater in Your Head* (1960).

Turner, Darwin T., ed. *Black Drama in America* (1971).

ELISE VIRGINIA WARD

Ward, Vera (6 Apr. 1902–6 Dec. 1964), blues, folk, and gospel singer, was born Adell Hall Ward in Livingston, Alabama, one of four children of Agnes Hall, a homemaker, and Efron "Zully" Hall, a farm laborer. Little else is known about her upbringing. It is not known whether she had any formal education, but her youth was a musical one, with an emphasis on the gospel songs that were favorites of her mother and father. As a youth, Hall won a reputation among the congregation at Old Shiloh Baptist Church for her beautiful voice and she appears to have been known around Livingston as someone with exceptional musical talents.

Sometime in 1917 Hall married a coalminer named Nash Riddle. The couple had a daughter, but Riddle was killed sometime in the early twenties, reportedly in a gunfight. Suddenly alone and facing tough economic times, Hall appears to have moved back in with her parents and made ends meet by doing chores like laundry and other kinds of domestic work. In 1940 her daughter, Minnie, fell ill and died of hepatitis. Sometime around 1937 (though some sources suggest as early as 1930) John Lomax, the Texas musicologist and father of the legendary ethnomusicologist Alan Lomax, heard rumors of Hall's singing and sought her out to make recordings for the Library of Congress Archive of American Folk Song project, which sought to document and preserve voices that might otherwise be lost. Hall performed both gospel and blues songs, and soon she had become something of a cause célèbre among musicologists and enthusiasts and students of folk and gospel music. Others sought her out to make their own recordings, and

when her version of "Another Man Done Gone" premiered during a 1943 BBC radio showcase of American folk music, Hall's beautiful voice was carried to a larger audience.

By this time, Alan Lomax had again sought out Hall and recorded a number of her songs. In 1945 she recorded an album with the musicologist and author of *Folksongs of Alabama* (1950), Byron Arnold. Three years later, she traveled with Alan Lomax to New York, where she performed during Columbia University's American Music Festival. Not long after, Hall again performed a number of her songs for yet another musicologist, Harold Courlande, after which she largely vanishes from the historical record. After she died in 1964, her simple grave appears to have been lost to a public works project.

Despite the paucity of personal information about her, Hall's most important legacy remains. Her music—powered by a voice both deep and gruff, full of spiritual passion, and punctuated by deep-well moans—resides in the Library of Congress. A number of modern-day pop stars have sampled her work, including the dance-pop producer and performer Moby. Ward's rendition of "Trouble So Hard" is familiar to many people who have never even heard of her, and her songs remain a treasure among enthusiasts of folk, gospel, and southern roots. She was inducted into the Alabama Women's Hall of Fame in 2005, and two years later a memorial was erected in her honor near the Sumter County courthouse.

FURTHER READING

"Adele 'Vera' Hall Ward." Entry in the online *Encyclopedia of Alabama*: http://www.encyclopediaofalabama.org/face/Article.jsp?id=h-1419

Arnold, Byron. *Folk Songs of Alabama* (1950).

Cohen, Ronald. *Rainbow Quest: The Folk Music Revival and American Society, 1940–1970* (2002).

JASON PHILIP MILLER

Ward, William (1840?–5 May 1895), soldier and political leader, was born in Charleston, South Carolina. Nothing is known of Ward's parents, and little of his early life, but he was raised a slave in Virginia, and became free during the Civil War. In January 1864 he enlisted in the First United States Colored Cavalry, a federal regiment organized in late 1863 in the Tidewater region of Virginia. A month after enlistment Ward was promoted to sergeant, a rank he held until his discharge in February 1866. Ward's service included duty in Virginia at Fortress Monroe, in Hampton, and in Richmond. During the war he received a bullet wound through the knee.

Following his discharge, he settled in Portsmouth, Virginia, where he worked as a carpenter. In October 1867 Ward reenlisted and served in the Thirty-ninth United States Colored Infantry. While stationed at Ship Island, Mississippi, he contracted a serious illness, most likely tuberculosis. He received a medical discharge in June 1868 and moved to New Orleans.

In 1870 a small group of veterans of the Thirty-ninth Colored Infantry, including Ward, moved to Grant Parish in rural north-central Louisiana where they rapidly became leaders of the radical wing of the local Republican Party. In 1871 Ward received a commission as a captain in the Louisiana State Militia. In September of that year a conservative mob attacked the home of two of Grant Parish's white radical Republican office holders, Judge William B. Phillips and Recorder Delos W. White, killing White in the attack. In response the administration of the Republican governor, Henry Clay Warmoth, dispatched a shipment of Enfield rifles to Ward with orders to keep the arms stored subject to further instructions. Despite these orders Ward distributed the arms and, in cooperation with Judge Phillips, arrested a number of suspects who were shipped to New Orleans to face federal civil rights charges. A board of militia officers sent to Grant Parish to investigate the situation recommended that Ward be suspended and placed under arrest. Though Ward was discharged from the state militia in 1872, he did not face charges, nor did he return the Enfield rifles.

Ward also played an instrumental role in the events that led to the April 1873 Colfax Massacre, the most deadly episode of Reconstruction-era political violence. The massacre stemmed from a contested November 1872 parish election in which a radical Republican slate, led by Ward as candidate for state representative, and a rival "fusionist" slate, made up of Democrats and disgruntled moderate white Republicans, both claimed victory. In January 1873 outgoing governor Warmoth appointed members of the fusionist slate to the local parish offices. In March, at the behest of William Ward (by then serving in the state legislature), incoming Governor William Pitt Kellogg appointed members of the Republican slate to the same offices. Late that month Ward and the radicals took possession of the parish courthouse in the village of Colfax. On 1 April an armed conservative party attempted to retake the courthouse but found it well defended by a small force, mainly African American, under Ward's command. Over the next two weeks armed conservatives from Grant and neighboring parishes converged on Colfax. After the murder of a black farmer by an armed white band, African Americans flooded into Colfax seeking mutual protection. At first, the radical forces held the upper hand, but the military balance eventually turned decisively against them. On 9 April Ward and the other radical leaders departed for New Orleans in a vain attempt to secure assistance from state and federal authorities. By 13 April, Easter Sunday, about 150 black men, many poorly armed, found themselves besieged at the Grant Parish courthouse by a conservative force about twice as large as theirs. In the battle and massacre that followed, between 70 and 100 black men are estimated to have died. Most of the dead were killed after surrendering, including roughly 40 who were summarily executed hours after the fighting had ended. Although the Colfax Massacre broke the back of the political and military insurgency that he had led, in 1874 Ward once again received the Republican nomination for state representative from Grant Parish, over the objections of moderate white Republicans. He narrowly lost the November election to the candidate of the recently organized White Man's Party. Four days after the vote, Ward was involved in an armed fracas with a group of white Republicans who blamed him for the party's electoral defeat. Indicted for his role in the affair, Ward fled Grant Parish and relocated to New Orleans. Despite his defeat at the polls Ward was nonetheless seated in the legislature after Louisiana's Republican state authorities threw out the results of the Grant Parish elections. Six weeks into the session, though, the Republican-controlled House of Representatives expelled Ward following a confrontation in which Ward pulled a revolver on the House floor.

Ward was married to Mary D. Staves of Richmond, Virginia. The couple lived together as husband and wife from at least 1870, but the marriage was not formalized until 1875 in a ceremony in New Orleans. In 1876, following the refusal of the Louisiana Republican Party to hire him as a campaign worker, a destitute Ward renounced his Republican affiliations and secured employment with the Louisiana Democratic Party. Ward campaigned openly for the Democratic state ticket in the 1876 state elections. In 1880 he returned to the Tidewater region of Virginia, and settled just outside the city of Norfolk. He lived out the remainder of his life in increasingly poor health and died in 1895. A fellow black legislator once described Ward as "a man of peculiar disposition, brave and determined, a good man" (*House Miscellaneous Documents*, Forty-fourth Congress, Second Session, No. 34, Pt. 2, 349). In contrast, a white army officer posted in Colfax following the massacre declared Ward to be "very generally hated" (*House Reports*, Forty-third Congress, Second Session, No. 261, Pt. 3, 161). Ward's life epitomized the militant black politics that emerged out of the experiences of emancipation and war. His personal and political unraveling reflects the collapse of those politics and the vision that inspired it.

FURTHER READING

William Ward's military pension file is housed in the Records of the Veterans Administration, Records Related to Pension and Bounty Land Claims, Record Group 15, National Archives, Washington, D.C.

Lemann, Nicholas. *Redemption: The Last Battle of the Civil War* (2006)

Sipress, Joel M. "From the Barrel of a Gun: The Politics of Murder in Grant Parish," *Louisiana History* 42 (Summer 2001).

Sipress, Joel M. "The Triumph of Reaction: Political Struggle in a New South Community, 1865–1898," Ph.D. diss., University of North Carolina at Chapel Hill (1993).

JOEL M. SIPRESS

Ward, William. *See* Kid Norfolk.

Ward Sears, Leah Jeannette (13 June 1955–), lawyer, community activist, and judge, was born Leah Jeanette Sears in Heidelberg, Germany, where her father, Colonel Thomas E. Sears, a young U.S. Army officer, and her mother, Onnye Jean (maiden name unknown), an elementary schoolteacher, were stationed. Colonel Sears would later become a Presbyterian minister; he died in 1989. Leah had an older brother, William Thomas, and a younger one, Michael Euric.

Military assignments kept the family moving; after leaving Germany, Thomas and Onnye moved several times, eventually settling in Maryland where Leah began school, at the height of the turbulent civil rights movement. Leah and her brothers, by integrating the schools they attended, became some of the youngest civil rights activists in their area. They lived in all-white neighborhoods and attended all-white public schools, first in Maryland and later in Georgia—circumstances that made for some difficulty but that also left an indelible impression upon the youngsters. It was not unusual for the Sears children to be greeted with the epithet "nigger" each day in school or in their neighborhoods, but the Searses did not let that deter them. Thomas Sears's military background and affiliation made it a little easier for the family to withstand taunts and other reprisals against the family. The family mantra was "Reach high," and the children were encouraged to assume that they were as good as or better than everybody else around them, white or black.

In the late 1960s the family was transferred to Savannah, Georgia. Leah was infatuated with anything having to do with the civil rights movement, especially the legal wrangling that occurred over various laws—the 1954 decision in *Brown v. Board of Education*, which invalidated school segregation, provided her with the greatest inspiration. She determined that she would be a lawyer because she wanted to argue the important legal issues and help African Americans in the tradition of one of her idols, THURGOOD MARSHALL, and the other justices on the Warren Supreme Court. Leah's parents expected nothing less than excellence, and after graduating from high school, she attended Cornell University to earn her B.S. in 1976.

In July 1976, just months after getting her degree, she married Love Collins III and took Sears-Collins as her surname. They had two children, a son named Addison and a daughter, Brennan. (Brennan was so-named because of Leah's regard for U.S. Supreme Court Justice William J. Brennan.) From 1976 to 1977 Sears-Collins worked as a reporter for the *Columbus Ledger* newspaper and as a summer associate in 1979 for the law firm of Sirote, Permutt, Friend, Friedman, Held, and Apolinsky of Birmingham, Alabama.

Sears-Collins enrolled at Emory University's School of Law in the fall in 1976, and in 1980 she obtained her law degree, which allowed her to pursue her long-held ambition to become a lawyer and a judge. During her first year of law school, working with Legal Aid of Georgia, she established the Battered Women's Project of Columbus, Georgia. From 1980 to 1985 she worked for Alston and Bird, a prestigious national law firm. She became founder and first president of the Georgia Association of Black Women Attorneys, an organization that began with meetings of approximately fifteen women in her living room and that grew to more than four hundred members.

She became a member of the Morehouse College School of Medicine's board of directors and of the Mercer College Law School board of visitors, chair of the American Bar Association board of elections, chair of the Atlanta Bar Association Minority Scholarship Program, and she served on the steering committee of the Georgia Women's History Month and worked with the Children's Defense Fund's Black Community Crusade for Children, both before and after she was appointed to a judgeship.

The former civil rights leader and United Nations ambassador ANDREW YOUNG became mayor of Atlanta during the late 1980s, and one of his stated goals was to bring more young African Americans into the judiciary, where real power could be had. Thus, in 1989, at the age of twenty-seven and only five years out of law school, Sears-Collins was appointed as a judge on the Atlanta City Court. She earned a reputation for doing her homework and for knowing the law. Because of her youth and intelligence, she became known around the state.

She was named an Outstanding Young Alumna at Emory University, and she received honorary doctorate of law degrees from Morehouse College, Mercer University School of Law, and LaGrange College of LaGrange, Georgia. She later returned to the University of Virginia and earned an LLM in 1995. She also studied at the National Judicial College during that time.

In 1992 Judge Sears-Collins tossed her hat into the ring to succeed a retiring justice on the Georgia Supreme Court. She did not think it was likely that she would gain the post, but she felt that it could not hurt to try. She was thoroughly surprised when she was called by Governor Zell Miller to come for an interview, and she was overjoyed and shocked when the call came a short time later informing her that Governor Miller was appointing her to fill out the term of her predecessor.

Sears-Collins and her husband divorced in 1995, and in 1999 she married Haskell George Ward, a former deputy New York City mayor under Mayor Ed Koch. Haskell Ward later became an African development expert who helped build hydroelectric power plants in countries like Guinea. Because Sears-Collins was becoming well known, the question of what her surname should be after her marriage to Ward presented some political problems. She considered the names Sears, Sears-Collins, or Sears-Ward, but felt that any of these could be potentially troublesome or confusing in the electoral arena. To address the issue, she adopted Leah Ward Sears, and her husband, in turn, became Haskell Sears Ward.

Georgia law requires Supreme Court justices to run in statewide elections at the end of each term, so in 2004, Ward Sears tossed her hat into the ring. Her white Republican opponent, G. Grant Brantley, made sure that everyone in Georgia knew that by electing her, they would be electing a black woman to the state's highest court. The Republican election mill labeled her an "activist judge" who needed to be replaced on the court. Conservatives demanded that Ward Sears fill out a questionnaire about her legal views, but she refused. Such questionnaires were designed to determine beforehand how she would vote, and Ward Sears similarly refused to fill out a questionnaire from the Christian Coalition on the grounds that she could then be required to do the same for every other interest group that made such a request.

Her opponents seriously underestimated how much Georgia had changed. Voters were no longer inclined to vote purely along racial or party lines. Brantley was found to have made false claims of having been nominated for a federal judgeship, and with her husband, Haskell, as her campaign manager, Ward Sears routed her opponent, winning 62 percent of the vote statewide, the highest majority ever in such a race, and taking 146 out of 159 counties. Ward Sears became the presiding judge of the Georgia Supreme Court in 2001, and in March 2005 the court unanimously elected her the first woman chief justice in the state's history.

FURTHER READING
"Sisters in the Spotlight," *Ebony* (March 2003).

LUTHER BROWN JR.

Ware, David S. (7 Nov. 1949–), jazz saxophonist, was born David Spencer Ware in Plainfield, New Jersey, the son of David Ware, a steelworker, and Lucille Moore Ware, a flat presser in the garment trade. Ware was raised in large part by his paternal grandparents, Spencer Ware, the owner of a wood and coal yard in Newark, and Elizabeth Garland Ware, homemaker. The Ware family had lived in the Plainfield area for several generations, and young David grew up in nearby Scotch Plains. He resided in his childhood home for much of his life.

As a child, Ware's family attended the local Emmanuel Baptist Church, and on occasion, the Hopewell Baptist Church in Newark. Though Ware found little satisfaction in the church, spiritual concerns would remain at the heart of his lifework. He states, "The essence of my life is to get closer to God" (Lang interview). Ware has pursued this through music and meditation. A demonstration of musical instruments in the fifth grade stirred an interest in drums, but his father, a fan of the saxophone, directed him toward the horn. He began lessons while practicing out of jazz books with the one other musician in the neighborhood, a young drummer. He listened intensively to late-night jazz radio and the records of his father. His parents took him to various performances, including one by Duke Ellington, but Ware found his primary inspiration in the new sounds and spiritual quest of John Coltrane and Sonny Rollins, who by the early 1960s were breaking with the limits of bop. Some critics at the time called their open approach to play "anti-jazz." Ware, on the other hand, discovered the basis of his style—"this is home, this is where I fit in" (Lang interview).

During his high school years Ware heard and met both Coltrane and Rollins in the New York clubs. He attended music camp at the University of Connecticut taught by Ron Carter, Charlie Mariano, and Alan Dawson and he played in his school's various all-white bands as well as in the New Jersey All-State band. In class, he was punished for failing to recite the Pledge of Allegiance. Little of the curriculum—taught by an all-white faculty—interested him, and his grades were poor. His music instructor, however, was entirely supportive and convinced Ware's other teachers to graduate him on the basis of his extraordinary talent.

In 1967 Ware began his course work at the Berklee College of Music in Boston, where he focused on the tenor saxophone. Many of the professors were uninterested in his style of music, but some offered valuable instruction. Herb Pomeroy, for example, taught harmonic tension and recognized its importance to Ware's play. His most significant connections, though, were with fellow students, especially Joe Hanna (later Abdul Hannan), who introduced Ware to a regular meditation practice. Under Hannan's name, they recorded the album *Third World* in 1968. Though an honors student, Ware left Berklee the following year and started the collective improvisational band Apogee with Gene Ashton (later Cooper-Moore), Chris Amberger, and Marc Edwards. At this time, Ware also occasionally practiced with Rollins, who taught him circular breathing and yogic philosophy.

Apogee remained in Boston until 1973 when they moved to an illegal rental in New York's lower eastside. This residence/practice/performance space was a magnet for free jazz improvisers, and Ware thus began jamming with like-minded players, including Raphé Malik and Rashid Bakr. The band also played at the Village Vanguard (opening for Rollins) as well as at Sam River's Studio Rivbea. In the same year, Ware lost both his paternal grandparents and began a lifelong commitment to Maharishi's Transcendental Meditation. Meanwhile, he worked an assortment of odd jobs as dish washer, messenger, and food deliverer until 1976, when the Cecil Taylor Unit hired him for its U.S. and European tour. Under Taylor's guidance, Ware moved away from emotional playing and toward greater development of motifs, as heard on the Unit's 1976 release, *Dark Unto Themselves*. Ware also increasingly toured and recorded with Andrew Cyrille's band Maono, from which he learned to focus more on the blues and on rhythm. The Taylor stint ended in 1977, and Apogee broke up that year as well, just after making its only studio recording, *Birth of a Being*, released in 1979 under Ware's name. Meanwhile, Ware was back to odd jobs while touring and recording with various players in addition to Cyrille, including William Hooker, Beaver Harris, and Cooper-Moore.

In 1981 Ware led a band on a European tour under his name, but despite the increased profile, Ware started to cut back on public performance. He found it necessary to rebuild his style; he slowed down his playing and applied meditative concentration to the note and chord components. By mid-1984 he emerged with a sound that one critic described as simultaneously "immense and vulnerable" (Ben Ratliff liner notes on David S. Ware, *Flight of i*. DIW/Columbia, 1992). The following year the David S. Ware Trio toured Europe, including a performance in East Berlin, and he married Setsuko Suzuki, whom he had known for several years. By the end of the decade, he had established the core of the David S. Ware Quartet, with William Parker on bass and Matthew Shipp on piano. A flurry of albums in the early 1990s garnered high praise and widening appeal. In 1995 Ware was involved in a serious automobile accident while driving a cab, work he had been doing since 1981. After the lay up, though, the quartet performed its first major jazz festival, in Vienne, France, where Branford Marsalis heard the set. Two years later Marsalis, as artistic director at Columbia Jazz, signed Ware to the label, which issued *Go See the World* in 1998 and *Surrendered* in 2000. The arrangement was short-lived, but Ware's following now expanded well beyond the avant-jazz circle, especially among young white audiences branching out from rock. In 2000 the Quartet performed to 10,000 listeners at a jazz festival in New York City.

Ware paid tribute to his great mentor with his extended arrangement and recording of Sonny Rollins's *Freedom Suite* in 2002. At this time, he also embraced popular deejay culture by allowing his material to be remixed. In his own work, he began experimenting with the use of strings and greater detailing in composition, for example on *Threads*, in 2003. Throughout his career, Ware has insisted on innovation as a reflection of God's creation. Like many American jazz players, Ware has struggled with the business of music. Nonetheless, he has consistently succeeded in elucidating jazz as a link between tradition and the ever new.

FURTHER READING

Ware, David S. Interview by Michael Lang. Tape recording at Ware home, Scotch Plains, New Jersey 1 April 2006.

Jacobson, Nils. "David S. Ware [interview]," in *All About Jazz*, available at http://www.allaboutjazz. com/iviews/dware.htm

Lopez, Rick. "The David S. Ware Sessionography," available at http://www.bb1ok.com/WARE.disc. html

Médioni, Franck, ed. "Sonny Rollins and David S. Ware: Sonny Meets David," in *All About Jazz*, available at http://www.allaboutjazz.com/php/ article.php?id=19423

DISCOGRAPHY

The Cecil Taylor Unit: *Dark to Themselves* (Enja 2084).

David S. Ware: *The Birth of a Being* (Hat Hut W).

Andrew Cyrille: *Special People* (Soul Note 1012).

David S. Ware Trio: *Passage to Music* (Silkheart 113).

David S. Ware Quartet: *Great Bliss, Volumes 1 and 2* (Silkheart 127/128).

David S. Ware Quartet: *Third Ear Recitation* (DIW 870).

David S. Ware Quartet: *Dao* (Homestead 230-2).

David S Ware: *Go See the World* (Sony/Columbia 69138).

David S. Ware Quartet: *Surrendered* (Sony/Columbia 63816).

David S. Ware Quartet: *Freedom Suite* (AUM Fidelity 023).

David S. Ware String Ensemble: *Threads* (Thirsty Ear 57137-2).

David S. Ware Quartet: *Live in the World* (Thirsty Ear 57153-2).

MICHAEL LANG

Ware, Wilbur (8 Sept. 1923–9 Sept. 1979), jazz string bass player, was born Wilbur Bernard Ware in Philadelphia, Pennsylvania, the son of Elijah Bernard Ware and Eleanor Broomfield. His parents separated when he was very young, and Ware went to Chicago to live with the family of a minister named Turner. Having already been exposed to African American gospel music, he began playing the drums in church at the age of eight or nine. Turner played a number of instruments, and when Ware was ten or eleven years old, Turner built him a string bass, which he began to play in what he called a "tramp band" composed of inexpensive or homemade string and percussion instruments. He also was a tap dancer during these years.

Ware worked locally in a five-piece band beginning in 1937, when he performed at the Tuxedo Inn, and he received lessons from the bassist Truck Parham. He was a member of the little-known Flip Benson band from the summer of 1939 to the summer of 1941. He married during this time, but his wife's name is unknown; they had two children. Ware joined a Works Progress Administration band in order to stay with his family in Grand Rapids, Michigan, when Benson's band went to the West Coast, but by 1942 he had returned to Chicago and resumed regional touring. Drafted into the Army Air Force, he played in a service band from September 1943 to January 1946, touring the Pacific.

After further work around Chicago, Ware traveled to Milwaukee to work briefly with the violinist STUFF SMITH and then with the trumpeter ROY ELDRIDGE and the alto saxophonist Sonny Stitt. At the decade's end he became involved with drugs, namely heroin, and alcohol; in the process he lost both of his string basses and consequently was obliged to work as a drummer. He was imprisoned in Chicago in 1952–1953 for a narcotics conviction.

In 1953 Ware joined the tenor saxophonist Johnny Griffin's group as a string bass player, and the following year he recorded a session released on the album *The Johnny Griffin Quartet*. As a member of the house band at the Flame Lounge in Chicago, he accompanied the singer JOE WILLIAMS (1953) and the pianist Junior Mance (1954). He played rhythm and blues in a band with the tenor saxophonist SONNY ROLLINS, and in 1954–1955 he played with the alto saxophonist and singer Eddie "Cleanhead" Vinson.

In 1955, at Chicago's Bee Hive Club, Ware sat in with the hard-bop group of the drummer MAX ROACH and the trumpeter Clifford Brown, playing a lengthy rendition of "Cherokee" at a blisteringly fast tempo. He performed so well that he was hired on the spot to lead the house trio. For his first job, visiting soloist THELONIOUS MONK took over the piano chair and Griffin was added, making it a quartet. Ware accompanied the trumpeter Art Farmer the following week, but within a couple of months he had fallen back into his drug habit and lost the job.

While working with the trumpeter and saxophonist Ira Sullivan in 1956, Ware had an opportunity to sit in with the drummer ART BLAKEY, who soon afterward sent for them to join him in New York City. Still troubled by drugs, Ware had a brief and chaotic affiliation with Blakey's Jazz Messengers in Atlantic City and Philadelphia in June 1956. Returning to New York, he held a brief job in the tenor saxophonist Stan Getz's quartet, playing alongside the pianist Wynton Kelly and the drummer Elvin Jones. In 1957, after playing briefly with the pianists Ray Bryant and HERBIE NICHOLS, he joined the tenor saxophonist JOHN COLTRANE and the drummer Shadow Wilson for Monk's historic quartet date at the Five Spot, until he was fired for getting sick and missing performances. He then worked as a freelancer, at one point leading his own band in Brooklyn that included the trumpeter Nat Adderley, the saxophonist CANNONBALL ADDERLEY, the pianist Wynton Kelly or Duke Jordan, and the drummer PHILLY JOE JONES. On 3 November 1957 he held a famous one-day job as a member of Rollins's trio in a performance at the Village Vanguard; the results were issued on two albums, including *A Night at the Village Vanguard*.

During this period Ware worked on approximately two dozen albums for Riverside Records and its subsidiary labels Jazzland and Judson, and he also recorded occasionally for the Blue Note label, but he wasted all the money he made on drugs. His studio sessions include the trombonist Matthew Gee's *Jazz by Gee!*, the trumpeter LEE MORGAN's *Lee Morgan Indeed!*, and the tenor saxophonist Zoot Sims's *Zoot!* (all 1956); *Monk's Music, Thelonious Monk with John Coltrane* (neither matching the quality of Monk's quartet in live performance), the pianist Sonny Clark's *Dial S for Sonny*, the baritone saxophonist Gerry Mulligan's *Mulligan Meets Monk*, a series of duos on American popular songs with pianist Kenny Drew, and Ware's own *The Chicago Sound* (all 1957); the harmonica player and guitarist Toots Thieleman's *Man Bites Harmonica* (Dec. 1957 and Jan. 1958); and *Johnny Griffin Sextet*, Griffin's *Way Out!*, and the trumpeter Blue Mitchell's *Big Six* (all 1958).

After working with Griffin, Clark, and the drummer Philly Joe Jones at the Bohemia in New York in about 1959 and with the tenor saxophonist J. R. Monterose in Albany in the summer of 1959,

Ware went to Chicago for a concert in October and was stranded there, lacking a local union card. He returned to New York just before the Newport Jazz Festival in July 1960 and participated in an alternative festival organized by the bassist CHARLES MINGUS at Cliff Walk Manor in Newport. Ware was then sentenced to ninety days in jail and stripped of his New York City police cabaret card for stealing a bass. Released early in 1961, he recorded three albums for Blue Note, with the tenor saxophonists Tina Brooks and Clifford Jordan and the guitarist GRANT GREEN; only Jordan's *Starting Time* was issued at the time.

In 1962 Ware was stricken with tuberculosis. After a lengthy stay at a veteran's hospital in Castle Point, New York, he returned to Chicago. While in the hospital, he transferred his addiction from drugs to alcohol. Ware worked only infrequently during this decade. In the summer of 1967 he performed in New York with Mitchell and in a band that included Elvin Jones. He accompanied the tenor saxophonist ARCHIE SHEPP at the Newport Jazz Festival in 1968, recorded a portion of Shepp's album *For Losers* in 1969, and continued working with Shepp intermittently into the early 1970s, including at the 1972 Newport festival. He also was reunited with Monk and Rollins (1969) in separate performances at the Village Vanguard. Occasionally thereafter he worked with Monk's quartets, including one with the saxophonist Pat Patrick and Philly Joe Jones.

In about 1972 Ware met Gloria Lewis, a schoolteacher. They married and settled in Philadelphia. He played in a trio with pianist Red Garland and Philly Joe Jones, and he worked with bandleader SUN RA in 1973. While suffering from emphysema and other ailments caused by his abuse of alcohol and his smoking, Ware worked with Jordan on and off until 1976, when his lung collapsed and he ceased performing. He died in Philadelphia.

In Ware's life story, a jazz stereotype is, for once, true: he was a drug addict and an intuitive artist, unable to read music but gifted with rock-steady timekeeping abilities and a tremendous ear for bop harmony. Ware held a traditional view of the function of the string bass and showed little interest in soloing; an exceptional example is his relaxed and spacious but cleverly disorienting sounding out of blues harmonies during a twenty-four-bar solo on "Blues March" from Mitchell's *Blue Six*. His importance, rather, is in the immaculate quality of the walking bass accompaniments that he supplied, as heard on any of the albums on which he worked.

FURTHER READING

A tape and transcript of Ware's oral history, recorded by his wife Gloria Lewis Ware on 18 Dec. 1977 for the Smithsonian Institution, is held at the Institute of Jazz Studies in Newark, N.J.

Litweiler, John. "Remembering Wilbur Ware," *Down Beat* 46 (1979).

Pekar, Harvey. "The Development of the Modern Bass," *Down Beat* 29 (1962).

Travis, Dempsey J. *An Autobiography of Black Jazz* (1983).

Obituary: *New York Times*, 13 Sept. 1979.

This entry is taken from the *American National Biography* and is published here with the permission of the American Council of Learned Societies.

BARRY KERNFELD

Warfield, George William (30 Apr. 1837–22 Jan. 1919), forced tobacco laborer, was born in Walnut Bottom, Henderson, Kentucky, the son of a slave woman and a free man; the latter was a Federal soldier in the siege of Petersburg and Richmond during the Civil War (1861–1865), carpenter, and land owner. Warfield identified his mother as Anna Warfield and his father as George Williams. Anna was living on the Kentucky farm of Marylander Richard Warfield when George was born. Eastern soil depletion drove many farmers and planters westward to Kentucky for fertile land, where slavery provided a free source of workers to cultivate the labor-intensive tobacco crops. Rich bottomlands formed by the confluence of the Green and Ohio Rivers were ideal for western Kentucky's tobacco economy. Annually the Ohio River flooded and revitalized the soil. When Richard Warfield died in 1838, George was sold to William Beverley (Beverly) at the time his estate was divided. Beverley moved from Virginia to establish a large, flourishing tobacco enterprise in Henderson County.

As the Secession crisis erupted in 1860, with Kentucky-born Illinois Republican Abraham Lincoln as president-elect, Kentucky held a crucial economic position in a cross-current of trade with the North and South. Kentucky remained in the Union, but also remained a slave state. As the war protracted, western growers got wealthier as the price and value of tobacco increased. Moreover, Kentucky fulfilled the growing demand of chewing tobacco for the Union Army. Slaves in the border states were exempt from military recruitment after legislation of the 1863 Emancipation Proclamation. Early in 1864 President Lincoln authorized the recruitment of slaves in Kentucky to fill the ranks of the Union Army. As recruitment began, slavery in the Commonwealth deteriorated considerably; however, the regime did not end until ratification of the Thirteenth Amendment to the U.S. Constitution at the end of the war in 1865. Kentucky did not ratify the Thirteenth Amendment until 1976.

At the age of twenty-five, George Beverly, enlisted under his slaveholder's name, at Owensboro, Kentucky, as a Private in the 118th United States Colored Infantry (USCI) Company H, 19 September 1864. George joined more than twenty-three thousand black Kentuckians who wore the blue uniform of the Federal Army. Kentucky had the second largest number of black recruits during the War. The 118th Regiment was organized at Baltimore, Maryland, 19 October 1864, with Newton S. Kirk as Captain of Company H. After muster in Baltimore, the 118th USCI moved to City Point, Virginia, in late October 1864. While stationed in Virginia, the regiment joined additional Union forces to perform offensive operations and laid siege against Petersburg and Richmond from November 1864 to 3 April 1865. Weeks of consistent battlefield maneuvers were compounded into one of the most complex and important campaigns that greatly reduced and weakened the Rebels. The Confederates were pinned inside their fortifications. Hence, the Confederate capital of Richmond fell and was captured by the Federal Army. As the Confederate government fled, they burned the city. Richmond had led the nation in manufacturing when the war began. Between June and July 1865, the 118th USCI headed for the United States–Mexico border, where they moved to Brazos Santiago, Texas, with duty at Brownville and various points on the Rio Grande until the regiment mustered out 6 February 1866, when George William Beverley was honorably discharged from White Ranch, Texas.

Following the war, George returned to Henderson County, seeking inclusion in American society. Self-assured by the reality of freedom, he began a new life based on familial and social relationships appropriate to the times as George W. Warfield. The local tobacco economy was still strong and remained so far many years after the war. George married Mary Ellen Broadwell, a beautiful mixed-race woman from Henderson on 25 August 1867 at the farm of William A. Hopkins in Spottsville precinct. Five boys and five girls were born to the couple in Henderson between the years 1868 and 1895. Lucy Warfield was born in 1868, the year Ulysses S. Grant was elected the eighteenth president of the United States. Grant served two consecutive terms. In 1878 and 1885, George purchased land for a homestead and family farm, where he raised tobacco and other subsistence crops. He applied for his military service pension in 1890 and received three periodic increases to the monthly allotments over twenty-nine years. Thirteen years lapsed before the War Department's Bureau of Pensions accepted George's identity. In 1903 his claim went to the Southern Division for a new face brief to change his name from George Beverly to George W. Warfield. George died in 1919 from heart failure at age eighty-two in the vicinity of his homestead. He is recorded in historical memory as a humble national warrior.

FURTHER READING

Hewett, Janet B., ed. *The Roster of Union Soldiers, 1861–1865, United States Colored Troops (Anderson, Henry to Jonte, Peter* (1997).

Howard, Victor B. "Slaves Go to War," in *Black Liberation and Freedom, 1862–1884* (1983).

Regosin, Elizabeth A., and Shaffer, Donald R., eds. *Voices of Emancipation: Understanding Slavery, the Civil War and Reconstruction through the U. S. Pension Bureau Files* (2008).

Smith, John David. "The Recruitment of Negro Soldiers in Kentucky, 1863–1865," *The Register of the Kentucky Historical Society*, Vol. 72, October 1974, pp 364–390.

CAROLYN L. WARFIELD

Warfield, Paul (10 Nov. 1941   ), football player, was born Paul Dryden Warfield in Warren, Ohio, son of Amelia Bell Fort and L. Dryden Warfield, who worked for Republic Steel. A gifted athlete, Paul grew up playing many sports, except football. His mother would not allow him to play football because he was so small (he did not reach 100 pounds until high school). When he was a freshman at Warren Harding High School, his mother finally relented, and Paul became the starting running back on Harding's team. He also lettered in baseball, basketball, and track, setting Ohio state records for the 100-yard and 180-yard hurdles and the long jump.

From more than seventy scholarship offers, Warfield chose to attend Ohio State University (OSU), where he played running back and defensive back on the school's football team. Head Coach Woody Hayes employed a power running offense, and though Warfield's size and speed did not fit this style, Hayes wanted Warfield on the field as much as

possible. He averaged forty minutes a game playing both ways. On offense, Warfield was often a decoy as opposing defenses had to respect his speed. Over his career at OSU, Warfield rushed for 1,074 yards, was named to the All Big-Ten Conference team in 1962 and 1963, and was named a *Time* magazine All-American in 1963. Warfield also played baseball and ran track at OSU. He turned down contract offers from six major league baseball teams because he wanted to stay in school. He was considered an Olympic prospect in the long jump, but he lost his chance to try out when he decided to pursue a professional football career.

In 1964 the Cleveland Browns of the National Football League (NFL) and the Buffalo Bills of the American Football League (AFL) selected Warfield in the first round of their respective drafts. Warfield signed with Cleveland because he grew up as a Browns fan and they offered him a chance to play offense. Warfield was considered too small (six feet, 185 pounds) to play halfback in the NFL, and the Browns were unsure what position he should play. At the first workout for rookies, Warfield so impressed coaches with his hands and pass routes that they named him one of the team's starting wide receivers even though he had never played the position. The Browns hired the recently retired Ray Renfro to teach Warfield the nuances of the position. The day before his rookie opener against the Washington Redskins, Warfield married Beverly Ann Keyes. They had two children, and she managed his business affairs.

Though Warfield had not played the receiver position before, he possessed speed, quickness, exceptional hands, and intelligence that allowed him to dominate the position. One Cleveland sportswriter compared him to an antelope because his movements were fluid and graceful. Even double coverage rarely stopped him because he had great leaping ability and almost always out-jumped defenders. During his rookie year Warfield caught fifty-two passes for 920 yards and nine touchdowns, helping the Browns win the 1964 NFL Championship over the Baltimore Colts.

He established himself as a team player, taking on any role the team asked—blocker, decoy, receiver—to help win. At the All-Star game following the championship, Warfield suffered a broken clavicle that caused him to miss most of the 1965 season. It was the only significant injury he suffered in his professional career. He helped the Browns make it to the NFL Championship in 1965, 1968, and 1969, but the Browns lost all three games. He had his best season with the Browns in 1968 when he caught fifty passes for 1,067 yards and twelve touchdowns.

In 1970 the Browns traded Warfield to the Miami Dolphins. Warfield was disappointed with the trade because the Dolphins were perennial losers and he was used to playing on a winning team. He went to Miami without complaint and became one of the team's starting receivers. Warfield was one of the major additions that enabled the Dolphins to become a championship-caliber team. In his five seasons in Miami, 1970–1974, Warfield helped the Dolphins to three Super Bowl appearances, winning two. He also played on the 1972 team that had the only perfect season in NFL history. During his time in Miami, Warfield also served in the National Guard, being discharged in 1973, and he completed his master's degree from Kent State in 1975.

Warfield left the NFL in 1975 to play for the Memphis Southmen of the fledgling World Football League. After one season he returned to the NFL and the Browns, playing two more seasons before retiring in 1977. His career statistics included 427 receptions, 8,565 yards, and 85 touchdowns. *Sporting News* magazine voted Warfield one of the top hundred players of all time. In 1983 he was inducted into the Pro Football Hall of Fame in his first year of eligibility.

After retiring as a player, Warfield worked as an announcer for NBC-TV as well as for the Browns as an assistant to the president. In 1981 the Browns named him director of player relations, a position he held until 1987 when he resigned to open an automotive supply business. In 1995 Warfield started Jamesco Sports Marketing in West Palm Beach, Florida, a company that sold NFL-licensed merchandise. Though he owned his own companies, Warfield wanted to return to football, preferably in an executive role. In 1998 he made an unsuccessful bid, with Calvin Hill, to buy the new Cleveland Browns franchise (the Browns team Warfield played for had since relocated to Baltimore). The Dallas Cowboys hired Warfield as a wide receiver consultant in 2000, and in 2004 he was back with the Browns working as a scouting and career-planning consultant.

As a football player and businessman, Warfield had been described as the epitome of class, from the way he treated people to his dedication to teamwork. Legendary Dolphins coach Don Shula called him a consummate pro and elegant pass runner as well as the type of personality you wanted to represent your team.

FURTHER READING

Coan, Howard. *Great Pass Catchers in Pro Football* (1971).

Liss, Howard. *The Making of a Rookie* (1968).

Pluto, Terry. *When All the World Was Browns Town: Cleveland's Browns and the Championship Season of '64* (1997).

MICHAEL C. MILLER

Warfield, William Caesar (22 Jan. 1920–26 Aug. 2002), vocal recitalist, concert artist, and university professor, was born in West Helena, Arkansas, the eldest of five sons of Robert Warfield, a minister, and Bertha McCamery Warfield. Because employment and educational opportunities in West Helena were limited, the Reverend Warfield moved his family to Rochester, New York.

Warfield became interested in performing and teaching when he was a high school senior. With the pianist at his church Warfield began piano lessons at age nine. He also sang in school choral groups. When he was a senior in high school, the 1937–1938 school year, he entered and won the regional auditions of the National Music Educators League Competition. He was the only African American competitor. Winning at the district level entitled him to enter the national finals, held that year in St. Louis. He was then working with Elsa Miller, his first voice teacher. He won first place at the national level and was awarded a scholarship to any American music school of his choice. The choice was easy. He lived in Rochester, site of the Eastman School of Music of the University of Rochester, one of the world's great institutions for the study of music.

Warfield entered Eastman in September 1939 as a voice major and embarked upon a vigorous curriculum that included languages and dialects, something for which he had already shown a particularly strong interest. On 18 November 1942 he presented his performer's recital. Warfield attended Eastman through 21 November 1942, at which time he discontinued study to join the military during World War II. His fluency in languages qualified him for special assignment in military intelligence, which kept him out of combat, enabling him to associate with higher-level personnel, and gave him time to explore popular music styles. He took his bachelor's of music degree on 19 December 1942, with distinction and performer's certificate.

On 11 March 1946, after completing military service, Warfield enrolled in "refresher" courses at Eastman in preparation for graduate study, and

William Caesar Warfield, photographed by Carl Van Vechten in 1951. (Library of Congress/Carl Van Vechten.)

entered the master of music degree program in performance and literature in June 1946. He remained in the program through 10 October 1946, withdrawing to take the male lead in the touring company of the Broadway hit *Call Me Mister*. The show's music was quite different from the concert and opera literature that had been Warfield's focus, but his successful musical involvement in the show and his interaction with other members of the cast prompted him to take a different perspective on his career. Warfield did not return to Eastman for graduate study, as he had originally planned. He continued with his performance career, making a stunning debut at age thirty on 19 March 1950 at New York City's Town Hall. Thereafter, for several decades without interruption, his career expanded and deepened. He became a consummate singing artist, performing to great acclaim internationally on stage and in concert and recital halls.

In the 1970s Warfield began to combine performance with university professorships in voice: first at the University of Illinois at Urbana-Champaign (1974–1990), retiring as department chair with the title professor emeritus; the University of Texas at San Antonio (1993–1994); and at Northwestern University from 1994 until his death in 2002. He also taught as a visiting professor at other universities within the Illinois university system.

Another Warfield strength was acting. Though he never studied theater formally, he read about acting and understood how theatrical skills could be applied to singing. Warfield's recitals were real theater pieces, expertly crafted and filled with intensity. In performances of Handel's *Messiah*, when he sang "The Trumpet Shall Sound," he wanted the trumpeter to stand alongside him. This placement created a setting that simultaneously emphasized the dramatic text and added a visual presence to the musical interaction between singer and instrumental soloist.

Warfield was married to LEONTYNE PRICE, prima donna assoluta, in 1952. They separated in 1958 and divorced in 1972. In 1984 Warfield won a Grammy in the spoken word category for his narration of Aaron Copland's *Lincoln Portrait*. He had first performed this work on tour in 1976 with Leonard Bernstein and the New York Philharmonic. In Paris he did the narration in French, and in Vienna, in German. Warfield received international acclaim as Porgy in Gershwin's *Porgy and Bess*, a character that he understood and for which he had tremendous passion.

Warfield remained a powerful presence long after his voice was past its peak. His performances were effective because he successfully compensated with artistry, with calculated decisions about repertoire, and by working with only the best people in carefully selected settings.

Warfield showed a commitment to activism through his involvement with the National Association of Negro Musicians, serving as the organization's eighteenth president (1985–1990); and as a board member, beginning in 1996, of the Schiller Institute, supporting a movement to establish a National Conservatory of Music. Warfield's seminars were always a highlight at National Association of Negro Musicians conventions, and through the Schiller Institute he worked with youth, trained voices, and gave master classes.

FURTHER READING

Warfield, William. *My Music and My Life* (1991).

Cheatham, Wallace McClain. *Dialogues on Opera and the African American Experience* (1997).

Gray, John. *Blacks in Classical Music* (1988).

McGinty, Doris Evans. *A Documentary History of the National Association of Negro Musicians* (2004).

WALLACE MCCLAIN CHEATHAM

Waring, Laura Wheeler (16 May 1887–3 Feb. 1948), portrait artist, was born in Hartford, Connecticut, to Robert Foster Wheeler, a railroad porter-turned-Congregationalist pastor, and Mary Christiana Freeman Wheeler, a graduate of Oberlin, Class of 1873. While known for her landscapes and portraits, Waring is best remembered for her work in the Harmon Foundation exhibition Portraits of Outstanding Americans of Negro Origin, which toured the United States in 1944.

Waring was a third-generation college graduate during an era when basic education for blacks, let alone a college education, was hard to get, particularly for girls and women. Waring graduated from Hartford Public High in 1906 and that same year entered the Pennsylvania Academy of the Fine Arts. She studied with painters Thomas Anschutz and William Merritt Chase, who also taught Georgia O'Keeffe. Black American artists studying with her included painters Lenwood Morris and Henry Jones and sculptors May Howard Jackson and META WARRICK FULLER.

Graduating with honors in 1914, Waring received a scholarship that allowed her to travel to Europe. She studied at the Académie de la Grande Chaumière in Paris. According to family lore, she returned to the States with the financial assistance of fellow Hartford resident, Mark Twain, just before the outbreak of war in Europe. After repatriating, Waring joined the faculty of Pennsylvania's State Normal School, later renamed Cheyney State Teachers College, the nation's oldest black college founded in 1837 as the Institute for Colored Youth. (She may have taught at Cheyney while at Pennsylvania Academy.) Here she met and married Walter E. Waring, who had been teaching at Lincoln University, in the late 1920s. She became director of the art department at Cheyney in 1925, a position she held for more than twenty years. In recognition of her exemplary service to the institution, a building on Cheyney's campus was named posthumously in her honor.

During visits to Europe, Waring met and befriended other artists, writers, and intellectuals of the African diaspora, such as HENRY OSSAWA TANNER and W. E. B. DuBois. Some of her friends and acquaintances sat for their portraits with Waring. Her art was displayed at the Harmon Foundation exhibition of works by "Negro artists" in 1927. Founded by the White real estate developer William E. Harmon, the Harmon Foundation's mission was to promote interracial cooperation and understanding. The foundation's executive director, Mary Beattie Brady, organized the exhibition Portraits of Outstanding Americans of Negro Origin in 1944. She commissioned Waring to work with the white artist Betsy Graves Reyneau on the series of notable Black Americans, and the exhibition traveled nationally.

Waring's contributions included her portrait of Harlem Renaissance writer JESSIE FAUSET, whom she had met in Paris thirty years earlier and with whom she remained friends. Waring traveled to the farm of opera singer MARIAN ANDERSON to paint her portrait. Her other Harmon portraits were of Judge RAYMOND ALEXANDER, lawyer SADIE ALEXANDER, musician HENRY T. BURLEIGH, educator DuBois, sociologist George T. Haynes, author and educator JAMES WELDON JOHNSON, and physician Dr. John P. Turner.

Waring was also a contributor and supporter of social change. Her work was frequently found in *The Crisis*, the official monthly publication of the NAACP, of which she was a member. Waring shared her skills and talent through education, particularly with black American students. Her dedication to education was honored when the Laura Wheeler Waring School was named in Philadelphia in 1956. After her death in 1948, her husband donated many of her papers to the Archives of American Art's Philadelphia Arts Documentation Project. A historical marker was erected at her home on North Forty-third Street in Philadelphia.

Waring's work reflected a traditional style gained through academic training: realistic and rendered with an impressionist attention to color, brush stroke, and detail. Her portraits had a dignified tone, creating an almost reverential attitude for her subjects. DuBois, Anderson, Fauset, and more, were depicted formally, at their best, to demonstrate the best—the New Negro—an ideological identification of that time. This traditional presentation of a subject was augmented by details specific to the subject's life or to African American culture or history. The paintings emphasized the emotional response to the subject and his or her contributions to society. Similar to her contemporary, painter Tanner, she emphasized biblical motifs and symbols, gained from her childhood sitting in the pew of her father's church, while known for her more traditional and academic style. Her work was exhibited at the Galerie du Luxembourg, Paris; Howard University, Washington, D.C.; Brooklyn Museum, New York; and the Newark Museum, New Jersey.

FURTHER READING

Driskell, David D., and Tuliza K. Fleming. *Breaking Racial Barriers: African Americans in the Harmon Foundation Collection* (1997).

Laura Wheeler Waring: An Appreciational Study (1949).

Patton, Sharon F. *African-American Art* (1998).

Taha, Halima. *Collecting African American Art: Works on Paper and Canvas* (1998).

ROBIN JONES

Warren, John Earl (16 Nov. 1946–14 Jan. 1969), soldier and Medal of Honor recipient, was born in Brooklyn, New York. Little is known about his life; he may have attended college and served as a cadet in an ROTC (Reserve Officer Training Corps), based on his subsequent service rank. He enlisted in the army at New York City prior to 1968 and later attended Officer Training School, graduating with the rank of second lieutenant in the infantry; by the time of his service in Vietnam, Warren had attained the rank of first lieutenant.

The service of John Warren as an army officer was indicative of just how far African Americans had progressed in the military in terms of career and leadership opportunities since World War I. While black officers like JOHN FOX and CHARLES THOMAS did serve in World War II and the Korean War, their career opportunities were generally limited due to the lingering effects of racism within the army. However, by the time of the Vietnam War these limitations had largely disappeared; not only were African Americans serving in the highest ranks of enlisted men as platoon sergeants, including such men as EUGENE ASHLEY JR., CLIFFORD SIMS, and MATTHEW LEONARD, but they were also given ample opportunity to advance at the officer level. That African Americans were equally capable of providing leadership in combat as officers, an idea that was held by only a minority of white officers just twenty years before, was demonstrated to the highest degree in Vietnam by such men as John Warren, RUPPERT SARGENT, and RILEY PITTS.

John Warren began his tour of duty in Vietnam on 7 September 1968, serving in Company C, 2nd Battalion (Mechanized), 22nd Infantry Regiment, 25th Infantry Division. On 14 January 1969 he was serving as a platoon leader during operations in Tay Ninh Province, moving through a rubber plantation to reinforce another unit when his men came under heavy enemy fire. Without any regard for his safety, Warren took several of his men and maneuvered through a hail of bullets toward the enemy position. When he was within short range of an enemy

emplacement, Warren was preparing to throw a grenade when an enemy grenade landed amid his group of men. He quickly fell on the grenade to shield his men from the ensuing blast; though he died as a result of the blast, Lieutenant John Warren's sacrifice saved the lives of three of his men and "was in keeping with the highest traditions of the military service and reflects great credit on him, his unit, and the U.S. Army (Hanna, p. 178). In recognition of his valor, John Warren was posthumously awarded the Medal of Honor, which was presented to his family during a White House ceremony on 6 August 1970 by President Richard Nixon. Warren was interred at the Long Island National Cemetery, Farmingdale, New York, where a Medal of Honor headstone marks his final resting place.

FURTHER READING

Hanna, Charles W. *African American Recipients of the Medal of Honor* (2002).

GLENN ALLEN KNOBLOCK

Warrior, John, aka John Ward (1848–24 May 1911), a Seminole Indian Negro Scout in the U.S. Army and Medal of Honor recipient, was born in Arkansas. Warrior's family background was a mix of Seminole Indian and African American heritage. This resulted when either his father or mother, like many who were enslaved in the pre–Civil War South, ran away from his or her master and found refuge and freedom with the Seminole Nation in Florida. Here they would stay and marry within the tribe. Beginning in the second decade of the nineteenth century, the Seminoles fought a series of wars with the Spanish and U.S. governments to retain their tribal lands; among those who fought in these wars were many Black Seminoles. It may be speculated that Warrior's family name was derived from their fighting abilities. When the second Seminole War ended in 1842, many among the Seminoles except for a few holdouts were forcibly removed to territory west of the Mississippi River, and it is likely that John Warrior's parents were among this group that traveled the Trail of Tears. Many Black Seminoles, fearful of being reenslaved, went further south to Mexico and formed their own settlements, and it may be that John Warrior was born during the forced migration from Florida. Whatever the case may be, by the late 1860s John Warrior was living in Mexico and earning a living as a farmer.

When John Warrior returned to the United States, enlisting in the army at Fort Duncan, Texas, in August of 1870, he arrived in the United States with ten other Black Seminoles, including their leader, John Kibbetts. These men were the first Black Seminoles to return to their native land after the army authorized the recruitment of Black Indians as scouts in the ongoing conflict with native peoples in the southwest. While little is known about John Warrior, who was enlisted under the shortened name of John Ward, he and the men who enlisted with him were highly skilled horsemen, trackers, and hunters, who well knew the native tribes the army was then fighting. Though Warrior and his fellow scouts spoke English and resembled in appearance the black soldiers serving in cavalry and infantry regiments at that time, the Black Seminole Scouts were anything but conventional soldiers; they sometimes wore Indian war bonnets along with their army uniforms and did not take kindly to the mundane soldier chores of everyday life, such as chopping firewood and standing guard. However, the army needed scouts, and the Black Seminoles were the best there were. By 1871, so many Black Seminole Scouts had joined the army that a settlement grew up at Brackettville, Texas, near Fort Clark.

In April 1875, having risen to the rank of sergeant, John Warrior was attached to the all-black 24th Infantry Regiment performing scout duty, along with fellow soldiers Isaac Payne and POMPEY FACTOR, under the command of Lieutenant John Bullis, a white officer who was loved and respected by his men. On 23–24 April they were searching for Indians near the confluence of the Pecos and Rio Grande rivers in an area now encompassed by the Seminole Canyon State Park, and the following day came across a Comanche war party consisting of nearly thirty warriors armed with repeating rifles. In the ensuing fight, which lasted nearly an hour, the Seminole Scouts under Bullis killed three men but were close to being surrounded and separated from their horses. In an effort to escape, the scouts made it to their horses, but soon noticed that their commanding officer was in trouble. With Indians rushing Bullis, his horse became spooked and he had no way to escape, but Sergeant Ward rallied his scouts, yelling to Factor and Payne "Boys, don't let us leave him" (Schubert, p. 36). While leading the effort to save Lieutenant Bullis, Warrior's rifle was shattered by enemy fire, but no matter. He galloped through the Comanche warriors, covered by the gunfire of Factor and Payne, and Bullis was able to jump on his horse and ride to safety behind him. For this action Lieutenant John Bullis recommended Warrior, Payne, and Factor for the Medal of Honor, commenting about all three that "they are brave and trustworthy" (Schubert, p. 36). As a result, all three men received the Medal of Honor in March 1876.

The service of Black Seminole scouts like John Warrior, Isaac Payne, Pompey Factor, and Adam Paine is significant for a number of reasons. Being Medal of Honor recipients alone makes these men worthy of remembrance. However, their Black Seminole heritage also makes them both interesting and somewhat contradictory figures in the U.S. Army's long-running battle to subdue the native peoples of the southwest in the last decades of the nineteenth century. That these men were brave and honorable soldiers is beyond question, but the fact that they were also the descendants of those formerly enslaved and of Native Americans driven from *their* homeland in an earlier age, and were now employed to drive Native Americans from their ancestral homelands is one of the many ironies that exist in the history of race relations in America.

Following the actions that earned him the Medal of Honor in 1875, John Warrior continued to serve as a scout, with only a few brief interruptions, for another twenty years. After spending a cold night as sergeant of the guard at Fort Clark in January 1878, Warrior contracted rheumatism, from which he suffered the rest of his life. So crippled by his ailments, Warrior could no longer mount a horse and subsequently received his final discharge on 5 October 1894. He continued to live in the Black Seminole settlement at Brackettville, Texas, with his wife Julia, and after his death in 1911 was buried there in the Seminole Indian Scout Cemetery.

FURTHER READING

Hanna, Charles W. *African American Recipients of the Medal of Honor* (2002).

Schubert, Frank N. *Black Valor: Buffalo Soldiers and the Medal of Honor, 1870–1898* (1997).

GLENN ALLEN KNOBLOCK

Warwick, Dionne (12 Dec. 1940–), singer, was born Marie Dionne Warrick in East Orange, New Jersey, to Lee Drinkard and Mansel Warrick. Her father was a gospel record promoter for Chess Records, and her mother managed and sometimes performed with the Drinkard Singers, a gospel group that featured four of Warwick's aunts and uncles, including Emily "Cissy" Drinkard, the mother of the pop singer Whitney Houston, and Ann Moss (née Anne Drinkard), who were both also members of the famed Sweet Inspirations.

Warwick's early years were spent singing gospel, first in the New Hope Baptist Church choir

Dionne Warwick, singing "I Say A Little Prayer" at the Air Jamaica Jazz and Blues festival in Montego Bay, Jamacia, 29 January 2005. (AP Images.)

in Newark and then, beginning in 1959, with the Gospelaires, which she formed along with her sister Dee Dee and her aunt Cissy. In the early 1960s the Warwick sisters joined the remnants of the Drinkard Singers to form the Sweet Inspirations and gained enormous success as one of the most used session and backup singing groups of all time. Warwick was on hand with the Gospelaires during a 1961 recording session with the Drifters when composer Burt Bacharach heard her and asked her to record some demos for songs he was writing with lyricist Hal David. The New York record company Scepter Records heard the demos and agreed to sign her. Bacharach and David composed and produced her first single, "Don't Make Me Over" (1962). It was a huge success, and owing to a typographical error in the credits, "Dionne Warrick" became "Dionne Warwick." Though retaining her stage name, in 1963 Warwick became Dionne Elliott with her marriage to drummer and actor William "Bill" Elliott II; they would have two sons, David and Damon Elliott.

Over the next ten years Warwick released eighteen albums, containing twenty-two Top 40 hits on *Billboard*'s Hot 100 chart. By the time she parted with Scepter in 1971, her string of classics, many of them written by Bacharach and David, had made her an international superstar. Among them were "Walk On By" (1964), "Message to Michael" (1966), "Alfie" (1967), "(Theme from) The Valley of the Dolls" (1968), "I Say a Little Prayer" (1967), "Promises, Promises" (1968), "This Girl's In Love with You" (1969), and "Make It Easy on Yourself" (1970). Two of her biggest hits, "Do You Know the Way to San Jose?" (1968) and "I'll Never Fall in Love Again" (1970), earned her Grammy Awards. In addition to her solo work, she occasionally stood in with the Sweet Inspirations and the Shirelles through the 1960s, most notably appearing on the Shirelles' 1961 classic "Will You Love Me Tomorrow," which she remade, along with the remaining Shirelles, on her 1981 album *Hot! Live and Otherwise.*

The masterful blend of pop, R&B, and showtunes that made Warwick a superstar was out of style by the end of the 1970s, except in England. Having signed with Warner Brothers Records in 1970, and having ended her collaboration with Bacharach in 1972, her subsequent eight albums charted only one number one hit: "Then Came You" (1974), which she recorded with the Spinners under the production guidance of the Philadelphia Sound architect Thom Bell. At what appeared to be the nadir of her career, the record executive Clive Davis signed Warwick to a contract with Arista Records and teamed her with singer-songwriter and producer Barry Manilow. Her next album, *Dionne* (1979) resurrected her from oblivion. Hugely successful, the album became Warwick's first platinum record, with two singles in the pop Top 20. "Dejá Vú" and "I'll Never Love This Way Again" garnered Warwick her third and fourth Grammy Awards for Best R&B Vocal Performance, Female, and Best Pop Vocal Performance, Female.

Warwick continued to figure regularly on *Billboard*'s adult contemporary charts throughout the 1980s and scored a pop Top 10 hit with the 1982 single "Heartbreaker" and an R&B Top 10 hit with "Love Power," a duet with the quiet storm star Jeffrey Osborne. Warwick's influence also extended into other arenas of popular culture during the 1980s and early 1990s. She hosted the pilot special for the Top 40 dance show *Solid Gold*, returning to host it several times over the course of the decade. She appeared on and hosted numerous TV series and specials, including the Grammy Awards and the Soul Train Music Awards. Perhaps less dignified but certainly more widely viewed, she aired a series of ubiquitous late-night infomercials for the Psychic Friends Network. In 1990 she hosted her own daytime talk show, *Dionne and Friends*, for one season. In the midst of her comeback, Warwick began to lend her talents to numerous philanthropic and social causes. In 1985 she organized a session to record "That's What Friends Are For" with STEVIE WONDER, Elton John, and GLADYS KNIGHT. The single went to number one and earned her a fifth Grammy for Best Pop Vocal Performance, Duo or Group. She donated the profits it generated to the American Foundation for AIDS Research. She also participated in the recording of the decade's most famous charity musical event, USA for Africa's "We Are the World" (1985) and happily donated her talents to the 1985 global concert "Live Aid." Further global recognition came in the form of being named a United Nations (U.N.) health ambassador (1987), gaining a star on the Hollywood Walk of Fame, becoming the first African American woman to appear in a command performance before Queen Elizabeth II of England (1968), singing with the National Opera Company of Japan, and being named a global ambassador for the U.N.'s branch of the Food and Agriculture Organization (2002). She was asked four times to perform at the Vatican's Christmas Concert and saw her elementary school, Lincoln Elementary, renamed the Dionne Warwick Institute of Economics & Entrepreneurship. The National Association of Record Merchandisers gave her the Chairman's Award for Sustained Creative Achievement (1998), while the R&B Foundation bestowed upon her their Lifetime Achievement Award (2003). She was honored by OPRAH WINFREY in her "Legends Ball" (2005) and with the Recording Academy's 2002 Heroes Award.

Although her recording career stalled again during the 1990s, Warwick had already achieved legendary status as a pop singer, a position confirmed by her 2006 appearance on *American Idol*, a show that repopularized the kind of R&B-influenced Brill Building pop that first made her a star. While planning an African American history book for schools, she penned her first book, *My Point of View* (2003), launched a skin-care line and fragrance, and formed a production company and an interior design firm. With forty-two albums, fifty-six *Billboard* Hot 100 hits, a hit single every year for nine consecutive years (1962–1970), a recording career spanning more than forty years, and a singing career approaching sixty years, by the late 2000s Warwick had become a true African American legend and role model.

DAVID DE CLUE

Washboard Bill. *See* Cooke, William E. "Washboard Bill."

Washboard Sam (5 July 1910–13 Nov. 1966), songwriter, singer, and washboardist, was born Robert Brown in Walnut Ridge, Arkansas, one of three children fathered by Frank Broonzy, a former enslaved black American from Lawrence County, a rural section of northeast Arkansas. Brown worked on a farm until he was a teenager; in the early 1920s he moved to Memphis, Tennessee, and began his professional career playing the washboard with local blues musicians. While in Memphis, Brown played for tips on street corners with vocalist "SLEEPY" JOHN ADAMS ESTES and blues harmonica pioneer Hammie Nixon (Nickerson). In 1932 Brown moved to Chicago, Illinois, continuing to work street corners with Estes and Nixon. Also, in that same year, he began playing gigs with guitarist and vocalist "BIG BILL" BROONZY, his older half-brother, who had already established himself in the budding Chicago blues music scene of the early 1930s, both as an early "race records" recording artist for the top labels in the recording industry—Paramount, Columbia, and Bluebird (a subsidiary of Victor)—and as a performer in the various clubs in Chicago's black community.

From 1932 to 1935 Brown recorded with Broonzy and other founders of Chicago blues including Jazz Gillum (WILLIAM MCKINLEY Gillum), TAMPA RED (HUDSON WHITTAKER), MEMPHIS MINNIE (LIZZIE DOUGLAS), MEMPHIS SLIM (JOHN PETER CHATMAN), and BUKKA WHITE (BOOKER T. WASHINGTON WHITE). These musicians played together in bands such as the State Street Swingers and the Hokum Boys.

It was during 1935 and 1936 that Brown established himself as one of the key session players of early Chicago blues. During this time, he started to record his own songs and impress audiences with his vocals, recording initially for the Vocalion Label under the names "Ham Gravey" and "Shufflin' Sam" before settling on the name Washboard Sam, the name used on his later Bluebird recordings. Through music industry connections of Broonzy and a business association with Lester Melrose, the record producer and talent scout most responsible for organizing and recording early Chicago blues musicians, Robert Brown was transformed into Washboard Sam, one of the most prolific and popular musical musicians performing in Chicago during the 1930s and 1940s. Washboard Sam was one of Melrose's primary recording artists, recording over 175 songs for Bluebird. When he was not cutting his own record tracks, Sam was backing many of the same Bluebird recording artists who ended up playing on his records, such as Broonzy, Jazz Gillum, and Tampa Red.

Washboard Sam was noted more for what critics have described as his "deep," "heavy," "powerful," and "rhythmic" vocals than for his washboard playing skills; yet it was his ability to keep strong, steady rhythms on the washboard (also known as the *frittoir*, scrub board, or rub board) and "modernize" the country blues sound that attracted Melrose and kept Sam busy recording with other Bluebird recording artists. Although the washboard was a common instrument among rural, farming black communities in the South during the 1930s and 1940s (and played a central role in zydeco music, a blues-based musical form popular among the black communities of southwest Louisiana and east Texas), the instrument was an anomaly in northern cities. Washboard Sam was one of a handful of performing washboardists in Chicago and the only one to gain fame there.

Of the numerous songs written and recorded by Washboard Sam, two Bluebird label recordings,

"Backdoor" (1937) and "Diggin' My Potatoes" (1939), were his most popular hits and the only two songs of his that Victor continued to promote after the demise of the Bluebird label in the 1950s. With menacing-sounding song titles like "Razor Cuttin' Man" (1936) and "Evil Blues" (1941), and songs about infidelity ("How Can You Love Me," 1941) and sexual escapades ("I'm a Prowlin' Ground Hog," 1936), Washboard Sam was one of the first recording artists to introduce risqué, even scandalous subject matter to popular audiences. In the process, he and other prewar blues artists challenged the conventions of the recording industry and subject matter that was publicly acceptable. And like other blues musicians of this time, Sam advanced unsettling social themes and human problems often ignored by the American white public, exposing the darker, more melancholy side of social reality and linking that reality to being black in America.

In 1941 Sam wrote "I've Been Treated Wrong," a semiautobiographical song that relates the sorrowful life story of a person who does not know their "real name" or "when they were born," whose "mother [has] died," and who is "treated just like an orphan" and "worked just like a slave." This song was more than just a lament, for it reminds audiences about the enslavement of blacks and that blacks were still being worked like slaves. Like many blues musicians, whether pre- or postwar, Washboard Sam was an early social critic and social historian.

Washboard Sam's popularity waned in the early 1950s as Chicago blues shifted from its acoustic, country-influenced blues sound established during the Bluebird years (1935–1949) to the electric, modernized blues sound of the 1950s engineered primarily by Chess Records and to a lesser extent Cobra Records. Accustomed to the acoustic-style blues, Sam never adapted to developments in Chicago blues during the 1950s. In many ways, however, he had paved the way for second-generation Chicago blues artists such as WILLIE DIXON, HOWLIN' WOLF (CHESTER ARTHUR BURNETT), LITTLE WALTER (MARION WALTER JACOBS), and MUDDY WATERS (MCKINLEY MORGANFIELD).

In 1953 Sam briefly recorded with Chess, but then he quit recording and performing for over a decade, declining invitations by fellow blues artists to reemerge. Sam started performing again in Chicago in 1963; in 1964, after a few performances in Europe, he recorded his last works with Spivey Records. Despite health problems associated with heart disease, Sam managed to play a few gigs around New York City in 1965 before his death the following year in Chicago. Washboard Sam, a key figure in the development of the blues, specifically the transition from rural to urban blues, was laid to rest with little fanfare at Washington Memorial Cemetery in Homewood, Illinois.

FURTHER READING
Harris, Sheldon. *Blues Who's Who: A Biographical Dictionary of Blues Singers* (1979).
Oliver, Paul, ed. *Blues Off the Record* (1984).

DISCOGRAPHY
Washboard Sam: Complete Recorded Works in Chronological Order, Vols. 1–7 (Document Records DOCD 5171–5177).

SEAN ELIAS

Washington, Augustus (1820 or 1821–7 June 1875), abolitionist, photographer, and Liberian statesman, was born in Trenton, New Jersey, the son of Christian Washington, a former slave from Virginia who operated an oyster saloon, and a woman who is identified only as a native of South Asia. She apparently died soon after his birth, for his father remarried in October 1821. Washington was raised in Trenton and until early adolescence attended school with white students. When access to such schooling ended in the face of growing racism, he was left to continue his education on his own. He worked for his father for several years, studied intermittently, and became an avid reader of Benjamin Lundy's *Genius of Universal Emancipation* and William Lloyd Garrison's *Liberator*. These papers aroused Washington's hatred of slavery and racial prejudice and inspired him to become an activist. Eager to contribute to the uplift of his community, he organized a debating society and, at the age of sixteen, briefly conducted a small school for black children. In 1837 Washington heeded the advice of a prominent abolitionist, most likely Lewis Tappan, and enrolled in the Oneida Institute, a progressive academy and college in Whitesboro, New York, that combined academics with a program of manual labor. He remained there for nearly a year and a half and completed both the preparatory course and his freshman year. When a lack of funds forced him to leave school and seek employment in 1838, he secured a teaching post at the African Public School in Brooklyn and also served as a subscription agent and correspondent for the influential *Colored American* newspaper.

An advocate for unrestricted black suffrage, Washington was a delegate to the Convention of the Colored Inhabitants of the State of New York held in Albany in 1840, and he afterward organized mass meetings in support of a petition drive to secure the franchise. Like other abolitionists he opposed the American Colonization Society's campaign to send free blacks and manumitted slaves to Africa. "I abhor with intense hatred the motives, the scheme, and spirit of colonization," he declared in the *Colored American* (31 July 1841).

With assistance from friends in the abolitionist movement, Washington resumed his formal education. In 1841 he was admitted to the Kimball Union Academy in Meridan, New Hampshire, and in 1843 entered Dartmouth College as its sole African American student. To support himself, Washington turned to the fledgling field of photography and became one of its earliest African American practitioners when he learned to make daguerreotypes during the winter of his freshman year. He parlayed his new skill into a profitable enterprise by daguerreotyping members of the Dartmouth faculty and residents of the town of Hanover, but he put his camera aside when his portrait business interfered with his studies. As a consequence, he was unable to keep pace with debts incurred at Dartmouth and left the college in the autumn of 1844.

Settling in Hartford, Connecticut, Augustus Washington took charge of that city's North African School. He taught classes in the basement of the Talcott Street Congregational Church—pastored by the Reverend JAMES W. C. PENNINGTON—until sometime in 1846 when he returned to the practice of photography and opened one of Hartford's first daguerrean galleries. Advertising his services in antislavery newspapers, including Connecticut's *Charter Oak* and New York's *Ram's Horn*, Washington initially sought the patronage of those sympathetic to the abolitionist cause. His success is reflected by the fact that soon after opening his gallery, he made the earliest known daguerreotype portrait of radical abolitionist John Brown. At a time when black businessmen faced enormous obstacles, Washington competed effectively against Hartford's white-owned daguerrean galleries and bested his early rivals. By offering quality portraits at attractive prices and astutely marketing his services, he attracted a large clientele that included citizens of all classes from Hartford and its environs.

In 1850 Washington married Cordelia (maiden surname unknown), who was ten years younger than he. The couple had four children. With the passage of the Fugitive Slave Act of 1850, Washington grew increasingly pessimistic about the long-term prospects for African Americans in the United States. Despite his success as a daguerreotypist, he could no longer reconcile his aspirations for the future with the harsh reality of racism in antebellum America. In 1851, after rejecting various emigration options within the Americas, he withdrew his opposition to the American Colonization Society and argued in favor of African colonization in a letter published in the *New-York Daily Tribune*. He announced his intention to emigrate in 1853, and, armed with sufficient photographic supplies to enable him to continue his career as a daguerreotypist, he sailed for Liberia with his wife and two young children.

Washington became one of the first resident photographers in West Africa. His surviving portraits constitute a unique visual record of the republic's early statesmen and business leaders. He later expanded his enterprise by visiting Sierra Leone, the Gambia, and Senegal, where he operated portrait studios on a short-term basis. Although he had planned to earn his livelihood as a daguerreotypist and by running a small store, Washington soon concluded that his future lay in agriculture. He acquired and developed substantial property along the St. Paul River to become one of Liberia's leading sugarcane growers. He also assumed a significant role in that nation's political affairs. First elected to the House of Representatives in 1863 and later chosen as its speaker, Washington won election to the Liberian Senate in 1871. Two years later he became the founding editor of the *New Era* newspaper. When he died in Monrovia, his passing was noted by the *African Repository* as "a severe loss to Western Africa."

As a pioneering African American daguerreotypist in the United States and later in West Africa, Washington occupies a singular place in the history of photography. Beyond his achievements in that field, his decision to break ranks with his fellow abolitionists and emigrate to Liberia makes him one of the more intriguing figures of the antebellum period.

FURTHER READING
Several of Washington's letters to officials of the American Colonization Society are housed in the American Colonization Society Collection in the Manuscript Division of the Library of Congress and are available on microfilm. For additional letters by Washington, excerpts from his articles for the *New Era* (Monrovia) newspaper, and reports from contemporaries detailing his activities in Liberia, see those issues of the American Colonization Society's *African Repository* published between 1851 and 1875. Washington offers revealing accounts of his early life and his struggles to obtain an education in two letters written to Reverend Theodore Sedgwick Wright on 1 Jan. 1846 and 15 Jan. 1846 and published in the *Charter Oak* (Hartford), n.s., 5 Feb. 1846 and 12 Feb. 1846, respectively.

Johnson, Carol. "Faces of Freedom: Portraits from the American Colonization Society Collection," *The Daguerreian Society Annual, 1996* (1997): 264–78.
Shumard, Ann M. *A Durable Memento: Portraits by Augustus Washington, African American Daguerreotypist*, the exhibition booklet published by National Portrait Gallery, Smithsonian Institution (1999).
White, David O. "Augustus Washington, Black Daguerreotypist of Hartford," *Connecticut Historical Society Bulletin* 39, no. 1 (Jan. 1974): 14–19.
White, David O. "Hartford's African Schools, 1830–1868," *Connecticut Historical Society Bulletin* 39, no. 2 (Apr. 1974): 47–53.
Willis, Deborah. *Reflections in Black: A History of Black Photographers, 1840 to the Present* (2000).

ANN M. SHUMARD

Washington, Booker T. (5 Apr. 1856?–14 Nov. 1915), educator and race leader, was born on the plantation of James Burroughs, near Hale's Ford in Franklin County, Virginia, the son of an unknown white father and Jane, a slave cook owned by Burroughs. Washington was never certain of the date of his birth and showed little interest in who his father might have been. His mother gave him his first and middle names, Booker Taliaferro; he took his last name in 1870 from his stepfather, Washington Ferguson, a slave whom his mother had married. In his autobiography *Up from Slavery* (1901), he recalled the poverty of his early years as a slave on Burroughs's plantation, but because emancipation came when he was around nine, he was spared the harsher experiences of the slave system. In 1865, at the end of the Civil War, his mother moved him, his half-sister, and his half-brother to Malden, West Virginia, where her husband had found work. Young Booker was put to work packing salt from a nearby mine and later did even harder work in a coal mine.

Two women were influential in Washington's early education. The first was his mother. He displayed an intense interest in learning to read; although illiterate herself, she bought her son a spelling book and encouraged him to learn.

While working in the mines, Washington also began attending a local elementary school for black youths. The other female influence was Viola Ruffner, wife of General Lewis Ruffner, owner of the mines. Probably around the age of eleven, eager to escape the brutal mine work, he secured a position as Viola Ruffner's houseboy. She had a prickly personality, was a demanding taskmaster, and had driven off several other boys, but in the eighteen months he worked for her he came to absorb and appreciate her emphasis on the values of hard work, cleanliness, and thrift; thereby an unlikely bond of affection and respect developed between these two people from very different backgrounds. Early on, Ruffner spotted the ambition in young Washington: "He seemed peculiarly determined to emerge from his obscurity. He was ever restless, uneasy, as if knowing that contentment would mean inaction. 'Am I getting on?'—that was his principal question" (quoted in Gilson Willetts, "Slave Boy and Leader of His Race," *New Voice* 16 [24 June 1899]: 3).

In 1872, at age sixteen, Washington entered Hampton Normal and Agricultural Institute in Hampton, Virginia; it turned out to be one of the most important steps of his life. Having overheard two miners talking about the school for young blacks, he had determined to make his way there and set out on the five-hundred-mile trip with a small sum of money donated by family and friends, barely enough to take him partway by train. The rest of the monthlong journey was on foot or via an occasional passing wagon. He arrived with fifty cents in his pocket and asked to be admitted. Ordered to clean out a room, and sensing that this might be his entrance examination, he swept and dusted until the room was spotless and was soon a Hampton student. While there he worked as a custodian to help defray his expenses.

Hampton Institute, only four years old at the time, was a monument to its principal, General Samuel Chapman Armstrong, probably the single most influential person in Washington's life. Born of missionary parents in Hawaii, Armstrong had led black troops in the Civil War. Convinced that the future of the freedmen lay in practical and industrial education and the instilling of Christian virtues, Armstrong had founded Hampton under the auspices of the American Missionary Association. In Booker Washington he found an extraordinarily apt and ambitious pupil. Washington not only learned agriculture, brickmasonry, and the standard academic subjects taught at Hampton, more importantly he absorbed the entire philosophy of character building and utilitarian education stressed by the handsome and charismatic Armstrong. After graduating in 1875, Washington returned to Malden for three years to teach in a black school and to spread the Hampton philosophy. Several months spent at Wayland Seminary, a Baptist institution, in Washington, D.C., in 1878–1879 convinced the restless young Washington that he was not cut out for the ministry. In addition, his exposure to the poverty and degeneracy of lower-class urban life instilled in him a lifelong dislike of cities. This prejudice would later weaken to a degree his message to his fellow blacks to remain in the rural South, at a time when far greater job opportunities were to be found in the nation's burgeoning cities.

Somewhat adrift in the late 1870s, having rejected the ministry, law, and public school teaching as viable careers, Washington was invited back to Hampton in 1879 by General Armstrong to run the night school and later to supervise the dormitory for Indian boys, who had recently been admitted. As usual, his performance was exemplary. In the spring of 1881 Armstrong received a request from three education commissioners in Alabama to recommend a white principal for a new Negro normal school to be established in Tuskegee. He wrote a persuasive letter urging them to accept Washington instead. They agreed, and the young educator was soon on the way to what would be his life's work. On arriving in Alabama, he learned that the state legislature had appropriated two thousand dollars for salaries only. There was no land, no buildings, no campus.

Plunging into unremitting activity, Washington won over local whites in the community, began to recruit black students who were hungry for education, and held the first classes in a shanty. One of his mentors at Hampton was the school's treasurer, James F. B. Marshall, an elderly and kindly ex-general who now began coaching Washington in the arts of financial management and extracting money from wealthy white benefactors. With a two-hundred-dollar loan from Marshall, Washington purchased land outside of town for a permanent campus. Student labor erected the initial buildings of Tuskegee Institute, and student farming supplied much of the foodstuff for the dormitory kitchen. Tuskegee would grow to two thousand acres and one hundred buildings, with a faculty of nearly two hundred and an endowment close to $2 million by the time of Washington's death.

In spite of Washington's national fame in years to come, Tuskegee never ceased to be his base of operations and the enterprise to which he devoted most of his time. Each morning began with a horseback ride to inspect the campus. He hired and fired faculty, admitted and expelled students, oversaw the smallest details of finances and purchasing, bought more land when he could, kept creditors at bay when he had to, and spent much time cultivating northern philanthropists for donations, at which he became extremely adept. Among the notable benefactors of Tuskegee were steel magnate Andrew Carnegie, oilman John D. Rockefeller, camera manufacturer George Eastman, and Julius Rosenwald, president of Sears, Roebuck, and Co.

In many respects Tuskegee was a "colony" of Hampton Institute, as Washington had imbibed General Armstrong's emphasis on industrial skills and character building. The vocational curriculum included some thirty-eight subjects, including printing, carpentry, cabinetmaking, and farming. Female students specialized in cooking, sewing, and other domestic skills. In addition to the standard academic subjects, from grammar and composition to history, mathematics, chemistry, and bookkeeping, strong emphasis was placed on personal hygiene and moral development and on daily chapel services. At the time of Washington's death the student body numbered more than fifteen hundred.

Unlike Hampton, however, Washington's faculty and administrative staff were all black, and many were graduates of Hampton and Fisk University. Notable among the staff were botanist and agricultural researcher GEORGE WASHINGTON CARVER and MONROE NATHAN WORK, the sociologist and bibliographer of black history and life who spent thirty-seven years at Tuskegee as head of the Records and Research Department. The highly capable OLIVIA DAVIDSON, a graduate of Hampton and the Framingham State Normal School near Boston, arrived in 1881 to serve as principal of the female students and came as close as anyone to being Washington's co-superintendent. For the last eighteen years of his life, Washington's personal private secretary, factotum, and alter ego was Emmett Jay Scott, an extraordinarily loyal, astute, and circumspect assistant who handled much of Washington's correspondence, supervised the Tuskegee office staff, and was privy to all of Washington's secret machinations at controlling black American politics.

Washington was married three times. His first wife, FANNIE SMITH [WASHINGTON], his sweetheart from Malden, gave birth to a child in 1883, the year after their marriage, but died prematurely

the next year. In 1885 Washington married Olivia Davidson; they had two children. This too was a short marriage, for she had suffered from physical maladies for years and died in 1889. Four years later he married Margaret J. Murray (MARGARET MURRAY WASHINGTON), a Fisk graduate who had replaced Davidson as lady principal. She remained Washington's wife for the rest of his life, helping to raise his three children and continuing to play a major role at Tuskegee.

As Tuskegee Institute grew, it branched out into other endeavors. The annual Tuskegee Negro Conferences, inaugurated in 1892, sought solutions for impoverished black farmers through crop diversity and education. The National Negro Business League, founded in 1900, gave encouragement to black enterprises and publicized their successes. Margaret Washington hosted women's conferences on campus. Washington established National Negro Health Week and called attention to minority health issues in addresses nationwide.

By the mid-1880s Washington was becoming a fixture on the nation's lecture circuit. This exposure both drew attention and dollars to Tuskegee and allowed the black educator to articulate his philosophy of racial advancement. In a notable 1884 address to the National Education Association in Madison, Wisconsin, Washington touted education for blacks—"brains, property, and character"—as the key to black advancement and acceptance by white southerners. "Separate but equal" railroad and other public facilities were acceptable to blacks, he argued, as long as they really were equal. This speech foreshadowed the accommodationist racial compromises he would preach for the rest of his life. During the 1880s and 1890s Washington went out of his way to soft-pedal racial insults and attacks on blacks (including himself) by whites. He courted southern white politicians who were racial moderates, arguing that black Americans had to exhibit good citizenship, hard work, and elevated character in order to win the respect of the "better sort" of whites. Full political and social equality would result in all due time, he maintained.

The apogee of Washington's career as a spokesman for his race occurred at the opening of Atlanta's Cotton States and International Exposition in September 1895. This was one of a number of such fairs held to highlight the South's progress since the Civil War. Blacks had their own, albeit segregated, exhibit space at the exposition, and the Atlanta leaders of the affair invited Washington to give a ten-minute address. He spent much time honing

Booker T. Washington, in a seated portrait, c. 1903. (Library of Congress.)

the speech, sensing its symbolic importance, and was uncharacteristically nervous as 18 September approached.

Dubbed the "Atlanta Compromise," the speech was a masterpiece of tact and ambiguity intended to impress all members of the integrated audience—northern whites, southern whites, and blacks from the South. It had all been said before by Washington but never as succinctly and before such an important gathering. Though acceding realistically to the deplorable state of race relations in the United States at that time, Washington seemed to accept the existence of segregation for his people and urged them not to push for integrated facilities and other civil and political rights. "The wisest among my race understand that the agitation of questions of social equality is the extremest folly, and that progress in the enjoyment of all the privileges that will come to us must be the result of severe and constant struggle rather than of artificial forcing." He urged southern blacks to "cast down your bucket where you are"—stay in the South, gain education, and through hard work win the economic

advancement that would also gain them the respect of their white neighbors. He reminded his white listeners that the blacks among them made up one-third of the South's population and that the fates of the two races were inextricably bound. The climax of the speech, which brought the audience to its feet in thunderous applause, was the memorable sentence: "In all things that are purely social we can be as separate as the fingers, yet one as the hand in all things essential to mutual progress."

The Atlanta Compromise speech unquestionably secured Washington's position as the leading spokesman for American blacks to the larger white community and particularly to the white power structure of American politics, and it was lavishly praised by white leaders. Symbolically the torch of black leadership had also been passed to a younger generation, inasmuch as FREDERICK DOUGLASS, the former slave turned abolitionist, orator, and journalist, who had been the most notable black American of his day, had died a few months before Washington spoke. Washington had tapped into the classic American myth that hard work, self-discipline, and economic independence would win for any citizen the respect of his neighbors. He conveniently ignored or chose to omit the fact that at the very time he spoke, American race relations were at their worst point since the end of the Civil War, with lynchings and other violence, grinding poverty, and legal and extralegal discrimination at the ballot box a fact of life for most American blacks. The U.S. Supreme Court's decision the very next year in PLESSY v. Ferguson would place the fiction of "separate but equal" on segregated public facilities.

Yet the decade after 1895 was for Washington the most influential period of his life, if that influence is measured by his demand as a speaker and the power he wielded among white political leaders. In 1898 President William McKinley paid a visit to Tuskegee Institute. McKinley's successor, Theodore Roosevelt, had been a friend of Washington's for several years. The relationship between president and educator began on an inauspicious note when Roosevelt, one month after taking office in 1901, invited Washington to dinner at the White House. Although other blacks had visited the executive mansion on occasion since at least the time of Abraham Lincoln, the Roosevelt-Washington dinner set off a firestorm of outrage, especially in the southern white press. Washington was chagrined by the whole affair; Roosevelt made light of it to his southern friend but privately called it a "mistake" and never again invited minorities to the White House.

The dinner aside, the relationship between the two men was unusually close. Roosevelt regularly though privately consulted Washington on matters involving race and southern policies, and almost all of the minority political appointments Roosevelt made as president were first cleared with the Tuskegeean. Washington's relationship with Roosevelt's successor, William Howard Taft, was cooler, given Taft's greater reluctance than Roosevelt's to make significant black political appointments; but Washington scored an occasional minor victory with Taft, and it was one of the many ironies of his career that while he urged ordinary blacks to eschew politics and humbly go about their daily work, he himself wielded more political power than any other black American of his day.

Washington's prolific writing also helped to spread his influence; moreover, much of the royalties from his books went into the coffers of Tuskegee. He wrote scores of articles and ten books, often with the help of ghost-writers, owing to his busy schedule. Among them were *The Future of the American Negro* (1899), a collection of his articles and speeches; *The Story of My Life and Work* (1900), the first of three autobiographies; *Up from Slavery* (1901), his most critically acclaimed autobiography, translated into some eighteen languages; *Working with the Hands* (1904); *The Negro in Business* and a biography of Frederick Douglass, both in 1907; *My Larger Education* (1911), the last of the trilogy about his own life; and *The Man Farthest Down* (1912), based on a European tour.

Washington's power involved not only close relationships with influential white political leaders and industrialists but also a secret network of contacts with journalists and various organizations. He schemed with white and black Alabamians to try to keep other black schools from locating near Tuskegee. He engineered political appointments for supporters in the black community as a way of solidifying his own power base. He planted spies in organizations unfriendly to him to report on their activities and at one time even used a detective agency briefly. Despite public denials, Washington owned partial interests in some minority newspapers. This allowed him to plant stories and to influence their news coverage and editorial stands in ways beneficial to himself. Beginning in the mid-1880s, and lasting for some twenty years, he maintained a clandestine relationship with T. THOMAS FORTUNE, editor of the *New York Age*, the leading black newspaper of its day. He helped support the paper financially, was one of its stockholders, and

quietly endorsed many of Fortune's militant stands for voting and other civil rights and against lynching. He also supported the Afro-American League, a civil rights organization founded by Fortune in 1887. Washington secretly provided financial and legal support for court challenges to all-white juries in Alabama, segregated transportation facilities, and disfranchisement of black voters. As black suffrage decreased nonetheless around the turn of the century, Washington struggled to keep a modicum of black influence and patronage in the Republican Party in the South. From 1908 to 1911 he played a major, though covert, role in the successful effort to get the U.S. Supreme Court to overturn a harsh Alabama peonage law under which Alonzo Bailey, a black Alabama farmer, had been convicted.

It is clear, from research in Washington's massive correspondence, that he supported the full agenda of civil and political rights put forward by Fortune, the Afro-American League, and later the National Association for the Advancement of Colored People (NAACP). But he refused to go public with such efforts, fearing, probably rightly, that to reveal his involvement would undercut if not destroy his support from white politicians and philanthropists and perhaps threaten his beloved Tuskegee. Emmett Scott was one of very few blacks who knew the full range of Washington's secret activities; certainly no whites did.

After about 1900 Washington came under increasing criticism from black opponents who questioned his measured and nonaggressive responses to legalized segregation, loss of voting rights, and violence against blacks. His critics referred disrespectfully to his enormous influence as the Tuskegee Machine. Among the most vocal were WILLIAM MONROE TROTTER, the militant editor of the *Boston Guardian*, and noted sociologist W. E. B. DuBois. In his *The Souls of Black Folk* (1903) DuBois launched a strong indictment of Washington's accommodationist philosophy toward the terrible racial climate of the time. DuBois and others also questioned Washington's emphasis on vocational and industrial education, claiming that the black race needed college-educated professionals in its fight against discrimination and injustice.

A series of setbacks after the turn of the century illustrated how little effect Washington's moderation had had in ameliorating the nation's tense racial climate. The uproar over the 1901 dinner with President Roosevelt was a harbinger of worse things to come. In September 1906 five days of frenzied racial violence rocked Atlanta, the supposedly progressive capital of the New South. After the violence subsided, at least eleven citizens, ten black and one white, were dead, many other blacks were injured, and black areas of the city experienced destruction. Washington gave his usual muted response, urging Atlanta's blacks to exercise "self-control" and not compound the lawless white behavior with violence of their own. He was, however, instrumental in bringing leaders of both races together after the riot to begin the healing process.

Also in 1906 occurred the notorious Brownsville affair. In August an undetermined group of people shot up an area of Brownsville, Texas, nearby Fort Brown, where black infantry soldiers were stationed. One white man was killed. The racial climate was already strained owing to previous attacks on soldiers by local residents. Townspeople assumed that the soldiers had done the shooting in retaliation for the previous attacks. All of the black soldiers vehemently denied their involvement, however, and there was no compelling evidence or proof whatsoever of their guilt. In spite of Washington's pleas not to do so, President Roosevelt dishonorably dismissed three companies of the black troops, creating an uproar among blacks and liberal whites.

Exasperated with Washington's low-key responses in the Atlanta and Brownsville cases, his old friend Fortune finally broke with him. More serious for Washington was the founding of the NAACP in 1909. Melvin J. Chisum, a northern confidant of Emmett Scott, had infiltrated Trotter's Boston Suffrage League and later the Niagara Movement, the forerunner of the NAACP, and reported the activities of both groups back to Tuskegee. Characteristically, Washington had a spy planted at the NAACP's founding meeting. Nonetheless, he was unable to prevent the creation of the NAACP, the membership of which included blacks, sympathetic white progressives, Jews, and even a few white southerners, or to influence its agenda, which included a broad-based call for a major assault on all fronts against racial injustice and white supremacy. Washington's old nemesis DuBois became editor of the organization's monthly magazine, *The Crisis*. Although Washington privately supported many of the goals of the NAACP, his concern was its threat to his own power within the black community.

An ugly incident that took place in New York City on the evening of 19 March 1911 illustrates how little protection was then afforded to a black person, even one as eminent as Washington, under certain circumstances. While scanning the residents' directory in the vestibule of an apartment building in search of a friend, Washington was assaulted and repeatedly struck on the head by Henry Ulrich, a white resident of the apartment. Ulrich first claimed that Washington was a burglar; the second version of his story was that the black educator was looking through the keyhole of a white woman's apartment and that he had made an improper advance toward Ulrich's wife. Washington charged him with assault, and the ensuing trial received much national publicity. Washington won considerable support from the black community, even from his critics. Ulrich's acquittal in the face of overwhelming evidence illustrated the difficulties that even a prominent black man could have with the American justice system in the early twentieth century.

Washington died of overwork and arteriosclerosis at Tuskegee, shortly after returning from New York City, where he had been hospitalized.

Assessments of Washington by his contemporaries and, later, by historians have been wide-ranging and contentious, revealing, if nothing else, his complexity and many-sidedness. In the 1960s his secret life emerged as scholars began to plumb the 1 million documents in his collected papers. They reveal a much more complex, manipulative, secretive, vain, and at times deceptive individual than the inspiring and benign image that Washington himself so assiduously cultivated in his own lifetime. Indeed, he likely enjoyed leading this "double life."

To most of his students and faculty at Tuskegee, and to millions of poor blacks nationwide, he was a self-made and beneficent, if stern, Moses leading them out of slavery and into the promised land. He tirelessly preached an upbeat, optimistic view of the future of his fellow blacks. "When persons ask me," he said once, "how, in the midst of what sometimes seem hopelessly discouraging conditions, I can have such faith in the future of my race in this country, I remind them of the wilderness through which and out of which a good Providence has already led us." When he also wrote that he would "permit no man, no matter what his color, to narrow and degrade my soul by making me hate him," he was undoubtedly sincere. His message to his fellow blacks that hard work, good citizenship, patient fortitude in the face of adversity, and love would ultimately conquer the hatred of the white man was appealing to the majority of whites of his time and foreshadowed the similar message of a later leader, MARTIN LUTHER KING JR.

Washington's hardscrabble "up from slavery" background made it difficult for him to communicate with his college-educated critics, such as

Trotter and DuBois. They in turn, from the comfort of their editorial offices in the North, were perhaps unable to fathom the pressures and constraints from the white community that southern educators like Washington had to deal with on a daily basis. Yet their point that the race needed lawyers and doctors as well as farmers and bricklayers was valid, and the growing crescendo of criticism against Washington on this issue made the last decade of his life probably his most difficult. The irony, of course, was that Washington was secretly supporting the campaign against legal segregation and racial violence and for full civil rights. But he was unwilling to reveal his covert role for fear that it would undercut his power base among blacks and sympathetic whites, and he was doubtlessly right.

Close analysis of Washington's autobiographies and speeches reveals a vagueness and subtlety to his message lost on most people of his time, whites and blacks alike. He never said that American minorities would forever forgo the right to vote, to gain a full education, or to enjoy the fruits of an integrated society. But he strategically chose not to force the issue in the face of the overwhelming white hostility that was the reality of American race relations in the late nineteenth and early twentieth centuries. In this sense, he did what he had to do to assure the survival of himself and the people for whom he spoke.

FURTHER READING

Most of Washington's papers are in the Library of Congress. A smaller but important collection is at Tuskegee University. The major published collection is *The Booker T. Washington Papers*, ed. Louis R. Harlan and Raymond W. Smock (14 vols., 1972–1989).

Harlan, Louis R. *Booker T. Washington: The Making of a Black Leader, 1856–1901* (1972).

Harlan, Louis R. *Booker T. Washington: The Wizard of Tuskegee, 1901–1915* (1983).

Hawkins, Hugh, ed. *Booker T. Washington and His Critics: The Problem of Negro Leadership* (1962).

Logan, Rayford W. *The Betrayal of the Negro* (1965).

Meier, August. *Negro Thought in America, 1880–1915: Racial Ideologies in the Age of Booker T. Washington* (1963).

Scott, Emmett J., and Lyman Beecher Stowe. *Booker T. Washington: Builder of a Civilization* (1916).

Obituary: *New York Times*, 15 Nov. 1915.

This entry is taken from the *American National Biography* and is published here with the permission of the American Council of Learned Societies.

WILLIAM F. MUGLESTON

Washington, Craig (12 Oct. 1941–), attorney and U.S. congressman, was born in Longview, Texas, to Roy and Azalia Washington. As a legislator, Washington was widely known for his brilliant political oratory and as a champion of civil rights and civil liberties. His career as a Texas legislator and U.S. congressman spanned the course of two decades.

After graduating from Fidelity Manor Senior High School in Galena Park, Texas, in 1958, he enrolled at Prairie View A&M University, where he graduated in 1966 with a degree in Biology. The path leading to Washington's career as a legislator did not run a straight course. While his involvement in student councils throughout high school and college seemed to prefigure a career in politics, his initial ambition upon graduating from Prairie View was to study medicine, but admissions had ceased by the time he applied to medical school. He somewhat fortuitously applied to Texas Southern University's Law School in Houston, Texas, with the idea of reapplying for medical school a semester later. However, law school appeared to be an excellent choice for Washington, as his debate skills and excellent classroom performance outrivaled his peers. He graduated number one in his class with honors, receiving his Juris Doctor in 1969. Upon graduating he joined the TSU Law School faculty as assistant dean and professor of law.

In 1970 he left the university to practice private law, cofounding Washington & Randle. Washington's path once again took a turn when, in 1972, the state of Texas began electing members of the state House of Representatives and State Senate by single-member districts. Dubbed the "People's Five," Washington, along with four other minority candidates, ran for the newly created seats in the Texas Legislature. Washington campaigned successfully, making him one of the first African American men to serve as a Texas legislator since Reconstruction. While serving as a representative of District 86 from 1973 to 1982, Washington continued to practice law, earning a good reputation among his urban constituents as a very effective criminal trial lawyer for those in need.

In April 1980 the African American Eroy Brown was accused of killing two high-ranking prison officials at Ellis prison, a death row unit located just north of Huntsville, Texas. Brown was accused of drowning the unit's new warden, Wallace Pack, and shooting its farm lieutenant, Billy Max Moore; his death by lethal injection appeared imminent. Bill Habern, then executive director of the Texas

Criminal Defense Lawyers' Project, was appointed to represent Brown, but realizing the two capital murder cases were too huge for one person to handle, he assembled a legal defense team that consisted of himself, Tim Sloan, Ken Schaffer, and, as lead counsel, Craig Washington. Brown pleaded innocent by reason of self-defense and was acquitted with thirty-five out of the thirty-six jurors believing him. This trial further revealed to the public the pervasive prison brutality sweeping Texas's prison industry and helped expand the sweeping reforms already being implemented. No doubt, Washington's reputation as an effective trial lawyer rose to higher heights.

From 1983 to 1989, Washington served as a senator for Senatorial District 13. During his career as a Texas legislator, Washington championed a wide array of liberal causes; he was an early and outspoken proponent of gay rights, and sponsored legislation for the elderly and disabled. His successes did not go unnoticed, as he was named one of the state's ten best legislators three times (1973, 1979, and 1981) by *Texas Monthly* magazine.

In 1989 Congressman GEORGE T. (MICKEY) LELAND and fifteen others were on a humanitarian mission to Ethiopia when their plane crashed about 300 feet below the tip of a 4,500 feet mountain, killing everyone aboard. Leland's death left the seat in Congressional District 18 (prior to Leland, Barbara Jordan held the seat) vacant, and a special election was held on 9 December 1989; Washington, a close ally of Leland's, was elected to the 101st U.S. Congress, defeating another Leland ally, Anthony Hall, as well as eleven other candidates. Washington's career as a congressman was not without controversy, however. While being sworn in, a Harris Country judge found him in contempt of court for abandoning his clients.

While in Congress, Washington sponsored 13 bills and co-sponsored 319. Bills ranging from the elimination of segregationist language from the Second Morrill Act, to terminating assistance to Algeria's military backed government, to one designed to curtail the damaging effects of mass incarceration on families, were sponsored by Washington, reflecting his progressive leanings. However, his votes against bills favoring NASA and the North Atlantic Free Trade Agreement (NAFTA) left him alienated from Houston's political elite.

Ken Lay, then Enron CEO, recruited SHELIA JACKSON-LEE to run against Washington in the mostly Democratic district. Enron employees bundled $24,000 into Jackson's campaign treasury, and Lay himself helped her campaign raise more than $600,000, more than three times as much as Washington spent during his previous campaign. In addition, numerous Republicans crossed over and voted in the Democratic primary, ensuring Washington's defeat. The fact that Washington had missed 869 of the 2,589 roll call votes during his career also weighed heavily against him. On 3 January 1995 Washington's colorful career as a legislator came to an unassuming end after being handedly defeated by Jackson-Lee in March of 1994.

After leaving office, Washington continued to practice law. In 2006, Tyrone Williams, a thirty-four-year-old truck driver, was convicted of fifty-eight counts for his part in leaving nineteen illegal immigrants to suffocate in an airless trailer. This was the nation's most deadly immigration-smuggling case to date, and Williams would all but surely receive the death penalty during the punishment phase of the trial the following year. Instead, he was sentenced to life in prison for thirty-eight counts of transporting illegal immigrants, as his lead attorney, Craig Washington, wiped away tears of joy.

FURTHER READING

Blumenthal, Ralph. "Jury Spare Driver in Smuggling Deaths Case." *New York Times*, 19 Jan. 2007.

Nowell, Scott. "A Guarded Past: Texas's Impressive Prison Museum Engages in a Little Escapism of Its Own." *Houston Press*, 9 Jan. 2003.

"Washington, Craig Anthony." In *Biographical Directory of the United States Congress, 1774–Present*.

LARVESTER GAITHER

Washington, Denzel (28 Dec. 1954–), actor and director, was born in Mt. Vernon, New York, the middle child of Denzel Washington Sr., a Pentecostal minister, and Lennis (maiden name unknown), a beautician and onetime gospel singer. Raised in a religious household in an integrated neighborhood just north of the Bronx, the Washington children were discouraged by their parents from watching television or movies. Instead, Denzel passed the time attending church, assisting his mother in the beauty parlor, and participating as a member of the Boys Club and the local YMCA. At age fourteen, when his parents divorced, Denzel helped his family make ends meet by working part time at the local dry cleaner and in his mother's barbershop.

Troubled by his parents' separation, Denzel developed a rebellious attitude and his schoolwork declined. Anxious to set him on the right path, his mother enrolled him in the largely white private school Oakland Academy in New Windsor, New York. His behavior problems eased as Denzel found other, more productive outlets, including playing baseball, track, football, and basketball. Off campus he played piano with a local blues band. After graduating from Oakland in 1972, Washington enrolled at Fordham University in New York City, where he began as a pre-med student, but eventually ended up as a journalism and drama major. Washington briefly dropped out of school owing to poor grades, and when he returned found success on the stage. Washington played the title roles in school productions of *The Emperor Jones* and *Othello* and his onstage work was strong enough to net him an agent prior to graduation and a small part in the television movie *Wilma* (1977) about track star WILMA RUDOLPH.

In 1977 Washington finally graduated from Fordham after which he entered the acting program at the American Conservatory Theater in San Francisco, leaving the program after the first year of a three-year program, in order to move to Los Angeles. Although he won minor stage roles and a small part in the television film *Flesh and Blood* (1979), Washington was financially and artistically frustrated in Los Angeles and he soon moved back to his mother's house in Mt. Vernon. Upon his return to the East Coast, Washington became reacquainted with Pauletta Pearson, an actress and singer he had met on the set of *Wilma*. The couple married in 1983 and had four children, later living in a house designed by PAUL REVERE WILLIAMS.

In 1980 Washington took a job teaching sports at a children's recreation center. Only one week before his job was to begin, Washington was cast as MALCOLM X in *When the Chickens Come Home* at Woodie King's New Federal Theater. Critics were impressed with Washington's performance, especially his willingness to physically transform himself to play the role, and he was awarded the Audelco Award for Excellence in Black Theater.

Washington then landed the lead role opposite George Segal in *Carbon Copy*, a comedic film universally panned upon its release in 1981. That same year Washington was cast as Private Peterson in the Negro Ensemble Company's Off-Broadway production of CHARLES FULLER's *A Soldier's Play*. Focusing on the investigation of a racially charged murder during World War II, the play won a Pulitzer Prize for Drama, an Obie Award for Best Ensemble Performance, and an Outer Circle Critics Award for Washington. Washington reprised the role in Los Angeles, remaining with the play until being cast as Dr. Phillip Chandler in the television drama *St. Elsewhere*, a role he played from 1983 to 1987. In 1984 Washington reprised his role as Private Peterson in Norman Jewison's film adaptation of *A Soldier's Play*, renamed *A Soldier's Story*. In 1986 Washington appeared opposite Richard Gere in the Sidney Lumet film *Power* (1986) and the television movie *The George McKenna Story*, a fact-based story about a school principal in a tough inner-city Los Angeles high school. The following year his performance as the martyred South African leader Steven Biko in Sir Richard Attenborough's film *Cry Freedom* (1997) earned him an NAACP Image Award and an Academy Award nomination. Proud to be recognized by his peers, Washington was nonetheless vociferous about the way the film emphasized the story of Biko's white liberal lawyer, played by Kevin Kline, at the expense of Biko. With his outspoken criticism, Washington emerged as a spokesman for increased visibility and better-quality roles for black entertainers. "The success narrows the roles you get to play, race narrows the roles you get to play," commented Washington (*Chicago Tribune*, 1 Feb. 1988).

In 1988 Washington made his Broadway debut in Ron Milner's comedy *Checkmates*. Later that year he starred in *For Queen and Country* and the Caribbean film caper *The Mighty Quinn* alongside ROBERT TOWNSEND. In 1989 Washington gave a searing performance in *Glory*, a film based on the letters of Colonel Robert G. Shaw (played by Matthew Broderick in the film), leader of the Fifty-fourth Massachusetts Volunteer Infantry, the unit of African American soldiers in the Civil War established in 1863. Appearing with MORGAN FREEMAN and Andre Braugher, Washington played Trip, a former slave who played a key role in the unit's attack on Battery Wagner, an important fortification of Charleston, South Carolina. For his performance Washington received an Academy Award for Best Supporting Actor.

In 1990 Washington emerged as a matinee idol following his work in SPIKE LEE's romance-drama *Mo' Better Blues*. He played the role of a self-absorbed jazz trumpeter, Bleek Gilliam, a character loosely based on MILES DAVIS. In 1992 Washington received the NAACP Best Actor Award for his performance in *Mississippi Masala*, a romantic drama about black and Asian relations in the American South. The same year he returned to the role of Malcolm X in Spike Lee's controversial biopic *X*. His startling performance garnered him a slew of accolades, including an Academy Award nomination, an NAACP Image Award, and the Chicago, Boston, and New York critics' awards.

Handsome and stirringly charismatic, Washington was voted one of *People's* "Fifty Most Beautiful People in the World" in 1994. One of the highest paid African American actors in Hollywood, he had become known for playing virtuous and heroic—if troubled—black men. Meanwhile, Washington continued to diversify as an actor, playing opposite Kenneth Branaugh and Emma Thompson in Shakespeare's *Much Ado about Nothing* (1993) and Tom Hanks in the AIDS drama *Philadelphia* (1993), and starring in the Hollywood thrillers *The Pelican Brief* (1993), *Crimson Tide* (1995), *Courage under Fire* (1996), *Fallen* (1998), *The Siege* (1998), and *The Bone Collector* (1999). In 1995 he starred as Easy Rawlins in Carl Franklin's film adaptation of Walter Mosely's book *Devil in a Blue Dress*, about a 1940s black private investigator. The following year he again worked with a black cast in *The Preacher's Wife* (1996) and re-teamed with Lee for *He Got Game* (1998) and *Bamboozled* (2000). In 2000 he netted another Best Actor Academy Award nomination for his portrayal of wrongfully imprisoned RUBIN CARTER in Norman Jewison's *The Hurricane*.

Over the course of his film career, Washington maintained his public image as a devout family man, even coaching his children's sports teams. On a summer trip to South Africa in 1995, Denzel and Pauletta Washington renewed their marriage vows in a ceremony officiated by archbishop Desmond Tutu. Denzel Washington, who has donated $1 million to the Children's Fund of South Africa, $2.5 million to the Church of God in Los Angeles, and time and money to the Boys and Girls Club, received the Whitney M. Young Award from the Los Angeles Urban League in 1997.

For his complex performance as a rogue cop in Antoine Fuqua's drama *Training Day* (2001), Washington became the first black actor since SIDNEY POITIER to win an Academy Award for Best Actor. The film revealed yet another side of Washington's remarkable diversity as an actor, since he was cast against type as the film's "bad guy." He emerged to great critical acclaim as a film director with *The Antwone Fisher Story* (2002), a psychological drama based on the true story of the title character, a Sony Pictures security guard who eventually gained fame as a writer and Hollywood producer. In 2004 Washington starred in the Frank Sinatra role in Jonathan Demme's remake of *The Manchurian Candidate*. Two years later he teamed up with Lee again in the crime drama *Inside Man*. In 2007 Washington showed his versatility by starring as drug kingpin and crime boss Frank Lucas in *American Gangster*, receiving a Golden Globe nomination for Best Actor, and as the famed Wiley University debate team coach, MELVIN B. TOLSON, in *The Great Debaters*. For the latter film, a rare Hollywood glimpse of life in a southern black college in the 1930s, Washington won a record ninth NAACP Image Award for Outstanding Actor in a Motion Picture. He repeated that feat in 2011 for his starring role as a post-Apocalyptic nomad in *The Book of Eli* (2010), but the film received mixed critical reviews. Washington also appeared in two high-grossing action thrillers, *The Taking of Pelham 123* (2009) and *Unstoppable* (2010); both involved runaway trains, and both were directed by Tony Scott. It was on the stage, however, that Washington enjoyed his greatest critical success in the 2000s. In 2005 he portrayed Marcus Brutus in Shakespeare's *Julius Casear* on Broadway, and in 2010 won the Tony Award for best lead actor in AUGUST WILSON's play *Fences*.

About his career as an actor, Washington once remarked, "I'm just trying to fulfill my part of the bargain, which is to give back, to be a positive influence on others" (*Jet*, 2 Oct. 1995, 32). One of the few African American men in the film industry with the power to pick roles and "greenlight" projects, Washington has remained in firm control of the destiny of his career.

FURTHER READING

Washington, Denzel. *A Hand to Guide Me* (2006).

Brode, Douglas. *Denzel Washington: His Films and Career* (1996).

Davis, Thulani. "Denzel in the Swing," *American Film* (Aug. 1990).

Hill, Anne E. *Denzel Washington* (1998).

JASON KING

Washington, Dinah (? Aug. 1924–14 Dec. 1963), singer, was born Ruth Lee Jones in Tuscaloosa, Alabama, the daughter of Ollie Jones, a gambler, and Alice Williams, a domestic. In 1928 her family moved to Chicago. As a teenager Washington achieved local fame as a gospel pianist and singer at St. Luke's Baptist Church. At age fifteen she won a talent contest at the Regal Theater and soon after was hired by SALLIE MARTIN to accompany her gospel singers on the piano. At age seventeen Washington married John Young, the first of her eight, more or less legal, husbands. She was the mother of two children, the older fathered by her second husband, George Jenkins (married in 1946), and the younger by her third husband, Robert Grayson (married in 1947). Her last husband, DICK "NIGHT TRAIN" LANE (married in 1963), was a professional football player.

In 1943 LIONEL HAMPTON hired Washington to sing with his big band. Hampton was one of several to take credit for suggesting that Ruth Lee Jones take the stage name of Dinah Washington. Later in 1943 in New York City she met Leonard Feather, who arranged for her to record some blues that he had written. "Evil Gal Blues" was Washington's first record. Two years later, the recording of Feather's "Blowtop Blues," with Hampton and a small ensemble, established Washington as a leader in the burgeoning market of rhythm and blues (R&B). She left Hampton's band in 1945 to venture out on her own, and in 1946 she began recording for Mercury Records, remaining with the company for fifteen years. Over that time Washington recorded hundreds of titles that fell primarily into two categories, blues and covers of popular songs.

With the end of World War II, advances in recording techniques, decentralization of the radio broadcast industry, cultivation and marketing of gospel music, and development of the electric guitar led to the growth and wide dissemination of popular, urban blues, a style epitomized by T-BONE WALKER. Washington entered this milieu, establishing herself as the "Queen of the Blues." Her blues records can be divided into powerful lamentations in the tradition of BESSIE SMITH and lighter, novelty material associated with R&B, such as "Fat Daddy" (1953), with its fashionable accompaniment of electric organ and bongos. Washington was equally well known, however, for her renditions of popular songs drawn largely from Broadway musicals and movies. Her recordings of standards such as "Smoke Gets in Your Eyes" (1955), often accompanied by a string orchestra, were intended by Mercury to be sold almost exclusively to African Americans. Indeed, Mercury expended little or no effort to publicize her outside African American communities.

The quality of Washington's voice was stunning, combining a reedy, almost nasal coarseness with wide, full vibrato on open vowels. Her treatment of lyrics included speechlike declamation, crystalline enunciation, and small ornamental squeaks at the ends of phrases—more identified with country and western singing than with R&B. Her phrasing

Dinah Washington, gospel, blues, jazz, and pop singer, in an undated photograph. (AP Images.)

was flexible and laid back, perhaps influenced by her idol, BILLIE HOLIDAY, and she infused all her songs with rhythmic swing. Fellow musicians June Christy and Bob Cooper, in a "blindfold test" for *Down Beat* magazine (1 Sept. 1960), noted that Washington made everything that she sang swing and sound like the blues. Eddie Chamblee, a musician and one of Washington's husbands, noted, "Dinah was like Judy Garland. She drew all the whores and pimps and losers…. She sang songs of losers" (Haskins, 124).

Throughout her career Washington toured relentlessly on the "chitlin' circuit," where she sang her blues and R&B numbers. According to the comedian REDD FOXX, "She wouldn't sing white, and because of that, she couldn't get the big, downtown jobs" (Haskins, 70). Although Washington had several R&B hits, she did not achieve general acclaim until late in her career, especially with "What a Diff'rence a Day Made" (1959), a romantic song accompanied by strings. It achieved widespread popularity, finished the year among *Billboard* magazine's top fifty, and won the Grammy Award for best R&B record. Duets with the singer Brook Benton, such as "Baby You've Got What It Takes" (1959), also enhanced her popularity. Washington was a remarkably versatile singer. Along with blues and romantic pop songs, she covered country and western hits such as Hank Williams's "Cold, Cold Heart" (1952). Some of her best work was done with jazz musicians, notably with her piano accompanist of the mid-1950s, WYNTON KELLY, on "Lover, Come Back to Me," recorded at the 1958 Newport Jazz Festival. Washington and Kelly often created a vocal-instrumental interchange similar to that achieved by Billie Holiday in the late 1930s with the tenor saxophonist LESTER YOUNG. Truly outstanding was a recording Washington made at a jam session in 1954 that included the drummer MAX ROACH and the legendary trumpeter CLIFFORD BROWN, the pinnacle of which is their rendition of Cole Porter's "I've Got You under My Skin." Throughout the latter part of her career, Washington frequently performed at jazz festivals and clubs.

Washington's lifestyle was flamboyant and her career tumultuous. Born in poverty, she sought riches and glamour throughout her life, a quest symbolized by her fascination with mink—stoles, coats, and even toilet-seat covers. During the latter part of her career she became especially concerned with her weight and employed drastic methods to control it, including diet pills, mercury injections, and water removal. She was noted for her coarse language, quick temper, and competitiveness. Washington was also noted for her spontaneous generosity to friends and strangers and for her promotion of young, aspiring singers and musicians. She was both vocally and financially supportive of the efforts of MARTIN LUTHER KING JR. in his battle against segregation and racism.

In 1962, with her popularity waning and her financial problems mounting, Washington's behavior became even more erratic and disorderly. She also became more dependent on alcohol, diet pills, and sleeping pills. She died at her home in Detroit, apparently from a combination of drugs and alcohol.

FURTHER READING

Haskins, Jim. *Queen of the Blues: A Biography of Dinah Washington* (1987).
Obituary: *New York Times*, 15 Dec. 1963.
This entry is taken from the *American National Biography* and is published here with the permission of the American Council of Learned Societies.

ANDRÉ BARBERA

Washington, Fanny Smith (18 July 1858–4 May 1884), educator and home economist, was born Fanny Smith in Malden, Kanawha County, West Virginia, the daughter of Samuel Smith and Celia. Historical accounts of Fanny Smith do not disclose much detail about her family, for instance whether or not she had siblings. Fanny grew up in Malden, West Virginia, where after the Civil War she became acquainted with BOOKER T. WASHINGTON, whose family settled there after emancipation. Washington began his studies at Hampton Institute in Virginia in 1872 and graduated in 1875. He returned to West Virginia and was Fanny's teacher in Malden, where he taught approximately eighty to ninety students in a day program from 1875 to 1878. Fanny and a few Malden schoolmates, assisted by Washington, gained admittance to Hampton Institute some time before 1878. This small group of students was known primarily as "Booker Washington's boys" (Harlan, 76). Fanny's acceptance by Hampton as a member of the Malden student group was thus significant, since she was the only female in a group designated as Washington's brightest students.

General Samuel Chapman Armstrong founded Hampton Institute (later Hampton University) in 1868 in Virginia to educate freed slaves. By 1878 the school had established a formal education program for Native Americans that continued for about forty years. The curriculum emphasized work-based education, teaching character, morality, agricultural and mechanical classes, cleanliness, discipline, and the dignity of manual labor. Sources do not document the year Fanny initially entered Hampton, but she was forced to leave the school in 1878 because she fell behind in tuition payments. She spent two years teaching school near Malden to settle her school account while also assisting with the financial support of her mother. By January 1880, when she made her final payment to Hampton, Fanny was earning $32.50 a month, most of which was required for living expenses. She returned to Hampton as a student in 1880 and graduated in June 1882.

Washington, in the meantime, returned to Hampton Institute as a teacher and director of the Native American dormitory in 1879. The relationship between Fanny and Washington grew stronger. In 1881 the state of Alabama requested that Armstrong name a white principal for Tuskegee Institute, a new school for blacks in Alabama, and he recommended Washington. Washington became principal of the school on 4 July 1881. After her graduation from Hampton, Fanny married Washington on 2 August 1882 in Rice's Zion Baptist Church in Malden. Fanny Washington became a member of the Tuskegee faculty immediately after their marriage. The state of Alabama initially apportioned two thousand dollars for salaries, but neither land nor buildings for the school was provided. The first building consisted of a one-room shanty provided by Butler Chapel African Methodist Episcopal (AME) Zion Church. The Washingtons rented a house, known as the Teachers Home, in which faculty members of the school also boarded. In addition to developing a home economics training program for female students, Fanny Washington also assumed the responsibility of housekeeper for the educational institution.

On 6 June 1883 Washington gave birth to Portia Marshall Washington, her only child and the first child born on the Tuskegee campus. Washington continued her devotion to and support of Tuskegee through her teaching as well as her responsibilities as housekeeper. She was meticulous in her upkeep of the institution and dedicated to setting a positive example for the students through her housekeeping and general work. Unexpectedly, Fanny Washington died at the age of twenty-six on 4 May 1884. The local newspaper stated that her death was due to consumption of the bowels; however, family members maintained the cause was internal injuries suffered after she fell from a wagon on campus. She is buried in the Tuskegee Institute cemetery.

FURTHER READING

Harlan, Louis R., ed. *The Booker T. Washington Papers*, vol. 2 (1972–1989).

Smith, Jessie Carney, ed, *Notable Black American Women, Book II* (1996).

DENYCE PORTER PEYTON

Washington, Ford Lee "Buck"

Washington, Ford Lee "Buck" (6 Oct. 1903–31 Jan. 1955), musician, actor, dancer, and singer, also known as Buck Washington, Ford L. Buck, and Ford Lee Buck, was born in Louisville, Kentucky. Little documentation exists of Buck Washington's youth. An orphan, at around the age of ten, while working as a bowling alley pin boy, Buck first met the younger JOHN "BUBBLES" WILLIAM SUBLETT, then six years old. The two young boys immediately bonded and using their respective nicknames, they formed the vaudevillian team, Buck & Bubbles. This friendship and artistic pairing would break color barriers and influence the entertainment industry for the next forty years.

After winning several amateur contests, the first in Indianapolis, the duo began touring in 1913, playing engagements in Louisville, Detroit, and New York. To circumvent societal prejudices, the two African American entertainers were occasionally required to perform in "blackface" when playing before some white audiences, especially in the South. Buck & Bubbles were heralded for their quick wit, amply displayed in their dancing, singing, and comedy routine that typically involved Bubbles reacting to Buck's rapid variation in tempo. Through their success and popularity they were among the first black vaudevillians to break into the "white" circuit, and in 1922, Buck & Bubbles headlined at the premiere vaudeville venue, the Palace Theatre in New York City. Their artistic achievements also translated into financial success; the duo reportedly earned salaries of up to $1,750 per week during the 1920s and 1930s. Primarily due to their immense popularity, as exemplified in their box office success, Buck & Bubbles were able to drop the forced "blackface" and began to headline the "white vaudeville circuit," breaking new ground for African American performers. Together they appeared on Broadway in such shows as *Lew Leslie's Blackbirds* (1930), *Ziegfeld Follies* (1931), *Porgy and Bess* (1935), and *Laugh Time* (1943). They are also noted for being the first African Americans to perform on stage at the Radio City Music Hall in 1931. Their career together spanned over thirty years and the two entertainers, equally regarded as musicians, dancers, and actors, were well respected in all areas of performance working on Broadway, in Hollywood, and on early American jazz recordings.

Not only breaking barriers on stage, Buck & Bubbles also adapted to the new era of recording technology with the advent of the motion picture industry. This led to another first, as the two are considered the first black artists to appear on television—in *The Buck and Bubbles Variety Show* in 1937. They would not be limited by the small screen, and the duo's visually exciting dance routines allowed them to become Hollywood regulars featured in over fourteen films such as *Calling All Stars* (1937), *Varsity Show* (1937), *Cabin in the Sky* (1943), and *A Song Is Born* (1948).

Buck was also highly regarded jazz musician, renowned for his skills as a vocalist, pianist, and horn player. He appeared as a studio musician on early recordings with LOUIS ARMSTRONG, BESSIE SMITH, and COLEMAN HAWKINS. Even in the recording industry, however, Buck's ethnicity prevented the early discographies of BILLIE HOLIDAY from listing him as the pianist. In the 1933 recording session of Holiday's "Your Mother's Son-in-Law,"

"Buck" Washington (l), with longtime dance partner and collaborator John "Bubbles" William Sublett. (Photofest.)

Joe Sullivan, Benny Goodman's white pianist, is named the studio pianist. This listing was contradicted by Holiday, who insisted in later interviews that Buck was her pianist on the first record. She recalled that before her first-ever studio recording Buck advised, "Don't let these white folks see you scared. They'll be laughing at you" (in Clarke, p. 61). She notes it was his advice that gave her confidence to record in a studio for the first time.

Buck died of a heart condition in New York at the age of fifty-one on 31 January 1955, but left behind a legacy of comedy, dance, and jazz piano, influencing future entertainers such as GREGORY HINES and MICHAEL JACKSON.

FURTHER READING

Clarke, Donald. *Billie Holiday: Wishing on the Moon* (2002).

Gottschild, Brenda Dixon. *Waltzing in the Dark: African American Vaudeville and Race Politics in the Swing Era* (2000).

Sobel, Bernard. *A Pictorial History of Vaudeville* (1961).

FILMOGRAPHY:
A Star Is Born (1948).
Cabin in the Sky (1943).
Laugh Jubilee (1946).
Varsity Show (1937).

HUGH K. LONG

Washington, Forrester Blanchard (24 Sept. 1887–24 Aug. 1963), social work educator, researcher, and social activist, was born in Salem, Massachusetts, the first of four children of Lucy August Wylly, originally from Darien, Georgia, and John William Washington, an artist and professional penman who also became a postal clerk in Boston after he moved his family there. Lucy was the daughter of a slave and her white owner, who sent her to Boston for her education. Washington graduated from South Boston High School in 1905 and from Tufts College in 1909. He is believed to have been Tufts' first African American graduate. Briefly he taught French at Howard University before resuming his studies. From 1912 to 1914 he pursued an economics degree at Harvard University and then attended Columbia University, where he graduated in 1917 with a master's degree in Social Economy. While at Columbia, he also completed training, supported by a National Urban League Fellowship, at the New York School of Social Work.

In 1917 Washington was also appointed the first director of the Detroit Urban League. This organization was one of many created by the National Urban League to provide services to the numerous African Americans relocating to the North in the great migration of 1910, a phenomenon that was stimulated by both the boll weevil's devastating attack on southern cotton crops and the availability of jobs in the North. Washington distinguished himself as director of the Detroit Urban League through his extraordinary success in job placements for migrants, his efforts to increase the broader community's understanding and tolerance for the influx of migrants, and his creation of social organizations and services to help migrants transition to urban life. On 18 May 1918 Washington married Sophronia Davis of Detroit, Michigan. They had one child who, like her father, became a social worker. Washington's role as director was cut short in 1918, when he was drafted into the army. In that same year GEORGE HAYNES successfully obtained Washington's release from the army so he could support Haynes in his leadership in the newly created Division of Negro Economics (in the U.S. Department of Labor). The goal of this office was to address the host of problems stemming from an insufficient number of jobs available to African Americans and the resultant militant response by some African Americans. Washington's work at the Division of Negro Economics was short-lived because the division was soon defunded after World War I, when a harmonious workforce that included African Americans was no longer a national priority.

In 1920 Washington returned to Detroit and became director of research for the Detroit Associated Charities, where he managed a research department and completed a major social survey that examined the social and economic conditions of African American newcomers to Detroit as well as African Americans in other urban environments. In 1923 Washington became director of the Armstrong Association of Philadelphia, a National Urban League affiliate charged with helping the city respond to the continuing influx of African Americans and the local government's challenges in responding to migrants' needs for housing and social welfare services. As director, Washington created programs to address deplorable health and housing conditions and problems of children and youth. He also worked to teach migrants and the African American community to become active in finding solutions to their social and economic problems and placed a strong emphasis on self-help.

Washington's work with African American migrants led him to understand the importance of preparing African American social workers to work with their own people. He began encouraging colleagues to relocate to the South, where he perceived a great need for education and social welfare programs. In 1927 he relocated to the South as well when he was appointed to the position of director for the Atlanta School of Social Work (ASSW). With limited resources and in spite of the challenges of running a school in the Jim Crow South, Washington sustained the development of the ASSW throughout the Great Depression, owing in large part to his persistent and skillful fund-raising. He was aided in his mission by many people, but notable was the support of the Atlanta University president JOHN HOPE and his friend Will Alexander of the Commission on Interracial Cooperation.

In 1934 Washington took a leave of absence from the ASSW to serve as director of Negro work in the Federal Relief Agency of Franklin Delano Roosevelt's New Deal administration. At the Federal Relief Agency, Washington argued for policies to remove barriers to equal employment and objected to the existing practice of placing African Americans on relief to serve economic interests of plantation owners and manufacturers. Washington resigned his position after six months when he realized that his recommendations were not being heeded; he thus forfeited his opportunity to advance his own career as a member of the "Black Cabinet." After his departure from the Federal Relief Agency, Washington returned to his post at the ASSW, where he oversaw significant growth in the school. In 1938 the school became affiliated with Atlanta University. This status change and accreditation from the American Association of Schools of Social Work provided ASSW with a national student body and an enrollment comparable to the top-tier white schools that were also members of the accrediting body. The renamed Atlanta University School of Social Work (AUSSW) was the only school of social work in Georgia at that time.

In 1939 Washington pioneered block social work field placements for African Americans when twenty-four students were placed for six-month periods in the most well-developed social service agencies in northern, eastern, and western states. This innovation was designed to ensure that the Jim Crow laws of the South would not inhibit these students from receiving the high quality education that was consistent with the AUSSW's mission. Washington engaged students in research commissioned by social welfare organizations in Atlanta to investigate the social problems experienced by their clients. He also articulated principles of culturally competent social work practice well before it was a widely acknowledged area of emphasis in social work education. Washington trained the first cadre of African American social workers to understand the importance of the scientific method and cultural sensitivity as requirements for skilled social work intervention. In recognition of his contributions to the social welfare field, Morehouse College awarded Washington the honorary degree of LLD in 1943. In 1947 the AUSSW was brought under the umbrella of Atlanta University and became the Atlanta University School of Social Work. Washington must be credited with its development for over a twenty-seven-year period, from the Great Depression until the dawn of the civil rights era. He advanced the development of this important African American institution so it could transcend social, cultural, and economic barriers.

Washington held memberships on the American Committee of the International Conference of Social Work, the Executive Committee of the National Conference of Social Work, and the Board of Directors of the Child Welfare League of America; he was a second vice president of the Southern Sociological Society and a member of the American Sociological Association. In addition he was a president of the Atlanta NAACP, an Elk, a member of the Republican Party, an Episcopalian, and a member of Alpha Phi Alpha fraternity. Washington died in New York City.

FURTHER READING

Barrow, Frederica H. "The Social Welfare Career and Contributions of Forrester Blanchard Washington: A Life Course Analysis," Ph.D. diss., Howard University (2002).

Ferguson, Karen. *Black Politics in New Deal Atlanta* (2002).

Kirby, John B. *Black Americans in the Roosevelt Era: Liberalism and Race* (1980).

Parris, Guichard, and Lester Brooks. *Blacks in the City: A History of the National Urban League* (1971).

FREDERICA HARRISON BARROW

Washington, Fredi (23 Dec. 1903–28 June 1994), dancer, actor, organizer, and activist, was born Fredericka Carolyn Washington in Savannah, Georgia. Washington was best known for her Caucasian features (pale skin, straight hair, and green eyes) which helped her to secure the original role of Peola, the sullen and dissatisfied daughter who attempts to claim the benefits of white privilege while passing in the 1934 film *Imitation of Life*. One of Robert T. Washington and Harriet Walker Ward Washington's nine children, Fredericka's early life was unsettled by the sudden death of her mother.

After the death of their mother, both Washington and her younger sister, Isabel Washington, were sent away to St. Elizabeth's Convent in Cornwell Heights, Pennsylvania, to be educated. In 1919 Washington moved to Harlem, New York, to live with her grandmother and later dropped out of school. Her exposure to show business probably began when she went to work as a typist and secretary for HARRY H. PACE at Black Swan Phonograph Corporation, whose slogan was "The Only Genuine Colored Record. Others Are Only Passing for Colored" (Kellner, 39).

Washington seemed to easily find show business opportunities. Her first stage appearance, in the early 1920s, was as a dancer in the chorus of NOBLE SISSLE and EUBIE BLAKE's legendary musical comedy *Shuffle Along*, then playing in Manhattan's Club Alabam. In 1926 she assumed the stage name of Edith Warren when she got a lead role opposite PAUL ROBESON in the play *Black Boy*, by Jim Tully and Frank Dazey. She toured Europe with Al Moiret as half of the dance team called Fredi and Moiret. According to the author Donald Bogle, they traveled to Paris, Nice, Berlin, Dresden, and Hamburg, and "in London, she taught the latest dance craze, the Black Bottom, to the Prince of Wales" (Bogle, *Bright Boulevards*, 130). She returned to the United States in 1928 prepared to resume her acting career.

During the 1930s Washington became familiar to audiences as an actor. In 1930 she starred in the musical play *Sweet Chariot* with FRANK H. WILSON and the blues singer CLARA SMITH. The play's theme was suggestive of the United Negro Improvement Association (UNIA) and the philosophy of MARCUS GARVEY. The play considered what would happen if a Garvey-type character (Marius Harvey) was able to transport a group of African Americans from the United States to the continent of Africa. Washington appeared in another musical in 1931, *Singin' the Blues*, which again starred Frank Wilson; Washington's younger sister, Isabel, was also in the cast. Washington continued to build her stage experience with the musical *Run, Little Chillun* in 1933.

Washington's movie career began in 1929 with an appearance in DUKE ELLINGTON's short sound feature, *Black and Tan Fantasy*. According to Washington's sister Isabel, the blues singer ALBERTA HUNTER, and the musician Mercer Ellington (Duke's son), the love of Fredi Washington's life was Duke Ellington (Bogle, *Bright Boulevards*, 131–132). In July 1933, however, Washington married LAWRENCE BROWN (1907–1988), a trombonist in Ellington's orchestra, and announced her retirement from show business. Their marriage would end in divorce in 1948.

During the 1930s Washington was politically active and participated in a number of boycotts and pickets to persuade Harlem businesses to hire African Americans. The protests were usually organized by ADAM CLAYTON POWELL JR., Washington's brother-in-law (Isabel's husband). Powell's weekly paper, the *People's Voice*, included a column by Washington, which focused on theater happenings and the struggles of black actors. She was also one of the cofounders of the Negro Actors Guild and served as its first executive secretary in 1937; the guild was formed to help black performers battle discrimination in show business. Her activism extended to the Joint Actors Equity-Theater League Committee that examined the problem of hotel accommodations for African American actors.

Washington's postnuptial retirement was short-lived, for in 1933 she appeared with Paul Robeson in the film *Emperor Jones*. Her light skin led the film's producers to darken her face with makeup for fear that audiences might think that the couple was interracial, a Hollywood taboo at the time (Bogle, *Bright Boulevards*, 130). The same year she also appeared in *Drums in the Jungle*, which was filmed in Jamaica. Washington's most famous film role came in 1934 in *Imitation of Life*, based on a novel by Fannie Hurst; she starred opposite LOUISE BEAVERS and Claudette Colbert. Her performance as Peola made her a celebrity and convinced many moviegoers that Washington, like Peola, passed for white. Unfortunately, Washington never had another opportunity to act in a movie that offered such wide exposure. Nevertheless, she went on to make other films during the 1930s, including *Mills Blue Rhythm Band* (1934), *Ouanga* (1936), and *One Mile from Heaven* (1937) with BILL ROBINSON and EDDIE ANDERSON. During the 1930s and 1940s she continued to work in theater, and some believe that her best work on Broadway was in *Mamba's Daughter* (1939), opposite ETHEL WATERS. In 1946 she performed on stage in *Lysistrata* with Etta Moten and a young SIDNEY POITIER; in 1948, *A Long Way from Home*; and in 1949, *How Long till Summer*. Her contribution to show business was honored in 1975 when she was inducted into the Black Filmmakers Hall of Fame.

Washington's political activism continued in the 1940s and 1950s through her work with the Cultural Division of the National Negro Congress and the Committee for the Negro in the Arts. Also, in 1952 Washington wed Hugh Anthony Bell, a prominent Connecticut dentist, and she retired—this time, permanently—from show business. Their marriage lasted until his death in 1970. Fredericka Carolyn Washington Brown Bell died of pneumonia in Stamford, Connecticut, after suffering a stroke.

FURTHER READING

Bogle, Donald. *Bright Boulevards, Bold Dreams: The Story of Black Hollywood* (2005).

Bogle, Donald. *Brown Sugar: Eighty Years of America's Black Female Superstars* (1980).

Kellner, Bruce, ed. *The Harlem Renaissance: A Historical Dictionary for the Era* (1987).

Newkirk, Pamela. *A Love No Less: More Than Two Centuries of African American Love Letters* (2003).

REGINA V. JONES

Washington, Grover, Jr. (12 Dec. 1943–17 Dec. 1999), musician and record producer, was born in Buffalo, New York, to Lillian Washington, a hairdresser and business owner, and Grover Washington Sr., a steelworker. Young Washington grew up in a family that encouraged creativity in music. His father played saxophone and was an avid record collector, and his mother sang in the church choir. Both of Washington's brothers were also musically inclined: Darryl played the drums and Michael played the keyboard. At age ten Washington began playing saxophone and by his teenage years was sneaking out of the house to watch and play in jazz clubs. His parents enrolled him in the Wurlitzer School of Music to study classical music. He took lessons on the piano, bass, guitar, and drums. By high school he was a member of the Buffalo all-city high school band as a baritone saxophonist. At age sixteen Washington left home to become a professional rhythm and blues musician. In 1963 he joined the

Grover Washington, Jr., performing at a news conference in the lobby of Radio City Music Hall in New York City, 13 July 1993. (AP Images.)

Four Clefs in Columbus, Ohio, and then, in 1965, the Keith McAllister Band.

In 1965 the U.S. Army drafted Washington, and he translated his musical abilities into a transfer into the Nineteenth Army Band playing the alto saxophone at Fort Dix, New Jersey. While at a gig off the military base, he met magazine production assistant Christine Bitner of Philadelphia, whom he married in 1967; the couple had two children, Grover III and Shana. That same year, following his discharge, Washington worked in a record store and tried to build his name as a performer. Renting a saxophone, he performed at gigs with several organists, including Charles Earland and Johnny "Hammond" Smith.

Washington's first big musical break came in 1971. He was twenty-eight. Creed Taylor, a record producer, had prepared to record a set of pop-funk sides with alto saxophonist Hank Crawford. Just before the recording sessions began, Crawford was jailed and Taylor needed an immediate replacement lead musician. He called Washington, who played the alto part. Within months, Taylor released the album *Inner City Blues*. The recording sold over two hundred thousand copies. The album focused attention on a new style of music, called fusion, a genre that bridged jazz, pop, soul, funk, and disco music.

New opportunities arose with the album's success. Washington found work as a sideman with Randy Weston, Don Sebesky, Bob James, and others. A 1972 solo release titled *All The King's Horses* and the follow-up 1973 *Soul Box* highlighted a blues-derived saxophone styling with distinctly jazz improvisations over a pop or contemporary beat. While he was not the first musician to explore an acoustical musical style with one that fused jazz, blues, soul, and pop sounds, he and his band attained unprecedented commercial success. Washington would record thirty-five albums over his career.

In 1980 Washington returned to school to seek a doctorate in Music Composition. Upon applying to Temple University in Philadelphia, the admissions staff informed him that he would first have to pass an audition. Washington was dumbstruck. He returned to the university the next day with a stack of his albums and told the staff they should listen for themselves and see if he could play. Temple University admitted him.

Also in 1980 Washington released what would become his most successful album, *Winelight*. This work propelled him to superstar status with the recording remaining on *Billboard* magazine's pop chart for 102 weeks. It also stayed on the jazz chart for thirty-one weeks. The album sold over one million copies and features a duet with the vocalist BILL WITHERS, "Just the Two of Us," which remains one of Washington's best known recordings. Over the next decade Washington maintained an exceptional pace of touring and recording. Thousands of performances around the world and dozens of studio sessions generated twelve separate albums in less than nine years.

During his career Washington inspired a great deal of criticism among his peers. Many disapproved of his style and tendency to borrow from various musical genres. Purists thought he was too commercial and not respectful of jazz traditions. Not solely a blues, jazz, pop, or soul musical performer, he frequently responded to such opposition by emphasizing his passion for all styles of music. His defenders often claimed that resentment by other musicians merely reflected jealousy of his enormous record sales. Washington responded to the jazz purists with *Then and Now* (1988) and *All My Tomorrows* (1994). Both followed traditional acoustic jazz.

In the 1990s Washington reduced his commercial output, although he did continue to perform for special occasions, such as the inauguration ceremony for President Bill Clinton in 1993. He collaborated with conductor John Williams and the London Symphony Orchestra to produce an album called *The Hollywood Sound* in 1996. He recorded his first Christmas album in 1997, *Breath of Heaven: A Holiday Collection*. As his fame and celebrity grew, Washington inspired numerous musical imitators, including Kenny G., Najee, Gerald Albright, and George Howard. His work had inspired a new category of music, and now it had a name: cool, or smooth, jazz.

In 1999 Washington, who had been debilitated by prostate cancer, collapsed and died of a heart attack following his recording of a segment for CBS television's *Saturday Early Show*. He was survived by his widow and children, who continued to support musical educational programs in his memory, including the Philadelphia-based Protect the Dream Foundation.

FURTHER READING
Palmer, Robert. "Newport Jazz—Grover Washington, Saxophonist," *New York Times*, 30 June 1979.
University of Pittsburgh Jazz Studies Program. Biography of Grover Washington, Jr. Available at www.pitt.edu/~pittjazz/individual_htmls/grover_washingtonjr.html.
Washington, Grover. The Best of Grover Washington Jr. (Musical Transcriptions) (2002).
Obituary: *New York Times*, 19 Dec. 1999.

DISCOGRAPHY
Inner City Blues (Kudu, 1972).
Winelight (Elektra, 1981).
Inside Moves (Elektra, 1984).
Anthology: The Best of Grover Washington, Jr. (Motown, 1996).
Grover Washington, Jr.—Prime Cuts: The Greatest Hits 1987–1999 (Sony, 1999).
Aria (Sony, 2000).

JAMES FARGO BALLIETT

Washington, Harold (15 Apr. 1922–25 Nov. 1987), politician and mayor of Chicago, was born on the South Side of Chicago, the son of Roy Lee Washington, a stockyard worker, and Bertha Jones, a domestic worker. Harold Washington attended a Benedictine boarding school in Milwaukee, Wisconsin, until the age of six. He was then enrolled in Chicago public schools but dropped out of high school after his junior year to take a job in a meatpacking plant. His father, who had become an attorney and a precinct captain for the Democratic Party in Chicago's largely African American Third Ward, secured a job for Washington at the Chicago office of the U.S. Treasury Department. In 1941 he married Dorothy Finch. They had no children and divorced in 1950.

Following U.S. entry into World War II in December 1941, Washington was drafted into the U.S. Army. He was stationed in the South Pacific with the Air Force Engineers, and he took enough correspondence courses between missions to receive his high school equivalency diploma.

After the war Washington enrolled in Roosevelt College in Chicago, an experimental new college that was one of the few in the country to be fully integrated. He excelled at Roosevelt and was the first African American elected senior class president. He graduated in 1949 with a bachelor's degree in Political Science.

After graduating from Roosevelt, Washington entered Northwestern University Law School,

Harold Washington, shown in his office in Chicago's City Hall, in an undated photograph. (AP Images.)

where he was the only African American in his class. He earned his law degree in 1952, then entered into practice with his father. When Roy Washington died the following year, Ralph Metcalfe, an alderman and Democratic Party committeeman, hired the junior Washington to replace his father as captain of his precinct.

Washington quickly won favor with the Chicago Democratic machine, effectively turning out the vote for Metcalfe and other Democratic candidates. As head of the Third Ward's Young Democrats, Washington became a valued member of the Chicago Democratic Party machine for his ability to cultivate young black party leaders. In return, he was rewarded with jobs as an assistant corporation counsel for the city from 1954 to 1958 and as an arbitrator for the Illinois Industrial Commission from 1960 to 1964.

In 1964 Washington campaigned for and was elected state representative for the Third Ward. Once in office, he began to establish his independence from the Chicago political machine, then dominated by Mayor Richard J. Daley. Washington first broke with city Democratic leaders in the late 1960s, when he sponsored a bill to create a police review board with civilian participation. At the same time he began to establish himself as a civil rights advocate, further distancing himself from the white-dominated Daley machine. As a member of the state legislature he supported the Equal Rights Amendment in the 1970s, worked to strengthen the Fair Employment Practices Act, and in 1969 helped establish the Illinois Legislative Black Caucus. In 1976 Washington was elected to the state senate despite opposition from a machine candidate.

In 1977 Washington made a decisive break from the Chicago Democratic organization by campaigning for the mayoralty in the special election that followed Daley's death. Despite a drubbing in the Democratic primary, in which he received less than half the black vote, Washington vowed to carry on the fight against the machine. "I'm going to do what maybe I should have done ten or twelve years ago," he announced. "I'm going to stay outside that damn Democratic organization and give them hell." True to his word, Washington returned to the state senate and continued to push reform legislation that was well to the left of the Chicago party's wishes.

In 1980 Washington successfully challenged a machine loyalist in the election for a seat representing Chicago in the U.S. Congress. In the House of Representatives he emerged as a leading figure in the Democratic Party's embattled liberal wing. He served as secretary of the Congressional Black Caucus and sponsored legislation that extended the Voting Rights Act of 1965, making it easier for African Americans to challenge discriminatory electoral practices. On foreign policy issues, Washington sought to reverse the military buildup championed by President Ronald Reagan. He supported an end to the production of nuclear weapons, opposed U.S. military intervention in Central America, and called for a 20 percent reduction in defense spending.

During his first term in Congress, Washington was approached by several Chicago political groups that were eager to draft a black candidate for the mayoral election in 1983. Washington agreed on the condition that a massive voter registration campaign be carried out before the election. The groups undertook the challenge, adding more than 130,000 new voters, many of them African Americans. Satisfied that the electoral base was now sufficient to make his campaign viable, Washington announced his candidacy. In the Democratic primary Washington faced the incumbent mayor Jane Byrne and State's Attorney Richard M. Daley, son of the former mayor. Washington won the primary with a plurality of 36 percent of the vote to Byrne's 34 percent and Daley's 30 percent. Washington's grassroots campaign earned him 85 percent of the votes cast by African Americans, who constituted approximately 40 percent of the electorate.

In the general election Washington's challenger was Republican Bernard Epton, an attorney and former Illinois state legislator, who capitalized on the wrath of a large segment of Chicago's white population. Washington nonetheless eked out a victory with 51.5 percent of the vote to become the city's first African American mayor. His support came overwhelmingly from black, Latino, and white liberal voters.

Washington's victory inaugurated a four-year period of factional struggle within the city council. The "Council Wars," as they came to be known, featured white opposition to Washington's attempts to reform Chicago's system of political patronage and diversify the city's political leadership. The white majority on the city council, led by Aldermen Edward Vrydolyak and Ed Burke, succeeded in blocking many of Washington's initiatives. Yet the new mayor was able to achieve passage of several laws that severely weakened the power of the white Democratic machine. His most important accomplishment was the Shakman Decree, which outlawed patronage hiring and firing of municipal employees. He successfully instituted a $1,500 limit on campaign contributions from companies with city contracts, and he added scores of women and minorities to the city administration, including Chicago's first black police chief. Washington effectively ended the system of political patronage that had dominated Chicago's governance for most of the twentieth century. Some of his critics, including television anchor Walter Jacobson and Aldermen Vrydolyak, Burke, and Richard Mell, though, charged that he only redistributed political spoils to a new elite of black and Latino politicians and bureaucrats.

In 1987 Washington was challenged by Byrne in the Democratic primary and by Vrydolyak, running as an independent, in the general election. With more than 99 percent of black voters casting their ballots for Washington, he easily out-polled his opponents, taking 54 percent of the vote in both races. Only seven months after his reelection, Washington died in Chicago.

A pivotal figure in African American politics, Washington initiated a wave of black electoral insurgency that resulted in the election of African American mayors in many of the largest cities in the United States. His success in dismantling the Chicago political machine made him a pivotal figure in the history of the city as well. Though he was a consummate politician and a product of the political system he ultimately dismantled, Washington destroyed an old system of urban governance and helped change the process as well as the face of American politics.

FURTHER READING
Dempsey, Travis J. *An Autobiography of Black Politics* (1987).
Kleppner, Paul. *Chicago Divided: The Making of a Black Mayor* (1985).
Rivlin, Gary. *Fire on the Prairie: Chicago's Harold Washington and the Politics of Race* (1992).
Obituary: *New York Times*, 26 Nov. 1987.
This entry is taken from the *American National Biography* and is published here with the permission of the American Council of Learned Societies.

THADDEUS RUSSELL

Washington, Harry (c. 1740–1800s), Revolutionary-era runaway slave, British Loyalist, and early settler in Sierra Leone, is believed to have been born in the Senegambia region of Africa. George Washington, then a colonel in the army of the British Empire, purchased Harry in 1763, along with Nan (believed to have been his wife) and four other slaves as a part of Washington's Great Dismal Swamp plan. According to this plan, Washington and five other planters would each provide five slaves to form a workforce to drain sixty square miles of the Great Dismal Swamp in Virginia and establish a rice plantation. By 1766 Washington had moved both Harry and Nan to work on his Mount Vernon Plantation in Virginia.

In 1771 Washington sent Harry to work on the construction of a mill approximately three miles from the Mansion House. Clearly not content with his lot as a slave, Harry made his first attempt at obtaining his freedom by fleeing from the worksite on 29 July 1771. However, he only remained free for a few weeks before being recaptured and returned to his owner as a result of advertisements of his escape posted by Washington. (This escape attempt is noted in Washington's *Diaries of George Washington*, vol. 3, 45.) Ironically, Harry's unsuccessful attempt at freedom mirrored much of the language of his owner and other Revolutionary leaders in their quest for independence from England.

With the rising tensions between Britain and her American colonies, the Loyalist governor of Virginia, Lord Dunmore, issued a proclamation offering freedom to those slaves able to cross over to his fleet. According to his proclamation issued on 14 November 1775, freedom would be granted to "all indented servants, Negroes, or others… that are able to bear arms" (Robert L. Scribner, *Revolutionary Virginia*, vol. 4, 334). On 24 July 1776 a small boat carrying three of General Washington's slaves offering their services to the British docked with the HMS *Roebuck*. Owing in part to an entry found in the Book of Negroes (which listed freedmen evacuated from New York by the British following the war), in which Harry states that he had run away from General Washington seven years earlier, Cassandra Pybus contends that Harry was among those brought aboard HMS *Roebuck* (Pybus, 19).

Lord Dunmore hoped to form what he called the "Ethiopian Regiment," a force of freedmen organized to fight in the southern colonies. However, depleting numbers, primarily due to smallpox epidemics among the freedmen, forced Lord Dunmore to leave Virginia for New York. On 7 August 1776 Harry and approximately two hundred to three hundred other surviving members of the Ethiopian Regiment and their families sailed along with Dunmore for New York. In New York, Harry worked for the Royal Artillery Department. Harry subsequently accompanied the British forces during their invasion of South Carolina, serving as a corporal in a corps of about sixty "Black Pioneers" with the Royal Artillery Department.

With the defeat of British forces and the surrender at Yorktown, an evacuation of the South became necessary. Those former slaves who could substantiate their role in aiding the British received a certificate of freedom and transport from Charleston. Harry had little difficulty proving eligibility for his certificate of freedom because of his many years of service with the Royal Artillery Department. As such, Harry took part in the final evacuation of Charleston and returned once more to New York. Terms of the provisional peace treaty, however, prohibited the removal of any slave property of Americans. Therefore, it became clear that if the British were to honor their pledge of freedom to escaped slaves they would need to be quickly removed from America. On 31 July 1783 Harry once again took part in an evacuation; this time leaving aboard *L'Abondance* destined for Nova Scotia.

The freedmen and women faced numerous problems in Nova Scotia and ultimately found residency there to be unacceptable. Among other concerns, whites denied blacks the right to vote and adequate protections from violence. In response to these complaints, the prime minister agreed to pay the expenses for those willing to relocate to the new colony of Sierra Leone in Africa. The Sierra Leone Company, interested in attracting settlers, promised to provide twenty acres for every man, ten acres for each woman, and five acres for each child. Harry was among the approximately twelve hundred who chose to venture to Sierra Leone in November 1791. Harry's distaste for life in Nova Scotia can perhaps best be seen in viewing what he was willing to leave behind: two town lots, a home, and forty acres (Records of the British Colonial Office).

Harry soon found trouble in Sierra Leone as well. Local blacks wanted the opportunity to select their own leaders as opposed to having them appointed by the Sierra Leone Company. As a result, in 1800 a number of men began considering ways to limit the authority of the governor solely to the affairs of the Sierra Leone Company. In response to appeals from the governor, British troops and Maroons from Jamaica arrived in order to quell the potential uprising. Harry and twenty-nine others ultimately surrendered to the British authorities. In October 1800 a military tribunal sentenced Harry to be exiled to the Bullom Shore, where the exile community elected him as their leader. He later received amnesty and may have returned to Sierra Leone. The date and location of his death was not recorded.

FURTHER READING

Frey, Sylvia. *Water from the Rock: Black Resistance in the Revolutionary Age* (1991).

Norton, Mary Beth. "The Fate of Some Black Loyalists of the American Revolution," *Journal of Negro History* 58, no. 4 (Oct. 1971).

Pybus, Cassandra. *Epic Journeys of Freedom: Runaway Slaves of the American Revolution and Their Global Quest for Liberty* (2006).

WILLIAM J. HARRIS

Washington, James Melvin (24 Apr. 1948–3 May 1997), scholar, preacher, and teacher, was born at the Colored General Hospital in Knoxville, Tennessee, to Annie Beatrice Moore Washington and James W. Washington. Raised with six siblings (Louise Hill, Helen Brown, Howard Moore, Willie Moore, Charles Washington, and Ray Washington) in the Austin Homes Project and at Mount Olive Baptist Church, Washington felt the call of God to preach in 1961 while attending a meeting of the National Baptist Young People's Union (*Conversations*, xxvii). In 1971 Washington married Patricia Anne Alexander, with whom he had a daughter, Ayanna Nicole Washington.

As a youngster from a working-class family in a segregated city, Washington's only source of books was a small library for "colored." After reading in the newspaper that Knoxville libraries were no longer segregated, he visited the "magisterial Lawson McGhee Library" with its "marble columns and a seemingly endless supply of books" (*Conversations*, xliii). The librarian, however, angrily ordered him to leave, attracting from the many library patrons "glares" that Washington recalled as seeking "to incinerate my soul." He considered the justice of burning the library, but instead he resolved to build his own library.

A bit older, Washington read about student sit-ins at lunch counters and immediately resolved to join those demonstrating against segregation. A protective older brother, however, detoured him away from any demonstrations by persuading Washington that he needed an assistant for his janitorial work at a synagogue—just at the times when demonstrations were scheduled. Washington learned more about American religion while working at the synagogue, and he also began following closely the ministry of the activist MARTIN LUTHER KING JR., his lifelong role model as an activist preacher. Like King, Washington felt the call of ministry while a college student and so began regular preaching at Riverview Missionary Baptist Church in Lenoir City, Tennessee. At the request of Washington's new congregation, in 1967 his home church, Mount Olivet, ordained him.

Washington graduated in 1970 with a B.A. in Religious Studies from the University of Tennessee at Knoxville, but not before joining the Black Power movement. He suffered arrest for demonstrating against the Vietnam War and the visit of President Richard Nixon to a Billy Graham crusade being held on the Knoxville campus. His jailing elicited feelings of "rejection, alienation, humiliation and defeat," Washington recalled, but he recovered after meeting with an elderly pastor who prayed over him, asking God to take away bitterness and make Washington "a mighty strong weapon in your warfare against evil!" (*Conversations*, xxxv).

From Tennessee, Washington went to Harvard Divinity School and in 1972 was awarded a master's degree in Theological Studies. He had focused his studies on social ethics but switched to church history when he realized that as a black church scholar he could tackle the major challenge set out by his professors in American church history, William R. Hutchinson and Charles C. Wright. That challenge was to find an "adequate interpretive scheme to

reflect the widest range of data" ("Craven Images," 143)—in other words, a religious history that included much more than the church life and theology of elites.

So he went to Yale to study with Sydney E. Ahlstrom, who believed that the new, more inclusive approach to understanding the variety of American religious experience would likely come from a scholar in black religious history. He earned a master of philosophy degree (1975) and a Ph.D. in Religious Studies (1979), with that dissertation later incorporated into his magisterial study *Frustrated Fellowship: The Black Baptist Quest for Social Power* (1986), an analysis of the origins of the black Baptist convention movement.

Washington showed that black Baptist churches and eventually conventions developed because of the unequal relationships between blacks and whites in the white-dominated churches and convention structures of the nineteenth century. In analyzing black and white churches together, Washington provided a successful and pioneering example of a broader kind of history, one that analyzed black and white churches together and that incorporated into his narrative both lesser-known individuals and the broader political and social issues of the times. The bibliographic essay included in his book is also a classic, providing detailed analysis of sources and early writings on the black church in America.

For twenty years Washington taught church history at Union Theological Seminary in New York City while at the same time preaching at churches around the country. He also lectured and occasionally taught at Princeton University and Columbia University, Oberlin College and Haverford College, and Yale Divinity School. He mentored numerous students, drawing many into his seminar on the religious history of the civil rights movement.

A prodigious scholar, Washington drew heavily but not uncritically from scholars of American religious history as well as from a broad range of writers on the human condition, including Sigmund Freud, Carl Jung, Herbert Marcuse, Mary Douglas, and Paul Ricoeur. He credited much of his spiritual and intellectual development to family, friends, and preacher colleagues in the black church, including Gardner C. Taylor and William T. Crutcher. He counted as close friends and major influences James Forbes of Riverside Church and colleague CORNEL WEST.

Washington was honored with several grants in support of his research on the civil rights movement. He melded his church and scholarly interests in his teaching, preaching, popular writings, and service as an officer of the American Baptist Historical Society and a leader at Riverside Church. Washington published numerous articles on the black church and on religion and politics. He also edited two collections of the writings of Martin Luther King Jr., *A Testament of Hope: The Essential Writings and Speeches of Martin Luther King, Jr.* (1986) and *I Have a Dream: Writings and Speeches That Changed the World* (1992). He compiled *Conversations with God: Two Centuries of Prayers by African Americans* (1994), including in his introductory essay a great deal of autobiographical material.

For his family, students, colleagues, and future readers, Washington's unexpected death from a stroke in 1997 was tragic. Assisted by a Lilly Foundation grant, he had just completed volumes of research on the civil rights movement and just begun writing his religious history of that movement.

FURTHER READING

The James Melvin Washington Papers are at Burke Library, Union Theological Seminary, Columbia University, New York City.

Washington, James Melvin. Introduction to *Conversations with God: Two Centuries of Prayers by African Americans* (1994).

Washington, James Melvin. "Craven Images: The Eiconics of Race in the Crisis of American Church Historiography," in *The Agitated Mind of God: The Theology of Kosuke Koyama*, eds. Akintunde Akinade and Dale T. Irvin (1996).

Obituary: *New York Times*, 8 May 1997.

DEBORAH BINGHAM VAN BROEKHOVEN

Washington, James W., Jr. (10 Nov. 1911–7 June 2000), painter and sculptor, was born in Gloster, Mississippi, the fourth of six children to Reverend James W. Washington, a cabinetmaker and an associate minister at the Gloster Baptist Church, and Lizzie, a homemaker. The birth year for Washington has been reported between 1909 and 1911. Washington made a futile effort to obtain a birth certificate and is reported to have rejected the notion of chronological age. In the rural, segregated town of Gloster, Washington endured poverty, unequal education, and racially fueled terrorism that propelled him into a lifetime fight for social justice. As a boy of six he saw his father, under threats from the Ku Klux Klan, forced to flee town in the trunk of a white friend's car. Wasington never saw him again. Without his father, Washington forged a greater bond with his mother, whom he credits for nurturing his natural talents in the creative arts. Washington knew early he had a gift for art and began to express his talent in drawing at age twelve. In an interview with Deloris Tarzan Ament for her book *Iridescent Light: The Emergence of Northwest Art*, Washington recalled how he would challenge his playmates to make random chalk marks on the sidewalk. He would then create unique images from the sketchy markings. "Even then," he told Ament, "I could utilize and observe the possibilities of anything" (154).

Washington worked as a deckhand on a Mississippi riverboat at age fifteen and taught as a Works Projects Administration (WPA) artist in Alabama in 1938. In 1942 he followed his mother to Little Rock, Arkansas, where he worked as a shoemaker. His passion for drawings and painting dominated his early artistic endeavors, which focused on the subjects and scenes of his life in southern towns, as in his painting *Arkansas River at Little Rock*. Many of his early paintings expressed his commitment to social justice, such as *Keeper of the Park*, 1945, illustrating a park groundskeeper reading a newspaper about discrimination against blacks, *Democracy Challenged, Lynching*, 1949–1950, depicting the unevenly tipped scales of justice dominate the center of the composition, and another 1945 painting, *The Making of the United Nations Charter*, in which he offered his personal protest against the omission of any provision in the United Nations Charter for the liberation of black Americans.

In 1943 Washington married Janie Rogella Miller (1908–2000), a native of Texas who was waitressing at a restaurant in his mother's Little Rock neighborhood when they met, and the couple moved to Bremerton, Washington, where he worked in the Puget Sound Navy Shipyard as a journeyman electrician. They moved in 1944 to Seattle, where Janie began a 35-year career in nursing and Washington associated with other area artists that formed the "Northwest School" of art. The group of mostly self-taught artists included the abstract artist Mark Tobey, who was Washington's friend and teacher, and the expressionist painters Kenneth Callahan, Guy Anderson, and Morris Graves. All were deeply affected by their common experience of poverty and by the beauty of the Northwest's low light, wildlife, and natural environment. In Seattle during the early 1950s, Washington began to book exhibits at small galleries and experienced some measure of success with his paintings, many of which were overtly Christian in theme. His religious series included his version of the Last Supper titled *The Passover* as well as *Nativity Scene* and *Christ in the Garden of Gethsemane.*

Washington used a variety of techniques and in varied mediums with his paintings, which were mostly small and medium scale, included soft-focus renderings of churches, street scenes from his youth, landscapes of the southern countryside, and focused on animals in nature, and universality and spiritual themes. Several of his paintings were done from the perspective of looking over the shoulder of someone, drawing the viewer into the scene.

On a trip to Mexico City in 1951, Washington visited the ruins of the pyramids of Teotihuacán. He was moved to pick up a small volcanic rock, which he bought home and put away. A few years later Washington said he heard the call of the stone and went to his basement to retrieve it. He believed God was commanding him to be a sculptor and he saw the face of a boy in the stone. He scarcely altered the shape of the stone and followed its natural lines to create his first sculpture, the *Young Boy of Athens.* His naturalistic approach continued with *The King* and *Head of Job*, followed by the 1956 Italian limestone *Young Queen of Ethiopia*, the 1957 driftwood piece *Nesting Bird*, and the small granite *Young Bird of the Swamp* (1959). Many of Washington's later paintings and early sculptures were similar in imagery and technique as those of other Northwest artists, particularly his 1947 series of tempera studies of seagulls with the chalky surfaces and feathery white lines familiar from Graves's bird paintings of the same period. However, Washington disavowed any direct influence from Graves or Tobey, under whom he studied.

Granite soon became his preferred medium. In 1969 Washington executed a series of six busts of historical figures, including Washington's heroes, MARTIN LUTHER KING JR. and GEORGE WASHINGTON CARVER, originally placed at the Rotunda of Achievements in Philadelphia. (This outdoor, open-access structure, which housed the sculptures, was raised ten years later after recurrent vandalism, and the works held for relocation.) For the 1980 pieces *The Golden Calf of Dan* and *Golden Calf*, and the 1981 *Arctic Hare*, Washington put his animal subjects, birds and squirrels, on stone altars, elevating them to symbols of religious significance. In the 1980 piece *Phoenix Reincarnated by Fire*, he symbolizes birth and the renewal of life with an animal emerging from an egg. Washington's repertoire in stone also portrayed classical and African American themes and religious symbolism, including the "eye of God,"

the Christian cross, and the Egyptian ankh. The 1982 *Obelisk with Phoenix and Esoteric Symbols of Nature* was commissioned for Seattle's Sheraton Hotel.

Paul J. Karlstrom, who extolled Washington's exceptional artistic vision in his book *The Spirit in the Stone: The Visionary Art of James Washington, Jr.*, praised his ability to animate the inanimate and find what Washington referred to as the "spirit in the stone." Scholars likened Washington's sculptures to prehistoric Mediterranean pieces, noting the power and simplicity of artistic expression he infused in them. His artistic renderings were reflective of his expression of religious faith and his view of the connectedness of God, nature, and man. Washington described his working process as the sublimation of himself to the subjects of his work and to the dictates of the medium he used to create them. "To me, art is a holy land, where initiates seek to reveal the spirituality of matter" (Ament, 152). In an interview with Regina Hackett for *American Artist*, he described his approach to sculpture:

> I wait until intuition moves me, and then I begin. I have to know the animal or individual before I can sculpt him. Not just know his features but feel them. I have to be him. Not until I get to the point where I am the animal can I release the spiritual force into the inanimate material and animate it. When this happens, I feel like I'm working with flesh rather than just stone (77).

Washington was not only a painter and sculptor of substantial repute but also a recognized poet. Active as a Thirty-third Degree Freemason and a member of the NAACP, he was a frequent spokesman for civil rights. A committed volunteer for his church, Mount Zion Baptist, Washington frequently made time to lecture young people and encourage their artistic interests. He continued to sculpt, teach, exhibit, and lecture over the next forty years of his career.

In 1990 the City of Seattle designated Washington's home and studio a historic landmark. In June 2000 he died in Seattle at the age of eighty-nine, having established himself as one of the nation's leading African American artists. Washington provided a personal account of his creative journey and his passion for the oppressed in his unpublished autobiography, which he titled "Passing the Torch." He left the legacy of his distinctive artistic creations in public and private collections, the Seattle Art Museum, the Smithsonian, and galleries worldwide. He ensured the protection and preservation of his legacy in founding, with his wife and a group of prominent Seattle businessmen, the James W. Washington Jr. and Janie Rogella Washington Foundation to provide teenagers with scholastic opportunity in the arts.

FURTHER READING

Ament, Deloris T. *Iridescent Light: The Emergence of Northwest Art* (2002).

Bearden, Romare, and Harry Henderson. *A History of African-American Artists: From 1792 to the Present* (1993).

Hackett, Regina. "James Washington: Secrets in Stone," *American Artist* (Nov. 1977).

Karlstrom, Paul J. *Spirit in the Stone: The Visionary Art of James W. Washington, Jr.* (1989).

Lucas, Patricia Latourette. "James Washington: A Sculptor of Stone and Spirit," *Seattle Times Sunday Magazine*, 6 July 1980.

J. DEBORAH JOHNSON STERRETT

Washington, Jerome (11 Jan. 1939–26 Apr. 2002), writer and activist, was born in Trenton, New Jersey, the second of three sons of Elizabeth Ernestine Bowman Washington. According to one of Washington's brothers, when he was young, his mother "cleaned white women's houses" (personal communication). Later in his life, she was a file clerk for the New Jersey Department of Labor and Industry. Nothing is known of his father, who was not present in Washington's life. In 1963 his mother married Cleveland Lewis and took his last name.

After graduating in 1957 from Hamilton High School West in Trenton and serving in the Ninety-seventh Signal Company, first in Germany and then in Vietnam, Washington became active in the civil rights, antipoverty, and antiwar movements of the 1960s and early 1970s. He became friends with the activists Paul Krassner, Abbie Hoffman, Phil Ochs, and Jerry Rubin, and he was considered the first black Yippie (Youth International Party) leader. In 1968 he participated in the Poor People's March in Washington, D.C. In that same year, prior to and during the Democratic National Convention, he negotiated with the Blackstone Rangers, the largest street gang in Chicago, not to oppose the presence of Mobilization Against the War (MOBE) in the city.

In 1972 in New York City, Washington was charged with second-degree murder and attempted murder following an altercation in a bar. He was found guilty of both charges, and in 1974 he began serving concurrent terms of 15 years to life and 8⅓ to 25 years in the Auburn Correctional Facility. Washington had married Ellen Maslow sometime

earlier, but, at his urging, she divorced him after his arrest.

Once in prison Washington quickly became editor of the *Auburn Collective*, an award-winning, inmate-produced newspaper. In 1978 he wrote an article for the *Cayuga Collegian*, a publication of Cayuga Community College, titled "Cold Duck," which was critical of prison guards. Consequently he was transferred from Auburn to Attica, where conditions were more brutal. Three years later, at his own request he was transferred to Green Haven Correctional Facility, located near Poughkeepsie, New York. In 1985 a federal grand jury found after an eight-day trial that Washington's First Amendment rights had been violated in his first transfer because people inside prison are allowed to criticize government officials. Washington referred to this case as his "Right to Write" lawsuit. In addition, the jury found that Washington should be paid five thousand dollars in damages by the prison's superintendent, because during the transfer to Attica his typewriter, writings, and manuscripts were confiscated and lost.

Despite the loss of his typewriter and his work, Washington continued to write. In 1981 he published a collection of essays called *A Bright Spot in the Yard: Notes and Stories from a Prison Journal*, which includes "Cold Duck." The book, which was highly praised by such critics and writers as Tom Wicker, Paul Krassner, Alan Sillitoe, and Allen Ginsberg, contains seventeen powerful vignettes of life inside the racist world of New York's maximum-security correctional facilities.

Washington also wrote plays, poetry, and fiction. In 1986 he became the first prisoner to receive a fellowship in the arts from the prestigious New York Foundation for the Arts for his play *The Boys in Cellblock "C."* While in prison he also wrote *Beanfields*, a short novel that is a recollection of picking beans during his childhood and that he self-published in 1990, and *One Crow One Buddha*, a series of poetic reflections on his daily meditative practice in his cell written between 1974 and 1988. In addition, Washington maintained long-standing correspondences with scores of people, most notably the author Kathrin Perutz, who started the Poets, Essayists, and Novelists (PEN) Prison Program to connect writers on the outside with writers on the inside, and with a bioethicist, Dr. Ruth Macklin.

On 1 November 1988 Washington was released from the Arthur Kill prison on Staten Island, New York, after serving fourteen years. At first he stayed in New York City, developing the workshop

Writing from Experience, which he gave at colleges and universities, and teaching meditation to Harlem youth. In 1989 Washington spoke out against the death penalty at the March Against State Killing (MASK) and in a series of readings that coincided with Amnesty International's Worldwide Week of Action for the Abolition of the Death Penalty in California. Shortly thereafter the writer John Fremont, who had corresponded with Washington while he was incarcerated, worked with his parole officer to help him move to Fort Bragg, California, and brought him into his men's writing group on the Mendocino coast. On 1 November 1991 Washington received his Certificate of Final Discharge from "further jurisdiction of the Board of Parole in accordance with the provisions of law" (Washington, *Bright Spot in the Yard*).

In 1994 Washington published *Iron House: Stories from the Yard* with QED Press as a hardcover book. It is an expansion of *Bright Spot*, and it includes an afterword about his life immediately following his release. The paperback rights to *Iron House* were subsequently sold to Vintage publishers. It, too, was highly praised, especially by PIRI THOMAS, author of *Down These Mean Streets*, and it won the Western States Arts Federation Book Award for Creative Nonfiction.

In 1997 Washington left California, returning to his mother's house in New Jersey, where he died five years later. He was a smoker and had long suffered from a respiratory illness. Upon hearing of his death Paul Krassner described Washington as having "a sweet idealism with a hunger for peace, justice, and compassion" (personal communication). Washington's writings both inside and outside of prison challenged people to rethink the senselessness and brutality that is often a part of prison life.

FURTHER READING

Washington, Jerome. *Beanfields* (1990)

Washington, Jerome. *A Bright Spot in the Yard: Notes and Stories from a Prison Journal* (1981)

Washington, Jerome. *Iron House: Stories from the Yard* (1994)

Washington, Jerome. *One Crow One Buddha* (1988)

THERESA C. LYNCH

Washington, Kenny (31 Aug. 1918–24 June 1971), football player, was born Kenneth Stanley Washington in Los Angeles, California, the son of Edgar Washington, an actor; his mother's name is unknown. He played football at Los Angeles Lincoln High School and was considered by some

Kenny Washington of the Los Angeles Rams, photographed on 3 September 1946. (AP Images.)

the best high school football player ever to play in Southern California. In one game against Garfield High School, he made headlines for throwing a sixty-yard touchdown pass.

Washington attended the University of California at Los Angeles (UCLA), intending to play football and baseball. He played baseball in the spring of 1937, hitting .454, and made the varsity football team in the fall of his sophomore year. The Bruins, coached by William H. Spaulding, compiled a lackluster 2-6-1 record, but Washington, a tailback in UCLA's single-wing offense, emerged from the season as the first great African American athlete on the West Coast. In the second game of the year, a 12-7 loss at Stanford, he carried the ball thirteen times for forty-six yards and played excellent defense. A week later, he intercepted a pass against Oregon State to set up the Bruins' only touchdown in a 7-7 tie.

Spaulding resisted pressure not to play Washington and WOODY STRODE, another black player, against Southern Methodist University (SMU). SMU won 26-13, but Washington, gaining 80 yards on fourteen carries, earned his opponents' respect. At the end of the season, the Mustangs voted him the greatest player they had faced that year. The

Bruins lost their season finale to the University of Southern California (USC), 19-13, but Washington stunned the Trojans by throwing two touchdown passes within twenty-nine seconds, both to Hal Hirshon. The second of these was adjudged the longest touchdown pass in college football history to that date. The play covered 72 yards, but Washington's effort was officially recorded as a 62-yard pass since the rules in effect at the time measured passes by the distance the ball traveled in the air. Washington played baseball in the spring of 1938 and hit .350. In his junior year the Bruins football team improved to 7-4-1; that season Washington scored ten touchdowns and rushed for 573 yards.

In 1939 UCLA hired a new head coach, Edwin "Babe" Horrell, and recruited a new backfield mate for Washington, JACKIE ROBINSON. The Bruins opened the season by defeating Texas Christian, the defending national champions, 6-2, and beat the University of Washington the next week, 14-7. In this game Washington rushed for a school-record 148 yards on twenty-five carries. He scored one touchdown to tie the game and threw a 5-yard touchdown pass for the win. UCLA tied Stanford and then beat Montana, 20-6, as Washington broke his own record by rushing for 164 yards. The Bruins then defeated Oregon, 16-6, to run their record to 4-0-1. Washington threw a touchdown pass to Robinson to erase a 6-3 deficit, and Robinson's 83-yard run clinched the victory.

UCLA extended its unbeaten streak by defeating California, 20-7, and tying nationally ranked Santa Clara and Oregon State. The Bruins beat Washington State easily, 24-7, and then ended their regular season with a scoreless tie against USC. As the game wound to its finish, the Trojans stopped the Bruins on three straight downs with the ball inside the USC three-yard line. On fourth down, UCLA eschewed a field goal attempt because both of the Bruins' kickers were injured, but Washington's pass, intended for Don MacPherson, was batted down in the end zone. For his spectacular season, leading the nation in total offense, Washington was named UCLA's first football All-American and Back of the Year by *Liberty* magazine. He finished sixth in the voting for the Heisman Trophy, given to the player considered the best in the country, but later evaluators have ranked his season, in which he played 580 out of a possible 600 minutes, one of the best ever in college football history. The National Football League (NFL), with a color line firmly in place since 1933, did not call on Washington after his college career ended. Instead he helped coach

the Bruins freshman team in 1940, graduated in 1941 with a degree in letters and science, and played semiprofessional football with the Hollywood Bears and the San Francisco Clippers for several years. He had one son, but it is not known whether or not he married.

After the 1945 season Dan Reeves, the owner of the NFL's Cleveland Rams, moved his team to Los Angeles. When he sought a lease to play home games in the Los Angeles Coliseum, officials of the publicly owned stadium refused unless he agreed to break with NFL policy and give Washington a tryout. Reeves consented, signed Washington to a contract on 21 March 1946, and the league's color line was broken. Strode, signed in May, joined Washington on the Rams, one season before Robinson began playing major league baseball with the Brooklyn Dodgers.

Washington played three seasons with the Rams, but in the seven years after playing college football his skills had been eroded by time, and his knees had been injured. Nevertheless, in 1947 he led the NFL in rushing average (7.4 yards per carry) and recorded the year's longest touchdown run, 92 yards, against the Chicago Cardinals. In the off-season, he worked in the juvenile department of the Los Angeles Police Department.

Washington retired after the 1948 season, and in 1950 he received a baseball tryout with the New York Giants. Having failed to make the Giants' roster, he became a marketing and public relations executive with a Scotch whiskey distillery and later was a part-time scout for the Los Angeles Dodgers. In 1955 the Helms Athletic Foundation named him one of the two greatest football players in Los Angeles history. He was also elected to the all-time Pacific Coast Conference team and was inducted into the College Football Hall of Fame. By 1970 he was suffering from polyarteritis, a circulatory and respiratory disease that had no cure. He died in Los Angeles.

FURTHER READING

Hurd, Michael. *Black College Football, 1892–1992: One Hundred Years of History, Education, & Pride* (2000).

Levy, Alan Howard. *Tackling Jim Crow: Racial Segregation in Professional Football* (2003).

Ross, Charles K. *Outside the Lines: African Americans and the Integration of the National Football League* (1999).

Obituaries: *New York Times*, 26 June 1971; *Sporting News*, 10 July 1971.

This entry is taken from the *American National Biography* and is published here with the permission of the American Council of Learned Societies.

STEVEN P. GIETSCHIER

Washington, Lowell, Jr. (?–?), a leading rank-and-file organizer of the Packinghouse Workers Organizing Committee in Chicago, and member of the subsequent United Packinghouse Workers of America, particularly instrumental in organizing the six "little" packers, providing a base from which to secure recognition at the dominant Armour, Swift, Cudahy and Wilson companies.

Details of Washington's birth have not been documented, but he grew up in Chicago, the son of a butcher at the Swift meatpacking company, who moved the family from Mississippi in 1915. Initially, Washington's father tried to obtain work in bricklaying and plastering, as he had in the Vicksburg area before moving north. Excluded from these occupations by the building trades unions' refusal to accept African Americans, he became a bitter opponent of unionization in the meatpacking industry, literally turning his back when representatives of the Stockyards Labor Council invited him to join.

Between the efforts of SLC to incorporate and advance African Americans from 1915 to 1921, and the efforts of packing companies to use blacks to undermine labor organization, many advanced to skilled jobs on the killing floor and in the cutting room. "My dad worked hard," Washington recalled, "but because of it we were pretty well off. To be a top man at Swifts or Armours meant that you could pay your bills, feed your family, have your kids in clothes and shoes, and have more than a little bit of respect from your neighbors" (Halpern, p. 78).

In 1930 the younger Washington was caught up in the "Don't Spend Your Money Where You Can't Work" campaign, led by the *Chicago Whip*, a smaller black newspaper than the well-known *Chicago Defender*. National chains with stores in predominantly African American neighborhoods were challenged to hire local residents or lose their patronage. A series of picket lines and mass rallies, sustaining an economic boycott, secured agreement from Woolworth's in October to employ twenty or more African Americans at a new store on 51st Street.

Still in his teens, Washington joined communist-led efforts to organize Works Progress Administration workers during the Depression, and the "flying squadrons" that prevented evictions. "Those guys really threw me," he later recalled,

"I mean here were these white fellas who were helping us out, really meaning it. I'd never seen anything like it." Few individuals or organizations were advancing the grievances of black workers and communities, but the active communists he knew "took up the things that really mattered—jobs, food, places to live. You might not agree with them all the time, but you had to stand with 'em when they was fightin' for you. You'd be a fool not to" (Halpern, p. 108).

Washington eventually got a job as a ham boner, a highly paid position, in one of the smaller packing houses. By 1930 one in three unskilled or semi-skilled jobs in the meat industry were filled by African Americans. As company officers candidly admitted to the researcher Alma Herbst, opening up unusually good opportunities for advancement was a form of "strike insurance" in case of future labor unrest. "We took the Negroes in as strike-breakers in 1921, and have kept them in ever since in order to be prepared for any kind of outbreak" (Halpern, p. 79). Fully aware of this management strategy, when demand for a union surged in 1937–1938, staff from the Congress of Industrial Organizations put unusual emphasis on interracial unity. But a good deal of the demand for a union came from long-established black employees like Washington.

Washington was a leader in organizing the Packinghouse Workers Organizing Committee among the "little six" meatpackers in Chicago in 1937–1940. Miller and Hart, P. D. Brennan, Reliable Packing, Roberts and Oakes, Illinois Meat, and Agar were more vulnerable to work stoppages than the larger Swift, Armour, Wilson, and Cudahy national companies. "Without us," Washington insisted, "it would have been years before the Armours and Swifts got organized" (Halpern, p. 138). Direct action on the job accomplished more than formal negotiations. In November 1937 at Miller and Hart, and later at Roberts and Oake, union shop stewards would halt production at strategic moments when two hundred or so freshly slaughtered hogs or cattle were hanging on the line—and would all have to be condemned if not processed and gotten into the cooler within an hour. The first action secured the first bargaining session from a reluctant management, and the latter secured the first signed agreement in the stockyards.

"You had to take it slow," Washington recalled years later, "to make sure that you was bringing everybody along with you." After getting management to talk to union representatives on the floor, workers who hadn't signed up think, "this union's gonna get some action and I better get on board so I can get a piece of it" (Halpern, p. 135).

Shortly after the Japanese attack on Pearl Harbor, 7 December 1941, Washington entered the military and served in the South Pacific. Like tremendous numbers of African American soldiers, Washington wrote to his brother-in-law, who worked at the Armour plant, his hopes that upon returning home from the war, they would have "given the crackers the same kind of licking" being given to the Japanese army. Meantime he instructed, "keep the bastards toeing the line" (Halpern, p. 214). Returning to find PWOC had become the United Packinghouse Workers of America, with government-imposed wartime contracts covering all three of the largest packing companies, Washington observed, "Guess they got along fine without me." He also observed "more black faces in there than I ever saw before. Black guys on jobs that whites used to hold down solid … and girls too" (Halpern, p. 167).

Washington apparently never served in a formal elected leadership or executive role. He was still alive on 28 April 1988, when the historian Rick Halpern interviewed him—the most detailed primary record of Washington's three decades in a variety of labor and community struggles. Like many who made history at the street and shop floor level, he then faded from the documented historical record.

FURTHER READING

Barrett, James R. *Work and Community in the Jungle: Chicago's Packinghouse Workers, 1894–1922* (1987).

Cohen, Lizabeth. *Making a New Deal: Industrial Workers in Chicago, 1919–1939* (1999).

Halpern, Rick. *Down on the Killing Floor: Black and White Workers in Chicago's Packinghouses, 1904–54* (1997).

CHARLES ROSENBERG

Washington, Madison (1815–?), was born into slavery in central Virginia, and his parentage and precise date of birth are unknown. Washington was the instigator of a slave revolt onboard the U.S. brig *Creole* in 1841. Very little is known about Washington's life before and after the *Creole* revolt. Married at the age of twenty, he escaped from slavery in 1839 and reached Canada in 1840 after traveling through either Ohio or New York State. He returned to Virginia to free his wife in 1841 and was helped on his return journey by abolitionists in Rochester. But when he reached Virginia he was recaptured, sold to a slave broker named Thomas McCargo, and placed on the *Creole* with 134 other slaves.

The ship left the port of Richmond, Virginia, on 25 October 1841 bound for New Orleans, Louisiana, where the slaves would be sold at auction. Also on board were thirteen crewmembers and six white passengers. Some sources mention that Washington's wife was on board and conclude that his desire to rescue her fuelled his role in the rebellion. Whether or not this is true, the *Creole* crew's depositions do reveal that the revolt began when Washington was discovered in the women's hold on the night of 7 November. The ship was near Abaco Island in the Bahamas, and Washington and eighteen other slaves seized pistols and knives, then subdued the crew. Only two men died, including John Hewell, who owned thirty-nine of the slaves on board. In both their individual and collective depositions in November and December of 1841, the crew members claimed that Washington—whom they identified as the leader of the mutineers—had prevented further violence and saved their lives ("The Mutiny," Senate Documents, 1842, 21–46).

After seizing control of the ship, Washington and the other rebels forced the crew to sail for British-controlled Nassau, a port in the Bahamas. The British Emancipation Act of 1833 had ended slavery in the British Empire, and the slaves may have assumed that they would be freed upon entering the port. The *Creole* reached Nassau on the morning of 9 November 1841, and on 12 November 1841 the nineteen insurrectionists were detained. U.S. Secretary of State Daniel Webster demanded that the British return the slaves and the ship, adding that the rebels were murderers and pirates; but British officials ruled that local laws applied to the *Creole*. The remaining 135 slaves were taken ashore and set free, and the *Creole* eventually reached New Orleans on 2 December 1841 without its cargo of slaves. The rebels were not deposed, but crew members—some of whom were interviewed six times—told British officials and the U.S. counsel in a collective statement that "the nineteen said, all they had done was for their freedom" ("The Mutiny," Senate Documents, 1842, 41). Washington remained in a British jail for five months, until 16 April 1842, when all the rebels were released. Some stayed in the Bahamas, but Washington probably went to Jamaica.

Attention soon shifted from the incident itself to the diplomatic struggle between Britain and the U.S. slave traders in the South who demanded compensation—southern journalists accused the British of attacking the domestic slave trade. Four other American ships had entered the waters of British islands before the *Creole* incident, and the British had freed the slaves on board each time. The argument over compensation continued for twelve years until 1853, when an Anglo-American claims commission awarded $110,330 to slave owners. The rebels themselves were pushed even further into history's shadows by controversial Congressional debates. On 21 March 1842 U.S. Representative Joshua Giddings introduced resolutions declaring that southern slave codes did not apply to the seas, and thus the *Creole* rebels had violated no law. Censured by the House, Giddings resigned and was immediately reelected.

Though the rebels' stories went unheard in the noise of diplomatic wrangling and Congressional controversy, the rebellion had an impact beyond the compensation claim and the censure of Giddings. By sparking a debate, Giddings was able to challenge the infamous gag rule, which silenced all discussion of slavery in the House between 1836 and 1844. And the *Creole* revolt gave abolitionists new material for their writings. Washington was invoked by Lydia Maria Child, and by former slave WILLIAM WELLS BROWN, who declared him to be "one of the handsomest of his race," with a clear "genius," and "created to guide his fellow men" (*The Negro*, 26). Then in 1853 the former slave and abolitionist FREDERICK DOUGLASS used elements of the *Creole* incident in his historical novella *The Heroic Slave*. Here, the character Madison Washington justifies his violence and claims his freedom with the words: "We have done that which you applaud your fathers for doing, and if we are murderers, so were they" (*The Heroic Slave*, 503).

Douglass's story came during a challenge to nonviolent abolitionism. The Fugitive Slave Law had passed in 1850, and in response some abolitionists advocated violent resistance. An abolitionist named JOSHUA B. SMITH circulated weapons at a meeting, and in the following half-decade other abolitionists endorsed slave violence. Although little blood was shed by the *Creole* rebels, the incident now helped to shift the abolitionist movement from the era of nonviolent resistance to one marked by violent means. The *Creole* incident was compared to DENMARK VESEY's plans for a slave insurrection in 1822, NAT TURNER's slave rebellion of 1831, and the *Amistad* slave revolt of 1839. And more widely, slave-ship resistance helped make the antislavery crusade a "precursor of the ... violent Civil War" (McKivigan and Harrold, 2): Africans had mutinied on slave ships 392 times by 1860—on as many as 10 percent of slave-ship voyages (Richardson, 72).

The abolitionist John Brown certainly saw the connection between Washington's revolt and his own violent action, taken on the eve of the Civil War. According to Brown's friend Franklin Sanborn, Brown sent for Washington while preparing his October 1859 raid on Harpers Ferry, as he needed him "as a leader among the colored recruits ... in his band of liberators" ("John Brown in Massachusetts," 423). It is unclear if this actually happened, and Washington certainly didn't join the Harpers Ferry raid, but Brown apparently took inspiration from the *Creole* revolt and hoped that his own raid would be accompanied by an armed slave rebellion.

FURTHER READING

Brown, William Wells. *The Negro in the American Rebellion* (1867).

Douglass, Frederick. *The Heroic Slave* (1853), in *The Life and Writings of Frederick Douglass*, ed. Phillip Foner (1950–1955).

Hendrick, George, and Willene Hendrick. *The Creole Mutiny: A Tale of Revolt Aboard a Slave Ship* (2003).

McKivigan, John R., and Stanley Harrold, eds. *Antislavery Violence: Sectional, Racial, and Cultural Conflict in Antebellum America* (1999).

"The Mutiny on Board the Brig *Creole*, and the Liberation of the Slaves who were Passengers in the Said Vessel, Jan 21, 1842." Senate Documents, 27th Congress, 2d Session, No. 51 (1842).

Richardson, David. "Shipboard Revolts, African Authority, and the Atlantic Slave Trade," *The William and Mary Quarterly* 58, 1: 69–92.

Sanborn, Franklin. "John Brown in Massachusetts," *Atlantic Monthly* (April 1872).

ZOE TRODD

Washington, Margaret Murray (9 Mar. 1861–4 June 1925), educator and clubwoman, was born Margaret James Murray in Macon, Mississippi, near the Mississippi-Alabama border, to Lucy (maiden name unknown), a washerwoman who was possibly a slave, and James Murray, who had immigrated to the United States from Ireland. After her father's death, seven-year-old Margaret left home to live with her northern-born, white siblings, the Sanders. The Sanders, who were Quakers, taught school in their community and encouraged their little sister to pursue a career in education. Margaret's Quaker surroundings fostered in the growing girl a sense of social responsibility, community building, self-help, and obligation. Taking the advice of her siblings, she passed the qualifying exam and began teaching local schoolchildren at age fourteen.

Margaret Murray Washington, educator and clubwoman, c. 1914. (Library of Congress.)

The ambitious young woman, known to her friends and family as Maggie, quit her teaching job and entered Fisk University in Nashville, Tennessee, in 1881, at the age of twenty. She shaved four years off her age and enrolled as a part-time student, working to support herself through preparatory school and college. Her experience as a struggling, working-class student typified the lifestyle of many black clubwomen at the turn of the century, most of whom came from humble beginnings. As the children and grandchildren of slaves, these young women learned early the importance of hard work, self-respect, thrift, and community consciousness in the face of adversity.

In addition to her studies and part-time work, Maggie found time for extracurricular activities as associate editor of the *Fisk Herald* newspaper, president of a literary society, and debate team member. Her classmates at Fisk included W. E. B. DuBois and Sterling Brown. Maggie met her future husband, BOOKER T. WASHINGTON, the principal of Tuskegee Normal and Industrial Institute (later Tuskegee University), on the day of her graduation

from Fisk in 1889. Washington, who gave the commencement address that day, offered her a teaching job after she persistently inquired about faculty openings. Although she had already accepted a teaching position at Prairie View College in southeastern Texas, she jumped at the chance to work alongside Washington.

Maggie Murray began her long career at Tuskegee in 1889 as an English instructor and, the following year, became lady principal and director of the Department of Domestic Service, which was later renamed Department of Girls' Industries and housed in the newly built Dorothy Hall. Murray oversaw the curriculum, which included lower-division and postgraduate courses in table setting, laundering, broom making, basketry, sewing, soap making, millinery, and cooking. Her other duties included supervising female coeds and faculty on campus, recommending faculty for merit raises, and writing letters of recommendation for job and college applicants. As dean, she organized fund-raisers and cultivated donors, including MADAM C. J. WALKER. Murray, whom graduates and coworkers remembered as a nurturing, yet intimidating administrator, also served on the governing committee that ran the campus in Booker T. Washington's absence. Washington took notice of Murray's leadership skills and commitment to Tuskegee. He proposed marriage in 1891, but Murray, who already felt uneasy around children, expressed some apprehension about marrying a man twice widowed with three children. Washington, who had a daughter, Portia, from his first marriage to FANNY SMITH [WASHINGTON], had married Tuskegee's cofounder, OLIVIA DAVIDSON WASHINGTON, in 1884, two years after the death of his first wife. Olivia died in 1889, following the birth of two sons, Booker Jr. and Davidson Earnest. Eventually, Murray's concerns eased, and the couple married on 12 October 1892. Years later, they took in her sister's children, Thomas and Laura Murray.

In addition to her work as wife, mother, and educator, Margaret Washington had a passion for community building. In March 1895 she and twelve other women formed the Tuskegee Women's Club, which opened a school on the Elizabeth Russell Plantation in Macon County, near Tuskegee. The rural school provided youngsters with a basic, rudimentary education; instructed wives and mothers on housekeeping and child care; held sewing classes; and developed reading seminars for men. With the assistance of Tuskegee graduates, the school soon held both day and night classes and helped many of the tenant farmers purchase their own farms.

The Tuskegee Women's Club also established Mother's Meetings for Macon County blacks. The group, which provided day care to its participants, taught classes on etiquette, housekeeping, and child care. Participation in the meetings swelled during the Tuskegee Institute's annual farmer's conferences, which brought five hundred southern farmers to the campus each year, but was closed to women until 1916. In 1910 the Tuskegee clubwomen formed the Town Night School, which provided courses in carpentry, bricklaying, painting, cooking, and sewing to the men and women of Tuskegee. Over the next few years the school expanded its curriculum to cover academic subjects, including African American history.

In 1899 Washington organized the Alabama Federation of Colored Women's Clubs. Led by the activist Cornelia Bowen, the club built a center for troubled youths, a nursing home for the elderly and indigent, and libraries for black Alabamians. It raised funds for the American Red Cross, supported black troops during World War I, encouraged good health and hygiene practices in the home, and established the state's first black YWCA.

Washington also worked with activists in the national clubwoman movement. In 1895, at the invitation of the civil rights activist and journalist JOSEPHINE ST. PIERRE RUFFIN, Washington traveled to Boston to aid in the formation of what became the National Federation of Afro-American Women (NFAAW). Washington served as the organization's first president. A year later, when the NFAAW merged with the Washington Colored League, headed by Mary Church Terrell, to create the National Association of Colored Women (NACW), Washington became NACW's membership coordinator, local and state-affiliated clubs organizer, and editor of the organization's magazine, *National Association Notes*. The NACW and its affiliates protested sexism, built kindergartens, created day-care centers, and opened libraries across the country. The organization, whose membership grew from 50,000 in 1914 to 300,000 in 1920, encouraged black educators to teach African American history, lobbied for prison reform, maintained settlement houses, supported women's suffrage, and campaigned with the NAACP and Urban League against lynching.

The NACW's efforts to develop coalitions with white women's organizations were the source of tension within the organization. Terrell and CHARLOTTE HAWKINS BROWN were often at odds with Washington and Jennie Moton, the wife of ROBERT RUSSA MOTON, after Booker T. Washington's untimely death in 1915. Tempers reached new heights, and Margaret Washington and Jennie Moton were blamed by some black clubwomen when white organizers of an interracial clubwoman convention in 1920 omitted portions of a seven-point statement issued by African American activists that called, in-part, for antilynching legislation. Washington's belief in interracial progress and cooperation was unquestionably rooted in her personal history. Similarly, her endorsement of black economic self-determination, which she viewed as both the final stage in the emancipation saga and a first step in the ongoing black civil rights struggle, was informed by her own experiences.

In her final years Washington became increasingly vocal about racial oppression in the United States and around the world. Inspired by DuBois's newly created Pan-African Congress, Washington, NANNIE BURROUGHS, MARY MCLEOD BETHUNE, and other NACW members founded the International Council of Women of the Darker Races (ICWDR) in 1920. The ICWDR brought together women of color from across the globe in fighting sexism, racism, imperialism, and global poverty. Although she was gravely ill by the time of the ICWDR's first convention in 1922, Washington continued to work with the organization as well as with the NACW and her beloved Tuskegee students. Washington died in 1924.

FURTHER READING

Washington's papers are located in the Hollis Frissell Library, Tuskegee University, Tuskegee, Alabama.

Lane, Linda Rochell. *A Documentary of Mrs. Booker T. Washington* (2001).

Rouse, Jacqueline Ann. "Out of the Shadow of Tuskegee: Margaret Murray Washington, Social Activism, and Race Vindication," *Journal of Negro History* 81 (1996).

Shaw, Stephanie. *What a Woman Ought To Be and Do: Black Professional Women Workers during the Jim Crow Era* (1996).

BERNADETTE PRUITT

Washington, Mary Helen (21 January 1941–), educator, literary critic, and anthologist, was born in Cleveland, Ohio, to Mary Catherine Dalton, a homemaker and mother of eight children, and David C. Washington, a bank guard at Cleveland National Bank. In 1962 she earned a B.A. from Notre Dame College, and she was a public school teacher of English from 1962 to 1964 before earning an M.A. in 1966 from the University of Detroit in Michigan.

Washington served as an instructor at St. John College of Cleveland from 1966 to 1968. She received her Ph.D. from the University of Detroit in 1976, and was an assistant professor there from 1972 to 1977 and an associate professor from 1977 to 1979. At Detroit, she served as director of the Center for Black Studies. From 1980 to 1988, Washington was an associate professor of English at the University of Massachusetts, Boston; in 1988 she achieved the rank of professor.

In 1990 Washington became professor of English in the Department of English at the University of Maryland in College Park, Maryland. To this position she brought scholarly interests ranging from race and ethnicity, gender and feminism, and history to African American literature and social movements. Washington lectured on the literature of the civil rights movement and twentieth-century African American literature, and served as affiliate faculty in the departments of American Studies, African American Studies, Women's Studies, and the Consortium on Race, Gender, and Ethnicity. She was a faculty contributor to the Life Writing Program, an organization composed of persons interested in the culture study of individual lives, and served as faculty adviser for *In Process*, a nationally distributed graduate student journal of African American literature.

Washington's scholarly writings and critical reviews appeared in publications such as *Massachusetts Review*, *Nation*, *Black World*, *Ms. Magazine*, the *Washington Post*, and *Of Our Spiritual Strivings: Recent Developments in Black Literature and Criticism*. In November 2006 her paper "Barbara Johnson, African Americanist: The Critic as Insider/Outsider" was published in the journal *differences*.

As a contributor to educational programming for television and film, Washington was an adviser for segments of the PBS documentary *Eyes on the Prize: America's Civil Rights Movement, 1954–1985*. She appeared in the 1992 production of *Literary Visions*, a twenty-four-part telecourse exploring literature and literary analysis, and in the Agee Films production *Tell about the South: Voices in Black and White* (1998–2000), a series of three feature-length films that tell the story of modern southern literature.

Washington's published volumes, spanning thirty years of scholarship, include *Memory of Kin: Stories about Family by Black Writers*, published by Random House in 1991. In this collection of nineteen stories and twelve poems, Washington explores the family as "a living mystery" and examines such features of family life as mothers and daughters, weddings, funerals, and the extended family—all through the work of African American writers including ALICE WALKER, CHARLES CHESNUTT, AUDRE LORDE, and LUCILLE CLIFTON.

A revised edition of her books *Black-Eyed Susans: Classic Stories by and about Black Women* (1975) and *Midnight Birds: Stories by Contemporary Black Women Writers* (1980) was published by Doubleday/Anchor in 1990. *Invented Lives: Narratives of Black Women 1860–1960*, published by Doubleday/Anchor in 1987, is an anthology that includes excerpts from the writings of ten African American women fiction writers including GWENDOLYN BROOKS, ZORA NEALE HURSTON, DOROTHY WEST, FANNIE BARRIER WILLIAMS, and HARRIET JACOBS, writer of the complex and thought-provoking slave narrative *Incidents in the Life of a Slave Girl*. In this volume, which includes an extensive preamble and critical headnotes for each chapter, Washington examines the history of black women's literary tradition, and as a focal point she discusses how and why the work of black women writers has often been marginalized while the work of black male writers has been extolled and positioned as "the" black literary tradition.

Washington's essays, introductory material, and prologues appeared in numerous published volumes, including "ANNA JULIA COOPER: The Black Feminist Voice of the 1890s," in *Black Women's Intellectual Traditions: Speaking Their Minds* (2007), edited by Kristen Waters and Carol B. Conaway; "'A Tenant of the World': Frank London Brown's Civil Rights Novel," an introduction to Frank London Brown's 1959 novel *Trumbull Park* (2005); "Alice Childress, Lorraine Hansberry, and Claudia Jones: Black Women Write the Popular Front," in *Left of the Color Line: Race, Radicalism, and Twentieth-Century Literature of the United States*, edited by Bill V. Mullen and James Smethurst (2003); "Declaring (Ambiguous) Liberty: Paule Marshall's Middle Class Women," in *Sister Circle: Black Women and Work*, edited by Sharon Harley and the Black Women and Work Collective (2002); and "Desegregating the 1950s: The Case of Frank London Brown, *Trumbull Park*, and Public Housing," in *Japanese Journal of American Studies* 10 (June 1999).

She wrote opening matter for volumes such as *Feminist Literary Theory: A Reader*, edited by Mary

Eagleton (1986); *Pioneer Spirit: Catherine Spalding, Sister of Charity of Nazareth*, by Mary Ellen Doyle (2006); *A Voice from the South*, by Anna Julia Cooper (1988); and *I Love Myself When I Am Laughing … And Then Again When I Am Looking Mean and Impressive: A Zora Neale Hurston Reader*, edited by Alice Walker (1979). In *The Memphis Diary of Ida B. Wells: An Intimate Portrait of the Activist as a Young Woman*, edited by Miriam DeCosta-Willis, Washington contributed an essay that serves to elucidate the "mystery and complexity" of Wells, who was at once a very private person and a very public crusading journalist. In the 1990s Washington began to focus her scholarship on the work of left-leaning black writers and visual artists during the cold war era of the 1950s, including ALICE CHILDRESS, LLOYD L. BROWN, LORRAINE HANSBERRY, PAULE MARSHALL, CHARLES WHITE, and ELIZABETH CATLETT.

Washington served as president of the American Studies Association in 1997–1998 and served on the board of the PEN/Faulkner Foundation from 1993 to 1996. She received five honorary doctorates and earned six fellowships, including the Ford Foundation Fellowship (1986) and the Mary Ingraham Bunting Fellowship, Harvard University (1979–1980); she also was a research fellow at the Wellesley Center for Research on Women. In 1996 she was a Smithsonian scholar in residence. Her citations include the Lyndhurst Prize (1994–1996), Chancellor's Distinguished Scholarship Award, University of Massachusetts (1988), Zora Neale Hurston Creative Scholarship Award (1906), and the Richard Wright Award for Literary Criticism, *Black World* (January 1974).

FURTHER READING

Davis, Bonnie M. "Feminizing the English Curriculum: An International Perspective," *The English Journal*, vol. 78, no. 6 (Oct. 1989).

Griffin, Farah Jasmine. "That the Mothers May Soar and the Daughters May Know Their Names: A Retrospective of Black Feminist Literary Criticism," *Signs: Journal of Women in Culture and Society*, vol. 32, no. 5 (2007).

Griffin, Farah Jasmine. "Thirty Years of Black American Literature and Literary Studies: A Review," *Journal of Black Studies*, vol. 35, no. 2 (2004).

PAMALA S. DEANE

Washington, Mary Parks (20 July 1924–), artist, teacher, and arts advocate, was born Mary Jeanne Parks in Atlanta, Georgia, the eldest of four daughters of Hattie Brookins and Walter Parks, owner of a shoe repair shop.

Washington began developing her artistic talent formally in an advanced art class in high school. While exhibiting her work at a school art fair, Washington met the artist HALE WOODRUFF, who would become her lifelong mentor and friend. After high school, Washington enrolled at Spelman College, where she majored in art, studying under Woodruff and the sculptors ELIZABETH PROPHET and WILLIAM ARTIS. While at Spelman, Woodruff encouraged Washington to spend the summer of 1945 at the Art Students League in New York, where she studied drawing under Reginald Marsh.

After Washington graduated from Spelman in 1946, Woodruff helped her receive a Rosenwald Fund scholarship to attend the Summer Art Institute at the experimental Black Mountain College in North Carolina. Washington took courses with prominent artists including Josef Albers, Jean Varda, Beaumont Newhall, and GWENDOLYN KNIGHT. The free-spirited and racially integrated environment of Black Mountain, where students sat on the floor during class and wore dungarees, was a stark contrast to the rigid rules and curricula of Atlanta's segregated schools. Washington credits her experiences at Black Mountain, particularly her work with Varda, for giving her ideas that she would later develop into the *histcollage*, an autobiographical collage form.

In the fall of 1946 Washington returned to Atlanta, where she taught for four years. She spent the summer of 1947 at the University of Mexico, studying Mexican art, folklore, and dancing. She also met Diego Rivera and other Mexican artists. Washington received financial assistance from the State of Georgia for her summer abroad. In an attempt to discourage the desegregation of higher education within the state, Georgia regularly paid the out-of-state tuition and traveling expenses for black students. Washington used this exclusionary policy to her advantage, becoming the first person to receive state funds to study outside the country.

Upon returning from Mexico in 1947, she married Samuel L. Washington, a psychiatric social worker in the armed forces and former Tuskegee Airman. During the 1950s Samuel Washington's career took the couple to Japan, providing an opportunity for Washington to study Japanese brush painting. In 1958 they settled in Campbell, California, where Washington taught art and raised the couple's two children. The couple divorced in 1971.

Despite the demands of work and family, Washington continued to create art although she did not receive public acclaim for her work until the 1970s. In 1971 the Johnson Publishing Company purchased Washington's painting *Black Soul* for display in its Chicago headquarters. Her first one-woman show took place at the San Jose Art Center three years later. Since then, Washington has exhibited extensively, including at the Asheville Art Museum, Atlanta University, Auburn Avenue Research Library, Oakland Museum, San Jose Institute of Contemporary Art, Spelman College, and Triton Museum of Art.

In 1978 Washington earned an M.A. in Art with a specialty in painting from San Jose State University. She continued to combine the study of art with travel including a trip to West Africa and a collage workshop with Romare Beardon in St. Martin. In 1988 Washington retired from the Union School District in San Jose, California, after twenty-seven years of dedicated service but continued as a district art consultant until 1990.

Beginning in the 1960s and increasingly after her retirement from teaching, Washington became a fierce champion of art in schools and a supporter of public art projects. She also advocated greater recognition of African American artists by chairing and serving on numerous committees, including California's Art Curriculum Criteria Committee and the advisory committee for the Fine Arts Museum of San Francisco. She served on the advisory board of the International Review of African American Art from 1990 to 1991. In 1995 the California Art Educator Association named Washington Distinguished Art Educator of the Year.

Washington uses a variety of media including drawing, painting, and sculpture. However, her works since the 1990s have displayed her preference for the *histcollage*, a mixed media assemblage through which she explores themes of history, memory, and omission by incorporating old family documents into her drawings and paintings. In *Georgia Out-of-State Tuition* (1996), the penciled outlines of three young women contrast with their bright hats and the texture of yellowed tuition receipts from the state of Georgia. For Washington, recording memories, both of triumph and of hardship, through art is an act of survival.

FURTHER READING

Mary Parks Washington's papers are housed at the Auburn Avenue Research Library on African American Culture and History in Atlanta, Georgia.

King-Hammond, Leslie. *Gumbo Ya Ya: Anthology of Contemporary African-American Women Artists* (1995).

KRYSTAL APPIAH

Washington, Mary Thelma (21 Apr. 1906–2 July 2005), first African American female certified public accountant, was born Mary Thelma Morrison in Vicksburg, Mississippi, to William Morrison, a carpenter, and Daisy Morrison (maiden name unknown). Her mother passed away when she was six, and she moved to Chicago to live with her maternal grandparents.

Morrison attended Wendell Phillips High School in Chicago, where she excelled, especially in mathematics. As a young woman, she joined the Douglas National Bank as a bookkeeper. She later moved to Binga State Bank, one of the two largest black-owned banks in the nation. Binga State Bank had been founded by JESSE BINGA in 1908, but it failed in 1930 at the outset of the Depression. Morrison worked as the assistant to the cashier and vice president, Arthur Wilson. Wilson was a certified public accountant; when he earned his CPA in 1923 he became only the second African American, after JOHN W. CROMWELL JR., to have achieved this distinction.

Morrison married Seymour Washington in 1927; they had one daughter, Barbara. Her career remained of paramount importance to her, and Wilson, recognizing Washington's talent and affinity for numbers, encouraged his employee to pursue a business degree at Northwestern University's downtown campus. As a student at Northwestern, she lived in Chicago's South Side, an African American section of the segregated city. Because Washington had fair skin, she was often mistaken for a white person. Washington feared poor treatment from her classmates and professors if it were discovered that she was black. Therefore, after her classes she would board the commuter train and head north, the direction of most white neighborhoods, to the very last stop. Then she would switch platforms and head back south to get home. She earned her bachelor's degree from the College of Business at Northwestern University in 1941.

Inspired and encouraged by Arthur Wilson, Washington wanted to become a certified public accountant. When Wilson become a CPA in 1923, the state of Illinois had not yet instituted a requirement that all prospective CPAs must work for a CPA, but when Washington wanted to pursue the credential she had to serve an apprenticeship in order to earn her license. At that time virtually no white CPAs would hire African Americans, so Washington was fortunate that Wilson was available to provide her with the requisite experience. In 1943 she became the first African American female CPA, and only the thirteenth African American CPA in the country. Wilson had been required to take the Illinois CPA examination behind a curtain in the testing room, but Washington did not have to suffer that indignity, though she told her daughter that the examiners were not too pleased to have a "lady" taking the examination. They did not realize that she was also African American.

Washington opened her own accounting firm in her basement in 1939, while she was still in school, and she soon counted many small black-owned businesses among her clients. Partly due to the pressure of her job, she and Seymour had divorced in 1935, and she married Donald Melvin Wylie in 1940. The couple adopted two children, Donald II (he already had a son named Donald Jr.) and Melanie. She continued to be known professionally as Mary T. Washington. Her second husband, who was a mechanic, was supportive of Washington's career: during tax season she and the brigade of ambitious young black men who became her employees would work late hours in their basement—often until midnight—and Wylie would make dinner for the entire group.

These young men had moved to Chicago from around the country for the opportunity to work for Washington. Because they needed to work for a CPA in order to earn the credential, and because apprenticeship opportunities for African Americans were scarce until the late 1960s, her first partner, Hiram Pittman, described her office as a kind of "Underground Railroad" for aspiring black CPAs (Pittman interview, 1992). Although some of the few male African American CPAs were reluctant to hire and train others because they worried that new black CPAs might "steal" their clients, Washington employed anyone with strong skills and the willingness to work hard. As a result of her self-confidence, generosity, and desire to help others, through the 1960s there were more black CPAs in Chicago than in any other city in the country. As the focal point for African Americans in the profession, she hosted an annual Christmas party for all the African American CPAs in town.

The fact that Chicago had a relatively large black middle class and several successful black businesses was a boon to her firm. The bulk of her work consisted of designing and maintaining accounting systems for small businesses and individuals, and tax preparation. Some of her major clients included Fuller Products, founded by the millionaire S. B. FULLER; the two major real estate companies on Chicago's South Side, Leon L. Motts and Company and Riley, Brown and Company; Parker House Sausage; Jackson Funeral Home; Seaway National Bank; and Continental Casket Co.

Washington was known to be exceptionally meticulous, and she drove more than one secretary to tears because she required that any report with a typographical error in it be completely retyped. No erasures were permitted. Her attention to detail and high expectations prepared her employees for successful and impressive careers. Two of these employees, Hiram Pittman and Lester McKeever, became named partners in her firm. Frederick Ford became the first African American to work in a major downtown real estate firm in Chicago, rising to the position of vice chair of the board at Draper & Kramer, Incorporated. Washington's first secretary, Willie M. Whiting, went on to law school and later became a circuit court judge in Cook County, Illinois.

Unlike the few other African American CPAs of the 1940s and 1950s, Washington had some white clients; her employees recall that she prepared tax returns for several Jewish individuals. This may have been because they did not perceive her as being African American, even though she was a leader in the black community. In 1957 her ability to "pass" caused some consternation within the mainstream of the profession. For example, she had planned to attend the American Institute of Certified Public Accountants (AICPA) national meeting in Texas (she had been the first African American female member of the AICPA), but she was discouraged by leaders of the Illinois Society of CPAs, who feared that her race would be discovered. Houston's Shamrock Hotel, where the meeting was to be held, was off-limits to black Americans. In the 1950s it was not uncommon for professional organizations to hold meetings in segregated hotels, although several major associations refused to do so.

Washington, Pittman, and McKeever, LLC, continued to flourish throughout the twentieth century, maintaining its place as one of the largest black-owned CPA firms in the United States. Its business expanded dramatically in the 1960s, when several social service agencies created under President Lyndon B. Johnson's antipoverty programs required the auditing and accounting expertise that her firm could provide. The rising boxing star MUHAMMAD ALI became a client of the firm, though he later moved to a larger, white-owned firm. The civil rights movement had a double-edged effect on black-owned accounting firms—as more opportunities arose for African Americans, black businesses such as Washington, Pittman, and McKeever saw their potential client base expand. Simultaneously, however, major white-owned firms started to seek out African American–owned businesses and black celebrities as clients. In 1983, when HAROLD WASHINGTON became Chicago's first black mayor, he mandated that minority firms be included in city contracts. Washington, Pittman, and McKeever subsequently became one of the auditors for the Chicago Public Library, the Chicago Housing Authority, and the City of Chicago.

Washington formally retired in 1985, at the age of seventy-nine, after having worked part time for a few years. She died at the age of ninety-nine in a Chicago nursing home. After her death, Washington, Pittman, and McKeever continued to be one of the largest black-owned CPA firms in the country.

FURTHER READING

Much of the information for this entry was gathered through interviews with Hiram Pittman (9 Dec. 1992) and Arthur Reynolds (10 Jan. 1992).

Drake, St. Clair, and Horace R. Cayton. *Black Metropolis: A Study of Negro Life in a Northern City* (1945).

Hammond, Theresa A. *A White-Collar Profession: African American Certified Public Accountants Since 1921* (2002).

THERESA A. HAMMOND

Washington, Mildred (1904/05?–7 Sept. 1933), actress, dancer, and producer, was born in Houston, Texas, the third of four children and youngest daughter of Lillie and Millard Washington, the latter having come to Texas from South Carolina. The family moved to Los Angeles in 1913, where they were active in the church at Eighth and Towne, and later at the Independent Church.

Little is known about Washington's early life. Legal documents indicate she was briefly married to a man whose surname was Youngae and gave birth to a daughter, Lillie June Youngae, in about 1923. An 8 September 1933 article in the *California Eagle* states that Washington "did not make her stage debut until 1924, remaining in school and graduating from Los Angeles High School." When she did appear onstage, the article continues, "she quickly attracted the attention of showmen because of her personal charms and unusual ability. She was headlined at the Cotton Club in New York City for one year."

Harlem in the mid-1920s was the center of a cultural renaissance in literature and the arts, including that big thing—jazz! Along with her talent as an entertainer, Washington had a deep appreciation of culture and literature. She combined energy and thoughtfulness in a way that affected people. Exceptionally beautiful, she could cut up the dance floor with joyful abandon. At the same time, the *California Eagle* reports: "she had a large library containing many rare volumes. She was a deep student of literature, Homer and Milton being among her favorites. She read extensively and included in her studies French and Latin" (8 Sept. 1933).

Washington returned to Los Angeles in 1926 and began to choreograph and produce her own floor shows at Frank Sebastian's Cotton Club in Culver City; she also performed at the Moulin Rouge Café and the Legion Café into the early 1930s. The *Los Angeles Times* carried advertisements for "Mildred Washington and Her Georgia Peaches" and "Mildred Washington and Her Humming Bird Café Creole Cuties, Consisting of 14 Performers … Together with Vernon & Hite Dixieland Jazz Band." An article about the all-black musical comedy *Struttin' Sam from Alabam'* described her performance of "The Ragtime Struttin' China Girl" (10 Oct. 1926).

In 1928 Washington began to work in Hollywood films, costarring with her sister Flora in *Tenderfeet*, a late silent movie in which the dancer James "Hambone" Robinson played himself. The following year *Hearts in Dixie*, one of the early sound pictures, was released by MGM and Fox Pictures. The film starred STEPIN FETCHIT, CLARENCE MUSE, Washington, Zack Williams, and Gertrude Howard, with a cast of 200, and was Hollywood's first feature film with an all-black cast. While the movie's presentation of life on a southern plantation after the Civil War was euphoric and patronizing, the dancing and singing had an exuberance and style that critics praised and audiences loved.

Hollywood generally offered only minor roles to African American actors and performers. Washington played the heroine's maid in *The Shopworn Angel* (1928), which starred twenty-seven-year-old Gary Cooper, and as a character named Purple in *The Thoroughbred* (a.k.a. *Riding to Win*), a British production from 1930.

Onstage, she starred in the musical *Lucky Day*, and was featured in Fanchon and Marco's *Ideas* between 1931 and 1933. She continued producing her own floor shows, including a burlesque marriage ceremony with a cast of fifteen at the Harlem Show Boat Café in Los Angeles. Her success as a producer can be surmised by the fact that she purchased several pieces of property, and the 1930 U.S. census lists her as head of a Pasadena home in which her young daughter, sister, brother, cousin, niece, and servant also resided.

It is a tribute to Washington's talent—and an indication of what might have been were it not for her untimely death—that in six years she appeared in more than a dozen films alongside unknown actors who later became famous: *Too Much Harmony* with Bing Crosby, *Blonde Venus*, starring Marlene Dietrich and Cary Grant (1932), *Only Yesterday* with Billie Burke (1933), and *Morning Glory* (1933), for which Katharine Hepburn won her first Oscar. Washington was a hardworking professional who earned the respect of entertainers, coworkers, directors, and producers—respect that can be seen in the role she was given in *Torch Singer*, starring Claudette Colbert (1933). Washington plays Carrie, the maid/confidante of the famous singer Mimi Benton (Colbert), and there is a genuine warmth and friendliness between them. This film is also remarkable for a scene in which Colbert and a black child actress speak to each other with depth and humanity. It also contains a notable, though brief, scene of Washington dancing.

Sadly, *Torch Singer* was Washington's last movie. In March 1933 an earthquake struck Los Angeles while she was rehearsing a spectacular dance number for the premiere of *King Kong*. As Washington fled Grauman's Chinese Theatre, she fell, injuring her right side. She continued working for several months but developed appendicitis and was taken to White Memorial Hospital. By the time doctors operated, peritonitis was irreversible. She died in 1933 at the age of twenty-eight.

The loss of Washington was deeply felt by African American entertainers. Many mourners viewed her lying in state at the Connor-Johnson funeral parlor, and hundreds attended her funeral. Pallbearers were musicians from Les Hite's orchestra. Albertine Pickens, Martha Ritchie, Pearl Jackson, and other notables of stage and screen were present. The respect and esteem had for Washington by both blacks and whites was evident in the eulogies given by Reverend Greggs, the family's minister for many years, and by John Bright, the Hollywood screenwriter (*Public Enemy*, 1931) known for his political activism and for reviving the Screen Writers Guild

in 1933. Bright said he was certain that "all who ever knew Mildred were made finer people by her acquaintance" (*The California Eagle*, 15 Sept. 1933).

FURTHER READING
Materials related to Mildred Washington can be found in the Los Angeles Public Library database and photo collection (www.lapl.org).
Obituaries: *California Eagle*, 8 Sept. 1933 and 15 Sept. 1933.

KAREN VAN OUTRYVE

Washington, Olivia Davidson (11 June 1854–9 May 1889), educator, administrator, and wife of BOOKER T. WASHINGTON, was born Olivia America Davidson in Tazewell County, Virginia, one of seven children of Elias Washington, a former slave, and Eliza Webb, a freeborn black woman, who was probably the daughter of Elizabeth Webb, a registered free woman of Tazewell County. There is also a possibility that Davidson was one of the fifteen slaves who were listed as the property of James (Joseph) C. Davidson, the former owner of her father. Her family lived in an area with fewer than ninety free blacks, with only one other Afro-Virginian family, probably her uncle's, Hiram Dorsey. In 1850, shortly after the passage of the Fugitive Slave Law and with the increasing pressure that was placed upon free and freed blacks as a result of the law, Davidson's family migrated to Ironton, Ohio. However, the family's hope for a better and more prosperous life was not fulfilled. In Ironton, the family's financial straits did not improve, nor did they purchase land in the area. Following the birth of her three siblings and the death of her father, her mother decided to move the family to Albany, Ohio, where she took work as the attendant and cook for the family of General George Custer. In an environment well-known for its educational opportunities for black people and its antislavery activities and sentiment, Davidson continued her education at Albany Enterprise Academy, a private school that was operated and run by black educators. There she came into contact with emerging and established black leaders and Oberlin College students, which no doubt fueled her desire to teach.

In 1872, after graduating and teaching for two years, Davidson moved to Mississippi to teach the freedmen. For many educated free blacks, this was an opportunity to assist in the federal Reconstruction efforts underway throughout the South. The Freedman's Bureau assigned her to work in Spencer, Mississippi, one of the largest black counties on the

Mississippi River. It was there that Davidson was first exposed to smallpox. When the outbreak forced her school to close, she decided nevertheless to remain and nurse a young student until he recovered. Further difficulties emerged due to problems within the local community itself, including the increasing corruption in the local government, white opposition toward black schools, high taxes, and postwar impoverishment. Partly because of the declining conditions in Spencer and because of her desire to be closer to Margaret, her older sister, and Joseph, her brother, who lived near Hernando, Mississippi, she relocated to Memphis, Tennessee.

In 1874, shortly after her move to Memphis, Davidson began working at Clay Street School for colored children, which was one of the first brick school buildings to be built in the city. Davidson, under the leadership of Principal J. H. Barnum, a white northern missionary, and along with three other black teachers and four white teachers, worked to meet the educational needs of close to five hundred black students. It was during this period that Davidson lost both her brother, who was murdered by the Ku Klux Klan, and her sister within four months of each other. When the school term ended as a result of ongoing financial difficulties, Davidson returned to Ohio to visit her family and to rest. While she was away, the yellow fever epidemic hit Memphis, and although Davidson offered to return as a nurse, her offer was refused and she decided to attend Hampton Institute.

In 1878 Davidson enrolled at Hampton and was immediately placed in the senior class. She graduated the next year and delivered her class commencement speech. Booker T. Washington also spoke, delivering his postgraduate address. Davidson gained a reputation as an intelligent, charming, and talented woman, and was subsequently offered funds to attend Framingham State Normal School in Massachusetts. She enrolled in a two-year course that provided her with additional pedagogical training. In 1881, shortly after graduating with honors and distinction, Booker T. Washington offered her a position at his Independence Day School. However, poor health led her to delay her acceptance, although she did later join the school, where, despite ongoing health problems, she worked tirelessly as a teacher, principal, and fund-raiser. Three years later, she suffered a relapse and moved to New Hampshire to recover.

Davidson returned in 1885, one year after Washington's first wife had died. One year later, she spoke at the Alabama State Teachers' Association on the subject of "How shall we make the women of our race stronger?" a speech in which she emphasized the need to establish and maintain physical strength before anything else. Shortly after that address, Davidson married Washington and became the stepmother to his daughter, Portia. By 1887 Davidson Washington had given birth to their first son, Booker Jr., and Washington named Rose Mason to replace her as "Lady Principal." Although she was both a wife and mother, Davidson Washington continued to work closely with the school until the birth of her second son, Ernest, eleven months later. One evening, while Washington was away, the chimney caught fire and Davidson Washington, along with the children, was forced to flee their home. This exposure to the cold, so soon after childbirth, greatly affected her health. She died three months later at Massachusetts General Hospital. Although the school survived because of her work and Washington's ongoing commitment, Davidson Washington's name in the oral history of the school has not.

FURTHER READING

Harlan, Louis R. *Booker T. Washington: The Making of a Black Leader 1856–1901* (1972).

Harlan, Louis R., ed. *The Booker T. Washington Papers, Volume 2, 1860–89* (1972).

Harlan, Louis R., ed. *The Booker T. Washington Papers, Volume 3, 1889–95* (1972).

Hine, Darlene Clark, ed. *Black Women in United States History: From Colonial Times Through The Nineteenth Century, Volume One* (1990).

Washington, Booker T. "Up From Slavery," in *The Booker T. Washington Papers, Volume 1, The Auto-Biographical Papers*, ed. Louis R. Harlan (1972).

K. WISE WHITEHEAD

Washington, Ora (16 Jan. 1899–28 May 1971), tennis and basketball player, was born Ora Belle Washington in Caroline County, Virginia, the daughter of John Thomas Washington, a farmer and house plasterer, and Laura Young. Ora, the fifth of nine children, attended the File School in Caroline County and the Chicago Presbyterian Training School. She lived on the family farm until she was in her teens, when she and an older sister moved to Philadelphia, Pennsylvania, where one of her aunts had settled and where many of her relatives would later go to live. The 1920 census recorded that Washington lived as a domestic worker in a Philadelphia home.

Although Washington did not travel to Philadelphia with dreams of athletic stardom, she arrived at an opportune time for gifted African American athletes. The prosperity of the 1920s sparked a boom in many sports, and because African Americans were barred from many mainstream sporting endeavors, they developed institutions of their own. Black colleges devoted increasing amounts of time and money to athletic programs. The Washington family was part of a wave of urban African American migration that encouraged the development of recreational facilities and provided spectators for black professional organizations, such as the New York Renaissance and Harlem Globetrotters basketball teams, and the baseball teams of the Negro National League. By the 1920s African American newspapers were eager participants in a nationwide explosion in sports coverage, offering detailed accounts of both men's and women's sporting events.

At some point in the 1920s Washington began playing tennis at the YWCA in Germantown, a Philadelphia suburb. She took to the game immediately. In 1925 she marked herself as a competitor to watch by upsetting Isadore Channels, the reigning national champion of the all-black American Tennis Association (ATA). Washington captured her first ATA singles title in 1929 and remained champion through 1935. In 1936 she lost the title to the former titleholder and fellow Philadelphian Lulu Ballard but won it for a final time in 1937. She retired from serious singles competition early in 1938. Along with her singles victories, she held the national women's doubles title for twelve straight years, from 1925 to 1936, partnering with Ballard, Blanche Winston of New York, and Anita Grant of Washington, D.C. (Ashe, 448–455).

After retiring from singles, Washington continued to compete in doubles and mixed doubles, winning the ATA mixed-doubles title in 1939, 1946, and 1947. In the latter contest, she and her partner, George Stewart, defeated R. Walter Johnson and his partner, an up-and-coming young star named ALTHEA GIBSON. Gibson went on to break Washington's record of eight singles crowns by winning nine straight titles between 1947 and 1956.

Washington was a superb tennis player. While she was not especially tall, she was powerfully built, with broad shoulders and sharply defined muscles. She became well known for her forceful ground strokes, her range on the court, and her skillful work at the net. "She was dynamic to watch," one tennis fan recalled, "and her overhead game was terrific" (Young, 195). She was also respected for her mental strength. "Courage and determination were the biggest assets I had," she once explained (Young, 195).

During her prime, Washington dominated black women's tennis so completely that in 1931 the *Philadelphia Tribune* reported, "Her superiority is so evident that her competitors are frequently beaten before the first ball crosses the net" (12 Mar. 1931). She did not, however, have the opportunity to test herself against top white players. Most white tennis clubs and associations barred African Americans, and the U.S. Lawn Tennis Association refused to admit African American players to its national championship until 1950, when Althea Gibson made her debut. Washington's reign coincided with that of the championship white tennis player Helen Wills Moody, but Moody rebuffed efforts to persuade her to play against Washington.

Washington's athletic talent was also evident in her basketball play. While she always preferred tennis, she was widely regarded as the best black female basketball player of her era. Washington began her basketball career in earnest in the fall of 1930, playing with the Germantown YWCA Hornets, which was coached by Lincoln University's track coach, Joseph Rainey. After a near-perfect season, against opponents representing black colleges, YWCAs, churches, schoolteachers, and hospital nurses, the Hornets claimed the national African American woman's title. Washington, who scored more than two hundred points in the season, was the undisputed star.

By the fall of 1932 Washington had moved to the team with whom she would make her greatest mark: the Philadelphia Tribunes, sponsored by Philadelphia's dominant African American newspaper. In 1931, under the leadership of the *Tribune* circulation director and former Negro League baseball star Otto Briggs, the paper had established the team to capitalize on the growing interest in women's basketball. In the spring of 1932 the Tribunes, led by Philadelphian Inez Patterson, won a five-game championship series, beating Washington and the Hornets to claim the national title. The following year Washington joined the Tribunes and remained with the team until it was disbanded in the 1940s.

The Tribunes were consistently the dominant team in African American women's basketball, rivaling the male Tribunes in popularity. Like many African American teams of the era, they usually played by full-court "men's rules" rather than the divided-court "girls' rules" that had become common among white teams. Besides playing a regular schedule of Philadelphia-area opponents, they also played outside the region. In 1934 they took trips to the Midwest, where they faced a series of white teams, and to the South, where they played African American opponents. They scheduled a second southern tour in 1938.

The Tribunes fielded many excellent players, among them Rose Wilson, Bernice Robinson, and Lil Fountaine, but Washington was almost always the featured attraction. In 1932 the *Philadelphia Tribune* sports editor Randy Dixon stated that Washington's "stamina and speed … make many male players blush with envy" (10 Jan. 1932). In 1934, when the Tribunes played the Bennett College team in Greensboro, North Carolina, the local newspaper touted Washington's tennis fame and her reputation as an "indomitable, internationally famed and stellar performer" (*Greensboro Daily News*, 9 Mar. 1932).

As in tennis, Washington and the Tribunes had few opportunities to challenge the best white teams. The Tribunes regularly played a handful of games against white northern and midwestern teams, winning some and losing others. But many of the best teams were in the South, where interracial competition was generally barred. The major national sponsor of competitive women's basketball, the Amateur Athletic Union, invited few African American teams to its national competitions, and professional clubs such as the Tribunes were not eligible for AAU play.

Athletic talent brought little financial remuneration in Washington's era. Tennis was an amateur sport, and semiprofessional basketball paid little more. Throughout much of her athletic career, Washington supported herself with the domestic service work that was the major option for wage-earning African American women of her era. In April of 1930, as she was preparing to defend her national tennis title for the first time, she was living as a lodger in a Chicago home and was listed in the census as a hotel maid.

After the Tribunes disbanded in the 1940s, Washington stayed in Philadelphia, where many members of her extended family had settled. She never married, and in her later years she supported herself mainly by working as a housekeeper. She maintained her interest in athletics and competition for the rest of her life. Her nephew James Bernard Childs recalled that on her frequent visits to family members in Caroline County, one of her favorite spots was a family croquet court, where she played almost every afternoon.

Despite her extraordinary accomplishments, especially in the field of tennis, Washington faded quickly into obscurity. In part, she suffered the fate of many early African American athletic stars, who were overshadowed by those athletes—in Washington's case, Althea Gibson—able to take advantage of postwar cracks in racial segregation. At the same time, Washington did not fit neatly into African American tennis circles. Black tennis was an elite sport. According to the historians David Wiggins and Patrick Miller, the ATA championships "were seemingly as much a grand social gathering for the upper reaches of black society as an opportunity to determine tennis supremacy" (105). Washington, who had grown up in the rural South and who had only a high school education, did not fit this mold.

In 1939, the year after her singles retirement, Randy Dixon called for broader appreciation of Washington's achievements, writing in the *Pittsburgh Courier*, "The land at large has never bowed at Ora's shrine of accomplishment in the proper tempo. She committed the unpardonable sin of being a plain person with no flair whatever for what folks love to call society" (21 Jan. 1939).

Washington spent her final years living with family members in Philadelphia while she contended with an extended illness. She passed away at the city's Mercy-Douglass Hospital in 1971 and was buried in Caroline County. Had Washington lived longer, her life and accomplishments might have been chronicled as part of the resurgence of interest in segregation-era African American sport that began in the 1970s. Instead, little has been written about her, and much of what has been published is inaccurate. As perhaps the greatest black female athlete of the early twentieth century, she deserves far more attention than she has received.

FURTHER READING

Ashe, Arthur R., Jr. *A Hard Road to Glory: A History of the African American Athlete, vol. 2, 1919–1945* (1993).

Grundy, Pamela, and Susan Shackelford. *Shattering the Glass: The Remarkable History of Women's Basketball* (2005).

Wiggins, David K., and Patrick B. Miller, eds. *The Unlevel Playing Field: A Documentary History of the African American Experience in Sport* (2003).

Young, A. S. "Doc," in *Negro Firsts in Sport* (1963).

Obituary: *Philadelphia Tribune*, 5 June 1971.

PAMELA GRUNDY

Washington, Sarah Spencer (6 June 1889–23 Mar. 1953), entrepreneur, was born in Berkley, Virginia, to Joshua Phillips and Ellen Douglass. At a time when Jim Crow was being established throughout the South and education for African Americans in the public school systems was made separate and clearly unequal, stemming from the Supreme Court's ruling in *Plessey v. Ferguson* in 1896, Mr. and Mrs. Phillips made sure that their daughter received the best education afforded to her. Sarah attended public schools in Berkley, and then went on to attend Lincoln Preparatory School in Philadelphia, Pennsylvania, and Norfolk Mission College for Negroes in Norfolk, Virginia. At some point, she went on to do advance work in chemistry at Columbia University.

Around the age of sixteen, Sarah became a dressmaker. Her parents encouraged her to become a school teacher, however, in 1913, at age twenty-four, Sarah decided to pursue an entrepreneurial path, opening a small hair dressing business in Atlantic City, New Jersey.

Shortly after slavery ended, entrepreneurship in the African American community began to flourish. Before the 1900s, many found success catering to whites with services that whites considered too menial, such as hotel keeping, local hauling/moving, and barbering. African American caterers in the North, for example, were so successful that W. E. B. DuBois documented in his study *The Philadelphia Negro*, that African Americans owned the city's leading catering firms. As more African Americans migrated to the North seeking better economic opportunities, racial hostilities in the North began to increase, and the demand for African American service providers declined sharply. Racism, coupled with competition from new immigrant groups, began to lock African American merchants out of the more affluent white marketplace, confining them to the less affluent African American market. Determined to succeed, African Americans decided to build their own communities within the larger, racist and discriminating society, and black merchants refocused their attention on the African American marketplace. It is within this cultural and economic context, that Sarah Spencer Washington built her fortune.

In the early 1900s, there was a dearth of beauty products in the marketplace for black women. Many women shared the problem of hair loss, scalp disease, and the inability to style their hair in a flattering manner. Two pioneers, most notably, MADAME C. J. WALKER, founder of the Madame C. J. Walker Manufacturing Co. and America's first self-made female millionaire, and ANNIE TURNBO

MALONE, founder of the Poro Company, took up the cause of solving this problem. They both made sizable fortunes developing and marketing hugely successful lines of beauty and hair products to the African American female consumer. They started colleges to teach their respective systems of beauty care to other women and employed them to teach that system and sell their products all over the world. At their peaks, Madame C. J. Walker and Annie Turnbo Malone are said to have employed upward of 25,000 and 75,000 sales agents, respectively, worldwide.

Sarah Spencer Washington modeled her business after these two icons, selling her products door-to-door, in the evenings, until she was able to open the Apex Hair and News Company in 1919. Sarah was the sole owner of the company and eventually opened Apex colleges and beauty stations, putting her in direct competition with Walker and Malone. When she opened a string of beauty parlors in the late 1920s along 7th Avenue in Harlem, an area dominated by Walker and Malone, a reporter for the *Pittsburgh Courier* claimed that Sarah Spencer Washington had initiated a "Beauty War."

When the rest of the nation was in an economic tailspin because of the Depression, in the 1930s, Ms. Washington was achieving her greatest success, surpassing Walker and Malone, whose companies were beginning to lose their luster. Washington preached to women, everywhere, that beauty care was a "recession proof business" and that they should join her and secure their futures. She built laboratories in Atlantic City, New Jersey, from 1937 to 1939, where more than seventy-five—and eventually more than two hundred—beauty products were manufactured and packed.

Washington's beauty colleges eventually spanned twelve states, and Apex employed upward of 45,000 agents worldwide, making her the founder of one of the oldest and largest internationally accepted systems of beauty culture in the world. In 1939, she was honored at the New York World's Fair as one of the "Most Distinguished Businesswomen."

Ms. Washington was a philanthropist and advocate for racial equality. She died in Atlantic City, New Jersey, at the age of sixty-three. Her daughter, Joan Washington Hayes, led the company until it was sold.

FURTHER READING
Blackwelder, Julia Kirk. *Styling Jim Crow: African American Beauty Training during Segregation* (2003).

Lommel, Cookie. *Madame C. J. Walker Entrepreneur* (1993).

KAHLIL GROSS

Washington, Valores J. (Val) (18 Sept. 1901–23 Apr. 1995), journalist and longtime Republican Party official, was born in Columbus, Indiana. His childhood and family background remain obscure. It is believed that his parents were James and Ella Patton Washington and his wife was Sarah Tyler. Working his way through school as a porter, Washington graduated from Indiana University in 1924 with a B.S. in Business Administration. It is believed that he also had an AB. He began his journalism career at the Chicago magazine *Reflections* before taking on the role of editor/publisher of the *Gary Sun* in Indiana between 1924 and 1926. Following a stint in the publicity department of Atlanta Casualty Insurance Company, Washington became general manager at the *Chicago Defender* in 1934. Washington now managed the operations of the most significant African American publication in the nation. The *Defender*, founded in 1905 by ROBERT ABBOTT SENGSTACKE, was a leading voice in favor of the Great Migration, against lynching, and for civil rights legislation.

Having established himself in Chicago, Washington left the *Defender* in 1941 to serve on the Illinois State Commerce Commission. During the 1940s he also became increasingly active in Republican Party politics on the national level. In 1944 he was cosponsor of a thirty-two-page booklet designed to demonstrate that the Republican governors of New York, Ohio, and Illinois had taken the lead nationally in recognizing African Americans and appointing them to important offices (*New York Times*, 17 Oct. 1944). In January 1948 Washington was appointed national political director of the Midwest Council of Negro Republican Clubs.

The year 1948 saw Washington's rise to national prominence as the director of "Negro activities" for the Republican National Committee (RNC). He also served as assistant campaign manager for the Republican ticket of New York Governor Thomas Dewey for president and California Governor Earl Warren for vice president. While the election marked a narrow loss for the Republican Party, Washington immediately went to work researching ways in which the GOP could reach out to minority voters. By 1949 he had completed studies showing that the black vote was sufficient to affect overall totals in sixteen states. In addition, he argued that under full suffrage conditions the majority populations of African Americans in 182 southern counties and large minorities in 278 additional ones would result in the election of at least eight black congressmen, with a "tremendous influence" exerted in at least twenty other congressional districts (*New York Times*, 17 Mar. 1949).

Washington remained the RNC's key minority relations director throughout the 1950s, operating under a variety of titles. During the Eisenhower years his position was at times on par with the very highest levels of Republican Party leadership. The *New York Times* reported, for example, that when planning for the 1954 midterm elections, Eisenhower met with RNC Chairman Leonard Hall, RNC Public Relations Director James Bassett, and Washington as minorities director. He met with some success in placing African Americans in key government positions, including Assistant Secretary of Labor J. Ernest Wilkins, United Nations Adviser Carmel Carrington Marr, and E. FREDERIC MORROW, the first black member of the White House staff. However, as the historian Robert Fredrick Burk described, Eisenhower's two terms in office were frustrating ones for African American civil rights activists in search of support. The administration helped institutionalize a pattern of limited federal response and public expectations of civil rights advances within a very narrow framework of political moderation and consensus—as symbolized by Eisenhower's famous comment before a black audience in 1958 that "you people have to be patient" (Burk, vi).

Despite the frustrations of working with a president whose viewpoint was, as Morrow put it, "essentially Southern" (Morrow, *Way Down South*, 121), Washington continued to articulate the importance of working through the party of Lincoln to advance civil rights. He served as "a tower of strength and encouragement" as pioneering government servants such as Morrow fought their way through the racism and obstacles of life in the GOP (Morrow, *Forty Years*, 89). Washington's comments to the press continually exposed the Democratic Party's legacy of racial injustices. He attacked the entrenched power of southern Democrats in Congress and labeled Democratic presidential nominee Adlai Stevenson's family background "more Copperhead than egghead," citing his namesake grandfather's Southern sympathies during the Civil War (*New York Times*, 7 Oct. 1956).

Washington continued in his leadership position with the RNC through Vice President Richard Nixon's 1960 campaign for the presidency, but even under Nixon's leadership the GOP proved an insufficiently supportive vehicle for black activists.

Nixon impressed Washington with his personal commitment to civil rights and such gestures as becoming the first vice president to visit an African American's private home when he visited ETHEL PAYNE in Washington, D.C., the bureau chief for the *Defender*, for a 1958 party (Nixon Pre-Presidential Papers, National Archives, Pacific Southwest Branch). By mid-1960, however, Washington was increasingly vexed by Nixon's failure to incorporate black leaders in his campaign. Morrow related in one of his memoirs how Washington was given almost no funding and the responsibility of coordinating a national campaign with only about five staff members (Morrow, *Forty Years*, 205). The baseball pioneer JACKIE ROBINSON was the only African American of any importance serving as a national campaign speaker for Nixon, and the campaign largely ignored the country's vibrant African American press (Burk, 258).

Washington resigned his position with the RNC in January 1961 and began an import-export business with several partners. For several years he also headed the BOOKER T. WASHINGTON Foundation, a nonprofit research organization headquartered in Washington, D.C. In 1981 *Ebony* columnist Simeon Booker lamented the Republican Party's failure to appreciate the important role Washington had played, calling his time in the RNC "an exciting chapter of personal devotion which could have long been a model for successors." Criticizing black Republicans of the 1970s and 1980s for failing to have regard for their history, Booker pointed out that Washington was "rarely invited as a guest or a speaker at meetings of the new breed of Black Republicans" (*Ebony*, July 1981).

This lack of institutional memory likely accounts for the dearth of information available on Washington's life and career, even as he maintained his party loyalty with a strong endorsement of Ronald Reagan in 1980. However, near the end of his long life Washington's work on behalf of the party was rewarded with a speaking appearance at the 1992 Republican National Convention as well as honors from the newly formed GOP Council in 1993.

FURTHER READING
Booker, Simeon. "Washington Notebook," *Ebony* (July 1981).
Burk, Robert Fredrick. *The Eisenhower Administration and Black Civil Rights* (1984).
Morrow, E. Frederic. *Forty Years a Guinea Pig* (1980).
Morrow, E. Frederic. *Way Down South Up North* (1973).
Obituary: *Jet*, 15 May 1995.

LAURA JANE GIFFORD

Washington, Walter E. (15 Apr. 1915–27 Oct. 2003), civil rights leader, housing administrator, and mayor, was born Walter Edward Washington in Dawson, Georgia, to William L. Washington, a millworker, and Willie Mae Washington, a schoolteacher. Two months after Walter's birth, the family moved to Jamestown, New York, where Washington would spend the next eighteen years. After the death of his mother, when Washington was six years old, his father and extended family cared for him. In 1933 he graduated from Jamestown High School and moved from his small, upstate New York town to attend Howard University, in the District of Columbia, a city he called home for the next seventy-one years.

Living in the nation's capital exposed Washington to the ugliness of segregation he had not experienced in Jamestown. But for District of Columbia natives, this was a way of life. The Jim Crow mores Washington encountered upon his arrival in the nation's capital in 1933 were rooted deeply in the institution of slavery that existed there from 1862 and through the policies of racial separatism supported by President Woodrow Wilson's administration during the World War I era. Nowhere was the stain of segregation more prevalent in the District than in housing, public education, and business. A bright, fiercely stubborn student of public administration and sociology at Howard University, Washington chose the racist hiring policies of downtown businesses as his first target, confronting the housing and public education issues later in his career.

As chairman of a student group linked to the New Negro Alliance, a grassroots organization founded in 1933 by JOHN A. DAVIS, Belford V. Lawson, and M. Franklin Thorne, Washington urged his Howard classmates and others to support a "Don't Buy Where You Can't Work" campaign. The effort paid off. In 1938 the U.S. Supreme Court in the *New Negro Alliance v. Sanitary Grocery Co.* decision ruled in favor of the group's campaign for fair hiring practices. THURGOOD MARSHALL, then a young attorney, worked on the case. Decades later as a U.S. Supreme Court justice, Marshall presided at the swearing-in ceremony when Washington became the District's mayor on 2 January 1975.

After graduating from Howard University in 1938 with a B.A. degree, Washington enrolled in a Ph.D. program in public administration at American University. Three years later he married the former Bennetta Bullock, daughter of a prominent D.C. minister named Reverend George O. Bullock. The couple had a daughter. Washington completed all his graduate course work at American University, but by the fourth year his desire to complete the doctorate waned and he became more interested in law. Washington returned to Howard as a part-time law student and earned a J.D. in 1948. While in law school he worked on a set of footnotes for the NAACP Legal Defense Fund that became part of the *Brown v. Board of Education* case.

During his tenure as a graduate student, Washington worked full time, mostly in the area of public housing. In 1941 he obtained a job as a junior housing assistant for the Alley Dwelling Authority. Washington's years of service to improve housing opportunities for the poor and working class did not go unnoticed. In 1961 President John F. Kennedy appointed him executive director of the National Capital Housing Authority (formerly the Alley Dwelling Authority), a position he held for five years. In 1966 New York City mayor John Lindsay recruited Washington to serve as chair of the New York City Housing Authority. The following year President Lyndon B. Johnson recruited Washington for a position back in the nation's capital, appointing him mayor-commissioner, a position created through the Reorganization Act of 1967 that became an elected position in 1973 with the passing of the Home Rule Act of the District of Columbia. This appointment made him the first black mayor of a major U.S. city.

Washington's honeymoon period as America's first black mayor was short lived. The 1968 riots that engulfed the city following the assassination of Dr. MARTIN LUTHER KING JR. tested the tenacity of his administrative leadership, which proved his mettle. For example, rather than give in to the passions of retaliatory violence echoed by U.S. Senator Robert Byrd of West Virginia, Washington commanded the D.C. police force and the National Guard not to shoot any looters. This decision, coupled with his wisdom and political dexterity, helped shepherd the city and its people through the riots, avoiding some loss of life and property that devastated other U.S. cities. In 1970 Princeton University awarded Washington with an honorary doctorate of laws, making him one of the first African Americans to receive this honor.

Because of Washington's administrative capability, President Richard M. Nixon twice appointed him mayor. But on 5 November 1974, in what would be the city's first mayoral popular election, Washington defeated Clifford Alexander to become the first elected mayor of the District of Columbia

in over one hundred years. During the nineteenth century Congress had approved the election of a mayor by the city council in 1812 and by the popular vote in 1820 of property-owning white men. But by 1871 the popular vote for mayor was taken away by Congress and replaced with an appointive system that remained in place until the popular election of Washington in 1974. As mayor, Washington supported full-voting rights for District residents and championed social and economic policies for his city. In 1978 he lost his reelection bid for mayor to MARION BARRY.

After a long and distinguished public service career, Washington turned his attention to law. He opened the District of Columbia office of the New York City–based Burns, Jackson, Miller & Summit law firm. As a prominent citizen of the District, he supported the opening of the National Museum of African Art and the City Museum of Washington, D.C. In 1994 Washington married for a second time to Mary Burke. Washington died in 2003 at Howard University Hospital at eighty-eight years of age.

FURTHER READING
Pacifico, Michele F. "'Don't Buy Where You Can't Work': The New Negro Alliance of Washington," *Washington History* 6 (1994).
Obituary: *New York Times*, 28 Oct. 2003.

GERARD ROBINSON

Washington, Warren Morton (28 Aug. 1936–), meteorologist, was born in Portland, Oregon, to Edwin Washington, a railroad porter, and Dorothy Morton, a homemaker. He became interested in science in high school, but his interests shifted during his senior year from chemistry to physics, which he majored in at Oregon State University in Corvallis. His interest in meteorology stemmed from a job he held as an undergraduate at a weather radar installation near Corvallis that tracked storms from the Pacific Ocean as they hit the Oregon coast. After receiving a B.S. in Physics in 1958 and an M.S. in Meteorology in 1960, he entered the graduate program at Pennsylvania State University, receiving a Ph.D. in Meteorology in 1964. That same year, he accepted a full-time position as a research scientist at the National Center for Atmospheric Research (NCAR) in Boulder, Colorado, where he had worked the previous summer.

As a graduate student, Washington became intrigued by the potential application of computers as tools for forecasting changes in the weather over extended periods of time. To a certain extent, his doctoral dissertation addressed this issue, but it was not until after joining the staff at NCAR that he wrote his first computer program for predicting the weather. He and an NCAR colleague, Akira Kasahara, collaborated on the development of a weather-forecasting computer model that simulated the general circulation of the atmosphere and the oceans. Not only was this program one of the first weather-forecasting programs, but it also was the first coupled-climate system in that it incorporated data for both the atmosphere and the oceans. As such, it was primitive compared to twenty-first-century programs, partly because of the primitive nature of the hardware available and partly because of the paucity of temperature, air pressure, humidity, and wind velocity data available for incorporating into the model. Nevertheless, the Washington-Kasahara program was a tremendous improvement over the weather-forecasting methods then in use. As equipment became more sophisticated, and as more and more weather observatories came to be located closer to oceans, where most weather events begin, Washington and his NCAR colleagues were able to develop coupled-climate computer models capable of providing increasingly accurate weather forecasts. Within ten years of the development of the Washington-Kasahara program, they had developed a model so sophisticated that it incorporated the effect of the Indian Ocean's annual monsoon on the jet stream, the high-speed air currents that flow eastward around the globe.

Over the next twenty years Washington devoted his efforts to writing increasingly sophisticated coupled-climate system models to be run on state-of-the-art supercomputers. In 1993 he was named director of NCAR's climate and global dynamics division. In this capacity, he oversaw the division's work in support of the development of long-range computer models for predicting the evolution of the Earth's climate such as NCAR's Community Climate System Model (CCSM), a general-circulation climate model made available in 2004 that incorporates phenomena ranging from the effect that volcanic eruptions have on temperature patterns to the impact of shifting sea ice on sunlight absorbed by the oceans. CCSM became one of the primary models by which scientists monitor the contribution to global warming made by carbon dioxide emissions into the atmosphere. His efforts in support of CCSM included becoming co-chair of its climate-change working group.

Washington and his wife Joan had three children. He served on a number of panels and commissions, including the President's National Advisory Committee on Oceans and Atmosphere, the National Research Council, the National Science Board, and the Secretary of Energy's Biological and Environmental Research Advisory Committee. He also cofounded the Black Environmental Science Trust as a tool for increasing the number of young African Americans who choose a career in one of the environmental sciences. His publications include *An Introduction to Three-Dimensional Climate Modeling* (2d ed., 2005). His honors include fellowship in the American Association for the Advancement of Science and election to a term as president of the American Meteorological Society (1994).

FURTHER READING

Climate Change Research Section, National Center for Atmospheric Research. "Warren M. Washington." Available at www.cgd.ucar.edu/ccr/warren.

Kessler, James H., et al. *Distinguished African American Scientists of the 20th Century* (1996).

Spangenburg, Ray, and Kit Moser. *African Americans in Science, Math, and Invention* (2003).

CHARLES W. CAREY JR.

Washington-Williams, Essie Mae (12 Oct. 1925–), gained fame in 2003 when she revealed that she was the illegitimate, biracial daughter of the late Strom Thurmond, U.S. senator from South Carolina. America knew Thurmond as a staunch segregationist, and he was the longest-serving and oldest senator in U.S. history, dying at age one hundred in June 2003. Her mother was Carrie Butler, who had a love affair with Thurmond when she was fifteen and employed as a domestic servant in his family home. At the time of their relationship, Thurmond was a single, twenty-two-year-old schoolteacher and football coach at Edgefield High School.

Born in Aiken, South Carolina, Washington-Williams was raised by her maternal aunt, Mary Butler Washington, in Coatesville, Pennsylvania. She met her real mother in 1938, when "Aunt" Carrie came to visit and revealed their true relationship. At age sixteen, in 1941, while in Edgefield, South Carolina, for a family funeral, Washington-Williams met her father for the first time, but she was sworn to keep his identity secret. Washington-Williams noted she maintained silence on the identity of her famous father until after his death out of respect for the Thurmond family.

Washington-Williams attended Scott High School in Coatesville and worked part time as a nurse's aide at Coatesville Hospital, hoping someday to become a nurse and live in New York. She was the hospital's first black nurse's aide; the nurses and doctors were white, and they treated black patients only in "welfare wards," never in private or semiprivate rooms. After high school graduation in 1945, Washington-Williams moved to Harlem, New York, and attended Harlem Hospital Nursing School. After only a few months, she quit school and moved in with her brother Calvin and his family. She worked various jobs while deciding what to do next. On a visit to South Carolina, Thurmond encouraged her to go to college, and with his blessing, and financial support, Washington-Williams began attending South Carolina State College, a historically black college, in fall 1946.

At a fraternity dance, she met Julius T. Williams, a World War II veteran and premedical student. They were secretly married during the summer of 1948, and Washington-Williams kept her marriage a secret for a year, until her first pregnancy forced her to quit school. In autumn 1949, Julius changed majors and enrolled in South Carolina State's first law school class. One of a class of only two students, he switched majors to prepare for a career that would enable him to earn a living more quickly and to support his new responsibilities. Washington-Williams went home to Coatesville to deliver their son, Julius Jr., returning in time for Williams's graduation in June 1950. After graduation, the family settled in Williams's native Savannah, Georgia, where he opened a modest law practice. The practice was not immediately profitable. Therefore, three years later, in 1953, the Williams family, including now two sons (Julius Jr. and Ronald) followed his sister to Los Angeles, California. A daughter, Monica, was born in Los Angeles in 1954, and another daughter, Wanda, was born in 1956. Williams could not practice law because he was not licensed in California, and the bar exam was expensive. He worked at the North American Aircraft plant to raise funds to take the bar. However, the lucrative income provided by the defense contractor led him to temporarily abandon his law career.

When Mary became terminally ill in 1959, the Williamses moved to Coatesville to care for her in her last days. By 1962, Washington-Williams and her family had returned to Savannah, where Williams resumed his law career. He worked for the local branch of the NAACP, handling its civil rights cases. Washington-Williams became her husband's secretary, and he served his own court summons to save

money. Many of their clients could not afford to pay. In 1964 Williams was severely injured in a conflict with the Savannah police, and he died later that year.

In 1969, widow Washington-Williams moved with her four children to Los Angeles, where she completed her B.A. in Business Education at California State College. Washington-Williams married James Stoner in 1970, and although he left her for another woman within a year, they were never formally divorced. Beginning in 1970, Washington-Williams taught for the Los Angeles Unified School District. Starting as a part-time business education teacher, she retired as assistant principal for Counseling Services in 1997 after twenty-seven years of service. After retirement, Washington-Williams earned her M.A. degree from the University of Southern California in 2003 and received an honorary doctorate in Education from South Carolina State College in 2004.

After Senator Thurmond's death, Washington-Williams revealed her secret and challenged his widow to claim her share of Thurmond's estate. She appeared on the television show *60 Minutes II*, taped on 16 December 2003, and was the focus of a press conference in Columbia, South Carolina, the next day. With her paternal parentage confirmed, she submitted applications to the National Society Daughters of the American Revolution (DAR), a predominantly white hereditary society for female descendants of Revolutionary War patriots, and the United Daughters of the Confederacy (UDC), a similar organization for women descendants of Civil War veterans. Washington-Williams says Lena Ferguson was her inspiration to join DAR. Ferguson was one of the first five known African American members of DAR when she joined in 1983. Ferguson (and her nephew, Maurice Barboza) successfully sued DAR for full chapter membership and to identify more black patriots ("Our Colorful Past," *New York Times*). In 2007, African American membership in both organizations remained *"a precious few"* (approximately 51 of over 164,000 members for DAR) ("Seeks Confederacy Group," *New York Times*). Washington-Williams published her autobiography in 2005 and, although she decided not to join UDC because of the distance required to attend meetings, she was active in the Hollywood chapter of DAR in 2006. She continued to live in Los Angeles, but planned to return to Columbia, South Carolina, to open a daycare center there in 2007.

FURTHER READING

Barboza, Maurice, and Gary B. Nash. "We Need to Learn More About Our Colorful Past," *New York Times*, 31 July 2004.

Dewan, Sheila K., and Ariel Hart. "Thurmond's Biracial Daughter Seeks to Join Confederacy Group," *New York Times*, 2 July 2004.

Thompson, Marilyn W. "Woman Claims Thurmond as Father …," *Washington Post*, 14 December 2003.

Washington-Williams, Essie Mae, and William Stadiem. *Dear Senator: A Memoir by the Daughter of Strom Thurmond* (2005).

KAREN E. SUTTON

Waters, Ethel (31 Oct. 1896–1 Sept. 1977), singer and actress, was born in a slum section of Chester, Pennsylvania, as a result of the rape at knifepoint of her twelve-year-old mother, Louisa Tar Anderson, by her white father, John Wesley Waters. She was raised by her grandmother in Chester and Philadelphia. Completing only the sixth grade, Waters could not read or write well and was unable to express herself verbally without often resorting to violence. She grew up with prostitutes, procurers, and thieves and stole in order to eat. Having begun to sing at the age of five, Waters became known as "Baby Star." In 1909, at the age of thirteen, she married Merritt "Buddy" Purnsley, who was twenty-three. He beat her and humiliated her frequently. They separated by the time Waters was fourteen. The unhappiness of her early years is poignantly addressed in Waters's autobiography, where she writes, "I was never a child. I never felt I belonged. I was always an outsider. I was born out of wedlock" (Waters, 1).

Waters worked as a maid before she began entering singing competitions. In 1917 she made her professional debut at the Lincoln Theatre in Baltimore, Maryland, for nine dollars a week. Because of their dark skin, both Waters and JOSEPHINE BAKER were rejected for the 1921 Broadway production of *Shuffle Along*. While Baker finally worked her way into the chorus and clowned her way into acceptance, Waters became bitter.

She began singing in Edmonds's Cellar in Harlem. "It was a sure enough honky-tonk, occupying the cellar of a saloon. It was the social center of what was then, and still is, Negro Harlem's kitchen. Here a tall brown-skin girl, unmistakably the one guaranteed in the song to make a preacher lay his Bible down, used to sing and dance her own peculiar numbers" (Rudolph Fisher, quoted in Krasner, 72).

Waters also toured with the Theater Owners' Booking Association (TOBA), a booking agency for black performers, often referred to as "Tough on Black Actors." Performers often rehearsed without pay and got no money if a show closed on the road. Frequently, they were denied hot or cold running water and other amenities in their dressing rooms. More than once, Waters dressed under a staircase, without even a curtain for privacy. She endured many of the difficulties of segregated America as well as the abuse of some in management and the police. She was very poorly treated in a black wing of a hospital in Anniston, Alabama, after she sustained a leg injury in a car accident while on a TOBA tour. For much of the 1920s and all of the 1930s, Waters sang at popular nightspots and recorded. Leonard Feather observed, "It is curious that the obituaries described Waters as a blues singer, which during almost all of her career she was not. In fact, she had been the first prominent black singer on records who was not primarily associated with the blues. While BESSIE SMITH … [was at her peak], Waters was lending her gracious touch to pop songs of the day" (*Los Angeles Times*, 3 Sept. 1977).

Waters sang with FLETCHER HENDERSON's and DUKE ELLINGTON's bands at the Cotton Club, the Plantation Club, and many other elegant establishments. When Earl Dancer implored Waters to leave the "colored time" and try the white clubs, she made him her manager and toured the Keith-Orpheum vaudeville circuit. In her early years Waters was tall and lean; audiences and critics dubbed her "Sweet Mama Stringbean." By 1927 she had made her Broadway debut as Miss Calico in the revue *Africana*. Following the early death of FLORENCE MILLS, Waters performed in Lew Leslie's *Blackbirds* in 1927 and 1928. Also in 1928 she married Clyde Matthews, with whom she adopted a daughter, Algretta. All her life Waters struggled financially, even when she made good money. Generous to a fault with her men and with considerable medical expenses, Waters declared bankruptcy in 1929, at the time of the great stock-market crash. That same year she appeared in a movie, *On with the Show*, wearing a bandana and carrying a large basket of cotton, and in *Rhapsody in Blue*, a revue at the Belasco Theatre in Washington, D.C. Several New York City theaters picked up the revue in 1930, and by 1931 Waters was a star.

Irving Berlin heard her sing "Stormy Weather" at the Cotton Club and cast her in the famous Broadway revue *As Thousands Cheer*, at the Music Box in 1933. Brooks Atkinson, critic for the *New York Times*, wrote of her performance: "Ethel Waters takes full control of the audience and the show whenever she appears. Her abandon to the ruddy tune of 'Heat Wave Hits New York,' her rowdy comedy … and her deep-toned song about a lynching give some notion

Ethel Waters, singer and actress, photographed in New York City (?) between 1938 and 1948. (Library of Congress/Gottlieb Collection.)

of the broad range she can encompass in musical shows" (*New York Times*, 2 Oct. 1933).

Four years out of bankruptcy, Waters became the highest-paid woman on Broadway. In 1933 she lived royally, for a season, while many stood in soup lines. She had an apartment on Harlem's "Sugar Hill," a regal wardrobe, a large earring collection, a Lincoln Town Car with a chauffeur, servants for her ten-room apartment—and a man to occupy it, though in 1934 she divorced Matthews.

In 1939, as the Depression lifted and World War II approached, Waters became one of the first African American women to star in a dramatic role on Broadway, in Dorothy and DuBose Heyward's *Mamba's Daughters*. (ROSE MCCLENDON had starred in LANGSTON HUGHES's *Mulatto* on Broadway in 1935.) Waters played Hagar, an unlettered woman on a South Carolina plantation. On opening night, she took seventeen curtain calls. Brooks Atkinson printed a lukewarm review, and many of Waters's friends took out a full-page advertisement in the *New York Times*, strongly suggesting that he return to the theater and review the play more objectively. He did. Waters also appeared in an experimental television broadcast by NBC in

1939, *The Ethel Waters Show*, which was the first ever television show to star an African American.

Following the close of *Mamba's Daughters*, Waters worked with the United Service Organization (USO), entertaining military men of color all over the world. In 1940 she starred in Lynn Root's *Cabin in the Sky* in New York City. KATHERINE DUNHAM, whose dance troupe was part of the musical, took over as choreographer when George Balanchine was fired. In *Cabin in the Sky*, Waters played a God-fearing woman whose husband, Little Joe, gambles and enjoys the women. Hollywood made a film of *Cabin in the Sky* in 1943, again starring Waters as Petunia, with LENA HORNE replacing Dunham as Sweet Georgia Brown, the other woman. The jealousy Waters displayed on both the stage and film sets became legendary. Waters's poor judgment, violent streak, and jealousy often eclipsed her talent. During the *Cabin* productions, she lived with Eddie Mallory, a handsome trumpeter who developed an eye for other women. Nevertheless, she gave him a large portion of her savings, set him up in business, and helped sponsor his musical career.

TALLEY BEATTY, a member of the Dunham dance company, observed that Waters removed Dunham from two dance numbers in *Cabin*, so that Waters herself could dance with the younger Archie Savage. Because Waters was better known than Dunham at the time, the producers bowed to her wishes. Waters's relationship with Mallory was in trouble, and she claimed Savage as her protégé, setting him up in her Los Angeles home, rent free, around 1943.

In 1944 Waters accused Savage of stealing ten thousand dollars in cash and thirty thousand dollars worth of jewelry, and he was convicted and sentenced to a year and a day in San Quentin Prison. Such a public display of revenge, coupled with publicity about her outbursts and language in the courtroom, did not help Waters's image in the media, which expected its female stars, at least, to show some propriety.

Waters claimed that, because of some anti-Semitic epithets she allegedly uttered on the set of *Cabin in the Sky*, she was unable to get employment for six years, except for an appearance on the *Amos 'n Andy* radio show on NBC. In 1949, however, her fortunes turned when she secured the part of Granny Dysey Johnson, in Darryl F. Zanuck's *Pinky*, a highly touted film about passing for white, starring the white actress Jeanne Crain as Pinky, a fair-complexioned black nurse who returns to Mississippi after passing in Boston. Though Granny was ostensibly another Mammy role, Waters, like HATTIE MCDANIEL before her, gave a performance that went beyond stereotype. In 1949 Waters was nominated for an Academy Award for Best Supporting Actress for her portrayal of Granny.

In 1950 Waters took on the servant role of Berenice Sadie Browne in the stage production of Carson McCullers's *The Member of the Wedding* at New York City's Empire Theater, giving over 850 performances on the stage, followed by a road tour. The critical acclaim she received for that role, which she reprised in a film version in 1952, was the greatest of her career. In 1950 Waters began to play a maid on the *Beulah* television show. Dooley Wilson, who had portrayed Sam, the piano player, in the film *Casablanca* (1942), played her boyfriend. Television historian Donald Bogle notes that "Waters's Beulah seemed a real person, trapped in an artificial world" (25). She did not use dialect, and came across as much sexier than larger, older women were supposed to on television. Nonetheless, Waters left the series after two years, because she no longer wanted a "white folks kitchen comedy role" (quoted in Bogle, 25).

Being typecast in Mammy roles and her constant financial troubles marred Waters's artistic success. In a letter to Floretta Howard, her secretary, Waters wrote on 8 December 1951: "It looks as if they [the IRS] are going to make me pay an extra $4,000.... They will take $625.00 weekly.... They still don't know what I have." After Dooley Wilson's death in 1953, *Beulah* was syndicated and withdrawn. Waters's career was all but over.

Waters sought solace in religion and in 1957 began touring with the Billy Graham Crusade, singing her signature song for this period in her life, "His Eye is on the Sparrow," which was also the title of her best-selling autobiography, which was first published in 1951. In 1959 Waters appeared in the film of William Faulkner's novel *The Sound and the Fury*, again playing a Mammy role, Dilsey. She was a favorite of President Richard Nixon and performed for him in the White House in 1971. Her tragic, though occasionally triumphant, life ended at age eighty, on 1 September 1977, in Chatsworth, California. She was a diabetic, suffered greatly from weight problems in her later years, and was living with friends, on Social Security, when she died.

FURTHER READING

Ethel Waters's letters to her secretary, Floretta Howard, are housed in the Performing Arts Section of the Library of Congress.

Waters, Ethel, with Charles Samuels. *His Eye Is on the Sparrow* (1951; repr. 1980).

Bogle, Donald. *Prime Time Blues: African Americans on Network Television* (2001).

Cherry, Randall. "Ethel Waters: The Voice of an Era" in *Temples for Tomorrow: Looking Back at the Harlem Renaissance*, eds. Geneviève Fabre and Michael Feith (2001).

Gill, Glenda E. *No Surrender! No Retreat! African American Pioneer Performers of Twentieth Century American Theater* (2000).

Krasner, David. *A Beautiful Pageant: African American Theatre, Drama and Performance in the Harlem Renaissance, 1910–1927* (2002).

Obituaries: *Chicago Tribune, New York Times, Washington Post*, and *New Orleans Picayune*, 2 Sept. 1977; *Los Angeles Times*, 2 and 3 Sept. 1977.

GLENDA E. GILL

Waters, Maxine (15 Aug. 1938–), politician, was born Maxine Moore Carr in St. Louis, Missouri, to Remus and Velma Lee (Moore) Carr. She was the fifth of thirteen children in a low-income family. She was raised by her mother following her parents' separation in 1940 in a St. Louis housing project, and supported by public assistance. In large part, it is this upbringing that she credited for her success as a representative for poor and working-class black and Latino constituents in California's Thirty-fifth Congressional District, which encompasses most of South Central Los Angeles as well as Inglewood, Gardena, Hawthorne, and Lawndale.

Waters is a graduate of Vashon High School in St. Louis. In 1956, at age eighteen, she married Edward Waters. The couple moved west to Los Angeles in 1961 in search of better wages and greater opportunities for their two children. To help support her family Waters worked in a garment factory and as a telephone operator. By 1972 Edward and Maxine had divorced.

Balancing a life overflowing with responsibility—two children, work, and school—was by no means an easy task. Waters found the support that she sorely needed in her community, among the informal network of black women who served as community "other-mothers" and sister-friends. It was this sorority of black women that encouraged Waters to initiate the Black Women's Forum, a nonprofit organization of more than 1,200 African American women in the Los Angeles area. It was also among this black sisterhood that Waters found what would continue to be her base of political support as she emerged as both a community and political leader.

In 1966 she began working as an assistant teacher in the Watts neighborhood of Los Angeles for the Head Start program (a program designed to

Maxine Waters, U.S. Congresswoman and House Judiciary Committee member, speaking to reporters on Capitol Hill during the impeachment trial of President Bill Clinton, 4 February 1999. National Organization for Women president Patricia Ireland looks on at left. (AP Images.)

provide preschool learning experience and support to children under five from low-income families). While working for Head Start, Waters enrolled in college, earning her bachelor of arts in Sociology from California State University, Los Angeles, in 1970. At Head Start the always outspoken Waters quickly emerged as a community leader, becoming a voice for frustrated parents and community members. This experience aroused her interest in local politics. She began her work in politics in 1973 as chief deputy to the Los Angeles city councilman David Cunningham. Her career as an elected official was launched in 1976, when she was elected to the California State Assembly. During her fourteen-year tenure in the assembly, she worked to support and strengthen the state's affirmative action programs and to encourage investment in public education.

In 1977, Waters married Sidney Williams, a luxury-car salesman and former professional football player with the Washington Redskins and Cleveland Browns; during the Clinton administration Williams served as U.S. ambassador to the Bahamas.

In 1991 Waters became the second African American woman to be elected to the United States Congress from California (YVONNE BRATHWAITE BURKE was the first), receiving more than 80 percent of the vote. She was reelected for each subsequent term. As a member of Congress she served on the Financial Services and Judiciary committees, chaired the Congressional Black Caucus from 1997 to 1998, served as deputy whip of the Democratic Party, and was a co-chair of the House Democratic Steering Committee.

Waters earned national recognition in 1992 as an advocate for programs and funding directed to impoverished areas of Los Angeles in the aftermath of the civil unrest following the verdict in the case of the beating of African American motorist RODNEY KING at the hands of four white police officers. Waters saw the "not guilty" verdict in the case as merely the spark that ignited a flame within poor black and Latino urban communities; the rebellion at its root was not about King or even a racist police force, but about the institutionalized racism and classism that keeps people of color at the bottom. The uprising was about a rage that simmered just below the surface among the underclass that has been denied basic human rights, such as a decent place to live, health care, nourishing food, education, and a livable wage. Waters pushed for greater funding for programs in impoverished communities, and, as a result of her efforts, Community Build, a nonprofit community development corporation, was founded in July of 1992 to provide vocational training, career counseling, and tutorial services to underprivileged youth and young adults. The Maxine Waters Employment Preparation Center also was established in 1989; both were established in the Thirty-fifth District.

In the mid-1990s Waters again gained national and international attention by leading the investigation of the alleged involvement of the Central Intelligence Agency (CIA) in the Contra cocaine drug trafficking in South Central Los Angeles in the mid-1980s. The illegal actions of the federal government in both financing an illegal war in Latin America and in denigrating black and Latino urban communities was first uncovered by the *San Jose (CA) Mercury* news reporter Gary Webb. An advocate of rehabilitative, as opposed to simply retributive, models of justice, Waters called for redirecting the resources of the so called war on drugs to prevention and treatment and advocated the repeal of mandatory minimum sentencing laws for minor drug offenses. Waters was long interested in fighting injustice abroad as well as at home. As a member of the California State Assembly, she led efforts to divest state pension funds from apartheid South Africa. She founded the Los Angeles Free South Africa Movement and served as an adviser to TransAfrica, an organization that focused on the conditions of the African world. Waters called for the granting of political asylum to Haitian refugees and, in 2004, advocated the restoration of power to the democratically elected Haitian President Jean-Bertrand Aristide.

Waters enjoyed easy victories in her five Congressional races after 2000, winning with around 80 percent of the vote each time. By 2011, she was the longest serving female member in the 112th Congress. Her solid support in the district—one of the hardest hit by the economic crises of the 2000s—may have emboldened her to vocalize her concerns that the administration of BARACK OBAMA had been too willing to compromise with Republicans, to the detriment of poor and working class Americans. Waters also urged Obama to directly address the economic problems that were specific to the African American community and to use his "bully pulpit" to rein in what she called "gangsta" banks. The White House, she said, should "bring the gangsters in, put them around the table and let them know that if they don't come up with loan modifications and keep people in their homes that they've worked so hard for, we're going to tax them out of business" (http://thehill.com/blogs/blog-briefing-room/news/179193-waters-obama-should-go-after-gangsta-banks). Waters, along with Congresswoman ELEANOR HOLMES NORTON and other lawmakers, also questioned the Obama administration's support for the NATO bombing campaign in Libya in the spring and summer of 2011.

In 2010 Waters faced a House ethics probe for allegedly arranging a federal bailout for the FirstUnited Bank in which her husband was a stockholder. However the investigation appeared to have stalled by the summer of 2011, when it emerged that members of the Committee investigating Waters's alleged malfeasance were found to have leaked information to Republicans in Congress. The Committee was then forced to hire an outside lawyer to investigate what the *New York Times* called "its own bollixed investigation into the conduct of Representative ...Waters". In September 2012 a House ethics panel cleared Waters of all charges.

FURTHER READING

"The House's Farcical Self-Investigation." *New York Times*. 24 July 2011.

Gill, LaVerne McCain. *African American Women in Congress: Forming and Transforming History* (1997).

MELINA ABDULLAH

Waters, Muddy (4 Apr. 1915–30 Apr. 1983), blues singer and guitarist, was born McKinley Morganfield in Rolling Fork, Mississippi, the son of Ollie Morganfield and Bertha Jones, sharecroppers. As a small child he enjoyed playing in the swampy puddles by the family home, so he was nicknamed "Muddy Waters" by his grandmother. In time he became better known by his childhood nickname than by his family name.

When Waters was three years old, his mother died, whereupon his maternal grandmother, Della Jones, brought him to her home at Stovall's Plantation near Clarksdale. Waters attended school only through the third grade. While still a boy, he began plowing and chopping cotton at Stovall's, and in those years he took up the harmonica as his first musical instrument. In 1932 he married Mabel Berry.

The musicians best known to blacks at Stovall's and around the Mississippi Delta region in the early 1930s were guitarists, including CHARLEY PATTON, SON HOUSE, Willie Brown, and ROBERT NIGHTHAWK (Robert McCollum). By the end of 1932 Waters had bought a guitar and began taking lessons from another teenager, Scott Bohanner. Whenever he could, Waters paid close attention to the playing of Son House, who specialized in the bottleneck style of slide guitar playing and who was even at that time a great influence on younger musicians, including ROBERT JOHNSON. Emulating House, Waters took up the older musician's bottleneck technique and songs. Often he played weekends in a musical group with Bohanner, guitarist Percy Thomas, and fiddler Henry "Son" Simms, performing string band favorites in the style of the Mississippi Sheiks. Sometimes Waters went to Memphis, Tennessee, to hear local and visiting musicians, including the jug bands and harmonica players.

For a few months in 1939 or 1940, Waters moved to St. Louis, Missouri, but he quickly returned to Stovall's in Mississippi, working in the cotton fields and performing on weekends. Briefly he ran a roadhouse where he sometimes featured guest musicians such as Aleck Miller (also known as SONNY BOY WILLIAMSON, not to be confused with John Lee Williamson of Chicago who recorded for RCA Victor under the same nickname) and ELMORE JAMES of Helena, Arkansas, and through which he served bootleg liquor. Indeed, when Waters first met Alan Lomax of the Library of Congress in 1941, he mistook him for a government agent investigating his bootleg operation. Lomax, however, was on a field recording trip seeking guitarists who could play in the manner of Robert Johnson, who had died in 1938. Since Waters had based his "Country Blues" on the "Walking Blues" melody previously played by House and Johnson, he was allowed a lengthy interview session by Lomax, who was sufficiently impressed to record Waters with his string band shortly afterward. Later that fall Waters received a test copy of two of his solo performances, a boost to his musical confidence. Lomax returned to Stovall's the following summer and again recorded Waters in solo and band contexts. By 1942 Waters had separated from his first wife. In December of that year

Muddy Waters, performing in a benefit for the New York Public Library at the Palladium Theater in New York City, 1 October 1977. (AP Images.)

he took a Stovall's resident, Sallie Ann Adams, as his second wife, and continued farming and driving a tractor. He took additional opportunities to perform, such as a couple of nights with the Silas Green of New Orleans vaudeville troupe when it was in the Clarksdale region. Forsaking the hard rural life and the racial bias against black Americans in Mississippi, Waters left Stovall's Plantation and the Clarksdale area for Chicago in May 1943.

Initially Waters worked at menial jobs, unloading trucks or driving them; he confined his guitar playing to weekend parties. Later, as a sideman for John Lee Williamson, Waters began playing in the Chicago clubs. The urban clubs being noisier than rural juke joints, Waters realized he needed something louder than his acoustic guitar to be heard through the crowd; toward that end he acquired his first electric guitar in 1944. The following year, during a return trip to Mississippi, he met harmonicist and guitarist Jimmy Rogers, who became an important musician in Waters's first Chicago band. By this time Waters's second marriage had ended, and in the mid-1940s he married Geneva (maiden name unknown).

Waters made his first commercial records in 1946 on the labels 20th Century and Columbia as a supporting band member, and the following year he assisted pianist Sunnyland Slim during an Aristocrat Records studio date. The owners of Aristocrat, Leonard Chess and Phil Chess, noticed Waters's talent and decided to record him in a session of his own. That next session, with bassist Big Crawford, resulted in Waters's first important release, "I Can't Be Satisfied" backed with "I Feel Like Going Home." Released in 1948, the initial pressing of three thousand copies was sold out within forty-eight hours. The success of this hit paved the way for additional Aristocrat sessions with the guitar and bass format, although for club appearances Waters backed himself with a band that included Jimmy Rogers, harmonicist "LITTLE WALTER" JACOBS, and drummer "Baby Face" Leroy.

During 1950 Waters continued working in the black clubs in Chicago and in the recording studio of the Chess brothers, who by then had renamed their label Chess Records. At the same time, the Chess brothers allowed Waters to use his club band in the studio. Thus began a series of records lasting through 1960 that are now considered his most important and popular records: "Long Distance Call," "She Moves Me," "I Just Want to Make Love to You," "Still a Fool," "Standing around Crying," "I'm Your Hoochie Coochie Man," "Mannish Boy," "Nineteen Years Old," and "Got My Mojo Working." These records document Waters's command of his voice and instrument, as well as the backing performances of his best sidemen, including pianist OTIS SPANN, who joined Waters in 1954.

Waters's Chicago music began with his adaptation of Mississippi acoustic blues technique with bottleneck slide to the amplified electric guitar. He then fit the electric guitar in the context of amplified harmonica, piano, and drums. The songs he played were rooted in the Mississippi blues tradition, employing the standard twelve measure form and blues chord progressions. On his early records, especially in the guitar and bass format of his Aristocrat sides, Waters wrote and developed his own material. Later in the 1950s he began performing songs by another transplanted Mississippian, BIG WILLIE DIXON, a composer/bassist who was a regular session musician for Chess and other Chicago-based record labels.

Waters as bandleader was a mentor for upcoming blues musicians. "Little Walter" Jacobs enjoyed a popular solo career after scoring a hit record, "Juke," which up to that time had been the Muddy Waters Band's signature tune. Other harmonicists who followed Jacobs included JUNIOR WELLS and James Cotton. Through his death in 1970, pianist Otis Spann enjoyed several solo recordings and bookings when he was not playing behind Waters.

By the late 1950s Waters was generating international interest. In 1958 he and Otis Spann toured England with the Chris Barber band. The following spring, in April 1959, Waters played at Carnegie Recital Hall in New York, and the year after that he performed at the Newport Folk Festival, where his show was taped and released on Chess Records. Before long Waters was developing a dual career: as an acoustic guitarist for the folk revival audiences, for whom he recorded the albums *Muddy Waters Sings Big Bill* and *Folk Singer*, and as the leader of an electrically amplified band, a format imitated by British ensembles, especially the Rolling Stones (who named themselves after Waters's song "Rollin' Stone"). By the end of the 1960s Waters's influence would be heard through white American bands such as the Paul Butterfield Blues Band.

In October 1969, near the end of a successful year, Waters was in a head-on car collision that killed his driver; Waters himself was in the hospital for three months and unable to play guitar for a year. After recuperation, he resumed his tours, retaining bookings at the large festivals such as the Ann Arbor Festival and the Montreux Jazz Festival. Meanwhile, Chess Records was recording Waters two different ways: either taping his live shows with his club band (such as *Live at Mr. Kelly's* in 1972) or having him lead studio ensembles composed of young white rock and blues musicians, such as *Fathers and Sons* with Paul Butterfield and Mike Bloomfield in 1969 and *The London Muddy Waters Sessions* with Rory Gallagher in 1972.

The mid-1970s brought changes in Waters's life. During the 1950s and 1960s he lived in a brownstone on Chicago's South Side, but in 1973 he moved to Westmont, a suburb. Also in 1973 his third wife died, after some three decades of marriage. In addition, Waters took on a manager, Scott Cameron, who advised him to set up Muddy Waters Productions/Watertoons Music to protect his composing rights. Then, Cameron, Waters, and Willie Dixon sued ARC Music Corporation for the return of their respective song copyrights. The suit was settled out of court in 1976 in the musicians' favor. In the meantime, in 1975 Waters taped his last session for Chess Records and parted company with the label after twenty-eight years.

Around that time Waters deepened his acquaintanceship with Texan guitarist Johnny Winter. They began an artistic collaboration resulting in an Indian-summer series of albums for Blue Sky, a Columbia Records subsidiary, between 1976 and 1980. In the wake of the renewed acclaim these records brought, Waters toured and performed with a band that included guitarist Bob Margolin and pianist Pinetop Perkins. The band performed concerts around the world, and among the highlights were the 1977 White House staff picnic (with an introduction by President Jimmy Carter) and the 1981 Delta Blues Festival near Greenville, Mississippi. In 1979 Waters took a fourth wife, Marva Jean Brookes, and subsequently continued living in Westmont. Waters had a total of seven children with his four wives.

From 1960 on, Waters was frequently filmed and televised. Most notable was a guest appearance in *The Last Waltz* (1978), a film by Martin Scorsese of the rock group The Band. Waters died in Chicago in his sleep.

FURTHER READING

Guralnick, Peter. *Feel Like Going Home* (1971).
Obrecht, Jas. "Muddy Waters: The Life and Times of the Hoochie Coochie Man," *Blues Revue* (Dec. 1995–Jan. 1996): 24–38.
Oliver, Paul. "Muddy Waters, 1960," *Blues Unlimited Collectors' Classic*, no. 1 (1963, repr. in *Back Woods Blues*, 1968): 13–19.
O'Neal, Jim, and Amy van Singel. "Muddy Waters," *Living Blues* (Mar.–Apr. 1985): 15–40.
Palmer, Robert. *Deep Blues* (1981).
Rooney, James. *Bossmen: Bill Monroe and Muddy Waters* (1971).
Welding, Pete. "An Interview with Muddy Waters," *American Folk Music Occasional*, no. 2 (1970): 2–7.
Obituary: *New York Times*, 1 May 1983.

DISCOGRAPHY

Wight, Phil, and Fred Rothwell. *The Complete Muddy Waters Discography* (1993).
This entry is taken from the *American National Biography* and is published here with the permission of the American Council of Learned Societies.

EDWARD KOMARA

Waters, Sylvia (22 Jan. 1940–), dancer, instructor, and artistic director, was born in the Washington Heights neighborhood of New York City to Benjamin Franklin Waters, a social worker and landscaper, and Brittania Rachel Waters, a beautician and homemaker. Raised in Harlem, Waters was an only child who grew up with a large extended family of cousins who lived with her family during different periods of her childhood. Her parents eventually adopted two of her cousins and raised them as their own. From the age of four she spent summers with her grandparents in Virginia, her mother's home. Every summer from the ages of seven through thirteen she was enrolled in a two-week summer camp where her father worked; at the end of the two weeks she would be sent back to her grandparents in Virginia for the remainder of the summer.

During her childhood Waters studied piano in Virginia and in New York with Howard Mann, the choir director of Convent Avenue Baptist Church. Although she loved piano, she was never given the opportunity to develop her skills because there was no piano at home on which to practice. On Saturday afternoons, while babysitting the Mann family children, Waters would take them to their dance classes with Mary Bruce in Harlem on 125th Street. It was there that she was first exposed to what became her life's passion and work.

Waters's earliest formal education in dance came during her freshman year at Evander Childs High School. On the first day of gym class students were given the option of enrolling in the modern dance program in lieu of taking general physical education. The instructor, a Ms. Newman, conducted the dance classes and brought in books with photos of KATHERINE DUNHAM, PEARL PRIMUS, and dancers from the American Ballet Theatre to share with the students. At Newman's urging that she seek outside training at a professional dance studio, Waters took her allowance and enrolled at the New Dance Group.

The New Dance Group faculty roster included ALVIN AILEY, Sophie Maslow, Donald McKayle, Murial Manning, Jane Dudley, GEOFFREY HOLDER, CARMEN DE LAVALLADE, and Nona Sherman. Waters began her training by taking one class per week. Eventually she became a scholarship student as her enrollment and participation at the New Dance Group increased. She often saw Ailey in passing, but it was not until he filled in as an instructor for one of her classes that she was formally introduced to him and the Lester Horton dance technique—the signature training technique of the Alvin Ailey American Dance Theater.

The decision to pursue dance study in college came after a visit to the Juilliard School in New York to observe classes. She auditioned, was accepted, and studied there with Anthony Tudor and Martha Graham. Waters earned her B.S. from the dance department in four years, attending summer sessions at the City College of New York and at Hunter College every summer to complete her academic requirements. She graduated from Juilliard in 1962.

In 1965 Waters performed in the seven-month European tour of LANGSTON HUGHES's *Black Nativity*. She remained in Europe and took up residence in Paris for approximately three years. While living in Europe she worked with different choreographers, including Donald McKayle, Milko Sparembleck, Maurice Béjart, and Michel Descombey of the Paris Opera Ballet. She returned to the United States in 1968 after performing at the Summer Olympic Games in Mexico with the Béjart Company. She was scheduled to continue on to Cuba with the group but encountered problems with her visa and was unable to complete the tour. In a sense it was a relief for Waters, who wanted to return home to be involved in the exhilarating world of American modern dance. As she later recalled, it was a time of new and exciting energy, funding possibilities, and flourishing dance companies.

Waters joined the Alvin Ailey American Dance Theater in 1968. During a performance at the Brooklyn Academy of Music, Ailey and Waters had run into each other, and Ailey invited her to join the company. The agreement was the culmination of numerous professional encounters on the American and European dance scenes. Her career as a principal dancer with the Alvin Ailey American Dance Theater lasted until 1973. During that time she toured the United States, South America, Europe, and the Soviet Union.

Waters married Chauncey F. Jones in 1981, and the couple remained together for seventeen years. Together they raised a son, Kenya Welsh, who was born in 1972. During the 1970s, maternity leave was unheard of in the American workplace. Nevertheless Alvin Ailey kept open a spot in his company for Waters. For three years she took her son on the road with her as she continued to tour with the company.

In 1975 Waters became the artistic director of the Alvin Ailey Repertory Workshop. The group evolved out of Ailey's plan to give dance students an opportunity to develop their craft by learning new choreography. At first the group did not have a name. It was at the onset of planning the "Ailey Celebrates Ellington" festival for America's bicentennial celebration, and with funding from the Ford Foundation, that the group became official. The initial performance for Ailey Celebrates Ellington was aired nationally and consisted of both students from the group and experienced dancers like Diane Harvey and FRED BENJAMIN.

Under Waters's direction the name was changed to the Alvin Ailey Repertory Ensemble, and it was again renamed Ailey II. She reportedly believed that the dancers selected were no longer just students, but young dancers on their way to becoming professionals. The Ailey II company comprised approximately eleven dancers who held two-year contracts to teach classes and perform Ailey repertory. In addition, they performed the work of other seasoned and emerging choreographers nationally and internationally.

In 1997 the State University of New York at Oswego awarded Waters an honorary doctorate, and in 2003 the Dance Theater Workshop presented her with a New York Dance and Performance ("Bessie") Award for Sustained Achievement in recognition of her outstanding commitment to young and emerging artists. In addition to having served on numerous local and national arts organizations, she served as a panelist for the National Endowment for the Arts and for the New York State Council on the Arts.

FURTHER READING
Dunning, Jennifer. *Alvin Ailey: A Life in Dance* (1996).
Long, Richard. *The Black Tradition in America Dance* (1995).

PRINCESS MHOON COOPER

Watkins, Julius (10 Oct. 1921–4 Apr. 1977), French horn player, was born in Detroit, Michigan. Details of his family, including the names and occupations of his parents are unknown. He began to play French horn in 1930 and developed a lifelong love for the instrument and a desire to be a soloist on the strength of having heard his teacher, Francis Hellstein, a member of the Detroit Symphony. He chose jazz, explaining that insufficient opportunities existed for soloing in the classical repertoire. No doubt a second reason was the racist barrier against African Americans in the classical music profession.

Watkins toured with Ernie Field's big band as a trumpeter in 1943 and left three years later to resume playing French horn. Moving from Detroit to Denver, he found work in a jazz sextet. After returning to Detroit, he joined the pianist MILT BUCKNER's big band in 1949. Buckner required that he play trumpet more often than his chosen horn. Recording that same year in New York with KENNY CLARKE and his Clique, Watkins was featured on "Don't Blame Me" and "French Licks." He quit Buckner's group in 1950 to attend the Manhattan School of Music. While studying under Robert Schultze of the New York Philharmonic for three years, he took classes in music theory and composition.

At a recording session in November 1953 Watkins found himself paired with SONNY ROLLINS in THELONIOUS MONK's quintet, to which he contributed imaginative solos on "Let's Call This" and "Think of One." He toured with Pete Rugolo in 1954 and joined OSCAR PETTIFORD's sextet, which included the tenor saxophonist CHARLIE ROUSE.

Subsequently, Watkins and Rouse led Les Modes—soon to be called Les Jazz Modes—a group that presented a gentle version of bop. Making its debut at Birdland in New York in 1956, it worked mainly as a quintet, with French horn, tenor sax, and a conventional jazz rhythm section (piano, bass, and drums). For recordings and concerts, Watkins and Rouse added a singer, a harpist, the Latin percussionist Chino Pozo, and—for the group's last studio session in November 1958—the baritone saxophonist Sahib Shihab. Les Jazz Modes had no work after January 1959. With the pianist Gildo Mahones leaving to join the then-popular vocal group Lambert, Hendricks, and Ross, and Rouse leaving for Monk's quartet, Watkins's career declined. He played briefly with a big band led by George Shearing in 1959, and he was a member of QUINCY JONES's orchestra in 1961 (plus recordings in other years).

In the 1960s and 1970s Watkins worked as a freelance musician in Broadway pit orchestras while also making albums in ad hoc ensembles accompanying prominent jazz musicians. More significantly, he recorded as a soloist with, among others, Benny Bailey's septet, which included Phil Woods, in 1960; JIMMY HEATH's sextet, which included Freddie Hubbard, in 1961 and 1962; and the Jazz Contemporaries in 1972. He was also a member of CHARLES MINGUS's octet in mid-1965 and sextet in late in 1971.

By 1976 he had settled in Montclair, New Jersey, where he variously taught horn, commuted to play in the Symphony of the New World, and continued to work in Broadway pit orchestras, an assignment he found boring and that he said led to his drinking too much. He died in Short Hills, New Jersey, survived by his wife, Harriette Davison (date of marriage unknown), and their two children.

The French horn has held a modest place in jazz, mainly in those ensembles oriented toward smooth and gentle sounds. Thus it is no surprise that Watkins regularly recorded with Gil Evans's sumptuous orchestras under the direction of MILES DAVIS, KENNY BURRELL, or Evans himself, from 1958 to 1964 and in 1969. But the instrument's pure tone and the perverse difficulty of playing it with virtuosic dexterity were at odds with the aesthetics of Watkins's chosen style, bop. Even at the relaxed tempo of Monk's "Let's Call This," Watkins's struggle to improvise in a fluid manner is obvious. He managed nonetheless to make a career as a soloist of note. This achievement has been of some consequence in scholastic circles, as young French horn players endeavor to play jazz, but it has had little influence on professional jazz performance.

FURTHER READING

Agrell, Jeffrey. "Jazz and the Horn: Julius Watkins," *Brass Bulletin*, no. 41 (1983).

Wilson, John S. "The Horn That Nobody Wants," *Down Beat*, 17 Sept. 1959.

Obituaries: *New York Times*, 8 Apr. 1977; *Down Beat*, 16 June 1977.

This entry is taken from the *American National Biography* and is published here with the permission of the American Council of Learned Societies.

BARRY KERNFELD

Watkins, Mark Hanna (23 Nov. 1903–24 Feb. 1976), by all available evidence the first American of African descent to earn a Ph.D. in anthropology, was a founding father of that science as it became an organized professional field in America, and a leading pioneer in the development of linguistics, doing field research in Haiti, Guatemala, Costa Rica, and southern Africa. His wide range of professional affiliations included the American Anthropological Association, the American Association for the Advancement of Science, the American Sociological Association, the International African Institute, and the International Linguistic Association. In 1933, he was one of the first three African Americans admitted to the Society of Sigma Xi (Wright, p. 889).

Born in Huntsville, Texas, he was the son of Walter Watkins, a Baptist minister, and Laura Williams Watkins (Wright), whose Republican politics are reflected in naming their son for the party leader and wealthy Ohio senator, Mark Hanna. He was the youngest of fourteen children; of those closer to him in age, by the time he was sixteen, three older brothers were farming, and two sisters were school teachers (Wade-Lewis, p. 183). The future anthropologist graduated from Sam Houston Industrial Training School, established in 1906 by Samuel Walker Houston, publisher of the *Huntsville Times*, a teacher determined to develop leadership within the state's black community, who had been born in 1864 to JOSHUA HOUSTON (then owned by former Texas governor Sam Houston) and Sylvester Lee (Lede, Naomi, "Paving the Way to Literacy," *Huntsville Item*, 12 June 2006).

Watkins earned a Bachelor of Science degree in Education from Prairie View State College, Texas, in 1926, then served as assistant registrar at Prairie View. A 26 August 1928 paper titled "An Outline of the Work at Pecos" (a Native American archaeological site in New Mexico) evidences an early interest in his future profession (Wade-Lewis, p. 186). Continuing his education at the University of Chicago, he earned a Master of Arts in Anthropology in 1930, and his Ph.D. in 1933, completing a dissertation entitled "A Grammar of Chichewa: A Bantu Language of British Central Africa." Widely praised by, among others, the linguistic anthropologists Benjamin Whorf and Clement Doke as a ground-breaking study (Wade-Lewis, p. 191), the dissertation was published in 1937 by the Linguistic Society of America. His primary informant was Kamuzu (later known as Hastings) Banda, a fellow student who later graduated from Edinburgh University in Scotland, and served as the first post-independence prime minister of Malawi.

Sometime in the early 1930s Watkins married Alma Taylor, a native of Louisville, Kentucky; records of the marriage are absent from published sources. Taylor taught at Roosevelt High School in Gary, Indiana, next to Chicago, from 1931 to 1934 (*Who's Who in Colored America*, 1950). Watkins accepted a position as assistant professor of sociology at Louisville Municipal College, 1933–1934. From 1934 to 1947, Watkins served as professor of anthropology at Fisk University in Nashville, Tennessee, his wife joining the faculty at Fisk in 1937 as an assistant in foreign languages (*Who's Who*, 1950). In a 1937 paper, "The Place of Anthropology in the Negro College," he advocated establishment of anthropology departments in what later became known as Historically Black Colleges and Universities, because it could serve as a laboratory equipping scholars to most frankly face the question of the worth of different groups of human beings (Wade-Lewis, p. 193).

In 1943 Watkins was one of six scholars associated at Fisk with the first attempt to form an African Studies Program in the United States, along with CHARLES S. JOHNSON, chair of the Department of Social Sciences; Robert E. Park, sociologist and professor emeritus from University of Chicago (full-time scholar-in-residence at Fisk); Edwin Smith, president and cofounder of the International Institute of African Languages and Cultures in Great Britain; Ina C. Brown, social anthropologist; and LORENZO DOW TURNER, with extensive research and teaching since 1910 at Howard, University of Chicago, and Harvard, known as the father of Gullah studies (Wade-Lewis, Margaret, *Lorenzo Dow Turner: Father of Gullah Studies*, 2007, p. 140). The program never materialized—Watkins was on leave for his own research with Indian languages in Guatemala, while student interest and funding were both limited (Gilpin, Patrick J., and Marybeth Gasman, *Charles S. Johnson: Leadership beyond the Veil in the Age of Jim Crow*, 2003, p. 103).

Although much of his research focused on people outside of North America, Watkins published papers on the African American experience as well, including "Racial Situation in Denver," which appeared in *The Crisis*, May 1945 (p. 139). Watkins published "The Social Role of Color in Haiti" (1946), and "Race, Caste, and Class in Haiti" (1948). In the second article, he asserts that "The clearly distinguishable divisions in Haitian society are the elite and peasants, not the 'mulattoes' and 'blacks,'" identifying social class as primary and race as a complicating factor (Wade-Lewis, p. 195).

He and Alma Taylor Watkins divorced in 1944 (Wade-Lewis, p. 215, fn. 20); she had begun teaching romance languages at Tennessee A & I University in 1943, later becoming known for her 1949 doctoral dissertation "Eroticism in the Novels of Felipe Trigo." Watkins obtained leave to teach at the University of Chicago, in 1944–1945, then took a sabbatical year as visiting professor at the Escuela Nacional de Antropología e Historia, Mexico, in 1945–1946. In September 1946, he spent a year working with the Guatemalan Institute on studies among the Cakchiquel Indians, financed by a State Department grant-in-aid. Returning to the United States in 1947, he resigned from Fisk to accept a position as professor of anthropology at Howard University, where he remained until his retirement in 1976. He returned to Guatemala in the summer of 1948 as a visiting professor of anthropology at the Universidad de San Carlos.

In 1951 Watkins married Dr. Charlotte Crawford, a Howard University English professor, 1933 graduate of Wellesley College, with a Ph.D. from Yale University. He was instrumental in founding the first African Studies Program to offer degrees at the bachelor's and master's degree levels in 1954. The program emphasized exchanges bringing African students to Howard and sending Howard students to receive part of their education in Africa. At least one-sixth and sometimes over one-fourth of the students enrolled in African studies courses were natives of the African continent from 1958 to 1962 (Wade-Lewis, p. 206). He also taught as a visiting professor in 1954 at Georgetown University, Washington, D.C. Four years later, he taught at the University of Natal, South Africa, in 1958—an exchange with Natal Professor E. G. M. Njisane, who taught for six months at Howard.

Watkins joined an informal Howard faculty social club, "Thinkers and Drinkers," led by the sociologist E. FRANKLIN FRAZIER, with fellow sociologists Harry Walker and G. Franklin Edwards, poet STERLING BROWN, and historians Sam Dorsey, Harold Lewis, and JOHN HOPE FRANKLIN. The only prerequisite for membership was that no member did or would play poker—they met for drinks and dinner, and talked (Teele, James E., *E. Franklin Frazier and the Black Bourgeoisie*, 2002, p. 18).

Retiring from Howard in 1972, Watkins continued to teach courses in anthropology and linguistics, until just prior to his death in 1976 at George Washington University Hospital, Washington, D.C. His colleague at Howard, Jerome W. Wright, eulogized him as a splendid teacher who generated in his students a great enthusiasm for anthropology, remembered for his sense of humor and concern for student welfare. Watkins, who had no children from either marriage, was survived by his wife Charlotte, who died 15 April 1997. A dissertation year fellowship and a postfield fellowship are offered by the University of Chicago Department of Anthropology, in memory of Watkins.

FURTHER READING

Wade-Lewis, Margaret, "Mark Hanna Watkins: African American Linguistic Anthropologist." *Histories of Anthropology Annual* 1 (2005).

Obituary: Wright, J. W. "Mark Hanna Watkins, 1903–1976." *American Anthropologist* 78, no. 4 (1976): 889–890.

CHARLES ROSENBERG

Watkins, Mel (8 Mar. 1940–), author and editor, was born in Memphis, Tennessee, to Pittman Watkins, a laborer, and Katie Watkins, a homemaker. When he was a young child the family moved to Youngstown, Ohio, following the second wave of the Great Migration. Watkins called it "that second large wave of Southern black emigrants" (*Dancing with Strangers*, 23). He chronicled much of this youthful journey in *Dancing with Strangers: A Memoir* (1998), in which he describes his family as "a Rainbow Coalition" (60).

His dark-skinned father had African and Native American ancestry; his mother, whose father was Irish, could have passed for white. Because of the variety of skin tones in his own family, Watkins didn't pay much attention to racial differences until he began school, when he first experienced racial discrimination from other students. After a rocky start in elementary school, the bright and energetic Watkins got mixed up with the "wrong crowd," engaged in petty thievery, and was expelled from second grade for making and selling drawings from French pornographic postcards. He recovered to become a scholar-athlete and was the first of five siblings to graduate from high school in 1958. In *Dancing with Strangers*, Watkins describes the many obstacles he overcame, but also describes some rich treasures from his upbringing, including the oral storytelling tradition passed on to him by his paternal grandmother, "Miss Aggie." He credits his mother's respect for education and her wise intervention after he failed second grade due to his disruptive behaviors with helping him to make a turnaround in his school career.

As his parents' marriage began to disintegrate during his middle-school years, Watkins found an outlet in sports. In high school he became a three-sport athlete, playing football, baseball, and basketball. Although he had ambitions of becoming a professional baseball player, it was his basketball skills that attracted college recruiters. In his senior year of high school, 1957–58, he was an All-State athlete and was awarded a War Memorial Scholarship. Offered scholarships by the University of Pittsburgh, Dartmouth, and Colgate, he chose to attend Colgate University, which had offered the scholarship because of his athletic and scholastic ability, in Hamilton, New York, from which he graduated in 1962 with a degree in Fine Arts History.

Watkins played basketball throughout his years at Colgate, but became increasingly interested in academics, in particular psychology and literature. During his senior year at Colgate, Watkins decided to become a writer rather than a professional basketball player, a decision that was reinforced when he received a severe and debilitating injury during a basketball game. The summer before his senior year, Watkins had worked as a copy boy for the *New York*

Daily News and lived in Harlem. When he returned to Colgate, he wrote a novella for a special study course, based partly on his experiences in Harlem that remains unpublished. By reading existentialist philosophers, such as Nietzsche and Sartre, and literary writers, such as T. S. Eliot, Thomas Mann, Kafka, and JAMES BALDWIN, Watkins gained a perspective that would inform his future writing.

After graduating from Colgate, Watkins worked for two years in New York City as a Social Security claims examiner. In 1963 he married Patricia M. Marsh, and the couple had one child, Kim Danielle. In 1964 Watkins took a position at the *New York Times* as a copy boy for the Sunday section. He began to write reviews for the *New York Times Book Review* on the side. When the *New American Review* offered Watkins a job as its new editor, the *Book Review* also offered him a job. Watkins became the first African American staff editor for the *Book Review* in 1968, and he remained in this position until 1986. Between 1967 and 2002, Watkins wrote more than two hundred editorials, reviews, and interviews for the *Times*. His first full-length feature, "Black Skins, White Skins, Thin Skins" (3 December 1967), chronicled the dilemmas of black families moving to the suburbs. He continued to contribute commentary on black issues and books by African American writers throughout his long career at the *Times*, during which time he helped to shape critical opinion about African American writers. He interviewed writers from LeRoi Jones (AMIRI BARAKA) to ALEX HALEY, and he wrote major reviews of fiction by Baldwin, ALICE WALKER, GLORIA NAYLOR, JOHN EDGAR WIDEMAN, and WALTER MOSLEY.

During the 1970s, Watkins emerged as an editor of several published collections that contributed to the Black Arts movement. *The Black Review, No. 1*, a literary and critical annual published in 1971 and edited by Watkins, received critical praise from noted literary critic Stephen E. Henderson (*NYTBR*, 28 March 1971). During the same year, he coedited with David Jay an anthology, *To Be a Black Woman*, a collection of essays. However, it was not until he left the full-time employ of the *Book Review* in 1986 that Watkins began his career as the author of several major books on African American humor, popular culture, and the entertainment industry.

After leaving the full-time employ of the *Times* to become a freelance writer in 1986, Watkins began a successful career as a popular historian of African American humor, entertainment, and popular culture. *On the Real Side: Laughing,*

Lying, and Signifying: The Underground Tradition of African-American Humor That Transformed American Culture, from Slavery to Richard Pryor (1994) received a positive, front-page review by Lawrence W. Levine in the *New York Times Book Review*. Initial research for this volume began when Watkins received a grant from the Alicia Patterson Foundation in 1979–1980 to research black humor. *Dancing with Strangers* was followed by an anthology, *African American Humor: The Best Black Comedy from Slavery to Today* (2002), and *Stepin Fetchit: The Life and Times of Lincoln Perry* (2005). Watkins also contributed stories and essays to a variety of periodicals, from *Penthouse* to the *Southern Review*, and he wrote introductions for the first six volumes of the Howard University Press Library of Contemporary Literature Series (1984). As both a witness to and a shaper of one of the most productive periods in African American literary history, Watkins has created, through his writing, a critical framework through which readers interpret the major contributions of African American culture.

FURTHER READING

Watkins's reviews and essays for the *New York Times* are available in back issues of the *New York Times* and in the Historical *New York Times* database.

Boskin, Joseph. Review of *On the Real Side: Laughing, Lying, and Signifying—The Underground Tradition of African-American Humor that Transformed American Culture, from Slavery to Richard Pryor*. *Journal of Southern History*, vol. 61 issue 2 (May 1995).

"Mel Watkins." *Contemporary Authors Online* (2003). Available at http://galenet.galegroup.com/servlet/BioRC.

"Mel Watkins." *The Black Journalists Movement: How They Got Their Start*. Robert C. Maynard Institute for Journalism Education, 25 July 2007. Available at www.maynardije.org/programs/history/collection/mel_watkins.

ANN HOSTETLER

Watson, Anthony J. (18 May 1949–), U.S. naval officer and submarine commander, was born in Chicago, Illinois, to Johnny Watson, who worked at a printing plant, and Virginia Watson, a community liaison and teacher's aide. One of six children, Anthony John Watson was raised in the Cabrini-Green public housing community and attended Chicago's Lane Technical High School, where he was a starter on the football team. Upon graduating in 1966 he entered the University of Illinois at Chicago Circle, and in June of that year he was recruited to the U.S. Naval Academy, where he became a "plebe" (first-year) midshipman.

Watson was one of only six African Americans to graduate in the class of 1970 at Annapolis. Indeed, at all of the nation's service academies by 1969 only 116 cadets were "nonwhite" (Foner, 211). Watson "remained engaged in spite of the distractions and challenges" faced by African American midshipmen at Annapolis in the late 1960s. He was twice elected class president, became a battalion boxing champion, and was the first black brigade commander as a third-year midshipman. His high standing at the naval academy is evidenced by the ceremonial sword he was awarded in 1968 by Academy Superintendent Rear Admiral Draper Kauffman for his leadership abilities.

Following his graduation he attended nuclear power school and subsequently saw his first submarine duty as a junior weapons officer. He later gained added experience aboard six submarines on deployments that carried him to places as distant as the North Pole and the Panama Canal. In his early career Watson was often the only African American on the submarines on which he served. Prior to the 1980s no African American had ever risen to command a submarine, and there were only a few black flag officers, a naval rank above captain. Seeking new opportunities in the private sector, he left active service in 1982 to work for an electric power company while remaining in the naval reserve. However, Watson soon found that he "missed the ultimate leadership challenge of submarines" and rejoined the navy on active duty in 1983, the same year that C. A. "PETE" Tzomes, a 1967 Annapolis graduate, became the first black submarine commander in the U.S. Navy when he took command of USS *Houston*.

Four years later Watson became the second African American to command a submarine when he was named skipper of the fast-attack boat USS *Jacksonville* (SSN-699). As the second member of a group later called the Centennial 7, the first seven black submarine commanders in Submarine Force history, Watson helped to create a wider range of opportunities for blacks in the Submarine Force. In the view of RICHARD RENARD BRYANT, a commander of the submarine USS *Miami*, Watson was "the bedrock and foundation" for those who came after him.

While in command of USS *Jacksonville* from 1987 to 1988, Watson and his crew excelled; his ship won the Engineering "E" award for excellence and was the first in twenty-five years to perform a live at-sea shock test to prove the submarine capability to withstand depth charge–like explosions under live fire conditions. Watson's later navy career was equally successful and even more groundbreaking. In 1988 he was named the Black Engineer of the Year in Government. From 1989 to 1992 he served as deputy commandant of midshipmen at the naval academy and from 1992 to 1993 as the commander of Submarine Squadron Seven in Pearl Harbor, in charge of thirteen fast-attack submarines. He was selected to the rank of rear admiral in 1994, becoming the first black submariner to achieve flag rank. He subsequently served as the deputy director of the operations on the Joint Chiefs of Staff while General COLIN POWELL was chairman.

Throughout his career Watson remained closely tied to his inner-city roots. For his efforts in promoting diversity within the navy, he received the NAACP's Roy Wilkins Meritorious Service Award in 1990 and in 1991 the Order of Lincoln Award from the State of Illinois, the state's highest honor. The Tony Watson/Chicago Youth Centers Math and Science Scholarship, founded in 1991, provided annual scholarship funding for inner-city youth in Chicago. In 1996 Watson was named commander, Naval Recruiting Command. He was the first African American to hold this post, which he held until his retirement from the navy in 1997.

Watson married Sharon Watson, and the couple had two daughters, Erica and Lindsay. In 2003 he founded the Alliance Leadership Group, a firm that specializes in helping companies achieve diversity within its senior executive positions.

FURTHER READING

The unsourced material quoted herein comes from the author's interview with Anthony Watson on 20 March 2007.

Foner, Jack D. *Blacks and the Military in American History* (1974).

Massaquoi, Hans J. "Rear Admiral Anthony Watson: From 'the Projects' to the Pentagon," *Ebony* (June 1994).

GLENN ALLEN KNOBLOCK

Watson, Barbara Mae (5 Nov. 1918–17 Feb. 1983), government official, was born in New York City, the daughter of James S. Watson, the first black elected judge in New York, and Violet Lopez. After receiving her B.A. from Barnard College in 1943, she served as an interviewer with the United Seaman's Service in New York from 1943 to 1946; as owner and executive director of Barbara Watson Models, a modeling agency, from 1946 to 1956; as a research assistant for the New York State Democratic Committee, from 1952 to 1953; as a clerk at the Christophers, a non-profit Catholic organization in New York, from 1956 to 1957; and as foreign student adviser at Hampton Institute in Virginia, from 1958 to 1959.

Watson, who was honored as "the most outstanding law student in the City of New York," received an LLB from New York Law School in 1962, graduating third highest in her class. She was admitted to the New York bar in that same year and served as an attorney on the New York City Board of Statutory Consolidation, in 1962–1963; as assistant attorney in the New York City Corporation Counsel law department, in 1963–1964; and as executive director of the New York City Commission to the United Nations, from 1964 to 1966.

Watson joined the Department of State in July 1966 as special assistant to Deputy Undersecretary of State for Administration William J. Crockett. In October 1966 she became deputy administrator of the Bureau of Security and Consular Affairs and acting administrator in April 1967. When President Lyndon B. Johnson appointed her administrator of that bureau in July 1968, Watson became the first woman and the first African American to achieve a rank in the Department of State equivalent to that of an assistant secretary.

Shortly before Watson left her post as administrator on 31 December 1974, she received the State Department's Luther I. Replogle Award for Management Improvement, established in 1973 to be awarded annually to the person who had most effectively contributed to sound management in the department during that year. The statement nominating Watson for the award noted that, among her achievements as administrator of the Bureau of Security and Consular Affairs, she had imp.roved consular facilities and service to the public by introducing better procedures, such as computerized visa and passport hookups, and had established a better and closer system of communications between the bureau and the officers in the field. She was also commended for achieving better career opportunities for consular officers, including opportunities for broader assignments, recognition of "consular interest posts," introduction of a mid-career consular management course, and more extensive training for senior consular officers. She was also cited for "outstanding professional leadership in administering the Immigration and Nationality Act fairly and in a humanitarian manner."

After two years as a college lecturer and legal consultant, Watson returned to the Department of State as administrator of the Bureau of Security and Consular Affairs in April 1977. The administrator's title was changed to assistant secretary of state for consular affairs in August 1977. Watson remained in that position until President Jimmy Carter appointed her U.S. ambassador to Malaysia in August 1980. She presented her credentials in Kuala Lumpur on 25 September 1980 and served at that post until 1 March 1981.

Following her return to Washington, Watson entered private law practice and became a senior associate at an international consulting firm. She also served on the boards of Fordham University, Barnard College, the Georgetown University Center for Strategic and International Studies, Radio Liberty/Radio Free Europe, and the Wolf Trap Foundation for the Performing Arts. She never married and remained in Washington, D.C., until her death.

Watson, who received many awards during her lifetime from black and women's organizations, was a pathfinder whose exceptional competence in her varied roles helped to pave the way for other women and blacks in professional positions. As the first woman and the first black to serve in the Department of State at the assistant secretary level, she was one of a handful of pioneers who helped to break down some of the psychological barriers and preconceptions that had prevented women and blacks from rising to positions of leadership in the department.

FURTHER READING

Calkin, Homer L. *Women in the Department of State: Their Role in American Foreign Affairs* (1978).

"Miss Watson Named Administrator, Security and Consular Affairs," *Department of State Newsletter*, no. 88 (Aug. 1968).

Obituaries: *New York Times*, 18 Feb. 1983; *Department of State Newsletter*, no. 254 (Mar. 1983).

This entry is taken from the *American National Biography* and is published here with the permission of the American Council of Learned Societies.

NINA DAVIS HOWLAND

Watson, Bob "The Bull" (10 Apr. 1946–), baseball player and executive, was born Robert Jose Watson in Los Angeles, California, the elder of two sons born to Eddie Watson and Wilma (Stewart) Watson, of whom little is known. The Watsons divorced in 1947, and Watson was raised by his mother's parents in a nearby section of South Central, Los Angeles. Watson developed his baseball skills by playing stickball with his younger brother, Arthur Sandoz, who lived next door with close friends of the Stewarts. Watson would later credit the difficulty of swatting bottle caps with turning him into a major-league-caliber hitter. He first became involved in organized baseball when he was eight years old, while on a visit to his great-aunt in eastern Los Angeles. He saw a group of boys playing baseball on a playground across the street and immediately signed up to join their summer league. Watson was assigned to play catcher, which became his regular position until he reached the major leagues. By the time Watson turned thirteen, he was already six feet tall and playing in three separate summer leagues.

Upon joining the Fremont High School baseball team, his coach told him that he was too big to adopt the nickname of his favorite player, the San Francisco Giant ORLANDO "BABY BULL" CEPEDA; he would simply be called "Bull," a name that stayed with him throughout his career. Watson was a standout player at Fremont and was named a second team All-City catcher during his senior year. This was an especially impressive feat in Los Angeles at the time; between summer leagues and high school Watson had played alongside such future major league stars as Reggie Smith, Roy White, Paul Blair, Dock Ellis, and George Hendrick. He attributed the explosion of local talent to year-round warm weather, the relocation of the Brooklyn Dodgers to Los Angeles in 1958, and the inspiration of JACKIE ROBINSON and other African American pioneers who were breaking the major-league color barrier.

In the fall of 1963 Watson began studying mechanical drafting at Harbor Junior College in Wilmington, California. A walk-on to the baseball team, he became its starting catcher and batted .371 to earn a spot on the All-Conference team. This attracted the attention of Houston Astros scout Karl Kuehl, who signed him to a $2,000 contract. In February 1965 Watson flew to the Astros' Florida spring training camp, where he was assigned the ominously high uniform number of 202 and given little chance of making the team. But Watson's batting skills were impressive enough to earn him an assignment to Houston's Class A affiliate in Salisbury, North Carolina. There he would have his first experience with overt racism, as he lived in segregated housing and ate in segregated restaurants. In September 1966 Watson was called up for a game in Los Angeles to make his major-league

debut. He spent 1967 shuttling between Double-A Amarillo and Triple-A Oklahoma City, reaching Houston for fourteen at-bats and a .214 average at the end of the season. The next year he was hitting .395 with Oklahoma City when he was called up mid-season, only to break his ankle soon after while running out an extra-base hit. This ended his season and put him in a cast until 4 October 1968, the day before he married Carol Le'fer. They would have two children, Keith and Kelley.

After honing his skills playing winter ball in the Dominican Republic, Watson became Houston's starting left fielder at the beginning of the 1969 season. He was returned to the minors to work on his catching skills, and he hit .408 at Oklahoma City. But Watson could not find a place on the field; he was the team's fifth outfielder, third-string catcher, and backup first baseman. During the off-season he agreed with his wife to stick out one more season in the major leagues, thereby qualifying for a pension. But in early 1970 starting first baseman Joe Pepitone was arrested for failing to make alimony payments, and Watson took over. At one point in June, he was named Player of the Week, and Pepitone was traded to the Chicago Cubs.

In 1972 Watson was moved to left field, and his place in the starting lineup was secured. He finished in the top five in the National League for batting average in 1972 and 1973, and he was named to the All-Star team in the latter year. He would again be selected for the team in 1975. That year he batted .324 and contended for the National League batting crown, before breaking his hand in September. Watson's career was often interrupted by injuries. His other obstacle throughout most of his career was playing in the pitcher-friendly Astrodome, which restricted his career power numbers.

In 1977 Watson enjoyed a career year with a .289 batting average, twenty-two home runs, and 110 RBI. But by 1979 he wanted to play for a more competitive team and was traded to the Boston Red Sox. In eighty-four games with Boston, Watson hit .337 with thirteen home runs and fifty-three RBI, splitting time between first base and designated hitter. On 15 September Watson became the first player to hit for the cycle—a single, double, triple, and home run in one game—in both the National League and American League. He had accomplished the feat against San Francisco on 24 June 1977. Boston finished the 1979 season eleven games behind Baltimore, and Watson, a free agent, signed a three-year, $2.1 million contract with the New York Yankees that November. With the Yankees

Watson finally reached the play-offs, although the team lost the American League Championship Series in three games to the Kansas City Royals. In 1981 the Yankees won that series before losing in six games to the Los Angeles Dodgers in the World Series. Over the two post-seasons, Watson distinguished himself as an outstanding clutch hitter, batting .500 in the 1980 ALCS, .438 in the first round of the 1981 play-offs, and .318 with two homers, including a game winner, and seven RBI against the Dodgers in the World Series. Early in the 1982 season Watson was traded to the Atlanta Braves. Nearing the end of his career, he platooned at first base and occasionally pinch-hit, batting only .212 in his final season, 1984. During these three years in Atlanta manager Joe Torre designated Watson as the Braves' unofficial assistant hitting coach.

After retiring as a player Watson signed on as the Oakland Athletics' minor-league roving hitting instructor. He would later become the hitting and bench coach for the Athletics' major league team, which won the American League Pennant in 1988. In November of that year Watson was hired by the Houston Astros to be their assistant general manager, the first African American ever to hold that position in Major League Baseball. On 5 October 1993 he was promoted to general manager, again the first African American to hold such a position. But in April 1994 Watson discovered that he had prostate cancer. Surgery that July was successful, and he went on to serve as a spokesperson for the National Cancer Institute, in addition to advocating successfully for increased cancer testing for Major League Baseball players. Watson, active in the financial industry since the early 1980s, also sought to help current Major Leaguers by starting an investment company geared toward encouraging savings and financial planning among ballplayers.

In late 1995 Watson returned to the New York Yankees as their general manager. A series of brilliant moves helped bring the Yankees their first world championship that year since 1978 and laid the groundwork for a dynasty that would continue to dominate baseball throughout the decade. For his efforts Watson was named the 1996 Executive of the Year. But in 1997, frustrated with meddling owner George Steinbrenner, he resigned his position with the Yankees, subsequently joining the commissioner's office as Major League Baseball's vice president of on-field operations, often referred to as baseball's "chief disciplinarian." In this position Watson was also active in international baseball endeavors, serving as assistant chairman of the Team Selection Committee for the 1999 USA Baseball Pan Am team, co-chair of the Team Selection Committee for the 2000 Olympics, and co-chair of the Steering Committee for the 2004 team.

FURTHER READING
Watson, Bob, with Russ Pate. *Survive to Win* (1997).
Hanks, Stephen, et al. *150 Years of Baseball* (1989).
Shatzkin, Mike, ed. *The Ballplayers: Baseball's Ultimate Biographical Reference* (1990).
Thorn, John, and Pete Palmer, eds. *Total Baseball* (1989).

CHRISTOPHER DEVINE

Watson, Diane (12 Nov. 1933–), member of the U.S. Congress, was born Diane Edith Watson in Los Angeles, California, the oldest of three children. Her parents divorced when she was seven years old, at which time her mother began working nights at a post office; her father was a Los Angeles police officer. She attended Birdie Lee Bright Elementary School (formerly 36th Street School), Foshay Junior High School, and Dorsey High School. Upon graduating, Watson studied at Los Angeles City College before transferring to the University of California at Los Angeles, where in 1956 she earned a Bachelor of Arts degree in Education. In 1967 she acquired a Master of Arts degree in School Psychology from California State University. Attending the Claremont Graduate School, in 1986 Watson earned a Doctor of Philosophy degree in Educational Leadership. Subsequently, Watson attended the Kennedy School of Government at Harvard University in Cambridge, Massachusetts.

Watson had begun working with the Los Angeles Public School System upon graduating from UCLA. In the early 1960s she taught at U.S. Army Schools in Okinawa, Japan, and France, and returned to L.A. public schools in 1963; she worked as a teacher, assistant principal, and school psychologist. She has lectured at California State University in Long Beach and Los Angeles. Watson worked with the California Department of Education Bureau of Industrial Education as a health occupation specialist. In 1975 she became the first African American woman to be elected to the Los Angeles Unified School District Board of Education; in this capacity she sought school integration and the elevation of academic standards. Watson, a democrat, was elected to the California State Senate in 1978, winning 70 percent of the votes; she is an advocate for health care, children, women, and consumer

Diane Watson (D-California) congratulates Bill Clinton after he spoke at the City of Refuge Church in Gardena, California, on Sunday, 3 February 2008. (AP Images.)

protection. In 1992 she was defeated in the election for Los Angeles County Board of Supervisors in a race against YVONNE BURKE, who was supported by Congresswoman MAXINE WATERS. Despite a loss in the L.A. County election, her tenure with the California State Senate was marked with a number of milestones and accomplishments; from 1981 to 1998 she chaired the Senate Health and Human Services Committee and served on the Senate Judiciary Committee; in 1993 she authored the California Birth Defects Monitoring Program Act and the Residential Care Facilities Act; in total she introduced over eight hundred bills to legislature, of which some were enacted into law. Her tenure with the State Senate ended in 1998 due to term limits, and in 1999 she was appointed by United States President Bill Clinton to serve as the United States Ambassador to the Federated States of Micronesia, where she spent eighteen months.

At age sixty-seven, Watson returned to California as a candidate in a special election on 5 June 2001 for the congressional seat that had been vacated by the death of Congressman JULIAN DIXON. She was accompanied on the campaign trail by her ninety-one-year-old mother and eventually won a sweeping victory in the 33rd Congressional District. Congresswoman Watson was reelected on 5 November 2002 to serve a full two-year term, and was reelected in 2004, 2006, and 2008.

Congresswoman Watson is a member of the House Oversight and Government Reform Committee, and chairwoman of the subcommittee on Government Management, Organization and Procurement. She is also the chair of the Congressional Entertainment Industries Caucus and a co-chair of the Korean Caucus. Watson defeated the Republican candidate David Crowley in the 4 November 2008 election for the United States House of Representatives. In the

Democratic primary of 2008, like many of her fellow black members of the House she supported candidate New York Senator Hilary Rodham Clinton for president of the United States; in the California Democratic primary, the 33rd Congressional District largely supported Illinois Senator BARACK OBAMA. Congresswoman Watson is a member of Alpha Kappa Alpha, Sorority, Incorporated, the first sorority for African American women in the United States.

FURTHER READING

Jet, 30 Apr. 2001, p. 4; 25 June 2001, p. 30.

Los Angeles Times, 6 Jan. 1996, p. 2; 25 Mar. 1998, p. 1.

San Francisco Chronicle, 9 May 1990, p. 12.

SAFIYA DALILAH HOSKINS

Watson, Ella, daughter, wife, mother, grandmother, and devoted Christian, was the primary subject of the famed African American photographer GORDON PARKS SR. In Parks's famous photograph *American Gothic*, a scathing reinterpretation of Grant Woods's classic painting of that name, Ella Watson, holding a mop and broom, stands in front of an American flag hanging on a wall in a government office. The photograph is a searing representation of the discrimination and segregation that many African Americans encountered regardless of their gender or class position. Behind Watson's famous image was a woman with a challenging, albeit obscure, life story. Parks recalled several details Watson shared with him during an informal interview:

> She began to spill out her life's story. It was a pitiful one. She had struggled alone after her mother had died and her father had been killed by a lynch mob. She had gone through high school, married and become pregnant. Her husband was accidentally shot to death two days before their daughter was born. By the time the daughter was eighteen, she had given birth to two illegitimate children, and then died two weeks after the second child's birth. What's more, the first child had been stricken with paralysis a year before its mother died (Parks, 230–331).

Parks took nearly one hundred photographs documenting Watson's life and career as a charwoman in the federal government's employ. These pictures depict Watson spending time with her adopted daughter and grandchildren, traveling to and from work, and participating in religious services at her church. The photographs show Watson's efforts to rebuild her family after the numerous difficulties she endured.

Ella Watson, pictured in *American Gothic* by Gordon Parks Jr., August 1942. (Library of Congress.)

In addition to her personal tragedies, Watson's professional life at the Farm Security Administration was rife with challenges. In 1942 Watson had to clean the office of a female employee who worked in a higher position than Watson, even though the two women had been hired at the same time and their résumés were similar. Additionally Watson was caring for her grandchildren and adopted daughter, all of whom subsisted on her yearly income of $1,080. Fortunately Watson had the support of her neighbors and her church. Watson's neighbors formed a sort of extended family who provided care for her children while she worked the late shift. Moreover Watson was a deeply religious woman who maintained a large prayer altar in her home and often received spiritual succor from Reverends Vondell Gassaway and Clara Smith, pastors of St. Martin's Spiritual Church in Washington, D.C.

Little else is known of Watson's life after she stopped being one of Parks's primary subjects. However, what is certain is that Watson's image has been indelibly woven into the tapestry of American history.

FURTHER READING

Fleischhauer, Carl, and Beverly W. Brannan, eds. *Documenting America 1935–1943* (1988); also available from http://memory.loc.gov/ammem/fsahtml/fadocamer.html.

Ham, Debra Newman, ed. *The African American Mosaic: A Library of Congress Resource Guide for the Study of Black History and Culture* (1993).

Natanson, Nicholas. "From Sophie's Alley to the White House: Rediscovering the Visions of Pioneering Black Government Photographers," *Prologue* 29, no. 2 (Summer 1997).

Parks, Gordon. *A Choice of Weapons* (1966).

Willis, Deborah, and Carla Williams. *The Black Female Body: A Photographic History* (2002).

EUNICE ANGELICA WHITMAL

Watson, George (14 Mar. 1914–8 Mar. 1943), a U.S. soldier and Medal of Honor recipient, was a native of Birmingham, Alabama. Federal Census records indicate that he is likely the same man who later resided in Possum Bend, Wilcox County, Alabama, with his uncle and aunt, Henry and Sue Brown, as well as his two brothers. Information on Watson's parents is unknown, but they may have died while he was still young. Nothing further of George Watson's early life is known.

George Watson enlisted in the U.S. Army at Birmingham on 11 September 1942, and was subsequently sent for boot camp training at Fort Benning, Georgia. After an initial training period that lasted from four to six weeks, Private Watson was assigned to the 2nd Battalion, 29th Quartermaster Regiment, which soon departed the states for the Pacific theater. Men like Watson serving in the Quartermaster Corps performed important though often underappreciated work as the supply arm of the U.S. Army. Because African American soldiers were not yet allowed to serve in infantry units in combat theaters at this point in the war, those that did serve at the front did so in supply and transportation units that were often in harm's way. Watson's unit was embarked on the *USAT Jacob*, a Dutch steamer, near Porlock Harbor, Papua, New Guinea, on 8 March 1943, when it was attacked by Japanese dive bombers. The ship quickly took a number of hits and was set afire and in danger of sinking when its captain gave the order to abandon ship, upon which men, Watson included, dove overboard and swam for the few life rafts that could be found. While swimming to the raft on his first attempt, Watson grabbed a soldier who could not swim and took him to the boat. Instead of joining the raft after his first rescue, Watson stayed in the water and continued to assist his fellow soldiers and sailors gain the safety of the life rafts. Watson probably saved at least three

men, but it would cost him his own life. The battered transport ship finally began to sink, and in its final plunge to the bottom, the suction of the sinking ship dragged Watson—weakened by his struggles in the water and while attempting to save yet another man—down with it, and he was drowned. For his courageous actions and ultimate self-sacrifice, Private Watson was subsequently awarded the Distinguished Service Cross, becoming the first African American to be so honored during the war.

The service and heroism of black soldiers and sailors in World War II, men like George Watson, JOHN FOX, DORIE MILLER, and LEONARD HARMON, is important for a number of reasons; not only do these men deserve to be remembered for their heroic deeds on their own merit, but by these deeds they also served to prove to the American military establishment and the American public at large, though it would be a long time coming, that African Americans could and should serve on an equal footing with white soldiers and sailors.

George Watson's name was inscribed on the wall of those missing at sea at the Manila American Cemetery in the Philippines after the war, but like many, his deeds seemed to have been largely forgotten. Watson might have remained a forgotten hero were it not for the army's reassessment of its wartime award policies toward Medal of Honor recipients and African American soldiers in the 1990s. In 1995, in collaboration with the army, researchers at Shaw University completed a 272-page study on overlooked black World War II heroes, concluding "that racism was the reason Black soldiers did not receive the top military award." Shaw recommended that ten servicemen receive the medal, including Private George Watson. In an unprecedented move, the Army Board of Decorations subsequently approved the nomination for seven of these men, and on 13 January 1997 President William Clinton made the presentation of their Medals of Honor at the White House; one surviving soldier accepted his in person, and the next of kin of five others received the medal in an emotional ceremony. Since George Watson had no known surviving family members, his Medal of Honor was accepted by Sergeant Major of the Army Eugene McKinney, who is also African American. George Watson's Medal of Honor now resides in the U.S. Army Quartermaster Museum at Fort Lee, Virginia.

FURTHER READING

Hanna, Charles W. *African American Recipients of the Medal of Honor* (2002).

U.S. Army Quartermaster Foundation. "Private George Watson, Medal of Honor, World War II."

GLENN ALLEN KNOBLOCK

Watson, James Lopez (21 May 1922–1 Sept. 2001), state senator and federal jurist, was the third of four children born to Violet M. Lopez and James S. Watson, who immigrated from Jamaica in the early 1900s. His father was the first naturalized person of West Indian descent admitted to the New York State Bar in 1914, and in 1922 he was appointed special assistant corporation counsel of New York City, in the Special Franchise Tax Division. In 1930 he was one of the first two justices of African descent elected to judicial office, serving as a municipal court judge. Watson's sisters were lawyers: Grace Watson worked with the U.S. Department of Education, and BARBARA MAE WATSON was ambassador to Malaysia and assistant secretary of state for consular affairs. His brother, Douglas Watson, was the first African American aeronautical engineer.

Watson was born in Harlem, where he lived all his life, and was known to neighbors and professional associates by his childhood nickname "Skiz," after a *Gasoline Alley* comic strip character. He attended DeWitt Clinton High School, graduating in the class of 1941. There he belonged to the Douglass Society, dedicated to scholarship and social justice, and was a star player on the basketball team that won the New York City championship. At age eighteen he was drafted and served during World War II (1942–1943) in the first unit of African American soldiers to fight in Europe: the Ninety-second Infantry "Buffalo Soldier" Division. Correspondence with his father during the war appears in the collection *I Hear a Symphony: African Americans Celebrate Love* (1994). Watson earned three Purple Hearts, the Battle Star, the Combat Infantry Badge, and other decorations, and he was hospitalized after being severely wounded in Italy. His sister Grace noted that years later, while her brother was serving as a jurist in Florida, Watson found and thanked the combat doctor responsible for saving his leg.

He attended New York University and Brooklyn Law School on the GI Bill and earned his bachelor of laws degree in 1951. On 14 July 1956 he married D'Jaris Ellyn Hinton, who served on President Kennedy's Equal Employment Opportunity Commission. They had two daughters, Karen and Kris, a large extended family, and a marriage of thirty-four years when she passed away in November 1989. Karen Watson said of her father: "He was one

of the most fair people I've ever met. When we were kids, if we had a gripe with our parents, he held a family meeting to hear each of us out…. Even if it didn't come out your way, you always felt like you had a fair hearing" (Bernstein, 71–72).

Watson's legal career began in private practice with Bruce Wright, Lisle C. Carter Jr., and Jacob Smith. Their clientele included DUKE ELLINGTON, COUNT BASIE, BILLIE HOLIDAY, and many others. In 1954 he was elected to the state senate representing the Twenty-first Senatorial District, serving until 1963, when he was elected to the New York City Civil Court. There he hired a young attorney, CHARLES RANGEL, to work for him.

In 1966 President Lyndon Johnson, with whom he was friends, appointed Watson to the U.S. Customs Court, later renamed the U.S. Court of International Trade. Judge Watson was chairman of that court's legislative committee, which developed the Customs Courts Act (1970) and Trade Agreement Act (1979). While serving there, Watson was also designated by the chief justice of the U.S. Supreme Court to preside over civil and criminal matters as a visiting judge in the First Circuit Court of Appeals and district courts throughout the United States, Puerto Rico, and the Virgin Islands. In that capacity he fulfilled over seventy assignments—a record that earned him the affectionate and humorous appellation of "circuit rider." He was the first black judge since Reconstruction to serve on a federal court in the South.

Throughout his career Watson had a reputation for fairness, humility, and the ability to bring opposing sides together in settling lawsuits. Daniel Katz, his law clerk for thirty years, said of him: "Many judges, after a few years, think they walk with gods. This man was a real human being [and] truly communicated with people" (Bernstein, 70).

Two matters of major significance during Judge Watson's lifetime were civil rights and the war in Vietnam. His support of civil rights was unquestioned: he knew many in the forefront of that struggle, including MARTIN LUTHER KING JR., ADAM CLAYTON POWELL JR., Basil Paterson, and MALCOLM X. In 1963, as a New York state senator, he sat on the platform with Dr. King at the March on Washington. As a lifelong Harlem resident with a keen interest in the community, Watson was keenly aware of the impact of the Vietnam War on African Americans, but research has revealed no statement of his position about this war.

In 1992 he cofounded the Just the Beginning Foundation, an organization of judges, lawyers, and others dedicated to improving the U.S. legal system and educating people about "the struggles and successes of African American lawyers and judges … from slavery to the Supreme Court." Judge Watson was a founding member and lecturer for the Judicial Council of the National Bar Association, aimed at eradicating racial and class bias from judicial and law-enforcement processes.

Watson was on the Board of Directors of 100 Black Men and the Board of Managers of Harlem YMCA. His friend Daniel Rose, a real estate executive and community leader, was instrumental in the late 1980s in bringing the Police Athletic League (PAL) to central Harlem. With Watson as chairman and Rose as vice chairman, Harlem PAL began an after-school tutoring component. This was so successful that in 1991 these men became founding board members of the Harlem Educational Activities Fund (HEAF), providing educational opportunities for young scholars from elementary school through college. In 2002 HEAF launched an endowment in Judge Watson's name and a yearly Watson Award. By 2007 over one thousand young people had entered HEAF programs, heading toward college, graduate school, and careers in the mainstream of American life.

Judge Watson died in New York City in 2001. In a ceremony held on 10 November 2003, the United States International Trade Court building at One Federal Plaza in New York City was renamed the James L. Watson United States Court of International Trade. He was among the first African American jurists for whom a federal court building was named.

FURTHER READING

Personal papers and photographs are included in his father's collection: James S. Watson Papers, 1913–1991, Schomburg Center for Research in Black Culture, New York City. James L. Watson's papers relating to the National Bar Association, and correspondence with African American lawyers and judges, are in the Damon J. Keith Law Collection of African American Legal History, Wayne State University, Detroit, Michigan.

Bernstein, Alice. "Court Building Named for Judge James L. Watson," in *Aesthetic Realism and the Answer to Racism* (2004).

Who's Who in America (44th–56th editions) (1986–2002).

Obituary: *New York Sun*, 19 Aug. 2001.

ALICE BERNSTEIN

Watson, Johnny "Guitar" (3 Feb. 1935–17 May 1996), singer, guitarist, and pianist, was born John Watson in Houston, Texas. His father taught him to play piano. At age eleven he inherited his first guitar from his grandfather, a preacher, who told him not to use it for playing blues. However, as Watson later admitted, that was the first thing he played. His early influences were T-BONE WALKER and Clarence "Gatemouth" Brown. As a teenager he made a name for himself in the Houston blues scene, playing with blues guitarists ALBERT COLLINS and Johnny Copeland and winning talent contests hosted by singer Johnny Otis. Watson left for Los Angeles when he was fifteen years old.

In the 1950s Watson became one of the most exciting blues guitarists on the West Coast. He played piano and sang on the saxophonist Chuck Higgins's "Motorhead Baby" in 1952 and signed his first record contract as Young John Watson one year later. His jump-blues piano playing and laid-back singing style were quite exceptional, but he did not make a lasting impact until he switched to guitar, changing his name to Johnny "Guitar" Watson after Nicholas Ray's movie western *Johnny Guitar* (1954) with Sterling Hayden. This ironic adaptation of Old West lore is also evident in the witty "Gangster of Love," which Watson originally cut in 1957 and successfully re-recorded in 1978. The twelve-bar blues features Watson rapping about himself putting "bad cats" such as Jesse James to shame; it became his signature song for years to come.

Watson's guitar technique, evident on 1950s tracks like "Space Guitar" and "Hot Little Mama," would influence players such as IKE TURNER, BO DIDDLEY, and, ultimately, JIMI HENDRIX. Watson did not use a guitar pick: he employed low-slung strings that he slapped against the fretboard and effects such as reverb, feedback, and later, wah-wah. Rock guitarist Frank Zappa, who hired Watson to sing on his albums *One Size Fits All* (1975) and *Them Or Us* (1984), called Watson's style "razor-blade totin' guitar." When playing live, Watson emphasized showmanship, using his teeth or playing the guitar behind his back. In an interview with *Guitar Player* magazine in 1982 Watson recalled how, using long guitar-amp cords, he would make his entrance into the clubs carrying fellow bluesman Guitar Slim on his shoulders, both musicians rapidly firing away on their guitars.

Ironically Watson had his first Top 10 hit on the R&B charts in 1955 with a cover of Earl King's slow piano ballad "Those Lonely, Lonely Nights." In 1962 he hit the R&B charts again with the string-accompanied "Cuttin' In." The 1960s saw Watson trying out different musical personas and showcasing his versatility with dwindling success. Watson played piano on a few jazz albums and went to Europe for rock and roll shows with Larry Williams. For these shows he was erroneously billed as "Elvis Presley's private guitar player" and invented stories about Presley to gain publicity. Watson's songwriting talents paid off when his "Mercy Mercy Mercy" became a Top 5 hit for the Buckinghams in 1967.

Watson's most successful reinvention came in the 1970s when, at age forty-one, he turned himself into a pimped-up funkster, replete with skin-tight suit, Panama hat, Afro haircut, feather boa, and gold rings and teeth. Watson had dabbled in some soul music when recording *I Don't Want to Be Alone, Stranger* for Fantasy Records in 1975, but the audiences in Europe still demanded the blues he had played in the 1950s. However, Watson's two funk albums *Ain't That a Bitch* (1976) and *A Real Mother for Ya* (1977) for DJM records signaled a huge comeback in the United States, striking a chord with black audiences back home. Both albums went gold, hitting both the R&B and pop charts. Watson's new sound was clearly influenced by funk musicians such as GEORGE CLINTON and SLY STONE and featured heavy bass lines, horn arrangements, and Watson's characteristic choppy, heavily reverbed wah-wah guitar. The playfully ironic vocals of songs such as "Ain't That a Bitch," "I Want to Ta-Ta You Baby," and "I Need It" commented on the recession of the 1970s (by which African Americans were hit particularly hard) and humorously boasted about Watson's sexual abilities in "Superman Lover." In relating to relevant issues in such a current fashion, critics argued that the blues-playing Watson had gained the allegiance of a young and predominantly African American disco-listening audience.

Watson continued to record successful funk albums for DJM, scoring R&B hits with *What the Hell Is This?* (1979), *Love Jones* (1980), and the rap song "Telephone Bill" (1980). After switching to A&M Records and releasing the album *Strike on Computers* (1984), Watson once again slipped into obscurity. He had drug problems and toured in Europe, earning the tag "Godfather of Funk" in France. His lasting impact, however, could be heard in the recordings of hip-hop artists such as ICE CUBE, SNOOP DOGGY DOGG, and DR. DRE, who sampled Watson's music. After a recording hiatus of almost ten years, he returned with *Bow Wow* in 1994, another funk album. In the opening track

he declared: "Johnny G. Is Back!" The album was nominated for a Grammy as Best Contemporary Blues Album and spawned the notable R&B hit "Hook Me Up," which introduced Watson to a new generation of funk fans. Watson also received the Pioneer Award from the Rhythm & Blues Foundation, an organization providing funding for black performers cheated of their royalties. On 17 May 1996 Watson suffered a heart attack onstage in Yokohama, Japan, and died later on the same day. He was survived by his mother, his wife, and two children. Watson's main contributions to popular music and African American history were his pioneering guitar work and his mixing of blues and funk, updating the former with a cocky attitude and irresistible disco rhythms.

FURTHER READING

Nathan, David. "'Guitar' Watson Finds a New Audience," *Billboard*, 18 Feb. 1995.

Obrecht, Jas. "Johnny 'Guitar' Watson: Razor-Blade-Totin' Guitar," *Guitar Player* (Feb. 1982).

Palmer, Robert. "Johnny (Guitar) Watson Plays Blues for Blacks," *New York Times*, 19 June 1977.

Vincent, Ricky. *Funk* (1996).

Obituary: *New York Times*, 19 May 1996.

DISCOGRAPHY

Ain't That a Bitch (DJM 3).

Bow Wow (Bellmark 51007).

The Very Best of Johnny "Guitar" Watson (Rhino 75702).

ULRICH ADELT

Watson, Lauren (1940–), antipoverty organizer and founder of the Denver, Colorado, chapter of the Black Panther Party, was born in San Francisco, California. He was one of three children born to Ruth Watson. Along with his sister Sandra (who became a journalist) and brother Clarke (later a journalist and energy entrepreneur) Watson moved to Denver after his parents divorced in 1950. They lived with Watson's uncle, "Private-Car-Reed," one of the many railroad porters who constituted the core of Denver's early middle-class, African American Five Points community. Lauren graduated from Manual High School in 1957 and then briefly attended the city's Metropolitan State College.

He moved to Los Angeles for a brief time and held odd jobs including work as a security guard at a medium-security prison. After being inspired by his tangential participation in the 1965 Watts riot, he convinced the editor at *The Denver Blade* to send him to interview the Black Panther leader HUEY NEWTON in jail. Energized by the riot and the interview, he returned to Denver and founded a local chapter of the Black Panther Party.

The first public appearance of Denver's Black Panthers was in the summer of 1967 at a joint demonstration with Rudolpho "Corky" Gonzales's Crusade for Justice to protest the deaths of two young men at the hands of Denver police—Eugene "Skijump" Cook, who was African American, and Louis Pinedo, who was Hispanic. The Party had a brief but sensational career, though its membership was a matter of some dispute (police felt there were no more than a dozen hardcore members, while Watson claimed up to one hundred).

After the assassination of the Reverend Dr. MARTIN LUTHER KING Jr., Watson and Gonzales formed the "Black-Brown Unity Council." They sought to reduce violence and promote minority political representation; they fought for reforms around economic justice and police brutality issues; and they raised awareness about the need for school curricula that included the history and cultures of their peoples. Watson proclaimed, "most of the education taught in Denver Public Schools is racist education teaching white supremacy" (*Denver Post*, 5 Apr. 1968).

His summer of 1968 included multiple arrests, involvement with the city's War on Poverty including participation in the Denver Model Cities program, and an 8 August marriage to the VISTA worker Mary Lou Brooks.

The arrests were at least in part a planned strategy of ongoing conflict with law enforcement and the existing power structure. Charges spanned the mundane, from failure to use his turn signal while driving to the standard trinity used against civil rights radicals: resisting arrest, refusing to obey police, or interference with an officer. But there were also charges related to violence, physical harm, and property damage. On 2 October, when Watson faced felony charges connected to the September "Dry Cleaning riot," the director of the Colorado Civil Rights Commission called the charges frivolous and said, "I think law and order has become a euphemism for a bit of racism" (*Denver Post*, 4 Oct. 1968). He was acquitted, but, while awaiting trial, Watson held an anti–Vietnam War rally with seven fellow Panthers dressed in black standing behind him. The crowd of 350 to 400 cheered as he accused the D.A. of using attacks on the Panthers to enforce white supremacy.

Run-ins with police often assumed a theatrical air. The morning after the 5 November election

of President Richard Nixon, Denver police officer Robert Cantwell shouted "White Power, now!" in front of Watson's home. A car chase ensued, with Watson arrested on multiple charges: all were dropped except a resisting arrest charge. Owing to widespread interest, National Education Television—the predecessor to the Public Broadcasting System—produced an award-winning documentary, *The City and County of Denver vs. Lauren Watson*. This was the first time cameras recorded a courtroom trial in its entirety. The all-white jury voted to acquit, but in the closing scene, Watson blazed in defiance: "I should've resisted arrest; I should've killed both of them when they came in the door; and that would have been justice to me."

Armed, wearing the Panthers' black uniform, and with a .50-caliber bullet around his neck, he intentionally portrayed a threatening image. However, he and wife Mary Lou spent time on multiple nonviolent community projects, including free breakfast programs for children, tutoring students in black history, and conducting other community outreach programs.

His community organizing work also included involvement with Denver's Model Cities program as an elected representative. Then U.S. Senator Peter H. Dominick and John McClellan, the "Senate's top crime buster," ordered "an investigation into reports that a Denver black power group is using federal funds to buy guns." Watson's response was a boast that he would continue to lead armed patrols "against murdering racist police and Minutemen" (*Rocky Mountain News*, 30 July 1968). Program organizers argued on his behalf that the aim of the program was "to solve the very problems that the militant complain about" and that their inclusion aims to find "constructive rather than destructive" answers. As Watson only received sixty dollars for his work, the accusation that federal funds were being used to buy guns for the Panthers proved unfounded, but Watson bowed out nonetheless. Adding further insult, in 1970 Watson either left or was purged from the Panther Party based on his nonsanctioned involvement with the War on Poverty.

In 1971 his first son, Hasira, was born, and then a second son, Kahlil, came two years later. Mary Lou reported that Watson was a wonderful father, one of a new generation of men who changed diapers and held their children in public. In need of a job, he returned to the Model Cities program and eventually led the Resident Participation of Denver Incorporated, a nonprofit arm of the larger program. At one point in that capacity he led a sit-in demonstration of Denver Mayor William McNichols's office—he was accompanied by future Denver Mayor Wellington Webb. However, under the Nixon administration the Model Cities program was ultimately defunded, and Watson found himself again seeking employment. Because of his former affiliation with the Panthers, he was ineligible for federal employment. He tried mainstream politics, including attendance at the first National Black Political Convention in Gary, Indiana. In 1975 he made an unsuccessful bid for City Council.

None of those efforts led to much substance. In 1978 he earned a degree in public management, only to quit a job after a few years with the state labor department. By 1980, he and Mary Lou divorced. He worked for the Urban League's weatherization program, ran a record store, and held other minor jobs, but eventually quit work after being diagnosed with narcolepsy.

In 1981 he was convicted of shooting an off-duty fireman, his only conviction (this has improperly been reported as the reason for his termination with the Model Cities program). After three months in prison he was released after then-state senator Regis Groff and city councilman Hiawatha Davis intervened on his behalf. He was arrested again in 1994, this time for dealing crack cocaine. After weeks in a holding cell, charges were dropped: a federal Drug Enforcement Administration officer testified that "He delivered on time and on schedule at least five different times" during a sting operation, but Watson claimed the evidence had been planted by police. Later in life he granted occasional interviews to researchers and guest-taught in college history courses, but little else is known of his later life.

FURTHER READING

Brown, Fred. "Rights Official Assails Charges on Panther." *Denver Post*, 4 Oct. 1968.

Carter, Charles. "Minorities Voice Demands at Metropolitan Symposium." *Denver Post*, 5 Apr. 1968.

Forster, James. "Senate to Probe Denver Model Cities Program." *Rocky Mountain News*, 30 July 1968.

Sanders, Denis. *Trial: The City and County of Denver versus Lauren R. Watson*, Video documentary produced by Robert M. Fresco, directed by Harold Silver (1970).

Stephens, Ronald J., and La Wanna M. Larson, and the Black American West Museum. *African Americans of Denver* (2008).

BRET A. WEBER

Watson, Samuel Codes (15 Aug. 1832–13 Mar. 1892), political activist, politician, and the first African American to matriculate at the University of Michigan, was born in Saint James Parish, near Charleston, South Carolina, to an elite family of free blacks. Reportedly orphaned as a youngster, Samuel was sent to Washington, D.C., as the ward of the white Presbyterian minister William McLane. The District of Columbia was home to a handful of private schools for blacks during the 1840s, though which Watson may have attended or for how long is unknown. His academic accomplishments and private support were such, however, that at the age of seventeen he enrolled at the prestigious Phillips Academy at Andover, Massachusetts. Watson studied in the English department, which emphasized teacher training, rather than in the academy's classics program, which prepared young men for study at elite colleges in New England. Reportedly disillusioned over southern slavery and unhappy at the prospect of becoming a teacher, Watson signed on to serve on a U.S. Navy ship that surveyed America's Atlantic coastline. Meanwhile his brother, whose name is unknown, reportedly enrolled at Oberlin College, in Ohio, one of the few American colleges then open to black students. Samuel then decided to study medicine, and he moved to Oberlin in the summer of 1853, only to learn that the college had no facilities for medical studies.

He briefly settled in Saint Thomas, a small town in Ontario, Canada, halfway between Toronto and Detroit, and about twenty miles south of London, Ontario, which was then known as "Canada West." Saint Thomas was one of dozens of small towns along the northern edge of Lake Ontario to which fugitive slaves and free blacks flocked in the early 1850s. There Watson began to focus his energies on the study of science and medicine, obtaining an apprenticeship with Dr. C. B. Hall. With Jesse Earl Wilson, also an apprentice of Dr. Hall's from Saint Thomas, Watson made his way to Ann Arbor, Michigan, where the University of Michigan had opened a medical school in 1850. Apparently unaware that the fair-haired, well-educated Watson was of mixed-race parentage, administrators at the medical school enrolled both Watson and Wilson on 1 October 1853, 2 of 154 medical students set to study medicine during the new fall term. Jesse Wilson's race is unknown, making young Samuel Watson the first black known to have matriculated at the University of Michigan.

In the 1850s the curriculum at Michigan's medical school emphasized anatomical study, dissections, and the study of surgery to heal serious injuries and correct severe birth defects. Watson was more interested in the competing philosophy of homeopathy, which emphasized applied chemistry, the compounding and administering of drugs, and the psychological well-being of patients, whose ills could be addressed by introducing drugs that produced similar but much less severe symptoms than those for which the patient sought treatment. The school's faculty adamantly rejected homeopathy. Students were taught that homeopathy was quackery, and some of them formed a student society and launched a student medical journal devoted to attacking homeopathy and its practitioners. Perhaps for this reason Watson did not complete his medical degree at the University of Michigan, although he was continuously enrolled there between 1853 and 1856.

Unlike most other medical students in Ann Arbor, Watson continued to travel between, and perhaps during, the academic terms. By October 1855 he had ceased listing his permanent address as Saint Thomas, Canada West, and instead gave his home as Washington, D.C. This may have been due to his growing involvement in emancipation politics. Watson had become the Ann Arbor–based correspondent in a network of black activists who recorded their observations on local antislavery feeling in Michigan and lower Ontario; the network included the black abolitionist leaders and newspaper publishers Thomas F. Cary and MARY ANN SHADD CARY, Thomas's wife, who later earned a law degree and was one of the period's most influential black journalists. Watson emerged as one of Mary Shadd Cary's closest friends and advisers. Unsettled in his medical studies, and perhaps unwelcome as a pro-homeopathy black student at the University of Michigan, Watson left Ann Arbor in the summer of 1856 for Cleveland. There he entered the widely respected Cleveland Homeopathic Medical College, which was part of the Cleveland Medical College. He graduated with an MD degree in March 1857.

For the next few years Watson moved frequently; he may have been in some legal trouble for his political activism with the Underground Railroad in southeastern Michigan and lower Ontario and for his associations with such abolitionists as Mary Cary, FRANCES ELLEN WATKINS HARPER, and John Brown. While in Ontario, he briefly practiced medicine in both Chatham and Toronto, and he traveled to the Frazier River area in British Columbia to try gold mining. Watson returned to the Detroit area in 1859 to work as a clerk on the passenger steamer *Whitney*, which operated between Detroit and Sandusky, Ohio. With the outbreak of the Civil War, Watson's political views evolved, from abolitionist activism to support for President Lincoln's Republican Party and Union strategy in the Civil War. In 1861 he married Sarah L. Cassey of Philadelphia, and in 1863 decided to establish his family in Detroit. Rather than practice medicine, however, he purchased a building at the corner of Jefferson Avenue and Beaubien Street, where he opened a drugstore and worked as its pharmacist. In 1867 he moved the business to the corner of Jefferson and Riopelle Street, where his clientele included both black and white customers. Watson began buying and renting out houses and commercial buildings across Detroit, and by 1867 one Detroit newspaper proclaimed him the city's wealthiest black property owner.

Watson's great passion, however, was for municipal and national black politics. In 1868 he helped Mary Cary obtain a teacher's license for Detroit's public schools, and in 1869 he sponsored her to represent Detroit's black workers at the Colored National Labor Union convention in Washington, D.C. Watson rented or arranged for large meeting halls in Detroit to be available to black speakers and often used his own drugstore to accommodate political meetings. In 1870 he was among the first blacks to be impaneled on a jury in the city of Detroit; the case was politically charged because the defendants, three white men, were accused of assaulting the black plaintiff. In a widely heralded decision said to illustrate black men's capacity to render justice, Watson and the all-black jury—which included black community leaders John D. Richards, Alexander Moor, George de Baptiste, James H. Binge, and Richard Gordon—found the white men not guilty.

In 1874 Watson's wealth as well as his influence with both blacks and whites spurred his decision to run for elected office. The Republican Party approved his nomination as a candidate for the Michigan state legislature. One optimistic Republican journalist claimed the party's decision would mark "the death of the last remains of colorphobia in Michigan." Although he was the first black to run for a state office, Watson was defeated—as were most Republican candidates that year. In 1875 the party nominated him to run for election to the Detroit Board of Estimates, a municipal taxation body. A suspicious printing error on the ballots invalidated hundreds of pro-Watson votes. The Democrat who "won" the race voluntarily resigned, allowing Watson to take the seat in 1876. Samuel Watson thereby became the first black Republican to hold office in the city of Detroit.

Watson again ran for the state legislature in 1876 and was again defeated. His interest in local politics had not obscured his awareness of the continuing discrimination against blacks in the late Reconstruction South. He accused the Democrats there of blocking "every measure looking toward the freeing and education of the colored people," and called for an immediate end to the "shotgun oppression of the colored people in Mississippi, Louisiana and South Carolina." In 1881 he organized the Oak & Ivy Club, which brought together Detroit's black intelligentsia and elite business-people to discuss race issues on both a local and national scale.

Although in 1882 Watson was elected to the Detroit City Council as a Republican, he was becoming disenchanted with his party's apparent neglect of blacks' political demands, both in the South and in Detroit itself. To placate him, local party officials nominated him to attend the national Republican Party convention in 1884. Watson thus became the first black delegate at a major national political convention. That year, he was also dispatched as Michigan's only black representative to the Louisiana World's Exposition, in New Orleans, where he oversaw the small exhibit on Michigan's black population.

However, his dissatisfaction with the Republican Party's policies on race issues was not assuaged. In 1888 Watson, a pillar of the black wing of Michigan's Republican organization, defected to the Democratic Party. Citing the Republicans' history of broken promises to blacks, particularly in the South, he formed a new association, the Independent Colored Democratic Club of Detroit. His goal was to provide Detroit's black voters with alternatives to the major parties' candidates. Most of his longtime political associates, both white and black, deserted him; some were so devastated that they appealed to FREDERICK DOUGLASS to intervene. Douglass, who had remained loyal to the Republican Party, was dismissive of his old ally, writing to the prominent Detroit lawyer D. AUGUSTUS STRAKER in August 1888 that Detroit's black voters would not follow Watson, not least because his fair coloring and light skin gave "not the slightest evidence of colored blood." Depressed and humiliated, but locally well regarded and very wealthy, Samuel Watson died in Detroit after several bouts of pneumonia in March 1892.

FURTHER READING
Calkins, Laura M. "Samuel Codes Watson," *Michigan History* 86, 1 (Jan.-Feb. 2002).
Katzman, David. *Before the Ghetto: Black Detroit in the Nineteenth Century* (1973).
Rhodes, Jane. *Mary Ann Shadd Cary: The Black Press and Protest in the Nineteenth Century* (1998).
Simmons, William J. *Men of Mark: Eminent, Progressive and Rising* (1887).

LAURA M. CALKINS

Watt, Mel (26 Aug. 1945–), attorney and U.S. congressman, was born Melvin Luther Watt in Charlotte, North Carolina, the son of Graham E. Watt and Evelyn Mauney Watt. His great-grandfather, Wesley Mauney, had been a slave in nearby Gaston County but became a successful businessman. Watt's parents were divorced when he was five, and his mother, who had her first child when she was thirteen and raised Watt and his two older brothers in a house with no electricity and no indoor plumbing, worked as a domestic and school janitor. She eventually earned her GED certificate and had a long career with the U.S. Postal Service.

As a student at York Road High School, Watt drove a school bus to help support his family. While there he won his first protest against racial discrimination by convincing school district authorities to give his still-segregated school a new bus, rather than, as had been the custom, the castoffs of predominately white schools.

Following graduation in 1963, he entered the University of North Carolina at Chapel Hill, and four years later earned his bachelor of business administration degree with the highest academic average in the business school and Phi Beta Kappa honors. He married Eulada Paysour in 1968, and, after completing his J.D. degree at Yale Law School in 1970, he returned to Charlotte to join the firm of Chambers, Stein, Ferguson, and Lanning, which was beginning to distinguish itself in the field of civil rights litigation.

During the next twenty-two years Watt practiced law, was elected to be the first black president of the Mecklenburg County Bar (1988–1989), and served as campaign manager for his friend HARVEY GANTT in his successful race to become the first African American mayor of Charlotte in 1983 and again in 1990 in Gantt's unsuccessful bid to unseat Jesse Helms for the U.S. Senate.

In 1984 Watt was appointed to fill a vacancy in the North Carolina state senate. His colleagues recognized him for his integrity and forthrightness, and Senator Charles Hipps (D-Haywood) described him as "the conscience of the Senate ... He said some things that needed to be said when everybody was afraid to say them" (Morrill). The memory of his own childhood without a father remained strong within him, however, and after serving only one term Watt decided not to seek public office again until his sons finished high school.

By 1992 Watt's elder son, Brian, had graduated from Yale, and his younger son, Jason, was a freshman there. At the same time, the 1990 census, the requirements of congressional redistricting, and intervention by the U.S. Justice Department led the North Carolina General Assembly to create two predominantly African American districts to represent the state in the U.S. House of Representatives. With his children grown, Watt decided to reenter politics and run for the new Twelfth District seat that covered parts of the highly urbanized Piedmont, including his hometown, Charlotte. In spite of the strength of the field—one of his opponents was a much better known African American state legislator—Watt won the Democratic primary and beat his Republican opponent by a margin of 70 percent to 28 percent. He and EVA CLAYTON, the winner of the First District seat in the mostly rural eastern part of the state, became the first two African Americans to represent North Carolina in the House of Representatives since GEORGE WHITE in 1901. In the years since his initial election, Watt has typically prevailed over his opponent by a margin of two to one.

When Watt entered Congress in 1993, his district ran 165 miles along Interstate 85 from Charlotte to Greensboro to Durham and was 57 percent black. Throughout the 1990s, critics of the unusually long and narrow shape of the district raised issues of racial gerrymandering and repeatedly contested its validity in federal court. Watt was not directly involved in the legal disputes, but he defended the district as being based on a community of interest, which, he argued, made better sense than defining congressional districts by geographic boundaries. After the boundaries had been changed twice by lower courts, the U.S. Supreme Court finally upheld the constitutionality of the plan in 2001. By 2006 the percentages of blacks and whites in the district were almost equal—45 percent and 47.2 percent—with approximately 7 percent Hispanic and 2 percent Asian.

Watt's district includes all or most of the city centers of Charlotte, Greensboro, High Point, and Winston-Salem and is home to two of the nation's largest banks—Bank of America and Wachovia. Consequently, he sought and won an appointment to the House Financial Services Committee in his first term, and, as a result of the Democratic Party's victory in the 2006 election, he became chairman of the Oversight and Investigations Subcomittee in the 110th Congress. He is the sixth ranking Democrat on the House Judiciary Committee, having served on that committee since his arrival in Congress. In addition, he was on the Joint Economic Committee from 2001 to 2004.

Watt's visibility in Congress and engagement with issues has led to his emergence as a leading spokesman for the Democratic Party. On the Financial Services Committee, he supported efforts to expand access to affordable housing and to increase corporate responsibility while at the same time being attentive to the needs of his business constituents. On the Judiciary Committee, he opposed the impeachment of President Clinton, was a major negotiator for the extension of the Voting Rights Act, and consistently defended individual liberties while seeking to balance the need to provide for greater homeland security following 9/11.

Watt opposed the USA Patriot Act of 2001 and he voted against the resolution to authorize the use of force against Iraq the following year. He was among leaders of the Congressional Black Caucus who spoke most forcefully in urging Ralph Nader not to run for president lest he dilute the Democratic vote against George W. Bush in 2004, and in 2005 he was unanimously elected chair of the caucus. He has also been on *Ebony*'s list of most influential blacks in America since his election in 1992.

FURTHER READING

Morrill, Jim. "Candidness of Freshman Mel Watt Drew Limelight, N.C. Senate's Notice," *Charlotte Observer* (6 June 1985).

Newsome, Melba. "Why Won't They Just LEAVE Mel Watt ALONE," *Charlotte* 6 (Sept. 2001).

Perlmutt, David. "Watt: 12th District Can Build Consensus," *Charlotte Observer* (30 Apr. 1992).

Perlmutt, David. "Watt's Success Fulfills His Mother's Wish," *Charlotte Observer* (28 Feb. 2007).

U.S. Congress. *2005–2006 Official Congressional Directory: 109th Congress* (2005).

Winick, Stephen. "We've Come This Far by Faith: An African-American Family Reunion Turns One Hundred," *Folklife Center News* 27 (Fall 2005).

ROBIN BRABHAM

Wattleton, Alyce Faye (8 July 1943–), nurse, organization executive, and reproductive and women's rights activist, was born in St. Louis, Missouri, the only child of George and Ozie Wattleton. Wattleton's mother was a charismatic preacher who traveled the revival circuit for the fundamentalist Church of God. As a result her father worked at an ever-changing series of construction and factory jobs, and Wattleton often lived with church members during the school year while her parents were on the road. Wattleton's childhood experiences of traveling with her parents taught her a great deal about the second-class status held by black Americans in the 1940s and 1950s. But she also learned important lessons about standing up for herself. One example she always remembered was that when her father stopped for gas in the South, he would ask the attendant if they had toilet facilities for blacks: "If the attendant said they did, Daddy instructed him to fill the tank. If they didn't we would drive on until we found a station that did" (Wattleton, 35). At a time when it was more than challenging for a black woman to excel in any profession, Ozie Wattleton was a strong role model for her daughter, standing on her own at the pulpit and preaching to congregations, both black and white, all over the country.

After completing high school in Port Lavaca, Texas, Wattleton enrolled at Ohio State University, where she graduated in 1964 with a bachelor of science degree in Nursing. As her mother did, Wattleton embarked on a career of service, but her calling took her in a different direction. Her lifelong involvement in women's health issues began immediately, when in August 1964 Wattleton became a nursing instructor at the Miami Valley Hospital School of Nursing in Dayton, Ohio. Two years later she traveled to Columbia University in New York City, earning her master of science degree in Midwifery and Maternal and Infant Health in 1967. While in nursing school Wattleton became pointedly aware of the suffering women were subject to following botched abortions, a procedure that was then illegal. When she worked at Harlem Hospital during her time at Columbia, she saw that poor black women had even more limited health-care choices, especially with regard to reproductive issues.

After completing her education in 1967, Wattleton returned to Dayton, where she soon became assistant director of the Montgomery County Combined Public Health District, in charge of overseeing child health programs and pregnant teenagers. Although no longer providing direct patient care herself, as a public health administrator she was able to serve a larger population. It was also in Ohio that Wattleton met jazz musician and social worker Franklin Gordon. The two were

married in 1972, and their daughter Felicia was born in 1975; the couple divorced in 1981.

Wattleton's involvement in women's health issues deepened further when she was named executive director of the Dayton–Miami Valley chapter of Planned Parenthood in 1970. Never one to stand on the sidelines, Wattleton quickly made her voice heard at Planned Parenthood, the oldest and largest family-planning organization in the United States. In 1973 the Supreme Court ruling in *Roe v. Wade* decriminalized abortion in America, and although the procedure was not provided at the Dayton branch of Planned Parenthood, Wattleton soon found herself at the center of the abortion controversy.

In 1978 she left Ohio for New York when she was named president of the Planned Parenthood Federation of America (PPFA). At thirty-four years old Wattleton was not just the youngest president ever, she was the first woman in the role since the organization's founder, Margaret Sanger, stepped down in 1942, and she was the first African American to hold that position. During Wattleton's tenure, PPFA greatly expanded the services it offered to women. Under her leadership PPFA grew to include 170 affiliates in forty-nine states and the District of Columbia and more than nine hundred clinics nationwide. Most significantly, her leadership of PPFA occurred during a time when a woman's right to choose was coming under aggressive challenge by fundamentalist religious and ultra-conservative political factions. Wattleton quickly became a familiar and striking media presence and a fierce, unyielding advocate for reproductive rights, pushing for more active political involvement on the part of PPFA in shaping the political debate and bringing the organization onto the front lines in the battle for abortion rights.

In 1977 the federal government began restricting funding for abortions, and hundreds of violent attacks were aimed at clinics that provided abortions, but Wattleton refused to back down. She fought to secure federal funding for birth control and prenatal programs, stressing their importance to impoverished women both in the United States and abroad. In 1989 the pro-choice movement suffered a severe setback when the Supreme Court decision in the *Webster v. Reproductive Health Services* case allowed states to restrict abortions. As the public face of PPFA's dedication to reproductive rights for all women, Wattleton used this event to further mobilize supporters. Her steadfast commitment to the cause at hand never wavered, but Wattleton often found herself on the defensive, and her years on the front lines in the public debate about abortion began to take their toll.

In 1992 she resigned from the Planned Parenthood Federation, announcing her plans to host a television talk show. However, although a series of test shows were produced, the program never materialized. The following year, Wattleton was among ten African American women selected for induction into the National Women's Hall of Fame in Seneca Falls, New York. She helped to found the Center for Gender Equality, which later became the Center for the Advancement of Women, an independent not-for-profit education and advocacy institution committed to women's issues and dedicated to advancing women's equal participation at every level of society. In 1995 Wattleton was named president of the center, serving as a worldwide consultant on family planning and women's issues.

FURTHER READING

Wattleton, Faye. *Life on the Line* (1996).

Summers, Barbara, ed. *I Dream a World: Portraits of Black Women Who Changed America* (1989).

ELLEN BASKIN

Watts, André (20 June 1946–), pianist, was born in Nürnberg, Germany, the son of Sergeant Herman Watts, a career soldier, and Maria Alexandra Gusmits Watts, a Hungarian refugee. Watts lived on army posts in Germany before the family moved to Philadelphia, Pennsylvania, in 1954.

Watts's mother, who came from a musical family, introduced him to the violin when he was four. At seven Watts switched to the piano, taking lessons from his mother. Maria convinced her son to practice through stories about the devotion to his art of her countryman Franz Liszt, who became Watts's hero. He entered the Philadelphia Academy of Music to study under Doris Bawden, Clement Petrillo, and Genia Robinor. When he was nine Watts made his first public appearance with a Franz Joseph Haydn concerto as part of a children's concert given by the Philadelphia Orchestra. When he was fourteen he made his official debut with that orchestra, performing César Franck's *Symphonic Variations*.

During this period Watts practiced three or four hours a day while attending Catholic and Quaker schools, graduating from Lincoln Preparatory School in 1963. His parents divorced in 1962, and Maria supported herself and her son by working first as a secretary and later as an art gallery receptionist. Watts's big break occurred while he was still in high school. He won an audition to play in a New York Philharmonic Young People's Concert conducted by Leonard Bernstein. The concert was videotaped and televised by CBS on 15 January 1963. The critical acclaim for his performance of Liszt's Concerto No. 1 in E Flat resulted in overwhelming demand for tickets to his student recital at the Philadelphia Academy of Music the following week. Later that same month Glenn Gould became ill two days before his appearance with the New York Philharmonic, and Bernstein summoned the prodigy from Philadelphia. The 31 January performance, again of the Liszt concerto, was another critical success, as Watts became the first black instrumentalist to appear as a soloist during a regular Philharmonic concert since the turn of the twentieth century.

Despite considerable acclaim Watts limited his public appearances during the rest of 1963. After graduating from high school, he enrolled at the Peabody Conservatory of Music in Baltimore, studying under Leon Fleisher. Watts's part-time studies allowed him to perform several times with the New York Philharmonic, the American Symphony Orchestra, and Washington's National Symphony Orchestra in 1964–1966, playing works by Chopin, MacDowell, Rachmaninoff, Nicolia Rimsky-Korsakov, and Saint-Saëns. He made his European debut on 12 June 1966 with the London Symphony Orchestra, followed by an appearance with Amsterdam's Concertgebouw Orchestra. His New York recital debut came on 26 October 1966 at Philharmonic Hall.

Watts celebrated his twenty-first birthday by playing Johannes Brahms's B Flat Concerto with the Berlin Philharmonic, conducted by Zubin Mehta. That fall he began a three-month tour, sponsored by the U.S. Department of State, of sixteen cities in Asia and Europe. At Bernstein's invitation in January 1968, Watts played Brahms's Piano Concerto in B Flat with the New York Philharmonic to mark the fifth anniversary of his debut. Watts gave sixty-nine concerts in 1968, earning $6,000 to $7,000 for each. He played at the Boston Symphony Orchestra's inaugural concert at Constitution Hall in May 1969, performing Liszt's Piano Concerto no. 1, with President Richard M. Nixon in attendance. Watts had played at Nixon's inauguration the previous January.

Because of the demands of his concerts, studies, and practice (up to eight hours a day), Watts devoted little time to recording early in his career, issuing only two records, with his first, *The Exciting*

André Watts photographed between 1960 and 1965. (Library of Congress.)

Debut of André Watts, earning a Grammy as most promising new classical artist in 1964. On his twenty-first birthday, he signed an exclusive, long-term contract with Columbia Records. He graduated from Peabody in 1972.

Watts received some criticism during the era of black militancy for not being political. He was nevertheless for many a symbol of the civil rights movement for his quiet grace in paving the way for other African American classical musicians. As he became older, Watts assumed a professorial demeanor and talked frequently about the artist's responsibility to society. His causes included Performing Arts against AIDS. He also taught music at the University of Maryland beginning in 2000.

In addition to becoming the first African American concert pianist to attract international acclaim, Watts accomplished several other firsts, including the first full-length piano recital in television history in 1976 on PBS's *Live from Lincoln Center*. He has made many television appearances as performer and host, including Philadelphia Orchestra's centennial in 2000.

Before a December 2002 concert in Costa Mesa, California, Watts was rushed to a hospital for emergency surgery for a ruptured vein on the surface of his brain. He recovered quickly and resumed his concert tour.

Watts was notable for the passion and spontaneity displayed in his performances. Some critics, however, complained that Watts's style was too emotional. They acknowledged his skill at bravura music, such as Rachmaninoff, but felt his interpretation for more lyrical pieces, as with Chopin, was lacking. With his large hands spanning twelve keys and a left hand as strong as his right, Watts excelled at powerful playing. Though some commentators felt that Watts's skills deteriorated with age, Allan Kozinn of the *New York Times* praised a 2006 Carnegie Hall performance of Brahms's Second Piano Concerto with the Philadelphia Orchestra as his most focused in years.

Watts received honorary doctorates from Yale University (becoming, in 1973, the youngest person ever to receive this honor), Albright College, the University of Pennsylvania, Miami University of Ohio, Trinity College, and the Juilliard School of Music. He was also awarded an arts medal by Philadelphia's University of the Arts, the Order of Zaire, the Lincoln Center Medallion, the Avery Fisher Prize, the Gold Medal of Merit from the National Society of Arts and Letters, and the Peabody Conservatory's Distinguished Alumni Award.

FURTHER READING
Current Biography Yearbook (1968).
Gillespie, John, and Anita Gillespie. *Notable Twentieth-Century Pianists: A Bio-Critical Sourcebook* (1995).
Mach, Elyse. *Great Pianists Speak for Themselves* (1980).
Smith, Jessie Carney, ed. *Notable Black American Men* (1999).

MICHAEL ADAMS

Watts, Frederick (1904–7 Apr. 2007), psychologist, was born Frederick Payne Watts to Charles Watts, who performed house repairs and worked as a farmer, and Harriett Watts, a homemaker in Staunton, Virginia. Watts was one of five siblings raised in a household where both parents valued and promoted education and learning and encouraged their children to excel academically and professionally. Following his graduation from Dunbar High School in Washington, DC, he attended Howard University in 1922, where he gradually found himself drawn to the field of psychology and away from his original interest in ophthalmology. One of his early mentors was Albert Sidney Beckham, who established the psychology laboratory at Howard.

Watts received his B.A. in 1926, having majored in Psychology and French. He remained at Howard University on a teaching fellowship, earning his M.A. in Psychology in 1927. Following a one-year stint teaching at Kittrell College in North Carolina, he became a full-time member of Howard's psychology department in 1928.

In 1936 Watts and his colleague at Howard University, F. C. Sumner, collaborated on a study appearing in the *American Journal of Psychology* entitled "Rivalry between Uniocular Negative After-Images and the Vision of the Other Eye." Their examination documented the "phenomenon" of afterimages experienced as a result of the human eye fixating on particular color objects for precise periods of time. In 1941 Watts completed his doctoral work at the University of Pennsylvania, becoming only the fourth African American to earn a Ph.D. in the field of Psychology in the United States. That same year he published an article based on his dissertation research, entitled "A Comparative Clinical Study of Delinquent and Non-Delinquent Negro Boys," in the *Journal of Negro Education,* analyzing the behavior and aptitude of ninety-two black adolescents assigned to Washington, DC's Industrial Home School for Colored Children by the city's juvenile court. He surmised that the youths' behavioral problems did not stem from developmental deficiencies, but were based primarily on environmental issues, particularly a dearth of guidance and support from family members, specifically their parents.

Watts's thriving academic career was temporarily stalled in 1942 with his conscription into the U.S. Army, where he was eventually promoted to the rank of captain in the Adjutant General's Office. Watts was assigned to the induction station in Baltimore, Maryland, where he assisted in preparing preinduction procedures, psychological examinations, and counseling services for new recruits. Even before being called to duty, Watts had enjoyed a long-standing relationship with the armed forces, having served in Howard University's Army ROTC unit, where he received training and scholarship money to help pay for his studies. Following the end of World War II he worked for the Veterans Administration in Philadelphia as the head clinical psychologist until 1948, when he resumed his position as professor of psychology at Howard.

From 1948 to his eventual retirement in 1970, Watts emerged as a leading figure in Howard University, serving a variety of roles including teacher, researcher, and administrator. His most important and permanent contribution was founding and overseeing the Liberal Arts Counseling Service, which provided psychotherapeutic counseling to students as well as guidance regarding their academic performance and course requirements. In 1961 the school's administration expanded his creation into a University Counseling Service with Watts serving as its director. During his final year at Howard, Watts and the clinical psychologist James Stanfiel, who also worked at the counseling center, published the article "Freshmen Expectations and Perceptions of the Howard University Environment," which analyzed students' overall experiences both positive and negative at the university during the peak of the civil rights era (1965–1966). The study found that Howard freshmen began their studies with very high, often unattainable expectations about college life and were particularly optimistic about their future employment and overall economic prospects, as well as the possibility of earning postgraduate degrees. Watts and Stanfiel concluded that their positive outlook was largely based on the belief that education represented a cure-all for young African Americans and would enable them to overcome discrimination and make a genuine impact on society. Both authors recommended that such lofty ideals needed to be tempered and that Howard's Counseling Center could go a long way in preparing freshmen for the challenges ahead.

Watts's legacy was further cemented through his training and mentoring of future generations of psychologists, most notably Kenneth Clark and Mamie Clark, who went on to establish the Northside Center for Child Development in Harlem. The Clarks' research on child development and their testimony in the case of *Briggs v. Elliott* was an important precursor to the seminal ruling in *Brown v. Board of Education* (1954).

Watts died of congestive heart failure at the age of 103 on 7 April 2007. Watts and his wife, Louise Armstead, who passed away in 1974, had four daughters.

FURTHER READING

Guthrie, Robert V. *Even the Rat Was White: A Historical View of Psychology* (1998).

Rose, Anne C. *Psychology and Selfhood in the Segregated South* (2009).

DÁLIA LEONARDO

Watts, J. C. (18 Nov. 1957–), athlete, minister, political leader, entrepreneur, and commentator, was born Julius Caesar Watts Jr. in Eufaula, McIntosh County, Oklahoma, the fifth of six children of Helen

Pierce and J. C. "Buddy" Watts Sr., a policeman, preacher, cattle owner, handyman, and local entrepreneur. The Eufaula area, part of the Creek Nation Indian Territory until 1907, had a historical tradition of Native American slaveholding, and racial segregation persisted there during Watts's youth. Only blacks were allowed to attend Watts's first elementary school, and Eufaula's only public swimming pool excluded blacks until his father and his uncle, Wade Watts, who later became head of the NAACP's Oklahoma chapter and a member of the U.S. Civil Rights Commission, successfully lobbied to open it to all races. Watts had other experiences with segregation. Until he was in high school, whites sat on the ground level of Eufaula's local movie theater, while blacks sat in the balcony. Transferring from the all-black BOOKER T. WASHINGTON Elementary two blocks away, Watts became one of two blacks to enter Eufaula's previously all-white Jefferson Davis Elementary School in 1965. After he was elected Eufaula High's first black junior-senior prom king, he and the white queen agreed to dispense with the traditional kiss because of local racial feelings.

A gifted all-around athlete, Watts starred as a running and passing quarterback for Eufaula High's football team, and he played basketball and baseball as well. He first gained statewide attention as a sophomore by running seventy-six yards for a touchdown as Eufaula routed Oklahoma's then top-ranked high school football team, the Sallisaw Black Diamonds, 41–7. During his senior year in 1975–1976, Watts was Eufaula's team captain in football and a starter on its basketball team. He was named the Oklahoma High School Football Player of the Year and Athlete of the Year as well as a high school football All-American. Also active in student government, Watts was Eufaula's second black student body president.

During his senior year Watts accepted a scholarship to play football for the University of Oklahoma (OU), turning down offers from other leading schools. In 1977, while at OU, he married Frankie Jones of Eufaula. They had five children. Watts also had a sixth child from a high school relationship. He was an outstanding college football player. As OU's starting quarterback in 1979 and 1980, Watts led OU to twenty-one wins and three losses. In both seasons OU was undefeated in the Big Eight Conference, defeated Florida State University in the Orange Bowl games, and finished ranked third nationally. Watts was named the most valuable player in both of OU's Orange Bowl games. While at OU, Watts preached with the Fellowship of Christian Athletes. He earned a degree in journalism in 1981.

After graduating from college, Watts played professional football in Canada, mostly for the Ottawa Rough Riders, where his mix of running and passing skills was more useful than in the National Football League and height was less important because of differences in the Canadian game. By that year five of the nine starting quarterbacks in the Canadian Football League (CFL) were black. Watts was named the most valuable offensive player in the CFL's Grey Cup championship game in 1982. He averaged 6.7 yards per run during his CFL career and more than 3,000 passing yards for Ottawa in 1984 and 1985.

Watts next became youth minister at Sunnylane Baptist Church in Del City, an Oklahoma City suburb, where he could both work with younger people and preach. He became the first African American elected to statewide office in Oklahoma when in 1990 he was elected to the three-member Oklahoma Corporations Commission, which regulated telephone, oil, gas, and trucking businesses. He became chair of the commission in 1993. Previously a Democrat, Watts had changed his political registration to Republican in 1989, explaining that he thought Democrats had taken black voters for granted without reciprocating and that his values of faith, family, hard work, small-scale entrepreneurship, and personal responsibility were closer to those of Republicans.

In 1994 Watts successfully ran for an open congressional seat in Oklahoma's largely white Fourth Congressional District, receiving 52 percent of the vote and becoming the second African American in a white majority district. During the campaign his white Democratic opponent used an old picture of Watts with an Afro in an unsuccessful attempt to portray him as a radical. Watts campaigned as a supporter of the Republicans' 1994 Contract with America, which promised to promote small business, reduce the size of government, and lower taxes while avoiding potentially divisive social issues.

Watts had received national notice as a political figure even before 1994, having seconded President George H. W. Bush's nomination at the 1992 Republican National Convention. Once in Congress, Watts made it clear that he intended to follow his own independent agenda, emphasizing private initiative and personal responsibility in dealing with social problems, declining to join the Congressional Black Caucus (CBC) because he wanted to be neither pro-CBC nor anti-CBC, and advancing an approach to affirmative action that included race-based preferences in college admissions. His profile remained high throughout his years in Congress. He spoke at the Republican National Convention in 1996, received the 1996 Junior Chamber of Commerce's Ten Outstanding Young Americans Award, and gave the Republican response to President Bill Clinton's 1997 State of the Union Address. From 1998 to 2002 Watts was chair of the House Republican Conference, the House Republicans' fourth-ranking leadership position.

As a congressman Watts's particular interests included community improvement and redevelopment, education, national defense, and African development. He was co-author of the American Community Renewal and New Markets Act, which provided tax and other financial incentives for private investment in low-income and distressed communities and finally passed in 2000 after years of effort. He promoted the use of school vouchers to enable students to escape poor schools; favored welfare reforms, including time limits on welfare benefits; voted for free trade; sought an increased role in social services for faith-based organizations; and pushed for food and medical aid for Africa. During his tenure in Congress he served as a member of the House Armed Forces, Banking, and Transportation and Infrastructure Committees and on such special committees as the House Select Committee on Homeland Security and the Special House Oversight Committee on Terrorism. Watts's reelection margins increased each year, to 58 percent in 1996, 62 percent in 1998, and 65 percent in 2000, before he chose not to run for reelection in 2002.

In early 2003, within weeks of leaving Congress, Watts cofounded the Coalition for AIDS Relief in Africa, became a fellow of the Mercatus Center (global economic development), was elected to the boards of directors of Burlington Northern Santa Fe Corporation, Clear Channel Communications, Inc., Dillard's, Inc., and Terex Corporation, and was appointed by President George W. Bush to the West Point Board of Visitors. Watts founded and chaired or became chief executive officer of a number of private companies, working in such areas as government relations, workforce training, low-income housing, project management, and farm equipment sales. In the nonprofit area, Watts cofounded the J. C. and Frankie Watts Foundation (youth training) and was elected a director of Africare and the Boy Scouts of America. He also became a syndicated newspaper columnist, a regular radio and television commentator, and a frequent guest preacher and speaker.

After Watts left Congress in 2003, there were no more African American Republicans in the House until 2011, when Representatives Tim Scott of South Carolina and Allen West of Florida were part of the GOP takeover of the House in the 112th Congress. In 2009 he contemplated a run for Governor of Oklahoma, but decided not to run, citing business commitments, including his efforts to launch a new African American focused television channel.

FURTHER READING

Watts, J. C., Jr., with Chriss Winston. *What Color Is a Conservative? My Life and My Politics* (2002).

Dozier, Ray. *The Oklahoma Football Encyclopedia* (2006).

Lutz, Norma Jean. *J. C. Watts* (2000).

Switzer, Barry, with Bud Shrake. *Bootlegger's Boy* (1990).

STEVEN B. JACOBSON

Wayans, Keenen Ivory (8 June 1958–), actor, comedian, writer, and director, was born in New York City, the second of nine children born to Howell and Elvira Wayans. Wayans's father was a supermarket manager and his mother a social worker.

Wayans attended Seward Park High School in New York. After graduation he won a scholarship to Tuskegee University but left prior to graduation to work in stand-up comedy in the late 1970s. He achieved some success in New York but moved to Los Angeles to pursue a career in television and film. He debuted in television on a pilot for a sitcom called *Irene* (1981) and then signed a development deal with NBC in 1981. During this time he also had bit parts on *ChiPs* (1982) and *Cheers* (1982). From 1983 to 1984 he appeared regularly on *For Love and Honor*, a military soap opera that appeared on NBC.

In 1983 Wayans made his first film appearance in Bob Fosse's *Star 80*. Soon after he met EDDIE MURPHY, and made a small, but impressive appearance in Murphy's live concert film *Eddie Murphy Raw* (1987), directed by ROBERT TOWNSEND. Then, with Townsend, he coproduced and cowrote *Hollywood Shuffle* (1987), a satiric film about the prejudice and typecasting faced by black actors in Hollywood. The following year Wayans wrote, directed, and starred in *I'm Gonna Git You Sucka* (1988), another satiric work that targeted 1970s "blaxploitation" films pervasive during Wayans's adolescence. The film featured appearances by a number of African American personalities from the 1970s such as JIM BROWN, Antonio Fargas, ISAAC HAYES, and Bernie Casey. It also included performances by other Wayans family members, including brother Damon Wayans and sisters Kim and Nadia Wayans.

After the success of *I'm Gonna Git You Sucka*, Wayans was courted by the Fox television network.

In 1990 he made his television breakthrough with *In Living Color*, a sketch comedy show, for which he served as the creator, executive producer, writer, and a cast member from 1990 to 1992. The show based its irreverent humor on explosive racial comedy and targeted black stereotypes by depicting the most outlandish caricatures in order to undermine their power. One of the most cutting-edge shows on television in the early nineties, *In Living Color* straddled a thin line between being culturally and politically progressive and offensive. Called "bright, fresh and generally outrageous" by the *New York Times*, the Emmy Award–winning show featured ensemble comedy sketches and dance routines by the "Fly Girls." It launched the careers of Jim Carrey, CHRIS ROCK, JAMIE FOXX, Jennifer Lopez, Tommy Davidson, David Alan Grier, and Wayans's siblings, Kim, Damon, Dwayne, Marlon, and Shawn, who served as the show's DJ. Wayans left *In Living Color* after a series of disputes with Fox over the show's content and the network's push for reruns. Called "*Saturday Night Live* with attitude" by Wayans, *In Living Color* was one of Fox's most popular shows until it went off the air in 1994.

After he left television, Wayans returned to writing, directing, and starring in feature films with *A Low Down Dirty Shame* (1994), which, like *I'm Gonna Git You Sucka*, parodied blaxploitation film. Continuing with his penchant for parody, he produced *Don't Be a Menace to South Central While Drinking Your Juice in the Hood* (1996), targeting the content of "hood" films such as *Boyz in the Hood* and *Menace II Society*. In 1997 Wayans returned to television with a short-lived, syndicated late night talk show, *The Keenen Ivory Wayans Show*.

With the horror film satire *Scary Movie* (2000), cowritten by his brothers Marlon and Shawn, who both starred in the film, Wayans directed a multimillion dollar blockbuster spoof of the teenage horror film genre. This success was followed by *Scary Movie 2* (2001). He once again directed his brothers (who also cowrote the film) in *White Chicks* (2004) and *Little Man* (2006), the latter of which won BET Comedy Awards for directing and writing. In 2006 Keenan, Shawn, and Marlon created *Thugaboo* for Nickelodeon, an animated television series that revisited their early years growing up in a large family in the inner city.

In 2001 Wayans married Daphne Polk. The couple had five children before divorcing in 2004.

FURTHER READING

Bogle, Donald. *Primetime Blues: African Americans on Network Television* (2002).

Grey, Herman S. *Cultural Moves: African Americans and the Politics of Representation* (2005).

Haggins, Bambi. *Laughing Mad: The Black Comic Persona in Post-Soul America* (2007).

ALLYSON N. FIELD

we Langa, Wopashitwe Mondo Eyen (21 May 1947–), minister of information for the Black Panther Party of Omaha, Nebraska, and political prisoner, was born David Lewis Rice in Omaha, Nebraska, to Vera (Black) Rice and Otis Rice. We Langa graduated from Creighton Preparatory School in 1965, and for the next two years he took classes at Creighton University. He was active for a short while in the Nebraska Democratic Party but grew increasingly discouraged over the continued oppression of African Americans in North Omaha, Nebraska, and soon began writing social commentary for alternative newspapers. Police violence in the segregated community led to protests by young African Americans in North Omaha, including we Langa. Amid mounting police violence in Omaha, during the 1960s a local branch of the Black Panther Party formed. Its leaders declared their intention to serve as surveyors of police activities, to document incidents of physical and verbal abuse, and defend Nebraska's African American community. Between 1966 and 1969 four unarmed African Americans in Omaha were shot by police. One of the slain was a fourteen-year-old girl named Vivian Strong. She was hit in the back of the head by a policeman's bullet while she was running down the street, and her death infuriated and sickened the African American community.

The young activist joined the Nebraska chapter of the Black Panther Party early in 1969. His views at the time included a Marxist evaluation of the causes of racism in America. Determined to use his energy and intellect constructively, we Langa joined other Panther Party members in running breakfast programs for Omaha children and in establishing courses in legal rights and free health clinics.

On 17 August 1970 Omaha policeman Larry Minard was killed when a suitcase bomb exploded in a vacant house where he and fellow officers were responding to a 911 telephone call. Prosecutors argued that the call was made by fifteen-year-old Duane Peak. After first swearing that he had no knowledge of the bombing, Peak later "confessed" to placing the 911 call and to making the bomb. We Langa and Poindexter, the most outspoken members of the local Black Panther Party, were charged and convicted of conspiracy to commit murder and were convicted of murder; the conspiracy charge had been dropped. Immediately after the trial the charges against Peak were reduced to juvenile delinquency. The youth entered a witness protection program and left Omaha.

In 1990 Amnesty International wrote to Nebraska attorney general Robert Spire that "there is evidence to suggest that the authorities may have acted improperly to secure a conviction." The organization called for the immediate release of we Langa and Poindexter. In 1993 the Nebraska Parole Board voted unanimously to recommend the commutation of we Langa's sentence from life to a specific number of years. The following year the Nebraska Pardons Board refused to hear we Langa's case. In 1996 the Lincoln Justice Committee (of Nebraska) sent a resolution to the International Association of Democratic Lawyers arguing against the continued imprisonment of we Langa. In 2006 Peak, who was the state's chief witness against the Black Panther Party members, was required to submit to a test comparing his voice against the voice on the original 911 call. A voice expert determined that the voice on the tape was not Peak's. The prosecution's case, after thirty-five years, was effectively destroyed. Yet, Nebraska's judicial system had not released we Langa from prison as of July 2007.

University of Colorado professor Ward Churchill argued that we Langa and Poindexter were the targets of an outlawed Federal Bureau of Investigation domestic intelligence program called COINTELPRO (Counter Intelligence Program) designed by the FBI's late director J. Edgar Hoover. COINTELPRO aimed to destroy the credibility of the leadership of political organizations that Hoover disliked, and its victims were the targets of campaigns to criminalize their leadership. Churchill maintained that we Langa and Poindexter were convicted on the testimony of a teenager who had been threatened and intimidated by police.

In the mid-1990s we Langa's case was adopted by the Jericho movement, a national group whose mission is to identify and aid political prisoners in the United States. Former Nebraska Governor Frank Morrison argued that we Langa and Poindexter were convicted for their rhetoric, not for any crime they committed. Amnesty International subsequently argued that the improprieties in obtaining the convictions of we Langa and Poindexter we so extreme that the men should be given a new trial or released. We Langa's supporters over the years have included a number of celebrities, activists, and scholars, such as DANNY GLOVER and ANGELA DAVIS.

In spite of the decades he spent in prison, we Langa continued to contribute to the intellectual Africana community, writing extensively and publishing regular news columns and several volumes of poetry. His articles and short stories have been published in the *Black Scholar*, *Pacifica Review*, *Obsidian*, and other periodicals. He published six volumes of poetry, including *The Black Panther Is an African Cat* (2006). His plays *Different Dances* and *We Dance in Our Neighborhood* were performed by Ujima Youth Theatre in Nebraska and in New York. We Langa is a contributing author to the book *The Race: Matters concerning Pan-Afrikan History, Culture, and Genocide* (1992) and was one of a handful of scholars forging a new diasporic history and writing within an African-centered paradigm. His poem "Great Batlatuer" was featured in MALCOLM X: *By Any Means Necessary* by Walter Dean Myers (1993).

A visual artist as well as a writer, we Langa created contemporary art with African motifs in several mediums, including sculpture, sketches, and paintings. He maintained his role in the liberation struggle by working to educate other prisoners. He carried out many of his activities through his leadership in the Harambee African Culture Organization, which brings in speakers from the community, maintains a prison library, and encourages men to contribute positively to the community upon their release from prison.

FURTHER READING

Churchill, Ward. "Wages of COINTELPRO Still Evident in Omaha Black Panther Case," *ZNET Commentary*, 10 Mar. 1999.

Marlette, Marj. "New Habeas Corpus Action to Be Filed in Court," *Lincoln (Neb.) Sunday Journal and Star*, 16 Apr. 1978.

TEKLA ALI JOHNSON

Weaver, Anna Bolden (?July 1859–?1939), teacher, assistant principal, and school and orphanage founder, was born Anna Bolden, a slave, in Cumberland County, Virginia, on the plantation of Blake Woodson, clerk of the court. Her parents were Daniel and Delia Bolden. Anna remembered vividly her early life and the Civil War. During the latter days of the war, Colonel Archibald Hopkins of the federal forces, a brother of Mark Hopkins, president of Williams College in Williamstown, Massachusetts, took Anna's uncle home with him to be educated. After a few years Anna's uncle sent for her father and mother, and in 1865 they moved to

Williamstown. Anna received her early education in Williamstown at an academy with white boys and girls. Her father had taught himself to read and write by candlelight in an old icehouse while he was a slave, and he attended classes at the academy. The family moved again when Anna's father gained employment as a waiter at the Wilmot House in Stamford, Vermont. Later the family moved to an estate located between Troy and Albany, New York, where Anna attended school for four years with Scottish, English, Dutch, and Irish children. She and her two brothers were the only African American students in their school. At the end of the four years Anna's teacher, who had been studying at night, left to become a doctor in Albany. Anna's two brothers were sent to the Hampton Institute, but her mother felt Anna was too young to go away.

In September 1876 Anna moved to Albany, New York, to live with Mrs. T. C. Cooper until she graduated in 1880 from Albany High School. After graduation, Anna was offered teaching positions in St. Joseph, Missouri, in Tennessee, and in North Carolina. Her uncle, who had been educated for a clerkship, urged Anna to come to St. Joseph, but her mother said she should return to Virginia, where she was born.

Anna returned to Virginia in 1881, after receiving a letter from WILLIAM B. WEAVER to become an assistant teacher at the Bethel School, which was founded in 1865 as a private school for African Americans in Sassafras, Gloucester County, Virginia. Anna and William were later married in 1884. In 1888 William and Anna Weaver founded and opened the Gloucester Agricultural and Industrial School, to help African American students prepare for Hampton Institute. The school began in a storehouse and moved to the Weavers' residence in 1889. On 27 October 1890 the school opened on land purchased with the assistance of the American Missionary Association in Cappahosic, Gloucester County, Virginia. Anna served as the assistant principal of the school and later retired from teaching in the classroom to raise their five children. She continued to teach children in her sitting room. The Weavers retired from the Gloucester Agricultural and Industrial School in 1899. The school eventually closed in 1933, after providing farm training and secondary education for many black students who would not otherwise have been able to receive such an education.

The family moved to Elizabeth City County, Virginia, near Hampton, and opened the Weaver Orphan Home in 1904. By 1905, the orphan home had forty-five children. Four of the children had been returned to parents and seven were placed in Christian homes. Children were educated at the facility and received religious instruction until they found homes or were returned to their families. Those children who were old enough were taught to cook, do laundry, general housework, farming, and gardening. The staff of four workers and teachers would lead the children in these duties and at the same time teach and train them.

Over the years Anna cared for about four hundred orphans, children who would not have had a chance otherwise. "I have always had great confidence in you and your Orphanage and have from time to time referred friends to you. You have my full permission to refer to me as a friend and admirer of yourself and work. And I sincerely hope you may succeed in securing all the money necessary for the Weaver Home," wrote Archdeacon JAMES S. RUSSELL, principal of St. Paul's Normal and Industrial School, Lawrenceville, Virginia, in 1929. Following the death of her husband in 1929, Weaver, with the help of her daughter Ruth Weaver Fagan and son-in-law Spillman Fagan, continued the work of the orphan home until her death. The Weaver Orphan Home operated until 1965.

FURTHER READING

Fairfax, Colita Nichols. *Hampton, Virginia*, Black American series (2005).
Heinegg, Paul. *Free African Americans of North Carolina and Virginia* (1997).
"Key to Virginia Historic Landmarks in Gloucester County." Available online at www.gloucesterva.info/HistoricalLandmarks.pdf.

DEBRA THOMAS TRUHART

Weaver, Robert Clifton (29 Dec. 1907–18 July 1997), government administrator, writer, and educator, was born in Washington, D.C., the second son of Mortimer Grover Weaver, a postal clerk, and Florence Weaver Freeman. Robert's grandfather, ROBERT TANNER FREEMAN, was the first African American to graduate from Harvard Dental School (in 1869), and he practiced in Washington, D.C. Robert grew up in the middle-class, integrated neighborhood of Brookland and graduated from the prestigious Dunbar High School in 1925.

Robert then enrolled at Harvard College, which his older brother, Mortimer, also attended. Among his friends in college were RALPH BUNCHE, WILLIAM HENRY HASTIE, RAYFORD W. LOGAN, and John P. Davis. Robert and his brother had intended to become lawyers and open a joint practice, but when Mortimer died suddenly at age twenty-three, Robert decided to pursue an economics degree. He received his bachelor's degree in 1929 and his master's in 1931.

Despite his credentials, Weaver was unable to secure a teaching job at a white college, and he taught briefly at North Carolina Agricultural and Technical College in Greensboro before returning to Harvard in 1932 to defend his dissertation, "The High Wage of Prosperity." In 1933, along with Harvard Law School graduate John P. Davis, Weaver founded the Negro Industrial League (NIL) to lobby the federal government for fair treatment of black workers under the National Industrial Recovery Act, passed in order to deal with the nation's economic crisis. The NIL represented black workers before the National Recovery Administration, testified at congressional hearings, and in 1934 solicited support from the NAACP, the National Urban League, and other black organizations to establish an NIL office in Washington, D.C. Weaver's lobbying efforts brought him to the attention of Interior Secretary Harold Ickes, who in 1934 created in his department an Office on Negro Affairs and appointed Weaver as assistant to Clark Foreman, the white Atlantan chosen to run the office. Weaver joined a small but increasing number of black professionals in the federal government, a group known to some as the "Black Cabinet." While MARY MCLEOD BETHUNE was the leader of the group, Weaver provided much of the organizational direction. He fought to include blacks in projects funded by the Public Works Administration and battled racial discrimination by white southern employers.

In 1935 Weaver married Ella V. Haith, of Washington, D.C., and the couple adopted a child. Three years later Weaver became director of the Office of Race Relations at the United States Housing Authority (USHA). Charged with overseeing the construction of public housing across the country, he focused on ensuring that blacks received employment opportunities in the construction and management of public housing. Weaver's work at USHA serves as an early model for federal affirmative action programs. So, too, did his efforts for the National Defense Advisory Commission (NDAC), where he worked to reduce racial barriers within the defense industry and supported African Americans' integration into labor unions. When the NDAC was later incorporated into the Office of Production Management, Weaver

Robert Clifton Weaver, photographed in the Cabinet Room in Washington, D.C., 4 March 1966. (Library of Congress.)

served as the director of the Negro Training and Employment Branch and the Negro Manpower Service, where he oversaw a dramatic increase in black participation in the industrial workforce.

Despite his success in creating new opportunities for black workers, Weaver grew increasingly frustrated with the obstructionism of other federal officials, particularly in Congress. In 1944 he left the federal government to become the executive director of the Mayor's Committee on Race Relations in Chicago, which was established to prevent the eruption of racial violence that had plagued Detroit a year earlier. The committee possessed little influence, however, and he resigned less than a year later to lead the American Council on Race Relations. There, he continued to push to lower discriminatory barriers to housing in Chicago and elsewhere.

Throughout his years in the federal government, Weaver was a prolific writer, publishing at least twenty-seven articles on labor, housing, and race relations between 1933 and 1944. In 1946 he published his first book, *Negro Labor: A Problem of Today*, which examined the structure of the black labor market and the role of discrimination in limiting economic opportunities for blacks.

Weaver's second book, *The Negro Ghetto* (1948), examined the creation, growth, and current status of black urban life and was widely praised as one of the definitive studies of modern black America. The volume's research in the area of housing discrimination was used that year by the NAACP's THURGOOD MARSHALL in his brief to the U.S. Supreme Court in *Shelley v. Kraemer*, a landmark case that struck down restrictive covenants that discriminated against blacks seeking to purchase homes in certain neighborhoods. Because of his role in *Shelley*, Weaver became a leader in the fair housing movement, becoming president of the newly created National Committee against Discrimination in 1949.

Weaver moved to New York in 1949 to take the position of director of the Opportunity Fellowships Program at the John Hay Whitney Foundation. This program provided financial support to promising minority candidates pursuing advanced degrees. Among the people Weaver supported while he was director, and who went on to distinguished careers, were the economist ANDREW BRIMMER, the jurist A. LEON HIGGINBOTHAM, and the political scientist MARTIN KILSON.

New York Governor Averill Harriman appointed Weaver deputy state housing commissioner in 1955 and, a year later, state rent administrator. As head of the state's controversial rent-control program, Weaver was the first black member of the cabinet in New York State. When Harriman left office in 1959, it was reported that Weaver would be appointed borough president of Manhattan. However, Congressman ADAM CLAYTON POWELL JR. opposed the appointment, because Weaver was not a member of Powell's political club. That year Weaver was elected chairman of the board of directors of the NAACP.

Shortly thereafter, President-elect John F. Kennedy selected Weaver to be administrator of the Housing and Home Finance Agency (HHFA), the bureau that managed the federal government's housing programs. Weaver's nomination brought cheers from civil rights leaders, but southern members of Congress actively opposed him. After several days of grueling hearings, in which Weaver was accused of being a Communist, his nomination was approved.

Weaver quickly became the Kennedy administration's primary adviser on housing and urban affairs. He crafted and pushed through Congress the Housing Act of 1961, which expanded the nation's public housing program and provided housing for seniors. But Congress rejected the administration's proposal to elevate the HHFA to a cabinet-level Department of Urban Affairs. Kennedy's statement that he intended to appoint Weaver as secretary of the department played an important role in the failure of the initiative, because once again it engendered strong opposition from segregationists in Congress. Weaver's other major success during the Kennedy administration was the issuance of the President's Executive Order banning racial discrimination in federal housing programs. The order was of limited scope, however, and Weaver regretted that it was not more influential.

Following Kennedy's assassination, Lyndon Johnson's administration entered the White House with substantial plans for urban America. Housing and urban revitalization were important parts of Johnson's Great Society, and Weaver played a crucial role in this program. In 1965, fresh from a landslide victory, Johnson advocated the creation of the Department of Housing and Urban Development (HUD). This time the legislation passed easily. Most people expected Johnson to appoint Weaver as secretary, but Johnson delayed for more than four months, stating that he was conducting an exhaustive search. Many thought that Johnson had disgraced Weaver, and Weaver considered resigning, but in January 1966 Johnson finally nominated him. The Senate overwhelmingly approved his nomination and Weaver became the nation's first African American cabinet secretary.

As HUD secretary, Weaver spent a great deal of time speaking around the country. In the mid-1960s, as inner-city riots exposed problems of urban decay and the increasing disillusionment of young African Americans, Weaver became an important administration spokesman. He played a crucial role in the development, passage, and implementation of several major pieces of legislation, including the Model Cities Act, the Housing Act of 1968, and the Civil Rights Act of 1968. Passed at the height of the urban crisis, the Housing Act of 1968 dramatically expanded home ownership opportunities for blacks and also increased federal support for rental housing. Weaver was particularly active in the effort to pass the Fair Housing Act, which was part of the 1968 Civil Rights Act. This law, the culmination of Weaver's three decades of struggle for fairness in housing, provided federal enforcement against racial discrimination in housing.

Weaver left HUD in the fall of 1968 to become president of Baruch College, a school in the City University of New York (CUNY) system. CUNY trustees had proposed making Baruch the center-piece of a dramatically expanded university system. A year later, however, the trustees revised their plan, and Weaver resigned in protest. Weaver spent the rest of his professional life as a distinguished professor at Hunter College. There, he mentored numerous graduate students and continued to be a prolific writer and speaker on issues of urban policy and race relations for more than twenty years. He was one of the original directors of the Municipal Assistance Corporation, the entity that was cre-ated to keep New York City out of bankruptcy in the 1970s, and he was active in many other national organizations. He died in New York City in 1997.

FURTHER READING

Weaver's papers are located at the Schomburg Center for Research in Black Culture of the New Public Library.

Gelfand, Mark. *A Nation of Cities* (1972).

Meyer, Stephen Grant. *As Long as They Don't Move Next Door: Segregation and Racial Conflict in American Neighborhoods* (2000).

Shipp, Sigmund. "Building Bricks without Straw: Robert C. Weaver and Negro Industrial Employment, 1934–1944" in *Historical Roots of the Urban Crisis*, eds. Henry Louis Taylor Jr. and Walter Hill (2000).

Obituary: *New York Times*, 19 July 1997.

WENDELL E. PRITCHETT

Weaver, William B. (7 Apr. 1852–? Sept. 1929), teacher, principal, school and orphanage founder, minister, and superintendent, was born William B. Weaver in Winton, Hertford County, North Carolina, the son of Willis Weaver and Sarah, both farmers. William was the sixth child born to the family. Ancestors of the Weaver family were recorded in Hertford County in the 1840 census and were described as free persons of color. Weaver attended public school in North Carolina before entering Hampton Normal School in October 1872. He taught four months of public summer school in North Carolina in 1873 and 1874. He completed his education and graduated in 1875.

In November 1875 General Samuel Armstrong, the founder of Hampton, sent Weaver to Mount Sidney, Augusta County, Virginia, where he taught three terms of five months each. In 1877 Weaver was sent by Armstong to Williamsport, Pennsylvania,

where he taught in the city school for one term. In 1879 Armstrong requested that Weaver go to Gloucester County, Virginia, where he taught at the Bethel School, founded to educate African Americans. Weaver reported that Bethel School, located in the Petsworth District of Gloucester County, was "very pleasant to say that the patrons of this school have not been entirely asleep to the work of education." Bethel School began in 1865, Lucy Lee was hired by its patrons to teach private school. In the later part of that year she opened the school in an old log cabin. Lee taught a few pupils for a part of two years for small compensa-tion. In the latter part of 1866 Lee was succeeded by Charlotte Ryley, who had taught at another loca-tion. Despite many disadvantages, Bethel School continued and received a boost in 1868, when the Freedman's Bureau began support. In November 1868 E. F. Jefferson opened the public school in the same log cabin that had housed the private school. By 1870 the school had closed, but in 1871 Rueben Berkley took charge of the school, and it continued to receive support from the Freedman's Bureau. After a few months the school was moved from the old log cabin to Bethel Church, and the next year the Freedman's Bureau ended its support. Berkley was employed by the state to teach pub-lic school, and in 1873 the Bethel Church opened as a public school. In 1876 William R. Guest, the only white person to teach at the school, suc-ceeded Berkley. Then patrons of the school wrote to Armstrong requesting a "colored" teacher. When Weaver arrived on 7 November 1879, he noted that he found "an anxious people for school and edu-cation, but no school house." Having to resort to the log cabin because Bethel Church was under repair, Weaver opened school on 13 November 1879 with twenty pupils and closed after eight months with close to one hundred pupils. During the sum-mer of 1880 Weaver and the parents petitioned the district school board for a schoolhouse. The board gave Weaver $275 to build a one-room schoolhouse of eighteen by twenty-four feet. A two-story addi-tion of twenty by twenty-six feet was quickly added with approval and funding by the school board. Bethel School opened for the first time in a school building in November 1880. An assistant teacher, Lucy Isabell, was hired at $20 a month because the school had 120 pupils. In 1881 Weaver wrote to Anna Bolden to request that she serve as an assis-tant teacher. Anna agreed to come to the school, and they married in 1884; they had five child-ren. By 1883 the school had 136 pupils and added another room. The school now had three rooms, three teachers, and 190 pupils. Money to support the growth of the school was raised through a network of northern friends.

On 18 February 1888 Weaver called a public meeting at the Gloucester County Courthouse to organize and establish a school for the higher education needs of the youth of Gloucester and the adjoining counties. A board of trustees was elected, and Weaver was selected as the principal of the Gloucester Agricultural and Industrial School. Money was raised to establish the school, and in October 1888 the school opened for only three months in a vacant storehouse. Work began on building the school on thirty-four acres in the Cappahosic District of Gloucester County. In the meantime the school opened in October 1889 at the residence of W. B. and ANNA WEAVER, who also served as teachers with little pay or reward. In May 1890 the work on the building began, and the outside of the building was completed on 7 October 1890 at a cost of $3,500. The school, though not fully complete, opened on 27 October 1890. Clubs were organized through black and white churches in Richmond, Virginia; Washington, D.C.; Philadelphia, Pennsylvania; and New York City to raise funds for the school. W. B. Weaver traveled to these cities and spoke about the mission and the needs of the school. In an article published in the *Philadelphia Weekly Standard Echo* (5 December 1891) Weaver said: "Up to the 20th of October we had neither chairs, beds, bed clothing, nor furniture of any kind for school use. Boarding students were expected, and some preparation had to be made. We nailed rough boards together for single beds, bought bed ticking and made straw mattresses. Kind friends of the North sent us some sheets, pillow slips and other bed clothes just two days previous of the arrival of the first boarding student."

In the spring of 1891, the American Missionary Society came to the rescue of the school and accepted and settled its debts of about $3,400. On 1 October 1891, the school opened under the supervision of the American Missionary Association, and it provided salaries for the first time for the principal and teachers.

FREDERICK DOUGLASS presented a benefit lecture on behalf of the Gloucester Agricultural and Industrial School at Bethel African Methodist Episcopal Church in Philadelphia on 22 March 1894. Supporters of the school paid twenty-five cents to hear "the old man eloquent." The program advertising the event included the following

commendation from R. C. Ogden of Hampton Institute: "It gives me very great pleasure to state that I have known you and your work very favorably for a number of years. Testimony concerning its efficiency has frequently been given by my friend, the late General Armstrong, and other persons of influence at Hampton Institute." The Gloucester Agricultural and Industrial School succeeded and eventually secured 140 acres of land, erected two large dormitories, and enrolled a hundred pupils.

In 1900 W. B. and Anna Weaver began formulating plans to address the needs of orphaned African American children. In the early spring of 1901 they left Gloucester for Elizabeth City County near Hampton, Virginia. W. B. Weaver purchased twenty-five acres of land in January 1902 for $2,800 by borrowing money, making payments, and securing a deed of trust. In August 1903 the Weavers began erecting a building. At the end of March 1904 they moved with their family into the new orphan home. A formal opening exercise for the reception of children was held on 27 June 1904. At the time of the opening there were no applicants to the home, but on 12 August 1904 two children were admitted. By 25 November twenty-two children had been admitted to the home.

Weaver served as the president of the board of trustees and superintendent of the home. Trustees included ministers, attorneys, educators, and others primarily from the African American communities in Hampton, Newport News, Phoebus, Gloucester, and Petersburg, Virginia. A lookout committee was formed, and an attending physician, W. E. Atkins, provided medical service free of charge. In its early days the orphan home was largely supported through contributions from churches near and far and donations of food and other supplies by farmers, citizens, and community groups. It was later organized under the Tidewater Orphan Association in 1913. Its board comprised leading black and white citizens.

When Weaver died in September 1929, his wife, daughter Ruth Weaver Fagan, and son-in-law Spillman Fagan operated the Weaver Orphan Home, which remained open until 1965. It housed up to forty orphans and gave instruction in religious subjects. Weaver Road in the Aberdeen neighborhood of Hampton, Virginia, was named in recognition of Weaver's contributions.

FURTHER READING

Fairfax, Colita Nichols. *Hampton, Virginia*, Black American series (2005).

Heinegg, Paul. *Free African Americans of North Carolina and Virginia* (1997).

"Key to Virginia Historic Landmarks in Gloucester County." Available online at www.gloucesterva.info/HistoricalLandmarks.pdf.

DEBRA THOMAS TRUHART

Webb, Chick (10 Feb. 1909–16 June 1939), jazz drummer and bandleader, was born William Henry Webb in Baltimore, Maryland. The identity of his father is unknown. He was raised by his mother, Marie Jones, and his maternal grandfather, Clarence Jones, a porter in a shoe store. Webb was a hunchback and often lived in pain. According to an oft-repeated but probably apocryphal story, he was dropped on his back in infancy, and several vertebrae were crushed, but another oft-repeated and entirely plausible account attributed his condition to tuberculosis of the spine (then common in the inner city), which dwarfed his torso while leaving his limbs intact. Webb never grew above four feet one inch tall. He acquired the nickname Chick in boyhood as a reference to his small size.

Webb was interested in music from age three and seemed a natural drummer, banging on household objects. This activity helped strengthen him, but clearly the inner motivation was musical rather than therapeutic. To help support his family, he began working at age nine. Three years later, by selling newspapers, he had earned enough to buy a drum set. He performed locally on the street and then with dance bands, including jobs with the Jazzola Band on excursion boats on the Chesapeake Bay. In this setting he met guitarist and banjoist John Trueheart, who became a lifelong friend and musical colleague.

Webb and Trueheart moved to Harlem in 1924 or 1925 and joined the band of Edgar Dowell. Webb's bandleading commenced for five months in 1926 at the Black Bottom Club, where his group also included the trumpeter Bobby Stark, the saxophonist Johnny Hodges, and the pianist Don Kirkpatrick. For a job at the Paddock Club he added the tenor saxophonist Elmer Williams and a trombonist. Webb's group performed at the Savoy Ballroom for the first time in January 1927, and it expanded further in size for an engagement at Rose Danceland from December 1927.

The next few years were a period of struggle during which Webb remained loyal to his sidemen, suffering with them through the lack of steady work in an effort to keep the band together. Stark joined FLETCHER HENDERSON's band early in 1928, and

Hodges joined DUKE ELLINGTON in May after a brief period with the pianist LUCKEY ROBERTS. In June 1928 Webb made his first recordings, "Dog Bottom" and "Jungle Mama," released under the name the Jungle Band, a studio name echoing Ellington's records, and indeed "Jungle Mama" could be passed off as Ellington's work. In 1929 Webb's band performed in the film short *After Seben*. He secured jobs at clubs and ballrooms such as the Strand Roof, Roseland, and the Cotton Club (July 1929). Late that year the saxophonist Benny Carter reached into the band's personnel, taking Trueheart and others temporarily to form a short-lived group.

After another stand at the Savoy, Webb was leading his band at Roseland in March 1931 when he engineered a celebrated trade: the trombonist BENNY MORTON and the alto saxophonist RUSSELL PROCOPE went to Henderson's orchestra in exchange for the superior musicians Jimmy Harrison and Carter. On 30 March they recorded Carter's song "Blues in My Heart" and Carter's arrangement of "Heebie Jeebies," on which the featured soloists include Williams, Kirkpatrick, and Harrison. But Harrison died from stomach cancer in July, and Carter left Webb in August to lead McKinney's Cotton Pickers, thus placing Henderson's seemingly disadvantageous trade in another light.

Late in 1932 Webb's big band embarked on a theater tour accompanying LOUIS ARMSTRONG in a revised version of the musical revue *Hot Chocolates*. The drummer reportedly was unusually attuned to the needs of the lindy-hopping dancers at the Savoy, where his group was resident from 1933 on, apart from theater shows and short tours. Late in 1933 the arranger and alto saxophonist Edgar Sampson joined Webb. When the big band began recording regularly in mid-1934, Sampson's contributions proved crucial in the achievement of a special sense of identity and creativity. Sampson brought in two compositions he had written for the cornetist REX STEWART's short-lived big band in 1933, "Stomping at the Savoy" and "Don't Be That Way," and even though these pieces did not become anthems of the swing era until Benny Goodman recorded his versions later that decade, Webb's 1934 versions are superior for their rhythmic drive.

Sampson also arranged others of the group's best instrumental recordings, including "Blue Minor," "What a Shuffle," "Blue Lou" (all from 1934), and "Go Harlem" (1936). Apart from the attractive ensemble work and catchy themes, these recordings feature a rhythm section—the pianists Joe Steele or Kirkpatrick, Trueheart, the bassists JOHN KIRBY or Bill Thomas, and Webb—that was probably the best in New York before COUNT BASIE's orchestra came east. It also spotlighted soloists such as Stark (who rejoined in 1934), the trumpeter Taft Jordan, the trombonist Sandy Williams, and the tenor saxophonist Elmer Williams. The group's finest instrumentalist was Webb, who figures prominently on "Go Harlem" and on further studio recordings made after Sampson's departure—"Clap Hands! Here Comes Charley," "Squeeze Me," "Harlem Congo" (all from 1937), and "Liza" (1938)—although by the testimony of many who heard him live, these recordings give only a small taste of his drumming for the Savoy's dancers.

During this last period of recordings, Webb engaged in celebrated battles of the bands at the Savoy, and on 11 May 1937 he faced Benny Goodman. This legendary event broke attendance records at the club, and Webb was universally acclaimed the victor. His group came off far less well in a contest with Basie's big band on 16 January 1938, but nevertheless the audience voted slightly in Webb's favor, the dancers' loyalty to their drummer outweighing Basie's musical advantages. Not even loyalty was enough for Webb in March 1938, when his big band was reportedly trounced by Duke Ellington's in all respects except drumming.

By conflicting accounts, the singer ELLA FITZGERALD somehow came to Webb's attention after winning an amateur contest at the Apollo Theater in Harlem in 1934. In 1935 she joined his orchestra. Fitzgerald was an orphan, and Webb became her legal guardian; Fitzgerald moved into his home. Her singing gradually reshaped the band's stylistic orientation. This shift became dramatic in mid-1938 with the success of "A-Tisket, A-Tasket," in which she rendered the nursery rhyme as a swing tune. At some cost to fans of Webb's instrumental jazz, Fitzgerald's hit song brought Webb more exposure on radio, including weekly performances on the "Good Time Society" network show, and it attracted offers of residencies at prestigious locations such as the Park Central and the Paramount Theater in midtown Manhattan, and Levaggi's in Boston.

Just as Webb began to achieve the commercial success he had sought for the past dozen years, his health failed. Hospitalized after a hugely successful summer tour, he resumed playing in November 1938. He was hospitalized again in January 1939. In June, after one final effort, he entered Johns Hopkins Hospital in Baltimore, where he died after a major urological operation. Webb was beloved by many,

and the published account of the usually irrepressibly cheerful Fitzgerald breaking down at Webb's public funeral is as moving today as it was in 1939. Webb was survived by his wife Sally; her maiden name and the date of their marriage are unknown. His orchestra continued under Fitzgerald's leadership until early 1942, when she disbanded it.

Webb's recordings document his unfailing sense of swing, explosive percussive force, and formidable technique. Such qualities are not at all unusual for a drummer. What set Webb apart was his ability to couple such extroverted playing to a keen and discreet musical sensitivity to questions of tuning, tone color, balance, and volume. From this sensitivity there resulted a handful of recorded examples of drum melodies in which he effortlessly combined the components of the drum set—assorted drums, cymbals, bells, and blocks—to create utterly original, kaleidoscopic sequences of percussion sounds. Insufficiently representative as these documents may be, Webb's recorded solos nonetheless argue that he deserves his reputation as the greatest jazz drummer of his era.

FURTHER READING

Charters, Samuel B., and Leonard Kunsttadt. *Jazz: A History of the New York Scene* (1962; repr. 1981).
Garrod, Charles. *Chick Webb and His Orchestra* (1993).
Korall, Burt. *Drummin' Men: The Heartbeat of Jazz: The Swing Years* (1990).
Schuller, Gunther. *The Swing Era: The Development of Jazz, 1930–1945* (1989).

This entry is taken from the *American National Biography* and is published here with the permission of the American Council of Learned Societies.

BARRY KERNFELD

Webb, Frank J. (21 Mar. 1828–7 May 1894), writer and educator, was born Frank Johnson Webb in Philadelphia, Pennsylvania. He may have been the son of Frank Webb, a china packer and community activist; his mother's name is not known. Little is known of Webb's life prior to his marriage to MARY WEBB, whose maiden name is unknown, in 1845. Webb apparently lived on the fringes of Philadelphia's black elite, and he seems to have been related to the Forten family by marriage.

Webb and his wife worked in clothing-related trades, and he participated in the Banneker Institute, an African American literary and debating society. When their business failed around 1854, the Webbs attempted to move to Rio de Janeiro, Brazil. Webb was denied passage because of his race, and this event was reported in several abolitionist newspapers.

In the meantime Mary Webb began giving dramatic readings. Harriet Beecher Stowe noticed her and wrote a dramatization of *Uncle Tom's Cabin* titled *The Christian Slave* "expressly" for her readings. This led to tours of the North in late 1855 and early 1856 and England in late 1856. Frank Webb seems to have managed both tours, and he wrote a biographical account of Mary that prefaced the British edition of *The Christian Slave.* Through Mary's readings, Frank Webb built connections with several abolitionists among the British aristocracy.

In 1857 George Routledge and Company published Frank Webb's novel *The Garies and Their Friends.* Prefaced by Stowe and Lord Brougham and dedicated to Lady Byron, *The Garies* was one of the first novels written by an African American. Though similar in its sentimentalism to *Uncle Tom's Cabin*, Webb's novel may well have perplexed Stowe's readers. *The Garies* focuses on free black life in the North, treats northern white mob violence in depth, considers issues like "passing" and black entrepreneurship, depicts a JAMES FORTEN–like wealthy black character, and arguably begins to assert an emergent black nationalist ethos. Phillip Lapsansky, a modern scholar, characterizes it not as an antislavery novel but as an antiracist work, "the first American novel to deal with race relations and colorphobia in the urban north" (29). It received positive notices from the British press but was all but ignored in the United States, and it fell into obscurity until the late 1960s.

When Mary Webb's health forced her to seek a better climate, friends among the British aristocracy secured a position for Frank Webb in the post office of Kingston, Jamaica, and the couple moved there in 1858. Though her health briefly improved, Mary died in Kingston on 17 June 1859. Frank Webb continued at the post office and eventually married a Jamaican woman, Mary Rodgers; the couple had four children between 1865 and 1869. Webb returned to the United States without his family sometime in 1869.

Settling in Washington, D.C., Webb tried to revive his literary career while clerking for the Freedmen's Bureau and attending law school at Howard University. He published two serialized novellas and a handful of poems and articles in an African American newspaper, the *New Era*, between January and April 1870. While his articles considered racial issues such as school integration, the novellas both focused on white characters in European settings. In his letters to the journalist Mary Wager Fisher, he also mentioned completing a second novel titled "Paul Sumner," which he claimed was superior to *The Garies.* Webb hoped a major house like Harpers would accept it, but the novel was never published.

The failure of the Freedmen's Bureau and his attempts to make a living through writing led Webb to leave Howard before completing his degree and move to Galveston, Texas, probably near the end of 1870. He secured work at the post office, became active in city and state politics, and edited a short-lived newspaper, the *Galveston Republican.* Webb actively supported the radical Louis Stevenson against the incumbent congressman William T. Clark, who was a close ally of Texas Governor Edmund J. Davis, claiming that, though Republicans, Clark and Davis had not sufficiently supported the black community. Webb's stand offended not only Davis but also Galveston's powerful black political boss GEORGE T. RUBY; at a public meeting in August 1871, Ruby actually called for Webb's arrest. Davis retained power in the Republican Party even though Clark eventually lost to Democrat Dewitt Giddings, and Webb's career as an editor ended. Ruby, though, left the state in 1873, and Webb's relationship with his successor NORRIS WRIGHT CUNEY seems to have been better; Webb attended the 1875 Republican state convention. Webb's family joined him in Galveston in early 1873, and the Webbs had two more children. For unknown reasons, Webb and his family moved to nearby Colorado County in the late 1870s.

Webb returned to Galveston in 1881 to become the principal of the Barnes Institute, one of the first public schools for blacks in Galveston. He continued as principal and teacher for the next thirteen years, during which the school grew significantly, was renamed the West District Colored School, and sent graduates on to the newly formed Central High School (one of the first black high schools in the state). Two of his children taught in the Galveston public schools. Webb was also active in St. Augustine's Protestant Episcopal Church, which was founded in 1884. When he died in Galveston, his colleagues placed a notice in the *Galveston Daily News* (8 May 1894) eulogizing him as "a teacher who was ever ready to proffer the hand of aid and the voice of sympathy to the needy."

Webb remains an enigma in many ways—arguably a "Renaissance man" without a renaissance. Prior to the 1960s his first novel was often dismissed (sometimes as a ruse by a white author), and the manuscript he considered his strongest work has never been found. Intimate with prominent abolitionists on both sides of the Atlantic, he never became an antislavery activist. Smart and talented—Stowe described him as "a gentleman of superior cultivation and refinement"—he nonetheless bounced from place to place until the last decades of his life. Generally neglected by scholars, his contributions to literature and education in the face of discrimination mark him as a significant figure among nineteenth-century Americans.

FURTHER READING

Two of Webb's letters are housed in the Mary Wager Fisher Papers at Duke University, Durham, N.C.

Crockett, Rosemary. "Frank J. Webb: The Shift to Color Discrimination," in *The Black Columbiad*, eds. Werner Sollors and Maria Diedrich (1994).

Gardner, Eric. "'A Gentleman of Superior Cultivation and Refinement': Recovering the Biography of Frank J. Webb," *African American Review* 35, no. 2 (Summer 2001): 297–308.

Obituary: *Galveston Daily News*, 8 May 1894.

This entry is taken from the *American National Biography* and is published here with the permission of the American Council of Learned Societies.

ERIC GARDNER

Webb, Jane (c. 1682–1764), litigant, born in Northampton County, Virginia, was the daughter of an indentured mother, Ann Williams, and an enslaved father, Daniel Webb. In accordance with a Virginia law that stipulated that children would be slave or free according to the status of their mother, Jane Webb was born a free person. However, because she was the product of a mixed-race, out-of-wedlock union and because her mother gave birth while under an indenture contract, the law also required that Jane Webb be bound out as a servant until she reached the age of eighteen. Throughout her lifetime she was variously referred to as Jane Webb (her father's surname), Jane Williams (her mother's surname), and Jane Left (her husband's first name). These variations reflect the uncertainty of her status in early-eighteenth-century Virginia, as the colony's lawmakers worked in earnest to both limit the numbers of free blacks in the colony and constrain their independence. In this context, Jane Webb, like other free blacks, was forced to fight legal battles in order to secure and maintain her own liberty and that of her family.

When Jane Webb was freed from indentured servitude in 1703, probably at the age of twenty-one, she married an enslaved man who is designated in the court records only as Left. Because Left was a slave and could not legally marry, Jane Webb approached his owner, Thomas Savage, and the two of them struck a detailed bargain that would control the fate of her family for more than two decades. In order to marry Left, Webb reentered indentured servitude and agreed to serve the Savage household for seven years. Any children born to Left and Webb during those seven years would be similarly indentured until the age of eighteen. In exchange, the contract stipulated that after Jane Webb's indenture ended, Left would be freed from slavery and that any children born subsequent to the termination of her indenture would bear no obligation to Savage. All told, Jane Webb bore three children during the term of her service, Dinah (1704), Daniel (1706), and Frances (1708), and four more children after her indenture ended, Ann (1711), Elizabeth (1713), Lisha (1716), and Abimelech (1720). All of these children were given Webb as their surname.

Although by the terms of the contract Left and Jane Webb were to be freed in 1711, he remained a slave, and, year by year, Savage successively bound to his service all of Webb's children. One can only speculate, but it seems likely that Webb embarked on a series of informal tradeoffs in hopes of eventually securing Left's freedom. By 1722, however, Jane Webb sought the formal protection of the law, as it was abundantly clear that Thomas Savage had no intention of keeping his side of their bargain. Thereafter, Jane Webb fought a series of legal battles in the Northampton, Virginia, County Court in attempts to force him to honor the provisions of their contract. She petitioned the court to secure the release of Dinah, her eldest daughter, who had served Savage for the agreed-upon eighteen years. The court sided with Savage; Dinah was finally released from his service in 1725, only after producing written evidence of her age from the church parish register. She had served him for twenty-one years. Meanwhile Savage attempted to detain Webb's two youngest children on the grounds that Webb could not support them; he also complained that she had hidden one of them. The court ordered that both be bound over to Savage.

In 1725, no doubt fed up with Thomas Savage and his attempts to possess her family, Jane Webb brought a suit in chancery against him. *Webb v. Savage* recited the original terms of the contract and argued that Savage had failed to perform the conditions of the bargain. Predictably, Savage successfully contested Webb's case and produced witnesses on his behalf. Unfortunately for Webb, the written contract had disappeared (Savage might have destroyed it). Frustrated, in a moment of unguarded speech, Webb reproached the court for its lack of justice; she was repaid with ten lashes at the public whipping post.

In 1726 she made one final attempt to prove her case and brought an unnamed free black person as a witness for her cause. The justices, although apparently divided on the matter, ruled that Virginia law debarred legal testimony from free blacks. *Webb v. Savage* was dismissed; Left remained a slave for the rest of his life, and all of the Webb children served Thomas Savage or his heirs for terms of twenty-one years. Jane Webb continued to be listed in county records variously as the head of her own household, as a member in the household of her daughter, Dinah, or as a part of the Savage household. She periodically reported on infractions of her children's masters to the local court, but the justices typically dismissed her complaints. After Thomas Savage died, his heirs continued to exercise ownership over Webb's family; Jane Webb contested their right to do so, and she successfully petitioned for the recovery of her grandchildren who, the court agreed, were illegally detained by the Savages.

In 1740 Jane Webb petitioned the court for the last time. Because of her age and infirmity, she could no longer labor in the tobacco fields, so she asked to be exempted from paying taxes. The justices agreed. By 1764, Jane Webb was dead. Her experiences and efforts reflect the precarious liberty of free blacks in the early American South. The local judicial system was hostile to her petitions and unsympathetic to her lawsuit, and, in this discriminatory climate, her success at court was unlikely at best. Yet, Jane Webb prevailed. Thanks to her determination and her legal acumen, her children and grandchildren enjoyed a circumscribed freedom as legally free blacks in the racially charged environment of eighteenth-century Virginia.

FURTHER READING

The petitions by Jane Webb and her children can be found in the Northampton County, Virginia, Court Records (Order Books, Judgments, and Chancery Suits), The Library of Virginia, Richmond, Virginia.

Deal, Joseph Douglas. "A Constricted World: Free Blacks on Virginia's Eastern Shore," in *Colonial Chesapeake Society*, eds. Lois Green Carr, Philip D. Morgan, and Jean B. Russo (1998).

Deal, Joseph Douglas. *Race and Class in Colonial Virginia: Indians, Englishmen, and Africans on the Eastern Shore during the Seventeenth Century* (1993).

Heinegg, Paul. *Free African Americans of North Carolina, Virginia, and South Carolina from the Colonial Period to about 1820* (2001).

Snyder, Terri L. *Brabbling Women: Disorderly Speech and the Law in Early Virginia.* (2003).

TERRI L. SNYDER

Webb, Mary (1828–17 June 1859), dramatic reader, was born in New Bedford, Massachusetts. Her parents' names and specific details of her youth remain unknown, though nineteenth-century accounts spin rich tales of her parentage and childhood. According to her husband FRANK WEBB, her father was "a Spanish gentleman of wealth" and her mother "a woman of full African blood" who escaped from slavery while pregnant with Mary and later died from anxiety produced by the Fugitive Slave Act. Other sources claim she was the child of a Cuban official, and a letter of introduction written by Harriet Beecher Stowe claims she was sent to Cuba as a child and was educated in a convent. There was even speculation that she was the daughter of the Spanish general and statesman Baldomero Espartero.

In 1845 Mary married Frank Johnson Webb, and the couple settled in Philadelphia, Pennsylvania, where they worked in the clothing trade until their business failed in 1854. The couple's financial need led Mary Webb to consider "turning her marked elocutionary powers to some practical account." She studied briefly with H. O. Apthorp, who ran a "vocal institute" in Philadelphia, and gave a private reading in early April 1855. This reading led to her public debut on 19 April 1855 in the Assembly Building in Philadelphia. Billed as the "Black Siddons," after the British actress Sarah Siddons, Webb attracted a racially diverse audience of several hundred, including Lucretia Mott. Webb's success in Philadelphia led to engagements in Boston and Worcester in May 1855. She read selections from Shakespeare, Richard Brinsley Sheridan, John Greenleaf Whittier, and "the favorite Irish, Negro, and French eccentricities."

While reviews were not uniformly positive and attendance was mixed, events surrounding the readings introduced Webb to a number of abolitionists, including Thomas Wentworth Higginson and Stowe. Stowe took the role of patron and apparently provided both lodging and a voice teacher for Webb during the summer of 1855. More importantly, though Stowe had resisted all requests to dramatize her blockbuster *Uncle Tom's Cabin* (1852), she compiled a selection of slightly revised scenes from her novel under the title *The Christian Slave* "expressly" for Webb's readings. Stowe's selection heavily emphasized black characters and especially black women; of the most interest, Cassy, whose role in the novel is relatively brief (albeit pivotal), has the longest soliloquy in the play and is arguably the center of its final act.

Webb gave the first public reading of *The Christian Slave* on 6 December 1855 in Boston's Tremont Temple as part of an antislavery lecture series set up by Samuel Gridley Howe that included such notables as Wendell Phillips. The event drew over a thousand people, ranging from the black abolitionist WILLIAM COOPER NELL to the poet Henry Wadsworth Longfellow. Attendees were encouraged to purchase an inexpensive edition of *The Christian Slave* published a few days before. By all accounts, though the text offers stage directions, Webb gave this reading and all subsequent readings standing behind a podium; she relied mainly on vocal variation for characterization and made few gestures. Reviewers from both the mainstream and the abolitionist presses agreed that the large audience regularly offered "marked applause" and that Webb had a "sweet voice" and "perfect self-possession."

The Boston reading was quickly followed by performances for large audiences in Worcester and Plymouth and smaller groups in New York City (where she appeared with the abolitionist Oliver Johnson) and Brooklyn. The Webbs' friendship with Nell and Mary Webb's early successes led Nell to introduce them to Amy and Isaac Post, white abolitionists, who helped secure subsequent engagements in Rochester and Buffalo. During the spring of 1856 Webb embarked on a "western tour" (including a reading in Cleveland), but few details of this trip are known. She gave another performance in Rochester on 5 May 1856 and a week later read at Touro Hall in Hartford, Connecticut. In these later performances Webb still read from *The Christian Slave*, but she also included extensive excerpts from Longfellow's *Hiawatha*, which she reportedly read in "full Indian dress." It seems likely that, as with the singer ELIZABETH GREENFIELD, part of Webb's appeal to audiences was as a curiosity; newspaper coverage consistently discussed her connection to Stowe and her race (often spending significant time commenting on her color). Like Greenfield, Webb both engaged in occasional spectacle (like the Native American costume) and struggled to prove her talent went beyond curiosity.

Soon after the Hartford reading, the Webbs traveled to Great Britain, armed with letters of introduction from Stowe and others. As she had three years earlier for Greenfield, Stowe's friend the duchess of Sutherland became Mary Webb's patron and opened her home (London's Stafford House) for Webb's first British reading on 28 July 1856. The event attracted several members of Britain's abolitionist aristocracy and was covered extensively by the London press; the *Illustrated London News* even carried a striking illustration of Webb giving the reading. The success of this reading (and the stamp of approval from luminaries like Sutherland) led to other engagements, and when Stowe's sister Mary Beecher Perkins visited London in July 1857, she reported that the Webbs were intimate with several British nobles.

Webb's health declined, though, and after a brief stay in the south of France, the Webbs returned to the United States in early 1858 before traveling on to Jamaica, where the Webbs' aristocratic friends had secured a position for Frank. The Webbs clearly had intentions of continuing Mary's career; she gave a semiprivate reading attended by Charlotte Forten (later CHARLOTTE FORTEN GRIMKÉ) and other abolitionists in March 1858 and a public reading in Kingston in May 1858, soon after her arrival in Jamaica. However, her health continued to decline, and she died in Kingston a year later.

Webb has generally been neglected by both historians and critics, perhaps in part because both her fame and her life were quite brief and because she left no personal narrative. Still, along with Greenfield, Webb is one of the few African American women who gained international fame before the Civil War. As one of the first African American women to take the public platform in both the United States and Britain, she paved the way for important events like SARAH PARKER REMOND's tour of Britain (1859–1861) and for a reconsideration of how black voices are represented in Stowe's work and the larger debates over slavery and race.

FURTHER READING

Mary Beecher Perkins's letters mentioning the Webbs are at the Harriet Beecher Stowe Center, Hartford, Conn.

Clark, Susan F. "Solo Black Performance before the Civil War: Mrs. Stowe, Mrs. Webb, and *The Christian Slave*," *New Theater Quarterly* 13 (Nov. 1997): 339–348.

Gardner, Eric. "Stowe Takes the Stage: Harriet Beecher Stowe's *The Christian Slave*," *Legacy: A Journal of*

American Women Writers 15, no. 1 (Spring 1998): 78–84.

This entry is taken from the *American National Biography* and is published here with the permission of the American Council of Learned Societies.

ERIC GARDNER

Webb, Rothchild Roscoe (3 May 1915–12 Sept. 2000), World War II soldier and Silver Star Medal recipient, was likely born in Marion County, Indiana, possibly in the city of Indianapolis. Little is known about the details of his life beyond his military service.

During World War II, Webb rose to prominence during his service in the 93rd Cavalry Reconnaissance Troop (mechanized), an element of the 93rd Infantry Division. This unit was one of two all-black divisions (along with the 92nd Infantry Division) activated by the army during the war, manned entirely by African American enlisted personnel and junior officers, and commanded by senior white officers. While the details of Webb's early service with the 93rd are unknown, the fact that he had attained the rank of sergeant by early 1944 tells us that he was a very capable soldier and a leader. Staff sergeants often commanded a squad, consisting of about ten men, while operating in the field, and most of the young privates at this point in the war were either teenagers or in their early twenties. At the age of twenty-nine years when he performed his heroics, Webb would have been an old man to those under his command, a knowledgeable soldier who could be depended on in times of battle. Indeed, Webb was likely an early soldier in the 93rd, probably assigned to the unit in the very beginning when it was activated at Fort Huachuca, Arizona, in May 1942 and subsequently trained in Louisiana and California before being sent for combat duty in the Pacific in January 1944.

The service of African American soldiers in the Pacific theater, men like Rothchild Webb, ROBERT J. PEAGLER, and TOMMIE HOLLOWAY is an important aspect of our military history that is largely forgotten even today. Because of the prevailing racist attitudes in army command that had been present for years, and the oft-stated belief by senior commanders that white soldiers were more skilled than black soldiers, the men in these segregated divisions had to "fight" just to be allowed to serve as combat infantrymen. Finally, when political pressure at home from groups like the NAACP mounted, and the need for more manpower was on the rise by late 1943, the army relented and sent its black soldiers into combat in early 1944. Even then, they operated under intense scrutiny, the 92nd in Europe and the 93rd Infantry Division in the Pacific. Closely evaluated, they were often unfairly criticized for their combat skills early on when they were newcomers with little training or service under fire to their credit. The stigma of these early, hasty judgments, in the case of the 93rd, would stay with the men of the division through the remainder of the war. However, the acts of valor by men like Sergeant Webb serve as a reminder that the fighting abilities of African American soldiers was every bit equal to that of their white counterparts.

Upon arriving in the Pacific at Guadalcanal in January 1944, Webb and the men of the 93rd underwent further combat training, and were then sent to Bougainville in April 1944 to take part in the battle to wrest control of the island away from the Japanese. Sergeant Webb's reconnaissance troop was subsequently attached to the Americal Division and was on patrol on 17 May 1944 when Japanese forces were encountered, resulting in a short but fierce battle that resulted in three American soldiers killed and four wounded. Among the wounded was the patrol's commanding officer; Sergeant Rothchild Webb and three other soldiers stayed with him and another wounded soldier after the battle and evaded capture in enemy-held territory for three days before finally making their way safely back to the American lines. For this valorous and successful action, Webb was subsequently awarded the Silver Star Medal on 20 July 1944; he was just one of seven black soldiers serving in the 93rd Infantry Division to be awarded a high-level combat decoration during the war.

Following his actions on Bougainville, Webb continued his service for the duration of the war and an unknown period of time afterward. Nothing is known of his personal life, except that he married, likely had at least one child, and lived in Indianapolis, Indiana. Upon his death he was interred at Crown Hill Cemetery in Indianapolis.

FURTHER READING

Converse, Elliot V., Daniel K. Gibran, John A. Cash, Robert K. Griffith, and Richard H. Kohn. *The Exclusion of Black Soldiers from the Medal of Honor in World War II* (2008).

Jefferson, Robert F. *Fighting for Hope: African American Troops of the 93rd Infantry Division in World War II and Postwar America* (2008).

GLENN ALLEN KNOBLOCK

Webb, Wellington Edward (17 Feb. 1941–), state legislator, federal appointee, and mayor, was born in Chicago, the son of Wellington M. Webb, a railroad porter, and Mardina Devereaux Webb. When he was seven, Wellington was sent to Denver to live with his grandmother, Helen Gamble. He suffered from asthma, and the dry mountain air was thought to be an improvement for his health. It was, and he excelled both in school and at sports, especially basketball. In 1960 Webb attended Northeastern Junior College in Sterling, Colorado, and was an all-conference basketball player. Four years later he obtained his B.A. in Sociology from Colorado State on a basketball scholarship. In 1969 he married Wilma Gerdine, a political activist. Webb received his M.A. in Sociology at the University of Northern Colorado in Greeley in 1971. That same year, while working in Denver as a forklift operator, he decided to seek career advice from his grandmother, who had been active in the Democratic Party. Helen Gamble had strong community ties and directed her grandson to reach into community work; Webb was hired at city hall in the social service system.

In 1972 Webb ran for state representative in his old neighborhood in northeast Denver and won decisively, serving three terms in the Colorado statehouse until 1977. During this time Webb was able to learn the legislative system, and he focused on health care, welfare, and social issues. One of his early major accomplishments was cowriting the state's first civil rights laws concerning people with disabilities. Though a Democrat, he took stances on issues that were not considered mainstream. In 1975 he protested Governor Richard Lamm's failure to appoint blacks to high-level state positions by staging a walkout at the governor's inauguration.

Webb was appointed in 1975 to head up Jimmy Carter's presidential campaign in Colorado. Following his election in 1976, President Carter appointed Webb to a senior position in the U.S. Department of Health, Education, and Welfare in 1977. This was a huge task, managing a $3 billion budget, and three thousand social service programs in six western states. Webb also focused on improvements for Native Americans throughout the West. When Carter lost to Ronald Reagan in the 1980 election, Webb returned to Colorado and was hired by Governor Lamm to oversee the Regulatory Agencies Department. He was the only African American appointed to a top leadership post. That same year his wife, Wilma Webb, was elected a representative to the Colorado legislature and would serve there for the next thirteen years.

Many recognized Wellington and Wilma Webb as one of Denver's political power couples.

In 1983 Webb ran for mayor of Denver. His efforts fell flat, and he finished fourth. Returning to Governor Lamm's cabinet, he then opted to seek the position of Denver city auditor and was elected in 1987. By 1990 Webb had developed citywide political organizing skills and ran again for mayor. His persistence meant going up against seven worthy challengers. Trailing badly in the polls, he implemented a unique strategy: he hit the streets and vowed to visit all areas of the city, on foot, taking the media with him to see Denver and its neighborhoods. He stayed with different supporters, night after night. Three hundred miles later he had lost twenty-five pounds and had gained voter confidence. Webb ended up in a runoff election and won the mayor's office with 57 percent of the vote, emerging from underdog status in a city of 467,000 that counted only 12 percent of its population as black. At his inauguration in 1991 he wore sneakers, which had become his trademark.

Webb knew that Denver was in an uphill battle to build itself economically. Roughly 30 percent of downtown buildings were vacant, and the city was $3 billion in debt. His first goal was to spearhead a "back to basics" strategy, to improve and enhance essential city services like parks, garbage pickup, social services, schools, and police and fire services. Webb's strengths as a charismatic power broker began to shine, and he realized that a diverse city infrastructure was central to Denver's success. He oversaw the completion of a new $4 billion airport (located away from the city for more space as well as to reduce city noise and air pollution). A new baseball field and National League Baseball team were landed. Major downtown renovations included a walking mall, a rebuilt library, a new indoor sports facility, an expanded art museum, and a convention center. With more than $7 billion invested, Denver became a magnet for development and growth, and its image as a healthy city flourished. Private investments poured new revenues into city tax coffers. Webb's fiscal conservatism had brought the city from debt to surplus, and accolades and national recognition came from many quarters. In 1993 Webb hosted a visit from Pope John Paul II and then one from President Bill Clinton.

Reelected mayor in 1995, Webb faced stiff criticism from whites that his city contract reward policies favored African Americans and Hispanics. Boycotts resulted, and the airport and convention center lost significant revenue. In 1999 Webb sought a third term with a platform to manage growth and solve traffic congestion, motivate redevelopment in poorer areas, and reduce unemployment rolls. He won decisively. As a sign of his strength and popularity, he reached the national level with his message. Years of his garnering funds from the state and federal government enabled the economic powerhouse that had become Denver to turn the tables. Webb's summer jobs program and improved after-school programs for youths paired with a tough stance on crime and gangs were the key drivers in a 40 percent reduction in the city's crime rate. Webb also led the transformation of the Denver Medical Health Center from a lagging city hospital to a state-of-the-art facility with $38 million less in debt and a $50 million cash balance for future investments. By 1999 Denver Health ranked in the top five hospitals in the United States for financial stability, low cost, and quality.

Upon leaving the mayor's office after twelve years in 2003, Webb set up a consulting company called Webb Group International. The group focused on economic development projects in downtown areas. Webb received awards from, for example, the National Trust for Historic Preservation, Americans for the Arts (for leadership), the French government (a Legion of Honor), and the U.S. Conference of Mayors (for distinguished public service).

FURTHER READING

A collection of Webb's work is accessible at the African American Research Library (Blair Caldwell Branch) in Denver, Colorado.

JAMES FARGO BALLIETT

Webster, Ben (27 Mar. 1909–20 Sept. 1973), jazz tenor saxophonist, was born Benjamin Francis Webster in Kansas City, Missouri. The names of his parents are unknown, and little is known about his early life. He was raised by his mother and his grandmother, both schoolteachers. Webster received his earliest music education in a Kansas City elementary school and from home violin and piano lessons provided by his grandmother. Webster began his career as a pianist, and his jazz sensibilities were shaped by the ragtime and blues traditions of the Southwest, as well as the fiercely competitive institution of Kansas City jam sessions. His early professional work, interrupted by studies at Wilberforce University in Ohio, from 1922 to 1925, consisted of jobs with regional bands based in Oklahoma, Texas, Missouri, and New Mexico. He first began to specialize as a saxophonist in 1930 with the Gene Coy and Jap Allen bands and made his first recordings with BLANCHE CALLOWAY in 1931.

Throughout the 1930s Webster worked with many of the period's finest black jazz musicians, among them BENNIE MOTEN from 1931 to 1933; ANDY KIRK in 1933; FLETCHER HENDERSON in 1934; Benny Carter in 1934; Willie Bryant in 1935; DUKE ELLINGTON briefly in 1935 and 1936; CAB CALLOWAY in 1936 and 1937; STUFF SMITH and ROY ELDRIDGE in 1938; and TEDDY WILSON in 1939 and 1940. Some specimens from this period are "Toby," with Moten (1932); "Dream Lullaby," with Carter (1932); his first recorded solo on a slow ballad, "I'll See You in My Dreams," with Wilson (1936); and "Sing You Sinners," with Henderson (1937). By the end of the decade Webster was regarded, along with Hershel Evans and CHU BERRY, as a major tenor saxophonist in the style established by COLEMAN HAWKINS. By his own account, it was at this time that he began to develop a personal approach. While working again with Duke Ellington, from December 1939 to August 1943, Webster found his own voice and emerged as one of the greatest jazz soloists of his generation. His solos are featured in nearly three dozen Ellington pieces, among them "Cottontail," "All Too Soon," "Conga Brava," "Bojangles," and "Sepia Panorama" (all 1940); "Blue Serge" and "Chelsea Bridge" (both 1941); and "Main Stem" and "What Am I Here For?" (both 1942).

For the remainder of his life Webster worked mostly as a freelance musician and leader of his own small groups. A good chronology has yet to be established, and at present one must often rely on various discographies that chronicle his recordings. From 1944 to 1949 he was active in New York and rejoined Ellington from November 1948 to June 1949 before moving back to Kansas City, where he remained until returning to New York in late 1952. Webster lived in Los Angeles for much of the 1950s and early 1960s but frequently recorded in New York and appeared there in nightclubs. Although Webster was widely admired for his sensitive performances of popular ballads and regarded by jazz cognoscenti as a giant of the tenor saxophone, he was often unemployed during the early 1960s. Seeking new audiences, he moved to Europe in December 1964. Using Copenhagen as a home base and working with European and expatriate American musicians, he remained creatively active in England and on the Continent until his death in Amsterdam.

Webster's music is preserved on approximately 1,400 recordings. Some 650 items from 1931 to 1944 present him with several of the larger ensembles already cited, as well as smaller units led by BILLIE HOLIDAY, in 1937; LIONEL HAMPTON, in 1939; BARNEY BIGARD, in 1940; and others. In all these he is working as a sideman and does not necessarily receive solo space. From 1944 to 1973 Webster recorded frequently as a leader (450 items); as coleader with Coleman Hawkins in 1957, Gerry Mulligan in 1959, Harry Edison in 1962, and others; and as sideman with BIG SID CATLETT in 1944, JOHNNY HODGES in 1952, 1953, 1958, and 1959, Benny Carter in 1946 and 1957, ART TATUM in 1956, Billie Holiday in 1956 and 1957, CLARK TERRY in 1963 and 1964, and others. The typical context features Webster as soloist with small jazz ensembles (quartet, quintet, or sextet including piano, string bass, drums, and occasionally guitar).

Webster's first recordings are best understood in historical context. The tenor saxophone had yet to outgrow its identification as a burlesque contrivance, and its first jazz master, Coleman Hawkins, was still struggling to refine its artistic potential. Thus, Webster's early solos—marked by a rough tone, many notes, and a lack of restraint—are specimens of both his individual immaturity and the generally crude standards of tenor saxophone playing at the time. His solos with Ellington present an entirely different picture. Webster had absorbed elements of the alto saxophone styles of Benny Carter and Johnny Hodges and mingled them with the Hawkins model. In addition to the intense rhythmic drive of the earlier work, his solos were not merely exciting and expressive but also logical and balanced in their dramatic, narrative design. Above all, Webster became a master of the handling of sound itself in his manipulation of a wide variety of tone colors, speech-like articulation, dynamics, vibrato, and inflection. As Webster continued to grow as an artist, new recording and playback technology permitted him to be more expansive and allowed the transmission of the increasingly subtle, multidimensional vocabulary of his narrative flow. Webster has long been considered one of the important saxophonists in the tradition established before, during, and after the swing era of the 1930s. Gunther Schuller's assessment is more appropriate: "One of the greatest and most consistent invincible artists in jazz."

FURTHER READING

De Valk, Jeroen. *Ben Webster: His Life and Music* (2000).

Schuller, Gunther. *The Swing Era: The Development of Jazz, 1930–1945* (1989).

DISCOGRAPHY

Delmarche, Y., and Iwan Frésart. *A Discography of Ben Webster, 1931–1973* (c. 1983).

This entry is taken from the *American National Biography* and is published here with the permission of the American Council of Learned Societies.

JAMES PATRICK

Webster, Milton Price (1887–1965), Pullman porter, labor leader, Brotherhood of Sleeping Car Porters (BSCP) functionary, political organizer, and Fair Employment Practices Committee (FEPC) panelist, was born in Clarksville, Tennessee, in 1887, two years after the birth of ASA PHILIP RANDOLPH, the visionary, charismatic, intellectual founder of the Brotherhood of Sleeping Car Porters. As the first vice president of the BSCP, his public profile is linked to that of Randolph, the BSCP, and the struggle for civil rights.

Webster went to Chicago as a working youth; there he became a porter on the railroad. By 1925 he was serving as a bailiff in Cook County and a ward leader who established strategic ties to the black Republican establishment. His work and political associations soon proved decisive.

Webster's reach extended to the powerful black Republican politician OSCAR DE PRIEST, as well as to present and past porters, who respected him for having been one of them. The combination of these factors granted Webster entrée into exclusive arenas, enormously benefiting the Brotherhood, Randolph, and by extension the black proletarian rank and file.

Pullman porters had taken their name from the Pullman sleeping cars designed and produced by the company owned by industrialist George Pullman. Offering a more luxurious and expensive traveling experience, the cars were manned by African American porters who saw to the needs of mainly white passengers. By race-typing the porter's position as African American, Pullman reinforced the belief in African American racial inferiority. Within decades the Pullman porter became a universal symbol of black subservience, as those who filled these positions were expected to provide all-purpose intimate attention as valets, cooks, and overall client-guardians of their white patrons on short- and long-term train trips. These employees lost individual identities, often being referred to generically as "George" after Pullman himself.

The first challenge to the authoritarian administration of the Pullman company came in the summer of 1925 when five senior-level people with porter experience approached radical journalist A. Philip Randolph, editor of the *Messenger*, to ask if he would ally himself with their struggle for recognition and improved wages and working conditions and act as a public and print spokesman. Randolph took on the roles, leading the union and devoting his periodical to their cause. Together they founded the International Brotherhood of Sleeping Car Porters. Webster became the principal BSCP leader in Chicago. His was a difficult position because he was in the city where the headquarters of the fiercely anti-union Pullman Company was located.

Pullman porter advocacy was further complicated by the perception that the job paid well; company publicity claimed over 10,000 porters drew $67.50 monthly wages. This meant that the base annual wage was $810; even adding an additional $600 in tips, the average porter fell well below the $2,088 needed to support a family in 1926. Out of this meager pay, porters were expected to purchase and maintain their uniforms and supply shoe polish and other incidentals for patrons. Clearly, there was a strong need for union advocacy.

Webster's rise was as remarkable as it was meteoric, occurring within the context of 1926. In a relatively short space of time, Webster became the BSCP's number two man. Whereas Randolph was sometimes perceived as aloof and haughty, Webster was direct and a no-nonsense organizer. So effective was he in reaching the rank and file of porters, that his leadership style became the model for local BSCP leaders. The BSCP confronted overt opposition from the Pullman Company whose Employee Representative Plan (ERP) and Benevolent Association (PPBA) were designed to make a union seem irrelevant. In October 1926 BSCP also campaigned to end using "George," agitating for name plates.

Between 1926 and 1937 Webster epitomized the challenges before the BSCP as a regional and local organization whose national strategy was dictated by its New York office, led by Randolph. Through a mixture of tough negotiating skills, implacable will, and deftly issued threats, Webster used armtwisting when necessary, cajoling when advisable, and intelligence and integrity. He dealt brilliantly if not always cordially with embezzlers, editors, company hacks, union defectors, overinflated egos, and ever tenacious Pullman opposition.

By 1928 Webster had secured a key agreement from the national office to make Chicago and New York equal in BSCP planning, making himself Randolph's indispensable deputy. Braving internecine feuds, company-induced violence against BSCP officials, fiscal scandal, and strikes, Webster became a stabilizing influence against tumultuous odds.

The critical period from the late 1920s through the 1930s saw BSCP strategy focus upon achieving recognition within organized labor. Appealing to the American Federation of Labor (AFL), the union fought hard to obtain support for their efforts. However, this campaign conflicted with longstanding AFL policies against interfering with racial bans practiced by local affiliates, adding another obstacle to the Brotherhood's objective. This was further complicated by AFL policy to accept charters from local chapters rather than national bodies like the BSCP, undermining the central structure on which the Brotherhood had been organized. From 1930 to 1933 the BSCP pursued a two-pronged strategy: steadily gaining legal recognition from Pullman through the courts; and persuading the AFL to back them up. Eventually the latter led to appearances by Randolph at AFL conventions and behind-the-scenes negotiations by Webster and others to buttress BSCP fortunes within the federation. After a dozen hard years the BSCP finally gained Pullman recognition on 25 August 1937.

Webster's public role in succeeding years pivoted around the reputation he earned in the BSCP. In 1941 when Randolph utilized the Brotherhood's network to forge a March on Washington movement aimed at forcing desegregation in war-related industries through a threatened protest march in the nation's capital, Webster was involved. Though the march itself was called off at the request of President Franklin D. Roosevelt, the threat had secured the significant concession of Executive Order 8802, desegregating defense-related industries and establishing a Federal Employment Practices Committee (FEPC), on which Webster was subsequently invited to sit. The March on Washington movement continued to exist for another decade and provided the impetus for the organization of the 1963 March on Washington. Milton Price Webster was a vital factor in every aspect of these campaigns. He died in 1965.

FURTHER READING

The Brotherhood of Sleeping Car Porters' records are held at the Library of Congress in Washington, D.C.

Anderson, Jervis. *A. Philip Randolph: A Biographical Portrait* (1973).

Arnesen, Eric. *Brotherhoods of Color: Black Railroad Workers and the Struggle for Equality* (2001).

Bates, Beth Tompkins. *Pullman Porters and the Rise of Protest Politics in Black America, 1925–1945* (2001).

Brazeal, Brailsford. *The Brotherhood of Sleeping Car Porters, Its Origin and Development* (1946).

Garfinkel, Herbert. *When Negroes March: The March on Washington Movement in the Organizational Politics of FEPC* (1959).

Harris, William H. *Keeping the Faith: A Philip Randolph, Milton Webster and the Brotherhood of Sleeping Car Porters, 1925–37* (1991).

Valien, Preston. "The Brotherhood of Sleeping Car Porters," *Phylon* 1, no. 3 (1940).

Wilson, Joseph H. *Tearing Down the Color Bar: A Documentary History and Analysis of the Brotherhood of Sleeping Car Porters* (1989).

DAVID H. ANTHONY III

Wedgeworth, Robert, Jr. (31 July 1937–), librarian, was born in Ennis, Texas, the son of Robert and Jimmie Wedgeworth, who both passed away when he was a teenager. He was raised with his six siblings in Kansas City, Missouri, where he attended the all-black Lincoln High School. During the summers he worked as a library page.

After graduation Wedgeworth received a scholarship to attend Wabash College in Indiana. Although he intended to pursue a career as a language interpreter, Wedgeworth worked as an assistant to the librarian, Don Thompson, whom he found to be an influential role model. After earning a bachelor's degree in English, Wedgeworth enrolled in the master's program in library science at the University of Illinois in 1959. Following graduation in 1961, his first job was as a cataloger at the Kansas City Library. He joined the American Library Association (ALA) in 1962 and helped to create the display at the Seattle World's Fair. The exhibit at the World's Fair featured a Univac computer, which was Wedgeworth's introduction to library automation and had a profound effect on his career. Wedgeworth left Kansas City in 1962 to become assistant librarian at Park College in Parkville, Missouri. In 1964 he moved to work as head librarian at Meramec Community College, a new college in Kirkwood, Missouri. After a brief stay Wedgeworth accepted the position of assistant chief order librarian at Brown University in Rhode Island.

While working at Brown University Wedgeworth developed a strong interest in advanced studies in librarianship. He enrolled in the doctoral studies program at Rutgers University in 1971. He also served on several committees in the ALA, including the panel investigating charges of discrimination against the Library of Congress. In 1972 he accepted a position as the executive director of the American Library Association.

When Wedgeworth took over the director's position, ALA was experiencing a period of unrest over issues of governance and whether the association should be more involved in public awareness and social issues. The association was also experiencing financial difficulties. Within two years Wedgeworth had balanced the budget and established a public information program to enable libraries to increase their visibility in communities throughout the United States.

Wedgeworth also worked with the ALA presidents to restructure the divisions of ALA by instituting a dues structure that made each division or unit self-supporting. Smaller units that were being supported by the centralized budget of ALA were disbanded because they lacked membership support. The ALA office simply tracked divisional balances. Although ALA had become a federation of divisions and units, the organization still shared professional goals, conferences, and a headquarters building in Chicago, Illinois.

As executive director during the 1970s, Wedgeworth led ALA through the construction of a new headquarters building. Despite concerns raised by the membership and trustees about the funding and construction of the new headquarters in fragile economic times, ALA moved its headquarters to its present location in Chicago in 1981. As Wedgeworth later reflected on the move, "The space expanded the operating capability and provided the opportunity for a major upgrade in technologies employed by several offices. While these kind of improvements are largely invisible to the membership (and extremely boring as well), they make a critical difference in what can be accomplished" (Wedgeworth, *American Libraries* [Feb. 2003]: 47–51).

The 1970s was also an era when the American Library Association sought to play a major role in championing intellectual freedom. ALA's Office of Intellectual Freedom made an agreement with a major film company to produce a film titled *The Speaker* to present a dramatic representation of the issues surrounding challenges to intellectual freedom and the First Amendment. The subject of the film was a high school activities committee that invites a white speaker to make a presentation about the inferiority of the black race. Controversy among ALA members about the film's content and subject matter followed the screening of the film at the 1977 annual conference. Many ALA members felt that the racial subject of the movie destroyed the progress of racial harmony and equality that had been made in the preceding years. Others felt that the film was sly in the way it tested people's commitment to free speech. Wedgeworth did not distance himself or the organization from the endorsement of the film. Wedgeworth saw the film as a powerful vehicle for teaching an important issue that was vital to libraries across the country. Despite the strong opposition and resistance, and the push to remove the association's name from *The Speaker*, ALA still owns the rights to the movie today.

Overall, ALA became a larger and more affluent association during Wedgeworth's leadership. From 1972 until 1984 membership in the organization increased from 31,580 to 39,477. Also, the annual budget of the association increased from $3.8 million to $9.5 million. When Wedgeworth resigned from the director's position in 1985 he was highly praised for his leadership abilities by many, including E. J. JOSEY, who said that Wedgeworth "works well with people and has shown the capability to walk a straight line in an organization where we have crosscurrents from various groups with different personalities" (Fischer, 215–218).

In 1985 Wedgeworth became dean of the Columbia University School of Library Service. At Columbia Wedgeworth faced a situation similar to the one he dealt with when he held the director's job at ALA; Columbia was in the midst of hard times, with declining enrollment and faculty departures. Within a few years, however, the school's budget had doubled to more than $2 million, and the master's program had expanded its course of study from one to two years. Wedgeworth revitalized the reputation of the library school and was influential as Columbia's highest-ranking black officer and only black dean. Despite his success at Columbia, the administration made the difficult decision to close the School of Library Studies in 1992 because keeping other programs was a higher priority.

In 1991 Wedgeworth was elected president of the International Federation of Library Associations and Institutions (IFLA). In that role Wedgeworth presided at conferences in New Delhi, Barcelona, Havana, Istanbul, Beijing, and Copenhagen. Under Wedgeworth's guidance, the IFLA leadership expanded the Preservation and Conservation Program to centers in Caracas, Tokyo, Canberra, and Moscow.

After the closing of the Columbia School of Library Service, Wedgeworth became librarian at the University of Illinois at Urbana-Champaign in 1993. He was credited with the establishment of the Library Systems Office at the University of Illinois.

He was also responsible for automation projects including the transition from a local online catalog to a commercial online system and was also at the forefront of the digital library initiatives that continue at the library. He retired as professor emeritus in 1999.

Wedgeworth continued to enrich the literacy community in the United States and abroad as president of ProLiteracy Worldwide, a literacy/basic education training and advocacy organization with programs in the United States and forty-seven developing countries in Africa, Asia, and Latin America. Throughout his life, he worked to bring resources to an information-conscious society. His efforts in working with libraries both in the United States and abroad led to innovative programs and technologies that reached out to those who were highly motivated to seek knowledge, were involved in educational programs, and strove to bring services to the communities in which they lived and worked.

FURTHER READING

A collection of materials from Robert Wedgeworth's tenure at the American Library Association can be found in the American Library Association Archives at the University of Illinois at Urbana-Champaign.
Baker, Joseph F. "Robert Wedgeworth," *Publisher's Weekly* (16 June 1975).
Dugan, Kieran. "Portrait," *Wilson Library Bulletin* (Feb. 1980).
Fischer, Russell G. "RW Steps Down," *American Libraries* (Apr. 1985).
"Thank You, RW," *American Libraries* (June 1985).
"Voice of 30,000 Librarians," *Ebony* (June 1973).
Wedgeworth, Robert. "The Seeds of Prosperity: ALA in the 1970s (Part 1)," *American Libraries* (Jan. 2003).
Wedgeworth, Robert. "The Seeds of Prosperity: ALA in the 1970s (Part 2)," *American Libraries* (Feb. 2003).

MARK L. MCCALLON

Weeks, James (1922–1998), painter and instructor, was born in Oakland, California, the son of Anson Weeks, a pioneering West Coast bandleader, and Ruth Daly Weeks, a classical pianist. When his father's band was booked for a seven-year engagement at the Mark Hopkins Hotel in San Francisco, the family enrolled Weeks at the Pacific Heights Grammar School in San Francisco and, a few years later, into children's art classes at the California School of Fine Arts. His junior high and high school years introduced him to fellow students and artists William Wolff and Richard Diebenkorn, who eventually would achieve celebrity as a woodcut printer and an abstract painter, respectively.

Following graduation in 1940, Weeks enrolled in evening painting classes at the California School of Fine Arts (CSFA), while supporting himself by working days at Wells Fargo Bank. He studied under traditionalist painter William Gaw, but he was drawn to the work of Paul Cézanne, Marsden Hartley, and Walt Kuhn. After a stint in the air force that took him to Ipswich, England, Weeks returned to California to study with Edward Corbett, Paul Forester, David Park, Hassel Smith, Clay Spohn, and Marian Hartwell. In 1948 he was instructing part time at CSFA and soon serving as Marian Hartwell's teaching assistant. Despite his first significant museum exhibition in the spring of 1950, Weeks's marriage and the birth of their first child required him to enter a more secure profession as a sign and billboard painter while developing his creative artistry during his leisure hours.

In 1957, Weeks's work was included in the Oakland Art Museum's Contemporary Bay Area Figurative Painting exhibit, defining for the first time a distinct school of figurative painting that centered around Weeks, Richard Diebenkorn, Elmer Bischoff, and David Park. It freed artists with conceptual tendencies, those influenced by European artists Matisse, Munch, Beckman, and early Picasso, rather than the Dadaists and Surrealists, to once again include the human form in their work, leading them to stage personal, spectacular defections from the established abstract expressionistic style. Weeks was as consistently committed to figuration as any artist in the Bay Area during those years. Many of his figurative works in the mid-1950s are marked by a powerful vigor of application, a brilliant sense of color, and an awareness for the monumentality of the human form. Unlike his peers, however, Weeks did not experiment publicly with nonobjective painting, nor did he incorporate sun-drenched landscapes and light-dappled interiors into his oeuvre. Influenced by his parents' musical forays, he portrayed the darker, grittier facets of American culture, such as nightclubs, jazz performers, and athletic stadiums.

The hallmark of Weeks's painting, a flattened style, differs greatly from the gesticulative approach employed by many of his peers. Harkening back to classical influences, his figures are revealed through economic, adroitly fashioned lines. The immensity of his canvases, the daring borders enclosing brilliant swatches of color, and the bold intermingling of forms are reminiscent of a variety of influences, including Modernists Henri Matisse, Max Beckmann, and Maynard Dixon, and Social Realist and Mexican muralist Jose Clemente Orozco. The artist's style had reached its apex by 1960, and his works from this period are highly prized by both collectors and curators. Weeks added landscapes to his subject matter at this time, probing the dynamic between light and space, color and form.

He turned his focus to teaching again in 1967, relocating to Los Angeles to teach with Diebenkorn at the University of California and then transferring three years later to assume the chairmanship of the art department at Boston University. In the ensuing years, Weeks's work took on a formality, with his switch from oil to acrylic paint giving his pieces a sheerer, veiled appearance. He continued to depict landscapes and figures, many of which featured blocky shapes evoking vistas and gashes of color suggesting chamber musicians. His style hardened, taking on an architectural feel. Simplified in a mode reminiscent of American artist Guy Pene duBois, Weeks's figures unfolded as mere components in larger schemes. They complement scenes of boating, walking, and instrumentalizing without animating them. These works illustrate apparent contradictions that become reconciled on the canvas. Comedians are rendered in a menacing, distinctly ill-humored manner. A gliding ferry sits disturbing still. Musicians clasp their instruments but not in positions that would allow them to generate music, depicting silence where tunefulness is anticipated. As Richard Vine notes, "Now pictorial space gets pushed and pulled to the artist's purposes in the manner of Cézanne. Those riders on the ferry, would they not be at home on Seurat's Grande Jatte? The trees above that man on a park bench bear a distinct resemblance to the ones that Picasso and Braque cubicized in 1908. The space around the two people at a piano is Giacometti's, filled with light." Weeks takes these familiar, stylized elements and maturely transforms them. His confidence is marked by the retention of his corrections, such as the remnants of a rock's image peeking through the desired solid strip of water in *Seascape II*. He also forgoes the specifics of posture and facial expression, preferring the emotionless, mask-like impersonality that defies psychological interpretation.

In 1988, Weeks retired from teaching and embarked on a series of solo exhibitions in New York and California. His paintings are held in several important collections, including the American Federation of Arts; Howard University; Museum of Fine Arts, Boston; San Francisco Museum of Modern

Art; and the Oakland Museum of California Art. Weeks's paintings illustrate the gesture of abstract expressionist leanings incorporated in the drawing of tangible forms, thus initiating one of the West Coast's most significant art movements. His spotlight on jazz venues paid homage to African Americans, like himself, whose innate desires to interweave traditional and abstract expressions gave birth to an explosion of color, texture, and intensity.

FURTHER READING

Jones, Caroline A. *Bay Area Figurative Art (1950–1965)* (1990).

Plagens, Peter. *Sunshine Muse: Contemporary Art on the West Coast (1945–1970)* (1974).

Vine, Richard. "James Weeks at Hirschl & Adler Modern—New York, New York—Review of Exhibitions," in *Art in America* (Dec. 1993).

ROXANNE Y. SCHWAB

Weeks, Seth (8 Sept. 1868–Dec. 1953), musician (mandolin, banjo, guitar), music teacher, composer, and bandleader was born in Vermont, Illinois. His father, an "elocutionist," recognized his son's musical abilities and encouraged him to commence his musical studies at the age of seven, besides attending school. Seth Weeks started with the violin, but soon abandoned that instrument in favor of the guitar, and eventually the mandolin. After playing and practicing for some fifteen years, he conducted a Mandolin and Guitar Orchestra in Tacoma, Washington, and became a music teacher with pupils in Chicago, Boston, San Francisco, and Salt Lake City. From the 1890s most of his compositions were published by Shaeffer and Lyon & Healey (Chicago), a typical example being the "Grand Concert Polka" for Mandolin, guitar/piano (Shaeffer, 1900). Besides teaching he made concert tours throughout the United States and Canada.

He was in Boston on the Keith circuit in 1900 when he decided to participate in the 1900 annual "Cammeyer Festival of the Banjo, Mandoline & Guitar" in Britain, where he arrived with his wife Carrie (age thirty-three) and daughter Hazel (age seven) in September of that year. His international reputation as "America's Greatest Mandoline Virtuoso" was such that, a few days after arrival and even before he performed at the festival (in December), he made recordings for Edison cylinders and Berliner discs.

Weeks made London his permanent home (his compositions, mainly vocal music, now being published by Francis, Day & Hunter), and from this base toured the United Kingdom and the continent with repeated returns to the London recording studios in 1901 and 1902 (Berliner discs, Edison and Pioneer cylinders): "Mr. S. Seth Weeks will soon gain a vast international reputation as a mandolinist, thanks partly to the phonograph. On his way to Russia this month, he is to visit both Paris and Berlin to make phonograph records" (*Anjo World*, Vol. VIII, No.81, 8 Jan. 1901, p.160; no surviving copies of these recordings have been found). Weeks travelled both as a solo performer and in troupes of varying sizes. The Sunderland People's Palace saw the "Weeks & Jones Trio, In Their Original Rag Time Dance" (May 1902); a series of postcards captioned "Cake Walk" and postmarked 1904 show him playing the banjo in a group of four (two ladies, two gentlemen); in Budapest in 1909 he was billed as "Week's Neger-Quintett"; in Berlin in 1910 theatrical contracts were for Week's American Singing Band (with Thornton Buckley, born 12 November 1875 at Fayetteville, Tennessee; and Russell Jones, born 29 Oct. 1892 at Tacoma, Washington); in Frankfurt's Krystall-Palast in 1911 he was advertised as "Weeks, Negerkapelle." His first wife Carrie is believed to have died during 1904. On 23 December 1905 Seth Weeks, widower, married Eleanor Jones, age thirty-two, from London. In 1912 Seth Weeks and his daughter Hazel witnessed the wedding of their fellow countryman Victor Joyner, musical entertainer. When war broke out in Europe Hazel and Seth Weeks, once again widowed, returned to New York; by 1919 he played mandolin with WILBUR SWEATMAN's Kings of Jazz in that city.

In January 1920 Weeks returned to Europe, this time directing his own jazz band to replace Mitchell's Jazz Kings at the Apollo, Paris. His musicians deserted him in August to reorganize as the "Red Devils" under the direction of pianist Eli Carpenter. Over the next few years Weeks played banjo as a sideman with bands led by drummers Hughes Pollard (1921) and BUDDY GILMORE (1924), and the "International Six" (up to 1926). His death was reported in the *New York Amsterdam News* (9 Jan. 1954, p. 9). His daughter Hazel had also returned to Europe and became a well-known personality in Berlin's black community, working as a German-English-French correspondent for the Greek legation.

Prior to World War One, almost all names in American mandolin history were of either Italian descent or had a Jewish background. As far as is known,

Weeks was the only black American soloist during the 'Golden Age of the Mandolin'. At first glance, his compositions are similar to those of other Americans ... with his use of difficult full-chordal writing. It seemed logical enough to assume that he was just writing in the style of the day, until we consider that he was born about ten years before Pettine, Abt, Siegel and Stauffer. Having studied the guitar for fifteen years before taking up the mandolin, it was probably his experience playing chordal music on the larger guitar fingerboard that led to his writing tour-de-force chords for the mandolin, so it is entirely possible that he was influential in establishing chord-melody writing as the American mandolin style. Although his influence on the American mandolin school is only conjecture, Weeks can be credited with writing the first known American mandolin concerto, in 1900.... Although the piano writing is rather weak, the mandolin writing is extremely difficult and advanced.... After beginning his career as a classical soloist, by 1919 Weeks was playing mandolin with jazz bands, possibly also making him the first jazz mandolinist, before Dave Apollon (Gladd, p. 14).

FURTHER READING

Bee. "Portraits. No.69. Mr. S. Seth Weeks," *The Banjo World* Vol. 8, No. 73, p. 20 (Dec. 1900).

Gladd, Neil. "Black Musicians in American *Mandolin History*," *Mandolin Quarterly*, Vol. 1, No. 1 (Winter 1966).

Heier, Uli, and Rainer E. Lotz. *The Banjo on Record: A Bio-Discography* (1993).

Lotz, Rainer E. *Black People: Entertainers of African Descent in Europe and Germany* With audio CD (1997).

Lotz, Rainer E. "Seth S. Weeks: A Bio-Discography," *Mandolin Quarterly*, Vol. 1, No. 1, pp. 4–13 (Winter 1996).

RAINER E. LOTZ

Weems, Carrie Mae (1953–), photographer and mixed-media artist, was born in Portland, Oregon. Nothing is known of her parents or early life. She began exploring issues of family life, memory, and narrative—concerns she held throughout her career—while studying at the California Institute of the Arts in Valencia. In 1981 she received a bachelor of arts degree from Cal Arts. In 1984 she both earned a master of fine arts degree from the University of California at San Diego and exhibited her first major work, *Family Pictures and Stories* (1978–84), at San Diego's Multi-Cultural and Alternative Space Galleries. She attended the graduate program in folklore at the University of California at Berkeley from 1984 to 1987.

Although photography was central to Weems's projects, her art most frequently consisted of complex mixed-media presentations in which photographs were enhanced with tints and through their juxtaposition with text and fabric. Inspired by the photographs of black American life in the 1950s made by Roy DeCarava, Weems often examined and contested documentary photography's claim of objectivity (hooks, 67). Like DeCarava before her Weems produced "images problematizing black subjectivity [which in turn] expand the visual discursive field" (hooks, 67–68). At the same time, her work transcended the boundaries seeking to restrict it to black contexts. She endeavored both to complicate hackneyed ideas of black collectivity, and to position the black experience as a universal one.

In the *Ain't Jokin'* series (1987–1988) Weems composed a pictorial narrative told through the presentation of original and re-photographed images juxtaposed with clever and acerbic text clips, both new and appropriated. Weems commented: "There will always be this kind of tension between what you see within the photograph and what you see beneath it, with the text always cutting through" (hooks, 82–83). *Ain't Jokin'* was followed by the well-known *Kitchen Table Series* (1990). In this project she staged a picture of home life centered on a black woman character. The female subject, played by the artist herself, assumed intricate and unabashed looks and gestures that directly engaged the viewer. Deceptively simple in composition the sparse silver print images were rife with emotional tension. Weems mused, "In most every black person's life today, home is where you find it, just where you find it" (hooks, 74).

After serving as a teaching assistant in the early 1980s at the University of California at San Diego, San Diego City College, and University of California at Berkeley, she took on assistant and visiting professorships at Hampshire College (1987–1991), Hunter College of the City University of New York (1988–1989), and the California College of Arts and Crafts in Oakland (1991). She was an artist-in-residence at the Rhode Island School of Design, Providence (1989 1990), the Cité des Arts, Paris (1993–1994), and was the Philip Morris Resident at the Künstlerhaus Bethanien, Berlin (1997–1998). In 2000 Weems was the STERLING A. BROWN and Class of 1922 Visiting Professor at Williams College, in Williamstown, Massachusetts, and a resident artist at the Skowhegan School of Painting and Sculpture in Maine. She later served as a visiting professor in Harvard University's Department of Visual and Environmental Studies in 2001.

Weems's metaphorical family album featured places existing in private and collective memories. In "Went Looking for Africa" (1993) she photographed contentious sites on the continent, including Gorée Island, the infamous holding area for slaves prior to their crossing of the Atlantic, which she captured with unsettling beauty. In so doing Weems questioned on the one hand, the endurance of the "slave forts," and on the other, the ephemerality of a black, racial collective based upon the black Atlantic diaspora. Of the project's evolution, Weems stated, "I was a subject in search of myself and attempting to map a new psychological terrain for myself and others ... 'searching, [to use James Baldwin's words] for the evidence of things unseen'" (Collins, *Projects 52*).

Weems's search for family and self was also addressed in other areas of her oeuvre. Out of an installation she created at the J. Paul Getty Museum emerged her *From Here I Saw What Happened* and *I Cried* series (1995–1996). The work involved her appropriation of Joseph T. Zealy's daguerreotypes of South Carolinian slaves, commissioned by Harvard geology and zoology professor Louis Agassiz in 1850, who hoped that Zealy's pictures of enslaved blacks would support the polygenetic rhetoric. However the daguerreotype portraits did not present the slaves as anthropomorphic specimens; instead, these images intimately depicted the slaves' humanity (Banta, 51). Weems enlarged and placed Zealy's pictures in a circular frame to highlight the act of looking. She also treated the glass frame with a red tint to evoke violence and passion, and she added provocative text that functioned as critical voice and image caption. Weems's adaptation of Zealy's photos intensified the emotive experience and drew attention to artistic creativity, recording and revisiting history.

In 2000 Weems added The Hampton Project to her archive of photo-based journeys into the limitations and possibilities of family histories. This Williams College Museum of Art exhibition was comprised of her responses to photographs from Frances Benjamin Johnston's Hampton Album (1900). Johnston's images documented student life at Hampton at that time when the school's primary mission was the education of newly emancipated slaves and Native Americans. Weems digitally remastered and transferred Johnston's original photographs to variously sized muslin and canvas supports while employing her characteristic method of accenting pictures with text. Following its display at Williams, The Hampton Project toured venues throughout the United States, although Hampton University opted out as an exhibition site.

Weems continued to expand notions of place and belonging, family and community with each new work created or exhibition mounted. Some included: Recent Work, 1992–1998, Everson Museum of Art, Syracuse (1998–1999); Ritual and Revolution, DAK'ART 98; Biennial of Contemporary Art, Galerie Nationale d'Art, Dakar, Pilkington-Olsoff Fine Arts, Inc. (PPOW Inc.), New York, University of California at Berkeley Art Museum, and Pacific Film Archive, Berkeley (1998); Who What When Where, The Whitney Museum of American Art at Philip Morris, New York (1998); The 2nd Johannesburg Biennial, Africus Institute for Contemporary Art, Johannesburg (1997); Projects 52: Carrie Mae Weems, Museum of Modern Art, New York (1995); and Carrie Mae Weems Reacts to Hidden Witness, J. Paul Getty Museum, Malibu (1995).

For her talents Weems has received numerous prestigious awards including The Louis Comfort Tiffany Award (1992); a National Endowment for the Arts Fellowship (1993–1994) and NEA Visual Arts Grant (1994–1995); The Alpert Award for the Visual Arts (1996); and a 47th Venice Biennial Commission (1997). She was awarded an honorary doctorate by the California College of Arts and Crafts in 1999.

FURTHER READING

Banta, Melissa. "Framed: The Slave Portraits of Louis Agassiz," in *A Curious and Ingenious Art: Reflections on Daguerreotypes at Harvard* (2000).

Collins, Thomas W., Jr. *Projects 52: Carrie Mae Weems* (exhibition pamphlet, 1995).

Friis-Hansen, Dana. *The Kitchen Table Series* (catalogue, 1996).

hooks, bell. "Diasporic Landscapes of Longing," and "Talking Art with Carrie Mae Weems," in *Art on My Mind, Visual Politics* (1995).

Patterson, Vivian. *Carrie Mae Weems: The Hampton Project* (2000).

Piché, Thomas Jr., and Thelma Golden. *Carrie Mae Weems: Recent Work, 1992–1998* (1998).

GENEVIEVE HYACINTHE

Weems, Renita J. (26 June 1954–), ordained minister in the African Methodist Episcopal Church, teacher, and women's advocate, was born in Atlanta, Georgia, the daughter of Willie James Weems Jr., a self-employed electrical contractor, and Carrie Baker. Weems and her two brothers began their early education at Haugabrooks Academy, a private black school in northwest Atlanta. Despite their meager income, her parents were determined that their children's learning would entail small classes and nurturing that elevated their sights. Haugabrooks lacked many resources. It did not have enough books for the students or a real library, the school bus was unstable, its buildings were dilapidated, and most parents were unable to pay the tuition in full or on time. Her parents' strain to pay tuition of twelve dollars per week for Haugabrooks proved well worth it for Weems. The academic challenges, nurturing, and strong educational base she received provided a substantial foundation, inspiration, and resolve that became an integral part of her career.

Weems graduated from West Fulton High School in Atlanta in 1972, earned her B.A. from Wellesley College outside of Boston in 1976, and earned her master of divinity from Princeton Theological Seminary in 1984. She earned her doctor of philosophy from Princeton Theological Seminary in 1989, becoming the first African American woman to earn a degree in Old Testament studies. Weems attributed her interest in ministry to something much larger than herself or anything within her, namely God. She decided not to become a full-time pastor or evangelist, however, and instead she became a professor of religion. As a minister, she explains, she can "operate in a number of different venues," speaking, preaching, writing, and full-time teaching (www.beliefnet.com/story/130/story_13035_1.html, 22). Weems's passion for teaching is grounded in the Haugabrooks learning experience imparted by her African American teachers, in particular Susie Skinner and Lewis Smith, the white guidance counselor, Ms. Flowers, who pointed her toward Wellesley College, and the white librarian, Ms. Culbreath, who discussed books with her. Her Haugabrooks teachers instructed her in obedience, courage, leadership, ambition, discipline, confidence, compassion, and conversation. They were dedicated beacons, teachers with a mission to educate and elevate the race.

Weems became professor of Hebrew Bible studies at Vanderbilt University Divinity School in Nashville, Tennessee, and she served as the 2003–2005 Camille and William Cosby Visiting Professor in Humanities at Spelman College in Atlanta. She emulated the teaching style of her Haugabrooks teachers, who understood that educators do not make one learn but simply create a space for learning. She understood that while intelligence is crucial, a student must be "ready from within" to engage in true learning. She aimed to teach

"students a reverence for learning, for mystery, for something to happen within and from within," to demonstrate "the power of thinking and the power of remaining open" (Weems, 13).

Weems wrote or contributed to several academic books and articles, including *Battered Love: Marriage, Sex, and Violence in the Hebrew Prophets* (1995), commentary for the book of Song of Songs for *The New Interpreter's Bible*, (1990), and a commentary on the book of Jeremiah for the *Global Bible Commentary* (2004). Her nonacademic books include *Showing Mary: How Women Can Share Prayers, Wisdom, and the Blessings of God* (2002) and *What Matters Most: Ten Lessons in Living Passionately from the Song of Solomon* (2004). Weems's nonacademic books focus on "womanist" theology, examining the religious standpoint of women of color. Her work in this area specifically challenges standard patriarchal images of women in the Bible, offering a reassessment and reinterpretation of them, along with the commonalities of struggles and passion shared by biblical and modern Christian women. In *Showing Mary*, Weems sees Jesus's mother as a matriarchal symbol possessing keen intuitive wisdom and powerful inner strength rather than a fragile woman who is overwhelmed by God's plan for her son. Likewise she reveals that the crises that confront Mary—her immaculate conception and possible damage to her reputation as an unwed mother—are similar to numerous relationship issues and career transitions that women encounter in the early twenty-first century. *What Matters Most: Ten Lessons in Living Passionately from the Song of Solomon* is a story grounded in Weems's lived experience and extensive Old Testament scholarship of Shulammite, a remarkable, passionate, strong-willed woman seeking to follow God's plan for her. Weems describes through the life of this protagonist how to discover one's passion and understand the essence of being passionate—dreams that inspire one's soul and choices that make one's spirit alive. From the text, women understand their feminist nature and decide who they are and what they want out of life. Weems's online newsletter *Something Within: For Women Seeking Balance and Wholeness* and bimonthly e-column "Beliefnet" reflect her passionate commitment to teaching and empowering women. Weems saw her nonacademic writings as a "confluence of conversations" (personal letter) that combine her voices of personal experiences and academic scholarship. They are a convergence of scholarship with her personal interest in ordinary

African American women readers, demonstrating that she was an informed writer in these works. Like others, she argued that there is a relationship between scholars and their scholarship. For Weems, that relationship is contextual. Her nonacademic writings are substantive works grounded in research but not necessarily intended to represent the value of her scholarship.

Weems was the keynote speaker for national religious, civic, and sorority organizations, local churches, community events, and radio and television programs. In 2002 she gave the keynote address "Women and Leadership" at the Delta Sigma Theta annual meeting in Atlanta and presented "Women, Spirituality, and Healing" at the annual Women's Council luncheon at the National Medical Association annual meeting in Honolulu. She served as a panelist for Bill Moyers's award-winning 1995 PBS *Genesis Project* and several A&E channel religious and biographical projects. For several years she was a featured speaker for the North Carolina State Substance Abuse Office's Addiction: Focus on Women Conference, held in Kanuga, North Carolina. She married and had one daughter.

FURTHER READING

Weems, Renita J. *I Asked for Intimacy: Stories of Blessings Betrayals, and Birthings* (1993).

Weems, Renita J. *Listening for God: A Minister's Journey through Silence and Doubt* (1999).

BLANCHE RADFORD CURRY

Weightman, Philip Mitchell, Jr. (13 June 1902–22 July 1991), a leading organizer and international vice president of the Packinghouse Workers Union of America, following a period as a respected organizer of the Swift Company's in-house welfare system, who later worked with the Political Action Committee of the Congress of Industrial Organizations (CIO), and with the merged AFL-CIO's Committee on Political Action (COPE).

Born in Vicksburg, Mississippi, Philip Mitchell Weightman Jr. was the oldest son of a man of the same name, born around 1859, equally skilled at brickmaking, bricklaying, and butchering, and the former Sara Lee Watts, born around 1870, both native to Mississippi. Weightman's paternal grandmother was one of several sisters born enslaved in Brunswick, Virginia, and brought to Vicksburg by owners who refused to break up the family group. His paternal grandfather was classified as "white" by the laws and customs of the nineteenth century; the elder Weightman's "white" cousin Frank Hall owned a meat market connected to a grocery store, which opened up opportunities to learn the trade. The family included his siblings Charles, Frances, and Philander.

Weightman attended St. Mary's Catholic School through fourth or fifth grade, then went to work at Burke Construction Company to help support his family. Plastering and bricklaying in Mississippi at the time were entirely black professions; he excelled in both. He became a frequent reader at a local library, and later took some summer high school night classes at Mrs. Johnson's School, achieving credit through eleventh grade.

In 1917 the family settled in St. Louis, arriving from Vicksburg at different times by way of short stays in Memphis. Father and son got jobs at American Car and Foundry Company, then worked together on a contract to unload two cars of coal a day into the boiler room at $10 per car. Within a year, both got jobs in meatpacking, at Armour and Company, one of the four largest meat processors and wholesalers in the country. In 1920 he married Lululia Mays. From 1920 to 1926, Weightman worked for Swift Dressed Beef, where, he later recalled, black and Polish American workers maintained a close working relationship in the face of exploitation by the packing industry.

Many grievances concerned safety: meat cuts were made on band saws without protection, so if the blade broke, operators could lose their fingers or limbs, or even be sawed in half. Without a union, Weightman often became the spokesperson for informal complaints to foremen. A member during 1920–1921 of the Amalgamated Meat Cutters, he walked out in disgust after a Labor Day parade, when he was waiting for a sandwich at the union hall, only to be redirected to a separate line for black members. The Amalgamated lost a 1921 strike in the industry, partly because, as Weightman recalled, "it was a paper union. They used to have booths, just like where they sell newspapers, where you come and pay your dues. No association with the workers, just a dues-collecting setup."

After walking out of Swift in a dispute with a foreman running 350 hogs an hour down the line in the butchering department, Weightman worked for the smaller Krey Packing Co. until 1929, moving to Chicago at the start of the Great Depression. Starting work at Armour, where a foreman was greatly surprised by his skill splitting hogs and facing hams, he soon moved on to a Swift plant, which already had a 25 percent black workforce. Impressed with the company's industrial relations department, and modest employee benefits, he was a "Swift-oriented company man," organizing baseball teams among Swift employees, and resisting the overtures of the new Packinghouse Workers Organizing Committee. He changed his mind after advocating for a Swift worker, terminated when the company doctor decided he was "too great a risk." That, Weightman asked a supervisor, "could apply to me. That could apply to anybody in here, right?" Soon after, he showed up at work with six union buttons on his cap, at a time when most union members were afraid to show it.

Proceeding to sign up other workers in his department, he found Polish American employees were afraid they would be fired and replaced by black strikebreakers. "I'll join when that guy joins" one told him—pointing to an older black worker. When the Packinghouse Joint Council was established in Chicago in 1939, Weightman successfully opposed establishing separate Polish, black, and other committees, arguing "we're going to have one union or we're not going to have a union at all." During that time, he was often asked to say the last words at funerals for deceased Polish union members. His coworkers elected him president of Local 28 at the Swift plant in 1939. In 1943, PWOC became the United Packinghouse Workers of America, electing Weightman as the union's first international vice president.

Repeatedly refusing overtures to join the Communist Party, Weightman gave communist organizers credit for exposing racial discrimination in hiring at Swift and Co., and contributions to organizing the union, but opposed the party's efforts to control the union. "In all I've said about the Communist Party," Weightman recalled, "I don't want to take anything away from them, because they contributed .... I may not have been as aggressive as I was if it hadn't been for them, you see. The fact that they were talking and urging this and the other, that I thought was for the wrong reasons, but they were good things they were suggesting. That makes the difference" (Cohen, p. 311).

In 1946 Weightman led mass rallies during the UPWA strike against the four largest packing companies, winning a pay increase of sixteen cents an hour after defying a federal return to work order when President Truman seized the industry under the War Labor Disputes Act. After UPWA lost a 1948 strike, although securing the return to work of workers fired during the strike, and a small wage increase, Weightman ran for reelection with the anticommunist "CIO Policy Caucus." He and the

rest of the slate were defeated. He served as field representative, and later as minorities director, with the CIO's Political Action Committee, and after merger with the American Federation of Labor in 1955, with the newly formed AFL-CIO's Committee on Political Education (COPE). In 1960 he was named assistant national director of COPE.

In 1958 Weightman directed successful efforts to defeat so-called right to work legislation in Ohio and California, which would have banned union shop contracts. The same year, supporting Wilbur B. Nolen in the Alabama Democratic primary against Representative George M. Grant, Weightman found the Montgomery Improvement Association, fresh from its victory in the campaign to integrate the city's local buses, "most cooperative." He particularly praised "the cooperation of MIA President Reverend MARTIN LUTHER KING," still relatively unknown, who showed "desire for complete cooperation between Labor and the Negro" (Fink, Gary, *Race, Class, and Community in Southern Labor History*, 1996, p. 216). The following year, he spearheaded voter registration drives in Alabama, Louisiana, and Texas. The National Institute of Labor Education (NILE), formed in 1957 to develop labor education as a component of university education, employed Weightman as an instructor at its first institute in North Carolina.

Weightman was a founding member of the Overseas Hunt and Fish Club, organized in 1958 in Washington, D.C., known among members as the "Godfather" (*Jet*, 14 Mar. 1974, p. 40), and served as treasurer in 1976 (*Jet*, 13 Mar. 1976, p. 40). In 1961 Weightman was assigned to aid Democratic Party efforts to prevent Richard Nixon's first attempted return to political office, as governor of California, in 1962 (*Jet*, 19 Apr. 1962, p. 12).

Weightman retired from COPE in 1967; although retirement at age 65 was mandatory, *Jet* magazine (17 Aug. 1967, p. 12) lamented, "Even with the importance of the Negro vote in next year's presidential election, the AFL-CIO refused to grant its political action ace" another year of work, which would have qualified him for twenty years of service and better pension benefits. He was promptly hired by the Office of Economic Opportunity, as a Supervisory Labor Management Relations Specialist, retiring from the Community Services Agency in 1980 (*Jet*, 27 Mar. 1980, p. 40).

After his second retirement, although he had lived for many years in Washington, D.C., he returned to Illinois. He was living in Calumet City, in Cook County, when he died in 1991. He was survived by his daughter, (Mrs.) Eulalia Luke and preceded in death by his son, Leonard.

FURTHER READING
Barrett, James R. *Work and Community in the Jungle: Chicago's Packinghouse Workers 1894–1922* (1987).
Cohen, Lizabeth. *Making a New Deal: Industrial Workers in Chicago, 1919–1939* (1999).
Draper, Alan. *Conflict of Interests: Organized Labor and the Civil Rights Movement in the South, 1954–1968* (1994).
Halpern, Rick. *Down on the Killing Floor: Black and White Workers in Chicago's Packinghouses, 1904–54* (1997).
Halpern, Rick, and Roger Horowitz. *Meatpackers: An Oral History of Black Packinghouse Workers and Their Struggle for Racial and Economic Equality* (1996).
Street, Paul. "The Backbone of the Union," *Chicago History* 29, no. 1 (Summer 2000): 4–21.

CHARLES ROSENBERG

Weir, Reginald S. (30 Sept. 1911–22 Aug. 1987), tennis player and doctor, was born in New York City, the son of Felix Fowler Weir, a concert violinist and member of the Negro String Quartet, and Ethel (Storum) Weir, daughter of noted Washington, D.C., educator James Storum. Weir first encountered the sport of tennis at the age of ten at nearby Mount Zion Baptist Church. Slender and quick, he readily learned the game and received his first formal instruction at Harlem's main courts on 138th Street from Edgar G. Brown, one of the first great black American tennis players. Weir entered the world of integrated tennis during his senior year at DeWitt Clinton High School. He became the first African American to compete for the school's varsity team in that year, but he also soon experienced the sport's racial inequities. For example, during summer breaks, Weir's white teammates honed their games on the meticulously maintained courts of New York's posh country clubs, while he continued to practice on Harlem's grittier municipal courts.

After graduating from high school in 1927, Weir entered the City College of New York (CCNY), where he won three varsity letters as the school's first black tennis player. During his collegiate years, Weir often played number one singles and competed without racial incident against many of the Northeast's leading colleges. While at CCNY he also received private instruction from white professional Allen Behr, who may have helped arrange a four-month trip to France in the summer of 1929, during which Weir trained with the French National Junior team.

In December of 1929 the United States Lawn Tennis Association (USLTA) held its annual National Junior Indoor Tournament at New York City's Seventh Regiment Armory. Weir and his friend Gerald L. Norman Jr., captain of the Flushing High School tennis team, sent in their one-dollar entrance fees. The USLTA, however, silently omitted the names of the two black entrants from the tournament draw. Norman's father, who coached the varsity tennis team at integrated Bryant High School, investigated, but ULSTA executive secretary Edward B. Moss explained that the organization did not permit black competitors. The elder Norman informed the national office of the NAACP, which promptly publicized the color line and sent an angry open letter to the tennis organization. "The action of the United States Lawn Tennis Association constitutes an action unfair, unsportsmanlike, and calculated to degrade the sport you profess to cultivate," wrote Robert W. Bagnall, associate secretary of the NAACP. "Patrons of sport in this country," he continued, "do not relish the administration of public contests by a spirit of caste and class snobbery" (*New York Age*, 4 Jan. 1930). The black press, along with some white commentators, joined in the harsh criticism, but the tournament's organizers held firm. The USLTA acknowledged its rejection of Weir and Norman and justified its position in a short press release. "In pursuing this policy," executive secretary Moss explained, "we make no reflection upon the colored race, but we believe that as a practical matter, the present method of separate associations for the administration of the affairs and championships of colored and white players should be continued" (*New York Times*, 28 December 1929).

Despite this disappointment, Weir continued to represent CCNY. His teammates recognized his ability and leadership and elected him team captain for his senior year. That season, Weir advanced to the singles finals of the New York state intercollegiate tennis championship, before losing a five-set thriller to a rival from New York University. He graduated from CCNY in 1931.

After college, the USLTA's restrictive policies effectively ended Weir's career in integrated tennis. He competed instead under the auspices of the American Tennis Association (ATA), a parallel organization of African American players founded in 1916. Like its white counterpart, the ATA held annual championships, and Weir quickly found success. A few months after leaving CCNY he won his first ATA National Men's Singles tournament. He successfully defended his title in 1932 and 1933, becoming the first man to win three consecutive ATA titles. Weir also won ATA singles titles in 1937 and 1942.

Off the court he received a medical degree from New York University in 1935 and started a lucrative family practice. As his business grew Weir had less time to devote to tennis, and he became a less frequent participant in ATA tournaments. His time in the spotlight, however, was not over. After World War II, many color barriers fell, and, after JACKIE ROBINSON and KENNY WASHINGTON had integrated professional baseball and football, respectively, in March 1948 Weir applied again for the USLTA-sponsored National Indoor Championship, which was back at the Seventh Regiment Armory. Alrick H. Man Jr., chair of the tournament committee and captain of the United States Davis Cup team, accepted the application based on Weir's performances in previous unsanctioned tournaments. Although Weir lost in the second round to another member of the American Davis Cup team, he had erased professional tennis's unwritten color line and paved the way for other pioneers like ALTHEA GIBSON and ARTHUR ASHE.

In 1952 Weir and his doubles partner, George Stewart, were the first African American men to play at the U.S. Open in Forest Hills, New York; and three years later Weir became the first black man to win a USLTA national championship when he captured the Senior (over the age of forty-five) Indoor Singles. Weir repeated as Senior Indoor champion in 1957 and 1958, and he added Senior Doubles titles in 1961 and 1962. Weir remained active in the sport, winning his last title at the New York State Indoor Clay Court Senior Singles competition in 1977 at age sixty-six. Although he never received the recognition of fellow trailblazers like Robinson, Washington, Gibson, and Ashe, he was a respected member of the metropolitan tennis scene. The *New York Times* routinely referred to him as simply "Dr. Weir," and, in 1970, the City College of New York inducted him into its Athletic Hall of Fame. Weir continued his successful family medicine practice until a few years before his death in Fairlawn, New Jersey.

FURTHER READING
Burrell, J. Mercer. "Hypocrisy in Tennis Color Line," *Amsterdam (NY) News*, 15 Jan. 1930.
Djata, Sundiata A. *Blacks at the Net* (2005).
Friedman, Charles. "Age Is Served," *New York Times*, 23 Nov. 1974.
George, Nelson. "Reginald Weir a Champ to Remember," *Amsterdam News*, 22 Dec. 1979.
"Negro to Compete for First Time in National Tennis Tourney," *New York Times*, 9 March 1948.
"U.S. Lawn Tennis Body Refuses to Allow Colored Players in Junior Tourney," *New York Age*, 4 Jan. 1930.
"Weir, Reginald," in *Total Tennis: The Ultimate Tennis Encyclopedia*, ed. Bud Collins (2003).

GREGORY BOND

Weir, Samuel (15 Apr. 1812–1887?), Brethren minister, was born a slave in Bath County, Virginia. Little is known of his early life. At age two he was moved with his family to Botetourt County, Virginia, when the family's owner, William Byrd, relocated. In 1824, at the age of twelve, Weir was sold to Andrew McClure, whom he served until 1843.

Following the death of his son in a riding accident, McClure and his wife applied to join the local Dunkard Brethren congregation. The Dunkard Brethren originated in 1708 near the village of Schwarzenau, Germany, and originally called themselves Neue Täufer (New Baptists) in order to better distinguish themselves from older Anabaptist groups, such as the Mennonites and the Amish. They were called Dunkers because they fully immersed, or "dunked," their baptismal candidates three times—in the name of the Father, the Son, and the Holy Spirit. One group under the leadership of Peter Becker came to America in 1719 to take up free lands offered by William Penn. The members settled in Germantown, near Philadelphia, from where they eventually spread across the country. Informed that the Brethren did not accept slave owners into membership, the McClures freed Weir, declining an opportunity to sell him for $1,500. Weir remained with the McClures as a free laborer and soon after also joined the Brethren. He was baptized on 14 May 1843 and became "the first colored member received by the [Brethren] church in that part of Virginia" (West in Sappington, 265).

Virginia law allowed emancipated slaves to be sold again into slavery if they were found within the state twelve months after receiving their freedom. This made it dangerous for Weir to remain in Virginia, and in October 1843 it was decided that he should accompany B. F. Moomaw, a member of the Brethren traveling to Ohio. McClure gave Weir "a good suit of clothes, a valuable horse, a saddle and bridle, with money and all things necessary for Sammy in his journey to Ohio; and they parted as Brethren, with their best wishes and prayers for each other's welfare. They met no more in this life" (West in Sappington, 267). On 29 October 1843

Weir and Moomaw reached Ohio, eventually traveling to Paint Creek in Frankfort County.

Weir was received into membership at the Paint Creek Brethren Church as the "first and only colored member in that church, and in that part of the State at that time" (West in Sappington, 268). He found work with William Bryant, with whose family he lived for the next two years. While living with the Bryants, Weir expressed a desire to learn to read. At the age of thirty-one he started informal evening lessons with the Bryant's ten-year-old granddaughter Catherine Long. Weir records the result: "We worked at it that way all winter, and I learned my letters" (West in Sappington, 269). After learning the basics Weir continued in his quest for education:

After this I went to school two winters, and to a colored teacher over in Highland County, where I studied spelling, reading and arithmetic, but I could never make any headway in writing. I stopped going to school too soon, for when I found that I could read the Bible I felt satisfied, and I gave up on all other books but that (Landon in Sappington, 269).

Weir's Highland County, Ohio, teacher was Jacob Emmings, a Baptist minister who was also responsible for encouraging Weir's public ministry. Weir records that his public ministry had an inauspicious start:

My teacher in Highland County was a Baptist preacher, and at their meetings, where I often went, he would urge me to get up and talk. At last I told him I would try; but when the day came I felt so very weak that I thought I could not, and did not get up. But I did not feel well over it, and I thought I would never do so any more (Landon in Sappington, 270).

Despite his unpromising start, Weir became an experienced preacher—though he was not yet accepted as such by his own Brethren church. He recorded:

I had been preaching around at the meetings of the colored people, and of other churches for four or five years; so when the Brethren heard that I was trying to preach, they told me to come out from town, and preach a sermon for the whites at the Bush Meeting House. And they said if they then thought I could preach, they would put me at it earnest (Landon in Sappington, 270).

In August 1849 Weir preached his first sermon at his local Brethren church, speaking for thirty-nine minutes on Hebrews 2:1–2. After the meeting, the members regathered and decided unanimously to grant Weir a charge as minister, and he was instructed to "go to his own race and hold meetings wherever opportunity was offered" (West in Sappington, 270). He continued to travel and preach with some success for many years. In 1872, at a Brethren meeting in Fairview, he was granted authority to baptize and conduct marriages.

The date of Weir's death is not known. Landon West records that Weir was interviewed on 23 February 1887, "during the time of his last affliction" (Landon in Sappington, 265). It seems reasonable to assume that he died shortly after this interview. A successful preacher, Weir made the most of his limited education and was well known for his comprehensive knowledge of the Bible:

Of his knowledge of the Bible, the whites say there was no one in the village or neighborhood who was better acquainted with the reading and sense of the Scriptures than was Sammy; and if any question or dispute arose among his neighbors as to a Bible subject, he was their reference, and his decisions satisfactory (West in Sappington, 271).

FURTHER READING
West, Landon. *The Life of Elder Samuel Weir (Colored)* (1909); reproduced as "The Life of Elder Samuel Weir: A Colored Brother," in *The Brethren in the New Nation: A Source Book on the Development of the Church of the Brethren, 1785–1865*, ed. Roger Sappington (1976).

JEFF CROCOMBE

Welch, Eileen Watts (March 28, 1946–), activist, educator, and business and administrative leader, was born Constance Eileen Watts in Durham, North Carolina, to Constance Merrick and Dr. Charles DeWitt Watts. Dr. Watts was North Carolina's first black surgeon, and it was his outspoken advocacy that would serve as a catalyst for the merger in 1976 of the all-black Lincoln Hospital and the all-white Watts Hospital into a single, multiracial entity, the Durham Regional Hospital. In addition to being the granddaughter of Dr. AARON M. MOORE, one of the founders of Durham Mutual Insurance Company and Durham's first black doctor, and JOHN MERRICK, a prominent black entrepreneur, Constance Merrick Watts was a public force in her own right, lecturing, speaking, and serving a notable term as the head of Moore's popular Durham Colored Library. "As an adult," said Welch in a 2004 speech, "I am much better able to understand and appreciate the accomplishments of my ancestors, of which there are many" (Welch, p. 7). These accomplishments in business, health care, and education would ultimately be echoed by achievements in her own life in those fields.

In 1964 Eileen Watts graduated from Hillside High School, which was, at the time, still an all-black institution. Four years later, while her father was fighting to make integration and the promise of the 1964 Civil Rights Act a reality in health care, Watts graduated from the historically black Spelman College in Atlanta, Georgia. She left Spelman, however, with the intention of pursuing a career as an elementary school teacher, rather than choosing a career in the medical professions like her father. Twenty-two years old, she returned to Durham briefly during the summer of 1968 to marry James "Jim" Welch; they were joined on 13 July 1968 at St. Joseph's African Methodist Episcopal Church in Durham. It was the beginning of a long, happy marriage; in later years, Mrs. Welch affectionately related how her family "adopted" Jim (Welch, p. 1). Shortly after the wedding, the young couple returned to their new home in Atlanta, where Welch began work. Her stint teaching the third grade was cut short, however, by Jim getting drafted into the army to serve in the Vietnam War, which forced the pair to uproot and move to Arlington, Virginia. The couple had two sons, born in 1970 and 1972, and Eileen Welch put her career on hold for a time to raise them.

However, it wasn't long before Welch refocused on a professional career. A few years after her second son was born, she decided to start her own small business in Virginia's Fairfax County, a move that kept her schedule flexible and put her communication skills to work. Book Art, Ltd., a for-profit bookstore, quickly grew into a chain, and it was not long before Welch began to reap a tidy profit. From this point on, she permanently altered the trajectory of her work, now focusing on her entrepreneurial talents. She began a second venture a few years later known as Publishers Network, Ltd., which worked closely with individuals and government agencies in its sale of "special-order publications." Local officials and businessmen took note of her deft aptitude; in 1983, it was her turn to be drafted, in this case as the manager for the Reston (Virginia) Employment Service. She served seven years in this position before being recruited by the INOVA Health System, based in Falls Church. In nearly no time at all, Welch came from being a stranger in town to being a leading and popular administrator. Her employers at INOVA encouraged Welch to work on her M.B.A. in her spare time. In 1995 she received her degree from George Mason University.

Just as Welch's plans had changed over the course of nearly two decades, so had her hometown. In 1996 she came back with her husband when Duke University offered her a position as a director of development for its small, ambitious nursing program. Over the next several years, she flitted through a variety of positions, from director of development to associate dean for external affairs to, finally, assistant dean for development, remaining in the same role: fundraiser. Like her great-grandfather Aaron Moore, she was not at all shy about forging partnerships and making connections, growing to be a close friend of Mary T. Champagne, the dean who "resurrected the school of nursing." Together, they worked tirelessly to raise funds for a new building to consolidate the nursing students and provide more training and communication with the nearby Duke University Medical Center. Proposed in 2002, the completion of the building seemed unlikely just over a year later, but like her father, Welch prevailed through ironclad perseverance. Like her mother, Welch also cleverly utilized community connections, inheriting her mother's position as head of the Standford L. Warren Public Library (formerly the Durham Colored Library) and involving herself as a member of organizations like the Triangle Community Foundation and the Rotary Club. Mary Champagne retired in early 2004, and the building was dedicated in 2005.

Shortly before the building dedication, in the summer of 2004, Dr. Charles Watts, Welch's father, passed away. In the wake of his death, Welch increasingly drew inspiration from her memories of him, a fact that echoed in her speeches and activities; since her return to Durham eight years earlier, she had become closer than ever to the man she affectionately dubbed "an old-timey doc." In 2005, shortly after the dedication of the new nursing building, Watts joined the North Carolina chapter of the Center for Child and Family Health as an Executive Director of Advancement. Using her connections at Duke, Welch helped to forge valuable partnerships between Duke, NCCU, and UNC, including the sharing of North Carolina Mutual company archives. Increasingly, she turned to the press to advocate for awareness and funds for young victims of mental illness and trauma. She has also worked as an Officer in Duke's Department of Child and Adolescent Psychiatry.

Welch's evolution from teacher to entrepreneur to administrator paralleled, in many ways, the strides and successes of more and more African American women at the turn of the twenty-first century. Her personal journey, like others, was inspired by the battles fought and won by her ancestors in the nineteenth and twentieth centuries. Her achievements are significant on a national as well as a personal level. "We all have talents," mused Welch in a 2009 interview, "and we have to use them for the best" (The History Makers).

FURTHER READING

The History Makers. "C. Eileen Watts Welch Biography." *The HistoryMakers.com.* 23 Jun 2009 (accessed 23 Feb. 2011).

Anderson, Jean Bradley. *Durham County: A History* (1990).

Welch, C. Eileen Watts. "Introduction of Family Members and History of Aaron Moore." *North Carolina Mutual Life Insurance Company Records,* 11 May 2004, pp. 1–8. Rare Book, Manuscript, and Special Collections Library, Duke University, Durham, North Carolina.

ALEC LOWMAN

Welch, Elisabeth (27 Feb. 1904–15 July 2003), stage and screen actress and singer, was born Elisabeth Welsh in New York City, the daughter of a Scotch-Irish mother, Elisabeth (Kay) Welsh, and an African American father, John Wesley Welsh (she changed the spelling of her last name from "Welsh" to "Welch" in the late 1920s). Her parents met around the beginning of the twentieth century as domestic workers on the estate of a New Jersey millionaire. Elisabeth described her mother as "a defiant woman" who married her father in spite of the prevailing legal and social prohibitions against interracial relationships in the United States. From the age of seven Welch sang in the choir of her neighborhood Episcopal church, St. Cyprian's, beginning a lifelong singing career that placed her in major stage productions and onto the silver screen. Her proclivity for music reflected her musical family; both parents sang, and John Welsh's brother played trombone. Elisabeth Welch and both of her brothers, Edward and John Jr., took piano lessons as children. John Welsh Jr. eventually studied piano in Berlin.

Welch attended Julia Richman High School, an all-girls school in Manhattan, where she made friends with an assortment of fellow students, including FREDI WASHINGTON. From her early days Welch cultivated the racially color-blind outlook that she maintained for much of her life. Her parents' unconventional relationship, the mixed neighborhood of San Juan Hill in which she grew up, and the panoply of racially diverse friends she collected in school all shaped her view of race as no boundary to the way she lived. Reflecting upon her childhood Welch wrote: "I never felt that I had to fight anything. My closest friends at school were a German and a Swede and they lived around the corner because it was a mixed neighborhood" (Bourne, *Elisabeth Welch,* 5).

Welch made her first show business appearances in the Broadway shows *Liza* (1922) and *Runnin' Wild*, both resulting from her membership in the St. Cyprian's choir. *Runnin' Wild* was a production of the celebrated black vaudeville duo Flournoy Miller and Aubrey Lyles. Welch appeared as Ruth Little, a notable role in which she performed the soon-to-be famous song "Charleston," which introduced the 1920s dance craze of the same name. Yet the success of Welch's first theatrical outings presaged a tragic change in the life of her family. In her late teens, when she first appeared onstage, Welch earned the support of her Episcopalian mother, who accepted the young woman's choice of a life in the entertainment business. Her Baptist father, however, hated his daughter's choice. According to Welch, her father "associated show business with low life and he thought I would become a whore, a streetwalker" (Bourne, *Soft Lights,* 8). Distraught and angry over what he felt was his only daughter's betrayal and his wife's collusion against him, John Welsh left his family and never returned. Though she mourned her father's abandonment, Welch grew more and more enamored with performing and did so now all the more out of the necessity to help support her mother.

In the mid-1920s Elisabeth appeared in NOBLE SISSLE and EUBIE BLAKE's *Chocolate Dandies* with a cast that included JOSEPHINE BAKER. Following this, Welch performed as a chorus member in Lew Leslie's *Blackbirds of 1928*, a noteworthy production that included ADELAIDE HALL, BILL "BOJANGLES" ROBINSON, and Aida Ward. This appearance proved fateful for Welch, for the show's success in the United States initiated European interest, and in 1929 the entire company traveled to Paris for an extended engagement at the Moulin Rouge. This trip marked the beginning of Welch's life as an American expatriate, and her presence in Europe shaped her career significantly. Only a year before Welch had married the trumpeter Luke Smith Jr. in a bid for greater independence from her family. But Smith wanted Welch to give up show business, and she was unwilling to compromise her life on the stage. Her departure for Europe with *Blackbirds* ended the brief marriage. According to her biographer Stephen Bourne, Welch rarely spoke about this particular chapter in her life.

Welch's talent as a singer had always brought her applause, and throughout her show business career she performed in many popular and critically acclaimed stage musicals and revues. Her signature performances set the bar for a number of songs that became standards. Besides "Charleston," Welch performed Cole Porter's "Love for Sale" and "Solomon." In 1933 she introduced the British to Harold Arlen's hit "Stormy Weather" in a wildly popular London revue called *Dark Doings* fully ten years before LENA HORNE popularized the song Stateside. Welch's London performances in *Dark Doings* and then later in that year in Porter's musical play *Nymph Errant* signified the beginning of her fifty-year sojourn in England. She remained there through World War II and beyond and did not appear on an American stage again until the 1980s, when her name, though fairly well known in Britain, was almost entirely forgotten in the United States.

Welch is perhaps best remembered for her British film roles with the African American actor, singer, and activist PAUL ROBESON: *Song of Freedom* (1936) and *Big Fella* (1937). Welch's roles in these films were fairly unconventional in the sense that they avoided the clichés of black women playing servants or prostitutes and were instead leading roles, sharing with Robeson's characters romance, kindness, humor, tenderness, and intimacy. Moreover both films (especially *Song of Freedom*) feature the Robeson and Welch characters as part of egalitarian, interracial communities. Complex and human portrayals of black characters were largely unseen onscreen in the 1930s, and it is not surprising that both of these films came out of Europe instead of the United States.

Although she spent the bulk of her show business career in Europe, Welch returned to the United States toward the end of her life, appearing in musicals and revues that celebrated the tradition of musical theater that launched her career. These included *Black Broadway* in 1980 (featuring BOBBY SHORT, HONI COLES, JOHN W. BUBBLES, and EDITH WILSON), a 1985 production staged in tribute to the composer Jerome Kern, and her own one-woman show *Time to Start Living*, which won an Off-Broadway Theater (OBIE) Award in 1986. Welch continued to perform and record regularly until her death in 2003. She died in Denville Hall, Middlesex, England, at the age of ninety-nine.

FURTHER READING

Bourne, Stephen. *Black in the British Frame: Black People in British Film and Television 1896–1996* (1998).

Bourne, Stephen. *Elisabeth Welch: Soft Lights and Sweet Music* (2005).

DISCOGRAPHY

Elizabeth Welch: Harlem in My Heart (Living Era CD CDAJA5376).

Elisabeth Welch: Soft Lights and Sweet Music (Pavillion Records: Flapper 7060PASTCD).

Miss Elisabeth Welch, 1933–1940 (World Records SH-328).

Paul Robeson and Elisabeth Welch: Songs from Their Films (Movie Star Series CD B000004C4R).

Obituaries: *New York Times*, 18 July 2003; *Variety*, 21–27 July 2003.

MIRIAM J. PETTY

Welcome, Verda Freeman (18 Mar. 1907–22 Apr. 1990), teacher, activist, and legislator, was born Verda Mae Freeman in the tiny North Carolina town of Lake Lure, the third child of the farmers John Nuborn and Ella Docia Freeman's sixteen children. Theirs was a lively household, one in which all the children were expected to shoulder a portion of the workload, rising early to pick, clean, and pack produce for sale at market each day. Verda thus learned from a tender age the value of communal enterprise and self-sacrifice—lessons that served her in good stead later in her life when her commitment to social justice was sorely tried.

Not until she was an adult, though, did Welcome encounter the racial and gender inequality that determined the course of her public life. Indeed, her childhood was a happy one. She was descended, as her maiden name implies, from a line of freemen. Her family had a history of land ownership and was respected by members of the Lake Lure community, both black and white. Welcome attended the Mary B. Mullen Institute, a school sponsored by the American Missionary Association where black pupils interacted freely with the largely white staff.

In 1929, Welcome moved north, against her father's wishes, to continue her education and climb the professional ladder. At first she lived with her distant cousins, Elmer and Florence Stubbs, in Wilmington, Delaware, working as a domestic servant by day and attending school by night. She earned a high school diploma, then moved in with another set of distant relatives, Dr. and Mrs. James White, to attend Coppin Normal School, a teacher preparatory college in Baltimore, Maryland. In 1932 she received a teaching certificate from Coppin.

But in Baltimore, Welcome came face to face with the harsh realities of racism. With no African Americans in the police or fire departments, and with even menial jobs allotted by preference to whites, racial strife was endemic. Welcome struggled to make her way in this difficult milieu, attending classes at Morgan State College and teaching full time in a segregated school while coming to grips with her circumstances.

A turning point in Welcome's personal and professional life came when a friend invited her to a series of forums for black college students on the topic of race relations in America. At these forums, she discovered the ideas of W. E. B. DuBois, Booker T. Washington, and Alain Locke. Their ideas, she later said, encouraged her to consider political leadership roles.

While at Morgan State College, Verda met an ambitious young medical student, Henry C. Welcome, and the two married in 1935. They had one child, Mary Sue. Welcome continued teaching at public schools across Baltimore, becoming increasingly distressed at the poor quality of the segregated schools. She also continued her education, earning a bachelor's degree in History from Morgan State College in 1939 and a master's in History from New York University in 1943. At the same time she began to take a more active role in the civil rights movement, joining the National Association for the Advancement of Colored People (NAACP), the National Council of Negro Women, and the Delta Sigma Theta sorority.

When her husband was admitted to the American College of Surgeons, allowing the family to live on his income alone, Welcome retired to take up activism full time. By 1946 she was president of the Northwest Improvement Association, an organization dedicated to cleaning up one of Baltimore's most overcrowded neighborhoods. She then joined the Citizen's Planning and Housing Association, one of the first racially integrated political groups in the city. For the better part of a decade she organized protests, voter registration drives, and boycotts for the NAACP.

Then in the late 1950s a battle over the location of a sporting arena set Welcome's mind on electoral politics. In 1958 she ran for a seat in the Maryland House of Delegates against a candidate who had the backing of the powerful political boss Jack Pollack. Drawing on grassroots organizing skills from her days as an activist, she put together a coalition known as the Valiant Women's Democratic Club and won a narrow victory. During her term in office she took part in the historic effort to ratify the Fourteenth Amendment, which Maryland had failed to do when it was first introduced.

In 1962, after a successful but brief stint in the House of Delegates, Welcome ran for the Maryland state senate, again challenging a powerful, Pollack-endorsed candidate, Senator J. Alvin Jones. And again Welcome won by a tiny margin, fewer than a hundred votes, but her triumph made history as she became the first black woman elected to the upper house of a state legislature. Welcome's proudest accomplishment during her long senate career was winning university status for Morgan State College, the historically black institution in Baltimore. But she was also a key figure in the passage of the Miscegenation Act, which legalized interracial marriage, a public accommodations statute that opened hotels and restaurants to African Americans, and an equal-pay-for-equal-work law. She also supported important gun control and voter registration bills and was an early and persistent advocate for a smoking ban in public places.

In 1964 a group of gunmen attempted to assassinate Welcome as she returned home from a meeting. Luckily, she received only minor injuries. Authorities quickly arrested three men—Charles Hall Jr., James McCall, and Harold Williams—and convicted them of conspiracy to commit murder. At their trials, the men claimed that they had been working for Delegate Ernest D. Young, an African American General Assembly member from Welcome's district who had long been a political rival. Young was arrested and tried but acquitted of all charges later that year.

When her husband died in 1979, Welcome was devastated. She competed to keep her state senate seat in 1982, but many commentators noted that she lacked the spirit and audacity that marked her earlier campaigns, and she lost the race. Soon thereafter her health began to fail, and her daughter, by then an attorney in Atlanta, returned to Maryland to care for her.

Welcome's dedication to public service did not go unrecognized, and she received honorary degrees from the University of Maryland and Howard University. In 1962 she was presented with the Woman of the Year Award from the Women's Auxiliary to the National Medical Association, and in 1988 she was inducted into the Maryland Women's Hall of Fame. Welcome died peacefully at home on a Sunday morning, just after her eighty-third birthday.

FURTHER READING

Maryland General Assembly. *Verda Freeman Welcome: A Person of Principle* (1991).

SUSAN J. MCWILLIAMS

Wells, Dicky (10 June 1907–12 Nov. 1985), jazz trombonist, was born William C. Wells in Centerville, Tennessee, the son of George Washington Wells and Florence (maiden name unknown). Around 1917 Wells's family moved to Louisville, Kentucky, where he began studying music; at age thirteen he was playing baritone horn in the Booker T. Washington Community Center band.

In 1923 Wells switched to trombone. He worked locally with Lucius Brown and Ferman Tapp until 1926, when he was hired by Lloyd Scott to join his Symphonic Syncopators in Springfield, Ohio. After some touring, the band went to New York in 1927 and worked at the Capitol Palace, the Savoy Ballroom, and other venues both in and out of New York through June 1929, when Lloyd's brother, the saxophonist Cecil Scott, took over as the band's leader. After leaving Scott in mid-1930, Wells jobbed around New York, replacing J. C. HIGGINBOTHAM in LUIS RUSSELL's band in the fall of 1931, then joining the banjoist ELMER SNOWDEN at Small's Paradise, where fellow sidemen included ROY ELDRIDGE and SID CATLETT. While Wells was with Snowden, the band appeared in *Smash Your Baggage* (1933), a Vitaphone short. On leaving Snowden, Wells worked briefly with Russell Wooding at Connie's Inn and, from August 1932 to June 1933, was a featured soloist in the Benny Carter Orchestra. A short engagement with Charlie Johnson at Small's preceded a June to December 1933 stay with the FLETCHER HENDERSON band and an appearance at the Lafayette Theater with CHICK WEBB's orchestra.

Wells rejoined Carter's band in early 1934 to work at the Savoy and Empire ballrooms. In September he returned to the Savoy and Connie's Inn with Teddy Hill. In the summer of 1937 he toured Europe with the Hill band, and after playing dates in London, Manchester, and Dublin, he made the first records under his own name while in Paris. In July 1938 he joined COUNT BASIE and remained with the band until early 1946, when he left because of illness. Opting to stay in New York for a while, Wells worked locally with the bands of LUCKY MILLINDER, J. C. HEARD, Willie Bryant, and SY OLIVER until the fall of 1947, when he rejoined the Basie orchestra. In January 1950 Basie disbanded, and Wells went with the blues singer JIMMY RUSHING into the Savoy for an extended stay. In October 1952 Wells began a European tour with the trumpeter BILL COLEMAN, but the combination of extremely cold weather and his excessive drinking took a noticeable toll on both his health and his playing. When he returned to the States the following February, he was still very ill, but by autumn he resumed regular work, this time with Lucky Millinder. A period of freelancing followed, during which he worked with EARL HINES, Buddy Tate, BUCK CLAYTON, Max Kaminsky, REX STEWART, ILLINOIS JACQUET, and Red Prysock.

In early December 1957, as a member of Count Basie's All-Stars, Wells participated in the widely praised CBS telecast *The Sound of Jazz* as well as joining two Rex Stewart–led reunions of Fletcher Henderson alumni in November 1957 and August 1958. In the fall of 1959 and the spring of 1961 Wells toured Europe with Buck Clayton's All-Stars, a nine-piece group including the former Basie sidemen Emmett Berry, Earle Warren, and Tate. Between these tours Wells worked in Tate's band at the Celebrity Club in Harlem. From October 1961 until June 1963 he toured with RAY CHARLES, and during the summer he played in Reuben Phillips's show band at the Apollo. In 1965 Wells returned to Europe to work as a featured soloist with Alex Welsh. On his return to New York, he resumed freelancing. In September 1967 he began working days for a Wall Street brokerage firm, but he remained active in music, touring Europe with Tate in late 1968 and appearing at the New Orleans Jazz Festival in June 1969 and the Newport Jazz Festival in July 1972 with Carter's all-star big band. Before the 1971 publication of his autobiography, Wells had been mugged three times: twice in Brooklyn, while attempting to collect rental income on property he owned, and once near his home in Harlem. A fourth, even more brutal attack took place in 1973, but he survived a long coma and began playing again in late 1976 with Earle Warren and CLAUDE HOPKINS. His last noted appearances were with his own combo at the West End Café in 1981 and with Bobby Booker's Big Band at Small's Paradise in 1984. In 1985, suffering from a complication of ailments, he was admitted to a rest home in New York, where he died.

Wells made his first records in January 1927 with Lloyd Scott and, although he had been influenced earlier by the trombonist Jimmy Harrison, a youthful idol in Louisville and later a major voice in Harlem bands, it is clear from Wells's solos on "Symphonic Scrontch" and the November 1929 "In a Corner" and "Springfield Stomp" by Cecil Scott's Bright Boys that his was a new and independent voice. Further growth toward stylistic individuality is apparent on Russell's August 1931 session, but his indisputable high points during this early period are on the April and May 1933 recordings of the Benny Carter Orchestra, under the leadership of the British arranger Spike Hughes. On almost all of the fourteen titles recorded, Wells is at his most distinctive. Even in the company of such widely regarded jazz soloists as Carter, HENRY "RED" ALLEN, and COLEMAN HAWKINS, the trombonist emerges as a totally matured stylist, as inventive and emotionally moving as any of his better-known colleagues. He conducts himself with similar conviction on Fletcher Henderson's "King Porter Stomp" from August 1933 and on Horace Henderson's "I'm Rhythm Crazy Now" and "Minnie the Moocher's Wedding Day" from October, but his major opportunity occurred in the spring of 1937 while he was with Hill. Strikingly fluent solos on "My Marie," "A Study in Brown," and "King Porter Stomp" were followed in July with twelve small band performances recorded in Paris under his own name. Here he is at his best on "Between the Devil and the Deep Blue Sea," "Lady Be Good," and "Dicky Wells Blues." In the four years since the Hughes recordings, Wells's style went from unbridled passion and restlessness, as evidenced in his pronounced vibrato and yearning declamations, into a more mellow, controlled virtuosity characterized by a broader tone and increased technical mastery.

Without question, Wells's most stylistically definitive work took place during his first years with Basie. Beginning in August 1938 he was featured on such groundbreaking records as "Texas Shuffle," "Panassié Stomp," "Taxi War Dance," and "Dickie's Dream" as well as several more on which he provided stirring backgrounds to Rushing's vocals. Wells made his second appearance as a small-band leader in December 1943, and on these records, in the company of Bill Coleman and LESTER YOUNG, he can be heard giving full rein to his unconventional ideas. Although evident in his solos on the big band records, the compact setting of the septet allowed him even more space to experiment with asymmetrical rhythmic phrasing, upper register glissandos, wide interval skips, and other devices uncharacteristic of the trombone. At this time Wells was also mastering diverse timbres, both with and without mutes and replete with burry sonorities and growling guttural moans. These he had used earlier in his obligatos behind Rushing, but here they are brought into prominence as integral elements in his jazz solos, particularly when he wished to express his humorous side. In March 1944 Wells also played an important role in two small band sessions under the group names of the Kansas City Seven and the Kansas City Six. Recorded within a week of each other, these dates feature Young

but are equally rewarding for the contributions of Wells, Clayton, and Coleman. From the mid-1940s on, Wells recorded prolifically with both big bands and jazz combos, the best of these under the leadership of Basie, Rushing, Clayton, Coleman, Rex Stewart, and Tate. In 1958 and 1959 he led fellow former Basie trombonists BENNY MORTON, VIC DICKENSON, and George Matthews on sessions for the Felsted label; the resulting albums, *Bones for the King* and *Trombone Four-in-Hand*, were among his personal favorites.

FURTHER READING

Wells, Dicky, and Stanley Dance. *The Night People: The Jazz Life of Dicky Wells* (1971; repr. 1991).

Allen, Walter C. *Hendersonia: The Music of Fletcher Henderson and His Musicians* (1973).

Coleman, Bill. *Trumpet Story* (1991).

Dance, Stanley. *The World of Swing* (1974).

McCarthy, Albert. *Big Band Jazz* (1974).

DISCOGRAPHY

Bruyninckx, Walter. *Swing Discography, 1920–1988*, 12 vols. (1985–1988).

Rust, Brian. *Jazz Records, 1897–1942* (1982).

This entry is taken from the *American National Biography* and is published here with the permission of the American Council of Learned Societies.

JACK SOHMER

Wells, Henrietta Bell (11 Oct. 1912–27 Feb. 2008), social worker and educator, was born Henrietta Pauline Bell near the banks outside Houston, Texas, known as the Buffalo Bayou. She was the daughter of Octavia Bell from the West Indies. Her father's name is not recorded.

Growing up in a single parent home in the Fifth Ward section of Houston, Wells knew the hardship and trials that came with being an African American woman in the post-slavery south. As a child, her home was ransacked during the 1917 riots over the treatment of black soldiers in World War I. She also endured Jim Crow–era-segregation, unable to eat in certain areas or try on clothes in some stores. Yet, in spite of the inhospitable racial climate, Wells was determined to succeed beyond what the conventions of the day would see as possible. In fact, she began her journey of participating in the making of history even in early childhood. At eleven years old, she became the first African American child baptized at Houston's former Saint Clement's Episcopal Church.

Wells attended the segregated Phyllis Wheatley High School, graduating as valedictorian in 1929.

She received a partial YMCA scholarship to Wiley College in Marshall, Texas, an historically black, liberal arts college founded by the Methodist Episcopal Church in 1873 to educate newly freed slaves. Wiley College has the distinction of being the first all-black educational institution west of the Mississippi River and it was at Wiley where Wells encountered for the first time poet, educator, and politician, MELVIN B. TOLSON, an unorthodox, yet compelling English professor and coach of the debate team. Tolson was known for challenging his students to think and read critically, and Wells learned quickly how to articulate various positions against an opposing view. Tolson later would become responsible for expertly leading the Wiley debate team on a ten-year winning streak and after some aggressive encouragement, Wells went on to become the first freshman, female member of the Wiley College debate team.

The Wiley debate team also boasted another significant team member, fourteen-year-old future civil rights leader and founder of the Congress of Racial Equality (CORE), JAMES S. FARMER JR. Farmer would go on to be pivotal in the organization of sit-ins and freedom rides during the 1950s and 1960s. He joined the team in 1935 and was the son of JAMES S. FARMER SR., the first black man in Texas to receive a PhD.

As a member of the team, Henrietta Bell Wells competed against and won matches against black colleges like Fisk University in Nashville, Tennessee, and Virginia Union in Richmond, Virginia. After defeating most of the all-black debate squads, Tolson sought competition from all-white universities, in spite of the racial tensions that existed at the time. The Wiley College debate team, with Wells, would later be successful in overcoming all-white teams such as the law students of University of Michigan, initially in non-decision matches.

However, the team, along with Wells, made history in 1930 by being the first all-black team to participate in the first interracial college debate competition held in the United States, holding their own against the more established and well-resourced teams of the University of Oklahoma and Texas Christian University. Due to financial hardships, Wells did not continue to participate on the debate team in her subsequent years at Wiley; deciding to work at the Wildcat Inn, a local college hangout, and as a housekeeper to pay for college instead. In 1935 the Wiley College debate team would later beat the University of Southern California in the national debate championship only to have their win not recognized because all-black teams were not officially recognized until after World War II.

An account of the Wiley College debate team's rise to prominence was depicted in the 2007 film *The Great Debaters*, directed by Academy Award–winning actor, DENZEL WASHINGTON. While many parts of the film were fictionalized, Washington based pivotal scenes on firsthand accounts and scrapbooks shared with Washington and Journee Smollett (the actor playing a composite character based on Wells) by Wells. The oldest living debater at the time, she encouraged Washington to play the role of the testy but prolific instructor Melvin Tolson.

After graduating from Wiley in 1934, Wells utilized her superlative communications skills in a number of different careers. After graduation, in Houston she met and married Wallace Wells, a minister and musician. The couple moved to Gary, Indiana, where she worked as a social worker and case supervisor for the state welfare department and he used his master's degree in music from the University of Southern California to land a position as organist at Saint Augustine's church. Their life in Indiana was abruptly interrupted by World War II when Wallace Wells entered the armed forces.

Upon his return from his last tour of duty, the Wellses moved to New Orleans where Henrietta Wells served as the dean of women at the historically black Dillard University. Finally, both moving and making history once more, Wells returned to her hometown of Houston, Texas, and became the first African American educator at Bonner Elementary School. Wallace Wells died in 1987.

Henrietta Bell Wells defied the popular view of African American women in the first half of the twentieth century. In a time period when women barely had the right to vote, African American's could not vote at all, and most of American society subscribed to the notion that African American women were mostly inarticulate and best utilized as maids and nannies, Wells treated education as her right and pursued excellence as a young orator and later as an educator. Wells died in Baytown, Texas, at the age of ninety-five of unknown causes. She had no immediate survivors.

FURTHER READING

Douyon Jessup, A. "Local Black Politics: Early Evidence from the Houston Case," A paper presented at the annual meeting of the Midwest Political Science Association, Chicago, 2007.

Farmer, James. *Lay Bare the Heart: An Autobiography of the Civil Rights Movement* (1998).

Farnsworth, Robert M. *Melvin B. Tolson 1898–1966: Plain Talk and Poetic Prophesy* (1984).

TRACEY M. LEWIS-GIGGETTS

Wells, James Lesesne (2 Nov. 1902–20 Jan. 1993), artist and educator, was born in Atlanta, Georgia, the oldest of three children of Frederick W. Wells, a Baptist minister, and Hortensia Ruth (Lesesne) Wells, a kindergarten teacher. The couple met while both were students at Wilberforce College in Ohio. When James was one year old, the family moved to the working-class town of Palatka, Florida, where Frederick Wells became pastor of the Mount Tabor Baptist Church. After Reverend Wells died, around 1912, Hortensia Wells opened a day-care center and a five-and-dime store, and James helped support his mother and two siblings by doing odd jobs. Wells's artistic skills were encouraged by his mother, and in 1914 he received a scholarship to the Florida Normal and Industrial Institute, a segregated Baptist high school in Jacksonville. As a teenager he won several awards for drawing and woodworking at the Florida State Fair. Wells deferred admission to Lincoln University in Pennsylvania, which had offered him a scholarship, in order to earn some money before beginning school. In 1919 he moved to Harlem, where he lived with an aunt until 1922. Working as a porter on the Hudson River Day Line, he visited art museums and galleries in his spare time and, in 1920 he took evening classes with George Laurence Nelson at the National Academy of Design.

When Wells entered Lincoln University in 1922 he was disappointed to find that the school had no studio art program. After two years of study he returned to New York and the evening classes at the National Academy of Design, which he continued after enrolling in the undergraduate department of fine arts at Columbia University's Teachers College in the fall of 1924. That same year he received his first solo show, at the 135th Street branch of the New York Public Library. At Columbia, Wells was introduced to the graphic work of Albrecht Dürer and the German Expressionists, both profound influences on his work. Private pilgrimages to the Metropolitan Museum of Art and the Morgan Library, as well as visits to a groundbreaking exhibition of African sculpture at the Brooklyn Museum of Art in 1923, furthered his training. Wells took his first printmaking class in 1927, a year before graduating, and almost immediately he began selling illustrations to the growing number of magazines and journals of the period, especially Harlem's two major publications, *Crisis* and *Opportunity*. A variety of books and publications, including the literary magazines *The Dial* (edited by poet Marianne Moore) and *The Golden Book*, and the political journals *The Survey, Annals of the American Academy of Political and Social Science*, and *New Masses*, also showcased Wells's graphic works. In 1929 Wells's flirty art deco prints with their Egyptian and African motifs were exhibited by the influential art dealer J. B. Neumann at his New Art Circle gallery.

Later that same year Wells accepted a post at Howard University, in Washington, D.C., teaching art alongside James V. Herring and James A. Porter, the school's only other art instructors until LOIS MAILOU JONES joined the department the following year. Wells remained at Howard for the next thirty-nine years, founding the graphic arts program and teaching several generations of African American artists, including ELIZABETH CATLETT, Lou Stovall, and DAVID DRISKELL. Upon his arrival in Washington, Wells moved into a house on R Street in the Logan Circle area, where his neighbors included the Grimké family, ALMA THOMAS, MARY MCLEOD BETHUNE, ALAIN LOCKE, and MARY JANE PATTERSON. Wells quickly became an integral member of Washington's thriving black community, contributing to a range of social, political, and creative pursuits.

After the publication of Alain Locke's anthology *The New Negro* in 1925, Wells heeded the author's call for black artists to focus on African and African American forms and themes. In Washington Wells became a close friend and collaborator of Locke's, who was now his colleague at Howard; he even illustrated later reprints of *The New Negro*. Almost immediately, Wells commenced a long affiliation with another Washington friend, CARTER G. WOODSON, for whom he illustrated books, including *The Negro Wage Earner* (1930) and *The Rural Negro* (1930), and the *Journal of Negro History* published under the auspices of Woodson's Association of the Study of Negro Life and History. He also illustrated books on black history, including Maurice Delafosse's *The Negroes of Africa: History and Culture* (1931), published by Woodson's company, The Associated Publishers. Other projects for which Wells contributed illustrations include the books of the Washington playwright WILLIS RICHARDSON and publications of the New Negro Alliance.

The graphic works, primarily wood block and linoleum-cut prints, that Wells produced for these publications during the early 1930s are characterized by their bold use of pattern and shape and their confident juxtaposition of negative and positive space, realized by intense areas of black and white. Enthusiastically indebted to both African and Egyptian art traditions, Wells often concentrated on African American subjects and themes, including the slave trade and contemporary black life. During his first years in Washington, Wells was also painting, in a style influenced by Cézanne's handling of paint and perspective and the Fauves' use of hot colors. In 1931 he sold two oil paintings, *Flight into Egypt* and *Journey to Egypt*, the first to the Harmon Foundation, which also awarded him their gold medal, and the second to Duncan Phillips, founder of the Phillips Collection. By the early 1930s, Wells was showing regularly in Washington and New York.

In 1931 Wells spent the first of many summers in New York working towards his master's degree at Columbia University's Teachers College. In 1933 he married Ophelia Davidson, a high school teacher and the daughter of a prominent Washington lawyer, SHELBY DAVIDSON, and the sister of Eugene Davidson, president of the NAACP's Washington chapter. The couple had a son, James Lesesne Wells Jr., in 1941. The summer after their wedding, Wells was appointed director of the Harlem Art Workshop, a Works Progress Administration (WPA)–sponsored program offering free art classes to Harlem children, including young JACOB LAWRENCE, ROBERT BLACKBURN, and brothers MORGAN and MARVIN SMITH, all of whom later became well-known artists. Located at the 135th Street branch of the New York Public Library (later the Schomburg Center for Research in Black Culture), the Workshop's faculty included CHARLES ALSTON, Henry Bannarn, and AUGUSTA SAVAGE, who went on to direct the Harlem Community Art Center. The WPA's support of printmaking through its workshops and exhibitions proved a great boon to the development of the graphic arts. Inexpensive to reproduce and distribute, prints played a key role in efforts to democratize both the creation and consumption of art, making it more accessible and affordable to the general public. These goals dovetailed with Wells's interests, and by the time he took another WPA position in the summer of 1935, teaching for the Civilian Conservation Corps in Renovo, Pennsylvania, Wells had turned exclusively to printmaking.

In 1936 Wells took a sabbatical from Howard, returning to Columbia University to complete his M.A. degree. During this year he also studied with the printmaker Frank A. Nankivell. Encouraged by the aesthetics, themes, and politics of Social Realism, Wells took up lithography, an even less expensive production medium, and shifted his focus to images of black workers and contemporary African Americans with works like *Negro Worker* (1938), *Asphalt Workers* (1940), *Portuguese Girl* (1940), and *Flower Vendors, Georgetown* (1940). He continued to teach at Howard, spending occasional summers in Provincetown, Massachusetts. He took a second sabbatical in 1947, which he spent studying at the innovative printmaking studio Atelier 17 in New York City, and after which he introduced engravings to his oeuvre. In the 1950s and 1960s Wells turned to themes from the Old and New Testaments, some inspired by medieval and renaissance art. In the 1960s he began reintroducing color to his work, producing several paintings, including *Salome* (1963), *Ascension* (1963), and *Calvary* (1964). In 1968, after almost four decades of teaching and more than a decade of civil rights work (for which he experienced some hostility—in 1957 a burning cross was placed on his lawn), Wells retired from Howard. In the early 1970s he switched to color linoleum-cut prints, many of which depicted African subjects and places he first encountered on an extended trip to West Africa in 1969. Wells continued working until his death in 1993, in Washington, D.C., from congestive heart failure.

During his lifetime Wells was included in over seventy-five group exhibitions and had solo exhibitions at the Delphic Studios (1932), the Barnett Aden Gallery (1950), the Smithsonian Institution (1948, 1961), Howard University Gallery of Art (1938, 1959, 1965), Spelman College (1966), the Smith Mason Gallery of Art (1969), and Fisk University (1972). Retrospectives of his work were organized by Howard University in 1977 and the Washington Project for the Arts in 1986, and remounted at the Studio Museum in Harlem two years later. Wells was the recipient of several honors, including the JAMES VANDERZEE Award given by the Afro-American History and Cultural Museum in Philadelphia (1977), a citation for lifelong contribution to American art from President Jimmy Carter (1980), and a Living Legend Award from the National Black Arts Festival (1991). In 1984, the mayor of Washington, D.C., MARION BARRY, declared 15 February James L. Wells Day. Wells's work is held in the collection of many galleries and museums, including the Smithsonian, the Metropolitan Museum of Art, and the Howard

University Gallery of Art, which boasts galleries named after two beloved teachers, Lois Mailou Jones and James Lesesne Wells.

FURTHER READING
Powell, Richard J., and the Washington Project for the Arts. *James Lesesne Wells: Sixty Years in Art* (1986).
Obituary: *Washington Post*, 23 Jan. 1993.

LISA E. RIVO

Wells, Junior (9 Dec. 1934–15 Jan. 1998), blues harmonica player and vocalist, was born Amos Blackmore in Memphis, Tennessee. His parents' names are not known. He was raised on a farm just outside nearby Marion, Arkansas, and attended grade school but did not pursue a high school education. Wells, as he was known by the late 1940s, began playing harmonica on the streets of West Memphis, Arkansas, where his family had relocated during World War II. Largely a self-taught musician, Wells was influenced by the recordings of SONNY BOY WILLIAMSON as well as a local resident, Herman "Little Junior" Parker, who later recorded for RPM and Duke records.

In 1946 Wells moved with his mother to Chicago, where he became attracted to the blues clubs, most of which were located in the city's predominantly African American West Side and South Side neighborhoods. Within two years Wells was sitting in with well-known local musicians, such as TAMPA RED, who enjoyed a protracted engagement at the C & T Tavern in the late 1940s. Wells, now using an electric amplifier to project the sound of his harmonica within the noisy clubs, impressed the more experienced musicians, and in 1950 he joined guitarist-vocalists Arthur "Big Boy" Spires and Louis Myers to form the Little Chicago Devils, later known as the Three Aces. When the drummer Freddy Below joined the group in 1951 they became known as the Four Aces and regularly played the local blues club circuit.

Wells's first major break came in 1952, when MUDDY WATERS's harmonica player, LITTLE WALTER JACOBS, left the band to lead his own ensemble, and the departing musician recommended Wells for the band. Although Wells began performing regularly with one of the genre's biggest names, he continued to play "side gigs" in Chicago. In 1953 he made his recording debut for the local States label. Accompanied by the Aces, who were augmented by the pianist Johnnie Jones and the slide guitarist ELMORE JAMES, Wells made a handful of superb recordings, including "Eagle Rock," "Cut That Out," "Junior's Wail," and "Hoodoo Blues."

Shortly thereafter the nineteen-year-old Wells was drafted into the U.S. Army, an event that slowed down but did not entirely stop his musical career. In April 1954 he went AWOL and recorded a second, equally artistically successful session for States. This time he was accompanied by Waters on guitar, the pianist OTIS SPANN, and the bass player and producer WILLIE DIXON. Forced to serve the rest of his two-year term in the army, Wells could not tour and perform regularly with Waters, and his tenure with the band ended.

Wells returned to the Chicago blues scene after leaving the army in late 1955, briefly rejoining Waters's band before re-forming the Aces—this time with guitarist Syl Johnson joining Below and Dave Myers. The group played for an extended period at the Du Drop Inn on Wentworth Avenue, which helped to solidify his place as a respected and popular blues musician in Chicago. Early in 1957 Wells returned to the studio, signing a recording contract with Mel London's Chief Records. The resulting recordings are not as compelling as the States sides, but they also feature Dixon.

In 1958 Wells began a lifelong affiliation with the guitarist BUDDY GUY, with whom he performed at Pepper's Lounge and at Theresa's, a South Side basement club. Wells recorded a handful of successful selections for London's newly formed Profile label in 1959, including the best-selling release "Little by Little." Four months later Wells recorded his initial (and perhaps strongest) version of what became his signature song, "Messin' with the Kid." The song's swagger and bravado appealed to Wells and his audiences. It is distinctive for its alternating rhumba rhythm and 4/4 sections, which give the song a somewhat unusual rhythmic character. His association with London continued for two more years until the company closed.

In the mid-1960s Wells's career shifted in three important ways. First, he began recording albums for Bob Koester's small but important Delmark label. Wells's 1966 *Hoodoo Man*, which owes an artistic debt to both Sonny Boy Williamson and JAMES BROWN, won the *Down Beat* award for the year's best rhythm and blues recording and remains a classic. Second, Wells's audience began to expand beyond its core of urban black listeners to encompass younger white listeners; by decade's end, the majority of his public appearances were on college campuses and in clubs. Third, he cemented his relationship with Guy (who appears on *Hoodoo Man*), and the two remained closely associated until Wells's death.

The period between 1966 and 1970 was one of Wells's strongest. He worked on a series of albums for Vanguard; the first was *It's My Life*, some of which was recorded live at Pepper's Lounge. His crowning achievement was *South Side Blues Jam*, recorded for Delmark, which is arguably Wells's best long-play recording. It included Spann and Guy. In 1970 the Junior Wells–Buddy Guy band also toured with the Rolling Stones, marking Wells's transition to a blues icon in the world of rock and pop music.

Wells spent the rest of his career touring and recording albums in the United States and Europe. The recordings, whose quality was wildly uneven, ranged from a lackluster *Buddy Guy and Jr. Wells: Alone and Acoustic* (1989) to a much stronger band effort in *Better Off with the Blues* (1993). When the band was not touring, Wells continued to perform at Theresa's, his Chicago home base, and at Guy's Checkerboard Lounge. Guy and Wells were often hailed as the "Original Blues Brothers."

Wells contracted cancer in the mid-1990s but continued to perform for two more years. One of his final recordings, *Come On in This House*, received a 1996 Grammy nomination for Best Traditional Blues Album. He died in Chicago.

FURTHER READING

Rowe, Mike. *Chicago Blues: The City and the Music* (1975).

Wilcock, Donald E., with Buddy Guy. *Damn Right I've Got the Blues* (1993).

Obituary: *New York Times*, 17 Jan. 1998.

This entry is taken from the *American National Biography* and is published here with the permission of the American Council of Learned Societies.

KIP LORNELL

Wells, Mary (13 May 1943–26 July 1992), singer and songwriter, was born Mary Esther Wells in Detroit, Michigan, into a single-parent household. Her mother worked as a domestic, but her name is unknown. As a child Wells survived spinal meningitis and tuberculosis, although she was left with temporary paralysis and permanent hearing and sight impairments. After years of struggle to regain her health, she tapped into her vocal ability; her featured solo performances in her uncle's Baptist church and Northwestern High School's choir in Detroit first showcased her warm, throaty voice. She soon began to sing with all-male vocal groups.

There are conflicting accounts of Wells's start at Motown. In 1959 or 1960 at age seventeen or eighteen she either went to Motown's open auditions or was introduced to Motown founder Berry Gordy by his assistant Robert Bateman to demo a song she had written for JACKIE WILSON called "Bye Bye Baby."

Gordy, sensing the potential of both the song and Wells's voice, signed her to a Motown contract as a singer, transformed her style from gospel to pop, and released "Bye Bye Baby" in 1961 on his newly formed Motown label. Motown was a small, two-track studio when Wells joined, but her success would help launch it as a formidable company. Her career as a singer took off almost immediately after Gordy paired her with songwriter Smokey Robinson, and her performances of "The One Who Really Loves You," "You Beat Me to the Punch," and "Two Lovers" made the top ten. Although still under twenty-one years of age, Wells's mature subject matter and soft vocal style set her apart from other popular female singers and "girl groups" such as the Marvelettes and Martha Reeves and the Vandellas. She cultivated a sophisticated and glamorous appearance and quickly gained star status among Motown's performers. In 1962 Gordy put her in his *Motown Revue*, a traveling bus tour that launched the Motown label and the careers of many other Motown stars, including Smokey Robinson and the Miracles, The Marvelettes, and The Supremes, among others, and was a major box-office success. Though the tour showcased Wells's polished stage presence, it was a grueling test of endurance. When the *Revue* played in the South, the performers encountered both segregation and the violence of the civil rights movement. Wells remembered it as a frightening ordeal that brought home the seriousness of the civil rights struggle.

Wells's distinctive voice and presence made her Motown's first solo star performer. Her biggest hit came in April 1964: "My Guy," cowritten with Smokey Robinson, was Motown's first number one single. She appeared on American Bandstand and the Ed Sullivan Show. Wells was the first Motown act to perform outside the United States; she toured with the then up-and-coming English rock group the Beatles, who thereafter cited Wells as their favorite female performer. When the Beatles sent her some of their new songs, she recorded the album *Love Songs to the Beatles* in 1965. While with Motown, Wells had ten Top 40 records as a solo performer and two of her duets with Marvin Gaye, "Once Upon a Time" and "What's The Matter with You, Baby?," were top twenty hits.

During her early career, Wells was married to Herman Griffin from 1960 to 1963, another ambitious Motown singer. Their relationship, however, was marred by discord. He influenced her to have two abortions, and in 1964, upon turning twenty-one and following the success of "My Guy," she acted on his advice and left Motown in search of greater

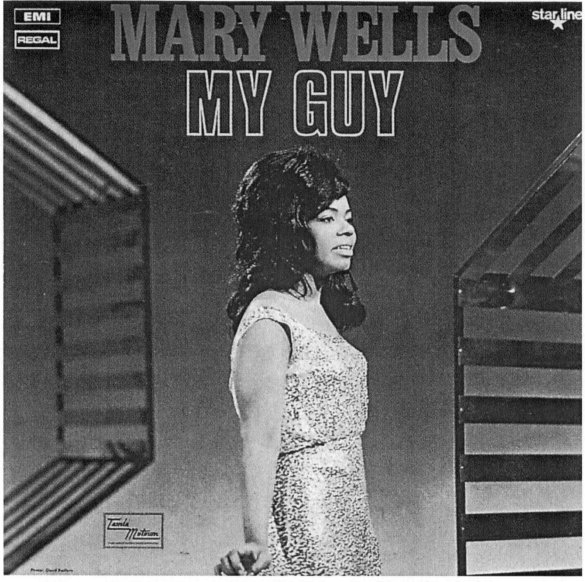

EMI
REGAL

MARY WELLS
MY GUY

star line ★

Mary Wells, on the cover of the 1970 EMI-Starline release "My Guy." (Photofest.)

fortune when her contract with Gordy was declared void because she was underage when she signed it. Wells acted against the advice of her own lawyer, whom she fired, and when she hired a new attorney she became the first artist to sue Motown. According to most accounts, Gordy tried to hold onto his star singer by influencing other labels not to hire her. Wells eventually signed with Twentieth Century–Fox in 1965, lured by a $500,000 recording contract and the possibility of a film career at the studio. Despite the early acclaim, her career was less successful following her departure from Motown. She had only one Top 40 hit with Twentieth Century–Fox, "Use Your Head," in 1965, and appeared in the little-remembered film *Catalina Caper* in 1967. During the next twenty years she had few hit recordings and largely unsuccessful albums with different record companies, including Atlantic-Atco and Jubilee.

During her second marriage, to guitarist Cecil Womack from 1967 to 1977, she took time off from her singing career to raise their three children. By the 1980s, she had once again emerged as a performer. Although disappointed by her subsequent career setbacks, Wells embraced a performance career in "oldies" revues. She also performed in Motown's twenty-fifth anniversary television special in 1983.

In 1990 Wells, a heavy smoker, was diagnosed with cancer of the larynx. Refusing to allow the removal of her larynx, which would have prevented her from ever singing again, Wells opted for radiation therapy. Wells, however, had no health insurance, and the high cost of medical treatments thrust her into poverty. The music industry rallied around Wells when the new Rhythm and Blues Foundation, founded in 1988, raised money for her medical bills. In addition, the American Federation of Television and Radio Artists (AFTRA) and individual admirers in the music industry, including Bruce Springsteen, Rod Stewart, and former Motown colleague Diana Ross, donated money to cover her medical expenses. In 1991 Wells appeared in front of a Congressional Committee to advocate funding for cancer research. She died in Los Angeles the following year, at age forty-nine.

Though the failure of Wells's post-Motown career has often been viewed as a tragic tale, one that necessarily subordinated the artist to the company, her early success as a hit maker established Motown as a record company. Her crossover success with white audiences contributed to the breakdown of racial segregation in the music industry and furthered the success of black performers among white listeners at the height of the civil rights movement in the 1960s. Known as "the First Lady of Motown," Wells also helped further possibilities for women in popular music as songwriters and performers.

FURTHER READING

Garr, Gillian A. *She's a Rebel: The History of Women in Rock and Roll* (1992).

"Mary Wells," in Ashyia Henderson, ed. *Contemporary Black Biography*, Volume 28 (2001).

Posner, Gerald. *Motown: Music, Money, Sex, and Power* (2002).

Stambler, Irwin. "Wells, Mary," in *Encyclopedia of Pop, Rock, and Soul* (1974, 1989).

Wild, D. "Support for Ailing Mary Wells," *Rolling Stone* (10 Oct. 1990).

DISCOGRAPHY

The One Who Really Loves You (Motown 1961).

Two Lovers and Other Great Hits (Motown, 1963).

Recorded Live Onstage (Motown 1963).

Second Time Around (Motown, 1963).

Together (with Marvin Gaye) (Motown 1964).

Mary Wells Sings My Guy (Motown 1964).

Greatest Hits (Motown 1964).

Mary Wells (Twentieth Century–Fox 1965).

Mary Wells Sings Love Songs to the Beatles (Twentieth Century–Fox 1965).

The Two Sides of Mary Wells (Atco 1966).

Servin' Up Some Soul (Jubilee 1968).

In and Out of Love (Epic 1981).

JILL SILOS-ROONEY

Wells, Willie (10 Aug. 1905–22 Jan. 1989), Negro Leagues baseball player and manager, was born Willie James Wells in Austin, Texas, the son of Lonnie Wells, a Pullman porter, and Cisco Wells (maiden name unknown). Willie Wells, the youngest of five children, honed his skills on the city's sandlots, and he began playing with the San Antonio Black Aces, a local African American team, in 1923. In 1924 he competed on a local African American All-Star squad that played exhibition games against the St. Louis Stars and the Chicago American Giants, Negro Leagues teams that held spring training in Texas. Both teams vied for Wells, but he signed with St. Louis.

Wells's new St. Louis teammates ridiculed the bowlegged young man, who stood only five feet eight inches and weighed 160 pounds. Wells was a right-handed thrower and a slick fielding shortstop, but his inability to hit the curveball limited him to a .264 batting average, with few extra base hits. After a disappointing season, he was signed by the Philadelphia Royals, an African American winter All-Star team, to replace its injured starting shortstop. Under the tutelage of veteran outfielder Hurley McNair, Wells learned to hit the curveball. In his sophomore season with St. Louis, Wells's batting average climbed to .295, with six home runs. In 1929 he led the league with twelve stolen bases, a .368 batting average, and twenty-seven home runs, a Negro League record; all accomplished in only eighty-eight games. He led the league in hitting in 1930 with a .404 average. Wells contributed greatly to the St. Louis Stars' Negro National League championships in 1928, 1930, and 1931.

When the Great Depression led to the collapse of the Negro National League after 1931, Wells had short stints with the Detroit Wolves, the Homestead Grays, and the Kansas City Monarchs. From 1932 to 1935 he played for the Chicago American Giants, leading his team to pennants in 1932 and 1933. He was selected as the West Squad's starting shortstop in the first annual East-West All-Star game in 1933, and he played in eight additional All-Star games.

Wells joined the Newark Eagles in 1936 as a player, and he eventually became a player-manager.

Always a keen student of the game, Wells compensated for his weak throwing arm by playing shallow and studying batters' tendencies. He wore the small infielder's glove common to this era, and he cut a hole in the middle of the glove to attain more feel for the ball. As a manager he called the pitches and positioned his defense. The Eagles had what was referred to as the "million dollar infield"—MULE SUTTLES at first base, DICK SEAY at second base, RAY DANDRIDGE at third base, and Wells at shortstop.

In 1940 Wells left Newark to play for Veracruz in the Mexican League, batting .345 in 1940 and .347 in 1941. He returned to Newark for the 1942 season, and he won the Negro League East batting crown with a .342 average, before going back to Mexico from 1943 through 1946. In a 1944 interview with the sportswriter WENDELL SMITH, who played a pivotal role in helping JACKIE ROBINSON break the major league's color line, Wells explained that the salaries were higher in Mexico and, more importantly, African American ballplayers were better accepted by Mexican society. "One of the main reasons I came back to Mexico," Wells explained, "is because I found freedom and democracy here, something I never found in the United States. I was branded a Negro in the States, and had to act accordingly. Everything I did, including playing ball, was regulated by my color. They wouldn't even give me a chance in the big leagues because I was a Negro.... Well, here in Mexico, I am a man" (Smith, 46).

Wells, a valuable player and a fierce competitor, was often targeted by the opposition's base runners and pitchers. After being knocked unconscious in a 1942 game, he returned to the next game wearing a modified construction worker's hardhat. This is one of the earliest recorded uses of a batting helmet. Wells's reputation as a great defensive player and competitor earned him the nickname "El Diablo." He batted .295 at Veracruz in 1944 and in 1945 became the player-manager of the Mexico City team, batting .294. His other Latin American baseball experiences included seven seasons of winter ball in Cuba with a .320 lifetime average and two home run titles, as well as two MVP awards. In the winter of 1941–1942 he played in Puerto Rico, where he batted .378.

When Major League Baseball was integrated in 1947, Wells was on the down slope of his long, distinguished career. His remaining years in the Negro Leagues corresponded with the decline of black baseball. In the early 1950s he went to Canada to manage and play for the Winnipeg Buffaloes. He finished his career in 1954 as the manager of the Birmingham Black Barons. Wells achieved a career batting average of .328 against Negro League competition, and in exhibition games against white major leaguers he batted .392 in 143 plate appearances. The diminutive shortstop put up impressive numbers during his long career and became the first shortstop, either black or white, to combine stellar defense with homerun power.

Wells retired to New York City, working in a delicatessen for thirteen years before returning to Austin in 1973, where he died of congestive heart failure. The Committee on Baseball Veterans voted him into the National Baseball Hall of Fame in 1997, and in 1999 the Society for American Baseball Research ranked Wells eighth on the list of best Negro League players. In 2004 Wells's remains were interred in the Texas State Cemetery in Austin near other famous Texans, including Confederate military heroes.

FURTHER READING

Holway, John. *Black Diamonds: Life in the Negro Leagues from the Men Who Lived It* (1989).

Holway, John. *Voices from the Great Black Baseball Leagues* (1975).

Riley, James A. *Dandy, Day, and the Devil* (1987).

Smith, Wendell. "Introducing 'El Diablo' Wells of Mexico," in *Black Writers/Black Baseball: An Anthology of Articles from Black Sportswriters Who Covered the Negro Leagues* (1994).

Obituary: *New York Times*, 25 Jan. 1989.

PAUL A. FRISCH

Wells-Barnett, Ida Bell (16 July 1862–25 Mar. 1931), antilynching reformer and journalist, was born Ida Bell Wells, the first of eight children born to James Wells, a carpenter, and Elizabeth Arrington, a cook, in Holly Springs, Mississippi. Her parents worked for Spires Boling, a contractor and architect, as slaves and then as free blacks until 1867, when James Wells, against the wishes of his employer, exercised his new right to vote. After returning from the polls to find his carpentry shop locked, Wells moved the family to a house nearby and went into business for himself. In Holly Springs, Ida Wells attended a freedmen's school, of which her father was a trustee, and Shaw University (later Rust College), founded by the Freedmen's Aid Society of the Methodist Episcopal Church and incorporated in 1870.

Ida Wells's early life as a "happy, light-hearted schoolgirl" (Duster, 16) was upended in 1878, when both of her parents and her infant brother died in a yellow fever epidemic that swept the Mississippi Valley that year. Wells, who was then sixteen years of age and the oldest of the five surviving siblings, dropped out of Shaw to support her family by teaching at a rural school in Mississippi. In 1880 or 1881, her two brothers went to live with members of her extended family. Around that time, one of her sisters died of a disease of the spine from which she had been suffering for several years. Subsequently, Wells's widowed aunt, Fanny Wells, invited Ida and her two younger sisters to join her in Memphis. Upon her arrival in the "Bluff City," as Memphis was called, Wells took classes at LeMoyne College and taught school in Woodstock, Tennessee, ten miles outside the city; subsequently she taught in the Memphis public school system.

Wells's activist career began in earnest on 15 September 1883, when she refused to leave a first-class ladies car on the Chesapeake, Ohio, and Southwestern Railway. After the U.S. Supreme Court overturned the 1875 Civil Rights Acts in October of 1883, Wells again attempted to ride a first-class car, so that her subsequent suit against the railway could challenge the Supreme Court's decision. Although Wells won her case in the lower courts in 1884, the Tennessee Supreme Court overturned the decision in 1887. Soon after the first court decision, Wells was asked to write about her protest for the *Living Way*, a Baptist weekly in Memphis. Her successful debut as a journalist came at a time when urbanization and the increase in black literacy rates helped propel the growth and independence of the black press. Taking the pen name of "Iola," she was soon invited to write about practical matters, black womanhood, and politics in black weeklies across the country and, occasionally, for the white dailies in Memphis. In 1887 Wells became the first woman elected as an officer of the Negro Press Association, which had been established in 1884. By 1889 she was anointed "The Princess of the Press" by her colleagues and became a co-owner of the *Free Speech and Headlight*, a militant weekly.

In 1891 a *Free Speech* editorial praising black men who set fire to buildings in Georgetown, Kentucky, in response to a lynching drew calls for the paper's extinction. In the same year, Wells was fired from her teaching position when she wrote an editorial criticizing the inadequacy of the segregated schools and the sexual exploitation of black woman teachers by white board members. With the opportunity to devote all her time to newspaper work, Wells continued writing and traveling throughout the Mississippi Valley to secure subscriptions for the paper.

When a mob murdered a close friend of Wells's and two of his associates in March 1892, Wells embarked on what became a lifelong crusade against the horrors of lynching. The victims—associated with the People's Grocery, a black-owned cooperative—were not killed for any criminal act, she editorialized, but because they took business away from a white competitor. The circumstances surrounding their deaths propelled Wells to call for a boycott of the Memphis trolleys, encourage thousands of blacks to leave Memphis for the newly opened Oklahoma Territory, and expose, as she put it, the "truth about lynching." Lynching had long been a common practice in rural America, especially in the South and West, but, beginning in the late 1880s, it began to take on a particularly racial character in the South. In 1892 alone, there were more than two hundred lynchings, most often of African Americans by whites. Southern white leaders routinely justified the practice by claiming that since emancipation black men had retrogressed to a savage state, and were raping white women. Lynching was primarily a problem in the South, but it was northern academics, at Harvard University, the University of Pennsylvania, and elsewhere, who were most responsible for promulgating theories of black retrogression.

Using the methods of investigative journalism (before there was such a category), Wells documented the fact that less than a third of black victims were even accused of rape, much less found guilty of it. Instead, she averred, it was black women who were the real victims of interracial rape and coercion. Blacks, she thought, were really being punished for their increasing militancy; for their ability to compete economically with whites, and, in particular, for the growing number of consensual relationships between black men and white women. Such assertions undermined the "scientific" racism of the period, the moral authority of white women and men, and the justification for the disenfranchisement of blacks. Her writings, replete with statistics and firsthand observation and interviews, provided the sociological framework that underpinned subsequent studies and antilynching strategies for the remainder of the twentieth century.

In 1892 Wells's campaign urged that blacks boycott the city streetcars and leave Memphis for the new territories opening in the West. Soon after, on 27 May 1892, the offices of *Free Speech* were destroyed, and Wells was exiled from the city upon the threat of death. She found refuge in Brooklyn, New York, where she wrote antilynching editorials for T. THOMAS FORTUNE's *New York Age*, widely considered the country's best black newspaper. Subsequently, her writings were compiled

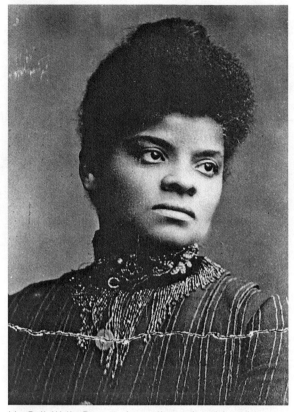

Ida Bell Wells-Barnett, journalist and activist who campaigned vigorously for civil rights and to expose the horrors of lynching, in an undated photograph. (Library of Congress.)

1894 resulted in the formation of the British Antilynching Committee, made up of influential journalists, members of Parliament, and such prominent figures as the Duke of Argyll and the Archbishop of Canterbury. Such attention pressed important liberal figures in the United States, including the labor leader Samuel Gompers and the Women's Christian Temperance Union President Frances Willard (who had earlier opposed Wells), to lend their names to the antilynching cause. Upon her return, Wells continued her campaign across the United States and in 1895 published the anti-lynching pamphlet *The Red Record*.

In June of 1895 Ida Wells married Ferdinand L. Barnett, a Chicago widower who had founded the *Conservator*, the city's first black newspaper, and who, in 1896, became the first black appointed as an assistant state's attorney for Cook County. Soon after their marriage, Wells-Barnett purchased the *Conservator* from stockholders and presided over the Ida B. Wells Club, founded in 1893, which helped establish one of the first black kindergartens in the city. While remaining active in many endeavors, Wells-Barnett and her husband had four children: Charles in 1896, Herman in 1897, Ida in 1901, and Alfreda in 1904. During this period, she campaigned for Republican candidates throughout the state, cofounded the interracial Frederick Douglass Club, worked with the settlement-house founder Jane Addams to thwart calls for segregation in the Chicago public schools, enjoined an interracial delegation to the White House to protest the lynching of a South Carolina postmaster, and mobilized protests against lynchings in her adopted state of Illinois.

In August of 1908, a riot in Springfield, Illinois—in which two blacks were lynched and businesses and homes destroyed—so alarmed a group of northern reformers that they called for the establishment of a new organization later known as the National Association for the Advancement of Colored People (NAACP). Although Wells-Barnett was one of its "Founding Forty" members, she later criticized the organization for its moderation. In response to the riot, Wells-Barnett established the Negro Fellowship League, a settlement house that provided employment and legal protection for the burgeoning number of blacks who migrated to Chicago from the South. In 1913, when women gained limited suffrage in Illinois, Wells-Barnett cofounded the first black women's suffrage club in Chicago, the Alpha Suffrage Club, which was instrumental in the election two years later of the first black city alderman, OSCAR DE PRIEST.

into a pamphlet, *Southern Horrors: Lynch Law in All Its Phases*, which was subsidized by a testimonial given to Wells by black women activists from New York, Boston, and Philadelphia, Pennsylvania. The gathering held on 5 October 1892 was the "real beginning of the club movement among colored women in this country," Wells wrote in her autobiography, *Crusade for Justice* (Wells, 81). In 1896 the movement coalesced into the National Association of Colored Women, the first secular, nationwide organization of African American women.

In 1893 Wells was invited to take her campaign to the British Isles by two editors of *Anti-Caste*, an anti-racist journal published in England. She returned to the United States to protest the exclusion of blacks from the 1893 World's Columbian Exposition in Chicago and to publish a pamphlet, *The Reason Why the Colored American Is Not in the World's Columbian Exposition*, with, among others, FREDERICK DOUGLASS, an ardent supporter of her campaigns. Wells's return to the British Isles in

During World War I, both Barnetts were associated with militant protest and, like others viewed by the federal government as "radicals," were the subjects of dossiers compiled by military intelligence. In 1917, despite warnings by government authorities that she was committing treason, Wells-Barnett protested the hanging of twelve black soldiers who were court-martialed for their alleged role in a riot in Houston, Texas, where the men were stationed. Although she was not arrested, Wells-Barnett was refused a passport to attend the Versailles Peace Conference in 1919 as a delegate of the National Equal Rights League, an organization headed by the Boston editor WILLIAM MONROE TROTTER. MARCUS GARVEY's Universal Negro Improvement Association had also selected Wells-Barnett as a delegate to the Versailles Conference.

The ending of the war in Europe coincided with an upsurge in racial violence in the United States, and Wells-Barnett again played a vital role in publicizing these events. She published on-site investigations of the 1918 East St. Louis Massacre, where at least forty black people lost their lives, and also covered the even bloodier Elaine, Arkansas, race riot the following year. The Arkansas riot was precipitated by local authorities when they attempted to break up a union meeting of black sharecroppers. Several of the farmers and a white deputy sheriff were killed in the melee, but the response by white planters and farmers was unprecedented in its barbarity. Over the course of seven days, local whites, aided and abetted by U.S. infantry troops, systematically chased down and killed more than two hundred African Americans in what historian DAVID LEVERING LEWIS has described as an American pogrom. More than a thousand black sharecroppers were rounded up and packed in a stockade. Wells-Barnett, the NAACP, and other organizations engaged in a multi-year effort to defend the sharecroppers, twelve of whom were sentenced to death. Sixty-seven others were given lengthy prison terms.

But the racial violence of the era was not restricted to the South. In her hometown of Chicago in 1919, an attack and subsequent drowning of a black youth, swimming in the "white side" of a beach area, escalated into urban warfare that resulted in the death of thirty-eight people, including fifteen whites and twenty-three blacks. The Chicago riot was distinguished by the militant response of blacks who fought back and, in some cases, took the offensive. In its aftermath, Wells-Barnett urged blacks to testify against white assailants. She also became active in civic organizations formed to ameliorate race relations and, with her lawyer husband, helped defend African Americans indicted for violent crimes and murder during the uprising.

Despite her declining health in the 1920s, Wells-Barnett continued to fight discrimination and racial violence through the Ida B. Wells Club. She also remained active in politics with the Cook County League of Women's Clubs and helped to establish an early Chicago branch of A. PHILIP RANDOLPH's Brotherhood of Sleeping Car Porters and Maids. In 1930, a year before her death of uremia in Chicago, she ran unsuccessfully as an independent for a state senate seat in Illinois.

Wells-Barnett left a rich legacy of activism. She helped to establish community institutions and organizations that aided poor blacks, empowered women, and defended those unjustly accused by the legal and extra-legal systems of law. Wells-Barnett's strategies, developed through her campaign against lynching, also anticipated future political movements. Her militant activism drew upon a long tradition of African American civil disobedience and self-defense, and her political journalism challenged the prevailing racial and sexual stereotypes of her times. Her essential radicalism, which focused on the interconnections of race, class, and gender discrimination, prefigured that of later black feminist activists and writers such as ANGELA DAVIS, ALICE WALKER, and BELL HOOKS.

FURTHER READING

The Ida B. Wells Papers, including her diary, are in Special Collections, Reggenstein Library, University of Chicago.

Duster, Alfreda M. *Crusade for Justice: The Autobiography of Ida B. Wells* (1970).

McMurry, Linda O. *To Keep the Waters Troubled: The Life of Ida B. Wells* (1998).

Obituaries: *Chicago Tribune*, 25 March 1931; *Chicago Defender*, 4 April 1931; *National Notes*, May 1931: 17; *Crisis*, June 1931: 207.

PAULA J. GIDDINGS

Wesley, Carter Walker (29 Apr. 1892–10 Nov. 1969), military veteran, attorney, civil rights advocate, and publisher, was born in Houston, Texas, the son of Harry and Mabel Green Wesley.

Carter Wesley lived with his mother, a public school teacher, after his parents separated. Attending early grades in Houston's racially segregated public schools, he graduated from Booker

T. Washington High School, then arrived at Fisk University in Nashville, Tennessee, by 1910.

Like many students at historically black colleges and universities at that time, he may have taken college preparatory classes at Fisk, but did not enroll in college level courses until 1913–1917, earning a bachelor's degree, magna cum laude. He was listed in the 1910 census twice, once at a Fisk dormitory, and also at his mother's home, 3200 Washington in Houston, where his older brothers Harry and Freeman were working, respectively, as a general laborer and a Pullman car porter.

Registered for the draft in Nashville, May 1917, Wesley volunteered for a segregated army officer training camp in Des Moines, Iowa. Commissioned as a second lieutenant in October 1917, he served with the 372nd and 370th infantry regiments in the battles of Argonne, Verdun, and Oise-Aise. By Armistice Day, when the war ended, he had been promoted to first lieutenant.

Demobilized from the army, Wesley entered Northwestern University Law School, in Evanston, Illinois, graduating in 1922. In 1920 Wesley was one of three roomers with the family of William and Carol Harris, at 3826 Vernon Avenue in Chicago. He moved to Muskogee, Oklahoma, where he formed a law practice with J. Alston Atkins, a friend from Fisk, who had graduated from Yale Law School. In 1923 Wesley married Gladys Dunbar, an Ohio native he had first met at Fisk; she died in 1925.

During the next five years, Wesley argued thirteen cases before the Oklahoma Supreme Court, winning eleven, according to Charles William Gross's unpublished dissertation, cited in at least two published books. The most controversial case has been widely misunderstood. Leonard D. Ingram, a minor child and member of the Muskogee (Creek) nation, received patents for a homestead of 160 acres in 1907, in connection with the former "Indian country" becoming a state. Like many Muskogee, Ingram was of partly African descent, which could have been from ancestors adopted into the nation, ancestors enslaved to other Muskogee, or both. In 1911 his mother, Minerva Ingram, was appointed guardian, and promptly executed three oil and gas leases for "as long as oil and gas were found in paying quantities." There appears to have been manipulation to arrange a deal advantageous to Prairie Oil and Gas Company.

Wesley and Atkins argued a case in 1926–1927 brought by both Ingram and his mother to void the leases. The case went all the way to the United States Supreme Court, where Justice Oliver Wendell Holmes noted they had argued it well. However, the court "declined to correct construction of state law by state courts," and found no federal constitutional violation, thereby leaving the leases in force. Wesley and Atkins's local reputation was tarnished over billing Ingram $40,000, motivating another African American attorney to file *Ingram v. Wesley* on Ingram's behalf (169 Okl. 248, 36 P.2d 720).

Wesley returned to his native Houston in 1927. For a time he moved back in with his mother, now a school principal, at 3210 Washington Avenue. Wesley and Atkins formed Safety Loan Brokerage, with two other partners, investing $25,000 in real estate and property management. This business failed as the Great Depression deepened. The two law partners were among the founders of Webster-Richardson Publishing Company, organized 6 April 1927 with Clif Richardson Sr., founder and publisher of the Houston *Informer*; S. B. Williams; and George H. Webster. Richardson received one hundred shares of the *Informer*, Webster the same for his print shop, and Wesley and Atkins fifty shares each for $5,000 cash investments.

After 1929, Atkins focused on the practice of law, while Wesley fought Richardson for control of the *Informer*. Wesley insisted on a sophisticated bookkeeping system, while Richardson was more relaxed; Richardson objected to tabloid-style content he found offensive, which Wesley considered good for business. Richardson was a local hero for risking his life documenting incidents of systematic racial discrimination since 1919. Wesley, however, wanted control, and got it. At the end of 1930, Richardson formed a new paper, the *Houston Defender*, and his name was dropped from the title of the publishing company.

Wesley merged the *Informer* with the *Texas Freeman* in 1932, taking positions as treasurer of the corporation and general manager and editor of the combined paper. He forced out George Webster in another clash. Wesley made the *Informer* the most successful black newspaper in Texas, and circulation grew from 4,764 to 44,024 in fifteen years, supporting the expansion of the paper's format from eight pages to twenty by 1941. Wesley published customized editions in Austin, Galveston, Beaumont, and other towns. He also owned the Dallas *Express*, and papers in New Orleans, Mobile, and San Diego.

Continuing to practice law, Wesley and Atkins, along with JAMES MADISON NABRIT JR., who joined the firm in 1931, played a long, and sometimes contentious, role in a series of cases challenging

Democratic Party primaries in Texas that were limited to voters classified as "white." Since Democrats routinely won every general election, the racially exclusive primary meant that those African Americans able to vote at all had no influence on who actually took office. Four decisions by the United States Supreme Court from 1927 to 1944 overturned the practice, which had first been challenged by Richard D. Evans in 1919.

Following the court's 1932 ruling in *Nixon v. Condon*, Wesley had some sharp debates with NAACP officers, who thought Wesley should give more credit to the NAACP in the *Informer*, while Wesley advocated a greater role for attorneys of African descent in handling the cases. In 1936 Nabrit left to join the faculty of Howard law school (later serving as president), where WILLIAM HENRY HASTIE and others on the faculty helped formulate strategy for further Texas voting rights challenges. The litigation was taken up by THURGOOD MARSHALL, NAACP chief counsel, ultimately reaching the United States Supreme Court in 1944, in *Smith v. Allwright*.

Wesley remarried in 1933, to Doris Wooten; the couple had three children. In 1940 Wesley and Frank L. Stanley Sr. formed the National Negro Publishers Association, which in 1956 changed its name to National Newspaper Publishers Association, growing to 120 members at the time of his death, and 148 by 1989. He provided financial and legal aid to HEMAN SWEATT, the *Informer*'s circulation manager, who secured enrollment in the University of Texas law school after a Supreme Court ruling, but clashed with Thurgood Marshall and other NAACP leaders, arguing that truly equal black schools would be acceptable, while Marshall pushed for full integration.

In 1954, weeks after the Supreme Court decided *Brown v. Board of Education*, Wesley urged an "easy does it" approach to desegregation of public facilities, focusing on libraries, parks, and golf courses, leaving swimming pools until later. He counseled black leaders in Beaumont, Texas, to "refuse any public statement" while quietly talking to "the people who control the parks and golf links" (Robertson, p. 87). Wesley died at home after a long illness.

FURTHER READING

Bessant, Nancy Eckols. "The Publisher: A Biography of Carter Walker Wesley." Unpublished Ph.D. dissertation, University of Texas, 1981.

Grose, Charles William. "Black Newspapers in Texas, 1868–1970." Unpublished Ph.D. dissertation, University of Texas, 1972.

Robertson, Robert J. *Fair Ways: How Six Black Golfers Won Civil Rights in Beaumont, Texas* (2005).

Smith, J. Clay, Jr. *Emancipation: The Making of the Black Lawyer, 1844–1944* (1999).

Obituaries: *Jet* magazine, 27 Nov 1969, p. 53; *International Library of Negro Life and History*, 1970, p. 369.

CHARLES ROSENBERG

Wesley, Charles Harris (2 Dec. 1891–16 Aug. 1987), historian, educator, minister, and administrator, was born in Louisville, Kentucky, the only child of Matilda Harris and Charles Snowden Wesley. His father, who had attended Atlanta University and worked as a clerk in a funeral home, died when Charles Wesley was nine years old. Wesley grew up in his maternal grandparents' comfortable home, completed Louisville Central High School in two years, and entered the preparatory division of Fisk University in Nashville, Tennessee, at the age of fourteen. He later enrolled in Fisk's collegiate division, where he developed a strong interest in music. He joined the famous Fisk Jubilee Singers, which had been organized in 1867 to raise much-needed funds for the fledgling school, founded two years earlier by the American Missionary Association. The Jubilee Singers secured funds from national and international tours to construct the university's first permanent building, Jubilee Hall, in 1875. Wesley was a baritone and sang in the group with ROLAND HAYES, later a renowned tenor.

Wesley excelled in the classroom, on the athletic field, and in debate and drama. He ran track, played baseball and basketball, and was quarterback of the football team. He graduated in 1911 with honors in classics and was later initiated into Phi Beta Kappa when the honor society established a chapter at Fisk in 1953. At nineteen Wesley entered Yale University with a graduate fellowship and earned a master's degree with honors in History and Economics two years later, while waiting tables to support himself. He then became an instructor of history and modern languages at Howard University and traveled to Europe, where he studied French history and language. He completed a year of law school at Howard University in 1915 and that same year married Louise Johnson of Baltimore, Maryland, with whom he had two daughters, Louise and Charlotte. Wesley's daughter Louise died in 1950, and his wife passed away in 1973.

Wesley became a minister in the African Methodist Episcopal (AME) Church and was presiding elder over all the AME churches in Washington, D.C., from 1918 to 1938. He later became a candidate for bishop but was not elected, as he refused to campaign for the position. Wesley, who had taught at Howard for seven years, took a sabbatical leave during the 1920–1921 academic year to pursue a doctoral degree in History at Harvard University, while returning regularly to Washington, D.C., to preach at several local AME churches. In 1925 he became the third African American to receive a Ph.D. in History from Harvard, following W. E. B. DuBois and Carter G. Woodson.

Wesley rose through the ranks at Howard University, where he was promoted to professor, chaired the history department, and was director of the summer school, dean of the College of Liberal Arts, and dean of the graduate school. Together with other influential faculty, he helped persuade the board of trustees in 1926 to appoint Howard's first black president, Mordecai Johnson. Wesley's first book, based on his dissertation, *Negro Labor in the United States, 1850–1925: A Study in American Economic History*, appeared in 1927. Carter G. Woodson, who reviewed the book in *The American Historical Review* in 1927, called it "the only scientific treatment of Negro labor in the United States." Wesley refuted biased accounts of black labor, which contended that African Americans were not capable of skilled labor and that they would not work after emancipation without coercion. He revealed early labor-organizing efforts among black Americans and their struggle for economic rights after Reconstruction. Wesley concluded that labor inequality during the early twentieth century resulted more from racial prejudice and discrimination against black workers than from any innate ability among whites. His work was the first comprehensive study of African Americans as laborers rather than as slaves.

Wesley published hundreds of articles and twelve books during his career. His book *The Collapse of the Confederacy*, published in 1937 by the Association for the Study of Negro Life and History, established him as an expert in the field of southern history. The study began as an essay written for a graduate course taught by Edward Channing at Harvard. In the expanded work, Wesley suggested a revisionist thesis that the South lost the Civil War because of internal social disintegration. He became the first black historian to receive a Guggenheim Fellowship in 1930, which he used in London to study slave emancipation within the British Empire. That work influenced his pioneering publications on the role of African Americans in the fight against slavery

in the United States. He sought to demonstrate that African Americans made important contributions to the struggle for their freedom. This was at a time when many mainstream historians argued that African Americans were given their freedom without much effort on their part.

During his long career, Wesley wrote extensively about the history of black fraternal organizations. He explored the group life of African Americans and what they did for themselves more than what was done to them. He published the first edition of the history of Alpha Phi Alpha, the first black college fraternity, in 1929 and became its national historian in 1941. He served as the fraternity's general president from 1932 to 1940, the longest tenure of anyone in that office.

In addition to histories of black fraternal organizations, such as the Prince Hall Masons, the Improved Benevolent and Protective Order of Elks, and the Sigma Pi Phi fraternity, Wesley published *The History of the National Association of Colored Women's Clubs: A Legacy of Service*, when he was ninety-two years old. Wesley was concerned with revealing the group life of African Americans and their achievements not only within their own communities but also in the context of the broader American society. In examining how teachers of U.S. history treated African Americans, he noted that revisions had taken place in interpreting American history and stated in the journal *Social Education* in 1943 that "This need of revision is also clear in relation to the study of Negro life in the United States." He believed in a conscious effort to set the record straight and to revise the errors, omissions, and distortions about black life and culture from the African roots through slavery, Reconstruction, migration, and urbanization.

Wesley became president of Wilberforce University in 1942, an AME-affiliated school that the Methodist Episcopal Church founded in 1856 to educate African Americans from Ohio and nearby free states. The AME Church had purchased the school in 1863. He clashed with church trustees over administration of the school and was asked to resign in 1947. The state of Ohio had financially supported the Normal and Industrial Department within Wilberforce since 1887. When Wesley left Wilberforce, he presided over the separation of the state-supported unit from the university and the establishment of Wilberforce State College, which, after an acrimonious court fight, became Central State University. Wesley served as president of Central State from 1947 to 1965, when he retired.

He was soon appointed executive director of the Association for the Study of Negro Life and History (ASNLH), which had been organized in 1915 by Carter G. Woodson, who had served as a mentor to him. Wesley had been president of ASNLH from 1950, after Woodson's death, to 1965, when he became executive director, a position that he held until 1972, when he again retired. During his tenure as executive director, he revised and republished many of Woodson's earlier works, such as *The Negro in Our History, Negro Makers of History*, and *The Story of the Negro Retold*. He also edited a ten-volume series, *The International Library of Negro Life and History*. Wesley again came out of retirement in 1974 to head the new Afro-American Historical and Cultural Museum in Philadelphia, Pennsylvania, until 1976. He married DOROTHY B. PORTER WESLEY, former head of the Moorland-Spingarn Research Center at Howard University, in 1979. Charles Harris Wesley, who at the time was known as the dean of black historians, died of pneumonia and cardiac arrest at Howard University Hospital.

FURTHER READING

Most of Charles Harris Wesley's papers are in the possession of his family. Some of his papers and publications are housed in the Archives of Dorothy Porter Wesley in Fort Lauderdale, Florida.

Conyers, James L., ed. *Charles H. Wesley: The Intellectual Tradition of a Black Historian* (1994).

Harris, Janette Hoston. "Charles Harris Wesley: Educator and Historian, 1891–1947," Ph.D. diss., Howard University, 1975.

Meier, August, and Elliott Rudwick. *Black History and the Historical Profession, 1915–1980* (1986).

Obituary: *Washington Post*, 22 Aug. 1987.

ROBERT L. HARRIS JR.

Wesley, Cynthia (30 Apr. 1949–15 Sept. 1963), schoolgirl and terrorist bombing victim, was one of eight children born to a poor family in Birmingham, Alabama. When she was six she was adopted by Claude Wesley, a grade school principal, and his wife, Gertrude, a nursery school teacher. The Wesleys had waited a long time for their first child, and they did their best to provide her with a financially secure, culturally enriched childhood. Cynthia took dance and music lessons and was regarded as a promising student at both the Wilkerson Elementary School and the Ullman High School in Birmingham, where she did well in math and played saxophone in the Ullman school band. A vivacious child, Cynthia made friends easily, but she did not forget the siblings she had left behind, passing on to them books and other gifts that she received.

Claude tried to shield his daughter from the harsh reality of segregation, though that was difficult since the Wesleys lived in the African American middle-class neighborhood of Smithfield, also known as "Dynamite Hill"—so named because of the large number of bombings of black homes, churches, and businesses in the area. After the Birmingham police did nothing to solve these crimes, Wesley joined several other black Smithfield residents who volunteered to serve in nightly patrols of the neighborhood. The bombers were widely believed to be members of Birmingham's large Ku Klux Klan, who had access to dynamite and other incendiary devices in the nearby coal mines. Already in 1963 the homes of a prominent black attorney and a wealthy black businessman had been firebombed.

When he dropped Cynthia off at Sixteenth Street Baptist at around ten on the morning of 15 September 1963, however, Claude believed that his daughter would certainly be safe in church, where she planned to attend Sunday school and sing in the youth choir at the main service. Twenty minutes later, as her father filled his car's tank with gas a few blocks away, Cynthia stood with her close friend CAROLE ROBERTSON and fellow choristers ADDIE MAE COLLINS and DENISE MCNAIR in the women's lounge of Sixteenth Street Baptist, where the girls were primping. Upon hearing a tremendous explosion, Claude rushed back to the church, where he found other anxious parents screaming and searching through the rubble for their children. As many as fifteen sticks of dynamite had ripped a large hole in the wall of the women's lounge and demolished a foundation thirty inches thick. Frantic and on the verge of collapse himself, Claude went to the local hospital, where the four girls killed in the blast had been taken. Together with his wife, Claude identified his daughter as one of the four victims. Although his daughter's face had been rendered almost unrecognizable by falling concrete and debris, Wesley recognized Cynthia's class ring and her patent-leather shoes.

Interviewed by the *New York Times* on the day following the blast, Cynthia's parents exhibited a remarkable forbearance in the midst of what must have been unspeakable grief. Claude believed that "this thing that engulfed our child and others is worldwide. Many are involved in this social change. I have not asked why this has happened to

Cynthia Wesley, age 14, is shown on the far right, along with (from left) Denise McNair, 11, Carole Robertson, 14, and Addie Mae Collins, 14. All four girls were killed in the bombing of the Sixteenth Street Baptist Church in Birmingham, Alabama, on 15 September 1963. (AP Images.)

us. I don't feel bitter about it. I'm just hurt that our daughter was plucked from us." Others less directly affected by the killings attempted to make sense of the four senseless murders. On 18 September a funeral service was held at Birmingham's Sixteenth Street Baptist Church for McNair, Cynthia, and Collins—Robertson was buried in a separate service. More than four thousand mourners heard the eulogy by MARTIN LUTHER KING JR., who declared the four girls "heroines of a modern crusade for freedom and human dignity" and argued that they "did not die in vain" (McWhorter, 538). "Good still has a way of coming out of evil," King added, before expressing his hope that the "blood of these girls" would "serve as a revitalizing force to bring light" to Birmingham. King also believed that the girls' sacrifice would finally spur into action "a Federal Government that has compromised on civil rights with a bloc of Southern Dixiecrats and Right-wing Republicans" (*New York Times*, 19 Sept. 1963, 17).

King's words proved somewhat prophetic. Within nine months of the murders the U.S. Congress finally enacted a meaningful civil rights act that ended segregation in all public accommodations. Within two years the 1965 Voting Rights Act finally brought America closer to achieving the democracy that it had long claimed to cherish. The Wesleys and the families of the victims had to wait until 1977, however, before any of those responsible for the bombing were brought to trial. That year Klansman Robert Chambliss, long believed to have been involved in the Sixteenth Street Church bombing, among others, was tried and convicted of the first-degree murder of McNair. When another Klansman, Thomas Blanton, was convicted of all four murders

in 2001, it emerged at his trial that he, Chambliss, and two other co-conspirators could all have been tried and convicted as early as 1965 had it not been for the obstructive tactics of the Federal Bureau of Investigation and local law-enforcement officials.

FURTHER READING
Hampton, Henry, and Steve Frayer. *Voices of Freedom* (1990).
McWhorter, Diane. *Carry Me Home: Birmingham, Alabama: The Climactic Battle of the Civil Rights Revolution* (2001).
Mendelsohn, Jack. *The Martyrs: Sixteen Who Gave Their Lives for Racial Justice* (1966).

STEVEN J. NIVEN

Wesley, Dorothy Burnett Porter (25 May 1905–17 Dec. 1995), archivist, bibliophile, scholar, and librarian, was born Dorothy Louise Burnett in Warrenton, Virginia, the daughter of Hayes Joseph Burnett, a physician, and Bertha Ball, a tennis champion. After her father graduated from Howard University's Medical School, the family moved to Montclair, New Jersey, where she was raised and graduated from Montclair High School in 1923. In 1924, she received a teacher's certificate from Palmer Method of Business Writing and in 1925 received a teaching diploma from Myrtilla Miner Normal School in Washington. She worked as a librarian at Miner Teachers College from 1925 to 1926. Her mentor Lula Allan, librarian at Miner, influenced her to change her field of interest from teaching to library service. In 1929 she married JAMES AMOS PORTER who became a well-known African American artist and art historian;

they had one daughter, Constance Burnett. Porter died 28 February 1970. After receiving her Artium Baccalauei from Howard University in 1930, Porter Wesley enrolled in the Columbia University School of Library Service and in 1931 received her B.S. degree, becoming the first African American woman to do so. A scholarship from the Julius Rosenwald Fund was awarded her in 1931–1932 to attend graduate school at the Columbia University School of Library Service and subsequently she received a master's of library science in 1932.

Porter Wesley devoted her life to the acquisition and collection of materials relating to the African and African American diaspora. She joined the library staff at Howard University in 1928, and in 1930 she was appointed to administer and organize a Library of Negro Life and History from a small collection of three thousand titles presented to Howard University in 1914 by JESSE MOORLAND. The doors opened in 1933 as the Moorland Foundation, and the collection grew to nearly 200,000 items by her retirement in 1973, when it became known as the Moorland-Spingarn Research Center. She became curator emeritus. In 1979 she married CHARLES HARRIS WESLEY, a noted educator and historian who also served as executive director of the Association for the Study of Negro Life and History.

For patrons of the library, Porter Wesley was an invaluable resource with a profound knowledge of black history and culture. Many scholars and authors, including JOHN HOPE FRANKLIN, ALAIN LOCKE, STERLING BROWN, LANGSTON HUGHES, ALEX HALEY, RICHARD WRIGHT, Marion Wright, LERONE BENNETT, John Blassingame, Peter Ripley, JOHN HENRIK CLARKE, Marilyn Richardson, and Roslyn Terborg-Penn, relied heavily on her bibliographic knowledge. In 1973 LETITIA WOODS BROWN said Porter Wesley "has the broadest understanding of Black bibliography of anyone living. If it has been written or even spoken about, Dorothy Porter knows" (Battle). That same year historian BENJAMIN QUARLES stated that "without exaggeration, there hasn't been a major history book in the last 30 years in which the author hasn't acknowledged Mrs. Porter's help" (Encarta). A "go-getter of raw material" (Ardes) is how Clarke, Hunter College professor emeritus, described Porter Wesley in her prime. She was known to frequent estate sales, acquiring trunks of old records, books, and personal correspondence. Clarke said Porter Wesley collected "things other people hadn't even thought about" (Blockson) and wrote of her as "my late mentor and friend ... whom I call the Queen

Mother of African-American bibliophiles and collectors." A dynamo of research and resourcefulness, Porter Wesley provided black bibliophiles and researchers with invaluable information in this area and many others.

In August 1940 Porter Wesley, SUE BAILEY THURMAN, and four other African American women traveled to Cuba as representatives of the National Council of Negro Women. Porter Wesley received the Fellowship for Research in Latin American Literature in 1944–1945, served on the Executive Council of the Association for the Study of African American Life and History, and held memberships in many organizations, including the Africanist Society, American Antiquarian Society, American Library Association, Association of African American Museums, African Studies Association, Bibliographical Society of America, Black Academy of Arts and Letters, Columbia University Library School Alumni, Delta Sigma Theta sorority, District of Columbia Historical Society Advisory Board, District of Columbia Library Association, Essex Institute, National Caucus and Center on Black Aged, National Trust for the Preservation of Historical Sites, Nigerian Historical Society, Phi Beta Kappa Society, the Society of American Archivists, the Library Advisory Committee for the White House, and the U.S. President's Committee on Employment of the Handicapped. In addition she worked on the editorial boards of the Black Abolitionists Papers, Beacon Press, Gale Research, and University Microfilms. From 1962 to 1964 the Ford Foundation sent her to Lagos, Nigeria, to serve as the acquisitions librarian to build the collection at the National Library of Nigeria.

In 1957 Porter Wesley received the Preservation and Administration of Archives Certificate from American University. She was inducted into Phi Beta Kappa Gamma of the District of Columbia on 21 May 1963 in recognition of her attainments in liberal scholarship. She received honorary degrees from the University of Susquehanna in 1971, the University of Syracuse in 1989, and Radcliffe College in 1990. In 1988–1989 she was a Ford Foundation Visiting Senior Scholar at the W. E. B. DuBois Institute of Afro-American Research at Harvard University.

In 1990 the Black Caucus of the American Library Association gave her its first Trailblazer's Award, presented once every five years in recognition of an individual whose pioneering contributions have been outstanding and unique and whose efforts have "blazed a trail" in the profession. In

1993 she received the Distinguished Service Award of the National Historical Publications and Records Commission, and she was awarded the Certificate of Recognition from the Alpha Phi Alpha Wives of Washington, D.C., on the occasion of the installation of their archives at Howard University, Moorland-Spingarn Research Center, on 10 June 1994. Harvard University's Department of Afro-American Studies, the W. E. B. DuBois Institute for Afro-American Research, and the Library Company of Philadelphia sponsored "A Celebration of the Lives and Works of Dorothy Porter Wesley and Dorothy Sterling on the Occasion of the Publication of *The Abolitionist Sisterhood: Women's Political Culture in Antebellum America*" in Cambridge, Massachusetts, on 18 May 1994. On 14 October 1994 President William Clinton, on the South Lawn of the White House, presented Porter Wesley with the National Endowment for the Humanities Charles Frankel Award, which honors Americans who have had outstanding success in bringing the insights of the humanities to wide public audiences. Clinton referred to her as:

> a preeminent archivist of African Americana. During her forty-three-year tenure as the principal compiler of the black studies collection housed at Howard University's Moorland-Spingarn Research Center, she has set national standards for collecting, preserving and making accessible thousands of books, pamphlets, manuscripts, portraits and artifacts relating to blacks in America and in Africa.

She received an award from the Association for the Study of African American Life and History in October 1995, and the latest honor was the 2000 National Advocacy Honor Roll. A plaque was given to the State Librarian and was displayed in the outer lobby of the MARTIN LUTHER KING JR. Memorial Library in Washington, D.C.

One of her earliest publications was a review of André Salmon's *Black Venus* in *Opportunity* in 1930. Two very important papers were published in 1936, a nine page bibliography titled "A Selected List of Books by and about the Negro," which was published by U.S. Department of Commerce, and "The Organized Educational Activities of Negro Literary Societies," 1828–1846, in the *Journal of Negro Education*. She wrote numerous biographies including "David Ruggles, an Apostle of Human Rights" (1943). Porter Wesley's writings and edited works include "Early American Negro Writings: A Bibliographical Study," published in the *Papers of the Bibliographical Society of America* (1945); *North American Negro Poets* (1945); *Early Negro Writing, 1760 to 1837* (1970, repr. 1995); *Afro-Braziliana: A Working Bibliography* (1978); *The Remonds of Salem, Massachusetts: A Nineteenth Century Family Revisited* (1986); and *The Negro in the United States: A Bibliography* (1970, repr. 1999). Her unpublished writings display the range of her academic interests. In 1945 she delivered a paper titled "Racial Heritage of Brazil and Afro-Brazilian Literature in the Colonial Period" at the Latin American Seminar at Wilberforce University.

Hundreds of articles, lectures, and speeches later, her last publication *William Cooper Nell, Nineteenth-Century African American Abolitionist, Historian, Integrationist; Selected Writings from 1832–1874*, was completed by her daughter, Constance Porter Uzelac, and printed posthumously. Other semiannual works by her include *North American Negro Poets; a Bibliographical Checklist of Their Writings, 1760–1944; Early Negro Writing, 1760–1837*; and *Afro-Braziliana; a Working Bibliography*.

Biannually, the Africana Librarians Council (formerly the Archives Libraries Committee) of the (U.S.) African Studies Association presents the Conover-Porter Award, named for her and Helen Conover, a Librarian at the Library of Congress, honoring an author for the most outstanding achievement and excellence in Africana bibliography and reference work. The W. E. B. DuBois Institute at Harvard University presents the Charles Harris and Dorothy Porter Wesley Scholarship in her honor. The Annual Dorothy Porter Wesley Forum and Lecture was initiated in 1989 and is held each Friday of National Library Week at Howard University under the sponsorship of the Moorland-Spingarn Research Center.

Porter Wesley died in Fort Lauderdale, Florida, where she had moved to be with her daughter and son-in-law.

FURTHER READING

The Dorothy Porter Wesley Collection is housed in the Special Collections Division of the African American Research Library and Cultural Center in Fort Lauderdale, Florida, and contains the major portion of her monographic and visual image collection, totaling forty-five hundred volumes and two hundred images and vertical files.

Bahn, Esme E. "Library Curator, Librarian," in *Notable Black American Women*, ed. Jessie Carney Smith (1992).

Battle, Thomas. "Dorothy Porter Wesley: Preserver of Black History—Afro-American Librarian," *Black Issues in Higher Education*, 15 January 1996.

Blockson, Charles L. *Damn Rare: the Memoirs of an African-American Bibliophile* (1998).

Britton, Helen H. "Dorothy Porter Wesley; A Bio-Bibliographic Profile," in *American Black Women in the Arts and Social Sciences: A Bibliographic Survey*, ed. Ora Williams, 3d ed. (1994).

Burkett, Nancy, and Randall K. Burkett. "Dorothy Burnett Porter Wesley," *Proceedings of the American Antiquarian Society* 106 (1996).

Findlay, James A., and Constance Porter Uzlec. Dorothy Porter Wesley (1905–1995): Afro-American Librarian and Bibliophile; an Exhibition 1 February–16 March 2001.

Madison, Avril Johnson, and Dorothy Porter Wesley. "Pioneers of *Public History*: Dorothy Burnett Porter Wesley: Enterprising Steward of Black Culture," *Public Historian* 17, no. 1 (Winter 1995).

Remarks by the President [William Jefferson Clinton] at the Arts and Humanities Awards Ceremony, the South Lawn. The White House, Office of the Press Secretary.

Obituary: "Museum Mourns Dr. Dorothy Porter Wesley," *National Afro-American Museum and Cultural Center Newsletter* 7, no. 2 (Spring 1996).

CONSTANCE PORTER UZELAC

West, Cornel (2 June 1953–), philosopher, educator, and social critic, was born in Tulsa, Oklahoma, the son of Clifton L. West Jr., a civilian air force administrator, and Irene Bias, an elementary school teacher. The West family eventually settled in the segregated city of Sacramento, California. The young Cornel's childhood was at first marked by much anger and rebellion. In the third grade, when his teacher slapped him, he hit her back and was expelled. He was taught at home for six months before being placed in a newly integrated school. At the age of eight he became a devout Christian. From then onward, the precocious Cornel became a conscientious student, and spent much of his youth reading biographies and philosophical texts from the neighborhood bookmobile and articles from the Black Panther newspaper.

West's family was Baptist, and he grew up with a sense of pride in the role of the black church in the spiritual and material survival of former slaves and their descendants. Two influential figures from his childhood were Theodore Roosevelt, a biography of whom West read at age eight, and the Danish philosopher Søren Kierkegaard, whose work he read when he was fourteen. The former inspired him to attend Harvard University and to seek a career in public life; the latter stimulated his philosophical commitment to grapple with the absurdities of modern civilization.

West studied philosophy at Harvard and later at Princeton at a time when both universities were highly influential in the development of American political philosophy. At Harvard, under the influence of the liberal philosopher John Rawls, West espoused the conviction that political institutions should be in the interest of the least advantaged members of society. West also attended many of the lectures of Peter Camejo, a Trotskyite public intellectual who used Harvard's space, and he benefited from the mentorship of MARTIN KILSON, the first African American professor of political science at Harvard. In 1973 West received his BA, magna cum laude, in Near Eastern Languages and Literature, reading biblical Hebrew, Old Testament Aramaic, and classical Greek. Although West's activism had begun in high school, where he served as student president and volunteered in Black Panther soup kitchens, his undergraduate years were marked by an intensification of his social commitments as he and fellow black students participated in antiwar protests and antiracist struggles. West went to Princeton University for graduate study, because he was told by his mentors that it was the best philosophy department in the country. There he came under the influence of Richard Rorty, the most influential advocate of American pragmatist philosophy. That philosophy, built on the thought of Charles Sanders Peirce, William James, John Dewey, and Clarence Irving Lewis, asserts the importance of experience and the value of effective action in social life. West earned his M.A. in 1975 and completed his doctorate in 1980. His dissertation, entitled *The Ethical Dimensions of Marxist Thought*, was published by Monthly Review Press in 1991.

West was a teaching assistant while at Princeton and also an instructor in the New York federal prisons. In 1977 he joined the Union Theological Seminary in New York City, where he taught philosophy of religion and ethics. His senior colleagues at Union included JAMES CONE, the highly regarded African American liberation theologian. While at Union, West began his preaching at Riverside Church as a lay preacher. West has taught at many institutions, including Union (1977–1984 and 1987–1988), Williams College (1982), Yale University Divinity School (1984–1987), and the University of Paris (1987). In 1988 West became Director of Afro-American Studies and Professor of Religious Studies at Princeton, before moving to Harvard in 1994, where he became the Alphonse Fletcher Jr. University Professor in 1998. He and WILLIAM JULIUS WILSON were the first African Americans to hold such professorships, Harvard's most prestigious accolade.

In 2002, after a controversial conflict with Harvard's President Lawrence Summers, West returned to Princeton as the Class of 1943 University Professor of Religion and African American Studies. According to *The Wall Street Journal* (11 January 2002) and *The Chronicle of Higher Education* (18 January 2002), Summers had criticized West for his politics and other nonacademic work, including his rap CD *Sketches of My Culture* (Artemis Records, 2001) and his support of AL SHARPTON's presidential campaign. Summers had also derided West's scholarship as not serious, and he accused West of grade inflation and missing classes. West responded that he would not tolerate the disrespectful way Summers addressed him. The incident received much press coverage, and many editorials appeared on both sides of the dispute. However, as GLENN LOURY reflected in his review of George Yancy's *Cornel West: A Critical Reader*, the many articles and growing number of books on West's scholarship attest to West's influence as a scholar. As for his activism, it is West's prerogative to have a civic life, as it is, ostensibly, for all Americans.

West's political work—marked by his concern about poverty, racism, sexism, and homophobia and by his belief in a radical participatory democracy—has led to his sometimes controversial association with many organizations and leaders, be they black nationalist, Christian, moderate Marxist, cultural leftist, or progressive. For example, West argued that he supported the Million Man March organized by LOUIS FARRAKHAN in 1995 because the march was consistent with his own Christian values and his commitment to black liberation causes. He saw working with Farrakhan to be no more problematic than working with the many white activists with whom he has had disagreements. On another front, West and Rabbi Michael Lerner, editor of *Tikkun* magazine, collaborated on *Jews & Blacks: A Dialogue on Race, Religion, and Culture in America* (1996), in order to address the division and tension between blacks and Jews and to affirm the historical commonality of the oppression faced by both groups. Some black critics have opined that West speaks more of black anti-Semitism than he does of Jewish racism. West has also been criticized for failing to address the fact that white Jewish communities and African American communities are not on an equal playing field in American society, and he has also been criticized for overlooking the existence of African American Jews. West has also been a spokesperson for the Democratic Socialists of America, of which he remains an honorary chairperson, and an adviser to Senator Bill Bradley's presidential campaign in 2000 and to Al Sharpton's in 2004.

West's reputation as the leading exemplar of African American philosophical and religious thought was established during the late 1970s through the late 1980s. His explorations in African American philosophy and his critical engagement with contemporary problems appeared in both Christian and Marxist journals and magazines. In 1989 West became more acceptable to mainstream white scholars in philosophy and religion with the publication of *The American Evasion of Philosophy: A Genealogy of Pragmatism*, which examines the thought of mostly white philosophers and social critics, as well as that of W. E. B. DuBois. In 1993 he achieved national and international acclaim with the publication of *Race Matters*, which received several influential book awards. West's message of building humanistic institutions on the basis of hope, faith, and love for humanity appealed to many readers. It was also popular because of its critical and at times controversial discussion of sexual politics, racial and class conflicts, and the failures of contemporary black leadership. West's professional, intellectual development could thus be constructed as a movement from producing works that focused on black audiences at one stage, to white academic audiences at another, and then speaking to all audiences from his understanding of black America. Since 1993 West has received more than twenty honorary doctorates and awards. Interviews of him have appeared in magazines, journals, documentaries, and news programs in Africa and Europe. His popularity is also attested by his appearance in the blockbuster films *The Matrix Reloaded* and *Matrix Revolutions*, both of which appeared in 2003.

There is, however, a negative side to West's fame. For example, he often receives death threats from white supremacists and other hate groups, especially after an appearance on television. On one occasion, a gunman broke into his home and held a gun to his wife's head, and on another the West family was accosted by an assailant with a rifle. The profound love for and faith in humanity he embodies in his lectures and writings in the face of such reaction reveal much about the man. West's Christian philosophical and ethical conviction is that every human being is valuable, including his enemy. He literally loves his neighbor, including those who might hate him.

West's philosophical originality rests in his unique formulation of what he calls, in his book

Prophesy, Deliverance! (1982), "Afro-American revolutionary Christianity." He argues that philosophy is a special type of critical writing on pressing social problems of "bondage to death, disease, and despair" (*Prophesy, Deliverance!*, 18). Such problems are a consequence of poverty and racism in American society, and they can best be addressed through three resources for African American revolutionary thought: pragmatism, Marxism, and prophetic Christianity.

West aligned himself with John Dewey's pragmatism, which he saw as making a difference through a commitment to historical criticism, and he views this pragmatism as the *American* component of African American thought. The Marxism West defends is in the tradition of democratic socialism, which rejects communism. He also draws on Antonio Gramsci's theories of "organic intellectuals," whose ideas reflect the interests of a particular community—which in *Prophesy, Deliverance!* is the black poor—and of "critical consciousness," which involves questioning our everyday presumptions and political assumptions. Finally, West argues for prophetic Christianity because he believes that it is the overwhelming spiritual legacy of most African Americans. He contends further that the *prophetic* aspect is expressed in the sermons of the African American clergy, many of whom provide insightful criticisms of American society, as found, for example, in the thought of MARTIN LUTHER KING JR. and MALCOLM X. But more importantly, West's formulation of prophetic discourse brings pragmatism and Marxism together in the figure of the cultural critic.

Although West claims to advance three intellectual resources in the book, he in fact advances several. Existentialism emerges throughout in his reflections on black suffering. He uses French and German postmodern thought to construct a "genealogy" of modern racism in European Enlightenment thought. And African American political thought emerges in his discussion of four classical responses to racism: assimilationism, exceptionalism, marginalism, and humanism. West advocates African American humanism. His Marxism, too, is influenced by the Black Panthers' class-based black nationalist thought, which he acknowledges by giving priority to the black poor over the black middle class in both *Prophesy, Deliverance!* and *Race Matters*, in which he advocates a class-based affirmative action remedy.

Since *Prophesy, Deliverance!*, West has consistently remained an existential humanist of the pragmatist variety, a position that he defends in such scholarly works as *The American Evasion of Philosophy* and *Keeping Faith* and in popular ones as *Race Matters, The War against Parents* (1998), and his controversial hip-hop musical tribute *Sketches of My Culture* (2001). In each of these works, he presents the intellectual's task as grappling with political and spiritual absurdity and human suffering. The ongoing thesis of all these works is that African Americans should maintain hope and continue to fight for freedom in a world in which the evidence on such matters as health and incarceration and the political disenfranchisement of black people suggests the contrary. He calls such hope in the face of seemingly hopeless situations a struggle against nihilism.

West's writings became noticeably less overtly Marxist after the fall of the Soviet Union and the Berlin Wall, but the egalitarian and humanistic spirit remains. The result is a body of work with a deep-rooted faith in the potential of American society to fulfill the promise of one day becoming a society that values people more than profits.

In 2009 West published *Brother West: Living and Loving Out Loud: A Memoir*. The memoir was published by Smiley Books, a company founded and owned by the radio and televison host TAVIS SMILEY. Since 2010 West and Smiley also worked together on a radio show, *Smiley & West*. Although he had been supportive of BARACK OBAMA's candidacy for the presidency, West has been among the president's sharpest critics since Obama's election. In West's view, Obama should have done more to help bail out working-class Americans, instead of the banks and other financial institutions. He has also criticized the president's foreign policy for maintaining high troop levels in Afghanistan. In the fall of 2011 West was strongly supportive of the Occupy Wall Street (OWS) movement to highlight corporate greed at a time of economic inequality, and was arrested twice in OWS demonstrations that October.

FURTHER READING

Cowan, Rosemary. *Cornel West: The Politics of Redemption* (2003).

Johnson, Clarence Sholé. *Cornel West and Philosophy* (2002).

Loury, Glenn C. "Review of George Yancy's Cornel West: A Critical Reader," *The A.M.E. Church Review* (April–June 2003).

Osborne, Peter, ed. *A Critical Sense: Interviews with Intellectuals* (1996).

Yancy, George, ed. *African American Philosophers: 17 Conversations* (1998).

Yancy, George, ed. *Cornel West: A Critical Reader* (2001).

Wood, Mark David. *Cornel West and the Politics of Prophetic Pragmatism* (2000).

LEWIS R. GORDON

West, Dorothy (2 June 1907–16 Aug. 1998), writer and editor, was born in Boston, Massachusetts, the only child of Rachel Pease Benson of Camden, South Carolina, and Isaac Christopher West, an enterprising former slave from Virginia who was a generation his wife's senior. Nicknamed the "Black Banana King" before his prosperous wholesale fruit business failed during the Depression, Isaac West provided his gifted daughter with a privileged, bourgeois upbringing. Dorothy's formal education began at the age of two when she took private lessons from Bessie Trotter, sister of the *Boston Guardian* editor WILLIAM MONROE TROTTER. Young Dorothy grew up in a four-story house in Boston with a large extended family made up of her mother's numerous siblings and their children. Although Dorothy tested at the second-grade level at age four, Rachel West insisted that her precocious daughter enter first grade at Boston's Farragut School. Years later West recalled, "When I was a child of four or five, listening to the conversation of my mother and her sisters, I would sometimes intrude on their territory with a solemnly stated opinion that would jerk their heads in my direction, then send them into roars of uncontrollable laughter.... [T]he first adult who caught her breath would speak for them all and say 'That's no child. That's a sawed-off woman'" (West, *The Richer*). Dorothy finished her elementary education in the racist environment of the Martin School located in the city's heavily Irish Mission District, graduated from Girls' Latin School in 1923, and later took courses at Columbia University, where she studied creative writing.

Dorothy always thought of herself as a short-story writer and began her literary career at age seven when, she said, "I wrote a story about a little Chinese girl, though ... I'm sure I had never seen a Chinese girl in my life" (McDowell, 267). From about age ten into her early teens, she regularly won the weekly short-story contest sponsored by the *Boston Post*. The *Post* published her first story, "Promise and Fulfillment," when Dorothy was ten, and the paper's African American short-story editor, EUGENE GORDON, encouraged her to join the Saturday Evening Quill Club, a black writers group. In response to a story submission, *Cosmopolitan's*

Dorothy West, photographed at her home in Oak Bluffs, Martha's Vineyard, Massachusetts, 20 January 1995. (AP Images.)

editor Ray Long—convinced that the writer was a forty-year-old spinster who knew nothing about love—wrote the fourteen-year-old Dorothy a scathing letter asserting that his magazine "had one Fanny Hurst and so didn't need another" (McDowell, 268). Far from discouraging her, however, this rejection had the opposite effect on Dorothy.

In 1925, shortly before turning eighteen, West entered a short-story competition sponsored jointly by *The Crisis* and *Opportunity*, the publications of the NAACP and the Urban League respectively. Her submission, "The Typewriter," tied for second place with ZORA NEALE HURSTON's "Muttsy" and was subsequently published in the July 1926 issue of *Opportunity*. West was then able to convince her family that she had the talent to launch a literary career in New York City alongside Harlem Renaissance stalwarts.

Almost immediately West's stories began to appear in print. "Hannah Byde," published in *The Messenger* (July 1926), was one of the earliest pieces of African American literature to use a jazz motif to explore the spiritual discord of urban life. Over the next few years she published "Prologue to a Life," "Funeral," and "An Unimportant Man." These early stories feature West's lifetime preoccupation with the ways in which children interact with and affect the adult world around them. They are suffused with West's characteristically ironic tone, inspired by Fyodor Dostoyevski, who, she said, "became my master, though I knew I would never write like him" (McDowell, 268). "Nine out of ten stories I write are real," West later said, of her keen observations of family, friends, and social milieus. "I change the situation, but they are something that really happened" (Dalsgard, 37).

When Hurston left New York, West and her cousin Helene Johnson, with financial help from West's father, took over her apartment. West continued to write short stories, although, for a variety of reasons, including the discontinuation of *Opportunity*'s writing contests in 1927, few were published, leaving the young writer dissatisfied with her literary prospects. In 1927 West and her new friend Wallace Thurman won minor roles in the stage production of *Porgy and Bess*, and her weekly earnings of seventeen and a half dollars helped keep her in New York during hard economic times. In June 1932 West sailed for the Soviet Union, along with twenty-two other African Americans including LANGSTON HUGHES, who had been commissioned to revise a movie script about black American life titled "Black and White." When the project fell through, West—and Hughes—remained in the Soviet Union for nearly a year, until word arrived that her father had died.

A more responsible, twenty-five-year-old West returned to New York in 1933, regretful that she had not lived up to her earlier artistic promise. Only "Funeral" and "The Black Dress" were published during the 1930s, although she produced the nonfiction pieces "Ghost Story," "Pluto," "Temple of Grace," and "Cocktail Party" while working for the Depression-era Federal Writer's Project, part of the Works Progress Administration.

In 1933, in an attempt to revitalize the Harlem Renaissance movement by providing an outlet for black authors, West founded *Challenge Magazine*, of which she published five issues. Under the pseudonym of Mary Christopher, West published her own work and that of Hughes, Hurston, ARNA BONTEMPS, CLAUDE MCKAY, COUNTÉE CULLEN, and PAULI MURRAY. The last issue appeared in June 1936, when RICHARD WRIGHT virtually took West's journal away from her. Wright wanted to shift the journal's focus toward a more socially conscious protest literature, a direction West found uncomfortable but against which she offered little resistance. As she explained later, unlike modern women, she was too passive, petite, and soft-spoken to stand up to Wright, his friends, and his lawyer, "who sent me a form to sign giving Wright the rights to something, I can't remember" (McDowell, 272). Moreover, she presumed Wright was acting as a pawn of communists. "I was never crazy about Richard Wright because he was too timid and afraid of white people. I guess it stemmed from his southern background" (McDowell, 272). West's own dry spell came to an end on 29 September 1940, when the *New York Daily News* published "Jack in the Pot," a story that captured the economic and spiritual strife of the Depression. For the next twenty years she wrote two short stories per month for the *Daily News*, a job that kept her writing and able to pay her bills. In the mid-1940s West left New York and moved to Oak Bluffs, Massachusetts, on Martha's Vineyard, the summer playground of her youth. There she wrote her first novel, the semiautobiographical *The Living Is Easy* (1948). The novel, a family drama told through the eyes of young Judy Judson, includes West's examination of black middle-class social pretensions in Boston. The novel was generally well-received although, in a move that deeply affected West, *Ladies Home Journal* eventually decided against serializing the book, which it felt might offend southern readers. When the Feminist Press reprinted *The Living Is Easy* in 1982, West was introduced to a whole new generation.

In the late 1960s West began a new novel, "Where the Wild Grape Grows." Although she had financial support from a Mary Roberts Rinehart grant and a Harper and Row contract, she stopped work on the book, feeling that black revolutionary politics conflicted with her theme of miscegenation. Instead, she resigned herself to writing for the *Vineyard Gazette*, focusing on countering the impression that the only blacks on Martha's Vineyard were in work uniforms. At first her "Cottagers Corner" columns showcased prosperous and affluent black families and their prominent friends and visitors. Later, she began to write more broadly, about people, places, and island happenings, even contributing sketches to the *Gazette*'s bird column. Her last piece appeared on 13 August 1993, when she left the paper to devote herself full time to completing the novel *The Wedding*, incorporating much of the earlier "Where the Wild Grape Grows" into it.

In the early 1990s, after reading West's *Gazette* articles, Jacqueline Kennedy Onassis helped West secure a book contract for *The Wedding*. The novel, about the spiritual price of assimilation and miscegenation, was published in 1995 and became a best-seller, drawing yet another generation to the door of the woman who became known as the sole survivor of the Harlem Renaissance. West's book, which centers on the wedding preparations of Shelby Coles, ends with a child's death and without a wedding, though Doubleday sent out review copies of the novel with an ending Dorothy West had not written. When this was discovered in the fall of 1994, the Harvard professor of African American studies, HENRY LOUIS GATES JR., championed her cause, and Doubleday delayed publication until West's own final chapter could be included. Unfortunately, a number of reviewers had already published their assessments of the novel with the spurious ending. In 1998 OPRAH WINFREY produced a television adaptation of the novel starring HALLE BERRY which transformed the story into a sentimental tale in which Shelby heads down the aisle with few racial concerns and which the critic John Leonard called "Soap Oprah."

West died at age ninety-one in 1998 in Boston. Her many short stories, two prominent novels, and nonfiction articles distinguish a literary career of eight decades that, in the final analysis, reflected the many expectations, failures, and achievements of its times.

FURTHER READING

West, Dorothy. *The Dorothy West Martha's Vineyard Stories: Essays and Reminiscences by Dorothy West in the Vineyard Gazette*, eds. James Roberts Saunders and Renae Nadine Shackelford (2001).

West, Dorothy. *The Richer, The Poorer: Stories, Sketches, and Reminscences* (1995).

Dalsgard, Katrine. "Alive and Well and Living on the Island of Martha's Vineyard: An Interview with Dorothy West, October 29, 1988," *Langston Hughes Review* 12 (Fall 1993).

Guinier, Genii. "Interview with Dorothy West (6 May 1978)," in *Black Women Oral History Project* (1991).

McDowell, Deborah E. "Conversations with Dorothy West," in *The Harlem Renaissance Re-examined*, ed. Victor Kramer (1987).

Obituary: *New York Times*, 19 Aug. 1998.

SALLYANN H. FERGUSON

West, Miguel S. (13 Sept. 1956–), transplant surgeon and associate professor of surgery, was born Miguel Samuel West, the second of seven children to Daisy and Joseph West in Chicago, Illinois. His mother was a social worker, and his father worked as an electrical engineer. His parents separated leaving him to be raised by his hardworking, determined mother. The West children drew inspiration from their mother's work ethic and also from the expectations of their paternal grandmother, who was a teacher. Born in 1913, West's grandmother retained the pins, school transcripts, and certificates belonging to their ancestors who had graduated from schools in the South during the 1860s. West grew up believing that "There is no reason that we [West and his siblings] can't go to school. Our ancestors went to school during slavery!" exclaimed West in an interview. Miguel West's wife Sandra, whom he had known since he was eight years old, became assistant comptroller for the City of Chicago.

West was raised with his brothers and sisters on the South Side of Chicago and became interested in a medical career through watching television programs such as *Marcus Welby, M.D.* and *Dr. Kildare*. West learned human anatomy by studying copies of pictures found in the *World Book Encyclopedia*, drawn for him by one of his friends. His mother helped him learn medical terms when she got home from work. Considered by most to be the smartest kid on the block, he made it through grade school with little effort and graduated fifth in his class at the highly competitive Lindblom Technical High School, a Chicago public school. Tall and athletic, West went to the University of Michigan on a football scholarship; there he completed both of the university's acclaimed premedical and medical programs. In medical school West won the prestigious Kaiser Foundation Scholarship.

In 1982, when two white, South African doctors tried to put up barriers that would have kept him from graduating from medical school, they found themselves in a fight with both Miguel and his strong-willed mother. One surgical residency program dismissed the only two enrolled blacks and suggested that West go into anesthesiology. The dismissals were done so skillfully that there was no legal recourse, so West transferred to a different residency program, refusing to settle for anything but surgery. West completed general surgery residencies at the University of Illinois and Mount Sinai Hospital/Chicago Medical School.

For some years West had a successful vascular surgery practice in Dayton, Ohio. At the age of thirty-nine, however, he decided to go into the transplant field. He completed a fellowship in transplantation and immunology at the University of Minnesota Hospital and Clinic, then worked five years with Dr. Clive Callender at Howard University as associate director of the transplant program, assistant professor of surgery, and chief of kidney transplantation. One of only nineteen African American transplant surgeons in the country, West specialized in liver, kidney, pancreas, and small bowel transplantation. He was an expert in advanced laparoscopic surgery and did extensive research in islet cell, pancreas, and small bowel transplantation.

West, in conjunction with other doctors, published many professional articles based on his work and was the first physician to describe the laparoscopic biopsy of transplanted pancreas grafts. Dr. Scott Gruber, director of the Detroit Medical Center pancreas transplant program, recruited West in 2002, the same year that West was voted one of the top one hundred African American doctors in the country.

West was acutely aware of the inequalities in the healthcare system for African Americans. He did research on blood pressure and other problems that plagued the African American community. Nearly half of the people awaiting transplants in Michigan were African Americans, and West dedicated himself toward ending such inequalities. Ironically, West did not consider his medical work as his greatest accomplishment. He was proudest of the work that he did with young people. Besides mentoring his godchildren, he spent as much time as possible motivating youngsters, including speaking at graduations and career days. He wanted to help them avoid the negative influences that prevent them from reaching their highest potential.

FURTHER READING

Anstett, Patricia. "Doctor on a Mission," *Detroit Free Press*, 25 Feb. 2002.

DEBORAH LOIS TAYLOR

West, Togo, Jr. (21 June 1942–), Secretary of the Army and Secretary of Veterans Affairs, was born in Winston Salem, North Carolina, son of Togo West Sr. and Evelyn Carter, both high school educators. As a youth West was a gifted student, encouraged by both parents to reach his full potential. He was active in the Boy Scouts of America, eventually earning the distinction of Eagle Scout with bronze palms. In 1959 he graduated valedictorian from Atkins High School where both his parents taught.

After high school West moved to Washington, D.C., to attend Howard University. As an undergraduate his campus life was steeped in the civil rights movement. West was involved in several service organizations and played an active role in the university community advocating for social justice. Upon graduation in 1965 West was commissioned a second lieutenant in the U.S. Army Field Artillery Corps. In 1966 he married classmate Gail Berry; they would have two daughters, Hilary and Tiffany.

West continued his studies at Howard, pursuing a law degree. He joined the *Howard Law Journal* and served as managing editor. During this time he pursued both private and public sector law internships. After graduation in 1968 West secured a yearlong judicial clerkship for the Honorable Judge Harold R. Tyler Jr. in the U.S. District Court for Southern District of New York.

In 1969 West was called up for active military duty and joined the U.S. Army Judge Advocate General Corps. West was well regarded among his colleagues. After serving four years, West was appointed by President Gerald Ford to the U.S. Department of Justice as an associate deputy attorney general. In 1973 West entered private practice as an associate attorney at Covington and Burling law firm before being appointed by President Jimmy Carter to general counsel for the Department of Navy in 1977. In 1981 President Carter appointed West to general counsel for the Department of Defense. With the succeeding Reagan and Bush Republican administrations, West returned to private practice as managing partner at Patterson, Belknap, Webb, and Tyler law firm. In 1990 he served as senior vice president for Northrop Corporation, an aircraft manufacturer with military contracts.

After nearly a decade out of public service, West returned in 1993 with a nomination to secretary of the army by President Bill Clinton. At the time there existed a leadership vacuum in the army; congressional leaders on both sides of the aisle agreed with President Clinton's belief that West could fill the void. His confirmation process went smoothly.

The army was facing serious financial challenges; military budgets were decreasing and there were pressures to downsize in light of a post–cold war environment. West developed an effective plan to deal with the financial problems. This work was overshadowed by revelations of sexual harassment of female soldiers at the Aberdeen Proving Grounds in Maryland. The scandal gained national attention and West did not shy away from the controversy; he was called on several occasions to testify before Congress. West took the issues seriously, carrying out high-level investigations and appointing a panel to revise sexual harassment policies. In the wake of the scandal, racial and gender discrimination claims also came to the surface. West was quick to address these issues and minimize damage to the army's reputation.

In 1998 President Clinton appointed West secretary of Veterans Affairs, making him the third African American in the president's cabinet and the third person to serve in the position created by President George H. W. Bush. Veterans Affairs faced many of the same challenges West dealt with in the army, but on a larger scale and with a greater level of bureaucracy—it was the second largest government department. West had several disagreements with veterans' groups and congressional members over the direction of the department. In light of criticisms about questionable expenses and oversight, West resigned in 2000; however, his reputation stayed intact and he remained a vocal advocate for the rights of veterans and minorities.

After leaving government West returned to private practice at Covington and Burling law firm and served as president of the Joint Center for Political and Economic Studies, a think tank focused on minority issues. He joined several corporate and nonprofit boards and traveled the country for speaking engagements. In 2007 West joined a commission, initiated by Secretary of Defense Robert Gates, examining the conditions at Walter Reed, a military hospital exposed for poor conditions.

FURTHER READING

Karmen, Al. "West in Line for Top Army Post," *Washington Post*, 16 Sep 1993.

McAllister, Bill. "Army Secretary is Choice for Veterans Affairs Helm," *Washington Post*, 8 Nov 1997.

Priest, Dana. "Army Probe to Focus on Top Level," *Washington Post*, 23 Nov 1996.

MICHAELJULIUS IDANI

Westbrook, Peter (16 April 1952–), international fencer and philanthropist, was born Peter Jonathan Westbrook in St. Louis, Missouri, the son of Ulysses Westbrook, an African American army corporal, and Mariko Wada, a school custodian. Peter's parents met while his father was stationed in Kobe, Japan, and married despite the objections of his mother's well-to-do Japanese Catholic family. Soon after his birth, Westbrook's family relocated to Newark, New Jersey, where they lived in near poverty in a housing project. When he was a toddler, Peter's parents separated and he rarely saw his father again. His tough surroundings and teasing because of his biracial background often compelled young Peter to get into fights. Seeing that her son needed a positive way to channel his aggressive energy and believing that the discipline involved in fencing would be good for him, Mariko Westbrook persuaded her 13-year-old son to join the fencing team at Essex Catholic High School by proposing to pay him five dollars a week to attend the practices. He was at first reluctant to participate in such an unconventional sport, especially one that was likely to be viewed as unfashionable and elitist in his inner-city neighborhood. He was swayed, however, by his mother's promise of the five-dollar weekly stipend. Years later Peter revealed that he had become so enamored with the swashbuckling sport that his mother stopped paying him soon after he started taking lessons.

Westbrook was an eager student and a quick learner. He soon began to specialize in the saber, one of the three disciplines in fencing. Surrounded by a sea of white faces, Westbrook often felt out of place, but his love of fencing spurred him on. By the time high school graduation loomed, he had become so proficient at the sport that he was awarded an athletic scholarship to attend New York University. Success continued at the collegiate level, with Westbrook earning the National Collegiate Athletic Association championship in the saber event in 1973. In 1974 he began a strenuous training regimen in anticipation of making it to the Olympics, working with renowned Hungarian coach Csaba Elthes seven days a week. It was also in 1974 that Westbrook won his first U.S. Fencing Association national championship, becoming the first African American (and one of the youngest competitors ever) to claim the title; he would go on to win the title another twelve times.

After graduating from college in 1975 with a BS, he worked in sales and marketing, first at IBM for three years and later for Pitney Bowes and North American Van Lines. While the completion of a degree would have spelled the end of an athletic career for most college athletes, for Westbrook it marked the beginning of the most competitive phase of his fencing career. He continued training and competing while working full time, and his hard work paid off when he was named to the 1976 Olympic team. However, Westbrook's dream of bringing home a medal went unfulfilled when he was injured just days before his event; he managed to compete, but finished thirteenth.

Though a disappointment, this setback did not deter Westbrook. For that matter, he was not put off by his next Olympic experience, either, which may be called more accurately a nonexperience. Because the United States boycotted the 1980 games in Moscow, eight years passed before Westbrook got another chance to go up against the best fencers in the world. When he did, he did not waste the opportunity. At the 1984 Olympic Games in Los Angeles, Westbrook claimed the bronze, becoming the first American to win a fencing medal in twenty-four years. Westbrook also competed in the games in 1988, 1992, and in 1996, when he was the oldest member of the fencing team.

Often referred to as a pioneer in his sport, Westbrook indeed broke new ground as the most decorated African American in fencing history. But in 1991 his career expanded when he founded the Peter Westbrook Foundation, an education-centered nonprofit organization that provided fencing instruction to low-income children. Westbrook's organization, for which he began using his personal savings, established a training facility in New York City to teach kids the art and discipline of fencing. The program started with just a handful of students that first year. By 2007 it routinely attracted more than one hundred students to its weekly Saturday morning sessions. Of those students, approximately forty of the most promising attended daily after-school sessions.

Much like Westbrook was when he first encountered the saber, most of his students were economically disadvantaged inner-city children with little or no knowledge of the sport. Because the cost of equipment and coaching made participating in fencing expensive, Westbrook's training facility, opened from September to May in conjunction with the school year, offered an annual tuition rate of just twenty-five dollars per child in the 2000s. And Westbrook sometimes reduced that fee even further so that families who could not afford the tuition could pay whatever they were able.

Westbrook's facility differed from most training institutes that worked with young children in that it did not dedicate itself solely to training athletes to compete on the most elite levels. Westbrook believed fencing to be a perfect medium for teaching the values of discipline, concentration, the ability to analyze and find solutions to difficult situations, and for practicing a healthy lifestyle. Westbrook's program also prioritized academic achievement. Students, ranging in age from nine to eighteen, maintained good grades in order to continue receiving fencing lessons. The foundation provided tutors and even sponsored bimonthly essay contests, awarding small cash prizes to the top

essayists. Over the years many of the children who benefited from the academic tutoring and rigorous training were awarded scholarships to colleges and private schools.

While Westbrook charged nominal fees, the foundation flourished on a shoestring budget using his savings, a donated space, and contributions from the likes of BILL COSBY and the United States Olympic Organizing Committee. Although the foundation toiled for a number of years in relative obscurity with little money, the organization slowly began to gain recognition for its work, perhaps in part due to the publication of Westbrook's memoir, *Harnessing Anger*, in 1997. The book was optioned by Disney for a future film. Westbrook was also the subject of *Passing the Torch*, a 2000 film produced by CNN. That same year, OPRAH WINFREY awarded Westbrook with a $100,000 "Use Your Life Award" to further the foundation's operation.

In 2000 the Peter Westbrook Foundation achieved what was then its crowning success: three fencers who got their start at the institute were named to the Olympic team. Four foundation athletes were part of the 2004 Olympic team. The foundation also received its largest single donation ever—$1 million—in 2004.

FURTHER READING
Westbrook, Peter, and Tej Hazarika. *Harnessing Anger: The Inner Discipline of Athletic Excellence* (1997).
Cooper, Carol. "Living by the Sword," *Village Voice* (15 July 1997).
Hall, Jeff. "From the Streets to the Piste," *The Atlantic Monthly* (Aug. 2000).
Jerome, Richard, and Nancy Matsumoto. "Man of Steel," *People* (16 June 1997).
Rhoden, William C. "Turning Underdogs into Fencing Champions," *The New York Times* (2 Aug. 2004).
                                    T. NATASHA TURNER

Weston, Maudelle Bass (c. 1908–11 June 1989), dancer, artist's model, and dance instructor, was born in Early County, Georgia, sometime in 1908. Information about her parents and childhood years is unavailable.

Known professionally throughout her career as Maudelle, Bass moved to California around 1933 and attended classes at the Gray Conservatory of Music and Art in South Central Los Angeles. Bass was the first black dancer to be trained by modern choreographer Lester Horton, and she later danced with her instructor as part of the Lester Horton Dance Group. Bass trained in the Mary Wigman and Bess Mensendieck dance techniques, which stressed interpretation and stark movement, often without music or to a simple drum or percussion instrument. Dr. Bess Mensendieck taught to liberate women from traditional movement and showcased the use of the natural body as a modern form.

Bass also joined a number of black dancers who were interested in studying the roots of native dance, particularly the part that the dances of Egypt, Brazil, Cuba, Mexico, and parts of Africa played in shaping the American modern dance movement. Bass enhanced her dance technique in classes at the Fowler School of African Culture in Los Angeles in the 1930s. She took classes in Nigerian dance with noted dance teachers including Modupe Paris and ASADATA DAFORA, and studied Liberian culture and dance with Tony Massaqua. Bass danced for several years with the Arte Folklorico de Mexico, performing with the troupe throughout Latin America in the late 1930s. It was during this time in Mexico that she studied Mexican culture, met well-known local artists, and posed for Mexican muralist Diego Rivera. *Dancer in Repose* (1939), one of several paintings completed by Rivera during this time, was exhibited throughout Mexico and in Europe. Bass became a well-known image as a result of the exhibit.

In 1939 she also posed for photographers Johan Hagemeyer and Sonia Noskowiak—establishing herself as a celebrated model as well as a dancer. The only black model used by noted American photographer Edward Weston, Bass posed for him in a 1939 session in sand dunes in the Carmel Highlands in California. Several of Weston's photographs of Bass were published in *U.S. Camera* in 1941. The images of Weston's Maudelle portfolio later toured the world in photographic exhibitions in the 1960s.

Bass also worked as a photography model for newspaper photojournalist Weegee in 1939 and the husband and wife photography team Manuel and Lola Alvarez Bravo in 1947. Manuel Alvarez Bravo's photograph *Espejo Negro* (Black Mirror) featured Bass. Bass also posed for painters Abraham Baylinson, Nicolai Fechin, and Robert M. Jackson, and sculptor BEULAH WOODARD in the 1930s and 1940s. Her image influenced the representation of black women in mid-twentieth-century art, showing a sense of pride in racial identity and African heritage that was in contrast with the popular stereotype of black females in the early 1940s that included advertising images of Aunt Jemima and film images of black mammies. Bass, through the use of her artistic images and dance chorography,

was in the vanguard of the movement that countered the racial discrimination of the time as illustrated in these stereotypes.

In 1940, impressed by Bass's dance technique, American chorographer Agnes de Mille selected her to dance the role of the "Black Priestess" in *Black Ritual*, a landmark performance made by American Ballet Theatre during its first season. Bass made dance history as one of the first blacks to play a principal role in a dance performance by a major company, and also worked as a member of what was sometimes called the "Negro Wing" of the American Ballet Theatre, an informal group of black dancers that de Mille used in various productions.

Noted photographer Carl Van Vechten's images of her performance as the priestess were outlawed as pornography under U.S. federal postal regulations at the time they were printed. Later in the 1940s, the images were exhibited by Edward Weston throughout the United States and helped establish photography as a legitimate contribution to the art world. Photographs had not been considered art; they were made by hobbyists. These exhibits showed the human form in poses and artistic forms as paintings had been exhibited for earlier generations.

Bass established her own dance academy in Los Angeles in 1948 and was hired to lecture as a member of the dance department at the University of California, Los Angeles. She appeared in various performances with premiere dancer and choreographer PEARL PRIMUS in the 1950s. Bass married the Antiguan dancer and the president of the United Negro Improvement Association (UNIA) George Weston in 1960. The marriage lasted until Weston's death in 1973. They had no children. Bass lectured about dance and taught movement well into her seventies. Dressed in native African clothing, she gave lecture and dance demonstrations in master classes at colleges and universities across the country, including the University of California, Los Angeles, in the 1970s. Bass also spoke at churches and museums about ethnic dance technique and history. Exposing audiences to African culture and heritage was the major goal of her teaching. She was presented an award in 1983 for her lifework at "A Celebration of Women in Dance" at the Thelma Hill Performing Arts Center in New York. She died in Plainfield, New Jersey, after a short illness in 1989.

FURTHER READING

The George and Maudelle Weston Papers are housed at the Schomburg Center for Research in Black Culture, New York Public Library.

Long, Richard A. *The Black Tradition in American Dance* (1995).

Sanders, Kimberly Wallace, ed. *Skin Deep, Spirit Strong: The Black Female Body in American Culture* (2002).

Williams, Carla, and Deborah Willis. *The Black Female Body: A Photographic History* (2002).

Williams, Carla. "Maudelle: An Artist's Model," in *Fotophile: The Journal for Creative Photographers,* no. 41 (2002).

Obituary: *New York Times,* 1 July 1989.

PAMELA LEE GRAY

Wharton, Clifton R., Jr. (13 Sept. 1926–), economist, educator, businessman, and diplomat, was born Clifton Reginald Wharton Jr. in Boston, Massachusetts, one of four children of CLIFTON REGINALD WHARTON, an ambassador, and Harriette B., a social worker in Boston and a French and Latin teacher at Virginia State University. His father was the first African American to pass the Foreign Service examination and became the first black career ambassador.

Wharton attended the prestigious Boston Latin School and graduated in 1943. The precocious Wharton enrolled at Harvard University at age sixteen. At the age of nineteen he served as an army aviation cadet and was stationed in Tuskegee, Alabama. However, with five weeks remaining to earn his aviator wings, he decided to return to Harvard to complete his undergraduate degree. He earned his AB in History in 1947. Wharton was the first African American to enroll in the Johns Hopkins School of Advanced International Studies (SAIS), where in 1948 he earned a master's degree in International Affairs. On 15 April 1950 he married Dolores Duncan; they had two children. In 1956 Wharton earned a second master's degree and in 1958 a PhD, both in Economics, from the University of Chicago, becoming the first black American to receive a doctorate from the university's renowned economics department.

From 1947 to 1957 Wharton's work focused on Latin American development. From 1957 to 1969 he held executive-level positions with the Agricultural Development Council, Inc., a private nonprofit international organization founded by John D. Rockefeller III. During his tenure with the council, Wharton's area of program responsibility focused on the nations of Southeast Asia, and he held visiting professorships at the University of Malaya in Singapore (1958–1960) and the University of Malaysia in Kuala Lumpur (1960–1964).

From 1966 to 1969 Wharton was a member of the State Department's East Asia Advisory Committee, which provided regular reviews and comments on U.S. policies in East Asia for Assistant Secretary of State William Bundy. Wharton's article "The Green Revolution: Cornucopia or Pandora's Box?" appeared in *Foreign Affairs* magazine, published by the Council on Foreign Relations, in April 1969. In 1966 he was also a member of the Presidential Mission on Agriculture to Vietnam headed by Secretary of Agriculture Orville Freeman. The purpose of the mission was to develop programs to win over the rural areas of Vietnam.

The year 1970 represented a watershed moment in the annals of higher education in the United States: for the first time a major research university had an African American president. On 2 January 1970 Wharton assumed office as the fourteenth president of Michigan State University (MSU). He served for eight years, concluding his tenure in 1978. Despite repeated budget reductions, Wharton successfully maintained the quality of MSU's academic programs while simultaneously expanding opportunities for racially, economically, and educationally disadvantaged students to pursue higher education at the institution.

From 1976 to 1983 Wharton was also chairman of the Board for International Food and Agricultural Development, a committee that advises U.S. AID, where he developed a wide range of new programs to offer greater involvement of U.S. universities in foreign development. From 1978 to 1980 he was a member of the Presidential Commission on World Hunger, which made major recommendations to President Jimmy Carter for strengthening U.S. efforts in foreign agricultural development.

Perhaps the most lasting contribution to the Wharton legacy at MSU was Dolores Wharton's efforts to establish a new center for the performing arts. The Clifton and Dolores Wharton Center for the Performing Arts, dedicated on 26 September 1982, was named in recognition of the couple's strong support of the arts.

After leaving MSU, from 1978 to 1987 Wharton served as chancellor of the State University of New York (SUNY). As chancellor of SUNY, Wharton designed a set of internal reforms necessary to minimize inefficiency in university operations and maximize value-added service delivery, an economic description of customer satisfaction. He accomplished this by implementing a system that transferred key decision-making authority back from the centralized headquarters to the local campuses and campus administrators.

In June 1982 Wharton was elected chair of the Rockefeller Foundation. This marked yet another groundbreaking achievement as Wharton became the first African American to serve as chair of a major U.S. foundation. This appointment enabled him to continue his lifelong dedication to philanthropic activities aimed at improving the quality of life both domestically and abroad for indigenous farmers, entrepreneurs, and workers in Southeast Asia and parts of Africa. He served as chair of the Rockefeller Foundation for five years while also serving as chancellor of-SUNY.

In January 1987 Wharton resigned his position as SUNY chancellor to become the chair and CEO of TIAA-CREF, the largest pension firm in the United States, with assets exceeding $250 billion. This position meant that Wharton was the first black American to serve as chair of a Fortune 500 company. During his time at TIAA-CREF, Wharton dramatically changed the company by restructuring it, developing several new investment options, introducing increased reporting, and making fund transfers possible. As a pension manager, Wharton was a key player in helping to provide a stable source of funds for equity markets and venture capitalists. These carefully planned investments encouraged capital formation and job growth in the United States.

In January 1993 Wharton stepped down as chair of TIAA-CREF to become President Bill Clinton's deputy secretary of state; he was the first African American to hold this position. Wharton's family roots, his long and prestigious career in international development during the 1950s and 1960s, and his long affiliation as trustee with the Council of Foreign Relations provided him with the necessary skills to effectively serve as the number two diplomat in the U.S. State Department. A smear campaign trying to impugn Wharton's fitness to serve as deputy secretary of state prompted him to resign from the position in November 1993 and return to the private sector, where he became active in public speaking, consulting, and advancing sustainable economic development.

FURTHER READING
Bennis, Warren. *On Becoming a Leader* (1994)
Hesburg, Theodore M., Paul A. Miller, and Clifton R. Wharton. *Patterns for Lifelong Learning* (1973).
"The Wharton School," *USA Today*, 12 Oct. 1991.

BILL DICKENS

Wharton, Clifton Reginald (11 May 1899–23 Apr. 1990), Foreign Service officer, was born in Baltimore, Maryland, the son of William B. Wharton and Rosalind Griffin. He received an LLB cum laude from the Boston University School of Law in 1920 and an LLM in 1923 from the same institution. Wharton was admitted to the Massachusetts bar in 1920 and practiced law in Boston until 1924. In August 1924 he received a telegram appointing him as a law clerk in the Department of State. In 1924 he married Harriette Banks; they had four children before divorcing.

In January 1925 Wharton became the first black to take the new Foreign Service examination established by the 1924 Rogers Act, which had created a career Foreign Service based on competitive examinations and merit promotion. Only twenty candidates passed both the written and the oral parts of the examination. In March 1925 Undersecretary of State Joseph Grew wrote to a colleague that the twenty included "one negro, who will go at once to Liberia" (Calkin, *Women*, 72). Wharton later recalled that when he decided to take the Foreign Service exam, his prospective associates were not enthusiastic.

The lack of enthusiasm Wharton sensed also existed at the highest levels of the department. Following passage of the Rogers Act, the Executive Committee of the Foreign Service Personnel Board prepared a memorandum on how to avoid appointing women or blacks. One alternative suggested was an executive order stating that persons in those groups were not eligible to take the examination. Another was to rate such candidates so low that they could not achieve a passing mark. Secretary of State Charles Evans Hughes, however, emphatically rejected both alternatives.

Wharton was appointed a Foreign Service officer on 20 March 1925, and on 21 March he was assigned to Monrovia, Liberia. Blacks had been receiving diplomatic appointments since 1869, but such appointments were almost always to Liberia, Haiti, or small consular posts in tropical countries. Wharton was the first black in the new career Foreign Service, and his career followed the same pattern for more than half of his forty years in the Department of State.

Wharton was not sent to the new Foreign Service School for instruction as were the other new appointees. Department officials later informed him that this was because he was needed so urgently at his new post. Despite this urgency, however, they initially planned to send him and his wife to Liberia on a cargo ship. When Wharton said that he did not need the job that badly, the department officials relented and arranged for passage on an ocean liner and a passenger ship.

Wharton served as third secretary and vice consul in Liberia until December 1929. In June 1930 he became consul in Las Palmas in the Spanish Canary Islands. In July 1936 he returned to Monrovia on the first of three temporary assignments. He served alternately in Monrovia and Las Palmas until April 1942, when he was appointed consul in Antananarivo in the French island colony of Madagascar, where he also represented the wartime interests of Great Britain and Belgium.

In April 1945 Wharton was appointed a member of the U.S. maritime delegation at Ponta Delgada in the Portuguese Azores. In July of that year he became consul at Ponta Delgada, where he served for the next four years. In 1949 he married Evangeline L. Spears; they had no children. In October 1949 Wharton's career took a new path when he was named first secretary and consul in Lisbon, Portugal. In 1950 he became consul general at that post. From 1953 to 1957 he served as consul general in Marseilles, France.

When President Dwight D. Eisenhower offered him appointment as minister to Romania in February 1958, Wharton flew to Washington to talk to Deputy Undersecretary for Administration Loy Henderson to make sure that the appointment was based on merit, saying that if race were one of the criteria, he would not accept the appointment. Henderson wrote later that he had been glad to tell Wharton that "race had not been a factor" (Calkin, "A Reminiscence," 28). As minister to Romania, Wharton became the first black career Foreign Service officer to serve as chief of mission and the first black to serve as chief of mission in Europe. In 1959 he was promoted to career minister, once again the first black to achieve that honor.

Wharton became the first black ambassador to a European country when President John F. Kennedy appointed him ambassador to Norway on 2 March 1961. Democratic majority leader Mike Mansfield praised Wharton to the Senate as a "highly skillful, understanding and tactful diplomat" and quoted a *Washington Post* editorial looking forward to "a day when the appointment of a Negro so well qualified as Mr. Wharton will have ceased to be a novelty" (Calkin, "A Reminiscence"). While ambassador to Norway, Wharton also served as a delegate to the North Atlantic Treaty Organization (NATO) Ministerial Council meeting and as an alternate delegate to the sixteenth session of the U.N. General Assembly.

Wharton was a genuine pioneer, and his career was full of "firsts," including the first black to pass the Foreign Service exam, the first black chief of mission to a European country, the first black career minister, and the first black ambassador to a European country. Such achievements took not only superior ability but also great patience, tolerance, and persistence in the face of what was often blatant racial discrimination. For most of his career, Wharton had to fight against such discrimination alone. By the time he retired in October 1964, however, a sea change had occurred. Thanks partly to his achievements, Wharton inspired and helped to pave the way for professional careers in diplomacy for other blacks, who began to enter the Foreign Service in ever increasing numbers during the 1960s. Wharton died in Phoenix, Arizona.

FURTHER READING

Calkin, Homer L. "A Reminiscence: Being Black in the Foreign Service," *Department of State Newsletter*, no. 198 (Feb. 1978): 25–28.

Calkin, Homer L. *Women in the Department of State: Their Role in American Foreign Affairs* (1978).

Trask, David. *A Short History of the U.S. Department of State, 1781–1981* (1981).

Obituary: *New York Times*, 25 Apr. 1990.

This entry is taken from the *American National Biography* and is published here with the permission of the American Council of Learned Societies.

NINA DAVIS DAVIS

Wheatley, Phillis (c. 1753–5 Dec. 1784), poet and cultivator of the epistolary writing style, was born in Gambia, Africa, probably along the fertile lowlands of the Gambia River. She was enslaved as a child of seven or eight and sold in Boston to John and Susanna Wheatley on 11 July 1761. The horrors of the Middle Passage likely contributed to her persistent trouble with asthma. The Wheatleys apparently named the girl, who had nothing but a piece of dirty carpet to conceal her nakedness, after the slaver, the *Phillis*, that transported her. The Wheatleys were more kindly toward Phillis than were most slaveowners of the time, permitting her to learn to read. The poet in Wheatley soon began to emerge. She published her first poem on 21 December 1765 in the *Newport Mercury* when she was about twelve. The poem, "On Messrs. Hussey and Coffin," relates how these two gentlemen narrowly escaped drowning off Cape Cod.

Much of her subsequent poetry deals, as well, with events occurring close to her Boston circle. Of her fifty-five extant poems, nineteen are elegies; all but the last of them are devoted to the commemoration of someone she knew personally. Wheatley herself and her career are the subjects of her last elegy. One possible explanation for her preoccupation with this genre may be that she recalled the delivery of oral laments by the women of her tribal group whose responsibility it was to make such deliveries.

In October 1770 Wheatley published an elegy that must be called pivotal to her career. The subject of this elegy is George Whitefield, evangelical Methodist minister, a close friend of Charles Wesley, and privy chaplain to Selina Hastings, Countess of Huntingdon. During his career Whitefield had made seven journeys to the American colonies, where he was known as the "Voice of the Great Awakening" and as the "Great Awakener." Only a week before his death in Newburyport, Massachusetts, on 30 September 1770, Whitefield preached in Boston where Wheatley very likely heard him. As Susanna Wheatley regularly corresponded with the countess, she and the Wheatley household may well have entertained the Great Awakener. Wheatley's vivid, ostensibly firsthand account in the elegy, replete with quotes the minister is alleged to have spoken, may, then, have been based on actual acquaintance. Owing to this evangel's extreme popularity, Wheatley's deft elegy became an overnight sensation and was often reprinted.

It is almost certain that the ship that carried news of Whitefield's death to the countess also carried a copy of Wheatley's elegy. It was this elegy that brought Wheatley to the sympathetic attention of the countess. Such an acquaintance ensured that Wheatley's elegy was also reprinted many times in London, giving the young poet an international reputation. This acquaintance also ensured that Wheatley's *Poems on Various Subjects, Religious and Moral* appeared in print, not in Boston where the project was rejected for racist reasons, but in London, printed in 1773 by the English publisher Archibald Bell and financed by the countess.

Wheatley's support by Hastings and her rejection by white male–dominated Boston signaled her nourishment as a literary artist by a community of women. While Wheatley received encouragement for the writing of her poems by prominent men of Boston such as the ministers Mather Byles (nephew of Cotton Mather) and Samuel Cooper, she was taught to read the King James Bible by Susanna Wheatley and probably as well by her daughter Mary. In addition, Susanna promoted Wheatley's publication of her poems in local newspapers.

Wheatley displays in her poems a sophisticated classicism. She knew Latin well enough to craft the excellent epyllion (or short epic) "Niobe in Distress ..." from book six of Ovid's *Metamorphoses*. Of Wheatley's twenty-two extant letters, seven are addressed to Obour Tanner, an African American who many have speculated may have been forced to make the journey of the Middle Passage with Wheatley; in any event, the intimacy of their relationship is self-evident from the tone and detail of Wheatley's letters to her (none of Tanner's responses are extant). Tanner must have been a close friend and probably a valuable counselor and confidante of the poet.

All these women (the countess, who encouraged and financed the publication of her *Poems*; Mary and Susanna Wheatley, who taught her to read and write; and Obour Tanner, who could empathize probably better than anyone with her condition as a slave) were much older than the poet and obviously nurtured her development. Their importance to Wheatley's development is virtually incalculable. It is not excessive to submit that without this community of women, Wheatley's poems may never have been printed. Although Anne Bradstreet's poems, Jane Turell's, and those of other women poets who preceded Wheatley were published by then, the publication of her poems through the efforts of women marks the first such occasion in the annals of American letters.

During the summer of 1773 Wheatley journeyed to England, where she assisted in the preparation of her volume for the press. While in London she enjoyed considerable recognition from such dignitaries as Lord Dartmouth, Lord Lincoln, Granville Sharp (who escorted Wheatley on several tours about London), Benjamin Franklin, and Brooks Watson, a wealthy merchant who presented Wheatley with a folio edition of Milton's *Paradise Lost* and who later became lord mayor of London. Wheatley was to have been presented at court when, owing to an illness of Susanna Wheatley's, she was summoned to return to Boston in August. It is significant that sometime before 18 October 1773 Wheatley was granted her freedom, according to her own testimony, "at the desire of my friends in England" (*Collected Works*, ed. Shields [1988]: 170). It follows then that if Hastings had not agreed to finance Wheatley's *Poems* and if the poet had not then journeyed to London, she probably would never have been manumitted.

When the American Revolution erupted, Wheatley's patriotic feelings separated her even more from the Wheatleys. After Susanna died on 3 March 1774, Wheatley's relationship with her Loyalist former master doubtless became strained. As her position in regard to independence has often been confused with the Loyalist position of John Wheatley and his son Nathaniel, her patriotism requires underscoring. Throughout her career she repeatedly celebrated American freedom, indeed rivaling Philip Freneau's claim to the title "Poet of the American Revolution." Her two most famous revolutionary war poems are "To His Excellency General Washington" (1775), which closes with the encomium "A crown, a mansion, and a throne that shine / With gold unfading, WASHINGTON! be thine," and "Liberty and Peace" (1784), written to celebrate the Treaty of Paris and containing the forceful line "And new-born *Rome* [i.e., America] shall give *Britannia* Law."

Another misunderstood contribution of Phillis Wheatley is her attitude toward slavery. Because major statements Wheatley made attacking the institution of slavery were recovered only in the 1970s and 1980s, she was earlier thought to have ignored the issue. In February 1774, for example, Wheatley wrote to Samson Occom: "In every human breast, God has implanted a Principle, which we call Love of Freedom; it is impatient of Oppression, and pants for Deliverance." This letter was reprinted a dozen times in American newspapers over the next twelve months. Certainly whites and blacks of Wheatley's time never questioned her attitude toward slavery.

Later in the same year Wheatley observed in a letter to John Thornton, the English philanthropist, "The world is a severe schoolmaster, for its frowns are less dang'rous than its smiles and flatteries, and it is a difficult task to keep in the path of Wisdom." This entire letter appears cast in the tone of the African American who has found her white would-be benefactor's motive to be less than philanthropic and indeed hollow or even destructive, much in the manner of the fictions of LANGSTON HUGHES, RICHARD WRIGHT, and RALPH ELLISON. In an elegy of July 1778 on the death of Major General David Wooster, who, according to Wheatley, "fell a martyr in the Cause of Freedom," Wheatley challenges the notion that whites can "hope to find / Divine acceptance with th' Almighty mind" when "they disgrace / And hold in bondage Afric's blameless race."

The year 1778 was a pivotal one for Wheatley. Soon after John Wheatley died, Phillis married John Peters, a free African American who was a jack-of-all-trades, serving in various capacities from storekeeper to advocate for African Americans before the courts. But Wheatley's fortunes began to decline. In 1779 she published a set of "Proposals" for a new volume of poems, probably in an effort to mitigate her worsening poverty.

While the "Proposals" failed to attract subscribers, they show that she had produced some three hundred pages of new poetry since the publication of *Poems* six years earlier. The volume never appeared, and, sadly, most of its poems are lost.

Wheatley's final proposal for a volume of poems in September 1784 went virtually unnoticed. This volume, whose title was to have been *Poems and Letters on Various Subjects*, would have included thirteen letters to dignitaries such as Benjamin Rush, the Earl of Dartmouth, and the Countess of Huntingdon. Once having carried a reputation of such distinction that it earned her an audience with General Washington in March 1776, Wheatley and her newborn child died alone in a shack on the edge of Boston. It is believed she died as a result of an infection from the birth.

Wheatley's end, like her beginning in America, was pitiable. Yet this genius of the pen left to the country a legacy of firsts: the first African American to publish a book, the mother of African American letters, the first woman writer whose publication was urged and nurtured by a community of women, and the first American woman author who tried to earn a living by means of her writing.

FURTHER READING

Carretta, Vincent, ed. *Phillis Wheatley: Complete Writings* (2001).

Gates, Henry Louis, Jr. *The Trials of Phillis Wheatley: America's First Black Poet and Her Encounters with the Founding Fathers* (2003).

O'Neal, Sondra A. "A Slave's Subtle War: Phillis Wheatley's Use of Biblical Myth and Symbol," *Early American Literature* 21 (1986): 144–65.

O'Neal, Sondra A. *Critical Essays on Phillis Wheatley* (1982).

O'Neal, Sondra A. "Phillis Wheatley," in *African American Writers*, ed. Valerie Smith (1991).

Robinson, William H. *Phillis Wheatley in the Black American Beginnings* (1975).

This entry is taken from the *American National Biography* and is published here with the permission of the American Council of Learned Societies.

JOHN C. SHIELDS

Wheatstraw, William Bunch "Peetie" (21 Dec. 1902–21 Dec. 1941), blues pianist, vocalist, and guitarist, was born in Ripley, Tennessee, the son of Nathan Bunch and Mary (Burns) Bunch, of whom nothing else is known. Little is known about Bunch's life, especially his childhood. It is believed that he left Ripley at a young age. He may have been raised in Cotton Plant, Arkansas, where he lived before migrating to St. Louis, Missouri, in 1929. St. Louis was a logical place for Bunch to settle. Although not as big an attraction as Chicago or Detroit, the city was a popular destination for African American migrants from the South searching for economic opportunities in northern cities. It also had a thriving blues community located in and around Deep Morgan and West Biddle Street, which were run-down, crime-ridden neighborhoods notorious for prostitution and bootlegging but also filled with blues clubs and juke joints that attracted talented musicians like Bunch.

The blues scene extended across the Missouri River into east St. Louis, Illinois, where Bunch settled with his wife, Lizzie, and son, Tango. How and when he met his wife, when they married, and when their son was born are all unknown. East St. Louis had not yet recovered from a 1917 race riot, considered the bloodiest in twentieth-century America. By the time the violence was over, thirty-nine blacks and nine whites had been killed. The Bunch family lived in the still burned-out Valley section, where a majority of the violence took place. The neighborhood was home to the poorest migrants in the city, and the hard economic times, class prejudice, and police brutality people faced there served as fodder for Bunch's music. He returned to these themes often in the songs he wrote and recorded.

Although it is not known where or how he received his training, Bunch was already a musician before he left the South, launching a professional career the same year the Great Depression began. When the stock market crashed in 1929, nearly everyone in the city fell on hard times; hundreds were without food and shelter. As bleak as the situation was, migrants searching for a good time somehow managed to make it to the many juke joints and barrelhouses in and around St. Louis. The music provided a release, if only briefly, from the troubles of the day. In this environment good blues musicians always worked, and Bunch saw his opportunity to perform. Billing himself as "Peetie Wheatstraw, the Devil's Son-in-Law," he launched a successful music career.

Wheatstraw based the re-creation of himself on a mythical character from African American folklore. The fictitious Peetie Wheatstraw was wicked and mischievous, creating chaos for his own enjoyment. He was someone to be feared, and his reputation fit well within a musical genre that flourished along the underbelly of African American society. Blues songs had sexually charged lyrics and told stories about crime and violence. The well-established African American middle class in St. Louis considered it music for the downtrodden and immoral. But playing the nine-string guitar and the piano, this new, deep-voiced Peetie Wheatstraw exploited these stereotypes to his advantage, looking to his audience of poor migrants like a hero strutting in the devil's clothing. In the only photograph of Wheatstraw known to exist, he looks more like a clean-cut minister than the devil's son-in-law, but the guitar he is holding provides a clue that he would not be considered a respectable member of the African American elite. His songs certainly did not put him in that category. He slurred his words when singing bawdy, sexual songs in a cool and idle manner, filling them with "ooh well, well," which became his trademark. The audiences loved it.

Wheatstraw often played at a juke joint over the barbershop on West Biddle Street or at a club called Lovejoy near east St. Louis. In the early days he worked mainly as a guitarist, but later he switched to piano. He was so successful that he did not need an alternative means of making a living. There was much debate among his peers as to which instrument he played better—some did not consider him a virtuoso on either. What made him popular were his lyrics and the way he sang them. Onstage Wheatstraw worked with many other well-known blues musicians, including Charlie Jordan, LONNIE JOHNSON, and ROOSEVELT SYKES. It was Jordan, while working as a scout in St. Louis for both Vocalion and Decca Records, who first brought him into the recording studio for a duet with a singer named "Neckbones." The song was titled "Tennessee Peaches Blues" and was recorded for Vocalion on 13 August 1930. Wheatstraw's singing was somewhat off-key and his piano playing was bland, but his performances improved a few months later when he returned to the studio alone to record "Don't Feel Welcome Blues," "Strange Man Blues," "School Days," and "So Soon." This was the beginning of a successful period for Wheatstraw, when he recorded twenty-one songs in two years.

During the fall of 1931 Wheatstraw went back to Chicago to record a few more songs, this time for Bluebird. Under the name Pete Wheatstraw he made *Devil's Son-in-Law* and *Pete Wheatstraw*. *Devil's Son-in-Law* is the first recording in which he proclaims himself a legend, announcing that "the next time you see me, I'll be the Devil's Son-in-Law." This was the only time he worked for Bluebird. A few months later he returned to Vocalion, traveling to New York to record "Police Station Blues," "All Alone Blues,"

"Can't See," and "Sleepless Nights Blues." After that session he did not make another record until 1934. Perhaps the national decline in record sales during the Depression slowed Wheatstraw's recording efforts; he did not seem to be in a creative slump. In 1932 only 6 million records had been sold nationally, dropping from 104 million sold in 1927. But when he returned to Vocalion in March 1934, Wheatstraw had enough material to make several recordings. He also came back with a new musical style. The biographer Paul Garon described his work as "superbly swinging piano, imaginative lyrics and an intensely emotive delivery" (Garon, 31).

Five months later Wheatstraw recorded a few songs for Decca, and in another two weeks he was back at Vocalion recording four more, including the popular "C and A Train Blues." To maintain his bad-boy image, he gave himself another nickname, the "High Sheriff from Hell." Days after recording "C and A Train Blues," he returned to Decca to record "Doin' the Best I Can."

Wheatstraw was now at the height of his career, having recorded nearly sixty songs. In 1936 he made his last recording for Vocalion and began working exclusively for Decca. During this final Vocalion session, he recorded one of his most popular songs, "Kidnapper's Blues." Tinged with humor and sarcasm, the song tells the story of Wheatstraw's baby, a black woman, who is kidnapped and ransomed for $10,000 at a time when virtually no one has money, and the police—perhaps of east St. Louis—searching the block desperately to find her. The song was so popular that he recorded another version for Decca just six days later. Soon after cutting his ties with Vocalion, Wheatstraw teamed up with the guitarist JAMES "KOKOMO" ARNOLD in a musical partnership that lasted several months. They recorded a total of twenty songs, including "Deep Sea Love," "When I Get My Bonus," and "Working on the Project." Arnold later said that he preferred working with the pianists Roosevelt Sykes and Joshua Altheimer than with Wheatstraw.

In 1938 Wheatstraw teamed up with Lonnie Johnson for seventeen songs. This was the last year Wheatstraw played accompaniment on his own recordings, although he continued to do so during performances. Decca replaced him with various studio pianists, including LIL ARMSTRONG and Sam Price, and it has been speculated that they felt that Wheatstraw's playing had become too repetitive. Blues critics feel, however, that even with new accompanists in place, his later records still lacked excitement.

His last recording session was on 25 November 1941, when he made "Mister Livingood" and "Bring Me Flowers While I'm Living." On 21 December, after a night of drinking, he was involved in a fatal car accident not far from his apartment building in east St. Louis. Lizzie Bunch saw the accident from their window but did not know who was in the car until she reached the scene. At 11:30 a.m. the car Wheatstraw was riding in slammed into a stationary boxcar on the train tracks along Third Street and Illinois Avenue. Two other passengers in the car died instantly, but Wheatstraw was taken to St. Mary's Hospital, where he died later in the day. The official record specified massive trauma to his head and body as the cause of death and also marked the day as his thirty-ninth birthday. His body was returned to Cotton Plant for burial.

Wheatstraw was considered an innovator who made more than 160 recordings—many more than most blues musicians of his day. Some performers billed themselves as the Devil's Daddy-in-Law or Peetie Wheatstraw's Buddy to boost their own popularity. Others took on his stage name, including Peetie Wheatstraw of Alabama. But following Wheatstraw's death his work sank into obscurity, even though RALPH ELLISON paid homage to him in the novel *Invisible Man* by introducing his main character to a fast-talking cart pusher named Peter Wheatstraw, the Devil's Son-in-Law. In the 1950s Wheatstraw's popularity began a postmortem ascent after the music critic Paul Oliver praised his work in various articles and eight of his songs were reissued on LP. In 1971 Garon published a biography of Wheatstraw; the entire collection of his recorded works is now available on compact disc.

Because Wheatstraw's music sounds much like that of popular artists, those unfamiliar with blues history may mistake him for a style emulator rather than an innovator. Had he been able to record music a decade or two longer, Wheatstraw may have received the widespread acclaim some critics feel he deserves as the popularity of blues music spread internationally.

FURTHER READING

Garon, Paul. *The Devil's Son-in-Law* (1971).
Oakley, Giles. *The Devil's Music: A History of the Blues* (1983).
Oliver, Paul. *Blues off the Record* (1984).
Rudwick, Elliott M. *Race Riot at East St. Louis, July 2, 1917* (1982).

LILLIAN BAULDING

Wheelan, Belle S. (10 Oct. 1951–), educator, was born in Chicago, Illinois, to Adelia Leonard Smith, an elementary school teacher, and Frank David Smith. Wheelan graduated from St. Gerard Catholic High School of San Antonio, Texas, in 1968. In 1968 Wheelan entered Trinity University of San Antonio, Texas, and graduated in 1972 with a double major in psychology and sociology. She became the first African American at Trinity to be included in *Who's Who in American Colleges and Universities*. It was to be the first of many milestones in a career that covered more than three decades. She went on to study at Louisiana State University and received a Master of Arts degree in Developmental/Educational Psychology in 1974. That same year, Wheelan became an associate professor at Alamo Community College District at San Antonio College. Recognizing the importance of advanced education, she left that position in 1984 to enroll in a doctoral program at the University of Texas, earning a doctorate in educational administration with an emphasis in community college leadership. Returning to the Alamo Community College District, San Antonio College, Dr. Wheelan eventually became director of counseling, later director of developmental education, and finally director of academic support services. Her postdoctoral training included the American Association of Community Colleges President's Academy as well as the Harvard University's Institute of Lifelong Learning.

Dr. Wheelan relocated to Hampton, Virginia, in 1987 when she accepted a position at Thomas Nelson Community College as dean of student development services. It was there that she began developing her focus on a comprehensive student programming strategy designed to enhance development of the "whole student." Her student development focus eventually raised her profile in educational circles around the country, garnering the attention of Virginia higher education leaders. Dr. Wheelan then received an appointment as Provost at Tidewater Community College's Portsmouth Campus in 1989. In addition to her duties as provost, she served as the chief administrative and academic officer of the local campus in a multicampus, comprehensive community college, roles that would position her to become president of Central Virginia Community College in 1992, making her the first African American woman to serve as president of a two- or four-year public institution of higher education in the commonwealth of Virginia. Dr. Wheelan left the Central Virginia campus in 1998 to take over as president of Northern Virginia Community College, becoming the first African American woman in Virginia to serve as president of not just one but two public higher education institutions. Northern Virginia Community College is the largest institution in the Virginia Community College System and the second largest in the nation. She served as its president until 2001.

In 2002 Dr. Wheelan was appointed the Commonwealth's Secretary of Education and was the first African American woman to serve in this capacity. Known for her efforts to diversify the student body, faculty, and staff of Virginia's higher education system, Wheelan came under fire for having what some critics called an excessive number of minorities on her staff. She refused to back down, pointing to the historical underrepresentation of minorities to justify a deliberately inclusive hiring policy. Since 2005 she served as president of the Commission on Colleges of the Southern Association of Colleges and Schools—again as the first African American woman in that capacity. Dr. Wheelan also served as the chief executive officer of the Regional Accrediting Commission for eleven Southern states and Latin America (Mexico, Costa Rica, and Venezuela).

Her numerous awards and recognitions include four honorary degrees from Virginia Seminary and College (1995), Marymount University (2002), Bridgewater College (2002), and Virginia State University (2006); and the Distinguished Graduate Award from Trinity University (2002) and from the College of Education at the University of Texas at Austin (1992). In addition, she was the recipient of the Pioneer Award from the National Council on Black American Affairs and the Award of Distinction from the American Association of University Women. Dr. Wheelan held membership with Rotary International, Alpha Kappa Alpha Sorority, Inc., the board of directors of American College Testing, Inc., the American Association of Community Colleges' board of directors, and the President's Roundtable of the National Council on Black American Affairs among others.

Despite an impressive career and a long list of accomplishments, Dr. Belle S. Wheelan is often quoted as saying her greatest achievement has been raising her son, Reginald.

FURTHER READING

Wheelan, B.S. *Making Public Education Work for Black Males* (1991).

Wheelan, B.S. "More teachers learning I.T." *Washington Business Journal*, 1999, p. 55.

Wheelan, B.S. *What's It Like Being the Only Black Woman Here?* (1995).

ADRIEL A. HILTON

Wheeler, Emma Rochelle (7 Feb. 1882–12 Sept. 1957), physician, health-care institution founder, and community activist, was born Emma Rochelle near Gainesville, Florida. Little is known about her parents except that her father was a farmer and a veterinarian. Her two siblings were William Rochelle and Ella Rochelle (later Stamps). Emma became entranced with medicine at age six when her father brought her to a white female doctor for eye disease treatment. After her schooling in Gainesville, Emma moved to Jacksonville to attend MARY MCLEOD BETHUNE's Cookman Institute. She graduated in 1899 and married Joseph R. Howard, a teacher, a year later. In 1901 her husband died from typhoid fever while she was pregnant with their son Joseph Howard Jr. The young widow moved to Nashville, Tennessee, with her son and enrolled in Walden University.

In 1905, as one of three women in a class of sixty-eight, Rochelle earned her MD from Meharry Medical, Dental, and Pharmaceutical College, then part of Walden. Meharry was the first southern medical school to train blacks. On 28 February 1905, during the same week as graduation, Rochelle wed another doctor, John N. Wheeler, in the Meharry auditorium, and their marriage lasted until his death in 1940. The couple had two biological daughters, Thelma Wheeler and Bette Wheeler (later Strickland), and an adopted son, George Wheeler, Emma Wheeler's nephew.

The couple relocated to Chattanooga, Tennessee, where for much of her career she worked as the only African American woman doctor Practicing together in their Main Street office, the couple grappled with the dire health consequences of segregation. Denied basic public health and clinical services, black Chattanoogans were left to substandard housing, poor sanitation, and high illness and death rates, especially from infectious diseases like tuberculosis. Inpatient care was unavailable except in the overcrowded basements of white hospitals. Refused privileges at these same hospitals, black physicians went without vital networking and training opportunities, particularly in surgery. Not only were black doctors scarce; most nursing schools excluded people of African descent.

Wheeler saved up her own money and after a decade purchased a double lot on the corner of East Eighth and Douglas streets. Her personal funds were enough to cover half the construction costs of the three-story brick building she started on the site. In 1914 she opened a nursing school that lasted for the next twenty years. Walden Hospital was officially dedicated at the same location on 30 July 1915. Even as Wheeler continued in private practice, she worked as superintendent of both the hospital and the nursing school. Although her husband held some clinical and teaching responsibilities, the creation, funding, and leadership of these two institutions were hers. The hospital proved so popular with patients and local black physicians that Wheeler was able to pay off the remaining half of the construction debt within three years of the opening. The thirty-bed Walden Hospital had departments of maternity, nursery, and surgery and was noted for its modern operating room. Walden employed in-house nurses and doctors but extended admitting privileges and learning opportunities to both white physicians and the members of the Mountain City Medical Society, an African American physicians' organization that met twice a month on Walden's premises.

In 1925 Wheeler established the Nurse Service Club. The affordable dues guaranteed each member and his or her family two weeks of free hospitalization in the event of serious illness, plus free in-home nursing care after discharge. Thousands benefited from this creative prepaid health-care plan, the only one in the city at the time. During the same year she also co-founded Pi Omega, the Chattanooga chapter of Alpha Kappa Alpha, the national African American sorority. Pi Omega launched a college scholarship program during the Depression. Because Wheeler actively supported their ambitions and otherwise acted as a foster mother toward many young people, the Chattanooga NAACP chapter eventually honored her in 1949 as Negro Mother of the Year. In fact Wheeler herself saw her professional and volunteer work as a natural extension of mothering her own children.

In 1931 Wheeler's hospital tried to remedy a human rights violation that had raised a national outcry among both black and white Americans, although similar incidents occurred regularly without such attention. Fisk University's dean of women JULIETTE ALINE DERRICOTTE and her student Edna Johnson were both severely injured in an automobile accident outside Dalton, Georgia, fifty miles from Chattanooga. The women were refused hospital care until Walden finally heard about their plight. The surgeon L. L. Patten ventured out with an ambulance. By the time the ambulance returned, nine hours had passed since the crash. Johnson was already dead, and Derricotte was near death.

In 1947 Hamilton County and the city of Chattanooga established the fifty-bed Carver Memorial Hospital, a publicly funded, segregated, and black-staffed institution. Four years later Wheeler retired from Walden because of her deteriorating health. A leadership crisis ensued. Walden shut down permanently on 30 June 1953, along with the Nurse Service Club. Reflecting on the past four decades, Wheeler was especially pleased about delivering more than two thousand babies, many of whom later wrote her grateful letters, and she rejoiced in their successes. These much-treasured letters gave her tangible evidence of her enduring legacy in the African American traditions of self-help and community service.

Wheeler died at age seventy-five in Nashville, Tennessee. She was buried in Chattanooga's Highland Cemetery, which she had served as treasurer and trustee board member. In 1962 the Chattanooga Housing Authority named its new housing project after her, and on 16 May 1990 the Chattanooga African American History Museum and the Tennessee State Historical Commission dedicated a marker at the site of the former Walden Hospital.

FURTHER READING

The Chattanooga African American History Museum and the Chattanooga-Hamilton County Bicentennial Library hold archival materials on Emma Rochelle Wheeler, John N. Wheeler, and Walden Hospital.

Savitt, Todd L. "Black Doctors: A Strong Medicine to Take in the New South," *New Crisis* (Jan./Feb. 2001).

"Walden Hospital Has Served Colored People for 24 Years," *Chattanooga News* (12 Aug. 1937).

Wynn, Linda T. "Emma Rochelle Wheeler," in *Notable Black American Women*, vol. 2, ed. Jessie Carney Smith (1992).

MARY KRANE DERR